# Platonic Patterns

# PLATONIC PATTERNS

A Collection of Studies by
**Holger Thesleff**

Las Vegas | Zurich | Athens

PARMENIDES PUBLISHING
Las Vegas | Zurich | Athens

© 2009 Parmenides Publishing
All rights reserved.

The seven works in this collection, three books and four articles, were originally published as follows:

1. *Studies in the Styles of Plato* (Acta philosophica Fennica 20), Societas Philosophica Fennica, Helsinki: 1967
2. *Studies in Platonic Chronology* (Commentationes Humanarum Litterarum 70), Societas Scientiarum Fennica, Helsinki: 1982
3. *Studies in Plato's Two-Level Model* (Commentationes Humanarum Litterarum 113), Societas Scientiarum Fennica, Helsinki: 1999
4. "**Theaitetos and Theodoros**," ARCTOS, Acta Philologica Fennica XXIV (1990), 147–159
5. "**The Early Version of Plato's *Republic*,**" ARCTOS, Acta Philologica Fennica XXXI (1997), 149-174
6. "**Plato and His Public**," NOCTES ATTICAE: Studies Presented to Jørgen Mejer on his Sixtieth Birthday March 18, 2002, Museum Tusculanum Press, University of Copenhagen (2002), 289-301
7. "**A Symptomatic Text Corruption: Plato, *Gorgias* 448a5**," ARCTOS, Acta Philologica Fennica XXXVII (2003), 251–257

This Collected Edition, with a new Introduction and Revisions,
published in 2009 by Parmenides Publishing
in the United States of America

ISBN: 978-1-930972-29-2

**Library of Congress Cataloging-in-Publication Data**

Thesleff, Holger.
  [Selections. 2009]
  Platonic patterns : collection of studies by Holger Thesleff / Holger Thesleff.
     p. cm.
  ISBN 978-1-930972-29-2 (pbk. : alk. paper)
  1. Plato. I. Title..
  B395.T488 2009
  184—dc22

2008056059

The Publisher would like to thank Professor Ilkka Niiniluoto of the Societas Philosophica Fennica, Professor Carl G. Gahmberg of the Societas Scientarum Fennica, Professor Olli Salomies of the Classical Association of Finland (Acta Philologica Fennica), and Dr. Birgitte Holten of the Museum Tusculanum Press for their kind permission to reprint the present works in this collection.

Typeset in Palatino and OdysseaUBSU (Greek) by 1106 Design
Printed by Transcontinental Printing in Canada

1-888-PARMENIDES
www.parmenides.com

# CONTENTS

Note to the Reader     xi
Introduction     xiii

## STUDIES IN THE STYLES OF PLATO     1

Preface     3
Abbreviations     5

**Introduction**     7
    Plato and style (7)—Stylometry (7)—Other studies of Plato's style (9)—The present task (10)—Notes on chronology and authenticity (10)—General observations on style and styles. Remarks on methods (21)

**Technique of Composition and Dialogue Structure**     27
    General observations     27
    A. Question and reply     29
       Origins (29)—Function (30)—Technique: Variation of formulae of reply (31)—Variation by means of expansion (31)—Change of dialogue partner (32)—Deliberate restriction (33)
    B. Discussion and conversation     33
       Origins (34)—Function (34)—Technique: The relation of B sections to A (D) (and E) sections (35)—Several persons joining in the conversation (36)
    C. Reported dialogue     36
       Origins (37)—Function (38)—Technique: Type C in relation to A and B (39)—Indirect report of replies (40)—Formulae of the type 'said I,' 'said he' (40)—Frame dialogue and report (40)
    D. Dialogue approximating to monologue     41
       Origins (41)—Function (42)—Technique: Relation of D to A, B, and E (43)—Stages of development (44)
    E. Monologue and continuous exposition     44
       Origins (45)—Function (46)—Technique (49)

| | |
|---|---:|
| **Style Markers and Classes of Style** | 51 |
| General observations (51)—Colloquial style (51)—Semi-literary conversational style (53)—Rhetorical style (54)—Pathetic ('affected') style (56)—Intellectual style (57)—Mythic narrative style (60)—Historical style (61)—Ceremonious style (61)—Legal style (62)—Onkos style (63) | |
| Lists of style markers | 65 |
| **Stylistic Analyses** | 83 |
| Analysis of the *Republic* | 83 |
| Conclusions regarding *R*. | 95 |
| Stylistic conspectus of the rest of the authentic works | 98 |
| *Hippias Minor* (99)—*Ion* (99)—*Laches* (99)—*Crito* (100)—*Apologia* (101)—*Menexenus* (101)—*Gorgias* (101)—*Meno* (103)—*Euthyphro* (105)—*Cratylus* (105)—*Lysis* (106)—*Charmides* (107)—*Protagoras* (108)—*Euthydemus* (109)—*Phaedo* (111)—*Symposium* (113)—*Parmenides* (115)—*Theaetetus* (116)—*Phaedrus* (118)—*Timaeus* (119)—*Critias* (120)—*Sophistes* (121)—*Politicus* (122)—*Philebus* (123)—*Epistula 7* (124)—*Leges* (125)—*Epinomis* (127) | |
| Notes on the dubia and spuria | 128 |
| **Conclusions** | 131 |
| Observations on the relation of style to the formal structure of the dialogues (131)—Observations on the function of style for characterization of the speakers (132)—Observations on the relation of style to the contents (135)—Observations on the rise of Plato's so-called "late style" (139)—Various concluding observations (141) | |

# STUDIES IN PLATONIC CHRONOLOGY     143

| | |
|---|---:|
| *Preface* | 145 |
| PART I | 147 |
| **The 'Platonic Question'** | 147 |
| Introductory notes (147)—Some trends (148)—Conspectus of chronologies suggested (153) | |
| **Critical Comments** | 165 |
| Preliminary remarks | 165 |
| External criteria: Biographical problems relating to Plato's youth (167)—The Megarian hypothesis (172)—The Corinthian war (173)—The first voyage outside Greece (174)—Theory of Parmentier (177)—Allusions by Plato to his contemporaries, and vice versa (177)—The pamphlet of Polycrates (177)—The Academy (178)—Plato and Isocrates (180)—Plato and Xenophon (180)—Plato and Aeschines of Sphettus (181)—Plato and Antisthenes (181)—Plato and Comedy (181)—Other contemporary persons (182)—The second voyage to Sicily (183)—The third voyage to Sicily (183)— | |

Contents

  Various references to contemporary events in Plato's works (183)—Plato
  and Aristotle (184)—Death of Plato (184)

| | |
|---|---:|
| References from one Platonic work to another | 185 |
| Ancient testimony regarding the publication of Plato's writings | 185 |
| Arguments from the contents | 186 |
| Literary criteria; dialogue technique | 199 |
| Linguistic criteria; 'stylometry' | 213 |
|  Test I (220)—Test II (222)—Test III (226) | |
| Revision | 230 |
| Problems of authenticity | 235 |

## PART II   245
## A New Model   245

### The 390s   249

The problem of the 'early *Republic*'   250
 Introductory (250)—The 'Proto-*Republic*' (251)—The separation of
 *Republic* I (256)

The *Apology*   259

Additional considerations; Isocrates XIII   262

### The Reported Dialogues and *Gorgias, Menexenus* and *Theaetetus*   265

General arguments for establishing a hypothetical order   265

Further arguments; introductory notes on the method   273
 *Gorgias* (274)—*Menexenus* (276)—*Protagoras* (276)—*Symposium* (283)—*The
 Respublica Rediviva* (285)—*Phaedo* (288)—*Euthydemus* (292)—*Lysis* (295)—
 *Charmides* (298)—*Theaetetus* (300)—*Parmenides* (304)

### The Rise of the Dramatic Dialogue   309

Introductory (309)—*Gorgias* (309)—*Meno* (310)—*Cratylus* (314)—*Phaedrus*
(317)—The adding of dramatic frame dialogues (326)

### Plato's 'Late Period'   331

Introductory (331)—The completing of the *Republic* (331)—The early portions
of the *Laws* (333)—*Theaetetus* and *Parmenides* (334)—*Timaeus* and *Critias* (335)—
The *Sophist* and *Politicus* (339)—*Philebus* (344)—The *Seventh Letter* (346)—'On
the Good' (347)—The completing of the *Laws* (348)—*Epinomis* (349)

### Dubia and Spuria and Semi-authenticity   351

Introductory (351)—*Clitopho* (352)—*Crito* (355)—*Laches* (357)—The *First
Alcibiades* (361)—*Theages* (364)—*Amatores* (365)—*Eryxias* (366)—*Hippias
Minor* (366)—*Ion* (367)—*Euthyphro* (369)—*Hippias Major* (372)—*Hipparchus*
(374)—*Minos* (375)—*Sisyphus* (375)—*Demodocus* (376)—*De Virtute* and *De Justo*

(376)—*Definitiones* (377)—The *Second Alcibiades* (377)—*Halcyon* (378)—*Axiochus* (378)—*Letters* (378)

## A Concluding Chronological Sketch   381

# STUDIES IN PLATO'S TWO-LEVEL MODEL   383

### *Preface*   385

### Introductory Remarks   387
Problems (387)—The present approach (391)—Who Speaks for Plato? (392)

### General Notes On Contrasts   393
Generally human and Greek attitudes (393)—Two-level contrasts (395)

### Pairs of Asymmetric Contrasts   397

Not two worlds   397

Compare 'divine / human'   398

Ten illustrative pairs in the 'earlier' dialogues   399
Divine / human (400)—Soul / body (401)—Leading / being led (402)—Truth / appearance (403)—Knowledge / opinion (404)—Intellect / senses (405)—Defined / undefined (407)—Stability / change (407)—One / many (408)—Same / different (409)

### Two Levels   411

Other examples   411

Two levels—and a third?   411

The two principal levels and their background in Greek thought   413

Characteristics of this vision   414
Orientation (414)—Eros (415)—The Divided Line (416)—A philosopher's vision (416)—Bridging the contrasts (417)

Examples of the function of the model   418
*Protagoras* (419)—*Charmides* (420)—The *First Alcibiades* (422)—*Apology* (423)—*Hippias Minor* (423)—The early Utopia (424)—Some general arguments (425)

### On Polar Opposites in Plato   427

Opposites and two-level contrasts   427
Examples: *Gorgias* (427)—*Republic* I (429)—*Lysis* (431)—*Euthydemus* (432)

*Phaedo*   433
Opposites (433)—Forms and opposites (434)

Contents

## On Ideas and Forms — 437
### The secondary status of the theory of Forms — 437
### Notes on the terminology — 438
### Forms in general — 439
Pre-Platonic background (439)—'Shape' rather than 'class' (440)
### Ideas — 441
Ideas as values (441)—Examples of Ideas of the αὐτό type (442)—Presence, participation (443)—Τὸ καλόν and the two levels (444)—Ideas 'as such' and as the focus of orientation (445)
### Notes on the interrelationship of the levels — 446
### Neutral and negative Ideas and Forms — 447
Forms treated as Ideas (447)—Artifacts (447)—Ideas or Forms for opposites? (448)—A unique Idea versus innumerable Forms (450)
### Forms as 'types' or 'kinds' — 450
'Kinds' in arts and crafts (451)—Forms as 'kinds' in two-way dialectic (451)—'Kinds' gradually more common? (452)
### Retrospect and partial conclusions — 452
Ideas, Forms as concepts, Forms as kinds (452)—The Divided Line and Ideas, Forms, and Phenomena (453)—Few and unique Ideas (455)

## Forms and Categories — 457
### The impact of younger associates — 457
### The interrelation of Ideas and Kinds — 457
*Parmenides* and new perspectives (457)—Two-level categories in the *Sophist* (460)—Categories versus Ideas and Forms (462)—*Politicus* (463)
### Categories and the Soul — 464
*Theaetetus* (464)—*Phaedrus* (464)—The World Soul in *Timaeus* and *Laws* X (465)—Human soul in *Timaeus* (467)—Anamnesis (467)
### Categories elsewhere — 469
*Cratylus* and *Republic* IV (469)—*Philebus* and πέρας / ἄπειρον (470)
### Concluding remarks on Categories — 471

## Forms, Categories, First Principles — 473
### The Principles as Categories — 473
An authentically Platonic theory? (473)—Notes on the sources (475)—The Principles and the two levels (476)—Principles and Categories (476)—Principles and Ideal Numbers (478)—Principles and Ideas (480)—A reduction of the Categories to mathematical concepts (481)
### Principles as Causes? — 483
### The relation of the First Principles to Categories, Forms, and Ideas — 483
### The status and chronology of the theory — 485
'On the Good' (485)—A late and tentative theory (486)—An episode? (488)

**Notes on Chronology**     **489**

   The coherence of the Corpus     489

   Problems with a refined analysis     490
      Eros (491)—Soul (491)—True Being (492)—Senses (492)—Definition (492)

   Forms and Categories as Criteria     493
      Forms and Ideas (493)—Terms (494)—Categories (494)

   Can chronological conclusions be drawn?     494

**Summary and Conclusions**     **499**

## ARTICLES

"Theaitetos and Theodoros"     509

"The Early Version of Plato's *Republic*"     519

"Plato and His Public"     541

"A Symptomatic Text Corruption: Plato, *Gorgias* 448a5"     551

*Bibliography*     557
*Index*     609

# NOTE TO THE READER

The present volume is a collection of seven works—three books and four articles—that were previously published separately and independently of each other (see the copyright page for details). They include some of the most significant of Holger Thesleff's works published from 1967 to 2003, thereby presenting scholarship from five different decades. Both as an homage to the original publications, and as a way of facilitating the looking up of references based on earlier editions, the pagination of the original books and articles is included here in the margins in square brackets.

Considerable effort has been put into streamlining and modernizing the various styles of expression and conventions of scholarship in order to present the reader with a volume that is both internally coherent and as up to date as possible. All Greek names and terms, with few necessary exception, have been rendered in the Latin spelling, e.g. Heraclitus instead of Herakleitos, and Lyceum instead of Lykeion. Furthermore, the Abbreviations for Platonic works listed at the beginning of the first book, *Studies in the Styles of Plato*, have been applied throughout the rest of the book.

The current Bibliography is a combination of all three bibliographies in the original works, and entries have been updated wherever possible and/or appropriate. Similarly, the present Index was compiled from the combined lists of index terms from the original indices, with additional new entries for the text of the four articles. Note that pages of particular relevance to a specific term are marked in boldface, and dashes following a page number are used to indicate that the respective term is discussed on the noted page as well as in the following pages. Last but not least, please note that Plato's works are indexed in a separate section titled Index of Platonic Texts, which follows the main Index.

# INTRODUCTION

The struggle to understand Plato, the Proteus of Western philosophy, continually takes new shapes. The heterogeneous masses of specialists and nonspecialists all over the world who find themselves involved in this struggle are assisted by ever better means of international communication. But the spread of better information means we must also face the problem of innumerable different, coexistent approaches. In fact, no other author or body of texts from Greco-Roman antiquity has appealed to so many different categories of readers. Anyone trying to get a serious grasp of Plato will, at some point or another, become bewildered not only by his dialogues but also by the chaos of interpretative efforts from different viewpoints or schools that surrounds them.

Yet one can see trends that are leading toward clarification. For my part, I would emphasize six shifts in recent attitudes. One is the growing conviction that the Platonic dialogues should be read as philosophy in a literary (or dramatic) disguise, and certainly not merely analyzed as philosophical tracts, however much a stringent analysis of terminology and logic (especially by 20th-century British and American scholars) has contributed to our understanding of Plato's explicit reasoning. Another shift has occurred, however gradually, from the 19th-century belief that the dialogues directly reflect a development of Plato's thought—and thus can be put in a chronological order—to skepticism regarding our ability to reconstruct the details of development and chronology. The differentiating of "Socratic" dialogues from the rest also seems more problematic than it did some decades ago. A third shift, related to the first two, concerns the unquestioned acceptance of the fact that there was a continuous oral discussion in Plato's circle that is only partly—and wryly—reflected in the written dialogues. A fourth shift is implied in the recent debates about a possibly coherent doctrinal basis in the oral discussions. A fifth shift, which I consider particularly challenging today, is the serious pondering of the questions of why Plato wrote as he did and for what audiences he wrote. And a sixth overall shift can be seen in the fact that both "historicists" (who try to understand Plato in his original context) and "modernists" (who read the dialogues in terms of, and for the benefit of, modern philosophy) have begun to profit from each other's ways of thinking.

In various ways, the texts reprinted in this volume happen to fit in with these trends, though more in the historicist aspect than the modernist. They are the result of a life's scholarly work. Originally published by academic societies in Finland (with one article published in Denmark), they have heretofore not been easily accessible outside the Scandinavian countries. They may be of interest specifically because my premises differ from the usual ones on which most Platonic research is based.

Step by step and by sidesteps, I entered into my struggles with Greek philosophy, at first with an orientation toward historical linguistics. My investigations began at grammar school, with the surprisingly easy style of the *Crito*. In silent periods during the War, Homer's *Odyssey* encouraged me to reflect on the colorful varieties of Greek imagination, so different from the Iliadic realities around me. As a university student, I found the reasoning in *Phaedo* a challenge, but a frustratingly difficult one, especially since I lacked appropriate teachers and commentaries on Plato. Aristophanes, my only classical companion on a sailing adventure around the world in the late '40s, offered fascinating parallels to Plato's use of Attic Greek. I had a philologist's schooling: my PhD thesis (1954) concerned certain idiomatic expressions used by ancient Greeks, including Plato. T. B. L. Webster's circle in London opened my eyes to the PreSocratics. A note in a book on Pindar led me to follow up on the problems of the Pythagorean texts and their relation to Plato's Academy. I have been trained to follow the international scholarly discussion, but I have never been associated with any particular authority or any philosophical school of Plato interpretation. Since the 1980s, however, I have had much contact with various members of the International Plato Society and with other philosophers. "Modernism" is not entirely alien to me.

I have written quite a lot on Plato over the years, but mostly from a historicist or philological perspective. Publications not reprinted here include two volumes on (pseudo)Pythagorean texts (1961, 1965); several specialist articles in English and German; commentaries on Plato's dialogues in Finnish and Swedish (since 1977); a comprehensive volume on Plato for general readers in Finnish (1989) and Swedish (1990); and together with my former student, Juha Sihvola, a large volume in Finnish on ancient philosophy and the history of ideas (1994).

*Studies in the Styles of Plato* (1967) is an ambitious attempt to describe from a formal perspective the stylistic shifts within the various writings of the Corpus Platonicum. As a case study, the linguistic structure of the *Republic* is analyzed in some detail. Though very much remains to be done to refine such analyses, the book has been considered an interesting step away from statistical stylometry (see below) toward the understanding of variations in style (sociolects, idiolects) in terms of modern text linguistics. The most manifest result of the interpretation of the dialogues is the tracing of some typical structural patterns, such as the tendency to "pedimental" composition.

*Studies in Platonic Chronology* (1982) is an even more ambitious effort to cope with the problems of dating the Platonic texts. Chronology had been the object of frustrating debates among Plato scholars since the 1860s. Statistics of linguistic phenomena, so-called stylometry (the term introduced by the Polish Platonist W. Lutoslawski in the 1890s), was in many quarters regarded as the definitive method of proving the existence of "early," "middle," and "late" Platonic works, and perhaps to ascertaining a chronological order within the groups and sorting out spurious texts. In spite of considerable opposition by some authorities, it seemed in the 1980s that the stylometrists had won the game. I tried to show that they had not. Though I admit that the use of electronic means has revolutionized even this issue, I point out the numerous complications that, taken together, exclude the possibility that the dialogues reflect a steady line of linguistic change. Such complications include the revision of the texts;

Plato's cooperation with younger friends ("semiauthenticity"); the oral discussion behind the texts, which may have affected even the choice of style; and, above all, the different audiences to whom the written dialogues were originally addressed. Instead, I suggest the importance of studying very carefully the external evidence we have of Plato's life and activities, as well as the change in the contents or emphasis of his philosophy that can be traced independently of linguistic or terminological variations in the dialogues. The book ends with a tentative sketch of a new chronology, open to further debate. The debate goes on, occasionally with secondary reference to my work; it may be useful for those who want to proceed with these questions to know what I have actually written.

Two of the articles reprinted here are dedicated to the question of Plato's alleged "development." In "Theaitetus and Theodoros" (1990), I produce rather definite proofs that Plato began to develop his theories of geometry before his first voyage to the West, in cooperation with his very gifted friend Theaetetus, who died young but left behind him a tradition developed in Plato's Academy under his name (cf. Euclid X). I also suggest that 'Socrates the Younger,' who reappears in later Platonic works, is not a historical person but a pseudonym for Plato. In "The Early Version of Plato's *Republic*" (1997), I expand my earlier arguments that Plato had presented a utopian "Proto-Republic" for an audience in Athens before 392 BCE, long before the written text we know gradually took shape.

The book *Studies in Plato's Two-Level Model* (1999) may be a stumbling block for those who are not acquainted with the problems of Plato's metaphysics. I am trying in this work to harmonize the different views of these issues, which have existed since the days of the early Academy and have again appeared in recent scholarly debates, notably in Germany, Italy, and the United States. I base my argument on an earlier assumption of mine (originally developed from an idea of Dutch scholar Cornelia de Vogel) that Plato had a deeply rooted vision of two ontological levels in constant interplay (for example, light and different shades of darkness). It is not a philosophical "system" in any sense, just a visionary model. This "two-level model" (TLM) can in fact be taken as an overall key to the understanding of Plato's thought and dialectic, as well as its literary expression. It underlies practically all dialogues. It includes a notion of a constant contrast (but not opposition) between the ideal and the imperfect, the abstract and the concrete, the stable elements of the universe and those that change, the divine and the human. The higher level is the more valuable and important object of the philosopher's orientation. The notorious theory of Forms (which was later extended to lower-level concepts, still taken as abstractions) is only one aspect of this model; the vexed theories of First Principles and basic all-round concepts ("kinds") cover it from another perspective. The theories of the soul, anamnesis, eros, hypothesis, the classifying method sometimes called dihaeretics, and the mediatory role of the philosopher are other bridge-building efforts within the frame of the model.

The article "Plato and His Public" (2002) and the brief note on "A Symptomatic Text Corruption" (2003) are part of my recent pondering about how and for whom Plato presented his dialogues. I have since returned to these questions (2007 and forthcoming). It is important for us to keep in mind the oral context of the written texts as a constant complication. And I am sure Plato did not on the whole intend his dialogues for general circulation, whatever countless generations of readers have thought.

I regret that it has been impossible, except on a few points, to update the statements of the texts printed here. As a brief summary of my interpretation of Plato, in these reprinted works and elsewhere, I want to make the following claims.

A detailed examination of the language of the Platonic writings reveals shifts of style, of dialogue technique, of terminology, and of allusive irony or thought-play (however difficult to ascertain) that give few signs of a chronological development but do present clues to the different situations and contexts in which the texts were originally meant to be presented. The persons involved and the interweaving of themes and subthemes may give hints about the original audience. Since the dialogues are not discursive tracts but often artistically composed wholes, their purpose is not just the argumentation around a single overt theme. Training and provocation to thinking ("protreptics") are in many cases the essential primary purposes of the dialogues. The intensive modern discussion of the alleged changes in Plato's views and logic has tended to ignore this idea.

The dialogues were read aloud by a single person (usually Plato or someone well acquainted with the text) to selected audiences. They were not intended for a general public (as the *Apology* was), but carefully composed for appreciation by connoisseurs; note the pedimental structure of most of them. The reported dialogues (such as the *Symposium*) could be copied for circulation among friends, but Plato preferred to authorize a single manuscript that could then be revised (by himself or, later, by his associates). Texts revised or rewritten in the Academy (after ca. 387 BCE) can in some cases be termed "semiauthentic." There was always an oral discussion accompanying the reading, and more or less important points could be left out from the written text. The end is normally left somewhat open (even in the case of the relatively systematic *Philebus*).

Because of these and several other facts, the dating of most dialogues is hazardous. A "late group" of dialogues (addressed to advanced Academic listeners) can be distinguished, but "Socratic" dialogues were also produced in the same period. It is doubtful if any Platonic dialogues have been preserved in their original shape from the time before 387 BCE. Various facts about the life of Plato can be sifted out from the sources available to us; the *Seventh Letter* is essentially an authentic and important document.

It seems certain that Plato had developed early on a personal vision of what he called "true philosophy," with ingredients of PreSocratic and Socratic thought (see the above notes on the TLM). The theory of a distinct "Socratic period" is untenable.

The chief function of the dialogues is to suggest points and provoke oral discussions in specific situations, under the leadership of a philosopher. This person (Plato's "Socrates" or somebody else) stands for Plato to a somewhat varying extent, but the directing of the dialectic must be said to be Plato's. Plato's "true philosophy" can be described as visionary, holistic, educational persuasion in two-level dialogue form, primarily intended to deepen and ennoble the ethics of the intellectual elite for the benefit of the entire society. The gradual growth of the *Republic* from an early utopia to reactions to Plato's Sicilian experiences reflects central parts of his personal philosophy. The three famous allegories in the center of the work as we have it give useful hints about the levels and directions of his thought and its orientation towards the ultimate good.

Together with his associates in the Academy, who tended to specialize in various branches, Plato made tentative (never dogmatic) pushes into specific areas of intellectual activity later called ontology and metaphysics, epistemology, Eleatic logic, mathematics, cosmology and physics, psychology, ethics, political science and legislation (though the *Laws* is predominantly semiauthentic), religion, and eschatology. But to Plato, "all is involved in all": he is not only a holistic thinker but also a "both-and" thinker (not an "either-or" one like the Eleatics).

Plato inclined to ethical reform from a pointedly theoretical and metaphysical perspective. His thought is not especially rooted in the varieties of practical experience (cf., for example, drama, rhetoric, medicine, history), or induction (cf. Aristotle), though he has a sensitive eye for human life and its emotive dimensions. His theories are chiefly founded in some basic human beliefs and impressions, which constitute his points of orientation. It can be claimed that he is obsessed by the power of "reason" (*nous, logos,* and derivatives) to a degree that may seem at first foreign to the romantic and post-romantic world and to modern readers who would expect more from the lower-level play in the dialogues.

Plato continually sets his focus on potential philosophers—their resources, attitudes, responsibilities, and training. In his own environment, he wanted to provoke such listeners. He is not really interested in the trivialities of everyday life. The dialogues ought not to be read as handbooks in ethics, or statesmanship, or logic, or religion, or any other line of thought, as posterity has too often tended to do.

His methods are essentially oral "dialectic," based on Socratic questioning, but they developed at an early stage into philosopher-led shared discussions, typically extending over both main levels of the TLM. Here refutations of opponents' points and apparent shortcomings ("aporias") are intermingled with constructive logical arguments, as well as multilevel ironical or playful ideas (including myths) supporting the latter. The rise of Platonic dialectic and its variants still requires much research, in spite of the enormous amount of work already done on the issue.

Plato liked to play the role of a "new Socrates," but it is actually his dialectic that reflects his own, always holistic, thinking.

Over the span of the last decades, more and more intellectuals all over the world are learning to read the Platonic dialogues in accordance with the new trends described above. Earlier generations' uncritical admiration or rejection of Plato are out of fashion. Purely "modernist" readings have become scarce. But a great variety of approaches will certainly persist, some of them very conservative. There is nothing wrong with plurality in a case as complicated as the interpretation of Plato. It is to be hoped, however, that ever more scholars will begin to think over the possibility of harmonizing the different approaches and analyze where and why they happen to be incompatible.

That would be a properly Platonic way to proceed. When we enter on a new research into a particular Platonic question, or into a particular dialogue, it is always good to consider what Plato seems to say on this question elsewhere, and how he does it, and what other interpreters have said on the issue. Admittedly, this is no easy task. I know that naive Plato students will easily be discouraged by such warnings. But naiveté is not needed here. Definitive, final answers will probably never be found; instead, they will become Platonically "suspended." But from Plato's point of view, I believe, orientation toward truth is more essential than reaching it entirely.

My thanks are due to innumerable colleagues, older and younger, who have aided me for more than sixty years with their suggestions, criticism, and encouragement. In addition, I have been surrounded by my wonderful family and my personal friends. Now I am particularly grateful to Parmenides Publishing who have taken the risk of reprinting these works, and especially to their managing editor, Eliza Tutellier, whose understanding attitude and support have been immensely helpful to me, and to her assistant, Karen Succi, and the rest of the staff, who have coped so excellently with all of the unexpected complications during the editorial process.

Helsinki, March 2009

# Studies In The Styles
Of Plato

# PREFACE

This book is concerned with patterns of style and their function in Plato's works.

In order not to lose sight of the relevance of stylistic studies to the interpretation of Plato, and because of the specific nature of Plato's prose—and indeed, in order to save space—, I have adopted an unconventional method of examination which, I hope, has been sufficiently justified in the Introduction.

My thanks are due to the Finnish State Commission for the Humanities, to Societas Scientiarum Fennica, and to the Finnish Philosophical Society. I also recall with pleasure many inspiring discussions, of style and styles and of Plato, with colleagues and friends in London, Mainz, Frankfurt, and my own country.

University of Helsinki, November 1966

# ABBREVIATIONS

For the letters A–E denoting different types of dialogue structure, *see* the chapter 'Technique of composition'; for the figures **1–10** (in bold type) denoting different classes of style, *see* the chapter 'Style markers.'

Bibliographical references in the text and notes are normally given only by the author's name, the year of publication, and the page number. For full references the Bibliography should be consulted. Some well-known monographs on Plato (Friedländer, Gauss, Taylor, Wilamowitz) and some handbooks (such as Schmid) have been quoted without the year of publication. KB of course means Kühner-Blass, KG Kühner-Gerth, and LSJ Liddell-Scott-Jones.

For the writings of the Platonic Corpus the abbreviations of LSJ have been adopted:

*Alc.* 1, 2 = *Alcibiades* 1, 2
*Amat.* = *Amatores*
*Ap.* = *Apologia (Apology)*
*Ax.* = *Axiochus*
*Chrm.* = *Charmides*
*Clit.* = *Clitopho*
*Cra.* = *Cratylus*
*Cri.* = *Crito*
*Criti.* = *Critias*
*Def.* = *Definitiones*
*Demod.* = *Demodocus*
*Ep.* = *Epistulae*
*Epin.* = *Epinomis*
*Erx.* = *Eryxias*
*Euthd.* = *Euthydemus*
*Euthphr.* = *Euthyphro*
*Grg.* = *Gorgias*
*Hipparch.* = *Hipparchus*
*Hp.Ma.* = *Hippias Major*
*Hp.Mi.* = *Hippias Minor*
*Ion* = *Ion*
*Just.* = *De Justo*
*La.* = *Laches*
*Lg.* = *Leges*
*Ly.* = *Lysis*
*Men.* = *Meno*
*Min.* = *Minos*
*Mx.* = *Menexenus*
*Phd.* = *Phaedo*
*Phdr.* = *Phaedrus*
*Phlb.* = *Philebus*
*Plt.* = *Politicus*
*Prm.* = *Parmenides*
*Prt.* = *Protagoras*
*R.* = *Respublica (Republic)*
*Sis.* = *Sisyphus*
*Smp.* = *Symposium*
*Sph.* = *Sophist*
*Thg.* = *Theages*
*Tht.* = *Theaetetus*
*Ti.* = *Timaeus*
*Virt.* = *De Virtute*

# INTRODUCTION

## Plato and style

Plato's mastery of style has been recognized since antiquity.[1] It is no exaggeration to state that he makes use of a stylistic register far wider and far more subtle than any other ancient prosaist. This mastery is, to some extent, a "mimetic" attitude which has something to do with his fascination by language and with his notorious *odi et amo* complex towards art and literature.[2] But it seems to be also reflecting shifts in his thought.[3] Thus the study of Plato's style can be expected to afford a clue to Plato, both as a writer and as a thinker.

It is, however, surprising how little has been done for studying Plato's stylistic practice systematically, except for the specific purpose of establishing a chronology for his writings.

## Stylometry

Since Lutoslawski (*see* note 4) this term has been applied to that special branch of study which aims at solving problems of chronology or authenticity by statistical

---

1. Admittedly the views taken by ancient critics were mostly based on conventional rhetorical theory and concerned what we are used to calling Plato's late style. The Neoplatonic commentaries opened the way for a wider appreciation of his style, and sometimes (e.g. in Hermogenes) the shifts of his style seem to have been connected with his ἠθοποιία, though we know of no comprehensive treatment of this subject. *See* Walsdorff 1927, who however does not give the whole material; cf. Orth 1933, Nock 1947: 170–173.

2. For the former *Cra.* and *Phdr.* are the most evident proofs. For the latter, *see* the discussion and references in Cherniss 1959: 246–248, 520–554 and Vicaire 1960 (especially 261–270); cf. below p. 28. To the impressive bibliography of Vicaire the following studies could be added: Vanhoye 1952, Webster 1952, Lodge 1953, Mazzantini 1953, Görgemanns 1960.

3. Plato himself was well aware of the relationship between form and content; *see* especially *Phdr.* 277bc and in general the discussion in Vicaire 1960: 352–362. The importance of studying this relationship in Plato's writings has been emphasized by D. Tarrant 1948 and Gigon in different connections, especially *Euthphr.* 1954, and it appears from the interpretations of numerous scholars, already in Schleiermacher (*see* Gaiser 1959: 10–11), and notably Stenzel, Wilamowitz, and

[8] accounts of the relative frequency of linguistic or other peculiarities in literary texts. Stylometry started with Plato's writings, and so far they seem to have remained one of its chief battlefields.

Naturally, stylometry can have but a very limited use in determining and interpreting an author's style. If the stylometrists give full references to the phenomena they are dealing with, other students of style may profit from their collections of material (cf. below p. 63). But mere statistics of occurrence of linguistic data can only indicate very general tendencies—if indeed anything at all. The subtleties of the author's change of style within brief units of text cannot be determined by statistical stylometry as hitherto practiced.

As for Plato, stylometry has established beyond doubt the category, of "late style," represented by *Ti.*, *Criti.*, *Sph.*, *Plt.*, *Phlb.* and *Lg.*, and the partial affinity with this style noticeable in *R.* II–X, *Prm.*, *Tht.*, and *Phdr.* But it is impossible to deduce from this a stylistic scale indicating the chronological place of each dialogue according to its degree of stylistic affinity with the *Lg.* Against any mechanical application of the "law of affinity" as assumed by Lutoslawski, it has to be remarked that Plato is particularly unlikely to have had a linear development, and that, because he is very likely indeed to vary his diction with deliberate purpose from dialogue to dialogue just as he does from section to section, the internal chronology of the late group of writings is as difficult to prove on stylometrical grounds as the internal chronology of the early group. Nor have questions of authenticity been settled with any more reliability by traditional stylometry, than by other stylistic or non-stylistic methods. But the application of computers to linguistic research will perhaps alter the conditions to some extent because of the large amount of phenomena they enable the stylometrist to study simultaneously.[4]

---

Friedländer; cf. further Schwessinger 1925, Willi 1925, Schaerer 1938, Hoffmann and Merlan 1947, Buccellato 1963. The rejecting of the relationship in *Grg.* by Duchemin 1943: 272–273 is badly founded.

4. Stylometry began by establishing some features in Plato's "late style" (*see* below p. 63). This was first done by Campbell 1867 (cf. 1894, 1896) and; independently, by Dittenberger 1881 (who observed variations in the use of particles throughout the whole Corpus). The history of Platonic stylometry and its results up to 1896 can be found in Lutoslawski's programmatic work 1897 (cf. 1898). After Lutoslawski the chief stylometrists were Ritter, whose work on Platonic chronology comprises the time from 1888 to 1935, and v. Armin, whose laborious calculations of the relative frequency of formulae of reply (1913) have been compared to logarithm tables (Geffcken II. A. 139). For complete references to Platonic stylometry up to the early 1920s, *see* Ueberweg-Praechter I[13] 69*–72*. The work up to the last War was summed up by Simeterre 1945 (some additions in Cherniss 1959: 62 n. 3). In later years only experiments and tentative suggestions have been made: Vanachter 1946, statistics on various aspects of linguistic usage in *Chrm.*, *Phlb.*, *Lg.*; Owen 1953, early dating of *Ti.* and *Criti.* on account of new stylometric criteria (but cf. Cherniss 1957); Brandwood 1956 and 1958 (with criticism of earlier work on the subject), principles settled for using electronic computers in stylometry; Díaz Tejera 1961 and 1965, confirmation of earlier stylometric conclusions, suggestions for comparing Plato's vocabulary to the standard of Hellenistic Koiné. Some observations and references to the latest literature concerning statistical stylistics in general in Janson 1964.—The objections of Natorp (1898, 1899–1900, 1911)

## Other studies of Plato's style [9]

A large-scale analysis of Plato's language[5] will probably never appear, because the labor involved would by far exceed the applicability of such a work. Indeed, we shall apparently have to wait long for a complete concordance, which is much more urgently desired by philologists and philosophers alike.[6]

There are two good characterizations of Plato's language and style in general: Campbell 1894: 165–340 and (much briefer and more subjective, but with important observations) Wilamowitz II 412–429.[7] Baron's thesis of 1891 is far too superficial and loose to be of real service. A good and fairly detailed introduction to the literary art of Plato, designed for the general reader, was provided [10] by Puech in a series of articles in 1932–1934.[8] Fine analyses of the all-pervading function of play in Plato's art have been performed by D. Tarrant in a number of articles published between 1926 and 1958, by Schaerer 1938, and in particular by de Vries 1949 whose book unfortunately was only published in Dutch[9]; D. Tarrant also considered dramatic devices, imagery, colloquialisms, proverbs, and the like. Witte 1949 propounded a peculiar theory about a hidden meaning in Plato's style which is of little use here. Observations on the style of Plato's myths were made by Harris 1892.[10]

Of the general works on Plato, those by Wilamowitz and Friedländer contain much scattered material of interest to the student of Plato's style. For the composition and structure of the dialogues, *see* also below p. 27 ff.

Particular phenomena have been treated in a number of studies of widely varying quality and range. I mention the following[11]: Riddell 1867, a large collection of

---

and Immisch (1899, 1915, 1924) to stylometry are still valid; cf. Warburg 1929: 31–61, Kretschmer, [Review of] Hans v. Arnim's *Die Sprachliche Forshung* (1932): 232, (the rather more eccentric) Lönborg 1939, and Vretska 1958: 31–36. Except for Ritter, who however is very cautious, first-rate Platonic scholars have been inclined to reject a detailed stylometry. The fact that Plato's deliberate and highly individual choice of words extends even to particles and formulae of assent has been stressed by Immisch 1915: 550–553, Denniston 1954: LXIX, Ojeman 1957, Benardete 1963.

5. Such as e.g. Gautier 1911 for Xenophon.
6. Some prospects have been announced: *see* Ueberweg-Praechter I$^{13}$ 73* and Lesky$^{74}$ 507. Dr. Brandwood informs me that he is preparing an index of words [appeared in 1976]. Meanwhile Ast and des Places 1964 will do some service even for stylistic studies.
7. Norden 1898: 104–113 and Ritter 1923: 847–867 have expositions on a somewhat comparable scale.
8. Similarly, but more briefly: Festa 1912, Austin 1921, Hoffmann 1947, Murley 1954, Laborderie 1960. Levinson 1964 attempts to apply New Criticism to Plato. Cf. also the articles of Greene (1920 to 1958).
9. Also e.g. Klein 1965: 10–20. Tracy 1937 in general terms compares the satire of Plato to that of Horace and Juvenal. Rezzani's attempt (1959) to contrast the styles of Gorgias and Plato remains unclear.
10. Cf. below, n. 152.
11. References to stylometrical works above n. 4. Further references in due place below; cf. also Ueberweg-Praechter I$^{13}$ 71*–73*, Cherniss 1959–1961, and (for the vocabulary) des Places 1964: IX–XIV.

instances where Plato breaks the rule of "normal" grammar or which are otherwise linguistically remarkable; in spite of his principles of selection and arrangement, Riddell's work offers much useful material. Campbell 1867, on Plato's "late" style (cf. above n. 4); unfortunately Campbell in part gives only statistics based on Ast's Lexicon. Schanz 1871, on points of grammar and rhetoric. Roeper 1878, on the dual. Droste 1886, on adjectives terminating in -ειδής, -ώδης. Walbe 1888, on πᾶς, παν-. Janell 1901, on avoidance of hiatus, v. Arnim 1913, on formulae of reply. Luise Reinhard 1920, on anacoluthon. Grace Billings 1920, on formulae of transition. Des Places 1929, on some particles. Louis 1945, on metaphors. Ammann 1953, on adjectives terminating in -ικός. Of books dealing with Greek language and style in general, the comprehensive work of Denniston on the particles ($^2$ 1954) is worth special mention here because of the importance of particles in Plato's linguistic usage.

## The present task

It is evident that the above-mentioned works, even if put together as a mosaic, only cover disparate parts of Plato's linguistic and stylistic usage. And what is more serious, the majority are purely descriptive.

Before further descriptive work is done, I believe it is worth while to attempt a new approach and ask whether the relation of Plato's style to his thought and his other intentions can be clarified in general terms. The present task will be to study *the structure and the function of style* in Plato's writings.

## Notes on chronology and authenticity

The stylometrists (p. 7) have established three main chronological groups of Plato's writings, and since this arrangement has been seemingly or actually confirmed by other observations, most Platonic scholars have accepted it. But there is little agreement on the internal chronology within the groups.[12]

Some scholars pay little attention to chronology, either because they think it cannot be solved, or because they incline to think with Schleiermacher and Shorey that Plato's writings arose from a unity of conception or even from a plan of work that remained essentially unchanged during his manhood.[13] I am personally

---

12. For the problems of Platonic chronology, *see* Ueberweg-Praechter I[13] 194–218, 68*–73*, Leisegang 1950: 2369–2376, Friedländer III[2] 415–423, Cherniss 1959: 62–68, 250–260. An intelligent criticism of many old arguments (some of them still in use) in Shorey 1933. For stylometry in particular, *see* above n. 4.

13. Both Schleiermacher and Shorey have been sometimes misinterpreted. For the former, *see* Leisegang 1950: 2372–2374; for the latter, Shorey 1933: 58–59, 66–67. A kind of compromise between the genetic and the systematic approaches was attempted by Stenzel 1917. *See* further

convinced of the importance of trying to arrive at a reliable chronology, but I am also convinced that the difficulties are almost insuperable.

First of all, there is indeed much to be said in favor of the theories of Schleiermacher and Shorey, or variants of them, at least regarding part of the dialogues. I only refer to three points. Since the "aporetic" character of many "early" dialogues is more apparent than real, it is probable that Plato does not in them produce his whole view, or his actual state of knowledge of the subject. One need not be a strict adherent of the recent theories of the "esoteric Plato" to find this assumption likely.[14] And this, as well as the didactic path hinted at in some dialogues,[15] suggests that part of the dialogues may have been intended for different stages of instruction, or even different degrees of esoterism. And if, as seems a priori probable, Plato deliberately adjusted his manner and style to such differences of level, the criteria of the conventional chronology may seem problematic.

These considerations lead to the very difficult questions of Plato's public relations and the part played by the Academy in propagating his doctrines and writings. I am sure these questions have not been taken into due account when discussing the chronology and authenticity of the dialogues.[16] In fact, it is unlikely that the texts we have always represent faithfully the actual words of Plato as they were successively written down by himself or taken down by his secretary or some other listener. I should like to draw attention to three problems in this connection.

The problem of authenticity is largely a question of degree: how much is authentic material in the spurious works, and how much is interpolation in the authentic ones?[17] The accumulation of semi-spurious material under the name of a master

---

Liebrücks 1948, Krämer 1959: 33–35, 481, with references, Manasse 1961: 54. v. Armin is the only adherent of the systematic theory (*see* especially 1914) who has considered chronology very important (cf. above n. 4).

14. Cf. e.g. Hoerber 1955. Jaeger (*see* especially II 94–106) and Friedländer interpret the early dialogues according to this conception. For the view that Socrates embodies the virtues seemingly to be defined, *see* Schaerer 1938: 170–171. Merlan 1947 points out that Plato's changes of approach may imply, not so much a development, as a need of viewing the problems from different angles; similarly Sinaiko 1965.—The theory that Plato had at an early stage developed an esoteric doctrine which is only indirectly reflected in his writings, has been combined with the systematic theory and put forward in voluminous studies by Krämer 1959 (*see* especially 249–486 with references), 1964, and Gaiser 1959: 18–19, 1963, 1964; cf. Oehler 1965.

15. The didactic path in *Smp.* 210a–212a (cf. *Hp.Ma.* 286ab, 292c–293a; Friedländer II² 99, 101, 104) is not essentially different from the educational program in *Lg.* (*see* e.g. I.636a–e, I.643–II.674c, VII.788a–818e); the education of the Guardians in *R.* (cf. Raven 1965: 120–124) is kept more austere, but nevertheless starts with μῦθος (II.376d–378e) and παιδιά (VII.536e–537a) and ends with λόγος (VII.534b–e) and ἀναγκαῖον (VII.540b). Cf. also *Sph.* 230b–d, on the elenctic method.

16. Some important remarks relating to this topic in Alline 1915: 2–6, 27–50.

17. Cf. Gigon 1955, Friedländer II² 142. The eccentric view of Zürcher 1954 that the entire Corpus Platonicum is spurious requires no serious consideration here, nor do the charges of plagiarism which sometimes in antiquity were brought against Plato (*see* E. Stemplinger, *Das Plagiat*, 1912: 25–27).

[13] of a School was normal in Greece down to the Hellenistic age, and no conscious "forgery" need be assumed in such instances. My personal impression is that the following works in the Corpus are predominantly or entirely spurious insofar as their stylistic form is concerned: the very artless *Just.*,[18] and *Virt.*,[19] the rather more elabo-
[14] rate *Hp.Ma.*,[20] *Hipparch.*,[21] and *Thg.*,[22] and the otherwise dubious compilations *Alc.* 1,[23]

---

18. This is probably a product of the early Platonic school (hardly Arcesilaic, as Schmeken 1950 thinks), and it represents the kind of argument referred to in *Clit.* 407d.

19. The connection with *Men.* is evident; see Souilhé 1930: 24–26. But if it were an imitation of *Men.* made for exercise in a rhetorical school, as Souilhé thinks, we should expect it to be more elaborate. It may be, like *Just.*, a product of Plato's teaching in the Academy about the times when he planned *Men.*; indeed, it may even be earlier, as the motif of inspiration in the *Ion* seems to suggest.

20. Considered spurious by the great majority of scholars who have penetrated the problem; see the reconsideration by Horn 1964. In recent years only Friedländer II² 97–107, Soreth 1953, Hoerber 1955 and 1964, and with some hesitation Gigon 1955, have defended the authenticity. The question is highly complicated, especially if one assumes (with Hoerber) that the dialogue was written as a specimen of Socratic method at a not very early date. To the indications of a date later than, say, 385 BCE. I would add the reference to Eudoxus 287e: the word εὔδοξος is poetical and so rare in Plato (twice in *Lg.*) that its occurrence in this connection must imply a special point. Hoerber 1964 regards as Platonic the triads and the interlockings noticeable in the composition. My impression is that the dialogue is a good imitation of Plato's art, but that it is somewhat too mechanically composed, and that the stylistic variation and the character-drawing is not sufficiently subtle, to be by Plato's own hand. Besides, Plato cannot really be expected to have written two Hippiases. For the anonymous critic appearing in the dialogue (from 286c onwards), see n. 114.

21. Considered authentic by Friedländer but by very few others; references in Friedländer II² 293 n. 1, 295–296. There seem to be no real linguistic or stylistic arguments against the authenticity (but note the unique ναίχι 232a). But on the other hand the contents and the manner of composition look suspicious, and Friedländer's interpretation has not convinced me. Possibly the dialogue could be taken as a very early work, rather the oldest in the whole Corpus, and then it would be a very important document. But the "historical" digression in *Hipparch.* 228b–229d recalls similar digressions in *Alc.* 1, *Alc.* 2 and *Min.* (see Dönt 1963), and they were probably modeled on the genuinely Platonic central vision (p. 47) rather than vice versa. So the priority of *Hipparch.* seems questionable.

22. In spite of Friedländer's eloquent defense of *Thg.* (II² 135–142 with notes) I hesitate to accept it as genuine. I agree with Friedländer that the affinities with other writings, notably *Ap., La., Smp.* and *Tht.*, do not necessarily indicate that *Thg.* is dependent on these. They may independently go back to the same oral traditions. The same may apply to the rather striking combination of a reference to the person of Theages with a reference to the δαιμόνιον of Socrates in *R.* VI.496bc. I also agree that the late date supposed by Souilhé (1930: 137–142) and others is very unlikely, and that *Thg.* is rather early Platonic in setting and spirit. Indeed, if the apologetic character of the dialogue is stressed it may be put in the environment of *Ap.* and *Cri.* Yet the ironical distance to the naiveties in the speech on the δαιμόνιον 128d–130e is not sufficiently clear to be Platonic, the careful stylistic characterization of the speakers seems to me somewhat overdone, and the idioms do not sound altogether genuine.

23. This is an old battlefield for attacks on Platonic authorship. The chief defendant in recent years has been Friedländer; note also Motte 1961. Among the arguments against the authenticity (for older references, see Ueberweg-Praechter I¹³ 87*, Dittmar 1912: 65–173, later Leisegang 1950: 2367f., Cherniss 1959: 71, Dönt 1964) I find the judgment of Gauss 1.2.13–14 particularly pertinent (in spite of Friedländer II² 317 n. 1): the dialogue looks like a compendium of Platonic philosophy. In fact this character extends even to formal matters such as the broad representation of typical Socratic attitudes and phrases. Yet the style is remarkably flat. It has certain

*Alc.* 2,[24] *Amat.*,[25] *Clit.*,[26] *Sis.*,[27] *Min.*,[28] and *Erx.*[29] But these works stand in various ways close to Plato's manner, and it will be necessary to consider them below for comparison. On the other hand, *Demod.*,[30] *Ep.* 1–6 and 8–13,[31]

[15]

[16]

---

un-Platonic devices such as μᾶλλά 114e (Denniston 1954: 5). The dialogue clearly has a didactic purpose and cannot be very early. On the other hand it is hardly later than the 380s (*see* the following note). I find it impossible that Plato would have produced such flat circumstantiality for such a purpose about the times when he wrote *Grg.* Various portions may of course derive from genuine drafts (cf. Clark 1955), so perhaps also the central historical speech 120e–124b the irony of which may have sounded more genuinely Socratic in a different context.

24. The early Academic and Socratic character of this dialogue has been emphasized by Souilhé 1930: 9–18, against the very late date assumed by some scholars. I am prepared to go as early as the 380s. Both *Alc.* 2 and *Alc.* 1 represent earlier stages of the stories current about Socrates and Alcibiades than *Smp.*; for instance, *Alc.* 2.151ab probably derives from the same source as *Smp.* 213e, and it shows that the author probably was not acquainted with *Smp.* For the affinities of the composition of *Alc.* 1, *Alc.* 2, *Hipparch.* and *Min.*, see Dönt 1963. *Alc.* 2 is more vivid in style than *Alc.* 1 (*see* p. 157), but it is also straightforwardly naive.

25. The similarity to *Chrm.* is generally recognized; cf. Souilhé 1930: 107–110 who (112) wants to refer the dialogue to the times of Polemon. I am not sure it is necessary to go later than the 370s. The dialogue is a harmless and fairly correct piece of imitation, including matters of composition and style. The fact that the interlocutors of Socrates remain anonymous indicates that the author has not attempted a forgery, but merely a specimen of Socratic and Platonic methods of thought; Isnardi 1954 in my opinion over-emphasizes the ambitions of the author.

26. *Clit.* has been considered authentic by several scholars, among them Souilhé 1930: 169–179 (where further references), Stefanini 1949: 1. 203 n. 3, Gaiser 1959: 140–147. Friedländer II[2] 45 avoids taking a definite view. I find the language slightly un-Platonic (e.g. συνεπιθυμητής 408c, δίδαγμα 409b, λεγέσθω 409d, γιγνέσθω 410d, θές 410d), though it is possible to regard the stiff rhetorical formality of Socrates as a conscious attitude. The composition is curious (*see* p. 157). But *Clit.* can hardly be very late (in spite of Ritter 1888: 93), and it is reasonable to suppose that the references to *R.* I (for which, *see* Souilhé) imply that *R.* I had been published, but not yet the rest of the *R.*

27. A fairly ambitious imitation of Plato; cf. Souilhé 1930: 62–65, with references. The style is literary, slightly artificial and clearly un-Platonic. I do not think Isnardi's (1954) early dating is possible and I prefer, with Souilhé, to put it in the latter part of the 4th century.

28. *Min.* is considerably different from *Hipparch.* and can hardly be coupled with it as is often done. Though there are little positive criteria of spuriousness, the author's naivety (cf. Souilhé 1930: 81–82) and lack of skill are obvious. Particularly un-Platonic I find to be the lack of balance between the definitory first part of the dialogue, and the protreptic second part, both regarding the contents, the composition, and the style; and the conclusion is probably intended to be aporetic in the manner of the typically Socratic dialogues. A post-Platonic, yet 4th century, date has been suggested by Souilhé and Isnardi 1954.

29. *Erx.* is a very ambitious imitation of Platonic method, composition, and style. Its post-Platonic origin cannot be doubted. There are some indications, such as possible Stoic reminiscences, the reference to the gymnasiarch 399a, and some late words, pointing to the 3rd century. *See* Souilhé 1930: 83–89 and Gartmann 1949.

30. Socratic and/or sophistic ἀπορίαι. There is nothing particularly Platonic about them, and the absence of Socrates' name suggests that Plato has nothing to do with them. An early date has been proposed by Isnardi 1954.

31. The spuriousness of the letters, except *Ep.* 7 and possibly *Ep.* 8, is now almost universally agreed upon; *see* the sensible analyses of Souilhé 1926. Taylor's (15–16) generous and "anti-authoritarian" acceptance of them all except *Ep.* 1 requires no serious refutation, nor Wilamowitz' (II 281) equally subjective judgment in favor of *Ep.* 6. Ritter, *Neue Untersuchungen über Platon* 1910: 327 ff., has not succeeded in defending *Ep.* 3. The majority of the letters seem to reflect the biographical and

[16] *Ax.*,[32] and *Def.* are totally irrelevant to a study of Plato's style. Possibly these restrictions of the material will exclude something that later research will prove to be Plato's ipsissima verba, but this would not alter the picture of Plato's use of style to any notable extent. I trust that the same will apply to those parts of the material included in my analysis, which are possibly interpolations by later hands.

Another difficulty arises from the question whether Plato himself (or some of his intimate pupils) revised his works in accordance with new achievements [17] or new intentions. There is a general likelihood that this was what happened, especially if his writings were continually used for exercise or instruction in the Academy already in his life-time. Dionysius of Halicarnassus (De comp. verb. 208–209) explicitly states that Plato continued to curl and comb the tresses of his dialogues to the last; and if this is true, it must have concerned matters of style as well as the contents.[33] A few of the dialogues bear fairly clear marks of revision. The best-known case is *R.*, for which many scholars since Hermann have assumed a successive expansion. Very many take the first book, sometimes called "Thrasymachus," to be a relatively early dialogue that, with some alternations, was made the basis for the rest.[34] Another much-disputed case is *Phdr.* which also looks curiously heterogeneous.[35] A revision of *Tht.* appears to be hinted at in the

---

Pythagorean interests of the Academy for the next few generations after Plato's death. Stylistically they are either somewhat flat and unambitious imitations of Plato's conversational manner (*Ep.* 2, *Ep.* 9, *Ep.* 12, *Ep.* 13), or rather more ambitious but even more unsuccessful pastiches of *Ep.* 7 (*Ep.* 3, *Ep.* 4, *Ep.* 10, *Ep.* 11; for *Ep.* 8 see below). *Ep.* 6 is overambitiously expansive and pathetic. *Ep.* 1 and *Ep.* 5 (cf. Socr. *Ep.* 31, Plato to Philip) are entirely different from the rest, with only remote echoes of Platonic biography and none at all of Platonic style.—*Ep.* 8 has fairly generally been regarded as authentic, partly because great scholars such as Wilamowitz, Taylor, and Friedländer have accepted it, partly perhaps because *Ep.* 8 seems to be so inseparably associated with *Ep.* 7. Even the cautious Souilhé (1926: LXI–LXVII) is inclined to accept *Ep.* 8. I find this impossible. Not only the banal considerations, the would-be wise tone and the character of the advice given seem to me entirely un-Platonic; but the rhetorical style, polished throughout, has little to do with what can be expected of Plato, especially in a letter written shortly after *Ep.* 7 and addressed to the same audience.

32. This compilation is essentially a speech of consolation, partly broken up into dialogue, and with a "frame" dialogue attached to it, though not consistently carried out. For the late style, the anachronisms, the influences (from Crantor among others), and the myth, see Souilhé 1930: 123–136, who would date the work in the 1st century BCE—Further, Ps.-Lucian's "Alkyon" has sometimes been ascribed to Plato; see Brinkmann 1891. Diog. L. 3.62 mentions 6 spurious dialogues which have not come down to us. Athen. 506d refers to a dialogue named Cimon.

33. Stenzel 1956: 335 assumes that Plato often used earlier drafts and even complete works when composing the dialogues as we have them.

34. The name "Thrasymachus" was first used by Dümmler (1891). For references to literature on the problem, see Ueberweg-Praechter I[13] 79*–81*, further Friedländer II[2] 283 n. 1, Cherniss 1959: 161–162. In later years Vretska (especially 1958) has advocated the unity of the *R.* But the differences in approach and style, and also the references to *R.* in *Clit.* (above n. 26), possibly *Ti.*, remain important indications of heterogeneous composition. Cf. below, p. 111.

35. Revision has been assumed by Gomperz and later by many others, often in connection with the vexed chronological problem; references in Ueberweg-Praechter I[13] 81*–82*, Friedländer III 466 n. 1.

36. An extensive revision was assumed notably by Chiappelli 1904 and later by e.g. Wilamowitz I 515–516, II 235–236 (cf. the cautious review of the problem by Diès 1927: 317–332),

text (143a–c).[36] The heterogeneousness of the *Lg.* is notorious and suggests a combination of many different layers, perhaps revision even during Plato's lifetime.[37] To assume a later revision would help to explain some anomalies of *Grg.*,[38] *Men.*,[39] *Prm.*,[40] and *Phlb.*[41] Is *Ly.* an adaption of a theme taken from an early dramatic dialogue?[42] Was *Smp.* originally a collection of speeches with a dramatic frame, like *Mx.* with its single speech (but a promise of more to follow, 249e), and the first part of *Phdr.*? And has *Phd.* expanded from a minor biographical and apologetic dialogue like *Cri.*? However all this may be, if the supposed revision was extensive and thorough, as in *Ly., Grg., Smp., Phd.* and *Phlb.*, there should be no hesitation in classing the dialogue according to the date of revision rather than the date of the first version; but the rest of the examples above may serve as reminders against an application of a rigid chronology to Plato's writings.

[17]

[18]

The third problem to be mentioned here is the possible chronological relevance of the use of reported dialogue. The reported form occurs with some variation in eight dialogues[43]: *Ly., Chrm., Euthd., Prt., Phd., Smp., R., Prm.* In *Tht.* 143ac the reported form is explicitly abandoned. It is really very tempting to infer that all eight belong closely together to the same period, and rather, perhaps, to the middle period.[44] But apart from the real or supposed results of detailed stylometry, there is a serious obstacle against this assumption in the fact that some dramatic dialogues, notably *Grg., Men.* and *Cra.*, appear to represent a considerable advance from the level of *Ly.* and *Chrm.*, yet without reaching the levels of *R.* and *Prm.* Most scholars solve the dilemma by thinking that the form of the dialogue is of no consequence to chronology.[45] I strongly disagree.

[19]

---

also by Cornford 1935: 1, 15, Gauss III 1. 74. In spite of Friedländer's (III² 131–132, 151–156, 171) arguments for unity, I find the theory of revision quite reasonable. It is true that if sections such as 147c–148b and 172c–177c have been later inserted, they have been carefully worked into the whole composition. Antiquity knew two versions of the introduction (*Anonymer Kommentar zu Platons Theätet*, Berliner Klassikertexte ed. Diels-Schubart, 1905). Cf. below p. 117.

37. Cf. Döring 1907, Billings 1920: 47–52, G. Müller 1951, Gigon, "Das Einleitungsgespräch der Gesetze Platons" (1954); Gauss III 2.209–210; Görgemanns' (1960) theory of an exoteric protreptic purpose of the *Lg.* does not contradict this view, nor do the occasional indications of a deliberate arrangement of the material (cf. Taylor 466, Friedländer III² 362–381, 508 n. 37, 509 n. 46).

38. Thus Gauss II 1.40–41, doubted by Dodds 1959: 16 n. 1.

39. The Anytus episode 89e–95a looks like a later insertion; cf. Koller 1948: 81–84.

40. In spite of Wyller's (1960) arguments for a coherent structure of *Prm.*, the contrast in form between the first and the second part of the dialogue is quite remarkable. *See* below, p. 139.

41. If this late tract is based on an early "Socratic" dialogue, the revision is very extensive, indeed almost complete. But here, as in *Prm.*, the first part has more touches left of Socratism than the second (main) part.

42. Cf. below n. 53.

43. For details, *see* below p. 36 ff.

44. The extreme positions of Schöne (1862, *see* Lutoslawski 1897: 80) who thought that the reported dialogues were the last that Plato wrote, and Teichmüller 1879, who thought that Plato began by writing them, cannot of course be held any longer.

45. Cf. e.g. D. Tarrant 1926: 107 who thinks that Plato chose the form according to his purposes and mood, and Schaerer 1938: 190–207, Andrieu 1954: 283–286. Only Stefanini 1949 (*see* especially

[19] In my opinion the differences between the reported and the dramatic dialogue are quite remarkable—here I follow Stefanini 1949–, and they include manners of composition and style which make shifts from one type to the other seem difficult. The fact that Plato formally preserved the reported form in the later *R*. and in the first part of *Prm.*, in spite of its obvious disadvantages, until he finally and expressively gave it up in *Tht.*, indicates a practice to which he had become accustomed and from which he did not find it altogether easy to free himself. The theory that the eight were really composed successively one after another may get some support from the above considerations of different audiences and possible revision. I shall return to the problem presently.

∘-∘-∘- 〇 -∘-∘-∘

Considering all this, as well as the unreliability of traditional stylometry for a detailed chronology, I feel myself free to propose a theory for the order of the dialogues which suits the present purpose better than the theories so far current. It should be noted that the following survey does not claim to be even a hypothetical chronology in all details, because as I see it this would require a thorough reconsideration of an enormous mass of data. Here I can only hope to make the order chosen look somehow reasonable both as an order for analyzing the style and as an internal chronological order. I trust that the results of the analysis will in general confirm the former aspect, even if they do not contribute much to the latter. Cf. p. 142.

I would begin with *Hp.Mi.* and *Ion*, for which an early date is fairly generally agreed upon. These two dialogues can be called *mimetic*, and they were probably addressed to a closed circle of friends in the mid-nineties.[46]

[20] There must be reasons other than the mere freshness of the impression why Plato later returned to the death of Socrates. I would assume that the public discussion of Socrates' person, of which the pamphlet of Polycrates is a sign, occasioned Plato in the late 390s to address a wider public than before, and to make a more clearly *apologetic* and protreptic approach to the role played by his master. *La.*

---

I.LXXIII–LXXXI) thinks that the reported dialogues belong together, but his arguments are partly different from mine. Cf. below p. 17.

46. This point was explicitly made by Alline 1915: 3–4; cf. the interesting inference of Andrieu 1954: 288–307 that the earliest Plato manuscripts lacked character sigla, which means that the dramatic dialogues cannot have been intended for unprepared reading. On the other hand it is clear that Plato in the 390s would not have introduced Socrates to the general public in a manner which would make him seem an "erist" and immoralist. Cf. also below, p. 17.—*Hp.Mi.* is somewhat less advanced than *Ion*. The only reason for putting it after *Ion* would be that it has three characters; but Plato wrote dialogues for only two characters as late as the Phdr.Ion can be dated about 394 BCE; *see* the reconsideration of the problem by Flashar 1958: 96–105 (cf. also Diller, "Probleme des platonischen Ion" 1955: 171–187, who regards *Ion* as semi-spurious, and Vicaire 1960: 10 n. 1, who however would not date *Ion* very early). I find it difficult to imagine, with Friedländer and others (notably M. Wundt, "Die Zeitfolge der platonischen Gespräche" 1949: 29 ff.), Plato writing Socratic dialogues during the life-time of Socrates.

perhaps opened this period.[47] *Cri.* and *Ap.* naturally belong here.[48] The *Mx.* can [20] perhaps be taken as Plato's ironical farewell to public life in Athens before he set out on his first voyage to the West about 386 BCE.[49]

After his return to Athens Plato is said to have begun teaching at the Acade- [21] meia. I like to think that the forcible and strongly protreptic *Grg.* opened this *early instructional* period. After *Grg.* it is customary to put *Men.*[50] After *Men.* I somewhat hesitatingly insert *Euthphr.* as a parergon.[51] Then Plato would have written the *Cra.* which was clearly not intended for a general public.[52]

Plato had thus by the late 380s passed through the 'mimetic,' 'apologetic' and first 'instructional' stages and ended in the ironical pose of *Cra.* He had secured his fame as a writer and teacher, and he started to face the problems that were to occupy him in his later age. This is the situation in which the period of the *reported dialogues* is likely to have originated (cf. Stefanini 1949: I 159–211). As I see it, his aim was at first to create a "Socrates glorified" and perhaps a course of "Protreptic to philosophy" for people who were unable to listen to him personally, that is to say, for the educated public outside the Academy. He adopted

---

47. Steidle 1950 argues that *La.* is Plato's earliest work because it is more concerned with political education than with polemics against the sophists. Though his arguments have been accepted by some scholars (e.g. Gaiser 1959: 111 n. 116, Nagel 1962), I cannot find them convincing. But I agree with Steidle that *La.* seems to belong together with *Cri.* and *Ap.*

48. The doubts of Friedländer II² 287 n. 2 (cf. III² 423) about the apologetic purpose of these and other writings are in my opinion unwarranted.—For *Ap.*, cf. in particular Coulter 1964; Alline 1915: 4 cannot be right in regarding *Ap.* as esoteric.—*Cri.* is probably close to *Ap.* in time. The connections between *Cri.* and *Grg.*, pointed out by Friedländer II² 164, seem to support my theory of a close association of the "apologetic" and "early instructional" periods but probably do not indicate that the dialogues come next to each other in the chronology, as Böhme 1959: 17–45 thinks. The connections between *Cri.* and *Phd.* (see especially Fox 1956) are clearly irrelevant to chronology. I have put *Cri.* before *Ap.* only because it is half-way between "mime" and "speech," but the order could equally well be the opposite.—According to my view (cf. below p. 18) early versions of later dialogues such as *Lysis* may also have originated in this period.

49. *Mx.* 244b–246a refers to the Corinthian war which ended in 386 BCE. In *Ep.* 7.324a Plato says that he was σχεδὸν ἔτη τετταράκοντα when he went to Sicily for the first time, and he was probably born in 427. But σχεδόν means "approximately," as it does two lines before. Is it possible that Plato should have risked such a voyage before the war was over?

50. In putting *Grg.* and *Men.* immediately after the founding of the Academy I agree with the opinion of most scholars. In recent years only Hoerber and Böhme have doubted the conventional date. Hoerber 1960: 78–82 prefers to remain skeptical regarding chronology. Böhme 1959: 79–89, 99–102 regards *Grg.* as very early. Though his many unconventional redatings do not prove a new chronology, his point that *Prt.* is later than *Grg.* can be conciliated with the rather indisputable fact (which he has not seen; though cf. Taylor 103) that *Grg.* is the more advanced of the two, by making the assumptions suggested below regarding the "reported" dialogues.

51. In spite of its seemingly "early" form *Euthphr.* is rather sophisticated. See Raeder 1905: 127–130, Gigon 1954, and Patzer 1965: 33–34.

52. *See* the extensive discussion by Luce 1964 who accepts the date 384/3 BCE; cf. Ilting 1965: 381. Some would go considerably later, notably Natorp 1900: 20, Warburg 1929: 31–61; cf. Gaiser 1963: 255–258. But the unmistakable points of contact between *Cra.*, *Tht.* and *Sph.* can be explained otherwise than by a chronological affinity; and when all is said stylistic reasons seem to exclude a late date for *Cra.*

the reported form of memoir literature (cf. below p. 45) which was better suited than the dramatic form for reading by a single unprepared reader and, therefore, more suitable for general circulation. He began by re-writing older material, until then existing in drafts or "published" only for friends or pupils: *Ly.*,[53] *Chrm.*,[54] *R.* I,[55] *Prt.*,[56] *Euthd.*,[57] *Phd.* and *Smp.*[58] Plato then for many years went on discussing and teaching the problems that had emerged from the *R.* I and from the theory of Forms, and so the original plan for the *R.* expanded to comprise all aspects of human life. During his work with *R.* he began to write the *Prm.*, but here the plan was soon changed to suit the more esoteric purpose of an appendix to the theory of Forms and of an exercise in Zenonian dialectic for internal use in the Academy.[59] Before the *R.* was finished he had also faced the new problems and approaches which led to the writing of *Tht.* and *Phdr.*, and to the final abandoning of reported dialogue.

The period after *Smp.* may be called Plato's *critical* period, and the internal order accepted here, *Prm.*, *Tht.*, *Phdr.*, rests primarily on the following considerations. *Tht.* arises from a similar need to clear up the conditions of knowledge and argument as the *Prm.*, but it is curiously different in many respects. The difference may be explained by assuming that *Tht.* is a revision of an earlier work or draft from the environment of *Cra.*, and written in the manner of *Ly.* and *Chrm.*; and the leaving out of the report was not only, as is sometimes assumed, a conscious reaction against the awkwardness of the first part of *Prm.*, but also perhaps due to a similar change of purpose as was suggested above for *Prm.* It should be noted that the terminus post quem usually given, 369 BCE, is probably too late

---

53. There are some possible indications that *Ly.* was originally a dramatic dialogue, notably the reoccurrence of the same mention in the narrative and in a following utterance in 203ab, 204bc. A comparatively late date has been assumed by Ritter 1888: 139–140, Hoerber 1959: 15–16.

54. While *Ly.* ends in a seemingly bewildered aporia, like *Ion* and *Hp.Mi.*, the conclusion of *Chrm.* contains a promise of future teaching, like *La.* and *Mx.*

55. Cf. above n. 34.

56. The advanced art of this work has sometimes been underrated, especially by Wilamowitz I.146, 153, Gigon 1946: 103–151, Koller 1948: 93–110; cf. Friedländer II² 324. Note in particular the gradual and ironical change of Protagoras' and Socrates' positions, the latter beginning as the pupil and ending as the teacher. The early date advocated by Wilamowitz seems to me out of the question. Cf. Martens 1954: 66 ff.

57. Note here the protreptic conclusion.

58. It can hardly be doubted that these two dialogues belong closely together, and after some hesitation I have decided to take *Smp.* 223d to indicate that their internal order of publication was *Phd.*—*Smp.* The motif and myth of *Phd.* develop ideas present in *Cri.*, *Ap.*, and *Grg.*; *Smp.* again proceeds on the lines of *Ion*, *Mx.*, and *Ly.* Both may be dated not later than the beginning of the 370s; see Dover 1965: 15. The very late date suggested by Lönborg 1939: 153 for *Smp.* is unthinkable.

59. The esoteric character of *Prm.*, especially of its latter part, is evident. *R.*, again, is regarded as a typical exoteric work by Gauss II 2.118–119. I find his observation interesting, in particular as regards the internal relationship of *R.* and *Prm.*, though he certainly goes too far in denying the philosophical relevance of *R.*—The problem of the really esoteric Plato (see above n. 14) is admittedly a great problem, but I think it is fair to say that the extant works represent different degrees of exoterism.

by some ten years or more.⁶⁰ The highly problematic *Phdr.* may have its roots in the environment of *Smp.*, perhaps even *Ion*, but the extant version points forward to the late period. *Phdr.* seems to attempt a reconciliation of philosophy and rhetoric under the formula of "psychagogy," and thus it is also concerned with the conditions of argument. But contrary to *Prm.* and *Tht.* it is not esoteric but addressed to Isocrates and his school, as the remark at the end appears to indicate.⁶¹

It may well be that *R.* was not completed until after the second voyage to Sicily about 366 BCE,⁶² but the bulk of the work must have been ready, and therefore it is convenient for the present purpose to put *R.* II–X before that date.

Plato's *late* period can reasonably be said to begin with his return from Sicily about 365 BCE. His experiences in Sicily had meant considerable disillusionment to him, but he tried to go on where he had left. I prefer to think that he began by writing to *R.* the "appendices" on the cosmic State and the State of ideal legend, known as *Ti.* and *Criti.* At the same time he perhaps made a final revision of the *R.*,⁶³ *Ti.* and *Criti.* were planned as parts of a separate trilogy. Plato then changed

---

60. Against the usual assumption that the writing of the dialogue, or its revision (cf. above n. 36), was occasioned by the recent death of Theaitetos in a battle at Corinth (142a–c; *see* in particular Sachs 1914: 18–40), it can be claimed that basing a dialogue on a recent event would be unique in the case of Plato. And since Plato as a rule does not introduce characters still living, the opening dialogue between Euclides and Terpsion seems to imply that they too were dead when the introduction was written. Now, the battle in question was not necessarily that of 369 BCE; it may have been the battle of 394 BCE or some battle in the Corinthian war (390–387 BCE), as Campbell 1883: LX II suggested. It should be remembered that mathematicians usually reach their peak of brilliance at a young age. But though the only certain terminus post quem is 394 BCE, *Tht.* is clearly later than the standard of *Grg.* and *Men.* On the other hand stylistic reasons suggest that *Tht.* comes at a considerable distance before *Sph.* and *Plt.*, i.e. before the second voyage to Sicily. Those who believe with Wilamowitz (I 525–526, 532, II 230–232) that the digression on philosophical life (172c–177c) could only have been written after the disappointments in Sicily, have to face the fact that this conflict occurs in many works beginning with *Grg.* The reasons why Plato revised *Tht.* (if he did it) remain unclear.

61. A date prior to the second voyage has been accepted by the majority of scholars; *see* especially Robin 1947: III–IX, Cherniss 1957: 231–233. A recent exception is Webster 1956: 58–60, who argues from the chronology of Theodectes, Isocrates and Aristotle that *Phdr.* is later than 362 BCE. I cannot see that his points really outweigh the difficulties of fitting in *Phdr.* among the late dialogues. Nor is the "pastoral" feeling of the introduction sufficient reason for assuming that it was written under recent Sicilian impressions; *see* Thesleff, "Stimmungsmalerei oder Burleske? Der Stil von Platons Phaidros 230bc und seine Funktion" (1967).

62. This has been suggested by e.g. Geffcken II 115. I find it difficult to think that *R.* III.544b–IX.592a was written in its present shape before Plato's experiences in Sicily. Cf. below p. 98.

63. On the themes of *Ti.* and *Criti.* and their connection with *R.*, see Friedländer III² 332 (cf. Muthmann 1961: 72–97 with references.). The much-discussed partial summary of *R.* at the beginning of *Ti.* may really imply that *R.* had been only partially published at the date when Plato began writing the *Ti.*—The date of *Ti.* and *Criti.* has been subject to much controversy. In recent years only Owen 1953 has advocated a very early date; but cf. Cherniss 1957, 1959: 65–66, Rist 1960. The common view is that they are later than *Sph.* and *Plt.*, or, as some think, even later than the third voyage to Sicily about 360 BCE (thus e.g. Wilamowitz I 586). Friedländer III² 417 and Brandwood 1958: 334–343 incline to date them before *Sph.* and *Plt.* I can find no really reliable criteria, but I think it psychologically probable that Plato was still deeply concerned with the State on his return to Athens about 365, but wanted to escape from it into myth and legend. The

[24] his mind and planned another trilogy, for a more esoteric and technical purpose, and linked it up with *Prm.* and in particular *Tht.: Sph., Plt.,* and "Philosophus" which was never written.[64]

[25] In order to place *Phlb.* at a considerable distance from both of the uncompleted trilogies, I would assume that Plato did not start working with it until after his final return to Athens in 360 BCE.[65] This would also agree with what we know of the Pythagorean bent of Plato's latest oral teaching.[66] *Ep. 7* was written soon after 354 BCE.[67] The *Lg.* certainly extend over a long period of time; they may contain parts written in the 360s, possibly even earlier, but they were still unfinished when Plato died in 347.[68] *Epin.* is closely related to *Lg.* and probably has to be regarded as substantially Platonic.[69]

---

combination of μῦθος and λόγος in *Ti.* and *Criti.* also somehow parallel the *Phdr.* The fact that *Criti.* is incomplete and *Ti.* lacks a final touch (thus e.g. Wilamowitz I 592, Geffcken II 141; the observations on the art of *Ti.* made by Shorey 1888: 408–409 and Friedländer III³ 353–355 have not convinced me of the contrary) proves that they were never published for a general public in Plato's life-time. But of course it is not necessary to assume that any dramatic event such as Plato's being summoned to Sicily for the last time occasioned the break (cf. p. 121). Perhaps Plato simply exhausted himself in myths and returned to philosophy.

64. Unless Philebus is an ironical substitute for the "Philosophus" (*Sph.* 217a); possibly Philebus was no real person. *Sph.* 217c not only explicitly mentions the *Prm.,* but also (note μακρῷ λόγῳ) seems to imply that the audience knew the existence of *Ti.* The dependence of *Sph.* and *Plt.* on *Tht.* is obvious from the choice of characters as well as the topic and approach, and some (among them Klein 1965: 27) speak of a "trilogy" *Tht.—Sph.—Plt.*; but stylistic reasons really exclude the possibility that *Tht.* and *Sph.* were written in close succession. It is customary to date *Sph.* and *Plt.* between the last two visits to Sicily (thus e.g. Friedländer III² 273). The objection of Taylor 371 that Plato did not have much time for writing before he finally returned to Athens in 360 is hardly pertinent; after all he was teaching in Athens for several years between the voyages, cf. Hackforth 1945: 1–2.

65. Date of the Olympic games mentioned in *Ep. 7* 350b. In putting *Phlb.* late I agree with the chronology usually accepted. *Phlb.* is complete in itself (in spite of the opening and concluding remarks), and it is the only Platonic dialogue actually constructed as a discursive tract (in spite of its returning to Socrates, the master of elenchus). It must come either before or after the two trilogies, and it is decidedly more likely to come after.

66. The material about the lecture Π. τἀγαθοῦ in Gaiser 1963. *Ti.* (and *Criti.*) is not distinctly Pythagorean, though the post-Platonic tradition thought so and some modern scholars (notably Taylor 1928) have tried to prove it.

67. Date of Dion's death; see Souilhé 1926: XXXVII. It is rather generally agreed now that *Ep. 7* is authentic; cf. Cherniss 1959: 92–93. Since Shorey (1933) few scholars have athetized the whole letter; G. Müller 1949 and Edelstein 1965 may be mentioned (a postscript reference to G. Ryle, *Plato's Progress,* 1966 may be added), but cf. Friedländer I² 354 n. 3 (add K. v. Fritz, "Die philosophische Stelle im siebten platonischen Brief und die Frage der 'esoterichen' Philosophie Platons." (1966): 117–153). The complicated composition and the subtle shifts of style seem to me entirely Platonic; cf. Souilhé 1926: XLI–XLV. Cf. above n. 31.

68. I do not find any reason to doubt the tradition of posthumous publication. The different layers of *Lg.* are open to dispute; cf. Döring 1907, Gauss III 2.209–210, Gigon 1954, Morrow ap. Düring 1960, Friedländer III² 417, 513 n. 86. Görgemanns' theory (1960) of a "popular," i.e. exoteric and protreptic, character of *Lg.* (contrary to e.g. *Sph., Plt.,* and *Phlb.*) clearly contains some truth but over-simplifies the matter: for instance, the practical purpose of the prooimia and the regulations and laws is different from the purpose of the sections on education and statesmanship, and the public in view was not the same.

69. This is the opinion of a large number of scholars, notably (Ueberweg-) Praechter I¹³ 326, Taylor, Raeder 1938, des Places 1952, Novotný 1960, Manasse 1961: 53 (against G. Müller).

## General observations on style and styles. Remarks on methods. [26]

It will be necessary here to deal at length with some theoretical questions which do not seem to have received much attention in classical studies.

For the present purpose we shall use the term "style" in the wide sense in which it is generally accepted to-day.[70] Thus "style" is not the equivalent of "good style" or of any "literary style." Also any piece of non-literary spoken language can have a "style."

Style is often viewed "impressionistically" as the sum of those features in a text which somehow strike the reader as being remarkable. When dealing with dead languages it is of course advisable to attempt an objectification of the stylistic criteria. The most common method then is to discuss the occurrence in an author of those linguistic phenomena which have been traditionally regarded as "stylistic," e.g. imagery, sentence construction, antithesis, assonance, repetition, rhythm, and so forth; perhaps also such features as the provenance of the vocabulary and the use of strengthening expressions. There are however several obvious reasons why this method is unsatisfactory for a general study of the function and the structure of Platonic style. It is clear that categories such as those mentioned are largely rhetorical and aesthetic in origin, and so they cannot cover the whole range of Plato's styles—in spite of the fact that a complete list [27] of such features in the Platonic corpus would fill a volume. A selection again of either some features or some passages would be hazardous. Furthermore, with an author such as Plato, who changes his style within very brief units of text, a successive record of the different phenomena would make little sense unless we also consider how and where they combine, and this would lead to an awkward system of cross-references. And similar combinations, suggesting similar patterns, would then demand a third approach. But as it is only through *patterns* that the function of style can be really grasped, the first analytic record would seem rather meaningless.

How then can stylistic patterns be studied in practice? The following considerations will perhaps help us a bit further.

---

Among those who think *Epin.* predominantly un-Platonic, Wilamowitz, Friedländer, Leisegang 1950: 2368, and G. Müller 1951 may be mentioned. I cannot see that the arguments from the contents prove anything, because Plato may have changed his cosmological conception considerably since he wrote the *Ti.* F. Müller 1928 tried to prove that the style of *Epin.* is imitating, but different from, that of *Lg.* but his arguments have been largely refuted by G. Müller 1951 (who thinks both *Lg.* and *Epin.* spurious). Without going into details I can see no notable differences (except at the end), and I find it unlikely that somebody could imitate the Platonic style of *Lg.* as closely, without overdoing it or introducing personal manners. But the problem requires a thorough investigation.

70. *See* the conspectus in Enkvist 1964. I am much indebted to Enkvist's considerations, though on some points my approach is different. I have also profited from Fowler 1966. Some more references in Hofmann-Szantyr, *Lateinische Syntax und Stilistik,* Handbuch der Altertumswissenschaft II.2.2 (1965): 686–688.

[27]　　I find it very important to make a distinction between generic and individual style, that is to say, between the *stylistic class or standard* as represented by a type of text or a genre, and the *stylistic structure or coloring* of a particular piece of text.

We may first discuss the stylistic coloring from a generic point of view and consider individual style as a *reproduction* of patterns.

To some extent, and particularly often in the conservative ancient languages and in authors like Plato who play with styles, the stylistic coloring can be determined by the degree of its approximation to one or several stylistic standards. This standard may in certain cases be the speaker or author himself; and in such cases we say that he uses his own typical style or "manner." More commonly we think at the same time, or solely, of a major stylistic class as the standard, such as, in 4th century Athens, e.g. dithyrambic poetry, epideictic rhetoric, historical narrative, educated conversation, or a combination of these standards; and in such cases we may say that the author uses dithyrambic style, rhetorical style, historical style, and/or conversational style.

Each stylistic standard is characterized by a number of peculiarities which, alone or in combination, make it stand out from other standards. Theoretically the number of peculiarities of each stylistic standard is very high, because a great part, probably the majority, of the existing linguistic units (forms, words, expressions, or types of expression) are preferably used in some classes of style and hardly used at all in others. Very many linguistic units thus have a more or less [28]　distinct *shade of style* owing to their habitual use in particular stylistic classes or genres. But difficulties may easily arise in determining this shade, because its presence and quality depends ultimately on the relative frequency of the expression in a particular type of context known to the author and/or reader. The peculiarities to be observed in stylistic studies may therefore for practical reasons be reduced to a few typical *style markers*.[71]

The stylistic coloring of a piece of text thus results, at least to some degree, from the combining of expressions carrying distinct stylistic shades, i.e. above all style markers. A stylistic shade usually extends to the whole of a passage (either because there is only one typical style marker and the rest is stylistically neutral, or because there are several style markers of the same class), and the passage may then be said to carry this shade. Often the same or similar shades cover large consecutive portions of a text, and then "shade" is in fact equivalent to "coloring." But there may occur considerable stylistic changes within very brief units of text. In an advanced cultural environment there are always a wide range of possibilities of reproducing styles, extending from a more or less consistent use of style markers of a certain class to a mixture of very different style markers, perhaps in a varying proportion to stylistically neutral expressions. And there is always a constant change of styles going on. The same linguistic unit may consequently act as a style marker for several stylistic classes successively[72]; and it may

---

71. I owe this term to Enkvist 1964: 34.
72. E.g. words such as οἶκτος or ἀνήκεστος which were adopted by orators like Gorgias from high poetry and later extended to rhetorical diction in general; or devices such as assonance

gradually alter its shade owing to a change of distribution, and the knowledge of the author and reader of this distribution. Which style it is the mark of—if it is the mark of any style at all—must be carefully pondered in each case separately.

Because mixture of styles is very common, and because many expressions act as markers of several styles, it is sometimes necessary to look for *leading style markers* in the first place, i.e. traits in principle characteristic of one style only, and according to these decide on the shade of other style markers in the context. And it is important to remember that isolated style markers may be only apparent: an over-attentive reader may find odd touches of style which are actually irrelevant for the author himself. On the whole, only the consecutive occurrence of two or more markers of the same style is a sufficiently reliable indication of the presence of this style.

It is also important to be able to check the shade of a style marker by considering its occurrence and distribution in the stylistic classes. But because of the limitations of the extant Greek material, mere numerical ratios will seldom suffice: other considerations must give cumulative support. And in practice persons with a reasonable knowledge of Greek will normally agree about the most distinct style markers without having to check their distribution any more than they need to check the use of common words to determine their meaning. Stylistic understanding is closely related to linguistic understanding. I am hoping for such inter-philological agreement on many points in the following.

We have so far considered the stylistic coloring of a text as resulting from a reproduction of standard patterns, or of some traits suggesting these patterns. From this point of view the individual character of the coloring depends on how the traits reproduced are combined. But this is obviously not sufficient as a determination of "style."

There is another approach to style which could be called "non-generic."

We sometimes speak of "style" as the entire linguistic form which a piece of text has taken (perhaps including extra-linguistic features such as the line division and the typography of a poem). This use of the term is of course vague and awkward and close to being meaningless; it is recommendable only if the text is viewed in contrast to another text or a set of texts which are somehow commensurable with it, because it is generally agreed that "style" should always imply a choice or at least the existence of alternatives.[73] It is rather more practical to concentrate on some features and say, for instance, that "style" is the collective characteristics af a text.[74] Then we are possibly not thinking of these characteristics as reproduced from a stylistic class or as reproduced in the author's own usage, but simply as features that we find somehow remarkable. By viewing "style" this way we may sometimes miss a point, the generic or "reproductive" aspect of style which may be evident to others and to the author himself. But sometimes

---

which the Gorgian style took over from old gnomic style but which later preserved its Gorgian mark in prose.

73. Cf. Enkvist 1964: 15–20, 35.
74. This is approximately the definition given in the *Concise Oxford Dictionary*.

[30] it is true, regarding at least some characteristics, that the approximation to a model or the idea of recurrence plays no part worth consideration. The more individual, dynamic and "in revolt" an author is, the more likely is he to put the traditional linguistic material in entirely new combinations, and to invent new linguistic expressions. In extreme cases the result would be a wholly individual and occasional blend, and an atomistic analysis of the traditional style markers accidentally occurring in it would be pointless. The character of such a piece of "style" has to be determined by other means.

It seems that a consistently non-generic approach to style raises in extreme form the same difficulties as the conventional treatment of separate stylistic phenomena referred to above (p. 21). It would demand either a complete description of the whole linguistic (and extra-linguistic) apparatus of the text, or a careful selection of really characteristic criteria viewed in their relation to one other. The first is theoretically possible, but hopelessly laborious and of questionable value if it cannot be reduced to a practical code; perhaps future computer programmers will find a solution. Here we have to note a fact which is of some importance if style is considered from this angle, namely that there are almost an infinite number of ways of expressing the same thing, and each of these ways can be said to be a style of its own. Consequently every single linguistic element contributes to the "style": every single element in a text exhibits a preference, or is a characteristic. The second method again is largely subjective, if the generic criterion of reproduction, i.e. of style markers in the above sense, is excluded. The random sampling method employed by the traditional stylometrists (p. 7) is worthless for other purposes than, possibly, problems of chronology and authenticity.

Fortunately however we are seldom concerned with extremely individual styles of an extremely occasional character. Every language is by nature more or less conservative, and so most speakers and authors tend to reproduce traditional patterns or their own modifications of such patterns. This is particularly true of the written ancient languages.

When considering the style of a piece of text we can safely begin by sorting out the typical style markers that suggest traditional classes of style or the
[31] author's own typical usage. Several style markers of the same class are a good indication that we are on the right track, whereas isolated instances demand caution. Having thus determined the *generic coloring* of the style we may be left with a series of linguistic phenomena which strike us as not being stylistically neutral but which cannot be reasonably referred to any existing stylistic class, such as a tendency to accumulation, notable emphasis, neologisms (except of course in contexts where word-coinage as such is a style marker), peculiar metaphors, or odd syntactic constructions. These may be said to constitute the *occasional traits* of the text. In this way the subjective factor in determining non-generically the characteristics of a piece of style is, though not eliminated, at least reduced. Both aspects of "style," the generic and the non-generic, have in fact been combined. And from a practical point of view, we are able to work with larger units—shades of style—instead of the countless atoma produced by conventional analysis.

The occasional traits to be analyzed separately are normally rather few and isolated. The special qualities of the style, which cannot be reached by the generic style markers, can be reached indirectly; indeed, they stand out clearer, if the traditional patterns are first envisaged.

As a result of these considerations we may state that the style (or more fully: the stylistic coloring) of a piece of speech or text consists normally of a basic generic coloring and a varying amount of additional occasional traits. The exceptional cases where occasional traits predominate can be left aside here.

If "style" is taken in a very large sense it will include such features as the technique of composition and the techniques of narrative and dramatization (and even extra-linguistic features, as was said above). It is clear that style in this sense can be satisfactorily observed only in large pieces of text or in a literary work as a whole. A study of *style proper* can be reasonably restricted to linguistic expressions and patterns which can be observed even in quite brief units of text. Yet it is often recommendable to consider them in relation to the technique of exposition.

∘∘∘ ◯ ∘∘∘

When applying these theoretical considerations to the study of the structure and the function of style in Plato's works, it is convenient to devote a preliminary chapter to Plato's technique of composition and the formal structure of his dialogue. These are likely to afford certain clues to his use of style in the strict sense. I shall then proceed to discuss the stylistic coloring and the shifts of coloring in the dialogues. It will be necessary first to make clear the criteria of generic style markers, and then to carry out an analysis of a typical text. I have chosen the *Republic* as the subject for a fairly detailed analysis, because it is sufficiently large in scope and varied in style to be representative of most of Plato's moods and manners, and because it is one of the best-known Platonic works. Having thus illustrated my method, I shall make brief comments on the stylistic coloring and the shifts of style in the other writings of the Corpus that are likely to be genuine, and some even more brief comments on the style of those dialogues which I consider of doubtful authenticity or obviously spurious.

Description of style is always problematic. In order to reach some degree of brevity and surveyability I refer to the generic style markers and shades by figures in bold type (cf. p. 51). Mere touches of style are denoted by brackets. Often it is necessary to give in a few words an additional qualification of the style and its occasional traits, and to exemplify notable features. This method of description is of course far from adequate in details, but I trust it will serve the present purpose reasonably well.

In the analyses and in the conclusions I shall pay special attention to four questions: (a) the relation of style to the formal structure of the dialogue, (b) the function of style for characterization of the speakers, (c) the relation of style to

[32] the contents, especially the changes of approach as reflected in the stylistic shifts, and (d) the rise of Plato's so-called "late style."

It probably goes without saying that the method here sketched out can only be a complement to other methods. Its main purpose, as was said above, is to indicate notable patterns and changes of style, and thus it can perhaps serve as a basis for further analysis and interpretation of particular passages.

# TECHNIQUE OF COMPOSITION AND DIALOGUE STRUCTURE

## General observations

In a much-quoted passage Socrates states that every λόγος should form a harmonic unity of different parts, like a living being: *Phdr.* 264c ἀλλὰ τόδε γε, οἶμαι, σε φάναι ἂν δεῖν πάντα λόγον ὥσπερ ζῷον συνεστάναι, σῶμά τι ἔχοντα αὐτὸν αὑτοῦ ὥστε μήτε ἀκέφαλον εἶναι μήτε ἄπουν, ἀλλὰ μέσα τε ἔχειν καὶ ἄκρα, πρέποντα ἀλλήλοις καὶ τῷ ὅλῳ γεγραμμένα. It is tempting to assume that this principle is somehow relevant to Plato's own dialogues. On the whole his dialogue composition appears to be a product of careful consideration and deliberate art though, as has often been emphasized, he was constantly experimenting with new forms and constantly introducing different approaches and moods.[75] Indeed, the simile of the living being in itself implies a great variety, and also flowing transitions between the different parts.

Without pressing the simile it is easy to observe a compositional rhythm in most writings. There are marked changes of weight and tone in the movement from the introduction to the main argument, to interludes and digressions, to visionary statements, and back to the main theme. This rhythm is clearly accompanied by external devices such as change of interlocutors and change of the formal character of the exposition. All this, however, has never been studied systematically.[76]

---

75. This is the line of interpretation followed, among others, by Hirzel 1895, Wilamowitz, and Friedländer, and by Hoerber in a number of recent articles on the early dialogues. For the application of *Phdr.* 264c, cf. Pfister 1922 and 1946. Billings' (1920) and Willi's (1925, especially 44–52) analyses of Plato's technique of transition lead to subtleties which cannot be really relied on.

76. On the relevance of the introductions and the interludes for the main theme, and the use of interludes for retardation before an important point, some observations have been made e.g. by de Vries 1949: 60–77, 84–91, Murley 1954, Martens 1954, Dodds 1959: 331, Muthmann 1961. For Billings 1920, *see* the preceding note.

[34]     Some scholars have compared Plato's art of composition to dramatic art, and have traced three or five "acts" in some dialogues.[77] Plato's dependence on drama cannot be doubted but, highly individual as his art is, he cannot really be expected to adopt consistently devices of dramatic composition any more than other conventional devices. It is, however, a very important fact that many of Plato's works, like Attic tragedy, obviously include a central "peripeteia" of some kind which is often combined with a culmination of the course of the argument: a κεφαλή and a μέσον at the same time. This principle of structure could be called *pedimental*.[78] In recent years it has been observed, and commented on, in some studies of Plato, though on the whole it has received very little attention.[79]

[35]     We shall here attempt to view Plato's art of composition from the formal angle. In order to make out the principles of the formal structure of his dialogues, we shall distinguish roughly between the following five types of exposition and consider some points in their function and in the formal technique of their use:

---

77. Thus already Thiersch 1837. Cf. further notably the following studies (most of which appear to be independent of one another!): Jowett 1892 (especially II 193–194), Hirzel 1895: 218–241, Dyer 1901, Wilamowitz I 275, D. Tarrant 1926 (and "Plato as Dramatist" 1955), Rivaud 1927, Stenzel 1956: 333–344, Geffcken I 57, 104, etc., Anderson 1935, Schaerer 1938: 218–234 (tragedy!), Rudberg 1939, Kühn 1941–1942, Hoffmann 1947: 472–476 (comedy!), Gaiser 1959: 22–23. More references in Klein 1965: 3–5. Some passages indicate that Plato himself regarded his dialogues as dramas, e.g. *Smp.* 212c (as if a choral interlude of Middle Comedy, cf. Murley 1954: 282), 223d. Puech 1940 makes an interesting comparison with Homeric composition, but here of course no dependence can be assumed. Vourveris 1954 (cf. Dodds 1959: 4–5) speaks of a "spiral" movement as a Platonic structural principle, as opposed to "rectilinear" movement in drama.

78. Cf. Myres 1953: 81–88 on the art of composition of Herodotus, with references to tragedy and to parallels in art. Cf. also Vretska, "Platonica I" (1956): 414: "Kompositionsprinzip des Tympanons."

79. This conception underlies implicitly many of the analyses in Friedländer, *see* especially III[2] 106–107 (*R.*), 171–172 (*Tht.*). Cf. further Kühn 1942 (peripeteia!), Koller 1948 (*Smp.*), Hornsby 1956 (*Smp.*); Vretska, "Platonica I" (1956): 406–414 (especially *R.*); Flashar 1958 (*Ion, Men.*), Wyller 1958 (*Ion*), Gaiser 1959 (especially *R.*), Krämer 1959: 482–485 (*Tht., R., Ti., Plt.*), Wyller 1960 (*Smp., Prm., R.*), Vretska 1962 (*Smp.*), Dönt 1963 (*Hipparch., Alc.* 1, *Alc.* 2, *Min.*)—The rules of "proportional composition" worked out for *Phdr.* by Pfister 1922 and for *Smp.* by Vretska "Zu Form und Aufbau von Platons Symposion" 1962 (cf. also Hoerber 1964 on *Hp.Ma.*, regarded by him as authentic) are more complicated but amount to a similar pedimental pattern. The "triadic" composition of *Ap.* may also seem pedimental (cf. Apelt 1922: 68 n. 40); in *Grg.* it is seemingly climactic, but cf. below p. 122. For triads in *Men., Ly.*, and *Hp.Ma., see* Hoerber 1959, 1960, and 1964. It is true that many dialogues seem to follow a principle of "rising accumulation," for which *see* in particular Schwessinger 1925 (cf. v. Sybel 1889, Archer-Hind 1894, and further e.g. Gauss II 2.17). But Schwessinger certainly goes too far in emphasizing the importance of the end of the dialogues; cf. below p. 59. Normally, as will be seen, the actual culmination comes closer to the center than to the end. Schaerer 1938: 135–143 (followed by Goldschmidt 1947) also takes little or no account of the central peripeteia when assuming, as a basic scheme for all dialogues, a kind of scale: "illusion—ignorance—connaissance—science" (of which the third point is often, and the last point mostly lacking). Gauss (especially III 1.184) attempts to show that Plato in his late works, instead of logical composition, arranged his material "aesthetically" according to the order and proportion in which he wished his readers to utilize it; but I am not sure this theory is of any other consequence to stylistic studies than that it emphasizes the complexity of composition of the late dialogues.

A. Question and reply
B. Discussion or conversation
C. Reported dialogue (with A, B, D, or E)
D. Dialogue approximating to monologue
E. Monologue or continuous exposition.

## A. Question and reply[80]

Sample text: *Hp.Mi.* 373c–376b (intentional wrong-doing is better than unintentional).

*Origins*

The sources of this type of dialogue are the old Greek arts of elenctic and eristic. The ἔλεγχος naturally had an important function in judicial practice, and this is probably where it originated, though Socrates and Plato are likely to have taken it over from some sophists and, perhaps, the Eleatics.[81] But it is essential to note the difference of ἔλεγχος from the ἀγῶνες and ἀντιλογίαι also practiced in courts and in politics, and by sophists in particular: the latter are an exchange of different views and arguments,[82] whereas the ἔλεγχος is a dialogue where one of the partners is leading the course of argument and the other is following, principally by answering only "yes" or "no". There seems to be no difference in the external form between elenctic (and διαλεκτική in its old sense, referred to in *Men.* 75d, *Euthd.* 290c, and probably *Cra.* 390cd, 398d)[83] and eristic.[84]

---

80. Cf. Schaerer 1938: 25–38.
81. Cf. the parody in Ar. *Nub.*, especially 478–494, which hardly concerns Socrates alone. It must be left undecided whether the Eleatics really practiced this method, though this is implied by Pl. *Prm.* and Arist. ap. Diogenes Laertius (Diog. L.) 8.57 (fr. 65 Rose). On the Eleatic contribution to the rise of argumentation in Greek prose, cf. Thesleff 1966: 92–93.—For Plato's use of the word ἔλεγχος, see des Places 1964; for a brief conspectus of the use of this word in Greek, cf. Waldenfels 1961: 52–55. Cf. also Robinson 1953: 7–19.
82. Cf. Aly 1929: 38, 95–104; cf. below, B.
83. Διαλεκτική in the sense of a philosophical method, from *Phdr.* 266c and *R.* VII.531e (cf. *R.* V.454a, etc.) onwards, does not imply a strict succession of questions and answers. Of the voluminous literature on the development of Plato's "dialectic" (cf. Cherniss 1959: 261–278, Sinaiko 1965: 18–20) I mention Stenzel 1917 and Robinson 1953 which also deal, though only in passing, with the formal aspect. But Goldschmidt 1947 only considers the contents; and the observations of Bezzel 1963: 48–60 on dialogue structure (in *Euthphr.*) are also insufficient for stylistic studies.— Plato also refers to the elenctic method as μαίευσις, μαιευτική (*Tht.* 150b, 210b, etc.), for which see Hirzel 1895: 78–79, Landmann 1950.—It is the elenctic and maieutic function of type A that Proclus is thinking of in *Alc.* p. 170–171 Creuzer (cf. Olymp. *Alc.* 51–57 Creuzer).
84. Parodied in *Euthd.* in particular, see the analysis by Sprague 1962: 1–33. Cf. Arist. *Soph. elench.* Sometimes, especially in early dialogues such as *Hp.Mi.*, Plato's elenctic is actually eristic in content.

[36]    *Function*

Plato apparently took type A to be typical of Socrates.[85] For instance, it is normally in A sections that the typical Socratic device occurs of illustrating a point with examples taken from various crafts and arts; in addition to the above-mentioned passage cf. e.g. *Ion* 537c.[86] The leader in A sections is normally Socrates. Very occasionally in the early and middle dialogues somebody else is made to lead the A. The most interesting cases are found in the exemplification of bad elenctic and μακρολογία in *Grg.*, especially *Grg.* 462b–e,[87] where Polus comes to Gorgias' assistance and tries to interrogate Socrates, though without success:
[37]    Socrates to all intents and purposes still conducts the questioning; cf. 447c–448d, 466a–467c, 468e–469c, 470c–471a (also 506c–507c where Socrates even takes over the answering). In *Prt.* 338e–339d Protagoras attempts to discuss the poem of Simonides by questioning Socrates. This turns out to be the wrong method. In *Euthd.* the erists give several farcical examples of their method by means of A dialogue. In the later works Socrates' successors sometimes lead A questioning. In *Smp.* 201e–207a Diotima introduces her teaching by a partial questioning of Socrates. In the latter part of *Prm.* (from 137c) Parmenides questions young Aristoteles; these sections are probably intended as specimens of Eleatic method. The questioning conducted by the Elean Guest in *Sph.* and *Plt.* is nowhere very strict, and it approximates to D dialogue (*see* below). This tendency is even more manifest in the questioning conducted by the Athenian Guest in *Lg.*, though in isolated passages there may occur a rather typical A (so e.g. in the dialectical passage X.900c–903a). An occasional brief A passage occurs in B in *Epin.* 981ab. It is significant that there is comparatively much distinct A dialogue in *Phlb.*, which is the only one of the late works where Socrates actually leads the argument.—In *R.* II 357a–358b Glaucon puts some critical questions to Socrates, but this passage cannot be regarded as a normal A section.[88]

The A sections carry much of the main argument, either by criticizing ironically or aporetically the common opinion, as very often in the early works,[89] or by searching positive answers "dialectically," "anamnetically" or "maieutically," which becomes more common later (especially from *Grg.* and *Men.* onwards).[90] The change from destructive to constructive A dialogue cannot be studied here, and it has little or no relevance to style. It is important, however, to observe two points. The A sections, whether destructive or constructive, are in all authentic works complemented by B sections and type E (cf. also D). And the gradual rise of the D type leads to a corresponding gradual loss of strict A. All early and

---

85. This and some of the following points have been made by Schaerer 1938: 25–28.
86. Gaiser 1959: 90 would derive this trait from sophistic "protreptic" speeches, but undoubtedly it is particularly typical of Socrates.
87. For the distribution of the dialogue, *see* Dodds 1959 ad 1. and Friedländer II² 321 n. 7.
88. In the spurious *Erx.* however there is a curious digression 397e–399a where Prodicus is questioned by an unnamed young man.
89. Cf. e.g. *Ion* 531a–533c, 536d–541b.
90. But rather distinct already in *Cri.* 46b–50a.

middle dialogues except *Mx.* include A sections of varying length; even *Ap.* has a brief section of elenchus (24c–28a). But after *Tht.* the tendency to D dialogue predominates; and in *Ti.* and *Criti.* (and *Ep.* 7) there is neither A nor distinct D. In general, cf. below, D, and the analysis.

*Technique*

Normally type A consists of comparatively brief questions put by Socrates (or his successor in the later dialogues) and of simple confirmative or negative replies by his dialogue partner. This *dialogue "tension"* between Socrates and a single interlocutor is normally not allowed to be broken in the same section, not even when many other persons are present listening, and thus the A has a tone of intension and fixity of purpose.

A sections are frequently introduced by *transitional phrases* such as καί μοι εἰπέ (e.g. *Ap.* 24c, *Ly.* 212a), λέγε πάλιν ἐξ ἀρχῆς (e.g. *La.* 197e).[91]

Often Plato avoids monotony in A sections by slight variation of different kinds; on the other hand he sometimes tends to strict uniformity for specific purposes.

*Variation of formulae of reply.* Plato employs a wide register of brief confirmative and negative formulae and other types of reply, and the special preferences adopted in different works are not very marked.[92] The recurrence of the same formula in two successive replies is notably rare. There are somewhat more examples of this in the earliest dialogues than later (e.g. *Ion* 537c–e, 538b, *Hp.Mi.* 373d, 374d, 375c); in the whole of the latter part of *Prm.*, in spite of its apparent monotony, successive recurrence of a reply is only found five times (140bc, 147d, 148b, 159c, 163a), and in the whole of *Plt.*, in spite of its size, only four times (261d, 283a, 287e, 292b).[93]

*Variation by means of expansion.* Questions very frequently expand, but in typical A sections (cf. B and D below) they usually preserve their character of questions. When glancing at the pages of the printed text it is easy to see that the questions tend to come in strings where the different questions have approximately the same size. An expansion usually marks a summing up, a change of approach, a new point made, or the like. Ultimately the fact that Plato avoids extensive sections of uniform A must be due to a need to vary the means of expression, rather than to the subject-matter which could be treated by a much stricter and more mechanical application of type A.—Replies do not expand as commonly within

---

91. Cf. Billings 1920: 54; but she has treated this phraseology far from exhaustively.
92. Cf. the material collected for a stylometrical purpose by v. Arnim 1913. He has considered only the formulae, and thus his collection does not give a real picture of Plato's use of brief replies. An important type never studied in Greek are the anaphoric replies, e.g. *Hp.Mi.* 375e.
93. Also the spuria avoid successive recurrence; in the simple and seemingly artless *Virt.* there is only one example, just at the end (375cd).

[39] the same A section. The questions are normally put so as to require a simple answer; if not, the answer may expand (e.g. *Hp.Mi.* 367a). Somewhat more often replies expand for the introduction of an additional point or objection, and then expansion is frequently combined with characterization of Socrates' partner or of the situation (e.g. *La.* 194ab). As can be expected, such expansions are comparatively common in *Grg.* and *Prt.* (cf. below, restriction).

*Change of dialogue partner.* Of the persons present in a Platonic dialogue[94] one is the chief interlocutor of Socrates (or of Socrates' stand-in) in A sections. Frequently however another partner is addressed in preparatory or less important A sections: such a change of interlocutor in A sections of rising significance occurs in *La.* (Laches-Nicias), *Cra.* (Hermogenes-Cratylus), *Chrm.* (Charmides-Critias), *R.* I (Polemarchus-Thrasymachus), *Smp.* (Agathon questioned by Socrates—Socrates questioned by Diotima), *Grg.* has three stages (Gorgias-Polus-Callicles). Alternative partners, of which the latter appears to be addressed in sections of greater importance, in *Ly.* (Lysis-Menexenus, cf. below), *Phd.* (Simmias-Cebes, once also Phaedon, 89c–90d, in connection with the "peripeteia" of the work) and *R.* II–X (Adimantus-Glaucon); in *Tht.* Socrates mostly questions Theaitetos, but in the visionary central section he turns to Theodoros. The arrangement of *Euthd.* is rather more complicated owing to the display of eristics in the work (*see* especially 294e–303a), but Clinias may be regarded as the chief partner of Socrates; also *Men.* where Socrates illustrates his point by questioning a slave (82b–86c), and *Prm.* with its display of Eleatic argument, are rather specific. In *Lg.* Clinias remains the chief interlocutor of the Athenian, but Megillus is occasionally addressed, especially in matters concerning Sparta. Except for some passages in *La.* and *Prt.* which will be discussed presently, the persons not habitually addressed in A sections join in the conversation in B sections only (*see* below). This fact emphasizes the fundamental difference between the types A and B.

[40] A change of interlocutor does not normally occur within the same A section. But here too Plato sometimes allows himself variation. In the preliminary A section in *La.* 184d–186a Socrates successively questions the two fathers and the two experts, and in the last section, *La.* 197e–199e, which is addressed to Nicias, there are occasional apostrophes to the other expert, Laches. In the two last A sections in *Ly.*, 212a–218c and 218d–222d, Socrates first addresses Menexenus, then Lysis, then Menexenus again, and finally (from 217a) both boys at the same time, though principally Menexenus; the reason for this is probably that the boys both together represent one aspect of friendship (cf. the brief preliminary questioning in 207bc, which is also addressed to both). In the concluding analysis of virtue in *Prt.* 349d–360e, where Protagoras is questioned, Socrates also addresses Prodicus and Hippias in the passage 358a–359a; perhaps, this is principally in order to add weight to the passage, which, I believe, includes a hidden reference

---

94. Disregarding *Ap., Mx., Ep.* 7 and the spuria, the following have only one character in addition to Socrates: *Ion, Cri., Euthphr., Phdr.* Altogether 3 characters: *Hp.Mi., Cra., Tht.* (the main dialogue), *Phlb., Lg., (Epin.).* The rest have 4 or more characters.

to the death of Socrates (358e). The change of interlocutor in *R.* IX.576b actually implies a change of section, though the B section to be expected is lacking.⁹⁵ *Lg.* does not follow the earlier rules of composition, and in its AD sections Megillus sometimes joins in though Clinias is chiefly addressed.⁹⁶ The special case of *Euthd.* was referred to above.

*Deliberate restriction.* Among the many references in passing to the technique of Socratic argument and the ideal of strict questioning and brief replies, there are some passages that illustrate this point more extensively. In *Grg.* Gorgias, Polus and Callicles find it difficult to submit to this requirement (especially 448e–449d, 461b–462a, cf. 466a, 468e, 494b–495b, etc.); similarly Critias in *Chrm.* (162e–163b, 163d–164c, etc.) and Protagoras in *Prt.* (especially 329a–332a), cf. Hippias in *Hp.Mi.* 364c–365d. All gradually learn to accept Socrates' method, Gorgias perhaps with less success than the others, and the passage in *Prt.* is followed by a show-piece of strict A dialogue (332a–333d). In *Men.* 82b–86a (cf. 75c) where Socrates exemplifies his method, the passages where the slave is questioned are kept rigorously strict whereas the questions somewhat expand when Socrates turns to Menon. The latter part of *Prm.* is kept in a seemingly very strict A dialogue. There are occasional and brief instances of strict A in some other early and middle dialogues (cf. especially *Hp.Mi.* 373c–376b, *Grg.* 497c–499a, *Cra.* 385a–390d with concluding reference to the art of dialectic, *Ly.* 212a–218c, cf. 211b ἐριστικός, *R.* I.349c–350c), but after the effusion in *Prm.* only some instances in *Phlb.*⁹⁷

It should however be noted that the strictness of the A dialogue in *Prm.*, and also in *Phlb.*, is to some extent only apparent. The argument does not proceed merely by question and reply, but also by successive statements supported or interrupted by assent or questions. The external structure of the dialogue with its fairly brief kola recalls early A dialogue, but the technique is influenced by the D dialogue. Cf. below p. 44.

## B. Discussion and conversation

Sample texts: Opening B section, *Cri.* 43a–44b. Brief B interlude, *Grg.* 497bc. Concluding B section, *La.* 199e–201c.

In its characteristic form this type of dialogue differs from the A type by distributing between the speakers the ideas to be expressed.

---

95. Cf. Wilamowitz II 210–211 who thinks that the change of partner denotes the return to the main theme. This part of the work may have received its final shape after Plato's drawbacks in Sicily, and a lack of B sections is not uncommon in his late works; cf. below, p. 36.— Cf. *R.* V.466d–471c which is rather loosely attached to the preceding CA section.

96. Such instances are sometimes open to textual criticism, e.g. *Lg.* III.696b.

97. The spurious writings have comparatively much strict A dialogue, evidently because it was regarded as a typical Socratic device.

[41] *Origins*

Exchange of speeches had occurred in Greek literature since Homer, but the main source of the type B, if we are to speak of sources, must be looked for in drama and mime where a varied and realistic conversation was largely current.

Unfortunately we do not know the mimes of Sophron sufficiently well to be able to judge the extent of Plato's debt to him.[98] This debt is usually taken for granted. But it is possible that the ancient tradition (chiefly Diog. L. 3.18) ulti-

[42] mately derives from Aristotle's theoretical comparison of Socratic dialogues with the mimes of Sophron (*Poet.* 1447b) and the speculations about "mimetic" art. Indeed it seems rather a paradox that Plato should have modeled his writings, or a type of dialogue in them, on such a low branch of literature. Were there any intermediate links, perhaps a "mime de salon" practiced in Megara where Plato lived the first months or years after the death of Socrates? What did Alexamenus of Styra or Teos write, who according to Aristotle (Diog. L. 3.48, fr. 72 Rose) was a predecessor of Plato? Was Plato's B dialogue as remotely related to mime as it evidently was to tragedy and comedy which he at any rate knew thoroughly well? However, what links it up with mime rather than with drama proper, is the realistic prose form used in it, and the possibility that it was originally intended for a closed public only (cf. above, p. 16). On the other hand the deducing of the B dialogue from early Σωκρατκικοὶ λόγοι is wholly uncertain.[99] It is true that Aeschines and Xenophon seem to make a somewhat more extensive use o f it than Plato, but the fact that Plato lays little primary weight on it rather contradicts such an assumption. For the ἀντιλογίαι, see below p. 45.

*Function*

Because the B dialogue imitates situations of ordinary life better than the A dialogue, and because it was not as distinctly intellectual or "philosophical" in origin as the A dialogue, Plato naturally uses it in particular for framework and interludes. In a sense the B sections correspond to the choral sections of drama. Plato's B sections carry most of the external setting and much of the characterization of the speakers and the situation,[100] and rather less argument than the A

---

98. Some material and references to the problem of Sophron having influenced Plato in McDonald 1931, especially 380–384, 396–399 (more substantial and elaborate than Reich's classical exposition 1903: 381–382, 405–413). McDonald's own view rests chiefly on the fact that Plato's character portraiture, like Sophron's, is both realistic and typological.

99. The Socratic literature is likely to have arisen after Socrates' death in 399 BCE, and Plato probably had a considerable part in its very earliest stages. The extensive literature on this subject clearly shows how little we know; cf. Hirzel 1895: 13–140, Bruns 1896: 224–236, Dittmar 1912, Wilamowitz II 22–31, Schmid I 3.219–235, Gigon 1947: 181–208, de Magalhães Probl. 1952: 321–353.

100. This has been observed in particular by de Vries 1949: 60–77. For *Chrm., Euthd., Smp., Tht.,* and *Ti.,* cf. Muthmann 1961. Cf. further the references above n. 77.

(and D) sections. They may however implicitly and secondarily take over an important philosophical function. They often state problems, they may contain serious objections, and normally they accompany the "peripeteia" and the central vision of the work (*see* below, p. 46 ff. and the analyses). They are also used for retardation before important arguments, as the above-mentioned *Grg.* 497bc, cf. 499bc, further e.g. *R.* IV.432b–e, V.471c–472b, *Phlb.* 22c–23b. The concluding B section of course has a function of its own.[101]

Very frequently the utterances in a B section tend to expand, but very frequently too B sections include extensive monologues. It is not always possible to draw a sharp distinction between expanded B utterances and monologues or speeches of type E, but on the whole the latter are characterized by a considerably greater length, a change of tone, and a comparatively loose relation to the preceding or following dialogue. The interrelation of B and E in B sections will be conveniently discussed in connection with type E.

## Technique

*The relation of B sections to A (D) (and E) sections.* Looking at the distribution and the length of the utterances it appears that the B sections, whether including distinct E's or not (*see* p. 49), as a rule stand out clearly from the surrounding sections.[102] There is also an evident interplay of distinct B and distinct A (or D or E respectively), as can be seen from the analyses below; and the difference in length between the sections differentiated by the B dialogue is seldom very remarkable. Thus the B dialogue on the whole seems to create a compositional rhythm.

The B sections normally occupy much less space in the writings than the A (or D or E). The only exceptions are *La.* and *Prt.* where the B sections (including E's) are comparatively extensive; and it is significant that Socrates in both works is

---

101. Plato on the whole did not attach much importance to the conclusions; cf. below p. 48. If there is a concluding B section at all, it is normally quite brief. Nowhere does it include a real "summary and conclusions"; it is significant that the only work that has something of the kind, *Phlb.*, puts it in the preceding AD section. A concluding B section is completely lacking (disregarding *Ap., Ep.* 7 and, because of the concluding speech, *Grg.* and *R.* X) in *Prm., Ti. (Criti.), Sph.,* and *Epin.* Rather brief aporetic or seemingly aporetic B: *Ion, Hp.Mi., Ly., Euthphr., R.* I. Statement of something to follow: *La., Mx., Cra., Chrm., Prt., Phlb., Lg.* Somewhat more visionary: *Men.* Fairly extensive protreptic: *Euthd.* (cf. *Tht.*). Description of background resumed: (*Euthd.*), *Phd., Smp., Phdr.* Brief statement of agreement or result: *Cri., Tht., Plt.* Most of the spuria have no concluding B; an aporetic concluding B in *Hp.Ma.*; statement of something to follow in *Thg., Alc.* 1, *Alc.* 2; description of background resumed in *Amat.*

102. It is usually not necessary to take occasional expansions of objections and comments as distinct B sections (e.g. *Cra.* 385d–386b). But if the expansion is accompanied by a manifest change in tone or the course of the argument it may be called B even if it is very brief (e.g. *R.* VI.509c). In a few instances however the alternative is difficult to decide upon (e.g. *Tht.* 148c–e), and in such cases the general rhythm of the composition may be taken into consideration. In the spurious *Erx.* there are some distinct anomalies in this respect, notably the insertion of an E in an A section (396a–e) and of A in a B interlude (397e–399a).

[44] conversing with people of higher social rank than himself, to whose views Plato wants him to listen.[103]

The opening B section is sometimes quite brief *(Hp.Mi., Ion, Men., Cra., Plt., Phlb., Lg., Epin.)* but it is nowhere wholly absent in the authentic works.[104] More often it is more extensive than the other B sections; sometimes when combined with C dialoge (p. 48) it consists of two distinct parts *(Ly., Chrm., Prt., Prm.,* cf. *Tht.).* Many dialogues have an important central B *(see* below, E). Some of the shorter works have no other interludes *(Hp.Mi., Ion),* nor has *Prm.* Some works that essentially consist of speeches have only an opening B *(Cri., Mx., Ti., Criti.).* Some of the more extensive works have a great number of interludes *(R.* II–X have altogether about 20). In the late dialogues they are scarcer (in *Sph.* 4, in *Plt.* 3,[105] in *Phlb.* 3 and all in the first part of the work, and in the whole of *Lg.* only 12). Later, different (A) D (or E) sections are sometimes attached to each other without an intermediate B (note *R.* IX.576b,[106] *Plt.* 285c ff. where the D actually takes the function of B's, *Phlb.* 31a, 55c, 59d, and quite commonly in *Lg.* and *Epin.).* From *Sph.* onwards the D dialogue extends its influence to the B sections (e.g. *Sph.* 236c–237b), which then differs formally from D only by a notable expansion of the replies and comments on the main exposition (cf. D). For B sections as conclusions, *see* above n. 101.

[45] *Several persons joining in the conversation.* Contrary to the A dialogue which is essentially a tension between two (above p. 38), the B sections very frequently include more than two speakers. In the works with more than two characters this principle is in fact almost a rule. It is regularly applied in the opening B sections;[107] more or less regularly in the interludes;[108] but not so commonly in the conclusions, which corresponds to the little weight that Plato attaches to them. For details, *see* the analyses. It should be observed that this technique contributes to the compositional rhythm referred to above, and it is also reflected in the style.

## C. Reported dialogue

Sample text: *Prt.* 310a–311a (beginning of Socrates' report).

---

103. In the somewhat similar situations in *Smp., Prm., Ti., Criti., Sph.* and *Plt.,* Plato makes other persons take over the teaching.
104. Among the spuria, *Just., Virt.,* and *Alc.* 2 have no opening B at all.
105. But the D sections 285c ff. correspond functionally to B interludes.
106. Cf. above n. 95. In a sense this applies also to the 8 (or 9) "hypotheses" of the latter part of *Prm.;* the highly technical character of this part excludes ordinary literary devices.
107. *Men.* makes no use of this principle at all, and this stresses the digressional (and perhaps secondary) character of the Anytus episode; the slave of course could not partake in B conversation. In *Cra.* and *Tht.* the third person does not take part in the opening conversation, but he is present and explicitly referred to.
108. Apart from *Men.* (*see* the preceding note), only the very technical *Sph.* and *Plt.* do not apply this principle after the opening section.

As was suggested above (p. 17), the eight works which wholly or mainly consist of reported dialogue do not belong to the beginning of Plato's literary career. This type of dialogue corresponded to a need of introducing Socrates and his environment to a wider public. It could also be used for increasing the historical distance to the situation reported, thus giving the author more licence, as in *Smp.* and *Prm.* in particular. But owing to a change of preferences, approach, and probably public, Plato virtually gave it up when writing *Prm.* and *R.*, and explicitly when writing *Tht.* The passage on διήγησις versus μίμησις in *R.* III.392d–394d may reflect to some extent this conflict.[109]

## Origins

The literary source of type C appears to have been story-telling and biographical memoirs. These branches of literature, which anticipate later novels, can be reconstructed from 5th century logography and especially from the fragments of Ion of Chios.[110] Considering the "exoteric" and tendentious character of Plato's reported dialogues, it is particularly interesting to note that Stesimbrotus of Thasus had made use of reported dialogue in his collection of anti-Periclean anecdotes (FGrHist 107 F 5, 7). Report thus was established long before Plato in public propaganda as well as in biographical narrative.

Plato may however have had nearer models than Ionian logography. Some other early Socratics also used the reported form, among them Aeschines, Antisthenes, and Xenophon. If Dittmar is right in dating Antisthenes' Κῦρος and Aeschines' Ἀλκιβιάδης in the late 390s and Aeschines' Ἀσπασία before Plato's *Mx.*,[111] and if my theory of a comparatively late date for Plato's reported dialogues is correct, it seems likely that Plato took over this practice from his Socratic friends and competitors. This hypothesis gets some support from the fact that the C dialogue of the latter is fairly simple and artless and shows no signs of attempts to imitate the literary brilliance of Plato, which could have been expected if they had used Plato as a model.

---

109. Note especially 394b, on removing τὰ μεταξὺ τῶν ῥήσεων It is true that the result would be strict μίμησις. But whatever Plato makes Socrates state in the matter, it is likely that Plato himself evaluates Socratic μίμησις higher than Socratic διήγησις. I am not sure Stefanini 1949: I.LXXIII ff. is right in taking the passage as an indication that Plato at this stage preferred the reported form.

110. F. Jacoby (ed.), *Die Fragmente der Griechischen Historiker* (FGrHist) 392. Cf. Bruns 1896: 50–55, 239–241, Pohlenz 1913: 4–7, Gigon 1947: 183–184, 199–201. Hirzel 1895: 65–66 also refers to Critias' Ὁμιλίαι as a likely source, but it remains doubtful whether they were memoirs (cf. Diels-Kranz II⁹ 88 B 40–41, p. 395). The symposiastic literature may have had an origin of its own, cf. Martin 1931: 292 ff., Aly 1921: 260–262 suggests Oriental sources.

111. For the reported dialogue of the Socratics, see Dittmar 1912: 49–50, 83, 157, 243–244; some additions to Aeschines' *Alcibiades* in Gaiser 1959: 77–95. See now also Ehlers 1966. In *Thg.* 128d–130e Socrates illustrates the intervention of his Daimonion with a few anecdotes with dialogue partly quoted, in the simple and straightforward manner of Xenophon and Aeschines.

[46]     As a matter of fact there occur some traces of this artless Socratic practice in Plato's early works. In the Euenus episode in *Ap.* 20ab Plato makes Socrates use a careless and inelegant colloquial tone which is very realistic but suggests that Plato had not yet adopted the technique of C dialogue as a routine.[112] In *Cra.* 383b there is a very brief piece of report whose purpose is merely to quote an enigmatic utterance by Cratylus. Cf. the anecdote with C dialogue reported in R. I.329bc, and the biographical report quoted in *Smp.* 218b–219b. In two isolated passages in the late works Plato returns to reported dialogue, and both passages are written with stylistic skill and a technique somewhat reminding of the great C dialogues: *Ti.* 21a–25e (legend of Solon and the Egyptian priests), *Ep.* 7.347c–350b (the circumstances of Plato's leaving Syracuse for the third time).

[47]     Type C should not be identified with the quotation of a single utterance, e.g. the proclamation of the hierophant in *R.* X.617de, or the speech of the Demiurge in *Ti.* 41a–d.[113] The dialogue and the background description, characteristic of C proper, are absent in such cases. Nor should type C be identified with the report of a fictitious objection or a fictitious complete dialogue for the sake of argumentation. Such ὑποφοραί were current in oratory (e.g. Andoc. 1.148, Lys. 22.11), and this is probably the ultimate source for the fictitious dialogue in Plato. It frequently starts from an objection introduced by a phrase of the ἴσως εἴποι ἄν τις type (cf. *Ap.* 20c), e.g. *Ap.* 28b–d, 29c–e, *Cri.* 50a–54d (the *Laws'* argument). There are abundant examples of it in Plato's works especially later, but most have a rhetorical touch,[114] and there are no signs of a real approximation to the technique of the C dialogue. *Cri.* 50ce is no exception, because the θαυμάζοιμεν and the two cases of φαίην ἄν have little to do with that technique.

In the following we shall only consider the reported dialogue in the eight works *(Ly., Chrm., Prt., Euthd., Phd., Smp., Prm.,* and *R.)* which use this principle of composition consistently.

## Function

It is generally recognized that these eight writings constitute the culmination of Plato's literary art. It is also evident to the attentive reader that the reported form has no philosophical relevance. Matters of factual importance for the argument are not on the whole discussed or even mentioned in the reporting narrative. The most notable exceptions are the elaborate central sections in *Euthd.* and *Phd.*

---

112. Note especially τοῦτον οὖν ἀνηρόμην—ἐστὸν γάρ αὐτῷ δύο ὑεῖ· Ὦ Καλλία, ἦν δ' ἐγώ, εἰ ...

113. Cf. also the partially quoted dialogue in *Clit.* 408c–410a which Plato would probably have written as a C dialogue proper.

114. E.g. *Grg.* 451a–452d, *R.* V.453bc, *Phlb.* 63b–64a, *Lg.* I.662c–e, X.893b–894a. But sometimes distinctly colloquial, e.g. *Prt.* 330c–331b. In the spurious writings this device occurs occasionally, e.g. in the somewhat rhetorical opening B section of *Alc.* 1 (105a–c). In *Hp.Ma.* the anonymous critic introduced in 286c later accompanies the dialogue in a rather peculiar manner and even receives some stylistic characterization (cf. p. 128); this procedure is without parallels in the genuine works but remotely recalls *Cri.* 50c–e.

The primary function of the C is description of the setting, the characters, and their reactions in a more plastic and extensive manner than what could be done by the means of the dramatic dialogue.[115] Such descriptions may help to determine Plato's intentions with a passage or a work (for instance, the description of happy old Cephalus R. I.328bc adds weight to the common-sense of his speech 330d–331b; and the reference to tragedy and comedy in *Smp.* 223d has a certain bearing on the whole work[116]), but they cannot be said to give actual clues to the argumentation. The description of Socrates' environment indirectly illuminates the personality of Socrates from various angles, and in the two great enkomia, *Phd.* and *Smp.*, light falls on him more directly. Thus the C dialogue can be said, more specifically, to give the overtones for an understanding of Socrates and the Socratic milieu.

[47] [48]

*Technique*

*Type C in relation to A and B.* The use of B and A (or D or E) sections remains essentially unchanged; this fact gives some support to the assumption that the C form is secondary.[117] Narrative and description of type C is chiefly concentrated to the B sections, and thus the variety and liveliness of these is further increased. Especially the opening B sections become elaborated. Disregarding the use of a separate frame dialogue (below) the opening CB section is sometimes divided into two rather distinct parts, in some works with a change of scene.[118] The other CB sections have commonly various descriptive remarks (such as *Chrm.* 159b καὶ ὃς μὲν πρῶτον ὤκνει τε καὶ οὐ πάνυ ἤθελεν ἀποκρίνασθαι, ἔπειτα μέντοι εἶπεν ὅτι οἱ δοκοῖ . . . , *Phd.* 77e καὶ ὁ Κέβης ἐπιγελάσας . . . ἔφη), but not much narrative. There is some vivid narrative in *Ly.* 223ab (conclusion), *Euthd.* 291b–d, 292c–293a (central sections, on the Kingly Art), *R.* I.344d (Thrasymachus angry, but persuaded to stay), *Phd.* 84cd (doubts of Simmias and Cebes), *Phd.* 116a–118a (death of Socrates), *Smp.* 212c–214e (arrival of Alcibiades), *Smp.* 222c–223d (end of the feast), but these are exceptional cases, and most of them are connected with particularly important points.[119] The biographical CB narrative in the speech of Alcibiades in *Smp.* 217a–219e (cf. 220c–221a) should also be mentioned here though it has little to do with the compositional rhythm of the work; cf. the brief anecdote about Sophocles in *R.* I. 329bc and the legend about Solon and the

[49]

---

115. Cf. *Grg.* 468c and d (τί οὐκ ἀποκρίνει;), 473e (γελᾷς;) Such references are never common in the dramatic dialogues. For a survey of some traits in Plato's use of description especially in the reported dialogues, *see* Murley 1954–1955.
116. Cf. above n. 58.
117. Cf. above p. 37.
118. *Ly.* 206c, *Chrm.* 156d, *Prt.* 316a, *Prm.* 127d; a somewhat less distinct division in *R.* I.328b, *Phd.* 61d, *Smp.* 175c, *R.* II.358b. The same device occurs in some dramatic dialogues though with less elaboration; cf. especially *La.* 180a, *Grg.* 448a (cf. Dodds 1959: 188), *Phdr.* 229a, *Ti.* 20c.
119. Brief passages of CB narrative in *Ly.* 210e, 218cd, *Prt.* 335c–336b, *Euthd.* 304c, *Phd.* 69e, 77e, 86d, 88c, 95e, 102ab, 103a–c, *Smp.* 180c, 185c–e, 189a–c, 198a, 199b, 207a, *Prm.* 136de, *R.* V.449ab, 451b. The elaboration of *Phd.* and *Smp.* in this respect is obvious.

[49] Egyptians in *Ti.* 21a–25e. In *R.* II–X there is hardly any narrative at all (only *R.* V. 449ab, 451b, introducing the chapter on the women), and only occasionally descriptive remarks in the CB sections; this corresponds to the abandoning of the C dialogue in the latter part of *Prm.* (below).

In CA (or CD or CE) sections narrative occurs only in some passages in the very vividly elaborate *Euthd.*, 276b, 276d, 295a–296d (for *Smp.* 217a–219e see above). Descriptive remarks are quite common in such sections in *Euthd.*, and not uncommon in *Prt.* (notably 358a–359a) but only very occasionally they are found in other works.[120]

*Indirect report of replies.* An indirect report of questions in a CA dialogue does not seem to occur. But quite commonly the replies alone are reported whereas the questions are quoted in full, e.g. *R.* I.342c–e, *Phd.* 93a. Brief reported replies take the shape of formulae, e.g. συνέφη, συνεδόκει ὡμολόγησε.[121]

*Formulae of the type 'said I,' 'said he.'* Such "inserenda" (εἶπον, ἔφη, καὶ ὅς, ἦ δ' ὅς, etc.) are common in all sections, also in rather strict CA, except in the latter part of *Prm.* where the dialogue after the opening φάναι 137c is kept as virtually dramatic.[122]

*Frame dialogue and report.* The C is chiefly, and originally, reported by Socrates. But (disregarding occasional anecdotes) in *Euthd.* 304c–305a Criton introduces an additional point in a report; and in *Phd.*, *Smp.* and *Prm.* the objective angle of approach requires reports by persons other than Socrates. In *Ly.*, *Chrm.* and *R.* I Socrates addresses an unnamed audience, and this can be regarded as the earliest stage of Plato's use of C.[123] In the rest of the reported dialogues Plato

[50] has complicated the structure of the composition by adding a dramatic frame dialogue or *(Prm.)* an opening section with a similar function.

*Prt.* has only an opening frame dialogue and the interlocutor of Socrates remains unnamed; he represents the audience of the first C dialogues (cf. the reference to an audience in 310a). In *Euthd.* the structure is considerably more elaborate:[124] a frame dialogue between Socrates and Criton not only opens but concludes the work, and it is resumed in the important central passage on the Kingly Art, 290e–293a (including an A section). In *Phd.* the frame dialogue between Phaedon and Echecrates is resumed at two important points, 88c–89a and 102ab, though not explicitly at the end (but there is a concluding apostrophe

---

120. *Ly.* 213cd, *Chrm.* 158e–162b, *Phd.* 101b, 102d, *Smp.* 202bc, 204d, *R.* IV.424bc. The spurious *Erx.* over-ambitiously uses narrative and description in all sections, e.g. 393ab (in A), 396a (introducing an E inserted), 397b–398c (in connection with an A inserted in an interlude).

121. Cf. v. Arnim 1913.

122. For Plato's use of these formulae, see Andrieu 1954: 316–319.

123. The same principle is employed in the two spurious C dialogues, *Amat.* and *Erx.* The former is very artless, almost a mere skeleton of the type represented by *Ly.*

124. The complicated but symmetrical structure has been studied by Friedländer II$^2$ 169–180 and Sprague 1962: 1–33.

to Echecrates). *Smp.* returns to the structure of *Prt.:* it has only an opening frame dialogue between Apollodorus and an unnamed friend. But on the other hand it adopts the device of second-hand report (Apollodorus-Aristodemus). *Smp.* also includes C reports by Socrates (201e–212c) and Alcibiades (215a–222b). In *Prm.* too the frame is merely opening, but a third-hand report is adopted (Cephalus-Antiphon-Pythodorus). Cf. the opening frame dialogue in *Tht.* where (143ab) reasons are given for abandoning the C type.

If thus the chronological order was as here assumed, it seems that Plato introduced the "frame" *(Prt.)* to give an additional dimension to the work, experimented with it as a throughout counterpoint *(Euthd., Phd.)*, then *(Smp., Prm.)* used it for justifying the increasing perspective of the second-hand and third-hand report, and finally *(Tht.)* for justifying his return to the dramatic form.

The oratio obliqua necessitated by the second-hand and third-hand report in *Smp.* and *Prm.* is not kept up strictly, and in *Prm.* the very awkward "Antiphon said that Pythodorus had said that . . ." occurs explicitly only twice (127a, 136e). Plato is never particular about matters of consistency.[125]

[50]

## D. Dialogue approximating to monologue

[51]

Sample text: *R.* VI.489a–497a (reasons why philosophers are not trusted).

It is a well-known fact[126] that type D is particularly common in Plato's later works: Plato tends to develop dialogue into monologue or "lecturing," and the comments of the lecturer's interlocutor tend to lose much of the factual importance which the replies have in elenctic (or eristic) of type A. But as will be seen below, type D occurs in connection with, or as a substitute for, type A.

### Origins

In real life a dialogue of the D kind has of course always occurred whenever one person gives consecutive information or instruction to another person. But it seems entirely improbable that Plato had had any literary models for his use of D. There are no distinct examples of it in the dialogues of Aeschines and Xenophon, and the only spurious Platonic dialogues where something comparable occurs, *Min.* (320d–321d) and *Erx.* (399e–406a), are clearly influenced by Plato's literary technique. Had the D dialogue been in any sense typical of Socrates' manner of argumentation there should have been traces of it in the dialogues of the other

---

125. Cf. also the oscillation between oratio obliqua and oratio recta in the myth of Er, *R.* X.614b–621d. Cf. D. Tarrant, "Plato's Use of Extended Oratio Obliqua" (1955).
126. Discussed notably by Campbell 1867: XX, Hirzel 1895: 240–241, Wilamowitz II: 213 ("Ermüdung"), Ueberweg-Praechter I[13] 213–214, Levi 1940: 110–118, Merlan 1947: 409–410, G. Müller 1951: 124–126.

[51] Socratics and in Plato's early "mimetic" works. The rise of Plato's D must be explained from the development of Plato's own stylistic practice and intentions.[127]

Like A, D is principally employed by Plato's Socrates or his successor in the later dialogues. In fact no other characters attempt to use it, except Theaitetos in a brief passage *Tht.* 147c–148b (inserted in B), and this seems to indicate that it is really a Platonic device.

## Function

The function of type D appears to be always to carry a positive and constructive argument or piece of information. Often the D dialogue amounts to a point or a view of particular importance. Owing to its weight it is more distinctly and [52] seriously persuasive than the strict A dialogue. There is not often distinct irony in it (rather a grim irony in *Grg.* 480a–481b, on the usefulness of rhetoric for evil-doing; for *Cra.* see below). A passage of D dialogue sometimes precedes the final argument or vision of Socrates, thus already in *Cri.*, and later in *Grg.*, *Phd.*, *Smp.* (Diotima), and *R.* X. The D is also used for partial or full conclusions, as in *Grg.* where each of the three main parts of the work is concluded with an AD passage (459c–461b, 478e–481b, 519e–522e, with growing force and weight); cf. *Men.* 93b–94e (conclusion of Anytus episode), *Prt.* 352a–360e (leading to concluding exchange of speeches), *Euthd.* 307a–c (concluding protreptic). An examination of the rest of the (A) D sections before *Phdr.* shows that all, except *Cra.* 391e–427d, and perhaps *Grg.* 449c–455a, have an important function in the course of the argument.[128]

Socrates' playful lists of etymologies in *Cra.* may however cast some light on Plato's own view of the function of D dialogue. Socrates begins after a reference to Homer (391d) by analyzing the names of gods and heroes (391e–396d). His speculations tend to expand to long coherent pieces of declamation, and after the passage on Zeus and Cronus Hermogenes remarks (396d) that Socrates seems to be inspired (ὥσπερ οἱ ἐνθουσιῶντες) and utter oracles (χρησμῳδεῖν). He has this inspiration from Euthyphron, Socrates replies. He then goes on with various etymologies, and Euthyphron or the "Muse" of Euthyphron figures from time to time (399a, 400a, 407d, 409d, 428c). The very extensive speculations about the origin

---

127. Schaerer 1938: 34–35 seems to think that the dialogue here called D was equally Socratic as the dialogue of type A, but he fails to give any reasonable support to this view.

128. *Grg.* 449c–455a (attempts to define rhetoric) belongs to the preliminary discussion, but Socrates here already has the impetus which is later in the dialogue characteristic of him. The following (A)D sections are of greater significance: *Grg.* 500a–501c (on true arts and empirical skill), *Grg.* 513c–515c (on political expertise), *Ly.* 219c–220e (on the highest love and the opposite of love), *Euthd.* 282a–d (importance of teaching wisdom), *Phd.* 63e–69e (a philosopher dies with confidence), *Phd.* 78b–84b (third argument for immortality), *Phd.* 89c–90d (on preserving reason), *Phd.* 102b–103a (consideration of the Forms), *Prm.* 134e–136c (Parmenides gives advice about method and exercise), *Tht.* 147c–148b (mathematical argument of Theaitetos), *Tht.* 148e–150b (Socrates as a midwife), *Tht.* 156a–457c (the nature of perception), *Tht.* 169d–179b (criticism of Protagoras and, in the center, digression on philosophical leisure). Cf. the analyses below.

of the word δικαιοσύνη (412c–413d) occasion Hermogenes to suggest that Socrates has perhaps heard all this from somebody else. And in the B section which closes the etymological chapter (428c) Cratylus admits that this was all really oracular (χρησμῳδεῖν), whether Socrates were inspired by Euthyphron or some other Muse. Now it is hardly possible to infer that Plato here has imitated the manner of speech of some oracular teacher (e.g. Euthyphron or Cratylus), because in fact the exposition with its inserted questions and its playful tone still remains quite Socratic. But what Plato means to say is that such a D dialogue has something of *divine inspiration* in it. In *Cra.* Plato only plays ironically with the idea. But from *Phd., Smp.* and *Phdr.* onwards he makes serious use of inspired D dialogue. [52] [53]

Indeed, in the later works from *Phdr.* and *R.* II (or rather, III) onwards type D becomes the proper medium for Plato's thought, and distinct A passages are few and brief (cf. above p. 37, and the analyses below). This also corresponds to the fact that Plato in his late works is principally delivering constructive teaching.

## *Technique*

*Relation of D to A, B, and E.* Type D clearly emerges from type A and it is frequently, especially in the middle period, combined with passages of strict questioning. Before the late period only one passage reminiscent of D is found in a B section: *Euthd.* 274d–275b (Socrates proposes that the sophists should teach Clinias). In fact this passage functions as a persuasive speech, and Plato has probably inserted some questions and replies in order to make it fit better in the vividly conversational tone of this work. It has little relevance to the general history of D. But from *Ti.* onwards the D dialogue tends to intrude in the B sections: note *Ti.* 17a–19b, all interludes in *Sph.* and *Plt.* (*see* the analyses), and *Lg.* I.632d–637b, VI.769a–771a, VII.818e–822d, X.885a–887c, XII.968b–969d (conclusion).

An occasional expansion of a question in A dialogue (above p. 31) should not be taken as D. Only a considerable expansion of several consecutive questions is a mark of this change. The difference can be seen clearly when comparing e.g. some passages in the examination of the nature of rhetoric in *Grg.* 449c–455a: the first approach is kept as fairly strict A, but ends in two somewhat expansive summing-up statements by Socrates (450ab) and an objection by Gorgias (450bc); but for the next approach Socrates employs a typical D exposition with much more force and weight. Agreement about what is to be called A and what D can hardly be reached in all cases, and thus a minute classification must remain subjective to some extent (cf. below, third stage of D). But characteristic instances such as the above-mentioned case are sufficiently obvious to justify the differentiation between the types. [54]

On the whole it is also possible to make a differentiation between D and E, because the monologues and speeches proper tend to come in B sections or otherwise they clearly stand out from the rest (cf. below, E); the anomaly in *Euthd.* 274d–275b was referred to above. In *Ti., Lg.,* and *Epin.* however this difference is not so clear. The introduction of Timaeus' exposition ends with a comment by Socrates (29d), as in D dialogue; and large parts of *Lg.* are virtually kept as a

[54] continuous exposition to which occasional comments lend a slight character of D. In *Epin.* the comments are restricted to the B sections.

*Stages of development.* Three stages may be distinguished:

In the early stage Socrates keeps a constant contact with his interlocutor. His utterances, though they expand, normally end in questions, and passages with more strict questioning of type A are inserted from time to time. This stage is represented by *Cri., Grg., Men.,* and the very brief passages of D in *Ly., Chrm., Prt.,* and *Euthd.,* and also on the whole by the first AD sections in *Phd.* (63e–69e, 78b–84b, 89c–90d).

The next stage implies a further expansion of the teacher's utterances, a further restriction of the questioning, and tendency of the interlocutor's replies to become mere assent or questions asking for further information.[129] This stage makes its first appearance in *Cra.* (393a, 396d, 379a, etc) and occurs to a varying extent from the central part of *Phd.* (96c) onwards in all dialogic works.[130] Also the brief mathematical passage *Tht.* 147c–148b, where Theaitetos takes the lead, represents this stage, though it is inserted in a B section.

The third stage can be said to imply a new approximation of D to A. The teacher's utterances become brief again but are rarely put as questions, whereas the interlocutor's assent and questions only serve the purpose of marking a vivid interest or, rather more mechanically, give a dialogic rhythm to a virtually coherent exposition. This stage occurs for the first time in *Smp.* (teaching of Diotima, 201e–202e, 204d–207a), and later it occurs together with a more distinct A in particular in *Prm.* (the 
[55] latter part) and *Phlb.*,[131] and together with a more distinct D of the second type in particular in *Sph.* and *Plt.*, and also elsewhere in the late works. It can be said to affect the A dialogue in such cases as *Tht.* 163c, 164c, *Phdr.* 266e, *R.* IV.429ab, *Lg.* X.902c.

## E. Monologue and continuous exposition

Sample text: *Ion* 533c–535a (Socrates on inspiration).

In all the authentic works (except *Sph.*) there occur passages that are not primarily links in the A(D) or B dialogue but that can be regarded as examples of continuous exposition. Such monologues or "dihegetic" passages vary in character and length from fairly brief deliberative utterances, e.g. *La.* 181d–182d (Nicias on the usefulness of teaching military skill), *Grg.* 456c–457c (Gorgias or rhetoric), or pieces of visionary imagery, e.g. the *Ion* passage above, or exhortative speeches, e.g. *Grg.* 526d–527e (concluding protreptic by Socrates), to rhetorical speeches, such as those in *Mx., Smp.* and *Phdr.*, and extentive myths, or systematic treatments of a subject, such as the "speech" of Timaeus in *Ti.*

---

129. Some observations on the last-mentioned technique in Billings 1920: 103.
130. See e.g. *Prm.* 135d, 136a, *Tht.* 171a, 172cd, *R.* II.373e, 377c.
131. For this usage in *Phlb.*, see Friedländer III² 286–287.

## Origins [55]

All E passages are formally speeches, except *Ep.* 7 which, however, can be said to function as a speech. But it is evident that their stylistic sources are widely different. Plato appears to have made use of all contemporary genres of literary non-dialogical prose, notably the different branches of public oratory (symbuleutic, dicanic, epideictic, encomiastic), but also myths and apodeixeis of sophists, historical narrative, scientific and technical tracts, and legal and ceremonious texts. Also branches of earlier prose are imitated, such as 5th century gnomic style and logographic narrative. This approximation to existing stylistic models will be considered more closely below in connection with the different stylistic shades.

It may be asked whether the insertion of speeches and other pieces of continuous exposition in prose dialogue was a practice invented by Plato, and, if not, what kinds of monologue were used by his predecessors. In spite of the scarcity of the material it can be stated with some certainty that Plato here too did have predecessors in Greek prose. First, there is the genre of ἀντιλογίαι. Traditionally, these consisted of antithetic speeches without support of a real dialogue, as often in Thucydides,[132] but to judge from Xenophon's account (*Mem.* 2. 1. 21–34, *Vors.* [56] 84. B. 2) Prodicus in his Ὧραι interspersed some dialogue between the antagonistic speeches of Arete and Kakia. There are traces of antilogies in Plato, as will be seen below. Second, the genre of ἐρωτικοὶ λόγοι, which was also practiced by 5th century sophists and which had a natural function in the symposion literature,[133] was taken over by the Socratics and may have included dialogue before Plato wrote *Smp.*, and *Phdr.*[134] Third, there existed a type of dialogic ὑποθῆκαι of which Hippias' Τρωικός (Ps.-Pl. *Hp.Ma.* 286ab, *Vors.* 86. A. 9) is the first example known: here Neoptolemus put at least one question to Nestor who answered it at length with a sophistic logos. A similar pattern is quite common in Xenophon's Socratic dialogues (*see* especially Socrates' pronouncements on various ethical concepts in *Mem.* 3. 9), and it is probable that other Socratics too employed it. Plato to be sure tries to avoid it, as he usually avoids depicting Socrates as a sophist, but in some of his works a speech of Socrates starts from aporetic questions or appeals and can thus be said at least to reflect the ὑποθῆκαι pattern, e.g. *Ion* 533c, *Hp.Mi.* 372a. And fourth, speeches on political, historical or mythical subjects seem to have been current in the Socratic dialogues, as is shown by

---

132. Cf. Aly 1929: 38 and 95–104. Some sophists, notably Protagoras, seem to have practiced "antilogies" of brief antithetic arguments; cf. Dissoi Logoi (Diels-Kranz II⁹ 90), Pl. *Tht.* 167d. The notice in Diog. L. 9.53 that Protagoras τὸ Σωκρατικὸν εἶδος τῶν λόγων πρῶτος ἐκίνησε may have something to do with his antilogies; cf. Gaiser 1959: 60.

133. For the λόγος ἐρωτικός, *see* Lasserre 1944; Ps.-Dem. *Erot.* is a typical independent specimen (cf. Gaiser 1959: 67–68). For the symposion literature, *see* Martin 1931.

134. It is usually assumed that Xen. *Smp.* is later than Pl. *Smp.*, but Xenophon is normally independent of Plato in matters of composition and may reflect older traditions. The context is unknown for a fragment of a speech of Euclides ap. Stob. 3 p. 302 Hense, which Hirzel 1895: 110 n. 4 assumes to be from an Ἐρωτικός. Gaiser 1959: 65–66 sees a reflection of this practice in *Ly.* 207d–210d, but this too remains uncertain.

[56] Aeschines *Alc.* fr. 8 Dittmar and some spurious Platonic works (*Hipparch.* 228a–229e, *Alc.* 1.120e–124b, *Alc.* 2.146e–150b, *Min.* 318e–320d).[135]

[57] It is worth particular notice that the deliverer of such speeches in the Socratic literature is largely Socrates himself. There must be some historical truth in this. Though the Socrates of Plato had a pronounced distaste for "macrology" (cf. above, p. 33), his occasional lapses into it are not entirely anomalous. These lapses make Socrates the sophist come somewhat nearer to us.

Gaiser (1959) has argued that the Socratic dialogue arose from a protreptic logos practiced by the sophists, and that the early Platonic dialogue essentially retained a protreptic character which is particularly conspicuous in some central and some concluding "paraenetic" speeches (p. 148–196). I am prepared to admit that the speeches principally reflect a sophistic practice, but I would stress the heterogeneous origins of the Socratic dialogue as a whole, as the above considerations on the various types of dialogue will have shown.[136]

## Function

The function of the E passages is on the whole not to carry the main argument, but to present a problem, or an important aspect of a problem, or a point or counterpoint or vision in connection with, but not solving, a problem. The stylistic analysis below will, I hope, illuminate this fact.[137]

Most *opening* B sections contain one or several introductory E's,[138] often in pairs and arranged as antilogies stating two contrary positions, as e.g. the speeches of Nicias and Laches in *La.* 181d–184c[139]; cf, above p. 44.

The important *central* section (with the "peripeteia," cf. p. 28) often includes, or consists of, a speech of Socrates or his stand-in.[140] There are roughly three types of such central E's.

---

135. See Dönt 1963. There are a few other traces of such speeches in the fragments of Aeschines, e.g. fr. 18 Dittmar; cf. de Vries 1963: 41–42.—For Phaedon and Antisthenes, cf. Hirzel 1895: 261.

136. Cf. Gottschalk's review of Gaiser, *Erasmus* 16 (1964): 419–422. It should be observed that Gaiser rather presses the term "protreptic." As he is not concerned with the external form of the works, he makes the term include both continuous exposition and dialogue proper.

137. Schaerer 1938: 143 seems to underrate the difference between questioning and continuous exposition.

138. Of the authentic dialogues, only *Hp.Mi., Sph., Plt., Phlb.* and *Lg.* wholly lack E passages in the opening B sections. In *Ion* and *Grg.* they are not very manifest.

139. Similarly in *Men., Euthphr., Cra., Prt.* (316c–317c/319a–320c, and especially 320c–328d/328d–329d), *Prm., R.* II (358b–368c); cf. *Cri.* Other pairs: *Ly.* (204c–206a), *Chrm.* (156d–158c), *R.* I (329a–331b), *Prt.* (313a–314b), *Phdr.* (228a–230a). Also *Thg., Alc.* 1.

140. Gaiser's "central parainesis" (1959: 148–187, 198–217; parallels in Homer and Pindar 225–226) is not identical with my "central speech," though there are many coincidences. In his search for paraenetic components Gaiser sometimes seems to lose sight of what is really central from the point of view of the argument and the composition; for instance, (201–207) he takes the "paraenetic" sections *R.* VI.487b–497a to be the central culmination of *R.* II–X (instead of VI.507a–VII.527c, the Sun, Line, and Cave).

The first is an ironical statement of the position to which the first part of the [58] argument seems to have led, as the two speeches of Socrates in *Hp.Mi.* 369d–373c or the (semi-ironical) examination of the poem of Simonides by Socrates in *Prt.* 342a–347a.[141] Cf. *Euthphr.* which however lacks a distinct E in the central B section.

The second type is a legend or a historical exposition illustrating the dialogue leader's belief. There are traces of this device in *Mx., Smp., Plt.,* and *Phlb.,* but with different alternations of the pattern. In *Mx.* the central E has expanded so as to become the main part of the work. In *Smp.* 201e–207a (preparatory myth of Eros, leading over to a visionary exposition of type three, below) as in *Plt.* 268d–274e (myth of Cronus), Diotima and the Elean Guest respectively use D dialogue instead of the E proper. In *Phlb.* 18b–d the legend of Theuth constitutes the center of the first part of the work, and though it is very brief and hardly more than an expanded B utterance, it pregnantly recalls the more elaborate myth of Theuth in *Phdr.* 274c–275b (below, p. 142).[142]

The third type of central E is a visionary speech of Socrates, which raises the argument to a higher level, as the two speeches on divine magnetism in *Ion* 533c–536d. In this type too there occurs considerable variation. For *Grg.,* see below p. 122. In *Men.* 81a–e the central vision of anamnesis comes as a kind of antilogy to a speech of Menon (79e–80d, simile of the torpedo); the Anytus episode (89e–95a) can in fact be regarded as a digression having its own ironical anticlimax in the center (91c–92a). *Chrm.* culminates in a brief visionary speech on moderation (173a–d), rather towards the end (but this arrangement is somewhat balanced by the introductory Zalmoxis legend 156d–158d). In *R.* I.347b–e the speech of Socrates on true leadership comes immediately after the significant introduction of Glaucon. In *Phd.* the argument turns upon the central D or E speech of Socrates [59] 96a–102a. In *Smp.* the central speech is the initiation of Socrates by Diotima, 208c–212a. *Phdr.* culminates in the second speech of Socrates, 243e–257b. In some of the later works[143] D passages seem to take over the function of the central E. In a sense this applies to the etymologies in *Cra.* (cf. above p. 52). *Tht.* has a preliminary "central speech" in 150b–151d (on maieutics), and various other culminations (cf. below p. 141), but the D passage on philosophical leisure in the absolute center of the work (172c–177c) may be regarded as the main culmination. *R.* II–X culminate in the D passages on the Line and the Cave at the end of the VIth book and the beginning of the VIIth.

It may be mentioned here that *Euthd.,* instead of a central E, has a very clearly marked brief A on the Kingly Art (291d–292e). Disregarding *Ap.,* which however

---

141. With allusions to mythology in *Hp.Mi.,* and to legends in *Prt.* (cf. type 2). Cf. *La.* 186a–189e (two speeches by Socrates), *Ly.* 211d–212a; and among the spuria, *Thg.* 127d–128b (though approaching the end), *Sis.* 390a–d, *Erx.* 396a–e.

142. Cf. the historical digressions in the spurious *Hipparch., Alc.* 1, *Alc.* 2, and *Min.,* discussed by Dönt 1963.

143. In *Criti.,* the speech of Zeus which was never written was perhaps intended as the central culmination of the whole trilogy, just as the Cronus myth in *Plt.* seems to mark the central point of the unfinished *Sph.* trilogy. Cf. below p. 148. Cf. further the "culminative" function of the so-called "digression" in *Ep.* 7.342a–344d, and the prooimion in *Lg.* V.

has the main weight in the center and *Epin.*, the only Platonic work that wholly lacks traces of a central E or a comparable section, is *Cri.*[144]

The *concluding* B sections normally lack the elaboration and stress of the opening and central sections. Yet they sometimes include E passages. In these cases too the speaker is always Socrates (or his stand-in), which indicates that Plato here followed a deliberate rule.[145] Whether originally Platonic or not,[146] this practice serves the tendency to make the end of the work incomplete in itself, by opening a new view with new perspectives (cf. below p. 138). The E passages at the end are nowhere "summaries and conclusions" of the previous discussion. They carry an additional point, either ironically and quasi-aporetically, as in *Ion* and *Cra.* (cf. *R.* I, *Prt.* and *Euthd.*),[147] or protreptically, as in *Chrm.* (cf. *Euthd.*), or more commonly on a visionary level with reference to superhuman matters: the great eschatological myths in *Grg., Phd.* and *R.* X have more or less remote parallels in the concluding speeches by Socrates in *Cri.* (the Laws), *Ap., Men., Euthphr.*, and *Tht.*[148]

Several of the above-mentioned passages have been classed as *"myths"* in the large literature on the subject.[149] The rest of the passages that have been called so occur in various other places in the dialogues. Usually they are attached to B sections and function as semi-playful "historical" illustrations of the argument:[150] *Prt.* 320c–322d (myth of Protagoras, pastiche), *Smp.* 189d–191d (speech of Aristophanes, partial pastiche), *Phdr.* 259a–d (cicadas), *Phdr.* 274c–275b (Theuth), *R.* II.359b–360d (Gyges), *R.* II.372a–d (origins of civilisation),[151] *Lg.* IV.713c–714b (Cronus). But some are inserted in the D dialogue (cf. above, p. 54), and they are considerably more heavy and serious: *R.* III.414d–415c (earthborn man),

---

144. But cf. below p. 49.—On the other hand several of the spuria have no central E or central culmination: *Just., Virt., Hp.Ma., Amat., Clit.*

145. In *Prt.* and the concluding frame dialogue of *Euthd.* Plato seems to experiment with a quasi-antilogical exchange of speeches between Socrates and his partner.

146. The concluding speeches in Ps.-Pl. *Virt.* and Aeschines fr. 11 Dittmar, and the sporadic occurrence of such speeches in Plato, suggest that Plato had not introduced the practice himself.

147. Cf. also *Hp.Ma.*

148. Cf. the concluding reference to piety in *Epin.*, and the brief prayer to Pan in *Phdr.*— Among the spuria, a similar concluding E passage occurs in *Virt.*; in *Alc.* 2 and *Min.* they are followed by a B and D passage respectively.

149. See especially Harris 1892, Stewart 1905 (both concerned with the most typical instances only), Willi 1925 (over-abstract and difficult), Reinhardt 1927 (subjective literary judgment), Frutiger 1930 (new classification, with abundant material and references; criticized by Levi 1946), Stöcklein 1937 (mythos as preparatory stage for logos), Friedländer I² 182–219 (three classes), Schuhl 1947 (complexity of associations), de Vries 1949: 281–330 (play and seriousness interwoven), Edelstein 1949 (classification according to function), Hartland-Swann 1951, v. Loewenclau 1958, G. Müller 1963 (all concerned with myth as a complement to dialectic). On the possibility of differentiating myths from legends and paradigms, *see* in particular Goldschmidt 1947. More references in Cherniss 1959: 240–244.

150. Cf. the second type of central E's above. *See* further Edelstein 1949, who differentiates such myths from the rather more serious, and at the same time more irrational, ethical and eschatological myths.

151. Cf. Frutiger 1930: 49–53.

R. VIII.546a–547a (nuptial number), *Lg.* X.903a–905a (eschatology).[152] The main exposition in *Ti.* (and *Criti.*) remotely corresponds to this last type.

For various *other purposes* which cannot be discussed here utterances by Socrates or his successor or his interlocutors sometimes expand into monologues or speeches of type E. This is comparatively common in *Grg.* and *Prt.* which are concerned with "macrology" (for details, *see* the analyses below). Complete formal speeches occur, disregarding the eschatological myths, in *Prt., Smp., Phdr.* and *Lg.,* but only in *Ap.* and *Mx.* does the main exposition consist of a formal discourse. The "speeches" of Timaeus and Critias in *Ti.* and *Criti.,* and large portions of *Lg.* and *Epin.,* are to all intents and purposes written tracts. *Ep.* 7 comes in a class of its own.

For the use of narrative and description in C dialogue, *see* above p. 47.

Thus it is clear that Plato makes a very considerable and varied use of monologue, and it is interesting to note that the speaker in the great majority of these passages is Socrates or his successor in the late works (cf. above p. 46 ff.). Type E is not a mere by-play to, but complements types A, B, and D.

*Technique*

As was noted above (p. 31 and 35) it is on the whole easy to differentiate E passages from merely expanded utterances in B and A(D) dialogue: a notable change of tone and extent, and a looser connection with the surrounding dialogue are usually marks of E. There are of course some border-line cases where the classification has to rest on subjective criteria. In the later works the D dialogue sometimes tends to lose its dialogue character and thus to approximate to continuous exposition (above p. 44), but a complete change into E does rarely occur. An apparent example of this can be seen in the early *Cri.,* 46b–47a, but here it is rather the opposite that has happened; the utterance of Socrates is virtually an antilogical E speech answering the preceding request of Criton, but it slips over into an AD dialogue. The first real examples of the tendency of D to approximate to E can be found in *Phd.,* 96e–102a, 107c–115a (myth); cf. the occurrence of the second stage of type D, above p. 44. Further e.g. *R.* VIII.546a–547a (nuptial number), the opening section of *Ti.* (where D is intermixed with B according to Plato's later practice, cf. above p. 43), and *Lg.* passim (for *Epin.,* see below).

E passages usually occur in, or are attached to, B sections (cf. above p. 35). Quite often an E passage concludes the work, but it rarely opens it, in spite of the common use of E in opening B sections. Disregarding *Ap., Ep.* 7 and the C

---

152. Friedländer I² 188–189 regards the second speech of Cephalus in *R.* I.330d–331b as "mythic" on behalf of its references to eschatology and poetry, but I do not think there are sufficient formal criteria for this. The same seems to me to apply to the following passages which Frutiger 1930 classes as myths: *Cra.* 388e–391a (p. 53–57), *R.* IV.434e–441c, X.611b–612a (p. 76–96), *Lg.* III.676a–702a (p. 49–53). The occasional references to death and retribution in the passages recorded by Frutiger 1930: 30–31 have little to do with real myths.

[62] dialogues, only *La.* (speech of Lysimachus), *Criti.* (speech of Timaeus) and *Epin.* (speech of Clinias) open with an E passage; and note the fact that the speakers in all three cases are minor characters, whereas the concluding speeches are normally by Socrates.[153]

Sometimes B sections are replaced by a single E speech.[154]

In A(D) sections E passages are only occasionally found. *Cri.* 46b–47a can be connected with the preceding B section (cf. above). A more obvious instance is *Grg.* 469c–e (Socrates on the lunatic). The rest of the instances arise from special conditions; some are quotations of fictitious speeches or apostrophes.[155]

E speeches stand for entire A(D) sections (disregarding *Ap.*, *Mx.*, and *Ep.* 7) in *Smp.*, *Phdr.*, *Ti.* and *Criti.* (for details, *see* the analyses below), and virtually in the whole of *Epin.*[156]

---

153. The opening speech of Socrates in *Alc.* 1 thus represents an anomaly.

154. *Grg.* 523a–527e (concluding myth and logos by Socrates), *Men.* 89e–90b (Socrates introduces Anytus), *R.* I.354a–e (concluding speech of Socrates), *Euthd.* 277d–278e (speech of Socrates to Clinias and the sophists), *Euthd.* 303c–304b, but framed by a C narrative (concluding speech of Socrates to the sophists), *Smp.* 201de (Socrates makes Diotima take over), *R.* X.614b–621d (concluding myth). For *R.* I.352b–d, *see* the following note.—In the spuria: *Virt.* 379cd (concluding speech of Socrates), *Alc.* 1.120e–124b (central speech of Socrates), *Sis.* 390a–d (central speech of Socrates).

155. Further *R.* 1.352b–d (Socrates on the importance of the problem under discussion, but the speech may be taken as corresponding to a B interlude), *Prt.* 350c–351b (extensive objection of Protagoras in the form of a speech), *Phd.* 66b–67b (fictitious speech of the philosophers), *Phdr.* 273d–274a (apostrophe to Tisias by Socrates), *R.* III.393d–394a (prose transcription of the beginning of the *Iliad*, by Socrates), *R.* VII.520b–d (speech of Socrates to the philosophers who are going to rule the State), *R.* VIII.546a–547a (nuptial number), *R.* X.599de (apostrophe to Homer by Socrates), *Lg.* I.631b–632d (plan of legislation by the Athenian), *Lg.* IV.715e–718e (fictitious speech of lawgiver), *Lg.* VI.772e–773e (speech to young men who are going to marry), *Lg.* VII.823d–824a (speech to young hunters), *Lg.* IX.854b–e (to a person prepared to make sacrilege), *Lg.* X.888a–d (to the atheist), *Lg.* X.899d–900b (to the believer in indifferent gods). Note the preponderance of such instances in *R.* and *Lg.*—In the spuria: note *Erx.* 396a–e (mediating speech of Socrates, probably representing a central speech).

156. Cf. also the speech of Clitophon in *Clit.* 407a ff.

# STYLE MARKERS AND CLASSES OF STYLE [63]

## General observations

It will be convenient to differentiate roughly between 10 generic classes of style whose style markers repeatedly occur in Plato's prose:

1. Colloquial style
2. Semi-literary conversational style
3. Rhetorical style
4. Pathetic style
5. Intellectual style
6. Mythic narrative style
7. Historical style
8. Ceremonious style
9. Legal style
10. Onkos style

In this list are approximately represented all prose styles (classes of style) which to our knowledge were used by Plato's contemporaries. In addition to them the list includes one more distinctly Platonic class, 10.

In the following, these ten classes, and the corresponding stylistic shades and style markers, will be referred to by *figures in bold type*. It should be noted here once for all that this classification of style is by nature inexact and vague in outline; it only indicates tendencies.

The discussion of each class will be followed by a brief illustrative analysis of a piece of text. In these sample analyses *square brackets* denote touches of other styles. Lists of all style markers referred to will be found on p. 65 ff.


## 1. *Colloquial style*

This is the common basis for Plato's normal diction in the early and middle works up to and including the *Tht.* Plato on the whole employs the style of

[64] cultivated every-day conversation; this can be regarded as reasonably evident a priori.[157] This style is not very markedly "colloquial," and leading style markers may be quite rare in it. Sometimes however his colloquial diction is more distinct and manifestly elaborated to suit the contents and the characterization of the speakers. Some details will be referred to in the analyses below. Only very occasionally does Plato introduce idioms of a considerably lower social stratum, and always with a very specific point, e.g. ἐπὶ κόρρης τύπτειν *Grg.* 486c, *Phdr.* 268d. Vulgarisms in phonology, morphology, or syntax do not seem to occur.[158]

For colloquial Attic there is abundant material to be found in Comedy and Xenophon, also to some extent elsewhere.[159] But difficulties arise when we look for general criteria of colloquial style markers.

It is customary to refer to certain general trends which would seem to be characteristic of colloquial speech in all languages at all periods,[160] namely (a) exaggeration: hyperbole, abundance, emphasis, strengthening, etc.; (b) understatement: irony, attenuation, approximation, etc.; (c) lively and picturesque forms of expression: imagery, quotations, proverbs, puns, etc.; (d) brevity and disorganization of expression: ellipse, anacoluthon, parataxis, etc.; and (e) mechanization: idioms, set phrases.[161]

[65] It is obvious however that these categories are only tendencies which occur somewhat more commonly in spoken language than in written language. They cannot on the whole be used as primary criteria for determining colloquialisms, because they are common in literary styles as well. It does not take much effort to find, for instance, hyperboles in high poetry, approximative expressions in scientific prose, vivid metaphors in rhetoric, parataxis in the language of decrees, and set phrases in the stylized diction of classical drama. The truth is probably that such tendencies are typical of language in general, though some styles suppress them to a varying degree.[162] For colloquial style, as for other styles, reliable

---

157. Explicitly pointed out by Campbell 1894: 260; cf. Lammermann 1935, Frank 1937, D. Tarrant 1946, 1958. The paper of I. v. Müller, announced in Sitzungsberichte der Königlichen Bayerischen Akademie der Wissenschaftern, Philosophisch-historische Klasse, München (1896), was apparently never published. For the philosophical usefulness of an easy-going style, cf. *Tht.* 184c.

158. For vulgarisms in the Old Comedy, *see* the references in the next note, in particular Setti 1885: 115–119. For the epigraphical material, *see* Schwyzer I (1950): 87–88.

159. Cf. des Places 1934 who emphasizes the fact that none of our sources are "purely" colloquial. There are many studies on the language of Comedy, but they do not differentiate between "vulgarisms" and "colloquialisms," thus notably Lottich 1881, Setti 1885, Selvers 1909. Gautier 1911 is insufficient for Xenophon's colloquialisms. Colloquialisms in tragedy have been recorded by Stevens 1937 (Euripides) and 1945 (Aeschylus and Sophocles).

160. *See* notably Wunderlich 1894, Bally 1909, J. B. Hofmann 1926; for Greek, *see* the studies of Setti and Stevens recorded in the preceding note.

161. The emotional aspect of colloquial speech was rather overstressed by Bally and Hofmann. But for the "dialogical situation,"and hence dialogical phrases in Latin colloquial speech., *see* Hofmann 1936: 9ff.

162. Thus it is natural that similar categories have been applied to language as a whole by language psychologists such as Havers 1931; *see* especially the chapter 'Triebkräfte' p. 144 ff.

criteria can only be found by carefully studying the distribution of the individual [65] expressions. As can be seen from the table below (p. 65) most of the colloquial style markers indeed belong to one of the above-mentioned categories; but it is not because of this that they can be taken as style markers.

In very general terms colloquial style, as opposed to other styles, can perhaps be characterized as having a light and easy tone with many shifts of emphasis and a tendency to brevity and slackness of exposition, and a marked use of idioms.

*Sample text. La.* 194c–196c: lively polemic between Nicias and Laches about the nature of courage, with interjected remarks by Socrates. ἴθι δή—imagery (Socratic)—τις—ὁρᾷς—πάλαι—[2 οὐ καλῶς]—word order expressive—οὗτος resumptive—d inconsistent [3 antithesis]—νὴ Δία—δῆλον ὅτι—ἤκουσας;—ἔγωγε—σφόδρα—ἀνήρ, krasis—ὅδε reference to person—e ἔγωγε—ἴθι δή—που—comical—οὐδαμῶς—δῆτα—πάνυ—οὗτος prepar.—ἔγωγε—[2 synonymy]—195a [3 polarization]—ὡς exclamatory—ἄτοπος—word order expressive—ὅ τι; in reply—δήπου—οὐ reply—μὰ Δία—τοι—καί climactic—ληρέω—οὐκ reply—krasis—μηδὲν λέγω—b πάνυ μὲν οὖν—οὐδὲν λέγω—ἐπεί explic.—αὐτίκα "e.g."—σύ redundant—οὐδ᾽ ὁπωστιοῦν—word order expressive—καίτοι—δήπου—ἅπας redundant—[2 synonymy, but [66] reference to 194e]—c οὐδέν τι μᾶλλον—λέγω τι—[5 abstract: subst. adj., -ώδης]—δήπου—τω—οὗτος prepar.—ί—οὗτος prepar.—σύ redundant—d ἔγωγε—word order expressive—ἔγωγε—οὗτος prepar.—σύ redundant—e ἔγωγε—ellipse—ὅτω—καίτοι—σύ redundant—τί δέ;—ἔγωγε—ὦ βέλτιστε—ἐπεί explic.—τω—[3 polarization]—196a τω—εἰ μή "except"—τις—γενναίως—οὐδὲν λέγω—b ἄνω καὶ κάτω—καίτοι—krasis—abundance—word order expressive—dat. comm.—τί; "why?"—[4 imagery]—c οὐδὲν οὐδέ—λέγω τι—ποτε—λέγω τι—[2 εἰ δὲ μή]—εἰ βούλει with inf.—ἴσως "probably"—οὐδὲν κωλύει—[4 πύστις]—πάνυ μὲν οὖν.

Other sample texts: *Grg.* 488b–491e, *Euthd.* 287e–288d.

## 2. *Semi-literary conversational style*

This is a mixed style, and it does not seem to have attracted the attention of scholars.[163] Its use however in semi-formal discussion, in particular by men of prominence, is shown by such passages in Plato as the opening section of *La.*, which is likely to reproduce real practice (though of the 4th century and not of the 5th). As will be seen it plays an important part as a basis for Plato's later diction.

---

Havers does not really distinguish between "vulgar" and "colloquial" speech, cf. 30 ff. and 52 ff.—Hofmann 1926: 4–5 maintains that he has used categories of the above-mentioned type as criteria of 'sermo familiaris' in Latin, but it is easy to see that he has not. His first criterion is in fact the stylistic environment of the expression to be discussed: his main sources are Comedy, Cicero's letters, and Petronius, and he has hardly considered at all "affective" expressions in higher literature.

163. Lammermann 1935 and Frank 1937 treat certain aspects of it, but both are more concerned with what is here regarded as style 1.

[66]    Apart from Plato style 2 is found mainly in the dialogues of Xenophon, notably *Oec.* and *Hier.*, and in less formal but not distinctly colloquial passages in the Attic orators.

Style 2 can be described as a compromise of colloquial (1) and formal rhetorical (3) diction. The speaker avoids idioms that are markedly and vividly colloquial, but he also avoids a continuous use of markedly rhetorical devices; yet he employs features from both sides. He is courteous and urbane, often circumstantial. His sentences expand: the number of ideas expressed in the same sentence, and the number and extent of words in that sentence, are considerably greater than in normal style 1. He often uses hyperbaton (systrophe) in word order and sentence structure, though his periods are not as a rule formally elaborated. Participles have a large use. Synonymy and similar pairs are common. The vocabulary and phraseology are conventional and suggest the usage established by early Attic oratory.—Thus style 2 can be said to draw on rhetorical diction in the same manner as a speaker of modern English, giving an informal non-technical contribution to a conference on some general subject, would draw on conventional "literary" diction.[164]

[67]    *Sample text.*[165] *La.* 178a–180a: monologue by Lysimachus on the question whether boys should learn military skill. In general expansive style, θεάομαι, perfect—(μὲν) οὐκ ... δέ—ἡγέομαι—χρή—παρρησιάζομαι—b στοχάζομαι, participle—ἡγέομαι, participle—participle—οὕτω apodotic—συμβουλή—179a [1 πάλαι]—προοιμιάζομαι—hyperbaton—[1 -ί]—participle—[1 krasis]—δοκέω "think good," perfect—ὡς οἷόν τε—hyperbaton—perfect—[1 νῦν δή]—καθ᾽ ὅσον οἱοί τ᾽ ἐσμέν—participle—ἡγέομαι—perfect—b εἴ τις ἄλλος—participle—πολλάκις "perchance"—perfect—[1 τὸν νοῦν προσέχω]—participle—χρή—participle—[3 isokolon]—abstract: subst. inf.—[1 anacoluthon]—δοκέω "think good"—χρή—[1 krasis]—compar. approx.—c hyperbaton—participle—παρρησιάζομαι—πολλὰ καὶ καλά—[3 anaphoric repetition, polarization]—participle—[3 anaphoric repetition, polarization]—[1 ὑπο-]—d participle—[3 isokolon, period]—ἀκλεής—τάχ᾽ ἄν—hyperbaton—synonymy—participle—ὅτι with superl.—e [1 οὗτος preparative]—θεάομαι—participle—[1 krasis]—θεάομαι—δοκέω "think good"—χρή—[1 ἀνήρ, krasis]—ἅμα μέν ... ἅμα δέ—synonymy—hyperbaton—περί common—ἐπιμέλεια—180a εἴτε ... εἴτε—δοκέω "think good"—χρή—hyperbaton—[1 τις].

Other sample texts: *Grg.* 457c–458b, *R.* II.376c–377e.

## 3. Rhetorical style

Plato's use of rhetoric in parody and imitation and, also especially later, in constructive argument has often been noticed though not so much studied. But there

---

164. This is not the place to discuss what style 2 would have been like before the rise of Attic oratory.

165. The occasional touches of style 1, though as a whole characteristic of style 2, are here denoted separately.

is a considerable literature on Plato's ideological attitude to rhetoric.[166] It is evident that Plato was fascinated by rhetoric, as he was by poetry, though he had certain moral objections to both. In *Phdr.* he appears to have settled his relations with rhetoric better than he ever managed to do with poetry.

Those rhetorical features in Plato's writings that have been mainly studied so far are: the avoidance of hiatus, the rhythms, and the periods. The two first seem to be concentrated to the late works: hiatus is clearly avoided in *Phdr., Ti., Criti., Sph., Plt., Phlb.,* and *Lg.*;[167] and certain types of clausulae, all including a tribrach ($\smile\smile\smile$) seem to be preferred in *Sph., Plt., Phlb.,* and *Lg.*[168] The Platonic periods have been shown to be distinctly rhetorical mainly in the inserted speeches, whereas the complicated sentence structure of the later works has to be connected with Plato's general tendency to complication (cf. below p. 139).[169]

When deciding on style markers for the present purpose, we shall have to make the standard of comparison sufficiently wide so as to include both early forensic oratory (e.g. Andocides 1–2, Antiphon, part of *Lysias*), early encomiastic oratory (e.g. 'Pericles' in Thuc. 2.35–46, Lys. 2), early symbuleutic oratory (e.g. speeches in Thuc., Andocides 3, Ps.-Hipp.V. M.), and polished 4th century rhetoric of the 'Isocratean' kind (Isocrates).

On the other hand Gorgian epideictic oratory stands out as a rather special and easily recognizable type owing to its excessive use of antithesis, isokolon, assonance (in the larger sense of the term),[170] poeticisms and neologisms. It will here be referred to as **3 Gorg.**[171]

Summing up the features that all these styles have in common, it may be said that style **3** in the sense here adopted has the following general characteristics: It shares with style **2** all features that are not at the same time colloquial **(1)**. With style **5** it shares a tendency to explicit argumentation (though with special devices such as τεκμήριον, μάρτυρα ἔχομεν, εἰκός which belong to the leading style markers of style **3**), a tendency to a pointed structure and pointed transitions

---

166. See Vicaire 1960: 276–361, with reference; add Hirzel 1871, Novák 1883, Saupe 1916, Lehnert 1935 (reference), Raeder 1956, Buchheit 1960: 84–108, Kucharski 1961, Th. Meyer 1962: 115–128, Coulter 1964.

167. First observed by Blass 1874: II 426 f. Statistics (for stylometry) by Jannell 1901, cf. Cherniss 1957: 230–233.

168. The clausulae in particular were analyzed by Kaluscha 1904 (following observations by Blass 1901: 152–154) and Billing 1920 (both for stylometry), cf. Brandwood 1958: 12–13. Rhythms have been observed in some speeches of Plato by Blass 1874: II 460 and 1901: 75–93 (also considering the dialogue section *Phdr.* 260a–261a), Harris 1892: 30–47, de Groot 1918 (cf. 1926), Kolár 1951. However, apart from clausulae, the question of Greek prose rhythm seems obscure (so Denniston 1952: 14).

169. Analyses of Platonic periods from the point of view of conventional rhetoric, by Engelhardt 1853 and 1864. Blass 1874: II 429 observed that *Criti.* has comparatively elaborate and polished periods. des Places 1951 points out the difference between rhetorical periods and the typically Platonic expanding sentences "à rallonges." Cf. Denniston 1952: 68–70. Some observations on Plato's tendency to a greater complication of the sentence structure by Campbell 1867: XXXVIII f., 1894: 61, Webster 1941. Saupe 1916 analyzes some of the pastiches.

170. Cf. Denniston 1952: 124–139.

171. A recent reconsideration of the "Gorgian" style by Zucker 1956.

[68] (with devices such as πρῶτον—δεύτερον, ἔτι δέ),[172] and a tendency to abstract ex-
[69] pression.[173] Among its proper features, which can be taken as leading style markers, we may note its inclination to balanced and rounded periods, or at least to isokola and similar parallelism, further antithesis (sometimes chiastic),[174] polarization, assonance (polyptoton), figura etymologica and other devices of expressive sonority (though a pointed use of these features is **3 Gorg.**), and in emphatic contexts enumeratio, climax, anaphoric (epanaleptic) repetition, and asyndeton. The avoidance of hiatus and possible rhythmical patterns (*see* above) will not be considered here. And the use of poetical expression and hyperbole will be regarded as embodying style 4.[175]

> *Sample texts.* 1. *Ap.* 17a–18a:[176] Opening of the first speech. In general periodic. ὅτι clause prothetic—ὦ ἄνδρες Ἀθηναῖοι—perfect—[1 οὕτω intensive]—πιθανός—[1 καίτοι]—ὡς ἔπος εἰπεῖν—hyperbaton—antithesis—χρή—[1 δεινός "good"]—participle—b abstract: subst. inf.—ἔργῳ—[1 μηδ'ὁπωστιοῦν]—[1 δεινός "good"]—hyperbaton—[1 ἔγωγε]—hyperbaton—perfect—[1 μὰ Δία]—ὦ ἄνδρες Ἀθηναῖοι—καλλιεπέομαι, perfect, participle—[1 καὶ μέντοι]—[1 πάνυ]—ὦ ἄνδρες Ἀθηναῖοι—[1 οὗτος preparatory]—synonymy—participle—synonymy—d [1 οὕτως preparatory, -ί]—[1 ἐγώ redundant]—perfect—hyperbaton—[1 ἀτεχνῶς]—ξένος adj.—λέξις—systematic arrangement—τῷ ὄντι—[1 τυγχάνω]—[1 δήπου]—synonymy—perfect—18a καὶ δὴ καί—[1 ὥς μοι δοκεῖ parenth.]—λέξις—ἴσως μέν ... ἴσως δέ—compar. approx.—[1 αὐτὸ τοῦτο]—synonymy—[1 τὸν νοῦν προσέχω]—antithesis. The comparatively great number of colloquialisms is of course intended to characterize Socrates.
> 2. *Mx.* 246a–c: Exhortation to the living. In general systematic arrangement. Participle—τελευτάω "die," perfect—πολλὰ καὶ καλά, hyperbaton—climax—participle—b polarization—abstract: subst. partic.—χρή—participle—πᾶς singular collective—πρόγονος—[1 krasis]—participle—patronymic address—polarization—λοιπός of time—[1 τῷ]—c synonymy—ἐν τῷ παρόντι—δίκαιός εἰμι—ἐπισκήπτω—hyperbaton—abstract: subst. partic.—ἡνίκα—κινδυνεύω "be in danger"—φράζω—synonymy—hyperbaton—τεκμαί-ρομαι, participle—χρή—hyperbaton.
>
> Other sample texts: *Smp.* 197c–e **3 Gorg.**, *Phdr.* 233d–234c, *Lg.* V.746b–d.

[70] **4. *Pathetic ('affected') style***

I have adopted this term[177] for an affective, at times indeed "affected," manner of speech which is quite common in Plato's early and middle dialogues. This

---

172. Cf. Thesleff 1966: 7.
173. Cf. KG I (1890): 267 f., Thesleff 1966: 104.
174. For antithesis, cf. Denniston 1952: 70–77, cf. Thesleff 1966: 97 n. 31.
175. The use of colloquial hyperboles and of other colloquial features such as aposiopesis or anacoluthon for a deliberate rhetorical effect (as often in Aeschines and Demosthenes) are artifices that need not bother us here. Though later rhetorical theory considered such devices as rhetorical, they will be regarded simply as colloquial (style 1) when occurring in Plato.
176. Th. Meyer 1962: 45–46, 51–52 calls attention to some of the rhetorical features of this passage.
177. Cf. Arist. *Rhet.* 3.7.1408b.

class does not exist anywhere in pure form, and normally in Plato as elsewhere in prose and in comedy it occurs as an accessory shade only; but Gorgias and his followers made a fairly marked and mannered use of a rhetorical variant of it. Its proper range is high poetry: epic, and especially choral lyric and tragedy, though here also it combines with other styles.

Style 4 can be described as an expressive and hyperbolical pitch on other styles, in Plato notably 1 or 3. Hence it is important to note the style employed with it. Sometimes pathetic idioms tend to become mechanized in the basic style (e.g. ὑπερφυῶς in 1, hyperbolic superlatives in 3), and then it is reasonable to take them as markers of both styles. The leading style markers of 4 are (a) non-mechanized hyperboles, and (b) otherwise striking vocabulary and imagery amounting to the same effect, but in principle having a literary origin.

It should be specially noted that the pathetic style, in Attic as in modern English, draws mainly on literary sources. It can therefore not be identified with expressive variants of so-called vulgar speech.

The style markers of Plato's style 4 are largely of a poetic origin. They may also be used as markers of Plato's style 10, but then their purpose is different: in 4 they raise the style hyperbolically to the point of the striking and the extraordinary, whereas in 10 they give weight and grandeur to the exposition. As an illustration of this difference I refer to English idioms such as "divine" or "most" which, though literary in origin, are used both in pathetic colloquial diction and (with a different intonation and shade of meaning) in high style.

Sometimes devices of styles 5 and (when 4 is applied to 1) 2 and 3 may amount to the coloring of 4. In such cases they can be regarded as secondary style markers of 4.[178]

*Sample text.* There is one single passage in Plato's writings where style 4 predominates over the basic style (1): *Phdr.* 230bc:[179] Socrates praises the attractions of the place chosen for reading the speech of Lysias. In general, note the sonority (e.g. opening η/α) and [3/4] climactic arrangement. [1 νή]— Ἥρα—2/4 καταγωγή—5/4 nominal clauses (several)—τε connecting sentences (several)—μάλα—ἀμφιλαφής—pairs (several)—5/4 abstract: subst. adj.—παν-—ὡς exclamatory—2/4 ἀκμή—εὐώδης, superl. hyperb.—χαρίεις, superl. hyperb.—μάλα—[2 τεκμαίρομαι]—expressive reference to nymphs and Acheloos—ἄγαλμα—[1 εἰ βούλει]—c 5/4 abstract: subst. adj., εὔπνους—ὡς exclamatory—ἀγαπητός—[1/4 σφόδρα]—5/4 θερινός—λιγυρός—ὑπηχέω, [1 ὑπο-]—imagery (poet.)—[1 κομψός], superl. hyperb.—5/4 abstract: subst. genitive—2/4 πέφυκε—participle—παν-—superl. adv.—2/4 dative with passive—2/4 ξεναγέω, perfect—2/4 ὦ φίλε.

## 5. *Intellectual style*

Like the pathetic style, the intellectual style in Plato normally occurs as an accessory shade only, but it is more common and more manifest than style 4, and in

---

178. The use of (originally) intellectual expressions in pathetic style is paralleled e.g. by English *extraordinarily, exquisite.*
179. Cf. Thesleff, *Arctos* N. S. 5 (1967).

[71] many passages, especially later, it clearly predominates. It is still more heterogeneous than style **3**. In general the qualification "intellectual" applies to various aspects of all Platonic styles, but for the present purpose we shall restrict it to a certain group of phenomena and to certain conditions.

Most clearly the characteristics of intellectual style are exhibited by advanced so-called "scientific" prose such as, in 4th century Greece, the Hippocratic Art. and Fract. or the prose of Aristotle. In such texts the following tendencies can be observed:[180]

(a) explicit argumentation,

(b) systematic arrangement of the exposition, composite qualification,[181] pointed transitions,

(c) strictness and matter-of-factness, lack of emotional coloring, of external ornament and of superfluous elements,

(d) exactness of expression, large use of technical terms,

(e) abstractness of expression.

It will be convenient to look for style markers within these tendencies.

[72] However, the "scientific" style did not come into being before the 4th century, and Plato was probably not very much influenced by it except, perhaps, in his late works; συγγραφικῶς *Phd.* 102d is likely to be the first explicit reference to this style.[182] The sources for Plato's use of **5** should on the whole rather be looked for in the earlier stages of the "scientific style": i.e. the "early treatise style" of Anaxagoras, Melissus and Diogenes of Apollonia (tendencies (a) and (b), occasionally (d) and (e), but seldom (c)), the discourses and the "pamphlet style" of the sophists (tendencies (a), (b) and (e), occasionally (c) and (d)), and various technai and hypomnemata (tendencies (c) and (d), occasionally (a), (b) and (e)). The influence of the sophists on Plato is evident, and presumably it was largely from and through them that he adopted the tendencies (a), (b), (d) and (e).[183] The tendency (c) is, without the other tendencies, present in Plato's strict A dialogue (e.g. *Hp.Mi.* 373c ff.); and this variant probably derives from eristics and ultimately from judicial elenchus. Together with other tendencies of intellectual prose the tendency (c) occurred in hypomnemata of sophistic logoi: Zenon, Gorgias, cf. Dissoi logoi (Diss. Log.).[184] Plato of course is not likely to have adopted the style of such hypomnemata in his literary prose except for parody (cf. *Grg.* 506c–507c), but they constitute one source of influence on his style **5**. He was probably also influenced by the diction of mathematical (geometrical) demonstration, which seems to have

---

180. For this and the following, *see* some additional observations in Thesleff 1966.

181. I did not discuss the "composite qualification" separately in my paper (1966). By composite qualification I mean, not only organized sentence periods, but also the tendency to accumulate different kinds of qualifiers to the same noun or verb, e.g. *R.* V.478e.

182. Cf. the reference to Hippocrates in *Phdr.* 270cd. Plato of course became early acquainted with medical theories (cf. Shorey 1933 on *Chrm.* 156e, Joly 1961), but he had no particular bent to contemporary medicine, as his occasional jokes with pedantic physicians indicate (Eryximachus in *Smp.*, Acumenus in the opening of *Phdr.*). Cf. below p. 87.

183. For these tendencies in sophistic discourses, *see* in particular Thesleff 1966: 100–105.

184. Cf. Thesleff 1966: 93, 97, 101 f.

been begun to be written down in his days by mathematicians such as Archytas and Eudoxus;[185] the passage *Men.* 86e–87c (below) suggests this directly. The possible influence of Democritus in stylistic matters remains entirely doubtful.[186] Finally, legal style provided Plato with some patterns of intellectual diction, but these are more easily distinguishable and will be treated separately (under **9**).

A practical difficulty thus lies in the fact that all the above-mentioned tendencies occur also in other Platonic styles, notably in style **3**. Ultimately the criteria of the style markers are again the distribution in the extant texts, and not the belonging to one of these tendencies (cf. above **1**); but it may be possible to get some first hand criteria by adopting the following premises: If in a certain passage there occur a number of phenomena representing only one of the five tendencies, the passage will not be regarded as colored by style **5** (e.g. *Hp.Mi.* 373c–376b, on account of its strictness; or *Grg.* 463a–c, on account of its terminology). Phenomena representing the tendencies (a)–(e) will be considered as style markers of style **5** only if at least two of the tendencies are clearly represented, and if they are not at the same time style markers of another style present in the context (e.g. argumentation, systematic arrangement, and abstract nouns in a distinctly rhetorical passage). The presence of a least some degree of tendency (c), notably the occurrence of abstract words, will be regarded as the leading style marker.

*Sample texts.* 1. *Men.* 86e–87c: Socrates on the application of the geometrical method. In general fairly strict, somewhat systematic, some argumentation. [2 ἔοικε "it is reasonable"]—-τέον—[1 τις]—[2 εἰ μή τι ἀλλά]—[1 σμικρόν]—[1 dat. Comm.]—[1 imagery]—ὑπόθεσις [2 εἴτε ... εἴτε]—διδακτός—[2 ὁπωσοῦν]—abstract: subst. adv.—ὑπόθεσις—χωρίον—87a κύκλος—χωρίον—τρίγωνον—[1 ὅτι introd. or. recta]—ὑπόθεσις—[2 προὔργου]—[2 hyperbaton] χωρίον—δοθείς—[2 hyperbaton]—[2 participles]—γραμμή—ἐλλείπω—χωρίον—abstract: subst. partic.—συμβαίνω—ὑποτίθεμαι—συμβαίνω, abstract: subst. partic.—b περί—ἔντασις—κύκλος—[2 εἴτε ... εἴτε]—οὕτω δή concl.—abstract nouns—[2 hyperbaton]—ὑποτίθεμαι—[2 εἴτε ... εἴτε]—διδακτός—περί abstract: subst. partic.—διδακτός—πρῶτον μέν—διδακτός—ἀναμνηστός—c διδακτός—[2 παντί δῆλον].

2. *Smp.* 186bc: Part of Eryximachus' speech on the nature of Eros. In general systematic, argumentative, fairly strict. -ικός—[2 πρεσβεύω]—φύσις "nature"—abstract: subst. adj.—abstract: subst. partic.—ὁμολογουμένως—[2 synonymy]—abstract: subst. adj. —[2 synonymy]—[3 antithesis]—abstract: subst. adj.—-ώδης—c [3 double antithesis, but reference to Pausanias]—[2 synonymy]—abstract: subst. adj.—-ικός—-ώδης—-ικός. This is a parody of medical style, with some rhetorical features appropriate to an enkomion.

Other sample texts: *Grg.* 464b–d (first example of the dihaeretic method),[187] *Phd.* 102c–103a.

---

185. For Hippocrates of Chios and others, *see* Thesleff 1966: 105.
186. In fact Democritus is not a typical exponent of intellectual style, *see* Thesleff 1966: 95–96. Plato's alleged dependence on Democritus (in *Ti.* in particular) is an open problem; *see* Taylor 1928 passim and Friedländer III² 335–338, 495 n. 11 (cf. 353–355).
187. Cf. Friedländer II² 234–235 and n. 9, Dodds 1959 ad 1. Cf. also *Prt.* 322b.

[74] **6. *Mythic narrative style***

Plato makes some use of this style in pastiche and play, especially in the lengthy myth of Protagoras (below), but also to some extent, as we shall see, in his own myths.[188] It seems to approximate to the narrative style of the 'logographers' and of the less sophisticated passages in Herodotus.

As Aly[189] has pointed out, it is not easy to find positive criteria of the Ionian mythic style as distinguished from other archaic styles. Nevertheless it stands out clearly from the 4th century Attic prose styles. The following general characteristics of it may be noted: vocabulary largely Ionic or else of the type of style 2, sometimes 4;[190] monotony, naive circumstantiality, much parataxis (including great use of particles such as καί and οὖν); occasionally but inconsistently the historical present; oratio obliqua sometimes extensive; resumptive repetitions (cf. below p. 69), especially by means of participles; great use of participles in prothetic apposition, also of genitive absolute; strings of descriptive adjectives in postposition; ideas in pairs; quotations of lengthy utterances or speeches. All these characteristics occur in other styles also; but the monotonous circumstantiality, the anaphoric repetitions, the strings of qualifiers in postposition, and the καί and οὖν parataxis seem particularly typical of style 6 and may be taken as leading style markers.

*Sample text. Prt.* 321c–322d: Part of Protagoras' myth. In general naive, simple, somewhat circumstantial; considerable use of parataxis, especially with καί and οὖν. Partic. proth. app.—hist. present—νομή—ἐμμελῶς—string of descr. adj.—[4 assonance]—ἄστρωτος—[7 ἄοπλος][191]—ἤδη narrative—εἱμαρμένος—lack of article—partic. proth. app.—d hist. 
[75] present—ἔντεχνος—ἀμήχανος—κτητός—[1 τῳ]—χρήσιμος—οὕτω δή apodotic—δωρέω—ταύτῃ—οἴκησις—[2 ἐγχωρεῖ]—πρὸς δέ introductory—φυλακή "guard"—φοβερός—φιλοτεχνέω—e partic. proth.app.—ἔμπυρος—hist. present—εὐπορία—322a ᾗπερ—lack of article—θεῖος—[5 πρῶτον ... ἔπειτα]—ἄγαλμα—[5 διαρθρόω]—οἴκησις—partic. proth. app.—b lack of article—[5 abstract: subst. inf., systematic arrangement, -ικός]—resumptive repetition—[5 -ικός]—partic. proth. app.—c hist. present—lack of article—[4 imagery]—συναγωγός—quot. of utterances—resumptive rep.—[3 antithesis, hyperbaton]—d [8 anaphoric repetition, imperat. 3 person]—[8 lack of article]—[9 inf. in regulation.] There is an intermixture of other styles towards the end of this passage, but on the whole it must be regarded as highly typical of style 6.[192]

Other sample texts: *Phdr.* 259b–d, *R.* II.359d–360a.

---

188. Cf. below p. 137.—The literature on the Platonic myths (*see* references above n. 149) treats style very briefly. Comparatively much stylistic material can be found in Harris 1892 whose approach however is "rhetorical."
189. Aly 1929: 63–64. This work contains many valuable observations on traditional "mythic" style; *see* also under the heading 'Der Stil der jonischen Wissenschaft' (p. 44 ff.).
190. Willi 1925: 56 calls attention to the fact that distinct poeticisms are not as common in the mythic style as is sometimes believed; admittedly he is thinking mainly of Platonic myths.
191. Cf. 320e. ἄοπλος is a military term, but owing to its ἀ- and its use in historical narrative it makes no striking dissonance in this context.
192. Cf. Geffcken II A.42 n. 3 where references.

## 7. *Historical style* [75]

This class of style has been included here for the sake of comparison and completeness. In spite of its very important position in Greek literature since the beginning of the 4th century Plato very rarely makes use of it, even more rarely than could perhaps be expected considering the fact that narrative and historical events do not play a wholly negligible part in his works.[193] It is however easy to understand Plato's attitude if it is remembered that the style of Attic historiography is in fact a variant of rhetoric. In Plato too style 7 only occurs in rhetorical contexts.

Style 7 can be described as an amalgamation of style 6 with style 3. The naive and archaic features of the former have been dropped but some patterns are preserved, such as the extensive oratio obliqua, the prothetic participles and the genitive absolute (the two latter occurring also elsewhere in style 3); and note the use of μὲν οὖν ... δέ instead of the recurrent οὖν of style 6. The vocabulary is of the type of style 2 and 3. Of the characteristics of style 3 notably the extensive periods (including hyperbaton) and the great use of participles are adopted. As a further style marker the employment of military terms may be mentioned: Attic historiography was largely concerned with the history of wars.

*Sample text. La.* 183d–184a: Laches tells the story of Stesileos in the naval battle. In general: [76] some periods, large use of participle, military terms. Genitive absolute—3/7 διαφέρων— μὲν οὖν ... δέ—3/7 οὐκ ... δέ—3/7 ἄξιος with infinitive [1 ἀνήρ pron., krasis]—e genitive abs.—[1 που]—[1/6 οὖν]—μὲν οὖν ... δέ—184a 3/7 synonymy—genitive abs.—[1/6 hist. present] —[1/6 τότ᾽ ἤδη apodotic]. Here the slight intermixture of styles 1 and 6 adds to the liveliness of the passage.

Other sample texts: *Mx.* 242cd, *Lg.* III.698c–e.

## 8. *Ceremonious style*

The formal style of solemn proclamations and prayers may be considered here as a single whole, though it would be more correct to speak of a type of style or a group of styles. This type is extremely rare in Plato. I refer to it mainly for the sake of completeness, and in order to show what influence it may possibly have had upon Plato's solemn diction (p. 139).

On the whole the early and classical Greek material is sporadic and scarce, especially if the style of solemn oaths and curses is assigned rather to the legal type 9 (below). There are some brief parodies of ceremonious style in comedy (e.g. Ar. *Ach.* 237–244, 1000–1002, *Av.* 448–450, rather a pastiche in *Th.* 295–311). The orators

---

193. Some scholars, among them de Romilly (*see* Cherniss 1959: 52–53) deny that Plato ever knew Thucydides' *History*, but I am inclined to agree with the current opinion that *Mx.* rather proves the contrary. For Plato and the historians, *see* also Vicaire 1960: 8 n.1 with references.

[76]  occasionally quote ceremonious passages (e.g. Demosthenes 21.52, a proclamation of the Delphic priests). Inscriptions offer some material (*see* the "Res sacrae" W. Dittenberger, *Sylloge Inscriptionum Graecarum*, Third Edition 1915–1924 [Ditt. Syll.,[3] e.g. 367, 590]). The defixionum tabellae form a special group which however offers some illustrative material (*see* especially the extensive Cyprian fragments in Defixionum Tabellae, collection A. Audollent (1904): nrs. 22–37).

The following features may be regarded as typical of ceremonious style: simple syntax, much parataxis; nominal clauses common; enumeratio, asyndeton, polarization; anaphoric repetition; patronymic references to persons; lack of article; use of 3rd person imperative and of infinitive in appeal; optative in wishes; solemn vocabulary (styles **2** and **3**, also distinctly archaic); very specific phraseology, including ritual phrases.

*Sample text*. R. X.617de: First proclamation of the hierophant. Nominal clauses, asyndeton—patronymic reference—lack of article (almost throughout)—κόρη—ἐφήμερος—θανατήφορος—e anaphoric repet.—imperative 3rd person—ἀδέσποτος—polarization.

Other sample texts: *Phd.* 117c, *R.* II.382e.

[77] **9. *Legal style***

Plato employs this special style very frequently in *Lg.* but only very occasionally elsewhere. It is known from innumerable inscriptional and several literary documents from the early classical time onwards. Apart from laws in the proper sense it is used in decrees, public oaths (e.g. Hp.Jusj.), public execrations (e.g. Dirae Teiae, Ditt. Syll.[3] 37–38), and similar texts.

Style **9** has some features in common with style **8**, notably the solemn vocabulary (though it is seldom distinctly archaic), the tendency to enumeratio and polarization, and some rather special devices such as the use of 3rd person imperative and infinitive in appeal. But it shares with style **5** the highly systematized and pointed sentence structure, especially with alternatives in εἰ clauses.[194] It has further a very marked tendency to precision and force which can be seen, apart from the polarization, in the use of synonymy and other pairs, and in accumulative devices such as polyptoton with negatives. The special phraseology and terminology is also manifest. Besides, style **9** is of course easily recognizable from the subject matter.

*Sample texts*. Two brief examples taken at random from *Lg.* may suffice as illustration. *Lg.* VIII.847bc: A law. In general systematic arrangement, terms. Polyptoton with negatives—infinitive in appeal—polarization—c pairs—genitive absolute—polarization—imperative 3rd person—polyptoton with negatives—genitive abs. *Lg.* IX.880b–d: A law. In general systematic arrangement, terms. Pairs—imperative 3rd person (several)— ἐάν ... ἤ accumulative—[**10** pleonasm] c pairs—d participle masculine with art.—[**10** -οισι].

---

194. It may in fact have influenced intellectual prose in this respect; cf. Thesleff 1966: 99–100.

## 10. Onkos style

This term[195] can be conveniently applied to the expansive, weighty and lofty diction typical of Plato's late works. Ancient critics quite often referred to this specifically Platonic manner and described it in various terms (ὄγκος, σεμνότης, μεγαλοπρέπεια, πολυτέλεια, διθυραμβώδη, etc.).[196] But a real discussion or analysis of it does not seem to have been attempted in antiquity, any more than of other Platonic styles.

The styles so far analyzed all existed outside Plato's writings, and his originality in treating them lies chiefly in his using them freely in new combinations. Style **10** is different. It appears to have been essentially Plato's own creation. Indeed it may be asked whether Plato here had any models at all in earlier or contemporary literature. We shall return to this question below (p. 139), but it can be preliminarily stated that a dependence on a single author or stylistic tradition, such as Homer, or Pindar, or Heraclitus, or Parmenides, or tragedy,[197] is entirely improbable. There are no parallels to Plato's onkos in the Greek prose of his age, unless the non-Attic peculiarities of Xenophon's prose and the lofty diction and expansive accumulations in late classical oratory—most manifest in Hyperides' *Epitaphios* (322 BCE)—are taken as representing remotely the same tendencies.[198]

Plato's 'late style,' which is largely the same as style **10**, has been studied, mainly for stylometrical reasons, by several scholars.[199] A fine general characterization of it with some important observations of details was made by Campbell 1867 and 1894 and, much more briefly, by Wilamowitz II 403–414, 424–429.

It seems to me that all the phenomena characteristic of style **10** can be connected with either or both of the following two main tendencies:

(a) The tendency to *expansion* and *weight*, e.g. expansive and complicated sentence structure, including large use of participles, genitive absolute, etc.;

---

195. Cf. Arist. *Rhet.* 3.1407b–1408a, cf. *De Subl.* 12.3, Hermog. p. 247.12 Rabe; LSJ ὄγκος II.3.
196. Cf. Walsdorff 1927 passim. Some observations in Wehrli 1946.
197. Antiquity sometimes referred to Homer as a source of Plato's "poetical" style, e.g. *De Subl.* 13.3, cf. Walsdorff 1927: 45, 70, Vicaire 1960: 81–103. A stylistic dependence on Heraclitus, though tempting to assume at first sight, is really out of the question because Plato hardly at all uses gnomes and twisted antitheses in the manner of Heraclitus. Plato's admiration of Pindar has often been observed; cf. des Places 1949, Hartland-Swann 1951: 11, Duchemin 1955: 29–36, Vicaire 1960: 139–148. For the alleged influence of Parmenides, *see* Diès 1927: 258. Plato's use of tragic words and expressions was studied by Campbell 1894: 53–59, 263–279, 286–288, and Gleisberg 1909, and his intimate acquaintance with tragedy has been pointed out e.g., by D. Tarrant 1955 and Vicaire 1960: 158–178 (cf. the references above n. 77). More references in Cherniss 1959: 35 ff.
198. Gautier 1911: 22–108 (cf. 16–19, 137) in his study of Xenophon's vocabulary accepts the common opinion that the non-Atticisms are due to Xenophon's having lived abroad most of his grown-up life. Part of them may however have a stylistic function.—Some Hellenistic authors tend to a kind of 'onkos,' e.g. Agatharchides (cf. Palm 1955: 27–55). In Hellenistic 'Pythagorean' texts Plato's onkos is sometimes imitated (though with poor result), *see* notably Pempelos De parent., Thesleff 1965: 141.
199. *See* the reference above n. 4. Some studies which are of interest here have been recorded in the list of style markers below.

[79]     anaphoric repetition, assonance, polyptoton (e.g. with the negative and with forms of πᾶς), synonymy, other pairs, and various other accumulative and amplificatory phenomena, such as pleonasm and periphrases; abstract nouns qualified; lack of article; heavy words (partly taken from other styles) such as compounds, extensive derivatives, archaic words, and poetical words.

The tendency to *variation*, e.g. rare words,[200] lack of balance, chiasm, intermixture of different styles, anacoluthon, and above all a twisted and complicated order of words (synchysis, interlacing).[201]

Now all of these devices, except a notable synchysis, occur in other styles as well, and hence a difficulty of classification arises in practice. Admittedly the subjective factor is greater with style 10 than with any other Platonic style. How can I be sure that a particular passage that I feel as predominantly colored by onkos, is not felt by another reader as composed of, say, rhetorical and intellectual style, perhaps with a touch of poetical pathos and combined with colloquial carelessness? I believe that the following principles of classification will reach a reasonable degree of common agreement, and at the same time bring out what is typical of Plato's manner:

[80]     The use of an archaic or in general heavy vocabulary and a synchysis in word order, combined with a general expansion of expression, will be taken as the leading style markers. In a passage where these devices occur all phenomena amounting to "weight" and "variation," no matter how common they are in other styles, will be considered as markers of style 10. Only if such phenomena form distinct patterns suggesting another style, the latter style will be considered as being present as a basic or additional coloring.

*Sample text. Plt.* 294e–295c: Part of the Guest's considerations about law-giving. In general expansion and synchysis, composite qualification, much participles. **2/10** ἅμα μέν ... ἅμα δέ—οισι—ἀγέλη—[**5** abstract: subst. adj.]—πέρι—**5/10** συμβόλαιον—259a pleonasm—**2/10** ἀκριβής—**2/10** προσήκει—τὸ γοῦν εἰκός—**2/10** ὡς ἐπὶ τὸ πολύ—[**1** οὕτως "simply," -ί, παχέως, compar. approx.]—polarization—ἀγράμματος—πάτριος—**2/10** ὀρθῶς reply—b periphrasis—**2/10** προσήκει—[**1** ἐπεί explic]—**2/10** ὄντως [**1** ποτε redundant]—[**1** ὦ βέλτιστε]—pleonasms—c **2/10** συχνός—μνημονεύω—**2/10** κάμνω.

Other sample texts: *Phdr.* 272d–273a, *Lg.* II.666d–667a.

---

200. The use of hapax legomena in Plato's late style has repeatedly been observed, e.g. by Campbell 1894: 60. The statistics of Fossum 1931 are far too mechanical.

201. This phenomenon differs from simple hyperbaton in changing the logical or habitual order of more than two words in the sentence. In extreme cases, well-known from Roman poetry, the effect is an interlacing of the sentence in a single complex whole. Regarding Plato, this device has been observed in particular by Campbell 1867: XLI f. who connects it with a tendency to obtain a sentence rhythm by successively placing emphatic and unemphatic words. Cf. Denniston 1952: 54–59 who suggests that the intention is to avoid the appearance of mechanical formality. *See* also below p. 98. It is important to note that the attempt to avoid hiatus (above p. 55) cannot account for this phenomenon, as is sometimes believed (e.g. Burnet 1928: 55). Blass 1874: II.315 has found some traces of it in Antisthenes, and he notes (141) that Isocrates, who is the main representative of the hiatus-avoiding style, does not employ synchysis. The problem clearly needs a thorough investigation.

# Lists of style markers

The lists include the style markers referred to in this and the following chapter. Account has been taken of their different shades insofar as they are relevant here. In most cases a brief reference to such handbooks as Ast[202] (1835), LSJ, or KG has been considered sufficient for enabling the reader to check the distribution, and hence the shade of style. Sometimes, when I have not been able to give any reference at all, I can only hope for subjective agreement from the reader.

|  | Shades (see p. 51) | | | | | |
|---|---|---|---|---|---|---|
| Abstract expression, in general. Above p. 58; Röttger 1937; Denniston 1952: 23–34; Palm 1955: 159–184 ....... |  |  | 3 |  | 5 |  |
| ——, abstract nouns qualified. Denniston 1952: 35–36 ............... | 2 |  |  |  |  | 10 |
| ——, substantival neuter adjective (or adverbial phrase or similar) with the article. KG I 267 f., Denniston 1952: 20 f., 36 f., Thesleff 1966: 101, 104 ......................... |  |  | 3 | (4) | 5 | 10 |
| ——, substantival infinitive with the article. KG II 2 f., Palm 1955: 121 ... | 2 |  | 3 |  |  |  |
| ——, plural of abstract nouns. Denniston 1952: 38 ..................... |  |  | 3 |  |  | 10 |
| Adjectives, strings of, in postposition, used for description. Trense 1901 ......................... |  |  |  |  | 6 | 10 |
| Anacoluthon. Reinhard 1920 ........ | 1 |  |  |  |  | 10 |
| Anaphoric repetition.[203] Chantraine 1951: 355 f.; Denniston 1952: 84–87 .... |  |  | 3 |  | 8 | 10 |
| Antithesis. Denniston 1952: 71–74; cf. *Grg.* 466 ab. ................... |  |  | 3[204] |  |  |  |
| Archaic vocabulary[205] .............. |  |  |  |  | 6 | 8 | 10 |
| Argumentation, systematic. Solmsen 1929: 272–293; Thesleff 1966 ..... |  |  | 3 |  | 5 |  |

---

202. As for the distribution in Plato, it is clear that a predominant occurrence in the late works or in speeches can be taken as a fairly good indication of a non-colloquial shade; but this rule of course must not be applied mechanically.

203. I use this term, with Denniston 1952: 84, for those different kinds of repetition which amount to emphasis. Cf. Resumptive repetition.

204. Especially **3 Gorg.**

205. *See* the references to studies of Plato's 'late style' above n. 4.

[81] | Article, lack of. KG I 604–610, Schwyzer II 23 n.1 ...................... | | | | 6 | 8 | 10

| | | | | | | |
|---|---|---|---|---|---|---|
| Assonance. Campbell 1867: XXXIX f.; Norden 1898: 106 f.; Denniston 1952: 124–139; cf. *Grg.* 467b ...... | | | $3^{206}$ | 4 | | 10 |
| Asyndeton. Denniston 1952: 99–123[207] .. | | | 3 | 5 | 8 | |

[82]
| | | | | | | |
|---|---|---|---|---|---|---|
| Chiasm. Denniston 1952: 74–76; cf. *Mx.* 246d, *Phdr.* 255b ............... | | | 3 | | | 10 |
| Circumstantiality ................... | | 2 | | | 6 | 10 |
| Clausulae, *see* Rhythm | | | | | | |
| Climax ........................... | | | 3 | (4) | | |
| Comical and burlesque effects. D. Tarrant 1946: 109 ................. | 1 | | | | | |
| Comparative approximative ("rather"). Thesleff 1954: 123 f. ............ | 1 | 2 | | | | |
| Compounds, large use of. Schubert 1893; G. Meyer 1923: 24–46; Chantraine 1951: 345; Denniston 1952: 19 f. Cf. Poetical compounds ....... | | | 3 | 5 | | 10 |
| Dative, dat. commodi (incommodi), ethicus, of personal pronouns. KG I 417–420, 423 ............. | 1 | | | | | |
| ——, resembling the agent with passive. KG I 422 ..................... | | 2 | | (4) | | |
| ——, cf. οισι | | | | | | |
| Diminutive. Cf. Setti 1885: 119; Havers 1931: 35 f. ...... | 1 | | | | | |
| Ellipse. Setti 1885: 125; Stevens 1945; Chantraine 1951: 351 f. ......... | 1 | | | | | |
| Enumeratio. Cf. Denniston 1952: 100, and Adjectives, Asyndeton ...... | | | 3 | | 8 | 9 |
| Expansion of sentences and words[208] ..................... | | 2 | 3 | | | 10 |

---

206. Especially **3 Gorg.**
207. Chantraine 1951: 353 f. rightly points out that asyndeton occurs on all levels of style (= classes of style). But regarding marked asyndeton this is obviously not so in Plato.
208. *See* the references to studies of Plato's 'late style' above n. 4.

# Studies in the Styles of Plato

| | 1 | 2 | 3 | 4 | 5 | 6 | 7 | 8 | 9 | 10 |
|---|---|---|---|---|---|---|---|---|---|---|
| Figura etymologica. Cf. Thesleff 1954: 195 | | | $3^{209}$ | | | | | | | |
| Genitive absolute | | 2 | 3 | | (5) | 6 | 7 | | 9 | |
| Gnomic expression | | | 3 | | | | | | | |
| Heavy words. *See* above p. 63 | | | | | | | | | | 10 |
| Hiatus avoided. *See* above p. 55 | | | (3) | | | | | | | 10 |
| Homoioteleuta, *see* Assonance | | | | | | | | | | |
| Hyperbaton, *see* Word order | | | | | | | | | | |
| Hyperbole, literary. *See* above p. 70 | | | | 4 | | | | | | |
| ——, superlative. Thesleff 1955 | | | 3 | 4 | | | | | | |
| Idioms. *See* above p. 65 | 1 | | | | | | | | | |
| Imagery, poetical. Louis 1945. Cf. Personification | | | | 4 | | | | | | |
| ——, Socratic. Cf. Billings 1920: 71–88; Schmid I 3.267 n. 7; McDonald 1931: 333; Louis 1945 | 1 | | | | | | | | | |
| Imperative, 3rd person | | | | | | | | 8 | 9 | |
| Inconsistency, *see* Anacoluthon | | | | | | | | | | |
| Infinitive in regulation. KG II 19–24 | | | | | | | | 8 | 9 | |
| Interlacing, *see* Word order | | | | | | | | | | |
| Ionic, *see* Archaic | | | | | | | | | | |
| Isocolon | | | $3^{210}$ | | | | | | | |
| Krasis, in general[211] | 1 | | | | | | | | | |
| Litotes. Palm 1955: 153–156 | | 2 | 3 | | | | | | | |
| Metabole, *see* Variatio | | | | | | | | | | |
| Monotony in narrative | | | | | | 6 | | | | |
| Neologism for striking effect | | | $(3)^{212}$ | | | | | | | |
| Nominal clauses, large use of Schwyzer II 623 | | | | (4) | 5 | | | 8 | | |

---

209. Especially **3 Gorg.**
210. Especially **3 Gorg.**
211. Though krasis, as KB I 218 f. say, mostly occurs in poetical texts, the instances in prose are obviously no poeticisms. The phenomenon needs investigation from a stylistic point of view.
212. Especially **3 Gorg.**

[83]

| Entry | | | | | | | | | |
|---|---|---|---|---|---|---|---|---|---|
| Optative in wishes. Schwyzer II 321 f. | | | | | | | 8 | | |
| Oratio obliqua, extensive. Cf. KG II 543–547[213] | | | | | 6 | 7 | | | |
| Pairs, Cf. Synonymy, and above p. 66 | 2 | 3 | 4 | | 6 | | | 9 | 10 |
| Parallelism in sentence structure, *see* Isocolon | | | | | | | | | |
| Parataxis. Schwyzer II 632–634; Chantraine 1951: 354 f. | 1 | | | | 6 | | 8 | | |
| Parisa, paromoia, paronomasy, *see* Assonance | | | | | | | | | |
| Participles, large use in general. Campbell 1867: XXXVI; Shorey 1888: 410 f.; Harris 1892: 44 f.; Palm 1955: 89–91, 117–119 | 2 | 3 | (4) | 5 | | 7 | | | 10 |
| ——, large use especially in prothetic apposition | | | | | 6 | 7 | | | |
| ——, masculine singular, with the article. Cf. *Prt.* 322d | | | | | | | | 9 | |
| ——, periphrastic. Campbell 1867: XXXIV; Riddell 1867: 159 f. | | | | | | | | | 10 |

[84]

| Entry | | | | | | | | | |
|---|---|---|---|---|---|---|---|---|---|
| Patronymic address or reference. Cf. *Ly.* 204b, *Smp.* 214b | | | | | | | 8 | | |
| Perfect, large use of. Cf. Schwyzer II 287 f.[214] | 2 | 3 | (4) | | | | | | 10 |
| Periods, complicated but balanced ... | | 3 | | | | 7 | | | |
| Periphrasis. Campbell 1894: 53; G. Müller 1951: 105–111, 114; Palm 1955: 93–99, 172–184[215] | | | | | | | | | 10 |
| Personification. Webster 1956: 38–43 .. | | | 4 | | | | | | 10 |
| Pleonasm, notable. Campbell 1867: XXXVI; Wilamowitz II 424–425 | 1 | | | | | | | | 10 |

---

213. D. Tarrant, "Plato's Use of Extended Oratio Obliqua" (1955), finds the extended oratio obliqua in Plato on the whole lively and natural, but she has not observed the literary artifice underlying it.'

214. Wilamowitz II 413 seems to me to underrate Plato's use of the perfect.

215. In Plato this is evidently not a colloquial trend, as sometimes elsewhere; cf. Chantraine 1951: 351.

| Feature | | | | | | | | |
|---|---|---|---|---|---|---|---|---|
| Poetical words, in general. Rutherford 1881; Gleisberg 1909. Cf. above p. 70 | | $3^{216}$ | 4 | | | | | 10 |
| ——, in particular compounds. G. Meyer 1923: 22–24 | | | | | | | | 10 |
| Polarization. Kemmer 1903 | | 3 | 4 | | | 8 | 9 | 10 |
| Polyptoton, in general, *see* Anaphoric repetition | | | | | | | | |
| ——, with negatives | | | | | | | 9 | 10 |
| Precision. Cf. above p. 62 | | | | 5 | | | 9 | |
| Present, historical, occasional and inconsistent use. Cf. Harris 1892: 45–47; Schwyzer II 271 f.; *Prt.* 310c, *Euthd.* 273a bis. | 1 | | | | 6 | | | |
| Proverbs. Setti 1885: 128 ff.; Grünwald 1893; D. Tarrant 1946: 112–114 | 1 | | | | | | | 10 |
| Puns. D. Tarrant 1946: 116 f., 1958: 60 | 1 | | | | | | | |
| Qualification, composite. *See* above n. 181 | | | | 5 | | | | 10 |
| ——, strings of qualifiers, *see* Adjectives | | | | | | | | |
| Quotation of poetry. D. Tarrant 1946: 111 f., 1951, 1958: 160[217] | | 3 | 4 | | | | | |
| Repetition, *see* Anaphoric r., Resumptive r. | | | | | | | | |
| Resumptive repetition.[218] Norden 1913: 369f.; Denniston 1952: 80, 92–98; Thesleff 1966: 99 | | | | | 6 | | | |
| Rhythm. *See* above p. 55 | | 3 | | | | | | |
| Ritual phrases | | | | | | 8 | | |
| Simple syntax | 1 | | | | 6 | 8 | | |
| Solemnity. Cf. Archaic | | | | | | | | 10 |

---

216. I.e. **3 Gorg.**
217. I am not prepared to stress, with D. Tarrant, the colloquial aspect of this feature.
218. With Denniston I use this term for the picking up of a word from the preceding sentence, mainly the resumption of a finite verb by a participle.

| | | | | | | | |
|---|---|---|---|---|---|---|---|
| Sonority, expressive. Cf. Assonance .. | | $3^{219}$ | 4 | | | | 10 |
| Strictness, marked. *See* above p. 58 ... | 1 | | 5 | | 9 | | |
| Structure of sentence pointed, *see* Systematic ................ | | | | | | | |
| Superlative, adverb. Cf. Thesleff 1955: 114 ........................ | 1 | | 4 | | | | |
| ——, cf. Hyperbole | | | | | | | |
| Synchysis, *see* Word order | | | | | | | |
| Synonymy. Cf. KG II 584 f.; Webster 1956: 13 ................ | | 2 | 3 | | (7) | 9 | (10) |
| Systematic arrangement of ideas in the sentence. Campbell 1894: 171; Thesleff 1966 ................ | | | 3 | 5 | | 9 | |
| Systrophe, *see* Word order | | | | | | | |
| Terms, in general. Cf. Campbell 1867. XXV–XXVIII and above p. 73$^{220}$ .. | | | | 5 | | | 10 |
| ——, legal ........................ | | | | | | 9 | |
| ——, military. *See* above p. 75 ....... | | | | | 7 | | |
| Traductio, *see* Anaphoric repetition .. | | | | | | | |
| Transition, *see* Resumptive repetition and Systematic arrangement .... | | | | | | | |
| Variatio. *See* p. 64 ................ | | | | | | | 10 |
| Weight ........................ | | | | | | | 10 |
| Word order, expressive$^{221}$ .......... | 1 | | | | | | |
| ——, hyperbaton, systrophe, and similar phenomena not merely amounting to occasional emphasis. Cf. Campbell 1867: XXXVII; Riddell 1867: 228 ff.; Trense 1901; J. de Vries 1938; Denniston 1952: 49–54 ........................ | | 2 | 3 | | | | 10 |

---

219. Especially **3 Gorg.**

220. The literature on Plato's terminology is enormous but of little interest for studies of style. *See* references in Ueberweg-Praechter I$^{13}$ 72*; add Baldry 1937, des Places 1964, Mannsperger 1965.

221. It has often been pointed out that Greek word order is fairly "free" and liable to changes according to the mood of the speaker; *see* e.g. Schwyzer II 697 f., Denniston 1952: 44–47. By "expressive word order" I mean a change of the logical order for the sake of emphasis.

# Studies in the Styles of Plato

| | | | | | | | |
|---|---|---|---|---|---|---|---|
| ——, interlacing, synchysis.²²² Campbell 1867: XLI f.; Denniston 1952: 54–59 .......... | | | | | | | 10 |
| ἄγαλμα. Ast ..................... | | 2 | | 4 | 6 | | |
| ἀγαπάω. Ast; LSJ ................ | | 2 | | 4 | 6 | | |
| ἀγαπητός. Ast; LSJ .............. | | | 3 | 4 | | | |
| ἀγέλη. Ast ...................... | | | | | | | 10 |
| ἀγράμματος. Ast ................ | | | | | | | 10 |
| ἀδαμάντινος. metaph. Ast²²³ ........ | | | | 4 | | | 10 |
| ἀδέσποτος. LSJ .................. | | | | | | 8 | |
| ἀκλεής. Ast; LSJ ................. | | 2 | | | | | |
| ἀκμή. Ast; LSJ ................... | | 2 | | (4) | | | |
| (ἀκούω) ἤκουσας; Ast I 82 .......... | 1 | | | | | | |
| ἀκριβής. Ast ..................... | | 2 | | | | | (10) |
| ἅμα μέν ... ἅμα δέ. Ast ............ | | 2 | 3 | | | | (10) |
| ἀμήχανος. Ast; LSJ ............... | | | | 4 | 6 | | |
| ἀμφιλαφής. LSJ .................. | | | | 4 | | | |
| ἀναμνηστός. LSJ ................. | | | | | 5 | | |
| ἀνήκεστος. LSJ .................. | | | | | | | (10) |
| (ἀνήρ) ἀνήρ like a pronoun. Ast I.174 f., cf. Ar. *Vesp.* 269 ................ | 1 | | | | | | |
| ——, (ὦ) ἄνδρες (Ἀθηναῖοι) ......... | | | 3 | | | | |
| ἄνω (καί) κάτω. Ast .............. | 1 | | | | | | |
| ἄξιος with infinitive. Ast I.200; LSJ II.3.a ........................ | | 2 | 3 | | | (7) | |
| ἄοπλος. LSJ²²⁴ .................. | | | | | 5 | 7 | |
| ἅπας, see πᾶς | | | | | | | |
| ἀπατεών. LSJ ................... | | | | 4 | | | |
| ἄρδην. Ast; LSJ ................. | | | | | | | 10 |

---

222. *See* above p. 64.
223. In *Grg.* 509a σιδηροῖς καὶ ἀδαμαντίνοις λόγοις it is probably the double hyperbole that is felt as ἀγροικότερον.
224. Cf. above n. 191.

| | | | | | |
|---|---|---|---|---|---|
| [86] | ἄρνυμαι. LSJ | | 4 | | |
| | ἄστρωτος. LSJ | | | 6 | |
| | ἀτεχνῶς. D. Tarrant 1946: 114 f.; Thesleff 1954: 160 | 1 | | | |
| | ἄτοπος. Ast; LSJ | 1 | | | |
| | αὐτίκα "e.g." Ast; Riddell 1867: 173 | 1 | | | |
| | βδελυρός. LSJ | 1[225] | | | |
| [87] | (βέλτιστος) ὦ. βέλτιστε. Ast; LSJ | 1 | | | |
| | βλακικός βλάξ. Ast; LSJ | 1 | | | |
| | (βούλομαι) εἰ βούλει and similar Ast I. 359; Lammermann 1935.72 f. | 1 | 2 | | |
| | βρῶμα. LSJ | | | | 10 |
| | γέμω. Ast | | 3 | | |
| | γενναῖος "good" Ast; LSJ | 1 | | | |
| | γηγενής. LSJ | | | 6 | |
| | γραμμή, geom. term | | | 5 | |
| | δεινός "skilled." Ast; LSJ | 1 | | | |
| | δεῦρο in command. Ast | 1 | | | |
| | (δῆλος) δῆλον ὅτι. Ast; KG II 368 A.l. | 1 | | | |
| | ——, παντὶ δῆλον. Ast | 2 | | | |
| | δήπου. Denniston 1954: 267 f. | 1 | | | |
| | δῆτα. Denniston 1954: 269–278 | 1 | | | |
| | διαρθρόω. LSJ | | | 5 | |
| | διαφέρω "be better" Ast; LSJ | 2 | 3 | (7) | |
| | διδακτός. LSJ | | | 5 | |
| | (δίδωμι) δοθείς, geom. term | | | 5 | |
| | δίκαιός εἰμι with infinitive. Ast; LSJ c | 2 | 3 | | |
| | (δοκέω) δοκεῖ, δέδοκται, etc. "it seems good." Ast I 551–553; LSJ II.4.b | 2 | | | 9 |
| | δωρέω. Ast; LSJ | | | 6 | |

---

225. Manifestly vulgar.

| | | | | |
|---|---|---|---|---|
| ἑ reflexive. Ast | 2 | | | |
| ἐάν. cf. εἰ | | | | |
| ἐγχωρεῖ "it is allowable." Ast; LSJ[226] | 2 | | | |
| ἐγώ redundant[227] | 1 | | | |
| ἔγωγε, especially in reply. Cf. v. Arnim 1913: 33. | 1 | | | |
| (εἰ) εἰ (or ἐάν) τις ... ἤ ... ἤ ... and similar | | | | 9 |
| ——, εἰ δὲ μή Ast I 602 | 2 | | 5 | 9 |
| εἰ μή "except." Ast I 601 f.; LSJ VII.3.a | 1 | | | |
| ——, εἰ μή τι ἀλλά. Ast I.602 | 2 | | | |
| ——, εἰ(περ) τις ἄλλος, etc. Thesleff 1954:190; cf. Thuc. 6.32.2 | 2 | 4 | | |
| ——, εἰ βούλει see βούλομαι | | | | |
| εἰκός "reasonable." LSJ II; Diès 1927: 413 | | 3 | | |
| ——, τὸ γοῦν εἰκός reply, v. Arnim 1913: 42 | | | | 10 |
| (εἴκω) ἔοικε "it is reasonable," Ast I.615; LSJ ἔοικα III.2 | 2 | | | |
| εἱμαρμένος. LSJ μείρομαι III | | 4 | 6 | |
| (εἶμι) ἴθι, see ἴθι | | | | |
| εἴτε ... εἴτε. Ast | 2 | | | 9 |
| ἔκγονος. LSJ | 2 | | | |
| ἐλλείπω geom. term | | | 5 | |
| ἐμμελής. Ast; LSJ | 2 | | 6 | |
| ἔμπυρος. Ast; LSJ | | 4 | 6 | |
| ἔντασις. LSJ | | | 5 | |
| ἐντέλλομαι. Ast; LSJ | 2 | | | |
| ἔντεχνος. Ast; LSJ | 2 | | 6 | |
| ἕξις. Ast; LSJ | | | 5 | |

---

226. A distinctly Attic usage, but above colloquial level in the 4th century.
227. KG I 556 calls this use poetical, but it is certainly colloquial.

[88]

| | | | | |
|---|---|---|---|---|
| ἐπακτός Ast; LSJ | | | | 10 |
| ἐπεί explicative. Ast; KG II 461 f. | 1 | | | |
| ἐπιμέλεια. Ast | 2 | | | |
| ἐπισκήπτω. Ast; LSJ | 2 | 3 | | |
| ἐράσμιος. Ast; LSJ | | | 4 | 10 |
| (ἔργον) ἔργῳ (... λόγῳ). Ast I 821 f.; LSJ I 4 | 2 | 3 | | |
| ——, προὔργου. Ast | 2 | | | |
| ἔτι δέ. LSJ II 1 | | 3 | | |
| (ἐτός) οὐκ ἐτός. LSJ | 1 | | | |
| (εὐδαίμων) ὦ εὔδαιμον. LSJ | | | 4 | |
| εὔπνους. LSJ | | | (4) 5 | |
| εὐπορία. LSJ | 2 | | | 6 |
| εὐώδης. Ast | | | 4 | |
| ἐφήμερος. LSJ | | | | 8 |
| ἤ, ἤπερ. Ast; cf. ταύτῃ | 2 | | | 6 |
| ἡγέομαι "think." Ast | 2 | | | |
| ἤδη, narrative. Jecht 1881 | 1 | | | 6 |
| ἡδύς, pejorative. Ast II 24; D. Tarrant 1946: 110, 1958: 158 | 1 | | | |
| ——, ἥδιστε. Ast | 1 | | | |
| ἡνίκα. Ast; LSJ | 2 | 3 | | |
| (Ἥρα) νὴ τὴν Ἥραν. Blaszczak 1932: 20 ff. | | | 4 | |
| θαμίζω. Ast; LSJ | 2 | | | |
| θανατήφορος. LSJ | | | | 8 |
| (θαυμάσιος) ὦ θαυμάσιε. Ast | 1 | | | |
| θαυμαστός (ὅσος etc.). Thesleff 1954: 188; D. Tarrant 1958: 159 | 1 | | 4 | |
| θεάομαι. Ast; LSJ | 2 | | | |
| θεῖος. | | | 4 | 6 |
| θερινός. LSJ | | | (4) 5 | |
| -ί. Cf. Setti 1885: 117 f. | 1 | | | |
| ἴθι (δή). LSJ εἶμι VI 1 | 1 | | | |

| | | | | |
|---|---|---|---|---|
| ικός. Ammann 1953; Chantraine 1956: 101–152 ....... | | 5 | | |
| ἰού. LSJ ......................... 1 | | | | |
| ἴσως "probably." Ast; Frank 1937: 36 ff. ....................... 1 | | | | |
| ——, ἴσως μέν ... ἴσως δέ. LSJ ....... | 3 | | | |
| καί copulative, large use in narrative. Trenkner 1960 ................ 1 | | | 6 | |
| ——, climactic. Denniston 1954: 316–323 ..................... 1 | | | | |
| ——, καὶ δὴ καί. Denniston 1954: 256 | 2 | 3 | | |
| ——, καὶ μέντοι. Denniston 1954: 413 ff. 1 | | | | |
| καίτοι adversative. Denniston 1954: 556 ff. .................. 1 | | | | |
| καλλιεπέομαι. LSJ ................ | 3 | | | |
| (καλός) οὐ καλῶς. Cf. *Smp.* 187a ...... | 2 | | | |
| κάμνω. Ast; LSJ .................... | 2 | | | (10) |
| καταγωγή. LSJ .................... | 2 | (4) | | |
| κινδυνεύω "be in danger." LSJ ....... | 3 | | | |
| ——, "may." Ast; LSJ 4.b; Frank 1937: 36 ff. .................... 1 | | | | |
| κομψός. Ast; LSJ ................... 1 | | | | |
| κόρη. LSJ .......................... | | | 8 | |
| (κόρρη) ἐπὶ κόρρης. LSJ κόρση I 2; D. Tarrant 1946: 111 ............ 1[228] | | | | |
| κτητός. Ast; LSJ ................... | | 4 | 6 | |
| κύκλος. geom. term ............... | | 5 | | |
| (κωλύω) οὐδὲν κωλύει τί κωλύει; Ast; LSJ κωλύω 6 ................. 1 | | | | |
| (λέγω) οὐδὲν λέγω, λέγω τι. LSJ λέγω III 6 ......................... 1 | | | | |
| λέξις. Ast ......................... | 3 | 5 | | |
| ληρέω. Ast; LSJ ................... 1 | | | | |

---

228. Manifestly vulgar, as the references in *Grg.* 486c, 508d, 527a indicate.

| | | | | |
|---|---|---|---|---|
| [89] | λιγυρός. LSJ ................ | | 4 | |
| | λιχνεία. Ast; LSJ (cf. λίχνος) ........ 1 | | | |
| | λοιπός "future." LSJ 3 .......... | 2 3 | | |
| | μά. Thesleff 1954: 166 .......... 1 | | | |
| | μάλα. Thesleff 1954: 56 .......... | | 4 | |
| | ——, καὶ μάλα. Thesleff ibid ........ 1 | | | |
| | μάλιστα, cf. τίς. | | | |
| | (μᾶλλον) οὐδὲν (τι) μᾶλλον Ast II 274; LSJ μάλα II 5 ............... 1 | | | |
| | (μάρτυς) μάρτυρα ἔχομεν and similar Ast | 3 | | |
| [90] | μὲν οὖν, see οὖν. | | | |
| | μεστός metaphorical Ast .......... | 2 3 | | |
| | (μικρός) (σ)μικρόν τι. Ast II 348, III 260 .................... 1 | | | |
| | μνημονεύω. Ast .................. | 2 | | 10 |
| | νή. Thesleff 1954: 166. .......... 1 | | | |
| | νομή "distribution, pasturage." Ast; LSJ .................... | | 6 | |
| | (νοῦς) προσέχω τὸν νοῦν. Ast II 397; LSJ προσέχω 3 ............... 1 | | | |
| | νῦν δή. Ast II 399 f.; Denniston 1954: 206 f. .................. 1 | | | |
| | ξεναγέω. LSJ .................... | 2 | (4) | |
| | ξένος adj. "unacquainted." LSJ B.III .. | 2 3 | | |
| | ὅδε. personal .................... 1 | | | |
| | οἴκησις. Ast; LSJ ................ | | 6 | 10 |
| | οἶμος. LSJ .................... | | | 10 |
| | οἷος exclamative. Ast II 424 ........ 1 | 4 | | |
| | ——, ὡς οἷόν τε. Ast II 425: LSJ ...... | 2 3 | | |
| | -οισι, -αισι. Ritter 1888: 9[229]; Campbell 1894: 52 f. .................. | 2 | (4) | 10 |

---

229. Ritter has not observed all instances, e.g. *Ion* 535d. Some cases, e.g. *R.* I.345e, indicate that the Ionic dative did not only belong to solemn diction in 4th century Attic, but could be used (very much like the inverted πέρι) in style 2 for obtaining emphasis.

Studies in the Styles of Plato 77

| | | | | | |
|---|---|---|---|---|---|
| ὄμμα. Ast; LSJ | | | 4 | | 10 |
| ὁμολογουμένως. Ast | | 3 | 5 | | |
| (ὄν) τῷ ὄντι. Thesleff 1954: 163²³⁰ | 2 | | | | |
| (ὄν) ὄντως. Thesleff 1954: 163 f. | 2 | | | | (10) |
| ὄναρ. Ast; LSJ | 2 | | | 8 | |
| ὅπου γῆς εἰμι. LSJ γῆ I 1 | | | 4 | | |
| ὁπωσοῦν. Ast; LSJ | 2 | | | | |
| (ὁράω) ὁρᾷς; Ast II 478; LSJ I 3–4 | 1 | | | | |
| (ὀρθός) ὀρθῶς in reply, v. Arnim 1912: 42 f. | 2 | | | | (10) |
| ὅσος exclamative. Cf. Schwyzer II 626 | 1 | | 4 | | |
| (ὅστις) ὅ τι; and similar in reply. Cf. Setti 1885: 125; KG I 310 f.; LSJ ὅστις III.1 | 1 | | | | |
| ——, ὅτου, ὅτῳ; Cf. KB I 612 | 1 | | | | |
| ὅτι. clause prothetic (hysteron proteron) | | 2 | 3 | | |
| ——, introducing oratio recta. KG II 367 | 1 | | | | |
| ——, with superlative. Ast II 486; LSJ ὅ τι III | 2 | | | | |
| οὐ, in reply, alone. LSJ A. II.1 | 1 | | | | |
| ——, οὐ ..., ... δέ. Cf. Denniston 1954: 167 | | 2 | 3 | (7) | |
| οὐδαμῶς. LSJ | 1 | | | | (10) |
| οὐδέ in strengthened expressions, e.g. οὐδ᾽ ἑνί, οὐδὲ οὐδέν, οὐδ᾽ὁπωστιοῦν. Ast; D. Tarrant 1946: 110–111, 1958: 158 | 1 | | | | |
| (οὐδείς) οὐδέν = οὐκ. LSJ οὐδείς A. III.1 | 1 | | | | |
| οὖν, narrative. Denniston 1954: 425 f | 1 | | 6 | | |
| ——, μὲν οὖν ... δέ Denniston 1954: 472 | | 2 | | 7 | |

---

230. τῷ ὄντι is always in Attic slightly literary; D. Tarrant 1946: 114 f. seems to be wrong about its colloquial tone.

[91]

| Entry | | | | | |
|---|---|---|---|---|---|
| οὗτος, especially τοῦτο, preparative. KG I 658 f. | 1 | | | | |
| ——, esp. τοῦτο, resumptive. Ast II 494; KG I 660 f. | 1 | | | | |
| ——, ταὐτὸ τοῦτο, αὐτὸ τοῦτο, etc. Cf. LSJ αὐτός I 7 | 1 | | | | |
| οὕτως intensive, without ὥσ (τε). LSJ III | 1 | | | | |
| ——, οὕτω (δή) apodotic. KG II 83 f.; Norden 1913: 369 n. 1 | | 2 | | 6 | |
| ——, οὕτω δή in conclusion. Cf. Ast II 496 | | | | 5 | |
| ——, "simply." Ast II 495; LSJ IV | 1 | | | | |
| οὐχί, see -ί | | | | | |
| παγίως. Ast; LSJ[231] | | | | 5 | |
| πάλαι "since a long time." Ast III 15, KG I 135 | 1 | | | | |
| παν-. Thesleff 1954: 139–141 | | | 4 | | 10 |
| πανοῦργος. Ast; LSJ | 1 | | | | |
| πάνυ. Thesleff 1954: 56–80 | 1 | | | | |
| παραθαρρύνω. Ast; LSJ | | | 3 | | |
| (πάρειμι) ἐν τῷ παρόντι. Ast III 53 | | 2 | 3 | | |
| παρρησιάζομαι. Ast; LSJ | | 2 | | | |
| πᾶς, singular, collective "all." Walbe 1888 | | 2 | 3 | (4) | |

[92]

| Entry | | | | | |
|---|---|---|---|---|---|
| ——, redundant with or for pronouns. Cf. Thesleff 1954: 136 | 1 | | | 6 | |
| πάτριος. Ast | | 2 | | | 10 |
| παῦλα. Ast; LSJ[232] | | | | 5 | |
| (παχύς) παχέως. Ast; LSJ | 1 | | | | |
| περί, large use of. Cf. Wilamowitz II 424 | | 2 | | 5 | |
| ——, πέρι. Baron 1897 | | 2 | 4 | | 10 |

---

231. παγίως seems to have been a phrase in vogue in style **5** about 370 BCE; some think it Heraclitan (*see* Adam ad *R.* IV.434d), but this remains very hypothetical.

232. A medical term?

| | | | | |
|---|---|---|---|---|
| πιθανός. Ast; LSJ | | 3 | | |
| πολλάκις "perhaps." Riddell 1867: 173, LSJ III | 2 | | | |
| (πολύς) πολλὰ καὶ καλά Cf. KG II 252 | 2 | 3 | | |
| ποτε in a weak sense. LSJ III | 1 | | | |
| που. Denniston 1954: 491 | 1 | | | |
| πρεσβεύω "make reverence to." Ast | 2 | | | |
| πρόγονος. LSJ | | 3 | | |
| προοιμιάζομαι. LSJ | 2 | | | |
| πρὸς δέ adverbial, introductory. LSJ D | | | 6 | |
| προσήκει. Ast; LSJ | 2 | | | (10) |
| προσκυνέω. LSJ | | 4 | | |
| προὔργου, see ἔργον | | | | |
| (πρῶτος) πρῶτον ... δεύτερον (ἔπειτα) etc. Cf. Thesleff 1966: 97 | | 3 | 5 | |
| πύστις. Ast; LSJ | | 4 | | |
| σέβομαι. Ast | 2 | | | |
| σκέμμα. Ast; LSJ | | | 5 | |
| σκοπιά. LSJ | | | | 10 |
| στοχάζομαι metaph. Ast; LSJ | 2 | | | |
| στραγγεύομαι. LSJ | 1 | | | |
| σύ redundant. Cf. ἐγώ | 1 | | | |
| συγγενής "brother." LSJ II | | | 6 | |
| συμβαίνω "follow." LSJ especially III 3 | 2 | | 5 | |
| συμβόλαιον. Ast; LSJ | | | 5 | (10) |
| συμβουλή. Ast | 2 | | | |
| συναγωγός. Ast; LSJ | | | 6 | |
| συχνός Cf. Ast; LSJ | 2 | | | (10) |
| σφόδρα. Thesleff 1954: 92–111 | 1 | 4 | | |
| ταμιεύω. Ast; LSJ | 2 | | | 10 |
| ταύτῃ. Ast; LSJ οὗτος C.VIII.4.c | 2 | | 6 | 8 |

[92]

| | | | | | |
|---|---|---|---|---|---|
| [92] | (τάχα) τάχ' ἄν. Ast III 363 | 2 | | | |
| | τε connecting sentences. Denniston 1954: 497, 499, 504–505 | | | 4 | |
| | τεκμαίρομαι. Ast | 2 | 3 | | |
| [93] | τεκμήριον. Diès 1927: 413 n. 2; cf. Thesleff 1966: 96 ff. | | 3 | | |
| | τελευτάω "die." Ast; LSJ | 2 | 3 | | |
| | -τέον (-τέος). Kopetsch 1860; Palm 1955: 91–93 | 2 | | 5 | |
| | (τίς) τί; "why?" LSJ B.I.8.e; cf. KG I 310 f. | 1 | | | |
| | ——, τί δέ LSJ B.I.8.f; Stevens 1937: 184; Denniston 1954: 175 f. | 1 | | | |
| | ——, τί μάλιστα; Thesleff 1955: 86 | 1 | | | |
| | ——, τοῦ, τῷ. KB I 612 | 1 | | | |
| | τις in a weak sense, denoting inexactness. Cf. KG I 663 f. | 1 | | | |
| | ——, του, τῳ; KB I 612 | 1 | | | |
| | τοι. Denniston 1954: 539 | 1 | | | |
| | τόκος. Ast; LSJ | | | | 10 |
| | τότε. apodotic | 1 | | 6 | |
| | τρίγωνον, -ος. geom. term | | | 5 | |
| | τυγχάνω in a weak sense. Ast III 420 f.; LSJ A.II.1 | 1 | | | |
| | ὕπαρ. Cf. Ast; LSJ | 2 | | | 8 |
| | ὑπερφυῶς. Ast; Thesleff 1954: 180; D. Tarrant 1958: 159 | 1 | | 4 | |
| | ὑπηχέω. LSJ | | | 4 | |
| | ὑπνώδης. Cf.-ώδης | | | 5 | |
| | ὑπο- diminutive. Cf. Ast; Riddell 1867: 167; Thesleff 1954: 194 | 1 | | | |
| | ὑπόθεσις. LSJ | | | 5 | |
| | ὑποτίθημι abstract LSJ | | | 5 | |
| | φαῦλος, often in litotes. Ast; LSJ | 1 | | | |
| | (φίλος) ὦ φίλε. Ast III 496 | 1 | 2 | (4) | |

| Entry | | | | | |
|---|---|---|---|---|---|
| φιλοτεχνέω. LSJ[233] | | 2 | | 6 | |
| φλυαρία. Ast; LSJ | 1 | | | | |
| φοβερός. Ast; LSJ | | 2 | | 6 | |
| φράζω. Ast; LSJ | | 2 | | | |
| φυλακή "guard." Ast III 516; LSJ I 2 | | | | 6 | |
| φύσις "nature." LSJ; des Places 1964 | | | 5 | | |
| (φύω) πεφυκέναι = εἶναι. Cf. Ast III 524 f. | | 2 | (4) | | |
| (χαίρω) χαίρειν ἐᾶν and similar Ast III 531 | 1 | | | | |
| χαρίεις. Ast; LSJ | | | 4 | | |
| χρή. Cf. Benardete 1965[234] | | 2 | 3 | | |
| χρήσιμος. Ast; LSJ | | 2 | | 6 | |
| χωρίον. geom. term. | | | 5 | | |
| -ώδης. Droste 1886 | | 2 | 5 | | |
| ὡς exclamatory. Thesleff 1954: 191 f.; cf. Ast III 581 f. | | 2 | 4 | | |
| ——, ὡς ἐγᾦμαι, ὡς ἐμοὶ δοκεῖ. | 1 | | | | |
| ——, ὡς ἐπὶ τὸ πολύ. LSJ ὡς Ab.III.e | | 2 | | | (10) |
| ——, ὡς ἔπος εἰπεῖν. LSJ ἔπος II 4, KG II 508 | | 2 | | | |

---

233. Perhaps a neologism modeled on φιλοτιμέομαι.

234. Benardete is concerned with distinctions of meaning, not with distinctions of style, but he presents a material which is of interest also for the stylistic approach. I feel that one of the important differences between χρή and δεῖ, insofar as they are approximately synonymous, is that the latter is more colloquial. A detailed stylistic investigation is needed.

# STYLISTIC ANALYSES

## Analysis of the *Republic*

This minute analysis will be carried out according to the principles discussed above p. 25 ff. Changes of style will be viewed in relation to changes in the course of the argument, change in dialogue structure, and change of speaker. The letters A–E denote the structure of the exposition (p. 29). The figures **1–10** (in bold type) denote classes or shades of style (p. 51); brackets denote mere touches.

*Republica*. On justice and on its realization in an ideal State.[235]

I. 327a–331d **CBE** Introduction. Socrates meets old Cephalus.
  *327a–328b* **CB** Socrates asked to come to the home of Cephalus. *Socrates* **1**. Natural opening narrative (327a–c) and seemingly casual conversation. The concluding decision to stay has a touch of **(2)**. *Slave, Polemarchus, Adimantus* **1**; *Glaucon* **1** with a touch of **(2)** at the end.
  *328b–e* CB Socrates meets Cephalus. *Socrates* **1, (2)**. Simple narrative and description, the address to Cephalus (328de) polite, reference to poetry. *Cephalus* **1, 2**, somewhat dignified and circumstantial (note θαμίζεις 328c).
  *329a–d* CE First speech of Cephalus on old age. Anecdote about Sophocles. *Cephalus* **1, 2, (4)**, fairly vivid, expansive.
  *329d–330d* CB Discussion of old age and wealth. *Socrates* **1, (2)** *Cephalus* **1, 2**, somewhat expansive and circumstantial.
  *330d–331b* CE Second speech of Cephalus on old age. Eschatology. *Cephalus* **1, 2, (4)**, vivid and intense (note θαυμαστῶς ὡς σφόδρα 331a), quotation of poetry, expansive.
  *331b–d* CB First approach to justice prepared. Polemarchus joins in. *Socrates* **1, (2)**. *Cephalus* **1**, *Polemarchus* **1**.
I. 331e–336a **CA** The opinion of poets about justice. *Socrates* **1**. In parts strict. Somewhat expansive and ironically hyperbolic **(4)** conclusions 335e–336a.

---

235. There is an immense literature on the problems connected with the structure of this work. *See* especially Wilamowitz II 179–213, Diès 1932, Friedländer II² 55–123, Vretska 1956: 406–414.

[96] *Polemarchus* **1, (2, 3)**, somewhat expansive; some antitheses and polarizations (e.g. 332d, 332e).[236]

I. 336b–339b **CB** Thrasymachus interrupts. Might is right.

*336b–337a* CB Objection of Thrasymachus and answer of Socrates. *Socrates* **1, 4**. Very lively description of Thrasymachus' attack, semipoetic imagery; ironically submissive **(2)** reply 336e–337a (cf. εἰρωνεία 337a). *Thrasymachus* **1, (3)**, very emphatic, also vulgar. Note enumeratio with anaphoric repetition 336d.

*337a–338c* CB Thrasymachus agrees to give his definition of justice. Glaucon intervenes (337d). *Socrates* **1**, vivid **(4)** description 337a, 338a; fictional dialogue quoted 337b. Note slight systematization 337e (on the Socratic method). *Thrasymachus* **1**, very emphatic, also vulgar (note pejorative ἡδύς 337d). *Glaucon* **1**.

*338c–339b* CB Thrasymachus gives his definition. Preliminary discussion of it. *Socrates* **1**, at the end slightly **(5)**. *Thrasymachus* **1**, very emphatic, also vulgar (note βδελυρός 338d); also argumentative **(3)** 338de.

I. 339b–e **CA** The opinion of Thrasymachus. *Socrates* **1**. *Thrasymachus* **1**, brief replies.

I. 340a–341c **CBE** Interlude. Objections, and discussion of the opinion of Thrasymachus.

*340a–d* CB General discussion. *Socrates, Clitophon, Thrasymachus* **1**. *Polemarchus* **1**, somewhat expansive 340ab.

*340d–341a* CE Speech of Thrasymachus. *Thrasymachus* **1, (3)**, intense, argumentative, also vulgar (340d).

*341a–c* CB Polemic between Socrates and Thrasymachus. *Socrates* **1**, very emphatic, but slightly **(5)**. *Thrasymachus* **1**, very emphatic, rude.

I. 341c–342e **CA** Thrasymachus refuted. *Socrates* **1, (2, 5)**, intense. Expanding force. Note abandoning of play and irony (ἄδην 341c). Description of replies 342cd. *Thrasymachus* **1**, brief replies.

I. 343a–345b **CBE** Thrasymachus enraged, persuaded to stay.

*343a* CB Reaction of Thrasymachus. *Socrates* **1**. Some narrative. *Thrasymachus* **1**, very emphatic and rude.

*343b–344c* CE Speech of Thrasymachus on his opinion. *Thrasymachus* **1, 3**, emphatic, expansive (note remark of Socrates 344d).

[97] *344d–345b* CB Thrasymachus decides to stay. *Socrates* **1, (2)**. Very vivid description 344d, more dignified addresses to Thrasymachus. *Thrasymachus* **1**.

I. 345b–347a **CA** A leader or a craftsman does not act for his own sake only. *Socrates* **1, 2**. Emphatic, somewhat expansive and literary (note -οισιν 345e). *Thrasymachus* **1**, brief replies.

I. 347a–348b **CBE** Glaucon intervenes.[237] On leaders and profit. The discussion to be continued.

---

236. The urbane tone of this section has been pointed out by Diès 1932: XIV.

237. It has been assumed that Glaucon is introduced here to make a connecting link to *R*. II; *see* Wilamowitz II 183, Friedländer III[2] 441 n. 5. But cf. 337d where a similar topic is

*347ab* CB Intervention of Glaucon. *Socrates* **1, 2**. *Glaucon* **1, 2**.
*347b–e* CE Speech of Socrates on true leadership. *Socrates* **2**. Intense and serious. Note repetition of negative 347b.
*347e–348b* CB The discussion to be continued. *Socrates* **1, 2**. *Glaucon* **1**.
I. 348b–350c **CA** New approach to the opinion of Thrasymachus. The just is good. *Socrates* **1**. Very vivid at first (note ἥδιστε 348c, burlesque 348d), from 349c more strict, conclusion **(2)**. *Thrasymachus* **1**. Some emphatic replies (note 348d), later strict (though cf. 350d).
I. 350c–e **CB** Brief interlude. Objections of Thrasymachus to the method of Socrates. *Socrates* **1,(4)**, very vivid description 350cd. *Thrasymachus* **1**, emphatic, rude.
I. 350e–354a **CA(E)** Last approach to the opinion of Thrasymachus. Justice is always more useful than vice. *Socrates* **1, (2, 5)**. Forcible, also some systematization (e.g. 350e–351a, 351e–352a); note the expansive statement of position 352b–d ("it is a question of life!"); later more strict. *Thrasymachus* **1**. Emphatic, some expanding replies; note the reference to feasts 352b, 354a (irritated conclusion).
I. 354a–c **CE** Socrates finished with Thrasymachus. *Socrates* **1, 2, (4)**, expansive, imagery.

∘·∘·∘ ◯ ∘·∘·∘

II. 357a–368e **CBE** New introduction. Objections of Glaucon and Adimantus to the preceding argument.
*357a–358a* CB(A) Glaucon objects, discussion. *Socrates* **1, (4)**. *Glaucon* **2, 5**, intense (cf. ἀνδρειότατος 357a). Note the contrasted statements about justice 358a.
*358b–362c* CE Speech of Glaucon: the limits of justice; Gyges myth (359d–360b) *Glaucon* **(1), 2, (3, 4), 5**, the myth slightly **(6)**. On the whole vigorous (cf. ἐρρωμένως 361d) and clear, without pointed mannerisms. The end (from 361d) notably emphatic, expansive and accumulative (note ἀγροικοτέρως introducing asyndetic enumeration of means of torture 361e–362a). *Socrates* **1, 4**, some descriptive remarks.
*362d* CB Adimantus prepared to take over. *Socrates* **1, 4**. *Adimantus* **1**.
*362e–367e* CE Speech of Adimantus: the limits of justice. *Adimantus* **2, 3**. Expansive, emphatic, more markedly rhetorical than the speech of Glaucon, frequent quotation and reference to poetry.
*367e–368e* CBE Reply of Socrates. New approach to justice decided upon. *Socrates* **1, (4)**. *Adimantus* **2**, matter-of-fact.
II. 368e–372a **CA** Main theme introduced. The State.
*368e–369b* CA Justice in the State. *Socrates* **2, (5)**. *Adimantus* **2**.
*369b–372a* CA The activities of man in a primitive society. *Socrates* **2, (3)**. Considerable accumulation (e.g. 369c with polyptoton) as if depicting variety. *Adimantus* **1, 2**, brief replies; expansive 371cd.

---

touched upon. If the Glaucon passages have been later inserted they have been carefully worked into the dialogue.

[98]   II. 372a–e **CBE** A primitive paradise. *Socrates* **1, (2, 4)**. A burlesque list of everyday particulars in accumulated participial clauses. *Glaucon* **1, 2**, sarcastic.
   II. 372e–376c **CAD** A civilized State and its Guardians.
      *372e–374d* CAD A civilized State. *Socrates* **(1), 2, (4)**. Expansive and somewhat burlesque list of particulars **(3)** 373a–c. More serious questioning about war 373d–374b, leading to emphatic and expansive statement about warriors 374b–d. *Glaucon* **1, 2**, brief replies.
      *374d–376c* CA Selection of Guardians. *Socrates* **(1), 2, (4)**. Vigorous, some violently expressive passages (note ἄρνυμαι 374e, σκύλαξ—φυλακή 375a, pairs and assonance 375b, imagery in a compressed sentence preceded by C description 375d, dogs as philosophers characterized as κομψόν 375e–376a, emphatic
[99]      concluding description of the Guardian 376c). *Glaucon* **1, 2**, brief replies.
   II. 376cd **CB** How should the Guardians be educated? Preparations for a long investigation. *Socrates* **2**, expansive, emphatic (note the position of θρέψονται 376c). *Adimantus* **2**.
   **II.** 376d–383c. III.386a–398b **CAD** Education of the Guardians. Poetry and mimesis.
      *376d–III.392c* CAD On poetry. *Socrates* **2, (3, 10)**. Expansive, emphatic and somewhat exuberant (notably much synonymy, e.g. 378b–e, frequently -τέος, -τέον, at times weighty words, e.g. 378c, 380e, 381de, 387cd, 390d; quotation and reference to poetry; -οισι 388d, 389b). Sometimes the exuberance sounds manifestly playful and **(1)**, e.g. 380bc (note pun on ξύμφορος, σύμφωνος and σύμψηφος), 390bc (note diminutive). There are also manifestly solemn passages, e.g. the description of god's truthfulness 382e (note accumulation of polarized expressions). *Adimantus* **2**, mostly brief replies.
      *392c–393d* CA On diegesis and mimesis. *Socrates* **2, (5)**. Rather strict and matter-of-fact. *Adimantus* **2**, brief replies.
      *393d–394a* CE An example: transcription of *Iliad*. I 12–42 in prose without oratio recta. *Socrates* **(2)**. The style is quite specific, deliberately compressed and matter-of-fact, with participial clauses and some oratio obliqua. Many Homeric words have been exchanged in order to obtain a prose vocabulary, but the equivalents are still manifestly literary (e.g. σέβομαι, ἐντέλλομαι 393e, note also reflexive οἱ and οὗ).
      *394a–397e* CAD On mimetic art. *Socrates* **2, (3, 5)**. The lack of exuberance is notable in emphatic passages such as 395c (note here asyndeton), 395d–396b, 397ab (accumulation), 397d (climax). *Adimantus* **2**. Some personal replies (note the point in ῥήτορος 396e).
      *398ab* CD The poet to be dismissed with full honors. End of section. *Socrates* **(1), 2, 4**. Expansive, vehement and slightly hyperbolical. The playfulness of this passage is underlined by the change of style. *Adimantus* **2**.
   III. 398c **CB** Brief interlude. Music next to be discussed. *Socrates* **2**. *Adimantus* **2**. *Glaucon* **1** (note ἐπιγελάσας).
   III. 398c–417b **CAD** Education of the Guardians continued. The leaders.
[100]      *398c–403c* CAD On music and love. *Socrates* **2, (3, 10)**. In parts very expansive and weighty (note e.g. accumulation and concluding asyndeton 399a–c; synonymy, antithesis and anaphoric repetition 401a; synonymy, other pairs,

assonance, imagery and personification 401b–d; accumulation of heavy words and polarization 402bc).[238] A playful remark (1) on the flute 399e. Some metrical terms as occasional traits 400bc. The concluding section on love is introduced by the key words κάλλιστον and ἐρασμιώτατον 402d, but is then kept more strict (also A) and somewhat intellectual **(5)**. *Glaucon* **2, (5)**. Musical terms 398d–399a, 400a.

403c–410b CAD On gymnastic, medicine, and being a good judge. *Socrates* **(1), 2, (3, 5, 10)**. The style is more vigorous than in the preceding passage and playfully complex. There are manifestly colloquial features (e.g. ὡς ἐγᾦμαι 403d, ὅπου γῆς ἔστιν, οὐχί 403e, κομψός 405d, χαίρειν εἰπών 406d, πανοῦργος 409c) and a play with medical style (e.g. ἕξις 403e, ὑπνώδης 404a, dietics 404b–d, terms 405cd, 406d) combined with rhetorical expansion and weight (e.g. heavy and expressive words and rhetorical features 405a–c, anaphoric repetition 406c, complex sentence with some synchysis 409b). *Glaucon* **(1), 2, (3)**, lively and personal, expanding replies at times (note pun on γῆρας 406b, further 407e, 408b, 409c). More rhetorical 408cd.

410b–412b CAD Music and gymnastic to be combined. *Socrates* **2, (4, 5, 10)**. At first rather abstract though expansive. From 411a more weighty, with very expressive vocabulary and much imagery. Very emphatic conclusion 412a. *Glaucon* **2**, mostly brief replies.

412b–414b CAD The leaders among the Guardians. *Socrates* **2, (5, 10)**. Weighty and expressive (note τραγικῶς 413b with reference to style).[239] The conclusion from 413d is very emphatic and expansive. *Glaucon* **2**.

414b–415d CDE "Phoenician" myth: men are not born alike. *Socrates* **2**. The introductory remarks are kept in a somewhat abstract **(5)** and twisted style (note ὀκνοῦντι 414c). The myth itself, from 414d, is more simple though expansive (note synonymy). Occasional touches of **(6)** (καί style 414de, γηγενής 414e, ξυγγενεῖς 415a as if resuming ἀδελφοί, οὖν 415ab). *Glaucon* **(1), 2**. Quite vivid comments (note οὐκ ἐτός 414e). These comments, as well as the twisted opening and the Φοινικικόν τι 414c, suggest an ironical trend in the passage.[240]

415d–417b CAD General considerations on the leaders and warriors. *Socrates* **2, (3, 10)**. Weighty, expressive, with imagery, and in the conclusion 417ab a notable rhetorical tone. *Glaucon* **2**.

IV. 419a–421c **CBE** Will the Guardians be happy?
   419a–420a CE Objection of Adimantus. *Adimantus* **2, 3**.
   420ab CB Comments. *Socrates* **2, (3)**. *Adimantus* **2**.
   420b–421c CE Reply of Socrates to the objection. *Socrates* **(1), 2, (10)**. A rather striking style, with both everyday (e.g. ὡς ἐγᾦμαι 420b, ὦ θαυμάσιε 420d) and

---

238. Adam 1920 ad 401b ff. notes Plato's "glowing language" in this section.
239. Cf. Wilamowitz II 146 n. 1. The following explanations show that Plato does not think merely of a special use of κλέπτειν, as is sometimes believed (Adam 1920 ad 1., Gleisberg 1909: 5).
240. Adam 1920 ad 414b denies this; Carter 1952 also regards this myth as very important for the argument.

[101] solemn (e.g. οἶμος 420b, ἄρδην 421a) elements. Note the burlesque 420c-e. The sentence structure and word order are partly complicated.

IV. 421c–427c **CAD** The realization of the State. The dangers of change and innovations.

*421c–425a* CAD The dangers of change and the importance of a good education. *Socrates* **(1)**, **2**, **(3, 10)**. Not without vividness. Note rhetorical features (e.g. anaphoric repetition 421e; antitheses and polarization 422e–423b, introduced by a joke; gnomic 424c with a playful reference to Damon) and occasional weighty vocabulary (e.g. 422a, 424e). *Adimantus* **2, (3)**, sometimes expansive (especially 424de).

*425a–427b* CAD No petty legislation. *Socrates* **(1), 2, (3)**. Emphatic, fairly vivid. Note accumulation (425b with plural of abstract nouns, 425cd, 426ab) and the strongly ironical and partly colloquial tone in 426ab. Imagery especially 426e (the Hydra). *Adimantus* **(1), 2**, fairly personal.

*427b c* CD The religious institutions have to be founded by Apollo. *Socrates* **2**. Notably solemn and expansive (note triads). *Adimantus* **2**.

IV. 427de **CB** Return to main theme: justice in the State. *Socrates* **2, (10)**. Heavy and twisted, as if searching for a new approach. *Glaucon* **(1), 2**, emphatic (note οὐδὲν λέγεις 427d).

[102] IV. 427e–432b **CAD** The different virtues present in the State. *Socrates* **2, 5**. Abstract and intellectual, gradually more expansive. Simile of dyeing 429d–430b technical. Accumulation 431bc (here also anaphoric repetition). *Glaucon* **2**. Personal remark to the simile 429e.

IV. 432b–e **CB** Tracing justice. *Socrates* **1, (2, 4)**. Vivid and expressive, with hunting imagery; yet slightly literary (note participles 432b, ταύτῃ 432c, synonymy 432c, etc.). The imagery changes into comical hyperboles when Socrates finds a "track" (ἰοὺ ἰού, βλακικόν, κυλινδεῖσθαι, καταγελαστότατοι). *Glaucon* **2**. The somewhat dignified and circumstantial replies are perhaps intended as a contrast to Socrates' exuberance.

IV. 433a–444e **CAD** On justice. The three parts of the soul.

*433a–434d* CAD Justice in the State. *Socrates* **2, 5**. Note the compressed style of the conclusion 434c (asyndeton). *Glaucon* **2**.

*434d–436a* CAD Analogy between the State and the individual. *Socrates* **1, 2, 5**. Fairly vivid and personal (note opening playful assonance 434d, imagery 435a, φαῦλον, ὦ θαυμάσιε 435c, γελοίου 435e), yet manifestly intellectual (e.g. systematization 435b; large use of abstract nouns, though σκέμμα 435c may be playful). *Glaucon* **1, (2, 4)**. Vivid and personal replies (note proverb 435c, ἀγαπητόν 435d).

*436a–441c* CAD The three parts of the soul and their relation to virtue. *Socrates* **(1), 2, 5**. Not without vividness (note χαριεντίζω, κομψευόμενος and simile 436d, θορυβήσῃ 438a, ὥσπερ θηρίον 439b, anecdote of Leontios 439e–440a, quot. of Homer 441b). *Glaucon* **2**, occasional personal (imagery 440d).

*441c–444e* CAD Justice and injustice in the individual. *Socrates* **2, (5)**. More expansive than above (note accumulation and synonymy especially in the conclusion about justice, introduced by simile 443b, and the very considerable accumulation of extensive words in the opening passage about injustice 444b). *Glaucon* **2**.

IV. 444e–445b CB Is it useful to be just? *Socrates* **2**, expansive. *Glaucon* **(1), 2**, emphatic, accumulative and solemn (in spite of γελοῖον 445a, repeated by Socrates 445b, and the σκέμμα of 435c repeated 445a).

IV. 445c–e. V.449a CD Brief remarks on the varieties of State corresponding to the varieties of vice in the soul.[241] *Socrates* **2, (10)**. Solemn (note σκοπιᾶς 445c, anaphoric repetition 445d, synchysis); but opening δεῦρό νυν **(1)**. *Glaucon* **2**.

V. 449a–451c CB Which will be the position of the women in the State? Socrates hesitates, but is persuaded to speak. *Socrates* **(1), 2, (3), 4**. Somewhat heavy (also in the brief C narrative 449ab), but playfully expressive (note exclam. οἷον and ὅσον 450a, ἀγαπῶν 450a, ὦ εὔδαιμον 450c, παραθαρρύνειν 450d, προσκυνῶ, ἀπατεών 451a, synonymy and mock-rhetoric 450d–451b, imagery 451bc), also manifestly colloquial (note τί μάλιστα 449bc). The style reflects Socrates' hesitation. *Glaucon* **2**, somewhat expressive 451b. *Polemarchus* **(2?)**. *Adimantus* **1, 2**, rather expansive 449c–450a. *Thrasymachus* **1, 2**, literary, but vehement 450ab (note proverbial χρυσοχοήσοντας, see Adam ad I.).

V. 451c–466d **CAD** On women and children.

451c–453e CAD Opening considerations regarding the equality of sexes. *Socrates* **2, 10**. Expansive onkos (much synonymy, heavy words, synchysis; note also abstract substantive adjective and participle 452d).[242] Successively more vivid passages which add a playfully artificial touch **(1)** to the basic style (e.g. ὦ θαυμάσιε 453c, burlesque imagery 453d). *Glaucon* **(1), 2**, more vivid 453cd.

453e–457c CA(D) New approach to the equality of sexes. *Socrates* **2, 5**. Not without vividness, ironical, with reference to everyday ideas (especially 455cd), but abstract and systematic. Note the playful approximation to eristics 454ab and the extensive use of A questioning. Concluding imagery (κῦμα 457b). *Glaucon* **2, (10)**. Onkos 455d in reply to burlesque.

457c–461e CAD Regulations about community of women and children. *Socrates* **2, (3, 10)**. Expansive, rather heavy, much antithesis. Opening with a clearly legal prescript **9** (457cd), also elsewhere sometimes legal rather than rhetorical, notably in the concluding passage 461a–e which has a manifest exuberance of style. Vivid imagery about mental feast 457e–458b, somewhat colloquial **(1)** when reference to the preservation of the breed in animals 459a–d. The variations of style seem to reflect the ambivalences and difficulties of the subject. *Glaucon* **2, (10)**.

461e–466d CAD The harmony and happiness resulting from this. *Socrates* **2, (10)**. Expansive, largely somewhat heavy. Occasional legal touches **(9)**, especially 465ab. Very emphatic and expansive 465cd; expressive imagery **(4)** and reference to Hesiod 465d–466c, leading to emphatic conclusion 466de. *Glaucon* **2**. Legal touch **(9)** 463c. Strong assent **(1)** 465d.

V. 466d–471c **CAD**[243] Military training. On war. *Socrates* **2, (4, 5)**. Somewhat expansive and weighty, expressive, (note especially imagery 467de, 469de, reference

---

241. The argument is interrupted and not resumed until VIII.543c.
242. Probably parody of sophistic jargon (cf. 454ab); Denniston 1952: 21.
243. As appears from the connection between 466d and 471c, this section is a digression.

[104]    to poetry 468c–469a), but also intellectual and systematic (note especially 470b). Slightly legal **(9)** 471c. *Glaucon* **2**. Legal touch **(9)** 468bc.

V. 471c–472b **CBE** Can this State be realized?

*471c–e* CE Problem stated by Glaucon. *Glaucon* **2, (3)**.

*472ab* CB Reply by Socrates and comment. *Socrates* **(1), 2, 4**, expansive, serious, but very expressive (note colloquial στραγγευομένῳ v. l., metaphor τρικυμία with referenceto 457bc, cf. 473c). *Glaucon* **2**.

V 472b–473e **CAD** The philosophers as leaders of the State. *Socrates,* **2, (5)**. Somewhat abstract (note compressed style 472de, 473a) and systematic (note 473b); but very expressive **(4)**, emphatic and expansive when introducing the main point 473c–e (note κῦμα 473c, παῦλα 473d, φῶς ἡλίου ἴδῃ 473e).[244] *Glaucon* **2**.

V. 473e–474c **CB** Comments on this remarkable theory. *Glaucon* **2, 4**, expansive and very expressive. *Socrates* **2, 5**, systematic.

V. 474c–480a. VI.484a–487a **CAD** On philosophy. On knowledge and opinion.

*474c–476c* CAD The philosopher. *Socrates* **2**. Expansive, expressive **(4)** especially at the beginning (note the exuberant passage on lovers 474d–475a). More strict but accumulative from 475e. *Glaucon* **(1), 2, (4)**, rather vivid, note expressive objection 475de.

*476c–480a* CA(D) Knowledge and opinion. *Socrates* **2, 5**. Systematic and clear, partly strict, occasional emphatic and expansive (note 478e–479a) and very occasional imagery (note opening ὄναρ / ὕπαρ 476c, κυλινδεῖται 479d). *Glaucon* **(1), 2**, fairly personal. Intellectual **(5)** comment 478ab, expressive reference to children's riddle 479bc (note here παγίως).

[105]    (VI) 484a–487a **CAD** The true philosopher as ruler. *Socrates* **2, (3), 5**, expansive, emphatic (note synonymy and polarization e.g. 485b, anaphoric repetition 486a, concluding asyndeton 487a). *Glaucon* **2**. Concluding emphatic **(4)** proverb.

VI. 487a–489a **CBE** Objection of Adimantus: inability of the philosophers to serve the State. Reply: the ship.

*487a–d* CE Objection. *Adimantus* **2, (3)**, expansive.

*487de* CB Comments. *Socrates* **2, (8)**. Slightly solemn (note the reply of Adimantus and σκώπτεις 487e). *Adimantus* **2**.

*487e–489a* CE Reply. Simile of the ship. *Socrates* **(1), 2**. Fairly expressive and intense accumulation. The simile introduced by νόησον 488a, then a string of participial clauses 488a–e.

VI. 489a–497a **CD** Reasons why philosophers are not trusted. *Socrates* **2, (3, 10)**. Partly accumulative, also very emphatic and expressive **(4)** (note the passages on philosophical love 490ab;[245] the influence of public opinion 492a–d; sophists 493a–c; conclusion about the isolation of philosophers 496c–e). *Adimantus* **2**, brief replies.

VI. 497a–d **CB** Interlude. Can the ideal State be ruled by philosophers? *Socrates* **2, (5, 10)**. *Adimantus* **2**.

VI. 497d–506b **CD** Rule of the philosophers. Education of the philosophers.

---

244. The importance of this section is generally recognized; cf. Wilamowitz I 447, II 202–203, Friedländer III² 96. On the "growing metaphor" of κῦμα, see Campbell 1894: 249.

245. Cf. *Smp.* 206c–e, 210a–212a.

497d–502c CD Rule of the philosophers. *Socrates* **2, (5, 10)**. Partly expressive (note imagery 498ab, extensive words 500b, chiastic and otherwise twisted word order 501e). *Adimantus* **2**. On the whole brief replies but important extensive remark 498c.

502c–504e CD Education of the philosophers. *Socrates* **2, 10**. *Adimantus* **2**, brief replies.

504e–506b CA The greatest mathema. The Form of Good.[246] *Socrates* **(1), 2**. Fairly vivid, though expansive. A very marked change of style. *Adimantus* **(1), 2**.

VI. 506b–e **CB** What is the Good? *Socrates* **1, (2, 4)**. Vivid, imagery (τυφλῶν 506c, ἔκγονος 506e). *Adimantus* **(1), 2**. *Glaucon* **1, 2**, taking over from 506d.

VI. 507a–509b **CAD** On sensible and intelligible Good. Simile of the Sun.

507a–508b CA The sensible image of Good. *Socrates* **2, (5)**. Fairly strict, occ. expressive words **(4)** (note τόκος, ἔκγονος 507a, ὄμμα 507d, 508b, ταμιεύω 508b). *Glaucon* **2**.

508b–509b CD The intelligible. The Sun. *Socrates* **2, (5, 10)** Intense. *Glaucon* **2, (4)** (note ἀμήχανον κάλλος 509a).

VI. 509c **CB** Retardation. Comments. *Glaucon* **1, (2), 4**. Very emphatic (note γελοίως). *Socrates* **1, 2**.

VI. 509d–511e. VII.514a–527c **CAD** Similes of the Line and the Cave, and their consequences for education. Arithmetics. Geometry.[247]

509d–511e CD The divided Line. *Socrates* **(2), 5, (10)**, accumulative. Partly carried by imperatives (νόησον, τέμνε 509d, τίθει 510a, μάνθανε 511b, etc.). Very little onkos in comparison to the passages on the Sun and the Cave. *Glaucon* **2, 5**. Extensive comment 511cd.

(VII) 514a–518b CD The Cave. *Socrates* **2, (5, 10)**. Very expansive, and considerable use of expressive vocabulary.[248] Imperatives as above (ἀπείκασον, ἰδέ 514a, ὅρα 514b, etc). Also colloquialisms **(1)** (note φλυαρίας 515d, σφόδρα γελοῖος 517d). *Glaucon* **(1), 2**, fairly vivid.

518b–521b CD(E) Consequences for education. Speech to the philosophers (520b–d). *Socrates* **2, (5)**. Expansive, expressive, also colloquial **(1)** (note ψυχάριον 519a, λιχνεία 519b). Imagery in speech. *Glaucon* **2**.

521c–522b CAD The use of mathemata for educating the philosophers. *Socrates* **(1), 2**. Fairly vivid, expressive imagery 521 cd. *Glaucon* **2, (5)**, extensive remark 522a.

522c–527a CAD Arithmetics and (from 526e) geometry. *Socrates* **2, 5**. But expressive reference to Homer 522d **(4)** (note παγγέλοιον), and occasional later

---

246. It is possible to take the transition to this section as a B interlude.

247. Though this section is very extensive and seemingly heterogeneous, stylistic reasons speak for the division here adopted. All the subjects treated in the VIIth book arise from a single general conception, introduced by the Line and the Cave, and vitalized anew by the passage on astronomy (529a–530c). Friedländer III² 106–107 refers to the successive resumptions of earlier sections after the Similes in order to obtain a circular structure. The central importance of the Similes has often been emphasized; see e.g. Adam 1921: 156–163, Gould 1955: 165–181, Sinaiko 1965: 119–190, Raven 1965: 129–187.

248. The rhythms detected in this section by Kolár 1951: 116–117 can hardly be labelled "rhetorical."

[106]  more personal (e.g. 525d–526a, 527a). *Glaucon* **(1)**, **2**. Fairly vivid and personal, note accumulation in 526d.

VII. 527c–528a **CB** Retardation. The application of science is not so important. *Socrates* **1**, **(2)**, **4**. Vivid, very expressive. *Glaucon* **1**, **2**.

[107]  VII. 528a–532b **CAD** The use of mathemata continued. Stereometry. Astronomy. Harmonics.

*528a–d* CAD Stereometry. *Socrates* **2**, **5**, expansive. *Glaucon* **2**.

*528d–530c* CAD Astronomy. *Socrates* **(1)**, **2**, **(4, 5)**. Vivid, emphatic, expressive. *Glaucon* **1**, **2**, vivid, personal.

*530c–531c* CAD Harmonics. *Socrates* **2**, **(4, 5)**. Emphatic, expressive. *Glaucon* **1**, **2**, **4**. Vivid, expressive.

*531c–532b* CAD All these sciences are preludial. *Socrates* **2**, **(5, 10)**. *Glaucon* **2**, **(4)**, emphatic.

VII. 532b–533a **CB** Retardation. Glaucon asks for initiation in dialectic. *Socrates* **2**, **(10)**. Solemn imagery with reference to the Cave, as if revealing a mystery (note ἀκολουθεῖν 533a). *Glaucon* **2**, expansive, also with imagery (532e).

VII. 533a–541b **CD** Dialectic and education.

*533a–535a* CD Dialectic. *Socrates* **2**, **(5, 10)**. Partly expressive **(4)** (note ἐν βορβόρῳ βαβαρικῷ 533d, chiasm 533e, anaphoric repetition 534a, imagery 534e). *Glaucon* **(1)**, **2**, intense.

*535a–541b* CD Dialectic and education. *Socrates* **2**, **(5)**. Expansive; in parts expressive vocabulary (note play with μόνιμος and νόμιμος 537d, vivid imagery 539b). Conclusion about the philosophers as rulers 540a–c more solemn **(10)**, accumulative (note reply 540c ὥσπερ ἀνδριαντοπιός). *Glaucon* **2** (peculiar word order 537a). More vivid **(4)** comments to conclusion 540c, 541b.

VIII. 543a–544b **CB** Summary of the considerations about the Guardians. Resumption of argument from the end of the 4th book. *Socrates* **2**, **(3)**, expansive. On the whole formal, but imagery 544b. *Glaucon* **2**, fairly expansive.

VIII. 544b–548d **CD** The four forms of government. Change of aristocracy into timocracy. 'Nuptial number.'

*544b–545c* CD Four forms of government. *Socrates* **2**, **(10)**. Emphatic, expressive. *Glaucon* **2**.

*545c–545d* CD Change of aristocracy into timocracy. *Socrates* **2**, **(10)**. *Glaucon* **2**.

*545d–547a* CE 'Nuptial number.'[249] *Socrates* **2**, **5**, **(10)**. Opening with expressive reference to the Muses and the "tragic" style of the passage (cf. also 547a, 548b). Intellectual, but heavy and gnomic.

[108]  *547a–548d* Further observations on this change. *Socrates* **2**, **(10)** (note resumptive participle 547c). *Glaucon* **2**.

VIII. 548d **CB** Change of approach. Adimantus takes over.[250] *Socrates* **2**, **5**. Compressed style. *Adimantus* **(1)**, **2**.

VIII. 548e–569c. IX.571a–576b **CAD** Character of the individuals in the different forms of government.

---

249. For the interpretation see Adam 1921 ad l. and 264–312, Brumbaugh 1954: 107–150, Denkinger 1955, v. Ehrenfels 1962.

250. Cf. below, IX.576b.

*548e–550c* CAD The timocrate. *Socrates* **2, (5), 10**. Emphatic, expansive and accumulative, also expressive. *Adimantus* **2**.  [108]

*550c–555b* CAD Oligarchy and the oligarch. *Socrates* **2, 5, (10)**. Somewhat more strict than above, brief utterances; but accumulation 552a. Simile of the drone introduced 552c, then more expansive and expressive (note especially 553bc, 554a–c). *Adimantus* **2**, fairly personal.

*555b–562a* CAD Democracy and the democrate.[251] *Socrates* **2, 5, (10)**, with much expansion and accumulation; also expressive, and much imagery (note e.g. accumulation of participial clauses 556c–e, 560de, of finite clauses 560cd, simile 557c, ironical litotes οὐ κομψή 558a, Λωτοφάγους 560c, -οισι 560e). Occasional slightly rhetorical **(3)** (e.g. anaphoric repetition 559b). *Adimantus* **2, (3)** (note antithesis 557a).

*562a–(IX) 576b* CAD Tyranny and tyrannic man. *Socrates* **(1), 2, (3, 4)**. Fairly vivid, very emphatic and expressive (note ironical tone in 562a, 563e, 567e, 574c, etc.; frequent imagery; proverbs 563c, 565d, 569b, 575c; asyndeton 567b, 575b; νὴ τὸν κύνα 567d). Occasional onkos **(10)** (note ξὺν αὐτοῖσι τοῖς κηρίοις 564c, ἐπακτός 573b, βρῶμα 574e). *Adimantus* **(1), 2, (4)**, rather vivid and personal.[252]

IX. *576b–592a* CAD[253] Tyrannic man possesses extreme misery and vice, the philosopher-king extreme happiness and justice.

*576b–580c* CA(D) First demonstration that tyrannic man is the most miserable: [109] tyranny is slavery. *Socrates* **2, (3)**. Emphatic, expressive (note vocabulary 578a, 579de, synonymy 578e, asyndeton 580ab; frequent γέμειν, μεστός). Ceremonious touch **(8)** in the conclusion 580bc. *Glaucon* **2, (3)**.

*580c–583a* CA(D) Second demonstration: three parts of the soul. *Socrates* **2, 5**, somewhat expansive (note synonymy 580e, 581a, etc.); occasional expressive (note 581d). *Glaucon* **2, (5)** (fairly systematic 582bc).

*583b–588a* CA(D) Third demonstration: pleasure. *Socrates* **2, (4), 5**. Expressive and pathetic opening 583b. Then partly strict (note use of abstracts 583c–584a), occasional expressive (note 584a). Later more expansive, and very expressive onkos **10** in description of the life of pleasure 586a–c (note χρησμῳδεῖς in Glaucon's comment 586b).[254] Then again more strict, but emphatic (e.g. 588a). *Glaucon* **1, 2, (4)**. Fairly vivid and personal at times (note important comment 586b).

*588b–592a* CAD On justice and vice in man. Simile of the Chimaera (588c–e). *Socrates* **2, (5, 10)**. The simile emphatic and intense (note imperatives πλάττε etc), later more expansive. *Glaucon* **2, (4)**. Personal 588cd, 589ab, 591d.

---

251. On the forcible style of this passage *see* Adam 1921 ad 559d and p. 313. On the structure of the passage *see* Vretska 1955: 407 ff.

252. Adimantus seems to have been fond of country life, *see* 563d. It is perhaps significant that the recurrent simile of the Drone occurs in a section where Adimantus is addressed.

253. The B interlude had been reduced to a minimum between the two last sections (VIII.548d), and it is here represented by a mere change of interlocutor. The topics treated in the VIIIth and IXth books arise from a single conception, like those treated in the VIIth book. Wilamowitz II 210–211 calls attention to the fact that the change of interlocutor corresponds to the return to the main problem: justice.

254. Probably with reference to style, cf. Adam 1921 ad 1. and Willi 1925: 31. A passage from 586a is quoted by *De sublim.* 13.1 as an example of Platonic ὕψος.

[109] IX. 592ab **CB** Brief conclusion. The ideal city modeled on heaven. *Socrates* **1, 2, (4)**, emphatic. *Glaucon* **2**.
X. 595a–608b **CAD** On poetry and mimesis.
595a–598d CAD General considerations. Mimesis. *Socrates* **2, (3)**, expansive (note anaphoric repetition 596de, asyndeton 598b). Playful reference to everyday ideas when discussing mimesis 596c–597d, also elsewhere occ. expressive. *Glaucon* **2, (4)**.
598d–601b CD(E) On Homer and other poets as educators. *Socrates* **2, (3)**, accumulative. Playfully solemn (note ironical anaphoric repetition 598e); note especially speech to Homer 599de. Also expressive and hyperbolical **(1, 4)** (note 600cd), and reference to mean crafts. *Glaucon* **1, 2**, personal.
601b–605c CA(D) Comparison of the arts of illusion. *Socrates* **2, (5)**. Somewhat expansive, also expressive (note 602cd, 603d). From 604a rising onkos **(10)** with accumulation and some rhetorical mannerisms **(3)** (note anaphoric repetitions and polyptoton 603ab, 604a). *Glaucon* **2**.
[110] 605c–608b CD The dangerousness of Homer and dramatic poets. *Socrates* **2, (10)**. Very emphatic, expansive and expressive. *Glaucon* **2**.
X. 608b–d **CB** Change of subject. Immortality of the soul. *Socrates* **2, (4, 10)**. Very intense. *Glaucon* **1, 4**, emphatic (note θαυμάσας 608d).
X. 608d–614b **CD** Immortality of the soul. Retribution.
608d–611a C(A)D Immortality of the soul. *Socrates* **2, 5**, gradually more expansive. *Glaucon* **2**. Emphatic and solemn **(10)** comment on retribution 610de.
611a–614b CD The soul freed from the body. Retribution. *Socrates* **2, (3, 5, 10)**. Accumulations and much expansion, also expressive, and imagery (note simile of Glaucus 611cd; reference to myths 612b; polarization 612cd, etc.). Later more vivid **(1)** (note burlesque 613bc, reference to punishments 613de, cf. above II.361e–362a). *Glaucon* **(1), 2**, sometimes personal (note 612d, 614ab).
X. 614b–621d **CE** Myth of Er. Conclusion of the work.
614b Introductory remark and narrative. *Socrates* **2, (4)**. Opening with a pun.
614b–615a Beginning of narrative of Er. **2, (4, 6)**, accumulative, and oratio obliqua.
615a–d The punishment of great criminals, introductory. **2, (6, 10)**, accumulative, and oratio obliqua.
615d–616b The punishment of great criminals, partly oratio recta by a witness. **2, 6, (10)**, accumulative, very expressive.
616b–617d Cosmology. **2, 6, (10)**, accumulative, and oratio obliqua. In parts detailed and systematic **(5)**.
617d–620d The choice of life. Proclamations of the Hierophant (617de, 619b). **(1), 2, 6, (10)**, accumulative, and oratio obliqua. Expressive (note apostrophe to Glaucon 618b; ἀδαμαντίνως 619a, ἀνήκεστα κακά 619a, etc.; vivid details 620a). The speeches of the *Hierophant* ceremonious **8, (10)**.[255]
620d–621b The plain of Lethe. **(1), 2, 6, (10)**, oratio obliqua. Very expressive.
621b–d Concluding apostrophe to Glaucon. *Socrates* **2, (3, 10)**. Accumulative, solemn and emphatic.[256]

---

255. Cf. Proclus in Pl. *R.* II p. 269.
256. The expression μῦθος ἐσώθη 621b is regarded as a colloquialism by Rose 1938, but this seems to me very doubtful.

## Conclusions regarding *R*.

There are great variations in style. Book I owing to its easy and mimetic tone stands apart from the rest. In books II–X there occurs somewhat more variation before the peripeteia (VI/VII) than after it.

Different aspects (cf. above p. 27):

(a) The BABAB rhythm of the dialogue structure has a marked correspondence in the changes of style. The B sections are usually more lively and varied (e.g. V.449a–451c), or else they stand out stylistically from the preceding and following A section (e.g. VIII.548d). There are very few exceptions to this rule, the most notable being I.347a where the change of section is formally denoted only by Glaucon's joining in. Shifts of style are also common within the A sections, but they are not on the whole as marked as the changes between the sections. Exceptions (such as VI.504e) always imply important points.

The C narrative mostly occurs in B sections and is not so common in the later books (cf. p. 18). It is kept in lively and natural style 1; cf. below under (b).

D passages have a tendency to expansion and onkos which corresponds to their formal structure.

E passages always have a distinct stylistic character of their own.

The central sections (VI/VII) are not markedly different from the preceding and following sections; but cf. below (c).

(b) The study of the characterization of *Socrates* by stylistic means presents special problems because Socrates is either represented mimetically as an approximation to the historical Socrates, or he is actually and merely the mouthpiece of Plato, or, and indeed mostly, he is both at the same time though rather more the latter than the former. It is sufficient here if we look only at those passages where the manner of the historical Socrates is evidently imitated. As a fairly reliable external indication of this we may regard the contrasting of the style of utterances by Socrates with the style of utterances by his interlocutors: it is reasonable to think that Plato, if he bothered to characterize Socrates' interlocutors by stylistic means, did not in the same passage leave Socrates uncharacterized. There may also occur other external criteria (e.g. the reference to εἰρωνεία I.337a). But when there is no evident mimesis the style of Socrates will be regarded as the style of Plato and will be considered under (c).—The mimetic passages are mainly found in book I and the beginning of book II. Here also most of the C narrative and description occurs. The Socratic C is in style **1** with much **4**. It is often contrasted to the utterances of others. Socrates versus Polemarchus, Glaucon or Adimantus uses **1, (4)** up to the first part of book II. Socrates versus Cephalus is **1**, though markedly polite. Socrates versus Thrasymachus, his chief interlocutor in book I, largely employs a quiet and restrained **1, (2)** (though the C is vivid), sometimes **(5)**, later occasionally triumphant **(4)**. But the grave intensity of the important sections I.341c–342e and 345b–348b may be rather Platonic; note the lack of stylistic contrast in the latter case. From the introduction of the main theme II.368e onwards there is no evident imitation of Socratic manner, except perhaps the almost burlesque CB section IV.432b–e (tracing justice). Possibly the occasional exuberance elsewhere is intended to be remotely Socratic: note the slight contrast

[112] to the style of the interlocutor in IV.420b, V.453e–457c, VII.521c–522b, 527c–528a, and the opening of the myth of Er X.614b. But the contrast between "Socrates'" rhetoric or onkos and some lively comments by his interlocutor (especially from V.473e onwards) clearly is not characteristic of Socrates; *see* under (c).

*Thrasymachus*, Socrates' chief interlocutor in book I (from 336b onwards), is given a very emphatic, also vulgar, style 1 with touches of (3). It is interesting to note that the only utterance of Thrasymachus after the end of the first book, V.450ab, is in style 2 and not clearly mimetic. Plato's realism is never consistent.

*Glaucon*, the chief interlocutor in books II-X, is manifestly characterized at the beginning of book II as also the remarks of Socrates show. His style is literary, but vigorous and vehement. In book I he is not clearly characterized. Later in book II the sarcastic remarks 372a–e are probably intended to be mimetic, and so are the musical terms III.398d–400a.[257] Further perhaps the literary dignity in IV.432b–e, V.453e–457c, 471c–e is characteristic of him as contrasted to Socrates, though the note of **10** V.455d–461e is probably a mechanical application of the onkos of the context. And probably the occasional lively comments from III.403c onwards are partly mimetic though their main purpose is to underline important points in the argument of "Socrates"; cf. below (c).

[113] *Adimantus*, the second interlocutor in books II-X, is attributed a rhetorical speech at the beginning of book II,[258] and hence it is reasonable to take the similar style of his utterances as mimetic in IV.419a–420a, VI.487a–d, VIII.557a (cf. III.396e). Elsewhere he is not characterized.

*Cephalus*, the type of the happy old man who is vignetted in the opening scenes of book I, is characterized by an expansive and somewhat circumstantial **1, 2, (4)**.

*Polemarchus*, a minor character in book I, has a somewhat expansive style **1, (2, 3)** in 331e–336a, cf. 340ab. But like Thrasymachus he is left unindividualized in the opening of book V.

Clitophon and the Slave who appear in the opening of book I are given no stylistic elaboration. The same of course applies to Er the Armenian. But the proclamations of the *Hierophant* X.617de, 619b are as one should expect ceremonious.

Thus it can be seen that stylistic characterization is mainly limited to R. I and the first part of R. II. But Plato's special affection for his brother Glaucon is probably reflected in the occasional touches of his lively manner in the later books.

(c) Naturally the shifts discussed under (b) also reflect shifts in the approach. The quality and relative importance of the mimetic utterances in the course of the argument depend partly on which position the character is given but also on other facts. The natural and lively style **1, (4)** of Socrates is largely playful and obviously serves as background or counterpoint when contrasted, as C narrative or as utterances, to the styles of Cephalus, Thrasymachus, Glaucon and Adimantus.

---

257. Glaucon contrary to Socrates is a specialist in music (III.398e). Wilamowitz II 192 thinks that this is why Glaucon intervenes in 398c.

258. The speech is evidently intended by Plato as a candid objection, but the fact that he makes Glaucon the chief interlocutor of Socrates in the following indicates that he lays more stress on the arguments of Glaucon. Taylor 271 thinks that the tone of Adimantus' speech is intended to display more of moral indignation than that of Glaucon.

Also the section I.331e–336a, where Socrates uses this style versus Polemarchus, may be taken as essentially playful. On the other hand the quiet **1, 2, (5)** which Socrates employs against Thrasymachus is more weighty, and it was suggested above that the sections I.341c–342e and 345b–348b rise above the mimetic level. As a matter of fact the latter section resembles a visionary central section and it may be a further indication that book I was originally a separate work. Of the other characters of book I Cephalus' speeches in **1, 2, (4)** are evidently intended to state the introductory commonsense position. Polemarchus then more vaguely represents the common opinion. It is interesting to note that he combines **1** with touches of **(3)**, like Thrasymachus whose emphatic vulgarity of course underlines the contrary position to Socrates. The complex and vigorous style of Glaucon at the beginning of book II reflects the importance of the objections put in his mouth. Here I should like to call special attention to the occurrence of shade **5**. Adimantus uses a more formal style **3**, and though his objections complement those of Glaucon, it is possible that Plato would keep a certain ironical distance to them.

After II.368e, however, it can be maintained that the mimesis fades away: Socrates is essentially Plato, and his interlocutors principally give the resonance and ornament required by the dialogue form.

The basic style of this Platonic "Socrates" is **2**. Deviations into **1** (and **4**) are mostly clearly playful (e.g. II.372a–e, III.398ab). Such deviations are not so common from the introduction of the theme of philosophers as leaders V.472b down to the conclusion of book IX and serve mainly as retardation before important points (note especially VI.504e–506e, VII.527c–528a).

Quite often the Platonic πειθώ employs shades of **(3)**. It would seem that this shade too, is, if not ironical, at least not wholly serious: in the central part of the work, after IV.427d, it occurs only in the mock-rhetorical and awkward passages V.449a ff., 457c ff., and in defense of the remarkable suggestion that the philosophers should be made rulers, VI.484a ff., 489a ff.

Shade **5** has a different distribution. It appears to be almost always serious. In book I there are some touches of it. Book II opens with a considerable use of it in Glaucon's speech, as we have seen, and correspondingly the Platonic "Socrates" uses it in particularly important passages: note especially IV.427e–432b (the different virtues in a State), IV.433a–444e (justice and the three parts of the soul), V.476c–480a (knowledge and opinion), VI.509d–511e (divided Line), VII.522c–528d (mathematics and stereometry), VIII.545d–547a (nuptial number), IX.580c–583a (three parts of the soul), X.608d–611a (immortality); but manifestly ironical V.453e–457c (equality of sexes).

Shade **6** occurs as ornament in some passages of considerable, but not central importance: II.359d–360b (Gyges myth in the speech of Glaucon), III.414b–415d ("Phoenician" myth about inequality), myth of Er. Shade **7** does not occur in *R*. Shade **8**, apart from the above-mentioned proclamations of the Hierophant, is played with in VI.487de but used for solemn emphasis in IX.580bc. Shade **9** occurs in some regulations concerning the community of women and children and military training V.457c–471c. Here it is seemingly appropriate to the subject, but actually somewhat playful (note e.g. 468bc and cf. IV.425a–427b).

[115]    Shade **10**, finally, for the first time appears as an accessory touch in the section on poetry II.376d ff., and later it accompanies large portions of the work. It is however remarkably often absent from passages of evident importance, such as the above-mentioned passages where shade **5** is used (except the "nuptial number"). And it often combines with playfulness or even burlesque. On the other hand it is manifestly serious in passages such as III.412b–414b (the leaders among the Guardians), IV.445c–V.449a (analogy between the State and the soul), VI.502c–504e (education of the philosophers), VI.508b–509b (simile of the Sun), VII.514a–518b (simile of the Cave), VIII.544c–548d (the four forms of government), IX.588b–592a (justice and vice in man). The truth probably is (cf. also below p. 140) that Plato's onkos is a vehicle for psychagogy, playful or serious, but it is not suitable for the very highest considerations: note here above all the fact that the three central similes of R., of which the middle one represents the actual point of culmination,[259] shift from **2, (5, 10)** (the Sun) over **(2), 5, 10)** (the Line, with very few touches of onkos) back to **(2), 5, 10)** (the Cave). Only very occasionally, and hardly outside book V, does shade **10** extend to Socrates' interlocutor.

As a common trend in all expansively emphatic passages, playful or serious, whether uttered by Socrates of by somebody else (e.g. II.363cd), there can be noted a tendency to accumulation. This is probably a proper Platonic manner.

In general this brief discussion of the relation of style to the contents in R. has shown the relevance of the theory of central culmination (cf. p. 28 and n. 79). In the A sections around the central similes the play is abandoned which is often manifest in more peripheric sections, notably the sections on mimesis and communism.

(d) The rise of Plato's "late style," to judge from R., was no uniform or consistent process. If this style is roughly identified with shade **10** (for which cf.
[116]    above (c)), it can be seen that books III–V are largely heavier than many portions in the later books. The constituents of this heavy style, notably a basic accumulative style **2** with addition of **3** or **5**, are present already from the beginning of the second book, and not very much later (II.376d) the first signs of style **10** appear. If the considerations above under (c) hold true, it was a personal manner that Plato at this stage did not employ mechanically. Therefore its distribution is not likely to help in settling the internal chronology of the different parts of the R.

## Stylistic conspectus of the rest of the authentic works

The analysis here is carried out in very general terms. An oblique line / between the figures denotes a marked change of style that will be commented on under (b) or (c).

---

259. Cf. Raven 1965: 131–187.

*Hippias Minor* On intentional wrong-doing.

363a–364c **B** Introduction. Comparison of Achilles and Odysseus. **1, (2, 4) / 2, (5)**.
364c–369b **A** Only the expert can be "true" and "false." **1 / 2**.
369b–373c **BE** Intentional wrong-doing implies greater skill and is better. **1, 2, (3, 4) / 2**.
373c–376b **A** Intentional wrong-doing is better. **1**.
376bc **B** Brief, seemingly aporetic conclusion. **1**.

(a) Stylistic shifts between the sections except at the end. The conclusion lacks elaboration. The central E's stand out.

(b) *Socrates* slightly contrasted to Hippias by **1, (4)**, also ironically polite **(2)**. *Hippias* pompous **2**, also **(5)** (e.g. 363cd, 364c). The second A and the end lack a notable stylistic characterization. *Eudicus* is neutral.

(c) The mimetic first part is fairly burlesque. In the central section Socrates' speeches strike an emphatic **1, (3, 4)** with quotations of Homer, though with considerable play and irony. The second A and the end, which seemingly drive the point home, are fairly strict and colorless. Central culmination of style.

(d) No signs of **10**.

*Ion* On inspiration.

530a–d **BE** Brief introduction. On Ion and on rhapsodes in general. **1, (4) / 2, (8) / 3, (4)**.
531a–533c **A** First examination of rhapsodic **1, (4)**.
533c–536d **BE** On the nature of poetry and inspiration **(1), 3, 4**.
536d–541b **A** Second examination of rhapsodic **1, (4) / 1, 2, (4)**.
541b–542b **BE** Ironical conclusion. The rhapsode is no expert, but inspired. **1, (2)**.

(a) Regularly stylistic shifts between the sections. The central E's are very clearly marked.

(b) *Socrates* mocking **1, (4)**, also **3**, in contrast to Ion especially in the opening BE. *Ion* here self-confident **2, (8)**, later frequently **4**. The central BE and the second A probably Platonic rather than Socratic.

(c) The opening and the first A largely mimetic. The second A is at first more weighty **(2, 4)**; note here the florid quotations of Homer 538b–539e; later **1** is resumed. The central BE (cf. p. 34 and n. 3) is rich and varied, especially Socrates' first speech on divine magnetism, with **3, 4**, dithyrambic imagery and references to poetry. Central culmination of style.

The considerable use of **4** corresponds to the main theme.

(d) No signs of **10**.

*Laches* On courage and on teaching.

178a–184d **BE** Introduction On teaching military skill. **2 / 3, (7)**.
184d–186a **A** On experts and teachers. **(1), 2**.
186a–189e **BE** On being a good teacher. **(1), 2, (3, 4)**.
190a–193d **A** First approach to courage as a virtue. **1, (2)**.
193d–197e **B** Aporetic interlude. **1, (4) / 1, (2)**.
197e–199e **A** Second approach to courage as a virtue. **1, 2**.

[117]  199e–201c **B** Conclusion. Socrates agrees to teach the boys. **(1), 2**.
   (a) Clear stylistic shifts between the sections. The E passages of the introduction and the central section also stand out.
   (b)[260] *Socrates*, in the first part including the central section, uses a polite **2** with some ironical touches of **(1)** and in his first speech (186a–187b) also **(3)**, which however may be Platonic. After the peripeteia he changes to a vivid **1, (4)** which is partly contrasted to Laches and Nicias. From 198c onwards he resumes a dignified **1, 2**. *Lysimachus*, the "honorary president" (in B passages only), is character-
[118]  ized by a circumstantial **2, (3)**. *Laches* impetuous **3, (7)** in his introductory speech, also **3** in his speech 188c–189b (with **4**), and later very emphatic and energetic **1**, especially in the aporetic interlude. Like the others he resumes a dignified **2** in the conclusion. *Nicias* **2, 3** especially in his introductory speech, more lively **1, (2)** in the aporetic interlude (versus Laches), and again dignified **2** in the conclusion. There is less characterization of others than Socrates in the two later A sections. Melesias and the boys receive no stylistic characterization.
   (c) The extensive employment of **2** and **3** seems to be on the whole mimetic and corresponds to the social status and the ambitions of the characters. But the speeches of Socrates with **2, (3, 4)** in the central section 186a–189e have a personal touch **(1)** and draw the attention to the personality of Socrates the teacher; cf. also the interjacent discussion. The following argument then is entirely dominated by Socratic **1**. The conclusion returns to the dignified style **2** of the opening, though Socrates plays with **(1)**. The central section acts as a peripeteia.
   (d) No signs of **10**.

*Crito* On the authority of the laws and on Socrates' decision.

43a–46b **BE** Introduction. Socrates in prison. Attempt by Criton to persuade Socrates to leave it. **1 / 2 / 1, 3**.
46b–50a **(E)A(D)** Reply of Socrates. The duties. **1, 2**.
50a–54d **E** Speech of the Laws. **(1), 2, 3, (4)**.
54d **B** Concluding remarks. **1, (4)**.

   (a) For the irregularity of the composition, see p. 48. No clear stylistic shifts between the sections, except that the speeches of Criton and the Laws form fairly homogeneous units. Note the tendency to D and E which is also reflected in the style.
   (b) *Socrates* light and easy **1** in the opening,[261] then rising dignity with **2**; in the end more lively **1, (4)**. *Criton* deeply moved and embarrassed **1, 2, 3**.[262] After the introduction he remains neutral. The authority of the *Laws* is emphasized by **2, 3**.
   (c) There is a gradually rising dignity and gravity of style which corresponds to the contents: **1–2–3**. Criton's speech of persuasion stands out in the introduction.
   (d) No signs of **10**.

---

260. A very detailed analysis of the characters, with some observations on the style, by Nagel 1962; cf. Friedländer II² 33–34. Bruns 1896: 268 oddly maintains that Laches receives no individualization.
261. Intentional characterization; cf. Friedländer II² 160 and n. 3.
262. Cf. Shorey 1933: 467, Friedländer II² 160–161.

*Apologia* The apology of Socrates.

17a–35d **E** First speech: apology with refutation of Meletus (**A:** 24b–28a). **3 / 1, (2, 4)**.
35e–38b **E** Second speech: after the verdict. **1, (3)**.
38c–42a **E** Third speech: to the jury. Protreptic and eschatology. **1, 2, 3**.

(a) Note the insertion of the fairly vivid A in the first speech. Cf. the brief CA passage 20ab.

(b) The style is probably intended to characterize an idealized *Socrates*, who is at the same time Plato.

(c) The three speeches display rhetorical features **3** to a varying degree.[263] The interaction of **1** (and very occasionally **4**) corresponds to the introducing of typically Socratic points or aspects. The central culmination of the work as a whole may be seen in the passage 30c–31c (the city of Athens, not Socrates, will suffer), and here the style is remarkably personal with similes and metaphors.[264] The conclusion also is intensely personal.

(d) No signs of **10**.

*Menexenus* An epitaphic speech to the citizens of Athens.

234a–236d **BE** Introduction. On epitaphic speeches. **1, 2, (4) / 3, 4**.
236d–249c **E** An epitaphic speech by "Aspasia." **3, 4, 7**.
249de **B** Concluding discussion and promise of further teaching by "Aspasia." **1, 2**.

(a) Stylistic shifts between the sections. The ironical speech of Socrates in the introduction is also clearly marked.

(b) *Socrates* fairly vivid **1, (4)** in the opening, later mock-pompous; cf. (c). *Menexenus* somewhat circumstantial **1, 2**,[265] slightly contrasted to Socrates. "*Aspasia*": a pastiche of a funeral speech.

(c) The burlesque is stressed by (the Platonic) Socrates' mock-pomposity **(1, 2), 3, 4** in the frame dialogue. The speech of "Aspasia" appears to follow conventional rules.[266] Here the address of the dead to the living (especially 247c–248d) and the speaker's conclusion are very emphatic, the latter notably heavy and apparently intended to carry the main weight.[267]

(d) No signs of **10** (in spite of the heaviness of the conclusion of the speech).

*Gorgias* On rhetoric and philosophy and on statesmanship.

447a–448e **B** Introduction. Preliminary discussion of the art of Gorgias. **1 / 2 / 3**.
448e–455a **AD** Socrates versus Gorgias. Attempts to define rhetoric. **1, 2, (4) / 3 / 1, (5)**.

---

263. Cf. Friedländer II² 143, Th. Meyer 1962: 45–65.
264. Cf. Bruns 1896: 218–223.
265. Yet probably the same character as in *Ly.; see* Friedländer II² 312 n. 6.
266. On the composition and the style of the speech, *see* Blass 1874: 430–441, Méridier Ménex. 1931: 66–73 (with reference), Loewenclau 1961: 42–126,149–150.
267. Kahn 1963: 229 interprets these passages as Plato's contemporary message.

[120] 455a–458e **BE** The orator is not an expert. Gorgias persuaded to continue. **1, 2, (3, 4) / 2, (3)**.
458e–461b **A(D)** Rhetoric requires ethical standards. **1, 2**.
461b–466a **BE** Intervention of Polus. Polemical testing of methods and definitions. **1, 2, (3, 4) / 2, 5**.
466a–470c **A(E)**[268] The power of rhetoric in politics. **1, (3, 4, 5)**.
470c–474c **BE** Can the wicked be happy? **1, (2) / 1, (3, 4, 6)**.
474c–481b **A(D)** Wickedness is the worst evil, and rhetoric cannot help the wicked. **1, (4), 5 / 2, 3, (5, 9)**.
481b–488b **BE** Intervention of Callicles. Practical life and philosophy. **1, (2, 4) / 2, 3**.
488b–491b **A** On being superior. **1, (5)**.
491b–494b **BE** Superiority and will. Simile of the leaking jar. **1, 2, (4), 5 / 2, (3)**.
494b–497b **A** Pleasure and happiness. **1, (2, 9)**.
497bc **B** Brief interlude. Callicles persuaded to continue. **1, 2**.
497c–499b **A** New approach to pleasure. **1, 5**.
499bc **B** Brief interlude. Callicles irritated. **1, (2)**.
499c–505b **A(D)** On true arts and empirical skills, and on good as the aim of the former. **1, 2, (3, 5)**.
505b–509c **BE** Callicles refuses to continue. Speech of Socrates summarizing the previous argument (as a fictitious **A** dialogue)[269] and (from 507c) insisting on moral sense, order, and the necessity of suffering. **1, (2, 5) / (1), 2, 3**.
[121] 509c–511a **A** On following the wicked in politics. **1, (5)**.
511a–513c **BE** On a good life and individual security. **(1), 2, 3**.
513c–522e **(A)D** The true function of a statesman. **1, 2, 3**.
523a–527e **E** Concluding myth and (from 526d) protreptic. **2, (3), 6, (8) / (1), 2, 3**.

(a) Probably owing to the vehemence of the work the stylistic shifts between the sections are somewhat blurred, and there are considerable changes of style within the A sections. But on the whole, as can be seen, the BABAB pattern has a certain correspondence in style. The tendency to D especially towards the end is reflected by an increase of the weight of style. The E passages clearly stand out.

(b) *Socrates* is given a lively and forcible style **1** in the introduction and often later (also with **4**), notably in the Polus episode and the first part of the Callicles episode; also the touches of **(1)** in the concluding speech can be regarded as Socratic. Sometimes Socrates is polite and quiet **2** in contrast to his interlocutors, notably in the Gorgias and Polus episodes. But on the whole the "Socrates" of this work is an orator able to reduce even Callicles to silence; cf. (c). *Gorgias* uses pompous and "macrological" **2** and **3** (though not pointedly **Gorg.**[270]) up to 458e. His occasional later utterances are not distinctly characterized. *Polus* has touches of **3 Gorg.** in the introduction (448c). Later he is given an excited pitch of **1, (3, 4)**, in partial contrast to Socrates, also **(6)** (on Archelaus 471a–d), until 474c; from

---

268. The simile of the Lunatic 469c–e must be regarded as an E, irregularly inserted in this lively A section.
269. Socrates supplies the replies instead of Callicles.
270. Saupe 1916: 35–37 and Vicaire 1960: 302 go too far in emphasizing this feature.

481b he withdraws. *Callicles* has a dignified and emphatic style **1, 2** in the opening of the work and when intervening (481b); then he turns more rhetorical **2, 3**, and at times uses a sarcastic **1**. It is notable that the latter shade is sometimes contrasted to the rhetoric of "Socrates" (e.g. 495d, 505cd, 521a–c). At 513d, with the beginning of the final DE, Callicles the rhetor has completely given way to Callicles the listener. *Chairephon* uses lively **1** in the introduction and at the intervention of Callicles, more dignified **2** in 458c.

(c) This work is very impetuous,[271] and its "Socrates" shows a force and even an aggressivity nowhere else displayed by him. In spite of the occasional mimetic passages (especially in the first part of the work) it is clear that the styles of Socrates on the whole express Plato's personal moods. The three episodes, as has been often noticed (cf. above n. 79), form a sequence of rising accumulation, and in general it can be said that "Socrates" becomes gradually more serious and emphatic and uses more and more of styles **2** and **3** (to which the **6, (8)** of the concluding myth give a specific touch), as if the despiser of rhetorical "macrology" (expressively criticized 449a–c, 461d, etc.) had decided to combat his opponents on their own ground (cf. the apologetic remarks 519de). But touches of expansive **2** and **3** occur in the style of "Socrates" already from the first AD section (450c) onwards. Contrary to Gorgias and Polus, who only offer background for the argument, Callicles is a serious opponent. Obviously his first speech 482c–486d, which fluctuates between **2, 3** and **1, (4)** is intended by Plato as a weighty objection; it is contrasted to the more colloquial **1** yet rich style of Socrates' framing speeches. Similarly 491b–494a. Later, and especially from 507c onwards when shades **2** and **3** become more predominant in "Socrates'" argument, Callicles sometimes uses style **1** in contrast, as was noted above. Socrates' use of style **5** is also interesting. It occurs as a touch in the definitions of rhetoric at the end of the first AD section and after the intervention of Polus 462e–463e, and it is then taken up, rather more manifestly, in the curious dihaeretic argument 464d–466a[272] and occasionally later, notably in 475e–478e (wickedness an evil), 492e–494a (superiority and will), 497c–499b (pleasure). It may seem as if shade **5** here, contrary to R., is not as serious and important as shade **3** (which indeed is the more appropriate one to use in this situation); but cf. below p. 136. Shade **9** sometimes also occurs as a touch (e.g. 480cd, 481a), but it is insignificant. A kind of culmination and final peripeteia is reached in the BE section 505b–509c.

(d) No signs of actual **10**, but some heavy passages in the myth (e.g. 525bc) may be taken as pointing towards it.

*Meno* On virtue and knowledge.

70a–72b **BE** Introduction. Can virtue be taught, and what is virtue? **1, 2, (4) /2, (3), 5**.

72b–79e **A** Attempts to define virtue. **1, (2, 5) / 4, 5**.

---

271. This note is struck already by the opening words πολέμου καὶ μάχης, as Friedländer II² 227 observes.

272. For this passage, *see* Friedländer II² 234–235 with notes.

[122] 79e–82b **BE** Menon bewildered: Socrates the torpedo. On Socratic method. Myth of anamnesis (81a–e). **1, 4 /1, 5 / 2, 6, (8)**.
82b–86c **A** Theory of anamnesis applied on Menon's slave. **1, (2, 5)**.
[123] 86c–87c **BE** Return to opening question. "Hypothetical" method. **(1), 5**.
87c–89e **A** Virtue is knowledge, aporetic. **1, (4), 5**.
89e–90b **E** Introduction of Anytus. **2, (3), 4**.
90b–91b **A** On the teaching of the sophists. **1, 2**.
91c–93b **BE** On the sophists and on teaching virtue. **1, (5) / 1, 2, (4)**.
93b–94e **AD** The great men have not been able to teach virtue. **1, 2, (3,4)**.
94e–95a **B** Anytus warns Socrates and withdraws from the conversation **2 / 1, 2**.
95a–96d **A** Virtue cannot be taught. **1, 2, (5)**.
96de **B** Interlude. New approach. **1, (5)**.
96e–99e **A** True opinion as a basis for virtue. **1, 5 / 1, 2**.
99e–100c **BE** Concluding remarks on the divine nature of virtue. **2**.

(a) Stylistic shifts between the sections. The E passages (and AD) are also clearly marked.

(b) *Socrates* largely uses a personal **1, (2)** in contrast to his interlocutors. His first speech to Menon (70a–71b) is more ironically serious **1, 2**, and the introduction of Anytus mock-panegyrical **2, (3), 4**, a Socratic burlesque. The playful attempt at definition 76c–e is apparently intended to be in a "Gorgian" style **4, 5**.[273] Also the gravity **2** of the conclusion may be intended as characteristic. For other instances of play with style, *see* under (c). *Menon* in the introduction uses a notably abrupt and systematic style **(3), 5** which seems appropriate to precocious learning (cf. ἀφόβως 70b).[274] Later he uses straightforward and emphatic **1**, in the simile 79e ff. also **4**, obviously in contrast to Socrates. After 82b he receives no stylistic characterization (cf. c). *Anytus* is given a violently affective **1, 2, (4)**, contrasted to the quiet irony of Socrates. The slave of course remains uncharacterized except by the brevity of his replies (82b ff.).

(c) Though the first part of the work is largely playful and mimetic Socrates sometimes tends to a serious matter-of-factness manifest in a touch of **(5)**. In the important central BE section 79e–82b (cf. p. 34 and n. 3) he plays with an abstract **5** just before the myth (note ἐριστικὸν λόγον 80e). This strict abstractness, though
[124] without play, partly accompanies his questioning of the slave, and then, with a marked note of the style of geometrical demonstration, his presentation of the "hypothetical" method in the following BE section (cf. above p. 59). In the latter part of the work shade **5** is used together with **1** and **2** in most of the argumentation, and it even extends to the replies of Menon (e.g. 97c), probably without mimetic implications. But in the Anytus episode this shade is not so manifest, and this fact stresses its digressional character.[275] The real culmination and the peripeteia of the work is constituted by the brief anamnesis myth which is kept in styles **2, 6, (8)**.

(d) No signs of **10**.

---

273. This style is here called τραγική (76e, cf. p. 100). See Wilamowitz II² 146, Klein 1965: 68–69.
274. Hoerber's explanation (1960: 92–94) seems to me too complicated. On the character of Menon, as opposed to Socrates, cf. Bluck 1961: 124–125 (cf. 199), Klein 1965: 38–40.
275. Cf. above n. 39.

*Euthyphro* On piety (and righteousness) and on Socrates' search of unchangeable truth.[276]

2a–5c **BE** Introduction. The lawsuits and the persons of Socrates and Euthyphron contrasted, Socrates wishes to learn from Euthyphron. 1 / 1, 2, (3) / 1, 2, (9).

5c–10e **A** Three definitions of piety. 1, (2, 5) / 1, (2, 4, 9).

10e–11e **B** Interlude. Simile of Daedalus. 1, (5) / 1, (4) / 1.

11e–15c **A** Fourth definition: piety as part of righteousness. What is the common action of gods and men? Return to beginning. 1, (2, 5) / 1, (2, 9).

15c–16a **BE** Seemingly aporetic conclusion: Euthyphron leaves Socrates unaided. 1, (2) / 1.

(a) The BABAB structure has only a very slight correspondence in style, the introduction and the interlude being somewhat more lively than the A sections. The brief E's of the introduction, however, stand out more distinctly.

(b) *Socrates* is characterized by an ironically naive **1** especially in B sections, partly in A, in the interlude also **(4)**. In the introduction he occasionally uses mock-solemn **2** and **(3)**. *Euthyphron* uses vigorous and self-confident **1**, occasionally **(4)**, tending to expansive **2** at times, and with touches of judicial **(9)**.[277] In the central parts of the work (6c–14a) he remains uncharacterized.

(c) The mimetic characterization (b), which is found especially at the beginning (up to 6c) and towards the end (from 14a), forms an outer frame for the rather more matter-of-fact **1** with **(2)** and **(5)** used by Socrates in the two A sections. The interlude with the simile (10e–11e) functions as a central section though it lacks E and though it differs in style from the surrounding sections only by its somewhat greater liveliness.[278] Socrates hints at the "circular" composition 15b.

(d) No signs of **10**.

*Cratylus* On language and etymology.

383a–384e **BE** Introductory account of the views of Cratylus and Hermogenes. 1, 2, (5) / (1), 2, (5).

385a–391a **A** First refutation of Hermogenes. (1), 2, (5).

391a–e **B** Interlude. The opinion of sophists and poets to be consulted. 1, 2, (5).

391e–427d **AD** Etymologies tend to prove that there exists a natural connection between thing and name. 1, 2, (4, 5).

427d–428d **B** Interlude. The view of Cratylus to be examined. (1), 2 / 2, (3) / 1, 2, (10).

---

276. It seems to me possible to bring all the different aspects of this ironical and anomalous work (cf. Gigon 1954, Hoerber 1958) under this heading. Note Socrates' words in the central passage 11d.

277. There cannot be any doubt (in spite of Taylor 146) that he is identical with the Euthyphron mentioned in *Cra.* (see above p. 42). It is interesting to note that Plato has not depicted him as an oracular ecstatic, but as a bigoted legalist, well-accustomed (contrary to Socrates) to legal procedure.

278. Cf. above p. 47. Friedländer II² 82 regards 14bc, where Euthyphron misses the decisive point, as the culmination of the work. But it is not so, considering composition and style; and in the B interlude the simile of Daedalus alludes to something more essential than Euthyphron's missing the point: the Socratic "moving around" the truth.

[125] 428d–440a **A** Refutation of Cratylus. **1, (2, 5)**.
440a–e **BE** Seemingly aporetic conclusion. **(1), 2, 5**.

(a) There are only very slight stylistic shifts between the sections, and some variation in the extensive central AD section. The formal and stylistic structure thus looks somewhat flat and careless.

(b) *Socrates* uses a slightly ironical **1, 2, (5)** in the introduction and the first interlude, in partial contrast to Hermogenes. In the central AD section the touches of **1, (4)** like the burlesque of the contents can be regarded as both Socratic and Platonic. The more dignified **(1), 2** tone of Socrates in the second interlude is probably intended to reflect an ironically polite attitude towards Cratylus. There [126] seems to be no stylistic characterization after this interlude. *Hermogenes* is manifestly literary **(1), 2, (5)** in the opening and, with **(3)**, in the second interlude. It is not clear whether he is intentionally characterized elsewhere. *Cratylus* does not partake in the conversation until the second interlude where he is given a peculiarly obscure and twisted style **1, 2, (10)**; it is probably meant to characterize his oracular manner of expression which was hinted at in 383b–384a.

(c) "Socrates" is here uttering everything of importance, and the slight characterization of his interlocutors and of himself in contrast to them looks only as a conventional device. This Platonic "Socrates" has a bent to shade **5**. In the central AD section he also plays with shade **4** (e.g. 395de, 403e–404a) as well as with various proportions of **1** and **2**.[279] It cannot be doubted that this "peripeteia" is meant to be playful and inspired at the same time (cf. above p. 42). A detailed analysis would probably detect some correspondence between variations in style and the contents (note e.g. forcible **2** on δαίμων 398bc, mock-pedantic **5** on Ἑστία—οὐσία 401b–e, expressive **1, 2, 4** introducing ethics 411bc).

(d) No signs of normal **10**; but note the twisted style of Cratylus (*see* b).

*Lysis* On friendship and love.

203a–206c **CBE** Introduction. Two lovers and two loves. **1, (2), 4 / 1, (2)**.
206c–207d **CB** Socrates meets the boys. **1**.
207d–210d **CA** Parents' love and education. **1, (2)**.
210e–212a **CBE** Socrates' passion for friends. **1, 4**.
212a–218c **CA** On friendship. **1, (5)**.
218cd **CB** Brief aporetic interlude. **1, 4**.
218d–222d **CA(D)** New approach to friendship. On the highest love. **1, (2), 5**.
222e–223b **CB** Concluding aporetic remarks. **1, (4)**.

(a) Clear stylistic shifts between the sections. The C is kept in a casual and unemphatic style **1**. The tendency to D towards the end has a reflection in style. There are no real speeches, but those passages that can be labelled E stand out by a hyperbolical **4** (cf. b).

[127] (b) *Socrates* is characterized almost throughout by a light and easy **1**, often with **4**; but the C narrative and description is not as personal. A touch of a more seri-

---

279. The curiously composite character of the style in this section was observed by Kiock 1913 who (p. 36) also traces some iambic rhythms here (cf. p. 36).

ous but naivistic style **(2)** when addressing Hippothales and the boys (e.g. 205e–206a, 210cd) may also be characteristic. But there is a certain distance to the real Socrates in the last A(D) section. *Ctesippus* uses a very impetuous and hyperbolical **1, 4** in the introduction; later he remains neutral. *Hippothales*, who only appears in the introductory scenes, is not clearly characterized by style unless the expansive **2** of 206bc is intended to express his romantic feelings. The brief and strict replies of *Menexenus* in 212a–218c are perhaps meant to be characteristic (cf. ἐριστικός 211b). Lysis is shy (207ab, 211a) and remains uncharacterized by style.

(c) The style is largely mimetic and reflects the playful and bantering feeling of the gymnasion milieu. The central culmination (210e–212a) is half playful. The later A sections have a serious undertone, and this is accompanied by a touch of Platonic **5**, especially in the last A(D); note in particular 220b–e (love implies opposition).

(d) No signs of **10**.

*Charmides* On moderation and self-knowledge

153a–156c **CB** Introduction. Presentation of the persons. Attractiveness of Charmides. **1, 4 / 1, 2**.
156d–158e **CBE** The remedy of Zalmoxis. Is Charmides moderate? **1, 2, (3) / 1, (2)**.
158e–162b **CA** On moderation. **1**.
162b–165b **CBE** Intervention of Critias. Moderation as "doing" and as self-knowledge. **1 / (1), 2, 5**.
165b–168e **CA** Examination of this view. **1, (5)**.
168e–169e **CBE** Aporetic interlude. **1, (5)**.
169e–171c **CA** Moderation as knowledge. **1, (5)**.
171d–173d **CBE** Pondering moderation as knowledge. **(1), 2, (3, 5) / 1**.
173d–175a **CA** On higher knowledge. **1, (5)**.
175a–176d **CBE** Conclusion. Socrates receives Charmides as his pupil. **1, 2, (4) / 1, (2) / 2**.

(a) Clear stylistic shifts between the sections. The E passages are also quite distinct.

(b) *Socrates* is characterized by a lively **1** in the first part, also in C, with **4** in the opening scene when he is confronted with Charmides. His speeches in the first BE section have a playful dignity **1, 2, (3)**. After the intervention of Critias Socrates only very rarely uses a personal style, but this is again more manifest in the conclusion. *Critias* is somewhat formal **1, 2** in the opening scenes. After his intervention (162b) he produces two speeches which reflect a self-conscious intellectualism, **(1), 2, 5**.[280] This stylistic characterization is partly kept up in the following A section in contrast to Socrates' more neutral **1**. Later it is not as manifest. *Chairephon* accompanies Socrates with some lively **1, (4)** utterances in the introduction. *Charmides* is given a polite and modest **1, 2** at the end of the first BE section and in the conclusion.

---

280. Cf. Wilamowitz I 190–191, Friedländer II² 66.

[128]      (c) In the mimetic first part the play of styles forms a series of slight contrasts to the moderation seemingly exemplified by Charmides. The curious Zalmoxis phantasy however is not so florid in style as should perhaps be expected; apparently it is intended to strike a semi-serious note. Critias is an authoritative opponent of Socrates, and his speeches on "doing" and self-knowledge are important contributions (though he of course may be said to symbolize the lack of the virtues in question), not very much exaggerated in style, and with the significant use of **2, 5**. "Socrates" then abandons play almost entirely and takes up a touch of **(5)** which accompanies the rest of the work except the conclusion. The central culmination comes fairly late (171d–173d) and includes two speeches by "Socrates" in a markedly expressive and visionary style **(1), 2, (3, 5)**.[281]

(d) No signs of **10**.

*Republica, lib,* I, *see* p. 83.

*Protagoras* On teaching virtue and on the sophists.

309a–310a **B** Introductory frame conversation. **1, (4)**.

310a–316a **CBE** Introduction. Socrates and Hippocrates meet Protagoras and other sophists. **1, 4 / 2, (3, 4, 6)**.

316a–329d **CBE** Opening discussion. What can a sophist teach? Myth and logos of Protagoras: a sophist can teach virtue. Reply by Socrates. **1, (2, 3, 4) / 2, (3, 5) / 6 / (1), 3, (5)**.

329d–333e **CA** First examination of virtue. **1, (5)**.

[129]   333e–338e **CBE** Aporetic interlude. On sophistic and Socratic manner of speech. **1, (4) / 1, 2 / 2, 5 / 3 / 3, 4, 5**.

338e–339d **CA** Poem of Simonides adduced. Protagoras attempts to question Socrates. **2, (5) / 1, 2**.

339d–349d **CBE** Criticism of Protagoras' interpretation of the poem. Socrates' own interpretation. Protagoras persuaded to continue. Resumption of previous argument. **1, (4) / 2, (3), 5 / 2, (5)**.

349d–360e **CA(D)(E)**[282] Second examination of virtue. **1, 2, 5 / 2, (3, 4, 5)**.

360e–362a **CBE** Concluding exchange of speeches. **1, (2, 4) / 2, (4)**.

(a) The dialogue structure of this work shows an exceptional preponderance of B and E, and correspondingly the style is very varied. The three comparatively brief A sections clearly diverge from the rest. The E passages too on the whole differ from the surrounding styles, thus also the extensive objection of Protagoras 350c–351b which is irregularly inserted in an A section. The tendency to D in the same section has a certain reflection in style.

(b) *Socrates* uses a vivid and ironical **1**, with **4** especially in the opening sections, also in C narrative and description. He is mock-solemn **(1), 2, 3, (4)** in his

---

281. Cf. Wilamowitz II 66.
282. For this anomaly, *see* below (a).

speeches about the sophists in the introduction,[283] in the ironical speech about possibility to teach virtue 319a–320c, and in his reply to Protagoras 328d–329b. The description of his meeting the sophists 314c–316a has playful touches of (6). In contrast to his interlocutors Socrates largely preserves a tone of natural **1**, so also in the conclusion. But in the central section and the last A(D) Plato clearly distances the historical Socrates; *see* under (c). *Protagoras* is characterized in the opening discussion by **2, (3, 5)** and then in the magnificent pastiche by **6** and **(1), 3, (5)**.[284] The first-mentioned shades occur occasionally later, notably in the aporetic interlude and the following attempt at questioning by A dialogue, and the objection 350c–351b; cf. the tendency to expanding replies in other A sections (e.g. 331de, 349d–350c) and Socrates' remarks on "macrology" 329ab, 334c–335c. In the conclusion Protagoras uses a courteous **2, (4)**. No other person except Socrates ever receives such an extensive stylistic characterization in Plato's works. *Hippocrates* accompanies Socrates in the introduction with a hyperbolic **1, 4** (cf. πτόησιν 310d). The company of Protagoras is playfully characterized in the aporetic interlude in partial contrast to Socrates: *Callias* matter-of-fact **1, 2**. *Alcibiades* dynamic and accumulative **1, 2** (cf. also 347a–348c), *Critias* symbuleutic **2, 5**,[285] *Prodicus* rhetorical **3**, and *Hippias* epideictic **3, 4, 5**.[286] The unnamed friend in the introductory frame dialogue remains stylistically neutral.

(c) The first and middle parts of the work are on the whole elaborately mimetic. They are dominated, even stylistically, by Protagoras to whom Socrates makes an ironical contrast. The occasional mock-solemnity of the latter (*see* above) is probably meant to harmonize with this burlesque symphony. But there is a sotto voce touch of **(5)** in the first A section which anticipates the rather more Platonic last part. The peripeteia comes comparatively late, from 339d onwards. It is clear that the speech of "Socrates" 342a–347a constitutes the central culmination of the work by driving the sophistic argumentation in absurdum, yet opening new views.[287] The style of this speech is a peculiar combination of **2, (3), 5** which must have suggested "sophistry" to Plato's readers. It anticipates the fact (cf. 360e–361d) that Protagoras and Socrates seemingly exchange their positions. The new approach to virtue that follows is manifestly more serious than the first, and "Socrates" here uses a more expansive style **1, 2, 5**. Note also the tendency to D dialogue.[288] The end however again returns to the mimetic level.

(d) No signs of **10**.

*Euthydemus* On eristic and teaching of true wisdom.

271a–272d **BE** Introductory frame conversation. **1, (3), 4**.

---

283. In accordance with his thesis that *Prt.* is a very early work Wilamowitz I 146 maintains that the un-Socratic style of these speeches is due to Plato's unexperience as a writer, but this is a flagrant misconception.
284. Cf. Bodrero 1903, Norden 1913: 368, Saupe 1916: 43–50, Aly 1929: 70ff.
285. For the tone of this passage, cf. Friedländer II² 279 n. 17.
286. Cf. Saupe 1916: 51–5 3, Wilamowitz I 140, Vicaire 1960: 301.
287. Cf. the interpretation of Friedländer II² 20–21.
288. Cf. above p. 42.

[130]  272d–275c **CB(D)** Introduction. On erists. Socrates meets his interlocutors. **1, (3), 4** / **1, 2**.
275c–277c **CA** First display of eristic. **1, 4**.
277d–278e **CE** Speech of Socrates who takes over the questioning **1, 2, (4)**.
[131]  278e–282d **CA(D)** On happiness and teaching of wisdom. **1** /**1, 5** / **2**.
282d–283e **CBE** Interlude. **1, 4/1, 2**.
283e–285a **CA** Second display of eristic. **1**.
285a–d **CBE** Interlude. **1, 2, (4)**.
285d–286b **CA** Second display of eristic continued. **1**.
286bc **CB** Socrates takes over. **1, 4**.
286c–287e **CA** Criticism of eristic. On teaching of wisdom. **1, (4)**.
287e–288d **CBE** Interlude. **1, 4**.
288d–289c **CA** Criticism continued. On acquiring knowledge and happiness as an art. **1, (2, 4)**.
289c–290d **CBE** Aporetic interlude. **1, 4** / **2, (5)**.
290e–291d **B** The art required is the Kingly Art. **1, (4)**.
291 d–292e **A** Can the Kingly Art transmit knowledge? **1**.
292e–293a **BC** Aporetic appeal to the erists. **1, 4**.
293a–294b **CA** Third display of eristic. **1, (4)** / **1, (2)**.
294b–e **CB** Interlude. **1, 4**.
294e–303a **CA**[289] Third display of eristic continued. **1, (4)** / **1, (2)**.
303b–304c **CE** Display concluded. Harangue of Socrates to the erists. **1, (2), 4** / **1, 3, 4**.
304c–305b **CB** The above performance seen from another angle by an anonymous person addressing Criton. **1**.
305b–307c **BE** Concluding frame conversation. Protreptic to philosophy. **1, 2, (3, 5)**.

(a) The complicated but pointed and highly artful structure of this work[290] has some reflection in the shifts of style. This correspondence however is not very marked owing to the use almost throughout of vivid **1, 4** and of C narrative and descriptive side remarks. The E passages are few in number and mostly brief but they regularly differ in style from the context.

(b) *Socrates* is characterized throughout, except the conclusion, by a lively and notably pathetic **1, 4**, also in the extensive C passages, and partly in contrast to the rather more straightforward styles of his interlocutors. His pathos has a mocking touch of **(3)** sometimes in the opening sections and in the concluding speech to
[132]  the erists 303c–304b. Shade **2** seems to be more serious when it occurs and it will be considered under (c). The erists, *Euthydemus* and *Dionysodorus,* sometimes, especially in the first part, use a self-conscious and somewhat solemn **1, 2** (e.g. 273d, 274a, 283b, 302bc), and later they are occasionally exuberant **1** on the verge of vulgarity (e.g. 287b, 294b), but on the whole they receive little stylistic characterization unless the 'elegant' strictness of their questioning is counted to style.

---

289. It is possible to analyze further the structure of this section, but this would have little stylistic relevance. Note however the aporia 300de which obviously has a retarding function before the important point that follows; cf. Wilamowitz II 157–159, Sprague 1962: 25–30.

290. For the symmetrical structure of this work, *see* the observations of Friedländer II² 169–180 and Sprague 1962: 1–33.

*Ctesippus* often uses a vivid and emphatic **1** which seems to be characteristic of him (e.g. 283e, 284e, 285d, and the second part of the third display of eristic; cf. *Ly.*). *Criton* uses an artless **1** as can be expected. *Clinias* is not really characterized by his style **1**; the sophisticated critical remarks 289c–290d are only put in his mouth by Socrates, as Criton observes (290e). The anonymous *friend* of Criton (304c–305b)[291] also remains remarkably neutral in style.

(c) The work is largely mimetic and in parts burlesque. Sometimes however the shifts of style seem to reflect a more serious approach. The speech of Socrates 277d–278e is kept in a personal style **1, 2, (4)**, and the following A section (on happiness and wisdom) passes from a fairly vivid **1** through more strict and abstract **1, 5** to an emphatic and expansive **2**.[292] The appeal 282de is still partly serious **1, 2**. A new serious approach is prepared towards the end of the A section that precedes the central part, with a curious touch of **2, 5** (on knowledge and happiness, especially 289c). This is continued in the objections of "Clinias" (*see* above, b) to which Socrates' excited **1, 4** is clearly contrasted. The central discussion of the Kingly Art (B and A, with resumption of the frame dialogue) is carried by vivid and natural **1, (4)**. Then Socrates again changes to a markedly pathetic **1, 4**. As was said above (p. 59) the central part as a whole can be taken as the peripeteia, though in this agonistic work Plato has chosen A dialogue instead of visionary E for his hints at the way to true knowledge. The following displays of eristic show no stylistic signs of seriousness, and the comedy ends with a mockpathetic speech by Socrates 303c–304b. But with Socrates' remarks to Criton 304b the style changes to **1, 2**, and this is resumed, after the neutral **1** of Criton's report, in the conclusion. Here notably the speech of "Socrates" 305c–306d has a touch of **(3, 5)** which must be regarded as Platonic. Thus the end receives a counter-stress comparable to the concluding myths of some dialogues.

(d) No signs of **10**.

*Phaedo*[293] On the soul and on the Forms.

57a–59c **BE** Introductory frame conversation. The external circumstances. **1, 2, (4)**.
59c–63e **CBE** Introduction. The friends' meeting Socrates. On death. **1, 2, (6) / 1, 2, (5)**.
63e–69e **CAD(E)** A philosopher dies with confidence. **(1), 2, 5**.
69e–70c **CB** Intervention of Cebes. Immortality of the soul. **1, 2, 5**.
70c–72d **CA** First argument for immortality of the soul. The opposites. **1, (2), 5**.
72e–73b **CB** Interlude. On anamnesis. **1, (2, 5)**.
73c–76e **CA** Second argument for immortality of the soul. Anamnesis. **1, 2, 5**.
76e–78b **CB** Interlude. Worth of the first two arguments. **1, (2, 4) / 2, (3), 5**.

---

291. For various speculations about his identity, *see* Friedländer II² 179.
292. The protreptic character of this section has often been observed. *See* Wilamowitz I 308–309, Taylor 90, 95, Gaiser 1959: 47 ff.
293. The artful structure of this work has often been analyzed, most recently by Hackforth 1955 and Bluck 1955. In order to clarify the BABAB rhythm the present analysis will on some points diverge from the conventional pattern. Schwessinger 1925: 231–281 analyses the dialogue according to her principle of "rising accumulation" which puts an excessive weight on the end.

[133] 78b–84b **CAD** Third argument for immortality of the soul. The divine nature of the soul. Metempsychosis. The philosopher's progress. **(1), 2, (4), 5, (10)**.
84c–88c **CBE** Aporia. Objections of Simmias and Cebes **1, 2 / 1, (2), 5**.
88c–89a **B** Resumption of frame dialogue. Comments. **1, (2)**.
89a–c **CB** Aporetic interlude continued. **1, 2**.
89c–90d **CAD** On misology and on preserving reason. **1, 2, 5**.
90d–92a **CBE** On using argument and on the objections of Simmias and Cebes. **1, (2, 5) / 1, (4)**.
92a–95a **CA** Refutation of the objection of Simmias. **1, 2, 5**.
95a–96a **CBE** Interlude. Preparation for refutation of the objection of Cebes. **1, (2, 4, 5) / 1, (2, 4)**.
96a–102a **CD(E)** On natural philosophy and on the development of the "hypothetical" method. The Forms. **1, (2, 4), 5**.
[134] 102ab **B** Resumption of frame dialogue. Comments. **1, (4)**.
102b–103a **CAD** Examination of the Forms continued. **(1), 5**.
103a–c **CB** Interlude. Anonymous objections. **1, 5**.
103c–107a **CA** Fourth argument for immortality of the soul. The theory of Forms. **(1), 2, 5**.
107ab **CB** Retarding interlude. **2, 5 / 2, 5, (8)**.
107c–115a **CD(E)** Myth of the destiny of the soul. **2, (3, 5, 6, 10)**.
115b–118a **CBE** Conclusion. Death of Socrates. **1, 2,(4, 5, 6, 8)**.

(a) Slight stylistic shifts between the sections. On the whole the changes of style are not distinct in this work. The C narrative and description is kept in a deliberately quiet, almost hushed, **1, 2**. The occasional instances of D and E do not differ notably from the BABAB pattern.

(b) *Socrates* uses basically a quiet and dignified but very personal combination of **1** and **2**. Very occasionally does his style get a touch of **(4)**, thus notably in the third argument (e.g. 80c) and the description of his earlier studies (e.g. 96a) with its preceding interlude, and also in the conclusion. More commonly his style tends to a distinct **5**. Obviously the Socrates of this work is largely above the mimetic level; cf. under (c). The report of *Phaedon* and his apostrophes to Echecrates are kept in a **1, 2** that sounds somewhat impersonal in contrast to Socrates and also Echecrates; but this simple matter-of-factness may be regarded as characteristic of Phaedon and it produces a great effect together with the seriousness of the contents. Only sometimes in the introduction (especially 58c–59a) is there a manifest touch of **(4)**; occasionally in the introduction and the conclusion **(6)** (e.g. 59e, 116b).[294] *Echecrates* (in the frame dialogue only) is characterized by a more energetic **1**, also **(4)**, apparently in contrast to Phaedon. *Cebes,* the leading interlocutor of Socrates, uses a combination of **1, 2** and **5** that differs from the style of Socrates only by being somewhat more lively (e.g. 62a, 77e, 92a, 99d). His objection 86e–88b stands out by a clear and sharp **1, 5**. *Simmias* remains more neutral **1, 2, (5)**, though not without liveliness (e.g. 76e, 92a). His objection 85b–86d is

---

294. Phaedon was reputed for the elegant style of his Socratic dialogues, *see* Gell. *NA* 2.18.5; but there is nothing to indicate that Plato has such dialogues in mind.

more expansive and literary in style than that of Cebes. The rest of the characters receive some personal traits in the introduction and the conclusion: *Criton* friendly and worried **1, (2)**, *Xanthippa* pathetic **4** (60a)[295], the *Servant* of the Eleven devotedly profuse **1, (2, 4)** (116cd), the *Poison-mixer* dryly matter-of-fact **1, (5)** (117ab).

(c) The three tones **1, 2** and **5** keep up a grave and intense, yet profoundly personal feeling through the whole work. Because there is little real mimesis and no marked play, the slight shifts of style in the utterances of Socrates and his main interlocutors are likely to reflect above all the varying importance that Plato attaches to the argument. Clues to these variations are given, apart from the contents, by structural devices such as the use of C narrative and the frame dialogue. The touch of **5** occurs already in the introduction in the utterances of Socrates and Cebes, and it also accompanies the concluding myth. The three first arguments for immortality are arranged in a rising sequence, and the style becomes gradually more expansive: **1, (2), 5–1, 2, 5–(1), 2, (4), 5, (10)**. Note also the tendency to D dialogue in the last of these sections. Plato is well aware of the fact that this sequence gives more of persuasion than of proof, and the reaction comes in the extensive central part (84c–103c) with its appeal to reason and the introduction of the theory of Forms. The objections of Simmias and Cebes, which open this part, are certainly meant to be taken seriously, and this is reflected in their matter-of-fact style, notably the clear **5** of Cebes. The work culminates with the D (or E) section 96a–102a. Here it is very interesting to note the preponderance of a limpid and personal (semi-Socratic) **1, 5** which is quite in accordance with the appeal to reason. Also the concluding AD of this part (102b–103a) is rather more intellectual **5** than expansive. Then the style of "Socrates" expands again, and the myth with its almost ceremonious **(8)** opening (107b) and its heavy and rich **2, (3, 5, 6, 10)** strikes a note of persuasion rather than reason.

(d) Touches of **(10)** in the third argument and the myth; cf. above (c).

*Symposium* On Love and pursuit of the Good.

172a–174a B(C) Introductory frame conversation. **1, (4)**.
174a–178a CBE Introduction. Arrival of Socrates. Beginning of the symposium. The evening's programm. **1, (4) / 1, 2, (3, 4, 5)**.
178a–180b CE Speech of Phaedrus. **2, 3, (4)**.
180c GB Interlude. **1**.
180c–185c CE Speech of Pausanias **3, 5, (10)**.
185c–e GB Interlude. Hiccup of Aristophanes. **1 / 1, 2, (5)**.
185e–188e CE Speech of Eryximachus. **(3), 5**.
189a–c CB Interlude. Aristophanes afraid of making himself a fool. **1 / 1, 2**.
189c–193e CE Speech of Aristophanes. **(1), 2, (3, 4), 6**.
193e–194e CB Interlude. Preparation for speeches by Agathon and Socrates. **1, (4) / 1, 2**.

---

295. Except the woman of Socrates' dream in *Cri.* 44b, "Aspasia," and "Diotima," Xanthippa is the only woman ever to utter a word in Plato's dialogues.

[136] 194e–197e **CE** Speech of Agathon. **3** Gorg., **4**.
198a–199c **CBE** Critical interlude. Socrates professes to be unable to compete with Agathon. **1, (4) / 1, 2, (5)**.
199c–201c **CA** On the nature of Love. **1, (4, 5)**.
201de **CE** Socrates prepares to make Diotima take over. **1, 2**.
201e–207a **CAD(E)** Preliminary teaching of Diotima. **2, 3, (5, 6, 8)**.
207a–208b **CBE** Retardation. Love and immortality. **2, (3, 5)**.
208c–212c **CE** Great speech of Diotima. Socrates' conclusion. **2, 3, (4, 5, 8, 10)**.
212c–215a **CB** Lengthy interlude. Arrival of Alcibiades. **1, 4 / 1, 2, (5)**.
215a–222b **CE(B)** Speech of Alcibiades. **1, (3), 4**.
222c–223d **CB** Concluding scenes. Revelry. **1, (4)**.

(a) Very clear stylistic shifts between the sections. The E passages are all distinct. The AD 201e–207a also has a character of its own. The C narrative functions as a background (cf. b).

(b) *Socrates* is characterized by an ironical **1, (4)** in the introduction, the interludes 193e ff., 198a ff., 212c ff., the speech of Alcibiades (218d–219a), and the conclusion. The A passage 199c–201c is rather more strict (though cf. 200ab), and the conclusion to Diotima's speech is Platonic. *Apollodorus* is lively and intense **1, (4)** in the opening frame dialogue (cf. the remarks μὴ σκῶπτε 173a, μανικός, μαίνομαι 173de), but his C narrative is kept in a neutral **1** except parts of the conclusion which again have a touch of **(4)** (especially 223b). *Agathon*: the speech is a pastiche of 'Gorgian' style, **3 Gorg., 4**.[296] Perhaps urbane and generous **1** in the introduction (e.g. 175b), elsewhere
[137] no distinct characterization. *Eryximachus*: the speech a pastiche of medical style **(3), 5**;[297] in the introduction and most of the interludes he is given a pedantic **(1), 2, (5)**. *Aristophanes*: the speech is a comic phantasy **(1), 2, (3, 4), 6**;[298] in the introduction (176b) and the interludes that frame his speech he uses a vivid **1**. *Phaedrus*: the speech is a conventional enkomion **2, 3, (4)**,[299] and his words quoted by Eryximachus 177a–c strike the same note. *Pausanias*: the speech may be a pastiche of the twisted, irregular and abstract style of early sophists such as Antiphon, **3, 5, (10)**,[300] but the careless **1** in 176ab is hardly intended to be characteristic. *Alcibiades* (from 212e) uses a drunken hyperbolic **1, 4** with touches of **(3)** in the speech; he thus makes a magnificent stylistic contrast to the others. *"Diotima"* of course is essentially Plato, but it is possible that she is modeled on an Eleusinian priestess.[301] The *Slave* in 175a uses a formal **2**

---

296. *See* Blass 1887: 86–88, 1901: 76–81, Robin 1929: LXVII–LXVIII, Vretska 1962: 149–152.
297. Cf. Friedländer III² 13 with reference. For the systematic "Thrasymachean" structure of the periods, *see* Saupe 1916: 28–31.
298. Cf. Friedländer III² 16 with reference.
299. Novák 1883: 523 thinks that this was the style of Sicilian rhetoric, but there is little positive evidence for this. Nor is there anything to suggest a connection with the "Lysias" of *Phdr.*
300. Cf. also the style of Thucydides. Pohlenz 1913: 394–399 and Saupe 1916: 24–28 point out the inconsistency of the rhetorical features of the speech. Some scholars have regarded it as a pastiche of Isocrates (cf. Robin 1929: XL–XLII), but though there are occasional advanced periods (cf. Vretska *Smp.* 1962), the polish of Isocrates is almost completely lacking. Vicaire's (1960: 307) 'Gorgian' theory is not convincing.
301. Cf. Geffcken II 96 and A.84 n. 15. For Diotima as an "Aspasia ennobled," *see* Ehlers 1966: 134–136.

which may be characteristic of servants. But the unnamed friend of Apollodorus [137]
in the frame dialogue remains stylistically neutral, like Aristodemus (174a–175b).

(c) The first part of the work including Agathon's speech is essentially mimetic, and the different speeches with their different styles, whatever their relative importance, are apparently intended to illustrate Love from different angles of 'opinion.' It is notable that even the manifest tone of **5** in Eryximachus' utterances is parody; probably it is for the aesthetical purpose of contrast rather than because of the importance of his views that he has been given a comparatively extensive role. There is a first touch of seriousness to the style of Socrates in the interlude following the speech of Agathon, and in the subsequent sections Socrates gradually rises above the mimetic level. Diotima, who begins to take over at 201e, passes from a fairly simple, **2, (5)** over more and more solemn styles [138] and shades of **3** to the great climax of the mystic passage 209e–212a, **2, (4, 5, 8, 10)**. At the same time the dialogue structure passes from AD to E. After this central culmination (cf. p. 28 and n. 79) comes "Socrates'" brief conclusion in **2, 3**. The following interlude, the speech of Alcibiades, and the conclusion form a violent contrast to the first and central parts of the work. It is clear that the style of Alcibiades is meant to reflect, by the principle in vino veritas, the reality of Socrates as an incarnation of Eros the daimon. In no other Platonic dialogue is the play with styles made as marked a structural principle as here.

(d) Touches of **(10)** in the speech of Pausanias, and, rather more Platonic, in the great speech of Diotima.

*Parmenides* On the Forms and on Being.

126a–127d **CB** Introductory frame conversation. Brief sketch of background, **1**.
127d–130e **CBE** Introduction. Plurality and the Forms. **(1), 2, 5 / 1, (2), 5**.
130e–136c **CAD** Parmenides criticizes Socrates' theory of the Forms. Remarks on method (from 135c). **2, 5**.
136c–137c **CBE** Interlude. Parmenides agrees to demonstrate his method on Aristoteles. **1, 2, (4, 5)**.
137c–166c **A(D)** Application of the "Eleatic" method on eight (or nine) "hypotheses" regarding Being.[302] **(1), 5, (9)**.[303]

(a) Clear stylistic shifts between the sections in the first part. Also in the seemingly vague transition 130e the change is emphasized by a contrast between the styles of Socrates and Parmenides. The brief E of Parmenides in the interlude is fairly distinct. The two E's in the introduction however have no specific peculiarities of style. The tendency to D proper in the first A section is reflected by a more [139]

---

302. For the systematic arrangement of these "hypotheses," cf. Friedländer III² 184, Robinson 1953: 241–242, Schaerer 1955: 200–204, Wyller 1960: 77 ff, Sinaiko 1965: 236–283.

303. The occasional tendency to expansion (accumulation, anaphoric repetition, polyptoton, polarization and similar devices), e.g. 141e–142a, serves the purpose of clarity and suggests to me a shade of legal style **9**. Kleve 1961 would connect this tendency with Plato's "mystical style," i.e. approximately shade **10**, but there are definitely no traces of onkos in the vocabulary or of synchysis in the word order.

[139] considerable use of **2** than in the A(D) of the latter part (cf. p. 41). The C narrative is impersonal and somewhat awkward and it is dropped after 137c. In the whole of the latter part there are no manifest changes of style corresponding to the transitions between the "hypotheses."

(b) *Socrates* is partially characterized, in contrast to Parmenides, by a comparatively vivid and emphatic **1, (2)** in the introduction and the interlude; note especially the youthfully emphatic **1** of 130d. But the intellectual features—**5**—of his style must be regarded as Platonic. In the AD section he remains stylistically neutral (cf. 132cd which is as literary and abstract as the style of Parmenides). *Parmenides* uses a somewhat expansive and very abstract **(1), 2, 5** in the first part, in partial contrast to Socrates and Zenon, in the interlude with a touch of **(4)**. The strict questioning of the second part is probably not intended to be particularly characteristic of Parmenides. *Zenon*, in the introduction and the interlude, makes another lively contrast to Parmenides, but his **1, 5** is somewhat less emphatic than the style of Socrates. The persons of the frame conversation, like young *Aristoteles* and the fairly colorless and circumstantial third-hand C report, remain stylistically unidentified.

(c) Apart from the brief and uninspired frame conversation in style **1**, the work has a marked tone of abstract and systematic **5** which corresponds to the subject. Though there is some stylistic characterization by means of **1** and **2** in the first part the criticism of the theory of Forms and the answers to it are of course essentially Plato's own. There is no central culmination, but the decision of Parmenides to illustrate his method 136e–137b may be said to represent a peripeteia;[304] this is emphasized by the fairly lively style and the imagery **(4)** of his utterance. In the strict latter part there is a close correspondence between contents and style, **(1), 5, (9)**.

(d) No signs of **10**.[305]

*Theaetetus* On knowledge, philosophy, and the maieutic method.

142a–143c **B** Frame conversation. On the following dialogue. **1**.
143c–144d **BE** Introduction. Theaitetos introduced to Socrates. **1, 2 / 1, 2, (4)**.
[140] 144d–145e **A** Opening examination of knowledge. **1, (2, 5)**.
145e–146d **B** Aporetic interlude. **1, (4) / (2), 5**.
146d–147c **A** New approach to knowledge. **1, (2, 5)**.
147c–148e **B(D)**[306] Mathematical illustration of the problem by Theaitetos (147c–148b). Theaitetos unable to find a generic answer. **(1), 5 / 1, (4)**.
148e–150b **A(D)** Socrates a midwife. **1, (2, 4)**.
150b–151e **BE** Speech of Socrates on maieutics. Theaitetos attempts to define knowledge as perception. **1, (4) / 2, 5**.
151e–160e **AD** On knowledge as perception. The view of Protagoras. **1, (2), 5**.
160e–163a **BE** Interlude. Protagoras would raise doubts. **1, (4) / 1, (2) / 2, (5)**.
163a–164e **A(D)** New approach to knowledge as perception. Aporetic. **1, (2), 5**.

---

304. Cf. Wyller 1960: 55 ff.: "Anabole." But Wyller would put the actual "Hyperbole" of the argument in 142ab.
305. Cf. above n. 303.
306. Cf. above, p. 42.

164e–169d **BE** Apology of Protagoras. **1, 2, (4), 5** / **(1), 2, 3, (5)**. [140]
169d–179b **AD** Refutation of the view of Protagoras. Digression on philosophical leisure (172c–177c). **(1), 2, (3, 4, 5, 10)**.
179b–181b **BE** Discussion of Heraclitan theory. **1, (2), 5, (10)**.
181b–183c **A** Criticism of Heraclitan theory. **1, (2), 5**.
183c–184b **B** Interlude. Objection of Theaitetos. **1, 2**.
184b–186e **A** Final approach to knowledge as perception. **1, (4), 5**.
187a–e **B** Interlude. Is knowledge true opinion? **1, 2, 5**.
187e–200d **A(D)** On knowledge as true opinion. **1, (2), 5**.
200d–202c **BE** The definition is insufficient. Reason (λόγος) should perhaps be added to it. **(1, 2), 5, (8)**.
202c–210b **AD** On knowledge as true opinion with reason. Aporetic. **1, (2, 4), 5**.
210b–d **BE** Concluding remarks. The power of the maieutic method. **1, 2, (5)**.

(a) In spite of the complicated structure of this work there are clear stylistic shifts between the sections. The E passages also differ from the rest. The AD dialogue however is not notably expansive in style except in the central section.

(b) *Socrates* is characterized almost throughout by a fairly vivid **1, (4)** with much lively, also burlesque, imagery. Often he has an additional tone of **2**, but it is probably not intended to characterize him except in his opening address to Theodoros 143c–e.[307] The shade of **5** which accompanies the dialogue from 144d onwards is [141] rather Platonic, and so is the complex style of the central section. *Theodoros* has a notably florid style **1, 2, (4)** in the introduction and in his speech 179e–180b, and a somewhat circumstantial manner **2** in some interludes (cf. 146b, 162ab) and in the central sections from 164e onwards;[308] here he even accompanies Socrates with **(10)**. Stylistically he is thus characterized as an old man and not as a mathematician. After the interlude 183c–184b he withdraws from the discussion. *Theaitetos*, the interlocutor of Socrates in the maieutic sections, evidently is characterized by the very marked exact **5** in the mathematical passage 147c–148b, cf. his successive definitions in **(2), 5**, 146cd, 151de, 187b, 201cd. Elsewhere too he has a bent to **(5)**, but also to a vital **1** (*see* e.g. 184b–186e, 202c–210b); he resembles a brilliant young Socrates (cf. 144de). The fictitious *Protagoras* of the central sections (162d–168c) is attributed distinct tones of solemn **2, 3, (5)**. Euclides and Terpsion in the frame dialogue do not receive any stylistic characterization.

(c) This work shows a curious combination of three stylistic trends, or four if the frame conversation is added, each having a fairly distinct function of its own. Apart from the frame conversation which is of little stylistic interest, there is first the mimetic trend (b) that gives a playful undertone to the discussion of the nature of knowledge. Secondly there is the slightly literary and abstract trend of **2, 5** which appropriately accompanies the discussion and contributes to its serious dimensions. The shade of **5** predominates in two passages: the mathematical 'paradigm' given by Theaitetos 147c–148b, and the almost ceremoniously **(8)** opened "vision" (ὄναρ) of λόγος 201d–202c following the last definition of knowledge.

---

307. Cf. Friedländer III² 134.
308. McDonald 1931: 315 points out the literary allusions in his utterances.

[141] The latter passage can be said to represent the peripeteia of the maieutic discussion. Thirdly there is the persuasive and profoundly serious trend of **2**, **(3, 4, 10)** which is first introduced by "Protagoras" but then taken up by "Socrates" in his refutation of the former (169d ff.) and in the central digression on the philosopher's detachment to practical life. This is evidently to be regarded as the culmination of the work as we have it.[309] A touch of this trend accompanies the following BE section, but then vanishes again.

A note of **(10)** in the persuasive central sections; *see* above.

[142] *Phaedrus* On persuasion, on the Beautiful, and on writing philosophy.

227a–230e **BE** Introduction. Socrates enticed to follow Phaedrus to the country. **1, 2, 4**.
230e–234c **E** Speech of "Lysias." Love as seduction. **3, (5)**.
234c–237a **B** Discussion of the speech. **1, 4 / (1), 2, (4, 5, 9, 10)**.
237a–241d **E** First speech of Socrates. Love as an irrational and destructive force. **(1), 2, 3, 4, 5, (6, 8, 10)**.
241d–243e **BE** The daimonion of Socrates. Need of a palinody. **1, 2, (4, 10)**.
243e–257b **E** Second (palinodic) speech of Socrates. The cosmic life of the soul and real Love. **(1), 3, (4), 5, (6, 8, 9), 10**.
257b–d **B** Interlude. Some do not like speech-writers. **2, (10)**.
257d–258d **AD** Speech-writing is not bad as such. **(1), 2, (10)**.
258d–259d **BE** Interlude. How should good prose be written? The cicadas. **(1), 2, (4, 6, 10)**.
259d–274b **AD(E)** On good prose. **(1), 2, (3, 4), 5, (10)**.
274b–275b **BE**[310] Legend of Theuth: the invention of writing. **2, (5), 6, (8, 10)**.
275c–278b **D** The written word inferior to the spoken. **2, (3, 5, 9), 10**.
278b–279c **BE** Conclusion. The philosopher and the literary author. Prayer to Pan. **(1), 2, (5, 8, 10)**.

(a) The three extensive speeches, and to some extent the other E passages, stand out from the context. But after the palinodic speech the division into sections becomes blurred and the corresponding changes of style are lacking.

(b) *Socrates*. The lively note of **1, 4** struck by Socrates in the introduction and the following two interludes is partially meant as a stylistic characterization, but partially too it is a Platonic burlesque with a different purpose; *see* under (c). *Phaedrus* accompanies Socrates with an urbane **1, 2, 4** in the same sections, but it seems doubtful whether he is stylistically characterized later (note the occasional touches of **(10)** in his utterances from 257b onwards). On the speech of "Lysias" *see* below.

[143] (c) This is from the point of view of style the most composite and extravagant of Plato's works. There is much deliberate play and experimenting with style that

---

309. A common opinion, cf. n. 79. Wilamowitz in a sense is right when he claims (I 525–526, 532, II 230–232) that the digression is inorganic, but I am not sure this has any bearing on the problem of revision (p. 14). Cf. Diès 1924: 149, Friedländer III[2] 131–132, 151–156, Capelle 1960, Muthmann 1961: 62.

310. On formal grounds this is no manifest B section. But the legend constitutes a digression and at the same time introduces the last part of the work; cf. Luther 1961: 531–532.

corresponds to the literary criticism expounded in the work. A detailed analysis would indicate a much more detailed correspondence between changes of topics and approach and changes of style, than what can be discussed here.

The burlesque pathos 4 of the introduction and the two following interludes probably serves at stressing the ideas of sensual seduction and "nympholepsy" from which the speech of "Lysias" and the first speech of Socrates arise.[311] The speech of "Lysias" is likely to be a pastiche of sophistic rhetoric, 3, (5).[312] In the first discussion of this speech "Socrates" soon (234e) changes from pathetic admiration to a semi-serious criticism which is reflected in the growing complexity of style; note here the touches of (5) and (10). His own speech then playfully passes through various levels, invocation (1), 4, (8), storytelling (6), treatise style (3), 5, and burlesque complication (10) (a "dithyrambic" style, as he remarks 238d), until it reaches the style of a fairly heavy rhetorical discourse 3, 5, (10). With the intervention of the Daimonion the playful feeling begins to vanish. In the palinodic speech the disparate features seem to be more closely interwoven into a solemn 10.[313] Here the demonstration of the immortality of the soul 245c–246a stands out by its archaic, yet abstract, style (4), 5. It can hardly be doubted that this passage, rather than the myth of the soul, constitutes the peak of culmination of the entire work.[314] In the latter part there are only small variations of style. The two interludes are marked by the shade of (6) in the "myths," with (8) in the legend of Theuth, but on the whole the exposition tends to a continuous lecture of AD type in a florid style with 3 and 10, also 5, and occasionally more playful 4 (e.g. 261a, 263d) and 9 (277d). Even the conclusion, in spite of its playfulness, is kept in this heavy style, and the prayer to Pan is slightly ceremonious (8). The palinodic speech has introduced a manner of expression for Platonic "psychagogy" which then accompanies the work to the end.

(d) A tendency to (10) from the first B section and especially the palinodic speech onwards.

*Respublica*, lib. II–X *see* above, p. 85.

*Timaeus* On the universe.

17a–27b **BDE** Introduction. Plan of the present work. Egyptian legend of early world history. **(2, 3, 5, 6, 8), 10**.

---

311. Cf. Thesleff, *Arctos* N.S. 5, 1967.

312. A surprising number of distinguished scholars, among them Blass 1887: 423–430, Taylor 301–302, and Friedländer III² 203, regard this as an authentic speech of Lysias. I find this entirely unlikely. Constructing a speech according to all conventional rules, and then destroying it, seems to me to be a rather more Platonic play with styles than quoting at length a piece of mediocre contemporary oratory.

313. Cf. the remarks on the style, 257a, 265bc. Blass 1901: 83–87 traced some rhythmical patterns in the speech. Wilamowitz I 461 compares the style with that of *Ti*. For the "late" vocabulary, *see* Rudberg 1924: 35–40 and 1956: 28.

314. Cf. above p. 28.—Wilamowitz I 461–462 suggests a connection with Alcmaion of Croton, cf. Denniston 1952: 4; Raven 1965: 196 thinks that this passage directly influenced Aristotle. Cf. also Sinaiko 1965: 45–49: the "proof" complements the myth. For an analysis of the apodeictic argumentation of the speech as a whole, *see* Solmsen 1929: 272–293, who however does not consider the differences in style.

[144]  27c–92d E Exposition of Timaeus. **(3), 5, (6, 8), 10**.

(a) No distinct relation of style to the formal structure of the exposition. For changes of subject, *see* under (c).

(b) No detailed stylistic characterization of the persons in the dialogue; but the trend of **5**, which arises principally from the subject (*see* under c), corresponds to the choice of *Timaeus* the scientist as the chief character. Cf. *Criti.*

(c) A marked though varying onkos **10** throughout. Occasionally in the introduction the tone becomes easier and approximates to **2**, notably in the anecdote opening the speech of Critias 21a–d (a kind of CB). Sometimes the style has a manifest touch of **3**, e.g. 19de (speech of Socrates), 25bc (speech of the Egyptian priests), often **5** when summing up and planning, occasionally **(6)** (notably 21e, in the opening of the legend of Solon in Egypt), and **(8)**.

In the exposition of Timaeus two main trends combine: a systematic intellectual style **5** and onkos **10**. After the very solemn opening in **8, 10** there follows a passage with prevailing **5**, on the theory and principles of universal creation (a προοίμον, as Socrates remarks 29d). In the exposition of the creation of the universe and of man 29d–47e shade **10** on the whole prevails, and here the speech of the Demiurge in a ceremonious style **(8), 10** is inserted (41a–d)[315] in a mythical
[145] context **(6)** (41a, 41d, 42e). The elaboration of this passage seems to indicate that it is meant to represent a central culmination. The section (or sections, because there is a change of approach in 53c) on the physical composition of the world 47e–68d is kept in a style of prevailing **5** which of course is appropriate to the subject and hardly has anything to do with a change of literary sources.[316] With the resumption of the myth of creation at 68e the shade of **10** again begins to predominate until 79a where a more distinctly physiological approach leads to a predominance of **5**. The section on the sufferings of the soul and the care of the soul and the body 86b–90d is rather rhetorical, **3, 10**, in accordance with its protreptic character. Then again shade **5** prevails in the brief section on sex and generation 90e–92c. The conclusion is kept in solemn and heavy **10**.

(d) Shade **10** accompanies the whole work but is more marked in visionary sections; *see* under (c).

*Critias* On early Athens and Atlantis.

106a–108c **BE** Introduction. Preliminary speech of Critias. Comments. **2, 3, (4), 10**.
108c–121c **E** Exposition of Critias. **3, (4), 5, (6), 10**.

(a) No distinct relation of style to the formal structure of the exposition. Cf. (c).

---

315. *See* the analysis of Wilamowitz II 425–427.
316. For references to the discussion of "Democritean influence" on Plato, *see* above, p. 59. The opening part of this section is remarkably personal and somewhat confused, as if Plato had found it difficult to conciliate the parts of the Demiurge and Necessity. As he did not finish the trilogy, he did not give himself time to polish the contents and style of this passage. But later commentators brought about a complete "conciliation," thus already Timaeus Locrus.

(b) No detailed stylistic characterization;[317] but the trend of **3**, which arises principally from the subject, corresponds to the choice of *Critias* the politician as the chief character.[318] Cf. *Ti.*

(c) The introduction has a shade of **2** beside **10**, and a fairly manifest **3** in the speech of Critias. Socrates' comment has a tone of **(4)**.

These constituents, except **2**, return in the main exposition of Critias, with an occasional addition of **(6)** (e.g. 109b, 114d) and a systematic **5** in some descriptive passages, notably 115c–120d (the city of Atlantis). A touch of **(4)** accompanies style **3** in various connections, notably in the description of the grove of Poseidon 117bc (cf. *Phdr.* 230bc). The main tones are **3** and **10**. The former apparently corresponds to the political and "historical" subject. The latter amounts both to dignity and to persuasion, but it is conspicuously less marked in descriptive passages with **5**. The extant work ends with the turn of the luck of the Atlantids (from 120d), and this peripeteia was apparently planned to be accompanied by a speech of Zeus as a central culmination, corresponding to the speech of the Demiurge in *Ti.* Did Plato on second thoughts feel it presumptuous to write a speech for Zeus, and was this the reason why he stopped here?

(d) Shade **10** accompanies the whole work, but is not so marked in passages of systematic description.

*Sophistes* On sophistry and on being and non-being.

216a–219a **B** Introduction. Plan of the present work. **2, (5), 10**.
219a–236c **AD** Definitions of sophistry by the dihaeretic method. **(2), 5, 10**.
236c–237b **BD** The difficulty of truth and falsity. Reference to the *Prm.* **2, (4, 5), 10**.
237b–241c **AD** On being and non-being. **(2), 5, 10**.
241c–243d **BD(E)** The views of earlier thinkers. **2, 5, 10**.
243d–249d **AD** Criticism of earlier dogmas of being and non-being. **(2), 5, 10**.
249d–250e **BD** The aporia concerns both being and non-being. **2, 5, 10**.
250e–260d **AD** Ontology and universals. **(2), 5, 10**.
260d–261c **BD** Possible relevance of "speech" and "belief" to the definition of the sophist. **2, 5, 10**.
261c–268d **AD** On the use of language. Dihaeretic conclusion regarding the nature of sophistry. **(2), 5, 10**.

(a) The B sections are not very marked (cf. p. 36), but there are slight stylistic shifts between the sections noted above.

(b) No distinct stylistic characterization of the speakers. It is natural that the anonymous *Guest* from Elea should represent both intellectualism and dignity,

---

317. Geffcken II 149 calls attention to the fact that the utterance of Hermocrates 108bc is somewhat less formal than those of Timaeus, Critias, and Socrates; but this may be simply because Plato is less interested in Hermocrates. Again, the answer of Socrates to Critias has a shade of **(4)**, but this is probably for emphasis and not for characterization.

318. Some scholars suppose this Critias to be the grandfather of the "tyrant" who figures in *Chrm.* and *Prt.;* see McDonald 1931: 353–356. But then Socrates would have been quite a young man in *Ti.* and *Criti.,* which evidently is not the case. Cf. further Rosenmeyer, "The Family of Critias." (1949): 404–410.

[147] but the trends of **5** and **10** occur also in the utterances of Theaitetos and (in the introduction) Theodoros and Socrates.

(c) The stylistic variations are very small. The somewhat greater liveliness of the introduction and the interludes (especially the first) corresponds to changes of approach. But the irony and play which is obviously inherent in the work[319] receives little expression in style apart from the grotesque neologisms of the dihaereses 219a–236c and the conclusion, and perhaps a rather striking imagery at times. A peripeteia and a kind of central culmination is reached in the BD(E) section 241c–243d,[320] but in spite of the playful reference to μῦθος and Muses 242c–e the style is not very different from the surroundings.

(d) A shade of **10** accompanies the entire work.

*Polticus*[321] On the statesman in theory and practice.

257a–258a **B** Introduction. Reference to the *Sph*. **2, (5), 10**.
258a–261e **AD** Preliminary dihaeretic definitions of statesmanship. **(2), 5, (10)**.
261e–263a **BD** On the dihaeretic method. **2, (5), 10**.
263a–268d **AD** Resumption of dihaeretic definitions. **(2), 5, 10**.
268d–274e **BDE** Myth of the age of Cronus. **2, (5, 6), 10**.
274e–277a **AD** Critical conclusion relating to the former argument. **2, 5, 10**.
277a–c **BD** Interlude. This is not sufficient. **2, (5), 10**.
277c–285c **AD** Dihaeretic method illustrated by simile of the weaver. Digression on measuring (283b–285c). **2, 5, 10**.
285c–287a **D** On method. On extensive arguments. **(2), 5, 10**.
287a–290e **AD** On the assistants of the statesman. **2, 5, 10**.
[148] 291a–c **D** Interlude. The sophists. **2, (4, 5), 10**.
291c–303c **AD** The best State is founded on real knowledge. On law-giving. **2, (3, 5, 9), 10**.
303c–304a **D** The truly auxiliary arts. **2, (5), 10**.
304a–311c **AD**[322] Examination of these (304a–305e). The interweaving of different virtues in the fabric of the State. **2, 5, 10**.

(a) Like *Sph*. In the last three "interludes" there are no signs of B at all, but a slight change of style corresponds to the change of approach.

(b) Like *Sph*. The counterpart of Theaitetos is here Socrates the Younger.

(c) On the whole like *Sph*. But there is less of manifest irony and play in this work, though the dihaereses in the simile of the weaver are almost as grotesque as the first dihaereses in *Sph*. The myth of Cronus in styles **2, (5, 6) 10** forms a peripeteia and a central culmination, and in spite of the references to μῦθος and

---

319. See in particular Diès 1925: 299, Friedländer III² 235–236, 248, de Vries 1949: 180–186.

320. Schaerer 1955: 200–210 does not consider the formal structure.

321. The structure of this work is more complicated and refined than *Sph*.; see Diès 1935 (notably the table after the introduction), Zeise 1938, Friedländer III² 262, 265, 273.

322. If the concluding utterance is given to Socrates the Elder, as most editors have done since Schleiermacher, the work could be said to end with a brief B section. But this is a very uncertain conjecture; cf. Friedländer III² 283.

παιδιά (268de etc.) it is fundamentally serious.³²³ The sections 291a–303c with their polemics against popular sophistry have interesting additional touches of **(4)** and **(3)**, also **(9)** in political and legal passages (e.g. 293a–e, 297de).³²⁴

(d) Like *Sph.*

*Philebus*³²⁵ On pleasure and intellectual life.

11a–12b **B** Introduction. Is pleasure the highest good? **2, (5), 10**.
12b–17e **D** Preliminary examination of what is good in life. Pythagorean metaphysics. Observations on method. **2, (3, 4, 5), 10**.
17e–20a **B(E)** Relevance of the method. Legend of Theuth. **2, (5), 10 / 5, (10)**.
20b–22c **AD** Neither pleasure nor intellectuality are good alone. **2, 5, (10)**.
22c–23b **B** Interlude. Preparation for long and difficult investigation. **(1), 2, 5, 10**.
23b–27d **AD** On the four classes of being. **(1), 2, (4), 5, (10)**.
27e–28b **B** Interlude. The views of Socrates and Philebus contrasted. **(1), 2, (5), 10**.
28c–67a **AD** On the nature of pleasure and pain and of intellectual activity. On a "mixed" life. Résumé (from 66c). **(1), 2, (3), 5, 10**.
67b **B** Brief concluding remarks hinting at a discussion to follow. **(1), 2, (5), 10**.

(a) In the first part there are slight shifts of style between the sections. Note however the occasional touches of **(4)** in AD and not in B sections. In the main part (from 28c onwards) there are no distinct B interludes. Here transitions are often marked by by-play or personal remarks (e.g. 30e, 34de, 55c, 58ab, 61bc; on the other hand e.g. the digression on ethics 39e–40a has no other transitional devices than an opening ἄγε δή), but they cannot easily be grasped in terms of style; and the replies of Protarchus often in non-transitional passages expand so as to resemble B dialogue (e.g. 56c–58e).

(b) No distinct stylistic characterization.³²⁶ It is true that the personal remarks of "*Socrates*" (cf. a) and the touches of **(1)** sound remotely Socratic, but they have little of natural playfulness to them, and the latter are not confined to Socrates. It should also be noted that the occasional touches of **(4)** are rather rhetorical (cf. c).

(c) Beside the all-pervading **10**, the shade of systematic **5** is fairly marked from the introduction of the main argument 20b onwards; this corresponds to the fact that *Phlb.* is more like a discursive tract than any other Platonic dialogue.³²⁷ From the last regular interlude (23b) onwards there occur occasional but unmistakable touches of **(1)** which give a certain stylistic liveliness to this

---

323. For the myth, cf. Harris 1892: 26, Willi 1925: 35, Diès 1935: XXX–XLI, Capelle 1939: 26–38.
324 The importance and special points of these passages have been discussed especially by Wilamowitz I 580–583 (cf. the remark on style p. 561).
325. The structure of this work is very complicated; cf. Stenzel 1956: 342, Isenberg 1940, Diès 1941: IX (cf. the table after the introduction), Friedländer III² 286–287, 292, MacClintock 1961. The analyses of Billings 1920: 26–32 amount to sub-sections of little interest here.
326. The style of young Protarchus does not differ to any notable extent from the intellectuality and dignity of "Socrates." Philebus, who appears only in the introduction and the interludes of the first part of the work, may seem somewhat more straightforward and uncomplicated (Taylor 1956: 11: "boyish"), but I am not sure Plato has attempted to characterize him by style.
327. Cf. Gauss III 2.75.

[149]
[150] "Socratic" dialogue. Important points are sometimes emphasized by **(3)** or a rather rhetorical touch of **(4)**, e.g. 16b–d (Pythagorean cosmology), 26b (excessive vice), 30cd (end of argument that νοῦς is a cause), 47a–d (end of argument about contrast and mixture of pain and pleasure). The reference to the legend of Theuth 18b–d (cf. *Phdr.* 274b–275b) may be said to correspond to a peripeteia though it comes very early in the work and though it gives hardly more than a hint at a vision, in a rather compressed style **5 (10)**.

(d) A shade of **10** accompanies the entire work, but it is not quite as manifest as in *Sph.* and *Plt.* Note also the interplay of **(1)**.

*Epistula* 7 To the friends of Dion.

323d–324b E Introductory remarks. **2, 3**.

324b–330b E First part: Historical account of Plato's first two visits to Syracuse. **(1), 2, (3, 7, 10)**.

330b–340a E Second part: The advice given to Dionysius II. The death of Dion. Plato coming to Syracuse for the third time. **2, 3, (5, 10) / (1), 2, (7)**.

340b–344d E Third part: On philosophy and on teaching philosophy. **2, (3), 10 / 5, (10)**.

344d–350d E(CB) Fourth part: Objections to the actions of Dionysius. Detailed account of Plato's third visit to Syracuse and his leaving it. **(1), 2, (4, 5) / 2, (5, 9)**.

350d–352a E Conclusion. Reflections about Dion and the Sicilian affair. **2, 3, (4, 10)**.

(a) A division into sections has been made above in order to facilitate the discussion of changes under (c). It has some correspondence in style. Note also the comparatively vivid style of the C narrative 347c–350b.

(b) Stylistic characterization avoided. Note the strictly formal style **2, (5, 9)** of the utterances quoted 346a–347c, 348c–e.

(c) There is remarkably much variation of style, and on the whole these variations closely correspond to changes in the contents. The introduction and the conclusion are distinctly rhetorical **2, 3**, the latter more heavy and pathetic **(4, 10)**, as often in oratory. The narrative passages are carried by a fairly light and personal **(1), 2**, sometimes with a touch of **(7)** (e.g. 329d) or vivid imagery **(4)** (e.g. 348a), and with trends of **(3)** and **(10)** only in meditative passages (e.g. 329ab). The deliberative passages in the second part are kept in **2, 3, (5, 10)**, and rather

[151] similarly are the deliberations in the beginning of the third part and 346d–347b, 350cd, whereas Plato's indignation is given a more vivid, even colloquial expression **(1), 2, (5)** in the reflections about Dionysius 344d–345c. The speeches quoted 346a–348e are curiously formal and remind of decree style, **2, (5, 9)**, perhaps because Plato here aims at historical truth. The much-discussed epistemological "digression" 342a–344d with its sophisticated style **5, (10)** can be regarded as the central culmination.[328]

(d) Touches of **(10)** occur in meditative and deliberative passages; *see* (c).

---

328. Cf. G. Müller 1950, Brocker 1963, Isnardi 1964, Edelstein 1965. I can see no reason why the digression should have been later inserted if the rest of the letter is authentic. Indeed, its function as a central culmination stresses the Platonic character of the whole letter.

*Leges,* lib. I–XII On a good State and its laws.

I. 624a–625c **B** Introduction. Opening discussion of legislation. Persons and situation introduced. **2, (4, 10)**.
I. 625c–632d **ADE** The purpose of legislation and a plan of the present work. **2, 3, (10)**.
I. 632d–637b **ABDE** The virtues as a condition of legislation. Courage and temperance. **2, 3, (10)**.
I. 637b–641a **ADE** On the possibility of moderate symposia. **2, 3, (10)**.
I. 641a–643a **BE** Symposia may be useful. The Athenian agrees to speak about education. **2, (5, 10)**.
I. 643a–650b. II. 652a–674c **AD** On education, music, and symposia. **2, (3), 5, (9, 10)**.
III. 676a–687e **AD** The development of states. The Dorian states. **2, (3, 5, 9, 10)**.
III. 687e–688e **BE** Knowledge a condition for constructive change. **2, 3, 5, (10)**.
III. 688e–702a **D** On the division of power and on the history of Persia and Athens. **2, 3, 7, (10)**.
III. 702b–e **BE** Interlude. This discussion may be of use for the founding of a particular new city. **2, (5, 10)**.
IV. 704a–712a **D** Searching a constitution. **2, 3, (10)**.
IV. 712b–714b **BE** The ideal city of Cronus. **2, (10) / 3, 6, 10**.
IV. 714b–721d **ADE** On the authority and the persuasive function of the laws. **2, 3, (8, 9), 10**.
IV. 721e–724b **BE** The importance of prooimia. **2, (3, 5), 10**.
V. 726a–734e **E** A prooimion to the Laws. **3, 5, (8), 10 / 3, 5**.
V. 734e–747e **D** The founding of the city and its organization. **(3), 5, (8, 9), 10**.
VI. 751a–768e **D** On the magistrates. **2, 5, (10) / 2, (3, 8), 9, (10)**.
VI. 769a–771a **BDE** The individuals have to be educated to future law-giving. **2, 3, (5, 9), 10**.
VI. 771a–785b. VII. 788a–818e **D(E)** Duties of the individual. Family life. Education. **2, 3, 5, (9), 10**.
VII. 818e–822d **BAD** The sciences of measuring and astronomy. **2, (3), 5, 10**.
VII. 822d–824a. VIII. 828a–842b **D(E)** On hunting. On festivals and exercise. On sexual relations. **2, 3, (5, 9), 10**.
VIII. 842b–850d **D** On agriculture, commerce, and industry. **5, 9, (10)**.
IX. 853a–857b **D(E)** General considerations of crime. On sacrilege and treason. **2, 3, 5, 9, 10**.
IX. 857b–858c **B** Interlude. Legislation also demands a consideration of the particular criminal cases. **2, 10**.
IX. 858c–864c **AD** On criminal psychology and the principles of legislation. **2, 3, 5, (10)**.
IX. 864c–882c. X. 884e–885a **D** Criminal code. **(3), 5, 9, (10)**.
X. 885a–887c **BED** On impiety and atheism. **2, (3, 10) / 3, (10)**.
X. 887c–890b **AD(E)** On atheistic cosmology. **2, 3, (5), 10**.
X. 890b–891e **B** Retarding interlude. **2, (5, 10)**.
X. 891e–907d **AD(E)** Refutation of atheism and impiety. On the soul. Eschatology. **2, (3), 5, (10) / 3, (6), 10**.

[152]   X. 907d–910e **D** Regulations against offenders of the gods. **5, 9, (10)**.
   XI. 913a–938c **D** Regulations concerning private security. **2, (3, 4), 5, 9, 10**.
   XII. 941a–960b **D** Regulations concerning public matters. **3, 5, 9, (10)**.
   XII. 960b–e **B** Reflections on preservation and stability. **2, (3), 10**.
   XII. 961a–968b **AD** The nocturnal council. Qualifications of the Guardians. **2, (3), 5, (10)**.
   XII. 968b–969d **BD** Conclusion. Education of the Guardians is a condition for a good State. **2, (3), 5, 10**.

   (a) The analysis above is based primarily on formal criteria, but on the whole the sections correspond to changes in the contents.[329] The slight changes of style
[153] probably are due to the contents and have no direct connection with the formal structure of the work.

   (b) No distinct stylistic characterization. Being the leader of the discussion, the *Athenian* of course has a wider register of styles than Clinias and Megillus, but none of the three is clearly individualized.[330]

   (c) The main stylistic trends in this vast work are **2, (10), 3**, and **9**, all generally appropriate to the old age and dignity of the speakers and the political and judicial subjects discussed. On closer inspection it is easy to see that shifts of style on the whole correspond to shifts of subject or approach. Here I only call attention to the following details:

   There is a touch of **(4)** in the description of the surrounding nature 625bc which remotely recalls *Phdr.* 230bc, but later this tone does not seem to return. The shade of **3** occurs with some variation in large portions of the work, but it is particularly manifest in some speeches of a distinct E character, notably IV.713c–714b, with **6** (myth of Cronus), 715e–718a (speech of a law-giver), V.726a–734e, with **5** (a prooimion), VI.770b–771a (speech to the magistrates), VII.823d–824a (speech to the young about hunting), IX.854bc (speech to a person prepared to make sacrilege), X.885c–e (fictitious speech of the impious), 899d–900b (speech to the believer in indifferent gods).[331] Shade **5** occurs occasionally in the first books, notably II.667a–670c (mimesis), III.687e–688e (knowledge a condition). It is combined with considerable rhetoric and violent effects in the extensive prooimion in the Vth book (whose end however is of doubtful authenticity); possibly this
[154] section can be regarded as the central culmination of the work.[332] In the following

---

329. The composition of this work has often been regarded as haphazarded and even chaotic; cf. Döring 1907, Billings 1920: 47–52, Wilamowitz I 654–656, Geffcken II 150 and A 127–128 n. 2–6, Gauss III 2.209–210. Others, among them Taylor (especially 466 with reference to the first books), Friedländer III[2] 362–381, 508 n. 37, 509 n. 46, Görgemanns 1960, find in it marks of a deliberate arrangement. Both views are true in one way or another, though I am inclined to stress the former. At least the formal structure, and notably the BABAB pattern, is largely blurred.

330. The "Spartan" attitude of Megillus, e.g. I.633bc, 638a (cf. Weil 1959), is not reflected in his style (contrast the lapidaric form of the Spartan quotation 642c). Wilamowitz I 660 thinks that Plato wanted to portray Clinias as somewhat naive, but it seems to me doubtful whether his naivety extends to style in passages such as I.642d–643a.

331. But the speech to the atheist X.888a–d is not so rhetorical. Cf. Taylor 490.

332. G. Müller 1951: 11 ff. finds the style of the end of the prooimion (732d–734e) particularly un-Platonic. It is true that the style changes. Possibly it is explicable from the change from

section and in the later books shade **5** is on the whole more manifest than before [154]
the prooimion, notably in legal contexts, in the section on science VII.818e–822d,
and in the important (note the retardation X.890b ff.) discussion of "atheistic"
cosmology and physics X.888d–899d. A distinct tone of **(6)** only occurs in the
myth of Cronus IV.713c–714b and in the eschatological passage X.903a–905c. **7**
again is appropriately used in the passages of historical narrative in III.688e–
702a. Speeches sometimes open ceremoniously **(8)**, so notably the prooimion
V.726a. Shade **9** accompanies all the laws quoted in the later books, but it occurs occasionally elsewhere, first in II.665c (importance of incessant educational
"hymns"). For shade **10,** *see* under (d).

(d) Shade **10** accompanies the whole work, but it is used with more manifest
elaboration in visionary and meditative passages, notably the sections from the
myth of Cronus (IV.713c) to the founding of the city (V.747e), large portions of
the sections on education and crime (VI.769a–IX.858c) and of the refutation of
impiety (X.887c–907d), the section on stability (XII.960b–e), and the conclusion.
Curiously, the regulations concerning private security (XI.913a–938c) have on the
whole more stylistic onkos than the subsequent regulations concerning public
matters which have more of formal **3**. The reason may be that the former admit
more of personal emotions than public matters.

*Epinomis* On the order of the universe.

973a–974d **BE** Introduction. What teaching is required for wisdom? Reference to
the *Lg.* **2, (5, 10)**.
974d–979d **E** Review of the various arts. Importance of the number. **(2, 3), 5, (10)**.
979d–981b **B** The plan of the present exposition. Priority of divine matters. **(1),** [155]
**2, (4, 10)**.
981b–986a **E** On the five elements and on divine and mortal beings. **2, (3), 5,
(10)**.
986a **B** Brief comments on astral religion. **(1), 2, (10)**.
986a–992e **E** On astronomy and mathematics. Their study will lead to proper
piety and wisdom (from 991b). **2, 5, (10) / 3**.

(a) Slight stylistic shifts between the sections. Note the use of **(1)** and **(4)** in
the interludes. The return to uniform composition after *Lg.*, and the formal and
stylistic emphasis of the BEBEB rhythm, may indicate post-Platonic revision;
cf. (c).

(b) No stylistic characterization of the speakers.

(c) Corresponding to the subjects treated, there is a marked use of **5** in the
main exposition. The touches of **3** and **10** resemble on the whole Plato's practice

---

θεῖα to ἀνθρώπινα (732e), and from the unfinished character of the work. But I am quite prepared to accept Philippus as the author of this conclusion. However, athetizing large portions, or the whole of the *Lg.*, as Müller does, is another question on which such isolated cases of "interpolation" have little bearing.—Willi 1925: 96 considers the sections on impiety and atheism (X.885a–907d) as the most philosophical part of *Lg.*; though there are no formal and little stylistic indications of this, he may be right.

[155] in *Lg*. But the protreptic conclusion sounds to me remarkably formal, flat, and un-Platonic.³³³

A touch of **(10)** accompanies the whole work except the conclusion.

## Notes on the dubia and spuria

The dubia and spuria form a fairly large category (cf. above p. 11 ff.) which is on the whole of little stylistic interest—indeed this fact as such makes an additional indication of spuriousness. None of these writings (with the possible exception of some letters) show any tendency to shade **10**.

*De justitia*
    (a) No formal structure.
    (b) No characterization.
    (c) **1** throughout.

*De virtute*
    (a) No notable change of style with the concluding speech.
    (b) No characterization.
    (c) **1** throughout.

[156]
*Hippias Major*
    (a) A distinct BABAB pattern, but a distinct corresponsion in style is lacking.

    (b) *Socrates* mock-dignified **2** in the introduction, later ironical **1**. *Hippias* very pompous **2, 3** in the introduction and occasionally later (e.g. 291a). The *Anonymous critic* (from 286c onwards) uses an emphatic and almost vulgar **1** (e.g. 288bc, 290d, 292a–d). From the fourth tentative definition (293c) onwards there is no clear characterization.

    (c) Basically **1**. The play with **2** and **3** in the first sections seems to be only mimetic. No central culmination.

*Hipparchus*
    (a) Tendency to BABAB, but no clear corresponsion in the style except a panegyrical note in the legend of Hipparchus (*see* under c).

    (b) The note of **1, (3)** in the legend may sound as a *Socratic* burlesque.³³⁴

    (c) Basically **1** with an addition of **(3)** in the legend 228b–229d. For the "central legend" in some spuria, *see* above n. 142.

---

333. The passage has occasional late Platonic devices such as τούτοισιν 992d, but it is natural that Philippus of Opous should have adopted such touches. Cf. the end of the prooimion in *Lg*. V (above, n. 332). For the question of the authenticity of *Epin.*, *see* above n. 69.

334. It is of course appropriate to the contents, and perhaps it is not intended as a stylistic characterization. The play with ἄξιος and the assonance in the introduction (cf. 225c) has no such function.

## Theages
(a) Tendency to BABAB, and some stylistic elaboration of the introduction and the BE 127a–128c.

(b) *Socrates:* On the whole natural **1**, also in the E passage on his daimonion (128d–130e). But mock-dignified adaption of the tone of Demodocus, **1, 2, (3)**, in 122bc and 127d–128b. *Demodocus:* Somewhat solemn and circumstantial **(1), 2, (3)** in the introduction 125b, and 127c. *Theages* sometimes has childishly vivid reactions, note **l, (4)** 125e–126a.

(c) Basically **1**. Play with **2** and **(3)** for a mimetic purpose. No central culmination, but cf. Socrates' speech on his daimonion immediately before the conclusion.

## Alcibiades 1
(a) A fairly clear BABAB pattern, but without a clear corresponsion in style except for the historical digression (*see* c).

(b) No clear characterization.[335]

(c) Basically **1, (2)** with touches of **(3)** especially in the introduction and the "digression" 120e–124b (on the education of Persian kings and Spartan leaders). This corresponds to the central culmination of the authentic writings (cf. p. 47).

## Alcibiades 2
(a) A curious ABAB pattern, and marked stylistic shifts between the sections.

(b) No clear characterization.

(c) **1, (2)** in A passages and the two last B's. The speeches of Socrates (also Alcibiades 143ab) are all manifestly rhetorical **3**. Regarding the speech immediately before the conclusion, cf. *Thg.*

## Amatores
(a) A clear BABAB pattern coupled with C, but without any corresponsion in style.

(b) The notably easy **1**, also in narrative, can be regarded as intentionally *Socratic*. But only once this style is contrasted to **2**: 135b, the *Intellectual young man*.

(c) **1** almost throughout (cf. b). No central culmination.

## Clitopho
(a) BE, but with CA inserted (408c–410a). The A section is kept in **1, 2** in contrast to the rhetoric of the rest.

(b) *Socrates* is perhaps deliberately made stiff and formal, **2, 3**, in the introduction and in the speech quoted 407a–c. Contrast the CA questioning in a "Socratic" manner **1, 2** (κατὰ σέ 408d). *Clitophon* is verbose and rhetorical **1, (2), 3, (4)**.

(c) This work consists essentially of a critical speech by Clitophon. It has the appropriate shade of **3**. I can find no stylistic indications of conscious burlesque in

---

335. The occasional attempts to vivify the style, such as βαβαῖ 118b, 119c, are of course irrelevant.

[158] the work, though the idea of Socrates the rhetor sounds nonsensical to us when it is not explained by particular circumstances (as in *Grg.*).

*Sisyphus*
   (a) Tendency to BABAB, but without corresponsion in style.
   (b) No characterization.
   (c) Rather literary **1, 2** throughout. The aporetic speech of Socrates 390a–d corresponds to the central culmination of the authentic writings.

*Minos*
   (a) Tendency to BABAB, but without a corresponsion in style except for the legend (*see* c).
   (b) No characterization.
   (c) Rather strict **1** except the concluding D section where the style appropriately expands, **(2)**, and the speech of Socrates about Minos, **2, 3**, immediately before this section. Cf. *Hipparch., Thg.,* and *Alc.* 2.

*Eryxias*
   (a) Tendency to BABAB, with C. No clear corresponsion in style except for the central speech.
   (b) No characterization.[336]
   (c) Basically **1**. But with the intervention of Eryxias (394a) the dialogue assumes a shade of formal **(3)**, and the mediating speech of Socrates 396a–e, the "central culmination," is kept in **1, 3**.

*Epistulae*
   Except for *Ep.* 7 (p. 124) these compilations deserve little consideration here. But it may be noted that *Ep.* 3, 4, 6, and 10 have occasional heavy twists of style that remotely recall style **10** of Plato.

---

336. In spite of the ambitious elaboration of the formal composition, the author has overseen the aspect of stylistic characterization. In 397c, for instance, Eryxias assumes the formality of Socrates, in 396e the colloquial tone of Critias.

# CONCLUSIONS

## Observations on the relation of style to the formal structure of the dialogues

Plato's art of composition appears to follow a number of general rules. But there is a considerable variation in details, and no two dialogues have an identical structure.

I have used the signs A (elenchus), B (conversation), D (dialogue tending to monologue), and E (monologue) for the different types of exposition habitually employed in Plato's works, and C for the reported dialogue (p. 28 ff.). The different types to some extent reflect the complex origins of Plato's art.

Basically the structure of Platonic dialogues follows a BABAB pattern which in its simplest form is present in e.g. *Hp.Mi.* and *Ion*. The commonest alternation of this pattern is extension by the insertion of several B sections.

Type D is a further development of type A. It is Platonic in origin, and often felt to be somehow inspired. It is more common in the later works.

E passages mostly occur in connection with B, especially opening and central B's, and also in the concluding section. Normally the opening section is most largely elaborated (by using different types of exposition, change of speakers, etc.); the central section is often so, but the concluding section rarely. This is also reflected in the use of C narrative and C description.

The main argument is usually carried by the A(D) sections, whereas the B(E) sections raise problems, open new aspects, or simply function as interludes. A(D) is proper to Socrates (or his stand-in), E (and C) are also preferably used by Socrates, but B commonly introduces the views of the interlocutors.

ooo O ooo

There are normally clear stylistic shifts between the sections. The B(E) sections, especially the opening section and the central section, are also stylistically more elaborate, and usually more lively and varied, than are the A(D) sections.

[160] The C report in the dialogues from *Ly.* to *R.* adds to this variation, sometimes as a counter-point. D is accompanied by an increasing expansion and weight of style. As a rule the monologic E passages stand out stylistically from their context.

The different types of exposition and the corresponding changes of style thus create a compositional "rhythm" or "pulse." This rhythm is always more marked and varied in the first part of the work than in the latter part. It may seem to reflect a gradual slackening of interest in matters of form and style. However this may be, it often contributes at the same time to the factual and sometimes formal and stylistic climax of the central section. It also corresponds to the principle of the unstressed end which is adopted in most dialogues. For the two last-mentioned features, *see* below under (c).

Notable irregularities of composition occur, apart from *Ap., Mx.* and *Ep.* 7, in *Cri.* and *Prm.* In the later works (latter part of *Phdr.,* central and latter part of *R.* II–X, *Ti., Criti., Sph., Plt.,* latter part of *Phlb., Lg.*) the BABAB pattern and the corresponding rhythm of style become obscured to a varying extent. In *Epin.* E sections take over the function of A(D) sections, but there are occasional instances of this much earlier.

## Observations on the function of style for characterization of the speakers

Characterization by means of style occurs in all the authentic writings of the early and middle periods. It is always more elaborate in the first part of the work, notably in the introductory BE section, than in the latter part. It is much more common in B sections than in A sections.

In the late works this trait is virtually absent. It already tends to become obscured in *Cra.,* then in *Prm.* and possibly *Tht.,* and, more obviously, it is on the point of vanishing in *Phdr.* and *R.* III ff. In *Ti., Criti., Sph., Plt., Phlb., Ep.* 7, *Lg.* and *Epin.* it plays no part worth consideration.

### Socrates

[161] It is generally recognized that the chief object of characterization in Plato's works is Socrates.[337] Bruns (1896: 238–239) observes that the other characters are never drawn as full portraits but only delineated so far as they would add to the picture of Socrates. As a matter of fact, the idea of *contrast* is essential for determining the stylistic characterization of Socrates too, because when there is

---

337. In addition to the classical discussion by Bruns 1896: 281–360, *see* the comprehensive, though uneven, treatment by de Magalhâes–Vilhena Probl. 1952 and Socr. 1952, with references (add Diès 1927: 161–181, McDonald 1931: 317–340). More references to the vexed problem of the historical Socrates in Cherniss 1959: 31–35.

no mimetic contrast of styles Plato's Socrates is likely to rise above the mimetic level and become merely the mouthpiece of Plato. Such a partial approximation of Socrates to Plato occurs in all authentic works where Socrates is present.

Most typical of the "real" Socrates is a casual colloquial style (class **1**, according to my classification), often with some affectation (**4**) or with burlesque traits. This occurs in all works from *Hp.Mi.* to *Tht., Phdr.* and *R.* IX, though in some works (notably *Ap., Phd., Prm.* and the central and latter parts of *R.*) there are only rare glimpses of it. Sometimes he is characterized as dignified (e.g. *La.*) or grave (e.g. *Phd.*) (**2**) in appropriate situations. Often he is mock-solemn (notably *Ion, Mx., Men., Euthphr., Chrm., Prt., Euthd.*), but he does not appear to use formal rhetoric (**3**) seriously except in *Ap.*, because instances such as the central speeches in *Ion* and the latter part of *Grg.* are rather Platonic (*see* p. 135 ff.). In *Cra., Euthphr.* and *R.* I what would appear to be the "real" Socrates is occasionally given intellectual traits of style (**5**), but then he comes close to a Platonic level; most instances of intellectual style are obviously Platonic rather than Socratic.

## Other persons

The interlocutors of Socrates are characterized by various stylistic means, always in partial contrast to Socrates. No actual stylistic characterization occurs in those works where Socrates is not the central character. Most of the stylistic means used are literary devices. Some persons however are characterized by a casual style that may be simple and straightforward (e.g. Criton), or vividly emphatic (e.g. Hippocrates), or rude (e.g. Thrasymachus). It may be noted that the intellectual style which is normally typical of Plato has a mimetic purpose when attributed to Eryximachus, Hippias, Critias, Menon, Pausanias, the Poison-mixer, and possibly Hermogenes and Protagoras, whereas it is likely both to characterize the speaker and to represent Plato himself when attributed to Diotima, Glaucon, Cebes, Simmias, Parmenides, and Theaitetos.

I give here an alphabetical list of those persons who receive stylistic characterization in the authentic works. The brief description added to each name is intended to cover roughly both the shades of style used (for details, *see* the analyses above) and the traits of character otherwise exhibited in the context. On the whole my interpretation agrees with the traditional interpretation of Plato's characters, which has, however, devoted little attention to style.[338]

---

338. Plato's characters have been discussed in most comprehensive works on Plato. Note further Bruns 1896, Rudberg 1928, McDonald 1931, Puech 1932–1934, de Vries 1949: 91–116, D. Tarrant 1955 (whose brief characterizations seem to me particularly to the point). For the persons in *Chrm., Euthd., Smp.* and *Tht. see* also Muthmann 1961, for *La. see* Nagel 1962. As can be expected, there is little disagreement about the interpretation. The eccentrical view of Rick 1931 (somewhat similarly Salin 1957 acc. to Cherniss 1959: 25) that all characters are masks for contemporary characters, hardly requires serious consideration.

[162] —— Adimantus, *R.* II ff. Vigorous and sensitive, inclining to rhetoric. **1**, **3**
—— Agathon, *Smp.* Indulgent in luxurious beauty. **3 Gorg.**, **4** / **1**
—— Alcibiades, *Prt., Smp.* Intelligent, practical, and intense; reckless *(Smp.).* **1**, **2** / **1**, **(3)**, **4**
—— Anytus, *Men.* Surly and indignant. **1**, **2**, **(4)**
—— Apollodorus, *Smp.* Enthusiastic admirer of Socrates. **1**, **(4)**
—— Aristophanes, *Smp.* Funny and fantastic. **(1)**, **2**, **(3, 4)**, **6** / **1**
—— "Aspasia," *Mx.* Patriotic orator. **3**
—— Callias, *Prt.* Matter-of-fact patron. **1**, **2**
—— Callicles, *Grg.* Successful man of the world. **1**, **2** / **2**, **3**
—— Cebes, *Phd.* Forthright and clear-headed. **1**, **2**, **5**
—— Cephalus, *R.* I. Urbane old man. **1**, **2**, **(4)**
—— Chairephon, *Grg., Chrm.* Enthusiastic and devoted friend. **1**, **(4)** / **2**
—— Charmides, *Chrm.* Attractive and good-mannered boy. **1**, **2**
—— Cratylus, *Cra.* Reserved and oracular. **1**, **2**, **(10)**
—— Critias, *Chrm., Prt.*[339] Intellectual and self-conscious. **1**, **2** / **(1)**, **2**, **5**
—— Criton, *Cri., Euthd., Phd.* Loyal, somewhat colorless friend. **1** / **1**, **2**, **3**
—— Ctesippus, *Ly., Euthd.* Eager and cheeky youth. **1**, **4**
—— Dionysodorus, *Euthd.* Farcical disputant. **1**, **2** / **1**
—— ("Diotima," *Smp.* Hierophantic priestess.) **(2, 3, 8)**
—— Echecrates, *Phd.* Keen truth-seeker. **1**, **(4)**
—— Eryximachus, *Smp.* Cautious and pedantic physician. **(3)**, **5** / **(1)**, **2**, **(5)**
—— Euthydemus, *Euthd.* Farcical disputant. **1**, **2** / **1**
[163] —— Euthyphron, *Euthphr.* Conceited fanatic and legalist. **1**, **2**, **(4, 9)**
—— Glaucon, *R.* II ff. Vigorous and clear-headed. **1**, **2**, **3**, **4**
—— Gorgias, *Grg.* Pompous and condescending. **2**, **3**
—— Hermogenes, *Cra.* Unimaginative dogmatic (?) **(1)**, **2**, **(5)** / **(3)**
—— Hierophant, *R.* X. Ceremonious. **8**
—— Hippias, *Hp.Mi., Prt.* Vain of omniscience and grandiloquent. **2**, **(5)** / **3**, **4**, **5**
—— Hippocrates, *Prt.* Eager admirer of sophists. **1**, **4**
—— Hippothales, *Ly.* Romantic lover. **2**
—— Ion, *Ion.* Vain and unintelligent artist. **2**, **4**, **(8)**
—— Laches, *La.* Impetuous soldier of reputation. **1**, **2**, **3**, **(4, 7)**
—— ("Laws," *Cri.* Dignified and rhetorical.) **(2, 3)**
—— "Lysias," *Phdr.* Cynical epideictic. **3**
—— Lysimachus, *La.* Circumstantial old man. **2**, **(3)**
—— Menexenus, *Mx., Ly.* Young intellectualist (?) **1**, **2**, **(5)**
—— Menon, *Men.* Eager and precocious admirer of sophists. **(3)**, **5** / **1**, **4**
—— Nicias, *La.* Dignified general of reputation. **1**, **2**, **3**
—— (Parmenides, *Prm.* Reputed philosopher.) **(2, 4, 5)**
—— Pausanias, *Smp.* Aristocratic pupil of sophists. **3**, **5**, **(10)**
—— Phaedon, *Phd.* Affectionate but controlled admirer of Socrates. **1**, **2**, **(4, 6)**.
—— Phaedrus, *Smp., Phdr.* Naive admirer of literature. **1**, **2**, **3**, **(4)**

---

339. For the Critias of *Ti.* and *Criti. see* above p. 121.

—— Poison-mixer, *Phd.* Dryly matter-of-fact. **1, (5)**
—— Polemarchus, *R.* I. Well-educated young man. **1, (2, 3)**
—— Polus, *Grg.* Impetuous and unintelligent pupil of Gorgias. **1, 3 Gorg., (4), (6)**
—— Prodicus, *Prt.* Hypochondriac rhetor. **3**
—— Protagoras, *Prt., Tht.* Bland and pontifical, but also argumentative. **2, (3, 4, 5) / (1), 3 (5), 6**
—— Servant of the Eleven, *Phd.* Devote admirer of Socrates. **1, (2, 4)**
—— Simmias, *Phd.* Sensitive, sometimes confused critic. **1, 2, (5)**
—— Slave of Agathon, *Smp.* Polite and formal (cf, the slaves in *R.* I. and *Men.*). **2**
—— Theaitetos, *Tht.* (not characterized in *Sph.*). Brilliant and promising young mathematician. **5 / 1**
—— Theodoros, *Tht.* (not characterized in *Sph.* and *Plt.*). Old man of some reputation. **1, 2, (4)**
—— Thrasymachus, *R.* I. Impetuous, pompous and rude careerist. **1, (3)**
—— Xanthippa, *Phd.* Woman tending to pathetic reactions. **4**
—— (Zenon, *Prm.* Versatile disputant of reputation.) **(1, 5)**

These portraits, of course, are widely different in scope and significance; most are bare sketches or glimpses.[340] Judging from the extent of stylistic elaboration, Plato was fascinated by the following characters in particular:

| | |
|---|---|
| Nicias | Protagoras |
| Laches | Alcibiades |
| Callicles | Theaitetos |
| Cephalus | Glaucon |
| Thrasymachus | Adimantus |

Protagoras in fact would top this list. Cebes and Simmias, though sympathetically depicted, have rather less individuality of their own and more of Plato himself. Parmenides in *Prm.* introduces the series of rather non-individual venerable teachers who dominate the late works.

## Observations on the relation of style to the contents

It is evident that there exists a close relationship between style and content in Plato's works, and the phenomena discussed above under (a) and (b) may provide some clues to it. The compositional and stylistic rhythm (a), as we have seen, reflects changes of approach. And the characterization of speakers by means

---

340. Nevertheless Plato's ἠθοποιία is far more differentiated and modulated than that of any other classical author, probably including comedy. Plato also had a theoretical interest in characterology, as appears from the discussion of ἦθος of man in states with different constitutions, *R.* VIII.544d ff.; cf. Vretska 1953. For the physiognomy of Meletus, *Euthphr.* 2b, see Geffcken II A.51 n. 171. Cf. the observations on the characterology of Lysias, by Usher 1965.

[164] of style (b) represents a mimetic frame or a by-play to which a more serious approach, often in the middle and later parts of the work, is contrasted.

Taking account of these facts and of various other facts and circumstances, it may seem possible to trace Plato's stylistic preferences when playing, or being serious, or both, in narrative, argument, and visionary passages. This would require, however, much more detailed analyses than it was possible to carry out here, and I am not sure whether we can hope ever to get a really reliable stylistic [165] instrument to be used for determining the tone of Platonic passages. On the following pages I can only indicate some very general features in Plato's stylistic preferences under different conditions and in different moods.

We shall first view separately the function of each of the ten classes or shades of style that were considered above.

1. *Colloquial style.* A playful, mimetic and neutral basic style in the early and middle dialogues (cf. below, 2). The use of colloquial style is deliberately restricted in some dialogues (notably *Ap., Phd.*). In *Tht.* it is still quite freely used, but in *Prm., Phdr.* and *R.* II–X it is proportionally less common and may at times sound artificial; in the "Socratic" *Phlb.* we meet with a clearly articifial revival of it.

2. *Semi-literary conversational style.* Often contrasted to the more vividly colloquial style for mimetic play, but also used with a serious undertone from the earliest dialogues. In the later dialogues, from *Prm., Tht., Phdr.* and *R.* II onwards, it functions as a neutral basic style.

3. *Rhetorical style.* There are traces of this style in all of Plato's works except *Ly., Prm.,* and (oddly enough) *Sph.* It is commonly employed for play and parody in the early and middle works, notably in *La., Mx., Grg., Prt., Smp.,* and *Phdr.* But commonly also, and indeed more often, it serves Platonic persuasion above the mimetic level. Then it naturally occurs mainly in monologues or speeches (D or E), though in most cases as a light touch of style only (e.g. *Hp.Mi.* and *Ion*). Passages of parody and pastiche are sometimes quite elaborate (notably in *La., Mx., Grg., Prt., Smp., Phdr.*). But only in *Cri., Ap., (Mx.), Grg., (Prt.), Criti., (Ep.* 7) and *Lg.* does Plato employ lengthy passages of formal rhetoric for a serious, or predominantly serious, purpose. And the cases last referred to are all conditioned by particular circumstances (the speaker addressing representatives of public life, or himself speaking as such a representative).

4. *Pathetic style.* Except for one passage in *Phdr.* this style occurs as an accessory shade only, mainly in the early and middle works including *Tht., Phdr.* and *R.* II–X. Its primary function is to add to the liveliness of the style, and hence it is particularly common in interludes. It is largely mimetic (*see* e.g. *Euthd.*). But it may also mark a deepening interest in connection with passages of special importance (*see* e.g. *Euthphr., R.* VI/VII).

[166] 5. *Intellectual style.* This is a very interesting style, or type of style, and it would deserve profound study. It is almost entirely absent from the early works (*Hp.Mi., Ion, La., Cri., Ap., Mx.*); only in *Hp.Mi.* do there occur occasional touches of it in mimetic play. Plato occasionally plays with it later too (*Grg., Men., Chrm., Prt., Smp., Tht., Phdr., R.* V.). But on the whole, it seems that it serves a serious purpose in Platonic argument, and also in visions (e.g. end of *R.* VI). From *Grg.* onwards

it is found in all works, though in varying proportions to other styles. It is significant that the intellectual style is particularly manifest in those works which develop the methods of Platonic philosophy, *Men., Phd., Prm., Tht., R.* VII–IX; and in all the late works it constitutes an important trait.

6. *Mythic narrative style.* This style functions from *Grg.* onwards as ornament in (mostly E or D) passages of a considerable visionary but not fundamental importance, such as the concluding myths, the preliminary teaching of Diotima in *Smp.*, or the speeches of Socrates and the myths of the cicadas and Theuth in *Phdr.* Sometimes the mimetic play predominates (Polus on Archelaus *Grg.* 471a –d, *Prt.*, speech of Aristophanes in *Smp.*, Glaucon on Gyges *R.* II.359d–360b, "Phoenician" myth *R.* III.414b–415d). Only in two works does the mythic style accompany the central culmination (for which *see* below p. 167): *Men.* and *Plt.* Indeed, Plato considered μῦθος as παιδιά.

7. *Historical style.* This shade accompanies the rhetorical style in appropriate connections in *La., Mx., Ep.* 7, and *Lg.* III.

8. *Ceremonious style.* A solemn style, mostly used (from *Grg.* onwards) to add loftiness to myths and visions and (in the late works) speeches. Only in *Ion* and, possibly, *Phdr.* (first speech of Socrates and end) does it occur in mimetic play.

9. *Legal style.* Apart from *Lg.*, where this style is naturally very common, it contributes to the solemn note of some isolated passages in *Grg., Prm., Plt.,* and *Ep.* 7. The instances in *Euthphr., Phdr.* and *R.* V are more playful.

10. *Platonic onkos.* This complex style, which makes its first appearance in *Phd.* and *Smp.*, will be discussed below, p. 139 ff.

It is clear that these styles can be used with varying emphasis, and this emphasis may correlate with the importance of the passage. This however raises various problems on which I have only been able to touch in passing. An easily recognizable kind of emphasis is the *accumulation* of corresponding expressions or clauses. This old device is very common in Plato, both in colloquial and in more literary styles, and in particular in summaries and conclusions (e.g. *Ion* 532e–533c, *R.* VI.487a).[341]

In spite of the complexity of style of many Platonic works, especially from the middle period, they often have a *predominant individual coloring* appropriate to the main theme. Thus, for instance, the pathetic style in *Ion* corresponds to the theme of inspiration; the deliberative tone in *La.* corresponds to the theme of education and the social status of the participants; the rhetoric in *Grg.* is closely interrelated with the antagonism of philosophy and politics; *Prt.* plays with sophistic devices, *Euthd.* with colloquial burlesque, *Phd.* has a restrained grave feeling, *Phdr.* with its literary criticism presents a florid mixture of almost all styles, and the "dialectic" works from *Prm.* onwards are predominantly intellectual. On the whole it can be said that, just as Plato's changes of style are usually appropriate to the shifts of approach within the different works, so the general stylistic character of each work

---

341. Some observations on this feature in Plato's styles are made by Baron 1891: 59, Campbell 1894: 168–169, des Places 1951, Kleve 1961. For accumulation in early prose, *see* Thesleff 1966: 90 ff.

[167] corresponds to the main themes discussed and to the general orientation of the work. Among the works before the late period only *Cra.* is an exception, because here the style is remarkably flat although we should expect the theme of etymological play to invite to burlesque or detailed stylistic elaboration. The specific manner of Plato's late works will be discussed below p. 139 ff.

We have found abundant evidence of the *pedimental structure* which some scholars have observed in some Platonic works (cf. above p. 28). Most works clearly culminate in one or several central sections, though these seldom come in the absolute center of the work.[342] The central section normally includes a turning point for the argument, a *peripeteia,* and one, often two, visionary speeches by Socrates (or his stand-in) which open things up to ideas outside the immediate theme (cf. p. 47). There is almost always a corresponding elaboration of style in the central sections; indeed, many works could be said to culminate stylistically in the center.

[168] The peripeteia leads to a change of aspect, and mostly to a different shading of style in the latter part of the work. Often it marks the change from tentative "opinion" to approximate "truth," and from the point of view of style this is reflected in a complete or partial abandoning of the play and mimesis characteristic of the first part of the work. On the whole there is more seriousness in the latter part of a Platonic work than in the earlier part. But very seldom, as in *Smp.* and *Phdr.,* does the peripeteia lead to a radical change of approach. In a sense such a change can be seen in *Prm.* which, however, in addition to its other anomalies lacks a central vision.

*Cri.* is the only authentic work that has no traces at all of a peripeteia or a central culmination; on the contrary its structure is clearly "climactic." This work perhaps represents a stage of experimenting with the principle of concluding protreptic. This experimenting then resulted in the combining of a central culmination with an extensive concluding appeal in *Ap., Grg., Euthd., Phd.,* and *R.*[343]

It is easy to overrate the significance of the *concluding protreptic,* whether combined with a myth or not, and however elaborate it may be in style. *Cri.* is an exception. Plato tends to leave the ends of his works open. Even in the discursive *Phlb.* he follows this fundamental rule, though with an artificial trick (n. 101). I am sure the concluding protreptic essentially corresponds to the principle of the open end. It does not conclude the argument; it only opens an additional view to something to come, and it merely presents the personal hopes and fears of "Socrates." In *Grg.* Callicles is eventually reduced to silence by the rhetoric of this "Socrates," but he is certainly not convinced; he returns in *R.,* not only as the caricature Thrasymachus, but also in the shape of Plato's dearest brother, Glaucon. The result of the concluding protreptic is that μῦθος σώζεται (*R.* X.621b); but the appeal to λόγος in these works reaches its culmination about the center of the

---

342. If we are to use Plato's own simile of the living being (p. 27) we can say that a human body in constant movement is symmetrical only in theory.

343. Among the spuria, cf. *Thg., Alc.* 2, *Clit.* and *Min.*

work. And accordingly, at least in *Grg.*, *Phd.* and *R.*, the central culmination is simpler, clearer, and more intellectual in style than the concluding sections.

As a consequence of these considerations it may be stated that elaboration of style is not as such an indication of the relative importance of a passage.

On the other hand we have seen in the style constant reflections of the interaction of three forces: play, emotional appeal, and intellectual argument.

## Observations on the rise of Plato's so-called "late style"

The most characteristic features of the style of Plato's late works are expansion and weight. This Platonic "onkos," as defined on p. 64 above, appears first in certain passages in *Phd.*, *Smp.* and *Tht.* Then it extends to large portions of *Phdr.* and *R.* II–X. From *Ti.* onwards it occurs as a basic coloring in all authentic works: *Ti.*, *Criti.*, *Sph.*, *Plt.*, *Phlb.*, *Ep.* 7, *Lg.* I–XII, *Epin.*

Principally onkos is introduced by the Platonic "Socrates" above a mimetic level, and by the venerable but impersonal teachers in the later works (in *Smp.* Diotima). Secondarily onkos extends to the style of the interlocutors as well: thus already in *Tht.*, the latter part of *Phdr.*, and (very occasionally) in *R.* V. This becomes normal from *Ti.* onwards.

It is clear that onkos is a specific Platonic manner which has little to do with the mimetic approach. It does not pretend to imitate 5th century Attic, as some scholars have thought.[344] We have also seen (p. 63) that onkos is not due to a gradually deepening influence from contemporary rhetoric or other contemporary linguistic tendencies.[345]

It is true that the expression of an artist tends to become more complex in the course of time.[346] In Plato's works it is also easy to trace preliminary stages of the onkos, notably in the inspired speeches of Socrates in *Ion*, in the climax of *Mx.*, in the myth of *Grg.*, in the "archaic" twists of Pausanias diction in *Smp.*, and in general in the growing complexity of styles from *Grg.* and *Men.* through *Prt.* to *Phd.*, *Smp.*, and *Phdr.* But this "development" is by no means as rectilinear and automatic as the orthodox stylometrists thought.

I find it very important to note that the onkos at its first stages is a *conscious* manner. It occurs quite appropriately in visionary contexts: the third demonstration of immortality and the myth in *Phd.*, Diotima's speech of initiation

---

344. Hirzel 1895: 249–250, cf. Bruns 1896: 288–289.
345. The observations of Diàz Tejera 1961 (cf. 1965) regarding an increase of Koiné vocabulary in Plato's later works principally indicate that Hellenistic prose sometimes had similar preferences as Plato in his later days. It seems to me misleading to speak of Plato being influenced by Koiné.
346. The development of Goethe's prose is often mentioned as a parallel to Plato. Indeed James Joyce, to whom nobody as far as I know has referred in this connection, had the same tendency. In the history of architecture it is well known: Frank Lloyd Wright, Alvar Aalto and Le Corbusier may suffice as examples.

[169] in *Smp.*, the central "digression" in *Tht.*, and the palinodic speech of Socrates
[170] in *Phdr.* Sometimes Socrates ironically comments on his onkos as a "tragic" or "dithyrambic" style.[347]

Wilamowitz (II 423–424) is probably right in taking the Platonic onkos to be an approximation to poetical diction. In fact most of its features (*see* p. 64) are at the same time proper to high poetry, and the tendency to rhythmical expression and the avoidance of hiatus also suggest poetry. Poetry is on the whole a more likely source of Plato's onkos than is archaic prose.[348] But poetry is certainly not the only "source." It is safer to state that Plato's onkos was as complex in origin as it is in expression. And since most of its features are already present in his earlier styles, the onkos implies no sudden change of models, only a slight shift from a prosaic to a poetic attitude.[349]

But Plato's onkos soon changed from a conscious manner to a semi-deliberate *mannerism*.[350] This change is obvious in *Phdr.* and fairly obvious in *R.* II–X. In *Phdr.* the introduction is florid and extravagant in style but has no onkos. Onkos comes in with the change to a more serious critical discussion at 234e, and it then accompanies the rest of the work, most manifestly in the palinodic speech and in the eulogy of the spoken word 275c–278b. Though it is properly used in the latter passages and in the first speech of Socrates (and possibly in the myth of the cicadas and the legend of Theuth), it may seem a rather odd device in the discussion of the qualities of good prose 259d–274b. In *R.* II–X onkos is present in many sections of a visionary character, but also, and notably in books III–V,
[171] in sections where we should expect an easy playfulness or a matter-of-fact style to be more appropriate; to be sure, the onkos occasionally sounds playful (e.g. II.376d–III.392c, III.403c–410b, V.451c–453e).—From *Ti.* onwards some correlation between increase of onkos and increase of visionary intensity can be traced; but such fluctuations are nowhere very marked except in *Ep.* 7; and in *Sph.* and *Plt.* they are almost non-existent. There is some degree of onkos present almost everywhere in the late works.

The early stages of Plato's onkos indicate that its primary function was Platonic persuasion, *psychagogy* (cf. *Phdr.* 261a, 271c). Plato felt it to be inspired; and hence it naturally occurs mainly in speeches and in dialogue of the monologic D type. The discussion in *Phdr.* suggests that Plato may have intended it as a

---

347. τραγικῶς *R.* III.413b, VIII.543de; cf. *Men.* 76e, *Cra.* 414c, 418d. εὔροια and πόρρω διθυράμβων *Phdr.* 238cd, cf. 241e. Note also the simile of the singing swan following the onkos of the third demonstration in *Phd.* (84–85b). Diotima is described as a hierophant (*Smp.* 209e–210a, cf. 208c); cf. χρησμῳδεῖν *R.* IX.586b, *Lg.* IV.712a (for *Cra.*, see above p. 52).

348. Denniston 1952: 5 seems to have in mind the latter possibility, but he refers only to *Phdr.* 245cd which has no onkos (*see* p. 119). The gnomic prose of Heraclitus does not really remind of Platonic onkos.

349. Cf. above n. 197. Homer and the tragedians offer only remote parallels to Plato's onkos, and so do naturally the dithyrambic fragments. In some respects Plato is not so far from Pindar, though Plato does not indulge in high style words nor in gnomes.

350. This has often been observed, before Wilamowitz notably by Campbell 1894: 49 and Natorp 1899: 44.

substitute for formal rhetoric.³⁵¹ Some other passages (*see* above p. 140) suggest that he played with the idea of onkos as a substitute for poetry. But it is interesting to note that intellectual argumentation, or approximately what is now called "dialectic," is not so commonly accompanied by onkos before *Sph.* and *Plt.* And onkos is absent from the very highest points in *Phd., Tht., R.* VI, and *Phdr.*

Onkos often combines with rhetorical features and features of intellectual style. In varying proportions all three constitute together Plato's so-called "late style," each contributing to its "psychagogical" character.

## Various concluding observations

The ten main classes of style discussed here, and their combinations, naturally provide no complete picture of Plato's use of style. Such occasional traits as accumulation or specific metaphors or peculiarities in the sentence structure have been considered only in passing. It also follows from Plato's highly personal play with styles that he sometimes introduces odd patterns which cannot be properly described by means of the ten main classes: the most remarkable case is the prose paraphrase of the opening of the *Iliad, R.* III.393d–394a; cf. also the speech of Pausanias *Smp.* 180c–185c, the demonstration of the immortality of the soul *Phdr.* 245c–246a, and the Nuptial Number *R.* VIII.545d–547a.

Such anomalies remind us of the elusiveness of stylistic criteria in determining the *inauthenticity* of particular passages or works. I have expressed my personal opinion regarding the spuria above, p. 12 f. The lack of stylistic traits normally found in Plato's dialogues affords some cumulative arguments for spuriousness, though such a lack has to be considered with the greatest caution. In general the writings here regarded as spurious show notable anomalies in the BABAB structure and in the corresponding shifts of style; a lack of central culmination (though *see Hipparch., Alc.* 1, *Sis., Erx.*); and a lack of subtlety in the variations of style, notably in stylistic characterization.³⁵² As a rule only the four first classes of style occur; and there are no traces of Platonic onkos, except in some passages in the letters, that remotely recall it.

In the Introduction I warned against a mechanical application of stylometry, and the subsequent pages should have made it abundantly clear that the conventional methods of statistical measurement are of little use with an author such as Plato, who constantly and deliberately changes his style from passage to passage and from work to work. Indeed, as we have seen, the stylistic range

---

351. Cf. the observations of Vicaire 1960: 352–362: Plato aimed at an 'ideal rhetoric.' Cf. also Morrow 1953.

352. Among the works here regarded as spurious stylistic characterization occurs in *Hp.Ma., Thg.,* and possibly as occasional traits in *Hipparch., Amat.* and *Clit.* In *Hp.Ma.* and *Thg.* this feature is rather overdone; in the former writing it even extends to an anonymous person. D. Tarrant 1938 points out that the Socrates of the spurious works is rather more "Socratic" than "Platonic."

[172] as a whole seems in most works to be a product of deliberate choice. It may therefore be asked whether the problem of Platonic *chronology* can receive any additional illumination at all from the study of style. To be sure, the "late group" that was established by Campbell and Dittenberger (*Ti., Criti., Sph., Plt., Phlb., Lg.*; add *Ep.* 7 and *Epin.*) stands out by its onkos mannerism. And assuming, as a general trend, a development towards an increasing complexity of style, it seems possible to assign the dialogues with the simplest style to an early period, and the more complex dialogues with no or little onkos to a middle period. But can we, by methods of stylistic analysis, proceed beyond these banal, long-since accepted considerations? I am not sure we can. Not even the relative degree of onkos present in a work is a sufficient criterion of its proximity to the late group. *Prm.* has no onkos, though both the contents and the literary and intellectual style indicate a fairly late date. And once we begin to reduce the importance

[173] of the traditional criterion of "affinity to the late style," and assume that Plato largely chose his styles at will, we have to face anew the question of the relative date of such anomalous works as *Cra.* and *Tht.*, and ultimately the relative date of all of Plato's writings. The order suggested above (p. 16 ff.) as a working hypothesis is only one of many possibilities at the present state of our knowledge. Platonic chronology is still quite unstable. Next we should need a reasonably solid hypothesis constructed primarily on considerations of the contents.

I have tried not to lose sight of the relevance of stylistic studies to the *interpretation* of Plato. The present work can give little aid in details, but I hope it will provoke a discussion of Plato's styles and lead to further analyses of them, with special regard to the understanding of what Plato wrote and why he wrote as he did. On one point, however, I believe the preceding pages have given sufficient evidence. The changes of style make it clear that Plato's dialogues up to the late period always imply a tension between two or several aspects, and at the same time tensions between reasoning and persuasion and play and seriousness. Even the central visions or the other seemingly serious non-mimetic passages do not represent unambiguously the whole truth as Plato saw it. To Plato, writing was play. His writings in fact are dramatic plays where the drama or the tension as such is often more essential than the position of the individual actors. In the late works the tension between the speakers and between the different aspects vanishes while the tension between Plato and his audience remains: they appeal to the reader through devices of psychagogy. If the study of Plato's styles can teach us something about the overtones and the undertones of what Plato said, it should also teach us something about the tensions from which his philosophy arose.

# Studies in Platonic Chronology

# PREFACE

The present book has grown out of an ever-increasing dissatisfaction with the conventional and current solutions as regards the dating of the Platonic dialogues. Since I published my *Studies in the Styles of Plato* (1967) I have revised my opinion in these matters very thoroughly.

'Stylometry' as it has been traditionally practiced, seems to me now more suspect than ever previously. And, as many scholars have seen and some admit, skillful 'interpretation' of the philosophical contents can be adduced to 'prove' or endorse almost anything and to 'indicate' almost any order for the Platonic dialogues. To this general skepticism of what have been regarded as important, basically sound and mutually independent criteria, I would add a series of theses of which the most controversial are probably the following: we have to accept partial 'revision' and 'semi-authenticity' for some dialogues; and the 'Socratic' tenor or brevity or simplicity of a dialogue is no sure indication of earliness.

Part I of the book is mainly concerned with criticism. Part II attempts to sketch a new model and test it from various angles. Here the juxtaposition of somehow related dialogues, two at a time, however tedious this may be, appears in some cases to provide useful suggestions as to the order of composition. But certainly this 'method of confrontation' is by no means more reliable than any other method applied in isolation.

I am well aware that very much of what I say has been said in print before, tens or hundreds of times; it is merely the conclusions that do not appear to have been drawn. I have attempted to record in the footnotes such studies as deal with the point in question in a fresh or comprehensive or, from my point of view, particularly interesting manner. Of one or several dozens of useful passages, one or two had to be selected. More aggravating than the inevitable subjectivity of this selection is the possibility that I may have missed essential counter-arguments or long-since published refutations of what I assert. If this should happen, I can at least comfort myself with the feeling of being in very good company.

If this book, with its 'critical' and its 'hypothetical' part, its recurrent patterns of analysis, its *non liquet's* (and, alas, its awkward style), suggests to the reader a bad imitation of the *Parmenides*, I may perhaps express the hope that it will also, somewhat in the manner of that dialogue, contribute to keeping alive a discussion about the fundaments of alleged truths.

University of Helsinki, September 1981

# PART I

## THE 'PLATONIC QUESTION'

### Introductory notes

The story of the earlier phases of what is sometimes called the 'Platonic Question'[1] has been told many times over. Taken in a wide sense, this question involves not only the chronological order in which Plato is thought to have written his dialogues—a problem not perceived or considered worth solving before Tennemann posed it in 1792—but problems of authenticity and interpretation as well. An essential aspect of the Question is connected with the old, and recently revived, discussion of whether the philosophy of Plato can be considered a systematic whole of which the dialogues and the indirect traditions provide different viewpoints, or perhaps different levels, or whether his doctrines underwent important changes reflected in the dialogues.

The best general surveys of the history of this discussion are the following:

— Lutoslawski 1897: 35–63, 73–140 (concentrating on the discussion of chronology and on studies of Plato's language and style).
— Raeder 1905: 2–19 (a much briefer but somewhat better balanced survey of the whole problem and its history).
— Chevalier 1914: 193–222 (rather similar to Raeder's exposé).
— Ritter 1921: 44–227 (a detailed presentation of 'stylometrical' research since Campbell 1867 and Dittenberger 1881, with criticism); 1922, 1933 (concentrating on more recent studies of chronology).
— Geffcken II A 1934: 137–144 (a well-informed, personally drawn sketch of the main lines).

---

1. As a slogan, 'Die platonische Frage' seems to have been first coined on the model of 'Die homerische Frage' (in fact very different); cf. Schöne (1862), and G. Teichmüller (1876) and A. Krohn (1878) in polemics against the authority of Eduard Zeller.

[2] —Leisegang 1950: 2365–2376 (a brief survey of the discussion from antiquity to Ritter (1935)).
—Tigerstedt 1974 (a learned exposé of the history of the interpretation of Plato from Augustine to Hegel); 1977 (polemics against tendencies, from the early 19th century to modern times, to interpret Plato systematically or esoterically).

Additional references can be found in Ueberweg-Praechter, Totok-Schröer, Guthrie IV–V, and the two recent bibliographical source collections which cover most of the ground from the 1940s onwards, viz. Cherniss 1959–1960 (a systematic presentation of the literature on Plato 1950–1957 including a great number of earlier works) especially 62–68, 249–260, and Brisson 1979 (alphabetical bibliography for the years 1958–1975, with a systematic index).[2]

## Some trends

A few words may suffice here to delineate the rise and, indeed, development of the 'Platonic Question' in the 19th century.

In Germany and countries under German cultural influence the discussion was dominated by reactions against the authority of Schleiermacher (1804) and later Zeller (from 1846 onwards) who both preferred a moderately systematic interpretation of Plato with little consideration of questions of chronology. Following Tennemann's hints, a new historical and genetic approach had been introduced by Socher (1820) and was developed by several scholars among whom K. F. Hermann (1839), F. Susemihl (1855–1860) and F. Ueberweg (1861) deserve particular mention. Especially when Dittenberger had shown (1881, without knowledge of Campbell 1867) that some dialogues—among them the *Sophist* and *Politicus* which had been classed by Zeller in the early 'Megarian' period—contained a number of linguistic characteristics in common with the *Laws* and, hence, were likely to be late, the more advanced and positivistically oriented scholars of the age felt that an independent, objectively traceable criterion of chronology had finally been discovered. The systematic interpretation of Plato now began to be regarded as definitely old-fashioned, and the genetic view—also otherwise typical of the century—gained the upper hand. Although there was not much agreement as regards the details, most scholars (including Zeller) accepted that there must have been a fundamental development in Plato's thought, and it was commonly believed that this development had found direct expression in the dialogues.

---

2. Among cumulative *bibliographies raisonnées* of a more limited or otherwise specialized scope, the following may be mentioned: the reviews by F. Susemihl in the first volumes of the *Jahresbericht über die Fortschritte der classischen Alterthumswissenschaft (Bursian)* 1873–1880 and C. Ritter ibid 161, 1913: (1) 1–72; 220, 1929: (1) 37–108; 225, 1930: (1) 121–168; cf. id. 1921–1923 (above); De Corte 1938; Simeterre 1945; Schuhl 1953; Paleikat 1956–1959; Rosenmeyer 1957; Manasse 1957, 1961, 1976; McKirahan 1973; Lasso de la Vega 1975. *L'Année Philologique* is of course an indispensable tool.

So the order in which Plato wrote his dialogues had become a problem both important and possible to solve.

Outside the German sphere of influence there was no 'Platonic Question.' Plato and Platonism were as a rule interpreted along inherited lines, and little attention was paid to questions of dating or authenticity. Even Grote's well-informed, historically founded and penetrating work on Plato and his environment reflects an obvious reluctance to deal with the problem of the chronological order of the dialogues (I 1865: 185–205, cf. 280). And when Campbell (1867), in a careful analysis of the language, form and contents of some of the dialogues, established the 'late group' by their affinity to the *Laws*—anticipating the results of Dittenberger in a much more substantial work—this was generally accepted, somewhat casually, as a fact which did not affect the interpretation of Plato very seriously. One exception is the rather influential series of articles by Jackson (1882–1886, 1897) on the development of the theory of Forms seen in the perspective of Campbell's discovery. On the whole, however, British scholars, like their French colleagues, were not interested in the ontogenesis of Plato's philosophy.

It is unquestionably due to the energetic efforts of one person, the πολυθρύλητος Pole Vincent Lutoslawski (1897),[3] that the 'Platonic Question' suddenly became a challenge to international scholarship around the turn of the century. At the same time, the problem received new dimensions. Whatever one thinks of Lutoslawski's curious method of 'stylometry' (below, p. 213), it inaugurated a prolonged debate and occasioned, directly or indirectly, a considerable amount of research into the problems of Platonic chronology and, also, authenticity.

Lutoslawski encountered severe criticism from the start. But basically his view won a fairly general acceptance. He had argued that it is possible to arrange the authentic dialogues in a chronological series in accordance with linguistic and other criteria, and that the linguistic criteria are on the whole to be given preference when other 'objective' indications are absent. This view gradually became a commonplace to students of Plato after it had received the sanction of the influential Th. Gomperz (1902), and since the large-scale investigations into Platonic chronology by Raeder (1905) and Ritter (particularly from 1910 onwards) tended to give it ever more backing. It is true that some further discredit was reflected on the mechanical application of 'stylometry' by the excesses of von Arnim (1912) whose laboriously worked-out statistics of Plato's use of formulae of assent puzzled and irritated contemporary scholars. However, even skeptics were not totally averse to the basic premises and results of stylometry. This can be seen for instance in the controversy between Pohlenz and von Arnim concerning

---

3. His main work on Platonic chronology, rather misleadingly called *The Origin and Growth of Plato's Logic*, was accompanied by a number of lectures and articles in Polish, French and German. It is in many respects sad to read the grossly unfair verdict of Wilamowitz (II 1920: 8):" ... Es kam auch einer aus dem baltischen Russland [!], fuhr durch die ganze Welt und suchte sich als den aufzuspielen, der mit seiner (d. h. der von den andern gefundenen und aufgewandten) Methode die "platonische Frage" auf einen Schlag lösen würde. Aber das war kein Meteor, sondern ein Papierballon, der nur so lange leuchtete, bis er abgebrannt war."

[4] the chronological order of Plato's early dialogues (1913–1921) where the former took the position of the skeptic and the latter that of the believer.[4]

Above all, the influence of Ritter's painstaking, detailed and very positivistic (though sometimes compromising) considerations of Platonic chronology in his book on Plato (1910) and in his later studies and presentations can easily be traced in much that was written on Plato during the following thirty or forty years. The reliability of Ritter's conception and of his results is on the whole taken for granted in the much-read German standard works of this period, Wilamowitz' book on Plato (1919, 1920),[5] Hoffmann's Appendix to the fifth edition of Zeller's *Geschichte* II 1 (1922),[6] Praechter's thorough revision of Ueberweg's presentation of ancient philosophy (1925), Friedländer's *Platon* (1930, 1954–), Geffcken's learned chapters on Plato in his *Griechische Literaturgeschichte* (II 1934), and Leisegang's article on Plato in the RE (1950, though apparently written much earlier). And Ritter's influence extended far outside Germany. It is manifestly present in the widely known books on Plato by Taylor (1926), Grube (1935), Stefanini (1932), and Robin (1938, cf. id. 1908). To a lesser extent the same applies to Diès (especially *Autour de Platon* 1927 which includes his important essay of 1913 on 'Transposition') and Schaerer (1938) and also to Guthrie (1975).

As a matter of fact, the dominant view among scholars of the 20th century up to the present day can be characterized as a general siding with the 'Lutoslawski-Raeder-Ritter thesis' which implied (a) that the dialogues reflect trends of development in Plato's thought, and (b) that a close study of Plato's style and linguistic practice offers important independent clues to the order in which Plato wrote his dialogues. But the emphasis is variously placed by various scholars, and there is little positive agreement with regard to the details of the chronological problems. Examples of unresolved points at issue are: the question of whether Plato wrote dialogues before the death of Socrates in 399 BCE (*see* p. 171); the grouping and the order of the earlier dialogues, and in particular the place of *Phaedrus* and *Lysis*, and also that of *Theaetetus* and *Symposium*; the unity of the *Republic*; the place of *Cratylus*;[7] the place of *Timaeus* and *Critias*[8] and in general the order of the late dialogues; and the authenticity of *Ion, Hippias Major, Alcibiades* I, *Laws, Epinomis*, the *Letters*, particularly the important *7th Epistle*, and occasionally of other works.

[5] Comparatively few extensive or penetrating new discussions of Platonic chronology have appeared since the Second World War. Apart from the *Timaeus*

---

4. The controversy was never solved. It is perhaps worth noting that both von Arnim and Pohlenz later deserted Plato for the study of Stoicism!

5. It is characteristic that Pohlenz, who was no friend of stylometry, in his review of Wilamowitz' book (1921) criticized details of the order of presentation, without, however, questioning the underlying general conception of chronology.

6. Zeller's own position of 1888 is still given here below, pp. 496–507.

7. Beginning with Warburg's attack (1929) on the comparatively early date assigned to it by the stylometrists.

8. Beginning with Owen's thesis (1953) that they are earlier than stylometry indicates; *see* the recapitulation of the controversy by Prior 1975 and below, p. 335.

controversy (above), the most interesting or original contributions are Brandwood's critical summary of stylometric research (1958), the studies of Vollenhoven (1948), Boehme (1959), and Ryle (1966), all very eccentric, Kapp (1968), and the sections on chronological problems in Guthrie's two volumes on Plato (IV 1975, V 1978). More commonly scholars tend to accept, more or less vaguely and without insisting on certainty as to details, the general lines of the chronology given in current reference works, i.e. essentially the three chronological groups implied by the Lutoslawski-Raeder-Ritter view (Early period—Middle period with the *Symposium, Phaedo, Republic, Phaedrus, Theaetetus*—Late period with the *Parmenides*, the *Sophist, Politicus, Philebus, Timaeus, Critias* and *Laws*), and to present or argue for various lines of development within this general frame. In this way the conventional chronology has received an appearance of a continuously growing solidity. The conspectus below (p. 154) will include typical examples of this approach.

The combination of a genetic approach with a fundamental disagreement with the results of stylometry, which was typical of some conservatives around the turn of the century,[9] has not, as far as I can see, recurred since the 1920s.

Against this general, often passive and tacit, acceptance of the genetic view of the dialogues as essentially reflecting Plato's 'development,' there came first the vigorous and intelligent unitarian attack of Shorey in his 'Unity of Plato's Thought' (1903, somewhat modified in 1933). So well-established and deeply-rooted, however, was the genetic conviction by now that Shorey's points met with very little response, even in English-speaking countries, before the 1950s. On the other hand, a kind of passive resistance against the predominant view was propagated by Apelt: in the widely read German translation of Plato, with extensive and well-informed commentaries, which was published under his editorship (1913–1919), he obviously attempted to avoid the problems of chronology.[10]

At about the same time a clear unitarian approach, minimizing the importance of chronology, was adopted by Stenzel (1916 and later studies), who also, in various connections, called attention to the problem of Plato's oral teaching being perhaps independent of the written dialogues. Somewhat similar attempts to return to a systematic interpretation of Plato were made or suggested by Jaeger (1928), Solmsen (1929a: 239 ff.), H. Gomperz (1921), Goldschmidt (1947) and other French scholars, Schilling (1948), and Lodge (1953).

In partial agreement with this unitarian party of 'opposition,' but drawing on many other sources as well, there arose in the 1950s the much-debated

---

9. Notably Windelband 1894 cf. 1923; Waddington 1904, Horn 1904, Joël 1907; cf. also Zeller who with some reluctance had accepted a genetic view of Plato, and Natorp 1900, also 1903. A somewhat later exponent is Parmentier 1913.

10. Cf. also his critical review (1908) of Raeder 1905. Apparently for similar reasons the original plan of the Budé edition did not agree with the Lutoslawski-Raeder-Ritter view; cf. M. Croiset 1921: 10–13; severe criticism by Raeder 1925. The ancient tetralogical arrangement adopted by Burnet (1901) probably reflects the general caution of the Oxford editors rather than a disbelief in the genetic view.—It may be noted here that von Arnim (*see* especially 1914: III–IV), in spite of his efforts to arrange the dialogues chronologically on stylometric grounds, was in sympathy with the unitarian view.

[6] 'Tübingen School.'[11] Its chief concerns have been (as every student of Plato knows today) the 'unwritten doctrines' of the First Principles and other metaphysical aspects of Plato's thought. The champions of this school, Gaiser and Krämer, began expounding their theories in works dealing with protreptic trends in Plato's dialogues (Gaiser 1955, 1959) and his conception of virtue (Krämer 1957, 1959). At first the full consequences of the Tübingen theories to the question of chronology were not clearly seen. Both Gaiser and Krämer adopted conventional datings for the dialogues, though they argued from a rather unitarian point of view.[12] If, however, Plato did in fact set forth a separate doctrine in oral communication, and indirect glimpses of it can be found even in supposedly 'early' dialogues such as *Lysis*, and if, therefore, Plato's 'development' may have followed other lines than that which the Lutoslawski-Raeder-Ritter view implies,[13] then the Tübingen theory seems to call for a total reconsideration of the 'Platonic Question.' Oehler (1965) was the first to argue this, and other scholars have been inclined to think in the same way (e.g. Findlay 1974: ix f.). But even if Gaiser and Krämer were wrong in suggesting a separate unwritten doctrine at a comparatively early date, they have at any rate collected sufficient evidence of oral communication in the Academy, and have evoked enough problems relating to the function of the written dialogues, to motivate a reassessment of the Question. As will be seen below, other reasons also exist to justify such an undertaking.

[7] Many 'neo-unitarians' seem to be to some extent dependent on the Tübingen school. This does not perhaps apply to Rosamund Kent Sprague who in an article (1976) expressed sympathy with Shorey's unitarianism.[14] More clearly it applies

---

11. The existence of an oral doctrine independent of, or not directly reflected in the dialogues, had been vehemently denied e.g. by Zeller (II 1$^5$ 484–487) and later notably by Cherniss (1944, 1945: 1–30). Among earlier believers in a separate oral teaching by Plato which would include the notorious lecture or lectures 'On the Good,' note Hermann 1849 (*see* Gaiser 1969: 34 ff.), Ueberweg 1861: 207 ff., Shorey 1903: 82 ff., 1933: 58 ff., Robin 1908, Stenzel and Solmsen (above), H. Gomperz 1931, Findlay (*see* 1974: IX), Wilpert 1941, Bröcker 1949, de Vogel 1949. For details, *see* the survey published by Wippern 1972; cf. below, n. 13, and Szlezák 1978, 1979.

12. Cf. e.g. Gaiser 1959: 106 ff., 160 ff., 1963: 15, Krämer 1959: 29 ff. But note the interesting admission of Krämer 1964a: 94 that the dialogues do not primarily reflect a development of thought: "Die Abfolge der platonischen Schriften steht primär unter anderen: didaktischen, protreptischen, künstlerischen Gesetzen, die in ihrer Eihentümlichkeit eine besondere Erforschung verdienen." The same has been later repeated e.g. Gaiser 1969: XI f., 1980a: 29 n. 6. For recent restatements of the Tübingen position, *see* Gaiser 1980ab, Krämer 1980, especially 33–38.

13. The, in part, excessively destructive criticism directed against the Tübingen school has not managed to refute these possibilities. *See* e.g. Happ 1971: 85–208 and the remarks of Szlezák 1978. Scholars who have found the theory fundamentally perverse include Cherniss (obviously, though he did not personally enter on polemics), Vlastos 1963, von Fritz 1966, 1967, Dönt 1967, Allen 1970: 130–145, Tack 1970, Graeser 1974, Tigerstedt 1977; Guthrie V 418–442 takes a pronouncedly circumspect attitude. Various points of detail have been discussed critically by Perpeet 1962: 262 ff., Voigtländer 1963a, Berti 1964, 1965, Ilting 1968, Isnardi Parente 1969, 1970, Niewöhner 1971, Thurnher 1975. *See* the reply of Krämer 1980.—For the specific problem of the 'On the Good,' *see* below p. 201.

e.g. to Gundert 1968,[15] Findlay 1974, Joly 1974, and some recent 'esoterists' of other colors such as Meissner 1978.

As a general trend in the interpretation of Plato in the last ten or twenty years, there is a clearly noticeable emphasis of the fact that Plato very often seems to 'know more,' and expects his audience to 'know more,' than what is actually said in the dialogue. And this of course is a fact of considerable consequence to the handling of the chronological arguments drawn from the contents of the dialogues.[16]

A post-script reference should be made here to the article of Kahn 1981, 'Did Plato Write Socratic Dialogues?'

## Conspectus of chronologies suggested

For the reader's convenience, and in order to illustrate the multifarious trends in the history of the Platonic Question, I shall give here a list of various chronologies suggested since Tennemann. From the 19th century I have only selected some typical examples. From Lutoslawski onwards the list is intended to include all original contributions where the chronological order of several dialogues is discussed with explicit argumentation; discussions of the place of only one or two dialogues will not be taken into account here. In addition, the list includes a strictly limited selection of (a) chronologies suggested rather by implicit argumentation (cf. p. 186), (b) chronologies given with little or no new or independent argumentation, and (c) other attitudes to Platonic chronology which might be of some interest for the present purpose.

It hardly needs pointing out that the list cannot aim at even approximate completeness except for the most important contributions of the first-mentioned kind. Anybody who has glanced at the sections on Plato in the *L'Année Philologique* will understand why.

For the same reason it should be obvious that the great majority of the scholars listed below have to a very limited extent taken account of earlier studies. Already Lutoslawski (73) complained that writers on Plato are "generally unaware of the work of their predecessors." The situation has not changed very much in the past ninety years. This fact, and in general the lack of cumulative linearity in the progress of research of this kind, perhaps will also justify the printing of the list here: a later study is not necessarily closer to the truth than an earlier one.

---

14. There also occur varieties of unitarianism, such as that of. K. Friis Johansen (1964, in Danish) who attempted to combine the ideas of 'unity' and 'development,' or that of Kahn (1976: 22 f.) who revived the old idea of regarding all of the 'early' dialogues as in various ways preparing the way for the *Republic* (*see* now id. 1981).

15. Though in his book of 1971 Gundert accepted the three traditional chronological groups.

16. This concerns above all the dialogues traditionally considered as 'early'; *see* below p. 191.

[8] In many of the instances below the order given is not meant to be strictly chronological, and the degree of an author's conviction of being right is not easily ascertainable. Hence, the list is intended only for a general orientation. If some dialogues are apparently or obviously included in a chronologically undifferentiated group, they are separated by a comma (,); if they are meant to follow in a certain chronological order, they are separated by a dash (—).

> Tennemann 1792 (according to Ueberweg 1861: 7–12): *Ly, La, Chrm, Hipparch, Ion, HpMi, HpMa, Euthd, Prt*, perhaps *Thg, Amat, Alc 1, Alc 2, Cra* (all before the death of Socrates)—*Ap, Cri, Phd, Men* (soon after the death of S.)—*Grg*—*Tht*—*Sph, Plt, Phlb, Prm*—*Smp, Phdr, Mx*—*R, Criti, Ti, Lg, Epin.*
> Considering mainly external events in Plato's life.
> Schleiermacher 1804: *Phdr, Prt, Prm*—*Ly, La, Chrm, Euthphr* (all before the death of S.)—*Ap, Cri*—perhaps *Ion, HpMi, Hipparch, Min, Alc 2*—*Tht, Sph, Plt, Phd, Phlb*—*Grg, Men, Euthd, Cra, Smp*—perhaps *Thg, Amat, Alc 1, Mx, HpMa, Clit*—*R, Ti, Criti*—*Lg.*
> Considering various criteria but emphasizing their unreliability; attempting to extract the "natürliche Folge" of the dialogues from a slightly unitarian point of view.
> Socher 1820: *Thg, La, HpMi, Alc 1, Virt, Men, Cra, Euthphr* (all before the death of S.)—*Ap, Cri, Phd*—*Ion, Euthd, HpMa, Prt, Tht, Grg, Phlb* (before the foundation of the Academy)—*Phdr, Mx, Smp, R, Ti*—*Lg.*
> Considering Plato's philosophical development.
> Hermann 1839: *HpMi, Ion, Alc 1, Chrm, Ly, La, Prt, Euthd* (before 399)—*Ap, Cri, Grg, Euthphr, Men, HpMa*—*Cra, Tht, Sph, Plt, Prm* (before 387)—*Phdr*—*Mx, Smp, Phd, Phlb, R, Ti, Criti, Lg.*
> Considering various points of contents, external reference, and hypothetical changes in Plato's activities.
> Susemihl 1855: *HpMi*—*Ly*—*Chrm*—*La*—*Prt*—*Men* (399)—*Ap*—*Cri*—*Euthphr*—*Euthd*—*Cra*—*Tht*—*Phdr*—*Sph*—*Plt*—*Prm*—*Smp* (soon after 384)—*Phd*—*Phlb*—*R*—*Ti*—*Criti* (before the second voyage to Sicily)—later teaching—*Lg.*
> Considering a wealth of external and internal evidence, and a hypothesis of stages in Plato's development.
> Ueberweg 1861: *HpMi, Ly, La, Chrm, Prt* (before 399)—*Ap, Cri, Grg, R* (first version) (before 387)—*Men, Mx, Phdr, R* (second version)—*Ti, Criti, Smp, Phd, Euthd, Cra* (before 366)—*Tht*—*Sph, Plt, Phlb, Lg.*
> Critical discussion of predecessors; proceeding on the same lines as Hermann.
> Schöne 1862: *Lg* (though posthum.publ.), *Cra, Tht, Sph, Plt, Phlb, Ti, Criti, Men, Phdr*—*Mx, Ap, Cri, Grg, La*—*Chrm, Prt, Smp, Prm, R, Phd.*
> Taking artistic 'perfection' as a sign of relative lateness.
> Ribbing 1863 (Swedish edition 1858): *Phdr, Prt, Chrm, La, Euthphr, Ap, Cri*—*Grg, Tht, Men, Euthd, Cra, Sph, Plt, Prm*—*Smp, Phd, Phlb*—*R*—*Ti, Criti.*
> Based on a reassessment of the views of some predecessors.
> Grote 1865: *Ap*—*Cri*—*Euthphr*—*Alc 1*—*Alc 2*—*HpMa*—*HpMi*—*Hipparch*—*Min*—*Thg*—*Amat*—*Ion*—*La*—*Chrm*—*Ly*—*Euthd*—*Men*—*Prt*—*Grg*—*Phd*—*Phdr*—*Smp*—*Prm*—*Tht*—*Sph*—*Plt*—*Cra*—*Phlb*—*Mx*—*Clit*—*R*—*Ti*—*Criti*—*Lg*—*Epin.*
> Considering external and internal evidence and generally siding with Hermann against Schleiermacher, but emphasizing that Platonic chronology admits of no solution.

[9] Campbell 1867: Linguistic and other evidence for separating the late group, tentatively with the following order: *Sph*—*Plt*—*Phlb*—*Ti*—*Criti*—*Lg.*

Teichmüller 1879: Reported dialogues, *Phd, R, Smp, Euthd, Chrm, Prt—Tht—Cra, Plt, Phdr,* [9]
*Phlb, Men, Sph, Grg (Prm)* and other dramatic dialogues.
  Taking the dialogue technique as a criterion.
Dittenberger 1881: Early dialogues, *Phd—Smp, Ly, Phdr, R, Tht—Prm, Phlb, Ti, Criti, Sph, Plt, Lg.*
  Considering use of μήν and καθάπερ.
Jackson 1882–1886: Early dialogues—*R—Phlb—Prm—Ti—Tht—Sph—Plt—Lg.*
  Following Campbell, considering the development of the theory of Forms.
Schanz 1886: Early dialogues, *Ly—Euthd, Smp, Phdr, R, Tht—Phlb, Sph, Plt, Lg.*
  Considering the use of various adverbs (ὄντως etc.); on the whole agreeing with Dittenberger.
Ritter 1888: Early dialogues—*Phd, Euthd, Cra, Smp, (Ly,* if genuine*)—R, Phdr, Tht, (Prm,* if genuine*)—Sph—Plt—Ti—Criti—Phlb—Lg.*
  Summing up results of earlier linguistic studies in Germany and adding new material.
Pfleiderer (1888) 1896: *HpMi* (?), *La, Chrm, Ly—Prt* (before 399)—*R* (1st version)—*Ap, Cri, Euthphr—Grg, Men, Phdr, R* (additions), *Tht, Cra, Sph, Plt, Euthd, Prm—R* (additions)—*Phd, Smp—Ti, Criti, Phlb, Lg.*
  Considering hypotheses of Plato's philosophical development and the gradual accretion of the *Republic*.
Campbell 1896: Early dialogues—*Phdr, Tht, Prm, R*—late group.
  Adding new linguistic and other evidence.
Baron 1897: *Chrm, HpMa, Cri—Prt, Alc 1, Ap—Ion, Cra, Phd, Euthphr, La—Smp, Grg, Men, Euthd—Tht, R, Phdr—Ti, Criti, Sph, Plt, Phlb, Lg.*
  Siding with stylometry (cf. Lutoslawski 1897); considering the use of περί.
Lutoslawski 1897: *Euthpr—Ap—Cri—Chrm—La—Prt—Men—Euthd—Grg—Cra—Smp—Phd—R—Phdr—Tht—Prm—Sph—Plt—Phlb—Ti—Criti—Lg.*
  Comprehensive criticism of earlier discussions of chronology; application of the new method of 'stylometry' (below, p. 213).
Immisch 1899: *HpMa—HpMi—Ion—Phdr* (403)—*Prt—Grg* (soon after 399)—*Ap—Cri—Euthphr—Men* (ca. 395)—*Cra—R* (1st version)—*La* (ca. 387)—*Euthd—Mx—Chrm—Ly—R* (additions)—*Smp* (after 384)—*Phd—R* (final ed. after 366)—*Tht—Prm* (after 361)—*Phlb, Sph, Plt, Ti, Criti, Lg.*
  Critical of Lutoslawski but accepting earlier linguistic arguments; various additional arguments including theories of revision.
Zeller 1900: Review of von Arnim 1896 (*see* id. 1912), critical of the results of stylometry.
Janell 1901a: Late group *Sph, Plt, Ti, Criti, Phlb, Lg* characterized by the avoidance of hiatus; traces of this tendency in parts of *Phdr* indicates revision.
Trense 1901: Late group *Tht—Sph—Plt—Phlb—Ti—Criti—Lg* characterized by high frequency of adjective attributes, particularly in the post-position; the percentages suggest the above order.
Benn 1902: Early dialogues—*R—Phdr—Prm, Tht* (?)—*Sph, Plt, Phlb—Ti, Criti—Lg.*
  Considering the development of ontology, accepting the results of Lutoslawski.
Bovet 1902: Development of theology tends to confirm the results of Lutoslawski.
Eberz 1902–1912: Order of late dialogues *Phlb—Prm—Tht—Sph—Plt—Ti—Criti—Lg.*
  Considering references to contemporary events.
Th. Gomperz 1902: *HpMi—La—Chrm—Prt* (before 399)—*Grg—Euthphr—Men—Ly—Smp—* [10]
*Phdr—Phd—Mx—Cri—R—Euthd—Prm—Tht—Cra—Sph—Plt—Phlb—Ti—Criti—Lg.*
  Accepting stylometry on the whole, but arguing mainly from the contents of the dialogues and external evidence, without insisting on a strict chronology.

[10] Blass 1903: Order of late dialogues *Phlb, Lg* (though posthum.ed.)—*Sph—Plt—Ti—Criti*.
Various considerations including inferences from the results of Janell 1901.
Natorp 1903: *Ap—Cri—Prt—La—Chrm—Men* (395/4)—*Grg—Phdr—Tht—Euthd—Cra—Phd—Smp—R—Prm—Sph—Plt—Phlb—Ti—Lg*.
Skeptical of stylometry, arguing mainly from a Neo-Kantian view of the development of Plato's thought, in particular of the theory of Forms.
Shorey 1903: A violent and well-documented attack upon the genetic approach and the methods of the chronological studies of Plato, minimizing their importance and possibilities.
Horn (1893) 1904: *Ly—Chrm—Euthd—Phdr—Men—La—Prt—Grg—Cra—Prm—Tht—Sph—Plt—R—Smp—Phd—Ti—Lg*.
Skeptical of stylometry, arguing loosely but with a wealth of details from a personal view of the development of Plato's thought.
Kaluscha 1904: Order of late dialogues *Ti—Criti—Sph—Plt—Phlb—Lg*.
Considering the rhythm patterns of clausulae.
Waddington 1904: *Ap* and most 'Socratic' works of the Corpus—*Cra—Tht—Prm—Sph, Plt—Phlb—Men—Phdr, Smp, Grg—Cri, Euthphr, Clit; Phd, R, Ti—Hipparch, Min; Lg*.
Mainly based upon the hypothesis of a Socratic period and considering the development of the theory of Forms.
Raeder 1905: *Ap—Ion—HpMi—La—Chrm—Cri—HpMa—Prt—Grg—Mx, Euthphr, Men, Euthd, Cra—Ly—Smp—Phd—R—Phdr—Tht—Prm—Sph—Plt—Phlb—Ti—Criti—Lg—Epin*.
Comprehensive discussion of various types of argument; the results of stylometry combined positivistically and by way of compromises with other considerations.
Apelt 1908: Critical review of Raeder 1905, expressing far-going scepticism of his compromising method.
Robin 1908a: *Ly—Smp—Phd—Phdr*.
Considering the advance in the theory of love and other points.
Goedeckemeyer 1909: 'Socratic' period—*Tht—Men—Phdr—Euthd—Cra—Smp—R* (1st part)—*Prm—Sph—Plt—Phd—R* (2nd part)—*Ti—Criti—Phlb—Lg*.
Considering mainly evolution of thought; skepticalof stylometry.
Olzscha 1910: *HpMi—HpMa—Ly—Chrm—La—Euthphr* (399)—*Ap—Cri—Prt—Grg—Men—Euthd (Cra?)—Tht—Phdr—Smp—Phd—R—Prm—Ti—Criti—Sph—Plt—Phlb—Lg*.
Considering evolution of theory of virtue.
Ritter 1910b (1923): *HpMi—La—Prt—Chrm—Euthphr* (399)—*Ap—Cri—Grg* (ca. 390)—*Men—Euthd—Cra—Mx, HpMa* (if authentic), *Ly—Smp* (ca. 384)—*Phd—R—Phdr—Tht* (369/8)—*Prm* (366)—*Sph—Plt—Ti—Criti—Phlb—Lg*.
Comprehensive discussion, adding a wealth of fresh observations; emphasizing the importance of stylometry.
von Arnim (1896) 1912: *Ion, Prt—La, R I, Ly, Chrm, Euthphr—Euthd, Grg, Men, HpMi, Cra—Smp (?), HpMa—Phd—R II—X—Tht—Prm—Phdr—Sph—Plt—Phlb—Lg* (not discussing the place of *Ap, Cri, Ti, Criti* owing to lack of material).
Considering statistics of the formulae of assent.
[11] Apelt 1913–1919: *Prt—La—Euthphr—Ap—Cri—Grg—Men—Cra—Phd—Phdr—Euthd—HpMi—HpMa—Ion—Alc 1—Alc 2—Smp—Chrm—Ly—Mx—Tht—Prm—Phlb—R—Ti—Criti—Sph—Plt—Ep—Lg*.
Skepticalof stylometry, preferring a conservative attitude to chronology; very little argumentation.
Beare 1913: *Ap, Ion, Cri, Min* (?)—*Euthphr—Ly—La, Alc 1* (?), *Alc 2* (?)—*Chrm—HpMi—Euthd—Thg—Men—Cra, Tht, Prm, Sph. Plt* (or possibly later)—*Phd—Grg—Prt—HpMa* (?)—*Phdr—Smp—Phlb—R—Ti, Criti—Lg*.

Considering solely the advance from 'Socratic' intellectual ethics to gradual acceptance of feeling.
Groag 1913–1915: Early dialogues, *Prt, La—Grg—Men, Phd—Smp—Phdr, R—Ti, Plt, Lg.*
Considering the development of psychology.
Kallenberg 1913: Order of late dialogues *Phlb—Sph—Plt—Ti—Criti—Lg—(Epin).*
Considering the use of ὡς and ὅτι in relation to the tendency to avoid hiatus.
Parmentier 1913: No dialogues before 399; *Phdr* after 380; criticism of stylometry; suggesting, as a new criterion, that Plato did not introduce living persons as characters in his dialogues.
Pohlenz 1913: Order of early dialogues *Ap—La—Chrm—HpMi—Prt—Grg—Men—R* (1st version ca 391)*—Mx—Phd—Phdr—Ly—Smp.*
Based on a personal view of Plato's development, considering the contents, external references, and the historical frame; skeptical of the application of stylometry to the early period.
von Arnim 1914: *Prt—La—R I—Ly—Chrm—Euthphr—Euthd—Grg—Men—Smp, Phd—R II—X—Tht—Prm—Phdr—Sph—Plt—Phlb—Ti—Criti—Lg.*
Criticism of Pohlenz 1913 and of the opponents of stylometry; arguments from the contents and hypothesis of the development of Plato's thought supporting order based on stylometry (v. Arnim 1912).
Wundt 1914: *La, Ly, Chrm, HpMi, Prt, Ion, Euthphr* (before death of S.)*—Grg, Men* (after voyages)*—Phdr—Smp.*
A personal view of Plato's development.
Stenzel 1916–1917: Emphasizing the unity of Plato's thought, skeptical of chronological research except for differentiation between dialogues earlier and later than the *Republic*.
Verdam 1916–1919: *Grg* (394/3)*—HpMi, Ion, Ap, Cri, Mx, Euthphr—HpMa* (388)*—Tht—Smp* (384/3)*—Men—Phd—Phdr.*
Considering the hypothetical relations of the writings of Lysias, Polycrates, Isocrates and Plato; followed up by various arguments from the development of Plato's thought.
Cauer 1917/1918: *Prt—Men—Grg.*
Various arguments from the contents, against Th. Gomperz 1902 and Pohlenz 1913.
von Wilamowitz 1919: *Ion—HpMi—Prt* (before 399)*—Ap—Cri—La—Ly—Chrm—Euthphr—R I—Grg—Mx* (386)*—Men—Euthd—Cra—Phd—Smp—R II—X—Phdr—Prm—Tht* (369)*—Sph—Plt—Ti—Criti* (after 360)*—Phlb—Ep 8–Ep 7—Lg—Ep 6.*
A roughly chronological order of presentation, based on a wide range of biographical, historical and literary facts and hypotheses and on a personal view of the development of Plato's personality and thought; on the whole sympathetic towards Ritter's results.
Billig 1920: Order of late works *Ti—Criti—Sph—Plt—Phlb—Lg, Epin, Ep 2, 3, 7, 8.*
Considering statistics of clausulae and some features of the vocabulary.
M. Croiset 1921: *HpMi—Alc 1–Ap—Euthphr—Cri—HpMa—Ly—Chrm—La—Prt—Grg—Men—Phd—Smp—Phdr—Ion—Mx—Euthd—Cra—R—Prm—Tht—Sph—Plt—Phlb—Ti—Criti—Lg—Epin.*
This is the order adopted in the Budé (Collection des Universitaires de France) edition; it is meant to be roughly chronological, though Croiset and most of his colleagues remained skeptical of establishing a detailed order.
Hoffmann 1922 (1950): *Ion—HpMi—Prt—La—Ly—Chrm—Ap—Cri—Euthphr—R I—Grg—Mx—Euthd—Men—Cra—Smp—Phd—R II—X—Phdr—Prm—Tht—Sph—Plt—Phlb—Ti—Criti—Ep 7—Lg.*
A roughly chronological order, on the whole agreeing with Wilamowitz 1919.

[12] Windelband-Goedeckemeyer 1923: *Ap, Cri, Ion, La, R I, Ly, Chrm, Euthphr, Prt, HpMi—Grg, Men, Phdr, Euthd, Cra, Mx, Smp, R* (new version), *Phd, R* (final version)—*Prm, Tht, Sph, Plt, Ti, Criti—Phlb, Lg*.

Ueberweg-Praechter 1925: *Ap—Cri—Prt—Ion—La—R I—Ly—Chrm—Euthphr—Grg* (ca. 390)—*Men—Euthd—HpMa—Cra—HpMi—Mx* (ca. 386)—*Smp—Phd—R II—X* (after 378)—*Phdr—Tht—Prm—Sph—Plt—Phlb—Ti—Criti—Lg—Epin—Ep 7, 8*.

Summing up the results of modern chronological research, emphasizing the uncertainty of some points.

Taylor 1926 (1927): *HpMa—HpMi—Ion—Mx—Chrm—La—Ly—Cra—Euthd—Grg—Men—Euthphr—Ap—Cri—Phd—Smp—Prt—R I—X* (before 387)—*Phdr—Tht, Prm—Sph—Plt—Phlb—Ti—Criti—Lg, Epin—Ep*.

Considering the earlier dialogues largely as historical documents, but skeptical of establishing a detailed order for the dialogues preceding the *Republic*.

Diès 1927: Skeptical criticism of various methods of establishing a chronology, especially of stylometry.

Singer 1927: *Grg—Euthphr—Cri—Prt—Chrm—Ly—Smp—Phd—R—Mx—Euthd, Cra—Tht—Prm—Phdr—Ti, Criti—Sph, Plt, Phlb—Lg*.

Giving a personal view of Plato's development.

Field 1930: Early dialogues—*R I, Grg, Men—Phd, Smp—R II—X, Phdr, Tht, Prm—Sph—Plt—Phlb—Ti—Criti—Lg, Ep*.

Accepting the results of stylometry.

Friedländer 1930 (1954): *Prt—La—R I—Chrm—Euthphr—Ly—HpMa—Hipparch—Ion—Hp. Mi—Thg—Ap—Cri—Euthd—Cra—Mx—Alc 1—Grg—Men—Smp—Phd—R II—X—Tht—Prm—Phdr—Sph—Plt—Phlb—Ti—Criti—Lg, (Epin)*.

A roughly chronological order based on a personal interpretation of Plato's philosophy and also on a wealth of philological data; on the whole accepting stylometry.

Rick 1931: Early dialogues—*Grg* (after 390), *Phdr—Men, Prt, Euthd—Smp—Euthphr, Cra, Phd, Ly, Mx* (before 383).

Considering mainly internal references and supposed polemics with Antisthenes and Isocrates.

Stefanini 1932: *Ap—Cri—La—HpMi—Grg—Alc 1—Men—HpMa—Ion—Cra—Euthphr—Prt—Ly—Chrm—Euthd—Clit—Smp—Phd—R—Phdr—Mx—Tht—Prm—Sph—Plt—Phlb—Ti—Criti—Lg*.

Comprehensive discussion; rough chronology based on considerations of dialogue technique, results of stylometry, and various arguments from the contents.

Hildebrandt 1933 (1959): *Ion, HpMi*—Prt (before 399)—*Ap, Cri—La—Chrm, Ly—R I, Euthphr—Grg* (389)—*Mx—Men* (?)—*Euthd, Cra—Phd—Smp* (379?)—*R II—X—Phdr—Tht* (368?)—*Prm—Sph, Plt—Phlb—Ti, Criti—Lg*.

Interpretation largely following the chronology of Wilamowitz 1919.

[13] Shorey 1933: *Euthphr—Ap—Cri—HpMi—HpMa—Ion—Chrm—La—Ly—Prt—Grg—Men—Euthd—Phd—Mx—Smp—Phdr—R—Cra—Tht—Prm—Sph—Plt—Phlb—Ti—Criti—Lg—Epin*.

A roughly chronological order given without much argument and with general skepticism of the results of chronological research (cf. Shorey 1903).

Geffcken 1934: *Ap—Cri—Ion—HpMi—Prt—La—Ly—Chrm—Euthphr—R I—Grg—Mx—Men—Euthd—Cra—Smp—Phd—R II—X—Phdr—Prm—Tht—Sph—Plt—Phlb—Ti—Criti—Lg—Ep 6—8*.

Comprehensive discussion, largely accepting the methods and results of Wilamowitz 1919.

Grube 1935: *HpMi—La—Chrm—Euthphr—Ap—Cri—Grg—Prt—Men—Euthd—Cra—Mx, HpMa, Ly—Phd—Smp—R—Phdr—Prm—Tht—Sph—Plt—Phlb—Ti—Criti—Lg*.
Largely relying on Ritter (1910–1923).

Ritter 1935: *HpMi—Chrm—La—Prt—Euthphr—Ap—Cri—Grg—Men—HpMa—Euthd—Mx—Cra—Ly—Smp—Phd—R I*.
Arguing from various points of language and contents that the series beginning with *HpMa* is later than the first group, though the internal order within the groups is not absolutely certain.

Robin 1938: *Ion—HpMi—Prt—Ap—Cri—Euthphr—La—Chrm—Ly—R I—Grg* (before 390)—*Mx—Men—Euthd—Cra—Phd—Smp—R II—X—Phdr—Tht, Prm—Sph—Plt—Ti—Criti—Phlb—Lg*.
On the whole accepting Wilamowitz 1919.

Schaerer 1938 (1969): *Euthphr—La—Chrm—Ly, R I—Prt—Grg—Men—Ion—Phd—Smp—Phdr—R II—X—Tht, Prm—Sph—Plt—Phlb—Ti—Criti—Lg*.
A roughly chronological order; skeptical of establishing a detailed chronology.

Demos 1939: Skepticism of chronological research.

Lönborg 1939b: *Ap, Cri, Mx*—the remaining 'early' dialogues (after 387)—middle group—late group, *Smp*.
Considering various aspects of the form and contents of some dialogues.

Moreau 1939a: Accepting three chronological groups, remaining skeptical of establishing a detailed order.

Brommer 1940: Early dialogues—*Euthphr—Men—Chrm, La, Ly, Euthd, HpMa—Phdr* 1st version), *Prt, Grg—Cra—Smp* (1st version)—*Phd—R—Phdr* (2nd version), *Smp* (2nd version)—*Tht* (revised), *Sph, Plt—Prm* (revised)—*Phlb—Ti—*(*Criti—*) *Lg—Epin*.
Based on a supposed development of the theory of Forms and on hypotheses of the revision of the dialogues.

Popper 1945: *Cri—Ap—Euthphr—Prt—Men—Grg—Cra—Mx—Phd—R—Tht—Sph—Plt—Phlb—Ti—Criti—Lg*.
Considering Plato's gradual 'betrayal' of the legacy of Socrates.

Simeterre 1945: Brief survey of chronological research, siding on the whole with Ritter 1910b.

Schmalenbach 1946: *Ion, HpMi—Prt* (before 399)—*La, Chrm, Ly—Euthphr, Ap, R I, Grg—Mx, Men, Cri*.
Considering the development of Plato's political thought.

Festugière 1947 (1973): Order of early groups *La, Ly, Chrm, Euthphr, Prt—Euthd—Cra, Grg, Men* (ca. 390).
Considering various points of contents and supposed external references.

Goldschmidt 1947–1950: Minimizing the importance of chronological research.

Jaeger 1947: Accepting three chronological groups, but abstaining from suggesting a detailed order.

Schilling 1948: Early dialogues—*Smp—Phd—R II—X—Phdr—Tht—Prm—Sph—*(*Plt—*) *Phlb—Ti—Criti—Lg—Ep*.
On the whole relying on Ritter 1910b, but emphasizing the unity of Plato's thought.

Vollenhoven 1948: Order of later dialogues *R II—X—Phlb* (ca. 370)—*Phdr—Prm—Plt—Tht—Sph—Ti* (after 361)—*Criti—Lg*.
Based on a personal view of the development of Plato's philosophy and occasional other data.

Liebrucks 1948–1949: Early dialogues, *Prt—Phd—R—Tht—Sph—Prm*—late dialogues.
Based on a personal view of the development of Plato's dialectic; polemics against Schilling 1948.

[14]  Wundt 1949: *Chrm, La, Ly, HpMi, Ion, Prt, Euthd, Cra* (? before 399)—*Euthphr, Ap, Cri, Grg*—*Men*—*Phd* (after 393)—*Phdr* (1st version)—*Smp* (385)—*Alc 1*—*R*—*Tht* (369)—*Prm, Sph*—*Phdr* (2nd version)—*Plt* (366)—*Ti, Criti, Phlb, Lg.*
Selective consideration of various old arguments, emphasizing the importance of external criteria.
Leisegang 1950: *Ion*—*HpMi*—*Prt*—*Ap* (?)—*Cri*—*La*—*Chrm*—*R I*—*Euthphr*—*Ly*—*Grg*—*Mx*—*Men*—*Euthd*—*Cra*—*Phd*—*Smp*—*R II*—*X*—*Phdr*—*Prm*—*Tht*—*Sph*—*Plt*—*Phlb*—*Ti*—*Criti*—*Lg*—*Ep.*
Largely accepting the results of Ritter 1910b and Wilamowitz 1919.
Ross 1951: Earliest works—*Chrm*—*La*—*Euthphr*—*HpMi*—*HpMa*—*Men*—*Cra* (?)—*Smp* (after 385)—*Phd*—*R*—*Phdr*—*Prm*—*Tht*—*Sph*—*Plt*—*Ti*—*Criti*—*Phlb*—*Ep 7*-*Lg*.
Considering mainly the development of the theory of Forms.
Gauss 1952–1967: *La, Ly, Chrm, R I, Euthphr, Ap, Cri, Prt, Ion, HpMi*—*Grg, Men, Euthd, Mx, Cra*—*Phd, Smp, R II*—*X, Phdr*—*Tht, Prm, Sph, Plt*—*Phlb, Ti, Criti, Lg.*
Accepting chronological groups, but remaining skeptical of establishing a detailed order.
Owen 1953: Early dialogues—*Phd, R, Ti, Criti*—*Phdr*—*Prm, Tht*—*Sph*—*Plt*—*Phlb, Lg.*
Criticizing the results of stylometry; arguing from the development of terminology and thought.
Friedländer 1954, *see* 1930.
Zürcher 1954: *Ap*—*Cri*—*Mx*—*Chrm*—*Ly*—*Euthphr*—*La*—*HpMa*—*HpMi*—*Ion*—*Euthd*—*Prt*—*Grg*—*Men*—*Tht*—*Smp*—*Phd*—*Phdr*—*Cra*—*Prm*—*Sph*—*Plt*—*Phlb*—*Alc 1*-*Alc 2*—*Ax*—*Erx*—*Sis*—*Demod*—*Hipparch*—*Min*—*Just*—*Virt*—*Clit*—*Amat*—*Thg*—*R*—*Lg*—*Ti*—*Epin*—*Criti.*
Selective consideration of various points of language, contents and supposed external references, arguing that most of the dialogues in the Corpus received their present shape c. 300 BCE
Gaiser 1955 (1959–1974): *La*—*Chrm*—*HpMi*—*Ion*—*R I*—*Prt*—*Ap*—*Cri*—*Euthphr*—*Grg* (?)—*Mx*—*Clit*—*Ly*—*Euthd*—*HpMa*—*Men*—*Phd*—*Smp*—*R II*—*X*—*Cra*—*Prm*—*Tht*—*Sph*—*Plt*—*Phdr*—*Phlb*—*Ti*—*Criti*—*Lg.*
Beginning with considerations of the development of protreptic, later emphasizing the existence of oral teaching; not particularly concerned with questions of chronology, though adding a few new points.
Lodge 1956: Minimizing the importance of chronological research.
Krämer 1957 (1959–1968): Early dialogues, *Prt, Ly, R I*—*Grg, Men*—*Euthd, Smp*—*R II*—*X*—*Prm*—*Tht*—*Sph*—*Plt*—*Ti, Criti, Phlb.*
Concerned mainly with Plato's oral teaching; emphasizing the unity of his thought; not discussing questions of chronology.

[15]  Wake 1957: Order *Grg*—*Phd*—*Phdr*—*Ti, Lg, Ep 7* suggested by statistical study of sentence length.
H. M. Wolff 1957: *Ion*—*HpMi*—*Prt*—*Chrm*—*Ly* (before 405)—*La*—*Prm* (1st version)—*Euthd, HpMa, Euthphr, Cra, Men, Mx* (early version) (all before 399)—*Grg, Ap*—*Phd* (1st version)—*Smp* (395)—*Phd* (2nd version)—*Cri* (ca. 390)—*R* (before 380)—*Phdr, Mx* (later version)—*Prm* (2nd version)—*Tht* (368)—*Sph*—*Prm* (3rd version), *Plt*—*Phlb* (after 360), *Ti, Criti, Lg.*
Based mainly on supposed external references, hypotheses of revision, and a personal view of the development of Plato's thought.
Brandwood 1958 (1976): *Ap, Chrm, Cri, Euthphr, HpMi, Ion, La, Prt*—*Cra, Euthd, Grg, HpMa, Ly, Mx, Men, Phd, Smp*—*R*—*Prm*—*Tht*—*Phdr*—*Ti*—*Criti*—*Sph*—*Plt*—*Phlb*—*Lg*—*Epin*—*Ep.*
Based on a comprehensive critical discussion of the results of stylometry.

Boehme 1959: Order of early works *Grg—Cri—Ap—La—Prt—Men—Phd.*  [15]
  Considering various points of contents; arguing for a new view of the development of Plato's philosophy.
Ries 1959: *Grg* (390)—*Euthd—R* (1st version)—*HpMa—Smp—Mx* (after 386)—*R* (2nd version c. 374)—*Phdr—Tht* (c. 368)—*Lg* (c. 346).
  Considering supposed polemics between Plato and Isocrates.
Mugler 1960: Early dialogues—*Cra—Phd—Smp—R—Phdr—Prm—Tht—Sph—Plt—Phlb—Ti—Criti—Lg—Epin.*
  Considering the development of physical doctrines.
Vicaire 1960: *Ap—Euthphr—Ly—HpMi—Prt—Grg—Men—Cra—Ion—Smp—Phd—R—Phdr—Sph—Plt—Phlb—Ti—Criti—Lg.*
  Considering the development in views of poetry.
Díaz Tejera 1961: Early dialogues, *R I, Grg, Prt, Men—R* (main part)—*Phdr—Tht—Prm—Phlb—Sph—Plt—Ti—Criti—Lg.*
  Considering the gradual increase in frequency of non-Attic (Koiné) words.
Gulley 1962: Early dialogues—*Men—Phd—Smp—R—Cra—Tht—Phdr—Ti, (Criti)—Sph—Plt—Phlb—Lg.*
  Considering the development of the theory of knowledge.
Crombie 1962-1963: Accepting the three chronological groups established by stylometry, but remaining skeptical of a detailed chronology.
Bröcker 1964: *Ap—Cri—Prt—Ion—HpMi—La—Chrm—Ly—Grg—Men—Euthphr—HpMa—Euthd—Smp—Phd—R—Cra—Tht—Prm—Sph—Plt—Phlb—Ti, Criti—Phdr.*
  Accepting unpublished arguments by Ilting (cf. id. 1965).
Ilting 1965: *Ap, Cri—Prt, HpMi, Ion—La, Chrm—R I, Ly, Grg* (before 388)—*Men, Euthphr, HpMa—Euthd, Cra—Smp, Phd, R II—X*—later dialogues, including *Phdr.*
  Selective arguments from the contents, references in Aristotle etc., for chronological groups prior to the middle period.
Kucharski 1965: Tracing changes in Plato's theory of knowledge according to a chronology apparently approximating to Ritter's (1910b).
Oehler 1965b: Emphasizing the need for a reconsideration of Platonic chronology in view of the recent theories of oral teaching.
Raven 1965: Early dialogues—*Prt—Grg—Men—Phd—Smp—R—Phdr—Prm—Sph—Plt—Ti—Criti—Phlb—Lg.*
  Considering the development of metaphysics, largely accepting the conventional chronology.
Ryle 1966 (1969): Early dialogues?—*Euthd* (after 380)—*Grg—Men—R I—Ap, Cri* (c. 370)—*Phd, Smp, Prm* (1st version)—*R* (2nd version)—*Ti, Criti*—'On the Good,' *Phlb, R* (3rd  [16]
version)—*Lg* (parts)—*Phdr—Tht* (358 or later)—*Sph—Plt—Prm* (2nd version).
  A comprehensive discussion, based mainly on supposed historical and literary allusions, hypotheses of revision, and a personal view of Plato's philosophical development; a wealth of new arguments.
Wichmann 1966: *Ap—Cri—La—Hipparch—Thg—Ion—Virt—Just—Chrm—Amat—Alc 1—Prt—Alc 2—Euthphr—Ly—HpMa—HpMi—Euthd—Min—Cra—Clit—Grg* (all before 388)—*Men—Phd—Phdr—Mx—Smp—R—Tht—Prm—Sph—Plt—Ti—Criti—Phlb—Ep—Lg*—'On the Good'—*Epin.*
  A personal order of interpretation, with little consideration of earlier research and accepting almost the entire Corpus as authentic.
Wyller 1966 (-1970): Order of late works *Cra—Tht—Sph—Plt—Prm*—'On the Good'—*Phlb—Phdr* (?)—*Ti—Criti—Ep 7—Lg—Epin* (?).

[16]     A tentative chronology based on a personal interpretation, considering *Parmenides* as the culmination of Plato's thought.
Thesleff 1967: *HpMi—Ion—La—Cri—Ap—Mx—Grg—Men—Euthphr—Cra—Ly—Chrm—R I—Prt—Euthd—Phd—Smp—R II—X, Prm—Tht—Phdr—Ti—Criti—Sph—Plt—Phlb—Ep 7—Lg—Epin.*
Considering various current arguments and also changes in the technique of composition.
Erbse 1968: *Ap—Cri—Grg* (before 388)*—Prt—Euthd—Chrm—La—Euthphr—Men—Phd.*
Largely following Kapp (1968), considering the development of thought.
Kapp 1968: *Ap—Cri—Grg* (before 390)*—Prt—Mx—HpMi—Ion—La—Men—Euthd—Chrm—Euthphr—Phd—Smp—Ly—Cra—R* (after 377)*—Phdr—Prm—Tht—*late dialogues.
Comprehensive discussion of points in the contents; considering mainly the development of the theory of Forms.
E. Wolff 1968–1970: *Ap—Cri—Ion—Euthphr—HpMi—HpMa—Prt—La—Chrm—Ly—Alc 1—Grg—Mx—Men—Euthd—Cra—R—Phd—Smp—Phdr—Tht—Prm—Sph—Phlb—Plt—Ti—Criti—Lg—Ep 6–8.*
A roughly chronological order, considering the development of the conception of justice.
Kube 1969: *Ap—Cri—Ion—HpMi—Grg—Prt—La—Euthd—Chrm—Ly—Men—Euthphr—HpMa—Phd—R—Smp—Tht—Cra—Sph—Phdr—Plt—Phlb.*
A rough chronology, considering conceptions of τέχνη and virtue.
Allen 1970: Early dialogues (rather from 390s) include *Ap, Cri, La, Ly, Chrm, Euthphr, HpMa, HpMi, Ion, Euthd* and *Prt.*
Considering the development of the theory of Forms; abstaining from a detailed chronology.
Randall 1970: Playfully skeptical remarks against chronological research; reluctantly accepting separation of the 'late group.'
Wishatt & Leach 1970: Order of later works *Phdr—R, Smp—Ti—Sph—Criti—Ep 7, Plt—Phlb—Lg.*
Considering statistics of rhythmical tendencies throughout sentences.
Gundert 1971: *Ap—La—Chrm—R I—Euthphr—Ly—Euthd—Prt—Grg—Men—Cra—Smp—Phd—R II—X—Prm—Tht—Sph—Plt—Ti, Criti, Phlb, Lg, Ep 7.*
Considering the development of the structure of dialectic, without a detailed discussion of chronology and with a certain preference for a unitarian approach.
[17]    Boder 1973: Order of some earlier dialogues *La—Chrm—Euthphr—Ly—Ion—HpMi—HpMa—Prt—Euthd—Men.*
Considering the tendency to more complicated forms of irony, but not insisting on a detailed chronology.
Martin 1973: Accepting the three chronological groups as indicating changes in the theory of Forms.
Findlay 1974: Siding with the theory of oral teaching; pointing out discrepancies between Plato's development as a thinker and conventional chronology, but not suggesting new dates.
Joly 1974: Unitarian interpretation.
Guthrie 1975–1978: *Ap, Cri, Euthphr, La, Chrm, Ly, HpMa, HpMi, Ion—Prt—Men—Euthd—Grg—Mx—Phd—Smp—Phdr—R—Cra—Prm—Tht—Sph—Plt—Phlb—Lg.*
Comprehensive discussion of various kinds of argument, attempting a working compromise.
Rist 1975: *Chrm, La, Euthphr, HpMa* (?), *HpMi, Euthd—Prt—Grg, Men, Cra—Smp, Phd, R—*late dialogues.
Considering preliminary stages of the theory of Forms; against Allen 1970.

Sprague 1976: A unitarian view.

Michaelson, Morton & Gillies 1977: Statistics of occurrences and position of some particles, as well as differences in contents, suggest a different authorship for the groups *Ap, Chrm, Cri, Euthd, Euthphr, La* and *Men, Phd, Phdr, R, Smp*, and also for *Ti* and *Prm*.

Violette 1977: Early dialogues—*Euthphr*—*Men*—*Cra*—*Smp, Phd*—*R*.

Considering the development of the terminology of the theory of Forms.

Laborderie 1978: Early dialogues (including *Alc 1, HpMa* and possibly *R I*)—*Mx*—*Euthd*—*Cra*—*Men*—*Phd*—*Smp*—*Phdr*—*R*—*Tht*—*Prm*—*Sph*—*Plt*—*Phlb*—*Ti*—*Criti*—*Lg*—*Ep 7–8*—*Epin* (?).

Considering various trends in the dialogues of the 'middle period' in particular.

Kahn 1981: *Ap*—*Cri*—*Ion*—*HpMi*—*Grg* (390–86)—*Mx*—*La*—*Chrm*—*Ly*—*Euthphr*—*Prt*—*Euthd*—*Men*—Middle and late dialogues.

Interpreting the 'early' dialogues as reflecting Platonic philosophy.

# CRITICAL COMMENTS

## Preliminary remarks

A glance at the list above can be seriously misleading. The reader must be warned against assuming that there has occurred, in the study of Platonic chronology, a steady progress towards ever more certain results with regard either to the general lines or to points of detail.

As a matter of fact, things are in a deplorable state of confusion.

Firstly, from a methodological point of view, it should be realized that current reference works and the standpoints of 'authorities' play a very substantial part in the forming of opinions concerning the order in which Plato wrote his dialogues. This is normally the case even if the writer has carried out new and independent research of his own, attempting to relate the opinions on Platonic chronology which he has taken over from somebody else to an inductively acquired personal view of changes in Plato's thought, activities, manners, motives etc. (or a lack of such changes). Because very few scholars are even tolerably fully informed of the discussion concerning the relevant points of Platonic chronology (not to speak of the whole complex of problems), there is a considerable risk involved here: views expressed originally as mere opinions may become established as solid facts by this process of being part of a widely accepted tradition, and what seems to be adding cumulative proof to such facts or opinions may simply be begging the question, since the basis of the latter is unknown. This is of course a risk familiar to many students of antiquity. The risk is comparatively great in Platonic studies where there are two different parties at work—philosophers and philologists—who cannot be expected to inform each other sufficiently well and who are susceptible to mutual misunderstanding.

Secondly, even if we are not under the illusion of taking opinions for facts, the relative reliability and relevance to chronology of such heterogeneous opinions as are current in the discussion is often very difficult to evaluate. Moreover, the varying degree of conviction with which different chronologies are advocated, also constitutes a source of error.

Thirdly, books on Plato often include not only explicit arguments or statements of facts or opinions relating to chronology, but also a kind of 'implicit

[19] argumentation': the points under discussion seem to fit into a certain chronology and thus, because they do so, they seem to give the reader, as a feedback, cumulative proof that the order accepted was correct.[17] The value of such 'proofs' can only be determined *in casu*. Skepticism is on the whole justifiable, since almost any order of the dialogues can be 'interpreted' to make some sort of sense.

Fourthly, in many cases the discrepancies reflect factual disagreement between two or several scholars who are relatively well-informed but who interpret or rank the available facts differently. Though such conflicts could perhaps be solved to the advantage of one party, or reduced to a *non liquet*, they have often been forgotten *qua* problems in the subsequent discussion, and opinions or problems raised by new parties have come to the forefront.

Thus it is no exaggeration to state, in general, that most pronouncements on Platonic chronology are not as well-founded as they may appear to be, viewed superficially. And this is also one of the reasons for the persistent discrepancies between the chronologies suggested.

After all, the general trend has been rather a negative one during the last fifty or sixty years. The present state of our knowledge of the order in which Plato wrote or 'published' his works justifies much less confidence even about the general lines, than was common in the heyday of genetic and historical interpretation and stylometry, from the 1890s to the 1920s. The ever-growing uncertainty concerning fixed points, trends of change or development, and methods to be employed, is sometimes explicitly admitted.[18] More often it is to be seen in a reluctance to take a definite stand on questions of chronology.

As a consequence of all this, and as will be even clearer later on, a comparatively large-scale reconsideration of the whole complex of problems relevant here is needed before we can state what we really know or have reason to believe about Platonic chronology.

The critical comments below are not, any more than the survey above, meant to be a real *Forschungsbericht*. Such a tedious task, even if theoretically possible, is hardly worth while in a case where similar arguments and traditional views have recurred again and again in slightly modified combinations, and where opinions have gradually fossilized into facts. Nor is it necessary to search systematically
[20] for isolated fresh and useful observations that have become submerged in the stream of placita, though sometimes we are fortunate enough to come across such items.

The main object of this chapter is to subject the actual foundations of our present view of Platonic chronology to a critical reassessment. The review will,

---

17. Immisch 1915: 550 went as far as to state that interpretation rather than analysis may solve the problems of Platonic chronology, and what he apparently meant was primarily this kind of 'implicit argumentation.'

18. *See* e.g. the ironically skeptical remarks of Randall 1970: 32–35, the works of French scholars such as Goldschmidt and Joly, and Findlay 1974: iv f. Guthrie, however, maintains a traditionally optimistic view (especially IV 41–56).

therefore, focus upon arguments current in the debate rather than upon a possible introduction of new arguments. [20]

⦁⦁⦁ 〇 ⦁⦁⦁

It has been customary to classify the various kinds of criteria or explicit arguments used for establishing Platonic chronology. The four classes adopted in the presentation below—(1) external criteria, (2) arguments from the contents, (3) literary criteria and dialogue technique, and (4) linguistic criteria—correspond on the whole to the typologies used by Raeder, Ritter and Guthrie.[19] This grouping and labeling is of course ultimately a matter of convenience. No class of criteria can have *a priori* claims to greater reliability than any other.[20] Elusive arguments occur in all classes. Since we have very few 'objectively' determinable facts that will function in isolation as criteria of chronology, every criterion adduced requires testing from as many angles as possible.

In addition it will be necessary here to consider various problems relative to (5) a possible revision of the dialogues and (6) questions of authenticity.

## External criteria

This class will include both chronologically relevant references in other ancient sources to Plato, and corresponding references in the Platonic writings to external events, contemporary persons, etc. In addition, the very few explicit cross-references that occur in the dialogues will also be discussed (p. 185).

*Biographical problems relating to Plato's youth.*[21] It can now be regarded as certain that Plato was born about 427, give or take not more than one year.[22] [21]

---

19. Raeder 30–87: language and style, dialogue technique, external reference, philosophical contents; Ritter 1910b: 199–280: ancient testimony, reference to contemporary events and authors, reference to earlier dialogues, differences in contents, differences in form and language; Guthrie IV 41–56: literary criticism, philosophical considerations, stylometrics and linguistic tests, external evidence and cross-references. For earlier typologies, see Ueberweg 1861: 27, 89; Immisch 1899: 440.

20. This is often admitted in theory (even by Lutoslawski 52), though most scholars incline to prefer one class of criteria. For instance Guthrie lists the classes in what he believes is an "ascending order of objectivity" (IV 42, with an important reservation in n. 1 with regard to the last class).

21. For full-scale presentations of the life of Plato, see in particular Wilamowitz I 13–14, II 1 ff., 82 f. (suggestive but highly conjectural); Field 1930 (1967): 1–48 (semi-popular, but with independent new considerations); Shorey 1933: 1–57 (firmly skeptical); Leisegang 1950: 2342–57 (with a good conspectus of the sources; additions especially regarding Plato's oral teaching in Gaiser 1963: 46 ff.); Davies 1971: 322–25 (discussion of various aspects with references); Guthrie IV 8–38 (generally good references); Riginos 1976 (discussion of anecdotes and legends).—Generally speaking, the most valuable sources consist of the *7th Letter* (supplemented by Plutarch's *Dion*) and some of the evidence contained in Diogenes Laertius' Chapter III (ed. with the parallel traditions by Breitenbach al. 1907). The late Vitae have little independent value.

22. For the relevant facts, see Davies 1971: 333.

[21] The aristocratic background of his family is also well attested. It is clear that he and his brothers received a good education, and also reasonably clear that they were expected to make their career in politics.[23] The catastrophes of the years 404 and 403, in which Plato's relatives Critias and Charmides were actively and prominently involved, put an end to such possible plans at least on Plato's part, and the *7th Letter* (324b–326d) and other sources testify clearly enough that he never took an active part in Athenian politics, being in fact rather antipathetic to it. This attitude of relatively passive and emotionally averse, even embittered opposition is a biographical fact of some consequence to the chronology of the writings, which has often been perceived but has been interpreted in different ways.[24]

Whether Plato was engaged in military service during the Peloponnesian war or not we do not know. The fact that our sources seem to refer only to the Corinthian war (below p. 173) rather suggests that he was not.

Instead, there is some positive evidence of his association with the Heraclitan philosopher Cratylus before he became personally acquainted with Socrates.[25] Cratylus, as can perhaps be seen from the dialogue which bears his name, was a
[22] sophist inclined to exclusiveness and to enigmatic utterances. Plato is also very likely to have studied Anaxagoras' Περὶ φύσεως in his early youth.[26] It is unknown whether he had listened to any of the great non-Athenian sophists; the picture drawn of such sophists in some dialogues, particularly the *Protagoras*, may suggest that he had.[27] The intellectually and literarily versatile Critias was a relative of his and must have made a considerable impression on him, not

---

23. The fact that his elder brothers Glaucon and Adimantus are made the chief interlocutors of Socrates in the *Republic* is a positive indication of this; cf. the remarks on Plato's stepfather Pyrilampes in *Charmides* 158ab, and the occurrence of his younger half-brother Antiphon in the opening of *Parmenides* which alludes to the *Republic* (p. 306). There is nothing to indicate that Plato was in any way handicapped from appearing in public, except for what would seem to be an exceptional shyness (cf. below p. 169) possibly to be explained psychologically. However, the Freudian speculations of Kelsen, Popper and others (*see* Levinson 1953, especially 16 ff., 466 ff.) have no relevance to the present theme.

24. A good exposé of the facts relating to Plato's political attitudes, in Guthrie IV 16 f.— For Plato's possible engagement in foreign politics apart from Syracuse, *see* below, pp. 177 and 334.

25. Diog. L. 3.5–6 evidently from different sources; in the second passage Diogenes implies that Plato turned to studying (προσεῖχε) Heraclitanism and Eleaticism after the death of Socrates, but this is probably a mistake as far as Cratylus is concerned. Aristotle (*Met.* 987a32 ff.) tells us that Plato knew Cratylus and Heraclitanism from his youth (ἐκ νέου) without mentioning his interests in Eleaticism. And to judge by the dialogue *Cratylus*, Plato did not later regard Cratylus as a 'master mind' (Guthrie IV 14 n. 1), and is, therefore, not likely to have been attracted by him after the death of Socrates.

26. Cf. *Ap.* 36d, *Cra.* 400a, 409ab, 413e, *Phd.* 72c, 97b ff. It is often thought that Socrates' exposé of his philosophical development in *Phd.* 96a–102a actually concerns Plato himself. If this is so, Plato must have reached a considerable intellectual and philosophical maturity at an early age; but this is all very conjectural.

27. But Protagoras himself had died when Plato was a boy; and the dialogues obviously also operate with written sources; for *Protagoras*, cf. p. 278, for *Hippias Major* p. 373.

only as a politician, but in other ways, too.²⁸ Hence, there are several indications [22] that when Plato came to associate regularly with Socrates at the age of 20, about 407 BCE,²⁹ he had already been open to philosophical and literary impulses from various quarters. And among the friends of Socrates he met many other persons likely to influence him. He also met two Pythagoreans, Simmias and Cebes.³⁰

As far as we know, Plato's character was marked by a tendency to shyness and seclusion.³¹

I think it is important to observe that although the profound impact of Socrates upon Plato's philosophical personality is unquestionable—indeed he may well have "burnt his tragedies" after he had listened to Socrates, as the story [23] goes (Aelian. VH 2.30, Diog. L. 3.5)—and though the trial and death of Socrates in 399 BCE must have come as a tremendous shock to him (*Ep.* 7.324e ff.), his relations with Socrates were not perhaps after all as intimate and personal as is often believed.³² The consequence of this perhaps somewhat surprising suggestion for chronology is that we should not necessarily expect Plato to have felt himself from the outset as the true philosophical heir of Socrates, and hence, to have started his literary career as a writer of Socratic λόγοι more or less exactly reproducing the Socratic mode of debate.

---

28. Note the sympathetic picture drawn of Critias in the *Charmides* and especially in the *Timaeus* (where the person in question is certainly the sophist and politician who was killed in 403, and not his grandfather as has been sometimes assumed).

29. Diog. L. 3.6 ... γεγονώς ... εἴκοσιν ἔτη διήκουσε Σωκράτους. There is no need to doubt this piece of information; it is likely to derive from Plato's pupil and biographer Hermodorus (who is mentioned a few lines later and who also recorded Plato's experiences at the age of 28 and 40; *see* below), and ultimately from oral information by Plato himself. Riginos 1976: 50 n. 42 suggests a connection with the recommendation in *R.* VII 537bc to start training the future philosopher at the age of twenty, after a few years of gymnastics and the χύδην μαθήματα of early youth; indeed, Plato may be thinking of his own experiences here as he probably does in *R.* VII 540a and *Lg.* XII 950d. It is customary to point out that Plato must have known Socrates earlier (e.g. Guthrie IV 13), but one should not forget that Plato was personally shy (below), and also that conservative families may have regarded Socrates and his circle as somewhat suspect company for a youngster who had not finished his education.

30. *Cri.* 45b and *Phd.*—But it may be noted that Alcibiades, who plays a considerable role in Socratic literature, was finally banished from Athens in the same year, 407, as Plato probably joined Socrates.

31. The fact that he remains so exceptionally anonymous in all his writings (except the *Letters*) is an indirect sign of this. Other signs are his avoidance of a public career in spite of strong political interests, and above all various traditions relating to what was thought to be Plato's arrogance or haughtiness: cf. e.g. Diog. L. 3.26, 39, 4.7, 6.26; Alexis fr. 180, Amphis fr. 13; Isocr. *Antid.* (XV) 84 f. The theory of Plato's oral doctrine being taught esoterically fits in well with this conception of Plato's character; cf. Gaiser 1980, especially 17–27.

32. Those who most actively offerred their assistance to Socrates in 399 were, according to old traditions, Aeschines (Diog. L. 2.60, 3.36) and Criton (*see Crt.*); cf. *Ap.* 38b (where Plato is mentioned together with Criton, Critobulus and Apollodorus), X. *Ap.* 23 (ἑταῖροι) cf. also Riginos 1976: 96 f. The list of persons present at Socrates' death (*Phd.* 59bc) includes many others. Socrates' favorite pupil at that time was perhaps Phaedon (*Phd.* 89ab), and this is probably one reason why Plato makes him his mouthpiece for the record of Socrates' last hours (below, p. 141). Plato was not present owing to ἀσθένεια (59b), whatever this excuse may imply (the old theory of Plato being in a state of depression has been recently revived by Lavely 1974).

[23] The old hypothesis of a 'Socratic' period in Plato's literary work relies partly upon this assumption of a very close personal relationship between Socrates and Plato. It also rests mainly on two observations. One is the fact that some, but not all, of the Platonic dialogues present ideas and approaches that cannot possibly derive from Socrates but must have been developed later by Plato himself; however, to collect the rest into an early Socratic group is not necessary, as we shall see. The other observation is that Socrates seems to 'fade away' in some or all of the writings which are usually considered to be later than the *Republic;* but extrapolating this trend backwards into an ever more manifest 'presence' of Socrates in the early writings, is dubious in theory and almost impossible in practice. The only external evidence that is sometimes referred to is Aristotle's statement in the *Metaphysics*[33] that Plato's philosophy arose from a combination of Pythagoreanism and Heraclitanism with Socraticism (such as Aristotle describes it); but this is really not conclusive at all as regards the chronology of his writings. Hermann and his followers in the 19th century believed that the more 'Socratic' a Platonic writing is in tenor and contents, the earlier it is likely to be. Since then the criteria of what is 'Socratic' have been subject to much dispute: neither Xenophon nor the other Socratics provide us with very reliable standards of judgment.[34] The curious theory of Burnet and Taylor (cf. especially Guthrie III 351) that most
[24] of Plato's 'early' works give a historically true picture of Socrates, has not met with much approval and begs the question. To be sure, the *Apology* presumably approximates to historical truth, since it would otherwise seriously misfire if some (general) readers were expected to recall what Socrates had actually said. But affinity with the tenor and contents of the *Apology* cannot automatically be regarded as a criterion of an early date, even assuming that the *Apology* is early.[35]

This hypothesis of a distinctly 'Socratic' period has been gradually discarded in this century, chiefly because of the 'advanced' Platonic traits found, or assumed to have been found, in different dialogues traditionally regarded as Socratic. However, it still indirectly influences the general conception of Platonic chronology, and it is explicitly maintained e.g. by Guthrie. Most scholars who accept the existence of an 'early' group of dialogues take for granted, explicitly or implicitly, that such works should be in various ways more 'Socratic' than the rest. As we have seen, such assumptions are precarious as primary criteria. The assertion recently made by Kahn that there are no properly Socratic dialogues except perhaps

---

33. *Met.* A. 987a29 ff., cf. M. 1078b12 ff.
34. For the 19th century views *see* references in Raeder 88–92. For the subsequent discussion, cf. Gigon 1947 and de Magalhães-Vilhena 1952 (bis). The coherent and clear picture of Socrates presented by Guthrie III 378–488 (with further references) probably relies somewhat too much on the Platonic dialogues.
35. For instance, this is Raeder's (88–92) chief argument for placing *Ion, Hippias Minor, Laches, Charmides* and *Crito* in close connection with the *Apology;* but he admits that *Alcibiades* I and *Euthyphro* present difficulties. Further difficulties are presented by, say, *Phaedo* and *Symposium* with their mass of historical and biographical details concerning Socrates, though neither of them can be very early. Note further manifestly late Socratica such as *Hippias Major* (p. 226), whether authentic or not.

the *Apology, Ion* and *Hippias Minor*,[36] is symptomatic in two respects: it represents the modern tendency to make away with the 'Socratic period,' and it shows that such dialogues as are not necessarily very early (cf. below on *Ion* p. 367, *Hp.Mi.* p. 366) can still be labelled 'Socratic.'

Did Plato write dialogues before 399 BCE, or should the death of Socrates be regarded as an absolute *terminus post querm*? Authorities who have backed the former position include Schleiermacher, Hermann, Ueberweg, Pfleiderer, Hirzel, Immisch, Windelband, Ritter, Wilamowitz, and Friedländer.[37] Such a view does not stand up to criticism, however. Apart from the general difficulties of separating a very early group of dialogues (some of these difficulties were touched on above, others will be reviewed later), it should be noted that the two chief arguments usually produced in favor of the theory of very early dialogues by Plato, are based on very shaky premises. First, there are some passages that have been taken to suggest the existence of a Socratic literature before 399;[38] but there is nothing to suggest that such passages refer to finished pieces of literature, as Plato's dialogues certainly are, and not merely to oral traditions or rough ὑπομνήματα possibly taken down of Socratic conversations (cf. below p. 204). And second, if a number of otherwise seemingly 'early' and 'Socratic' dialogues may appear to depict Socrates as a sophist and to put him in a company of sophists and political adventurers hardly acceptable to an Athenian public soon after 399, it is for various reasons easier to argue that such dialogues are considerably later, than to argue that they were written for a general public (as they must have been) by a very young man (as they must then have been) in Socrates' lifetime.[39] As a matter of fact, every single one of Plato's so-called early dialogues can be said to convey a certain protreptic, or laudatory, or sometimes even apologetic tendency. With all his oddities, his irony, mockery and sophistry, Socrates is the

[24]

[25]

---

36. Kahn 1976: 21; 1981.

37. *See* e.g. Immisch 1899: 552–560 (also *Phdr.*), Ritter 1910b: 56, 95, 1922: 97–99, 105–107 (against Pohlenz), Wilamowitz I 131 (against Bruns and others), 139, II 22. Similarly, e.g. Mutschmann 1911 (arguing an early date for *Chrm.*), Wundt 1914, 1949: 40–48 (also *Euthd., Cra.*), Schilling 1948: 35, Hoffmann 1950: 23 f. (though reluctant), H. M. Wolff 1957: 10–13, 37 f. (death of Socrates led to a crisis in Plato's thought which is first reflected by the *Gorgias*, as already Ast and suggested), Fischer 1969: 29, 62 n. 4 (also *Hp.Ma.*). Some additional references and some pondering of the pros and cons in Guthrie IV 54–56.

38. Notably *Ap.* 23c (Socrates states that there are many who imitate his manner of asking questions), cf. 39cd; *Smp.* 173b (Apollodorus has asked Socrates for confirmation of the story of Aristodemus), cf. *Tht.* 143a; *Smp.* 215d (Alcibiades says everybody is impressed by the λόγοι of Socrates, even if they are retold .by someone else). The anecdote relating what Socrates had said when he had had the *Lysis* read to him (Diog. L. 3.35, cf. *Anon.Proleg.* 3) is practically worthless as evidence, as most scholars agree; cf. Riginos 1976: 55.—In fact the passage *Ap.* 39cd (the young followers of Socrates will prove after his death that he was right) has often been taken to imply that the Socratics had not published anything by 399: cf. e.g. Pohlenz 1913: 22 f., Parmentier 1913: 153 f., Gauss 1/2.12.

39. This has been thought to apply to *Hippias Minor* and *Ion* in particular, also to *Charmides, Lysis, Protagoras* and *Euthyphro*. If so, the catastrophe of 404 BCE is rather a *terminus ante quem* for all of them except *Euthyphro*.

[25] real and ultimately triumphant hero in all of them. This literary attitude is much more acceptable if they were written after his death, than before it.[40]

Again, the different ways of alluding to the trial and death of Socrates in some Platonic works have sometimes been taken to imply differences in time.[41] But this poses serious problems. The *Phaedo* in particular should remind us that an intense involvement in the fate of Socrates does not necessarily imply a very early date.

For the alleged 'youthfulness' of the *Phaedrus, see* below p. 319.

*The Megarian hypothesis.* After the death of Socrates, Plato together with some other Socratics went to Megara to stay with Euclides.[42] The foremost reason [26] for this appears to have been the political and moral antipathy to the Socratics in Athens.[43] This Megarian episode should probably be dated very soon after the death of Socrates (in May, 399),[44] and as far as we know or can infer it was not a particularly prolonged one.[45]

The hypothesis that, during his stay in Megara, Plato came under the influence of the 'school of Euclides,' was introduced by Tennemann and became quite common among 19th century scholars. In consequence, it was assumed that Plato's most 'Megarian' dialogues, *Theaetetus*, the *Sophist* and *Politicus*, and perhaps *Parmenides* and also *Euthydemus*, should be dated in the 390s. Since this seemed to become increasingly impossible on other grounds, especially to the stylometrists, the hypothesis was generally discarded around the turn of the century.[46]

---

40. Some or all of these points have been emphasized, against the very early dating, by many scholars including Bruns, Gomperz, Natorp, Raeder, Maier, Parmentier, Pohlenz, Geffcken, Gigon, Gauss, Ryle, Field, and Guthrie (IV 54–56).

41. This concerns notably (in alphabetic order) the *Apology, Crito, Euthyphro, Gorgias, Meno, Phaedo* and *Theaetetus*. For this reason the *Apology* and *Crito* have often been dated to the early 390s, whereas the more 'irreverent' *Euthyphro* is placed either considerably later or, sometimes, in its dramatic context just before the trial.

42. Diog. L. 2.106, 3.6 (Plato 28 years old); cf. Academicorum Index col. X 5 ff. p. 6 M, Cic. *de fin.* 5.29.87, *de rep.* 1.10.16, Apul. *de dogm. Pl.* 1.3. The common source appears to be Hermodorus relating oral information by Plato: cf. the notices on Plato's age when he met Socrates (above p. 168) and Dion (*Ep.* 7.324a). For Megara as a safe place, cf. also *Cri.* 53b, *Phd.* 99a.

43. According to Diogenes (2.106) Hermodorus said that the Socratics were "alarmed at the cruelty of the tyrants" by whom the radical democrats are perhaps meant (cf. Diog. L. 3.6 ὑπεχώρησαν); *see* Zeller II 1[5] 402 n. 2, Immisch 1899: 442 n. 3. No explicit mention of these events occurs in the *7th Letter*, but here the phrasing (especially 324d, 325c) makes it reasonably clear that relatives and former associates of the Thirty Tyrants did not feel safe in Athens.

44. The year seems to be established by independent evidence: cf. Diog. L. 2.44, from Demetrios of Phaleron and Apollodorus. The yearly theoria to Delos which delayed the execution of Socrates must have taken place in Thargelion, the month of the Delian Apollo. For reasons unknown to me, Unger 1891: 201 and others have suggested Munychion (March/April).

45. Cf. the silence of the *7th Letter*, above n. 42; for Plato and the Corinthian war, *see* below p. 27. Several years later the pamphlet of Polycrates (below p. 173) again aroused strong feelings, but considering how Plato reacted upon it in his dialogues, there is nothing to indicate that this had occasioned him to go, or stay, abroad.

46. *See* the discussion in Waddington (1886) 1904: 138 f., Lutoslawski 42–50, Horn 1904: 160 f., Raeder 62 f., Wilamowitz I 569 n. 1.

Even so, of course, it seems reasonable to assume that Plato received new and [26] fruitful impulses from the friends who assembled in Megara. Euclides, his host, appears to have been well acquainted with the writings of Parmenides and Zenon.[47] Be this as it may, it is not unimportant to note that Plato was in all likelihood well informed, in the early 390s, about both Heraclitan and Eleatic thought, and that he had had considerable opportunity to discuss and think over both these and other philosophical approaches to reality.

No manifest support has been found for the assumption sometimes made, partially as a corollary to the Megarian hypothesis, that Plato began his literary career in Megara.[48] On the contrary, writings such as, say, the *Apology* or the *Crito* [27] clearly imply a larger audience than Plato could possibly have had there.

*The Corinthian war.* The somewhat confused notes of Diogenes Laertius (Diog. L.) certainly do not imply that Plato went on extensive voyages abroad directly from Megara.[49] He may well have returned home after a few months. On the other hand, we have some positive evidence to suggest that he took part in certain Athenian (presumably cavalry) campaigns during the Corinthian war. It is true that the passage in Diogenes (3.8) concerning his military service is also rather confused and refers in part to Socrates and not to Plato, but it has been argued fairly convincingly that Aelianus (VH 5.16 and 7.14) faithfully reproduces the original and trustworthy text of Aristoxenus according to whom Plato had joined the Athenian forces twice, namely at Tanagra (possibly in 395) and at Corinth (in 394 or later).[50]

Plato's experience in this war may have some bearing upon the genesis of the *Menexenus* (p. 266) and *Theaetetus* (p. 302).

---

47. Diog. L. 2.106, cf. 2.30. For some modifications of older views of the relation of the Megarians to the Eleatics, see Guthrie III 500 f. If the person who introduced Plato to the philosophy of Parmenides really was Hermogenes who is coupled with Cratylus in Diog. L. 3.6 (cf. above p. 168 and the dialogue *Cratylus*), Plato must have been subject to these influences before the death of Socrates, since Hermogenes was an intimate friend of the latter (*Phd.* 59b). *Anon-Proleg.* ed. Hermann p. 199 has Ἑρμίππῳ for Ἑρμογένει. Cf. also Krämer 1959: 531.

48. For instance, Hirzel (1895: 86 n .1) noted that Aeschines is said to have presented one of his dialogues in Megara (Diog. L. 2.62, cf. Socr. *Ep.* 15.2 Hercher); and if this was the 'Miltiades' (cf. Diog. L. 2.61) its theme may have been related to Plato's *Laches*, which is generally taken to be very early; but such constructions are not very reliable as will be seen below.—Maier (1913: 107) suggested that the *Apology* was written in Megara but failed to provide convincing arguments.—For my own part, at one time (1967) I played with the thought that the Socratic dialogue, as a dramatic prose genre, may have received impulses from a local mime tradition in Megara; but there is little to prove the existence of an early Megarian mime (see Breitholz 1960).

49. This is sometimes believed; see e.g. Ritter 1910b: 65 f. But note the fact that Diog. L. 3.6 has εἰς Μέγαρα and ἔπειτα εἰς Κυρήνην but κἀκεῖθεν εἰς Ἰταλίαν ... ἔνθεν τε εἰς Αἴγυπτον. Cf. below p. 176.

50. Ritter 1910b: I 82, Wilamowitz 1919: II 4. On the other hand, Riginos 1976: 51 f. follows Cornford (1935: 15) in assuming that Aristoxenus had fabricated his story from references in the *Theaetetus*. But it is hard to see why Aristoxenus with his strong anti-Platonic bias, would not have fabricated a somewhat less laudatory piece of information, if he did not operate with facts.

[27] *The first voyage outside Greece.* Here the first and main problem is the documentary value of the *7th Letter*. Whatever position one takes in the debate regarding its authenticity (below p. 347) one has to admit that the evidence it gives demands careful testing by comparing it to whatever other evidence and considerations there can be produced. As far as I can see, such considerations tend to favor the reliability of the letter. At any rate the extreme skepticism towards its source value which was expressed in particular by Zeller and his followers,[51] is clearly unwarranted, since the author (whether Plato or not) is well informed and—what is even more important—expects his readers to be so.

According to the letter (325c–326b), Plato left Athens in a mood of resentment and with the feeling that the political afflictions of Greece could only be cured [28] by the assumption of power by philosophers. It is probably important to bear in mind that his dominant interests at that time were politically orientated.

Almost certainly this voyage was a single journey of not many years' duration. The most significant part of it was a visit to southern Italy and Sicily. The old theory of an extensive period of 'Wanderjahre' has no solid foundation and should in fact be abandoned.[52] The confused information given by Diogenes Laertius (3.6–7, 18) together with various other scraps of evidence are usually taken to imply that Plato's first voyage abroad brought him over Egypt, Cyrene, and Italy, to Sicily. There is not much evidence to support the view that Plato stopped in Egypt except possibly for a brief transit visit to Naucratis or some other place on his way to or from Cyrene. Stories of prominent Greeks' visits to the East tend to become elaborated in legends. And it should be noted that in order to study Egyptian institutions, geometry, astronomy, and 'secret wisdom' in general, any visit would have required a considerable length of time (and this not only due to linguistic difficulties) and would have left much clearer traces in the biographical tradition and in Plato's written works.[53] The tradition of Plato's stay in Cyrene is somewhat better founded, though this too must have

---

51. Zeller II 1⁵ 405 n. 1; more recently e.g. Ryle 1966: 55 ff., Finley (1968) 1972: 74–87.

52. Th. Gomperz II (1902) 208 ff. was probably the last to produce a detailed argument in favor of it. Our main (but not only) sources consist of the relevant passages in Diogenes Laertius and the *7th Letter*. The Academicorum Index col.X 5–11 p. 6 M (*see* now Gaiser 1988) mentions only the voyage to Italy and Sicily, but dates it immediately after the death of Socrates "when Plato was 28 years old," obviously owing to some confusion with the statement of Hermodorus (above n. 42); the Index is flatly contradicted by *Ep.* 7.324a where the notice that Plato was 40 years old receives additional support from the phrasing in 325c ὅσῳ ... ἡλικίας ... προύβαινον; cf. also *Lg.* XII 250d, where it is said that 40 years is a suitable age for ἀποδημία and cf. similar semi-self-biographical references in the *Republic*, cf. above n. 29. For details of the discussion of Plato's first voyage, see further Guthrie IV 10 n. 1, 16–19; Riginos 1976: 61–92.

53. The myth of Theuth in *Phaedrus* 274c ff. (cf. *Phlb.* 18b), and the Egyptian traits in the prooimion of the *Timaeus*, must be considered a meager result of Plato's supposed studies "with the prophets" (Diog. L. 3.7); one might almost think it was fortunate that a war prevented Plato from going on "to the Magians" (id. 7). For various elaborations of the legends of Plato's Egyptian visit, *see* Dörrie 1973: 99–118, Guthrie IV 14–16, Riginos 1976: 64–69. Geffcken II A 55 f. offers some good skeptical arguments; cf. also Raeder 63, Leisegang 1950: 2478. Even so, recently, the Egyptian hypothesis has again found a supporter (Nawratil 1974).

been a brief episode and we cannot be very sure of the details and the date. Plato probably knew the sophist and geometrician Theodoros from the latter's stay in Athens, and so he might well have paid him a visit if he landed in Cyrene when Theodoros was still alive.[54]

[28]

At any rate, whatever way he came, I believe that Plato arrived in southern Italy and Sicily during the same sailing season as he had left Athens. Diogenes has him coming to Italy in order to meet Pythagoreans; this is quite possible since he had known Pythagorean associates in Athens.[55] If, as will be argued below, Plato arrived in southern Italy before the wars of 388 BCE, he may have spent some time in Locri which was an ally of Syracuse, and so it is easily understandable that he received an invitation to the court of Dionysius I.[56] The Platonic Timaeus, the chief speaker of the dialogue bearing his name, whether a fictitious character or not, was a native of Locri. Note also, however, that Locri was more famous for its laws than for its Pythagoreanism, and this is a particular reason why it may have attracted Plato in those days. And it is clear, and important to note, that Plato, in Italy and in Sicily, saw less of a Pythagorean way of life than of the 'dolce vita.'[57]

[29]

From Italy Plato crossed to Sicily.[58] He came as a tourist,[59] but his meeting with Dion was the most significant and far-reaching result of this trip, as can be gathered from the *7th Letter* in particular. Plato need not have stayed for a long time even in Syracuse. I find it quite likely that he left the city in the same autumn, because in *Ep.* 7.330b (cf. 337e ff.) ὁ πρῶτος χρόνος refers to Plato's second visit

---

54. Theodoros seems to have been a middle-aged man when he visited Athens around the end of the 5th century; cf. *Theaetetus* and X. *Mem.* IV 2.10. But it is doubtful whether Plato went to Cyrene to see Theodoros, as Diogenes puts it; cf. the somewhat ironical tone in *Tht.* 143c, 161b, 162a, 164e, and Riginos 1976: 64. Plato may have passed by way of Cyrene on some of his other voyages to Sicily. After all Diogenes' (or Hermodorus') record of places visited by Plato may well reflect some facts, but the order given suggests an attempt to sketch Plato's philosophical development: Athens—Megara—geometry with Theodoros—Pythagoreanism in Italy—Egyptian wisdom—(Magic given up). Note the fact that the three visits to Sicily are not mentioned by Diogenes here but in a later connection, 3.18–24.

55. Simmias and Cebes, above p. 169. The names Philolaus and Eurytus, mentioned by Diogenes 3.6, are probably taken from a post-Platonic legend; *see* the references in Thesleff 1965: 87 f., 147 ff. and below n. 57.

56. Dionysius had married Doris of Locri before 397 BCE: Berve 1957: 18. For the possible invitation, *see* below.

57. This is v. Fritz' interpretation of *Ep.* 7.326b; cf. Guthrie IV 17 n. 4. Note the reflection of these experiences in *Ep.* 3.360ab. In *de fin.* 5.87 Cicero mentions as Plato's teachers the 'Locrians' Echecrates, Timaeus and Arion.

58. *Ep.* 7.326b εἰς Ἰταλίαν τε καὶ Σκελίαν ἦλθον. Cf. Academicorum Index col.X 5–11 p. 6 M.

59. *Ep.* 7.326de κατὰ τύχην. According to various sources, including Diogenes (*see* Riginos 1976: 73 n. 16) he came to see Aetna. It is possible that he was invited to the court of Dionysius, as Nepus (2.2) and others suggest (Berve 1957: 19); and it is not unthinkable that he was already well-known, even in the West, as an author and philosopher (Harward 1932: 16). But Nepus' statement that he was invited from Tarentum is probably based upon the (wrong) assumption that Archytas was at this time the dominating political leader in southern Italy and the central figure in Pythagoreanism (cf. below p. 182).

[29] which lasted about a year, as if the short duration of the first visit was not worth taking into account.

The circumstances of Plato's return to Athens are variously elaborated in our sources. It is rather irrelevant to chronology whether or not he was sold as a slave in Aegina and his freedom bought by a Cyrenean, and so the details and general reliability of the legend are not worth discussing here.[60]

[30] In order to reconstruct the dates of the first voyage, we have to consider the important testimony of *Ep.* 7.324a according to which Plato was σχεδὸν ἔτη τετταράκοντα γεγονώς when he first came to Syracuse. A close reading of the passage will reveal that Plato's (or the author's) point here is to state that at least he was old enough to understand young Dion's intentions when they met for the first time, and so σχεδὸν τετταράκοντα must mean "nearly 40" (allowing for, say, 38 or 39), not "about 40" (allowing for 41 or 42).[61] This suits what we happen to know about the political situation in the West: after the war with Carthage, c. 398–392 BCE, there was a comparatively peaceful period in Italy lasting until 388 when Dionysius began his Italian campaigns which by 386 had secured him domination over most southern Italian cities; then also began the rise of the power of Tarentum under the rule of Archytas who later became a friend of Plato.[62] From this point of view it seems probable that Plato left Athens in the spring of 389 or 388 and arrived in Syracuse in the summer of the same year. The main difficulty here is the development of the 'Corinthian' war in Greece and the East. Considering the increasingly severe naval blockade of Athens since 391 and the Spartan occupation of Aegina,[63] it may seem unlikely that Plato, who had obviously little inclination towards leading an adventurous life, would have taken the risk of a long sea voyage before, say, 387. But there is room for much speculation here. We simply do not know what connections Plato's family or his friends may have had with Sparta or her allies so as to enable him to travel by land and take a safe ship from some Peloponnesian or north-western Greek port.

---

60. For the details, see Riginos 1976: 86–92; cf. Gaiser 1968 and later. The former is more skeptical than the latter. Further arguments for accepting the story are given by Harward 1932: 18 f., Berve 1957: 20, Guthrie IV 19 and n. 1; against it are e.g. Geffcken II A 62 f., Leisegang 1950: 2349. The fact that not the slightest hint at those events exists in the *7th Letter* seems the more natural the more one is inclined to believe in the authenticity of the letter.—The only point in the story which has a possible relevance here is the additional information found in *Anon.Proleg.* p. 193 f. Hermann, referring to the second voyage, that Anniceris the Cyrenean who bought Plato's freedom, was on his way to the Olympic games; if these were the games of 388 BCE, as has been suggested by Ritter 1910: 83–86, cf. Wilamowitz II 82 f., Plato must have returned from Sicily in the early summer of that year; and this would presumably imply that he had spent the winter abroad which, as we have seen, is not particularly likely. Also the help received by Plato from (presumably) an ancestor of Anniceris the hedonist, looks rather like a *ben trovato* anecdote.

61. I took a different view in 1967 (above, p. 16 f.). For the 40 years, see above n. 29.

62. *See* below p. 182. For the historical situation in the West, *see* further details in Bengtson 1960: 279 ff.

63. Xen. *Hell.* 4.8.20, cf. Aristoph. *Plut.* 174.

It is not unimportant to note in this connection that Plato's voyage brought him principally to 'Dorian' cities with Spartan sympathies. [30]

So one or the other of the years 389 and 388 seems an acceptable date for Plato's first voyage to Italy and Sicily.

This first voyage abroad must have meant for Plato a considerable widening of horizons, beside the personal attachment to Dion and the engagement in Syracusan politics which it involved later on. However, one must not over-emphasize (as has very often been done) the suddenness or the scope and depth of these impressions. The involvement with Syracusan affairs followed gradually, and presumably through contact with Dion during his subsequent visits to Athens. In a similar manner, Pythagorean influences certainly reached Plato gradually, both before the voyage, and especially later, through contact with Archytas (below p. [31] 182). The *7th Letter* (especially 326b) rather reads as if the Italy of the 380s was a disappointment to him. Consequently, the dating of various Platonic dialogues by supposed reminiscences of the first voyage, or by the lack of such reminiscences, is much more hazardous than many scholars seem to believe. Details will be discussed below in connection with several dialogues, notably *Gorgias, Meno, Phaedo* and the *Republic*.

*The Academy.* It is practically certain that Plato settled down in the Academeia soon after his return from Sicily.[64] The gymnasium at the Academeia had long been frequented by young men and their teachers,[65] so moving out there was natural for Plato if he had educational plans and did not want to participate in the busy life in the city. Indeed, the choice of this place is rather a sign that his focus of interest had shifted from politics to education (cf. below p. 277). But there is really no evidence to suggest that Plato's Academy was from the start a 'school' or even a θίασος with regular activities and ceremonies.[66] It is often thought that some southern Italian Pythagorean community provided a model for the Academy, but this is in fact very doubtful considering the disintegrated state of Italian Pythagoreanism before the rise of Archytas to power. As a matter of fact the school which Isocrates had opened c. 390 BCE (below p. 180) presented a model closer at hand. At any rate, it is probable that the

---

64. The main sources are various passages in Plutarch and Diog. L. 3.20, cf. 37; cf. Gaiser 1963: 446. Extensive literature exists on the founding and the organization of the Platonic Academy; see the references in Gomperz II (1902): 560, Geffcken II A 73, Guthrie IV 19–24; the anecdotes in Riginos 1976: 119–150.

65. Cimon had laid out a park here, cf. Plut. *Cim.* 13; cf. Ar. *N* 1002 ff., *Lysis* 203a (below p. 296). Plato of course is likely to have known the place well before he decided to settle down there; cf. Diog. L. 3.5 and (for the financial support he received) 3.20.

66. This has been sometimes assumed (e.g. by Ritter 1914: 331) on rather shaky grounds and mainly because of the alleged influences from southern Italian Pythagoreanism. Skepticism about an early date of the 'founding' of the Academy has also been quite common, e.g. Gauss I/2.201 f., Ryle 1966: 222–225 (with hypothetical new interpretation of the evidence, suggesting a date c. 370 BCE), Randall 1970: 11, 22 f.; also implied by Gaiser 1980a: 24. In fact Diog. L. 3.5 (from Alexander Polyhistor) reads as if Plato had *not* founded his own school (in the 'garden') very soon after having started teaching in the Academy (gymnasium?).

[31] organization of Plato's school—whatever its models—took shape only gradually as Plato's fame as a philosopher and teacher grew. It is possible that Plato and some of his pupils in the Academy were engaged in foreign affairs before Plato was asked to Syracuse (below);[67] but we have no means of knowing the degree of Plato's interest in such projects. External contemporary evidence concerning the Academy—such as the notorious lecture 'On the Good,' references in Middle Comedy, the date of persons known to have belonged to Plato's circle, etc.[68]—on the whole point to the 360s or later. The internal evidence adducible from Plato's own writings is, apart from the equally 'late' features of dialogue technique (p. 211), even more scarce, and it begs the question in cases such as the *Meno* (p. 310). Choosing this or any other dialogue as the 'Programmschrift' of the Academy has not provided sufficiently solid hypotheses on which to build.

[32] *Theory of Parmentier.* Parmentier suggested (1913), as a new criterion for dating the dialogues, that Plato probably avoided introducing characters who were still living.[69] He admitted, however, that Callias (who lived in 371 BCE, cf. Xen. *Hell.* 6.3.2) belonged to the tradition which Plato followed in the *Protagoras* and so did not provide a *terminus post quem* for that dialogue. In my view the possibility has to be taken into account that Plato as a rule avoided using living models. But again the *Phaedo* should warn us against applying this theory automatically. It is hardly conceivable that Plato would have written his account of Socrates' last day in the name of Phaedon after the latter's death, if the traditions are to be trusted that Phaedon published dialogues of his own (below p. 205) and even founded a 'school' (Diog. L. 2.105).

*Allusions by Plato to his contemporaries, and vice versa.* This is an extremely intricate complex of problems which has caused endless speculation and controversy due to the scarcity of explicit and dateable references and the abundance of alleged or ambiguous allusions. In spite of the frustrating difficulties involved here, a review of the most important or controversial points is unavoidable.[70]

*The pamphlet of Polycrates.* The rhetor Polycrates is known to have published an attack on Socrates (and indirectly the Socratics) in the name of Anytus, the instigator of the trial of Socrates. Much ingenuity has been spent on reconstructing this pamphlet from references in Xenophon, Libanius and elsewhere, dating

---

67. Dušanič 1979, arguing from Plut. *adv. Col.* 32.1126c and other evidence that such activities took place soon after Leuctra 371 BCE. But his connecting (342 ff.) the finishing of the *Republic* with these incidents is not convincing; cf. Wörle 1981.—On the other hand it is highly probable that the Academy incurred a fame, among ordinary Athenians, of elitism and antidemocratic tendencies; cf. Gaiser 1980a: 20–24.

68. For this material, see Guthrie IV 21–24, and below. For the lecture 'On the Good,' see p. 347.

69. This had of course already occurred to others. Doubts were expressed by e.g. Wilamowitz I 127 n. 1, 131, 212; Taylor 176, 321 n. 2.

70. Further references and criticism can be found in Lutoslawski 57–59, Shorey 1903: 4 and n. 4, Ritter 1910b: 203 ff. Among later allusion-hunters note in particular Eberz 1902–1912 (criticized by Diès II 1927: 332–351), Verdam 1916–1919, Zürcher 1954, and Ryle 1966. Guthrie (IV 42 n. 1), following Field, is prepared to "dismiss altogether" this source of information.

it, and relating it to various Platonic works.[71] It was almost certainly published after 394 BCE because, as ancient authors had noted (Favorinus ap. Diog. L. 2.39), it contained an anachronistic mention of the walls that Conon had built in 394; but a definite lower limit is not found before 380 or later (the death of Lysias who answered it). If the anachronism was not a deliberate one, a relatively late date would be preferable (say, 385 or later); but we do not know anything of its context, and several facts seem to point to a date c. 392.[72]

In this pamphlet the specific charges against Socrates appear to have been as follows: Socrates was the teacher of persons of dubious character and of the rich (Lib. *Declam.* I 13, 16, 23–24, 38, 129), notably such politicians as Alcibiades and Critias (Lib. 136–149, cf. Isocr. *Bus.* 5, X. *Mem.* I 2.12–47, Aeschin. 1.173); he despised Athenian law and democracy (Lib. 13–14, 38, 48, 53, 162–166, cf. X. *Mem.* I 2.9); he criticized great poets (Lib. 62, 82, 92–95, 121–126; X. *Mem.* I 2.56–60) and yet relied on them in his argumentation (Lib. 98); he led an impious life (Lib. 153, 162) and taught the Athenians not to swear by the gods of their fathers (Lib. 109–113); he must have taught even more dangerous things secretly (Lib. 114), such as the right of clever young men to despise their relatives and punish even their fathers (X. *Mem.* I 2.49–55); he did not wish to hold discussions with the old and wise, nor to appear in public (Lib. 117, 133); he made people lazy (Lib. 127); he was not able to earn his living (Lib. 133–134); the Spartans (Lib. 134, 159) and great Athenians such as Themistocles and Aristides have had nothing to do with sophists [such as Socrates] (Lib. 155–160), and Damon was banished [c. 445] from Athens for less serious offenses (Lib. 157).

Some of these points, notably the political aspect, Socrates' association with Alcibiades and Critias, the example of great men, and Socrates' censure of poetry, seem to have been elaborated on after the Platonic *Apology* was written since they are not answered or even mentioned there. On the other hand, they have interesting parallels in various other Platonic works. Whether dialogues such as

---

71. In addition to Xenophon, who (at least partially) answers Polycrates in *Mem.* I 2, and Isocrates' *Busiris* 4–6, the main source is the *Apology of Socrates* by Libanius, *Declam.* I, Vol.V p. 13–121 Foerster; cf. also Themistius *Or.* 23.296bc. The first comprehensive collections of the evidence were made by Markowski 1910 and Mesk 1911; detailed discussions by Wilamowitz II 95–105, Humbert 1931, Hackforth 1933, Geffcken II A 63–65, Treves 1952, Chroust 1955 and 1957: 69–100, Gebhardt 1957 (cf. Kühn 1960), Erbse 1961.

72. Treves 1952: 1739 f.; often accepted, e.g. by Gebhardt 1957: 14. Among the additional clues adduced for dating, the pamphlet, the death of Anytus is sometimes referred to: according to Themistius, *Or.* 20.239c (cf. Diog. L. 2.43, 6.9), he died soon after 399; this is often taken to be a (moralizing) legend, but it may be implied by Xen. *Ap.* 31. Lysias 22.7–9 hardly refers to this Anytus. I find it probable that Anytus the opponent of Socrates was dead when Polycrates wrote his pamphlet, and that this appeared somehow from the latter, because later critics argue against Polycrates and not against the supposed speaker, Anytus. M. H. Hansen 1980: 58–64 (in Danish) is rather over-critical of the attempts to reconstruct the pamphlet, but his inference from the anachronism of the walls, that the text was (partly?) an essay and not a speech in Anytus' name, is probably correct. Note the fact that the walls of Conon symbolized national identity to the Athenians in the negotiations with Sparta and her allies from 392 onwards (Bengtson 1960: 260). Polycrates was a supporter of Thrasybulus and Conon (Chroust 1957: 73, 96), and lived together with the latter at the court of Euagoras of Cyprus about 390 BCE.

[33] *Charmides* or *Protagoras* may have occasioned the pamphlet, and other dialogues such as *Gorgias* or *Symposium* may have answered it, are questions still regarded as unsettled today. They will be discussed in greater detail below.

*Plato and Isocrates.* Plato and Isocrates obviously made allusions to each other in their written works, and were possibly involved in some kind of polemics. The details, however, are highly controversial. It is notoriously difficult and in many cases impossible to ascertain where references occur (because
[34] both authors, each in his own manner, prefer indirect hints), which works they concern, and often, to find independent evidence for dating the works of Isocrates.[73]

At the present state of our knowledge the main points of relevance to Platonic chronology are as follows: Isocrates opened his school in Athens about 390 BCE and soon discarded his former occupation of writing forensic speeches for others (λογογραφία). It is commonly thought (in fact on reasonably certain grounds)[74] that Speech XIII (Κατὰ τῶν σοφιστῶν was written soon after the opening of the school as a kind of 'Programmschrift'; whether it refers to, and is referred to by Plato (notably the *Apology, Gorgias, Euthydemus* and *Phaedrus*) will be discussed below. Speech XI (Βούσειρις) has been dated to the 380s or 370s by its references to Polycrates, and its possible interrelation with Plato's *Republic, Phaedrus* and *Symposium*;[75] we shall consider it in connection with the problems relating to the *Republic* and the *Timaeus*. Furthermore it seems possible to take some account of Speech X (Ἑλένης ἐγκώμιον), late 380s?; IV (Πανηγυρικός), 380; II (Πρὸς Νικοκλέα), c. 373; IX (Εὐαόρας), soon after this; III (Νικοκλῆς), from the 370s?; XIV (Πλαταϊκός), 373; *Letter* I (to Dionysius), not long before 367; Speech VI (Ἀρχίδαμος), 366/5; VIII (Περὶ εἰρήνης), 357/56; VII (Ἀρεοπαγιτικός), soon after 355; and XV (Περὶ ἀντιδόσεως), 354/53, with its several references to Plato.

*Plato and Xenophon.* Here the situation is somewhat similar. There is practically no explicit reference by Xenophon to Plato, and none at all by Plato to Xenophon, but allusions and even influences are likely to occur (and as a rule it is Xenophon who is considered to be dependent on Plato, rather than vice versa);

---

73. Isocratean chronology has not been subject to a detailed scrutiny since Münscher's article, "Isokrates (2)" (1916): 2146–2227, where the earlier discussion is summed up (including the interesting but eccentric analyses by H. Gomperz 1905–1906). Münscher is sometimes overconfident with regard to Platonic chronology which he often adduces for dating Isocrates' works. The later discussion (*see* notably Rick 1931, Ries 1959, Erbse 1971, de Vries 1971, Davies 1971: 245–248) has produced little new evidence. It should be noted that even when a reference in Plato to Isocrates, or vice versa, can somehow be made probable, it does not necessarily concern a recent work: a well-known example is Isocr. *Antid.* XV 13, written in 354, but referring to Plato's *Apology* which was almost certainly published very much earlier; cf. also Raeder 70 f., Ritter 1910a: 192–194.—The special much-debated problem of the exact nature of the antagonism between Plato and Isocrates is on the whole irrelevant to chronology; for references, *see* Ritter 1910b: 129–136, Shorey 1933: 32–35, Howland 1937, and the much too confident reconsideration by Ries 1959.

74. *See* H. Gomperz 1905: 168 f., Münscher 1916: 2171. *Antid.* 193 f. is rather explicit.

75. *See* H. Gomperz 1905: 192–197, Münscher 1916: 2179 f.

and the chronology is in a deplorable flux.[76] At any rate it is practically certain [34] that none of Xenophon's Socratic works was written before the early 380s when he had settled down in Skillous. And though he later (c. 370) moved to Corinth, there is nothing to suggest that he was able, or wanted, to partake in the latest de- [35] bate among the Socratics. He rather draws on existing (mainly written) sources than enters on polemics. Details will be discussed in various connections below, notably with the *Apology, Hippias Major, Ion,* and *Symposium.*

*Plato and Aeschines of Sphettus.* Though the Socratic Aeschines very probably began writing dialogues before Xenophon, the details and dates are even more obscure owing to the fragmentary material.[77] The relationship between Plato and Aeschines presents a wide range of problems;[78] cf. below on *Alcibiades* I, *Charmides, Crito, Gorgias, Ion, Menexenus, Meno, Protagoras* and *Symposium.*

*Plato and Antisthenes.* The interesting and enigmatic character of Antisthenes and his literary work unfortunately casts very little light on Platonic chronology. His impact on Xenophon is beyond doubt. Very probably there was a considerable animosity between him and Plato. Though he probably played a central role in the early history of the λόγοι Σωκρατικοί, the remnants of his philosophical writings are so scarce, and the dates so controversial, that the conjectural considerations relating to Plato's dialogues, which have been suggested by some scholars, must be handled with great caution.[79] Cf. notably *Charmides, Clitopho, Euthydemus, Symposium,* and p. 366 ff. For Antisthenes' use of dialogue, see p. 206.

*Plato and Comedy.* The possible parody of Plato's communistic City in Aristophanes' *Ecclesiazusae,* and Plato's relations with the author of the *Clouds,* present interesting problems which will be discussed in connection with the *Republic* (p. 251) and *Symposium;* cf. also the *Apology.*

The references to Plato in Middle Comedy fragments are not very helpful except for suggesting that Plato was known to have an 'esoteric doctrine,' and a fragment

---

76. The very comprehensive article "Xenophon (6): Xenophone von Athen" (1967) by Breitenbach is firmly skeptical regarding most points (partly against Maier 1913, Delebécque and others). Breitenbach (contrary to Emma Edelstein 1935: 78 ff.) thinks that the Memorabilia in particular has gradually grown by accretion; it was not finished before the 360s (see 1776, 1806, 1809–1811, 1902); cf. also Gigon 1953, Erbse 1961.

77. The reconstruction and discussion of the fragments by Dittmar 1912 is ingenious but hypothetical and relies partially on points of Platonic chronology taken for granted. His inferences have far too often been taken as established facts.

78. Plato is likely to have had more to do, personally, with Aeschines than with Xenophon. Aeschines was present at the death of Socrates (*Phd.* 59b) and also lived in Syracuse after 367; cf. Diog. L. 2.63, Suid. s.v. Αἰσχίνης ὁ τοῦ Λυσανίου, Luc. *Par.* 32.

79. For the assumption that Antisthenes in fact originated the genre of λόγοι Σωκρατικοί, cf. Chroust 1957: 135 ff., Rossetti 1975b: 378. The testimonies and fragments have been recently collected by Caizzi (1966). Examples of obvious over-interpretation of alleged allusions to Antisthenes by Plato, Xenophon and others, occur in various works by Dümmler (especially 1889) and Joël; cf. also Maier 1913, Rick 1931. Taylor (1926: 86 n. 1) thinks that Plato did not refer to Antisthenes before the *Parmenides,* but this is equally conjectural. For the legends relating to the controversies of Plato and Antisthenes, see now Riginos 1976: 98–101.

[35] of Epicrates which suggests that dihaeretic exercises such as those seen in the *Sophist* and the *Politicus* were current in the Academy (p. 342).[80] For Theopompus *see Phaedo*; for Alexis *see Symposium*; for Anaxandrides *see Hippias Major*.

[36] *Other contemporary persons.* References in Platonic works to Gorgias (*see* notably *Gorgias, Meno, Symposium*), Hippias (*see Hippias Major, Hippias Minor, Protagoras*), Prodicus (*see* notably *Protagoras*), Lysias (*see* notably *Phaedrus*), and various other persons who were active in Athenian public life in the 4th century, provide very few overt clues; the most obvious anachronism of this kind is one found in the *Sisyphus* (p. 375); more disputable are the alleged anachronisms of *Ion* (p. 367).

The biographical facts relating to the pupils and friends of Plato who are known to have joined or otherwise been in contact with the Academy, provide very little that would illuminate events before, say, the 360s.[81]

The first and foremost of these friends is Dion (above, p. 175) who is very likely to have visited Athens and stayed with Plato on several occasions before Plato's second voyage to Sicily, though we know nothing of the details.

Plato's relations with Archytas of Tarentum are likewise unclear. It is possible that Plato had already met him on his first visit to Italy. However, we hear of contacts between the two only after Archytas' rise to the position of political and spiritual leader of the Tarentinian confederation some time after 386 BCE. The legends about Archytas assisting Plato in acquiring some Pythagorean manuals are possibly based to some extent on fact.[82] The Pythagorean trends in Plato's later philosophy (*see* notably *Timaeus* and *Philebus*) and other evidence indicate a gradually deepening interest in southern Italian Pythagoreanism which, towards the mid-fourth century, was represented above all by Archytas. As far as we know, there was a mutual give and take between the 'schools' of Plato and Archytas; indeed, it may well be that Archytas on the whole owed more to the Academy than the Academy owed to him.

Other friends and contemporaries of Plato will be discussed in various connections below, notably Phaedon (p. 289), Theaitetos (p. 301), Heraclides of Pontus (p. 315), Philip of Opous (p. 349), and Eudoxus (p. 372). For Aristotle, *see* below p. 184.[83] For Hermodorus and other early biographers of Plato (including detractors such as Aristoxenus), *see* p. 167 ff.[83] For the discussion of Plato's lecture 'On the Good,' *see* p. 347.

---

80. Amphis fr. 6 (II 237 K) seems to allude to Plato's τἀγαθόν, but so does Philippides fr. 6 (III 303 K) about the end of the 4th century; cf. Theapompos fr. 15 (I 737 K) and Alexis fr. 112 (II 359 K); *see* Gaiser 1963: 446 and later. For other references, *see* Düring 1941: 137–142, Webster 1970: 50 ff.

81. Zeller II 1$^5$ 982 ff. gives a comprehensive list of such persons (the references attached are of course partly out-of-date).

82. The first reliable evidence of such contacts, *Ep.* 7.338c (cf. 350a), refers to the year 366 BCE. Wilamowitz I 545 suggests that Plato had not known Archytas before, but I find it perfectly possible that Archytas had by then visited Athens and Plato's Academy. Further references can be found in Burkert 1962 (passim) and in Thesleff 1965, especially 45–47.

83. For the other members of the Academy, *see* above n. 61.

*The second voyage to Sicily.* As far as the evidence goes, Plato had been living in Athens for more than twenty years when Dionysius I died in the spring of 367 and Plato was invited to Sicily by Dion.[84] Dion was banished from Syracuse three or four months after Plato's arrival, but Plato stayed for a considerable time after this and apparently was not allowed to leave for Athens until the following spring when there was a state of war in Sicily.[85] It is less clear whether Plato departed for Sicily in 367 or 366, and consequently whether he returned in 366 or 365. Both alternatives have had several advocates; the earlier one seems to me slightly preferable.[86] The second voyage was a failure, as has been eloquently described in many modern biographies of Plato. It is very reasonable to infer that there occurred a change in Plato's orientation and philosophical activities after this return, though there is little agreement as to what these changes consisted of and how Plato's later works should be arranged in relation to these events. See the discussions of *Phaedrus* (p. 319), *Parmenides* (p. 305), the *Republic* (p. 332), *Theaetetus* (p. 334) and *Timaeus* (p. 335).[87]

*The third voyage to Sicily.* This voyage can be exactly dated: the visit lasted from the summer of 361 BCE to the early summer of 360.[88] The complete failure of this voyage is a biographical fact of importance, though its implications for the chronology of the writings of Plato are again controversial;[89] *see* notably the discussions of 'On the Good' (p. 201), *Timaeus* and *Critias* (p. 189) and the *Laws* (p. 186). The subsequent chaotic development of Sicilian affairs and the murder of Dion in the summer of 354 BCE[90] must have cast a long shadow over Plato's last years.

*Various references to contemporary events in Plato's works.* Much inventiveness has also been expended on detecting allusions of this kind, but they are for the

---

84. References in Guthrie IV 24 and n. 3. Harward 1932: 12 argues that there was in Athens about 367 a markedly favorable attitude to the Dionysii, which of course would have made Plato's decision easier.

85. *Ep.* 7.327c–330b, 337e–340b; cf. Diog. L. 3.21; Academicorum Index col.X 22 ff. p. 9 M is very fragmentary. On the war, *see* also Plut. *Dion* 16. Berve's argument (1957: 34 n. 1, 41 f.) that Plato stayed only for one summer (366 BCE) is hardly acceptable.

86. For the earlier alternative, *see* e.g. Unger 1891: 210 f. (a war with Carthage), Skemp 1952: 15; for the later one, e.g. Wilamowitz I 545 (the Lucanian war of 365; but this would not necessarily have affected the conditions in Sicily), Guthrie IV 26 and n. 1. The issue largely depends on whether Dionysius the elder died sufficiently early in 367 for the news to reach Plato in the spring or the early summer at the latest. It seems that Plato would not have delayed his departure, and also that Dion would not have been banished after the sailing season was over.

87. Even the development of the theory of Forms has sometimes been seen in relation to his experiences in Sicily, e.g. by Kapp 1968: 78 f.

88. *Ep.* 7.330c, 337e, 340b–341a, 345c–351e; Academicorum Index col.X 35–43 p. 9 f. M, cf. col.Z 9–15 p. 11; Diog. L. 3.23. The date can be inferred from two events: Plato's meeting Dion at the Olympic games on his return journey; and the solar eclipse of 12 May 361 (Plut. *Dion* 19); cf. Guthrie IV 24 n. 1, following Wilamowitz; the eclipse was formerly dated in 360 (cf. Raeder 1906: 436, Ritter 1910b: 139 f., 146 f.).

89. Pfleiderer 1896: 535 f. n. thought that Plato was suffering from a serious nervous breakdown (cf. Sen. *Ep.* ad Luc. 58); cf. Hackforth 1945: 1, Raeder 1950 (in Danish). Note on the other hand the description of mental exhaustion in *Ti.* 88a.

90. For references to the life of Dion, *see* Berve 1957 and 1963 [sic!].

[37]

[38]

most part highly debatable.[91] The best-known and most unanimously accepted anachronistic allusions occur in *Menexenus*, implying the peace of Antalcidas in 386 BCE (p. 265), and *Symposium*, implying an event in 385/4 BCE (p. 266). Both are quite obviously deliberate. Other examples of anachronism are the possible allusions to the bribery and trial of Ismenias after 395 BCE in *Meno* and *Republic* I (p. 258 n. 266). Some further instances will be discussed below. The mention of the defeat of Locri in the 350s in the *Laws* I 638b is strictly speaking not an anachronism, since the dramatic date of the dialogue is not clearly located in the past; but it is a useful *terminus post quem* for at least part of the *Laws* (p. 334). For references to contemporary events in the *Letters*, see p. 379; *Ep.* 7, whether authentic or not, must have been written fairly soon after the death of Dion in 354.

*Plato and Aristotle.* Aristotle came to the Academy as a youngster of seventeen in 367 BCE.[92] His comments on Plato's doctrines, notably in the *Metaphysics*,[93] seem to imply discrepancies with what is written in the dialogues—the most important discrepancies concern the mathematical foundations of the theory of Forms—which have been explained in various ways. Insofar as we are able to reconstruct from Aristotle's report a reasonably reliable picture of changes in Plato's philosophy, this is of course extremely relevant to the question of Platonic chronology. Unfortunately, again, there are few or no independent clues from which to begin. The whole of this vexed problem is involved with the question of Plato's 'unwritten doctrines.'[94] The occasional direct references to Platonic works in Aristotle cannot be used for dating the dialogues, except for the note on the relation between the *Republic* and the *Laws* (p. 186).[95]

The most important apparent allusion to Aristotle in Plato occurs in the *Parmenides* (p. 305); others have been found in *Republic* X (p. 332) and, even more conjecturally, elsewhere.

*Death of Plato.* Plato's death occurred without any doubt in 347 BCE.[96] There has been some speculation as to whether his death was the reason why the *Critias* is unfinished (p. 337), or why the dialogue 'Philosophus' was never written

---

91. Examples from the earlier discussion in Hirzel 1895: 182–189, Raeder 64 ff. Later especially Eberz 1902–1912, Verdam 1916–1919 and H. M. Wolff 1957 have traced allusions of this kind. Wilamowitz declared in 1897 that there are no anachronistic allusions at all in Plato, but later changed his mind.

92. Ritter 1923: 134 suggested that he did not meet Plato until after the latter's return from Sicily (above p. 183), but this is quite conjectural. References to the anecdotes concerning Aristotle and Plato in Riginos 1976: 129–134.

93. All explicit or otherwise clear references to Plato have been recorded by Bonitz, Ind. Arist. 598 f.; cf. Zeller II 1⁴ 448 ff., Cherniss 1944 (lacking an Index), Tack 1970.

94. There are references to the earlier discussion in Raeder 72 f. Later the problem has been ventilated especially by Cherniss (1944 etc.) and the participants in the controversy about Plato's unwritten doctrine; cf. above p. 152.

95. Aristotle's references, or lack of references, have sometimes been used as arguments for, or against, the authenticity of the Platonic works. But such arguments have little value; cf. below p. 116 n. l, 220 f.

96. *See* the testimonies and references in Davies 1971: 333.

(p. 341). It can be stated with much more confidence that the *Laws* was published posthumously, and that the same editor probably published the *Epinomis* (p. 349).

[38]

**References from one Platonic work to another.** Explicit references of this kind are extremely rare in Plato. Also references to earlier or later passages in the same work are rare; and since they are normally irrelevant to the present study, there is no reason to discuss them here.[97]

[39]

The only unambiguous instances of cross-reference between different dialogues occur between the *Sophist* and *Politicus*, perhaps implying also a forthcoming 'Philosophus' (p. 341). And in the *Timaeus* we have a fairly certain reference to *Critias* and perhaps a 'Hermocrates,' both supposed to follow (p. 336 n. 574).

A much-disputed problem is whether the introductory section of *Timaeus* refers to the *Republic* as we have it, to an earlier version of it, or to a fictitious or real discussion (p. 251). Some of the *Letters* contain a mention of some dialogues; these instances are on the whole not relevant to the dating, but *see* p. 341.

Rather more implicitly, various passages in the *Laws* refer to the *Republic*;[98] and the *Epinomis* clearly purports to be a continuation of the *Laws*, as *Critias* continues the *Timaeus*, and as the *Sophist* and *Politicus*, more cryptically, appear to link up with the *Parmenides* and *Theaetetus*.

For other alleged linkages, sometimes taken as implicit references, *see* below p. 186.

**Ancient testimony regarding the publication of Plato's writings.** The tetralogical arrangement adopted in the manuscripts aims at grouping together works with related contents; obviously it is not based upon any genuine knowledge of the order in which they were originally written. Moreover, the earlier trilogical arrangement, supposed to have been introduced by Aristophanes of Byzantium, was almost certainly irrelevant to Platonic chronology. Both arrangements may possible reflect Academic practice and may derive, ultimately, from Plato's own grouping of some of his later works: the *Republic* is supposed to be followed (at some 'distance,' to be sure) by *Timaeus, Critas* (and 'Hermocrates,' p. 336); *Theaetetus* is supposed to be followed by the *Sophist, Politicus* (and 'Philosophus,' p. 341).[99] For the early history of the Corpus, cf. below p. 230 ff.

We know of various more or less untrustworthy anecdotes and traditions relating to the publication of some Platonic dialogues.[100] The most persistent of

---

97. The dialogue situation of course does not normally permit references like "As was said above," "See below," though the type "As we have agreed" is not uncommon. Geffcken II A 128 n. 5 notes some references in the *Laws* to passages that do not exist in our text, as indications that the work was left unfinished by Plato.
98. *See* Ritter 1910b: 216, and below p. 348.
99. This has been argued in some detail by Robin 1938: 32 f. Others have argued that the terralogical arrangement cannot possibly derive from the early Academy, e.g. C. W. Müller 1975: 27–41, Tarán 1975: 6.
100. References in Leisegang 1950: 2329 f. Some points will be discussed below.—*Anon.Proleg.* 26 p. 219 f. Hermann proposes a 'correct' order for reading the dialogues.

[39] these is the belief that the *Phaedrus* was a very early, or perhaps even Plato's first dialogue (*see* below p. 319). *See* also *Gorgias* (p. 275), *Lysis* (p. 296), *Phaedo* (p. 288), *Timaeus* and *Critias* (p. 337). The only piece of evidence which is manifestly reliable is Aristotele's statement (*Pol.* II 6.1264b24–27) that the *Republic* was written before the *Laws*.

[40] **Arguments from the contents**

In this chapter I shall consider a wide variety of arguments, or types of argument, which are taken from the contents of the dialogues and which are traditionally believed to indicate, implicitly, the chronological order in which the passages in question were written.

This heterogeneous group of criteria has been thought by most students of Platonic chronology to supply highly important additional evidence. Many scholars, notably in the 19th century but also in later times, have been inclined to prefer arguments from the contents ('thematic criteria') to the linguistic criteria (below, p. 213). Indeed, indications of the former type are sometimes regarded as a kind of 'implicit cross-references' between the dialogues.

In principle, the category here discussed does not of course involve any theory of 'evolution' in Plato's thought, though most of the users of this type of argument have held such a theory. Basically and theoretically, this chapter should be concerned with all kinds of general lines, or points of detail, or aspects of the contents of the Platonic writings that can be interpreted to speak in favor of a certain chronological order. In practice, however, we can discuss only a very limited selection of such thematic points or aspects. In this connection it will be sufficient to focus on some general problems and to give a few examples.

In the first place, it is reasonable to start from the assumption that a study of the treatment of the same idea in different dialogues may provide clues to the chronological order. Also the lack of an idea, or a different combination of ideas, can be regarded as significant, though here we are facing the notoriously difficult complex of arguments *ex silentio*.

Since there is no evidence that dialogues other than the *Sophist*—*Politicus*, and *Timaeus*—*Critias*, and *Laws*—*Epinomis* form coherent sets (above p. 185), Plato's methods of developing an idea or a series of thoughts within the frames of one work are not of particular interest here. In the great majority of cases a Platonic work can be considered as an independent whole.[101] And so the relations of the dialogues is a question of the relation between different entities.

A very common approach since the early days of genetic interpretation has been the tracing of general trends in Plato's doctrines or, more generally, his philosophy. Often the argument has been, at least in appearance, cumulative: a

---

101. The theories of early tetralogies have no factual basis; cf. below p. 213.

certain chronological order suggested by other criteria or otherwise taken for [40] granted, is thought to receive further confirmation from the trend of development or change found in Plato's way of reasoning or the focusing of his interest. The fact that this approach to the chronological problems often begs the question accounts for some of the discrepancies between the results at which different scholars have arrived.

The most frequently discussed ideas or areas of thought considered as revealing such trends are the following: the cardinal virtues;[102] teach- [41] ing and education;[103] anti-hedonism;[104] political theory;[105] physics and cosmology;[106] religion;[107] psychology, immortality of soul and reincarnation;[108] the theory of Forms and, in general, metaphysics;[109] logic in a narrow [42]

---

102. Plato's doctrine of virtues and their internal relations was a much-discussed topic up to the 1920s. For details, cf. Olzscha's extensive but superficial discussion (1910). Shorey of course denied all trends of change here (1903: 9–27). Very often the system of virtues in the *Republic* has been thought to result (in various ways) from the discussion in the 'earlier' dialogues; a special problem has been seen in the position and possible dropping of ὁσιότης. One of the unsuccessful solutions attempted was to connect closely those dialogues which purport to seek a definition of one of the cardinal virtues (*Laches, Charmides, Euthyphro, Republic* I). It has also been suggested that Plato in his early works intended to make his Socrates an incarnation of each of these virtues (e.g. Wilamowitz I 186 f., 209). Cf. also Kube 1969.

103. These questions are approached in different manners in very many dialogues; finding clear trends is a frustrating task if the chronological order cannot be ascertained on other grounds. Cf. e.g. the 'maieutics' theoretically discussed in the *Theaetetus* and applied in practice in the *Meno*.

104. It is sometimes thought that Plato gradually abandoned a rigid anti-hedonistic position; this was argued rather too one-sidedly by Beare 1913. For instance, the *Protagoras* (cf. Shorey 1903: 20–25, 38 n. 597) and *Phaedo* do not fit very well into this 'trend.'

105. The main problem here is the possibly gradual development and decline of the doctrine of the Ideal State; these trends are often seen in relation to Plato's experiences in Sicily.

106. Notably the relation of the 'earlier' dialogues, including *Phaedo* and *Phaedrus*, to *Timaeus*.

107. Here the problems include the presence of 'Socratic' agnosticism and 'daemonism' in 'later' dialogues; the rise of astral religion; and the earlier stages of the theocratic view of the *Laws*.

108. The extensive earlier discussion (cf. e.g. Groag 1913–1915) is now covered by Guthrie (1957). There are many controversial problems involved such as the possibly gradual development of the notion of a tripartite soul, the rise of the doctrine (or doctrines) of immortality, and the anamnesis doctrine (sometimes seen as particularly problematic, cf. Cobb 1973). It is generally believed that the doctrinal trends in Plato's psychology (especially in the eschatological myths) indicate the chronological order *Gorgias—Meno—Phaedo—Republic—Phaedrus—Timaeus—Politicus* (?)—*Laws*. Shorey (1903: 40–42) denied the existence of all trends here too. Cf. p. 312.

109. This is a topic really πολυθρύλητος, as it was even in the days of Plato (*Phd.* 100b). Most serious writers on Plato have expressed an opinion of how the theory arose, whether it contained notable changes, and why there are seemingly no traces of it in some of the dialogues. For some of the difficulties, *see* the clear-cut discussion by Ritter 1910b: 564 ff. Particularly controversial points of issue have been whether the theory is somehow implied in the 'early' or 'Socratic' dialogues (this is traditionally denied by the geneticists, e.g. Lutoslawski, Raeder, Ritter and Wilamowitz, also Natorp, and more recently by e.g. Bluck 1949, Rist 1975; affirmed by e.g. Shorey, Stenzel, Regenbogen (1950: 207–210), Crombie (II 252–261), Allen 1970, Martin 1973, Findlay 1974, Gundert 1977: 178 ff.), and whether and in what respects Plato changed it later, or perhaps even abandoned it. Since the establishment of the 'late' group of dialogues, it has very often been argued (partially following Aristotle) that there occurred essential changes in the theory of Forms,

[42]   sense;[110] epistemology;[111] dialectic and dihaeretic method;[112] mathematics;[113] theory of love;[114] theory of poetry and aesthetics;[115] and Plato's attitude to sophists and the great men of Athenian history.[116]

---

though agreement on the details has not been reached (cf. notably Jackson 1882–1886, Lutoslawski 424–434 (also id. 1949), Benn 1902, Raeder 84, Ueberweg-Praechter 284–286; more recently e.g. Cherniss 1944, 1945, Ross 1951, Kamlah 1963, Raven 1965, Kapp 1968, Guthrie V (especially 427 f.), Shiner 1974, Violette 1977; cf. the articles collected by Allen 1965). The unitarian position implies little or no change in the theory of Forms, but further complications may seem to arise from the hypothesis of Plato's unwritten doctrines on the ultimate principles (in addition to Gaiser and Krämer, see notably Runciman in Allen 1965: 149 ff., de Vogel 1960, Ebert 1974: 7 f., Findlay 1974, Gadamer 1974). One of the basic reasons for this persistent diversity of views is the fact that Plato is not on the whole very explicit as regards his doctrine of the Forms; and the implications of the criticism of Aristotle and of Plato himself in the *Parmenides* (cf. also *Republic* X) are not very clear.

110. Lutoslawski considered the 'development of Plato's logic' in a very large sense as involving all kinds of modes of thought, but he also argued that Plato became more and more aware of logic in the strict (rather more Aristotelian) sense. This view has been severely criticized, and many scholars have pointed out that apparent errors or irrationalities in Plato's logic may often be intentional or at least may not indicate trends of development (e.g. Ritter 1910b: 228 f., Apelt Prt 4 f., Ueberweg-Praechter 211 f.; and especially Cohen 1962, Sprague 1962; Hintikka 1973: 3–5 warns against anachronistic approaches). Another problem is whether the very different manners of handling logic in, say, *Hippias Minor* and the *Sophist* necessarily indicate different periods.

111. As can be seen from the *Republic* in particular, Plato's theory of knowledge is largely connected with the theory of Forms. To many scholars the 'trend' of development of Platonic epistemology is in keeping with the results of stylometry (below, p. 216); this conception was strongly opposed by Shorey (1903, especially 14 n. 76, 43 f., 48 n. 357). The special problems relevant here include the question of the relations of *Charmides, Cratylus, Meno, Republic* and *Theaetetus*, and the possible development of the theory of anamnesis (for this see especially Bluck 1961: 50–52 and the discussion of Plato's psychology, above n. 108). Some scholars have been inclined to assign a comparatively late date to the *Cratylus* (cf. below p. 314). The linear trend from 'Socratic' ἐπιστήμη to a later gradual acceptance of αἴσθησις, as suggested by Beare 1913, is clearly an oversimplification.

112. The controversies have concerned interpretation rather than chronology, although problems of the chronological order of the dialogues are usually involved. See notably Shorey (1903: 31 n. 200, 50 ff.), Regenbogen 1950 (206 f., arguing for a late date of *Phaedrus*), Goldschmidt (1947) 1971, Gundert 1971, Moravcsik 1973 (158–167).

113. Here the main points of issue have been the date of *Meno*, the influence of Pythagorean ideas (p. 182), the date of the death of Theaitetos (p. 302) and the date of Eudoxus (p. 372). Cf. also Brumbaugh 1954, Wedberg 1955 (probably over-interpreting the evidence). It is doubtful whether and in what respects the metaphysics of mathematics implied in the theory of Plato's unwritten doctrine, are in any sense reflected in the mathematical passages of *Meno, Republic, Theaetetus, Timaeus* and other dialogues.

114. Robin's comprehensive discussion (1908) has not settled the issue. The doctrinal and chronological relations of *Lysis, Phaedrus* and *Symposium*, together with some passages of the *Republic*, present controversial problems still today. 'Psychologizing' approaches such as the attempt of Brès 1968 are easily misleading. Cf. below p. 319.

115. The most comprehensive discussion is Vicaire 1960 who follows the main lines of conventional chronology. However, the trends are far from clear. The problems include the rise of Plato's critical attitude, the position of *Ion*, and the relation of the *Republic* (especially Book X) and the *Laws* to the apparent modification of aesthetics represented by the *Philebus*.

116. Apparent changes in these attitudes have often been noted, but there is little agreement on trends (though the explicit criticism of Protagoras in the *Theaetetus* is now universally thought to be later than the rather implicit one in the dialogue *Protagoras*). A close study of the different ways of characterizing and describing various persons in the Platonic dialogues may reveal some clues both to problems of authenticity and to chronology; some notes on this will be made below.

Many of the difficulties involved here have often been realized, or at least [43] stated in words even by ardent believers in trends of development in Plato's philosophy, including of course Lutoslawski. For instance, Raeder (74–87) lists the following points:

—— risk of arbitrary subjectivism in the interpretation;
—— risk of vicious circle in arguing an order for the dialogues from a trend in the contents which is derived from a certain order taken for granted;
—— a 'mythic' (Schleiermacher) or implicit vision does not necessarily precede rational reasoning or vice versa;
—— positive doctrines and criticism may be interwoven in the dialogues, and so the alleged tendency from skeptical criticism to positive statement of doctrinal facts (Hermann) is unreliable as a criterion of chronology;
—— a brief or compressed discussion is not necessarily earlier than an extensive one, or vice versa;
—— though Plato's logic is likely to have developed, a greater precision is not necessarily a sign of a later date;
—— the information supplied by ancient authors, notably Aristotle, on trends in Plato's philosophy is to some extent controversial.

Yet very many scholars who profess to being aware of the difficulties, or apparently are aware of at least some of them, have used arguments from the contents with a surprising degree of assurance. And if such scholars are regarded as authorities, such assurance can have far-reaching consequences.

A few examples of obviously arbitrary interpretation may be given here.

Zeller II $1^5$ 511 insisted that *Parmenides* 129c must refer to the *Sophist* 251a which he considered rather early; but the well-founded (though not entirely unanimous, cf. p. 343) opinion of modern scholarship is that the *Sophist* follows the *Parmenides* chronologically. Similarly, Zeller II $1^5$ 548 n. 2 argued that the passages *Republic* VI 505b and IX 583b ff. refer to the *Philebus*, whereas the consensus now is that *Philebus*, as belonging to the 'late group,' must be later than the *Republic*. Christ 1886: 489, accepting Zeller's early dating of the *Sophist*, thought that the mention in the *Sophist* 217c of a discussion between Parmenides and Socrates in the early youth of the latter refers forward to the *Parmenides* to come, whereas most scholars now take this passage to indicate the opposite order.

Lutoslawski 1897: 355 thought that the mere mention of Polemarchus' inclination to philosophy in *Phaedrus* 257b is likely to refer to the *Republic* where, it is true, Polemarchus has a minor role in the first book.

Natorp 1903: 118 stated that *Euthydemus* 286c and 288a "mit voller Sicherheit" [44] refer to the refutation of the position of Protagoras in the *Theaetetus*, but modern scholars usually place *Theaetetus* after *Euthydemus*. Natorp also (116 f.) found a 'clear' forward reference from *Theaetetus* 190e to the supposed criticism of Antisthenes in *Euthydemus* 285a–288d ("wenn je Plato in einer seiner Schriften die nächstfolgende voraus angekündigt hat, dann hier").

[44]     In the *Republic* IV 430c Socrates says he is prepared to discuss courage more fully another time. This was taken by Siebeck to indicate that the *Laches* was written later; Ritter 1910b: 219 and others who believe that *Laches* is earlier think that the passage in the *Republic* is irrelevant for dating the *Laches*; but Apelt (Staat, p. 468 n. 38) in spite of his usual skepticism in chronological matters, wanted to interpret it as indicating that the *Laches* was already published.[117]

Th. Gomperz II 1902: 231 is careful to point out that, although the development of an author ("der Fortschritte eines Autors, der Fortgang vom Unvollkommeneren zum Vollkommeneren") is—as was the conviction of his age—a reliable criterion of chronology (indeed, "das sicherste Merkmal der zeitlichen Abfolge seiner Werke"), it cannot be derived automatically from the texts. Even so, he is apparently under the illusion that arguments from the contents can be given primary importance: "Wenn am Schluss eines Gespräches ein Problem als ungelöst gilt und dieses in einem anderen Dialoge seine Lösung findet; wenn eine Frage hier in spielender und gleichsam tastender, dort in tief eindringender Weise verhandelt wird; wenn einmal eine Grundlage gewonnen, ein andermal auf dieser Grundlage fortgebaut wird; wenn Platon jetzt eine Untersuchung in Aussicht stellt und sie dann thatsächlich in Angriff nimmt; wenn der Dialog A auf B klärlich voraus- oder das Gespräch D auf C deutlich zurückweist—in all diesen Fällen kann über das Zeitverhältnis den fraglichen Schriften kein Zweifel bestehen." Unfortunately this is the kind of foundation upon which chronological research has largely been based, to some extent even in this century.

Ritter 1910b: 223–231 was the first to argue consistently that such alleged implicit 'references,' or indeed any 'line of development' in Plato's philosophy, cannot be trusted as the primary criteria of chronology; instead, he advocated a cautious application of stylometry (below, p. 213). Yet Ritter himself, and many after him, have rather too easily resorted to arguments from the contents when other criteria are not readily available. The juxtaposition of the books of Pohlenz 1913 and von Arnim 1914 gives a good illustration of how precarious and ambiguous arguments from the contents may be: both were good scholars, and they had a wealth of material at their disposal; yet they managed to argue two considerably different chronologies for Plato's earlier writings by using the criteria differently (von Arnim admittedly intended his book to be a secondary support for his primary stylometrical arguments of 1912).

[45]     At the beginning of this century, the warner *par préférence* against using chronological arguments of any kind frivolously was of course Shorey (1903) whose book, however, received little attention on the continent of Europe. It was rather the creed of Ritter that won general acceptance, or to which lip-service was paid. As was mentioned above (p. 150), his influence has been very considerable. For various mediating positions between the extremes of preferring one-sidedly either

---

117. The fact that the 'promise' at the end of the *Menexenus* is never carried out (at least literally) should warn us not to take passages such as *Prt.* 357b εἰσαῦθις σκεψόμεθα too seriously. Cf. below p. 359.

arguments from the contents or arguments from the style, *see* (after Raeder 1905) Ueberweg-Praechter[13] 1953: 211 f., Cherniss IV 1959: 249–260, Guthrie IV 1975: 45–48. But even compromises of this kind are of doubtful methodological value (cf. Apelt 1908).

[45]

The most generally accepted frame for the trends to be traced in Plato's philosophy is the old hypothesis of a first 'Socratic stage' followed by one or two earlier 'Platonic stages' (the later of these, the environment of the *Republic*, is often called the 'mature stage' of the 'middle period'), and a 'late stage.' This is the frame for the 'Lutoslawski-Raeder-Ritter' view of Platonic chronology. It is symptomatic, however, of the growing skepticism that doubts regarding the reliability of this conception have begun to spread outside the 'unitarian' circles. Notably the 'Socratic' dialogues have been shown to contain a considerable number of 'Platonic' features.[118]

Moreover, the often-realized truth that Plato 'knew more than he said' in his written works, may have a fundamental importance for the discussion of Platonic chronology, if consistently applied as a touchstone to the arguments from the contents. This aspect is primarily independent of the question of whether he had a separate oral doctrine. The irony of the aporetic passages in particular has often been pointed out.[119] But this is only a minor part of a large complex of problems.

New and far-reaching difficulties may seem to follow from the recent theories of Plato's 'unwritten doctrine' of metaphysical principles beyond the Forms (cf. above, p. 152). Determining whether and to what extent such a doctrine ran parallel with the written works, is bound to remain largely hypothetical; and in fact almost all the evidence comes from Plato's 'late period' whereas the earlier stages of the 'unwritten doctrine' are almost entirely obscure.[120] Still, when all is said and pace Cherniss, nobody has managed to prove that there was no esoteric discussion going on in the Academy or, else, that Plato's written works give a faithful picture of his philosophical development.

[46]

---

118. Cf. above p. 170 and the discussion below, passim. Early non-unitarian skeptics include Immisch 1899: 561, 612 ff., 1915: 549 and Joël 1906a: 310 ff. Since the 1940s skepticism regarding a distinct 'Socratic' period in Plato's philosophy has become increasingly common, Jaeger's clear-cut position against this hypothesis (e.g. II² 150, 155 f.) was probably at one time highly influential (cf. also Friedländer III² 417, though he inclines to accept a conventional grouping of the dialogues). Very much unlike Jaeger, Popper 1947: 258 ff. (cf. 183 n. 5) saw in the dialogues a gradual 'betrayal' of Socrates and arrived at an order not very different from Lutoslawski's.

119. With greatly varying emphasis: cf. e.g. De Corte 1938: 505 ff., de Vries 1949, W. Schulz 1960, Cohen 1962, Erbse 1962, 1968, Witte 1970, Martin 1973, Detel 1974.

120. Apart from the denunciation of writing for constructive philosophical purposes in the *Phaedrus* (and clearly late sources such as the *7th Letter*), and various notices deriving from Aristotle and other pupils of Plato, the *Philebus, Politicus*, and *Parmenides* in particular, and also the *Republic*, have provided material for Gaiser and Krämer; cf. Krämer 1964b, 1968: 111 and n. 21, 123 f., 128–135. However, certain passages in *Charmides, Gorgias, Lysis, Meno* and *Protagoras* have also been adduced. Gadamer 1968: 16 and n. 9 argued from a possible reference to a Platonic ἑν/δυάς doctrine in a fragment of the comedian Theopompus (fr. 15, I 737 K, Diog. L. 3.26) that Plato's oral teaching on the principles may reach back at least to the 370s.

[46]　　　At any rate, we are now aware more clearly perhaps than ever before of the possibility that the apparent changes in the doctrinal contents of the dialogues, or the shifts of emphasis, do not necessarily reflect directly trends of development in Plato's thought. On the contrary, it seems more and more reasonable to assume that the question of the chronological order of the dialogues should not be identified with the question of Plato's development.[121] A doctrinal 'advance' ('trend,' 'progress,' 'development,' 'evolution,' whatever term is preferred) turns out to be an unreliable and elusive criterion of chronology, if one accepts that the dialogues with their various purposes only give partial expression to complexes of thought which Plato preferred to communicate orally.

　　　It is certainly impossible to invent a single method, or set of methods, to ascertain solely on the evidence of internal factors the order in which two related passages in two different dialogues were written.[122] And indeed, interpretation can be manipulated to 'indicate' almost anything.

　　　I shall attempt here to illustrate the almost frustrating difficulties that arguments from the contents may involve, by a detailed consideration of the passages on ἀνδρεία in the *Laches* and the *Protagoras*. The relation of these passages is a much-debated question which is still apparently unsettled, though the last active participants in the debate (Hermann 1972 and de Romilly 1980) have argued for the
[47]　priority of *Laches*. Scholars who have tried to demonstrate, with special consideration of the ἀνδρεία passages, that *Laches* is the earlier dialogue include Horn 1893: 22, 54, 740–144; Pfleiderer 1896: 136 f., Lutoslawski (206), Raeder (110 f.), Mutschmann 1911: 474 f., Pohlenz 1913: 78 f., 94, 112; 1916: 250 f.; Stefanini I 1932: 167 n. 3, 169; Festugière 1946, Steidle 1950: 134 f., Boehme 1959: 97–99 and A. Hermann 1972: 21–26. In general, many scholars have preferred to take *Laches* as the earlier dialogue for various not particularly clear and often unspecified reasons (cf. p. 358). These include Taylor 1926, Schaerer 1938, Gaiser 1959, Gauss 1952, Guthrie 1975, Rist 1975. Some prefer to leave the question open because the relation of the ἀνδρεία passages is not clear, e.g. Immisch 1899: 615 f., Ritter 1922: 80–103, Shorey 1933: 499, Geffcken II 58, Friedländer II 285 n. 7, III 418; Hinske 1968. Others, again, incline to think that the *Protagoras* is the earlier dialogue, in which case the ἀνδρεία passages are usually interpreted to indicate this. Such scholars are notably Natorp 1903: 19 f., von Arnim 1914: 1–37,

---

121. Cf. Shorey, Stenzel and others, above p. 5; Goldschmidt 1950: 27 f.; Krämer 1964a (quoted above p. 152 n. 12).

122. Cf. the criticism by Raeder, above p. 189. Yet clues of general applicability have sometimes been produced even in recent literature. For instance, Crombie I 1962: 10 regards as a fairly reliable criterion "the unintelligibility of something in one dialogue to anybody who has not read another." I doubt whether this is generally true, since the frame of reference of a reader belonging to the public for whom Plato wrote was so very different from that of a modern reader. And against Moore's suggestion (1973: 54) that "contextually inappropriate passages refer to contextually appropriate ones" it can be said that most readers of Plato will find it extremely difficult to know when a passage really is contextually inappropriate.

Wilamowitz I 1920: 151, Schneider 1922: 12 (unusually confident), Ueberweg-Praechter[13] 1953: 229 f. and Erbse 1968: 25–28. Needless to say, the discussion implies that both dialogues are authentic or at least that the writer of the later passage is aware of the earlier one (but cf. below, p. 359).

At the outset it should be remembered that the scope and aims of *Laches* and *Protagoras* are very different, though both dialogues discuss the condition of education and of teaching virtue in particular. The *Laches* seemingly takes for granted that virtue can be taught if one knows what it is; the *Protagoras* (implicitly) leads over from the Protagorean view of teaching virtue to the Socratic one of knowing virtue. The whole of *Laches*, some 24 Stephanus pages, is implicitly or explicitly concerned with ἀνδρεία, and some 10 pages in the latter part of the dialogue discuss the nature of this virtue. Of the altogether 54 Stephanus pages of *Protagoras*, only some 4 pages towards the end, divided into two parts by an extensive digression, concern ἀνδρεία. The object of the later portion of the *Laches* (the 10 pages referred to) is to define ἀνδρεία, taking for granted that it constitutes a part of virtue which is not identical with virtue as a whole. Three successive definitions are offered, the last being ἡ τῶν δεινῶν καὶ θαρραλέων (also μὴ δεινῶν) ἐπιστήμη, which leads to aporia since it would either apply only to a part of ἀνδρεία or to virtue as a whole. Socrates conducts the argument, and Nicias and Laches refute each others' suggestions. The object of the 4 pages of the *Protagoras* is to demonstrate that Protagoras is wrong in asserting that ἀνδρεία differs substantially from the rest of virtue by admitting ἀμαθία; the argument amounts to a definition of ἀνδρεία as ἡ τῶν δεινῶν καὶ μὴ δεινῶν σοφία (and so it cannot admit ἀμαθία). Socrates conducts the argument, but Protagoras raises important objections. The complications are different in *Laches* and *Protagoras*, but there are a great many similar and even identical points.

The main lines of the argument run as follows:

|  | *Laches* |  | *Protagoras* |
| --- | --- | --- | --- |
| Ia 190ab | Socrates: We need a definition of virtue if we are going to teach it. | Ia 349d | Protagoras comments on Socrates' suggestion (349b, cf. 329c ff.) that virtue consists of 5 parts (σοφία, σωφροσύνη, ἀνδρεία, δικαιοσύνη, ὁσιότης): ἀνδρεία is very different from the rest because an ἀνδρεῖος does not necessarily possess the other parts of virtue. |
| 190c–e | We may here consider a part of virtue: ἀνδρεία. What is ἀνδρεία? |  |  |
| 190e | Laches (1st definition) gives an example. |  |  |
| 190e–192b | Socrates asks for a common feature in different examples, their common δύναμις. |  |  |
| 192b | Laches (2nd definition): ἀνδρεία is καρτερία τῆς ψυχῆς. |  |  |

| | | Socrates argues: | | Socrates argues: |
|---|---|---|---|---|
| [48] | 192c | — not all kinds of καρτερία! | 349e | — ἀνδρεῖοι are θαρραλέοι ("daring, trustful"); Protagoras: even ἴται! |
| | 192d | — ἀνδρεία is καλόν, | | |
| | | — so rather φρόνιμος καρτερία, | | — virtue is καλόν, not αἰσχρόν, |
| | 192e–193a | — but not all kinds of it, | 350a | — diving in wells θαρραλέως implies ἐπιστήμη; so does riding (θαρραλέως) and being a peltast, |
| | 193b | — and even ἀφρονεστέρα καρτερία may be ἀνδρεία: | | |
| | | — a rider who καρτερεῖ without ἐπιστήμη of riding is more ἀνδρεῖος; the same applies to the lack of τέχνη of slinging, archery etc., and to diving in wells without being δεινός ("a specialist")? | | —so having ἐπιστήμη makes one θαρραλεώτερος, |
| | | | 350b | — yet there are people not having ἐπιστήμη who θαρροῦνται; they are μαινόμενοι, |
| | 193c | | | — if such θαρραλέοι are ἀνδρεῖοι, ἀνδρεία would be αἰσχρόν, |
| | 193d | —but ἄφρων τόλμα or καρτέρησις are αἰσχρά. Aporia | 350c | — but if the σοφώτατοι are θαρραλεώτατοι and so ἀνδρειώτατοι, ἡ σοφία would be the same as ἀνδρεία. Aporia. |
| | Ib 193d–194e | Interlude. Nicias: it follows from what Socrates uses to argue that an ἀνδρεῖος must be σοφός. | Ib 350c–351b | Protagoras objects: — all θαρραλέοι are not ἀνδρεῖοι, |
| | 194e | Socrates: What kind of σοφία or ἐπιστήμη, then, is ἀνδρεία? Nicias (3rd definition): ἀνδρεία is ἡ τῶν δεινῶν καὶ θαρραλέων ("things to be trusted") ἐπιστή μη καὶ ἐν πολέμῳ καὶ ἐν ἄλλοις ἅπασιν. | | — θάρρος comes from τέχνη (and from θυμός and μανία), ἀνδρεία from φύσις (and εὐτροφία). |
| [49] | 195a–c | Laches objects: — σοφία and ἀνδρεία differ, — some specialists know the δεινά τε καὶ θαρραλέα of their trade but are not ἀνδρεῖοι. | | (351b–358b Digression on μετρητικὴ τέχνη as applied to pleasure and virtue: the 'hedonistic calculus.') |
| | 195c–196a | Banter of Nicias and Laches on doctors, prophets etc. consequently being ἀνδρεῖοι. | | |

|  |  |  |  |
|---|---|---|---|
|  | (195d Nicias resumes his definition in the form τῶν δεινῶν καὶ μὴ δεινῶν ἐπιστήμη). |  |  |
| 196b | Aporia. |  |  |
| II 196c–197a | Socrates: apparently ἀνδρεία does not belong to animals. | II 358d | Socrates defines δέος (and φόβος) as προσδοκία κακοῦ. Accepted by Protagoras, Hippias and Prodicus (who does not want to apply it to φόβος). |
| 197a–c | Nicias; ἄφοβος and ἀνδρεῖος are not the same thing; ἀνδρεία and προμηθία are different from θρασύτης and τόλμα. |  |  |
| 197de | Socrates agrees and suggests that Nicias has received this σοφία from sophists such as Damon or Prodicus. |  |  |
|  | Socrates argues: |  | Socrates argues: |
| 197e–198a | — virtue consists of parts such as ἀνδρεία, σωφροσύνη and δικαιοσύνη, | 358e | — nobody wants to go ἐπὶ ἃ ἡγεῖται κακά, |
|  |  | 359ab | — resumption of Protagoras' statement (349d), |
| 198bc | — definition of δεινά and θαρραλέα (meaning "things to be trusted"): δέος is προσδοκία μέλλοντος κακοῦ, and so δεινά are μέλλοντα κακά; θαρραλέα are ἀγαθὰ μέλλοντα, | 359cd | — there is a saying that the δειλοί go ἐπι τὰ θαρραλέα ("things to be trusted"), the ἀνδρεῖοι ἐπὶ τὰ δεινά, |
|  |  |  | — but evidently both δειλοί and ἀνδρεῖοι go ἐπὶ ἃ θαρροῦσιν, |
|  |  | 359e | — the δειλοί do not want to go to war though it is καλόν and ἀγαθόν and ἡδύ; but they do not know this, |
| 198c–199c | — but ἐπιστήμη must also concern present and past conditions, | 360a | — the ἀνδρεῖοι go to what is κάλλιον, ἄμεινον and ἥδιον, |
| 199c–e | — so Nicias' definition either does not apply to the whole of ἀνδρεία or, if it is made to include all things κακά and ἀγαθά, it applies to the whole of virtue, not to one of its parts (199d | 360bc | — the ἀνδρεῖοι θαρροῦσιν καλὰ θάρρη, the δειλοὶ θαρροῦσιν κακά and they do this because of ἄγνοια and τῶν δεινῶν ἀμαθία, |
|  |  | 360c | — so ἡ τῶν δεινῶν καὶ μὴ δεινῶν ἀμαθία is δειλία, |

[49]

[49] | includes ὁσιότης in the list). Aporia. | 360d | —and consequently ἀνδρεία is ἡ τῶν δεινῶν καὶ μὴ δεινῶν σοφία, and Protagoras was wrong in asserting that an ἀνδρεῖος can be ἀμαθής.

[50]  It can be seen that in both dialogues the argument proceeds in two general stages of which the first can be subdivided into two parts. In the section Ia in *Laches*, that portion of the argument which has its closest counterpart in the *Protagoras* starts with the second definition, at 192b. But whereas the *Laches* operates with καρτερία and καρτερεῖν, the *Protagoras* has θαρραλέος (in the sense of "daring, trustful") and θαρρεῖν. I can think of three reasons why the *Laches* would have introduced καρτερία if it is the later dialogue, but none why the *Protagoras* would not have used it if it was written later.[123] In *Laches* a noun is needed for the definition, and obviously θάρσος would not do. Being a more neutral word, καρτερία serves well the gradual development of the paradoxical idea that ἀνδρεία is not only φρόνιμος καρτερία but even more, perhaps, ἀφρονεστέρα καρτερία (192d–193b). And θαρραλέος is used in two senses in *Protagoras*: first in the common meaning of "daring, trustful," then (from 359c, with reference to "what people say") in the curious and rare sense of "to be trusted, safe."[124] The latter sense is adopted in *Laches* in the third definition (194e) alternatively with τὰ μὴ δεινά, and it accompanies the subsequent discussion, whereas the common active meaning of θαρραλέος occurs in *Laches* only once, in a different context (182c, where in fact it suggests *Protagoras* 350a). It would seem that, when writing the ἀνδρεία argument of *Laches*, Plato (or whoever the author was) wanted to reserve θαρραλέος for being used in the special sense that was introduced at the end of the argument in *Protagoras*.

Particularly interesting, however, is the set of three examples, riding, using arms, and diving in wells (*La.* 193bc, *Prt.* 350a). The fact that practising such activities implies both courage and art must have been a generally recognized truth, and the *Protagoras* goes no further. For the following idea, that one can also be θαρραλέος without ἐπιστήμη, no examples are given. *Laches* on the other hand introduces the quasi-paradoxical and obviously secondary idea that καρτερία without ἐπιστήμη in such circumstances may involve even more courage than a specialist needs. The elaboration of this 'paradox,' with the example of diving in wells as an expansive climax at the end (note also the pun on δεινός in the sense of "specialist"), suggests to me that the *Laches* passage is the later one.

---

123. In fact derivatives of the stem καρτερ- are not very common in Plato, and they do not occur in the *Protagoras* at all.
124. In addition to *Laches* and *Protagoras* it occurs four times in the Plato corpus (*R.* V 450e, *Phlb.* 32c, *Lg.* XII 959b, *Def.* 412a).

In *Protagoras* (Ib) there follow the objections of Protagoras to the application of θαρραλέος (and θάρσος); the use of the adjective in this sense is then dropped (though θαρρεῖν occurs 359c ff.). The extensive digression on the 'hedonistic calculus' is loosely appended to the objections of Protagoras (cf. below). It may be noted in passing that the combining of θάρσος with τέχνη in the 'Protagorean' antithesis of τέχνη/φύσις (351a) has its counterpart in *Laches* 195b where θαρραλέα in the passive sense, which does not occur in *Protagoras* at this stage, is substituted for θάρσος. In *Laches* (Ib) there follows the 'Socratic' definition that is propounded by Nicias, and the objection of Laches. The definition is essentially the same as the definition reached at the end of the argument in *Protagoras*, section II. It is significant, I think, (1) that Nicias hints that it derives somehow from Socrates, (2) that there is a glide in *Laches* 194e from σοφία (cf. *Prt*. 360d where it is appropriate) to ἐπιστήμη (which is needed in *Laches*), and (3) that θαρραλέα in the new, passive sense (introduced in *Prt*. 359c) occurs instead of τὰ μὴ δεινά which, however, appears in passing at 195d.

Section II of the argument in *Protagoras* starts with a definition of δέος as προσδοκία κακοῦ which is approved by the sophists present. Possibly the point was suggested by the digression which is of course concerned with "things to be expected" (though the terms προσδοκᾶν, προσδοκία, do not occur there); but I would prefer to think that it was not.[125] There are other similar points of semantic distinction made by Protagoras in 350c–351b. Socrates needs the point of προσδοκία since he is going to consider ἀνδρεία as a kind of endeavor, a "going somewhere" (which is clearly connected with the idiomatic ἴται so emphatically prominent in the argument 349e, repeated at 359ab). But it is important to note that this definition of δέος may well have been current outside Platonic circles, as Socrates' playful seeking of the sophists' approval seems to suggest. Could it have been taken from the *Laches* (198bc)? I do not think so: the *Laches* passage sounds like an abbreviation of a larger argument.

The προσδοκία passage in *Laches* (198b ff.), seemingly, is better prepared for. From the very beginning this dialogue, more explicitly than the *Protagoras*, is concerned with 'planning,' with συμβουλεύειν and, indeed, προμηθία (note 185a), whatever the connection may be with Προμηθεύς of *Protagoras* (320d ff., cf. 361d). And stage II of the ἀνδρεία argument begins with Nicias' separating ἀνδρεία and προμηθία from θρασύτης and τόλμα (197b). Yet προσδοκία is introduced only after Socrates' ironical remarks on sophists (197de), and the rest of the argument is really quite 'sophistic.' In particular, I find that the addition of the word μέλλοντος, which is required for destroying Nicias' definition, points to a secondary elaboration of a formula which occurs in its primary form in *Protagoras*. And, again, the adoption of θαρραλέα in the passive sense ("things to be trusted") suggests *Protagoras* as the model. The whole argument is switched round in the

---

125. Manuwald 1975 has argued rather convincingly (against Hermann 1972) that the digression may have been secondarily inserted and that the subsequent argument in the *Protagoras* is really quite independent of it.

[51] Laches, as was the order of the examples at 193bc. But more important, I think, is the fact that the argument in Laches employs a combination of a refined version of what the corresponding argument in Protagoras starts from (προσδοκία κακοῦ) with an elaboration of a rather occasional use of a saying ("the δειλοί go ἐπὶ τὰ θαρραλέα") in order to refute the very definition that results from the argument in Protagoras. Here, too, the priority of Protagoras seems to me more easily acceptable than the reverse relation.

The fact that the section on ἀνδρεία in the Republic IV 429a–430c rather corresponds to the final position of the Protagoras than to the final position of the Laches, [52] is as such of little consequence to the relative date of Laches and Protagoras. Nobody today believes that the final aporia of Laches is seriously meant. Apparently with some variation of what he has done in the Protagoras, Socrates in the Republic defines ἀνδρεία as δύναμις ... δόξης ὀρθῆς ... δεινῶν πέρι καὶ μή (430b, cf. 429c). The δόξα ὀρθή is of course part of the epistemological terminology of the Republic, but it is tempting to see behind it a contamination of the ideas of προσδοκία and ἐπιστήμη (reduced to δόξα ὀρθή) which in fact would imply a combination of the arguments of the Protagoras and the Laches; and the introduction of δύναμις (cf. Laches 192b) may suggest the same. Sometimes the words of Socrates at 430b, αὖθις δὴ περὶ αὐτοῦ ... ἔτι κάλλιον δίιμεν have been thought to refer to the Laches (as yet unwritten, or indeed written and 'published,' if one wants to assign to it an earlier date); but such references are no reliable criteria.[126]

While all these considerations seem to point to the internal order Protagoras—Laches, with Republic IV following at some distance, I am prepared to admit that this conclusion is not certain. As can be seen from the discussion of this vexed problem, it is possible to argue that the Laches is the earlier dialogue, though I am convinced that this is much more difficult than some scholars have thought. And then there is the possibility that not all of the passages in question are by Plato's own hand (cf. p. 359).

What emerges from all this, then, is a simple warning: though arguments from the contents, if carefully pondered, may provide various indications as to which of two dialogues is the earlier one, such indications are on the whole not to be trusted unless they can be supported by other, and independent, arguments.

And if we accept, as indeed we have to, that there was a continuous oral discussion going on around Plato, we must always take account of the possibility that two passages which seem to stand in direct relation in fact refer to a common source unknown to us and perhaps never written down.

Arguments from the contents can easily be misused. If one bothers to look more closely into the history of the 'Platonic Question,' of which I have tried to furnish some glimpses here, it can be seen how almost any order of the dialogues can be made somehow 'probable' by means of a 'prudent' interpretation of their contents. To a very large extent the much-used and much-discussed arguments from the contents amount to little more than a *non liquet*.

---

126. Cf. above, p. 189.

And yet, when all is said and the complications have been not only stated but [52] taken into account, it may still be possible to sort out some useful arguments, or support for other kinds of argument, for Platonic chronology—though not primarily for Plato's 'development'—by a careful and cautious interpretative analysis of thematic parallels. Some further attempts to use such a 'method of confrontation' will be made below (p. 245 ff.).

## Literary criteria; dialogue technique [53]

This aspect has not received very much attention. As a matter of fact Plato's literary art and his dialogue technique have been surprisingly often neglected in discussions of the finer qualities of ancient literature.

Scattered remarks and opinions about these questions can of course be found in the literature on Plato from antiquity onwards.[127] Hirzel's 'Der Dialog' (I 1895) unfortunately is hardly more than 'a literarhistorischer Versuch' as regards Plato, though he supplies a wide range of useful comments on the background in particular. Among later comprehensive studies of Plato, the books of Wilamowitz 1919, Taylor 1926 and Friedländer (1930, 1954–) deserve mention for their sensitivity to the literary aspect. Recently Dalfen 1975 has noted various literary points without applying them to the question of the chronological order of the dialogues. Very occasionally such observations have been made systematically in relation to the study of Platonic chronology. For earlier attempts, *see* the clear but very incomplete and over-simplifying conspectus of Raeder 44–61;[128] cf. further Thesleff 1967 (above, a tentative typology of Platonic styles with additional references), Guthrie IV 42–44.

One thing is very commonly agreed on and often tacitly accepted as a fact ever since the stylometrists' position began to be established: a simple style together with a simple and artless structure of the dialogue is taken to indicate an early date if there exist no other criteria to contradict this. This principle also seems to agree with the fact that many of the most 'Socratic' dialogues appear to be rather artless in style and structure. Plato's 'mature' periods are then thought to be characterized by a greater variety of styles and more complex structures. In the 'late' period the structures again become looser and more simple whereas the dialogue technique changes and the diction grows heavy and tortuous.

However, the validity of this hypothetical conception, especially as regards the early period, is highly questionable. Already the theory of 'development' that it seems to imply is, in principle, disputable. And since the notion of a 'Socratic

---

127. References in Thesleff 1967, above, especially 7 n. 1.
128. For instance Lutoslawski has some notes and references in various connections, all of which have not been observed by Raeder.

[53] period' has begun to evaporate (above p. 171), one of its supports has vanished. 'Socratica' such as the *Hippias Major* and the *Sisyphus* have been recently dated in the 360s or 350s.[129] And if it is objected that the trend from a more simple to a less simple form can apply only to authentic writings, the generally accepted relative chronology of, say, the *Protagoras* (if taken as early) and *Theaetetus* (if taken as not very late) would seem to be an anomaly. But authenticity is perhaps not needed to justify the drawing of conclusions from the literary form of the dialogues.

[54] On the other hand, it is a fact that almost all of the most artistic dialogues in the Corpus have the indirect, *reported* (narrated, 'dihegematic') form—eight apparently authentic dialogues, *Charmides, Euthydemus, Lysis, Parmenides, Phaedo, Protagoras, Republic, Symposium* (and add *Theaetetus* where this form has been dropped), and three dubia, *Amatores, Demodocus* and *Eryxias*—whereas the majority of the dialogues, including the 'late group' (except *Parmenides)* are of the direct, *dramatic* type. This is usually considered more or less irrelevant to problems of interpretation or chronology (cf. the survey above p. 154 ff.). Apparently this was also the opinion of ancient writers.[130] The cryptic remarks of Plato in *Republic* III 392c–396e on the reported ('dihegematic') versus the dramatic ('mimetic') type of exposition, have sometimes been adduced to show that Plato at this period preferred or recommended the use of the reported type of dialogue, though in *Theaetetus* (143b) he explicitly abandons it.[131]

Very occasionally attempts have been made to group the reported dialogues together and assign them all to Plato's late, early, or middle period. Such attempts have so far been unsuccessful.[132]

[55] However, in the view of the present writer this difference in form is after all quite remarkable and if it cannot be related to chronological facts or inferences, calls for a general explanation.

---

129. See below, p. 372 and 375. The even more 'primitive' *Just.* and *Virt.* would afford still better examples if a late date could be ascertained for them; cf. below p. 376.

130. Diog. L. 3.50 "I am not unaware that there are other ways in which certain writers classify the dialogues. For some dialogues they call dramatic, others narrative (διηγηματικούς), and others again a mixture of the two. But the terms they employ in their classifications of the dialogues are better suited to the stage than to philosophy" (translation by R. D. Hicks). Cf. Anon.Proleg. 20, p. 213 f. Hermann.

131. For the relevance of the *Republic* passage, cf. Pfleiderer 1896: 307 n., Immisch 1899: 621, Andrieu 1954: 284–286 (dramatic form more expressive), Thesleff 1967: (above) 37, Laborderie 1978: 396 f. Crain 1905: 17–19 argued that it is wholly irrelevant. Note the fact that dithyramb turns out to be of the 'dihegematic' type (394c), and Plato's own reported dialogues are of course highly 'mimetic.' After all it would be easier to argue that Plato in *Republic* III recommends the dropping of such μίμησις of human matters as most of the reported and dramatic dialogues actually present, and that he has in mind something like the exposition of Timaeus in the *Timaeus*.

132. Though Ueberweg 1861: 73 ff. had declared that the difference between reported and dramatic form does not seem to afford criteria for chronology, Schöne 1862 suggested that all the reported dialogues might be later than the dramatic ones; but this hypothesis was easily refuted by stylometry and other considerations. Teichmüller (1879) who was the first to see clearly the problem of the form (especially p. 10), argued with some force that all the reported

Studies in Platonic Chronology

There is, therefore, some justification for a reconsideration of the formal aspect. [55]

In order to acquire a general picture of the variations in the structure of the different writings in the Corpus Platonicum, it is convenient to distinguish five types of exposition; I shall use here capital letters as sigla as I did in my book on the styles of Plato (1967, above especially 29 ff.):

A = Question and reply; notably 'elenchus' or similar strings of relatively brief questions or statements by the dialogue leader, followed by very brief replies.
B = Discussion or conversation; two or more speakers exchange ideas, and the questions or remarks are of varying length.
C = Narrative connected with report of dialogue.
D = Dialogue approximating to monologue; the dialogue leader is 'lecturing,' and the comments made by the interlocutor are of little factual importance.
E = Speech or continuous exposition of other kinds.

The details of the combination and distribution of such passages in the various dialogues were mapped out and discussed in my book (though the 'spuria' were dealt with very briefly).

Though minor variations always occur (no two writings are really identical in form), it may be possible to make a rough typology of the texts in the Corpus (excluding of course the *Definitions* and the *Epigrams*) according to the dialogue technique employed, as follows:

| | | | |
|---|---|---|---|
| I | a | simple A throughout | *Just., Virt.* |
| | b | d⁰ in C form | *Demod.* (III–IV) |
| II | a | simple BAB pattern | *Euthphr., Hp.Ma.* |
| | b | d⁰ in C form | *Amat.* |
| III | a | BAB pattern with central E | *Alc.* 1, *Hipparch., Hp.Mi., Ion, Sis.* (cf. Va *Min.*, VIIIa *Phdr.*) |
| | b | d⁰ in C form | *Erx.* |
| IV | a | BAB pattern with various E's | *Alc.* 2, *La.* |
| | b | d⁰ in C form | *Chrm., Ly.* |
| | c | d⁰ & d⁰ with B frame | *Euthd., Prt.* |
| V | a | BAB pattern with tendency to D | *Cra., Men., Min.* (cf. IIIa), *Phdr.* (2nd part), *Phlb.*; cf. *Prm.* (2nd part) |
| | b | d⁰ in C form | *Prm.* (1st part) |
| | c | d⁰ & d⁰ with B frame | — |
| VI | a | BAB pattern with E and D and concluding E | *Cri., Grg., Thg.* |
| | b | d⁰ in C form | *R.* |
| | c | d⁰ & d⁰ with B frame | *Phd.* |

[56] VII a BDB pattern with E        *Lg., Plt., Sph.*
     b d⁰ in C form                  —
     c d⁰ (& d⁰) with B frame        *Tht.*
    VIII a BEB pattern                *Phdr.* (1st part; cf. IIIa)
     b d⁰ in C form                  —
     c d⁰ & d⁰ with B frame          *Smp.*
    IX a E throughout                 *Ap.* (some A, also with C, inserted), *Demod.* (I), *Ep.* 1–13 (some AG in *Ep.* 7)
     b E with B frame                *Clit., Criti., Epin., Mx., Ti.*
    X a anomalous structure without C *Halcyon*[133]
     b d⁰ with C                     *Ax., Demod.* (II)

The occasional instances of a fictitious C dialogue inserted in a dramatic context are not included in the survey but will be commented on below (p. 203). Similarly the occasional instances of a report of an earlier discussion in contexts of dramatic dialogue are not marked separately.[134] Even so, we can see that almost all classes recorded above include a dramatic and a reported (C) variety.

The coexistence and interrelations of these types are worth examining in the light of what is known, or can be inferred, about the early history of prose dialogue.[135]

The roots of the reported type go back to very ancient traditions of storytelling current all over the world. In Greek literature, the Homeric manner of reporting an exchange of speeches can also be traced in lyrics (notably Archilochus and Sappho). More realistic pieces of reported conversation occur in Herodotus beside the more formal (Homeric) type which is also adopted by later historians from Thucydides onwards,[136] and in some fragments of other early historians,

---

dialogues perhaps with the exception of *Parmenides*, are to be placed first, but this too seemed unacceptable (cf. p. 170). Christ 1866: 497–500 more cautiously attempted to group together only *Protagoras, Symposium, Euthydemus* and *Phaedo* which have dramatic frame dialogues. Somewhat different groupings were suggested by Pfleiderer and Immisch (above n. 131). Raeder 44–61 discusses the subject but thinks that little stress should be placed on the literary criteria. Andrieu 1954: 307 suggests that a study of this aspect might provide useful clues to chronology, but he does not follow up this idea. Stefanini, especially I.LXXIII–LXXVIII, LXXX f., 158 f., and Thesleff 1967, above, have argued that the eight reported dialogues were composed successively in Plato's middle period; but this is obviously at variance with the general opinion of the dates of, say, *Gorgias* and *Meno* in relation to *Protagoras* and *Phaedo*. Laborderie 1978: 385–407 attempts, conjecturally, to explain the difference in form from Plato's purpose in each case.

133. *See* below p. 378.

134. The most notable instances occur in *Euthydemus, Symposium* and *Theages, see* below n. 155.

135. Apart from scattered remarks by various scholars, we have the learned but somewhat unsystematic, wordy and antiquated exposition of Hirzel 1895, especially 26–174; cf. Bruns 1896: 50 ff.; additional observations by Pohlenz 1913: 4–7, Geffcken II 42 f., Gigon 1947: 179–208, Thesleff 1967: 29 ff. (I have reconsidered my position since then), and Laborderie 1978: 13–50 (who overrates Plato's originality).

136. For dialogue in the historians, *see* Hirzel 1895: 38 ff.

notably Ion of Chios and Stesimbrotus of Thasus.[137] It is perhaps possible to distinguish an Ionian literary genre of biographical memoirs and anecdotes to which such passages belong. Alexamenus of Styra or Teos, who is sometimes regarded as the originator of the Socratic type of dialogue, is entirely obscure to us; but at least he was an Ionian, and so may have been a representative of the memoir genre.[138] If Critias' Ὁμιλίαι were philosophical memoirs somewhat similar to the Ἐπιδημίαι of Ion,[139] they bring us closer to the world of Plato and other Socratics.

Reported dialogue also appears to have occurred sometimes in sophists' λόγοι. The pastiche of a Protagorean μῦθος in *Protagoras* has a partially indirect report of dialogue (320d, 322b–d) in the manner of the early historians. Prodicus' myth of Herakles (X. *Mem.* II 1.21–34) provides an exchange of speeches in the Homeric manner. In Hippias' Τρωικός young Neoptolemus asked Nestor for advice which the latter gave, apparently, as a single λόγος (*Hp.Ma.* 286ab, cf. DK [Diels and Kranz, *Die Fragmente der Vorsokratiker*] 86 A 2, p. 327.1); the words, of Hippias in the *Hippias Major* (especially 286a7–8) indicate that there was a frame narrative. It is of some interest to note here that Gaiser (1959) has tried to trace the background of Platonic dialogue in the protreptic speeches of sophists; but he was thinking of the contents rather than dialogue technique.

Pieces of reported dialogue can in fact be found in other genres of public speech as well. It is important, however, to distinguish the common rhetorical device of introducing a fictitious objection, the εἴποι ἄν τις type (so-called ὑποφοραί), which may sometimes develop into a kind of dialogue.[140] This device is very probably the ultimate starting point for the elaboration of the specific sort of fictitious dialogue of which the best-known example is the argumentation of the *Laws* as reported by Socrates in the *Crito* (50a–54d). Other examples are found in *Alcibiades* I (105a–d), the *Apology* (28b–d, 29c–e), *Gorgias* (450e–451c), *Hippias Major* (286c ff., introducing an anonymous critic who accompanies the dialogue

---

137. FGrHist 392 and 107.

138. Aristotle fr. 72 Rose (Athen. 11.505c) seems to have thought that the first Socratic dialogues were written by this Alexamenus, but the formulation of the notice in Athenaeus (τοὺς Ἀλεξαμενοῦ τοῦ Τηίου τοὺς πρώτους γραφέντας τῶν Σωκρατικῶν διαλόγων) is open to doubt, and the fact that the name of Alexamenus does not occur anywhere in the Socratic traditions is a further point of uncertainty. Favorinus (VH fr. 17 Mensch, Diog. L. 3.48) seems to have understood Aristotle to imply that Alexamenus was the first of all (prose?) dialogue writers (cf. now Oxyrhynchus Papyri [P. Oxy.] 3219 fr. 1). Another source (Diog. L. ibid.) considers Zenon the Eleatic the first to write dialogues, but this is evidently based on a misinterpretation of Aristotle (fr. 65 Rose, Diog. L. 8.57, cf. DK 31 A 19) who said that Zenon "invented" dialectic.—Adducing Aesopean fables and even Indian prose dialogue (Fries 1933) is clearly irrelevant for explaining the genesis of the Platonic dialogue.

139. For Critias, see DK 88 B 40–41a, also 45; cf. Hirzel 1895: 65 f., Pohlenz 1913: 51. At any rate in B 40 a 2nd person is addressed; and as the definition of σωφροσύνη given by "somebody" in *Chrm.* 16bc has a clear reference to Critias, though he tries to deny it, one explanation is that the Ὁμιλίαι included dialogue where some other person had given this definition. Dihle 1956: 47 f. somewhat unexpectedly suggests that Plato was influenced by Ion of Chios.

140. Cf. Hirzel 1895: 50–53. As Hirzel notes (52), the extensive use of this device in Ps.-Xenophon's Athenian Constitution has even led to the wrong assumption that this pamphlet was originally a dialogue. Cf. further e.g. Andocides 1.148, Dissoi Logoi 1.12–13.

[57] to the end; but cf. *Euthd.* 304c–305c), the *Laws* (II 662c–e, X 893b–894a), *Philebus* (63a–64a), *Protagoras* (330c–331b), and the *Republic* (V 453a–c). This is evidently a secondary mannerism, though it may have been influenced by the technique of ordinary reported dialogue (C);[141] obviously it cannot be used for explaining the genesis of the latter.

[58]  On the other hand, oratory also exhibits examples of reports of a discussion which is said to have taken place earlier. An interesting instance is found in Andocides (*de Myst.* 40–42,399 BCE) where the speaker records a story by Diocleides with quotation of dialogue in partially indirect form. Here the connection with the 'memoir and anecdote' genre is rather obvious. It should be noted, however, that Plato's *Apology* also includes such a piece of reported dialogue (20ab, the Euenus episode). Possibly it reflects a technique already current in Socratic literature.[142] But what is important in this connection is the fact that such reports did exist in early oratory, and that this practice may explain the occurrence of the piece in the *Apology*.

There is much less evidence for the existence of written 'dramatic' (i.e. direct) prose dialogue before the 4th century. Formal traditions of some kind are likely to have been developed early in the forensic practice of questioning witnesses or delinquents; and this was very probably the practice from which the ἔλεγχος methods of sophists, erists, and Socrates (i.e. dialogue type A, above) arose. The details are of course obscure to us. An early parody of sophistic elenchus is Aristophanes' *Clouds* 478–494 (which hardly concerns Socrates alone). It must be left undecided whether the Eleatics also practiced this method, though this is implied by Plato's *Parmenides* and a fragment of Aristotle's (above, n. 138).

Sometimes pieces of direct elenchus are quoted in the specimens of Attic oratory preserved to us: note Lysias XII 25 (403 BCE), Andocides I 14, 101 (399 BCE) and, again, Plato's *Apology*, 24a–28a (Socrates questioning Meletus). It is possible that such passages originally and on the whole derive from notes taken down at the actual speech situation. More commonly the questioning of witnesses is only marked Μάρτυρες in our manuscripts (this is already the case in the early speeches V and VI of Antiphon).

We do not know whether the friends of Socrates wrote down specimens of his elenctic λόγοι during his lifetime; it would be surprising if this was never done.[143] Obviously, however, mere hypomnematic notes could not have been intended for general circulation. Before one can begin to argue that, for

---

141. This would probably be easy to demonstrate, cf. Thesleff 1967: above, 38. Especially the very 'rude' critic in *Hippias Major* (Socrates' alter ego) is even given some light characterization, and is introduced as a real person (286c, 304d), though most of his objections are dealt with as anonymous ὑποφοραί; but the anonymous critic at the end of *Euthydemus* (probably Isocrates, cf. p. 294) is treated as a real person throughout, and so this dialogue really corresponds to the ordinary C type.

142. In 1967: 38, I suggested that this piece might indicate that Plato had not yet got used to writing C dialogue; this is doubtful, of course.

143. This possibility was touched upon above, p. 171. Cf. Guthrie III 343 f.

instance, the Platonic *De Justo* can be regarded as a very old example of such [58] authentic notes—which would not appear altogether impossible, prima facie (p. 376)—it is reasonable to ask how it found its way into the Academic Corpus which consists almost entirely of texts intended for publication or instruction, and whether it is not easier to explain *De Justo* as an Academic piece of exercise. But as we have seen, early extracts of dramatic dialogue could have been quoted in speeches.

Plato's dialogue technique seems to have little to do with sophistic ἀντιλογίαι, in the sense of antithetic speeches or arguments without the support of a narrative or a real (dramatic) dialogue,[144] except in special cases such as the speeches [59] in the *Phaedrus* (p. 318).

Plato's and the other Socratics' possible debt to the mimes of Sophron remains almost entirely obscure. Unfortunately Sophron seems to be very difficult to catch.[145] It is feasible that the ancient tradition about Plato's knowledge of and reliance on Sophron (chiefly Diog. L. 3.18) ultimately or partly derives from Aristotle's theoretical comparison of Socratic dialogues with the mimes of Sophron (*Poet.* 1447b) and from the discussion of 'mimetic' art. Indeed it seems rather a paradox that Plato or any Socratic should have modeled a specific type of philosophical dialogue (B, above) on that curious branch of literature. Was Plato's dialogue technique after all as remotely related to mime as it evidently was to Attic tragedy and comedy (with which he obviously was familiar)? And was the only feature that Socratic dialogue had in common with mime, perhaps the very stylistic realism employed? It is true that the mime genre of Sophron is the only literary genre of dramatic prose dialogue known to have existed in the 5th century. But the mimes were in fact prose dramas. Without any doubt they were intended for performance on a stage. Is there really any indication that the early Socratic λόγοι were intended for performance rather than for reading by one person only? It is a problem that I shall return to later (p. 209).

A fact of some importance here is that the other Socratics preferred to use the reported dialogue form. This is the only form used by Xenophon and, apparently, by Aeschines; and these two authors are likely to have been conservatives rather than experimentalists in formal matters. Xenophon did not begin writing Socratic dialogues before the 380s (above p. 181). Some of Aeschines' dialogues have been dated to the 390s by Dittmar,[146] but his inferences are highly hypothetical and involved with Platonic chronology. Phaedon of Elis also used the reported form, as

---

144. Cf. Thesleff 1967: above, 44 f. with references.
145. In spite of the interesting papyrus fragment PSI XI 1214, very little is known of Sophron's use of dialogue. For a discussion of the hypothesis of Sophron having influenced Plato, *see* McDonald 1931, especially 380 ff. (more comprehensive than Reich 1903: 381 ff.), cf. P. Oxy. 3219 fr. 1. McDonald points out that Plato's character portraiture, like Sophron's, is both realistic and typological. But so is character portraiture in Attic drama. Guthrie (III 332 f.) is rightly skeptical.
146. Cf. above p. 181. The term ἀκέφαλος which is applied to some of Aeschines' dialogues Diog. L. 2.60 does not denote "without dramatic frame dialogue" but refers to some alleged sign of spuriousness (cf. Diog. L. 3.62), possibly "without full title" (cf. Oświecimski 1979 who suggests that the ἀκέφαλοι formed a separate collection of Socratica of unknown authorship).

has been shown by Hirzel and, recently, with additional material by Rosetti.[147] We have no clues for dating his dialogues apart from the general consideration that he was probably dependent on Plato: the latter is not likely to have written his account of the death of Socrates in the name of Phaedon if Phaedon had at the time published dialogues of his own and perhaps even opened a 'school.' The dialogues of Euclides, who was clearly older than Plato, cannot be reconstructed or dated; and the same applies to various minor Socratics.[148] But then there is the notorious and always elusive Antisthenes (cf. p. 181). Most, or possibly even all, of Antisthenes' enormous output—insofar as it was authentic—consisted of speeches, and since he was older than Plato he probably started writing earlier. Among his fragments, two pieces of dialogue are to a certain extent traceable. One is from the 'Herakles,' and Hirzel 1895: 120 and n. 2 has pointed out that since we are confronted here with different mythic places, there must have been a frame story linking the pieces together; and if this is so, the dialogue was apparently quoted in reported form. Formally, the work may have been a speech; the speaker is unknown. The other piece, from an unknown writing, is quoted as a dramatic dialogue by Athenaeus; it was probably written later than Plato's *Symposium*.[149] The existence of a frame story in this case too is of course possible; in fact bits of reported dialogue without 'inserenda' occur frequently in Platonic writings of the type C (e.g. *Chrm.* 159cd).

What does all this amount to then? Can we say anything at all of the influences affecting Plato in matters of dialogue technique when he started writing his dialogues? To what extent was he an innovator?

I believe it can be regarded as almost certain that Plato did not 'invent' the reported form of Socratic dialogue. Aeschines, in whose dialogues the report-giver is Socrates, cannot have been wholly dependent on Plato;[150] and Xenophon who gives the report in his own name, also largely represents pre-Platonic and extra-Platonic traditions.[151] Generally speaking, the speech form was widely used, and in the early

---

147. Hirzel 1895: 111 ff., Rossetti 1973, 1980: 183 ff. In Phaedon's 'Simon' the report-giver may have been Socrates himself; cf. *Eryxias*, below p. 366. Rossetti has shown that the 'Zopyros' had a report narrative in the 3rd person and a myth.

148. For Euclides, cf. above p. 173 and below n. 161; for the fragments, see Rossetti 1980: 198 ff. (the fact that Panaetius ap. Diog. L 2.64 doubted their genuineness has little weight as such).—The details and authenticity of the dialogues attributed to Simon, Glaucon, Simmias, Cebes, Criton, Polyaenus and Aristippus (S:r) are doubtful; see Hirzel 1895: 102–110.—The reported form can still be traced among Plato's pupils, notably Heraclides Ponticus and Aristotle, and in some unidentified papyrus fragments of 4th century philosophical dialogue (P. Oxy. IV 664, PSI XI 1215, cf. Bartoletti 1959).

149. Athen. 5.216b, fr. 33 Caizzi, from Herodicus; the latter's manner of quoting Plato (e.g. Athen. 217b–d, 219e–220a) indicates that the text of Antisthenes did not have 'inserenda' of the ἔφη type. The brief quotation implies that Socrates had declined the ἀριστεῖα, and offered it to Alcibiades, not only at Potidaea (as Plato, *Smp.* 220e records, and as was generally believed, cf. Diog. L. 2.23), but also at Delium (cf. Socrates and Laches at Delium, *Smp.* 221a, *La.* 181b), which looks like a secondary elaboration of the story given by Plato.

150. This can be seen e.g. from his treatment of themes such as δαιμόνιον and ἔρως.

151. I have argued this (1978) for Xenophon's 'Symposium' in particular. Gigon 1953 and Breitenbach 1967 emphasize Xenophon's dependence on literary sources. Obviously he was fond of the writings of Antisthenes.

4th century it was the normal form for 'publishing' one's ideas. Plato was deeply [60]
interested in speech-writing, as his many pastiches and his criticism indicate.

So Plato had the reported dialogue form, and the speech form without dialogue, at his 'disposal' when he established himself as a writer. However, I do not think it can be demonstrated[152] that the dramatic prose dialogue was as readily [61] available to him. He may of course have had hypomnematic notes at hand. But when did it occur to him, or to anybody, that they could be 'published' as dramatic dialogue pieces for a wider public?

As a matter of fact, there are several points that can be adduced in favor of a hypothesis that the dramatic dialogue type intended for wider circulation was an innovation of Plato's Academy.

The 'late group' (*Critias, Laws, Parmenides, Philebus, Politicus, Sophist, Timaeus*) consists almost entirely of dialogues of the dramatic type, and the only exception, the *Parmenides*, reflects in a significant way the trend towards abandoning the reported form: only the first part of *Parmenides* is retained as a report, and the latter part (from 137c onwards) is written in a dramatic form throughout.[153] The same trend can be seen in the *Theaetetus* where we are informed in the frame dialogue (143bc) that the main dialogue has not been written down in such as manner as it was retold (διηγούμενον) by Socrates, but that the 'inserenda' such as καὶ ἐγὼ ἔφην or καὶ ἐγὼ εἶπον or συνέφη or οὐκ ὡμολόγει have been dropped for convenience. The obvious conclusion to be drawn from this is that there existed an earlier reported version of the dialogue where Socrates was the speaker; or at any rate, if there did not exist an earlier version (cf. p. 301), that Plato thought the reader might expect a reported dialogue. Also in the *Republic*, the technique of the reported dialogue is applied somewhat consistently only in the first book and the beginning of the second; it is then gradually dropped, and from Book VII to the end there is little more left of it than an occasional use of inserenda.[154]

Moreover, pieces of dramatic dialogue seem in many cases to have been secondarily attached to bodies of reported dialogue or speeches, whereas instances of the secondary attaching of reported dialogue to originally independent dramatic pieces do not seem to occur.[155] Most instances of dramatic 'frame' dialogues (noted in the conspectus p. 201 under IVc, VIc, VIIc, VIIIc and IXb) can be explained as such secondary additions. This point will be further developed below (p. 326). Note here, however, as a fairly clear example the opening

---

152. As Immisch 1899: 627 f. and others have believed.
153. Without speakers' sigla, though; cf. below p. 210. It is almost certain that the latter part is later 'appanded' to the first part (cf. p. 305).
154. Details in Thesleff 1967: above, 83 ff.
155. I.e. the secondary addition of a reported frame or the like to a dramatic dialogue, with specific reference to the latter. The occasional including of a report of a separate discussion in a direct speech that functions as a part of a dramatic dialogue, as in the opening of *Symposium*, or *Euthydemus* 304de (cf. above p. 204), or *Theages* 129d–130e, is of course irrelevant: as we have seen, quoting a dialogue in a speech is a traditional device. For the doubling of a motif in the opening of the *Lysis*, which I took in 1967 as a possible indication that the report has been added secondarily, *see* below p. 296.

[61] dialogue of the *Protagoras* which, apparently, has no other function than to connect secondarily the main dialogue with the discussion of Socrates' relations with Alcibiades.

[62] It has sometimes been noted that those reported dialogues which lack a dramatic frame *(Amatores, Charmides, Demodocus* II–IV, *Eryxias, Lysis, Parmenides, Republic)* do, however, imply an audience addressed by the speaker (who is Socrates except in *Parmenides);* sometimes there even occurs a direct address *(Chrm.* 154b ὦ ἑταῖρε, 155c ὦ φίλε, d ὦ γεννάδα). And since similar addresses occur in those reported dialogues that have a dramatic frame (e.g. *Euthd.* 275c, 283a, *Prt.* 339e), it could be argued that there is no fundamental difference between the type with and the type without a dramatic frame.[156] I believe it can be shown that the difference lies precisely in the adding of an explicit dramatic frame dialogue with a purpose of its own. But it is certainly an important fact to keep in mind that the reported dialogue tradition which Plato followed purports to be a speech by Socrates. Plato does not primarily follow the memoir tradition. And the introduction of report-givers other than Socrates (Phaedon in the *Phaedo,* Cephalus of Clazomenai in the *Parmenides,* Aristodemus in the *Symposium)* is likely to be a secondary device.

Whether or not the whole genre of Σωκρατικοὶ λόγοι arose from the fiction of speeches or 'stories' put in the mouth of Socrates himself and containing reports of earlier conversations,[157] Plato's adopting of this manner may have occurred at a comparatively early date. If we make this assumption, the connection between the speeches of, say, the *Apology,* the *Menexenus* (without its frame), and *Symposium,* and the reported dialogue, become more natural. To the young Plato, Socrates may have been a protreptic speaker (though not of course a public speaker), a persuader and a story-teller, rather than a participant in dramatic antilogies.

Still, of course, the fact that Aeschines, Plato and probably other Socratics as well wrote in the name of Socrates, pseudonymously, may seem somewhat odd from our point of view, and one that requires further explanation. I suggest that it was no more odd to a Greek of Plato's day than the fact that the 'Homerides' published epics in Homer's name or the Hippocratics wrote treatises in Hippocrates' name—or indeed, that members of Plato's Academy wrote in Plato's name (cf. below, p. 237). Using the mask of one's Master was common in Greek literary practice down to the Hellenistic age.[158]

The next question to be asked in this connection is this: supposing that there existed early dramatic dialogues (apart from mere ὑπομνήματα), how were they

---

156. This point has been made notably by Apelt *(see* his commentary on *Charmides* p. 60 n. 2 and *Protagoras* p. 121 n. 1, 131 n. 94, 133 n. 105).

157. But the fact that Aristotle *(Poet.* 1447b11) and others (cf. *Smp.* 215d) employ the term Σωκρατικοὶ λόγοι and not διάλογοι hardly indicates that it refers primarily to some sort of 'Socratic stories'; Plato often uses λόγοι in the sense of 'discussion' (e.g. *R.* II 365d, *Phd.* 67b).

158. Cf. *Ep.* 2.314c ". . . and no treatise by Plato exists or will exist, but those which now bear his name belong to a Socrates become fair and young" (translation by R. G. Bury); but it is unclear precisely what the author of the letter means. Cf. in general below n. 229 and p. 242.

'published'? Attic and Syracusan drama and Sophron's mimes of course were intended for acting, for performance on a stage, and certainly not for reading.[159] We can perhaps imagine a group of Socratics performing a 'Socratic mime' for an audience of friends. But writing down a dramatic dialogue for wider circulation—and most of the dramatic pieces in Corpus Platonicum are very obviously not intended for performance in a closed circle only—presumably implies a public accustomed to reading dramatic prose dialogue. This can hardly have been the case in Athens about 400 BCE. It seems to me that a necessary condition for writing such dialogues must have been some kind of institutionalization of Socratic dialectic.[160] The first institution which presented a suitable frame for this was Plato's Academy.[161] I suggest that after, but only after, the reading and perhaps acting of Socratic dialogues had become a practice in the Academy, were such texts circulated outside the Academy, too. After all, Plato's Academy had ambitions to influence public opinion with methods different from Isocrates' rhetoric. And I repeat: the majority of the dramatic pieces in the Corpus Platonicum are (as indeed are the reported pieces) rather exoteric in style. This assertion will be discussed further below.

It should also to be noted that a speech or a reported dialogue is better suited for publication in written form and for reading unprepared by a single person, than a dramatic piece. The narrative of the report gives the necessary hints regarding the characters speaking in the dialogue, and the background; no 'performance' or institutionalized dialectical situation is required. When the reader has received some information about the background and the persons, descriptions and inserenda (of the ἔφη type) can be dropped; this occurs frequently in the reported dialogues, e.g. *Chrm.* 159b–160a, *R.* I 332d–333c. Though such passages approximate to dramatic dialogue, they are clearly secondary products, and not primary cores around which the report has been woven. They would not be intelligible without the preceding (or surrounding) report. Also the frequent use in some reported dialogues of indirect replies such as ὡμολόγει, συνέφη (e.g. *Euthd.* 276a4, 277a3, 4, 6, etc.; 274d1, 276a7, etc., cf. *Tht.* 143c) indicates that the dialogue was originally written as a report and was not just inserted in a piece of narrative.

---

159. There is not much evidence that dramas, before the Hellenistic age, could be composed for reading only and not for performance. Dover 1968b: XCVIII suggests this for the second version of the *Clouds*; but ἀδίδακτα in Athen. 6.270a to which he refers, only implies that some dramas were never performed. At any rate this was not common (cf. the case of Chairemon, Arist. *Rhet.* 3.12.1413b12; I owe this reference to Maarit Kaimio).

160. Ryle (1966: 32–44) has seen this, but his suggestion that the Platonic dialogues were acted at public festivals in Athens is a somewhat whimsical solution; however, Crombie (1969: 363 f.) rightly insists that Ryle's assumption of performance is basically sound.

161. The Megarian 'school' of Euclides appears to have been pronouncedly esoteric. And even the Megarian dialect must have been an obstacle to a wider circulation of its possible literary products. The authenticity of the dialogues of Euclides himself perhaps need not be doubted (cf. above, n. 148), though they may have been rather late and written in Attic. Hirzel 1895: 110 n. 4 thinks that Plato would not have ascribed his *Theaetetus* to Euclides if the latter had not been known as a writer; I believe he had other reasons for the ascription (below p. 329).

[64]     In his interesting book on the classical and later traditions of dialogue literature, Andrieu (1954, especially 209–229, 283, 307 f.; cf. Turner 1971: 15) has argued in detail that the texts of drama and prose dialogue were originally written without names or sigla (ΣΩ etc.) for the persons engaged in the dialogue. The sigla of our manuscripts are comparatively late additions. If this is so, Plato's dramatic dialogues must have made quite heavy demands upon extra-Academic unprepared readers. The Academic reader, however, normally knew what to expect and was usually put in the picture by vocative addresses (e.g. *Hp.Mi.* 363a1 ὦ Σώκρατες, a 6 ὦ Εὔδικε; 373a6 ὦ παῖ Ἀπημάντου [cf. 363b1], a 9 ὦ Σώκρατες). To an Academic, the chief speaker was so obviously Socrates that the whole of the *Sisyphus* can manage without a single explicit mention of his name (though ὦ Σίσυφε occurs in the first sentence, and often later).

Moreover, it is interesting to note that the great majority of the dubia and spuria of our Corpus Platonicum represent the dramatic and not the reported type. I shall return to the problems of authenticity below: it may be noted here, however, that many of the dubia, e.g. *Alcibiades* I, *Hippias Major* and, again, *Sisyphus*, are certainly not very early works. Such instances indicate positively that the Academy regarded it as quite normal to write Socratic dialogues in a dramatic form.

The trend away from the preference for the reported form towards the preference for the dramatic form can be seen in several individual cases which will be commented on below (p. 309). For instance, as has already been shown (p. 198), we have reason to believe that the dramatic *Laches* is later than the *Protagoras* where the main dialogue is in the reported form. The *Clitopho* with its dramatic frame probably refers back to *Republic* I which has the reported form. And *Gorgias* may have been originally written in the reported form (p. 234).

So we are again facing the possibility that Plato began his literary career by writing speeches and reported dialogues, and that the dramatic form was introduced later. This position is not identical with that of Teichmüller (1879), although some of his arguments still hold good.

○

A study of other aspects of the formal structure of the dialogues, notably the BABAB pattern (above p. 201) and the 'pedimental' composition, may possibly provide further clues to chronology, though several complications occur here.[162]

The use in the dialogues, or apart from dialogue, of coherent speeches (type E in the conspectus p. 201) is not, as such, very helpful for deciding chronological problems. Plato must have been well acquainted from his early youth with various methods of using continuous speech (cf. above p. 203 and 206), and the *Laws*
[65]     and *Epinomis* still include such sections. Insofar as patterns of development have been traced here, they do not concern formal matters (apart from the linguistic

---

162. In 1967 I probably over-emphasized the 'authentically Platonic' nature of such structural features; cf. below p. 351 ff.

form) as much as the contents of Plato's speeches, and especially his 'myths.' [65]
Here again the premises are partly of a disputable validity, but some changes
in the manner of approach and the doctrinal contents seem beyond reasonable
doubt.[163]

The tendency to 'lecturer's monologues' interfoliated with occasional questions or comments (type D in the conspectus) is a different matter. Since this type is evidently preferred in the 'late group,' and it is likely to be connected with Plato's teaching habits in the Academy, a study of the possibly gradual emergence of it may present new clues to chronology. This possibility was in fact noted by Zeller, and has been taken into account by some, stylometrists and other geneticists, though no systematic analysis for chronological purposes has been made so far.[164]

Though it can, apparently, be argued that Plato 'invented' the dramatic prose dialogue and perhaps the D type, it is not probable that the dubious ancient tradition which ascribed to him the invention of prose dialogue in general, has anything to do with this. It is likely to derive from a literary evaluation of his dialogues as representing the perfection of the genre.[165] Whether there is any truth in the legend that Plato began his literary activities writing tragedies, we cannot tell;[166] at least this legend implies early literary inclinations and ability in Plato.

Many of Plato's dialogues, notably the reported ones, display remarkable literary qualities, including a variety of styles, vivid settings and characterization of persons, and both pathos and play.[167] It is doubtful what, if any, chronological conclusions can be drawn from this, or from other variations of style, except the (possibly gradual) emergence of the 'late style' (p. 216). A talented writer in [66] his thirties may certainly produce very 'mature' literary products. On the other hand, though the 'late' group of dialogues are marked by a heavy and tortuous

---

163. Cf. above p. 187 f. Schleiermacher's belief in the priority of mythic vision to logical elaboration is useless as a criterion of Platonic chronology (cf. also Raeder 76–78). Lönborg again argued (1939b: 145–151), equally wrongly, that the occurrence of several speeches in the *Symposium* is a sign of late date. In the considerable special literature on the Platonic myths the chronological order *Gorgias—Phaedo—Republic—Timaeus* (the position of *Phaedrus* being controversial) is on the whole taken for granted; cf. Reinhardt 1927, Frutiger 1930 (with consideration also of the short pieces, but without interest in the chronological problems), Edelstein 1949; also Friedländer I³ 186–219.

164. Cf. Zeller III 139–141, 150 n. 1; Lutoslawski 417, 438 f., 486 f. (over-emphasizing the linearity of the development), Gomperz II 1902: 465, Robin 1938: 24 (on *Lg* X 892e ff.), Ryle 1966: 220 f.; I made in 1967 a somewhat more detailed analysis; cf. below p. 315. It may be noted here that not only the 'late group' (including the latter part of the *Republic*), but also *Alcibiades* 1, *Cratylus* and *Laches* have the characteristic τὸ ποῖον; as comments by the interlocutor (or rather, audience).

165. *Anon.Proleg.* Pl. *Phlb.* I 5.44 ed. Westerink: εὗρεν δὲ καὶ εἶδος συγγραφῆς τὸ διαλογικόν. Cf. Diog. L. 3.48 and Hathaway 1969: 39 n. l.

166. Diog. L. 3.5. Plato's familiarity with dramatic art has often been emphasized; cf. especially Pfleiderer 1896: 119 f., 126.

167. Some attempts to typologize these features can be found in my book of 1967. Cf. also Laborderie 1978. Rudberg's attempt (1928) to trace lines of development in Plato's characterization of persons is a typical example of arbitrary interpretation.

baroque style ('onkos') they also reveal a notable lack of interest in external settings, characterization of persons and mimetic play. Yet there are some anomalous cases, of which the most obvious ones are the *Parmenides*, which in spite of the reported form of its first part lacks stylistic liveliness (an anomaly usually taken as a sign of a comparatively late date), the *Phaedrus* which despite its dramatic form exhibits both a vivid setting (presented through references in the dialogue) and a variety of styles including 'late' features (perhaps a sign of revision, cf. p. 318), and the dramatic *Hippias Major*, which is stylistically quite elaborate (though without signs of 'late' style) but structurally simple.

Changes in literary methods and dialogue technique may be somehow connected with the different functions which the dialogues presumably have. A change of purpose or audience has often been thought to have resulted from events in Plato's life, notably the voyages to Sicily and the foundation of the Academy.[168] The former is of little use as a primary criterion, as was noted above (p. 176); the relevance of the Academy is more obvious. However, changes of purpose may in fact constitute a complicating factor for determining the chronological order of the dialogues. For instance, Plato may have been writing for different audiences at approximately the same time, and his didactic, protreptic, apologetic etc. intentions may have varied from time to time.[169] Yet there is no direct relation between purpose and dialogue technique: e.g. *Meno* and *Parmenides* are obviously more esoteric than *Crito* and *Phaedo*, whereas *Meno* and *Crito*, and *Parmenides* and *Phaedo*, on the other hand, are formally related. Again, different dialogues seem to contain different degrees of laudatory, apologetic or even biographical tendencies concerning Socrates; we shall have to return below to this aspect and its possible relevance to chronology. Note here, however, that there is no simple relation between form and purpose in this case either: e.g. *Charmides* and *Protagoras* which are reported dialogues present a more esoteric picture of Socrates than do the dramatic dialogues *Crito*, *Laches* and *Gorgias;* but the opposite relation is true of, say, *Phaedo* (reported dialogue) and *Cratylus* or *Hippias Minor* (dramatic dialogues). It is clear at any rate that the Platonic works were not written in the order in which the events described took place, as an 'ideal biography' of Socrates, which would imply very odd changes of form, such as *Theaetetus—Euthyphro—Apology—Crito—Phaedo*.[170] And not even the well-known distancing or 'fading away' of Socrates in the 'late' period is consistent, since he makes an interesting come-back in the *Philebus*.[171] It is difficult to follow linear trends here.

---

168. A detailed elaboration of this point was made by Raeder 1950 (in Danish).

169. Note the possibility of various degrees of esoterism implied in the theory of oral teaching; above p. 152.

170. This has been sometimes suggested; references with criticism in Lutoslawski 50 f., Raeder 52–54; Robin 1938: 24–27, against Burnet's and Taylor's theory (above p. 170) in particular. Note the rise of the obviously secondary many-stage report in *Symposium* and *Parmenides* (cf. *Theaetetus)*; Bruns 1896: 335 f. wanted to connect this with the 'distancing' of Socrates; Immisch 1899: 623, 625 f. considered it irrelevant.

171. For a complicated and very hypothetical view of this 'fading away' of Socrates, *see* Ryle 1966: 28–37.

The same applies to formal details relating to the structure of the argument;[172] [67] methods of opening and concluding a dialogue;[173] details of the setting;[174] the choice of characters;[175] or the degree of irony or play present.[176] These aspects will also receive some further consideration below.

Since Plato seems to have intended some of his later works to be grouped as trilogies (or tetralogies), there has been some discussion as to whether such tendencies can be traced in his earlier works. Nothing but mere speculation has emerged from this.[177]

## Linguistic criteria; 'stylometry'

As was noted above (p. 149), and as can be seen from the table of chronologies (p. 154 ff), the linguistic criteria were given particular weight in the theory of Platonic chronology which has been dominant since Lutoslawski, Raeder and Ritter.

Lutoslawski 1897 gives references to all important contributions to the [68] study of Plato's language and style up to the mid-1890s,[178] and Ritter 1921–1935,

---

172. The fact that the structure is rather similar in those dialogues which purport to seek a definition of one of the cardinal virtues, *Charmides, Euthyphro, Laches, Republic* I (cf. Detel 1974), really demands an answer to the question why two of them are reported and two dramatic dialogues. Cf. below p. 357.

173. Some supposedly 'early' dialogues conclude with a reference of the type 'we shall return to this' *(Charmides, Euthydemus, Laches, Menexenus, Meno, Protagoras, Theages)*, but so do the 'late' dialogues *Philebus* and *Theaetetus*.

174. A lively description of the scenery is sometimes thought to be characteristic, not only of the 'mature' works, but also of 'early' ones (e.g. Ueberweg-Praechter 223 f., cf. 204, 253 f.: Plato began as a 'poet-philosopher') but this 'criterion' of course begs the question. The details may however be worth looking at. For instance, the motif of meeting somebody after a public performance of some kind or other, is notably common (cf. p. 270). The opening settings of *Parmenides, Republic* and *Symposium* are clearly related (cf. p. 267 ff.) and suggest the internal order *Republic* I—*Symposium* (frame)—*Parmenides* (first part). Details such as Socrates being *extra muros* (openings of *Lysis* and *Phaedrus*, also the *Republic* and *Parmenides*) are interesting.

175. The allegedly symbolic use of characters is on the whole an elusive criterion; cf. above p. 183. But we sometimes seem to get more manifest *termini post quos* out of this; for instance, in the case of Cephalus of Clazomenai in the opening of *Parmenides* or Aristoteles in the latter part of the same dialogue. The number of characters is no reliable clue (cf. Immisch 1899: 618 f.): the fact that Socrates has only one interlocutor in *Hippias Major* and *Phaedrus* does not indicate that they are earlier than, say, *Hippias Minor* or *Cratylus*.

176. There are, in this respect, considerable but elusive differences between the dialogues; cf. above p. 191. *See* especially the fine analyses of de Vries 1949 (in Dutch); cf. Eckert 1911, Plass 1967, Boder 1973.

177. Cf. above p. 185 and below p. 325. On the trilogies and tetralogies, cf. also Raeder 59, Ritter 1910a: 180–182. Haslam 1976 has argued that the *Critias* and *Politicus* were perhaps not intended as separate dialogues at all. Various loose hypotheses have been proposed by Christ 1886: 462–465, Stefanini II 70–74, Boehme 1959: 105 f., Ryle 1966: 253 f.

178. The conspectus provided by Lutoslawski is supplemented by Ritter's very comprehensive discussion in the 'Bursian' 1921: 44–227 (including criticism of Lutoslawski's method, p. 112–134).

[68] Brandwood 1958, Cherniss 1959–1960 and Brisson 1979 cover most of the ground for later periods. It will suffice here to sum up very briefly the general trends in the post-Lutoslawskian discussion of Platonic stylometry in the narrow sense of the 'statistics of language.'[179] Only original contributions and comprehensive reassessments will be noted. Of course, almost every serious writer on Plato in the 20th century has had something to say about stylometry and the general reservations as well as the praise for it occasioned by Lutoslawski's work, have recurred again and again.

In the rather heated debate around the turn of the century, the authority of Zeller supported the conservative position; his last article against stylometry was written in 1900.[180] Other more or less competent specimens of criticism were produced by Th. Gomperz 1887: 751–767 who later took a more favorable view (II 1902: 232 f.), Pfleiderer 1896: 299 f., n.; Natorp 1898, Immish 1899: 443–451, Heikel 1900, Shorey 1903 (4, cf. 88), F. Horn 1904, especially 407; Joël 1906–1907, Apelt 1908, and others, and by Ritter himself in various contexts (summed up in 1910a–b). Ritter's criticism was directed mainly against Lutoslawski. He supplied, however, more statistical evidence in support of his earlier study (1888), in which he had followed and developed the stylometrical ideas of Dittenberger and Schanz. His views later became largely normative for the conception of Platonic chronology even outside Germany (cf. above p. 149) because of his apparently careful weighing of the pros and cons, and his 'demonstration' that the study of the language of Plato offers, in general, more reliable, objective and unambiguous criteria for dating the dialogues than the study of the contents.[181]

[69] Apart from Ritter, new and constructive contributions to Platonic stylometry were made, in the period before the First World War, by Baron (1897, on πέρι), Janell (1901, on the avoidance of hiatus), Trense (1901, on the use of adjectives), Blass (earlier studies and 1903, on rhythm, particularly clausulae), Kaluscha 1904 (on clausulae), Raeder 1905 (attempting to combine the results of various

---

179. Lutoslawski himself employed, and probably coined, the term 'stylometry' to denote the application of his own method which included (as Campbell had also included) the observation of various non-linguistic characteristics of the dialogues in addition to the linguistic data. He classed the whole of his extremely heterogeneous material according to relative importance and relative frequency and subjected it to a numerical scale which he attempted to employ as a 'measure' of the 'relative affinity' of all Platonic works to the *Laws*.

180. A review of von Arnim 1896/7; cf. also Zeller 1887, and still II $1^5$ 512–516. In fact Zeller's 'last word' is not so one-sidedly averse as is sometimes believed, and his judicious remarks on the usefulness of linguistic analyses are well worth reading even today.

181. Scholars seem to have been particularly impressed by Ritter's tables 1910b: 230 f. and 254 f. which purport to show how divergent were the results reached by earlier methods in comparison to the general agreement of the stylometrists. Sometimes he is notably critical against the application of a detailed stylometry (e.g. 1910a: 208); but his testing of the method on the prose of Goethe and Zeller (!) appears to have given him a new confidence (1910a: 210–217, 223–226). The more detailed test promised 1910b: 273 was never carried out, as far as I can see. There is, however, an unmistakably apologetic and self-centered approach in much that Ritter has written which should warn the reader not to trust his 'objectivity' blindly. He was after all a partisan.

approaches), Kallenberg 1913 (on ὅτι and ὡς); and von Arnim published his statistics of various formulae of assent (1912, following up an earlier study of 1896). Though von Arnim himself seems to have lost some of his former confidence during the process of his work,[182] his 'quotients of affinity' provoked a new debate concerning the usefulness of stylometry; critics include Shorey 1912, Maier 1913, especially 125 n. 2; Parmentier 1913: 148–151, Pohlenz 1914, Immisch 1915 and, again, Ritter (see especially 1921: 166–183). For later critics, too, von Arnim is often the chief target. Others, including Wilamowitz II² 1920: 8 took a more sympathetic view, though nobody was enthusiastic and most scholars regarded von Arnim's tables with deep distrust.[183]

At any rate, the Raeder—Ritter 'compromise' had become normative since the 1920s. The later history of Platonic stylometry is characterized by a more widespread passivity and, perhaps, an increasing skepticism. Occasional tentative tests have been made in order to adjust the picture: we may list Billing 1920 (on clausulae), Fossum 1931 (on hapax legomena), Ritter 1935 (on various particles, and ἕτερος, ἄλλος, πᾶς, ὥσπερ and οἶον, Ritter's last contribution), Vanachter 1946 (the relative frequency of word classes), des Places 1951 (period structure), Humbert 1954 (sentence structure), Brandwood 1956 (arguing for the use of electronic computers), Wake 1957 (the theory of statistics of sentence length, an approach suggested by Webster 1941), Cox and Brandwood 1959 (stylometrical tests in support of Owen's early dating of Ti.; cf. above p. 160 and Brandwood 1958: 316–333, against Cherniss 1957), Díaz Tejera 1961, 1965 (on Koiné words); Wishart and Leach 1970 (statistics of rhythm of five syllable groups independent of position in clause), and various minor contributions by A. Q. Morton and S. Michaelson.[184]

Predominantly critical approaches have been made notably by the following: Ueberweg-Praechter (215–217), Diès II 1927: 250–265, Warburg 1929 (on *Cratylus*), Kretschmer 1932: 232 (a brief note against von Arnim 1912), Stefanini 1932: I.LXVII–LXXII, Robin 1938: 37–40, Owen 1953: 79–84 (opening the controversy on the position of the *Timaeus*, cf. p. 335), Benardete 1963, 1965; Mainz 1967 (chiefly against von Arnim 1912), Thesleff 1967, above, 7 ff.; Dover 1968a: 94–147 (on stylometrical methods in general), Kapp 1968: 79, and Tarán 1975: 14–19; and above all in the (unfortunately) unpublished dissertation of Brandwood 1958 which discusses critically and very fully the more important previous studies down to Ritter 1935, and where an attempt is made to establish the few positive facts resulting from these studies (cf. below p. 218). Brandwood's new Word

---

182. The modest results (recorded as results in the book) are totally disproportionate to the work accomplished. von Arnim did not publish the rest of the collected material (see 1912: 8–10), and in his book of 1914 he turns to other types of criteria.

183. Defenses of (chronological) stylometry such as those produced by Chevalier 1914 and Nolte 1914 have remained on a very superficial level; cf. Brandwood 1958: 431.

184. Most of them are of very limited value, such as the statistics of καί in some dialogues (Morton and McLeman 1966, Table 17); for this 'one word test' see also Ep. 7, below p. 347. The most interesting one is Michaelson, Morton and Gillies 1977, on the frequency and position of some particles, together with other considerations.

[70] Index (1976) is now an indispensable tool for every potential student of linguistic usage in the Corpus Platonicum.

∘∘∘ ◯ ∘∘∘

One result of this stylometrical research, already arrived at in the 19th century by the first stylometrists Campbell and Dittenberger independently of each other, is valid beyond any reasonable doubt: there exists a distinct group of dialogues (in alphabetical order, *Critias, Laws, Philebus, Politicus, Sophist, Timaeus*) which are characterized by certain linguistic mannerisms and various other features of form and contents; and because one of these is the *Laws* which is known to be one of Plato's last works, the group as a whole can be safely assigned a comparatively late date. Hence, it is customary to refer to these dialogues as the 'late group,' and to their style as Plato's 'late style.'[185] This result has been corroborated again and again by later research. Whether these are in fact Plato's last dialogues, i.e. the only works of the 'late period,' as is usually believed, or whether the Corpus includes other Platonic works of approximately the same date, is a special problem which will concern us later.

Moreover, more loosely but still with some degree of confidence, it can be stated that dialogues which appear to approximate stylistically to the 'late group' should be given a relative date not very far from it, especially if there is an affinity of contents or approach to support this association. This is commonly said to apply to the *Parmenides, Phaedrus* and *Theaetetus*, and to *Epinomis* (which is clearly an appendix to the *Laws*); and the same seems to apply to some parts of the *Republic*, perhaps the whole of the *7th Letter*, and possibly various parts of other works.[186] It is doubtful, however, to what extent the linguistic evidence as such is trustworthy in these cases. There are in fact little or no traces of the most characteristic 'late style' features ('onkos') in *Parmenides* and *Theaetetus*.[187] The assigning of these two dialogues to the context of the 'late group' partly depends on the occurrence in them of various expressions such as formulae of reply and philosophical terms which are current in the late works but are not current in dialogues considered 'early' on other grounds; and in the first place this classification is due to considerations of the contents. On the other hand, *Phaedrus*, parts of the *Republic*, and 

[71] occasional passages elsewhere undoubtedly have 'late style' features to a varying extent, although not a great deal of attention has been paid to this fact, either because it is not so obvious (statistics being based upon each dialogue as a whole) or because it does not fit in very well with our picture of Plato's later philosophy.

At any rate a reconsideration of the linguistic criteria is needed in order to determine the late group associates' and the 'middle' and 'early' dialogues. Before

---

185. For the characteristics of this 'late style' ('onkos'), and further references, *see* Thesleff 1967: above, 63–64, 139–141.
186. Notably *Phaedo* and *Symposium*, cf. Thesleff 1967: 111 ff., 139.
187. Slightly more in *Theaetetus*, cf. Thesleff 1967: 115 ff.

this is done, we should examine somewhat more closely three theses which will be elaborated on below: (1) the thesis of partial revision of some of the dialogues (p. 230), (2) the thesis that Plato relied on the assistance of a secretary who knew how to write 'late Platonic style' (p. 242), and (3) the thesis that 'authenticity' is not in Plato's case a strictly definable concept (p. 235 ff.).

For the present, let us consider what is meant by 'trends of change' or 'development' in Plato's style.

It is important to note that accepting a 'late Platonic group' of dialogues chiefly on linguistic grounds, and also accepting more vaguely perhaps a group of 'late group associates,' does not mean an automatic acceptance of any general theory of 'development' of this or any author's linguistic or stylistic usage. Such a theory, however, is more or less tacitly implied by most scholars who have tried to arrange Plato's dialogues in a detailed chronological order in keeping with linguistic evidence. Whether based upon Lutoslawski's curious 'Law of Affinity' or not,[188] such theories should, in the view of the present writer, be treated with the utmost suspicion. And applying them to the Corpus Platonicum in particular does in fact involve one in a whole range of specific problems.

It is a truism to assert that any author's manner of writing undergoes change. And it is probably true, though by no means certain, that with the majority of artists and thinkers the general tendency is towards a richer expression and register and towards greater complexity.[189] Every writer will occasionally adopt new expressions and mannerisms. But some will soon drop some of them, others stick to some mannerisms longer, or return to them after an interval of time.[190] At any rate, rules of general applicability can hardly be abstracted from such changes.

So it does not seem to me likely, even in theory, that the direction of the change in individual style normally follows a distinct trend which could be characterized quantitatively as a steady increase in certain features ('style markers')[191] and a steady decrease in others. And it is even less probable that the characteristics of such a trend, if it does exist, could be somehow derived by interpolation or extrapolation from two separate works of an author for which the chronological order is known—say, the *Republic* and the *Laws* in the case of Plato—so that the remaining works could be arranged in a correct chronological sequence according to their degree of stylistic affinity with or distance from the two points known, before, between, or after them. Do such consistent and manifestly traceable

---

188. Cf. above p. 213. The conception of a gradual 'development' of individual style corresponded of course to the genetic method of approach typical of the 19th century; e.g. Schanz (1886) had adopted this view, and it is still clearly implied by von Arnim and Ritter and even by Wake 1957, Brandwood (below), and later stylometrists (above). It is interesting to note, however, that neither Campbell not Dittenberger attempted to ascertain the internal order within the 'late group' on linguistic grounds.

189. This is apparently true of Goethe, James Joyce, Frank Lloyd Wright, Alvar Aalto and Le Corbusier, as I noted in 1967 (above, p. 139 n. 346).

190. Dover 1968: 87 ff. has some good observations on the caprices of writer's choice of words.

191. In 1967 (above, p. 22) I employed this term for the specific selected characteristics of individual or generic style.

[72] trends ever occur in literature? The burden of proof rests with those who assert this. Lutoslawski did not succeed in proving it.

Consequently, any attempt to determine stylometrically the internal chronological order of the dialogues in the 'late group,' not to mention the 'middle' and 'early' groups, rests methodologically upon precarious premises. It is regrettable that this fact was not clearly envisaged by Brandwood (1958), whose well-informed and prudent criticism of earlier Platonic stylometry is in most respects of great value. After a comprehensive discussion of various arguments produced by the stylometrists, and a careful sifting of the evidence, Brandwood rejected all attempts so far to establish the internal chronology of the 'early' and 'middle' groups on linguistic grounds; but he did not find the method inapplicable in principle. And for the 'late group,' certain apparent linguistic trends, notably in the use of clausulae and the avoidance of hiatus, led him to accept the order *Timaeus—Critias—Sophist—Politicus—Philebus—Laws* (especially 311–343). Whatever one thinks of the reliability of clausulae and hiatus as Platonic style markers,[192] the method is not basically sound.

Very much more has been said, and could be said, against the use of language statistics for determining a detailed chronology of the Corpus Platonicum. In my earlier book (1967), I expressed certain reservations about such applications of stylometry, but I was still inclined to think that measurable trends could be used for determining a rough chronology; but since then I have become much more skeptical. Most of the arguments which I now consider relevant have in fact been current, or at least implied, in the debate on this subject since the 19th century (cf. above p. 214), and it would be a profitless task to trace their origins or the varying emphasis attached to them by different scholars. But as far as I can see nobody has yet stated clearly or given reasons for the difference between what stylometry cannot possibly be expected to 'prove' or indicate in the case of Plato, and where it might be of some help. I shall try to do this here.

In addition to the two principal difficulties already mentioned—the difficulty of assuming distinct linear trends in an author's style, and the difficulty of ex-
[73] tracting such trends from a body of texts where only a few segments can be regarded as chronologically fixed—the following considerations have particular relevance to the Corpus Platonicum.

It is abundantly clear that Plato was fond of playing with styles, and that he deliberately varied his manner of expression in different works, and in different passages within the same work, for a variety of reasons some of which are more obvious to us than others.[193] And such choices and partly hidden preferences are likely to disturb considerably the picture of evenly developing trends which chronological stylometry presupposes. Indeed, we cannot even be sure that within the

---

192. Much has been said on this topic in various connections; for instance, Friedländer III² 513 n. 86 makes a pertinent observation against Billig's typology of clausulae which is accepted by Brandwood 1958: 294 ff.

193. Cf. in general Thesleff 1967. It is also noteworthy that the use of the formulae of reply is normally deliberately varied even in rather artless pieces of dialogue; e.g. consecutive strings of ναί:s are sometimes found (notably in *Alcibiades* I) but are not common.

same 'period' Plato did write with the same general purposes in mind or for a similar audience and, hence, preferred the same general style at any given time. Furthermore, we do not know very much about the stylistic motivations for Plato's linguistic choices or his potential linguistic register at various periods; and so the distinction between a deliberate choice more or less independent of time and a choice motivated by his linguistic usage at a certain period is often impossible to make. Drawing conclusions from the occurrence or non-occurrence of rare words is notoriously difficult anyway.[194] Even more disastrous for chronological stylometry would be to admit that some dialogues have undergone successive revision,[195] and that the line between wholly authentic and wholly spurious dialogues and passages is not easily drawn. As will be shown below, we can hardly avoid making such assumptions.

Thus, we have to face the fact that stylometry, however extensively used and with whatever degree of refinement, cannot be expected to yield reliable results or even indications as to the precise order in which Plato's dialogues were written. And confronting this negative fact, as well as the *non liquet's* of the preceding chapters, we may begin to see one of the basic reasons why it has been possible to argue for so many different chronologies for Plato.

On the other hand, stylometry is obviously useful in determining different manners of writing or, at least, for the objectification of subjective impressions relating to style. Consequently, stylometry can be expected to present criteria for distinguishing groups of dialogues other than the 'late group' and its 'associates.' Attempts to distinguish groups have in fact been made by several stylometrists, though on a very modest scale.[196] The different stylistic groups thus separated are usually taken to be chronological groups, analogously with the 'late group.' This inference, however, is methodically disputable as an *a priori* principle for reasons already stated. Unless there exists ample independent evidence, stylistic groups should not be identified with chronological groups. It is wiser not to trust chronological stylometry at all as a primary criterion, whether it is concerned with the relation of individual works or with groups of works.

Instead, considering the problems of authenticity involved with the Corpus Platonicum (below, p. 235), it would seem reasonable to apply stylometry in the first place to the question of whether we can distinguish wholly authentic Platonic

---

194. Wilamowitz II 68 has referred to the fact that one of the crucial instances of ἀλλὰ τί μήν; in *Lysis* (208c) does not appear in a papyrus fragment of the text (P. Oxy. VI 881 verso).

195. Ritter (1910a: 227, 1910b: 247 f.) insisted that revision normally would not have affected the essential qualities of style; similarly e.g. Ueberweg-Praechter 216, Robin 1938: 40 n. l. This is a highly debatable assertion.

196. The critical assessment of earlier work made by Brandwood 1958 conveys less confidence than what would appear from the preface of his Word Index 1976, especially XVI f.: "It can be taken as reasonably established on the basis of stylistic investigations that all works of Group I. were written before those of Group II with the possible exception of *R*. I, and that these in turn were written before those of Group III. It is also reasonably certain that Group IA as a whole is earlier than IB as a whole, although one or two works may be included in the wrong group. As regards the chronological sequence of individual works, nothing definite can be said. . . ." As for the order of the 'early' groups, this is very far from certain (cf. also 1958: 402–406).

[74] texts—or portions of texts—from semiauthentic and wholly spurious ones. This question has engaged A. Q. Morton and his followers, but not many others.[197]

The statistics produced by Morton and Michaelson are clearly insufficient because they are restricted to very few words, and because they do not take account of differences due to genre (e.g. the fact that common particles are likely to have a different occurrence in speeches, letters and different kinds of dramatic or reported dialogue).

In order to test the applicability of stylometry to distinguishing different groups in the Corpus and, hence, perhaps different hands at work, and possibly to prepare the way for a more systematic study of this complex, the present writer has made some further statistics of the Platonic vocabulary from Brandwood's Word Index. Though the results of these preliminary tests were not particularly encouraging, a brief account of them is appropriate here.[198]

**Test I.** The statistics concerned a total of approximately 200 words and expressions occurring in the Corpus. The words chosen included (1) philosophical terms such as derivatives of ἀγνο-/ἀγνω-, αἰσθ-, διαιρ-, θεωρ-, καρτερ-; (2)
[75] comparatively rare words and hapax legomena semantically suited to ordinary conversation such as βδελυρός, βλακεία, ἐξαπίνης, ἰδιολογέω; (3) pairs of approximate synonyms such as ἄγαν/λίαν, βούλομαι/ἐθέλω, δεῖ/χρή, δοκεῖ/ἔοικεν; and (4) common particles and combinations of particles. High style words typical of the speeches and/or the 'late style' were not taken into account.

From the distribution tables it appeared, in general, that there are considerable differences between the dialogues, even between dialogues commonly thought to belong closely together such as *Charmides/Laches/Protagoras*, or *Crito/Euthyphro* (and indeed the *Sophist/Politicus*!). On the other hand the difference between dialogues commonly considered spurious, and those considered authentic, is not on the whole more marked than the difference between various authentic works, to judge by this material; the only exception is *Axiochus* which really stands somewhat apart linguistically (as it does philosophically). Obviously the body of material considered was not large enough to confirm such impressions of 'un-Platonic' style as most readers acquire from, say, the *Hipparchus* ('clumsy'), *Hippias Major* ('artificially exuberant'), *De Virtute* ('unimaginative imitation of the Meno'), or *Eryxias* ('overdone imitation of the *Charmides*' or 'mannerisms in the use of participles'). In general, the dialogues usually accepted as authentic seem to have a richer vocabulary than the dubia and spuria; but the former include dialogues that are linguistically rather 'meager' such as *Crito, Hippias Minor* and *Ion*.

---

197. *See* the Bibliography, Morton and Michaelson. Note here again Dover's interesting application of stylometry to questions of authenticity in the Corpus Lysiacum (1968a).

198. It so happened that soon after I had written this (in October, 1980), I was contacted by a professional statistician, Mr. Kalevi Loimaranta, who has worked on stylometry as a hobby and was interested in carrying on with Plato. We collaborated in a fresh approach to 'cluster stylometry' (cf. n. 202). The results will be published separately, but it may be stated here that so far (October, 1981) nothing has appeared to contradict the chronology suggested in Part II of this study.

Studies in Platonic Chronology                                                                221

Occasional hapax legomena occur in almost all works in the Corpus, and hence [75] little primary weight can be attached to such instances as ἰδιολογήσασθαι in *Theages* 121a. Only *Hipparchus* and *Alcibiades* II (in addition to the *Axiochus*) have a relatively high frequency of curious hapax legomena.

Obviously the chance of a rare word being used increases with the length of the text (though notably in *Alcibiades* I the vocabulary is rather 'meager'): in fact the great majority of the words and expressions studied occur somewhere in the *Republic*. Consequently arguments *ex silentio* are not particularly valid for short texts. And an examination of words current only outside the *Republic* does not reveal very much (since no account was taken of 'late style' words).[199]

How precarious such statistics of mere occurrence or non-occurrence of words in different dialogues are can be easily illustrated. In the occurrence lists of some 115 comparatively infrequent words there were counted separately the number of instances when *Charmides* shared an occurrence of a word with another dialogue, and when a word occurred only in one of the two dialogues. The following picture emerges:

*Table 1* [76]

|  | a<br>number of words occurring in both dialogues | b<br>number of words occurring in one of the dialogues only | c<br>a minus b | d<br>number of words occurring in neither dialogue |
|---|---|---|---|---|
| Chrm. ~ Alc. I | 18 | 34 | −16 | 63 |
| ~ Cra. | 22 | 41 | −19 | 52 |
| ~ Euthd. | 22 | 32 | −10 | 61 |
| ~ Grg. | 25 | 47 | −22 | 43 |
| ~ Hp.Ma. | 19 | 38 | −19 | 58 |
| ~ La. | 18 | 29 | −11 | 68 |
| ~ Ly. | 16 | 39 | −23 | 60 |
| ~ Men. | 18 | 38 | −20 | 59 |
| ~ Prt. | 29 | 39 | −10 | 47 |
| ~ R. I | 19 | 33 | −14 | 63 |
| ~ Sph. | 24 | 49 | −25 | 42 |

Even though in these cases the points of positive agreement were less in number than the points of difference, the figures may suggest that the 'style' of *Charmides* is more closely related to *Euthydemus*, *Laches*, *Protagoras* and *Republic* I than to

---

199. For instance, these words include philosophical terms such as ἀλογία (*Ep. 7, Epin., Hp.Ma., Lg., Ly., Men., Phd., Phlb., Smp., Tht.*), ἀνάμνησις (*Lg., Men., Phd., Phlb., Phdr.*), δήλωσις (*Cra., Lg., Min., Plt.*), εἰρωνικός (*Amat., Euthd., Lg., Smp., Sph.*), καρτέρησις (*La., Lg., Smp.*); but their occurrence in the *Laws* is not of course a sufficient indication that the work in question should be placed with the *Laws* rather than with the *Republic*. Whatever the explanation of these instances, they cannot be used for determining chronology or authenticity.

[76] *Gorgias*, *Meno* and the *Sophist*; and this may appear reasonable at the first sight. But then the relatively great divergence from *Lysis* looks suspicious. For *Laches* versus *Lysis* the corresponding figures would be

|  | a | b | c | d |
|---|---|---|---|---|
| La. ~ Ly. | 15 | 29 | −14 | 71 |

which again suggests an affinity contradicted by the former table. A test with the same material of the closely related *Sophist* and *Politicus* gives a significantly positive result:

|  | a | b | c | d |
|---|---|---|---|---|
| Sph. ~ Plt. | 42 | 30 | +12 | 43 |

But one's confidence in the method is again seriously shaken by the figures for *Protagoras* versus the *Sophist*:

|  | a | b | c | d |
|---|---|---|---|---|
| Prt. ~ Sph. | 40 | 39 | −1 | 36. |

Is it possible that *Protagoras* is more closely related to the *Sophist* than to *Charmides*?

In fact such statistics are inadequate because they show only a very limited number of points of similarity and points of difference, and give only the sum of those points, without showing what points are shared in each case of contrast: a comparatively high number may include very different points in different cases. If one wishes to proceed along these lines, one has to work out, from detailed [77] occurrence and non-occurrence profiles, or rather 'isoglosses,' for several thousands of words, a general picture of the distribution of the vocabulary of the Corpus Platonicum. This is of course best done with the aid of an electronic computer. And as things stand I am not sure whether such an enormous task would be worth embarking upon. As has already been stated, the non-occurrence of a word is not a reliable criterion for classification of a Platonic dialogue; and the mere occurrence of a word hardly constitutes a more reliable basis except in special cases such as new terms or demonstrably un-Platonic idioms. Possibly, however, modern statistical methods could be used for differentiating groups of dialogues with material of this kind.

**Test II.** Another, more promising approach would be to take account of the relative frequency of words. In this case only comparatively common words, such as von Arnim's notorious formulae of reply, present a sufficiently broad population for reliable statistics. The use of some particles in the Corpus was chosen for this test II. In order to avoid the mistake of Morton and some other stylometrists, the relative frequency was studied only in dialogue passages (of types A and B,

above p. 201) of approximately the same length (owing to the brevity of certain [77]
short dialogues, 6–7 Stephanus pages had to suffice). Works with very little or
no dialogue (*Apology, Clitopho, Critias, Definitions, Demodocus, Epinomis, Epistulae*
*1–13, De Justo, Menexenus, Sisyphus, Timaeus* and *De Virtute*) were not utilized.[200]

Two somewhat different approaches were made.

First, the relative frequency of certain particles (ἆρα solitarium, γάρ solit., γε
solit., δέ solit., δέ γε, δὲ δή, δή solit., δῆτα solit., καίτοι, μὲν οὖν, μέντοι, μήν
solit., ναί, που solit., τε solit., τοίνυν, ὦ) and at the same time some other common
words (αὖ, βούλει, δεῖ, δοκεῖ, inf. εἶναι, ἔοικεν, κατά c.acc., μάλα, μάλιστα, οἴει,
οἶμαι, πάνυ, περί c.gen., χρή) was mapped out. The figures for the number of occurrences of each word in each piece of dialogue considered were classed, roughly,
as relatively 'high,' 'medium' and 'low' (including non-occurrence in the passage studied) in relation to the average occurrence. An attempt was then made
to group together dialogues which have approximately the same distribution
of frequency 'profiles.' The most obvious result was that the 'late group' again
looked rather coherent and distinct from the rest (though *Critias* and *Timaeus*
were not considered). But little more can be said with any reasonable degree
of confidence. If, according to this test, the dialogues *Crito, Hipparchus, Hippias
Minor, Ion, Protagoras* and *Theages* appeared to belong somehow together, this
is chiefly because of the low frequency of various characteristics which the passages studied share, and this is no reliable basis for conclusions, especially since
there are remarkable differences in details. Somewhat more interesting is the fact
that *Lysis* again stands somewhat apart from e.g. *Charmides*, in addition to the obviously very 'different' *Axiochus* (whereas *Eryxias* again rather approximates to [78]
the general Platonic standard), and that *Euthyphro, Hippias Major* and *Laches* bear
a slightly greater resemblance to *Alcibiades* I and *Gorgias* than the rest. However,
the differences are on the whole almost as marked as the affinities noted in each
combination. A partial reason for this may be the brevity of the passages examined. Another reason may be the highly diversified types of word chosen.

In order to adjust, if possible, this manifestly inadequate and unreliable picture, a second test was carried out with only a few of the most frequent particles.
The result appears in *Table 2*. The figures denote the number of occurrence in
the passages examined; the profiles of distribution can, I think, be visually extracted from the figures. An attempt was made to group the dialogues so that approximately similar profiles and at the same time interesting combinations come
together. Seemingly anomalous figures are easily discernible. Naturally various
other classifications are possible, but as far as I can see they would not significantly reduce the number of anomalous figures.

The first fact to be noted is that the 'late group' (classes VI and VII in the table,
cf. *Prm.* and *R.* IV in class IV, *Tht.* in class II and *Phdr.* in class V) does not now

---

200. It was noted, however, that the *Menexenus* (and also to some extent the *Apology*) shows
a markedly high degree of affinity with *Timaeus, Critias* and the *Letters* with regard to the use
of particles; this can probably be explained from the fact that a continuous exposition (type E,
above p. 201) demands another kind of employment of particles than dialogue.

Table 2

| | | ἀλλά solit. | δέ | ἄρα solit. | ἄρ᾽ solit. | αὖ | γάρ solit. | γε solit. | δή solit. | δῆτα | ἤδη | μὲν γάρ | μὲν οὖν | μέντοι solit. | ναί | οὐκοῦν | οὖν solit. | τότε solit. | του solit. | τε καί | τοίνυν solit. | Σ |
|---|---|---|---|---|---|---|---|---|---|---|---|---|---|---|---|---|---|---|---|---|---|---|
| I | Hp.Ma. 287c–294c | 23 | 31 | 6 | 4 | 2 | 26 | 34 | 13 | 2 | – | 5 | 6 | 6 | 2 | 8 | 14 | 3 | – | 8 | 7 | 63 |
| | Euthphr. 5c–11e | 36 | 38 | 12 | 9 | 3 | 21 | 35 | 10 | 2 | 2 | 2 | 3 | 2 | 3 | 7 | 4 | 5 | 2 | 7 | 3 | 45 |
| | La. 193d–199e | 24 | 13 | 6 | – | 5 | 17 | 28 | 21 | 4 | 1 | 4 | 9 | 6 | 1 | 7 | 9 | 2 | 2 | 15 | 4 | 53 |
| | Men. 72b–79e | 29 | 38 | 6 | 3 | 3 | 22 | 27 | 11 | 7 | 2 | – | 3 | 1 | 5 | 10 | 11 | 4 | – | 4 | 8 | 38 |
| II | Cri. 43a–50a | 32 | 24 | 8 | 2 | 3 | 13 | 10 | 12 | 1 | 3 | 2 | 2 | 1 | 2 | 4 | 5 | 2 | – | 4 | 2 | 38 |
| | Grg. 461b–468e | 29 | 22 | 5 | 2 | 2 | 18 | 14 | 9 | 3 | 3 | – | 10 | 3 | 3 | 10 | 12 | 1 | 1 | 9 | 3 | 26 |
| | R. I 331e–338c | 31 | 18 | 15 | 3 | – | 20 | 24 | 14 | – | – | 1 | 4 | 4 | 7 | 2 | 13 | 3 | 2 | 13 | – | 28 |
| | Smp. 198a–207a | 25 | 30 | 9 | 3 | 3 | 29 | 26 | 22 | 4 | 4 | 4 | 5 | – | 3 | 4 | 20 | 6 | – | 15 | 4 | 30 |
| | Tht. 179b–186e | 25 | 21 | 7 | 5 | 8 | 19 | 21 | 8 | – | 1 | – | 6 | 1 | 4 | 6 | 12 | 8 | 1 | 18 | 2 | 27 |
| III | Thg. 121e–127c | 23 | 35 | 1 | 6 | 3 | 17 | 17 | 7 | 2 | 2 | 3 | 4 | 3 | 15 | 5 | 19 | 2 | 1 | 8 | – | 26 |
| | Alc.1 106c–113b | 23 | 21 | 5 | 7 | 2 | 20 | 34 | 10 | – | – | – | – | 2 | 18 | 12 | 20 | 2 | 2 | 10 | – | 17 |
| | Alc. 2 138a–146e | 24 | 46 | 8 | 5 | 1 | 12 | 25 | 9 | 5 | 3 | 4 | 9 | 11 | 6 | 18 | 11 | 8 | – | 20 | 3 | 19 |
| | Hipparch. 225a–232b | 28 | 18 | 12 | 4 | 6 | 15 | 28 | 4 | 8 | 2 | 1 | – | 2 | 14 | 9 | 17 | 4 | 1 | 3 | 4 | 13 |
| IV | Ly. 212a–218d | 24 | 30 | 18 | 2 | 4 | 26 | 15 | 15 | 1 | 3 | 2 | 6 | 1 | 7 | 5 | 6 | 3 | 4 | 10 | 4 | 16 |
| | Chrm. 165b–171c | 27 | 23 | 9 | 4 | 6 | 18 | 15 | 14 | 4 | 1 | 3 | 3 | – | 5 | 10 | 10 | 5 | 5 | 7 | 6 | 16 |
| | Prm. 130e–137c | 24 | 41 | 10 | 2 | 14 | 19 | 19 | 11 | 1 | – | – | 1 | 1 | 6 | 5 | 10 | 1 | 2 | 5 | 1 | 22 |
| | R. IV 433a–440a | 24 | 33 | 11 | 6 | 8 | 13 | 25 | 13 | – | 2 | 1 | 6 | 6 | 5 | 9 | 5 | 8 | 1 | 22 | 5 | 6 |
| | Erx. 392a–399e | 20 | 73 | 6 | – | 3 | 17 | 20 | 3 | – | 1 | 1 | 1 | 7 | 3 | 9 | 16 | 3 | – | 8 | – | 14 |

|   |   | | | | | | | | | | | | | | | | | | | | | |
|---|---|---|---|---|---|---|---|---|---|---|---|---|---|---|---|---|---|---|---|---|---|
| V | Prt. 349d–355e | 18 | 29 | 2 | 4 | 6 | 12 | 13 | 11 | — | 2 | 4 | 2 | 2 | — | 7 | 12 | 4 | 1 | 17 | 3 | 17 |
|  | Euthd. 278e–285a | 9 | 34 | 9 | 4 | 1 | 12 | 18 | 5 | 6 | 2 | 1 | 5 | 2 | 6 | 7 | 16 | 3 | 1 | 25 | 1 | 32 |
|  | Hp.Mi. 363a–369b | 13 | 28 | 7 | 2 | 1 | 17 | 19 | 6 | 2 | 1 | 1 | 1 | 2 | 13 | 6 | 10 | 4 | 2 | 15 | 2 | 29 |
|  | Cra. 428d–435a | 18 | 30 | 5 | 9 | 5 | 15 | 18 | 5 | — | 1 | — | 2 | 4 | 10 | 11 | 7 | 4 | 2 | 8 | 5 | 25 |
|  | Phd. 69e–76e | 16 | 21 | 13 | 10 | 2 | 13 | 29 | 8 | 3 | 2 | — | 9 | 4 | 5 | 12 | 9 | 3 | 14 | 5 | 2 | 29 |
|  | Amat. 132a–139a | 13 | 21 | 14 | 3 | 1 | 12 | 23 | 9 | 2 | 3 | — | 2 | 4 | 7 | 7 | 19 | 2 | 1 | 11 | — | 13 |
|  | Phdr. 259d–266e | 18 | 18 | 3 | 1 | 4 | 6 | 22 | 12 | 1 | 3 | — | 2 | 5 | 5 | 5 | 6 | 5 | 4 | 17 | 2 | 15 |
|  | Ion 536d–542b | 16 | 13 | 3 | 2 | 1 | 5 | 15 | 8 | 4 | — | 2 | 2 | 1 | 2 | 10 | 3 | 1 | — | 3 | 3 | 24 |
|  | Min. 313a–319a | 15 | 17 | 17 | 3 | 3 | 13 | 14 | 6 | 2 | 3 | — | 4 | 1 | 26 | 15 | 13 | 3 | 2 | 9 | 2 | 8 |
| VI | Sph. 243–250e | 15 | 21 | 6 | 7 | 9 | 22 | 28 | 22 | 1 | 3 | — | 6 | 2 | 9 | 2 | 7 | 8 | 6 | 7 | 6 | 14 |
|  | Plt. 274e–281e | 9 | 21 | 2 | 1 | 11 | 14 | 19 | 14 | — | — | 5 | — | 3 | 2 | 3 | 5 | 2 | 7 | 10 | 4 | 9 |
|  | Phlb. 20b–27d | 15 | 42 | 2 | 5 | 9 | 24 | 23 | 16 | 5 | 2 | 2 | 8 | 2 | 2 | 9 | 2 | 8 | 8 | 9 | 5 | 18 |
| VII | Lg. III 676a–683a | 4 | 14 | 1 | 4 | 4 | 18 | 16 | 16 | — | 5 | — | 6 | 1 | 2 | 8 | 2 | 9 | 6 | 15 | 1 | 5 |
| VIII | Ax. 364a–372a | 16 | 12 | — | — | — | 28 | 2 | 1 | — | 5 | 2 | 2 | — | — | — | 8 | 4 | — | 7 | — | 15 |

For the passages examined, *see* above p. 223.

[78] stand out as clearly as it does in the other tests; and the internal difference between the *Sophist* and *Politicus* is in fact almost as great as between, say, *Politicus* and *Charmides* (class IV). But *Axiochus* (class VIII), contrary to the other 'spuria,' does maintain its divergent character.

In general, the differences between the various dialogues in the Corpus do not appear very marked in this test. After all it is extremely doubtful whether or to what extent the profiles of the different classes really betray different hands or even very different moods. Great caution is justified in interpreting such divergences. The profiles of many dialogues present such compromises as to blur the picture of separate classes almost completely: for instance, *Laches* (I) in spite of its characteristic high frequency of ὦ and its lack of ἆρα rather approximates to *Theaetetus* (II) or, because of δή, to *Symposium* (V); class III would seem closely related to class 1 were it not for the low frequency of ὦ (and various other 'anomalies' in *Alcibiades* (II); on the other hand, class III suggests class IV in various ways; *Alcibiades* II (III), *Eryxias* (IV) and *Minos* (V), all notorious 'spuria,' do indeed present anomalies, but so do notably *Ion* (V), *Phaedo* (V), *Symposium* (II) and *Laches* (I). On the other hand, again, many scholars would probably find it easy to accept the close similarity of the profiles of *Crito* and *Gorgias* (II), although *Gorgias* has a large number of μέν οὖν, οὐκοῦν and οὖν and of *Lysis* and *Charmides* (IV) respectively; and it may be interesting to note the very remarkable similarity of the profiles of *Hippias Minor* and *Cratylus* (V). But a considerable distrust of such apparent affinities is surely awakened by the figures for *Amatores* (V) if read in relation to those of its neighbors in the table: there must be other things to separate *Amatores* from *Phaedo* and *Phaedrus* respectively, than a somewhat high frequency of the particle οὖν!

[80] Considering once more the divergences to be found in the profiles of the *Sophist* and *Politicus* (VI), it is clear that even this table is not particularly helpful with regard to a stylistic classification of the dialogues. Disregarding again the *Axiochus* (VIII) and the 'late group' (VI–VII), it seems that there are a series of manifest differences between some individual dialogues of classes I–III on the one hand, and some from classes IV–V on the other, and notably between *Hippias Major, Euthyphro, Laches, Meno* and *Alcibiades* II on the one hand and *Amatores, Phaedrus, Ion* and *Minos* on the other. The obvious consequence is that these two groups can hardly be assigned, *en bloc*, to the same author. But for the rest, the answer must remain *non liquet* until more reliable evidence is found.

**Test III.** It may be of some interest to compare Table 2 with some of the statistics of the formulae of assent which were worked out by von Arnim (1912). His method need not detain us here.[201] However, his material can provide 'profiles' of occurrence for the most frequent formulae, corresponding to the profiles of Table 2.

---

201. It has been criticized many times over, as was noted above (p. 215); cf, Brandwood 1958: 372: "a waste of time and effort."

*Table 3* gives the most frequent formulae of von Arnim's 'Tabelle II' (p. 47 ff.), sections A and B. I have reduced his figures to three symbols: a = relatively most common in this dialogue; b = not unfrequent in this dialogue (3 or more instances); c = occasional occurrence (1 or 2 instances). An attempt was again made to group the dialogues according to the profiles thus formed. Note, however, that this material is not comparable throughout with that of Table 2. von Arnim considered only those works which he thought to be authentic. And some apparent oddities in the profiles of, notably, *Ion* and *Crito* (cf. also *Protagoras, Phaedo* and *Symposium*) may be due to the fact that the dialogue portions of these works are relatively brief and, hence, not representative.

The column on the right lists the three closest 'relatives' of each dialogue according to the complicated affinity calculations of von Arnim ('Tabelle V,' p. 211 ff.).

Although the profiles seem to form distinctly similar patterns only in classes I and II of this table, it is easy to detect far-reaching discrepancies between the affinities suggested by the profiles and the results of von Arnim. The main reason for this must lie in the fact that the *abc* profiles of my table place emphasis on the distribution of proportionally common formulae, whereas von Arnim's figures of affinity derive from a broader consideration of the occurrence in each dialogue of very different, occasional as well as common, expressions. Since von Arnim's method seems to allow a great many more or less accidental occurrences to disturb his statistics, the *abc* profiles of my Table 3 are likely to provide a picture of the affinities which is at least as reliable as von Arnim's results.

As the table shows, the 'late group' and its 'associates' (classes IV–VI) present somewhat similar profiles marked also by the occurrence of typical 'late style' formulae, παντάπασι μὲν οὖν, τί μήν;(though these are occasionally current elsewhere), ὀρθῶς, ἀληθέστατα (and a number of others not noted in the table).

A further, perhaps more interesting fact is the relative homogeneity of class I and its association with class II rather than with the other classes. Here we seem to have an independent indication of a relationship also suggested by Table 2: the dialogues *Euthyphro, Hippias Major* and *Laches* may somehow belong together. Although the position of *Euthydemus* in class I and the position of *Cratylus* and *Phaedo* in class II again complicate the picture and perhaps warn us not to trust it, we shall have to return to this association below (p. 358).

As for the rest, Table 3 suggests little more than *non liquet*.

As a preliminary conclusion it may be stated that the tests so far made have not succeeded in indicating any very distinct linguistic (or 'stylistic') groups within the Corpus, apart from the long since identified 'late group.' It may seem that the dialogue style of the Corpus Platonicum can (with the exception of *Axiochus*, and the *Halcyon* which was not considered here) be regarded as a fairly homogeneous linguistic 'flow.' The varieties, and possibly different patterns and hands, could perhaps be distinguished by a careful philological study of the text, if such a study were carried out systematically. Traditional chronological stylometry cannot be expected to yield useful results.

[81]

Table 3

| | ναί | πάνυ μὲν οὖν | πάνυ γε | ἔγωγε | ἀληθῆ λέγεις | ἀνάγκη | φαίνεται | ἔοικεν | πῶς γὰρ οὔ; | ἔστι ταῦτα | ἔοικέ γε δοκεῖ | παντάπασι μὲν οὖν | τί μήν; | ὀρθῶς | ἀληθέστατα | Closest 'relatives' (acc. to von Arnim) | | |
|---|---|---|---|---|---|---|---|---|---|---|---|---|---|---|---|---|---|---|
| **I** | | | | | | | | | | | | | | | | | | |
| Euthphr. | b | b | a | b | b | c | — | b | b | c | — | — | — | — | — | Chrm. | Ly. | Euthd. |
| La. | b | b | a | b | b | c | — | c | b | c | b | c | — | — | — | R. I | Grg. | Euthphr. |
| Euthd. | b | b | a | b | b | c | c | — | c | c | c | — | — | — | — | Men. | Euthphr. | Grg. |
| Hp.Ma. | b | b | a | b | b | — | c | c | c | b | b | — | — | — | — | Phd. | Grg. | Euthphr. |
| **II** | | | | | | | | | | | | | | | | | | |
| Grg. | a | b | a | b | b | b | b | b | b | b | b | — | — | — | — | Men. | Euthd. | Hp.Ma. |
| Men. | a | b | a | a | b | c | b | b | c | b | b | — | — | — | — | Grg. | Cra. | Euthd. |
| Cra. | a | b | a | b | b | c | b | b | b | b | b | — | — | — | — | Men. | Phd. | Grg. |
| R. I | a | b | a | b | c | b | b | c | b | c | c | — | — | — | — | Ly. | La. | Chrm. |
| Phd. | a | a | a | b | b | b | b | c | b | b | — | — | — | — | — | Hp.Ma. | Euthphr. | Cra. |
| **III** | | | | | | | | | | | | | | | | | | |
| Ion | a | — | b | — | b | — | — | b | — | — | — | — | — | — | — | Prt. | Grg. | Men. |
| Hp.Mi. | a | b | b | b | b | c | b | c | — | c | c | c | — | — | — | Men. | Grg. | Cra. |
| Prt. | a | b | b | — | c | c | c | — | — | — | c | — | — | — | — | Ion | R. I | Euthd. |
| Ly. | a | b | a | b | b | c | b | b | b | — | c | — | — | — | — | Euthphr. | Chrm. | R. I |
| Chrm. | b | c | b | c | c | c | c | b | c | — | — | — | c | — | — | Euthphr. | Ly. | R. I |
| Smp. | b | c | b | c | b | c | — | b | c | — | — | — | — | — | — | Euthphr. | La. | Men. |

|     |       |   |   |   |   |   |   |   |   |   |   |   |   |   |         |       |       |
| --- | ----- | - | - | - | - | - | - | - | - | - | - | - | - | - | ------- | ----- | ----- |
| IV  | Tht.  | a | a | b | b | b | b | b | b | b | b | a | c | b | Prm.    | R. X  | R. V  |
|     | Prm.  | a | b | a | — | — | b | b | b | c | b | b | b | b | Tht.    | Ly.   | Lg. XII |
|     | Sph.  | a | b | b | c | b | c | — | b | — | b | b | b | c | Plt.    | Phlb. | R. V  |
|     | Plt.  | a | a | b | — | b | b | c | b | — | b | a | b | b | Phlb.   | Sph.  | Phdr. |
|     | Phlb. | a | a | b | b | b | c | c | b | — | a | b | a | b | Plt.    | Sph.  | Lg. VII |
|     | Phdr. | b | c | c | c | c | — | — | c | c | b | c | — | b | Lg. III | Plt.  | Tht.  |
| V   | R. IV | a | b | c | b | b | c | b | c | b | b | a | — | — | R. III  | Tht.  | R. V  |
| VI  | Lg. III | c | a | a | — | — | — | c | — | b | — | a | — | — | Lg. VII | Phdr. | Lg. IV |
| VII | Cri.  | c | c | c | — | — | c | c | c | c | — | — | — | — | Cra.    | R. II | La.   |

[82]   On the other hand, this evidently comprises a field for a very broad 'cluster stylometry,'[202] applicable to a very large body of lexical and syntactical material by means of electronic computers and modern statistical methods.

[83] **Revision**

The modern view of Platonic chronology rests to some extent upon premises concerning methods of publication which are probably anachronistic. It is taken for granted or implied that the finishing of a manuscript for a dialogue was in most cases the result of a single effort within a relatively short space of time. It is thought that once a dialogue had been written down in a form suitable for publication—but not before—identical copies were taken of it that were put into circulation, perhaps sold in book-shops in Athens and elsewhere, and copied again. So the archetypus prepared and preserved by the author was a once-for-all product, and all the copies in circulation tended, in principle, to be identical reproductions of it. On the other hand, it is thought that the author had no means of controlling this process of distribution since there were no copyright or royalty laws and no bibliographical information. If on second thoughts he wished to make important changes or additions, preparing a revised edition was a rather

---

202. I use the term 'cluster stylometry' in the sense of the application of statistical methods of cluster analysis to a body of linguistic data.

*Postscript, October, 1981.* In cooperation with K. Loimaranta (above, n. 198) I have, during the last year, applied various cluster tests to the Platonic corpus. The variables consisted of (1) altogether 115 formulae of reply used in elenchus passages and similar dialogue sections, and (2) altogether 107 particles and combinations of particles used in strict elenchus sections, free dialogue sections, and monologue sections respectively. For studying (2), magnetic tapes of the Burnet text of Plato and, for control, of the Marchant text of Xenophon were acquired from the Theasaurus Linguae Graecae (Irvine, California). The work was done, partly, in the Computing Center of the University of Helsinki, partly by Loimaranta with the aid of a desk size computer. The most notable results are as follows:

(a) All tests place Xenophon distinctly apart from the Corpus Platonicum.
(b) All statistically reliable tests clearly place the 'late group' of Platonic dialogues in one or two separate clusters.
(c) Most tests separate *Phdr., Prm.* (the first part), *R.* II–X and *Tht.* into one or two distinct clusters close to the 'late group.'
(d) The differences in the use of particles are on the whole greater between the three types of exposition studied under (2), than between the various works in the Corpus.
(e) The differences in the use of (1) and (2) are greater between 'obviously' authentic works such as *Chrm., Grg., Phd.* and *Smp.*, than between the authentic works *en bloc* and various dubia or spuria.
(f) No statistically reliable dialogue clusters were found apart from the works mentioned under (a)—(c), although even *Alc.* 2, *Erx.* and *Ax.* were included. In the light of points (a)—(e), we interpreted this to corroborate the theories propounded in the present book of a rather undifferentiated linguistic 'flow' in the Corpus Platonicum, of 'revision,' and of 'semi-authenticity.'
(g) Many tests indicate a certain affinity between *Euthphr., Hp.Ma.* and *La.* and, on the other hand, oddities in *Cra., Grg.,* and *Phd.,* and also the second part of *Prm.*

useless undertaking. If the author was Plato, he would probably prefer to write a new dialogue. [83]

All of these points are in fact debatable. If, as was suggested above, Plato began as a writer of λόγοι, whether in his own name or in Socrates', these λόγοι were of course intended for oral communication. We know that, in *Phaedrus* and elsewhere, he emphasized his preference for the spoken word over the written.[203] We can also infer from what we know of his life and character (above p. 169) that he usually avoided appearing in public. His λόγοι were in all likelihood intended, in the first place, for reading in closed gatherings of friends, Socratics or others. If copies were taken of his early manuscripts and were distributed outside these circles, he might have been quite happy provided he thought them suitable for reading by the public at large. It is tempting to regard the *Apology* as such a case (p. 259).

But it is open to serious doubt that he generally speaking intended his early manuscripts for 'publication,' and it is in fact doubtful whether any of the dialogues, as we have them, are from the time before the founding of the Academy. We shall have to return to this problem below (p. 250). At any rate, once the Academy had become somehow institutionalized, it was comparatively easy for Plato as its head to keep a check on views and texts purporting to be his, but to which he was not prepared to subscribe. The Academy would authorize only what Plato himself accepted as his words (or what was thought 'worthy' of Plato). Spurious texts (or texts declared to be so) would not have much chance of remaining in circulation for long, or of being copied as 'authentically Platonic,' since the Academy exercised a function analogous to that of a modern copyright-supervising body of publishers.[204]

However, more important for chronological research is the fact that inconvenient or out-of-date pieces of λόγοι could also be remodeled or supplied with new settings. This, I suggest, is what happened for instance to some early speeches on Love (the first speech of Socrates in the present version of the *Phaedrus*, here followed by a παλινῳδία, and one or several of the speeches in the *Symposium*), to the 'Epitaphios' (now in the *Menexenus*), and to the notorious 'first version' of the Ideal State (now to be found in the *Republic*, Books II–V). For the details, *see* below. [84]

Considering the fundamental importance of oral discussion and 'dialectic' in the life of the Academy, Plato must have felt a constant need to recast 'his' dialogues.

If, as seems likely, earlier dialogues were 'performed' anew as part of the routine of the Academic discussion (cf. above p. 209), and new dialogues gradually

---

203. *Phdr.* 274b–378e, cf. *Ep.* 7.341a ff, These, and some corresponding passages elsewhere (e.g. *Prt.* 329ab, cf. 347b–348c) have often been commented on in the discussion of Plato's 'unwritten doctrines.' As far as I know only Bruns (1896: 226) has argued that it was Socrates, but by no means Plato, who preferred the spoken word to the written; but Bruns does not seem to have convinced anybody.

204. Cf. *Ep.* 7.341b, implying the existence of 'forgeries'; cf. Immisch 1915: 563, and below p. 88. Cf. also Aristotle's concept of ἐκδεδομένοι λόγοι *Poet.* 1454b18.

[84] took shape in a similar manner as a result of the oral communication between Plato and his friends and pupils,[205] the formulating and fixing of a text for general circulation—in cases when this was Plato's intention or met with his approval—was on the whole a slow and secondary process. If this is so, many of our dialogues and notably the longer ones, are indeed likely to contain different chronological 'layers.'

The theory advanced here, which implies that some of the works of the Corpus Platonicum are products of a successive revision, is naturally not a new one. But its consequences have not apparently been fully realized, or have led to uncritical nonsense (as in the extreme case of Zürcher 1954, above p. 160). Obviously theories of revision have not been popular among students of Plato. The vehemence with which some scholars have tried to refute such theories especially in the much-debated cases of *Phaedrus* and the *Republic* leads one to suspect that this antipathy rises not only form an anachronistic view of Plato's manner of publishing his dialogues, but from a genuine fear of the confusion which the theory of revision may create in Platonic chronology.

But—apart from minor dialogues which are probably or obviously homogeneous—what arguments can in fact be put forward against revision, if there is a general likelihood that revision did occur? Here the burden of proof actually rests with those who assert that the theory of revision is not helpful or even acceptable. I have not seen such proof. It is of no consequence here to point out, for instance, that the structure of the *Republic* in its present form is a well-balanced and well-deliberated whole (for the *Phaedrus* this is not so easy to demonstrate), or that the 'hedonistic calculus' of the *Protagoras* fits into its context, because there is no reason why Plato (or his 'secretary') should have lost his sense of logic and his artistic judgment when recasting a composition. On the contrary, is it not probable that a revision may sometimes even improve a work?

There is in fact some external direct evidence of revision in some dialogues.

Dionysius of Halicarnassus tells us in so many words that Plato used to "curl and comb" the tresses of his dialogues (De Comp. Verb. 208 f. Reiske), and he was
[85] known to have been pondering different openings for the *Republic* (Euphorion and Panaetius ap. Diog. L. 3.37, Quint. 8.6.64).[206] It is difficult to imagine why such pieces of information would not be based upon an authentic tradition deriving from Plato's Academy.

Moreover, we happen to know that there existed another version of the frame dialogue of the *Theaetetus* (the Anonymous Commentary, ed. Diels-Schubart 1905: 3.28 ff.), and since this piece of information has come to us by mere chance in a papyrus, it is quite possible that there existed parallel versions to parts of other dialogues of the Corpus which the Academics later managed to get rid of.

---

205. The possibility of taking the notorious lecture Π. τἀγαθοῦ as a dialogue *in primo statu nascendi*, was suggested by Ilting 1968; this has been denied by Gaiser 1980a. Cf. below p. 347.

206. Riginos 1976: 185 f., on insufficient grounds, regards this as, an unreliable anecdote. Gaiser, in his review of Riginos, *Gnomon* 51 (1979): 109, thinks that it applies to the style only.

The curious passage in the *Theaetetus* which informs us that the 'inserenda' have been omitted (143bc) is in fact easier to explain as indicating the existence of an earlier generally-known version of the main dialogue that had reported form, than as suggesting that Plato is abandoning, merely 'for convenience,' a form of dialogue which his readers expect him to use.

The following are the most interesting theories of revision that have been suggested since the turn of the century:

—— Successive revision of the *Republic*, after earlier theories argued in considerable detail by Horn 1893 (1904) and Pfleiderer 1896; for the later vicissitudes of this vexed problem, *see* below p. 250 and 519.
—— Revision of *Phaedrus* as explaining the anomalies of the dialogue and the different opinions as to its date: Immisch 1899: 549–561 (cf. 452–465, accepting the theory of revision of the *Republic*), 1915 (the theory revised); Janell 1901a: 307 f., Diès II 1927: 250–257, and others (cf. below p. 172).
—— Fundamental revision of *Theaetetus:* Chiappelli 1904.
—— Revision of *Parmenides, Phaedrus, Symposium* and *Theaetetus*, also other dialogues, suggested as part of an eccentric theory of chronology: Brommer 1940.[207]
—— Gigon, after arguing that the *Protagoras* is somewhat un-Platonic (1946), tended to accept the possibility of the revision of several dialogues; cf. Gigon 1954a, 1954b, 1955: 14 f.
—— Zürcher 1954 argued, on very flimsy grounds, that the whole of the Corpus was revised and edited about 300 BCE.
—— Pamela Clark 1955 attempted to demonstrate that the first part of *Alcibiades* I was written by a pupil of Plato but that Plato himself finished the dialogue.
—— Diller 1955 suggested that the *Ion* was begun by Plato but finished by a pupil.
—— On very insufficient grounds, H. M. Wolff 1957 argued for a very extensive revision of a large number of dialogues.
—— Kesters 1959 reintroduced the theories of successive publication of the *Phaedrus* and the *Republic*, adducing evidence from Themistius Speech 26.
—— Ryle 1966 accepted successive publication and revision of the text of the dialogues as a basis for a rather arbitrarily argued new chronology.[208]
—— Revision of some dialogues has sometimes been suggested as a possibility by adherents of the theory of Plato's 'unwritten doctrine,' e.g. Findlay 1974: 16 (*Phaedo*), Gaiser 1974: 95 (*Cratylus*).
—— Revision of *Protagoras*: implied by Manuwald 1975.

---

207. This Utrecht dissertation has been severely but somewhat unfairly criticized for obscurity and confusion; *see* Cherniss, [Review of Brommer] (1947): 126–133; Manasse 1976: 444–450.
208. Cf. above p. 151. To 'anti-revisionists' Ryle's arguments would seem to be a most typical example of the confusion and anarchy to which theories of revision may lead. It is indeed easy to criticize Ryle, as many reviews have shown; *see* e.g. Hathaway and Sesonske 1969 (Ryle produced no real defense in this book), Lafrance 1971. However, some of Ryle's inferences are fresh and interesting and will be taken into account below. Randall's (1970) ironically skeptical attitude to questions of chronology and authenticity appears to have been inspired by Ryle.

[86]  Furthermore, as was suggested above, it seems probable that the dramatic frame dialogues, at least in some cases, have been added later to the main text; cf. below p. 326.

Nobody seems to have noticed that there are slight indications of the *Gorgias* having been originally written in a reported form, a fact which would of course conform to the general trend discussed above (p. 207, cf. 551). Note the following points: unlike most of the dramatic dialogues, the opening of *Gorgias* lacks clear indications as to who the interlocutors of Socrates are. Taking for granted, as Andrieu has argued (above p. 210), that early manuscripts did not normally contain marginal or other notations of the persons in a dramatic dialogue, the ancient reader did not receive this necessary information until the fourth utterance (447a7 ὦ Καλλίκλεις, Χαιρεφῶν ὅδε). In other respects the first utterances also sound somewhat cryptic to an unprepared reader until the straightforward explanation comes: πολλὰ γὰρ καὶ καλὰ Γοργίας ἡμῖν ὀλίγον πρότερον ἐπεδείξατο (which in fact looks like a secondary insertion, since τούτων a7 does not refer to πολλὰ καί καλά but to a3–4). Most modern readers are certainly inclined to interpret this opening as a particularly dramatic and intentional *tour de force*. But then again, who can tell at b1, without being given the sign ΧΑΙ in the margin, that it is Chairephon and not Callicles who answers Socrates? Or at the beginning of the three next utterances, who the speakers are? At any rate, even if Andrieu's theory does not apply to this text, we should expect Plato to follow the normal practice in the Corpus of indicating in the dramatic dialogues important changes of speakers by explicit forms of address.[209] It has to be assumed, I think, that the background narrative originally belonging to the opening of the *Gorgias* has been

[87] dropped at a moment when the principal readers of this important dialogue who studied and perhaps 'performed' it again and again—presumably Plato's friends and pupils in the Academy—knew the setting sufficiently well to be able to dispose of it.—At 447b–d there are also some traces of an original change of the scene, a trait well known from most of the reported dialogues.[210] The company apparently does not move on to the house of Callicles (as suggested at b7; but cf. c3 εἰσαῦθις); but Chairephon's first question to Gorgias at d7 is really quite abrupt, devoid as it is in our present text of any hints of how the friends (presumably) had to force their way through the crowd that still surrounded the orator.— Then again at 448a6 Polus joins the conversation quite abruptly and without the text indicating in any way who the speaker is; his presence has not even been

---

209. Cf. e.g. *Hp.Mi.* 363a1, a6, c4, c6; at 364a1, it is true, Socrates comes in only with a characteristically ironical μακάριόν γε πάθος a7, b1; 373a6, a10, b3, etc. *Ti.* 17a2, a4, 20d2, d6, etc.; at 20c4 the fact that Hermocrates is the speaker follows more indirectly from 20a7, c4–5 and c7.—In the *Cratylus* the formal arrangement of the dialogue and the contents make it clear that the work was not written for the general public, cf. p. 315. The Academic reader probably knew at the outset that it was Hermogenes who put the problem to Socrates, and that the enigmatic Cratylus was listening silently (until he was addressed at 427e1).

210. Note in particular how Socrates gradually approaches Protagoras in *Prt.* 310b–316a, Cephalus in *R.* I 327a–328c, and Agathon in *Smp.* 174a–175c. In the dramatic *Phaedrus* the change of scene is commented on in the dialogue, 227a–230e, and similarly in *Lg.* I 624a–625c.

mentioned before.—Similar oddities which can be best explained as resulting [87]
from the omission of the background narrative, occur from time to time in the
text: note 458c4 where Chairephon refers to the θόρυβος properly belonging to
the background description (cf. 468cd, 473e, 475d); the repeatedly abrupt change
of interlocutor at 448c2, 461b3 and especially 481b (and cf. in *Republic* I 336bc the
vivid description of how Thrasymachus prepares himself to jump in like a wild
beast); and at 527c7 the concluding vocative ὦ Καλλίκλεις, intensely dramatic,
but odd enough as it stands, unanswered.

For the abrupt opening of the *Meno*, and the introduction of the slave boy
(82b) and of Anytus (89e) from a background about which we do not receive any
information at the outset, *see* below p. 310. Cf. also *Cratylus*, p. 315.

Extensive revision of the Platonic dialogues, however, is not particularly likely
to have occurred after the death of Plato. The late Master of the Academy had a
semi-divine status,[211] although his followers were not so interested in the doctrines of the dialogues except for the *Timaeus*. It is probable that the body of texts
regarded as authentically Platonic (cf. below p. 238) was preserved in the library
of the Academy as a normative standard collection, no alterations being permit-
ted. Tarán 1975: 131 and n. 550 has made the point that the publication of the
*Critias* and the *Laws* indicates positively that the Academy did not tamper with
Plato's text. It has also been argued (by Philip 1970) that this standard collection
was formed before the end of the 4th century BCE; I feel we can safely accept the
340s as the date of the collecting of the main body of the Corpus.[212]

# Problems of authenticity [88]

The Platonic Corpus has come down to us in a tetralogical arrangement that was
apparently adopted or introduced by Thrasyllus of Alexandria in the 1st century
BCE,[213] and which is still followed by Burnet in his Oxford edition (1901). The
tetralogies are as follows:

    I  *Euthyphro, Apology, Crito, Phaedo*
   II  *Cratylus, Theaetetus, Sophist, Politicus*
  III  *Parmenides, Philebus, Symposium, Phaedrus*
  IV  *Alcibiades* I, *Alcibiades* II, *Hipparchus, Amatores*
   V  *Theages, Charmides, Laches, Lysis*

---

211. Apparently Speusippus was one of the first to contribute to the belief that Plato was the
natural son of Apollo; cf. Diog. L. 3.2.
212. Cf. C. W. Müller 1975: 22–41 and below, p. 378. This would not of course exclude a
later polishing or normalising of the language; cf. Gomperz 1887: 766 f., Heikel 1900: 12, Ritter
1910a: 41 n., 1913: 69–71. Geffcken II A 27 f., on insufficient grounds, doubts that there existed a
standard text at all.
213. Though Thrasyllus' arrangement probably followed an earlier model (*see* Chroust 1965)
his edition seems to have been very influential.

[88]
    VI  *Euthydemus, Protagoras, Gorgias, Meno*
    VII  *Hippias Major, Hippias Minor, Ion, Menexenus*
    VIII  *Clitopho, Republic, Timaeus, Critias*
    IX  *Minos, Laws, Epinomis, Epistulae*

To these nine tetralogies there are appended in several manuscripts the *Definitions*, and the following dialogues marked as νοθευόμενοι: *De Justo, De Virtute, Demodocus, Sisyphus, Eryxias*, and *Axiochus*. To *Ep*. 12 (but not to the last letter, *Ep*. 13) the note ἀντιλέγεται ὡς οὐ Πλάτωνος is added.

We do not know who was the first to separate, or add, the alleged spuria. We know, however, that there existed in antiquity several other dialogues wrongly attributed to Plato. Diogenes Laertius 3.62 lists (in addition to *Erx., Sis., Ax.* and *Demod.*) the Μίδων ἢ Ἱπποτρόφος,[214] the Ἀλκυών, the ἀκέφαλοι[215] ἢ . . . Φαίακες . . . Χελιδών, Ἑβδομή, Ἐπιμενίδης. Of these only the *Halcyon* has come down to us. It occurs in some manuscripts of Plato and Lucian and has been edited as Pseudo-Lucian. It is a brief dramatic dialogue. Quite clearly it reveals no trace of Plato's hand.[216] Herodicus of Babylon (2nd century BCE) ap. Athen. XI 506de refers to a dialogue called Κίμων as 'authentic' evidence of the meanness of Plato's character; the fact
[89] that it is not included in the Corpus suggests that it was not accepted as authentic by the early Academy.[217] Five or six odd *Letters* purporting to be by Plato have been published in Hercher's Epistolographi.[218] Finally, the Greek Anthology and some other sources attribute altogether 32 *Epigrams* to Plato.[219] These are mostly trifles, and the great majority are obviously spurious. Since all of them are, in my view, completely irrelevant to the present purpose I shall not consider them in this study.

Occasionally in antiquity the authenticity of some of the tetralogical dialogues in the Corpus was doubted. The grounds were hardly reliable, and the

---

214. Wilamowitz II 1920: 325 n. 3 wishes to identify this dialogue with a secondary (?) version of *Meno* from which the *De Virtute* also derives; but this is all very vague.

215. Oświecimski 1979 argues that the ἀκέφαλοι formed a separate collection including dubia such as *De Virtute* and *De Justo*; it was also attributed to Aeschines. This seems possible, though the details are very uncertain. At any rate the term ἀκέφαλος does not appear to denote here 'without opening frame dialogue,' and certainly not 'without background narrative'; cf. above p. 201. Could it denote 'without a list of the dialogue persons' such as was helpful for unprepared reading of dramatic dialogues (cf. above p. 209)?

216. Diog. L. l.c. mentions, with reference to Favorinus, a certain Leo as its possible author; cf. Athen. XI.506c, with reference to Nicias of Nikaia (of unknown date). It is doubtful whether the person in question is Leo of Byzantium, an orator and politician who was a member of the Academy about the middle of the 4th century (Plut. *Phoc.* 14.4).

217. Düring 1941: 76 f. suggests that Herodicus, who is notoriously unreliable, invented the title since the same ideas as he refers to occur in *Gorgias* 503c, 515d, *Theages* 126a; but this is not a necessary inference.

218. Letters of Plato 14–15, Letters of Socrates 24–26 (add possibly nr. 36), p. 626 ff. Hercher. Cf. Ritter 1910a: 415–418, Sykutris 1931: 981 ff.

219. E. Diehl, Anthologia Lyr. Gr., accepts 17 out of the 32 *Epigrams*; see references in Beckby's index (Anthologia Graeca, Griechisch-Deutsch ed. H. Beckby, Tusculum-Bücherei, München 1957). Wilamowitz I 1920: 457 f. and Geffcken II A 31 f. certainly take too liberal a view regarding the question of the authenticity of the epigrams. Guthrie IV 1975: 13 makes the surprising assertion that they "are generally accepted as genuine."

sources are sometimes disputable, as can be gathered e.g. from the tradition that [89]
Panaetius declared the *Phaedo* spurious.²²⁰

As a matter of fact we are left with very little direct evidence as to which writings are certainly genuine. It is clear that the manuscript tradition and other pieces of evidence deriving from antiquity are not to be taken at their face value. Few scholars would today regard, say, *Alcibiades* II or *Minos* as equally and in the same sense genuine as *Phaedo* or the *Republic*. On the other hand, apart from lectures and discussions not intended for publication in written form—such as the now famous 'On the Good' (p. 347)—it seems that no authentic works by Plato have been lost.²²¹

It is more or less certain that the Corpus is the result of an accretion of spurious texts around an authentic core. In delimiting this core we are in a somewhat better position than we are in the case of Homer or Hippocrates: the authenticity of several of the Platonic works is after all beyond reasonable doubt, and so we are—theoretically—provided with a standard against which the acceptability of doubtful dialogues can be tested. We may safely take it for granted that, say, *Gor-* [90]
*gias*, *Phaedo*, the *Republic* and *Symposium* represent this genuine core or, at least, that they are the closest that we can expect to come to Plato's *ipsissima verba*.

Yet in practice this task of testing and sifting is not very easily done. The history of the controversies over the Platonic authorship of different texts shows that, in a large number of cases, there has been little agreement as to the criteria to be used.²²²

Since the turn of this century the common opinion which is also established in the current reference works, largely and silently follows the views of Lutoslawski, Raeder and notably, again, Ritter (cf. above p. 150). According to this view, the whole of the fourth tetralogy (*Alcibiades* I and II, *Hipparchus*, *Amatores*) is regarded as spurious (though the Budé edition has introduced a complication by accepting *Alc*. 1), as are *Theages* from the fifth tetralogy, *Hippias Major* from the seventh (though here opinions are divided), *Clitopho* from the eight, and *Minos*, *Epinomis* (which is however accepted by many) and most of the *Letters*

---

220. Asclepios ad Arist. *Met*. A 9.991b3 p. 90.23 ff. Hayduck; cf. AG 9.358; various speculations about Panaetius' reasons can be found in Zeller II 1⁴ 441 f.; cf. Guthrie IV 40 n. 2. In fact the tradition may have originated in a misunderstanding of the fact that Panaetius questioned the authenticity of the dialogues of Phaedon of Elis (Diog. L. 2.64).—Proclus rejected the *Republic* because it was not a real dialogue, according to *Anon.Proleg*. 26 p. 219 Hermann (cf. below p. 101.—For Thrasyllus (Diog. L. 9.37) the *Amatores* was suspect.—According to Aelianus VH 8.2 and Athen. ll.506c, the authenticity of *Hipparchus* and *Alcibiades* II was questioned.

221. Apart from the Π. τἀγαθοῦ complex, ancient summaries of Plato's doctrines (such as Alcimus ap. Diog. L. 9–17 and Albinus' Διδασκαλικός ed. Hermann) sometimes include points which do not occur as such in the dialogues, but this of course does not indicate that anything has been lost.

222. Good general surveys of the problems of authenticity in the Corpus, with references to earlier discussions, have been provided by Grote I 1865: 132–211 (extensive argumentation for accepting the canonic tetralogies as being based upon an old and reliable tradition), Heidel 1896, Raeder 20–30, Ritter 1910a: 217–219, Leisegang 1950: 2365–2369, C. W. Müller 1975 (concentrating upon the νοθευόμενοι), Guthrie V 383–417 (very cautious).

[90] from the ninth. Writings from outside the tetralogies are not usually accepted. Few scholars today would adopt the excessively liberal position of Grote 1865 or Waddington 1886 who accepted as genuine almost all writings preserved to us under Plato's name (Wichmann 1966, a veteran scholar, is an exception). On the other hand, the arbitrarily over-critical view of some 19th-century scholars such as Ast and his followers has not been popular in this century: they tended to stamp as 'un-Platonic' everything that did not fit their conception of Platonism, or tended to regard the re-occurrence of the same idea or formulation as the work of a forger, or the lack of references in Aristotle as negative evidence.[223] The general tendency today is rather for the liberal and inclusive view. Friedländer's tentative acceptance of *Hipparchus* and *Theages* is symptomatic, though it has not met with much approval.[224] All extremist positions are of course rare.[225]

[91] After all, however, the whole question of authenticity is much more problematic than is generally believed.

If the 'genuine core' that is to be taken as a standard (starting from, say, *Gorgias*, *Phaedo*, the *Republic* and *Symposium*) is enlarged to comprise 'early Socratic' writings such as the *Apology* or *Crito* and seemingly aporetic dialogues such as *Laches*, *Euthyphro* or *Protagoras* on the one hand, and the 'late group' on the other, the result is a very wide register of notions, techniques and styles which will allow most of the works of the Corpus to fit in with it somehow. If this is so, the most sensible approach is to start at the other end: it is better, then, to begin by separating from the Corpus all texts containing such ideas, words, phrases or anachronistic references as an Athenian could not have used or written before, say, 350 BCE.

The result of this first sifting is not very impressive, however. Only the *Axiochus* proves to be unambiguously Hellenistic in contents and style;[226] the *Definitions* are clearly post-Platonic;[227] and the *Halcyon* (which is of practically no philosophical interest), some of the *Letters* and most of the *Epigrams* look more

---

223. Ast and others were criticized by Ueberweg 1861: 171–201, Lutoslawski 198; cf. the references in n. 222, above. With characteristic frankness and considerable unfairness Shorey declared (1933: 58) that the opinions of the 19th-century atheticizers "are not of the slightest significance except as part of the history of the aberrations of the human mind."

224. Crombie I 12, 225 was eccentric enough to accept the *Amatores*; he is followed by Guthrie with some hesitation (V 390–392) who is also inclined to accept *Theages* (392–394); Wichmann 1966 accepts *Hipparch., Thg., Virt., Just., Amat., Alc.* 2, *Min., Clit.* and *Ep.*; Fischer 1969: 62 n. 4 would also accept *Alcibiades* II and *Minos*; Oświecimski 1967–68 (cf. 1978: 31) tends to accept *Eryxias*; Evans 1976 (I have not seen this dissertation) accepts *Amatores, Hipparchus, Minos* and *Theages*.

225. Recent extremists on the exclusive side are Zürcher 1954 who put forward the remarkable view that the whole of the Corpus is spurious; Randall 1970 who argued that the so-called 'late group' of dialogues are by another hand (especially 32–35, 172–187, 220–237; his argument is playfully ironical, but cf. below p. 243); and Michaelson, Morton and Gillies (1977) who on the basis of a very meager material suggested that several of the so-called 'early' dialogues and parts of some later works were not written by Plato (*Ap., Chrm., Cri., Euthd., Euthphr., La.* spurious, *Prm., Ti.* partly so). Other eccentric views of spuriousness have been advocated by e.g. Döring (1903: 122–129: *Phlb.*), Natorp (1903: 38 n. 1: *Euthphr.*), Rick (1916: *Chrm.*) and Gigon (1946: *Prt.*).

226. See the comprehensive discussion by Souilhé in the Budé edition 1930b: 123–136.

227. Not earlier than Speusippus, *see* Souilhé ibid. 155–158.

than doubtful.²²⁸ But for the rest, including those writings which are now generally regarded as spurious, no obvious or manifest signs of a post-Platonic date can be found. And this furnishes some corroboration for the important observation sometimes made, that the spuria do not on the whole represent intentional fraud but are Socratic or Academic texts that have been incorporated into the collection of Platonica.²²⁹ Some comments on this will be made below. [91]

We are now faced once again with the highly questionable type of criterion which has been preferred since the early 19th century for determining spuriousness in the Corpus: do the contents of certain dialogues contain such features as would not fit very well into the standard chosen? The subjectivity of this criterion becomes the more obvious the more liberal and inclusive the norm. Friedländer's arguments for accepting *Hipparchus* and *Theages* (II² 1957: 114–116, 301–304; 137, 141 f., 309–311) show that if *Hippias Major*, *Laches*, *Lysis* and *Alcibiades* I are regarded as genuine, the step to *Hipparchus* (if it is given a very early date) and *Theages* (where the doctrine of the δαιμόνιον is somewhat more elaborate) is not a very long or very difficult one to take. Should *Hipparchus* and *Theages* be excluded simply because they are a little too naive to be 'worthy' of Plato? Another illuminating example of the difficulties involved here is the *Alcibiades* II. This dialogue has not had many supporters,²³⁰ but since earlier theories of influence from Stoicism or Arcesilaus have been successfully refuted by Souilhé (1930a: 9–18) we are left with very few passages that contain really questionable notions or motifs. Of these the point about the presumptive conqueror of the world 141a–c (cf. Archelaus of Macedonia 141d, the oracle of Ammon l48e) does not necessarily imply a reference to Alexander the Great, but could perhaps be an expansion of *Alc.* 1 105a–c (combined with *Grg.* 470d ff., cf. *Thg.* 125e–126a, etc.); and Socrates' siding with allegorists and admirers of Homer in 147bc is not so very different from his position in *Protagoras* or *Ion*, though it is not so obviously ironic. If we accept *Alcibiades* I, *Ion* and *Protagoras* as authentic, is it not possible to accept *Alcibiades* II as written by Plato in a somewhat different mood? [92]

The answer to the last question is probably no, for various reasons. But I think we have to accept as a fact that, if we look solely at arguments from the contents, we are facing a sliding scale of 'genuineness' extending from writings or passages of seemingly authentic value, to writings and passages less and less so. Where are we to draw the line as to what is possibly Platonic?

The problem is quite similar when we consider arguments from literary and linguistic criteria.

From a literary point of view, the suspect texts reveal a wide range of different solutions, from the carefully composed and carefully written reported dialogue *Eryxias*, to the exuberant dramatic dialogue *Hippias Major*, and from more careless

---

228. For the *Letters*, see below p. 378. For the *Epigrams*, see above n. 219. Letters and epigrams were particularly liable to pseudepigraphy from the Hellenistic age onwards. Cf. n. 229.
229. Cf. C. W. Müller 1975: 12–21. On 'school accumulation' under the name of a Master, without intentional fraud, cf. the discussion in *Pseudepigrapha* I (*see* Gulley 1972), especially p. 86.
230. Cf. below p. 377.

[92] and awkward compositions such as *Clitopho, Minos* and *Sisyphus*, and odd letters such as *Epistula* 2, 8, and 13, to the extremely jejune pieces of elenchus *De Justo* and *De Virtute*. It is often thought that Plato simply would not have written unimaginative or 'bad' prose—such flat, or blunt, or overdone pieces as some of these are. But can we be so sure of this? The *Charmides, Crito, Gorgias, Ion, Laches, Parmenides* and the *7th Letter* really open a wide register of potentialities. Also, more formal criteria, such as variations in the dialogue pattern and the use of speeches in the center or at the end,[231] are difficult to apply consistently to the problems of authenticity, if all the writings mentioned above are included in the standard: e.g. *Ion, Alcibiades I* and *Hipparchus* have a distinctly 'pedimental' structure, *Crito* has not; *Laches* has extensive speeches at the beginning, *Crito, Gorgias* and *Mino* at the end, *Theages* both at the beginning and at the end; there are traces of a BABAB pattern (p. 201) in most of the dubia; and so forth.

From a more narrowly stylistic and linguistic point of view, the dubia also seem to represent a gliding scale extending from the very Platonic to the less Platonic in style. It was noted above (p. 227) that such stylometric tests as have been applied to the dubia so far do not reveal very remarkable differences between the dubia and dialogues usually considered authentic: there are in fact greater
[93] internal discrepancies between various 'authentic' writings, and also between various 'dubia' (notably *Alcibiades* II and *Minos*), than between the 'authentic' and 'spurious' dialogues on the whole. Such stylometric tests are obviously inadequate, however. It is possible that in the future, by the application of some statistical method upon an extensive computerized body of material, we shall be able to sort out different groups of texts and hence, perhaps, different hands. The same results could possibly be reached by traditional philological methods, if we had the patience and succeeded in mapping out the occurrence in the Corpus of common or rare or otherwise remarkable words, phrases and syntactic constructions.

At our present state of knowledge it would seem that there is a somewhat higher proportion of 'un-Platonic' linguistic traits in some 'dubia' than in others. Disregarding again the *Axiochus*, the *Definitions, Halcyon*, the *Letters* and the *Epigrams*, the following five dialogues stand out: *Alcibiades* II, *Eryxias*,[232] *Hipparchus*,[233] *Hippias Major*[234] and *Sisyphus*.[235] But then it should be borne in mind that rare constructions and hapax legomena do occur in the 'authentic' writings too.[236]

---

231. *See* above p. 210 and the discussion in Thesleff 1967.
232. For *Alc.* 2, see Souilhé 1930a: 7 and below p. 231. For *Erx.*, note the peculiar use of participle constructions 392d11, 393a8, etc.; *see* further Souilhé in the Budé edition 1930b: 88 f.
233. Note ὦ γλυκύτατε 227d, οὔτι 230a, 231c, d, ναίχι 232a, ὁπωσδή 232b.
234. *See* Thesleff 1976: 106 ff.
235. *See* Souilhé 1930b: 64 f.—To be sure, there occur oddities in other dubia, too: e.g. a breathless opening καί in the narrative parts of *Amat*.
236. Some (insufficient) observations on hapax legomena in some Platonic writings were made by Fossum 1931. It is easy to see from Brandwood's Word Index (1976) how frequent hapax legomena are.

Still other criteria exist, of course. To most scholars the general tenor of a text [93] is a criterion of considerable importance. If for instance *Hippias Major* or *Sisyphus* can, on other grounds, be dated about 360 BCE, they can be said to be spurious already because almost everything we know about Plato makes it highly improbable that he would have written such pieces in his old age. But this kind of argument is easily open to misuse, and approaches very close to the fallacious question of what is, after all, 'worthy' of Plato.

Inconsistencies or contradictions constitute another category of criteria which are easily misapplied and were exaggerated by some 19th-century critics. Yet it is clear that if flagrant discrepancies cannot be easily explained as due to a change of position (as in the notorious case of the theory of Forms, above p. 187) or as resulting from a change of purpose, emphasis, irony, *jeu d'esprit*, etc. (such as certain variations in the attitude to poetry, cf. above p. 188), they may be taken as revealing different hands. For instance, although the apparent inconsistencies found in the portraiture of Alcibiades in *Alcibiades* I and II as opposed to that in *Protagoras* and *Symposium* can somehow be analyzed as representing different stages in the discussion of his relations with Socrates, it would nevertheless be more natural to assume different authorship. And it is even more difficult to explain away the fact that the author of the *Laches* inclines to depict Socrates [94] as a fairly young man, still unknown to Lysimachus who was a friend of his father (180d–181a), and yet the discussion takes place a considerable time after the battle of Delium in 424 BCE (181ab); at that date Socrates was middle-aged, and a well-known character in Athens, a fact which the author of the speech of Alcibiades in the *Symposium* is clearly aware of.[237] In this case the *Laches* passage is somewhat more likely to be spurious than the *Symposium* passage, but obviously this criterion is not sufficient in itself.

A rather similar kind of criterion is imitation wherever, or if ever, it is possible to trace a clumsy or overdone replica of an authentic piece of work. For instance, the *Eryxias* is clearly suspect because it is in various formal respects an imitation of the *Charmides* (below p. 366); and the *2nd Letter* with its 'digression' on secret doctrines (312d–213c, cf. 314a, 314c) seems to be imitating the *7th Letter* (cf. 342a–344d, and 341c), and since it purports to have been written some ten years before the latter (below p. 379) it is probably a forgery. But since Plato may indeed have repeated himself, or may have elaborated passages used before in another context—such as the ἀνδρεία passages in *Laches* and *Protagoras* perhaps show (above p. 192 ff.)—this criterion is as shaky as all the rest if applied mechanically and without careful discrimination.

Then there is the problem of the posthumous publication of the *Laws* and *Epinomis*, and its possible consequence for the authenticity of the text (cf. below p. 349). The *Critias*, which is only a fragment, was very probably not 'published' by Plato; and if this is true, who published the *Timaeus*, and did the editor follow Plato's 'manuscript' closely?

---

237. Cf. below p. 358. Chronological inconsistencies occur elsewhere in Plato, but apart from the intentional anachronism of *Menexenus* (p. 276) they are nowhere as flagrant as in the *Laches*.

[94] In the face of all these difficulties, it is wiser for the present to refrain, in principle, from making *a priori* distinctions between what is authentically Platonic and what is not. Most texts that can be labelled 'Platonic' will be included in the discussion below—with a few obvious exceptions, namely, because they have no relevance to the history of the Corpus, some of the *Letters* and all of the *Epigrams* (cf. above p. 236).

It is in fact highly probable that the difficulties mentioned above, and the lack of agreement between scholars as regards the details, are symptomatic of a deeper complication inherent here: it is possible that the Platonic Corpus—even its central 'core' which is commonly believed to be above suspicion—represents in fact a varying degree of authenticity. Possibly only few, if any, of the Platonic texts were written down by Plato exactly as we have them.

If the remarks made above (p. 230 ff.) on the 'publication' of Plato's dialogues hold good, it seems quite reasonable to assume that many of them are after all 'semi-authentic.' After the founding of the Academy and the establishment of some kind of routine, it is more than natural that the friends and pupils of Plato began to participate in the production of the texts which have come down to us.

[95] Revisions of the texts and interpolations may have been carried out by pupils with the consent or later approval of Plato; or a dialogue may have been composed by somebody else from a draft or oral suggestions made by Plato; or a text begun by somebody else may have been finished by Plato (or by somebody else who knew his intentions).

Pseudepigraphical 'school accumulation' (cf. above, n. 229) was after all normal in antiquity down to the Hellenistic age. And it is to be remembered that Plato himself chose the mask of Socrates—when he did not chose to appear pseudonymously as 'Apollodorus,' 'Phaedon' or 'Euclides' (cf. Xenophon's appearing under the name of 'Themistogenes of Syracuse' as the author of the *Anabasis, Hell.* 3.1.2).

Theories of semi-authenticity in this vague sense have been propounded now and then since Schleiermacher,[238] though obviously they have been even less popular with students of Plato than the theories of revision have been. However, I see no reason why semi-authenticity should not deserve serious consideration.

In addition to the general reasons mentioned, I can see two specific reasons for assuming that several writings of the Corpus are not entirely from Plato's hand, though Plato and the Academy would have considered them 'Platonic.'

One is the fact that there were semi-authentic Platonic texts in circulation in antiquity, even though we cannot identify them. Some passages in the *7th Letter* (341e–342a, 344d–345a) imply that Dionysius II had published a text on a subject

---

238. Schleiermacher (1804) thought that the following dialogues might be semi-authentic: *Ion, Hp.Mi., Hipparch., Min., Alc.* 2; *Thg., Amat., Alc.* 1, *Mx., Hp.Ma., Clit. See* also e.g. Clark 1955 on *Alcibiades* I, Diller 1955 on *Ion*.—On somewhat different premises Dover 1968a has argued that several or most of the speeches in the Corpus Lysiacum are semi-authentic.—And recently Oświecimski (1978) argued that *Demodocus* and *Sisyphus* may represent semi-authentic texts written for a didactic purpose in the Academy. Were Speusippus' Ὑπομνηματικοὶ διάλογοι (Diog. L. 4.5) notes of Academic disputations?

concerning which he had received instruction from Plato, although in this case [95]
Plato denies his own authorship. And we are told elsewhere (Cic. *ad Atticum*
13.21.4, cf. Index Academy p. 34 Mekler) that a certain Hermodorus (presumably the writer of Plato's βίος) used to publish λόγοι of Plato without the latter's consent; cf. the traditions about Leo (above n. 216) and Pasiphon (Diog. L. 2.6, cf. Plut. *Nic.* 4) as supposed authors of Socratica. Quite obviously, on the other hand, λόγοι produced under the supervision of Plato or published with his consent, would have been considered as authentic.

The other reason is connected with the authorship of the *Epinomis*. The author of this work was very probably Philip of Opous, the astronomer and pupil of Plato, who acted as his secretary (ἀναγραφεύς), and who revised the *Laws* for publication after Plato's death.[239] However, it is not only the *Laws* and *Epinomis* that are closely related, stylistically and in other respects.[240] As a matter of fact [96] the whole of the 'late group' of dialogues is characterized notably by its stylistic affinity with the *Laws* (and *Epinomis*). Could it be that the 'late style' with its peculiar choice of words, its tortuous word-order, its avoidance of hiatus (an Isocratean mannerism unlikely to have been adopted by the aged Plato!) and its rhythmic clausulae, is largely a 'secretary's style'? In this case it is feasible to ask, with Randall 1970: 172–187, whether the 'late dialogues' really represent Plato's own words throughout.[241]

---

239. Diog. L. 3.37, cf. Academicorum Index Col. III 35 ff. p. 13 Mekler. *See* the comprehensive discussion by Tarán 1975, especially 132 f. Szlezák 1978: 26 ff. questions this but emphasizes the fact that the author of the *Epinomis* was well acquainted with Plato's doctrines. Whether Philip or not, the editor of the *Laws* and *Epinomis* is likely to have been the same person.

240. For this stylistic relationship which has been interpreted in various ways, *see* Fr. Müller 1928, G. Müller 1951 and the references in Dönt 1967, Thesleff 1967 (above, p. 20, 127), and Tarán 1975.

241. In order to give this last hypothesis some additional corroboration, let me remind the reader of the fact that middle-aged presbyopic persons who have no spectacles or other optical aids at their disposal tend to rely upon other people's help when reading or writing ordinary handwriting. I doubt that Plato, being a literary artist, had always done this. And if Plato was one of those unfortunate beings, and was the head of a reverent Academy with younger persons prepared to render him every possible assistance, we may take it for granted that he did not normally bother to write down himself what he found worth recording. If seen in this (long-sighted) perspective, Plato's notorious condemnation of writing is somehow understandable even from a practical point of view.

# PART II

# A NEW MODEL

The results arrived at so far in the present study are for the most part negative. The sad and perhaps irritating truth is that the strict, reliable and elegantly linear Platonic chronology dreamed of by earlier generations of scholars, seems to be today even more remote than ever.

Should we give up?

It is true that we may seem, today, somewhat better equipped than the 19th century was: we can (probably) profit from the enormous numbers of observations, opinions and mistakes that have accumulated since the days of Tennemann; we are (probably) comparatively free from biases such as an excessive trust in stylometry or a belief in a steady evolution which must be somehow reflected in Plato's works, or a trust in intuitional interpretation or a trust in authorities; we are aware of a series of complications (such as the probable relevance of oral teaching and discussions in the Academy, revision, and semi-authenticity) which earlier students of the problem did not consider important or did not consider at all; and we are in general prepared to apply more skepticism and less confidence than earlier generations of scholars. And yet, embarking once again on a critical reassessment of the various chronologies suggested, on a selection of the most plausible criteria and arguments to be used for dating each dialogue both in isolation and in relation to the rest, and on a careful sifting and weighing of the pros and cons—this is what Lutoslawski and Raeder and Ritter tried to do, and what very many others have tried on a smaller scale—all this would obviously be a waste of time, unless a new method or a new theory or model can be found which would supply the framework for a fresh discussion.

I shall attempt here to outline such a new model, and to construct from it, albeit very tentatively, the details of a new chronology.

My model comprises six principal components:

(a) The 'external criteria' which were classed and analyzed above (p. 167 ff.) provide some reasonably solid clues (such as close *termini post quos* for the speech

[98] of *Mx.* and the speech of Aristophanes in *Smp.*; the relative order *Sph.*—*Plt.* and *R.*—*Lg.*; and a date c. 360 for *Hp.Ma.*) and a great number of possible indications to be used with utmost caution.

(b) Changes in literary technique. Plato was apparently not the first Socratic to publish Σωκρατικοὶ λόγοι. The traditional forms which he adopted in his first writings were the speech form and the reported dialogue form (p. 210). It was suggested above that the dramatic dialogue form as a literary genre was developed in Plato's Academy. Also a consideration of various structural facts, such as the choice of persons and settings, and the use of the dialogue type approximating to a lecturer's monologue (p. 201), will in some cases lend independent support to assumptions of a relative order.

(c) The dialogues have different purposes and, hence, varying degrees of explicitness.

(d) The short dialogues are not early.

(e) Some of the longer dialogues have undergone one or several revisions by Plato himself, or with his consent (p. 230 ff.).

(f) With very few exceptions, the Corpus Platonicum came into being in Plato's lifetime. It includes works that are of varying degrees of 'semi-authenticity' (p. 236 ff.).

As can be instantly seen, these components are mainly 'external'; or 'formal': they are not concerned in the first place with 'internal' trends in the philosophical or otherwise thematic contents of the dialogues. Stylometry, however, does not form an integral part of this model either, apart from its only indisputable achievement, the delimiting of a 'late group' of dialogues.

The elusiveness of the two traditionally predominant criteria or kinds of argument, the supposed trends of development in style and the supposed development of Plato's philosophical opinions, methods and approaches, was discussed above. Hence, I consider it methodically important to attempt, for once, a construction of a chronology which is not primarily based on these two criteria.

However, it will of course be necessary to test this 'formal' model by applying to it 'thematic' considerations. And I shall try to do so here to some extent. This testing can be conveniently done in the form of a confrontation of thematically related passages in two dialogues at a time (cf. above p. 192 ff.). In some cases the assumption of one chronological order will turn out to be much more natural than the reverse one, but in many cases the result of the confrontation will simply be a *non liquet.* I shall try to select for this thematic testing various much-discussed or otherwise notable points in the contents. It hardly needs emphasizing that the selection is a very limited one, but I have not deliberately manipulated it in accordance with any preconceived view. As far as it goes, it does in fact show that what can be plausibly regarded as 'earlier' or 'later' approaches or formulations in the thematic contents, is not on the whole at variance with the chronology arrived at on formal grounds in the first place.

However, in order to avoid expanding the exposition with an account of all the impasses that I have encountered in the labyrinths of Platonic chronology, I

[99] present the arguments with an eye to what I have found to be the final way out.

This inevitable bias will, I hope, not be taken as a suppressing of counter-evidence.

When all is said and done, the hypothetical nature of the chronology to which all these considerations amount (cf. p. 381) should be evident to any reader. I hope, however, that it will not only provoke a much-needed discussion of the fundaments of Platonic chronology, and provide the reader with some useful facts and references, but that its main issues will also stand up to further testing, much as I am aware of the uncertainties as to details.

# THE 390s

There is some external and internal evidence to suggest that Plato's chief orientation before the first voyage to Sicily was towards a reform of society and man.[242] Considering on the other hand the implications of the theory advanced here, that his earliest written works were speeches or dialogues in reported form, we are left with very little that would meet these double requirements. The *Apology* is the only work which might have been composed in this early period exactly as we have it.

For most of the reported dialogues a somewhat later date is clearly preferable, as we shall see. For instance, taking the formally primitive and sketchy *Demodocus* (p. 376) as authentic and early would, apart from other difficulties, make early Plato an erist. And making the series of reported dialogues start with the comparatively small but subtle and refined pieces *Charmides* and *Lysis*, would introduce several complications of which the first and foremost is the fact that such seemingly (but not really) aporetic manifestations of Platonic play are understandable as didactic and semi-esoteric products of a well-established teacher or of the Academy, but not really understandable as written at a time when Plato is not likely to have been active as the head of a School.[243] Connecting them with dialogues such as *Theaetetus* or, on the other hand, *Laches* will seem more feasible.

Of course Plato is likely to have written, in the 390s and perhaps even earlier, speeches other than the *Apology* and pieces of Socratic dialogue. Apart from the general improbability of a literary genius remaining silent for so long, we have the evidence relating to the early version, or versions, of the *Republic* (below); the *Apology* seems to imply earlier writing activity by Plato (*see* p. 262); and the high

---

242. Cf. above p. 174. The *7th Letter* is explicit on this point (324b–326b); more evidence was adduced notably by Pfleiderer 1896: 247 ff.

243. For the problem of considering the (seemingly) aporetic dialogues as written for a general public, cf. Immisch 1915: 548 f., Moreau 1939: 8. Classing them as 'protreptic' (cf. Gaiser 1955, 1959, Krämer 1959: 33, T. M. Robinson 1970: 130) is to stretch the term. And in fact it is easier to detect in some of the major dialogues reflections of Plato's supposed early attempts as a dramatist (p. 169).

[101] literary quality of the dialogues from the 380s is explicable as resulting from an extensive period of experiment and exercise. However, it seems to me extremely doubtful that Plato would have later considered such early attempts, written presumably for reading at gatherings of small audiences, worth publishing as such, or at all. The *Apology*, being a 'historical' document, may constitute an exception. Plato and his Academy surely were in a position to authorize only such texts as they approved of (cf. above p. 231).

Consequently I suggest that what remains to us of Plato's earliest output is the *Apology* and, in addition, perhaps some speeches that have been incorporated in later works—such as the two first speeches of the *Phaedrus* and some of the speeches of the *Symposium*—and various indirect remains of early sketches developed and elaborated in later dialogues. The most interesting and most easily traceable case of the latter type is the 'early *Republic*.'

## The problem of the 'early *Republic*'

### Introductory

The view that I shall try to vindicate here and further below is a rather extreme variety of the often expressed opinion that the *Republic* is Plato's main work. I believe, not only that it took shape during different periods in Plato's life and that it includes most of the central facets of Plato's philosophy (except for the last stage), but also that it was constantly present to Plato, from the early 390s right down to the 350s when, I presume, it was finally 'published' as a complete whole. The *Republic* is indeed in some ways and senses heterogeneous, and this may have been the ultimate reason why Proclus is said to have atheticized it.[244]

The debate as to whether and in what sense the *Republic* forms a unity was initiated by German scholars (Boeckh, Hermann and Zeller) in the 19th century and it is still unresolved.[245] It is easy to censure extreme analysts (as e.g. Shorey has done) for making too much out of apparent inconsistencies or matters left unsaid in various parts of the *Republic*, or obscure hints in other authors. It is equally easy, however, to refute varieties of extreme unitarianism, implying for instance that both the contents and the general structure (e.g. the symmetrical

[102] pedimental composition) prove the *Republic* to be a solidly coherent whole, with

---

244. *Anon.Proleg.* 26. There are formulations in Proclus' commentary on the *Republic* (p. 6.5 Kroll, cf. 14.16 f.) which suggest that he believed that Plato did not give to the dialogue its final shape.

245. For the early history of the debate, *see* Raeder 1905: 182–198. Reflections of it can be found in most comprehensive books on Plato, especially the German ones. Among very decided unitarians in recent times, note Vretska 1958 and Harrison 1967 (who probably over-interprets Book I as an integral and necessary part of the whole work). I hope I have not missed any of the major arguments used in the debate. *See* now below, p. 519 ff.

the first book as its προοίμιον (cf. II 357a)—interpretation can indeed be manipulated to show almost anything—or that, because similar doctrinal ideas and similar principles of formal structure and a similar average style occur in dialogues which seem to be otherwise dateable to Plato's 'middle period,' and because at VII 540a the suitable age of the philosopher-king is said to be 50 years, the whole of the *Republic* should be dated to the mid-370s.

[102]

The analytical point of view includes four groups of problems which are partly independent: (1) the separation of a 'Proto-*Republic*,' (2) the separation of Book I, (3) the successive genesis of the present main body of the work, and (4) the separation of Book X or parts of it.

In this section I shall deal with problems (1) and (2); for (3) and (4) *see* p. 285 and 331.

## The 'Proto-*Republic*'

The two main arguments for the existence of an earlier version of the *Republic*[246] are the 'summary' in the opening of the *Timaeus* (17b–19b) of a set of λόγοι by Socrates, purporting to have been presented 'the day before' in Athens to Timaeus, Critias and their company but actually corresponding to large portions of *Republic* II 369b–V 466d (cf. also VII,) and the parody in Aristophanes' *Ecclesiazusae* 571–710 (392 BCE) of a theory of communism and community of women and children with possible allusions to parts of the same section of the *Republic*. The other topical arguments have a less obvious bearing on this early version.

We may first examine somewhat more closely the summary in *Timaeus*.[247] Some kind of fiction and deliberate mystification is very probably involved.[248] But it is at any rate obvious that the opening of the *Timaeus* is intended to connect the discussion of a Cosmic Order with the discussion of the Ideal State as reflected in the *Republic* (cf. also the opening of the *Parmenides*, below p. 307). And hence it is particularly interesting that the summary deals only with a specific part of the present *Republic* and, moreover, that it does not correspond exactly even to this part even though it is explicitly said to be complete (19b). Hence, a summary of our present *Republic*, i.e. an exposition by Socrates for Glaucon, Adimantus and the rest of his audience in Piraeus, is not intended in the *Timaeus*. On the other hand, if Plato had operated with pure fiction, it would have been easy for him to create a summary of a previous discussion which would have

---

246. For the earlier theories relating to this problem, *see* Hirmer 1897: 592–598; the hypothesis of the 'Proto-*Republic*' was elaborated on notably by Pohlenz 1913 and Haack 1917; varieties of it occur sporadically in the later discussion, e.g. Ryle 1966: 230 f., 244 ff. *See* below, p. 519.

247. Haack 1917: 3–14 gives a detailed synopsis of this and the corresponding passages in the *Republic*.

248. The missing 'fourth man' (*Ti.* 17a) remains obscure to us; cf. Plato's ἀσθένεια *Phd.* 59b. The Panathenaean festival (*Ti.* 21a) now replaces the festival of the Thracian Bendis in Piraeus (*R.* I 327a, 354a).

[103] fitted his present theme much better than the summary given in the *Timaeus* actually does. I find it difficult to avoid the assumption that Plato is referring to an existing version of the Ideal State which for some reason he wishes to keep apart from its later accretions, the discussion of Justice and Soul, the theory of Forms, etc., perhaps in order to make a fresh start; cf. below p. 337. Yet the fiction of the lecture having been given 'the day before' to the same company seems to imply that the earlier version had not been published in the manner of the exoteric dialogues and, consequently, that it did not have a fixed literary setting. It is also important to note that the style of the relevant portions of the present *Republic* II–V corresponds somewhat to the later Platonic style (cf. Thesleff above p. 83 ff.): the *Republic* has not merely incorporated an earlier dialogue.

It appears from the summary in *Timaeus* that the 'Proto-*Republic*' was a 'monologizing' dialogue conducted by Socrates in the manner of the corresponding portions of the present *Republic* (cf. notably 17c τῶν ὑπ' ἐμοῦ ῥηθέντων λόγων περὶ πολιτείας), but this may be part of the fiction. It is even somewhat probable, considering the parody in Aristophanes (below) and the absence of references in the pamphlet of Polycrates (cf. above p. 179) that Plato had originally expounded these ideas in his own name. The κεφάλαιον of the 'Proto-*Republic*' was οἷά τε καὶ ἐξ οἵων ἀνδρῶν ἀρίστη κατεφαίνετ' ἄν μοι γενέσθαι (sc. ἡ πολιτεία) The contents correspond to R. II 369b–374d (~ *Ti.* 17cd), 374d–376c (~ 17d–18a where the inner control of the State is somewhat more firmly emphasized, though cf. R. III 405bc), a very brief version of R. II 376c–III 412b and VII 521c–531c (~ 18a, enumerating the subjects of the education of the Guardians in the more natural order of γυμναστική, μουσική, μαθήματα),[249] III 416d–417b (~ 18b, without mention of the 'Phoenician tale'; cf. 19a), V 449b–457c (~ 18c; there is no mention of the contents of R. IV,) 457c–461e (~ 18c–19a, presenting 459c–460a separately and combining it with the point of III 415c), and more loosely 461e–466d (~ 18b, without elaboration of the harmony and mutual responsibility said in R. to result from communism).

The parody in the *Ecclesiazusae* is introduced with references which make it fairly clear that Aristophanes has in his mind ideas suggested by a contemporary philosopher.[250] The 'reforms' proposed by Praxagora concentrate on points suitable to the burlesque required here, but the contacts with our hypothetical 'Proto-*Republic*' are unmistakable and have often been noted though interpreted in different ways. Praxagora speaks at length about the community of property and land [104]

---

249. The *Timaeus* does not here make any reference to the extensive discussion of poetry in Books II and III of the *Republic* where μουσική precedes the more unambiguously useful γυμναστική; but there is an indirect reflection of it in *Ti.* 19de.

250. Note 571 πυκνὴν φρένα ... φιλόσοφον φροντίδα, 577 σοφοῦ τινος ἐξευρήματος, 579 μήτε δεδραμένα μήτ' εἰρημένα πω πρότερον, 581 ἅπτεσθαι, ... ταῖς διανοίαις, 583–585 χρηστὰ διδάξω (cf. R. V 458b), πιστεύω/δέδοικα, 589 ἐπίστασθαι τὴν ἐπίνοιαν. See the detailed discussion by Adam[2] (1965: 345–355). Some of these references were detected by Bergk and Meineke who added 427 εὐπρεπής νεανίας and 995 (wrongly, and refuted by Adam) τὸν τῶν γραφέων ἄριστον. Note on the other hand that the *Euthyphro* several times (3b, 5a, 16a) plays with the idea of καινοτομεῖν which is ironically introduced by Aristophanes (584, 586; cf. Aristotle *Pol.* II 6.1265a12, 7.1266a35).

(590 ff.),²⁵¹ and then proceeds to the proposal of a community of women (614). [104] This point is developed in its own way, but the problem of fathers being unable to recognize their offspring is solved in a practical manner and explained as a positive innovation, as in Plato (*Ec.* 636 ff., cf. *R.* V 457c–461e, 463c). Whether the notorious Aristyllus (647) has something to do with Plato may remain an open question.²⁵² In the Ideal State of Praxagora there is a lower class (slaves) doing the heavy work (651). A large portion of Praxagora's speech (656–672, cf. 560–567, 641–643) is devoted to the praise of communism because it disposes of lawsuits and quarrels (cf. *R.* III 405bc, V 461e–466d).²⁵³ And finally she mentions certain regulations regarding the recital of Homeric poetry (679–681, cf. *R.* V 468cd, etc.); cf. also the mention of ξυσσιτία (719 f., cf. 675 ff., *R.* V 458c).

The possibility of seeing here a reflection of an early version of the *Republic* has been dealt with in many different ways, ranging from hypotheses of an early edition of the work (Usener, Rohde, Krohn, Pohlenz, Haack and others, more recently Webster 1970: 34) to hypotheses of common sources or a skeptical acceptance of Plato's joining, in the 390s or later, in a discussion of the merits of communism (Chiappelli, Hirmer, Adam, Raeder, Jaeger and others, more recently Krämer 1968: 134, Ussher 1973) and to emphatic denial of all connections between the passages in the *Ecclesiazusae* and the *Republic* (Shorey, Wilamowitz, Diès, Geffcken and others). A full discussion of the evidence has not appeared since Pohlenz' work of 1913 (207–237, supplemented by Haack 1917 and the third edition of Adam's *Republic*). For my part, I think it is reasonable to infer that Aristophanes is in fact referring to the same proposals as those we find in the opening of the *Timaeus*; as far as I know, the arguments of Pohlenz have not been refuted on this point. But we need not assume that Plato's proposals were published in written form. If he had set forth these remarkable ideas, reading from a manuscript at small gatherings where good friends and less good friends were present, it is natural that they would soon become sufficiently well known in Athens to be susceptible to parody.

---

251. The phrasing at 606 suggests Plato's 'primitive paradise' *R.* II 372ab. Community of land (597) was of course an old dream; one of its advocates was Phaleas, who is mentioned by Aristotle (*Pol.* II 7.1266a39) as the first theorist apart from the Platonic Socrates to propose such reforms.—If it is accepted that Plato had developed a doctrine of Principles at an early date (cf. now Krämer 1980: 16–18), it is perhaps tempting to see reflections of Platonic 'henology' in Eccl. 591, 594, 673 ff., and 690 ff. (cf. *R.* V 462ab).

252. It has sometimes been observed that *Etym. Magn.* s.v. (referring in fact to Aristophanes; also Eustatheus, cf. Adam² 1965: 348) explains this name as hypocoristic for Aristocles, and this was said to have been Plato's original name (Diog. L. 3.4). But the context of Plutus 314, where apparently the same Aristyllus occurs, does not sound particularly Platonic. An intentional ambiguity is not unthinkable: Plato's aristocratic background may have inhibited Aristophanes from mocking him personally and directly (cf. Plato's attitude to Aristophanes in the *Symposium*.) And does the εὐπρεπὴς νεανίας λευκός τις (Praxagora in disguise, 427 f.; cf. above n. 9) allude to Plato? To be pale is to be like a philosopher, according to Aristophanes (cf. *Clouds* 503 f.).

253. It is curious that the only instances in Aristophanes of the late Platonic (or Socratic?) idiom τὸ ποῖον; and of τἀγαθόν; should occur in *Eccl.* 646 and 426.

[105] The evidence of Aristotle that Plato's Socrates was the first philosopher to propose a community of women and children[254] is quite important. And against those who assert that Book V of the *Republic* is a philosophical elaboration of Aristophanes' whimsical suggestions in the *Ecclesiazusae* (cf. the reference to comedy in *R.* V 452de, etc.)[255] it has to be said that the reluctance of the Platonic Socrates to speak of these matters (V 450a ff., etc.), as well as the references to comedy, are better understandable if 'he' has already been the target of ridicule in this respect also.

Perhaps Plato's deeply rooted distrust of the public (cf. above p. 169) has something to do with such experiences.

A further argument sometimes referred to is a passage in Gellius (Gell. *NA* 14.3.3–4) according to which Xenophon is said to have opposed Plato's view of the State, *lectis ex eo* (sc. *opera*) *duobus fere libris, qui primi in volgus exierant*, and have expressed his own view in the 'Cyropaedia' to which Plato answered by declaring (in *Laws* III 694c) that Cyrus had not received any education at all. Some scholars (among them Haack 1917: 33 f.) have thought that the 'two books' may really be the 'Proto-*Republic*,' whereas others assume that, unless the story is wholly unreliable, the present *Republic* was written out successively and Xenophon got hold of the beginning (cf. e.g. Wilamowitz II 181 f., Diès 1932 XXXIX–XLIII). Since Xenophon not only deals with the 'education' of Cyrus and his military training, but also with the organization of the Persian State (especially in Book VIII), he is somewhat more likely to have read the 'Proto-*Republic*' than the first books of our present *Republic*, provided, that is, his reactions were as Gellius informs us. This would imply that a text of the 'Proto-*Republic*' had been circulated (presumably without the author's consent), and this is perhaps not so improbable after all. But I would not attach much weight to this argument.

Certain passages in Isocrates' *Busiris* (XI) have sometimes also been adduced; the most detailed argument is again to be found in Pohlenz 1913 (215–223, cf. Ries 1959: 51–55). In §§ 15–23 Isocrates sketches briefly his view of the well-organized Egyptian State with its specialization of the trades and professions, and mentions in passing that there are well-known philosophers who have used it as their model (17). Very probably Plato is meant, or at least included. In *Republic* II 369b–371e this kind of specialization is supported, though Egypt is not mentioned (for an analysis of the parallels, *see* Pohlenz l.c.); and *Timaeus* 21a ff. with its explicit introduction of the Egyptian model (cf. notably 24ab), can be taken as answering and perhaps correcting the hints of Isocrates. The main problem here is the date of the *Busiris*. Pohlenz argued that since Isocrates answers both Polycrates' praise of Busiris and at the same time his attack upon Socrates (mentioned in this order in *Bus.* 4), and since he can refute Polycrates by stating that no[106] body has heard that Alcibiades was the pupil of Socrates (*Bus.* 5) though this was

---

254. Aristotle *Pol.* II 7.1266a33–36, cf. 1265a11, II 12.1274b9–11, and above n. 10. Cf. Adam² 1965: 346. The perspective of Aristotle does not exclude the possibility that Plato may have expressed these ideas in his own name.

255. Chiappelli's list of references is criticized by Adam 349. This point was argued by Susemihl II 1857: 294–303, and later by e.g. Diès 1932: XLIX–LII.

apparently commonly accepted at least in Plato's Academy after the *Symposium*, [106] the *Busiris* cannot be dated later than 385, and so the 'Proto-*Republic*' (without, or rather perhaps with an explicit reference to Egypt) must be what Isocrates has in mind. This may sound reasonable. Yet it is far from certain, and a considerably later date is still possible for the *Busiris*. At any rate, the latter is more likely to refer to an oral discussion and perhaps to the 'Proto-*Republic*' or to writings by other philosophers, than to the present *Republic* where the 'Egyptian' scheme is not particularly prominent among the profusion of themes.[256]

Then there is the much-discussed passage in the *Seventh Letter*, 326ab. Plato states, in phrasing very similar to but not identical with *Republic* V 473cd (cf. also *Lg.* IV 712a), that when visiting Sicily for the first time (cf. 324a–c) he had already arrived at the conclusion that there will be no end to man's woe unless true philosophers become political leaders (εἰς ἀρχὰς ... τὰς πολιτικάς in the *Letter*, βασιλεύσωσιν in the *Republic*) or vice versa. Whatever one thinks of an early version of the *Republic*, or of the authenticity of the *Seventh Letter*, there is really no positive reason for believing that the *Letter* does not report the truth here. Moreover—and this is particularly interesting if we regard, as I think we must, the *Letter* as an important historical document—Plato says he felt himself compelled to speak about this.[257] Since the *Letter* is greatly concerned with the problem of communicating philosophy in public, it is difficult to avoid the impression that Plato is referring to some kind of lecturing activity in the 390s, i.e. primarily the 'Proto-*Republic*.' And when in the *Republic* Socrates introduces his statement of philosophers as rulers by admitting that this will produce a great deal of laughter and ἀδοξία, this sounds very much like the same kind of hesitation he expresses in connection with the chapter on women (at the beginning of Book V and elsewhere) and which apparently reflects Plato's own experience of Aristophanic parody.[258]

Finally, there is the tradition that Plato was known to have altered the beginning of his *Republic* several times (above p. 232). At least this does not contradict the hypothesis of a 'Proto-*Republic*.' [107]

---

256. Those who date the *Busiris* after the *Republic* usually emphasize that Isocrates writes as if both he himself and the εὐδοκιμῶν φιλόσοφος were well-established teachers; cf. H. Gomperz 1903: 192–197, Wilamowitz II² 103. An allusion of Isocr. *Bus.* 49 to *R.* VII 536c is suggested by Shorey 1935 ad l. (who normally scorns allusion-seeking). Others, among them Diès 1932: CXXVIII–CXXXIV, argue that the *Busiris* does not refer to the *Republic* at all.—Since the *Busiris* refers to two speeches of Polycrates, and the point about Alcibiades should not be pressed (Isocrates has παιδευόμενον), a comparatively late date is perhaps to be preferred.

257. *Ep.* 7.326a6 ff. The verb λέγειν actually suggests oral communication (cf. Jaeger 1928: 9 f.). Some scholars think that ἠναγκάσθην refers (anachronistically) to Socrates' reluctance in *R.* V 473c, for which *see* below.

258. Cf. above p. 254. Note the 'waves' met by Socrates *R.* V 457bc, 472a, 473c. Now, Aristophanes does not exactly parody the idea of philosophers as political leaders, and this is probably one reason why scholars have been reluctant to accept the theory of the 'Proto-*Republic*.' But *Eccl.* 571 (cf. 581, 589, etc) does in fact imply political activity by a philosopher, so Aristophanes has not entirely missed this point; and presumably Plato did not speak of a sole ruler in the 'Proto-*Republic*.' It is more remarkable that, as far as we know, Plato's utopian 'rule of the philosophers' never became the target of Middle Comedy mockery.

[107] The separation of *Republic* I

This problem is really quite different from the question of the 'Proto-*Republic*.' Because the first book of the *Republic* is structurally and stylistically and even thematically different from the rest of the work and corresponds rather to the *Gorgias* and minor dialogues of the *Charmides* type, many scholars beginning with K. F. Hermann have been of the opinion that it was originally a separate sketch or even a separate dialogue (sometimes since Dümmler called the 'Thrasymachus').[259] It is in fact easy to detect breaks in the structure and the setting that may indicate that Book I, or substantial parts of it, had existed separately and later become combined with the main body of the work beginning with Book II.[260] In spite of the emphatic rejection of this view by some scholars (cf. Guthrie IV 437 with references; Harrison 1967: 39: "The sooner the 'Thrasymachus' theory goes onto the scrap-heap, with other relics of nineteenth-century separatism, the better for Platonic scholarship"), I still find it worth serious consideration (and not only because scrap-heaps seem more worth utilizing today). The main arguments against it, produced repeatedly by the unitarians, are that Book I does function as an introduction, and that many of the ideas dealt with in the later books are 'foreshadowed' in it. But surely we underrate Plato if we consider him unable to transform a separate sketch into an introduction.

Dating this early text, however, introduces additional difficulties. As regards both form and content, *Republic* I has chiefly two points of reference: the *Gorgias*, and the dialogues of the *Charmides* type. As will be argued below (p. 295), *Lysis* and *Charmides* come rather late in the reported dialogues series, and after *Gorgias*. And it may be noted here that *Republic* I corresponds more closely to *Gorgias* than to the *Charmides* type in introducing three discussion partners for Socrates in an order of ascending importance (the characters Thrasymachus and Callicles [108] being related in several respects), in dealing with political ethics, and in laying less stress upon definition.[261] The chief issue is whether *Republic* I precedes or follows *Gorgias* chronologically. Though there are many good scholars who support

---

259. See the references to the discussion in Geffcken II A 52 f. and Friedländer II 286 f. More recent supporters of this view include Krämer 1959, Ilting 1965, Ryle 1966 and Gundert 1971. Outside Germany, scholars have been generally skeptical towards this separation; cf. Harrison 1967: 37–39 and the references below.

260. Notably the change of the chief interlocutors of Socrates (cf. Friedländer II 47 and below p. 119; Wilamowitz II 783 thought that Glaucon and a new theme have been secondarily introduced at 347a in order to provide a link with Book II); the somewhat compressed and inconsistent ending at 353e–354c; the description of the previous discussion as having been, contrary to expectations, merely a προοίμιον, II 357c; the surely very strange fact that a single evening's conversation in a metic's house in Piraeus should provide, from the outset, an acceptable setting for the enormous theme of the Ideal State as presented from Book II onwards; and the probable fact that *Clitopho* takes account of Book I but not of the subsequent ones (below, p. 353). Cf. Friedländer II 45 ff., III 56 ff., 287 n. 1.

261. For this last point, cf. Raeder 201. The detailed arguments of von Arnim 1914: 97 ff., 136 ff. for the order *Republic* I—*Charmides*, *Lysis* are not very conclusive but, in part at least, better founded than the counter-arguments of Pohlenz 1916: 262, Ritter 1935 and Kratzsch 1964.

both views,[262] it should be pointed out that the order *Republic* I—*Gorgias* is the [108] natural one to accept if the first book of the *Republic* is separated from the rest. I would stress the following arguments:

*Gorgias* is in most respects the richer dialogue, and the comparative meagerness of *Republic* I is not only due to thematic concentration (as in the case of *Lysis* and *Charmides*), assuming that it had existed separately in roughly its present shape and had ended with a refutation of Thrasymachus' view: owing to the relative absence of sophistication and of implicit allusions, *Republic* I really looks more 'primitive' than *Gorgias*. The relatively broad opening conversation of *Republic* I might have become somewhat elaborated at a later (though hardly the final) stage of the growth of the present composition, although *Gorgias*, too, seems to have originally had a frame story (p. 234), and the 'chat' with Cephalus is more loosely connected with the main theme than is the discussion with *Gorgias*. Several of the approaches and views in *Gorgias* can be considered as more advanced than the corresponding ones in *Republic* I.[263] In both dialogues Socrates is discussing successively with three partners, but the choice of the characters in *Gorgias* seems to be somewhat more to the point, and can be seen as developed out of the group of chief characters in *Republic* I: whatever may have been Plato's reasons for choosing Cephalus and his son Polemarchus as conversation partners of Socrates for a λόγος concerning τὸ δίκαιον,[264] the addition of Thrasymachus of Chalcedon to this company looks like a rather artificial trick, whereas the famous rhetor Gorgias, his pupil Polus, and their host, the Athenian politician Callicles form a coherent group and one that is natural to the wide register of themes (rhetoric and persuasion versus philosophy, and both political and personal ethics). Although the game of detecting symbolism in Plato's choice of characters and names is admittedly a risky one, I find it tempting to take 'Thrasymachus' [109] to stand (partly) for Thrasybulus and 'Callicles' to stand for one of his most important successors in Athenian politics, Callistratus son of Callicrates.[265]

---

262. *Republic* I—*Gorgias*, e.g. Pfleiderer, von Arnim, Wilamowitz, Humbert, Geffcken, Schaerer, Friedländer, Krämer; *Gorgias*—*Republic* I e.g. Zeller, Lutoslawski, Th. Gomperz, Raeder, Pohlenz, Taylor, Vretska, Guthrie.

263. This is of course a very controversial subject. *See* especially v. Arnim 1914: 77–87: even his opponent Pohlenz admits (1916: 262 ff.) that he has made a good case (cf. 1921: 10). Note, for instance, that the idea ὁ ἄδικος ἄθλιος is only introduced in the final section of *Republic* I, 354a, but functions as one of the main themes in *Gorgias* (468e ff). The 'doctrine' of Thrasymachus, τὸ δίκαιον = τὸ τοῦ κρείττονος συμφέρον (R. I 338c) is introduced in the *Gorgias* in an ironical context, in the first speech of Callicles (483b), as the doctrine of the weak majority (i.e. democracy); but the tendency of *Republic* I to discuss ἀδικία from the aspect of what is useful, is implicitly present in most of the argument in *Gorgias* (458e ff.).

264. A play with the names, 'Head,' 'Beginner of struggle,' is not unthinkable.—At any rate Plato may have felt it safer to produce indirect criticism of current views of justice among metics known to sympathize with Athenian democracy; note also that the discussion takes place 'extra muros' (cf. *Phaedrus*).

265. The latter possibility was argued in some detail by Rick 1931: 23–26; for the allusion to Callias, cf. below.—As to Thrasybulus, note the fact that 'Thrasymachus' in *Republic* I is not characterized as a rhetor, though this was the main profession of the historical Thrasymachus (as Plato acknowledges in *Phaedrus* 261c, 266c, etc.); nor is he really a 'sophist' (cf. *Clitopho*, below p. 352). Also

[109] This would also provide some clues for absolute dating. Thrasybulus died in 388 (Xen. *Hell.* 4.8.30), but was presumably living when *Republic* I was written since Plato conceals him behind a mask; similarly Callistratus was alive when *Gorgias* was written, since he was politically active from the late 390s and did not die until the 350s (cf. below, p. 375).

Yet I am not so sure that *Republic* I can be shown to have preceded the pamphlet of Polycrates;[266] on the contrary, Socrates' first words to Cephalus, χαίρω διαλεγόμενος τοῖς σφόδρα πρεσβύταις sound like an intentional refutation of one of Polycrates' points (above p. 179); but this may of course have been a later addition.

The motif of Socrates and a younger friend of his arriving together at a patron's house where they meet several Important Persons, occurs variously in the first book of the *Republic*, *Protagoras* and *Symposium* as well as *Gorgias*. Since this motif was perhaps a *locus communis* of early Socratic literature, Plato may be following models unknown to us.[267] Comparing these four dialogues in isolation, one gets the impression that, although Callias was probably the traditional host at such meetings (Eupolis already has him perform this function), and whatever secondary changes the opening of the *Republic* may have undergone, this theme occurs in a rather more simple, straightforward and (presumably) original form in *Republic* I (327a–328c) and in *Gorgias* (since the lost frame story cannot have [110] been very extensive) than in *Protagoras* (310a–316e) and *Symposium* (174a–177e) where it has obviously been elaborated with Platonic overtones.[268]

However, since Plato apparently did not feel satisfied with the conclusion of *Republic* I (though we cannot tell exactly how the first version ended) and decided to rework it into a larger composition which came to include the 'Proto-*Republic*,'

---

e.g. Harrison 1967 argues, from a unitarian point of view, that Plato has 'manipulated' the character of Thrasymachus. Although the historical Thrasymachus, like his friend Clitophon (cf. below p. 353), had apparently been a sympathizer of the Four Hundred (and if Ps.-Herodes Atticus Π. πολιτείας really is by him, as Sordi tried to demonstrate in 1955, it rather shows oligarchic sympathies), Plato makes him symbolize a type of politician with whom he disagrees profoundly. Here, in the environment of Lysias, he presumably stands for the 'might is right' principle of democracy, as Plato saw it; note his crude brutality R. I 336b–d, 337a, 343a, 354a, and his inclination for tyranny, 344a (normal for an active 'democrat' in Plato's view). I do not think the historical Thrasymachus can be entirely harmonized with Plato's Thrasymachus, as e.g. Guthrie III 294–298 has tried to do. Quincey 1981 rightly sees in Plato's picture a caricature, but he probably overemphasizes the criticism of rhetoric inherent in it.

266. This was argued by Humbert 1931: 67–69. Another anachronistic reference has been seen in the mention of Ismenias in 336a which, according to some scholars, would be understandable soon after 395 BCE (Xen. *Hell.* 3.5.1) but less so after 382 BCE (id.5.2.35, Plut. *Pelop.* 5.2); cf. Adam ad 1.; but Hirmer 1897: 660 f. and others have thought this wholly irrelevant.

267. Apart from Eupolis' 'Colaces' (421), possibly 'Autolycus' (420) and Aeschines' 'Callias,' note Xenophon's 'Symposium,' below, n. 269.

268. Focusing on the teaching of sophists in *Protagoras*, and on the odd behavior of Socrates in *Symposium*. Some of the details in the corresponding section of *Republic* I seem to have little to do with the main theme. The ingenious argumentation of von Arnim 1914: 1 ff., 97 ff. produces the order *Protagoras—Republic* I by implication, but it has not convinced me on this point.

it is reasonable to assume, with the majority of the separatists, that *Republic* I     [110]
existed only as a sketch not suitable for publication in written form.²⁶⁹

## The *Apology*

A much-debated question regarding the *Apology* is whether, on general and specific grounds, it should be placed in its 'natural' environment soon after the trial and death of Socrates, or to what extent the indications of a considerably later date are relevant. The traditional and still largely current view is to accept a very early date.²⁷⁰ Against this view various assertions have been made. The following seem to me particularly valid: the *Apology* should be interpreted as a reaction, not so much to what many considered a judicial murder of Socrates, as to criticism of Socrates and the Socratics; and as Socrates is very unlikely to have said all this, in this manner, at the actual trial, the *Apology* would have missed its point seriously if it had been published very soon after the event, when hundreds of Athenians remembered more or less clearly what Socrates had said.²⁷¹ Even so, it is hardly possible to argue that the Platonic *Apology* is pure fiction. Presumably it approximates to historical truth somehow, and for this assumption the same reasons are valid: the *Apology* would indeed have missed its point if the readers who remembered the trial felt it to be manifestly untrue. So the closer to what Socrates     [111]
actually said the Platonic *Apology* is, the earlier it is likely to be, and vice versa.²⁷²

No stylometrical test is capable of indicating a date for this highly specific set of speeches with their special features of structure and style.²⁷³ The inserting of two

---

269. If Plato used to read it to his friends, its contents may have become more largely known; the *Clitopho* (p. 352) seems to imply this, and it also suggests that the early version of *Republic* I was slightly different from the present one. But this hardly provides an adequate explanation for the odd fact that Xenophon's 'Symposium' has an opening which in several respects reminds one of the opening of *Republic* I. It is *a priori* highly improbable that Xenophon would have used the extant version of the *Republic* of Plato as a model for his *Symposium*; and the main part of the latter is in fact likely to be rather early, as I have argued elsewhere (cf. below p. 267). I am now inclined to think that the settings of *Republic* I and Xenophon's 'Symposium' had a common model in the earliest Socratic literature or oral traditions.

270. Cf. e.g. Guthrie IV 72–80.

271. These are old points (cf. e.g. Pfleiderer 1896: 247 ff., v. Arnim 1923), recently argued again by Erbse 1975. Erbse's list of anachronisms (41–45) seems to me partly disputable, however.

272. Those who interpret the *Apology* as representing merely 'early Plato' run the risk of overlooking this historical aspect, e.g. E. Wolff 1929, Steidle 1950, Kapp 1968: 79 ff. Among those who think that the *Apology* approximates to historical truth, note Guthrie III 478 and pm.

273. Cf. Hackforth 1933: 9 f.; Ritter 1923: 869 Nachtr. is clearly wrong. The statistics which Michaelson, Morton and Gillies have produced (1977) to indicate that the *Apology* and *Meno* are not by the same hand, have much too narrow a basis. The somewhat uneven use of rhetorical figures (cf. Th. Meyer 1962: 45–65) in interplay with personal features of style (cf. Thesleff above p. 101) can be taken as characterizing Socrates or as reflecting the author's lack of practice, or both. For some possible reminiscences of Gorgias' 'Defense of Palamedes,' *see* Chroust 1957: 216 ff., Coulter 1964; such a dependence would also suggest a comparatively early date.

[111]  different types of dialogue in the first speech is not unparalleled in oratory (cf. above p. 204) but it is alien to Plato's practice. The lack of a setting or a frame dialogue (cf. *Mx.*, *Phdr.*, and *Smp.;* also Xen. *Ap.*) is interesting. Though readers perhaps did not require an introduction at the outset, the new situations encountered at 35c and 38c are quite unintelligible without an explanation by the performer of the speech. Since such indispensable comments would hardly have been dropped if they had existed as part of the text from the beginning (cf. *Phdr.* again), it seems feasible to assume that Plato had not intended the *Apology* for wider circulation in written form and hence, that it belongs to a very early period of his literary career when he presumably read his 'publications' himself to a chosen audience.

It is also reasonable to date the Platonic *Apology* before the pamphlet of Polycrates. It has been often observed that the *Apology* does not appear to take account of all the points of Polycrates.[274] In fact it is chiefly directed against Meletus, and Anytus, in whose name or from whose point of view Polycrates wrote, and also Lycon are kept more in the background.[275] Certainly there was much debate and discussion about Socrates in the early 4th century. One of the reasons that occasioned Polycrates to publish his attack may well have been the unconventional and by ordinary standards odd and haughty attitude of Socrates in Plato's *Apology*, but this cannot have been the only or even the chief inducement.

[112]  The main complication arising from this comparatively early dating of the *Apology* is that it conflicts with the theory of the priority of Xenophon's *Apology*, which was argued notably by von Arnim (1923) and Hackforth (1933). However, the independent evidence for this order is quite flimsy compared with the indications of the priority of Plato's *Apology*, and thus I am inclined to accept, with the majority of scholars, the latter alternative.[276] Aristophanes and Lysias have sometimes been adduced for dating Plato's *Apology* but can offer little direct help.[277] For Isocrates, *see* below p. 262.

---

274. *See* especially Humbert 1931: 67–69, Geffcken II A 64 f.; Verdam 1917 did not succeed in proving the contrary, and those who argue a late date for the *Apology* (e.g. Ryle 1966: 146 ff.; 221 f., Erbse 1975) usually overlook the problem of Polycrates. M. H. Hansen 1980 remains skeptical against the reconstruction of the pamphlet, since he emphasizes the political aspect of the historical trial of Socrates, but he does not take account of the full evidence. However, there are several unclear points in the history of the discussion about Socrates in the early 4th century, such as the position of Lysias' 'Apology' (usually regarded as a reply to Polycrates, cf. e.g. Rossetti 1975b: 87 ff.).

275. Note 36a, also τοὺς ἀμφὶ Ἄνυτον 18b, cf. 29c, 30b, 31a. Themistius, *Or.* 23.296bc, alludes to this fact.

276. The very complicated argument of v. Arnim 1923 for the order Xen. *Ap.*—Plat. *Ap*—Xen. *Mem.* is ingenious as usual but far too conjectural, and many of its premises are easily questionable. One of the interesting points, and perhaps the most important one, is that Xenophon's 'Apology' appears to take no account of Polycrates, whereas his 'Memorabilia' rather explicitly does. However, Xenophon's 'Apology' is mainly concerned with the specific and obviously secondary question of why Socrates chose to adopt a haughty attitude (μεγαληγορία) at the trial, and various passages suggest a considerable distance in time from the events of 399 BCE (cf. 1 γεγράφασι καὶ ἄλλοι, 29–32). Cf. Chroust 1951: 18 ff., Breitenbach 1967: 1889–1891, 1893.

277. There is no substantial ground for dating a 'revised edition' of Aristophanes' *Clouds* at late as the 380s (Geissler 1905, Morr 1929); cf. Dover 1968b: LXXX ff.; for the *Ecclesiazusae*,

Are there any Platonic dialogues that could with some degree of plausibility [112] be dated prior to the *Apology*? An examination of the evidence produces a rather negative answer. It has often been observed that the concluding vaticination with regard to the friends of Socrates following up his work (39cd) is likely to be a *post eventum* one, implying that some Socratics, presumably Plato among them, had already published Socratic λόγοι. On the other hand, it has been noted that the extant Platonic dialogues do not correspond exactly to the situations described in *Ap.* 21e–22e where Socrates tells us how he has been searching in vain for the 'wisdom' of politicians, poets and craftsmen.[278] On the other hand the *Protagoras*, for instance, may present itself as a concentration and a further development of some of the ideas propounded in *Ap.* 19d–20c (and the *Ion* similarly as a development of *Ap* 22a–c, but cf. below p. 367). As a matter of fact the picture which the *Apology* gives of Socrates' activities and the activities expected from his followers, is concerned first of all with such political and social ἀρετή and φιλοσοφία as are also implied by the reforms suggested in the 'Proto-*Republic*': cf. e.g. the emphatic pronouncements on φιλοσοφεῖν 28e, 29d, ἀρετή 20b, 30b, 31b, 41e, and notably the idea of Socrates and his followers criticizing and irritating the Athe- [113] nians, 30e, 36c, 39cd. The words (32a) ἀναγκαῖον ... τὸν τῷ ὄντι μαχούμενον ὑπὲρ τοῦ δικαίου ... ἰδιωτεύειν sound as if they reflect Plato's own experience after the 'publication' of the 'Proto-*Republic*.' And a more direct reference to this work can be found in 36c: Socrates says he has tried to make people understand that they should not concern themselves with external matters before making themselves as 'good' as possible, nor concern themselves with politics (τῶν τῆς πόλεως) before they have thought of the State itself (αὐτῆς τῆς πόλεως).[279]

The reasons sometimes given for dating some of the extant dialogues before the *Apology* have little independent value and can be easily refuted.[280] The dialogues

---

cf. below.—The possible points of contact between the *Apology* and some speeches of Lysias (Laudien 1914, Verdam 1917) are irrelevant.—The possible reminiscences of the *Apology* in Isocrates' 'Antidosis' (XV, 353 BCE; cf. H. Gomperz 1906a: 1–3, Ries 1959: 150 f.) are of no use for dating the former; H. Gomperz 1905: 170 f. also argued that Isocr. *C. Soph.* (XIII) 11 refers to *Ap.* 20c, but this is highly questionable.

278. For the vaticination, *see* now especially Erbse 1975: 38–41. As to the 'wisdom' of politicians and others, the examination of Alcibiades in *Alcibiades* I, Critias in *Charmides*, Callicles in *Gorgias*, Anytus in *Meno*, Thrasymachus in *Republic* I and Agathon in *Symposium* really does not correspond to the situations mentioned in the *Apology*. Surely we would expect Plato's Socrates to give as examples also, or at least, sophists, rhetors, religious men, rhapsodes and soldiers, if Plato had already published, say, the *Protagoras*, *Euthydemus*, *Hippias Minor*, *Gorgias*, *Euthyphro*, *Ion* and/or *Laches* (cf. Raeder 92).

279. This is sometimes taken as an early variant of the theory of Forms, cf. Erbse 1975: 25 f. However this may be, there is obviously no other Platonic text than the 'Proto-*Republic*' that would fit this picture (cf. Pfleiderer 1896: 26 f., 252). Note also the curious γνησίως in a similar context in *Ap.* 31e4 and *R.* V 473d2 (Morrison 1958: 212 rightly points out that the order of the extants texts is *Ap.*—*R.*).

280. Cf. above n. 278. Apart from those who date some of the dialogues before 399 (above, p. 171), note the following attempts: *Charmides*, Schmalenbach 1946, Kratzsch 1964; *Euthyphro*, Erbse 1975: 43 (but *see*, on the other hand, Hammer-Jensen 1905/6: 116–119); *Ion*, Flashar 1958: 101 f.; *Meno*, Erbse 1975: 43; *Protagoras*, Hammer-Jensen 1905/6: 120, Kratzsch 1964; *Theages*, Friedländer II 310 n. 7.

[113] which appear to offer the closest points of contact are *Crito, Gorgias* and *Phaedo*. For *Crito*, cf. below p. 355.[281] Though *Gorgias* and *Phaedo* are normally taken to represent an advance in various ways from the position of the *Apology*,[282] some scholars have been inclined to place *Gorgias* closer to the events of 399 BCE than the *Apology*, considering the emotional intensity of the former and certain other facts. The chief exponents of this view are H. Gomperz 1924 (followed by Boehme 1959) and Erbse 1975.[283] Gomperz suggested (cf. Boehme 99–102) that *Gorgias* (especially 521c–522e) looks as if it represents an earlier stage of the apology of Socrates; but other difficulties aside, it can be easily maintained that in *Gorgias* Plato preferred to concentrate on certain aspects, especially if Polycrates' pamphlet was fresh in his memory (cf. p. 179). Erbse again asserts (29–38) that
[114] Socrates' statements in the *Apology* (especially 36d) of his activities as a benefactor are difficult to understand unless the reader keeps in mind passages such as *Gorgias* 521d (Socrates the true statesman) or 513e (his εὐεργεσία); but surely we cannot expect Plato's original readers to be as badly informed as we are; and after all there are passages in the *Apology* which might have provided sufficient clues (notably 28a ff., especially 30a), and the possibility of the 'Proto-*Republic*' being in Plato's mind has also to be taken into account. The other arguments of H. Gomperz and Erbse are in my view even less reliable.

So it seems feasible, as far as the evidence goes, to assume that the *Apology* was composed after the 'proto-*Republic*' and possibly after Aristophanes' *Ecclesiazusae* but before the pamphlet of Polycrates, i.e. about 392 BCE or shortly afterwards. If it was partly occasioned by the parody of Aristophanes, it is at the same time understandable as an apology of Plato himself.

## Additional considerations; Isocrates XIII

As was suggested above, it is not unthinkable that other parts of later Platonic works derive from early sketches from the 390s. However, except for the portions

---

281. *Crito* is normally placed after the *Apology*. Whether the passages *Cri.* 45b, 52c refer to *Ap.* 37d, 30cd or to the historical events is not easy to decide. The apparent change from agnosticism in the *Apology* (40c–41c) to a religious attitude in the *Crito* (54b) has been explained as irrelevant to chronology (Shorey 1903: 40; Wilamowitz II 55 f., arguing that the personified Laws express the conventional view in *Crito*); but *see* below p. 355.—The reverse order sometimes suggested is not based on specific arguments (e.g. for Boehme 1959: 99–102 it is mainly a consequence of his very early dating of *Gorgias*; for Erbse 1975: 28 f. it follows from the late dating of the *Apology*).

282. For *Gorgias*, cf. also below p. 274 and the fact that it seems to take account of the pamphlet of Polycrates. A much-discussed problem is the relation of the apparent agnosticism of the *Apology* to the more religious attitudes in *Gorgias* and *Phaedo* (cf. e.g. Gauss 1/2.10 f., Erbse 1975: 23 f.); at any rate the position of the *Apology* cannot be taken as more 'advanced' in the sense of a chronological argument (as H. M. Wolff 1957: 101 f. and Ryle 1966: 219 f. do).

283. Also Immisch 1899, Taylor 1927, Ryle 1966 and some others have dated *Gorgias* before the *Apology*.

of the *Republic* already discussed, the direct traces of this are not particularly clear.²⁸⁴ [114]

Some indirect additional information can be gathered from Isocrates' speech 'Against the Sophists' (XIII), the documentary importance of which has often been underrated. Although Isocrates of course is not very explicit, this is the only large-scale testimony we have of the activities of rhetors, sophists and philosophers in Athens about 390 BCE (cf. above p. 180). Isocrates criticizes two categories of 'educators,' sophists in general (1–8), and rhetors (9–13), who he thinks have brought 'philosophy' into disrepute (1, 11, 14). The arguments are somewhat similar to those known from Plato, notably *Gorgias* and *Protagoras* (which are both likely to be later, cf. below p. 274 and 276). The interesting question here is whether Plato is included among the targets of Isocrates. Obviously he does not belong to the rhetors (the producers of πολιτικοὶ λόγοι 9 are described as teachers of rhetoric; one is inclined to think of Thrasymachus and Lysias as examples). The 'sophists' on the other hand are characterized as erists (1, cf. ἐναντιώσεις 7), and Isocrates is in the first place thinking of teachers of ἀρετή who take a (rather too modest!) fee for their teaching (3–6). At the end of this section (8), however, he contrasts the δόξαι of intelligent persons (cf. also 17, and *Antid.* 271) with the alleged ἐπιστήμη of the sophists in a manner that suggests the well-known Eleatic and Platonic terminology. Is he here polemicizing against Plato?²⁸⁵ I do not think so. At any rate he can hardly be referring to any of Plato's written works, because the contrast δόξα/ἐπιστήμη is explicitly discussed in such works as are most certainly later [115] (*R.* IV, V 476c ff., *Meno*, etc.); and in dialogues often considered 'early' it occurs only in the form of occasional hints in passing (e.g. *Prt.* 358c, *Chrm.* 168a, *R.* II 362a, III 412e–413b), and such hints could not have provided Isocrates with a sufficient basis for his polemics. Probably the δόξα/ἐπιστήμη point refers vaguely to the Socratics in general. If this is so, and the Socratics are included here among the 'erists,' some of whom teach for money, it would seem, either, that Isocrates is not very well informed about Plato, or that he knows him only as a representative of respectable 'philosophy' which has suffered from the bad reputation inflicted on it by sophists and rhetors. The former seems the more probable alternative, since Isocrates makes no mention of the revolutionary ideas of the 'Proto-*Republic*,' as he perhaps does later in the *Busiris* (above p. 254). Apparently Plato has not as yet had any public dealings with rhetors and sophists. I consider it fairly obvious that Isocrates has not so far seen any of the great dialogues of Plato.

He may, however, have seen the *Apology*. First, there is an interesting correspondence between *Ap.* 19c and Isocr. § 11 which has been sometimes noted but variously interpreted (cf. Ries 1959: 33): both Socrates and Isocrates profess to appreciate a certain kind of knowledge (ἐπιστήμη in Plato, φιλοσοφία in

---

284. For the possibility of an early doctrine of Principles, cf. above n. 251.
285. This has been sometimes argued, for instance by Ries 1959: 21–35 who (on flimsy grounds) infers that Isocrates has in mind various minor dialogues and in particular *Gorgias*. We shall see (below p. 275) that *Gorgias* is likely to be later than the 'Against the Sophists.'

Isocrates) which they do not pursue themselves, and the addition of φλυαροῦντες in Isocrates indicates that it is he who operates with a reminiscence of the *Apology* (19c4 φλυαροῦντα) rather than vice versa, especially since the following passage in the *Apology* (19d–20c) on sophists teaching for money seems to be echoed in §§ 3–6.[286] And secondly, the statement of Isocrates in § 14 that many philosophers have lived their whole lives as ἰδιῶται includes of course Socrates and sounds like an echo of Plato's forcible (and personal) argumentation in *Ap.* 31e–32a (cf. above p. 113). Cf. also Isocr. § 8 ψυχῆς ἐπιμέλεια and *Ap.* 29e.—The echo of the *Apology* in the 'Antidosis' (XV, 354/3 BCE, cf. Ries 1959: 150 f.) is remote and irrelevant for dating the former.

In conclusion, I suggest the following:

Before 388 Plato did not write for the general public. However, he seems to have delivered some of his sketches before audiences who made them more widely known. The most important instance of this was the 'Proto-*Republic*,' possibly a speech which Plato gave in his own name; it was parodied by Aristophanes in 392 and hence it is not likely to have been written very much earlier. Plato then wrote the *Apology* around 392. It was followed by Polycrates' attack upon Socrates. Somewhat later Plato wrote a dialogue on τὸ δίκαιον which largely corresponded to the present Book I of the *Republic*.

---

286. The 'three or four minae' in § 3 are intended as a trivial sum, and so this is perhaps an understatement of the 'five minae' in *Ap.* 20b9 where the idea is that Callias is prepared to spend a lot of money (cf. 20a5). Cf. also H. Gomperz 1905: 170 f.

# THE REPORTED DIALOGUES AND *GORGIAS*, *MENEXENUS* AND *THEAETETUS*

## General arguments for establishing a hypothetical order

If the inferences made in the preceding chapter are correct, all of the reported dialogues received the shape in which they have been preserved to us after Plato's first voyage abroad, i.e. after 388 BCE. The *Gorgias* originally belonged to this category, as was argued above (p. 234); so apparently did *Theaetetus*. Moreover, the speech of the *Menexenus* belongs to the same chronological context.

It would be convenient here to begin with those two works which can be given an approximate absolute date, the *Menexenus* and the *Symposium*.

The authenticity of *Menexenus* has sometimes been doubted merely because the absurdities of the speech and its setting have not been thought explicable on a hypothesis of Platonic origin.[287] It is easier, however, to argue that the speech is in fact Platonic, and this view will be taken for granted here. On the other hand, the possibility that the dramatic frame dialogue between Socrates and Menexenus is a secondary addition made in the Academy should be taken into account.

The funeral speech itself is obviously dateable to soon after the peace of Antalcidas which was concluded in the spring of 386 BCE (*Mx.* 245e–246a). As has been often repeated, the speech would have been pointless (since it is not merely a piece of rhetorical exercise artificially placed in a certain historical setting) if it had been written much later.[288]

---

287. Skeptics in this century include Beare 1913, Momigliano 1930, Bluck 1949 (193 n. 64) and Tigerstedt 1965: 537 f.; further references in Pohlenz 1913: 256–258, Huby 1957: 104–108, Guthrie IV 312–323. The fact that Aristotle (*Rhet.* I 9.1367b8–9, III 14.1415b30–31) refers to a passage in the frame dialogue (235d) as 'Socrates in the Epitaphios' indicates that Aristotle at least considered the *Menexenus* an authentic Academic text (for Aristotle's manner of quoting Plato, cf. Schwarz 1900: 125 n.). The factual correspondence between *Mx.* 240a–e and *Lg.* III 698c–e to which Pohlenz 1913: 278 ff. refers, proves nothing. It is more natural, however, to argue that the peculiarities even of the speech itself (disregarding the frame) are indeed Platonic.

288. This is the common opinion among modern scholars (*see* in particular Pohlenz 1913: 290–292, 305). Occasional dissidents (e.g. Stefanini II 125 n. 1) have not found much support, nor has Ritter who suggested (1910b: 201) that the peace negotiations of 390 BCE are the real

[117]     Plato's exact intentions with regard to the speech can only be the subject of guesswork. It is practically certain, however, that taken in isolation, the speech is at the same time a political pamphlet and a rhetorical pastiche: it includes ironic criticism of Athenian political machinery and propaganda and of the emptiness and even dangerousness of public oratory.[289] The contents can be fairly easily interpreted to correspond to Plato's attitude to Athenian democracy and rhetoric as expressed in the *Gorgias*.

For my part I believe that the speech was originally written for delivery, without a frame dialogue, to a selected audience. In this respect it would be a counterpart to the *Apology*. Possibly, however, Plato wrote it in his own name (as he perhaps did in the case of the 'Proto-*Republic*'). The addition of the frame dialogue and its function will be discussed below (p. 327).

The *Symposium* or at least the main part of it can with reasonable confidence be dated to c. 384 BCE or somewhat later. This date had already been largely accepted in the 19th century on account of the anachronistic reference in Aristophanes' speech (193a) to the διοικισμός of the Arcadians in 385 BCE (Xen. *Hell.* 5.2.1 ff.); and in spite of the doubts expressed in various quarters, this view has been reinforced by several additional arguments, last ventilated in some detail by Dover (1965).[290] Apart from the fact that the playful anachronism was very probably written shortly after the event, we may note here the following points: in Phaedrus' speech (178e–179a) the reference to a city or an army of lovers and their beloved is likely to be earlier than 378 BCE;[291] in the speech of Pausanias (182b) the implication is that Ionia is dominated by Persia, which probably reflects the feelings among conservatives in Athens soon after the peace of Antalcidas (cf. Isocr. *Paneg.* 176); Diotima is almost certainly a transformation of Aspasia known

[118]     from Socratic legends (p. 283), and this fiction points then to a not very early nor very late date, and the name may also include a reference to Plato's recent friendship with Dion (above p. 175);[292] and the explanation of Socrates' relations with Alcibiades indicate a date later than Polycrates' pamphlet (p. 179) but before Antisthenes fr. 33 Caizzi which seems to develop one of the points of the

---

*terminus post quem*. It should be noted that the ironical tone of *Mx.* 246a1–2 is hardly thinkable before 387 BCE.

289. For a conspectus of the very multifarious earlier discussion of Plato's intentions, *see* Loewenclau 1961, cf. Guthrie IV 321–323; also Thurow 1968, Loraux 1974, Bloedow 1975, Henderson 1975; in recent times only very few scholars (most expressively Stern 1974) have tried to minimize the irony of the speech, although with little success. My own view approximates to that of Thurow.

290. Dover also provides some references to the earlier discussion; add Morrison 1964: 44–46 (preferring an early date), Rosen 1968 (siding with Dover). For Moore's late dating of *Symposium* (1973), *see* below p. 322.

291. But Xenophon, Symp. 8.32–33 applies this to the Theban ἱερὸς λόχος which probably existed at that date (Dover 1965: 11–15; somewhat differently, but implying a similar chronology, Tigerstedt 1965: 164 ff.). Those who see in *Smp.* 178e a hidden reference to the battle of Leuktra, 371 BCE (e.g. Ryle 1966: 38), have not produced convincing arguments.

292. Suggested by Th. Gomperz II 319 and others; for *Phaedrus*, cf. below p. 319.

legend (above p. 206 n. 149),[293] and Antisthenes is not likely to have been active as a writer later than the 370s. As for the much-discussed interrelations of Plato's and Xenophon's Symposia, I have argued elsewhere (1978) that Plato made some use of an earlier, mid-380s, version of Xenophon's dialogue, but that in the 370s Xenophon added his Chapter 8 where he refers to Plato.[294]

How, then, should Plato's two great dialogues on rhetors and sophists, *Gorgias* and *Protagoras*, be placed in relation to these two 'fixed' points? And what general clues are there for the order of the remaining reported dialogues?

I shall tentatively argue for the order *Gorgias* (early version)—*Menexenus* (speech)—*Protagoras*—*Symposium*—*Republic* I (new version) combined with *Republic* II—*Phaedo*—*Euthydemus*—*Lysis*—*Charmides*—*Theaetetus* (early version)—*Parmenides*—the completed *Republic*.

This order would correspond to a shift in Plato's interests from (Athenian) politics and political ethics to education and philosophical teaching and training. The funeral speech of *Menexenus* would be Plato's final attempt (before the *Laws*) at a δημηγορία (*Grg.* 519d) however limited his audience; indeed it would be his funeral speech to Athenian politics. Like the *Symposium*, the *Protagoras* would inaugurate teaching in the Academy (p. 277 f.). Also, *Gorgias* would find its 'natural' place soon after Plato's return from Sicily in 388.[295]

Moreover, this order would reveal certain trends in the development of the choice of persons and settings for the dialogues, which turn out to be quite interesting on closer inspection.

Starting from the hypothesis sketched above (p. 258) that the setting of *Republic* I reflects a traditional Socratic motif, the following changes are worth noting in *Gorgias* and the reported dialogues:

— *Republic* I, report by Socrates: (a) Socrates and a younger friend are invited 'post festum' to the house of [Callias→] Cephalus.—(b) Change of scene: in the

---

293. On the other hand, as Coulter has argued (1963), Antisthenes' 'Herakles' may have influenced the Alcibiades episode in *Symposium*. Other supposed interrelations with the writings of Antisthenes (cf. Rick 1931: 223–228) are irrelevant to chronology.

294. It is reasonable to assume that Xenophon is dependent on various early Socratic sources such as Aeschines 'Callias' (cf. Allmann 1972) and Antisthenes, and perhaps Eupolis' 'Autolycus.'

295. This has very often been argued, though the indications are not particularly obvious. The alleged 'Pythagorean' ideas include nothing that Plato could not have picked up in Athens before the voyage to the West, notably the religious trend (Dodds 1959: 18–30 but cf. Shorey 1903: 40 f.), doctrines of a cosmic order and its relation to the human soul (Pohlenz 1913: 152–157, Groag 1915: 123–127), and the importance of mathematics (Geffcken II A 66 n. 16–17); yet of course his visit to the West may have 'activated' these aspects, though cf. above p. 177. The choice of the Sicilian orator Gorgias as the first interlocutor of Socrates would be another slight indication. The attitude of the dialogue to tyrants and hedonism may reflect recent impressions. Epicharmus (505e) and Mithaecus (518b) are Sicilians. According to the scholiast (ad 450b) χειρούργημα and κύρωσις are Sicilian terms. Cf. further Ritter 1910b: 84 n. 1 (95 f., 105 n. 1, 1922: 213 f., slightly skeptical) and Guthrie IV 284 f. Most of these arguments have been seriously questioned by Morrison 1958: 200–215; cf. Raven 1965: 54 ff., 86 f., Kapp 1968: 79 ff., 98 ff.

[119] house they meet several prominent persons.—(c) Socrates converses or debates successively with the host, his son, and Thrasymachus.

— *Gorgias* [report by Socrates dropped): (a) Socrates and a younger friend are invited 'post festum' to the house of [Callias →] Callicles.—(b) [Change of scene, meeting of other persons dropped, cf. above p. 234.]—(c) Socrates debates successively with Gorgias, one of the pupils of Gorgias, and his host.

— *Protagoras* (without frame dialogue), report by Socrates: (a) Socrates and a younger friend decide to approach Protagoras ['post festum'] in the house of Callias.—(b) Change of scene: in the house they meet several prominent persons, listed and described at length.—(c) Socrates debates with Protagoras, and the others including his host form a background which is activated from time to time.

— *Symposium* (without frame dialogue), report by a younger friend of Socrates: (a) Socrates and a younger friend are (successively) invited 'post festum' to the house of [Callias →] Agathon.—(b) Change of scene: in the house they meet several prominent persons, some of whom receive a preliminary characterization; the flute girl is dismissed.—(c) Some of the guests are presented successively and become characterized through their speeches; Socrates debates with his host, relates a discussion with Diotima, and becomes the object of a speech by Alcibiades; at the end he debates with a pair of interlocutors, Aristophanes and Agathon [note this symbolic δυάς!], before he returns to Lyceum.

(— *Republic* II: the plan of *Republic* I is altered so as to make Socrates debate with a pair of interlocutors, the two brothers of Plato.)

— *Phaedo*, frame dialogue depicting situation, report by a younger friend of Socrates: (a) The friends approach Socrates in the prison, 'invited' by the guard.—(b) Change of scene: in the room they meet Socrates; Xanthippa and the boys are dismissed.—(c) Socrates debates with a pair of interlocutors, Simmias and Cebes; the others form a background which is activated only at the beginning and the end; comments in frame dialogue at central points.

— *Euthydemus*, frame dialogue depicting situation and discussing theme of the main dialogue, Socrates 'inviting' Criton to attend teaching of the erists; report by Socrates: (a)—(b) Socrates about to leave Lyceum, prevented by his δαιμόνιον; several persons appear; Socrates joined by a younger friend.—(c) Complicated patterns of elenchus formed by Socrates, the pair of erists, Euthydemus and Dionysodorus, and their two victims, Clinias and Ctesippus; comments in frame dialogue at central points, extension of this dialogue at the end.

[120] — *Lysis*, report by Socrates: (a) Socrates on his way from the Academia 'extra muros' to Lyceum falls in with several persons, among them a younger friend (Hippothales) who invites him to a new palaestra.—(b) Change of scene: in the palaestra they meet ['post festum'] Lysis and Menexenus.—(c) Socrates debates with a pair of interlocutors, Lysis and Menexenus; the others form a passive background; at the end the boys are taken away 'as by daimons.'

— *Charmides*, report by Socrates: (a) Socrates, returning from the war, enters the palaestra of Taureas.—(b) Here he meets a younger friend (Chairephon) and several others, including a prominent person (Critias); later Charmides enters.—(c) Socrates debates with a pair of interlocutors, Critias and Charmides.

— *Theaetetus* (without frame dialogue) [report by Socrates dropped]: [(a) Description of Socrates entering a palaestra dropped?]—(b) Socrates meets Theodoros and later Theaitetos, and a 'younger Socrates' (cf. p. 302).—(c) Socrates debates with a pair of interlocutors, Theodoros and Theaitetos.

— *Parmenides*, report by Cephalus of Clazomenai: (a) Cephalus meets Plato's brothers and is invited to the house of Antiphon.—(b) Change of scene: report by Antiphon from Pythodorus of meeting between Parmenides, Zenon and Socrates and several others in the house of Pythodorus 'extra muros.'—(c) Socrates debates with the two Elean sophists, Zenon and Parmenides; Socrates (who is a young man) questioned by Parmenides; young Aristoteles the elenchus partner of Parmenides in the latter part of the dialogue.

Apparently there are two basic patterns: Socrates in the house of Callias, and Socrates in Lyceum. Varieties of the former are represented by the *Republic* 1, *Gorgias, Protagoras, Symposium, Phaedo* and *Parmenides*, and varieties of the latter by *Euthydemus, Lysis, Charmides* and *Theaetetus*. The Lyceum pattern may at first sight appear to be the simpler and more original one; and perhaps we expect Socrates to be more 'at home' in a gymnasium than in a wealthy man's house. However, several points suggest that the Callias pattern is in fact the earlier of the two at least in Plato's literary work. First, it seems that Plato adopted this pattern from Socratic traditions at an early date (cf. p. 258 and *Symposium*, below), whereas the Lyceum pattern has no parallels at all in the extant Socratic literature outside Plato.[296] Note also the fact that the discussions to which Socrates refers in the *Apology* (20a–c, 21b–22e, 23c) could hardly have taken place in gymnasia. Second, even the simplest of the gymnasium dialogues, *Charmides*, includes formal features which are more naturally explained as due to the influence of the Callias pattern, than as originally belonging to the Lyceum pattern: Socrates is welcomed, invited, and brought to sit with Critias as with the host of the place (153c); Critias and Charmides in fact represent very 'prominent persons' whom we should rather expect to meet at a party in the house of 'Callias'; and the encomium of Charmides at 157d–158b (however playful or ironical) belongs to such a party rather than to a palaestra. Third, Plato's chosing the gymnasium milieu for some dialogues fits in with the discussion of Socratic erotics and philosophical education which is reflected in the *Symposium* (where at the end Socrates returns to Lyceum) and in later writings but which is not traceable in demonstrably earlier works. Fourth, with the order adopted above, we can see that the series of successive interlocutors of Socrates in the earlier dialogues is later substituted by pairs of opponents or discussion partners: such pairs appear in *Symposium* (at the end only), *Republic* II and *Phaedo*, and they occur in all of the gymnasium dialogues. This is most probably a secondary device.[297]

---

296. The reconstructable settings of Aeschines' dialogues rather correspond to the Callias pattern as does Xenophon's 'Symposium'; the fragments of Antisthenes and the other Socratics are not helpful. Xenophon's 'Memorabilia' has only very peripheral references to the gymnasium milieu (such as III 12).

297. I have sometimes toyed with the idea that Socrates versus Two is like 'One' versus the 'Unlimited Dyad' (in some cases even the 'Great-and-Small') in the oral doctrine of Principles,

[121]  If we accept the above order provisionally, some further trends in the formal patterns are discernible. The narrator is Socrates except, secondarily and for specific reasons, in *Symposium, Phaedo* and *Parmenides*.[298] As regards the three sections of the setting, note the following trends:—(a): The young friend who accompanies Socrates remains a subordinate character in *Republic* I, *Gorgias, Protagoras* and *Symposium*; with the change of plan in the *Republic* he becomes one of two interlocutors of Socrates in *Republic* II; in *Phaedo* where the pattern is altered so as to make Socrates the object of the approach, the young friend, Phaedon, who is the narrator (as the young friend is the narrator in *Symposium* also), is given a further function at certain important points of the dialogue (88c–89b, 102ab, 117c); in *Euthydemus*, where the pattern has become twisted, the young friend (Clinias) joins Socrates after a while and becomes one of the chief disputants; in *Lysis, Charmides, Theaetetus* and *Parmenides* the 'young friend' theme seems to recede and is substituted by the theme of a 'young object of elenchus' (who in a curious way is also a 'Socrates rejuvenated' in the two least-mentioned dialogues, cf. p. 307). The theme of being invited 'post festum' or after a performance of some kind, in *Republic* I and *Gorgias*, is changed into 'uninvited intruders' in *Protagoras* and a combination of the two in *Symposium*;[299] reminiscences of the 'post festum' idea occur in *Phaedo* and *Euthydemus*; but *Lysis, Charmides* and *Parmenides* contain the invitation theme without 'post festum.' Why Plato chose to vary the name of the host in *Republic* I, *Gorgias* and *Symposium* is easy to imagine, and substituting in *Symposium* a 'Pseud-'Agathon for the ψευδόκαλλος of Callias is really a magnificent piece of manipulation; but it is not so clear why he decided to retain

[122]  Callias in *Protagoras:* was Callias' house the only place in Athens where all the prominent sophists of the old days could possibly meet? At any rate this 'anachronism' does not constitute a sufficient reason for placing *Protagoras* at the beginning of the sequence, of dialogues.—(b) and (c): The change of scene, which in *Republic* I probably represents a traditional pattern and which has been dropped in the present version of *Gorgias* (p. 234), has become extensively elaborated in various ways in *Protagoras* and *Symposium*. In *Protagoras* this elaboration is rather loose, in *Symposium*. it is carried out carefully and amounts to an emphasis on esotericism which is also underlined by various significant traits such as the dismissing of the flute girl.[300] In *Phaedo* the dramatic frame dialogue was originally

---

but this parallel is admittedly fanciful. Note, incidentally, the curious 'splitting' of Socrates into two characters in *Theaetetus*—the *Sophist*—*Politicus* (where 'Socrates the Younger' gradually emerges), in *Parmenides* (where 'Aristoteles' replaces the 'Young Socrates'), and in *Hippias Major* (below p. 374).

298. Also in *Gorgias*, I take it, the narrator was originally Socrates; and this was evidently the case in *Theaetetus* (143b).

299. Aristodemus is in fact an ἄκλητος though the receives an invitation from Socrates (174ab); the dialogue has another ἄκλητος too, Alcibiades. Cf. the one, probably traditional, uninvited guest in Xenophon's 'Symposium,' 1.11–16.

300. Note also Socrates in meditation before (175ab) and after (220a–d) the central story of the 'mystery of Love'; and the 'mutilation' of the 'herm' of Socrates (215ab) and the profanation of the mysteries by Alcibiades.

part of the composition (cf. below p. 288), and it contributes to a skillfully built change of scene, a concentration upon Socrates, and an esotericism to which the dismissal of Xanthippa furnishes a final touch. The structure of the opening of *Euthydemus* can be analyzed as a further development of these trends: the frame dialogue with its comments on the main dialogue has become an extensive piece of counterpoint (used not only in the center, as in *Phaedo*, but also at the end), containing also several changes of scene; and the introduction of the δαιμόνιον is (perhaps) a reminiscence of the esotericism of *Symposium* and *Phaedo* though it probably at the same time alludes to the discussion of Socrates the teacher (cf. below p. 353 ff.). The structure is, however, complicated and twisted in various ways. Examining *Lysis, Charmides* and *Theaetetus* then, it is in fact possible to regard the very much more simple structure of these works as due to secondary concentration. The themes are far more limited than in the series of dialogues beginning with *Gorgias* and ending with *Euthydemus*, and thus *Lysis, Charmides* and also *Theaetetus* could have been planned as rather short dialogues without a frame (though ὦ ἑταῖρε *Chrm.* 154b, etc., cf. 155d, imply the fiction of a frame dialogue), somewhat in the manner of *Republic* I. The explicit change of scene, still manifest in *Lysis* (206e) is dropped in *Charmides*. In the opening of *Lysis* the emphatically repeated 'from the Academy to the Lyceum' is certainly symbolic in some way or other.[301] In *Charmides*, however, Socrates' returning from the war in Thracia to the happy, sequestered world of an Athenian palaestra sounds like a variation on the theme of esotericism. Unfortunately we do not know why Plato here chose the palaestra of Taureas instead of Socrates' usual dwelling place, Lyceum.[302] And as was suggested above, Socrates' meeting in the gymnasium with a younger friend who becomes, or is replaced by, one of his chief interlocutors, also indicates a trend continued from *Euthydemus* to *Lysis* and *Charmides* and to *Theaetetus* and *Parmenides*. In *Parmenides* the structure is quite obviously due to a secondary development of earlier trends: there are two changes of scene, yet a very brief and concentrated description of the situation, amounting to young Socrates' meeting the prominent sophists in a wealthy man's house 'extra muros.' Though Socrates is still confronted with a pair of disputants, he has in fact rather taken over the role of *Charmides, Lysis* and *Theaetetus*, and is succeeded by the enigmatic 'Aristoteles' (cf. p. 306). The choice of persons at the opening also alludes to *Republic* I–II.[303]

Furthermore, this order is reflected in some easily explicable changes in Plato's dialogue technique. Plato operated from the outset with two different genres, speeches such as the *Apology* and the speech of *Menexenus*, and dialogues

---

301. Perhaps Plato means that he is returning to a Socratic theme from his Academic preoccupations. To Zürcher (1954: 33) 'Lyceum' of course symbolizes the 'Peripatos.' For the idea of 'extra muros,' cf. p. 324.

302. Cf. *Smp.* 223d, *Euthd.* 272a, 303b, *Euthphr.* 2a, etc.

303. For Cephalus of Clazomenai, who has succeeded the Syracusan Cephalus, cf. below p. 307. Glaucon and Adimantus are being 'replaced,' through the intermediaryship of their stepbrother Antiphon, by the Elean pair of sophists.

[123] reported by Socrates, such as *Republic* I. He probably had predecessors among the Socratics.[304] In *Republic* I the dialogue (B and A, cf. above p. 201) is fairly realistic, and the brief speeches (E) are not particularly stylized (cf. Thesleff 1967, above 83 ff.). In *Gorgias* the rhetorical pathos extends to Socrates himself and the dialogue tends, especially later, to approximate to a lecturer's monologue (D), although this is the result of emotional force rather than habit (as in the later works). We can see from *Menexenus* that at this period Plato was deeply concerned with rhetoric; for the *Phaedrus*, cf. below p. 318. The setting of *Gorgias*, which I assume was dropped later together with the report (p. 234), is likely to have been a brief one, corresponding to that of *Republic* I: an extensive setting like that of *Protagoras* or *Symposium* is not so easily omitted. On the other hand, the eschatological myth of *Gorgias* is a stylistic anticipation of the great myth of *Protagoras*.[305]—I presume that soon after 386 and the *Menexenus* Plato established himself as a teacher at the Academy. At this point, or when he had definitely settled down there (cf. above p. 179 and n. 66), he also became more interested in the artistic elaboration of his dialogues. The *Protagoras*, and in particular the very carefully composed *Symposium*, contain several magnificent pastiches and a good deal of playfulness, and here the principle of pedimental structure (p. 210) is carried through more explicitly and consistently than in *Republic* I and *Gorgias* (cf. Thesleff 1967). I assume that both received their frame dialogues later (p. 326). The fitting into the dialogue of extensive characteristic speeches by opponents of Socrates occurs again in *Republic* II where the brothers of Plato seem to take over parts of the roles of Thrasymachus and Callicles; and speeches are used in the *Phaedo* in a rather similar manner. From *Republic* II and *Phaedo* onwards, however, Plato operates with less stylistic variation (for details see again Thesleff 1967) though with considerable stylistic skill. For the *Republic*, see below p. 285. *Phaedo* reveals throughout a grave and restrained tone very appropriate to the theme; this dialogue is no doubt a highly refined piece of literary craftsmanship. Curiously enough, the *Euthydemus*, however different, is in several respects a

[124] counterpart of *Phaedo*. Both have a dramatic frame dialogue which is interwoven with the main dialogue and underlines its central point, and the frame dialogues of *Euthydemus* has been expanded into a background discussion. I find it reasonable to assume that these frame dialogues were written as part of the composition. The serious tone of *Phaedo* is replaced in *Euthydemus* by a gay and colloquial brilliance which is by no means due to carelessness but answers to the theme as appropriately as the opposite tendency does in *Phaedo*: the *Euthydemus* functions as a satyr play in relation to *Phaedo* (cf. *Menexenus* in relation to *Gorgias*). In *Euthydemus*, however, Plato no longer indulges in extensive speeches. The same tendency appears in *Lysis* and *Charmides*. As was argued above, the simple structure of these dialogues does not indicate a comparatively early date, and the same seems to apply to the dialogue structure and to style in a restricted sense. Both

---

304. The part played by Antisthenes here is obscure to us, but may have been important; cf. above p. 181.

305. *Grg.* 523a ff.; *Prt.* 320c ff. Cf. below p. 282.

dialogues contain reminiscences of the principle of 'central culmination.'[306] The lack of a frame dialogue is probably due to the restricted theme in the first place (above, p. 267). It may well be that Plato did not intend them for 'publication' in the same sense as the major dialogues. On the other hand, there is an additional indication of their relative lateness in the fact that *Theaetetus* as well as various dubia and spuria such as *Laches*, *Amatores* and *Eryxias* follow their model (cf below p. 357 ff.). *Theaetetus* has obviously been expanded from a pattern considerably reminiscent of *Charmides*. Note in particular the motif of Socrates debating in a gymnasium with a well-known sophist and his protégé (who turns out to be 'related' to Socrates, physically and mentally, just as *Charmides* is in fact a relative of Plato), as well as the common theme of ἐπιστήμη. For the change of *Theaetetus* into a dramatic dialogue, and the addition of the opening frame dialogue, cf. below p. 328. However, in many respects the dialogue technique of *Theaetetus* points forward to the late period (cf. p. 301). And the same applies to some extent to *Parmenides*, which is actually composed of two different parts: the three-step report of the first part as a further development of a device adopted in the present version of *Symposium* (p. 326), and the simple dramatic pattern of the latter part probably reflects dialectical exercises habitually carried out at the Academy (p. 306).

## Further arguments; introductory notes on the method

Having established in the preceding chapter, mainly from a consideration of formal facts, a hypothetical order for the reported dialogues, I shall attempt to test it by discussing (or referring to) various additional arguments which have been used or can be used for the dating. The following chapters will, I believe, provide some cumulative support for the order accepted here.

In the present and following chapters, the arguments will be normally grouped in three classes: 'General Considerations' (G.C.), 'External Criteria' (E.C., cf. above p. 167), and 'Internal Criteria' (I.C). This last group consists of arguments for the relative order of two dialogues extracted from a confrontation of the dialogues; most of these arguments are in fact concerned with the philosophical contents (cf. above, p. 186). A confrontation of every dialogue in the Corpus with every other one would of course be a profitless waste of time. Here I shall attempt to restrict the confrontation to the most important or vexed cases of relationship between somehow comparable dialogues. To find the relevant confrontations, the reader is advised to consult the Index.

Though I may well have missed essential arguments or important relations, I have not intentionally omitted anything that would speak explicitly against the hypothetical order accepted here. Hence I find it somewhat significant that on the whole the test results are positive, or *non liquet*. On some points, obviously,

---

306. *Ly.* 210e–212a, *Chrm.* 171d–173d; cf. Thesleff 1967 above, 106 f. Stylistically these dialogues are far from unsophisticated.

[125] the chronology proposed is less well supported by these additional arguments than on other points, but as far as I can see they never patently conflict with the basic theory. Or is this simply because 'interpretation can prove anything'?

## Gorgias

G.C. For the proposed date soon after the first voyage to Sicily, cf. above p. 267. This would conform with the generally accepted view that *Gorgias* is 'not very early.' It is true that this view relies partly on the assumption, which will be disputed here, that some of the minor dialogues are earlier. But it is nevertheless clear that *Gorgias* is not a beginner's work. Plato may indeed have practiced dialogue writing in various experimental pieces besides *Republic* I, though they cannot be traced with any degree of certainty. I repeat that I find it absolutely unlikely that Plato would have later authorized early specimens of Socratic dialogue which he found immature (p. 230). *Gorgias* is a very extensive and somewhat heterogeneous dialogue, and it may well include portions conceived, or even written, in the 390s, before the Sicilian voyage.[307] And the change from reported to dramatic form (below, p. 234) bestowed on the text a pointedly dramatic character, which makes it appear more 'advanced' in style than perhaps the original text was.

On the other hand, *Gorgias* is commonly considered 'earlier than the middle period.' I am not sure that the glimpses in *Gorgias* of, notably, the theory of Forms, the doctrine of Principles, the dihaeretic method, or mathematical ideas, can be proved to represent early or preliminary stages, though I find it rather probable that they do so.[308] But at least it is fairly obvious that the doctrine of Soul, such as it appears in *Grg.* 493a–d and the final myth, does not yet bear the implications given to it in *Meno, Phaedo, Phaedrus, Republic* IV (and X) and *Symposium.*

[126] E.C. There is some sound evidence that certain passages in *Gorgias* answer or otherwise reflect the pamphlet of Polycrates and not vice versa.[309] Since the pamphlet was probably published about 392 BCE (above p. 178), and echoes of it in this and other Platonic works are rather distant, a date c. 387 BCE again seems

---

307. The report, in 506c–507c, of a fictitious piece of elenchus without inserenda, may in fact represent an early type of dialogue text. Cf. above p. 204.

308. These points have been discussed at length. For the theory of Forms, *see* now Ilting 1965: 388–390, Guthrie IV 307 f.; for the Principles, *see* Gaiser 1963: 221 f., Krämer 1964a: 87; for the dihaeretic method, *see* Moravcsik 1973: 158–167.

309. *See* the discussion by Markowski 1910: 58–66, followed up by Geffcken 1930, Humbert 1931: 67 ff. and others; cf. Treves 1952: 742–1744, Chroust 1955, 1957 (especially 69, 98, 201). The reverse order has been occasionally argued, mostly on flimsy grounds (Natorp 1900b: 399 ff., Verdam 1917: 189 ff.; also Pohlenz 1913: 63 ff.); the points made by Wilamowitz (I 260, II 95 ff.) were refuted by Geffcken (cf. II 75–77, A 63–65). Dodds (1959: 28 f.) and Bluck (1961: 115–120) cautiously avoid adopting a definite position. Contrary to what is sometimes believed, there is some irony in the treatment of Socrates' relations with Alcibiades in the *Gorgias* (esp. 482a, cf. 481d, 519a); and since irony occurs in most passages that can be taken as directed against Polycrates (e.g. the quotation of Pindar 484b, 488b, explained by Geffcken), it seems that Plato did not take a very serious view of Polycrates at all (though e.g. Humbert and Chroust think so); cf. also *Protagoras*, below p. 278.

possible for *Gorgias*. The vehemence and ethical pathos of the dialogue are, then, occasioned principally by circumstances other than the attack of Polycrates.— The points of contact that *Gorgias* has with Isocrates' 'Against the Sophists' (XIII, c. 390 BCE) have been variously interpreted.[310] For my part I am convinced that the speech of Isocrates is the earlier of the two, bearing in mind the following facts: Isocrates states at § 17 that a good rhetor needs a ψυχὴ ἀνδρικὴ καὶ δοξαστική (which agrees with his doctrine of δόξα, e.g. 8); this is ironically echoed by Plato's Socrates who at 463a (cf. 464c) speaks of a rhetor's ψυχὴ στοχαστικὴ καὶ ἀνδρεία which amounts to κολακεία. At 5–6 Isocrates develops at length the 'ridiculous' fact that sophists who profess to teach virtue (cf. 1, 3–4) do not trust their pupils, but demand that the fees due to them be deposited with a third party; he then proceeds to criticize them for looking out for contradictions (ἐναντιώσεις) in words but not in facts, and for various other things, and from this (9) goes on to discuss from another angle the bad teaching of rhetors who are concerned with πολιτικοὶ λόγοι. Plato at 519cd equates the πολιτικοί (in the sense of 'politicians') with sophists because both are accused or prosecuted by their pupils whose situation they profess to improve; the phrasing is reminiscent of Isocrates (cf. also παιδεύειν εἰς ἀρετήν 519e, συνθέμενοι αὐτῷ μισθόν 520c); there is the specific point of δημηγορεῖν versus ἀποκρίνεσθαι (519d, cf. ἐναντιώσεις in Isocrates), and the emphatic statement at 520a ταὐτόν, ὦ μακάρι', ἐστι σοφιστὴς καὶ ῥήτωρ suggests that Plato has in mind Isocrates' differentiation of the two in this speech. Certain other details in *Gorgias* also suggest allusions to Isocrates C. Soph.[311] The relation of *Gorgias* to other works of Isocrates has less or no relevance to chronology.[312]—As to the supposed reflection in *Gorgias* of the recent founding of the Academy,[313] I find it rather more significant that the dialogue is hardly concerned at all with problems of teaching or education. This would indicate a date preceding initiation of regular teaching at the Academy.—For the possible

---

310. For the approximate date of this speech, see above p. 180, 363. The most recent comprehensive discussion of its relation to the *Gorgias* is Ries 1959: 21–35 who argues that *Gorgias* is earlier; others who have taken this view include Pohlenz 1913: 200 ff., Wilamowitz II 108–112 and Rick 1931: 44 ff. The reverse order has been argued by Shorey 1903: 77 n. 596 (and 1933: 503, with rate conviction), Raeder 123 f., Bluck 1949: 76 and a few others. Dodds 1959: 27–30 again avoids making up his mind.

311. Cf. Isocrates criticizing (8, 19–20) the practical uselessness of the studies of sophists (probably including the Socratics) with Callicles' attack in *Gorgias* 485e–486d: Isocrates' ψυχῆς ἐπιμέλεια seems to be echoed in 485e. But the reference to δόξα as opposed to ἐπιστήμη in Isocrates § 8, which is sometimes adduced for dating *Gorgias* (cf. Raeder 124 n. 3), is probably irrelevant: this Eleatic and Socratic terminology (cf. above p. 363), though it is not explicitly employed in *Gorgias*, is sufficiently clearly implied in 454de where πίστις (cf. πείθειν) is substituted for δόξα.

312. I think that the 'Encomium to Helen' (X, late 380s?) 7–8 and 'Panegyricus' (IV, 380 BCE) 11–12 may well refer to *Gorgias* in particular (for the former, cf. Ries 1959: 47 ff., Ryle 1966: 217, with a later dating); but this is quite conjectural. For even more uncertain references to *Gorgias* in various later Isocratean writings, see Raeder 124 f., Münscher 1916: 2211, Ries 82–85, Ryle ibid., Guthrie IV 308–311 (on p. 310 Isocr. *Antid.* is dated too early).

313. No very obvious signs have been found; cf. e.g. Hoffmann 1922: 1057, Rick 1931: 36 ff., Dodds 1959: 24 n. 3.

[127] allusion to Callistratus, cf. above p. 257. Various attempts to relate *Gorgias* to other contemporary persons or events have been wholly unsuccessful.[314]

I.C. For the order *Apology—Gorgias*, see p. 262. For *Republic* I—*Gorgias*, see p. 257.

## Menexenus

G.C. and E.C. For the date of the speech (without the frame dialogue) c. 386 BCE, *see* above p. 265. I can see no other clues for dating it than the reference to the peace of Antalcidas as a recent event.[315] Thus, the speech is connected with the discussion of rhetoric and politics in *Gorgias*.[316] The *Menexenus* may be said to
[128] conclude Plato's involvement in Athenian politics, and inaugurate a period of literary play and experiment.—For the addition of the frame, *see* below p. 328. Cf. *Phaedrus*, below p. 317.

## Protagoras

G.C. A very early date has often been accepted, mainly because of the apparent absence of traces of Plato's mature philosophy; Wilamowitz and some others have gone as far as to date *Protagoras* before 399 BCE.[317] The elusiveness of this kind of reasoning was discussed above (p. 171). In fact several scholars, among whom Taylor is probably the most influential, have argued to the contrary that the dialogue is a fairly advanced specimen of Plato's thought and art both as

---

314. For Aeschines, *see* the critical comments of Dodds 1959: 27 ff.; for Antisthenes, cf. the loose speculations of Rick 1931: 8–22; for the story about the Corinthian farmer who turned to philosophy after reading the *Gorgias*, cf. Riginos 1976: 185; for the probable fact that Gorgias was still living when the dialogue was written (cf. p. 174), cf. Wilamowitz I 212 f., Riginos 1976: 93 f.; for Lysias, cf. Verdam 1917: 191; for Xenophon, cf. Maier 1913: 53 f.

315. The possible allusions to, or in, Aeschines, Antisthenes and Xenophon concern the frame dialogue; cf. p. 327 f. It is irrelevant to chronology whether the model of the pastiche is Thucydides (cf. Pohlenz 1913: 244 ff.), Lysias (cf. Méridier Introduction 1931: 80 f., Lattanzi 1953), or some other author (cf. Taylor 44). Gorgias (sometimes suggested, cf. Raeder 127) is clearly out of the question as Plato would not have missed the chance of parodying the very typical stylistic mannerisms in Gorgias' 'Epitaphios' (DK 82 B 5). It has also been argued that Isocrates' 'Panegyricus' (IV, 380 BCE) includes references to the *Menexenus* (Pohlenz 1913: 306 ff., Ries 1959: 64 ff.), but this seems very debatable.

316. On regarding *Menexenus* as a 'satyr play' or an appendix to *Gorgias*, cf. Méridier Introduction 1931: 77, Geffcken II 82, Dodds 1959: 23 f.; cf. also Gauss II/1.101.

317. Wilamowitz (I 127, 151 f., II 431) regarded the dialogue as a superficial satire and a review of ideas adopted from others; and he also pointed out (I 140, cf. Pfleiderer 1896: 136 f.) that, as the examples of Michelangelo, Shakespeare and Goethe show, gifted young men may indeed be able to produce remarkable works of art. In recent times only Fischer 1969 has been inclined to follow Wilamowitz.

regards the contents and the literary form.³¹⁸ No doubt *Protagoras* is somewhat [128] heterogeneous.³¹⁹ The notorious 'criterion' of the theory of Forms is as difficult to apply as ever because Plato obviously eschews any kind of metaphysical approaches in the main part of the dialogue.³²⁰ But the 'digression' on the application of measuring 350c (351b)–358e, which may have been inserted later, seems to include at least some hints as to the oral doctrine of Principles;³²¹ and there has been considerable discussion of the implications for Plato's ethics of the 'hedonistic calculus' contained in this section.³²² Plato has made no point of dialectic in *Protagoras*, though several sections reveal a rather subtle play with logic.³²³ One [129] gets the impression, as the apparent interchange of the positions of Protagoras and Socrates also indicates (cf. 361a–c), that Plato has chosen to combat sophistry on its own ground.

This approach, as well as the interest Plato now takes in the traditional theme of the teachability of virtue, would suit a date soon after Plato had instituted some kind of teaching activities at the Academy, i.e. c. 385 BCE.³²⁴

The fact that the dialogue displays a considerable literary artistry in its setting, composition, characterization and stylistic register,³²⁵ may also seem to correspond to a situation when Plato has, so to speak, settled down. As I see it, he is unlikely to have had the time and leisure for such relaxed experimentation during the stormy years that preceded his first voyage abroad. Yet the composition

---

318. Taylor 235, following Grote and Burnet. For this point of view, cf. in general Shorey 1903: 3, Beate 1913, Boehme 1959, Raven 1965, Saupe 1967, Witte 1970. Many others (e.g. Lutoslawski 194 ff., 220, Pohlenz 1921: 7 f., Guthrie IV 214) consider the *Protagoras* as relatively advanced among the 'Socratic' dialogues.

319. The apparent anomalies and the widely divergent possibilities of interpreting the dialogue made Gigon 1946 declare it partly spurious. Admitting that it is heterogeneous will probably provide a sufficient basis for solving the problems.

320. Of the possible glimpses of the theory of Forms which are sometimes referred to (e.g. 330c–e, 349b, cf. Shorey 1903: 29 and n. 185, 31 n. 195, Taylor 257, Ilting 1965: 287 f., etc.), the playfully presented but very essential distinction between εἶναι and γίγνεσθαι in the central speech of Socrates is perhaps the most important one; cf. notably Gundert 1952: 82 ff., 90 ff. Cf. the following note.

321. For the digression, cf. Manuwald 1975, against A. Hermann 1972. For the Principles notably in 356d–357b, *see* Krämer 1959: 24, 490 ff., Gadamer 1968: 13 ff., Witte 1970. The εἶναι/γίγνεσθαι contrast (above, n. 320) can of course also be interpreted in this light.

322. The interpretations range from 'banal and early' (e.g. Pohlenz 1916: 244 ff., Friedländer II 282 n. 24, de Vogel 1973: 18 ff.) to 'advanced play' (e.g. Shorey 1903: 20 ff., von Arnim 1914: 14 ff., Raven 1965: 46 ff.) and to 'advanced and rather late' (e.g. Beare 1913, Taylor 1926, Rehork 1972, Gundert 1977: 161 ff.).

323. Those who point out logical fallacies in the dialogue (e.g. Lutoslawski 206, Raeder 109 f., and recently again Vlastos 1973: 221 ff.) usually overlook the peculiarly playful character of the work. Cf. Sprague 1962, Gagarin 1969 (especially 147 f., 154) and in general, for the 'underlying' dialectic, Ritter 1922b: 144 Nachtrag to 122.

324. It is not unimportant to note that the *Protagoras* is ultimately concerned with education in a social (and political) context; cf. Kapp 1968: 104 f. versus Pohlenz 1913: 110 ff., Dodds 1945: 17.

325. Cf. above p. 108 f., 268. The dialogue obviously has many features in common with comedy.

[129] of *Protagoras* is somewhat 'loose' and not at all as carefully accomplished as *Symposium*. Evidently Plato did not allow himself the time to polish it.

E.C. Placing the *Protagoras* after the pamphlet of Polycrates seems reasonable bearing in mind particularly the whimsical elaboration at 342a–e of the idea that sophists abound in Sparta, whereas Polycrates had asserted that there are none (Lib. § 134, cf. 159; above p. 179).[326] It is also natural to place it after the 'Callias' of Aeschines which was probably rather early.[327] Placing it after Isocrates' 'Against the Sophists' but before the 'Encomium of Helen' (X, late 380s?) also seems reasonable: *Prt.* 328bc (advance deposits of the fee in a temple) looks like a development of the point in Isocr. *C. Soph.* 5–6 (where the third party concerned is not necessarily to be trusted, cf. above p. 275); the question of the teachability
[130] of virtue which is touched upon and answered in the negative by Isocr. *C. Soph.* 21, is dealt with in a peculiarly fresh manner in *Protagoras*; and it is precisely this position of the Platonic Socrates which appears to be the target of Isocrates' remark in 'Helen' § 1 about philosophers who argue that all virtues are identical (ἀνδρία is mentioned first in the sequence) and can be acquired, not φύσει, but by a single ἐπιστήμη.[328]—Xenophon and Antisthenes are sometimes adduced but are not very helpful.[329]—Among the supposed anachronisms detected in *Protagoras*, I would attach some weight to the mention of peltasts as examples of skilful bravery at 350a; though the idea is earlier, it was Iphicrates who during the Corinthian war, in 393/2 BCE, introduced organized mercenary troops of peltasts, and there must have been much discussion of them in the subsequent years.[330]

I.C. The order *Republic I—Protagoras* appears to me quite reasonable, though it is difficult to discover positive clues other than the formal matters discussed

---

326. At 337d Hippias seems to refer to the same misquotation of Pindar as Callicles in the *Gorgias* (cf. above n. 309; this may, of course, be a sophistic commonplace, cf. Antiphon *Soph.* 87 B 44 A Col.2.10–30). For a further possible allusion to Polycrates, see Raubitschek 1955: 78 f. For Alcibiades in the frame dialogue, see below p. 327. It has often been thought that Plato could not possibly have presented Socrates as a sophist among sophists after Polycrates' attack, but then one probably overrates the importance Plato attached to the latter, and at any rate one misses the humour of the dialogue.

327. For a new reconstruction of this dialogue (which in fact has several thematic parallels with *Protagoras*) and the dating of it to about 392/1 BCE, see Allmann 1972. The setting of *Protagoras* has sometimes been placed in direct relation to Aeschines' 'Callias' and/or Xenophon's 'Symposium' (cf. e.g. Dittmar 1912: 210 ff., Maier 1913: 19 f.), but the pattern is clearly inherited (cf. above p. 268) and the lines of influence are probably very complex.

328. Cf. Howland 1937: 151 f., Bluck 1949: 34, 66 f., Ryle 1966: 269. The arguments of Wilamowitz II 108–112 for the order *Protagoras—C. Soph.* have convinced few scholars.

329. Cf. above n. 327. The relationship of the section on ἀνδρία in *Mem.* IV 6.10 f. to the corresponding sections in *Protagoras* and/or *Laches* is unclear; at any rate Plato is not the borrower (as is sometimes suggested, cf. Lutoslawski 207; but see Gomperz II 568, Ritter 1910b: 210).—For the alleged influence of Antisthenes on *Protagoras*, see Joël II 2.1901.732, Rick 1931: 130 ff.

330. Plato had probably seen the peltasts in action (cf. above p. 173).—Some other possible anachronisms and historical inconsistencies are listed by Geffcken II A 36 n. 16; at least they indicate a distance in time from the dramatic date of the dialogue (which is not later than 419 BCE but probably is much earlier, as Pericles is living, 319e, and his sons are present, 328d).

above. On flimsy grounds the opposite order is often taken for granted, also by those who separate the first book of the *Republic* from the rest.³³¹

The order *Gorgias—Protagoras* proposed here may seem much more difficult to accept. These two great dialogues are obviously related in various respects, and the great majority of students of Plato have adopted the view that *Gorgias* is the more advanced one of the two, and hence also the later one. It seems to me that this view is debatable and that there are other than the general considerations made above (p. 268 ff.) that point positively to the relative order *Gorgias—Protagoras*.

The impression that *Gorgias* is more 'advanced' is due partly to a preconceived view of Plato's development as an author and thinker, partly to the all-round series of themes in the *Gorgias*, and partly to the fact that *Gorgias* is more intense and penetrating owing both to its grasp of polemics and, probably, to the secondary change into dramatic dialogue form. If we acknowledge that seriousness and profundity are not necessarily, in Plato's case, a sign of greater maturity or a later date than is a somewhat careless, gay and superficial approach, combined with a certain restriction of theme, we should look elsewhere for criteria for the relative dating of these two dialogues.

Disregarding the 'hedonistic calculus' (below), a confrontation of various passages of a similar content would provide the following result:

In *Gorgias* 447d ff. as well as in *Protagoras* 311a ff. (316b ff.), 318a ff., the method of approach to the characterization of the profession of the sophist is somewhat indirect. In *Gorgias* it is not Socrates who addresses the (possibly genuinely Socratic) question τί(ς) ἐστιν; to the sophist, but Chairephon, asked by Socrates to do so. In *Protagoras* Socrates addresses the corresponding question first to Hippocrates in the preliminary discussion, and combines it from the beginning with a second question, viz. what will become of a pupil of the sophist; and only this latter question is later addressed to Protagoras.³³² Obviously Plato's concern in the *Gorgias* is with the nature and effect of professional public speaking in Athens, and not so much with the teaching of this profession (though this aspect occurs from time to time, cf. 447c2, 455cd, etc.). The whole of the first part of the dialogue with its definition of rhetoric as κολακεία amounts to proving that the rhetor lacks the ἐπιστήμη required for influencing public opinion constructively and imparting to the public δικαιοσύνη. At the end of the dialogue (521d), Socrates turns out to be the only true 'politician.' Plato seems to take it for granted that virtue can be imparted by a person who possesses the ἐπιστήμη required. This position is ostensibly the result of the discussion in *Protagoras* (and this is

---

331. One commonly used approach is to regard the general discussion of virtue in *Protagoras* as preceding the separate treatments in *Laches, Charmides, Euthyphro* and *Republic* I (cf. e.g. von Arnim 1914: 1–37, 97 ff., Ueberweg-Praechter 228 f.); but in my view Plato had specific reasons for starting from δικαιοσύνη. For other even less useful points, *see* von Arnim ibid., and Lutoslawski 284 f., Geffcken II 68 f.

332. The same question occurs in passing in a later context in *Gorgias*, 455cd. It has been suggested (Pohlenz 1913: 13 f.) that it reflects *Protagoras* 318a, but the reverse view seems equally possible to me.

[131] one of the reasons why it is sometimes thought that the *Gorgias* 'builds' upon the *Protagoras*), but here it has ironic overtones not always perceived. In fact on this point the *Gorgias* is somewhat closer to the so-called Socratic doctrine of 'virtue is knowledge' than is *Protagoras*; and *Meno* and other later dialogues show that Plato was not satisfied with it for very long. *Protagoras* is concerned with the teaching of the individual (παιδεία) and the imparting to him of virtue (ἀρετή). But the actual definition of the sophist *qua* professional teacher of virtue (cf. *Grg.* 519c), though the question is asked (311b, 312de), is passed over and replaced by Socrates' somewhat playful characterization of the sophist (313a–314b), followed later by the question in its renewed form and Protagoras' self-characterization (316c–317c), whereupon we are finally brought to face with the main question of whether virtue can be imparted at all, a question which is answered by a (as mentioned above, slightly ironic) variety of the thesis 'virtue is knowledge.' Apart from the possibility of finding a thematic advance in this respect in the *Protagoras*, this arrangement would seem to indicate that the simple definition pattern from which both dialogues (as well as *Republic* I) start, is more consistently maintained in *Gorgias* than in *Protagoras*. The fact that Chairephon is made to put the first question in the *Gorgias* (Socrates takes over at 448d) is of course a secondary trick, too. Explicit reasons for this may have been given in the lost background story; otherwise, also, the opening discussion of the *Gorgias* may have become somewhat abbreviated (cf. p. 234).

[132] The examples of doctors and artists given immediately after the opening question (*Grg.* 448bc, *Prt.* 311b–e) may also provide a clue to the relative order. The *Gorgias* obviously has Herodicus because he happens to be the brother of Gorgias, and this introduces with it another well-known pair of brothers, Aristophon and Polygnotus; the *Protagoras* ingeniously substitutes Hippocrates, the namesake of Socrates' interlocutor and, to represent the artists, adds not one but two equally famous names, Polyclitus and Phidias. It is easier to understand the series of examples in *Protagoras* as modeled on *Gorgias* than vice versa, especially since, as Socrates goes on to explain (312ab), a sophist is really not a technician at all from whom the pupil learns the teacher's profession: thus, the examples of doctor and artists are not really relevant in *Protagoras* (although the idea is ironically resumed at 318a–319a).

The fact that there is no mention of Gorgias among the sophists in the *Protagoras* is no more remarkable than the fact that Protagoras and the other sophists are not mentioned by name in the *Gorgias*.[333] *Gorgias* refers to sophists in two contexts: in the dihaeretic list of arts, 464b–465d, where sophists are grouped roughly together with rhetors (465c); and, with the same implications and with reference to the former passage (and probably to Isocrates, cf. above p. 275), in 519c–520e. I find it difficult to believe that Plato could have written the sweeping and condescending generalization of the latter passage soon after he had made

---

333. It is of course possible that Plato knew that Gorgias did not visit Athens until after the dramatic date of the *Protagoras* (above, n. 330).

the full-length and not so unsympathetic portrait of Protagoras.[334] It is interesting [132] that the *Gorgias* passage includes (250e2–4) a brief description of what the sophists try to do (and what Socrates in fact does, cf. 251d) in terms which have been thought to echo Protagoras' proud description of his own profession in *Protagoras* 318e f.;[335] but apart from the fact that the *Protagoras* passage can more naturally be regarded as a rhetorical expansion of a current commonplace, it should be noted that it is precisely this πολιτική τέχνη of which the teachability is doubted by Socrates in the next passage in *Protagoras*, whereas in *Gorgias* the problem of διδακτόν is not encountered at all.

The *Protagoras* refers explicitly to rhetors on only one occasion, and then in passing. This rather odd fact may require an explanation. The reference occurs in an ironic passage, 329a, where Socrates says he is sure that Protagoras, unlike rhetors who tend to give endless answers, will be able to answer briefly if he wishes. This problem of μακρολογία versus βραχυλογία is faced in both dialogues in various connections,[336] probably as a well-known Socratic topic. I do not think either approach should be seen as being developed out of the other, [133] although the ῥήτορες of *Protagoras* 329ab may contain a reminiscence of the *Gorgias*. More important is the absence from *Protagoras* of even the slightest reference to the main theme of *Gorgias*, the dangers of public oratory. After all, the misuse of rhetoric must have been an intense reality to Plato from his earliest years as a philosopher (it is implicitly present in *Republic* I in the person of Thrasymachus), and after *Gorgias* and *Menexenus* he returns to it in the *Republic, Phaedrus* and the *Laws*. Protagoras of course was no politician, but he was a public speaker. This aspect, the problem of rhetoric, must have been deliberately omitted from the *Protagoras*. And it is tempting to see two reasons for this: Plato felt he had nothing further to say about rhetoric for the time being; and the realities of Athenian demagogy seemed somewhat removed from the comparatively peaceful angle of vision of the newly founded Academy.

As a matter of fact, *Protagoras* is a rather more specialized work than the *Gorgias*, which encompasses most facets of Plato's philosophy (as do the *Republic* and the *Laws* later). This somewhat careless but apparently deliberate restriction to certain themes and the omission of others (including metaphysics), although the all-round activities of the sophists present might have invited to a thematic universalism, is certainly not a sign of the precedence of *Protagoras* in relation to *Gorgias*; on the contrary, most of Plato's dialogues are specialized.

The much-debated problem of the 'hedonistic calculus' in *Protagoras* and its relation to the ethics of *Gorgias* is perhaps not directly relevant to the dating of

---

334. Cf. also the rather respectful treatment of Protagoras in the *Theaetetus* 152a ff.; and even in the *Sophist* the 'art of sophistry' is difficult to 'catch.' For the development of the theme of pupils of sophists cheating their teacher (which is the point of the latter passage in *Gorgias*), cf. above p. 278.

335. Cf. Pohlenz 1913: 131, Geffcken II A 66 f.

336. Note *Grg.* 448c, 449c, 461d, 465a, 519d; *Prt.* 328e f., 334c–336d, 343b. Pohlenz 1913: 130 of course interprets the *Protagoras* passages as primary.

[133] the main part of *Protagoras*.³³⁷ In most respects the attitudes to ethics in the two dialogues are rather different and not easily comparable. Two points, however, deserve attention. The *Gorgias* represents and develops the conventional view that just punishment improves people, 476d–477a, 507c ff., etc. (though there are incurable cases in Hades, 525bc); the same conventional view is presented by Protagoras in *Protagoras* 324a, 325a–c as indicating that virtue can be taught, but the whole argument of the dialogue shows that 'Socrates' no longer agrees with this point of view; at least one does not educate by punishing.³³⁸ And whereas Socrates in the *Gorgias* argues polemically against Callicles (and, in fact, Polycrates) that prominent politicians such as Themistocles, Cimon, Miltiades and Pericles have in fact made the Athenians worse (503c, 515c–516e, 519a), in the *Protagoras* he mentions Pericles as an example of a prominent man who was unable to teach his speciality to his sons or anybody else (319e–320b). The latter is probably a
[134] commonplace (cf. *Laches* p. 360), and it recurs, combined with the assertion made in the *Gorgias*, in *Meno* (93c) and *Alcibiades* I (118c–119a); but Plato makes Protagoras return to it and expound it at length at the end of his λόγος, 326e–328b, with arguments that may seem more refined than those of Socrates in *Gorgias*.³³⁹

The passages on φύσις versus νόμος (*Grg.* 482e–484c, *Prt.* 337cd) and δειλοί versus ἀνδρεῖοι (*Grg.* 498a–c, *Prt.* 359c–360d) are taken by Geffcken II A 66 to indicate the precedence of the *Protagoras*. I can find no such clues here.

Finally there is the interesting fact that the eschatological myth of *Gorgias*, unlike the later Platonic myths, partly adopts the same story-telling style as Protagoras in his myth of the rise of civilization, *Protagoras* 320c ff.³⁴⁰ These are perhaps the first myths Plato wrote. Which of them is earlier? The principal criterion normally used for arguing the precedence for the myth of *Protagoras* is to regard the myth of *Gorgias* as more 'Platonic.'³⁴¹ In fact both are Platonic in the sense that they present an approximate, unproved but visionary truth beyond the scope of λόγος. The briefer myth of *Gorgias* starts from Homer and keeps within the framework of conventional mythology; and it is given its natural place at the end of the argument. The myth of *Protagoras* is evidently more unconventional and much more elaborate (note, too, that Prometheus, the god of forethought,

---

337. Cf. above p. 277 and notes 321 and 322. Many scholars have considered that the ethical arguments of the *Gorgias* are meant to refute the (possibly ironic) 'hedonism' of *Protagoras* 351b ff., cf. e.g. Pohlenz 1913: 100 ff., Jaeger 1928: 5 f., Moreau 1939a: 159 ff. Others emphasize the differences in approach (e.g. Shorey 1903: 78 n. 597, Ritter 1940b: 426 ff., Guthrie IV 304 f. The precedence of the position of *Gorgias* has been argued e.g. by Beare 1913: 51 f., Rick 1931: 138 ff., Boehme 1959: 81 ff., and especially Kapp 1968: 81 n. 30 (accepted by Erbse 1968, Kahn 1976: 24) and Rehork 1972. *See* now also Kahn 1981.

338. It may be that the position of the *Laws* rather approximates to that of the *Gorgias* in this matter; but Pohlenz 1913: 145 n. 1 wrongly asserts that the *Protagoras* passage must be earlier than *Gorgias*.

339. This is of course not the opinion of those who place the *Protagoras* earlier; cf. Horn 1893: 356 f., Lutoslawski 214 f. In more recent times nobody seems to have attached much importance to this point.

340. Cf. Thesleff 1967, above, 103, 109.

341. Cf. Edelstein 1949: 475 f., Rudberg 1953: 34 f., 39 f., Friedländer I 186 ff.

who also figures in the *Gorgias* myth, but alone, 523d, is coupled with his brother in *Protagoras*); and placing it as an introduction to the great λόγος of Protagoras which is balanced by Socrates' corresponding λόγος, reveals a higher degree of artistry, and anticipates the pedimental principle of composition with a playfully visionary speech at the center, which is so eminently clear in the *Symposium*.

Thus, there are several both general and specific indications—most of them admittedly not immediately obvious—of the order *Gorgias—Protagoras*. I can see no unambiguous signs to the contrary. In this question of the relative order, Taylor 1926, Stefanini 1932, Boehme 1959, Kahn 1963, 1976, 1981; Kapp 1968 and their (very few) followers seem to be right, although the problem cannot be regarded as solved.

Owing to the difference in approach and mood, *Protagoras* is not likely to have followed very soon after *Gorgias*. Dating *Protagoras* about 384 BCE would allow for a sufficient lapse of time. As already noted, it is a somewhat careless composition and probably did not take very long to write.

For the opening frame dialogue, *see* below p. 327.

## Symposium

G.C. For the dating of this dialogue to about 384 or somewhat later, *see* above p. 266. I would tentatively suggest 383 BCE in order to allow for some elapse of time from the composition of *Protagoras*.

*Symposium* is a carefully composed and brilliantly written work which must have taken a considerable time to complete. Some of the speeches may have been written earlier: as the pastiches of *Menexenus* and *Protagoras* indicate, Plato had been experimenting with literary styles at least since completing the *Gorgias*; cf. *Phaedrus*, p. 317.

*Symposium* is also the first of the works so far considered where Plato presents more or less explicitly some of his original contributions to philosophy: the theory of Forms, and a theory of Love.

E.C. In addition to the arguments considered above p. 267 ff., note the following external chronological indications:—It has often been said that by now Plato is likely to have settled down at the Academy, and that the dialogue reflects the high spirits and protreptic tendency of the early Academic συνουσίαι.[342]—Since Diotima is very probably a transformation of the Aspasia of Socratic legends who had taught Socrates 'erotics,'[343] not only Xenophon's 'Symposium' (above p. 266) and its (Antisthenean?) sources, but also other Socratic treatments of the theme such as Aeschines' 'Aspasia' were presumably written before Plato's *Symposium*. Plato felt he had literary rivals, and this may explain this somewhat odd combination of esoterism, protreptic and apol-

---

342. E.g. Lutoslawski 242, 414, Wilamowitz II 169–176. For the tradition of formal συμπόσια in the Academy, cf. Gaiser 1963: 448.
343. First argued in some detail by Dittmar 1912: 40 f.

[135] ogy in a literarily brilliant form.³⁴⁴—The relevance of Isocrates' *Busiris* (XI) 5–6 is questionable (cf. above p. 254).³⁴⁵—Aristophanes was probably dead by 383 BCE. It is an interesting though not fully explicable fact that Plato's portrait of Aristophanes in *Symposium* is quite sympathetic, in spite of the *Clouds* and the *Ecclesiazusae*, and considering the contempt with which he treats writers of comedy in the *Republic* (e.g. III 395e, V 452d, X 606c) and the *Laws* (e.g. XI 935e). The *Symposium* represents the same gentlemanly mood as the *Protagoras*.

I.C *Gorgias—Symposium.* This order is usually accepted both because of the 'general advance' found here, and also of various points of detail.³⁴⁶ Although much of what has been said in this respect remains controversial, it seems clear to

[136] me that the application, in the central section of *Symposium*, of an evidently new theory of Love to a combination of ontology, metaphysics, ethics and the teaching of ethics (note τίκτειν 212a3–5), really implies a step forward from the position of *Gorgias*.³⁴⁷ Particularly illuminating here is a comparison of the brief discussion of beauty in *Gorgias* 474c–475a with the ἐπαναβασμοί of Diotima, *Symposium* 210a–d, cf. 211bc. In *Gorgias* Socrates argues that what is common to all beautiful things (καλά) is that they are useful (χρήσιμα, ὠφέλιμα, also ἀγαθόν) or pleasant (ἡδέα, κατὰ ἡδονήν τινα) or both.³⁴⁸ The examples of 'things' given are σώματα, χρώματα, σχήματα, φωναί and ἐπιτηδεύματα which become soon differentiated into νόμοι, ἐπιτηδεύματα (proper), and μαθήματα. The process described by Diotima begins with σώματα (first one, then ἕτερον, then many and all) and passes through ψυχαί (omitted in the recapitulation 211c) to ἐπιτηδεύματα and νόμοι, to ἐπιστῆμαι, and finally to the one ἐπιστήμη of τὸ καλόν (μάθημα for ἐπιστήμη in the recapitulation). It is clearly the matter-of-fact list of examples in the *Gorgias* which is primary, and the presence of the aspect of ἡδονή here has made possible the consistent application of the gradually more metaphorical ἔρως to the series of examples (objects of Love) in *Symposium*; vice versa is hardly conceivable. Because of the ἔρως metaphor, and also owing to the background themes of ethics and teaching, Diotima can dispose of χρώματα, σχήματα and φωναί, but adds ψυχαί.

For Aspasia in the frame dialogue of *Menexenus*, see below p. 328.

---

344. For the Callias theme, cf. above p. 267 f. Cf. Rossetti 1974 on various Socratic writings dealing with themes of symposia and erotics.

345. Other supposed parallels in Isocrates are clearly irrelevant; cf. e.g. Isocr. *Hel.* (X) 12 (*Smp.* 177b), *Euagoras* (IX) 8.

346. See notably Lutoslawski 238 ff., Raeder 163, 166, 290, Krämer 1959: 233 ff., Ilting 1965: 388 ff. The arguments for the reverse order sometimes produced have little weight. For instance, Morrison's point (1964: 42–46) that the doctrine of immortality is more advanced in the *Gorgias* is untenable: the general theory of love in the speech of Diotima rather constitutes a fresh alternative to the conventional view of Hades or the Isles of the Blessed.

347. Cf. also e.g. Gaiser 1963: 221 f.

348. The 'looking' (ἀποβλέπειν 474d5) for a common feature is often regarded as implying an early stage of the theory of Forms, but cf. e.g. R. VI 484c10. For the use of ἀγαθόν in this context in the *Gorgias*, note the (possibly ironic) remark 475a3 ἡδονῇ τε καὶ ἀγαθῷ ὁριζόμενος τὸ καλόν. For the similar view of beauty in *Hippias Major*, cf. below p. 372.

*Protagoras—Symposium.* Much the same can be said about this relation as about the order *Gorgias—Symposium.* Moreover, *Protagoras* is more closely related to *Symposium* in formal respects (cf above p. 267 ff.), and so here, too, the trends of development can be studied in detail. Most points, including the pedimental composition, the motif of a reception at a wealthy man's home and the ἀγών of speeches (cf. *Prt.* 336b–338b), even, the choice and portrayal of persons, demonstrate rather unambiguously that *Symposium* is the later work.[349]

For the opening frame dialogue of *Symposium, see* below p. 327. I consider it quite possible that the dialogue was originally written as a direct report by Aristodemus[350]—Socrates could not of course report an encomium of himself—somewhat in the manner of the main dialogue of *Phaedo.*

For the relation to *Phaedrus,* cf. below p. 322.

## The Respublica Rediviva

G.C. According to the hypothesis put forward here, the 'Proto-*Republic*' and the first version of *Republic* I existed in the late 390s in draft copies not intended for publication. Since (perhaps) the *Gorgias* and (probably) the *Protagoras* had become known to a larger public and were read and studied outside the Academy,[351] and since the *Symposium* is quite likely to have been an immediate success, Plato may have decided to rework those earlier sketches into a larger whole, suitable for extra-Academic readers and yet containing a fuller review of his philosophy than that provided by the rather specialized *Protagoras* and *Symposium.*

We have no means of determining how many years the writing of the present *Republic* required, how many times Plato changed his plans, and how the final composition materialized. In spite of the formally coherent plan, and its symmetrically pedimental arrangement, the work is clearly heterogeneous.[352] I consider it practically certain that the *Republic* took shape gradually over a long period of time, and that it reflects many phases of Plato's experiences as a thinker, teacher and writer in the Academy and in Syracuse.

This impression of heterogeneity is confirmed by a closer examination of the style of the present *Republic.*[353] The most important fact in this connection is that various parts reveal obvious touches of Plato's typical 'late style' ('onkos'),

---

349. This is the generally accepted view. Taylor's insisting on the reverse order is mainly due to his theory of the 'maturity' of the *Protagoras.*

350. For Aristodemus, cf. Xenophon *Mem.* I 4. It is tempting to infer that he has something to do with Antisthenes.

351. The legend of the Corinthian farmer (above n. 314) is not so implausible after all.

352. Cf. the discussion and references above p. 250 ff.

353. Cf. Thesleff above, 83 ff. for a general conspectus of the various stylistic clusters in the *Republic;* cf. also above, n. 202. Traditional stylometry, wrongly, tends to consider Books II–X as a whole. Lutoslawski 153 ff. endeavored to test his 'law of stylistic affinity' on the various books of the *Republic,* but the scope of data used by him was too restricted.

[137] and that these parts are interspersed with passages written in a more easy-going dialogue style. The first touches of the onkos style appear at the end of Book II (376b, on poetry), and there is more evidence of it from the latter part of Book III onwards (403c ff., beginning with gymnastic) through the first part of Book IV (up to 427e, the 'founding' of the Ideal State). The rest of Book IV, which is concerned with justice and soul, is remarkably vivid in style. But the chapter on women and communism in Book V (up to 466d) again includes onkos, and so do various (but not all) parts of the argument in the center and the latter part of the work, among them the section on dialectic (VII 532b–541b). This suggests that the 'Proto-*Republic*' was not worked into its new context until comparatively late (cf. below p. 331).

On the other hand, as was noted above (p. 270), Plato perhaps introduced the probably somewhat symbolic idea of a pair of interlocutors of Socrates at approximately the time he wrote the *Symposium* (which ends with such a pair) and the *Phaedo* (which contains such a pair).

From this the following hypothetical picture would emerge: some time after the *Symposium* had been written and published (still without its opening frame
[138] dialogue), Plato began to re-write *Republic* I and to continue it according to his new plans.[354] Seen in its new context, the *Republic* I required a fresh and better answer to Thrasymachus' attack on the Socratic position (which had meanwhile been renewed by Callicles), and so Plato made his two brothers, Glaucon and Adimantus, take over as 'opponents' of Socrates: Book II opens with their exposition of their common-sense arguments in two speeches. Socrates' first answer to the speeches (367e–368d) is an inherent part of them and must have been written consecutively. Obviously, however, this was just a fresh start to what Plato envisaged as a huge task. How did he proceed?

What I would like to suggest here is that during the subsequent years— roughly the 370s—Plato drafted various portions of the future Books II–X but did not finish the composition. Judging by the style, among other things, such portions may well have been the following: the end of the present Book II (notably 372a–374d, on a primitive and civilized State), the section on mimetic art in Book III (392c–397e),[355] the latter portion of Book IV (425a–427c, notes on institutions; 432b–445b, on justice and the tripartite soul), the main portion of Book VII (518b–532b, education of the philosophers), and the final myth in Book X. All this is very conjectural, however.

E.C. Some not particularly obvious external criteria have been found for dating various sections of the *Republic*. It is doubtful whether V 471a–c can be regarded as having been written under the recent impression of internal warfare in Greece in 474 BCE.[356] It is more probable that the remark in VII 540a that the philosopher-king must have reached the age of 50 was written not very much

---

354. Cf. *Clitopho*, below p. 352.
355. Else 1972 has argued with some force that the corresponding section in Book X, 595a–608b, though written earlier, was placed here as a reply to Aristotle's criticism.
356. Suggested by Christ 1886: 489 ff. and others, questioned by Adam ad l.

later than 377 BCE since it has an autobiographical ring.³⁵⁷ For the possible re- [138]
flection of the Sicilian events, see below p. 332.—The relation of the *Republic* to
various works of Isocrates has been much discussed. Although it seems likely
that some sections dealing with philosophy in the *Republic* were written with
Isocrates and particularly the 'Panegyricus' (IV, 380 BCE) in view, no direct references or allusions have been detected;³⁵⁸ and except for the *Busiris* which may
refer to the 'Proto-*Republic*' (above p. 254), there seem to be no references to the
*Republic* in Isocrates until the 'Antidosis' (XV, 354 BCE).³⁵⁹ This is in keeping [139]
with my hypothesis that the *Republic* was not completed and 'published' before
the 350s.—There is little or no auxiliary support for this from Xenophon or the
other Socratics.³⁶⁰

I.C. The precedence of *Gorgias, Menexenus, Protagoras* and *Symposium* over
the later books of the *Republic* is generally accepted today and seems quite certain.
Note in particular the following points:

*Gorgias—Republic* II—.³⁶¹ This order corresponds to fairly obvious trends in
the conception of ethics, the theory of Soul,³⁶² the theory of knowledge, metaphysics, and eschatology.³⁶³ The mathematics of the *Republic* are also commonly
regarded as more advanced.³⁶⁴

*Menexenus—Republic* II—. Whatever else can be said of this relationship,³⁶⁵
I am prepared to infer from the 'promise' of presenting more πολιτικοὶ λόγοι by

---

357. Very often suggested, cf. Raeder 244 with references, Kapp 1968: 89. Among the skeptics, note Shorey 1935 ad l. Cf. the other 'autobiographical' remarks, above n. 52.

358. See, however, Adam II 77 f., Raeder 243 f., and in general Ries 1959: 68–82. For other
supposed (and still more uncertain) parallels, cf. Raeder ibid., H. Gomperz 1905: 204 ff., Ries
1959: 82–87.

359. For *R.* III 411e ff. being reflected in *Antid.*, see Ries 1959: 151–153; for *R.* V 474c, cf.
Pohlenz 1913: 362 ff.; for *R.* VI 498d, cf. Wilamowitz II 120 ff.; for *R.* VI 500b, cf. Raeder 244,
Wilamowitz l.c., Ries 1959: 159 ff. (cf. 82 ff., 143 ff.; questioned by H. Gomperz 1906: 11 f. only
because of the supposed distance in time); for *R.* VIII 526b, cf. Ries 1959: 159.

360. Maier 1913: 57 n. 2, 61 n. 2 refers to some extremely doubtful parallels in Xenophon's
'Memorabilia.' For the 'Cyropaedia,' cf. above p. 254. I do not find it very likely that the commonplaces about tyranny in Xenophon's 'Hiero' are inspired by the forcible passages in *Republic* IX,
as is sometimes believed (references in Breitenbach 1967: 1742 ff., Nickel 1979: 90).

361. Shorey has listed several interesting parallels in his notes ad ll. (1930–35). Cf. also
Pohlenz 1913, especially 160 ff., Diès 1932: CXXXIV ff., Krämer 1959: 77–83.

362. The fresh and systematic treatment of ethics in the *Republic* is noteworthy, and details
such as *Grg.* 491d versus *R.* IV 430e (on σωφροσύνη) suggest clearly the precedence of *Gorgias*; cf.
Raeder 211 f., Pohlenz 1913: 157. And there is no Tripartite Soul in the *Gorgias* (493ab does not
imply this), cf. Groag 1913, Pohlenz ibid., T. M. Robinson 1970: 39 ff.

363. The *Gorgias* reflects the doctrine of reincarnation only indirectly (492e–493b), and this
is not included in the final myth, as it is in the myth of Er. The curious detail of the κόσκινος,
which is elaborated on in *Grg.* 493b, is passed over with a brief mention in *R.* II 363d. It would
seem that Plato did not accept the doctrine of reincarnation in his philosophical 'system' until
the period of the *Phaedo* (below p. 292).

364. Cf. Morrison 1958: 213 ff. An interesting detail is the addition of ἐρωτικαὶ ἀνάγκαι to
the γεωμετρικαί in *R.* V 458d (cf. *Smp.*); cf. *Grg.* 508a.

365. Gaiser 1963: 250 f. probably exaggerates the idea of a political 'paradigm' inherent in
the *Menexenus*.

[139] Aspasia, at the end of the frame dialogue of *Menexenus* (249e), that the *Republic* had not yet been published when that passage was written, whenever that may have been (cf. below p. 328).

*Protagoras—Republic* II—. A 'general advance' as in the case of the relation *Gorgias—Republic* is easily recognized. In addition various details point to the precedence of the *Protagoras*, e.g. the conception of the primeval State as presented by Protagoras 320c ff. and by Socrates in the *Republic* II 369b ff., and the introduction of δόξα instead of ἐπιστήμη in the characterization of courage in *Republic* IV 429b–d (cf. Raeder 1905: 210 f., 216). Note also the fact that the brief reference in the speech of Protagoras (326ab) to the use of music in education contains no such ironic or critical distance as would be expected had it been written after the comprehensive treatment of this point in *Republic* III 398c–401a.

[140] *Symposium—Republic* II—. In this case the combination of ethics and the teaching of virtue with the metaphysical aspect and a clearly hierarchic theory of Forms may suggest a closer affinity in time, though the trend of 'development' is normally taken to indicate the precedence of the *Symposium*. The opposite order has been argued very occasionally and with little success.[366] In my view the most weighty argument is the presence albeit in an atrophied form, in the *Republic* of the same theory of Love as was introduced as, apparently, a new idea in the *Symposium*.[367] Also, the severe attitude to poetry, still maintained in the *Laws* (p. 203), appears to be one which Plato has not yet adopted in the *Symposium*.[368]

## Phaedo

G. C. *Phaedo* is normally taken to represent the mature phase of Plato's philosophy except in the field of cosmology and, perhaps, that of psychology. The authenticity of the dialogue is beyond doubt even though Panaetius is said to have questioned it.[369] The fact that its dramatic date connects it with the *Apology, Euthyphro* and *Crito* has little or no relevance to chronology.

---

366. After Bötticher (1894), Pfleiderer 1896: 247 f., 414, 566 considered the speech of Diotima as developing further some of the central ideas of the *Republic*; Lönborg 1939a, and recently again Moore 1969, 1973, have considered the theory of Love in the *Symposium* as being very advanced (but cf. below p. 322).

367. Cf. notably R. III 403a–c, V 474b, 475b ff., 479e f., VI 484b, 490ab (implying the speech of Diotima), IX 573b; cf. also Wilamowitz II 169 ff., Leisegang 1950: 2450. Shorey 1903: 19 is manifestly wrong in denying any conceivable change in the Platonic theory of Love. Cf. below p. 319.

368. In the *Symposium*, Aristophanes and Agathon are' treated with a respect (however ironical) which would not be so natural after the censure of comedy and tragedy in the *Republic*; note also the differentiation of the arts of the tragedian and comedian in R. III 394e f. (recurring in *Ion* 534c) versus *Smp*. 223cd. Cf. Raeder 167, Geffcken II A 95 n. 32. Shorey 1903: 81 f. wrongly denies the relevance of this argument, though he is probably right in seeing a kind of irony in the attitude to Homer and Hesiod in *Symposium* 209cd, an irony which is not always noticed by modern critics.

369. Cf. above p. 237.

In formal respects the *Phaedo* displays considerable artistry. Various layers have sometimes been seen in its complicated structure[370] but I do not think it can be proved to be really heterogeneous. On the contrary, even the dramatic frame dialogue was, I believe, written together with the rest, which was not the case with *Protagoras* and *Symposium*. It contains important background information, and is also used for giving structural emphasis to the central section (cf. Thesleff above, 111 ff.); and Echecrates, the interlocutor of Phaedon in this frame dialogue, is a Pythagorean like Cebes and Simmias, the chief interlocutors of Socrates. If the frame dialogue is not a secondary addition, we have to assume that a dramatic dialogue technique had already been developed in the Academy when *Phaedo* was composed (cf. below p. 309).

[140]

[141]

E.C.   Phaedon of Elis was a very young man in 399 (*Phaedo* 89b), and it is, therefore, highly unlikely that Plato would have made him the narrator of a conversation which at the very outset obviously involved much of Plato's own philosophy had he written an early version of the dialogue in, say, the 390s. On the other hand, it seems certain that Phaedon later founded a school of his own in Elis and even wrote Socratic dialogues (above p. 205). To assume that Plato at that time would have published his account of Socrates' last hours under Phaedon's name, is even more problematic. Hence, Plato is most likely to have written the *Phaedo* before Phaedon returned to Elis, which probably took place soon after the battle of Leuctra in 371 BCE.[371]

There are no other external criteria applicable to the dating of *Phaedo*.[372]

I.C.   *Apology—Phaedo*. The *Phaedo* is commonly thought to follow the *Apology* at a considerable distance in time. This is a reasonable view which it is hardly possible to refute.[373]

---

370. H. M. Wolff 1957: 120 f. argued that the first version was written soon after 399 BCE, and a second version after the *Symposium*. Ryle 1966: 227–229 thought (eccentrically) that the geophysics of 108c–113c were inserted after 367/6 BCE. Findlay 1974: 16 connected the 'Ur-Phaedo' with the supposedly early *Crito*. See however below p. 357.

371. Dušanič 1979: 327 f. The violation of the 'Law of Parmentier' means little. The somewhat similar problem of Euclides figuring as the 'narrator' of the *Theaetetus*, though he had published dialogues of his own, can be solved by assuming that he was Socrates' interlocutor in the original version of the dialogue; cf. p. 169 n. 32.—For anonymity and pseudonymity in general, cf. above p. 208.

372. It is possible, but by no means certain, that Aristotle considered the *Phaedo* a fairly recent work when he joined the Academy in 367 BCE: cf. Diog. L. 3.37 and *Ep.* 13.363a; but cf., on the other hand, Ueberweg-Praechter 200, Leisegang 1950: 2369 f., Ryle 1966: 38. At any rate, Aristotle's dialogue Εὔδημος ἢ Περὶ ψυχῆς, written after the death of Eudemus, c. 354 BCE, followed the model of the *Phaedo*. The pointed τὰ νῦν *Phd.* 57a8 has been thought to refer to the period soon after 379 BCE (Xen. *Hell.* V 3.21 ff.), Christ 1886: 491 f.—Since the description of Socrates' physical reaction to the κώνειον is probably embellished by fictitious traits (Gill 1973), this description at any rate was not written soon after the events.

373. The only reason for placing the *Apology* later than *Phaedo* would be the assumption that unlike the *Phaedo* it is intended to give a true-to-life picture of Socrates; but then we should expect an explanatory apparatus in the *Apology*, or even polemics, of which there is no trace.

[141] *Gorgias—Phaedo.* This is the order normally accepted, though scholars vary as to which criteria are to be trusted. It is difficult to deny that *Phaedo* is metaphysically more 'profound' and in various respects more 'advanced.'[374] A trend of development has been seen notably in the eschatology and psychology,[375] the theory of Forms,[376] and the criticism of hedonism.[377] I would agree with those (e.g. Wil-
[142] amowitz I 231) who see in the final eschatological myths and their implications (cf. also *Phd.* 80d ff. on reincarnation) clear signs of the *Phaedo* being the later dialogue.

*Protagoras—Phaedo.* These two dialogues have little in common, and though most scholars agree in regarding *Protagoras* as the earlier one,[378] it is only the attitude to hedonism that furnishes any kind of extensive basis for comparison. Now, the 'hedonistic calculus' may have been inserted in the *Protagoras* later (cf. above p. 281), and I am not sure that the corresponding passages in *Phaedo* can reasonably be interpreted as being later still.[379] On the other hand, the remark in *Phaedo* 68cd on courage seems to presuppose the discussion of this virtue in *Protagoras* (329d ff., 359c ff.).

*Symposium—Phaedo.* Here the affinity is obvious: it ranges from the distancing 'objective' report and the slightly idealizing picture of Socrates, to doctrinal points such as the presentation of the theory of Forms and the introduction of the problem of the immortality of the soul. Even so, the dialogues do not necessarily belong very closely together in time.[380] *Phaedo* is somewhat more commonly regarded as the later one than vice versa, but there is no substantial agreement on the criteria to be used.

The arguments propounded for the order *Phaedo—Symposium* do not bear close examination, however. To begin with formal considerations, the two-step report in the *Symposium* is probably a secondary device, and it may have been applied together with the opening dramatic dialogue (cf. below p. 327).[381] Socrates' identification of the arts of the tragedian and comedian in *Symposium* 223d has

---

374. Only Beare 1913: 49 f. has argued that the attitude of the *Gorgias* to ἐπιθυμία, αἴσθησις etc. is more 'advanced.'

375. Cf. Groag 1913, Crombie I 302 f., T. M. Robinson 1970: 21 ff., 50 ff.; but Shorey 1903: 40 f. took a decidedly skeptical view (cf. also Guthrie 1957: 5 f.): it is true that *Grg.* 493a may seem closer to the doctrine of the tripartite soul than any passage in the *Phaedo*.

376. Cf. Robin 1938: 100 ff., Ilting 1965: 388 ff.

377. Cf. Horn 1893: 305 ff., Pohlenz 1913: 325 n. 2, Crombie I 248 f.; but cf. Beare, above n. 374.

378. Beare 1913 and Taylor tend to accept the reverse order owing to the excessive emphasis they put on the 'maturity' of the *Protagoras*.

379. Cf. notably *Prt.* 352d ff., 354c ff. versus *Phd.* 68e ff.; cf. Horn 1893: 305 ff., Pohlenz 1913: 325 n. 2, Boehme 1959: 91 ff.., Crombie I 242. Boehme made the point that the simile of νόμισμα in *Phd.* 69a implies the μετρητικά in *Prt.* rather than vice versa.

380. This has been rightly pointed out by Raeder 169, Groag 1915: 120 n. 1.

381. An interesting detail is the portrait of Apollodorus ὁ μανικός (rather than μαλακός) in *Symposium* 173d (the frame) versus *Phaedo* 59ab, 117d. Robin 1929 (*Phd.* p. VII, *Smp.* p. VIII) thinks that the passages in the *Phaedo* presuppose the *Symposium*. For my part I should think that the words πλὴν Σωκράτους come more naturally in their context in *Phd.* 117d than in *Smp.* and that for other reasons, too, the opening of the *Symposium* can be regarded as modeled on the opening of the *Phaedo*.

sometimes[382] been taken to imply that Plato had already written the *Phaedo*, but it is very unlikely in fact that Plato had regarded the *Phaedo* as a tragedy or the *Symposium* as a comedy. Moreover, it is highly doubtful whether the slightly different attitude to the sensible world in the two dialogues is of any use as a chronological criterion.[383] In fact, the theme and argument of the *Phaedo* preclude such approaches to αἰσθητά as occur in the *Symposium*, and of course we should not expect to encounter here any mention of Diotima's ἔρως doctrine.[384] The psychology and eschatology of the *Symposium* do not seem to me to have advanced very much beyond the *Gorgias*, whereas the *Phaedo* goes considerably further.[385] The view that the theory of Forms in the *Symposium* must represent a later stage than the *Phaedo* has been recently argued in some detail.[386] It is perhaps irrelevant to chronology that the *Symposium* considers only one aspect of the theory and one Form, and does it through the ἔρως imagery, whereas the *Phaedo* presents a more greatly differentiated picture. But unlike the *Symposium*, the *Phaedo* takes it for granted that the reader has heard of the theory before (76d, 100b), and employs a somewhat consistent terminology. Much more could be said in favor of the precedence of *Symposium* in this respect.[387] Those who tend to place it later (e.g. Guthrie IV 389) have also overlooked the fact that no doctrine of anamnesis or reincarnation is actually implied in the *Symposium*. The philosopher's contact with absolute truth and eternity is here explained in a very different way. It is precisely this absence of what became later (cf. *Phaedo*, *Meno*, *Theaetetus*, *Phaedrus*, *Timaeus*) an important part of Plato's philosophical system, which is in my opinion after all the most weighty argument in favor of the order *Symposium—Phaedo*.

*Phaedo and the Republic.* Nowadays, there is almost universal agreement that *Phaedo* precedes the final publication of the *Republic*;[388] and all who separate the first book of the latter place it before the *Phaedo*. From the point of view of the present theory it would be more important to know whether any portions of *Republic* II–X can be shown to be earlier than the *Phaedo*.

---

382. Pfleiderer 1896: 530 ff., Natorp 1903: 166, and others.

383. This has been argued, after Beare 1913, e.g. by Gulley 1962: 52 f. and Raven 1965: 105 ff. But Bal 1950 has pointed out that the supposed 'asceticism' of the *Phaedo* is easily over-emphasized.

384. The idea of φιλο-σοφία = ἔρως τῆς φρονήσεως (*Phd*. 66e, etc.) is a commonplace; the ἔρως τοῦ καλοῦ is a very different thing which leads to a theory of Socratic παιδεραστία and teaching, and to a tentative but not very advanced theory of transcendent metaphysics and immortality.

385. This is not the opinion of Groag 1915: 120 n. 1, Grube (1935) 1958: XIII, Hackforth 1950, Crombie I 362 f., Guthrie IV 387 ff., and certain others. But the view that the *Symposium* is more advanced in this respect has been sufficiently refuted by Horn 1893: 278 f., Shorey 1903: 40 n. 279, and especially Morrison 1964: 42–46. Others (e.g. Natorp 1903: 166 ff., Dover 1965: 16–20) prefer to leave the question open. Cf. below.

386. Kapp 1968, especially 60 f., 109–130, following Dittenberger and others. Cf. Pfleiderer 1896: 566, Lönborg 1939a, Gulley 1962: VIII, Raven 1965: 105 ff.

387. Kapp (cf. n. 80) has not considered all of the evidence, not has he refuted all of the traditional arguments, e.g. Lutoslawski 245 ff., 338 ff., Gomperz II 577, Raeder 171 ff., Robin 1908: 118 ff. The doctrine of Principles affords an additional complication.

388. Earlier theories of the precedence of the *Republic* (e.g. Pfleiderer 1896) are not well founded.

[143]   One possible clue can be found in the speech of Adimantus in the opening of *Republic* II. Its critical attitude to naive Orphic and similar beliefs in retribution and reward after death (notably 363cd) appears to imply a certain advance from the position of the *Gorgias* where such ideas are only played with (492e–493e) and where the final myth concentrates upon retribution in the setting of a Homeric Hades (cf. above p. 282). The *Phaedo* goes two steps further: first, the 'Orphic' beliefs are explained symbolically so as to make the philosophers the true βάκχοι (62b, 68ab,
[144]   etc., and especially 69cd), and then (70c ff.) the doctrine of reincarnation is introduced. The latter doctrine is then, in the final myth (note 107de, 108c, 114bc), combined with the ideas of retribution found in the final myth of the *Gorgias*. The same combination, with considerable elaboration of cosmological details, too, occurs in the final myth of the *Republic*. All this would suggest the relative order *Gorgias*—*Republic* II—*Phaedo*—*Republic* X.[389]—Otherwise I can discover no signs of any portion of the *Phaedo* being later than any portion of the present version of *Republic* II–X.[390]

Hence, it can be assumed here that, having begun re-writing the *Republic* and having formulated the objections of Glaucon and Adimantus (and Socrates' answer to them), Plato shelved this project and returned to teaching (and perhaps wrote the *Meno*, cf. p. 310). Somewhat later he wrote the *Phaedo*, in which he attempted to present his revised views of the soul, metaphysics, cosmology, and a true philosopher's attitude to earthly life. The absence of the social aspect, so prominent in most of Plato's writings, is noteworthy.[391] I can see at least one hypothetical reason for this. Plato perhaps wished to reserve the social aspect for the *Republic* he was planning. The ethical and intellectual integrity and orientation of the ideal philosopher was to be depicted more fully than in the *Symposium*, before the philosopher's State could be described. This explanation would fit in well with the chronological pattern adopted here.

The teaching of ἀρετή to future philosophers now appears to have become central to Plato's interest.

## Euthydemus

G.C.   This gay and (seemingly) whimsical dialogue is usually placed 'rather late in the early period,' though there is little agreement on its exact position.

---

389. The order *Gorgias*—*Phaedo*—*Republic* is commonly accepted in view of the psychology and eschatology; for the details cf. e,g. Lutoslawski 314 ff., 329 ff., Groag 1913, Leisegang 1950: 2450, T. M. Robinson 1970: 39 ff., Else 1972: 10 ff. The possibility of inserting *Republic* II after *Gorgias* but before *Phaedo* does not seem to have occurred to anybody. I do not think Gomperz II 580 is right in regarding the different attitudes to 'Orphic' beliefs completely irrelevant to chronology.

390. Pohlenz 1913: 228–236 argued that the 'Proto-*Republic*' included a doctrine of a Tripartite State which is reflected in the *Phaedo* (notably 68c, 82c) though the Tripartite Soul of the later *Republic* does not occur in the *Phaedo*. This is very fanciful, to say the least, but it would agree with the hypothesis set forth above.

391. The didactic aspect is of course present in many ways, e.g. in the remarks on μισολογία in the center, 89d.

Scholars have been somewhat intrigued by the mixture of the supposedly 'early' [144] and 'mature' features it contains, and also by its rallying, satirical tone.³⁹² This tone is accompanied by an exceptional number of colloquialisms in the style (cf. Thesleff, above 109 ff.). I can find no reason to doubt the authenticity of this curious [145] work either on these or any other grounds.³⁹³

Dating the *Euthydemus* after, and not very long after, the *Phaedo* may seem an odd solution, but there-are facts other than the formal ones discussed above which favor it. And after all, if we accept that *Menexenus* followed *Gorgias* (and indeed, that Alcibiades is made to 'profane' the mysteries in the *Symposium*) we may safely trust Plato to have brought Socrates back to Lyceum from his death cell.

With regard to the dialogue technique (cf. above p. 268), it is tempting at first sight to look for two or more layers in the complex interweaving of the dramatic frame and the reported main dialogue.³⁹⁴ On closer inspection, however, it appears that the dialogue must have been planned and composed like this from the beginning.³⁹⁵ It is quite natural, I think, that in this respect *Euthydemus* should follow the model of *Phaedo* (cf. below). The only curious thing about the opening frame is that Socrates (273a) should need to introduce Ctesippus to Criton as if he were a completely unknown person; both were present at the death of Socrates (*Phaedo* 59b), and Plato must have known even before he gathered his information for the *Phaedo* that Ctesippus as well as Criton belonged to the circle of Socrates. Rather than to suppose that Plato is aiming at a dramatic date when Criton had not 'yet' made the acquaintance of Ctesippus, I prefer to think that the presentation of this minor character is intended for the general reader's information. The *Euthydemus* clearly has a protreptic function (cf. the end).

Owing to the playful tone of the dialogue, the allusions to central facets of Platonic philosophy are easily underrated. It is not safe to state that, just because they are mere allusions, passages such as 301a do 'not yet' imply a fully developed theory of Forms, or 290c, 291c, 292ac a fully developed theory of dialectic, etc.³⁹⁶ In particular the elusive Royal Art and its 'use' with which the central section (288b–293a) is concerned, very probably also involves, besides dialectic, the

---

392. For the earlier discussion, cf. Ritter 1922: 158 ff. The general tendency now is to emphasize the 'advanced' traits of the dialogue. Only Wundt 1949: 40 ff. and H. M. Wolff 1957: 45 have ventured to assign to it a very early date (about 400 BCE), on quite inadequate grounds.

393. Earlier theories of spuriousness have been refuted by Lutoslawski 210, Immisch 1899: 441 and Natorp 1900a: 1060 ff.

394. Ritter 1910b: 456 suggested this, but nobody seems to have followed him.

395. Note the ironic play with the motif of receiving instruction from the erists at the beginning (frame 272cd, main dialogue 275ab, etc.) and the end (main dialogue 304ab, frame 304bc); and especially the very subtle artistry by which Plato makes 'Clinias' gradually grow out of his role and lead the discussion towards the Royal Art (291b, cf. 289d ff.) which forces Criton to interrupt the report (290e). There are references from the main dialogue to the frame (notably 295d to 272c; cf. 283c).

396. Among the minimizers, note Zeller II 1⁵ 531 n. 2, Lutoslawski 217 f., Raeder 142 f., 261, Festugière 1973: 55 ff. But many scholars have seen that a great deal may be implied by such allusions (e.g. Shorey 1903: 31 and n. 199, Geffcken II A 77 n. 71, Allen 1970: 105 ff., Guthrie IV 266).

[145] political art of the true philosopher. And this brings us again into proximity with the *Republic*.

E.C. The most interesting of the external chronological criteria concerns Isocrates. It has often been argued that Isocrates is the target of the references at
[146] the end of *Euthydemus* (289d–290a, 304d–306d) to a certain unnamed λογοποιός (though a very typical indefinite plural is mostly used), who is also politically and 'philosophically' active (cf. notably 305cd). I find this practically certain considering also the parody of Isocratean style (304e, 305c–306d). And, as has sometimes been observed, these allusions imply that Isocrates had already published other political and cultural essays in addition to the 'Against the Sophists' (about 390 BCE).[397]

The possible allusions to Antisthenes have little chronological relevance for us.[398] And certain parallels to the *Euthydemus* in Xenophon's Memorabilia are also probably of little use, although the mention of βασιλική τέχνη in Socrates' discussion with Euthydemus in *Mem*. IV 2.11 is quite interesting and worth noting.[399]

I. C. *Gorgias—Euthydemus*. This order is now more often argued or taken for granted than the reverse order.[400] The criteria are not particularly clear, but details such as the play with παρουσία *Euthd*. 301a (cf. *Grg*. 497e) and with the definition of rhetoric *Euthd*. 289e (cf. *Grg*. 462e ff.) speak rather unambiguously for the precedence of the *Gorgias*. Those who regard the *Euthydemus* as earlier have been misled by stylometry, the references to Isocrates, or the allegedly 'preliminary' stages in the *Euthydemus* of the theory of Forms, dialectic, statemanship, etc.[401]

*Protagoras—Euthydemus*. *Euthydemus* is normally taken to be more advanced in various respects, and this seems generally plausible.[402] For my part I should like

---

397. See the discussion and references in Ritter 1910b: 29–32, 210 f., Ueberweg-Praechter 252 f., Geffcken II A 77 n. 66, Ries 1959: 35 ff., Festugière 1973: 159 ff., Guthrie IV 282 f. The doubts expressed by H. Gomperz 1906: 29 ff., v. Arnim 1914: 129 f., Wilamowitz II 165 ff. and some others are not convincing. Adducing the 'Helen' (X) because of its polemics against erists is not particularly helpful (Ritter 1910b: 210 f.). More pertinently, Mathieu 1932: 558 ff. argued that the 'Panegyricus' (IV, 380 BCE) must precede the *Euthydemus* (the objections of de Strycker 1935: 239 have little force in this connection); cf. Ryle 1966: 217. But to assume that the 'To Nicocles' (II), of 373 BCE, occasioned Plato's ironical comments on the Royal Art, would probably produce too late a date.

398. Cf. Raeder 138 ff., Rick 1931: 160 ff.; serious doubts by Wilamowitz II 158–165.

399. Cf. Maier 1913: 56 f., Geffcken II A 78 n. 80–81. This Euthydemus is not the erist, but the son of Diocles, a follower of Socrates who is mentioned by Plato in *Smp*. 222b. Xenophon does not refer to the erist anywhere, but Dionysodorus, the former teacher of strategy (cf. *Euthd*. 273c) is mentioned in *Mem*. III 1.1. In this case (contrary to the 'Symposium,' above p. 118) it is very much more probable that Xenophon is operating with Platonic reminiscences than vice versa. Or is Antisthenes again the common source (cf. below n. 684)?

400. Cf. Ritter 1914: 338 ff., Méridier Introduction 1931: 140 f., Ries 1959: 35 ff., Gaiser 1974: 137 (abandoning his earlier belief in the reverse order).

401. This seems to apply to Horn 1893: 179 ff., Lutosławski 194 ff., v. Arnim 1914: 129 f., Dodds 1959: 22 f., Bluck 1961: 115, Festugière 1973: 159 ff., and to a less degree to Beare 1913, Taylor, Friedländer, Gundert 1971 and some others.

402. Through many of the criteria are doubtful as such; *see* e.g. Ritter 1922b: 135 n. 112 and p. 144 (Nachtrag to n. 122) on dialectic. Only those who (like Taylor or Gundert 1971) think the *Protagoras* is a very advanced work tend to place it later; cf. also Crombie I 241–245.

to emphasize, in addition to the formal details discussed above, the fact that the teaching of virtue in the *Euthydemus* is approached from a more specific angle and is at the same time combined with a confrontation of a specific variety of sophistry, 'eristic,' with true philosophy.

*Symposium—Euthydemus.* The reverse order is normally taken for granted, but on quite inadequate grounds as far as I can see.[403] We actually have no reason to expect reminiscences of the theory of Love or the Form of καλόν in *Euthydemus*, if Plato wrote it after *Symposium*. The formal criteria discussed above point strongly to the order *Symposium—Euthydemus*.

*Republic* versus *Euthydemus.* There are no acceptable reasons for dating the *Euthydemus* after the whole of the *Republic*, but placing it in the period when large portions of the *Republic* were being planned or written seems feasible—however, Plato's dealings with the erists are really a side-track rather than a 'preliminary stage' for the *Republic*.[404] Those who separate *Republic* I normally place it before *Euthydemus*, admittedly on uncertain grounds.[405]

*Phaedo—Euthydemus.* The possibility of accepting this order, odd as it seems at first sight, was argued above p. 293. As in the case of *Symposium, Euthydemus* is normally regarded as the earlier dialogue on general and quite inadequate grounds.[406]

## Lysis

G.C. On the hypothesis advanced here, the *Lysis* and the largely similar *Charmides* have been wrongly assigned a place among the earliest works of Plato. Some 'advanced' features in the doctrinal contents and the approach which have been sometimes noted will be discussed below in connection with the internal criteria.[407] Several scholars in the 19th century considered *Lysis* spurious, among

---

403. Cf. Lutoslawski 238 ff., 282 ff., Ritter 1923: 869, Métidier 1931: M6–48, Moreau 1939: 27 n. 10, Goldschmidt 1940.

404. The above-mentioned allusions in the *Euthydemus* to the theory of Forms, dialectic, and the Royal Art, etc., though often adduced, give no real clues to the internal order; cf. Ritter 1910a: 278 ff., v. Arnim 1914: 135 f. The theories of Pfleiderer 1896 and Immisch 1899 implied that large portions of the present *Republic* preceded the *Euthydemus*. Gomperz II 590 f. tends to place *Euthydemus* after the *Republic*. In fact some details, notably the point about 'making and using' *Euthd.* 289a ff., *R.* X 601cff. (cf. Raeder 1905: 238), suggest the priority of the *Euthydemus*.

405. Among the specific arguments adduced, note the apparent development of the conception of virtue; v. Arnim 1914: 136 ff. (versus Lutoslawski 284 f.).

406. For various signs of a supposed doctrinal advance, *see* e.g. Lutoslawski 282 ff., Ritter 1910a: 278 ff., Méridier 1931b: 46–48, Festugière 1973: 86 f. The literary art of the *Phaedo* is sometimes considered more advanced, cf. Geffcken II 104. The only one who, to my knowledge, has argued specifically for the order *Phaedo—Euthydemus* is Rick 1931: 366 f., but I do not find his contribution very illuminating either. This is a typical case of *non liquet*.

407. For the *Lysis*, see the conspectus of Ritter 1923: 1–29 (reviewing also the controversy of v. Arnim, who argued for a relatively early date, and Pohlenz); cf. Begemann 1960, Versenyi 1975. But Guthrie IV 134 f., 143 ff. argues emphatically for an early date.

[147]
[148]
them Zeller, and Lutoslawski tended to follow them (cf. 340); *see* the refutation of this view by Kuiper 1909: 1–44. The limited size and scope and the didactic tone suggest that *Lysis* and *Charmides*, contrary to the large dialogues discussed above, were written in the first place for internal use in the Academy, and yet—as the finished literary form shows—with a larger public of young potential pupils in mind (cf. below p. 300). The ambiguities and obvious fallacies of the logic in *Lysis*, which have often intrigued commentators and contributed to the theory of spuriousness (note Guthrie IV 143–154), are probably explicable as intentional didactic exercises rather than as lack of maturity on the part of the author. This is not to say that the *Lysis* need have been a success with its readers (cf. Guthrie 143).

E.C.   The legend that Socrates himself had *Lysis* read to him and commented on it cannot be trusted.[408] And the possible allusions to Antisthenes[409] are not helpful as far as the dating is concerned. Rather more interesting, in my opinion, is the emphatically double reference in the opening (203ab) to Socrates walking from the Academy to Lyceum. This must have a symbolic function somehow (as Immisch 1899: 614 notes; Zürcher 1954: 33 of course thought that Lyceum refers to the Peripatos), though it is not pointedly anachronistic because we know that even in the 5th century young intellectuals used to gather in the Academia (cf. above p. 177). I would assume that this is a playful hint that the Academic reader will now be faced with a more Socratic theme than he, perhaps, expects.[410]

I. C. *Gorgias*—*Lysis*.   Most scholars have tended to regard *Lysis* as earlier, but several arguments have also been propounded for the order *Gorgias*—*Lysis*.[411] The two dialogues are in fact quite different. As far as I can see, the only important point of comparison is the treatment of παρουσία in *Gorgias* 497e ff. versus *Lysis* 217b ff., and here I am sure the more detailed discussion in *Lysis* is later.[412]

For the character of Menexenus in the frame dialogue of *Menexenus* and in the *Lysis*, see below p. 328.—For the order. *Protagoras*—*Lysis*, which is more often preferred than the reverse one, there seem to be no clear criteria.[413]

*Symposium*—*Lysis*.   This is a much-debated problem which, in spite of much disagreement as to details, is usually solved by explaining the *Lysis* as 'preliminary'

---

408. Diog. L. 3.35, *Anon.Proleg.* 3. This story has sometimes been accepted as true and has been combined with the highly suspect argument that the *Lysis* is too 'frivolous' to have been written after 399 BCE (cf. Ueberweg 1861: 210, 296); but cf. Leisegang 1950: 2369, Riginos 1976: 55.

409. *See* especially Wirth 1896 on οἰκεῖον 221e. For Antisthenes' 'Menexenus' *see* below p. 328.

410. Cf. Socrates 'returning' to the Lyceum at the end of the *Symposium*.

411. For *Lysis-Gorgias*, see e.g. Horn 1893: 118 f., 179 ff., Ueberweg-Praechter 243; for *Gorgias-Lysis*, *see* Raeder 153 ff., Kuiper 1909: 73 ff., Kahn 1981. Gaiser 1974: 137, too, has been inclined to place *Lysis* later.

412. *See* notably Raeder 155 for this point.

413. Cf. Kuiper 1909: 77 and the rather over-ingenious line of argument presented by von Arnim 1914: 97–109. Supporters of the order *Lysis*—*Protagoras* (e.g. Pfleiderer 1896, Taylor, Bluck 1949, Guthrie) have not produced any specific arguments of importance. And against Boder 1973 it could be asserted that the irony of the *Lysis* is certainly at least as 'complicated' as that of the *Protagoras*.

(or more cautiously as a 'satellite': Gomperz) to the *Symposium*.[414] The point of fundamental importance here is whether the doctrine of ἔρως as presented by 'Diotima' is somehow reflected in the *Lysis*. For my part, I am now more or less convinced that various allusions in the *Lysis* can really be read as implying the ideas of the *Symposium* (cf. notably *Lysis* 204bc, 205a, 206a, 211e, 216cd, 218ab, 219c–222a, 223ab with the doctrine of Diotima); obviously, however, Plato's intention is not to correct or even discuss the views of the latter.[415] All other arguments adduced for determining the relation between these two dialogues seem to me unimport or irrelevant.[416]

*Lysis* versus *Republic*. No real arguments have been produced for dating the *Lysis* even in relation to *Republic* I, although most of the scholars who separate the latter agree on the order *Republic* I—*Lysis*.[417]

*Phaedo—Lysis*. The common view of course is that because *Lysis* is more 'Socratic' and 'simple' it must be earlier. It is clear that where these two very different dialogues seem to have points of contact, notably in the logic concerning relation and opposites and the glimpses of the theory of Forms, *Lysis* is inconsistent and obscure. I do not think, however, that it can be proved to be earlier on these grounds any more than on the general grounds just mentioned. No positive criteria have been found.[418]

*Euthydemus—Lysis*. Here at least the bantering attitude and the play with logic provide some points of contact. The introduction in *Lysis* of Ctesippus the ὑβριστής without further characterization is interesting.[419] Those who have argued for the precedence of *Lysis* have not in my view come up with any substantial evidence,[420] whereas there are several specific arguments favoring the order *Euthydemus—Lysis*.[421]

---

414. Cf. notably Robin 1908, Pohlenz 1913: 368 ff., 1916: 251 ff., 1917, 1921: 9 f., v. Arnim 1914: 59 ff. (and Ritter 1923: 1 ff.), Friedländer II 94 ff., III 13 ff., Duncan 1969, Guthrie IV 143.
415. This has long been a controversial question; cf. e.g. Robin 1908 versus Kuiper 1909 and Rick 1931: 346 ff. In recent times the relative lateness of the *Lysis* has been accepted by Kapp 1968: 90, 131 f., Peters 1968: 60, Versenyi 1975, and some others.
416. Cf. Horn 1893: 289 f. on the aim of life, Wilamowitz II 69 ff. on the theory of Forms, Ueberweg-Praechter 261 on epistemology. The most common argument is of course that *Lysis* is simply 'more primitive.'
417. For various more or less unreliable criteria of the order *Republic* I—*Lysis*, see v. Arnim 1914: 97–109, Ritter 1922: 140 (who changed his view in 1935), Peters 1968: 170 ff. But many others, including Raeder, Wilamowitz, Geffcken, Krämer 1959 and Gauss (who yet separate *Republic* I,) tend to put *Lysis* before *Republic* I. The treatment of φιλία in R. I 332e, 335a, which is often referred to in this connection, is totally irrelevant as far as I can see.
418. The order *Phaedo—Lysis* was adopted by Pohlenz 1913 (who regarded *Smp*. later than *Phd*.), Stenzel 1917, Rick 1931 (346 ff., on very unreliable grounds), Kapp 1968: 131, and Peters 1968: 173 n. 284 (with doubts). A *non liquet* case again.
419. Cf. above p. 293. This was used as an argument for the order *Euthydemus—Lysis* by Kuiper 1909: 77 f.
420. After Horn (1893: 179 ff.) and other early believers in this order, note v. Arnim 1914 (especially 68, 110 ff.), Peters 1968: 142 ff. (with doubts again, cf. 151 n. 67), Boder 1973: 42 n. 2.
421. See Raeder 1905: 155 f., Kuiper 1909: 73 ff., Ritter 1910b: 265 ff., 1923: 869, 1929: 67. Note in particular the question of παρουσία (cf. above p. 296) and the κτῆσις/χρῆσις argument *Euthd*. 280c ff., 288e ff., which seems to be implied in *Ly*. 207d ff., cf. 220a.

[150] *Charmides*

G.C. The case is much the same as with the *Lysis;* but the belief in a very early date for the *Charmides* has been even more widespread.[422] Since the 1950s, however, some scholars have emphasized the 'advanced' features found in *Charmides*.[423] As an additional formal indication of a comparatively late date, one could refer to the 'myth' of Zalmoxis, 156d–157c, which is clearly of the same pseudo-exotic type as the 'Phoenician' tale in *Republic* III 414b–415d, the myths of Theuth in *Phaedrus* 274b–275b and *Philebus* 18b–d, and the Egyptian story *Timaeus* 21e ff.[424]

E.C. The fact that Plato's relatives, the oligarchic extremist Critias (as in *Protagoras*) and Charmides, are presented here in a rather favorable light has intrigued many scholars; and this is why some (among them Wilamowitz and Friedländer) place *Charmides* before 399 BCE, or at least before the pamphlet of Polycrates.[425] Since a very early date seems to me out of the question, I consider it reasonable to regard the introduction of these controversial characters as indicating a considerable distance in time from the trial of Socrates and the pamphlet. At any rate every attentive reader, and certainly all of Plato's friends and pupils in the Academy, would realize that neither Critias nor Charmides did in fact possess the qualities of σωφροσύνη, self-knowledge and 'minding one's own business,' which they are supposed to have; and many knew of course that the teaching of Charmides, which is 'forced' upon Socrates by Critias at the end of the dialogue (176cd), was a failure (cf. *Smp.* 222b, *Thg.* 128de; Crombie I 214).—The possible [151] relationship of *Charmides* with various works by Antisthenes, Aeschines and Xenophon is difficult to evaluate for the purposes of chronology.[426]

I.C. Though *Charmides* is commonly considered 'early' on general grounds, no reliable specific clues have been discovered for its relationship with *Gorgias, Protagoras, Symposium* or *Phaedo*.[427]

---

422. In more recent times, it has been maintained by e.g. Tuckey 1951, Dieterle 1966, Detel 1975 and also Guthrie IV 68 f.—The authenticity of *Charmides* was doubted (on quite unsufficient grounds) by Zeller and others (cf. Lutoslawski 203 n. 162) and Rick 1916. The traces of typically Platonic doctrines such as the theory of Forms, whether accepted at all, have usually been explained as representing a very early stage; cf. Shorey 1903: 18, 31, 45, 53 n. 384, Ritter. 1910b: 567 ff., Guthrie IV 155, 163 f.

423. Cf. Masaracchia 1950, Luce 1952, Krämer 1959: 503, Cohen 1962, Untersteiner 1965, Witte 1970, G. Müllet 1976. *See* now especially Kahn 1981.

424. Zalmoxis had been connected with Pythagoras as early as the 5th century (Hdt. 4.95 f.), and Plato may be alluding to Pythagorean traditions.

425. Treves 1952: 1748 f. and others assume that *Charmides* was one of the Platonic writings which occasioned the attack.

426. The most interesting of these possibilities is the suggestion made by Effe 1971 that the *Charmides* takes account of Aeschines' 'Alcibiades' which was very probably written after the pamphlet of Polycrates (Dittmar 1912: 152–159; the lower terminus proposed by Dittmar, Plato's *Meno*, is not so certain, and Dittmar dates it to 390 BCE which is obviously too early).—For Antisthenes and Xenophon, cf. Raeder 99, Chroust 1957: 204 f.

427. It is characteristic of the ambiguity of arguments from the contents that (Critias'?) definition of σωφροσύνη as τὰ ἑαυτοῦ πράττειν in *Chrm.* 161b ff., which occurs as a mere hint in *Grg.* 526c, has been used to vindicate the precedence both of *Charmides* (Pohlenz 1913: 149 n. 1) and

*Charmides* and the *Republic*. The *Charmides* is often placed before *Republic* I even by separatists. The somewhat parallel treatment of τέχναι (and ἐπιστῆμαι) in *Republic* I 346a ff. (cf. 349c ff.) and *Charmides* 161d ff. (leading into the main theme of ἐπιστήμη) has been interpreted to imply either the precedence of the former or the latter.[428] In my view, the more differentiated (though partly implicit) discussion in the *Charmides* is rather obviously more advanced and later. On the other hand, the manner in which the idea of 'minding one's own business' is introduced in *Republic* IV 433a ff. may presuppose the discussion in *Charmides* 161b ff.[429]

*Euthydemus—Charmides*. Although the reverse order is more often accepted or taken for granted, there is some disagreement as to how the points which these dialogues share should be interpreted, notably the glimpses we get of the theory of Forms and various epistemological details.[430] The main problem here is whether the discussion of the Royal Art in the *Euthydemus* (290a ff.) necessarily "founders on arguments used in the *Charmides*" (Guthrie 281), or vice versa, or whether there is a common (oral) source, and whether this can prove the precedence of either dialogue. I find it impossible to make a decision merely on the basis of these criteria alone since the arguments include, in both dialogues, playful and implicit hints; for instance, is the βασιλικὴ τέχνη more 'advanced' than the knowledge of τὸ ἀγαθόν which we are suddenly confronted with in *Charmides* 174b? If the *Euthydemus* is regarded as more explicit, and the trend of didactic exercise is emphasized in the *Charmides*, it is more natural to take the latter as the later one.

*Lysis—Charmides*. Here we are confronted with the intricate question of whether the close formal and structural resemblance of these dialogues is a sign of close proximity in time or rather not. Unlike many scholars,[431] I am inclined to

---

of *Gorgias* (Stefanini I 78 n. 3); the 'definition' was probably well known in Socratic circles (cf. R. IV 433a), and the two passages may well be independent.—For *Protagoras—Charmides*, cf. notably Natorp 1903: 19 f., v. Arnim 1914: 110 ff., Friedländer II 257 f.; for *Charmides—Protagoras*, Horn 1893: 128 f., 140 ff., Raeder 110 f., Pohlenz 1913: 1–13. In support of the precedence of *Protagoras* it could also be argued that *Charmides*, like *Symposium*, gives a more detailed and differentiated picture of characters mentioned as present in the *Protagoras* (315a, 316a, 336de).—As for *Symposium* and *Phaedo*, the common argument that the theory of Forms and epistemology are more advanced in these dialogues than in *Charmides* has little importance in view of the implicitness of the latter.

428. See notably v. Arnim 1914: 104 ff., 136 ff. for *Republic* I being earlier, and Pohlenz 1916: 262 and Kratzsch 1964 for *Charmides* being earlier.—Note the fact that the 'encomium' of Plato's family *Chrm.* 157e–158c is somewhat paralleled by R. II 367e f. and *Ti.* 20d–21a.

429. This is commonly accepted, cf. e.g. Raeder 212.—However, the more implicit occurrence of the same idea in R. II 369e ff. could be earlier than the *Charmides*; indeed, it may belong to the 'Proto-*Republic*' (cf. also above, n. 427).

430. For *Charmides—Euthydemus*, see especially Horn 1893: 179 ff. v. Arnim 1914: 110 ff., Festugière 1973: 159 ff., Guthrie IV 266 ff.; for *Euthydemus—Charmides*, Immisch 1899: 626 f., Erbse 1968: 36 f., Kapp 1968: 90 n. 51.

431. Ritter 1923: 9 even went so far as to suggest that formal identity may be a sign of chronological distance.

[152] think that it is. After much experimenting, Plato is about to fix a 'standard dialogue type' for semiesoteric use (cf. also *Theaetetus, Laches, Amatores* and *Eryxias*,) although he soon abandons this and later begins to plan trilogies of identical dialogues (cf. p. 335).

The *Lysis* is more commonly regarded as the later dialogue chiefly because *Charmides* is regarded as very early and *Lysis* is thought to approximate to the *Symposium*.[432] Those who argue that the *Lysis* is earlier attempt to prove that it is even less 'mature.'[433] Neither of these lines of argument fits in with the hypothesis adopted here. In fact there are no real thematic clues to be found. If it is assumed that the *Lysis* was intended for a somewhat younger category of pupils but did not prove to be a success, then the slightly more sophisticated and more carefully presented ideas of the *Charmides* suggest a later date. However, I would attach more weight to the formal facts discussed above (p. 267 ff.).

## Theaetetus

G.C. With regard to *Theaetetus*, the general opinion has veered from an insistence on a very early date[434] to an almost universal acceptance of a date in the early 360s.[435]

[153] It can be regarded as fairly certain that the dialogue was subjected to revision (cf. above p. 232).[436] However, separating two layers and dating them is no easy task. Considering the presence almost throughout of features in the contents and the style which must be regarded as fairly late,[437] one must assume that the revision

---

432. For this and various other arguments, *see* notably Kuiper 1909: 64–73, Maier 1913: 126 ff., Pohlenz 1913: 1 ff., Ritter 1922: 128–130, 140, Peters 1968, Boder 1973.

433. Cf. Beare 1913: 44 f., v. Arnim 1914: 63 ff., 110 ff., 1916 (against Pohlenz' later dating of *Lysis*), Geffcken II 65, Guthrie IV 134 f.

434. Whether connected with the theory of Plato's 'Megarian period' or not, the form and contents of the dialogue were thought to point to an 'aporetic' or 'preliminary' phase. After Zeller and his followers (references in Raeder 279 ff.) this view was still maintained by Windelband 1900, Natorp 1903, Waddington 1904 and Goedeckemeyer 1909 (*see* especially 435–438; but he discarded it in his new edition of Windelband 1923).

435. This view, taken by the 19th-century stylometrists, has been reinforced with various arguments in the subsequent discussion; cf. below. An even later date has been occasionally suggested; Vollenhoven 1948 tried to place *Tht.* after *Plt.* (cf. p. 194 n. 44), and Ryle 1966: 275–280, on equally shaky grounds, proposed a date after 358 BCE.

436. The main arguments are as follows: the explicit statement in the frame dialogue that the reported form has been dropped (143bc; if considered together with the other arguments this cannot be regarded as a mere fiction); the discrepancy between Euclides' statement in the frame (143a) that he has several times consulted Socrates about the details of the λόγος, and the end where the death of Socrates (the supposed reporter of the λόγος) is imminent (210d, but cf. also 142c); and the combining of apparently 'early' and 'late' traits in the contents and the style. Cf. Ueberweg 1861: 232–234, Chiappelli 1904, Wilamowitz II 230–237. Opponents to the theory or revision include Ritter 1910b: 247–249, Geffcken II A 112 n. 29 and Friedländer III 458 n. 75, but their objections are not convincing.

437. Cf. Shorey 1903: 33 f., Ritter 1910a: 228 ff., Robinson 1950: 3–19, Martin 1973: 32, Guthrie V 66 n. 1, 121 on the controversial question of the theory of Forms in *Theaetetus*; further,

was a thorough one. A reasonable hypothesis to start from seems to be as follows: Plato began by writing a reported dialogue in the style of the *Charmides*, yet probably with a frame dialogue in the manner of *Euthydemus*, presenting Socrates in conversation with Euclides (cf. *Tht.* 143b ἐμοί ... διηγούμενον).[438] It was concerned with ἐπιστήμη, more constructively perhaps than the *Charmides*, and with 'maieutics' (developed out of Socratic 'erotics').[439] The easy-going style of the first scene with Theaitetos, 144b–146c (but not the more formal opening exchange of speeches between Socrates and Theodoros), Socrates' presentation of maieutics 150b–151d, and the conclusion 210b–d, may represent the earlier layer.[440] The text was read at the Academy as an exercise, like *Lysis* and *Charmides*, and Plato found the problems it raised sufficiently interesting to be worth reconsidering, and he began to rewrite it at a later occasion. At this later stage the dialogue was considerably expanded, the background narrative was dropped, and the opening frame dialogue which survives was added. The date of this operation will be discussed below (p. 328).

Are there any means available to us for dating the earlier, reported version of *Theaetetus*? I do not think very much more can be said with reasonable confidence, than that it was probably written soon after the *Charmides* and that it was somehow connected with the renewed discussion of the role of 'Socrates' as a teacher (or rather, instructor) which is reflected in several dialogues that can be dated, roughly, to the 370s (cf. p. 351 ff.).

E.C. The specific, much-debated problem of the date of the death of Theaitetos does not necessarily have such a bearing upon the date of either of the two versions as is commonly believed today. It is fairly clear (though not absolutely certain) that Theaitetos died of his wounds and the dysenteria mentioned in 142b.[441] Whether the situation depicted refers to the Corinthian war (rather perhaps

---

the refutation of the opinions of earlier philosophers (cf. Raeder 297 f., Ueberweg-Praechter 290); and the systematic and sophisticated discussion of a single theme (cf. Taylor 323). For the 'maieutics,' cf. below n. 439. The style lacks the intensity of the *Gorgias* and the spirited ring of *Euthydemus* and *Charmides*; large portions even at the beginning (e.g. 143d–144b) approximate in fact to the 'late style' (cf. Brandwood 1958: 402 f., pointing out anomalies; Thesleff 1967: above, 116 ff.; Ritter 1910a: 247 f., 263 thinks that *Theaetetus* lacks stylistic peculiarities; Cornford 1935: 1 suggests that on the whole the latter part is more 'late' in style: evidently the problem of the style of *Theaetetus* would require reassessing; cf. p. 216.

438. This assumption would explain the role of Euclides in the frame dialogue preserved to us, and especially the fact that Plato makes him 'write down' the dialogue (143a). Euclides had published dialogues of his own (above p. 206; cf. the *Phaedo*, p. 289). Cf. also below p. 328 f.

439. There seems to have been some banter in early Socratic circles about mental 'delivery' after mental erotic contacts; cf. Aristophanes, *Clouds* 137, 695–740 (Taylor 1911: 131 ff., especially 148, 172), Xenophon, *Smp.* 4.56–64 (μαστροπεία, considered authentically Antisthenic, cf. Caizzi 52 f., 115). The anamnesis doctrine was perhaps implied in Plato's μαιευτική from the start (cf. *Tht.* 209c); see now Burnyeat 1977.

440. An earlier layer cannot be distinguished by means of traditional stylometry (cf. above n. 437); but to an attentive reader some sections give the impression of being 'earlier' than others.

441. Formulations such as 142b6 οἷον ἄνδρα, d2–3 εἴπερ εἰς ἡλικίαν ἔλθοι suggest this; and Euclides says (143a) that he has consulted Socrates several times about the discussion; but Theaitetos has not been consulted. Possibly there is a symbolic parallel between the death

[154] 390 B.G, cf. Xen. *Hell.* 4.5.19) or to the Isthmian war of 369/8 BCE (cf. id. 6.5.49–52, 7.1.18–19, Diod. 15.68) is still in fact an unsolved problem. Most scholars have now accepted the later date, originally suggested by Munk (1857), especially since it appears to fit in better with the results of stylometry and with our picture of the history of Greek mathematics.[442] Disregarding stylometry, I find it quite credible that the mathematical discoveries concerning irrationals and regular solids, which are attributed to Theaitetos by later authorities, could have been made or suggested by a brilliant mathematician in his early twenties; and indeed, should we not have heard more about this remarkable contemporary of Plato's had he really 'written' Books X and XIII of Euclid's *Elementa*? In particular, against the commonly accepted view that Theaitetos made his discoveries between the publication of *Republic* VII 528d, in which Plato speaks of the deplorable state of stereometry, and *Timaeus* 54d ff. where he presents the regular solids, it could be said that it is somewhat odd that the gifted geometrician Theaitetos should not have studied stereometry until he was middle-aged, if Plato who was not an active geometrician himself, was aware of the potentialities of this field of study; after all it is more natural to think that the suggestions made by the young Theaitetos, but never followed up by anybody, had opened Plato's eyes 
[155] to the possibilities of stereometry and occasioned the remark in the *Republic*. In fact, this may be implied by Eudemus who states (about Hermotimus) τὰ ὑπ' Εὐδόξου προυπειρημένα καὶ Θεαιτήτου προήγαγεν ἐπὶ πλέον (Proclus in Euclid. I p. 66 f. Friedländer); this is sometimes wrongly taken to mean that Theaitetos was a contemporary of Eudoxus. In *Theaetetus* 142d2 ἡλικίαν of course implies military age, but nothing more. It is true that Xenophon (*Hell.* 6.5.49) mentions that Iphicrates in 369 camped with his troups in the Academeia for one night. But was a 45 year old intellectual really likely to have joined his mercenary peltasts,[443] especially since this was by no means a war of national prestige for Athens?

For my part, I think it much more probable that Theaitetos died in 390 BCE. And I would assume that Plato wrote the first version of the dialogue some 15 or 20 years later. As a matter of fact, the whole setting, and the treatment of the character of Theaitetos in this dialogue (in the *Sophist* he is a stereotype, and in *Politicus* his transformation into a 'young Socrates' has been carried out completely)[444]

---

of Socrates, referred to at the beginning (142c6) and the end (210d2), and the death of his young 'counterpart' (for Theaitetos as a 'young Socrates,' cf. p. 307). But the main reason for making a point of the death of both in the introduction is probably the revision of the text so as to make it the 'last word' of Socrates on the concept of ἐπιστήμη.—*See* now below, p. 509 ff.

442. This was argued in particular by Vogt 1909/10 (especially 117–131), 1913/14, Sachs 1914, 1917 (especially 88–119), v. Fritz 1932; cf. Guthrie V 63 n. 1. The various other arguments adduced for the later date (cf. Christ 1886: 494 ff., Ritter 1910b: 111 f., 200, Wilamowitz I 513–515, II 21, Diès 1924: 120 ff., Taylor 320, Geffcken II A 112 n. 26) have little weight. After Zeller, Campbell (cf. Thesleff 1967: above, 18) and Shorey (1903: 66 n. 516), few have accepted the earlier date for the death of Theaitetos.

443. Cf. above p. 278.

444. I cannot agree with Gauss III/1.185 f. who thinks that Theaitetos is depicted as a full-grown man in the *Sophist*.

suggests a person whom Plato remembers many years later as a young man, [155]
rather than a person with whom Plato has been in constant touch for 30 years.
In this sense, too, the *Theaetetus* is reminiscent of the *Charmides*. But Euclides of
Megara (cf. above p. 301 and n. 438) appears to have been still living and active
about 370 BCE since his pupil Eubulides was a contemporary of Aristotle (Diog.
L. 2.108 f.); so the 'law of Parmentier' again seems difficult to apply.[445]

The other external criteria that have sometimes been adduced are not particularly clear, and may in fact apply to the second version only.[446]

I.C.   A later date for the *Theaetetus* in relation to *Gorgias, Protagoras*,[447] *Symposium*,[448] *Phaedo*,[449] *Euthydemus*,[450] *Lysis* and *Charmides*[451] is taken for granted nowa- [156]
days and can be accepted here without further comment, although many of the
arguments employed may in fact concern the later version, and not so much can
be said positively of the position of the hypothetical early version.

The relation between the *Republic* and *Theaetetus* is more problematic. Since
the theory of the early date of *Theaetetus* was gradually abandoned at the beginning of this century, nobody seems to have argued that the present version

---

445. Of the various explanations given of the choice of a Megarian setting for at least the second version of the dialogue, I find it quite reasonable that Plato wished to prepare for a constructive confrontation with Megarian philosophy; cf: Raeder 290 f., and below p. 329.

446. It is possible that the mention in *Tht.* 174d–175b of encomia of kings and tyrants and the playful remark (175a) that some boast of a pedigree of 25 generations from Herakles imply a real person: Zeller (II 1$^5$ 406 n. 1) thought of the Spartan king Agesipolis, who was active in the Corinthian war, others have thought of Agesilaus (cf. Ueberweg-Praechter 209, Ries 1959: 129 ff.) and have noted that Isocr. *Euagoras* (IX), from the late 370s, appears to have initiated the genre of prose encomia to living persons (8); but cf. the doubts expressed by e.g. Raeder 296.—It is also possible that κυλινδόμενοι *Tht.* 172c9 alludes to Isocr. *C. Soph.* (XIII) 20 and is alluded to by Isocrates in the *Antidosis* (XV) 30 (Ries 1959: 132 f.) but the frame thus obtained, c. 390–354 BCE, is of little use here.

447. Note the detailed criticism of the sophist in *Theaetetus*, versus the sweeping portrait in *Protagoras*.

448. At the beginning of his century some scholars still followed Zeller in considering the epistemology of *Smp.* 202a more advanced than that of *Tht.* (so did also Shorey 1903: 71 n. 554, and Verdam 1916: 287 ff.); but this view does not stand up to criticism and has now been abandoned. And it is much more natural to regard the play with epistemological 'maieutics' as secondary in relation to the 'erotics' of Diotima, than vice versa; cf. Burnyeat 1977.

449. Zeller and his followers (even Verdam 1919: 180 ff.) used to argue that *Phaedo* is in various respects more 'mature.' This view has perhaps never been refuted in all its details, but it can hardly be seriously maintained today. However, I have found no specific indications that the earlier version of *Tht.* was later than *Phd.*, because the relatively advanced ideas of *Tht.* concerning the theory of knowledge (disregarding maieutics), sense perception, the philosopher and the world, criticism of earlier philosophy, and eschatology (note *Tht.* 176e f.) may belong to the later version.

450. The remarkable confidence with which Natorp 'stated' the precedence of *Theaetetus* over *Euthydemus* (above p. 189) remains a curious incident in the history of the interpretation of Plato. The last to argue this order appears to have been Goedeckemeyer 1909: 435 ff.

451. It is difficult to avoid the impression that the early version of *Theaetetus* was one of the many dialogues (cf. below p. 357 ff.) that followed the model of the *Charmides*. A detail such as the ugliness of Theaitetos (143e, 209c) is probably an intentional contrast to the beauty of Charmides.

[156] of *Theaetetus* precedes the present version of the *Republic*.⁴⁵² A great many indications have accumulated to show the precedence of the *Republic*: apart from stylometry and the direct references sometimes detected in the *Theaetetus*, chronological trends have been noted particularly in the attitude to the theory of Forms, epistemology in relation to sense perception, the conception of soul, the philosopher's duties, and various details such as the doctrine of δύναμις and of change.⁴⁵³ Yet, accepting the hypotheses of an early version of the *Theaetetus*, and of a successive genesis of the *Republic*, we cannot be very sure about the internal order of these different stages. Does, for instance, Socrates' playful hint at his ability to match pairs so as to generate the best offspring possible, *Theaetetus* 149d, contain a reference to the eugenics of the 'Proto-*Republic*,' or to the present *Republic* V 458d ff, or is there no such connection? The terminology used in *Theaetetus* 143c (αἱ μεταξὺ τῶν λόγων διηγήσεις) does indeed suggest that the present prologue was written later than the discussion of μίμησις and διήγησις in *Republic* III (cf. notably 394b4), but this provides no clue as to the position of
[157] the early version of *Theaetetus*, or even the new version of the main dialogue, in relation to the *Republic*. The fact that there is no reference or allusion to Socratic midwifery in the *Republic* (cf. e.g. VI 490b which obviously alludes to the doctrine of Diotima in *Symposium*) is no indication that the first version of *Theaetetus* must have been written after the *Republic*: the midwifery of Socrates is likely to have been an old joke, and in any case no later work refers to it.⁴⁵⁴ I should prefer to think that Plato did not start writing the later portions of the *Republic* (cf. below, p. 331) until he had finished his experiments with *Lysis*, *Charmides* and the early *Theaetetus*, but this view remains purely conjectural.

## Parmenides

G.C. The authenticity of this anomalous work, though frequently questioned in the 19th century,⁴⁵⁵ is generally accepted today and need not be discussed here as a separate problem; even if not entirely by Plato, the dialogue must have been written by a member of his 'inner circle.'

It is also accepted now that the *Parmenides* must be a relatively late work, and that its attitudes to the theory of Forms, Principles and epistemology reflect a later stage of Plato's thought than the period of *Symposium*, *Phaedo* and the *Republic*; yet the exact implications of the dialogue are still highly controversial.⁴⁵⁶

---

452. The last to argue this in considerable detail were Natorp 1903 and Verdam 1919 (with criticism of Raeder's arguments in particular), but the points they made are manifestly inadequate and partly mistaken.
453. In addition to Lutoslawski and Raeder (passim), see especially Wilamowitz II 179, Robin 1938: 100 ff., Krämer 1959: 128 f., Mugler 1960: 124 ff., Peters 1968: 170 ff.
454. Cf. above n. 439 and Guthrie III 444 n. 3, V 73 n. 2.
455. See references in Lutoslawski 400 f., Raeder 305; the last of the skeptics (except for Zürcher 1954) appears to have been M. Schneidewin 1916.
456. The old problem of whether and to what extent the criticism of the theory of Forms implies a fundamental change in Plato's views has often in recent discussion been combined with

*Parmenides* consists of two formally and thematically distinct parts, the first recording (through an awkward three-stage report) young Socrates' meeting with the Eleans and Parmenides' criticism of his theory of Forms, the latter (from 137c) giving Parmenides' examination of eight ontological hypotheses relating to henology, as an elenctic exercise (cf. 136c γυμνασάμενος) of young Aristoteles (in a strictly dramatic dialogue form, though without the speaker's sigla in our manuscripts). It has sometimes been argued that the two parts did not originally belong together.[457] I find it quite plausible that Plato (or whoever wrote the first part) did not originally plan to add the second part such as we have it, and that the appending of this Academic exercise reflects a shift of purpose: initially intended for a somewhat larger circle of readers, perhaps as apology and/or polemic against critics of the theory of Forms, the dialogue now became a purely esoteric text. The second part may, however, have been composed before the first part of the dialogue.[458]

[157]

[158]

Stylistically, the *Parmenides* is anomalous and, apparently, heterogeneous.[459] The curious three-stage report of the first part, whatever Plato's reasons for choosing it,[460] indicates a further development (indeed, a *reductio ad absurdum*) of the trend of the *Symposium* (the final version, p. 327) and *Phaedo*; cf. also the *Republic* (below).

E.C. I cannot find sufficient grounds for connecting the supposed 'crisis' reflected in the *Parmenides* with the Sicilian events,[461] except for the possibility that Plato might, during his second visit to Sicily, have met Polyxenus, who perhaps introduced or at any rate propagated the τρίτος ἄνθρωπος argument.[462] But the slightly condescending attitude to young men in the dialogue, and notably the very precise piece of information that Parmenides was an old man of about 65

---

the problem of whether and to what extent the dialogue reflects other metaphysical doctrines; cf. notably Krämer 1959: 137 f., Wyller 1960 and later (arguing for a very late date), Crombie II 257 ff., Barford 1978, Rochol 1975, Gerson 1977, and Guthrie V 1978: 33 ff. To be able to fix the chronological place of this dialogue would obviously be useful.

457. Cf. notably Horn 1904: 279, Apelt Parm. 36–41 (arguing that the second part is actually the older one), H. M. Wolff 1957: 216 ff. (an unreliable conjecture that the first part is from 402 BCE, the second younger than the *Sophist*), Gauss II/1.75, Ryle 1966: 287 ff. (first part from the late 360s, second part about 356 BCE). The strict unity of the *Parmenides* has been argued recently, although not very convincingly as far as I can see, by Wyller 1966, 1969, 1970 and Gerson 1977, cf. Niewöhner 1971: 71 ff.

458. Cf. Apelt's suggestion, above n. 457.

459. Cf. Brandwood 1958: 154 ff., cf. 41 f., 102 f. The tests referred to above, n. 202, clearly indicate the same. Shorey 1903: 57 ff. did not fail to point out that *Parmenides* is not 'late' in style but in contents.

460. The need for distance and a 'young Socrates' was probably one reason, cf. Raeder 300 f. More difficult explanations have been suggested by Shorey 1903: 58 ff. (the reader warned not to take the dialogue too seriously), Ritter 1910b: 127 f. (Plato wrote the dialogue in Syracuse in 367/6 BCE), Alrivie 1971, Panagiotou 1981.

461. This has often been done, cf. e.g. Lutoslawski 412, Eberz 1907, Ritter 1910b: 265 ff., Taylor 1927: 371, Raeder 1950.

462. Cf. Gomperz II 438, Raeder 1905: 305 f.; Leisegang 1950: 2485 f., with further references. Cherniss 1944: 292 f. expresses serious doubts.

[158] years (127b), suggests to me (as it has suggested to some others) that Plato was himself of the same age when the first part of the dialogue was being written: this would mean an absolute date of around 362 BCE.[463]—And I would regard it as almost certain that the character of Aristoteles in the *Parmenides*, besides being a 'Charmides redivivus' (127d2), also represents Plato's famous pupil. It is important to note that Aristotle himself (*Met.* A 9.990b17) uses the 'third man' argument against the 'friends of Forms,' and that Plato must have been impressed by this pupil of his (cf. Aelian. VH 4.9). Note also the somewhat parallel play with the historical character of 'Socrates the Younger' in *Theaetetus*, the *Sophist* and *Politicus*. I can see no point in introducing the long-since forgotten 5th century
[159] politician Aristoteles, other than the desire to refer to the philosopher.[464]—Other supposed references to contemporary persons are less helpful to us.[465]

I.C. It is generally agreed today, and on substantial grounds, that the *Parmenides* must follow *Gorgias, Protagoras, Symposium, Phaedo*,[466] *Euthydemus, Lysis* and *Charmides*.

There is also fairly universal agreement that the *Parmenides* is later than the *Republic*, chiefly because the criticism made in the *Parmenides* of the theory of Forms and of ontology is thought to presuppose not only the presentation of these themes in the *Republic*, but also the general conception of this work.[467] Disregarding for the moment Book X, I believe this view is fundamentally sound. I find it more than unlikely that Plato would have presented his theory of Forms in this manner, and arranged it hierarchically as he does in the middle of the *Republic*, after the criticism of the *Parmenides*. Among additional arguments for a later date of the *Parmenides*, I would attach some importance to the play with names and characters at the beginning of the dialogue. 'Cephalus' meeting Adimantus and Glaucon provides a clear association with the opening of the *Republic*; and this reminiscence is less formal and superficial than the corresponding association

---

463. Cf. Lutoslawski 407 f., Ryle 1966: 287 ff.

464. This is a very controversial point, however. Among the adherents of this 'identification' (which of course cannot be more than an ambiguous allusion), note Lutoslawski 401, Eberz 1907, Wundt 1949: 37, Düring 1956: 112 f., Ryle 1966: 109, Kapp 1968: 89 f. The skeptics include Horn 1904: 158 ff., Raeder 305 f., Cherniss 1944: 29 f., Friedländer III 127 and Guthrie V 36. Most skeptics, unnecessarily, find difficulties in the chronology. Guthrie l.e. finds a possible indication that the philosopher is not meant in the fact that "Plato takes the trouble to point out . . . that he was the Aristoteles who became one of the Thirty Tyrants"; I would have thought this a rather strong indication that Aristotle indeed was in Plato's mind, and feel tempted to believe that Plato happened to have thirty pupils at the time (he writes in fact τὸν τῶν τριάκοντα γενόμενον).

465. Antisthenes, Taylor 86 n. 1; Eudoxus, v. Fritz 1927: 20 ff., Friis Johansen 1964: 193 ff., Schofield 1973 (but cf. Allan 1960: 143 f.); alios alii. With very little plausibility, Zeno the Stoic, Zürcher 1954: 76 ff.

466. Following Zeller, some conservatives around the turn of the century placed *Parmenides* before *Symposium* and *Phaedo*; the last to argue this in some detail was Pfleiderer 1896, especially 394 f., 477 ff. This order was still accepted by Goedeckemeyer 1909 (but abandoned in 1923).

467. This has been argued innumerable times since Jackson 1882; cf. e.g. Ross 1951, Kapp 1968: 55 ff. Zeller's old idea (II¹ 185 f.) that substantial parts of the *Republic* are later than *Parmenides* was maintained and supported with additional arguments by Pfleiderer 1896 and Horn 1904, but few were convinced, and even Goedeckemeyer finally abandoned it in 1923.

at the beginning of the *Symposium* (cf. p. 326), since 'Cephalus of Clazomenai' [159] is probably an intentional transformation of Cephalus of Syracuse: perhaps this name ('Headman from the Land of Screamers') is a symbolic fiction somewhat in the manner of 'Diotima of Mantineia'? And since the critical theme of the *Parmenides* has nothing to do with Books I–II but very much with the basic premises of the central part of the *Republic*, this 'linking up' with the opening of the latter work suggests that the present *Republic* was more or less complete when the *Par-* [160] *menides* began to take shape.[468]—For Book X, cf. below p. 332.

The relation to *Theaetetus* has been subject to considerable debate. The dialogues clearly belong together somehow, because both tackle somewhat similar problems in a critical manner,[469] and both are in their own way 'preliminary' to the *Sophist* and *Politicus*; stylometrists place both in the 'late middle group' or 'early late group' on somewhat dubious grounds. In spite of considerable differences there are also very similar formal traits such as the presentation of a 'young Socrates' as a contrast to an elderly teacher, and the reading of a manuscript (*Prm.* 127d, *Tht.* 143bc; cf. also *Phdr.* 230e). Though a majority of scholars would prefer to place *Parmenides* later, there is no real agreement as to the relative order of these two dialogues.

If the hypothesis of an earlier version of *Theaetetus* is accepted, it seems that many of the arguments for the precedence of *Theaetetus* would in fact apply to this version. However, I am inclined to side with the majority in thinking that the final version also preceded *Parmenides*, though the positive criteria are not very clear. The doctrinal contents and the difference in method do not seem to offer reliable clues: for instance, the approach to epistemology in *Theaetetus* was originally planned without an explicit discussion of the theory of Forms, and so Plato could do without it in the later version also;[470] and the dialectic is from the outset more 'Elean' in *Parmenides* and hence may give the impression of being more advanced, although the method of *Theaetetus* is in fact highly sophisticated too (as e.g. Cornford's analysis shows).[471] Certain other details sometimes taken as signs of *Parmenides* being later than the second version of *Theaetetus*

---

468. Various other arguments adduced for the precedence of the *Republic* seem to me more ambiguous: for instance, the 'henology' in *R.* VII 524e ff. is not necessarily more primitive than that of *Parmenides* (Raeder 229); the fallacy of non-being, though perhaps not taken into account in the *Republic* (Benn 1902), is taken into account in the *Euthydemus* and *Cratylus* (cf. Shorey 1903: 54 f.); the 'longer way' alluded to in *R.* IV 435d does not foreshadow the *Parmenides* (Raeder 213) but rather refers to the higher education described in the *Republic* (cf. Shorey ad *R.* VI 504b) and, of course, to Academic συνυσία; the dialectic implied in the *Republic* is not necessarily less sophisticated than the method presented in the latter part of the *Parmenides* (cf. Ickler 1973 against R. Robinson and others). For stylometry, cf. above n. 202c.

469. Often pointed out, e.g. Shorey 1903: 57 n. 424, Raeder 303, Taylor 348 f., Stefanini II 69–74.

470. It is often thought that Plato would have taken account of the criticism in the *Parmenides*, if he had written the *Theaetetus* later (cf. e.g. Lutoslawski 408 f., Natorp 1903: 220 f., v. Fritz 1927: 20 ff.), but the approach is really quite different.

471. A trend in this respect has been argued notably by Lutoslawski 405 ff., etc., and Liebrucks 1949. Note the secondary frame of *Theaetetus* which gives it a 'Megarian' touch.

[161] are also debatable.[472] On the other hand, the change in tone and the general trend from criticism of epistemology in *Theaetetus* to criticism of ontology in *Parmenides* (cf. *Timaeus* p. 338) strongly points to the correct chronological order being *Theaetetus—Parmenides*. The main difficulties are really formal ones. The mention in passing in *Theaetetus* 183e that Socrates had once, when he was very young, met the old and 'venerable' philosopher Parmenides (similarly, but more explicitly referring to the dialogue *Prm.*, in *Sph.* 217c) must, I believe, be taken to imply that the dialogue *Parmenides* had already been planned or existed in a draft form.[473] Although the *Sophist* and *Politicus* link up with both *Theaetetus* and *Parmenides* (p. 339), the fact that they are in formal respects more closely related to *Theaetetus* can be explained as due to their 'epistemological' (rather than ontological) themes. And there are probably specific reasons for maintaining an awkward three-stage report in *Parmenides*, in spite of the abandoning of the report in *Theaetetus*.[474] Various other arguments that have sometimes been adduced for the precedence of *Parmenides*, are easily refuted.[475]

---

472. Stylometry has been taken to suggest this (cf. Lutoslawski 189, 410 ff., v. Arnim 1912, Rudberg 1924: 121 ff., Diàz Tejera 1965), but the grounds are shaky to say the least. The explicit differentiation of qualitative change and motion in *Tht.* 181b ff. probably belongs to the second version, and it is taken for granted in *Prm.* 138bc; but it is also implied in *R.* II 380e, IV 436c ff., *Cra.* 439e, and as it seems rather unlikely that Plato argued it for the first time in the *Theaetetus*, it is no strong argument (as some believe, e.g. Raeder 316) for the priority of *Theaetetus* to *Parmenides*. Wyller's very late dating of the *Parmenides* (1968, etc.) depends essentially on his view that it represents the 'Philosophus' (below p. 195).

473. Note also the ἐπεισκωμιάζοντες λόγοι *Tht.* 184a5 which Socrates fears would keep him from his theme if he were to consider the points of Parmenides. I can see no reason for referring to the awkward fiction of Socrates meeting Parmenides unless the dialogue with its artificial setting was at least being planned (cf. Raeder 298 ff. with references). Some scholars take this as a strong argument that the *Parmenides* had already been 'published' (e.g. Wilamowitz II 222, Cornford 1935: 1, Guthrie IV 53 and n. 2, V 33); for the majority it is irrelevant, however (cf. Shorey 1903: 57 n. 424).

474. E.g. Diès 1924: 120 f., Geffcken II 122, Ross 1951: 6 f., and others believe that the report was omitted from *Theaetetus* because of the complications to which it had led in the *Parmenides*; others doubt this (e.g. Raeder 301, Ueberweg-Praechter 214). At any rate the twists in the report of the *Parmenides* were an intentional device emphasizing the distance; but no such distance was required in the *Theaetetus*. For a somewhat different theory, see Panagiotou 1981.

475. For such arguments, *see* Horn 1904: 275 ff., 341 ff., Vollenhoven 1948: 6 ff., H. M. Wolff 1957: 243 f., Mugler 1960: 124 ff.

# THE RISE OF THE DRAMATIC DIALOGUE

## Introductory

One of the basic hypotheses of this study is that the dramatic dialogue form intended for 'publication' springs from a secondary development. At any rate, a narrative by Socrates or somebody else is likely to have framed such early Socratic λόγοι as were written for circulation outside a selected audience (for whom hints regarding the setting and the characters participating in the discussion could be supplied orally and ex tempore). Cf. in general above, p. 207 ff.

In Plato's Academy, I take it, such λόγοι were habitually performed as part of the process of philosophical instruction and exercise. In this situation, no external setting was needed. In the written text of such λόγοι the change of speaker was indicated by the vocative addresses used or by simple notations in the manuscript; in commonly used texts the change of speaker gradually became known through rehearsal. This is what I believe happened to the *Gorgias* when the original reported form was dropped (p. 234), and to the *Theaetetus* after the revision.

Dialogues composed in a dramatic form throughout then began to be written for wider circulation; cf. e.g. *Crito* p. 208, *Ion* p. 221. The *Phaedrus* is a good example of an authentically Platonic dramatic dialogue of this semi-exoteric character. But, the *Meno, Alcibiades* I and *Cratylus* are examples of dialogues obviously not written for a general audience. The purpose and address of each dramatic dialogue must be considered separately.

The dramatic frames for reported dialogues and speeches form a specific problem (cf. below p. 326).

## Gorgias

I can discover no direct clue for dating the rewriting of the *Gorgias* in dramatic form. Regarding the new version of the *Theaetetus* as an absolute *terminus post quem* for all dramatic dialogues, as Teichmüller suggested we should do (above p. 155), involves particular difficulties in the case of *Gorgias*. We can see from

[163] the *Theaetetus* that the recasting of the text into a dramatic form offered an opportunity for up-to-date revision. The final version of the *Gorgias*, however, is concerned with Socratic ethics as challenged by rhetors and politicians, and thus suggests the environment of *Menexenus, Protagoras, Republic* I and *Euthydemus* rather than the later phases of Plato's thought. The final myth seems to represent a stage earlier than the *Phaedo* (above p. 290). And Plato had probably not yet made the new approach to δικαιοσύνη which is reflected in the introduction of the arguments of his brothers in *Republic* II.

Tentatively, then, it can be inferred that the reported form of *Gorgias* was dropped at a relatively early date, perhaps about 380 BCE, after the *Symposium* (but before its frame was added), at a date when Socrates as a teacher and an ideal philosopher is likely to have become the subject of special interest at the Academy. And the lack of frame dialogue is possibly significant: it may indicate that Plato had not yet acquired the habit of adding such frames and also suggests a date preceding *Phaedo* and *Euthydemus*.

## Meno

G.C. The *Meno* is best explained as written for internal use at the Academy at a fairly early date; this is also the opinion of most modern scholars.[476] The themes of teaching ἀρετή and ἐπιστήμη assign to it a place roughly in the same context as *Protagoras, Euthydemus* and the first version of *Theaetetus;* the anamnesis doctrine connects it with the *Phaedo;* and there are several points of contact with the *Gorgias*.

As far as I can see, the dialogue was written in dramatic form from beginning.[477] There is nothing remarkable about the style except that it displays little variety and is clearly not 'late'; whether in fact it represents Plato's *ipsissima verba* may be regarded as an open question.[478]

E.C. In addition to the didactic theme and tone suggestive of problems discussed at the Academy, at least one external criterion can be adduced for dating the *Meno:* the pamphlet of Polycrates is unmistakably, and again rather playfully, alluded to in the Anytus episode. The episode opens (90a) with Socrates' apparently nonsensical combining of the wealth of the father of Anytus with the
[164] bribery of Ismenias (he was known to have received Persian money in 395 BCE,

---

476. *See* the discussion and references in Hoerber 1960: 78–82, Bluck 1961. Verdam 1916, eccentrically, suggested a very late date.—No theory of spuriousness to be taken seriously has been suggested in this century as far as I know.

477. The opening is abrupt but perfectly clear (as in *Cratylus*, but unlike *Gorgias*, p. 234). There is no need for a setting since the insertion of the episodes with a slave boy (82a–85b) and Anytus (89d–95a) are easily dealt with by means of references in the actual conversation.

478. Cf. below p. 351. For the style, cf. my conspectus above 103 f. implying some typical but not very marked Platonic mannerisms. Pohlenz 1921: 11 f. on vague grounds considers the style 'early.'

four years after the death of Socrates, and was indicted for it some ten years later) and the riches of 'Polycrates'(implying of course, albeit ambiguously, the Samian tyrant as well);[479] and in the episode, Anytus himself, whom Polycrates had presented as exalting the great men of the past and denouncing the sophists (cf. above p. 179), is introduced as an 'apparently'well-educated man (90b, cf. 95a) whom Socrates forces to face the fact that the only teachers of ἀρετή appear to be the sophists, and that great men have been unable to impart education. This ironic reminiscence of the pamphlet clearly does not imply a temporal proximity. The tone of the *Meno* is less apologetic than the tortuous irony of *Protagoras* (cf. p. 278) and the Alcibiades episode in the *Symposium*. On the contrary, introducing Anytus as if 'accidentally'(89e) when this rather esoteric discussion has reached the problem of exactly who are the teachers of ἀρετή, suggests a commonplace (Anytus the hater of sophists) long since familiar to the audience.

The possible relation of *Meno* to various writings of Antisthenes, Isocrates, Aeschines and Xenophon does not provide us with any useful clues.[480]

I.C. *Apology—Meno.* The later date of *Meno* has usually been taken for granted, and *Meno* 99c may in fact allude to *Apology* 22c (deliberately omitting φύσει τινί).[481]

*Gorgias—Meno.* The features and points these two dialogues have in common have normally been interpreted as indicating that *Meno* is the later one; this view seems to me reasonable.[482] This order has very often been inferred from the passages on the Athenian statesmen and the sophists as presumptive educators (*Grg.* 503c, 515c–520e, Socrates versus Callicles; *Men.* 90b–95a, the Anytus episode).[483] The apparent advance in epistemology is also commonly thought

---

479. The implications of these references have often been discussed; cf. Ueberweg 1861: 225 ff., Markowski 1910: 58 ff., Pohlenz 1913: 189, Apelt *Men.* 85 n. 37, Wilamowitz II 104 f., Morrison 1942, Bluck 1961: 118 f. all of whom place the emphasis somewhat differently. Pohlenz, Wilamowitz and Morrison have not succeeded in explaining away the anachronisms; indeed, they can be taken as a rather typical Platonic side glance at Polycrates. At the same time the name 'Poly- crates' may be an intentional misspelling for 'Timocrates' (who according to Xenophon *Hell.* III 5.1 supplied Ismenias with the Persian money).

480. For Antisthenes, *see* Rick 1931: 90 ff.; for Isocrates, Bluck 1961: 118 f.; for Aeschines, Pohlenz 1913: 182 ff., Gigon 1947: 74 ff. (cf. below n. 483); for Xenophon, Maier 1913: 57 n. 2.

481. Cf. Pohlenz 1913: 182, Hackforth 1933: 50 n. 1. Erbse 1975: 43 does not produce any weighty counter-arguments.

482. Those who accept the order *Meno—Gorgias* have argued from very limited evidence such as a supposed advance in political ethics (Horn 1893: 356 f.), a greater literary refinement (Lutoslawski 213), or a growing religious feeling (Natorp 1903: 36).

483. Cf. Th. Gomperz 1887: 743 ff. and (with additional, partly debatable evidence) Cauer 1918: 287–306, Geffcken II A 74 n. 14, 75 n. 37. Sometimes Aeschines' dialogue 'Alcibiades' is inserted between *Gorgias* and *Meno* (Pohlenz 1913: 181 ff.; Allmann 1972, adding Aeschines' 'Callias' before *Gorgias*.) Although the approaches are different (*Gorgias* concentrates on describing the statesmen and sophists as corrupters of the Athenian people, whereas *Meno* is concerned with their inability to educate their sons, cf. Bluck 1961: 12, 115–117), I still think the details point to the order *Gorgias—Meno*. The idea of the shortcomings of politicians as 'teachers,' though not mentioned in *Gorgias*, is of course a commonplace (cf. the treatment of this topic in *Prt., Men., Alc.* 1, *La., Tht.* and *Virt.*).

[165] to indicate this order.[484] It is doubtful whether the metaphysics and eschatology of *Meno* can be said to represent a later position.[485] But there are various other details suggesting this order rather than the opposite one.[486] I would conjecture that the *Meno* was written soon after the rewriting of *Gorgias* in dramatic form.

*Protagoras—Meno.* Much the same arguments as for the *Gorgias* have been produced to show the precedence of *Protagoras;* only few scholars have considered *Meno* the earlier dialogue.[487] In this case, and taking all the evidence in consideration, there can be little doubt that *Meno* is later. Since both dialogues are primarily concerned with the teaching of ἀρετή, a confrontation is easily made; and it is hard to avoid the impression that the *Meno* represents a real advance, both generally, and as regards specific questions such as epistemology, teachability and teaching methods, the concept of virtue (note e.g. *Men.* 88b, on ἀνδρεία, as compared with the discussion in *Protagoras,* above p. 192 f.) and politicians as educators (cf. *Prt.* 319e–320b, *Men.* 93d ff.).[488] The fact that *Meno* only contains a conventional reference to the sophist Protagoras (91de) but several detailed references to Gorgias (cf. also n. 486) is best explained as due to the familiarity of the dialogue *Gorgias* (now perhaps in dramatic form) to the Academic reader. And Protagoras the teacher belonged to history.

*Symposium—Meno.* The *Symposium* is very often regarded as the later dialogue owing to the explicit doctrine of Forms and the doctrine of Love in the
[166] speech of Diotima.[489] It is easily understandable, however, that the 'mystery of Eros' is not reflected in a technical dialogue such as the *Meno;* and the ἕν τι εἶδος *Meno* 72c (cf. pre-existence 81a ff.) may well imply as much of the theory of

---

484. Notably the introduction of ὀρθὴ δόξα a in *Meno,* cf. Bluck 1961: 110 ff. Cf. also ὑπόθεσις (*Grg.* 454c, followed by μάθησις/πίστις 484d; *Men.* 85c ff.), Geffcken II A 75 n. 35; and the anamnesis doctrine below, p. 313. This advance, however, is more apparent than real because *Meno* obviously is more technical and esoteric than *Gorgias.*

485. This has often been asserted, e.g. Raeder 411 f., Ueberweg-Praechter 249, Rudberg 1953.34 ff., Morrison 1958: 212 f. But *see* the weighty counter-arguments of Shorey 1903: 40 f. For the anamnesis problem, cf. below p. 313.

486. For instance, the reference in *Men.* 71c to Socrates having met Gorgias when he visited Athens, which reminds of the similar allusion to the dialogue *Parmenides* in *Sph.* 217c; cf. Bluck 1961: 112 f. It is somewhat unclear why Plato chose to approach the problem of teaching virtue from a reference to the influence of Gorgias (*Men.* 70b) rather than Protagoras; he probably felt Gorgias and his followers (including Isocrates) were his most dangerous rivals. For other supposed allusions in *Meno* to *Gorgias, see* especially Pohlenz 1913: 168 ff., also Raeder 130, 290, 411 f., Wilamowitz I 275, II 114.

487. Notably Beare 1913, Taylor and Crombie I (241 ff.) in accordance with their conception of *Protagoras* as a very advanced work; Stefanini I 161 n. 1 mainly because of his theory of the lateness of the reported dialogues (I took the same position in 1967); and some others chiefly because the conception of virtue and teaching virtue is thought to be more 'mature' in *Protagoras* (cf. Horn 1893: 356 f., Rick 1931: 119 ff., and recently again S. M. Cahn 1973).

488. These points have often been made, cf. e.g. Lutoslawski 207 ff., Pohlenz 1913: 178 f., Cauer 1918, Friedländer II 257, III 421 f., Erbse 1968: 25 ff. The interpretation of Cahn 1973, amounting to the reverse order, seems very far-fetched.

489. Cf. e.g. Ueberweg-Praechter 262–264, Robin 1938: 100 ff. Other arguments have little weight: if e.g. ὀρθὴ δόξα *Smp.* 202a9 is thought to refer to *Men.* 97a ff., one could ask why it does not refer to the discussion in *Theaetetus* (cf. 161d5) as well, as Zeller II I⁵ 491 n. 3 implied.

Forms as does the Form of Beauty in the *Symposium*.[490] The two dialogues really have very little in common, a fact which renders a confrontation between them less meaningful.

*Meno* and the *Republic*. The *Meno* is usually placed after *Republic* I by the separatists, but before the main bulk of the *Republic*, and this seems reasonable on general grounds. Although there are no positive indications of the order *Republic* I—*Meno*, the position of *Meno* is taken for granted in the later books of the *Republic*.[491]

*Meno* and *Phaedo*. The treatment of the anamnesis doctrine, the theory of Forms, and eschatology justifies a comparison of these two very different dialogues. It is generally thought that *Phaedo* reflects an advance in these three respects. In fact it has often been said that the *Meno* is the first dialogue to introduce the (Pythagorean) theory of metempsychosis which has brought along with it a belief in transcendent Forms and ἀνάμνησις,[492] and thus it would have something of a pivotal position in Plato's thought. I feel (with e.g. Shorey 1903: 78 n. 601) that these ideas may have been current in Academic discussion for some time before they were actually written down, but I agree that it is much more natural to explain the *Phaedo* as developing thoughts implicit in the *Meno*, than vice versa. There are also certain additional arguments which have sometimes been adduced for the precedence of the *Meno*.[493]

If we accept the order *Symposium*—*Meno*—*Phaedo*, we have an indication that the dramatic dialogue form was adopted for internal use at the Academy around 380 BCE.

*Meno* and *Euthydemus*. In spite of certain thematic parallels in these dialogues, notably a similar aporetic attitude to the teachability of virtue, there is

[166]

[167]

---

490. Cf. v. Kleemann 1908, especially 62–75, who (following a suggestion by H. Gomperz) argued that *Meno* is really the more sophisticated dialogue in this respect also. The *Meno* passage is often taken to imply a preliminary stage of the Theory, e.g. Pohlenz 1913: 310 ff., Kapp 1968. 61 ff.; cf. Allen 1970: 154–163.

491. For epistemology, cf. Lutoslawski 285, Raeder 218 f.; for mathematics and the 'hypothetical' method, Raeder 411 f., Leisegang 1950: 2463, (but note the skeptical remarks by Ickler 1973); for dialectic, Geffcken II 118 f.; for the theory of Forms, Robin 1938, Ross 1951. R. VI 506c has been taken to refer directly to *Men.* 97ab, de, cf. Bluck 1961: 108. In R. VI 491b–493a the problems of teaching virtue are viewed in a perspective reminiscent of the *Meno* (cf. also θεῶν τύχη 492a5).

492. *Phd.* 72e ff. appears to quote *Men.* 81c ff. This view is inherent in most modern interpretations, cf e.g. Lutoslawski 209; 260 ff., Pohlenz 1913: 190 ff., Friedländer II 265 f., Bluck 1961, Vlastos 1966, Allen 1970: 154 ff., T. M. Robinson 1970: 21–33. It has been sometimes suggested (recently again by Cobb 1973, Ebert 1974: 96 ff.) that the anamnesis doctrine is not meant to be taken absolutely seriously; and cf. the objections of Szlezák 1978: 20. Here again the problem is one of emphasis. There is always some intellectual 'play' involved in Plato's myths, but some anamnesis is implied in Plato's later philosophy, e.g. the 'maieutics' (partly playful!) of *Theaetetus*, and the myth of the 'physical' composition of the soul in *Timaeus* (e.g. 37a, 41de).

493. For trends in the development of the 'hypothetical method,' cf. Geffcken II A 88 n. 80, Robinson 1941, Raven 1965: 62 f., 93 ff.; doubts by Ickler 1973. For other methods of argument, cf. Raeder 290, Pohlenz 1913: 310 ff., Geffcken l.c., Crombie II 144.

[167] little agreement among scholars as to which dialogue is the earlier one. The precedence of *Meno* has been somewhat more often argued than vice versa, although both views have authoritative supporters.[494] I can find nothing particularly concrete to support either view, and though the precedence of *Meno* seems to me on the whole better founded,[495] the differences in theme, approach and mood are actually more substantial than the points of contact. If, as is here assumed, the *Meno* and *Euthydemus* belong to approximately the same period, they must have been written for widely different purposes and different audiences. The protreptic character of the *Euthydemus*, which is completely absent from the *Meno*, provides a hint of how the differences should be understood and explained.

The *Meno* also lacks a common basis of comparison with *Lysis* and *Charmides*.[496]

*Meno—Theaetetus*. It is now universally agreed that the *Theaetetus* is in several respects more advanced than the *Meno*, and since this cannot be explained on the basis of a difference of purpose, it is natural to regard *Theaetetus* as much later. Since also the 'maieutics' as presented in the *Theaetetus* implies a real development of the anamnesis idea, *Meno* is likely to have preceded the early version of *Theaetetus* (cf. above p. 301).[497]

## Cratylus

G.C. The place of *Cratylus* in Plato's work is notoriously problematic. There are several thematical features, especially the criticism of the fundaments of language and thought, and the discussion of the views of earlier thinkers, which
[168] seem to connect it with Plato's later philosophy; and other features, such as the rather implicit and not necessarily very 'advanced' metaphysics, the fairly easygoing style and the humorously playful tone, which suggest a comparatively early date. A fairly late date was preferred by some scholars in the 19th century (cf. Shorey 1903.75 f.); and since Warburg in 1929 attempted to argue positively for a late date, several others have followed suit, whereas the majority have

---

494. *Meno—Euthydemus*, e.g. Lutoslawski, Th. Gomperz, Raeder, Ritter, Pohlenz, Wilamowitz, Geffcken, Shorey, and more recently Krämer 1959, Bröcker 1964, Ilting 1965, Kapp 1968. *Euthydemus-Meno*, e.g. v. Arnim, Taylor, Friedländer, Bluck, and Erbse 1968, Gundert 1971, Gaiser 1974: 137.

495. Cf. e.g. Wilamowitz II 150 ff. (and Méridier 1931a: 141) against v. Arnim's argument that *Men.* 87e ff. 'recapitulates' *Euthd.* 280d ff., and Pohlenz 1916: 261 n. 1 on ὀρθὴ χρῆσις. Shorey 1903: 14 n. 76 rightly remarked that there was no need, in the *Euthydemus*, for the crucial ὀρθὴ δόξα.

496. It is worth noting that the *Charmides* deals with epistemology from a very specific point of view, and thus does not need the apparatus of the *Meno*. And everybody knew that Socrates in fact was unable to impart σωφροσύνη to *Charmides* (p. 298). Could the 'Thracian medicine' 156d ff. have something to do with anamnesis?

497. Although the 'delivery' of a thought from a pupil seems to have been an old Socratic joke (cf. above p. 304), the illustration of it in the *Theaetetus* probably involves anamnesis; cf. Burnyeat 1977, Guthrie V 73 n. 2. For the trends in Platonic epistemology in general, cf. Gomperz II 446 f., 594.

remained cautiously skeptical.[498] For my part, I do not think it can be shown that [168] the doctrinal basis of the dialogue is in any sense 'early' or 'preliminary' by the standard of, say, the *Republic* (cf. below).[499]

Stylometry is, as usual, of uncertain value except insofar as it shows that there are practically no 'late style' features;[500] in this case this is quite an important fact. The almost complete absence of a setting links up with the *Meno* and corresponds to the probable fact that this dialogue was also written for internal use in the Academy; but this is not very helpful, since the *Sophist*, too, lacks a setting and yet indulges in absurd play. The systematic disposition of the *Cratylus*, again, suggests a rather late date. And there is a tendency to lecturer's monologue which Plato makes Socrates himself comment upon.[501]

We have to look elsewhere for more useful clues.

E.C. The only external point of reference which may be helpful for the dating, is Warburg's suggestion (1929) that Heraclides of Pontus is alluded to in the dialogue. It is often believed that von Arnim 1929 and Wehrli 1953 refuted this argument completely. This is not true, however. Warburg's points are still worth serious consideration, if one accepts that playing with anachronistic allusions was after all not alien to Plato and the Academics. Warburg argued from a large number of details and certain passages in later sources (including the grammarian Orion) that some of the etymologies in the *Cratylus* had been originally sug- [169] gested by Plato's pupil Heraclides. To make this chronologically plausible he attempted to minimize the results of stylometry, which immediately brought him into conflict with the consensus of scholarly authorities of the period; in the same year he was answered by von Arnim. After the war, Wehrli 1953: 117–119 tried to prove that the late sources adduced by Warburg in fact refer to the grammarian Heraclides of Pontus the Younger (1st century BCE) who may have used Platonic material. I do not think Wehrli succeeded in proving this conclusively, especially

---

498. Warburg received support from Weerts 1931, and though his arguments have been considered unreliable (below), various variants of the late date theory have been propounded by Shorey 1933, Hoffmann 1950: 130 f., Allan 1954, Crombie I 13, II 254, Sease 1966, Ryle 1966, Schadewald 1971, Derbolav 1953 and 1972: 25–31 (with bibliography on *Cratylus* p. 221 ff.), Gaiser 1974: 95 ff. H. M. Wolff (1957: 64 f., 73) suggested a fanciful theory of revision. The skeptics include Luce 1962 (a detailed reassessment), Kahn 1973: 154, Guthrie V 1 ff.—The authenticity has not been questioned since the 19th century (cf. Lutoslawski 230 with references), except by Zürcher 1954.

499. This has been often asserted with regard to the theory of Forms in particular, cf. Ritter 1910a: 262 ff., Ueberweg-Praechter 258, Geffcken II A 81 n. 139, Hackforth 1955: 9 ff., also Guthrie V 1f.; but cf. Shorey 1903: 33, Ross 1951: 4 f., Luce 1964: 143 ff., Gaiser 1974: 96 f.; also for epistemology (e.g. Horn 1904: 275 ff., but cf. Gulley 1962: 68 ff.), dialectic (Lutoslawski 421 f., but cf. Shorey 1903: 74, Bolton 1973), and the 'dihaeretic method' (which Guthrie V 27 thinks must have been familiar to Plato from the start, though he later developed it); but cf. Shorey 1903: 51 f., Friedländer III 444 n. 35.

500. Thesleff above, 105 f. Warburg's criticism went too far (cf. v. Arnim 1929), but the supposed evidence for a relative date in the 'environment of *Gorgias, Phaedo* and *Symposium*' (Brandwood 1958: 404 ff., cf. 379; cf. Wundt 1949: 44 ff., Luce 1964: 142 f.) really rests on a very restricted basis.

501. *Cra.* 396d, etc., 428c; cf. p. 65 and Thesleff above, 42 f., Gaiser 1974: 96.

[169] since there is independent evidence of at least one of the etymologies having really been used by Heraclides the Elder (as Wehrli admits). And Wehrli passes far too lightly over the curious fact that this Heraclides' father's name was Euthyphron, and that Socrates in the dialogue several times remarks that in producing his etymologies he seems to be carried away by the inspiration of Euthyphron. The latter passages have often been taken to allude to the dialogue *Euthyphro*, but this is in fact not plausible at all (cf. below, p. 371). That the *Cratylus* operates with playful mystification with Heraclides of Pontus in mind would, in my opinion, be very tempting to assume, if it were chronologically possible. Normally, however, it is thought that Heraclides of Pontus was born about 390 BCE and arrived in Athens about 365.

I would put the problem as follows: Taking for granted (as I think we have too)[502] that *Cratylus* is authentically Platonic in the same sense as, say, the final version of *Theaetetus* is (i.e. that it was written or at least dictated by Plato himself), it could hardly have been written as late as this chronology would imply. It cannot belong so closely with *Parmenides* and *Theaetetus* (or the *Sophist* and *Politicus*), apart from the difficulty of the absence of late style features. And I find it extremely unlikely that Plato had the time and was in the mood to produce the exuberant etymological fireworks of *Cratylus* between, say, 365 and 361 when, for all we know (cf. also below p. 332, on the *Republic*,) he was involved in the ever more confused Sicilian adventure. So either there is no reference to Heraclides—as in fact most scholars tend to think—or Heraclides should (following Warburg) be dated slightly earlier than is usually the case.

Perhaps the latter solution is after all the more natural one (provided Heraclides the Elder really was an etymologist, as Warburg argued). As far as I can see,[503] the main reason for dating Heraclides' first arrival in Athens to the mid-360s is the remark in Diog. L. 5.86 that he first became an associate ($\pi\alpha\rho\acute{\epsilon}\beta\alpha\lambda\epsilon$) of Speusippus, and it is thought that Plato must have been in Syracuse since Heraclides did not come to him. But in fact it seems quite possible that Heraclides was born about 400 and came to Athens about 375—and yet approached Speusippus first. This assumption would make it possible to date *Cratylus*, if it alludes to Heraclides, to the late 370s.

[170] I.C. The order *Protagoras*—*Cratylus* may be suggested by the fact that the latter contains references to Protagoras' writings (385e–386c, 391c, cf. *Tht.*) instead of parody.—The order *Symposium*—*Cratylus* (and *Phaedo*—*Cratylus*) has been argued only by those who assign to *Cratylus* a comparatively late date;[504] I find this reasonable, however, and I would add that the combined reference to eschatology

---

502. Cf. above n. 498 (the end).
503. Cf. Gottschalk 1980: 4 f. who however prefers the later dating. On p. 160 ff. he is overcritical of Warburg; the crucial point is the word for 'moon' (*Cra.* 409b, Wehrli 119), not 'virtue.'
504. Note, for instance, Kapp 1968: 131 ff.: the theory of Forms is extended to artifacts in *Cratylus*. For the (out-of-date) view that *Symposium* is more 'advanced' than *Cratylus*, see Lutoslawski 235 ff. 254 ff., 282 ff., Goldschmidt 1940. On similar, very flimsy grounds, the *Phaedo* has been regarded as representing a later stage of Plato's thought than *Cratylus* (cf. also Mugler 1960: 64 ff., especially 71).

and love in *Cratylus* 403b–404a may really imply the speech of Diotima (and note [170] in particular the τέλεος σοφιστής *Smp.* 208c1, *Cra.* 403e4).

It is possible to find in *Cratylus* various allusions to the later books of the *Republic*, such as 'user's knowledge' *Cra.* 390b, μίμημα *Cra.* 430b etc., the Form of artifacts *Cra.* 389a etc., and other metaphysical ideas, and notably the very interesting ἀγαθοῦ ἰδέα *Cra.* 418e; yet such allusions do not indicate that the *Republic* had already been 'published.'[505]

*Euthydemus—Cratylus.* This order is normally taken for granted, though the arguments used are not particularly conclusive as such; the dialogues are in fact quite different, apart from their indulgence in the absurd. The most reliable argument is perhaps the reference in *Cratylus* 386d to the erist Euthydemus and at the same time, apparently, to the dialogue (*Euthd.* 293b–294e, 297a ff.).[506]

*Meno—Cratylus.* This order is more often accepted than the reverse one, but here again no clear criteria have been found. Obviously, however, there is some advanced metaphysical play in the *Cratylus* (cf. above p. 215), and since *Cratylus* is also in various other respects more sophisticated, it is natural to consider it to be later.

*Cratylus—Theaetetus.* The *Cratylus* is now generally thought to precede the *Theaetetus* with which it seems to share various features, such as a somewhat similar theory of flux and change, of knowledge, and of language; cf. also the criticism of earlier philosophy in both dialogues. These points have often been discussed[507] and I agree that on the whole they seem to indicate the precedence of *Cratylus* to the later (but hardly to the earlier) version of *Theaetetus*.

So perhaps after all the *Cratylus* can be dated to the late 370s, between the two [171] versions of the *Theaetetus*.

## *Phaedrus*

G.C. This is another of the notoriously problematic dialogues.[508] Partly in accordance with ancient models (below), Schleiermacher and his followers in the 19th century considered *Phaedrus* 'juvenile' and 'mythic' and, therefore, early. Towards the end of the 19th and at the beginning of this century the stylometrists'

---

505. The implications of these, and especially the last point, have often been minimized (e.g. Raeder 153, Luce 1964: 152), but cf. Gaiser 1974: 96 f. I regard it as almost certain that Plato in the context of *Cra.* 418e plays with allusions to the Principles ἕν/ὄν (τὸ δέον can be read τόδε ὄν or even τὸ δὲ ὄν), δυάς ('δυογόν') and στάσις/κίνησις, ταὐτόν/θάτερον. See now below, p. 469 f.

506. Considered a very important argument by Luce 1964: 137 f., but questioned by others. For other more debatable arguments, see Lutoslawski 225 ff., 282 ff., Raeder 238, Méridier 1931b: 46 ff., Gauss II/1.204 f., 213, Wyller 1970: 44 f.

507. E.g. Gomperz II 450, 595, Shorey 1903: 33 n. 218, 55, 75, Raeder 280 ff., Weerts 1931, Haag 1933, Gulley 1962: 68 ff., Luce 1964: 148 f., Gaiser 1974: 96. One of the somewhat doubtful points is the possible reminiscence in *Tht.* 155d of the play with εἴρειν in *Cra.* 398d, 408b (regarded as a very important evidence by Luce 1964: 138, following Cornford).

508. For general histories of the controversy regarding the date of this dialogue, see Christ 1886: 501 ff., Raeder 245 ff., Robin 1908: 63 ff., Ritter 1914, de Vries 1969: 7 ff. Cf. above p. 233.

[171] view of a comparatively late date gradually won acceptance, in spite of the resistance of authorities such as Zeller, Immisch, Natorp and Pohlenz. Reinforced with various arguments from the contents, the late date theory became part of the Lutoslawski-Raeder-Ritter doctrine. Regenbogen (1950) argued for a very late date, chiefly on thematic grounds, but few have been inclined to follow him. It is now customary to interpret the doctrinal contents of *Phaedrus* as representing a *post-Republic* but pre-'late period' stage, but there are still dissenters and, as will be seen below, there is little agreement as to the value of the various arguments.

Both structure and style are rather odd. Although the pedimental composition with a visionary speech in the middle is reminiscent of the *Symposium* (and, more faintly, of *Phaedo* and certain other dialogues), the structure is not coherent. The restriction to two persons (as in some minor dialogues to be considered later) is in this case an important specific device connected with the theme. Although the dialogue is of the dramatic type, the setting is vividly depicted through remarks included in the actual discussion: this is a technique which Plato does not employ elsewhere (but there are reflections of it in the *Timaeus* and notably the *Laws*). The refined artistry which the dialogue displays indicates that it was written for a larger audience than the *Meno, Cratylus* and the late dialogues. The stylometrists have noted a mixture of 'early' and 'late' features of style, but then the various sections have not usually been kept apart.[509]

[172] A convenient way of explaining at least some of the anomalies is to accept some variant of the old theory of revision of this dialogue (cf. above p. 233).[510] I would propose the following hypothesis: in the mid-380s, when Plato was obviously interested in rhetorical pastiches, witness *Menexenus, Protagoras* and *Symposium,* and when love may also have affected him personally (cf. p. 177), Plato composed a first version of the *Phaedrus*. It was perhaps provided with a brief narrative report by Socrates, which (with some variation of the standard setting motif, cf. above p. 268) contained a description of how Socrates and Phaedrus met after Lysias' performance of his speech at Morychos' (227b) and decided to take a walk *extra muros,* during which Phaedrus presented the contents

---

509. The literary unity of the work is clearly over-emphasized by Helmbold and Holther 1952 and Dorter 1971; cf. Thesleff 1967, above 118 f. For the traditional stylometrical point of view, *see* Ritter 1914: 355–373 and the reassessment by Brandwood 1958 (especially 18–20, 35, 41 f., 102 f., 247 ff., 275 ff). Wishart and Leach 1970 suggested that the prose rhythm of *Phaedrus* is of a rather 'early' type; obviously it is not 'late' on the whole. The relevance of the 'late style' characteristics have often been minimized since Zeller; cf. e.g. Pfleiderer 1896: 543 n., Natorp 1900b: 386 ff. and especially Pohlenz 1913: 356–361; and adherents of the late date theory have also sometimes noted that the oddities can in this case be explained as a deliberate playing with style (cf. Robin 1908: 75 ff., Regenbogen 1950: 199 ff., Owen 1953: 81 f., de Vries 1963). Wilamowitz I 461 suggested that the second speech of Socrates (243e ff.) in fact initiates Plato's 'late style.'

510. The chief champion of this theory was Immisch (1899, etc., especially 1915). It was accepted by Gomperz II 577, Brommer 1940, Wundt 1949, and others but most students of the *Phaedrus* have remained skeptical (*see* especially Ritter 1910b: 247 f., 1914: 270 ff., Pohlenz 1916: 272 ff., Rick 1931: 88 f.). Kesters 1959 (especially 114–125), on shaky grounds, argued that the end of *Phaedrus* was added later as a reply to an unknown Socratic who is represented by Themistius *Or.* 26.

of Lysias' speech,[511] and Socrates produced a counterpart to it, but—warned by his δαιμόνιον—proceeded with a palinody. This palinodic speech was much briefer than the extant one. It concentrated upon the theme of erotic μανία as a divine power, and may have included the simile of the wings of the soul, and the pun on Δῖος and Dion (252e1, cf. 250b8), but it did not have the horses[512] or the proof of immortality, or the other metaphysical and cosmological ingredients of the present version of the speech. The dialogue ended with this speech of Socrates. The first version of the *Phaedrus* was written before regular activities got under way at Plato's Academy, and since Plato somewhat later wrote the much more spectacular *Symposium* with its new theory of love and metaphysics, the three speeches of the *Phaedrus* were superseded and subsequently forgotten. Some twenty years later, when the 'mystery' of love as expounded by Diotima did not after all seem so satisfactory, and the question of the spoken versus the written word became an acute problem for Plato, he decided to remold the *Phaedrus* into a discussion of beauty and persuasion. In this later version the frame story, now in dramatic form, was expanded, as was the palinodic speech, and the subsequent discussion of prose and of reasoning was added so as to create a pedimental composition resembling *Symposium*. I repeat, however, that this sketch of the genesis of the *Phaedrus* is only a conjecture.

[172]

E.C.  *Phaedrus* is the only Platonic dialogue whose date was apparently discussed in antiquity, and this fact may have something to do with the two versions suggested above. Some sources state that *Phaedrus* was Plato's first work, whereas Cicero implies that he was not very young when he wrote the dialogue. Neither tradition is very reliable as such.[513]

[173]

The 'Egyptian' myth 274c ff. is probably quite irrelevant for the dating.[514] The first Sicilian voyage and Plato's meeting with Dion in 388 is very likely to be a close *terminus post quem* for the first version.[515] If the theory of revision is accepted, the

---

511. It is irrelevant here whether this was an authentic speech by Lysias; cf. below p. 320. At any rate, the point about the speech having been written before it was read may not have belonged to the first version of the dialogue.

512. Cf. Immisch 1915: 555 ff

513. The reasons given for the former conception look suspicious and may derive from rhetor school traditions: the *Phaedrus* (which polemizes against formal rhetoric and writing) is said to be 'juvenile' and 'dithyrambic' (Diog. L. 3.38, Olymp. *V. Plat.* 3 p. 192.13 H., *Anon.Proleg.* 24 p. 217. 34 ff. H); cf. Ritter 1914: 321 ff., de Vries 1969: 8; Immisch 1904: 248–251, however, argued that there might be some biographical foundation for this view. Cicero's comment (Orator 13.42) strictly speaking does not imply more than that Isocrates was already well known when Plato wrote the passage about him; Hackforth 1952: 3 perhaps over-interprets it.

514. Cf. Leisegang 1950: 2478. Scheidweiler 1955: 120 suggested the possibility that 'Theuth' may refer to King Thamus (Tachos) in 362/1 BCE but rightly doubted whether there were sufficient indications of so late a date.

515. Cf. above p. 175 and 266, and Bruns 1900: 24 f., Pohlenz 1913: 40 f. The pun on Dion's name is often also accepted by late date adherents, e.g. Wilamowitz I 537, Rudberg 1956: 35 ff. But connecting the 'pastoral setting' of the *Phaedrus* with Sicilian topography and milieu (Rudberg 1924: 77 ff., arguing that Plato finished *Phaedrus* in Sicily in 366 BCE) and even with supposedly early Sicilian traditions of literary pastoral (Murley), is extremely far-fetched. The Academy, too, was a very idyllic place (Aristophanes, *Clouds* 1005 ff.). The hippological and sporting terms in

[173]  vexed problem of the speech of Lysias loses much of its chronological relevance.[516]
The 'greetings' sent to Isocrates at the end of *Phaedrus* (278e–279b) and other pos-
[174]  sible allusions to Isocrates probably belong to the later version, but provide no very
obvious clues.[517]

An unclear but interesting relation seems to exist between Socrates' remarks on writing and on 'play' towards the end of the dialogue (275d, 276de, 277c) and certain passages in Alcidamas' speech 'On the Sophists' (Περὶ τῶν τοὺς γραπτοὺς λόγους γραφόντων ἢ περὶ σοφιστῶν, 27, 35). Is is now often assumed that Plato alludes to the speech rather than vice versa, though it may appear odd that Plato had taken these rather central ideas from a rhetor; the speech is, on vague grounds, dated in the 380s.[518]—For the second version of the dialogue, a date later than

---

Socrates' second speech (note 256b) have also been explained as reflecting Plato's experiences in 360 BCE in Olympia where he met Dion (*Ep.* 7.350b), cf. Immisch 1915: 568, Ryle 1966: 259 ff.; but surely Plato was familiar with horses and wrestling (Diog. L. 3-4!) before that.

516. For references to the earlier discussion of the authenticity of the speech, see de Vries 1969: 11–14 who, in my view rightly, tends to think that the speech was composed by Plato; so does Panagiotou 1975, but others have again argued for authenticity, among them Dover 1968: 69–71, Wishart and Leach 1970, Guthrie IV 433. Whether Lysias or not Lysias, it seems to me clear that, as the speech is presented in the extant version of the dialogue, the implication is that Lysias is dead; otherwise he or his supporters would have answered the criticism, and such polemics would have constituted a *cause célèbre*; compare also Plato's much more 'considerate' attitude to Isocrates at the end of the work. The year of Lysias' death it unknown; it is normally taken to be somewhat later than 380 BCE (cf. Dover 1968: 43–46), and Panagiotou's recent (1975) suggestion of the mid-360s is probably too late. However, the setting for the speech may have been different in the first version. If, for instance, Phaedrus made a free report of the speech (as he promises to do at 228d; and indeed, the opening scene suggests that Phaedrus comes straight from the performance without having had time to write all of the speech), it would not have been as easy for Lysias to protest, as if the dialogue had given, or purported to give, Lysias' ipsissima vetba. Or Phaedrus may have presented the speech as his own (though attentive listeners would have recognized the voice of Lysias in it).

517. The 'greetings' are presumably sent by the Head of the Academy to the Head of the Rhetors' School; there is some irony in the praise (not seen by some commentators, see references in de Vries 1969: 15–18), and certainly it does not imply acceptance of rhetoric (a sign of an early date to Wundt 1949: 50 f., of a late to Erbse 1971). There are no clear reminiscences of Isocrates in the first part of the dialogue (the theory of Brown and Coulter 1971 that Socrates' first speech parodies Isocrates is far from convincing). Some allusions to Isocrates seem to occur in the discussion which follows the palinodic speech. Of these, the quite commonly accepted reminiscences of 'Against the Sophists' (about 390 BCE) 17–18 in 269d ff. and of 'Panegyricus' (380 BCE) 7 in 267ab are interesting as *termini post quos* (for the former, cf. Raeder 272 ff., Rick 1931: 41 ff., 80 ff.; Ries 1959: 78 f., 121 f., de Vries 1969: 16; for the latter, Raeder 273 f., Ritter 1922b: 5 f., 142 f.). The 'Helen' (X, from the 370s) would be more interesting as a point of reference especially if it could be demonstrated that Plato's story of the palinody (243a) was suggested by this speech (de Vries 1969: 16; for other possible reminiscences of the 'Helen,' cf. Howland 1937: 152 ff., Bluck 1949: 66 f., 112 f., Ries 1959: 103 f.). However, Plato very probably introduced the palinody independently of Isocrates (a dependence of Isocrates on Plato, argued by Verdam 1916: 389 ff., is equally improbable). For alleged, more or less doubtful references in *Phaedrus* to still later works of Isocrates, see H. Gomperz 1906: 32 ff., Münscher 1916: 2179 f., Howland 1937: 152 ff. (but cf. Hackforth 1952: 5 ff.), Bluck 1949: 112 f., de Vries 1969: 10.

518. Th. Gomperz II 341, 575 f. (following Zycha) and Pohlenz 1913: 351 n. 2 argued that Alcidamas alludes to Plato, but since Raeder 278 and H. Gomperz 1906: 32 f. it is customary to

the death of Gorgias about 376 BCE can be inferred from Socrates' words at 267a Γοργίαν... ἐάσομεν εὕδειν.—The 4th Book of Xenophon's 'Memorabilia' appears to contain some references to the *Phaedrus*, but this book was probably written in the 360s.[519]—*Phaedrus* seems to take no account of Polycrates.[520] Some supposed references to other contemporaries of Plato, including of course the ever-present Antisthenes, have been detected but are of no chronological value.[521]

Hence, the external evidence does not contradict the hypothesis of a date in the mid-380s for the first version of the dialogue, and the early 360s for the second version.

I. C. *Gorgias—Phaedrus*. It is impossible to relate the hypothetical first version of the *Phaedrus* to the first or second version of the *Gorgias*, except that an affinity of time is suggested by the fact that both criticize, rather indirectly, the ethics of a famous rhetor. The precedence of *Gorgias* as we have it to the extant version of *Phaedrus* has been argued by many scholars and can be accepted here without further discussion.[522]

*Menexenus—Phaedrus*. Here the play with rhetorical pastiche points to the same period for the early versions. And provided we accept the relative order *Gorgias—Menexenus—Protagoras—Symposium*, the natural place of the first version of the *Phaedrus* is after *Menexenus* rather than before it.[523]

*Protagoras* and *Phaedrus*. There are no real points of contact apart from the interest in stylistic pastiche together with various details in the setting, such as the performance of speeches in somebody's home (cf. also *Gorgias*) and the enthusiasm of the young admirer of sophists. The precedence of *Protagoras* to the extant version of *Phaedrus* is now universally taken for granted though very few

---

accept the precedence of Alcidamas, cf. Ries 1959: 95 ff., Coulter 1967: 232 ff. Some scholars prefer to leave the question open (Ueberweg-Praechter 209, Friedländer I 117 f.). After all Alcidamas was a friend of improvisation and an opponent of Isocrates, so a play with ideas borrowed from him is quite possible in the *Phaedrus*.

519. *Phdr.* 262ab / Xen. *Mem.* IV 6.1; 265e, 273d (266b) / IV 5.11–12; cf. Maier 1913: 58 f., Geffcken II A 105 n. 93. For the dating of *Mem.* IV, *see* Breitenbach 1967: 1830 ff., 1902. The supposed reminiscences of *Phaedrus* in Xenophon's 'Symposium' (Raeder 249, Wundt 1949: 50 ff., Rudberg 1956: 18 ff.) are too superficial to be taken seriously.

520. Though cf. 257d and Natorp 1900b: 399 ff.

521. For Archinus, *see* Immisch 1899: 552 f., Raeder 268 f.; for Antisthenes, Raeder 249, Rick 1931: 62 ff.; for Eudoxus, Vollenhoven 1948: 5; for Aristotle, Ryle 1966: 96. For Kester's theory of the anonymous Socratic, *see* above n. 510.

522. An advance can be seen in almost every doctrinal, methodological and formal respect, as has been often noted and was accepted even by Natorp 1903 and Shorey 1903 (though the latter of course remained somewhat skeptical, cf. 31 n. 200, 40 f., 51 f.). There seem to occur even direct allusions in *Phaedrus* to *Gorgias*, notably *Phdr.* 260e to *Grg.* 462b, cf. Gomperz II 574, Raeder 260. The arguments of Horn 1893 and Immisch 1899 for the precedence of *Phaedrus* are out of date.

523. The arguments produced normally concern the dialogues as we have them: cf. e.g. Pohlenz 1913: 260, 263, Ritter 1914: 338 ff. Friedländer II 204 f. notes some interesting parallels in the diction of the speeches. The precedence of *Phaedrus* over *Menexenus* has been taken for granted without specific arguments by those who place the former early (e.g. Immisch 1899, Rick 1931). The arguments of Stefanini for this order (I 96 n. 2, II 67 n. 2, 125 n. 1, accepting a very late date for *Menexenus*) are not convincing.

[175] specific arguments have been found.[524] However, the manner of characterization of some persons in the dialogues may imply that the early version of *Phaedrus* preceded the *Protagoras:* in the first part of *Phaedrus,* Phaedrus is merely a lover of λόγοι (cf. Simmias, n. 533) and a friend of Lysias and the physician Acumenus (227a); in *Protagoras* (315c) Phaedrus is found in the company of Eryximachus [176] son of Acumenus and is said to be an associate of Hippias;[525] and in *Phaedrus* 268a, which presumably belongs to the later version, Eryximachus is the friend of Phaedrus, with Acumenus' name somehow added secondarily to connect the passage with 227a (cf. 269a).

*Symposium* and *Phaedrus.* The obvious relationship of these two dialogues has been the subject of a good deal of discussion. Although the Lutoslawski-Raeder-Ritter model and especially Robin's highly comprehensive study of 1908 made the order *Symposium*—*Phaedrus* (the present version, of course) seem fairly certain, scholars have raised objections to it from time to time.[526] The greater 'maturity' of the theory of Love in *Symposium* is emphasized as one of the chief arguments by the dissenters, and it is true that μανία is implied but distanced in *Symposium,* but the 'ladder of sublimation' is not to be found in *Phaedrus.* The respective approaches are, however, really quite different (the *Phaedrus* being concerned with love between individuals); and since the picture of love is more realistic in Socrates' palinodic speech than in the generalized metaphors of the speech of Diotima, and since Plato at any rate appears later to have abandoned the theory which he produced an *Symposium,* the force of this argument is not so cogent after all.[527] Many of the other arguments propounded for the precedence of *Phaedrus* are obviously weak and have been refuted in subsequent discussion, but those points that can be taken seriously (note Moore's argumentation, slightly modified by Dillon) are easily explained by the theory of revision.[528] I find it natural to assume that the first version of *Phaedrus* was written not very long before *Symposium,* whereas the new version is much later, as we have seen.

---

524. Cf. Ueberweg 1861: 293 ff., Groag 1913, Friedländer I 186 ff. To earlier stylometry add the observations of Díaz Tejera 1965. The reverse order has been argued by some supporters of an early date for *Phaedrus,* note Horn 1893: 218 f., Immisch 1899, Rick 1931, Brommer 1940: 31 f., 95; but these arguments are very weak.

525. Plato may have chosen Eryximachus instead of his father for the *Symposium,* because his name could be taken to mean "combating hiccup" (cf. *Smp.* 185c-e, 189a); and the background characters in the *Protagoras* may somehow reflect an early conception of the *Symposium;* cf. above p. 285.

526. For references to this discussion, *see* notably Ritter 1914: 348 and de Vries 1969; among the dissenters, note Crain 1905, Pohlenz 1913, Rick 1931, Lönborg 1939ab, Moore 1969, 1973, Dillon 1973.

527. Since Plotinus it has been customary to try to harmonize the theories of Love as presented in *Phaedrus* and *Symposium;* I have elsewhere pointed out the difficulties involved here (1980: 101 ff.).

528. For instance, μανία and ὕβρις (Moore 55 f.), the acceptance of violent desire (57), φθόνος (59), ἔρως as a god (64), the concentration upon love between individuals (65) may have occurred in the early version of *Phaedrus;* and when operating with the character of Phaedrus in the *Symposium,* Plato may have had the first version of *Phaedrus* in mind (cf. Moore 67 f.).

*Phaedrus* and the *Republic*. The general tendency now is to place *Phaedrus* [176] in the environment of the *Republic*, though there is no agreement on the exact relationship. With the establishing of the late date theory for *Phaedrus* it has been more commonly argued that *Phaedrus* followed the completion of the *Republic* than vice versa, but analysts of the *Republic* have also tried to place *Phaedrus* between various sections of the latter.[529] Most arguments concern the cosmology, [177] eschatology, metaphysics and psychology in the palinodic speech, or the dialectic and criticism of literature presented in the second part of the dialogue (269d ff.), and consequently (as assumed here) they apply to the later version. I can see nothing to prevent us from regarding the first version as having been written long before the *Republic*, but neither can I find any real clues to its relation to *Republic* I.[530] As for the later version of *Phaedrus*, there is abundant evidence to suggest that it reflects such ideas as are presented or implied in the later books of the *Republic* (disregarding of course the political and social aspects which are almost wholly absent from *Phaedrus*), but nothing to indicate that the *Republic* was published roughly in its present shape before the *Phaedrus*.[531] For general reasons, and considering the approach and tone of *Phaedrus*, I would prefer to assume that Plato wrote the new version of the dialogue at the same time as he was working on the themes of the *Republic* (cf. p. 286), before the second Sicilian voyage.

---

529. Lutoslawski, Raeder, Ritter, Robin, Wilamowitz, Taylor and their followers prefer to date *Phaedrus* after the *Republic*. Those who put it before the *Republic* include Natorp, Shorey 1933, Sinaiko 1965, and Guthrie. For various theories of insertion of *Phaedrus* between portions of the *Republic*, see notably Pfleiderer 1896: 462 ff., Immisch 1899, Pohlenz 1913, Groag 1915, Schaerer (1938) 1969, and Erbse 1972.

530. Lysias of course is present in *Republic* I (328b4), but silent, and the dialogue is not concerned with rhetoric or love at all; the remarks of Cephalus on love at 329a–d are part of the characterization of this wise old gentleman. For Thrasymachus, cf. below p. 353.

531. The position of *Phaedrus* is commonly regarded as more advanced than the *Republic* on various doctrinal points. Note the following: the theory of Forms (R. VI 508b ff., 516a ff. / *Phdr.* 247a–c, cf. Robin 1938: 100 ff.); theory of dialectic (R. IV 435a ff., V 454c, VII 531d ff., IX 580c ff., X 611b ff. / *Phdr.* 265c ff., 270d ff., cf. Raeder 261, v. Arnim 1914: 197 ff., Raven 1965: 190 ff., Szlezák 1978: 28 f); epistemology (R. IV 440a ff., V 477b / *Phdr.* 248b, 253c ff., cf. Raeder 255, v. Arnim 159 f.); cosmology and eschatology (note the more consistent combination of the theory of reincarnation with cosmology in the *Phaedrus*, cf. Robin 1908: 83 ff., v. Arnim 1914: 161 ff., Else 1972: 15; in particular it is thought that *Phdr.* 249b2 cannot be properly understood without consideration of R. X 617d ff.; and the proof of immortality in *Phdr.* 245c–246a is much more sophisticated than R. X 608d ff., and it is adopted again in *Lg.* X 894b ff., cf. de Vries 1969: 9); the theory of the tripartite soul (believed to be introduced for the first time in R. IV, and then illustrated by the simile of the horses and the driver in *Phdr.*, cf. Robin 1908: 81 ff., v. Arnim 1914: 156 ff., accepted by Pohlenz 1921: 19 f. and most later students of Plato); the theory of Love (Robin 1908: 81 ff., debatable; cf. above, *Symposium* versus *Phaedrus*); the theory of literature (discussed in detail especially by Vicaire 1960, but really quite questionable; cf. the hypothesis of Else 1972 that R. X 595a–608b is later than *Phdr.*); and several minor points (cf. Raeder 268, v. Arnim 1914: 205 ff., Taylor 299 f., Krämer 1959: 23 n. 22). For the treatment of Thrasymachus as a political theorist in R. I but as a rhetor in *Phdr.*, cf. above p. 257 f. The objections to some of the arguments recorded above, *qua* chronological criteria, by Natorp, Groag, Pohlenz, Shorey, Verdam 1918, Diès 1932, Gaiser 1963: 270 ff., and others, make the cautious attitude of Guthrie to the question of the interrelation of the *Republic* and *Phaedrus* (cf. also 1957: 9–12) seem highly motivated.

[177] *Phaedo—Phaedrus.* Even though these two dialogues are not really related at all, the theory of Forms and of Soul together with various details provide some
[178] basis for a comparison. The precedence of *Phaedo* is more or less accepted today.[532] I find it fairly clear that the theory of Soul and eschatology in particular have undergone a real change from *Phaedo* to (the later version of) *Phaedrus.* I also consider it feasible that the first version was written long before *Phaedo.*[533]

*Meno* and *Cratylus* versus *Phaedrus.* The implications of the above considerations are that the new version of *Phaedrus* is later than *Meno*, a view which is also universally agreed on today.[534] The relation of *Phaedrus* to *Cratylus* is not so clear, and the contents do not provide a sufficient basis for comparison.[535] The absence of late style features in the *Cratylus*, however, is an indication of its precedence.

*Euthydemus* and *Phaedrus.* Here the points of contact are even less obvious. It is reasonable, on general grounds, to place the final version of *Phaedrus* later, but the specific criteria sometimes adduced are far from sound.[536]

*Lysis* and *Charmides* versus *Phaedrus.* The theme of love vaguely unites *Lysis* and *Phaedrus*, however different they are in most respects. It has sometimes been argued that *Phaedrus* precedes *Lysis*,[537] but the opposite is now usually taken for granted. In particular, if it is accepted that *Lysis* is somehow dependent on *Symposium*, the realism of the theory and love and friendship in the new version of *Phaedrus* can naturally be seen as being even later.[538] But the ἔξω τείχους in the opening of the new approach to love made in *Lysis* (203a1–2 where the addition
[179] ὑπ' αὐτὸ τὸ τεῖχος may convey a point) may be a reminiscence of the first version

---

532. The only opponent worth mentioning after Natorp is Rick 1931, but his doubts are not very convincing. For various points in support of the prevalent view, see Pohlenz 1913: 28 ff., Robin 1938: 100 ff., Owen 1953: 95, Manasse 1961: 91 f., Crombie I 341 ff., Else 1972: 10 ff. But Shorey, Apelt and some others have remained skeptical.

533. The playful mention in *Phdr.* 242b of Simmias as inspiring many λόγοι perhaps implies the *Phaedo* and the discussion of eschatology which it probably initiated both within and outside the Academy. In that case the passage has been added when the dialogue was rewritten. It should be noted that the same passage (242b2) may include a reference to Phaedrus as being πατὴρ τοῦ λόγου in *Symposium* 177d5.

534. There can hardly be any doubt of the precedence of the eschatology as presented in the myth of *Meno* (81a–e), and the objections of Rick 1931 can be easily refuted.

535. Against the prevalent view, the precedence of *Phaedrus* has been asserted by Pohlenz 1913: 361, Shorey 1933 and Findlay 1974, but on flimsy grounds.

536. The passages on dialectic have sometimes been compared, but it is not true that *Euthd.* 290c ff. is more 'advanced' than *Phdr.* 265c ff., 276e, as Natorp 1903: 63 f., 407, asserted (also Pohlenz 1916: 268, against v. Arnim). On the other hand, it could be argued that since the explicit reference to Isocrates at the end of *Phaedrus* reflects a higher degree of self-esteem, it must be later than the corresponding implicit reference at the end of *Euthydemus.*

537. This was the opinion of the adherents of an early date for *Phaedrus*, e.g. Immisch 1899 (refuted by Robin 1908: 54 f.); Pohlenz 1913: 367, 371, Rick 1931. The specific arguments have little factual basis, considering especially the very different approaches to love in the two dialogues, even if no account is taken of revision.

538. The arguments, of Pfleiderer 1896: 538–543n. are in my opinion still pertinent. Various other trends of development which have been detected are rather more doubtful, e.g. the changes in the attitude to literature asserted by Vicaire 1960.

of *Phaedrus* where it is indeed better motivated. For the relation of *Charmides* to *Phaedrus* I can find no specific clues.[539]

*Theaetetus* and *Phaedrus*. The chronological relation of these two dialogues is highly problematic, although interesting from the point of view of Plato's philosophical development.[540] They have often been associated together on account of various points of contact in the contents, the dramatic form and supposed stylistic affinity, and generally because both are interpreted as somewhat preliminary to the 'late period.' Since the early date theories for both dialogues have been abandoned, the tendency has been to place both soon after the *Republic*. But there is little agreement on the criteria to be used. In fact the dialogues are widely different in theme and general tone; to call *Phaedrus*, *Theaetetus* and *Parmenides* a 'trilogy'[541] is certainly misleading.

The best way to approach the problem is in my view to accept that both dialogues have been revised and rewritten. If the original context of *Phaedrus* was the discussion of love and rhetoric in the 380s, and that of *Theaetetus* the discussion of teaching in the 370s, it is understandable that the new version of *Phaedrus*, which was written perhaps around 370 BCE, should replace 'maieutics' with dialectic (which had been given a firm place in the educational system reflected in the *Republic*) and combine this with a new theory of anamnesis where the problem of persuasion is provided with a cosmic and metaphysical framework. The cosmic aspect of the second speech of Socrates points forward to the *Timaeus* (cf. p. 338), but the subsequent discussion of writing belongs rather to the context of *Cratylus* and *Theaetetus* (where the discussion of language and στοιχεῖα 201e ff. is of course more technical and sophisticated). The *Theaetetus* then went a step further by introducing a criticism of the fundaments of knowledge. Is is also important to note that the *Theaetetus* as we have it is more closely related to *Parmenides*, the *Sophist* and *Politicus* as regards both form and contents, than the final version of *Phaedrus* is to *Timaeus*. Stylometry provides no certain indication of which of the two dialogues is later.[542] The only large-scale specific argument for the order *Theaetetus*—*Phaedrus*, that of von Arnim's 1914: 155–224, was dissected and shown as unreliable by Pohlenz 1916: 266 ff. and other critics. The relative precedence of *Phaedrus* is usually accepted today.[543] It may seem odd that Euclides

---

539. Manasse 1961: 90 f. argues that the myth of Zalmoxis in *Chrm.* must be earlier than the psychology in *Phdr.*, and this may be true; but after all the former is a playful introductory myth.

540. The specific problems involved here have often been seen and pointed out, cf. e.g. Natorp 1903: 118, Rudberg 1924: 103 f., Dies II 1927: 414–432.

541. Stefanini II 66 n. 2, 69, 70–74.

542. Ritter 1888 and v. Arnim 1912 concluded that *Phaedrus* is later; but Lutoslawski 189, 397, Trense 1901: 29 f., Ritter in a later study of *Phdr.*, 1922: 4 ff., and Díaz Tejera 1965 have put *Theaetetus* later; note the doubts of Brandwood 1958: 137. I have the impression that the latter part of *Phaedrus* has somewhat more of 'onkos' reminding one of Plato's late style (cf. my study above, 116 ff.), but this may be due in the first place to a playful tendency to 'write literature'; cf. above p. 318.

543. Cf. also Robin 1938, Ross 1951, Gauss II/2.12–13, 255 f. and Kapp 1968: 9 f. on the theory of Forms. Cf. further the play with σχολή *Phdr.* 258e, *Tht.* 172d; the hint at the self-moving soul (*Phdr.* 245c) in *Tht.* 185de; and the prosaic and down-to-earth discussion of μανία in *Tht.* 157e ff.

[180] in *Theaetetus* 142d–143b is said to have taken such trouble in writing down the whole λόγος of Socrates, after all that was said about writing in *Phaedrus;* but surely Plato did not reject writing altogether, and the *Theaetetus* passage may convey a special point (below, p. 329).

*Phaedrus* and *Parmenides.* It is now usually thought (except by those who follow Regenbogen's very late dating of *Phaedrus*) that *Parmenides* represents a later stage in the development of Plato's philosophy. This was also the position taken by Lutoslawski, Raeder and Ritter, and it has been argued in detail especially by those who regard the criticism of the theory of Forms in the *Parmenides* as finally decisive.[544] The ironic reference in *Phaedrus* 261d to Zenon as the 'Elean Palamedes' rather suggests that the *Parmenides* had not yet been written.[545] For the reported form of *Parmenides* in spite of its more esoteric character, cf. above p. 305. For my part I find the precedence of the final version of *Phaedrus* over *Parmenides* quite plausible.

Thus, the hypothesis that the first version of the *Phaedrus* was written in the 380s and that the dialogue was finished in the early 360s, before Plato's second voyage to Sicily, fits in fairly well with the evidence deducible from the other dialogues discussed so far.

## The adding of dramatic frame dialogues

It was suggested above (p. 268) that the dramatic frame dialogue, and its resumption at the important center of the work, constituted a device which belonged to the composition of the *Phaedo* from the outset, and that this model was followed in the *Euthydemus* where the frame dialogue was also resumed at the end (p. 272). This theory implies of course that Plato and his readers had become accustomed to prose dialogue in dramatic form before the *Phaedo* was written. In the preceding chapter we have adduced some evidence for this (p. 309 ff.).

In four cases, *Menexenus, Protagoras, Symposium* and *Theaetetus,* the opening dramatic dialogue appears to be rather more loosely attached to the main bulk of the work. I shall argue here that, in these cases, the frame was added secondarily in order to make or explain a particular point. The fact that there existed two
[181] different versions of the frame dialogue of *Theaetetus* (below p. 329) is a further indication that the frames were felt to be secondary and of minor importance.

The frame dialogue of *Symposium* is perhaps the earliest of the four. It may have been added fairly soon after *Phaedo* had been written in order to emphasize, in a similar way, the distance from the events described (cf. *Smp.* 172c–173b); at

---

The very late date occasionally suggested for *Phaedrus* (e.g. Rudberg 1924: 103 ff., 1956: 44 ff., Regenbogen 1950, Gulley 1962: 108, Wyller 1970) and by implication, the order *Theaetetus—Phaedrus,* is based on insufficient evidence.

544. E.g. Robin, Ross, Raven, Kapp (1968: 89 f.); cf. Guthrie V 50–52. For other arguments, also against v. Arnim's assertion of the reverse order (1914: 191 ff.), see Pohlenz 1916: 171, Ueberweg-Praechter 284, Stefanini II 80 n., Sinaiko 1965.

545. Cf. Pohlenz 1916: 265 f. (against v. Arnim), v. Fritz 1927: 20 ff.

the same time the main dialogue probably received its somewhat awkward two-stage obliquity.⁵⁴⁶ Plato is not interested in the conversation partner of Apollodorus, and consequently he remains anonymous (unlike the partners in the frame dialogue of *Phaedo* and *Euthydemus*). But there are some unmistakable echoes of the opening scene of *Republic* I which Plato had presumably been concerned with not long before he wrote the *Phaedo* (above p. 286): as in the *Republic*, there are two parties meeting on the road leading to one of the harbors of Athens (Apollodorus, who is from Phaleron, suits the theme for this reason too); cf. also R. I 327b4–5 κελεύει ... περιμεῖναι and *Smp.* 172a5 οὐ περιμενεῖς; and the presence of Plato's brother Glaucon in both passages (R. I 327 al, *Smp.* 172c3).⁵⁴⁷ [181]

The brief opening frame dialogue of *Protagoras*, where Socrates is having a conversation with an anonymous friend, is rather odd because it seems to exercise no other function than to emphasize that Socrates is, after all, not as fascinated by Alcibiades as he is by Protagoras, and possibly, to make the dialogue structurally more like *Symposium*, *Phaedo* and *Euthydemus*. It seems that the main dialogue was written with no particular consideration of Socrates' relations with Alcibiades in mind (cf. 317d, 320a, 336b–d, 347b, 348bc); the remark 316a with its reference to the frame could have been added later though, as was noted above (p. 278), Plato was apparently acquainted with Polycrates' pamphlet. Probably the discussion of these relations, which occasioned Plato to write the Alcibiades episode in *Symposium* (cf. also the reference in the frame dialogue, *Smp.* 172b), had begun at the Academy after the main dialogue of *Protagoras* was composed. The appended frame of *Protagoras* may reflect these discussions. I am not so sure, however, that Plato wrote it himself. It is of some interest here to note that the opening of the 'pseudo-Platonic' *Alcibiades* I implies a situation similar to the frame of *Protagoras* (309ab): Alcibiades has grown up and Socrates keeps away from him. But the author of *Alcibiades* goes on to explain that Socrates, having avoided the company of Alcibiades, is now prepared to approach him. So here is an indication (though a slight one) that the frame of *Protagoras* is to be dated between the *Phaedo* and *Euthydemus* (and the frame of *Symposium*) on the one hand, [182] and *Alcibiades* I on the other (cf. below p. 361 ff.).

*Menexenus* is in my view more easily explained if it is assumed that Plato wrote the speech without a (written) frame, as a bitter satire and a 'farewell' to Athenian politics (above p. 276). Also, from a stylistic, and perhaps from a psychological, point of view I find the switch from the absurdities of the opening conversation to the rhetorical pathos of the speech and then back again to the absurd, somewhat hard to accept. I prefer to think that the frame dialogue was

---

546. Cf. above p. 285. Apollodorus, the notorious μανικός who also figures in the *Phaedo* (59ab, 117d, note here the similar phrasing) is well suited to presenting a dialogue on love, especially if it includes polemics. The correct reading at *Smp.* 173d8 is almost certainly μανικός, cf. μαίνομαι e2. Perhaps this is also meant to connect with the μανία theme dealt with in the first version of *Phaedrus* (above p. 172), and to Antisthenes who played a central role in Xenophon's version of the story. In the opening scene of *Charmides* (perhaps written later than the frame of *Symposium*) it is Chairephon who is μανικός.

547. Cf. Friedländer III 55.

[182] added later by Plato or, rather, a pupil of Plato, in order to bring out the irony of the speech quite clearly and to link it up with a current discussion of the teaching of Socrates and its sources. This discussion was obviously reflected in Aeschines' dialogue 'Aspasia';[548] cf. also *Clitopho*, below p. 352. The role played by Antisthenes in this discussion is again irritatingly unclear. Antisthenes wrote a (speech?) Μενέξενος ἢ περί τοῦ ἄρχειν which is likely to have been one of the targets of the irony of the frame dialogue of the Platonic *Menexenus*.[549] The character of Menexenus in this dialogue is quite different from that of the young boy who figures in the *Lysis* (note however *Ly.* 211b ἐριστικός), and this indicates slightly that both Antisthenes' writing and the frame of *Menexenus* are later than *Lysis*. It is also unclear what is implied by Socrates' promise at the end *(Mx.* 249e) to deliver more political λόγοι which he has learned from Aspasia.[550] At any rate it seems reasonable to place the frame dialogue of *Menexenus* in roughly the same context as *Clitopho* (cf. p. 354).

The opening dialogue of the *Theaetetus* is interesting for other reasons. The extant version of this frame was most probably written for the revised version of the dialogue, and thus it is important to note its easy-going style and the somewhat broad setting presented here, both of which resemble the openings of certain dubia and spuria such as *Ion* and the two *Hippias* dialogues, rather than the somewhat heavy and abstract latter part of the main dialogue of *Theaetetus*. In fact the introduction may give the false impression of being 'early.' I am inclined to believe that the frame was not written by the same person who completed the main dialogue.

[183] Now, the points which the author of the introduction wants to make are not absolutely clear to the modern reader.[551] I would interpret them as follows: Theaitetos was in all respects a virtuous young man (unlike, say, Charmides), and potentially an ideal philosopher; unlike the reader, Euclides knew him and Socrates well; hence, Euclides is able to give a true report of their discussion of

---

548. Dittmar 1912: 16, 20 ff., suggested that the frame dialogue of *Menexenus* playfully criticized the idealized portrait of Aspasia which Aeschines had created (cf. also Diotima in Plato's *Symposium)*; and this has been accepted by many scholars, whereas Wilamowitz II 147 (followed by Friedländer II 202) thought that it was Aeschines who corrected the picture of *Menexenus*. For chronological reasons, I would prefer the former solution. And because Plato had already 'refined' Aspasia into Diotima, it is perhaps reasonable to think that he did not himself write the frame of *Menexenus;* this assumption would explain some of its anomalies.

549. Rick 1931: 372–390 represents the speculations of the 'Pan-Antisthenians,' but the sad truth is that we do not know anything about the contents of Antisthenes' 'Menexenus.' Aspasia may of course have figured in this work, cf. fr. 34–35 Caizzi and id. p. 86.

550. Is this a hint that all that Antisthenes writes is just as unreliable as this speech? Cf. the preceding note.

551. The most common assumption, refuted above p. 301 ff., is that the introduction was occasioned by the death of Plato's friend Theaitetos. Some scholars have assumed that the introduction was written as a compliment to Euclides, either before or after his death (cf. Ueberweg 1861: 235 f., etc.), and since Schleiermacher (cf. Natorp 1903: 92) it has sometimes been believed that the introduction prepares for a confrontation with Megarian philosophy. Among other explanations, note the suggestion of Alrivie 1971 that, unlike the *Parmenides*, the *Theaetetus* is intended to represent written tradition; this agrees to some extent with my interpretation.

ἐπιστήμη; this was a very important discussion, superseding all that Socrates [183]
had said before on the subject; the Academy is lucky to possess an exact written
copy of this λόγος (143a); Plato's old friend Euclides is a very reliable witness
(unlike, perhaps, later Megarians).[552] Euclides, I take it, was dead at the time the
fiction of this introductory dialogue was written, but he was not necessarily dead
when the main dialogue was composed (cf. p. 303).

The alternative version of the opening dialogue, which we know of by a
happy chance (p. 232), was approximately of the same length and was attached
to the same dramatic dialogue text that we have, but was inelegant (ψυχρός) and
regarded as spurious; it began with the words "Would you bring, boy, the dialogue on Theaitetos!" It has been suggested that this was perhaps an earlier draft
of the introduction we have,[553] but since the existence of a written text to be read
by a slave boy is gradually explained in the extant version, it seems to me rather
more probable that the lost version was later. It may have been substituted
for the extant one which was perhaps not properly understood, felt to be irrelevant, and considered too pro-Megarian. This must, however, remain a matter of
conjecture.

---

552. The extent of Plato's debt to the Megarians is an old subject of controversy. Plato's early
association with the Megarians (p. 172 f.) and their well-documented Elean interests indicate a
common basis. For the Megarian background of e.g. the στοιχεῖα theory *Tht.* 201e f., cf. Aristotle
*Met.* H 3.1043b23 ff., Raeder 1905: 290 f.

553. Cf. Apelt, *Tht.* 147 f., Diès 1924: 121 f., Cornford 1935: 15.

# PLATO'S 'LATE PERIOD'

## Introductory

The fact that the *Sophist* and *Politicus* (and their 'associates,' *Parmenides* and *Theaetetus*), *Timaeus, Critias, Philebus,* the *Laws* and *Epinomis* form a separate late group of dialogues, can be regarded as incontrovertibly proved (cf. above p. 213 ff.). It is also commonly believed, and very reasonably, that this period essentially covers the time between Plato's second voyage to Sicily (366 BCE) and his death (347 BCE).

As was suggested above (p. 243), the typical mannerisms of Plato's 'late style' are not perhaps entirely Plato's own. And so, perhaps, the texts are not entirely authentic in the same sense as the works so far discussed are for the most part.

The internal order of the dialogues of the late group is still much more controversial than many scholars and reference books seem willing to admit. The *Laws* and their appendix, the *Epinomis,* are likely to represent on the whole a comparatively late phase, though the *Laws* must have taken a long time to write; and the *Philebus* is normally assigned a fairly late date also. But there is not so much agreement on the relative or absolute dates for the rest. For the genesis of *Theaetetus, see* above p. 300 and p. 328; for *Parmenides* p. 304.

For various reasons to be given later I would conjecture that Plato finished the *Theaetetus* before 366, and devoted the years between the second and the third visit to Sicily mainly to finishing the *Republic* and to preparing parts of the *Laws,* and also to the ontological questions embodied in the *Parmenides,* whereas the rest of the dialogues of this group were composed later.

## The completing of the *Republic*

On the preceding pages we have been several times faced with *non liquet* with regard to the date of the composition of the later books of the *Republic.* Although some portions may have been written in the 370s (cf. especially p. 286) I do not find it likely at all that the work as we have it was finished before the period of *Euthydemus, Charmides* and the first version of the *Theaetetus.*

[185]     As a matter of fact there are several positive indications that notably Books VI and VIII–X received their present shape after Plato's second voyage to Sicily, i.e. after 366 BCE.[554] The following points deserve special attention: At VI 496b Socrates lists examples of different kinds of people who might become philosophers; the examples are specific enough to suggest real cases (presumably members of the Academy); and it is fairly likely that the 'noble man' living in exile is Dion after his banishment from Syracuse in 366 BCE.[555] At VI 499b–d (cf. 502ab, IX 592ab) the pessimism both with regard to the philosopher's likelihood of reforming the State (if an ἀνάγκη τις ἐκ τύχης comes, 499b5) and as regards a real love of philosophy being kindled in the sons of kings, sounds like an echo of Plato's experiences in 366 (cf. also *Ep.* 7.327e4 θείᾳ τινὶ τύχῃ and 328c4 τόλμῃ).[556] In Books VIII and IX the description of the tyrant is infused with an intensely personal tone, and at IX 577ab 'Socrates' hints that 'he' has been living in a tyrant's house and has seen his private life. This is usually taken to refer to Dionysius I, although some scholars have noted that Plato really did not know him very well at all (cf. above p. 175 f.).[557] The pathos of these passages actually suggests a recent experience, and so Dionysius II may seem a more likely model. It has also been observed (by Joël 1907: 303 f.) that it is not likely that Dionysius II would have invited Plato to Syracuse if he had known the contents of the later books of the *Republic*. And at the end of Book IX (592ab) Socrates says that the true philosopher will concern himself rather with the cosmic State—is this a sign of Plato's disappointment with the events in Sicily, and of his planning the *Timaeus* (cf. p. 337)?—It has sometimes been thought that the *Republic* contains traces of influence from Eudoxus; this is very debatable, however, except for Book X.[558]

The somewhat heterogeneous Book X with its curious appendices on μίμησις and the theory of Forms, has quite often been interpreted as being a later addition,
[186]     or as containing later portions.[559] Recently Else 1972 has argued in considerable detail that the portion 595a–608b (on Forms and μίμησις) was written in the 350s, after the *Sophist* (and after the *Parmenides* with its 'third man' argument), and in reply to Aristotle's view of poetic μίμησις; further, that 608d–612a also constitutes an odd piece though it is earlier (cf. p. 286); but that the end of the book

---

554. For Books VI and VIII–IX *see* especially Immisch 1899: 624 f., Adam ad l., Joël 1907b: 295–315. Little attention has been paid to this evidence because the dominant 'Lutoslawski-Raeder-Ritter' doctrine implies that the *Republic* belongs to Plato's 'middle period;' cf. Ueberweg-Praechter 277.

555. Cf. 496c–497a and Adam ad l. Shorey ad l. ironically suggest Anaxagoras, Xenophon or Plato himself as alternatives, but unlike Dion none of these is really to the point.

556. Hirmer 1897: 667 f. and others have wrongly asserted that 499b7 νῦν must imply that Dionysius I is still living: it means rulers of the ordinary human type (cf. e.g. VII 540d5).

557. Cf. Pfleiderer 1896: 214n., Wilamowitz I 437 n. 1. For *Grg.* 510b, cf. Guthrie IV 284 n. 4.

558. Hirmer 1897: 667, referring to *R.* VII 529e f., 530e; but doubted by Apelt *R.* 530 n. 47, and others. It is rather more probable that the new cosmology presented in *Timaeus* had been influenced by Eudoxus.

559. The idea was suggested by Zeller (II I⁴ 566) and others in the 19th century, and it was partly accepted or modified by e.g. Lutoslawski 313 ff,, Apelt *R.* 534 n. 10, Ueberweg-Praechter 270, and more recently by e.g. Else (below). The unitarians have often insisted that Book X is an integral part of the composition, e.g. Rohatyn 1975.

(the myth of Er) belonged to the original body of text. For my part I find Else's argument largely convincing.

If the considerations made here and above hold good, the following general picture of the genesis of the *Republic* would emerge: After appending the objections of Glaucon and Adimantus to a new version of *Republic* I (perhaps about 380 BCE), and then having drafted various portions of the larger composition which he planned, including perhaps the final myth (which seems to develop further some of the ideas of the myth of *Phaedo* but perhaps is earlier than the central myth of *Phaedrus*),[560] Plato laid aside the work. He returned to it after the first version of *Theaetetus*, about 370 BCE, and then composed the main part of the present text, adding various sections to it after 366 BCE, and working into it the 'Proto-*Republic*.' The work still remained unknown to a wider public. In the mid-350s the first part of Book X was inserted, and the composition took its final shape, very probably with the aid of a secretary.

Could it be that Plato's eventual decision to compose this body of texts, which were largely personal documents of his development as a philosopher, was occasioned by the death of Dion and the final collapse of all hopes for an ideal State on this earth?

## The early portions of the *Laws*

Although the *Laws* were probably published posthumously and at any rate not by Plato himself (p. 348), they form a heterogeneous mass of texts which were certainly not written consecutively in a relatively short space of time. The fact that all of these texts have 'late style' characteristics to a varying degree,[561] has little bearing on chronology since such features may, wholly or partly, be due to the editor's revision of the work. On the other hand the difficulties of relating the doctrinal contents of the *Laws* to other Platonic works have sometimes been pointed out; obviously the purpose and potential public of the *Laws* are largely different from those of most of Plato's writings, and especially from the esoteric writings of the late period.[562] At any rate, those scholars who stress the homogeneity of the work have produced less convincing arguments than those who are of the contrary opinion.[563]

---

560. This is commonly accepted today, cf. Leisegang 1950: 2450, Crombie I 302 f., T. M. Robinson 1970: 50 ff., Else 1972: 10 ff. Cf. above p. 323.
561. For various observations, *see* the references in Lutoslawski and the critical discussion by Brandwood 1958: also Vanachter 1946. Cf. Thesleff 1967, above p. 125 ff.
562. Cf. notably Egermann 1959, Görgemanns 1959, Hentschke 1971; also Wilamowitz I² 634 n. 1. Shorey 1903: 85. pointed out that the *Laws* often represent the true Platonic position without irony or dramatic attitudes.
563. For inconsistencies and various signs of a lack of disposition, *see* Pfleiderer 1896: 715 ff., F. Döring 1907, Apelt *Lg.* p. XVI ff., Wilamowitz I 655 and n. 2, 658 ff., Geffcken II A 128 n. 5, Morrow 1960b: 161 f., Gauss I/1.204, III/2.209 f., Tarán 1975: 131 and n. 550; cf. also the analytic

[187]   Apart from the general likelihood that some portions of the *Laws* were originally intended for the reforms planned in Syracuse and may have existed in drafts as early as the 360s, or even earlier,[564] we have the statement of Diogenes Laertius (3.23, from Pamphila) that Plato was invited to write the laws for Megalopolis in Arcadia, presumably in the early 360s.[565] The technique of the opening scenes, preparing for a long walk and referring to the surroundings in remarks included in the actual discussion (notably 625a–c), reminds one of the *Phaedrus* and suggests a date not very much later than this dialogue. A clue to an absolute date can be found in I 638ab, which is believed to refer to Dionysius II capture of Locri in 356 (or 352),[566] but this is not very certain as the other example given in the same passage, the defeat of Ceos by Athens, may refer to Chabrias' activities in 376 (Demosth. 20.77, cf. SEG XIX 50). For a supposed reference in the *3rd Letter* to Book V, see n. 564.[567]

[188]   *Theaetetus* and *Parmenides*

The interrelations of these two dialogues was discussed above (p. 307).

To account for the differences between *Theaetetus* and *Parmenides,* and to explain the fact that the latter more clearly amounts to a confrontation with some of the central doctrines of the *Republic,* I prefer to think that *Theaetetus* was written down in the shape preserved to us (except perhaps for the introduction, cf. p. 328) about 367 BCE, shortly before Plato's second voyage to Sicily. This would agree roughly with the conventional dating, though I would not agree with all of

---

interpretation of Book I by Gigon 1954. Essential homogeneity has been advocated by Ritter 1910b: 279, G. Müller 1951 and some others; cf. Leisegang 1950: 2513 f., Friedländer III 504 n. 17, Görgemanns 1959. I have elsewhere (1972) pointed out that the editor partly followed Plato's compositional principles by varying the structure of the dialogue and style.

564. This has been often assumed, though it is difficult to demonstrate in detail. Thus, for *Lg.* IV 708d ff. as implying Dionysius II before 361 BCE, Ueberweg 1861: 221 and many others; but as implying Dion after that date, Ritter 1910b: 160, Leisegang 1950: 2513. For the 'mixed constitution' of *Lg.* III 693de, VI 756e as implying Dion's activities after 357 BCE (cf. Plut. *Dio* 53), Raeder 396f., 405, F. Döring 1907: 40 ff. (but questioned by Leisegang l.c. and others). The actual law texts may have been written at different dates for different purposes. And if the προοίμια νόμων in *Ep.* 3.316a imply Book V of the *Laws,* and since the letter apparently purports to be written during Plato's second visit to Sicily and the author is rather well informed, we have a possible *terminus ante quem* for this portion; this is debatable, however; for the pros and cons, *see* Raeder 1906: 518 f., Ritter 1910b: 123, Taylor 465 (suggesting 360 as the dramatic date of the letter); Wilamowitz II 279.

565. Cf. Ritter 1910b: 109 ff., Morrow 1960a: 8 and n. 11; the doubts of Wilamowitz I 490 seem unwarranted. Several Academics were concerned with law giving; *see* the references in Guthrie IV 23 f. and Wörle 1981.

566. Ueberweg 1861: 221, following earlier suggestions; Guthrie V 322.

567. For other, more debatable external criteria, *see* Pfleiderer 1896: 867 ff. (supposed polemics of Plato against Aristotle; cf. Ueberweg-Praechter 324); Ueberweg-Praechter 200 (a supposed reference in *Lg.* III 694c to Xenophon's Cyropaedia, cf. Diog. L. 3.34 and Athen. 11.504 f., Gell. *NA* 14.3.4); Gomperz II 574 f. (a supposed reference in Isocr. *Philipp.* (V) 12, written in the autumn of 346 BCE, to the *Laws;* doubts by Zeller II 1⁵ 443 n. 1 and others, including Guthrie V 321 n. 4).

the conventional arguments (cf. p. 303 and 308). This new and serious reconsideration of the fundaments of knowledge may well be situated in the context of the genesis of the *Republic,* though the exact relationship between *Theaetetus* and the *Republic* remains unclear.⁵⁶⁸ The famous digression on philosophical σχολή in *Theaetetus,* 172c–177c, cannot then, of course, be interpreted as reflecting Plato's negative experience of practical politics in Sicily, but surely he had had such experiences in Athens.⁵⁶⁹

It was suggested above (p. 306) as a somewhat reasonable possibility that the *Parmenides* (or at least the first part of the dialogue) is to be dated about 362 BCE, when the *Republic* had received approximately its present shape.

[188]

## *Timaeus* and *Critias*

G.C. The old controversies regarding the relative and absolute date of these texts were revived by the interesting suggestion of Owen (1953) that *Timaeus* should be dated soon after the *Republic,* possibly before *Phaedrus,* and at any rate before the critical dialogues *Parmenides, Theaetetus,* the *Sophist* and *Politicus.* The tendency had been to place *Timaeus* and *Critias* in Plato's latest period, that of the *Laws,* and this view had received support from stylometry.⁵⁷⁰ Owen based his thesis on a minimizing of the stylometrical evidence, on the close contacts between the *Republic* and *Timaeus-Critias,* and on the fact that the theory of Forms appears to be (as yet?) quite unchallenged in the latter. His view was tentatively accepted by some scholars notably in the Anglo-Saxon world.⁵⁷¹

[189]

As far as I can see, the Owen controversy has at least shown up the unreliability of the traditional stylometrical approach more clearly than hitherto.⁵⁷² The peculiar style of *Timaeus* and *Critias* is perhaps to some extent intentionally 'mythic.'⁵⁷³ Quite obviously, however, it has not been polished for 'publication,'

---

568. Cf. the references above p. 303 f. It seems *a priori* unlikely that Plato would have had the time and leisure to rewrite the *Theaetetus* in the years between 366 and 361 BCE.

569. The *Phaedrus* also refers to such σχολή above n. 543.

570. Some scholars have preferred to put *Philebus* later, and there has been little agreement on the place of *Timaeus* in relation to the *Sophist* and *Politicus* (especially since Kaluscha 1904, v. Arnim 1912 and Billig 1920 had adduced stylometrical arguments for the precedence of *Timaeus*); but since the establishment of the Lutoslawski-Raeder-Ritter position very few (e.g. H. Gomperz 1905: 193 n. 1) would place dialogues such as *Parmenides* or *Phaedrus* later than *Timaeus.*

571. Among them Gould 1955: 202 f., Crombie I 13, Shiner 1974; cf. also Guthrie V 243; and Brandwood 1958 attempted to reinforce this view 'beyond doubt' by a reconsideration of the linguistic criteria (notably clausulae, 316–343). The thesis was opposed by Skemp 1952: 237–239, 1954/55, Field 1954, Vlastos 1954: 334 f., Gulley 1962: 108 ff., and with particular vehemence by Cherniss (1957 etc.) supported by Rist 1960 and Prior 1975. On the whole the controversy did not affect the views of continental scholars.

572. Cf. above p. 215. I cannot see that even the clausulae, which are the strongest criteria produced by Brandwood in his very comprehensive discussion of the evidence (1958), have any particular importance in this connection: the style of *Timaeus* is odd anyway.

573. Cf, Wilamowitz I 628 f., Thesleff 1967, above 119 f. Cf. also the palinodic speech of the *Phaedrus,* above p. 318.

[189] since the 'trilogy' is left unfinished.[574] Plato cannot have intended the work for general consumption in its present shape.

E.C. The introduction of Critias as a representative of good ancient Athenian traditions seems to imply political conditions very different from those in which Polycrates' attack was written and perhaps reflects, indirectly, the same conservative trends in Athenian political life in the 350s as can be seen in Isocrates' 'Areopagiticus' and 'On Peace.'[575] The presence of persons and ideas connected with the West has been variously interpreted as reflecting Plato's second or third Sicilian voyage; from this point of view a date after 360 also appears slightly preferable to an
[190] earlier date.[576] Later pythagorizing Platonists took Timaeus to be a Pythagorean, but if he is a historical person, Plato's picture of him has probably borrowed traits from various quarters; and at any rate the allegedly Pythagorean elements of this picture and of the lecture of Timaeus cannot be used for dating the dialogue.[577] Neither do

---

574. Cf. below p. 337. It is somewhat unclear whether Plato had planned a real 'trilogy' (cf. *Ti.* 17c, 20bc, 27ab, *Criti.* 107ab; Ueberweg-Praechter 211) with a 'Hermocrates' as the third part (cf. *Ti.* 20b, *Criti.* 108ab), or even a 'tetralogy' (Ritter 1910a: 180 ff., referring to the mysterious fourth person mentioned in the opening of *Timaeus*), or a 'tripartite dialogue' (Haslam 1976), or any such complex series at all. Earlier theories of the genesis of *Timaeus-Critias* are discussed by Raeder 378. Hammer-Jensen's theory (1910) that the apparent break at *Timaeus* 45b is due to Plato's fresh studies of atomism, has been sometimes accepted (cf. Sachs 1917, Wilamowitz II 258 ff., Guthrie IV 37) but others have doubted it (*see* Leisegang 1950: 2509, Friedländer III 495, Fackeldey 1958). A complicated theory for the first part of *Timaeus* having originally belonged together with *Critias* (written before 366 BCE) was put forward by Ryle 1966: 232 ff. Obviously there is not sufficient evidence for reconstructing Plato's original plans and intentions. On the other hand, the arguments sometimes produced for regarding the composition of *Timaeus* and *Critias* as artistic and carefully carried out (Ritter 1910a: 175, 1929: 72, cf. Fackeldey 1958, Muthmann 1961: 93 ff.) are subjective and rather groundless in my opinion.

575. Jaeger's dating of the 'Areopagiticus' in 357 BCE is accepted by Bengtson 1960: 300.— The identification of this Critias with the tyrant's grandfather (Taylor 1928: 23) is hardly possible; cf. Davies 1971: 325 f.

576. Connecting the myth of Atlantis somehow with Plato's experiences in Sicily, as sometimes suggested (e.g. Ritter 1910b: 203), seems to me reasonable in principle, though there is room for much speculation (cf. Wilamowitz I 596 n. 1). The fact that Plato's sympathies are after all with Athens, though he had planned a detailed description of Atlantis, may indicate a date after 360 for the text as we have it. The same may be implied by the silent presence of Hermocrates of Syracuse.—It is often assumed that Plato was influenced for the sections on physiology by Philistion of Locri whom he probably met in Athens in the 360s and/or in Syracuse in 361: cf. Wilamowitz II 258, Taylor 1928: 9, Jaeger 1938: 7 ff., 211 ff. (but doubts by Cherniss 1959: 209). For the person of Timaeus and 'Pythagoreanism,' cf. below.—It is highly improbable that Plato would have found in Syracuse the time and leisure to write this work, as some scholars believe (e.g. Crombie I 13: 361 BCE; Ryle 1966: 63 ff., 238 ff.: 366 BCE). Rather, I think, it is an 'escape' into myth and universe *after* the break-down of the Sicilian project.

577. For later conceptions of 'Timaeus the Pythagorean,' *see* the references in Thesleff 1961: 102 ff., 1965: 202 ff. In my view the legends about Occelus and Philolaus represent earlier stages of this 'pythagorizing' process (for which *see* Burkert 1962 passim). The identification of the Πυθαγόρεια mentioned in *Ep.* 13.360b with the *Timaeus* (so Christ 1886: 482 ff. and others, also R. Adam 1909: 49 f.) is highly improbable and thus does not give 365 BCE as a *terminus ante quem* even if the historical frame of the letter is correct. After all the exposition of Plato's Timaeus is not typically Pythagorean in content (*pace* Taylor), and Timaeus cannot be said to 'stand' for Archytas. For Plato and Pythagoreanism, cf. above p. 182.

the Egyptian ingredients of the opening section of *Timaeus* provide any clues for [190] dating.[578] If it could be proved that the cosmology of the work is influenced by the astronomical conceptions of Eudoxus,[579] this would give us an important chronological checkpoint since Eudoxus very probably did not become a member of the Academy before the mid-360s (cf. below p. 372) and Plato would not of course have written the *Timaeus* immediately after he had become acquainted with the theories of Eudoxus; consequently, this would constitute an independent indication of a date after the third Sicilian voyage. A *terminus ante quem* has been seen in Aristotle's 'Protrepticus' (about 354 BCE) which may have used the *Timaeus*.[580] Other supposed contemporary references are even more conjectural.[581]

A specific problem is why *Critias* breaks off so abruptly, so that the whole [191] work in fact remains a torso. A long series of reasons have been suggested, extending from the dramatic events of Plato's Sicilian adventure in the 360s, to self-criticism, and to the death of Dion or of Plato himself.[582] The truth is not accessible to us. If a date after 360 is accepted on other grounds, then a combination of weariness, self-criticism (cf. below p. 341) and the development of the political situation in the West during the first half of the 350s may perhaps suffice as a hypothetical explanation.

I.C.    The *Republic* and *Timaeus-Critias*. It was argued above (p. 251) that the opening of the *Timaeus* operates with the 'Proto-*Republic*' in a fictitious setting. Since it must be regarded as certain that other portions of the present *Republic* already existed when the *Timaeus* was written (cf. below), this linking up with an early draft may seem odd. And why should Plato want to refer to his theory of the ideal πόλις at all in this connection? A possible explanation is that he still felt himself to be first and foremost a political philosopher and, hence, wished to view the idea of a well-organized State as a projection both into the physical universe and into myth and history (cf. *Timaeus* 19b ff.), but that he considered

---

578. Immisch 1899: 627 n. 1 noted that Athens had political contacts with Egypt in 362 BCE; but surely Plato may have received such 'information' at any date. Cf. Isocrates' *Busiris* (p. 254) and above p. 319.

579. This was argued in some detail by Friedländer I 291-299; cf. Gaiser 1965: 193, 200. Owen 1953: 86 f. begged the question by denying influence from Eudoxus on chronological grounds.

580. Düring 1956. But Pfleiderer's suggestion 1896: 659 f. that *Timaeus* 62c ff. refers to Aristotle is based on very loose evidence. And equally loose are the assumptions that the philosophical passages in the *Seventh Letter* (notably 341a ff., 344d ff., e.g. Ryle 1966: 238 ff.) have something to do with *Timaeus*.

581. Cf. H. Gomperz 1906: 11 on possible references in Isocrates' *Antidosis* (XV, 354 BCE); Ritter 1910b: 267 f. and Gauss III/1.228 on the question of whether Dion was still living; Eberz 1910, dating *Timaeus—Critias* between 357 and 353 BCE; Maier 1913: 57 n. 2 on alleged reflections of *Timaeus* in Xenophon's 'Memorabilia.'

582. At any rate, the manuscript tradition should probably not be charged with the incompleteness of the *Critias*, cf. Christ 1886: 464 n. 2. The opinions regarding the reason for Plato's stopping have no independent value; but the belief that the reason was Plato's own death has been somewhat persistent because it is partly based on Cicero's statement (Cato 5) that Plato *scribens mortuus est* (cf. Plut. Sol. 32, and Lutoslawski 490 f., Raeder 376, Ritter 1910b: 160 f., Geffcken II A 126 n. 130); doubts in Ueberweg-Praechter 201; indeed, Cicero's information may merely represent the tradition of Plato's 'curling and combing' his dialogues (above p. 232).

[191] some of the ideas and doctrines expressed in the *Republic* to be out of date; besides, he wished to attain more 'ancient' wisdom than what a discussion with Glaucon and Adimantus could possibly have achieved.[583] If this explanation is approximately correct, it is clear that the *Timaeus* represents a certain distancing of the *Republic* complex which would seem more natural after Plato's final return from Sicily than before it.

Most scholars agree that the *Timaeus* is essentially later than the *Republic*.[584] Disregarding stylometry and the various points of association with the *Sophist* and *Politicus* (below p. 339), the explicit arguments normally adduced are of widely differing validity. I would attach particular importance to the advance in the cosmological conception and the theory of Soul, whereas the advance (or change) in the theory of Forms is perhaps not so obvious.[585] The relative lateness of the
[192] portion 595a–608b of Book X of the *Republic* remains, however, a possibility to be taken seriously.[586]

*Phaedrus—Timaeus.* The cosmological conception and the metaphysics and psychology in the palinodic speech of the *Phaedrus* afford some points of contact with the *Timaeus*. Even if one ignores matters of dialogue technique and style, it is difficult to avoid the impression that *Timaeus*, with its explicit details especially concerning the World Soul, represents a later stage. The occasional attempts to assert the relative lateness of *Phaedrus* have not found much response.[587]

*Theaetetus—Timaeus.* For Owen (1953) the relative lateness of *Theaetetus* followed rather by implication, and much the same can be said against it as in the case of *Parmenides* (below).[588] The precedence of *Theaetetus* can be accepted here without further discussion.

---

583. And perhaps the hint in Isocrates' *Busiris* (p. 254) that he had taken his ideas from Egyptian sources called for correction. Cf. Joël 1907: 323 and Gomperz II 603, referring to Crantor ap. Procl. *Comm. Pl. Tim.* 24e, who seems to imply this. Cf. further Guthrie V 245.

584. Also analysts of the *Republic* are mostly of this opinion; among recent writers only Ryle (1966: 244 ff.) has argued that essential portions of what did not belong to the 'Proto-*Republic*' were composed after the *Timaeus*. I am rather more convinced by Else's argument (below n. 586).

585. Cf., however, *Parmenides*, below. For the theory of Soul in particular, cf. Groag 1913, T. M. Robinson 1970, and Szlezák 1976.

586. Cf. above p. 332. In particular, if the conclusions of Else 1972 can be accepted, it seems reasonable to assume that this portion was added when the text of the *Republic* was being prepared for final composition. And this, I believe, happened after Plato had finished with the *Timaeus* and *Critias*, in the mid-350s.

587. Among earlier attempts, note Immisch 1915: 565 (part of his argumentation for the *Phaedrus* being revised). For Owen 1953: 94 f, this is rather an implication of his placing *Timaeus* closely after the *Republic*, and for Bröcker 1964 a consequence of an extremely late dating of the *Phaedrus*. Only T. M. Robinson 1970 has argued the precedence of *Timaeus* at length. I find the considerations of Groag 1913, v. Arnim 1914: 174 ff., Stenzel (1914) 1956: 1 ff. and Wilamowitz I 470 ff. still largely pertinent and more acceptable. Cf. also Benn 1902, Regenbogen 1950: 212 ff. (placing *Sph.* and *Plt.* earlier, but *Ti.* still later than *Phdr.*), Ross 1951, Mugler 1960.

588. *See* notably Cherniss 1954: 130, 1957, 1965, Rist 1960. An old additional argument for the order *Theaetetus—Timaeus* is that in *Theaetetus* Plato shows an awakening interest in the physical world and αἴσθησις, which is elaborated in the *Timaeus* (cf. Zeller II 1⁵ 491 n. 3, Lutoslawski 374 f., etc.). In this respect *Timaeus* does in fact stand closer to the *Theaetetus* than to the *Parmenides*.

*Parmenides—Timaeus.* Here the precedence of *Parmenides* is usually taken for granted and Owen's theory of the reverse order has been refuted, on this point rather convincingly as far as I can see, by Skemp 1954/55, Rist 1960 and Cherniss 1965.[589] It seems practically certain now that in *Timaeus* the complicated process of creation is intended to account for some aspects of the relation παράδειγμα/ εἰκών which appeared so problematic in *Parmenides* 132c ff. Note also the mythical version of 'henology' in *Timaeus* 31ab which is perhaps directed, partly, against the 'third man' argument as expressed in the *Parmenides*.

Thus, a date not earlier than the first half of the 350s seems after all preferable for the unfinished torso of *Timaeus-Critias*. So far, we have found few manifest lower termini. The *Sophist* and *Politicus* will, however, provide some.

## The *Sophist* and *Politicus*   [193]

G.C. The place of this (unidentical) twin pair of dialogues in relation to the other works of the late period has been even more debated than that of *Timaeus-Critias*, ever since Campbell in his edition of them (1867) had launched the late group theory.[590] The problem of their chronological position is no doubt interesting and important. Their authenticity can be taken for granted here though, as in the case of the other late works, we cannot be so sure that Plato actually 'wrote' them personally or even intended them for publication.[591]

In formal respects the *Sophist* and *Politicus* are related both to *Parmenides* and *Theaetetus*, and to *Timaeus* and *Critias*, though thematically they are connected rather with the former. The net of associations is curiously complex, as has often been seen, and to which the different interpretations with regard to chronology bear abundant witness. Considering first only matters of form, such as the setting, characters, structure, dialogue technique and style, the following facts may be noted here: Like *Timaeus-Critias*, the *Sophist-Politicus* purport to be the first and second part of a planned trilogy (*Sph.* 217a) or 'tripartite dialogue' the third part of which was perhaps never written (for the problem of the 'Philosophus,' see below p. 341); both trilogies are (by way of a fiction) connected with an important earlier dialogue and purport to continue the discussion of 'the day before,' but the association of the *Sophist* with *Theaetetus* is somewhat less explicit than that of *Timaeus* with the *Republic*, although, on the other hand, the reader can more easily accept the fiction of the *Sophist* than the clearly untrue one of the *Timaeus*; the setting is reduced to a minimum in both; Socrates is present, but only as 'Ehrenpräsident' (Gomperz II 451); the central characters in both trilogies

---

589. Shiner 1974, especially 30 ff., has produced a reconsideration of the problem and renewed the arguments for the precedence of the *Timaeus*. A reconsideration was probably necessary, but I find the results negative.

590. The last to date the *Sophist* and *Politicus* early was probably Waddington 1904; cf. the theory of a Megarian period, above p. 172.

591. Cf. above p. 331. In the 19th century, several scholars considered the *Sophist* and *Politicus* spurious; cf. Lutoslawski 434 f., 453 ff. with references.

[193] are old venerable teachers from the West (but the *Timaeus* trilogy also introduces Critias who bears some resemblance to the Athenian of the *Laws*); the Elean Stranger of the *Sophist* trilogy is as unindividualized as the Athenian Stranger of the *Laws*, whereas Timaeus has received some characterization in the manner of the earlier dialogues; both trilogies, and the dialogues within them, are structurally loose and contain substantial digressions;[592] from the point of view of dialogue technique, large portions of the *Sophist* trilogy may give the impression of being, to all intents and purposes, a continuous lecture like the main expositions of *Ti-*
[194] *maeus* and *Critias*, even though it is artificially chopped up into dialogue;[593] and stylistically both trilogies have typical 'late style' characteristics throughout.[594] The formal association of the *Sophist* and *Politicus* with *Theaetetus* and *Parmenides*, again, is brought about by implicit references to the latter dialogues, notably by using the same persons but making some significant changes: Socrates and Theodoros appear only in the introductions, the Elean Stranger who leads the discussion somehow stands for Parmenides, and Theaitetos (whose counterparts in *Parmenides* are young Socrates and 'Aristoteles') remains as the interlocutor of the Stranger in the *Sophist* but is replaced in the *Politicus* by the curiously vague character of Socrates 'the Younger.'[595] And the same dialogue technique as in *Theaetetus* and *Parmenides* is explicitly chosen in the *Sophist* (217cd).

There can be little doubt that the *Sophist* and *Politicus* follow *Theaetetus* and the *Parmenides*; but the differences in tone, and also the 'fusion' of *Theaetetus* and *Parmenides* into a common background, suggest some distance in time.

The *Sophist* and *Politicus* clearly belong even more closely together than *Timaeus* and *Critias*. In addition to the formal and thematic correspondences, there are several explicit cross-references, contrary to Plato's normal practice.[596] Most probably the dialogues were written consecutively in a relatively short period of time.[597]

---

592. I believe this is rather the editor's 'fault,' since Plato probably did not intend to 'publish' the dialogues as such. The *Sophist* and *Politicus* are usually, and rightly, considered esoteric from the outset (cf. Ritter 1910b: 271 n. 1; also Wilamowitz I 561 who, eccentrically, thought that the *Timaeus* was intended to be exoteric). Against those who blame Plato's old age for the looseness of the composition, Geffcken II 133 f. rightly notes that the *Politicus* is in fact rather lively and energetic.

593. This is not as strong a connecting link between the trilogies as is sometimes believed (Shorey 1903: 57 n. 420 clearly pointed out the differences). The specific dialogue technique of the 'monologizing dialogue' occurs in manifestly earlier works also (even in the *Gorgias*), especially in *Cratylus*, *Phaedrus* and the *Republic* (cf. Thesleff 1967, above 42 ff., arguing that a later variety of this technique can be traced since *Phd.* and *Cra.*), whereas the continuous lecture of Timaeus corresponds to the set speeches and myths on the one hand and various sections of the *Laws* on the other.

594. For the different interpretations of the stylometrical evidence, see below p. 197.

595. He is first mentioned in *Tht.* 147d1. He was probably a historical person (though it is not absolutely certain that *Ep.* 11.358de actually refers to him and not to Plato's teacher). At any rate, there must have been some joking in the Academy about this 'doubling' of Socrates; cf. above p. 270. But see now below p. 466 n. 142.

596. Cf *Sph.* 217a, *Plt.* 257a, 258bc, 266d, 284bc, 286bc (quoting ὁ Σοφιστής as a book!).

597. The dissenting theories of some scholars have little weight. Ast and Rohde thought that *Plt.* 283b–287a answers some censure of the dihaeretic excesses of the *Sophist* (but cf. Raeder 337),

The specific problem of what became of the 'Philosophus' which Plato appears to have planned as the third part of the trilogy (*Sph.* 217a, cf. 253e, *Plt.* 257a) has little chronological relevance. Because the *Sophist* and *Politicus* belong closely together, formally and thematically, it is to be expected that the 'Philosophus' would be more or less similar to them. Evidently, however, such a dialogue was never written. There is little firm evidence for the speculations concerning Plato substituting some other work for it.[598]

E.C. The attitude to political leadership, the characterizing of it as a kind of 'weaving,' and notably the description of the true despot in *Politicus* 292a ff., 296b ff., has been variously interpreted to reflect the development of the situation in Sicily.[599] Though the details are somewhat ambiguous it is clear to me that, since the *Politicus* is rather ironically distanced from the art of politics, as the *Sophist* is from the art of sophistry, and since the emphasis in the *Sophist* and *Politicus* is on logic and method, not on polemics or reform, these dialogues should on general grounds be more naturally placed after Plato had withdrawn from practical politics altogether.

The διαιρέσεις mentioned in the *13th Letter* (360b) as being sent to Dionysius II together with the Πυθαγόρεια, are not likely to refer to the *Sophist* and *Politicus* any more than the Πυθαγόρεια refer to the *Timaeus* (above n. 577). There is obviously no reason for mystification in the case of the *Sophist* and *Politicus* whose διαιρέσεις could not have been regarded as imparting any profound wisdom; and after all the dialogues contain much more than mere διαιρέσεις. But because

[194]

[195]

---

and Skemp 1952: 14 n. 4 suggested that the quotations in *Plt.* 284b and 286b imply that the *Sophist* had already been published. Pfleiderer 1896 inserted *Euthydemus* between the *Sophist* and *Politicus*, E. Wolf 1968–70 preferred to insert the *Philebus*. The stylometrists on the whole (also v. Arnim) tend to place the *Politicus* after the *Sophist*, but Billig 1920: 238 ff. argued from the use of clausulae (a very weak basis in fact) that the 'digression' *Sph.* 236c–260e is later than the rest and was written under the influence of *Politicus*; cf. on stylometry below, p. 343. The very eccentric attempt of Vollenhoven 1948 to place the *Politicus* before *Theaetetus* but the *Sophist* after it does not bear critical examination at all.

598. *Parmenides*: Zeller, Stallbaum, argued again by Wyller 1966 etc., especially 1970: 7 f., 90 ff. *Symposium* and *Phaedo*: Zeller (II 1⁵ 549). *Republic* V–VII: Spengel, Pfleiderer (1896: 495 ff.). *Epinomis*: Raeder 1938. *Philebus*: Skemp 1952: 17, 80. *Timaeus* and *Philebus*: Krämer 1959: 316 f. Most scholars argue, however, that Plato changed his plans, and some think that he never planned a 'Philosophus' at all. For references to the earlier discussion, see Raeder 1905: 352 ff. (and 1938, in Danish); cf. Guthrie V 123.—Apparently the 'lost' Third Book on True Wisdom already constituted a problem for the later Academy, to judge by the 'Tripartitum' and the Λόγος τρίτος attributed to Pythagoras (cf. Thesleff 1965: 245, 170; more remotely relevant is perhaps the medieval 'Liber Quartus' attributed to Plato, cf. A. Badawi, *La transmission de la philosophie grecque au monde arabe*, Paris: Vrin, 1968: 42 f.).

599. A date after 366, when the hopes for a Philosopher-King were first seriously shaken, is commonly taken for granted; cf. e.g. Ritter 1910b: 148, 207 f., Hackforth 1945: 1 f. But some think that the Royal Art of Weaving implies new hopes of a leader able to handle more practical political methods, and that this indicates a date before the debacle of 360 (cf. e.g. Wilamowitz I 557 ff., Skemp 1952: 17 f., Owen 1953: 89 ff.). More commonly, however, it is believed that Plato's experiences in 361/0 BCE have also influenced his attitude in the *Politicus* (e.g. Lutoslawski 1896: 441, Gomperz II 432, 590, suggesting that *Plt.* 296b–e refers to Dion's activities in the 350s; Geffcken II 135, Gauss III/1.234).

[195] this letter belongs to those which are well informed about Plato and his circle (cf. below p. 380), the passage points to the existence in the mid-360s of some kind of dihaeretic tables which were in esoteric use at the Academy. The διαιρέσεις of the *Sophist* and *Politicus* may derive from, or playfully allude to, such tables.[600]—
The διαίρεσις method is ridiculed in the well-known fragment of the comedian
[196] Epicrates (fr. 11 K, II p. 355 ff. Edmonds, from Athen. 2.59d)[601] where we hear of a group of students at the Academy applying it to biological studies under the supervision of Plato, Speusippus and Menedemus. The fragment can be roughly dated to the 360s.

Of the alleged allusions to contemporary persons, the words τῶν γερόντων τοῖς ὀψιμαθέσι θοίνην παρεσκευάκαμεν in the *Sophist* 251b, which almost certainly refer to Antisthenes, have been thought to indicate a date not later than the 360s since the allusion, it is believed, would be pointless if Antisthenes were not living; I doubt, however, whether anything can be built upon this.[602]

I.C. The *Republic*—the *Sophist-Politicus*. This order—with the possible exception of the first part of *Republic* X as argued by Else (above p. 332)—has been proved against Zeller and his followers beyond any reasonable doubt and need not be discussed here.[603] The order *Phaedrus*—the *Sophist-Politicus* follows by implication, but it is not as clear as such; and the opposite order has also been argued in recent times, though on insufficient grounds.[604]

*Theaetetus, Parmenides*—the *Sophist, Politicus*. From a formal point of view, this chronology is practically certain (cf. above p. 339). It is now generally accepted

---

600. Suggested by Raeder 1906: 514f. (who had before, 1905: 351 f., belonged to those who identify the διαιρέσεις of the *13th Letter* with the *Sph.-Plt.*). Cf. the γεγραμμέναι διαιρέσεις criticized in the opening of Aristotle's *Part. An.*; Speusippus published a collection of διαιρέσεις (Diog. L. 4.5).

601. Cf. Diès in the Budé edition of *Plt.*, 1935: XXVI ff., who quotes the fragment.

602. Cf. Raeder 326 f., 331; for Antisthenes as ὀψιμαθής cf. Arist. *Met.* Δ 29.1024b32 ff.—The other supposed allusions are even less useful. For various theories, *see* Raeder 323, H. Gomperz 1906: 23 (Isocrates); Maier 1913: 59 ff. (alleged reflections in Xenophon, *Mem.* IV 5.11 f., almost certainly refutable since Xenophon hardly bothered to read and use the *Sophist* and *Politicus*); Apelt *Sph.* 2–4, Raeder 351 n. 2, Düring 1956 (Aristotle). Even more conjectural is the argument of Eberz 1909, indicating a date between 360 and 357 BCE.

603. In addition to the (not always cogent) observations of Lutoslawski, Raeder and Ritter, note especially Groag 1913, Robin 1938: 100 ff., Rist 1960: 211 ff., T. M. Robinson 1970, and the references in Leisegang 1950: 2501 f. The general skepticism of Shorey 1903 (e.g. 54 f., 62 f.) does not affect the fundamental fact that the critical and ironically distancing attitude of the *Sophist* and *Politicus* is very much more natural after than before the *Republic*.

604. Chiefly by Regenbogen 1950, for whose very late dating of the *Phaedrus* see the doubts and objections of Cherniss 1959: 65. For the relation *Phaedrus~Sophist~Politicus*, his theory was accepted by e.g. Bröcker 1964, Wyller 1966, 1970, and also Gaiser 1974 (137); cf. also Hoffmann 1950: 144 f. (a loose suggestion). Regenbogen's chief argument in this case (202–207) was that Plato in *Phaedrus* (especially 265a–266c) describes and uses the dihaeretic method in a more advanced manner than in the *Sophist* and *Politicus*; but he did not take into account the fact that the latter dialogues tend to play *in absurdum* with what must have been a well-known Academic method (cf. above n. 499). In most respects the precedence of *Phaedrus* is easy to argue; cf. e.g. Groag 1913 (conception of soul; note that the theory of self-motion is implied in all later works), Ross 1951 (theory of Forms), Hackforth 1952 (various points), Guthrie IV 47 (more emphasis on method).

on thematic grounds also, and occasional dissenters have not found any convincing arguments for the reverse order. For *Parmenides*, note, in addition to the various allusions in the *Sophist*, the almost explicit reference to the latter part of *Parmenides* in *Sophist* 217c where Socrates asks the Elean Stranger whether he prefers to give a continuous lecture (cf. *Timaeus*) or to use a questioning method such as Parmenides once used "when I was present as a young man, and he was very old."[605] For *Theaetetus* Cornford's interpretation (1935) has adduced sufficient additional evidence.[606]

*Timaeus-Critias* versus the *Sophist-Politicus*. The chronological relation of these 'trilogies' is a vexed problem which must be regarded as still unsolved, although the results of the Owen controversy (above p. 335) tended to confirm the widely accepted view of considering *Timaeus* and *Critias* later. Firstly, it should be stated that stylometry provides little or no aid.[607] Secondly, it is very doubtful whether there are any real doctrinal differences between the trilogies. The old view that there are was reinterpreted by Owen to imply that the critical discussion in the *Sophist* and *Politicus* also concerns *Timaeus*;[608] but some of Owen's opponents, notably Cherniss (1965), insisted that there are no essential differences.[609]

---

605. Cf. *Prm.* 127b2, c4–5; stating the age of both is motivated in *Parmenides* but not in the *Sophist*. I find it particularly important to note that the really typical example of the method δι' ἐρωτήσεων is the latter part of *Parmenides*, and that παρεγενόμην Sph. 217b implies exactly the situation of the second part of the dialogue, and not a discussion between Parmenides and Socrates. Cf. the less explicit 'foreshadowing' of *Parmenides* in *Theaetetus*, above p. 308. For the order *Prm—Sph., Plt.* in general, cf. Lutoslawski and Raeder pm., Ueberweg-Praechter 294, 296; the objections of Shorey 1903: 57 n. 424 are not pertinent; and the theories of a final edition of *Parmenides* after *Sph.*, whereas *Sph.* refers to an earlier edition (Brommer 1940: 152 f., H. M. Wolff 1957: 216 f., and others), lack a factual basis.—To what extent the *Sophist* and *Politicus* represent a modification of the theory of Forms is an unsettled question, but the view of Lutoslawski and others (still maintained by Kucharski 1949: 325 ff.) that the theory was virtually abandoned is not accepted today; cf. notably the conception of Ross 1951. Liebrucks 1949 argued that *Parmenides* is later chiefly because its dialectic appears to be more subtle (but he did not notice the play of logic in *Sph.* and *Plt.*). Wyller (1966, 1970) would place *Parmenides* after the *Sophist* and *Politicus* chiefly because he sees in it the dialogue 'Philosophus'; cf. above p. 194.

606. But Cornford probably somewhat underrates the formal and thematic differences in bringing *Theaetetus* and the *Sophist* closely together. The αὔριον at the end of *Theaetetus* is no reliable 'foreshadowing' of the *Sophist* (cf. Friedländer III 224). Lutoslawski and Raeder supply more points and references. For the theory of Forms, see Ross 1951. Vollenhoven's (1948: 6 ff.) theory of *Theaetetus* following *Politicus* but preceding the *Sophist* does not work in practice.

607. This was in fact argued by Owen 1953: 79 ff. against the prevalent view. His opponents have not been able to refute this point altogether, and Brandwood's attempt to support Owen's arguments for the order *Ti., Criti.—Sph., Plt.* by an examination of the use of clausulae (1958: 270 ff., cf. Kaluscha 1904, Billig 1920) has much too narrow a basis. The tone is very different in the two 'trilogies,' and the fact that *Timaeus* is more obviously lacking final polish than the *Sophist* and *Politicus* may be reflected in the clausulae and the avoidance of hiatus in the latter (cf. Janell 1901 on the hiatus).

608. This had been suggested before, especially as regards the theory of Forms, by Ueberweg 1861: 169 ff. and others; cf. also Wilpert 1953 and Friedländer III 417.

609. Similarly Skemp 1952. Before this, others had attempted to harmonize the differences, e.g. Rivaud 1925: 21 ff. It is interesting that Lutoslawski 486 rather minimizes the divergences

[198] However, to assume that the two trilogies were written alongside of each other, as some have suggested (e.g. Rivaud, Skemp), is an unsatisfactory makeshift bearing in mind the widely differing themes and approaches.

Apart from the much-debated theory of Forms, the points at issue include cosmology, especially the myth of Cronus in *Politicus* 268d–274e, and psychology. Considering these aspects, I find it more natural to regard the *Sophist* and *Politicus* as having been written later; in particular *Politicus* 269c–270a would be much more difficult to explain if the *Timaeus* had not preceded it, and the description of Universe as a living being in the *Sophist* 248d ff. seems to imply the idea of a World Soul.[610] And after all, is not the alternative provided at the *Sophist* 217c, αὐτὸς ἐπὶ σαυτοῦ μακρῷ λόγῳ διεξιέναι, almost as clear a reference to the *Timaeus* as the δι' ἐρωτήσεων of the same passage is to the *Parmenides* (above n. 605)? And why should not the remarks in *Politicus* 277bc on the excessive expanding of myths have a bearing on the *Timaeus* and the unfinished *Critias*? So the odds seem to me to favor the order *Timaeus, Critias*—the *Sophist, Politicus*.

It has been noted that certain thematically related passages in the *Politicus* and the *Laws* may indicate trends of philosophical development; thus, especially *Plt.* 271d/*Lg.* IV 713cd (Cronus); *Plt.* 295a ff., 301e/*Lg.* IV 709d (the despot and the laws); *Plt.* 279b ff./ *Lg.* V 734e (weaving); *Plt.* 310b ff./*Lg.* VI 773a–d (matchmaking). For my part I believe that at least in these cases the passages in the *Laws* can be reasonably interpreted as later, though various other sections may have been written before the *Politicus*.[611]

Thus, I am inclined to think that the *Sophist* and *Politicus*, like *Timaeus* and *Critias*, took shape in the first half of the 350s, and that the *Timaeus* torso was written somewhat earlier than the unfinished 'trilogy' of the *Sophist* and *Politicus*.

## Philebus

G.C. The late date and the authenticity of the *Philebus* have not been seriously questioned since the beginning of this century.[612] Among the criteria adduced for [199] a very late dating, the most important ones, apart from stylometry (which is no

---

though he argues that *Timaeus* and *Critias* are later, and curious that Shorey 1903: 38, 56 for once accepts an 'advance' in suggesting that when the *Timaeus* applies the categories of 'same' and 'other' to the creation of the soul, this indicates influence from the *Sophist*, whereas T. M. Robinson 1970: 72 f. has argued vice versa (in fact, as the Tübingen school in particular has shown, these Principles are likely to be much older).

610. T. M. Robinson 1970, especially 132–139, makes some good points regarding the relative precedence of the psychology of the *Timaeus*. This is not the common opinion, however; but the grounds for asserting the precedence of the *Sophist* and *Politicus* in these respects are generally weak, cf. e.g. Pfleiderer 1696: 656n., 646, Lutoslawski 476 ff., Raeder 339 f., 347, 382, 390, Leisegang 1950: 2500.

611. Cf. above p. 186. For the parallels, *see* the list in Raeder 403–405. Crombie I 170–173 seems to me to exaggerate the difficulty of reconciling the positions of *Politicus* and the *Laws* regarding the despot versus laws and the Golden Age: the attitude of *Politicus* is after all slightly ironic.

612. Waddington 1904 still followed Zeller's old view of the relative earliness of the *Philebus*. Horn 1893: 359 ff. and A. Döring 1903: 122 ff., following earlier suggestions, tried to demonstrate

more reliable here than elsewhere), are the rather systematic structure of the exposition, the metaphysical approach which includes the doctrine of Principles and, probably, Pythagorean ideas but largely dispenses with the theory of Forms, and in general the sophisticated and abstract discussion of the ethical theme, and the ideas of a μέσον or a 'third way' which accompany the discussion.⁶¹³

Yet Socrates leads the discussion, not a normal procedure in the 'late works.' I can see no reason for the reappearance of Socrates 'the teacher' in this dialogue, in which he is in fact as abstract and impersonal a character as Philebus and Protarchus, other than the author's lack of interest in his characters: Socrates, the traditional leader of Academic discussions, automatically comes in where there is no need for a foreign Stranger or an Athenian Guest.⁶¹⁴

E.C. The only criterion of this kind which is clearly useful here is the fact that the dialogue almost certainly takes account of doctrines of Eudoxus of Cnidos.⁶¹⁵ This indicates a date in the 350s (cf. below p. 372). Other supposed contemporary allusions are more conjectural or irrelevant.⁶¹⁶

I.C. It can be accepted here without discussion that the *Philebus* is later than the *Phaedrus*,⁶¹⁷ the *Republic*,⁶¹⁸ *Theaetetus*,⁶¹⁹ and *Parmenides*.⁶²⁰ The chronological

---

that *Philebus* is un-Platonic; cf. the defense of Rodier 1926: 74 ff. In my view the question of strict authenticity is wrongly posed for the late dialogues (cf. above p. 331); cf. also the interpretation of Guthrie V, especially 223–225, 238–240, amounting to the impression that the *Philebus* is indeed somewhat 'un-Platonic.'

613. Cf. already Ueberweg 1861: 202 ff. (against Zeller), Jackson 1882, Shorey 1903: 36 f., Wilpert 1953, Gulley 1962: 108 ff., Kapp 1968: 55 ff., 149 f.; for the Principles in particular, cf. Stenzel 1933: 68–70, Dönt 1967: 33 ff., Krämer 1959: 187 f., 193 f., 1968: 111 and n. 21. For the systematic approach, cf. Pfleiderer 1896: 402, 411n., 590 f. (on recapitulations); MacClintock 1961.

614. It is often said that the 'Socratic' theme suggested the use of Socrates as leader, e.g. Taylor 372; somewhat differently Hackforth 1945: 7. I am not convinced. And Friedländer III 287 ff. certainly over-interprets the implications of the characters and the presentation of them.

615. Cf. Wilamowitz I 630, II 266–277 (unnecessarily assuming that Eudoxus was already dead), Philippson 1925, Taylor 1956: 23 f., Gaiser 1965: 197 ff.

616. Cf. the speculations of Eberz 1902, 1903 (dating *Philebus* as early as 367 BCE). Allusions to Antisthenes, Aristippus and Speusippus are possible (cf. Raeder 307 f., 365, Philippson 1925) but of no consequence to chronology. Maier's theory (1913: 57 n. 2) of reflections in Xenophon's 'Memorabilia' is as improbable as for the *Sophist* and *Politicus* (above, n. 49). The possible references to *Philebus* in Alexis fr. 149, 152 Kock (II p. 351–353; cf. Cadiou 1952) is more interesting but very uncertain. The parallels with Aristotle (notably the μέσον doctrine) have often been noted; cf. Lutoslawski 464 f., Ueberweg-Praechter 306.

617. Regenbogen's (1950) view of the precedence of *Philebus* over *Phaedrus* has been wholly or partly refuted in the subsequent discussion; cf. above n. 587. In the case of *Philebus* his arguments are rather implicit.

618. It is hardly thinkable today that the complicated metaphysics of *Philebus* would be implicitly present in the exposition of the *Republic*, although this is what Zeller and his followers thought; cf. Gomperz II 600 ff., Geffcken II A 117 n. 4. It is also clear that the attitude to feeling and pleasure in the *Philebus* represents a real doctrinal advance (*pace* Zeller, Pfleiderer, and Beare); cf. Raeder 364–366, Ryle 1966: 249.

619. Notably the discussion of αἴσθησις indicates that *Philebus* is later, cf. Raeder 364; against Ryle's later dating of *Theaetetus* there are some pertinent remarks by Crombie 1969: 372.

620. Even Zeller (II¹ 202) thought that *Phlb.* 15a–16e "almost quotes" *Prm.* 129b ff. Though this is somewhat doubtful in fact, all serious interpretations point to the precedence of *Parmenides*.

[200] interrelation of the *Philebus* and the *Laws* are unclear, owing to the highly abstract approach to ethics in the former.[621]

The relation of *Philebus* to *Timaeus* and *Critias* on the one hand and to the *Sophist* and *Politicus* on the other, is also somewhat problematic, although certain pros and cons can be produced. The almost complete lack of a setting and characterization for the persons in the *Philebus* corresponds to the trend begun in *Theaetetus*, the *Republic* and *Parmenides*, and points to a relatively late date. The cosmogony of *Timaeus* seems to be implied in *Philebus* 30a, cf. 26d, 27a ff., 32b, etc.[622] The emphasis placed on Principles in dealing with metaphysics indicates an advance from the positions of *Timaeus*, the *Sophist* and *Politicus*.[623]

I can find nothing to invalidate the assumption that *Philebus* was written later than *Timaeus-Critias* and the *Sophist-Politicus* and, therefore, not earlier than the mid-350s. And since *Philebus* seems to require some distance from both 'trilogies,' I am inclined to believe that it should be dated some time after Dion's death (in 354, cf. below p. 347) rather than before it.

The *Seventh Letter*

Since this is the only letter which in my view can possibly have been 'written' (or dictated) by Plato personally, I shall consider it here; for the other *Letters*, see below p. 378.

---

621. Traditional stylometry provides little assistance (and the additional observations of Vanachter 1946 to show that the style of *Lg.* is later than that of *Phlb.* are practically worthless). Some thematic parallels have been noted by Raeder 401, but nothing very clear emerges from them. The fact that the attitude to the arts is more moralizing in the *Laws* (II 645a–656c, 667c–672d, III 700a–701a, VII 790c ff., IX 935d ff.) than in *Philebus* (47d, 51c, 64d–65a) is of course due to the different approaches. But could the '5 classes' *Phlb.* 23d, 66a ff. have something to do with the 'fifth element' in *Epin.* 984b (cf. *Ti.* 55c)? Cf. also *Ep.* 7 342a–d.

622. This is accepted by many scholars, e.g. Shorey 1903: 65 n. 510, Wilamowitz I 276 f., also Vlastos 1954: 334 f. The arguments of Lutoslawski 487 etc. and Raeder 381, 384, 394, 411 f. for the precedence of *Philebus* are ambiguous, and some of them rather indicate the contrary (and Raeder later, 1906: 449, discarded this view, only taking into consideration the avoidance of hiatus in *Philebus*). Regenbogen 1950 based his argument for the precedence of *Philebus* chiefly on his theory of a very late date for *Phaedrus*, which would imply an association of this dialogues with *Timaeus* and the *Laws*; but this is in clear conflict with much of the evidence. Considering the 'pythagorizing' trend at the Academy in the mid-fourth century and somewhat later (much of the evidence can be found in Burkert 1962, cf. Thesleff 1961) I find it important to note that the evidently Pythagorean doctrine of πέρας/ἄπειρον has a central function in the metaphysics of *Philebus* but is not (yet!) explicitly included in the system of *Timaeus*.

623. The opposite view of Raeder 394, 411 f., Leisegang 2507 and others can be considered outdated. Other arguments for the precedence of *Philebus* (e.g. Stefanini II 216 ff., Geffcken II 140 f., Vollenhoven 1948, Kucharski 1949: 285 ff.) have even less weight.—Very occasionally has it been argued that the *Politicus* includes more advanced ideas than the *Philebus*; this was implied by Ryle 1966: 285 for the μέτρον argument *Plt.* 283c ff., but the precedence is not so obvious if it is assumed that both dialogues reflect oral discussions at the Academy.

The vexed problem of the authenticity of the *Seventh Letter*[624] is really of minor importance in this connection: if not by Plato, the letter was evidently written by somebody who knew Plato and his life, thoughts and intentions very well; and the letter would have been pointless if it had not been published within a few years after the murder of Dion in 354 BCE. It was most probably written in 353 or 352 BCE. It is an 'open letter,' a pamphlet of apology, and at the same time it attempts to clarify some misunderstandings with regard to Plato's activities and his philosophy.[625]

Unlike some students of the letter, I am convinced that it did not include any gross distortions of the biographical or historical facts, because these could be easily controlled by other close associates of Plato. I believe the letter's historical value is quite considerable.

The only specific problem of some importance here is whether the 'philosophical digression' (340b–345b) represents *in toto* Plato's philosophical position in the late 350s. For many scholars the digression constitutes the main stumbling-block in the letter; for instance, Ritter 1910a: 404–410 considered it a spurious interpolation, and Bröcker (1963, 1965) argues that it is partly authentic (the section 342b–344b being spurious). Recent studies of Plato's oral doctrine of the Principles (cf. above p. 6) have made the digression appear more interesting and also more Platonic than hitherto.[626] To some extent the digression operates with the same conceptual apparatus as the metaphysical passages of *Philebus*;[627] cf. also below, 'On the Good.'

## 'On the Good'

The problem of whether this notorious piece of teaching, as reconstructed from Aristotle and later sources, consisted of a single lecture or of a 'course' repeatedly given by Plato, has been the subject of much discussion since the Tübingen

---

624. Writing the history of this controversy would require a separate monograph. For its earlier phases, see the conspectus of Raeder 1906: 428–435 (cf. id. 1915); see further Leisegang 1950: 2522–35, Friedländer I 249–259. Since the 1960s, supporters of the authenticity include Crombie, Gadamer, v. Fritz 1966, 1968, Gundert 1968, Brandwood 1969, Deane 1973, Thurnher 1975, Guthrie (V 399–402), de Blois 1979. Spuriousness and (partial) unreliability have been argued by, for instance, Ryle 1966, Edelstein 1966, Morton and Winspear 1966/67, Levison al. 1968, Finley 1972: 74–87, Gulley 1972, Vlastos 1973: 202 f., Caskey 1974. Stylometry is of little help except for tracing elements of Plato's 'late style': for such elements, cf. Ritter 1910a: 410 ff., Billig 1920, Geffcken II 159, 162, Morrow 1935: 17, Thesleff 1967, above 124. But Levison al. 1968 and Michaelson and Morton 1972 have (on insufficient grounds) argued that the style is decidedly un-Platonic.

625. Cf. Isocrates' *Antidosis* (of 354 BCE) and similar Isocratean (semi-)public pamphlets and letters; cf. Raven 1965: 23.

626. See especially Krämer 1968: 123 f. and Szlezák 1978, 1979. Earlier theories of direct allusions to the *Timaeus* (e.g. Ryle 1966: 238 ff.) or the *Phaedrus* (e.g. Rudberg 1956: 29 ff., Friedländer I 252) are less convincing.

627. This has sometimes been noted, cf. Stenzel 1933: 68 ff., Gauss III/2.146 ff.; in fact it is a further indication of the relative lateness of the *Philebus*.

[202] school posed afresh the question of Plato's oral doctrines (above, p. 152). The latter position was adopted from the start by the Tübingen scholars,[628] but recently Gaiser 1980a has changed his view and argued that 'On the Good' was in fact a single public lecture to be dated soon after the *Seventh Letter*, i.e. about 352 BCE Krämer 1980:16–18 n. 33 on the other hand maintains the traditional Tübingen view and asserts, with some modification of his earlier position, that the first (and famous) public lecture was given by Plato at the beginning of his teaching career, whereupon the oral doctrines became part of his esoteric instruction. This is an interesting controversy. Though I am rather inclined to side with Gaiser in this question, I am not averse to the idea that Plato appeared in public in the 390s (cf. above p. 251 ff.). [*See* now below, p. 485.]

At any rate, whatever the truth is about the Περὶ τἀγαθοῦ, the evidence given in particular by the *Seventh Letter* and the *Philebus*[629] indicates that the oral doctrines were much discussed within and outside the Academy around 350 BCE.

### The completing of the *Laws*

Although we have Aristotle's testimony that the *Laws* are later than the *Republic*, and reliable evidence that they were published not by Plato himself but by Philip of Opous and, very probably, posthumously,[630] we have very few clues for dating the various portions absolutely or relatively (cf. above p. 333). It has sometimes been thought that the main bulk of the *Laws* originated at the time of Dion's attempts to seize power in Syracuse, about 357–354 BCE, but this is a precarious basis for argument; and it is equally probable that Plato preferred not to concern himself with affairs of state at that time.[631]

Lutoslawski (1896 passim) and Raeder 1905: 395–413 have collected a good deal of evidence to suggest that the doctrinal contents of the *Laws* either correspond to the other late works or (in very many cases) represent a slightly later stage of trends present in these. Although all of these points are not of course of [203] equal value, and some can be easily refuted,[632] it is reasonably clear to me that large portions of the *Laws* must have originated after the period of *Timaeus-Critias* and the *Sophist-Politicus*. The relation to *Philebus* is more uncertain. For instance, with their tendencies to trichotomy and 'middle way' solutions (notably in ethics)

---

628. They were on this point opposed by e.g. Vlastos 1963, Voigtländer 1963b: 194 ff.; cf. also Guthrie V 424–426.

629. Also some Middle Comedy fragments; cf. Gaiser 1963: 446 ff., 1980a: 11 f.

630. Arist. *Pol.* 1264b26; Philip as editor: Diog. L. 3.37, Suda s.v. φιλόσοφος, *Anon.Proleg.* 24 f. Blass 1903: 62 correctly remarked that only Proclus (Proleg.) says that the edition was posthumous, but its heterogeneity and the appending of the *Epinomis* (below p. 349) support this inference. For various hypotheses regarding the editing, *see* the references in Raeder 398 n. 1, Guthrie V 322 n. 4. Guthrie's own verdict is that the *Laws* "is a work of old age, but definitely . . . the old age of Plato." I have argued elsewhere (1972: 226 f.) that even the principles of composition are Plato's.

631. For the date 357–354 BCE, cf. Raeder 396 f., 405. Morrow's (1960a) interpretation on the whole implies a comparatively late date, although he avoids taking a definite view of chronology.

632. Cf. the interpretation of Friedländer III 360–414.

the *Laws* and *Philebus* bear a basic resemblance to each other that has often been noted (cf. e.g. Raeder 400 f.). It is possible that a careful examination of the points of contact would reveal which way the trends of 'development' go. For the time being, I would content myself with the guess that the *Laws* took their present shape about the same time as *Philebus* and somewhat later, i.e. during Plato's last years. The difference from the other late works, and notably from the *Philebus*, can be largely explained as being due to the rather more exoteric character of the *Laws*.[633]

[203]

## Epinomis

The *Epinomis* was from the outset intended as a cosmological and astronomical appendix to the *Laws*, and was most probably written by Plato's pupil and 'secretary,' the astronomer Philip of Opous. It is reasonable to assume that it was written not very long after Plato's death and published together with the main body of the *Laws*.[634]

The much-debated problem whether, or to what extent, it represents Plato's own view in his last years is of no direct relevance to the chronology of the other works. Obviously none of the 'late works' manifests a later stage of Plato's thought; and again, to arrange the latter in an order corresponding to their relative affinity to or distance from the *Epinomis* is hardly recommendable or even possible.[635]

---

633. This of course conforms with the view of very many scholars. Recently Gaiser 1980a: 17 has pointed out the fact that the end of the *Laws* can be understood as Plato's philosophical testament.

634. This has been the opinion of the majority of scholars since the 19th century, mostly accepted also by those who believe that the *Epinomis* reproduces essentially Plato's own ideas (eg. Gomperz II 563 f., Raeder 1906, 1938, Ueberweg-Praechter[13] 325–327, Taylor 1926, 1935 (1956), des Places 1938, 1952, 1956, Specchia 1967). See now the comprehensive discussion by Tarán 1975, and the references above p. 243.

635. For the general unreliability of linear interpolation or extrapolation, cf. above p. 218. The thematic concentration of the *Epinomis* constitutes an additional difficulty. *Epinomis*, for instance, emphasizes mathematical σοφία (977c ff.) in a manner somewhat paralleled by the cosmological sections in the *Timaeus*, but this is no real indication of the *Timaeus* being closer in time to *Epinomis* than *Philebus* is (as Raeder 416 suggests). The 'pythagorizing' trend of *Philebus* is manifestly different from that of *Epinomis*. And the earlier Platonic phases of the 'fifth element' in *Epinomis* (981b ff., cf. *Ti.* 39e f., 55c, etc. and above n. 621) are notoriously problematic.

# DUBIA AND SPURIA AND SEMI-AUTHENTICITY* [204]

## Introductory

One of the basic premises of the present study is that no very sharp line can be drawn between wholly authentic and 'semi-authentic' Platonic texts (above p. 235 ff.). It seems to me quite possible that some of the writings considered in the preceding sections were not 'written' by Plato exactly as we have them; for the dialogues of the 'late period' this is rather probable in fact. Even so, to judge by the standard of undoubtedly genuine dialogues such as *Gorgias, Symposium, Phaedo* and the *Republic*, they can all be (with the exception for *Epinomis*) safely considered 'predominantly authentic.'

The dialogues which I have reserved for this last section form a more heterogeneous group. They include writings (notably *Laches, Euthyphro,* and *Hippias Major*) which are most likely to reproduce Plato's own thoughts very closely and which were perhaps somehow directly inspired by him. They also include writings (notably *Demodocus,* the *Second Alcibiades, Halcyon, Axiochus* and some of the *Letters*) which are only remotely related to the Platonism of Plato's time. And there are several varieties between these extremes. The only common characteristic of these texts is that the manuscript tradition assigns them to Plato although Plato probably did not 'write' (or dictate) or even, perhaps, personally 'tutor' the writing of them. The reasons for this atheticizing must be considered separately in each case.

If these texts are not by Plato, it would be of considerable interest to know whether two or several of them were written by the same person. Some preliminary stylistic tests and considerations of dialogue technique and contents indicate that *Laches, Euthyphro* and *Hippias Major* may be by the same author; and *Ion* and *Hippias Minor* (possibly including *Hipparchus* and *Minos*) likewise belong

---

*Postscript addition 2009: I am prepared to emphasize now that some of the dialogues discussed in this chapter should preferably be classed as 'genuinely Platonic' with only a slight touch of semi-authenticity due to manipulation or revision by another hand in the Academy. This applies to *Crito, Laches, Hippias Minor, Ion, Euthyphro,* and *Hippias Major; see* above, p. 239 ff., Thesleff 1989, and the reconsideration below, p. 489 ff. The exact proximity to Plato is impossible to determine from case to case—as with the 'late dialogues' (p. 331 ff.).

[204] together, as do some of the *Letters*. But the rest all seem to have separate authors with preferences of their own.⁶³⁶

[205] It is clear that no internal formal or thematic trends can be deduced from a material so heterogeneous; or that any hypothetical general trends can be applied to the chronological arrangement of these dialogues. The construction of a chronology must rely on other considerations.

I shall start from the following assumptions: the *Clitopho* reflects an early stage of the genesis of the *Republic;* the *Crito* reflects (like *Phaedo,* but with more explicit apology) the discussion of what Socrates' friends did, or did not do, during his last days in prison; the *Laches, Alcibiades* I, *Theages, Amatores* and *Eryxias* are all in different ways related to the *Charmides* and reflect the discussion of Socrates (alias Plato?) as a teacher, a discussion which can be followed in many Platonic works from *Symposium* and *Meno* onwards; the play with logic makes it seem probable that *Hippias Minor, Ion, Euthyphro, Hippias Major, Hipparchus, Minos, Sisyphus, Demodocus, De Virtute* and *De Justo* were written for the purpose of exercise at the Academy, and the absolute dates found for *Hippias Major* and *Sisyphus* indicate that there were Academics in the 360s and 350s who enjoyed playing with Socratic elenchus and aporias; the *Definitiones, Alcibiades* II, *Halcyon* and *Axiochus* are post-Platonic; the *Letters* form a tradition of their own which was largely inaugurated by the *Seventh Letter.*

It may be noted that some of these dialogues were hardly written for extra-Academic readers (this applies to *Amatores,* perhaps to *Clitopho, Alcibiades* I, *Hipparchus* and *Minos,* and certainly to *De Virtute* and *De Justo*) whereas the rest are composed for a somewhat more general public as can be seen from the literary ambitions of their authors.

## Clitopho

The genuineness of this curious little piece has been more often questioned than accepted by modern scholars, although authoritative defenders have appeared from time to time.⁶³⁷ Admittedly there is nothing unambiguously un-Platonic about the style or the contents, but very much that looks suspicious: words such as 408d3 προτροπή (hapax), 409b6 δίδαγμα (hapax), 409e3 ὄντως ('late Platonic'), 410d6 θές (idiomatic, elsewhere in Plato only R. IV 424c7, Tht. 209b3, Phlb. 13e2; cf. further Souilhé 1930a: 179 with references); the complete lack of irony and humor (here I
[206] disagree with Souilhé), although the side-attack on Socrates is left unanswered;

---

636. This is the impression I have acquired from a repeated reading of these texts, although the linguistic tests referred to above p. 213 ff. and n. 202 are obviously not sufficient.

637. See the discussion with references in Souilhé 1930a: 161–180 (include among the active supporters Maier 1913: 42 ff., 283 ff.). Souilhé himself tends to regard the dialogue as genuine, and so have later e.g. Stefanini, Kesters 1959, Gaiser 1959, Wichmann 1966, E. Wolf 1968–70, Fischer 1969. New arguments for spuriousness were produced by Geffcken 1933, cf. II (1934) 186, A 159 f., Shorey 1933: 657 f., Carlini 1962. Friedländer (III 287 n. 3) and Guthrie (V 387 ff) remain cautiously skeptical.

and in the selection of Socratic examples and arguments the placing of the emphasis somewhat differently from Plato's normal practice—to mention only a few points. Obviously the *Clitopho* is somehow connected with *Republic* I. Rather than strain one's imagination so as to believe that this piece was meant as an introduction to the *Republic* (this is what Souilhé suggests), it is much more natural to accept that it is spurious.

In order to understand the intentions of the author, I think it is important to note that the picture of Socrates which he criticizes is both that of Antisthenes and that of Plato and possibly that of some other Socratics (of course the historical Socrates is not addressed). It has sometimes been suggested that the focusing on protreptics and δικαιοσύνη in *Clitopho* must have something to do with Antisthenes' three protreptic speeches Περὶ δικαιοσύνης καὶ ἀνδρείας (Diog. L. 6.16, fr. 17–18 Caizzi), but few have noticed that the speech of 'Socrates' 407a–408b which the author discusses as an example of good though inadequate protreptic reasoning, is in fact quoted more fully by Dio Chrysostom 13.16–17, very probably from Antisthenes.[638] Plato's Socrates, on the other hand, enters notably in the latter part of the speech of Clitophon (409b ff.) with what appears to be some references to Book I of the *Republic*. Souilhé 1930a: 173–177 attempts to interpret them differently, bur the last one (410ab) in particular indicates, in my view quite clearly, that the author is operating with a text in which the points are made in the same order as in *Republic* I. Clitophon says that he finally asked Socrates himself what δικαιοσύνη is, and received the answer δικαιοσύνης εἶναι τοὺς μὲν ἐχθροὺς βλάπτειν, τοὺς δὲ φίλους εὖ ποιεῖν. It is true that the first definition of δικαιοσύνη in *Republic* I (332d), τοὺς φίλους εὖ ποιεῖν καὶ τοὺς ἐχθροὺς κακῶς is not strictly speaking Socrates' own, but is extracted by Socrates from Polemarchus. But later (R. I 342e), just before Thrasymachus joins the conversation, Socrates arrives at the conclusion that the just man would never do harm to anybody, or as *Clitopho* 410b puts it, ὕστερον δὲ ἐφάνη βλάπτειν γε οὐδέποτε ὁ δίκαιος οὐδένα. πάντα γὰρ ἐπ᾽ ὠφελίᾳ πάντας δρᾶν. I consider the words ὕστερον δὲ ἐφάνη in *Clitopho* highly significant, because they imply a discussion precisely of the kind which is interrupted by Thrasymachus in the *Republic*. There are other signs, too, of the author of *Clitopho* operating with reminiscences of *Republic* I. The presence in both dialogues of Socrates, Thrasymachus, Clitophon and (peripherally) Lysias may of course derive from a common source, but I consider it plausible that the Thrasymachus whom Clitophon is now, in *Clitopho*, prepared to ask for advice, is Plato's Thrasymachus of *Republic* I. For all we know, the historical Thrasymachus was a rhetorician with political inclinations.[639] Plato may have had specific reasons for making him Socrates' opponent in *Republic* I (above p. 258). The author of *Clitopho*

---

638. The identification was made by v. Arnim in 1898; for this and other suggestions see Cohoon's introduction to the Loeb edition of the speech (Vol. II 89). Souilhé 1930a: 178 very nearly hit the mark without apparently knowing the Dio passage.

639. Cf. DK 85, and above p. 257. Being a non-Athenian, he is very much a parallel to Lysias. In fr. B 1 (DK II 324.1) he argues for the πάτριος πολιτεία (in 411 or 404), as also the historical Clitophon did (Arist. *Resp. Ath.* 29.3, 34.3). The later traditions which characterize him as a sophist (e.g. the probably fictitious *Epigram* A 8) may be secondary.

[207] is not interested in rhetoric (though the historical Clitophon was, cf. Souilhé 1930a: 167 f. who however over-interprets καγκάλως 408b6). To him Thrasymachus is a sophist with ambitions to teach ethics (410c7, e7) like Protagoras, and Clitophon is his potential disciple. I believe he may have taken his conception from Plato's partly fictitious portrait: Plato's Thrasymachus of course 'knew' what δικαιοσύνη is, and he could be taken for a sophistic teacher by a reader who did not know or realize that he was first and foremost a λογογράφος.

It is apriori unlikely that a text as odd as *Clitopho* would have found its way into the Corpus Platonicum if it had not been written by an Academic. Note also the occurrence of δικαστική and πολιτική as 'aspects' of δικαιοσύνη (cf. *Clit.* 408b) in the clearly Academic *Amatores* (137d–138c).

I can think of only one reason for such a criticism of the 'Socratic' Socrates, written by an Academic, namely, that the author hopes for a more constructive teaching in political ethics by Plato. But who, then is the competitor of Plato whom 'Thrasymachus' stands for? Could he be Bryson who is coupled with Thrasymachus in a Middle Comedy fragment alluding apparently to the Academic opposition to teaching for money?[640] This is just a guess, of course.

An independent external criterion for dating *Clitopho* is supplied by Xenophon who very probably refers to this dialogue in *Mem.* I 4.1.[641] This passage must have belonged to the earlier portion of the Memorabilia.

These considerations would agree with the rough dating of *Clitopho* between Book I and the rest of the *Republic*, as commonly assumed by separatists. Obviously no pupil of Plato who was acquainted with the main parts of the *Republic* could have blamed 'Socrates' for concerning himself merely with protreptics in political ethics. This censure could, however, apply not only to Plato's *Apology* and *Republic* I, but also to *Gorgias* and *Protagoras*: the reader of these dialogues is actually left in uncertainty about what is δίκαιον in politics. The *Symposium* and *Phaedo* are of course irrelevant to a person who is mainly interested in δικαιοσύνη.[642] But the *Euthydemus* brings us closer to what would seem to be the context of *Clitopho*: note here the play on the ideas of teaching, the Royal Art, and protreptics (at the end). Apparently the *Clitopho* is connected with the Academic discussion of Socratic (and/or Platonic) teaching as reflected in the dialogues from *Meno* and *Euthydemus* onwards, according to the chronology suggested here.

The promise of more πολιτικοὶ λόγοι (by Aspasia) to follow, at the end of the frame dialogue of *Menexenus*, probably belongs to the same discussion (cf. above p. 328). And the brief opening dialogue in dramatic form in the *Clitopho* seems to conform to a pattern adopted at the Academy at this time.

[208] The relationship of *Clitopho* to *Meno* can perhaps be inferred from its attitude to the question of teachability of ἀρετή. In the quotation 407a ff. (presumably

---

640. Ephippus, Ναυάγος fr. 14 K (Athen. 11.509c). Webster's interpretation (1970: 51) implies that the young man from the Academy sides with Bryson.—For Bryson, cf. also K. Döring 1972.

641. Quoted, but not convincingly explained by Souilhé 1930a: 178.

642. The complicated hypothesis of Kesters 1959 that *Clitopho* answers the anonymous Socratic (reflected in Themistius Or. 26—could he be Antisthenes?) who had censured the first version of the *Phaedrus*, is interesting but highly conjectural.

from Antisthenes) the author of *Clitopho* inserts a conditional comment (which is absent from the corresponding passage in Dio Chrysostom): "if ἀρετή can be imparted"; but somewhat later, 408b7, he takes it for granted that Socrates used to argue ὡς διδακτὸν ἀρετή. This attitude (general doubts amounting to a Socratic assertion of teachability) roughly corresponds to the position of the *Protagoras*. But *Clitopho* contains no traces of the complicated discussion in the *Meno*, and of the θεία μοίρα 'solution.' I believe the chronological order is *Clitopho—Meno*. However, I do not, of course, think the *Meno*, or any single Platonic work, is the 'answer' to this not very intelligent pamphlet. It is part of a general discussion, largely no doubt an oral one, of which we can see only occasional hints.

Thus *Clitopho* would be one of the earliest, if not the earliest, example we have of a Pseudo-Platonic dialogue—or better, since the writing was probably not from the start fathered on Plato, of an Academic text not written by Plato himself.

## Crito

G.C.  *Crito* is normally associated with the *Apology*, and it is interpreted as typically Socratic.

However, the singularly heavy emphasis laid on the absolute authority of the laws (of democratic Athens!), and on Socrates' willingness to die for them, sounds somewhat odd and can hardly be satisfactorily explained without adducing a specific apologetic aspect.[643] The *Crito* not only defends Plato's friends from the charge of having missed their chance to help Socrates; and here the explicit refutation of Criton's arguments in fact gives Criton the honor of having tried his best and suggests a previous discussion of who had urged Socrates to escape.[644] But *Crito* also defends Socrates himself from a charge of ὑποψία τῶν νόμων. We happen to know that this was one of the charges produced in the pamphlet of Polycrates (above, p. 179). In *Crito*, Socrates is depicted in colors which Polycrates (and Anytus) would have largely approved of, though of course *Crito's* attitude to οἱ πολλοί (47a ff.) is not exactly that of an orthodox democrat. This indicates a considerable distance from the *Apology*.[645]

Elsewhere Plato seems to have taken the attack of Polycrates quite lightly (cf. above p. 274 and 278); why should he have felt Socrates' loyalty to the laws of Athens worth a particular, weighty and serious defense against what must have been his own conviction (cf. above p. 174 and e.g. *R.* VII 517de)? This last-mentioned point was one of the arguments which Meiser 1891 used against the

---

643. This has often been done, but in a variety of ways; cf. e.g. Pfleiderer 1896: 247 ff., Verdam 1917, Ryle 1966: 146 ff. Others deny the apologetic aspect, e.g. Harder 1934, especially 46–51 (arguing that *Crito* is esoteric, which can hardly be the case), Friedländer II 159, III 420.

644. There were different traditions about this: Diog. L. 2.60, 3.36 mentions Aeschines; Xenophon, *Ap.* 23 speaks vaguely about ἑταῖροι; cf. Riginos 1976: 96 f.

645. Among those who argue explicitly for a separation of *Crito* from the context of the *Apology*, note H. and Th. Gomperz, Raeder and Harder.

[209] authenticity of *Crito*. His article was soon forgotten among the mass of hypercritical atheticizings of Plato's dialogues produced by German scholars in the 19th century; in my view, however, it is quite an important contribution to be taken seriously.

The style of the opening could be considered a good imitation of Plato's easygoing dialogue style, but the speech of the *Laws* has a pathos of its own.[646] The structure of the work is rather more anomalous, with the fictitious speech of the *Laws* gradually intruding into the conversation and taking over; thus the general structure somewhat resembles the *Gorgias*.[647]

E.C. Apart from Polycrates (above), note the following: The reference to the 'good constitution' of Thebes, *Crito* 53bc, is typically ambiguous; from the Platonic point of view, it could imply a date before 395 BCE, or the 370s.[648] In *Crito* 52b it is said that, unlike others, Socrates never wished to visit other countries and study other forms of government. Probably these 'others' include Plato, and this would indicate a date after 388 BCE.

I.C. For the *Apology*, cf. above.—Many points of contact have been noted between *Gorgias* and *Crito*. They are normally interpreted as indicating the precedence of *Crito*,[649] but the opposite is quite possible and actually preferable especially if the *Crito* is regarded as not being by Plato. A detailed argument for dating *Crito* after *Gorgias*, *Republic* I, and even *Meno* and *Phaedo*, was published by H. Gomperz in 1896. Although his points are of varying validity, and only few scholars have been prepared to accept them, I feel that above all his view of [210] *Crito* as dependent of *Gorgias* and of its association with *Phaedo* (also argued by others) is worth serious consideration.[650] It is normally explained that *Phaedo* is

---

646. For the opening words, cf. *Prt.* 310ab. At the end, Socrates comments on his reaction upon the speech of the *Laws* as being 'Corybantic,' without much trace of the irony which normally accompanies this word in Plato. There are some occasional idioms which sound un-Platonic, such as 43c2 ἐπιλύεται, 44e2, 45a4 προμηθοῦσθαι, 46e3 ὅσα γε τἀνθρώπεια, and note the preference of ἐπαίων for ἐπιστήμων 47b ff. The stylometrical considerations of Ritter 1935 are practically worthless.

647. For these anomalies, cf. Maier 1913: 120n. (who regards them as indicating a very early date), Gomme 1958, Thesleff 1967 above, 48, 100. For the problems of interpreting *Crito*, cf. also Milobenski 1968 (referring to an article by Broemser), Kahn 1981: 308 n. 8.

648. Wilamowitz II 55 n. 1 suggested the former date, Ryle 1966: 221 the latter. Guthrie IV 93 notes that the problem relating to Megara (mentioned in the same passage) is similar.—For other doubtful external criteria, see Ritter 1910b: 95, 1922.201 ff., Humbert 1931: 73, Ryle l.e.

649. E.g. Ritter 1910b: 265 ff., Leisegang 1950: 2398. Note especially *Cri.* 46bc/*Grg.* 473cd, *Cri.* 48ab, 49ab, de, 54b.

650. For the reminiscenses of *Gorgias*, cf. above n. 14. H. Gomperz' late dating of *Crito* was accepted by Th. Gomperz II 359 and some others (e.g. Schmalenbach 1946 who added some unreliable arguments, and Ryle 1966: 220 f.). Apelt 1901 (who otherwise adopted a skeptical attitude) thought it tempting to find a reminiscence not only of *Gorgias* but also of *Republic* I 334b ff. in *Crito* 49bc, but Dodds 1959: 22 preferred to regard *Crito* as the earlier dialogue. Boehme 1959: 18–45, 125 n. 143 revived the argument for the order *Gorgias*—*Crito*, but he accepted Wilamowitz' early dating of *Crito* and thus placed the *Gorgias* at the beginning of the 390s. Pfleiderer 1896 and other adherents of an early version of the *Republic* have tended to place *Crito* after it (the objections of Ritter 1910b: 228 are not directly pertinent).—For the chronological association

more explicit on the details of Socrates' last days because it is written for a wider public than the *Crito*, but it is after all quite probable that the author of *Crito* expects his readers to know the *Phaedo* but wishes to place the emphasis somewhat differently.[651]

Perhaps the author of *Crito*, for specific reasons of his own, wrote the dialogue as an apology of Socrates and his old companion Criton, soon after the publication of Plato's *Phaedo*. *Crito* is part of the same discussion of 'Socrates in prison' as *Phaedo* is. It is interesting to note here that, in addition to the references in the *Apology* and the opening and concluding scenes of *Phaedo*, Criton appears as a discussion partner of Socrates only in *Crito* and in the frame dialogue of *Euthydemus*, and that we have dated *Euthydemus* not very long after *Phaedo*. It is also worth noting that Criton in the *Euthydemus* is a somewhat colorless ἑταῖρος who has problems with the education of his boys (306d ff.), whereas in *Crito* he is the old and intimate family friend who cares very much for the education of Socrates' sons (45cd, cf. 54ab). Apparently Plato did not find the character of Criton as interesting as the author of *Crito* did.

## Laches

G.C. As was demonstrated above (p. 198) there is some evidence that the *Laches* was written later than the *Protagoras*. Moreover, *Charmides* and *Laches* are in certain formal and also thematic respects very closely related, although the one is a reported and the other a dramatic dialogue.[652] And *Laches* is even more obviously than *Charmides* concerned with Socrates as an apparent yet elusive teacher of ἀρετή: the gradual panegyrical introduction of Socrates as the leader of the discussion is slightly apologetic[653] and amounts to demonstrating that the Socratic method is actually not teaching at all but συμβουλεύεσθαι (180ab, 184cd, etc. pm.) and κοινῇ ζητεῖν (note 201a). This method in fact corresponds to an Academic συνουσία, and the implication is that if one does not for some reason attend to it, one loses the contact with ἐπιστήμη (as happened to Charmides, and to the boys of Lysimachus and Melesias, as everybody knew).

---

of *Crito* with *Phaedo*, cf. Meiser 1891, Harder 1934, H. M. Wolff 1957: 149 ff. (dating *Phaedo* very early), Ryle 1966: 146 ff.

651. Notably the incident with the ship landing at Sunion and the dream of Socrates, *Cri.* 43c–44b, appear to be additions to the story in *Phd.* 58a–c.

652. Both are concerned with one of the cardinal virtues; both appear to seek a definition, and after some unsuccessful attempts both appear to end aporetically; both are 'Socratic' dialogues written in the playful, easygoing manner normally regarded as 'early Plato.' In both dialogues several persons partake in the discussion, and two of these are the chief interlocutors of Socrates (cf. above p. 270). In both, the two pairs of 'opponents' of Socrates are well known public figures in Athens who are, ambiguously, experts and yet fail in the virtues discussed. And both dialogues end with Socrates being asked to take over the teaching of the virtue concerned, to which he reluctantly agrees, while the reader is expected to know that the pupils in each case were not successful at all.

653. Note also the very respectable company in which Socrates now, for once, appears. Anytus and Polycrates would have had nothing to object to. Cf. below p. 358.

[211]    These preliminary considerations, together with the theory advanced here of the relative lateness of the dramatic dialogue type, provide a basis for the assumption that *Laches* was written later than *Charmides*, in the period when Socratic method was discussed in the Academy.

Traditionally, however, *Laches* is regarded as a very early dialogue. The grounds for this view consist of little more than negative evidence, the supposed lack of 'advanced' features, the Socratic tenor, and so forth. For the unreliability of such criteria, cf. above p. 170 f. Steidle 1950 attempted to discover some positive support for this conception by interpreting *Laches* as representing, together with the *Apology* and *Crito*, Plato's plans for an ethical and political reform in Athens in the 390s. Although many scholars seem to have accepted Steidle's arguments, they have little weight in comparison with the indications of a later date.[654]

The style has been classed as 'early' by most stylometrists, but some have noted anomalies.[655] The structural contrast between the heavy and expansive introductory part and the lively dialogue of the latter part (from 190b onwards) is remarkable and without parallels. Perhaps it is deliberate; at any rate, it is a new technique: the expansiveness of the speeches in the first section largely results from an attempt to describe the situation and the characters by means of dramatic dialogue instead of employing the introductory background story of the reported dialogues. I believe this is another indication that *Laches* was secondary in relation to the *Charmides* type.[656]

No serious doubts regarding the authenticity of *Laches* have been expressed since Ast, Madvig and early Zeller (II¹ 158 n. 3). For my part, I should like to draw
[212]    attention to the following points: The close resemblance with *Charmides* also with regard to the conception of Socrates is somewhat suspect as such; *Laches* only produces a philosophically less interesting argument and denies more explicitly (and apologetically) that Socrates is able to teach anybody; somewhat artificially, Socrates is appearing in the best company of the old Athenian establishment (cf. Polycrates, above p. 179, and *Crito* p. 355); Plato should have been better acquainted with the biographical details relating to Socrates, Lysimachus, Nicias and Laches than the author of the *Laches* was;[657] and the application of the

---

654. See e.g. Erbse 1968: 25–28. Various 'advanced' ideas, such as reflections of the theory of Forms, have sometimes been noted also by supporters of an early date such as Ritter 1910b: 567 ff., Geffcken II A 46 n. 79, Detel 1973: 28 f.; others have tried to advocate a later date from the existence of such points, thus Immisch 1899: 614 ff., O'Brien 1963, Ingenkamp 1967b, Kapp 1968: 62 f., Witte 1970, Allen 1970: 105 ff.

655. Cf. v. Arnim 1896/7, 1912, Immisch 1899: 449, 617. The list of anomalies could be easily expanded; note e.g. the occurrence in *La.* of 'late' Platonic ἐπίσκεψις, τὸ ποῖον etc.

656. The literary technique of *Laches* in particular has been studied by Nagel 1962 and Hoerber 1968; cf. Thesleff 1967, above 99 f. The explanation suggested above has not been proposed before to my knowledge.

657. Socrates is repeatedly described as fairly young (180d, 181d, 186d, 189ab, cf. above p. 194), much younger than Nicias and Laches, which cannot have been historically true (Nicias could only have been a few years older, cf. Davies 1971: 404). For the idealizing portrait of Nicias, cf. Marasco 1975. Laches says he 'remembers' Socrates from the battle of Delium (181ab, cf. *Smp.* 221a) and Plato must have known that Socrates was middle-aged then, in fact about 47 years

new dialogue technique has proved rather clumsy. Bearing this in mind, Plato [212] is perhaps not so likely to have written the dialogue himself. The variation of the ἀνδρεία a theme of *Protagoras* would also indicate this since Plato normally does not operate with extensive self-quotations.[658] And there are some signs of a stylistic affinity between *Laches*, *Euthyphro* and *Hippias Major*,[659] and the last-mentioned dialogue at least is very probably not by Plato.

It also seems fairly clear to me, on formal and stylistic as well as on thematic and doctrinal grounds, that the *Laches* was not written by the same author as *Crito* or as *Hippias Minor* (cf. below p. 366). But play with logic is of course not alien to the author of *Laches*.

E.C. No manifest external criteria can be found.[660]

I.C. The *Republic* and *Laches*. There are no grounds for placing *Laches* before Book I.[661] The ἀνδρεία passage in *R*. IV 430a–c has been normally interpreted as being later than *Laches*, and I agree that it seems to combine the aspects of *Protagoras* and *Laches* with the doctrine of ὀρθὴ δόξα, though the sources may of course be those of oral discussion at the Academy; αὖθις δέ 430c4 is certainly no promise of the *Laches* to come.[662] It is also interesting that *Laches* 188cd contains some [213] thoughts on being a μισόλογος, followed by some play on musical terminology (very curious in the mouth of Laches, in fact); the word μισόλογος appears in *R*. III 411d8 in a very similar context, which presumably operates with allusions to the musicologist Damon (cf. 400bc) with whom the author of *Laches* also appears to be acquainted (180cd, 197d, 200ab; for the chronological mistakes here, cf. Davies 1971: 383). Obviously the *Republic* passage is not dependent on *Laches*. Here again oral discussion at the Academy may be the common source, and this would indicate the period when Book III of the present *Republic* was taking shape.

For the relation to *Gorgias* no clear indications exist.[663] For *Protagoras-Laches*, see above p. 192 ff.

---

old. Lysimachus appears as a very old man (180de), a contemporary and friend of Socrates' father, which is of course possible though his boys are quite young (181a, cf. *Tht.* 150e, *Thg.* 130a; the later story about Socrates having a relationship with Lysimachus' sister Myrto, Arist. fr. 93 R (perhaps from Aristoxenus), *Halcyon* 8, etc., is not very reliable); but it is odd that he should not have met Socrates until now. *Meno* 94a gives a different picture of Lysimachus and Melesias, their age, and the attitude of their fathers to their education (cf. *La*. 189cd).

658. This was demonstrated by W. Eberhardt in an unpublished dissertation (1923), cf. Krüger 1935: 33.

659. Cf. above, p. 227 and n. 202.

660. For Steidle's attempt to relate the *Laches* to Athenian events in the 390s, see above. Its relation to the writings of Antisthenes (Joël 1906: 311 ff.) and Xenophon (Maier 1913: 57 n. 2) is more than unclear.

661. The order *Laches—Republic* I was argued notably by v. Arnim 1914: 97 ff., 136 ff., ingeniously but not convincingly. On the other hand, e.g. the 'post festum' pattern of the opening of *Republic* I is implied in *Laches* (178a) as in many Platonic dialogues; cf. above p. 267 ff.

662. Cf. above p. 198. See the discussion in Lutoslawski 1896: 288 (criticism of earlier theories of the order *R*. IV—*La*.), Hirmer 1897: 670 f., Gomperz II 567, Raeder 210 f., Pohlenz 1913: 112 n. 1.

663. Indications of the order *Laches—Gorgias* have been seen in the treatment of Athenian politicians and of ἀνδρεία (e.g. Pohlenz 1913: 149, 163, cf. Geffcken II A 67 n. 33, Dodds 1959: 22), but in fact the approaches are very different in the two dialogues. On equally shaky grounds *Laches*

[213] *Symposium—Laches.* The brief statement of Laches concerning Socrates' behaviour at Delium, 181ab, may at first sight look primary to the elaboration of the incident by Alcibiades in *Symposium* 221a, but since the author of *Laches* is not clear about chronology (cf. above p. 358) and Plato is, the former may have received the impulse from the latter; and perhaps he bears in mind, and expects his reader to remember, that Plato in the *Symposium* had characterized Socrates as more ἔμφρων than Laches. Considering this, the passage *Laches* 182a–c can be read as a (playful?) reminiscence of the ἀναβασμοί of Diotima, *Symposium* 210a–d, 211bc, rather than of *Gorgias* 474c ff. (cf. above p. 284).

*Meno* and *Laches.* The different treatment of Lysimachus and Melesias in *Meno* and *Laches* was noted above n. 657. The differences, as I see it, are partly due to different authorship of the dialogues. A significant detail, sometimes used for dating,[664] is that in the *Meno* (94a–c) Socrates states as a commonly known fact that Aristides and Thucydides had done everything possible (which is rather ironic, of course) for the education of their sons, but with little result, whereas Lysimachus in the *Laches* (179d1) says his and Melesias' fathers (that is, Aristides and Thucydides) did not have time for them but let them τρυφᾶν, whatever this verb implies. Clearly the author of *Laches* does not operate directly with the *Meno* passage, but rather with the old commonplace (cf. Eupolis fr. 9 K, Diss. Log. 6.4 ff., cf. p. 133 f.) that great men have been unable to impart their ἀρετή to others. But neither does *Meno* build upon *Laches*. In both dialogues, the background idea is that ἀρετή is not teachable by ordinary means. If it is accepted that the *Laches* [214] is intended as a more concentrated and restricted specimen of Socratic reasoning than the *Meno,* and that the κοινῇ ζητεῖν solution, which it amounts to, is essentially Academic, it is understandable that the author felt no need to introduce the more sophisticated Platonic apparatus of *Meno* with its theory of Forms, anamnesis, hypothetical method, ἀληθὴς δόξα, and so forth. And thus he may have missed the point about the 'education' of Lysimachus and Melesias, even if he knew the *Meno*. The usual method of reasoning, to be sure, is that since both dialogues are concerned with the teaching of virtue, and the *Meno* is the more 'advanced' one, it must be later.[665] However, apart from the fact that the advance is not a direct one in this case, I find it very important to bear in mind that *Meno* is of a rather more esoteric nature than *Laches.*

For similar insufficient reasons, *Euthydemus, Lysis* and *Charmides* are generally considered as more 'advanced' than *Laches* and, therefore as later.[666] For *Charmides,* cf. above p. 357 f.

---

is placed after *Gorgias* by Immisch 1899, Boehme 1959: 95 f., Kapp and Erbse 1968, Kahn 1976: 24, 1981: 314 ff.

664. Cf. Raeder 130, Cauer 1918: 286 f.

665. Cf. e.g. Ueberweg-Praechter 228 f., Friedländer II 257 f.—Another detail sometimes adduced is the ἀνδρεία passage in *Men.* 88b which is supposed to reflect the discussion in *Laches,* cf. Pohlenz 1913: 112 n. 1., Wilamowitz I 275, II[2] 150. More probably, again, oral discussions are the common source.

666. For *Euthydemus*, see notably v. Arnim 1914: 110 ff.; for *Lysis,* id. 97–109, Geffcken II 59 ff., Gauss I/2.75 ff. (the portrait of Socrates is regarded by Leisegang 1950: 2410 as more refined

Laches and *Theaetetus.* This relation is interesting because in *Theaetetus* (150e) [214]
Socrates mentions one of the boys whose education is discussed in the *Laches,*
Aristides son of Lysimachus, as an example of a person for whom the συνουσία
with Socrates turned out to be fruitless; the context is the presentation of the
μαίευσις method which is likely to belong to the earlier version of the dialogue
(cf. p. 301). Was the author of *Laches* acquainted with this passage? He might
have been. He knew of course that young Aristides was a failure as a 'pupil' of
Socrates (as indeed young Charmides was), and he may have substituted his
Academic recommendation of κοινῇ ζητεῖν for Socrates' δαιμόνιον and divine
'pregnancy' and 'delivery' which perhaps sounded a bit too fantastic to his taste.
We have already noted his apologetic tendency. The author of the *Theages* (below
p. 364) chose another way. However, this is not a very clear criterion, and it is
wiser, therefore, to conjecture that the *Laches* somehow belongs with the first version of *Theaetetus.*

If *Laches* is later than the *Clitopho,* it can be said to contain a negative answer
to the latter: one should not ask 'Socrates' for simple instruction at all.

## The *First Alcibiades*

G.C. This lengthy dialogue with its broad register of approaches and doctrines, or hints at doctrines, has been read as a convenient introduction to Plato
ever since antiquity; the Neo-Platonists' interest in it in particular is well documented. Although the prevailing trend since 19th century criticism has been [215]
to atheticize it, Friedländer's vigorous and eloquent defense of its authenticity
(1921–23, and repeatedly later) has produced some new adherents, especially
since the 1960s.[667] My impression is that the defenders have at least proved that
a post-Platonic date is out of the question, and that the 'degree' of authenticity is
particularly difficult to determine exactly in this case. There is very little in the
dialogue that can be regarded as decidedly un-Platonic, even though the style is
flat and unimaginative, the composition is over simple (with the 'central legend'

---

in *Lysis;* the irony as more complex by Boder 1973, and so forth); for *Charmides,* cf. Beare 1913: 43 f., Pohlenz 1913: 56 f., v. Arnim l.c., Gauss I/2.92 f. (but Ross 1951: 11, somewhat surprisingly, thinks that *Laches* 191e f. implies an advance towards the theory of Forms in relation to *Charmides.*

667. For references to the earlier discussion, *see* Heidel 1896: 61–71, Lutoslawski 196–198, Pavlu 1905 (all arguing against the authenticity) and Friedländer II 317 n. 1; for a useful summary of the chief points at issue, *see* Geffcken II A 156–157. After Stefanini 1932 and Vink 1939 had given Friedländer their support, spuriousness was vindicated again by many scholars including de Strycker 1942, Bluck 1953 and Gauss I/2.204–207; and Pamela Clark 1955 proposed a somewhat surprising compromise by claiming that the first part of the dialogue was written by a pupil though Plato himself finished it. The defensive position was revived by Motte 1961 and followed up by Kratzsch 1964 in a comprehensive dissertation; and further arguments for authenticity were produced by Weil 1964, Humbert 1967: 119 ff., and some others. Recent opponents include Dönt 1964 and Bos 1970 (a Dutch dissertation). Guthrie, though expressing himself very vaguely (V 387 n. 1), seems to regard the dialogue as spurious.

[215] somewhat artificially imitating Plato's mythic visions)[668] and tends to expand strings of elenchus at tedious length with little play or irony; and occasional odd ideas do in fact occur.[669] The author (or authors!) apparently knew Plato and his philosophy well. The most weighty arguments against full authenticity are the lack of brilliance (admittedly a dubious argument) and the fact that the dialogue reads as a 'textbook of Socratic and Platonic philosophy' (Burnet and others).

If it is accepted that *Alcibiades* I is 'semi-authentic' and written as a link in the internal Academic discussion about teaching, we have some premises for finding a place for it in our hypothetical chronological sequence.

In spite of the arrangement of the setting—Socrates and Alcibiades are alone and prepared to speak frankly—the dialogue is not manifestly apologetic. This is of little consequence to the dating, because *Alcibiades* I is after all rather more esoterically Academic than, say, the *Symposium*. As a matter of fact, Socrates' relations with Alcibiades do not interest the author particularly, though he considers them and makes some specific points at the beginning and end of the dialogue. Basically 'Alcibiades' stands for any ambitious, gifted and promising student of the Academy upon whom the elenctic method can be tested. The dialogue appears to me to be essentially a specimen of this method applied on the the-
[216] matic complex of philosophy as self-knowledge and control of others. Hence, the environment of the *Charmides* and the background of the *Republic* suggest themselves. However, the elenchus has a constructive and not an aporetic aim. Socrates, whether standing for Plato or not, is really a teacher here.

E.C. There is a slight indication of a date before 371 BCE; but the external criteria adduced by those who advocate a very late or a post-Platonic date are not reliable.[670]

I.C. *Symposium—Alcibiades* I. The most obvious problem here is the relation of *Alcibiades* I to the full-length portrait of Alcibiades in the *Symposium*. It seems practically certain to me that *Alcibiades* I relies on the latter although there are details which may have been taken from an earlier tradition.[671] The situation of the

---

668. The simple compositional rhythm is broken in the center (120e–124c) by a quasi-historical lecture by Socrates on education in Persia and Sparta with lessons to be drawn from it. This central 'myth' is of no very fundamental importance to the rest of the argument (as Plato's central myths normally are); it is rather a formal device, modeled on the central speeches in *Protagoras, Symposium, Meno* and *Phaedo* (for which cf. Thesleff 1967, above).

669. Note e.g. the ἐπιφάνεια of the δαιμόνιον 124c, the eye as the mirror of the soul 132d–133d, the stork's love 135de.

670. Friedländer II 214 argued that *Alcibiades* I must have been written before the battle of Leuktra (371 BCE) because Sparta is still described as wealthy (123ab). The romantic interest in Persia is characteristic of the first half of the 4th century, but does not provide an exact clue. For Aeschines and Isocrates, *see* below. Influence from Eudoxus has been seen notably in the passage on the mirror (132e ff., cf. Clark 1955: 234 f., Dönt 1964: 38 ff.), but this seems very debatable.

671. Such as Alcibiades' words ἐνοχλεῖς με *Alc.* 1 104d3 (cf. 103a3) to which Friedländer has called attention (II 224); possibly they represent an older variant of the Socratic tradition than the emphatic ἐλλοχῶν αὖ με ἐνταῦθα κατέκεισο in *Symposium* 213b; but note that Xenophon *Smp.* 8.4 (who in this chapter certainly relies on Plato's *Smp.*) makes Socrates say to Antisthenes in a similar situation μὴ νῦν μοι ἐν τῷ παρόντι ὄχλον πάρεχε. Perhaps a writing by Antisthenes is here the common source. Most of the other parallels listed by Friedländer have been usually, and

Alcibiades episode of the *Symposium* has been turned around. It is now Socrates [216] who actively approaches Alcibiades (who has lost all other 'lovers'), hardly a point which anybody could have made soon after the publication of Polycrates' pamphlet when "nobody had heard of Alcibiades having been the pupil of Socrates" (Isocr. *Bus.* (X) 5), or before Plato's *Symposium;* and Socrates has now become a 'daemonic' teacher whose δύναμις (explicitly denied in *Smp.* 218de) is his δαιμόνιον (*Alc.* 1 103a, 105de, 124c, 127e).

As noted above (p. 181), the secondary added frame dialogue of *Protagoras* seems to belong to the same context as *Alcibiades* I. On the other hand, the 'exchange of positions' at the end of *Alcibiades* I (135d8) corresponds to the similar situation at the end of the main dialogue of *Protagoras* (360e–361c).

The *Phaedrus* stands very far apart from *Alcibiades* I, but it is possible that the idea of 'breeding' a winged ἔρως, at the end of the latter dialogue (135e2), is a reminiscence of the first version of the former dialogue (cf. p. 319).

Though *Alcibiades* I is in various ways connected with the Academic discussion of the Philosopher-Statesman, I can see no clear points of contact with the various parts of the *Republic*.[672] This is possibly an indication of a relatively late [217] date of the latter. It is rather more interesting, however, to note that the author of the *Clitopho* was apparently not acquainted with the picture given in *Alcibiades* I of Socrates as a teacher of ἀρετή and notably δικαιοσύνη. Perhaps one of the aims of *Alcibiades* I is to supply an answer to the charges of Clitophon. The order *Clitopho—Alcibiades* I seems quite plausible.

The θεία μοίρα solution, played with in the *Meno,* is actually developed in the *Alcibiades* into a religious theory of 'instructing with god's help' (cf. the references to the δαιμόνιον above, and e.g. 132d–134d, 135d5). Rather than to assume with some supporters of the authenticity of *Alcibiades* I that the dialogue represents an earlier stage of Plato's thought, I am inclined to think that it follows a side-track. As far as I can see, it deviates somewhat from the main lines of dialectic and anamnesis that can be traced from the *Meno* onwards. The *Laches* with its down-to-earth recommendation of κοινῇ ζητεῖν perhaps follows another side-track. The discussion in *Alcibiades* I 118c–120e of the ideal qualities of a teacher which were lacking in great men like Pericles, suggests to me that the *Alcibiades* was written later than the *Laches,* but I would not insist on the value of this single criterion. Placing *Alcibiades* I after the first version of *Theaetetus* seems natural at any rate because *Alcibiades* develops the idea that Socrates can actively influence a pupil with the help of his δαιμόνιον once it permits him to start a συνουσία with somebody, and the possibility that Socrates would take advantage of such a situation

---

rightly, interpreted to indicate the precedence of the *Symposium*. Note e.g. the emphasizing of Socrates and Alcibiades being strictly alone, much more natural in the context of *Smp.* 218b than in *Alc.* 1 118bc; or the somewhat unexpected exclamation of Alcibiades in *Alc.* 1 114d ὑβριστὴς εἶ ὦ Σώκρατες (cf. *Smp.* 215b7).

672. R. Adam 1901 argued that the picture of the young potential ruler in *R.* VI 494a–e is taken from the opening section of *Alc.* 1; but in fact the historical Alcibiades may have served as a model for the former passage. Cf. also Friedländer II 222 ff. for supposed reminiscences of *Alcibiades* I in the *Republic.* This is all quite vague and arbitrary in my view.

[217] in the manner described in the opening of *Alcibiades* is obviously not implied in *Theaetetus* (151a) and is very probably a secondary invention. The fact that the Socratic art of 'maieutic' is not mentioned in the *Alcibiades* creates no problem: it does not occur anywhere in the Corpus outside the *Theaetetus*.

The fact that Zenon of Elea is treated as an ordinary sophist in *Alcibiades* I 119a indicates that the author has not yet seen the first part of *Parmenides*.

All this then would point to a date not very long after the first version of *Theaetetus*. The *Alcibiades* I still belongs with *Charmides*. More clearly than the latter, *Alcibiades* I shows what Socrates (or Plato) expects, of a potential 'tyrant,' and how instruction of a future philosopher can come about.

## Theages

After the broad treatment of the theme of Socrates (or Plato) as the teacher *dei gratia* in *Alcibiades* I, it seems reasonable to consider the more specialized little dialogue *Theages* which develops the same theme a bit further.

[218] The *Theages* has been normally considered spurious since the 19th century, and there is overwhelming evidence that it is not by Plato, in spite of Friedländer's somewhat hesitant attempt to prove the authenticity. The pros and cons need not be discussed here.[673]

Recently G. W. Müller (1969) has attempted to interpret the *Theages* as being written by a pupil of Plato in the period between 369 (the supposed date of *Theaetetus*) and 345 BCE (the supposed date of the Eudemian Ethics). I believe most of his points can be accepted.[674] A somewhat more precise dating could be conjectured from the following considerations:

*Theages* can be seen as producing a kind of thematic contamination of *Laches* and *Alcibiades* I, yet at the same time remotely following the formal pattern of *Crito*.[675] A father seeks Socrates' advice in the education of his son, who as we know from elsewhere (*R.* VI 496bc, cf. *Ap.* 33e) was prevented by his bad health from becoming a politician, and in fact was no success as a pupil of Socrates. It turns out that the boy expects Socrates to help him to power and influence (and in fact immortality). Socrates is reluctant to start a συνουσία with him and proceeds to explain the secret with his teaching. It all depends on ἡ τοῦ δαιμονίου δύναμις (129e) which works better the closer, even physically so, the contact is between Socrates and the pupil (130e3). He gives several examples intended to illustrate, without any trace of irony, this curiously naive thought. The examples and various other details elaborate the Socratic traditions about unsuccessful 'pupils' of Socrates that we know from *Charmides, Laches* and, notably, *Theaetetus* (151ab

---

673. *See* the details in Heidel 1896: 53–56, Ueberweg-Praechter 197 f., Souilhé 1930a: 137–142, Krüger 1935, D. Tarrant 1958, C. W. Müller 1969. Friedländer's position (II 137, 141 f., 309 ff.) has been adopted without much manifest support, by Wichmann 1966, E. Wolf 1968, Fischer 1969, Evans 1976, and—surprisingly—Guthrie V 392–394.

674. In my view, Müller rightly sees a reflection of *Thg.* 125e f. in EE 2.10.1225b32–35.

675. The emphasis is on the end with its extensive speeches.

where the terminology is very similar to *Theages*). It would probably be wiser, Socrates adds (130e), if Theages went to the sophists. The idea of sending to the sophists 'pupils' not accepted by the δαιμόνιον also occurs in *Theaetetus* (151b) and it may of course derive from a common source. However, since the point so emphatically made in the *Theages* is that during the 'erotic' (cf. 128b) συνουσία with Socrates it is the god who actually effects the teaching, it seems plausible to place *Theages* in the same 'side-track' as *Alcibiades* I. *Theages* seems in fact to correct, with more religious zeal and more naivete, the somewhat shockingly burlesque imagery of μαίευσις which Plato had played with in the *Theaetetus*.[676]

I would, therefore, prefer to date the *Theages* fairly soon after the first version of *Theaetetus* and in the context of *Alcibiades* I, i.e. in the 370s.

## Amatores [219]

This dialogue (Ἐρασταί, or better Ἀντερασταί) is reminiscent of *Lysis* and *Charmides* in other respects than *Laches* is reminiscent of them. Formally it is a reported dialogue with Socrates as the narrator. He moves again among young boys and their lovers, as in the *Lysis*. He holds discussions again with a pair of youngsters, now with two rivals who represent the intellectual and the unintellectual type. The theme is 'philosophy' as self-control and control of others, as if developing certain ideas from *Charmides* in the direction of the *Republic* (cf. also *Alcibiades* I.) Yet the dialogue is curiously meager, almost skeletal, in its setting and content: for instance, none of the acting persons except Socrates is mentioned by name.

The *Amatores* is an example of 'Plato simplified' (also linguistically).[677] Its authenticity was sometimes questioned in antiquity (Diog. L. 9.37), and it has been generally denied in modern times though somewhat surprisingly it has found some defenders recently.[678] I am sure the dialogue is not by Plato, but I can see no reason for accepting a post-Platonic date.

With its thematic association with the Academic discussion of philosophy as statemanship, which probably accompanied the genesis of the *Republic*, and its formal and thematic association with the *Charmides*, the *Amatores* can most naturally be dated to, or about, the 360s.

Unlike the *Charmides* type, however, the *Amatores* brings the Socratic elenchus to a definite result, which even wins applause at the end (καὶ οἱ ἄλλοι ἐπήνεσαν τὰ εἰρημένα). It is concerned with method, but does not discuss it. The problems relating to Socrates as a person and a teacher do not interest the author; it is worth noting that in spite of the setting ἔρως plays practically no

---

676. For the much-discussed relation between *Theaetetus* and *Theages*, see Souilhé 1930a: 140 f.
677. Among the stylistic peculiarities, note the high frequency of opening καί, also of οὖν. Otherwise the use of particles and formulae of reply corresponds to the 'Platonic' standard; cf. above p. 226 and n. 202.
678. For some arguments against authenticity, see Werner 1912, Souilhé 1930a: 108–112 and Carlini 1962. Defenders in recent times: Crombie I 12, 225, Wichmann 1966, Fischer 1969, Guthrie V 390 ff., Evans 1976.

[219] role at all.[679] The dialogue was probably written as a specimen of constructive Socratic dialectic, an example of an Academic seminar, for internal use in the Academy. Although it has a slightly protreptic tone ('philosophy is worth pursuing'), the dialogue cannot have been intended for the general reader in its present form. Why the author has chosen the reported form remains a mystery to me.

[220] *Eryxias*

The *Eryxias*, 'On wealth,' is a more ambitious imitation of the *Charmides* type of dialogue. The author, who cannot be Plato,[680] has made Socrates report a fairly complicated discussion pattern, and Socrates also brings the debate to a constructive conclusion. In this respect the dialogue reminds one rather of *Amatores* (and *Alcibiades* I). Clearly this is again intended as a specimen of positive Socratic elenchus, but with its elaborate literary apparatus the *Eryxias* addresses a wider public than the Academy could provide.

The aim of the dialogue is to prove that those who are wealthiest in external matters are the unhappiest, and that only the wise man is truly rich. This can be taken as an Academic doctrine, and it certainly does not prove Stoic influence.[681] I can see no certain indication of a post-Platonic date.

There are no obvious signs of influence from Platonic dialogues other than the *Charmides*.[682]

A slight clue for dating the dialogue to the 360s rather than later, would be the fact that Sicily still symbolizes to the author a world of wealth and external happiness (392a–393a). And this date would somehow explain why he chose *Charmides* as his formal model: the latter was a recent work at that time.

*Hippias Minor*

This is, I believe, the first in a sequence of small, apparently aporetic dialogues in dramatic form where the emphasis is placed upon logical play on the level of δόξα.

---

679. At 133a there is a formal reminiscence of *Lysis*; Guthrie (*see* n. 678) overinterprets the function of the ἔρως theme in the dialogue.

680. This is almost universally accepted: some linguistic peculiarities such as mannerisms in the use of participles could constitute additional proof. Oświecimski (1978: 31 f.) has failed to demonstrate that the dialogue is genuine, but he has contributed to showing that a post-Platonic date is hardly acceptable.

681. *See* Guthrie V 397, against Souilhé and others. The other points adduced by Souilhé 1930b: 87–89 to indicate a Hellenistic date have little or no weight. The only apparent exception is the mention of a γυμνασίαρχος Erx. 399a in the sense of a 'director of a gymnasium.' It is true that this special sense of the word is not found in classical Greek texts (though cf. Arist. *Pol.* 1323a1 where γυμνασιαρχία is ranked in the same category as γυναικονομία, νομοφυλακία and παιδονομία), but one wonders what other title a 4th century Athenian would have used for a person in charge of a gymnasium.

682. Gaiser 1959: 62 f. suggests influence from Phaedon's dialogue 'Simon'; but a common source seems more natural to assume.

For *Hippias Minor* an early date is usually taken for granted, though many scholars have observed that the dialogue is not so 'Socratic' after all. Doubts concerning its authenticity have been expressed from time to time, but a reference in Aristotle is usually thought to prove it genuine.[683] I am not prepared to take a definitive view of the question of authenticity, but I feel that such a minor piece with clear reminiscences of some major dialogues is better explained as written by a pupil of Plato.

The only external criterion worth noting is a fairly obvious allusion to Antisthenes, 364c ff., on Odysseus being πολύτροπος.[684] The reference is playfully polemical and therefore does not seem to suggest a very late date; but it should be remembered that allusions to Antisthenes occur as late as the *Sophist* (above, p. 342).

In formal and even linguistic respects there are a large number of reminiscences of the *Gorgias*, most of which have not been noticed so far. Note, for instance, the parallels in the opening scenes; the arrangement of the discussion as a formal 'disputation' in the presence of an audience (*Hp.Mi.* 364b, 369c, 373c) with a third part (here Eudicus) as 'arbitrator' (373ab, cf. *Grg.* 458d, etc.); and details such as the thematic and terminological corresponsion between *Hp.Mi.* 372e–373a and *Grg.* 519a,d (καταβολή, παρεῖναι, αἰτιᾶσθαι, δημηγορεῖν). Clearly it is the dramatic version of the *Gorgias* which constitutes the model. The character of Hippias may have been taken from the *Protagoras*, though he is somewhat differently treated.[685] But the wild play with logic at the expense of the sophist rather suggests the world of the *Euthyphro*.[686]

I would not venture to suggest a more precise date than this.

## Ion

The *Ion* is in various respects closely related to the *Hippias Minor*, and is possibly by the same hand. I discuss it here because it can also be associated with the *Euthyphro*. Both imply in their own way, as I see it, a reaction to the religious interpretation of Socratic 'teaching.'

For very much the same unsubstantial reasons as *Hippias Minor*, the *Ion* has been commonly placed among Plato's earliest works. Some scholars (most recently

---

683. No specific arguments for a very early date have been produced, but e.g. Wilamowitz. I 127, 313 f., etc. thought that because it is a 'satire' of Socrates it must have been written before his death. Those who question the authenticity include Pfleiderer 1896, Lutoslawski, v. Arnim 1914, and Bluck 1949: 133 n. 64. It is true that Aristotle's reference in *Met.* Δ 1025a6 ff. to ὁ ἐν τῷ Ἱππία λόγος does not really prove anything except that the *Hippias Minor* was an Academic text anterior to this passage in the Metaphysics (cf. *EN* 1140b21–25, 1144a22–36).

684. Cf. Antisthenes' 'Odysseus' fr. 51 Caizzi (Schol. Od. 1.1 p. 9.25 ff. Dindorf); Geffcken II A 42 n. 120.—Note also Xen. *Mem.* IV 2.1 ff. (from Antisthenes?), cf. Guthrie IV 197.

685. Various other parallels with the *Protagoras* have been listed by Pohlenz 1913: 81–85, 95n.; he interprets them as indicating the precedence of *Hippias Minor*, but in my view the reverse order is more natural.

686. For the logic of *Hippias Minor*, cf. Hoerber 1962, Hintikka 1973: 29 f.

[221] Flashar 1958, 1963) have dated it to the late 390s owing to certain external references and supposed anachronisms (*see* the conspectus of the discussion in Moore's study of 1974). Moore would prefer to date it considerably later and, apparently, declare it spurious (though he does not actually do so). Doubts regarding the authenticity have often been expressed before, more often than in the case of *Hippias Minor*.[687] For my part, I agree fully with most of Moore's arguments against an early date. Some indications of a stylistic affinity with the *Hippias Minor* and various linguistic oddities[688] add to my impression that the dialogue was not written by Plato himself.

[222] In formal respects *Ion* clearly resembles the *Hippias Minor*, though Socrates and Ion are alone, and the *Ion* is provided with a central section (533c–536d) of a more visionary kind.[689]

The degree of play and/or irony present in the central 'myth of the magnet' has been the subject of much debate.[690] I am sure the ironic note should be listened to, and this may have some consequences for the dating. If in fact the point the author is trying to make is to declare all so-called inspiration θεία μοῖρα somewhat suspect since it occurs independently of τέχνη and νοῦς, and since it produces such dubious things as Homeric poetry (!), dithyrambs (534c), the paian of Tynnichus (534d), and the even more dubious and secondary performing of all this (536a), including corybantic dance (536c), then he is criticizing not only the common Socratic conception of θεία μοῖρα,[691] but he is also censuring the Academic conception of philosophical teaching as functioning actively θεία μοῖρα through the teacher's δαιμόνιον. Such a conception was only toyed with in the *Meno* (99c ff., the end),[692] but it was developed into a kind of religious doctrine in *Alcibiades* I and *Theages*. But, the author of *Ion* seems to think, how can we know when Socrates is right or wrong, if divine inspiration is so irrational? The same question is implicit in the playful remarks about the 'Muse of Euthyphron' in the *Cratylus* (above p. 316). In the *Phaedrus* (the second version), Plato himself chose another way to explain epistemological irrationalism: the cosmic flight of the soul on wings recovered by love (although of course μανία is unable to bring

---

687. The skeptics include Schleiermacher, Zeller, Lutoslawski and Ritter, further, Moreau 1939b, Bluck 1949 (193 n. 64), and especially Diller who argued in considerable detail (1955) that Plato could only have made a sketch for this dialogue which was finished by a pupil.

688. Some of the tests referred to above p. 223 ff. and n. 202 indicate affinity. For the oddities, cf. Ritter 1910a: 354 and n. 38, but on the other hand Gomperz II 564, Wilamowitz I 134 f., II² 32 f.; in fact the notorious τί μήν; 531d is really interrogative.

689. Cf. *Alcibiades* I. In fact the compositional pattern of the *Ion* is remarkably symmetrical, perhaps too balanced to be 'authentic'; for details *see* my notes 1967 above 99 (I did not at that time question the authenticity). Wyller 1958 probably makes too much of the pedimental principle followed in the *Ion*.

690. See now Tigerstedt 1969 (with references), who stresses the ironical aspect.

691. This has sometimes been suggested, e.g. by Pohlenz 1913: 182 ff., referring notably to Aeschines' 'Alcibiades' (fr. 11c Dittmar). But many other scholars, beginning with Wilamowitz II 35 f., and especially Humbert 1967: 224, have thought that Aeschines was influenced by the *Ion*. Here again the priority has to be determined on other grounds.

692. It has been occasionally argued that *Ion* in fact develops the ideas of the end of *Meno*, cf. Pohlenz 1913: 188, Stefanini I 113 ff. However, a direct relation should perhaps not be assumed.

the soul directly to the world of Forms, as Plotinus thought it could).⁶⁹³ But I find [223] it quite possible that the first version of the *Phaedrus* contained essential parts of the passage on μανία (244a–245c, cf. above p. 319), including Μουσῶν κατοκωχή (245a1) which then provided the author of *Ion* with one of his starting points.

These conjectural considerations would assign to the *Ion* a place between the *Theages* and the final version of the *Phaedrus*, possibly in the context of the *Cratylus*.

If this interpretation is approximately correct, the *Ion* of course indirectly (in fact like *Hippias Minor*), sides with the criticism of poetry in the *Republic*, Books II and III, whether or not they had received their present form at the time.

Like *Hippias Minor*, the *Ion* also includes a series of reminiscences of a writing of Antisthenes: the passages *Ion* 530cd, 536e f. and 538c contain the same points as are made by Antisthenes about silly rhapsodes in Xenophon's 'Symposium' 3.5–6, 4.6–7, and the same quotation from Homer. Since a direct dependence of Xenophon on the *Ion*, or vice versa, is not very probable (although several scholars have thought so), the best solution seems to be to accept Antisthenes' Περὶ ἐξηγητῶν (Diog. L. 6.17) as a common source.⁶⁹⁴

I am unable to find any other absolute or relative clues for the dating.

## Euthyphro

G.C. Though this dialogue is not merely an aporetic discussion of ὁσιότης, its playfully critical attitude to conventional religion puts it in a very different category from, say, *Crito* (with which it has often been associated since antiquity, chiefly because of its dramatic date) and rather in the same category as *Ion*. I am inclined to think, however, that *Ion* and *Euthyphro* were not written by the same person. It is not only the difference in tone and doctrinal details which suggests this, but also stylistic considerations.⁶⁹⁵ Perhaps *Euthyphro* has the same author as *Hippias Major* with which it has a close resemblance in various respects; and this is in fact one of several indications of a fairly late date.

There are few actual grounds for the traditional assumption of an early date for *Euthyphro*; this relies chiefly on theories of a 'Socratic' or 'aporetic' stage in the development of Plato's thought (cf. p. 171) and on the fact that it is concerned with the trial of Socrates.⁶⁹⁶ The mixture of supposedly 'early' and later' features

---

693. E.g. Enn. IV 7.35. This is a common misapprehension among later Platonists.

694. Xenophon is usually thought to have quoted the *Ion*, cf. Geffcken II 40, Méridier 1931a: 25 f. But with an early dating of Xenophon's 'Symposium' (cf. Thesleff 1978) and a later dating of the *Ion*, and considering the importance which Antisthenean sources generally have for Xenophon, the inference made above is natural.

695. Some of the stylistic tests referred to above p. 223 ff. and n. 202 seem to indicate this, though they are obviously insufficient as such.

696. Stylometry (except Michaelson, Morton and Gillies 1977, cf. above p. 238) seemed to confirm an early date (cf. Ritter 1910a: 228 ff., 1935, v. Arnim 1912). The chief reason why Shorey 1933 treats *Euthyphro* as the first dialogue is probably his systematic tendency; but I am surprised to find that Guthrie (IV 68) still puts *Euthyphro* together with *Laches*, *Charmides* and *Lysis* in an 'early group.'

[224] in the contents, and glimpses of a sophisticated terminology and methodology,[697] have led some scholars to suggest a later date or propose various theories of interpolation, revision or spuriousness.[698] For my part, I believe the dialogue is best explained on the assumption that it was written by a pupil of Plato in close association with his teaching and his intentions. In my view, it is skilfully composed in the Platonic manner,[699] but it is somewhat too artificial and full of allusions to be by Plato himself.

E.C. Whatever other sources the *Euthyphro* may have, it appears to build (3e) on a suggestion made by Antisthenes in a speech: it is right (ὅσιον) to prosecute one's parents if they have done wrong.[700] In this respect *Euthyphro* corresponds to *Hippias Minor* and *Ion*. And again, little can be inferred from this: in fact this speech of Antisthenes is likely to have been rather early. On the other hand, however, there occur in the dialogue some pointless historical mistakes which indicate a considerable distance in time from the dramatic date, the spring of 399 BCE; the most obvious mistake is the reference to the Naxian cleruchy as still existing (4c) though as we know, and as Plato must have remembered in, say, the 380s, all cleruchies (except Salamis) were finished before 404 BCE.[701]

I.C. *Apology—Euthyphro.* This order has been argued more often and with better success than the opposite one.[702]

[225] *Meno—Euthyphro.* Various points of contact exist, such as the question of the relation and nature of the virtues, glimpses of the theory of Forms, the ὑπόθεσις, (*Men.* 86d, *Euthphr.* 11e), etc. These points are usually interpreted as indicating

---

697. The position of ὁσιότης among Plato's 'cardinal virtues' was much discussed before Wilamowitz II 77 f. (cf. also Shorey 1903: 12) took a skeptical view of this criterion. Since the 19th century, the implications in the *Euthyphro* of ἰδέα, εἶδς, αὐτό, παράδειγμα, οὐσία, πάθος, ὑπόθεσις, etc., and the mathematical terminology (12d) have been much debated. Though many scholars still interpret such details as representing 'early' or 'preliminary' stages (e.g. Allen 1970, Guthrie IV 114–121, Rist 1975: 336 ff., Violette 1973), others rightly note that the high number of them is suspect as such, and take them as indications of a comparatively late date (e.g. Stark 1952, Krämer 1959: 519 f., Kapp 1968: 107 f.).

698. The theory of inauthenticity was advocated in the 19th century by e.g. Schleiermacher and Ueberweg, and it was still accepted by Natorp (1903: 38 n. 1), though it was later abandoned (but cf. Buchmann 1936: 51 n. 127, and Zürcher 1954: 34 who of course thinks that the opening references to Λυκεῖον and ἡ τοῦ βασιλέως στοά imply Peripatetics and Stoics). Lutoslawski 1896: 198, Heidel 1900: 176 ff. (and also Guthrie IV 101) think that the authenticity is proved beyond doubt. Leisegang 1950: 2407 assumed that some passages have been interpolated, Gigon 1954 that the dialogue has been revised.

699. Cf. Thesleff 1967, above 105, for various literary niceties, and Hoerber 1958, S. A. Saunders 1974.

700. This must have been the point made in Antisthenes' 'Apology of Orestes,' cf. Chroust 1957: 129, 149. Cf. also Polycrates ap. Xen. *Mem.* I 2.49 ff., above p. 179.

701. Cf. Geffcken II A 51 n. 173, Guthrie IV 102 n. 1. Cf. further Gauss 1/2.132 f. The details of the (physiognomically interesting) presentation of Meletus (2b) would also seem odd in the 390s. Moreover, it has sometimes been suggested that the attitude of the author to the trial of Socrates implies a great distance in time; cf. e.g. Gomperz II 570, Stefanini I 148 n. 1.

702. For internal indications of this order, *see* notably Heidel 1902, Hammer-Jensen 1905/6. 116–119. For the reverse order, *see* Erbse 1975: 43 (presupposing a comparatively late date for the *Apology*).

the precedence of *Euthyphro*, but especially Kapp 1968: 65-67 has argued with [225] some force the reverse order, and I am convinced he is right.⁷⁰³ A specific detail of some interest is the treatment of the myth of Daedalus: In *Meno* 97d ff. Socrates illustrates his doctrine of δόξα with a joke about the running statues of Daedalus; in *Alcibiades* I 121a Socrates answers Alcibiades' boast about his pedigree by stating (with little or no irony) that he himself (i.e. his father, who was a sculptor) is a descendant of Daedalus; and in *Euthyphro* 11b-e (cf. 15b) the two ideas are combined so as to illustrate the running away of the Socratic argument. I feel fairly certain that *Euthyphro* here relies on *Meno*,⁷⁰⁴ and possibly it relies on *Alcibiades*, too.

*Cratylus* and *Euthyphro*. A relation between these two dialogues appears to exist because of the joke about the flow of etymologies being inspired by the 'Muse of Euthyphron,' *Cratylus* 396d, 399e, 407d, 409d, 428c (cf. above p. 368).⁷⁰⁵ Now, in the dialogue *Euthyphro* Euthyphron does not really appear as 'inspired' at all though he is (or thinks he is) a 'holy man'; only once (2bc) does he refer to situations where he has used his divinatory powers, and this occasional passage cannot have given rise to the repeated joke in *Cratylus*. Nor can the latter alone have provided a model for *Euthyphro*. Obviously both dialogues operate with a common (oral?) source. If, as seems possible (above p. 316), Euthyphron in *Cratylus* somehow stands for Heraclides of Pontus, the *Euthyphro* presumably also alludes to him. We know that this Πομπικός (Diog. L. 5.86) was interested in religious questions. At any rate, we have here a slight indication of a date not earlier than the mid-370s.

*Theaetetus* and *Euthyphro*. It should be noted that the dramatic situation of the *Euthyphro* immediately succeeds the situation depicted in *Theaetetus* (210d). It is hard to avoid the impression that there must be some intentional connection. Probably the rather odd reference to Μελήτου γραφή at the end of *Theaetetus* is a remnant of the lost background story (cf. 142c and above p. 301). And very probably it would not have occurred to Plato to create the fiction of two extensive philosophical discussions in the morning of the very day when Socrates went to take the γραφή, if he knew the *Euthyphro*; on the other hand, the author of the latter with his predilection for artificial tricks, might well have thought it worth while to insert a discussion of ὁσιότης on the δόξα level after the discussion of ἐςπιστήμη in *Theaetetus*.⁷⁰⁶ Possibly (though this is perhaps not a necessary infer- [226] ence) he knew the final, dramatic version of the *Theaetetus*. And this would bring us down to the 360s (not very far from the *Hippias Major* in fact).

---

703. Pohlenz 1921: 12 also adopted this position, against Wilamowitz and others, as did e.g. Taylor, Stefanini, Bröcker (1964), Ilting (1965), whereas the majority (including Erbse 1968: 24 f.) take the precedence of *Euthyphro* for granted.

704. This is also the opinion of Rick 1931: 294 f.

705. The order *Cratylus—Euthyphro* was argued by Ueberweg 1861: 251; but generally it is thought that *Cratylus* refers to *Euthyphro* (cf. Friedlander II 189, Luce 1964: 138, etc.), on flimsy grounds however (cf. below).

706. This was approximately what Ueberweg 1861: 251 argued.

[226] *Hippias Major*

In an article published in 1976, I attempted to demonstrate that the *Greater Hippias* was written by a pupil of Plato about 360 BCE. I also gave some references to the almost hopelessly extensive discussion of the authenticity of this dialogue, which has not so far led to any substantial agreement among scholars.[707] It is not necessary to repeat all the details here; my main points regarding the date were, and are, as follows:

The contents abound in evidence that *Hippias Major* is not an early dialogue, and the allusive play in which the author indulges makes it difficult, not to say impossible, to rank it as a missing link in any hypothetical chain of 'development' of Plato's doctrines, e.g. of the theory of Forms, as is often done. Thus, for instance, it is more probable that the manipulation of the words τὸ καλόν, τὸ ἀγαθόν, αἴτιον, ἔκγονον and ἰδέα in *Hippias Major* 279b alludes to the central section of the *Republic* (VI 506d –507b, 508bc) than that it 'foreshadows' it as, for instance, Friedländer asserts (II 103); and the καλὰ ἐπιτηδεύματα and νόμοι which recur in *Hippias Major* in various connections (286b, 294c, 295d, 298b–d, etc.) are rather a reminiscence of *Gorgias* 474d–475a (cf. above p. 284) and *Symposium* 210c, 211c (though the theory of Love does not seem to interest the author of *Hippias Major*) than a preliminary stage to these passages. The correspondences between *Hippias Major* and *Euthyphro* are obvious, and I would now add that *Hippias Major* can perhaps be shown to be somewhat later *Euthyphro* rather than vice versa.[708] An
[227] important *terminus post quem*, overlooked so far, is the pointed and unique εὐδόξως in Socrates' answer to Hippias' attempt to define καλόν as a παρθένος καλή (287e). I am sure this conveys an allusion to Plato's younger contemporary, the astronomer Eudoxus of Cnidos who was known for his theoretical hedonism, though he was also a man of exceptional temperance and love of the 'plausible' (τὸ ἔνδοξον according to Aristotelian terminology). Since, for all we know, Eudoxus lived as a member of the Academy for some years after the later 360s,[709] this is one

---

707. Among recent students of the dialogue, Liminta 1974 and Guthrie IV 1975 again side with the defenders of its authenticity.

708. The correspondences between *Hippias Major* and *Euthyphro* extend from dialogue technique and style to the playfully tricky tone, the mass of doctrinal and other allusions, and to the fact that, although the theme of both dialogues is a central one from the point of view of Platonism, it is treated on the δόξα level. The contacts have often been observed by those who consider both dialogues authentic, but there is no agreement as to which is the earlier one unless, for independent reasons, the *Euthyphro* is placed very early. Notably Soreth 1953 and Malcolm 1968 (*see* further my references 1976: 108) have produced some detailed argumentation for the order *Euthyphro—Hippias Major*, but while some of Soreth's points were refuted by Malcolm (194 n. 12), his own points rely too much upon a preconceived view of the development of the theory of Forms. I can see no internal grounds for vindicating the precedence of either of the two except that the *Hippias Major*, being a more elaborate piece of comedy around a still more vital theme, by following the *Euthyphro*, may correspond to a growth of ambition in the author. Also the association of *Euthyphro* with *Theaetetus* (above p. 371) may point to the order *Euthyphro-Hippias Major*.

709. I am here siding with Merlan's (1960: 98–108) chronology rather than with Lasserre's (1966: 137–146; cf. Toomer 1968: 334–337) except that I think (with de Santillana 1947 and Lasserre) that Eudoxus is likely to have visited Egypt in 365/4 BCE and not in 373/2.

indication of a date about or somewhat later than 360 BCE for *Hippias Major*. [227]
Among the large number of reminiscences of comedy and comic diction which
can be traced in the dialogue (cf. notably D. Tarrant 1928), there is one, the censure
of Socrates' 'chopping up' (κρούειν, κατατέμνειν) the διανεκῆ σώματα τῆς οὐσίας
(301b, cf. e3 and χύτρα 288c, 290d, etc., and especially 289b1–2 with αἰσχρά) which
seems to have been taken from a parody of Timotheus the lyric poet in Anaxandrides' comedy Αἴσχρα ('The Ugly Woman') fr. 6 K; and Anaxandrides was active
about this time.[710] The same passage in *Hippias Major* (301b) is also partly paralleled
by a reference in the *Sophist* 246ab to the idealists' 'chopping up' (διαθραύειν) the
σώματα of the materialists. Apparently both dialogues go back to oral discussions
and allusions employed at the Academy, which of course belong chronologically
to the context of the *Sophist*. Several indications exist of *Hippias Major* operating
with reminiscences of *Theaetetus*, notably *Tht.* 184a–185b/*Hp.Ma.* 300a–e. But
common Academic sources probably again lay behind Socrates' definition of τὸ
καλόν as τὸ δι' ἀκοῆς τε καὶ ὄψεως ἡδύ in *Hippias Major* 297e–298a (cf. 303e) and
the examination of 'pure pleasure' as restricted in the first place to sight and hear-
ing in *Philebus* 51b, 52c, etc.; though rather obviously the treatment of the theme
is more sophisticated in the *Philebus*. In the Topics 6.146a21–32, Aristotle seems to
quote somewhat freely, as an example of a faulty definition and the criticism of
it, the contents of *Hippias Major* 298a–300b; and since this portion of the Topics is
likely to be early (from the 350s?), it seems that Aristotle quotes from memory the
*Hippias* which was then a recently published text. I am not, however, as sure as
I was in 1976 that Xenophon in *Oeconomicus* 8.19–20 (however late this text may
be) quotes *Hippias Major* 288cd; after all, it is more probable that Antisthenes
is being alluded to in both passages, as Joël already suggested (especially II
1–2.1901.746 ff.). The curious διὰ χρόνου which opens the discussion with Hippias
about τὸ δίκαιον in Xenophon's 'Memorabilia' IV 4.5, and which sounds so much [228]
more appropriate at the opening of *Hippias Major* (281a1–2), is perhaps also taken
from some work of Antisthenes: it is worth noting that Hippias in Xenophon's
story (IV 4.9) seems to be discussing with an Antisthenean Socrates who does not
wish to instruct τὸ δίκαιον positively (cf. *Clitopho*).[711]

I find this evidence for a date of about 360 BCE or the early 350s fairly convincing. The role of Antisthenes is here again, as usual, the more mysterious the more
one comes to think of it. Could it be that the very odd Third Man, the arrogant

---

710. In Anaxandrides the simple word χύτρα is contrasted with the bombastic language
of Timotheus.—When I made this reference in 1976, I was not aware of the probable fact that
Polycrates wrote an encomium of χύτρα (Alex. II. ῥητορ. ἀφορμῶν III p. 3.19 Sp. = Polycrates
fr. 9 Radermacher) which may have been answered, or commented on, by Antisthenes in his
'protreptic' work II. δικαιοσύνης καὶ ἀνδρεία (cf. Joël II 2.1901: 708 ff.). If this is true, the author
of *Hippias Major* may of course allude to Antisthenes too (cf. below p. 228), though the διανεκῆ
σώματα come in the first place from Anaxandrides.

711. Breitenbach 1967: 1831 and others think that Dio Chrysostom 3.26–42 (note here the
opening διὰ χρόνου) with its discussion of δικαιοσύνη is a free quotation of Xenophon, but after
all Antisthenes again suggests himself; cf. the preceding note, and *Clitopho*, above p. 352.—For
same other alleged borrowings of Xenophon from *Hippias Major*, see Guthrie IV 178 n. 4.

[228] and rude Anonymus, whose objections and comments Socrates begins to introduce at 285c and who accompanies the discussion to the end (when it turns out that he is a kind of *alter ego* of Socrates, 304d), somehow stands for Antisthenes? In fact it is this Anonymus who adduces the famous χύτρα at 288c.[712]

Finally a word must be said about the relationship of *Hippias Major* to *Hippias Minor*. Although the majority of scholars prefer to date the more 'advanced' *Hippias Major* later, it has sometimes been thought that the epideixis on a Homeric theme which Hippias announces at the instigation of Eudicus, in *Hippias Major* 286c, is in fact the epideixis from which *Hippias Minor* starts.[713] But apart from the fact that the idea of a discussion 'after the show' is an old one as we have seen, and that I do not believe the two dialogues can have the same author, it seems to me that it did not occur to the author of *Hippias Minor* (note 363cd) that the sophist two days previously (note *Hp.Ma.* 286b5) had a lengthy, awkward and confusing conversation, with Socrates. Moreover, a close study of the details used for characterizing Hippias as a person and a sophist would also reveal, I believe, that although the author of *Hippias Major* may have known *Hippias Minor*, and not vice versa, the two pictures are largely independent.

## Hipparchus

The author of this little dialogue about τὸ φιλοκερδές, unlike most of the authors so far discussed, is not interested in character drawing. As in some dialogue frames (above p. 327), Socrates is conversing with an anonymous friend. However, the dialogue has often been regarded as typically 'Socratic,' and its light and playful style, its simple dialogue pattern and somewhat naive content have been [229] taken by some scholars to indicate a very early date, including some who think the dialogue spurious. Several scholars, among them Friedländer and Crombie, have accepted it as genuine.[714]

I find it impossible to accept Platonic authorship for this dialogue. Among the various points adduced by the atheticizers I should like to draw particular attention to the linguistic oddities[715] which, seen in connection with the general theory of the development of the Platonic dialogue which has been propounded here, cannot be explained on the grounds of youth, inexperience, or use of idioms later dropped.

---

712. Cf. above, n. 710. Cf. the 'splitting' of Socrates in some later Platonic dialogues, above n. 297.

713. This is expressively the opinion of Guthrie IV 191 n. 3.

714. The authenticity was also questioned in antiquity (Aelian. VH 8.2), and since the 19th century the *Hipparchus* has been commonly considered spurious; *see* especially the arguments of Souilhé 1930a: 47–51, 57 f. (with early dating), Geffcken II 181, 185, A 158 f. Arguments for authenticity have been produced by Eckert 1911: 46 ff., Friedländer II 114–116, 301–304, cf. III 304 n. 17, 419 and some others. It has been considered genuine also by Wichmann 1966 and Evans 1976.

715. Cf. above p. 240.

As a matter of fact, this author—who can hardly be identified with other authors in the Corpus—is fond of a mock-aporetic play with logic and allusions, in a manner somewhat reminiscent of the *Euthyphro* and the *Hippias Major*. There occur many allusions to τἀγαθόν in particular (noted and explained as *pre-Republic* by Friedländer) and other reminiscences of central Platonic doctrines (note e.g. τὸ αὐτό and περιτρέχειν 230d–231c). The central legend (228b–229e, formally and thematically adopting perhaps the model of *Alcibiades* I) is obviously ironic, but its implications, including the murder of a somehow spurious philosopher-king (Hipparchus), are largely obscure to us.

I would venture to suggest that the *Republic* is in fact implied in the allusions, and that the central legend has something (I am not sure what exactly) to do with the murder of Dion in 354 BCE.

## Minos

The *Minos* is in certain formal respects related to the *Hipparchus*, but as has been often noted, it is doubtful whether they have the same author. The *Minos* is not particularly playful or ironic, and there are no very obvious extrathematic allusions. Very few modern scholars have accepted this dialogue as authentic, although since the 1960s some have taken this view, among them Morrow.[716] For my part, I find that the association with Plato's *Laws*, commonly agreed on by the critics, is both a specific indication of spuriousness, considering the formal and stylistic details, and a sign of a date rather before than after the completion of the *Laws* (for this latter point, *see* Morrow 1960: 35–39).

## Sisyphus

In this case it is sufficient to refer to the competent discussion of C. W. Müller 1975: 94–104 who demonstrates, in my opinion convincingly, that the dialogue was written at the Academy during Plato's lifetime, probably in the 350s. Among the arguments, two are anachronistic allusions such as we noted in *Hippias Major;* one is to Callistratus hiding after his condemnation to death (*Sis.* 388c), the other is to Eudoxus (388e; Müller assumes an unnecessarily late date as a *terminus post quem* for this allusion).

The author of *Sisyphus* cannot be easily identified with any of the other authors in the Corpus. At any rate his Socrates is rather more fond of paradoxes than of aporias.[717]

---

716. *See* the references to the discussion in Souilhé 1930a: 81–85 and Guthrie V 389 f. Those who accept the dialogue as genuine also include Wichmann 1966, Fischer 1969 and Evans 1976.

717. Oświecimski 1978 suggests that *Sisyphus* is a didactic work designed for internal use at the Academy. Obviously, however, the author has some literary ambitions.

[230] *Demodocus*

This collection of four sets of sophistic paradoxes can be conveniently discussed here because, apart from the author's interest in self-contradictory statements, the general theme is the same as that of *Sisyphus*, συμβουλεύειν. Souilhé 1930b: 41 f. thinks that both the linguistic form and the contents point to a rather early 4th century date, and possibly to a Megarian origin, whereas C. W. Müller 1975: 268–271) (following earlier suggestions) dates texts II–IV to the Hellenistic (Arcesilaic) period, but argues (126–128) that text I could be dated to the early Academy, though after 350 BCE. I cannot see that there are very strong indications of a post-Platonic date for any of the four texts.

It is important, however, to consider the fact that these texts have nothing of Plato and very little of Socrates in them. The first text is a speech addressing a certain Demodocus; this is the name of the father who is seeking Socrates' advice (συμβουλεύεσθαι) in the dialogue *Theages*. The remaining texts are impersonally reported dialogues. The name of Socrates does not occur anywhere. There must have been strong and specific reasons why these odd pieces were incorporated into the collection of dialogues believed to be Platonic. The best reason I can think of is that they already belonged to an Academic collection of 'exercise books' before the death of Plato. We can see from the *Sisyphus* (and we can infer from many Platonic works, and certainly from Aristotle) that sophistic paradoxes interested various members of the Academy.

A reasonable *terminus post quem* for this collection is the dialogue *Theages*. Possibly, however, some of the texts are older.[718]

[231] *De Virtute* and *De Justo*

These two brief and colorless specimens of Socratic reasoning could perhaps at first sight be taken as very early ὑπομνήματα of Σωκρατικοὶ λόγοι. They are written for the purposes of exercise or in order to memorize pieces of Socratic elenchus, but surely not for 'publication.'

The *De Virtute* at any rate turns out to be taken from the *Meno*. Apart from the fact that it copies some portions of that dialogue (*see* Souilhé 1930b: 25 f.) it also produces occasional examples of terms such as θυμοειδές (378d) which prove that it is not an early text. And the conclusion, which includes the idea of θεῖος ἀνήρ (without irony), suggests that the author has studied the *Ion* (or similar Academic texts) rather unimaginatively.

For *De Justo*, it is perhaps possible to find some stylistic parallels with the *Amatores*.[719]

Both pieces probably reflect Academic training, and since we have seen various traces of Socraticism in the Academy in the 350s, they can be tentatively

---

718. The concluding appeal to a single listener in texts II and IV is interesting; cf. 'Lysias' ap. *Phdr.* 234c4–5.

719. I hope to be able to demonstrate this in another connection.

placed in that period. I am far from convinced by C. W. Müller's arguments [231] (1975: 187–191, 249–260) for dating them to the period of Arcesilaus.[720]

Definitiones

The collection of the Ὅροι is of very peripheral interest here. Regarding them as authentically Platonic is completely out of the question, and it has been argued that the collection took its final shape not earlier than the first century BCE.[721]

However, there is some evidence for Speusippus having collected such definitions, and so perhaps the oldest parts of the present text derive from the early Academy; cf. Souilhé 1930b: 156.

The *Second Alcibiades*

The author of this dialogue again has greater literary ambitions, and is evidently writing for an extra-Academic public. This is the first of the dialogues so far discussed where I am inclined to see definite traces of a post-Platonic date.[722] The earlier theories of Stoic or Arcesilaic influence have been refuted by Souilhé [232] (1930a: 10–13)[723] who finishes his comprehensive reassessment by concluding (18) that the *Alcibiades* II should be dated towards the end of the 4th century BCE. I have little to add to this.

The author's dependence on *Alcibiades* I is obvious to any reader. There are various other reminiscences of Platonic dialogues, some of them quite superficial, such as the idea of Alcibiades bewreathing his teacher and 'lover' Socrates, at the end (cf. *Smp.* 213e). The theme is a pronouncedly religious one, namely, the ethical conditions of prayer and sacrifice, and Socrates conducts the discussion in a quite un-Platonic manner in a somewhat floscular style, illustrating his points with quotations from poetry (in which he finds a deeper meaning). It is true that the idea of a World Conqueror (141a–c) also occurs in *Alcibiades* I (105a–c, and in *Theages*, cf. C. W. Müller 1969); but in *Alcibiades* II Archelaus of Macedon (141d) and the oracle of Ammon (148e) appear in contexts which suggest allusions to Alexander the Great.

Among the linguistic oddities it may be noted that *Alcibiades* II is the only dialogue in the Corpus which, according to our manuscripts, uses the varieties οὐθείς, μηθείς fairly consistently (*see* Brandwood's Word Index).

---

720. As a matter of fact, I can see no grounds for the largely current theory that the Academy of Arcesilaus also produced written 'Socratica.'
721. Ingenkamp 1967a; Souilhé (cf. below) would prefer an earlier date.
722. The only scholars who to my knowledge have accepted it as genuine in recent times are Wichmann 1966 and Fischer 1969: 62 n. 4. Both are highly uncritical and, apparently, badly informed.
723. Carlini 1962 revived the theory, but with little success; cf. above n. 720.

[232] To date this *Alcibiades* to the time of Xenocrates seems to me a feasible, although conjectural, solution.

## Halcyon

This dialogue (Ἀλκυών, Ἁλκυών) has no philosophical content at all, although the speakers are Socrates and Chairephon. It is of peripheral interest here only because it shows how the pattern of a Socratic dialogue could be applied to literary fiction and entertainment.

As to dating it, the tradition that it was written by a certain Leo, who could have been one of Plato's pupils,[724] is not very reliable. I believe C. W. Müller 1975: 272 ff. has said all that is necessary from the present point of view in favor of a Hellenistic date.

The fact that some manuscripts include the *Halcyon* in the Corpus Platonicum, though it normally appears as Pseudo-Lucian, is due to a mistake made outside the Academy.

## Axiochus

For the *Axiochus* a Hellenistic date is unquestionable, considering language and style in particular (cf. Souilhé 1930b: 125 ff.). I agree with Guthrie V 394–396
[233] that Souilhé's dating of it in the first century BCE is probably too late, but I am not sure the paradise vision of the eschatological myth can be said to be simply Platonic or pre-Platonic. The acceptance, into a philosophical frame, of the world of the mysteries (yet excluding Pythagoreanism) on such a scale and with such argumentative force, is certainly alien to Plato and his immediate followers.

The consolatory theme (cf. also the parallels recorded by Souilhé 1930b: 130 f.) faintly suggests that the author may have been inspired by Crantor's famous Περὶ πένθους, and so a date in the first half of the 3rd century BCE seems possible. At any rate this was apparently the last Academic dialogue to be included in the Corpus Platonicum.[725]

## Letters

Disregarding the *Seventh Letter* which was considered above (p. 346), very much has been written on the Platonic *Letters* in general, and notably the authenticity of

---

724. Diog. L. 3.62, cf. Athen. 11.506c; Plut. *Phocion* 14.4.
725. It is reasonable to ask why it was added to a Corpus consisting mainly of 4th-century texts and presumably considered 'authentically Platonic' by 3rd-century Academics. Perhaps this was an anonymous text, and anonymous Socratic dialogues with an Academic content were perhaps not common.

the separate pieces.⁷²⁶ In modern times very few scholars have been prepared to accept *Ep.* 1, 4, 5, 9, 10, 11, 12 and the 'odd' pieces *Ep.* 14–18 (for which cf. above p. 236). The most able defense of the genuineness of the whole set of *Ep.* 2 –13 *en bloc* is Harward's (1932: 59–96, cf. the notes 162 ff.). There is fairly large support for *Ep.* 2, 3 and 13 and, especially since Wilamowitz added the weight of his authority, *Ep.* 6 and 8; but no one who does not accept *Ep.* 7 has to my knowledge declared for the authenticity of any of the other letters.

I can see no pertinent reason for accepting the authenticity of any of the *Letters* except the *Seventh Letter*; some arguments will be found below. A few of the letters, however spurious, have a biographical and chronological and even, remotely, philosophical relevance, and these will be considered here separately. The rest can be regarded as extra-Academic additions to the Corpus, quite irrelevant to the present study, and will be omitted from the discussion.⁷²⁷

The *2nd Letter*, though obviously spurious and modeled on the *7th Letter* (cf. e.g. *Ep.* 7.341c / *Ep.* 2314b), is of some interest as it operates with Platonic mystifications and references to secret doctrines and oral teaching (note 312d–313c, 314c). It purports to be written in 365 (rather than 360, as Harward 1932: 164 ff. argued). A date of c. 350 BCE, when there was some discussion of the oral doctrines, seems reasonable.

The *3rd Letter* belongs to the same context as the above and, apparently, is quite well informed about Plato and his activities. The fictitious date is soon after Plato's third visit to Sicily; the actual date of composition is not necessarily very much later. As to the authorship, I am rather more inclined to side with Wilamowitz who thinks that *Ep.* 2–4 were written by the same person, than with Ritter who finds the style of *Ep.* 3 as Platonic as that of *Ep.* 7 and 8.⁷²⁸ The reference to prooimia of laws in this letter (316a) is probably historically correct, and may imply the present Book V of the *Laws* of Plato (above p. 334).

The *4th Letter* can be regarded as a fairly uninteresting appendix to the *3rd Letter*.

The *6th Letter*, though accepted as genuine by many authorities, including Wilamowitz, Geffcken, Field and Leisegang, is decidedly suspect owing to its mystifications and what can be regarded as Platonic reminiscences.⁷²⁹ It purports to be written about 350 BCE, and again its true date is probably not much later. It is of some interest to note that the *6th Letter* seems to have some stylistic affinity with the *7th Letter*.⁷³⁰ Apart from suggesting influence from the *7th Letter*, which

---

726. A rather sweeping argument that all *Letters*, including the *7th*, must be considered spurious, was propounded by Gulley 1972. The last who to my knowledge was prepared to accept *Ep.* 2–13 as genuine was Wichmann (1966, *see* especially 531 n. 61).

727. I.e. *Letters* 1, 5, 9–12, and the additional ones referred to above p. 236.

728  Wilamowitz II 279, Ritter 1910a: 410 ff. A curious example of the mechanical application of 'stylometry' is Michaelson and Morton 1973 who argued on linguistic grounds that *Ep.* 3 is the only one of the *Letters* likely to be genuine, taking the *Apology* as standard.

729. A detailed defense was produced by Brinkmann 1911; but *see* especially Ritter 1910a: 372 ff., Souilhé 1926: XCII ff.

730. Cf. Geffcken II 159, 162, des Places 1940: 132, Neumann-Kerschensteiner 1967: 182 ff. (who consider this a sign of genuineness).

[234] is also probable in other respects, such parallels remind us that Plato's 'late style' was not restricted to Plato personally (cf. above p. 243).

For the *7th Letter, see* above p. 346.

The *8th Letter* forms a kind of continuation to the *7th Letter* and it is fairly commonly accepted as written either by Plato or by the same person as the latter.[731] Although the style of the two letters is often said to be roughly identical (as Ritter 1910a: 410–415 tried to prove), my impression is that it is definitely not so: the *8th Letter* is more rhetorical in tenor.[732] But it should probably be dated fairly soon after the *7th Letter*, i.e. about 350 BCE.

The *13th Letter*, again, is closely related to the *2nd* and *3rd Letter* and may have the same author.[733] Here again the mystifications, biographical intimacies and trivialities tend to exclude a Platonic authorship, although several scholars have
[235] accepted it without question.[734] Wilamowitz (I² 646) thought that it was written by a pupil of Plato as early as about 359 BCE, but I find it hard to believe that any of the Pseudo-Platonic epistles can be assigned a date before the *7th Letter*. Again 350 BCE or thereabouts fms to be a plausible solution. Hence, the mention in the *Letter* (360b) of Πυθαγόρεια and διαιρέσεις is not directly relevant to the dating of *Timaeus* and the *Sophist* (cf. above p. 336 and 341).

---

731. Note e.g. Ritter 1910a: 404 ff., Wilamowitz II 299 ff., Souilhé 1926: LVIII ff. There has been little independent argumentation against the authenticity, but note R. Adam 1909: 32 f., Baer 1957, v. Fritz 1968: 110 ff. On the other hand, Aalders 1969 has argued for authenticity.

732. I argued this in the discussion following Aalder's paper (1971) 1972: 182.

733. Argued notably by Ritter 1910a: 364 ff. For various arguments against authenticity, *see* further Ritter ibid. 328 ff., 366 n. 49, Wilamowitz I 645 f., II 278, Souilhé 1926: LXX ff., Neumann-Kerschensteiner 1967: 221 ff.

734. E.g. Christ 1886, Gomperz II 565, Raeder 1906, Taylor, Field, Harward, des Places and Leisegang.

# A CONCLUDING CHRONOLOGICAL SKETCH

As with my *Studies in the Styles* (above), one essential underlying question of interpretation has been in the present work: for whom were the dialogues originally written? *See* also below, p. 541 ff.

The chronology deducible from the considerations made in the above chapters is, as has been repeatedly stated, a theory. It requires much additional testing, and confirmation or refutation as to detail, before it can be taken as a basis for a fresh interpretation of Plato's work.

Even so, I trust it is no less reliable than any other theory of Platonic chronology so far produced.

∘∘∘ ◯ ∘∘∘

In the table below the place of each dialogue is approximate to a varying degree. The relative order is on the whole better founded than are the absolute dates.

To find the relevant arguments for each case, the reader is advised to consult the Index. *See* also p. 351*.

| BCE | Exoteric | Esoteric | Dubious & spurious |
|---|---|---|---|
| 427 Birth of Plato | | | |
| — | — | — | — |
| 400 Death of Socrates | | | |
| 395 | ('Proto-*Republic*') *Apology* | | |
| 390 Sicily I | (*Republic* I[1]) | | |
| | *Gorgias*[1] *Menexenus*[1] | | |
| 385 | (*Phaedrus*[1]) *Protagoras*[1] | | |

(Continued)

| BCE | Exoteric | Esoteric | Dubious & spurious |
|---|---|---|---|
| | *Symposium¹* | | |
| | *Republic* | | |
| | I—II—begun | | |
| 380 | | *Gorgias²* | |
| | | | *Clitopho* |
| | | *Meno* | |
| | *Phaedo* | | *Crito* |
| | *Symposium²* | | |
| 375 | *Euthydemus* | | (*Protagoras²*) |
| | *Lysis*, *Charmides* | | (*Menexenus²*) |
| | *Theaetetus¹* | | *Laches* |
| | | | *Alcibiades* I |
| | | | *Theages Hippias Minor* |
| 370 | | *Cratylus* | *Ion*   *Amatores* |
| | *Phaedrus²* | | *Eryxias* |
| | | *Theaetetus²* | *Euthyphro* |
| Sicily II | | | |
| 365 | | *Laws begun* | |
| | *Republic* approx. completed | | |
| | | *Parmenides* | |
| Sicily III | | | |
| 360 | | | *Hippias Major* |
| | | *Timaeus*, *Critias* | |
| | | *Sophist*, *Politicus* | |
| 355 | | | (*Republic* edited) |
| Death of Dion | | | *Hipparchus* |
| | *Seventh Letter* | | *Sisyphus* |
| | 'On the Good' | | |
| | | *Philebus* | |
| 350 | | | *Minos* (*Demodocus*) *Epistulae* |
| | | | *De Virtute*, *De Justo* |
| | *Laws* approx. completed | | |
| Death of Plato | | | |
| 345 | | | (*Laws* and *Epinomis* edited) |
| 340 | | | (*Definitiones* begun) |
| Late 4th century | | | (*Alcibiades* II) |
| Early 3rd century | | | (*Axiochus*)   (*Halcyon*)? |

# Studies in Plato's Two-level model

# PREFACE

The present work attempts to combine some new and slightly eccentric approaches to Plato with the determining of an elderly philologist's positions arrived at successively over the past fifty years or more. Plato has intrigued me ever since, in the 1940s, I first became aware of the extraordinary wealth of his thought and its linguistic expression. Later more specific Platonic challenges have come into the foreground.

For practical (or 'technical') reasons, I have not read as much of the recent literature on Plato as I had wanted to in ambitious moments. I trust, however, that I have observed all or most of the significant trends in today's Plato interpretation. At any rate, I am deeply conscious of my debt to international scholarship. Colleagues and friends who bother to look into this book will easily see what I owe to them and their 'schools,' and those whose advice I have especially consulted know how grateful I am for their help. No names need mentioning here.

Helsinki, December 1998

# I

# INTRODUCTORY REMARKS

## Problems

It is no exaggeration to state that Platonic studies are at present in a more unstable flux than ever before. Hence also repetitions and overlaps abound. This is not only because scholarship tends to grow wild around any classic. It would be easy to enumerate several specific reasons why this Proteus of philosophy appeals to such a heterogeneous mass of readers, representing so many different languages, schools, and manners of interpretation, and why so little of reliable consensus has been reached.[1]

Although there is little hope of detailed agreement, it would be helpful if the various 'schools' and scholars would enter on a thorough reconsideration of the premises and principles of their Platonic interpretation. Possibly, then, a new general frame for what is reasonable and what is not would take shape. Possibly we would arrive at new general theories of how the dialogues and the indirect evidence reflect Plato's tenets and methods, new theories of play and dramatic art in his dialogues, and new theories of the purpose, the original character and function, and the chronology of the texts—or arrive at a gradually wider acceptance of old theories.

'En attendant': let us proceed, like Plato, by thought experiments. This study is an attempt to elaborate and ground more firmly some basic theses which

---

1. For overall pictures of recent trends in Plato studies, *see* notably Gonzalez (ed.) 1995: 2–13 and Press 1996 (abundant references). The emphasis is put differently in, say, German, Italian or French works dealing with rival schools (more references in the notes below). Philosophers focusing on the 'late' dialogues easily neglect what has been said about Plato's 'early' philosophy, notably in more 'philological' works; and vice versa. *See* also the frustratingly extensive lists in *L'Année Philologique*.

[1]  I have propounded in various contexts before. A number of issues have intrigued me, particularly:

[2]  (1) The shortcomings of 'developmentalism' and 'stylometry,' and hence the problems of Platonic chronology.[2]
(2) No 'early Socratic' stage?[3]
(3) The apparent lack of dogmaticism and of a doctrinal system in Plato's thought.[4]
(4) How to deal with Plato's ontology ('metaphysics')?[5]
(5) The problems of 'esotericism.'[6]

---

2. In recent years the traditional 'developmentalist' view of Platonic chronology has been challenged from various quarters: see Thesleff above and 1989, Howland 1991, 1998, Press (ed.) 1993, Nails 1995, Kahn 1996. In spite of new attempts to refine 'stylometry' (note Ledger 1989, Brandwood 1990), the weaknesses of this method, except for Plato's 'late style,' are largely admitted. Extreme 'unitarianism' (such as Shorey's) hardly exists today, but a unitaristic tendency is not uncommon, involving adherence to some theory of doctrinal system and intentional withholding of information on Plato's part (cf. below, notes 4 and 6). A vague, non-committal grouping of the dialogues in the corpus as 'early—middle—late—spurious' is still generally accepted, also by 'semi-unitarians' such as Kahn 1996 who combines his theory of 'prolepsis' (cf. below, n. 11) with developmental 'epicycles' (as one critic has put it). These complex issues are all connected with the problems ventilated in the following.

3. This is a thesis more or less vaguely implied by most unitarians, also the Tübingen school, and argued recently, especially against Vlastos, by many scholars, notably by Kahn (since 1981) as a modification of 'developmentalism,' and by myself (since 1982) in connection with reconsiderations of Platonic chronology. Cf. also e.g. Kühn 1977, Montuori 1981 (and later), Sparshott 1992, Nails 1995. The relative sophistication of dialogues such as *Hippias Minor* was argued by Sprague 1962. Other recent authors (also e.g. Irwin 1995: 240 ff.) have taken a modified Vlastosian position, with doubtful success. The problem is involved with the much-debated issue of what we know or believe about the historical Socrates; for references, cf. Kleve 1986, Montuori (ed.) 1992, Brickhouse and Smith 1994, Vander Waerdt (ed.) 1994, Rutherford 1995: 10 ff., 39 ff., Kahn 1996: 1 ff. The young Plato certainly was not influenced only by Socrates or Socratics, and Plato's entire philosophy seems to have been regarded in the Academy as a variant of Socraticism: from this perspective, the boundaries between Socrates and Plato become really blurred (cf. Jatakari 1990, Thesleff below 509). Plato's interests in mathematics (which he apparently did not share with the other Socratics except Euclides) must date at least from the 390s; *Laws* VII 819d only suggests that he did not learn to appreciate mathematics in his early youth. Cf. below, n. 56.

4. Few scholars have in modern times believed that Plato had a rigid doctrinal system, though a tendency to 'dogmaticism' occurs among unitarians or esotericists of various shades. More commonly, the dialogues are taken to prove that Plato had no coherent philosophic 'system,' but that he developed a number of doctrines which he perhaps successively changed. From time to time, doubts have been raised against what are regarded as too 'dogmatic' interpretations of Plato; see e.g. Tejera 1984, 1997 (with important notes, in somewhat eccentric contexts, on the post-Platonic dogmatization of Platonism), Schmitz 1985, Nails 1995, Freydberg 1997, and several of the contributions to Press (ed.) 1993, Gonzalez (ed.) 1995. The premises of such skepticism vary from case to case, but one common basis is the emphasis on the Socratic / Platonic πλανᾶσθαι as a prerequisite of constructive knowledge, known from e.g. *Meno*, *Alcibiades* I and *Parmenides*.

5. This question is faced by most Plato scholars in terms of doctrines, notably the theory of Forms; this work tries to approach it from the perspectives of a background 'vision.'

6. The assumption that important aspects of Plato's philosophy were never committed to writing occurs in recent times in two very different 'schools': (1) the adherents of the

(6) Limits of the 'literal' analytic method of interpretation.[7]  [3]
(7) Advantages of 'literary' and philological methods taking account of the context and artistic, dramatic, playful and ironic elements in the dialogues.[8]
(8) To what extent do the various characters in the dialogues speak for Plato?[9]
(9) The character of Platonic 'dialectic.'[10]  [4]

---

the (chiefly political) philosophy of L. Strauss with its reflections in modern American scholarship (*see* e.g. Bloom and Griswold and now especially Hyland 1995, Ausland 1997 Howland 1998); and (2) the 'Tübingen position' with its reflections especially in Italy (*see* below, n. 158). Kahn's theory of Plato's 'proleptic' withdrawing of doctrines (*see* 1996) is non-esoteristic, but the notion of prolepsis has for long occurred among the Tübingenists.

7. While the methods of analytical philosophy as applied to Plato have produced a wealth of interesting and important observations, the risks have been often noted: if a passage is analyzed out of context or on disputable developmentalist or anachronistic premises, one may easily miss the historical truth or Plato's real intentions (which some find less interesting, to be sure). This has been very often said or implied (though the full consequences are seldom realized), especially by German scholars (e.g. Friedländer, Heitsch, Szlezák, Ferber, Erler), also by Guthrie, several of the contributions to Klagge and Smith (eds.) 1992, and Halliwell 1994 (on Kraut (ed.) 1992); Kahn 1996: 41 f. refers to what he calls the 'fallacy of transparency' (not consistently avoided by himself). The contrasts between 'analytic' and 'anti-analytic' interpretations tend to become less marked today; yet a general tendency prevails to interpret the dialogues 'literally' (cf. the next note).

8. The necessity for a correct and full interpretation to take account of the entire apparatus of Platonic dialogues, including (if possible) the context, has often been emphasized; in recent years the target of criticism has often been the excessively 'literal' or 'analytic' readings (cf. above, n. 7). The focus is put very differently, however. For the 'literary' aspect in particular, cf. the 'Straussian' approach (above, n. 6), Rosen 1985 and elsewhere, Szlezák 1985, and now notably Erler 1994, Shankman (ed.) 1994, Hyland 1995, Nightingale 1995, Rutherford 1995, Zuckert 1996, Kahn 1996, Ausland 1997. The impact of dramatic art on Plato has often been noted; *see* Arieti 1995, Sansone 1996, and especially for comedy, Clay 1994: 37 ff., Nightingale 1995: 172 ff. Following German practice, I have (since 1967) found it important to try to combine 'philological' and 'philosophical' approaches. Press 1993 and 1996 has some good remarks on the 'holism' needed, including abundant references. Unfortunately this vast issue cannot be covered by a single Platonic interpretation. Very much remains to be studied and said about, say, dramatic artistry, the structure of the dialogues (for 'pedimentality,' cf. Thesleff 1993), the characterization of settings and persons, shifts of style (above, 83 ff.), allusions, play (cf. now Freydberg 1997), and irony. In general, however, it can be claimed that the literary artistry of the dialogues serves the treatment of the themes, and not vice versa. The complexity of Plato's thinking, his dialogue style, and its context has been sometimes grasped by modern authors in suggestive formulations. I quote at random: Schmitz II (1985) XIX "Platon ist . . . ein Meister suggestiven Zusammenführens, Pointierens und Zündens von Gedanken, dessen Meisterschaft auf einer unhegeuer breiten Anregbarkeit und Reaktionsfähigkeit beruht; er entwickelt sich nicht folgerecht, beharrt aber auch nicht, sondern reagiert, experimentiert, eignet sich an, moderiert als Präsident die akademische Diskussion . . ."; Kahn 1996: XIII "Plato is the only major philosopher who is also a supreme literary artist. There is no writer more complex, and there is no other philosopher whose work calls for so many levels of interpretation." For the recently realized openness of the discussion in Plato's Academy, *see* especially Schmitz II 1985: 369–375, Nails 1995.

9. *See* now a volume ed. by G. A. Press (2000); also Howland 1998. The role of Socrates in Plato's dialogues has been a major question in the recent discussion referred to above, n. 3.

[4]     (10) Problems of the 'function' and 'publication' of the dialogues; authenticity, revision.[11]
[5]     (11) The growth of the *Republic*: Plato's magnum opus?[12]

---

10. To my knowledge, no systematic study of what Plato understands by 'dialectic' has appeared since the classical monographs of R. Robinson ([2] 1953) and Goldschmidt ([3] 1971), but a wealth of observations have been made on his use of dialogue as a means of logical reasoning. Plato's notion of διαλέγεσθαι (διαλεκτική) slightly differs from earlier uses of the 'method' (some sophists and Zenon) and also from later uses (beginning with Aristotle) which normally imply 'discussions' or oral argumentation where one set of arguments is refuted by another. Plato (following Socrates) saw the 'art of dialectic' as philosopher-conducted reasoning (in what became Academic συνουσία) proceeding in two directions, while the partner is made successively to accept the leader's pushes and moves: an analytic ('diacritic') direction which may include the demonstration of the partner's ignorance, and a synthetic ('synoptic') direction; cf. below p. 451 and my notes in Press (ed.) 2000. For Plato's method of self-testing the arguments, cf. Casertano 1996, Nails 1997. The dialogic principle is here essential, including the criticism, reflection, and new starting points (ἐπιβάσεις, ὁρμαί, cf. *Republic* VI 511b) offered both by the leader and his less well-informed partner (and indeed the reader of the dialogue). Dialectic in this sense is probably Plato's invention though philosophic elenchus may be Socrates' (Murray 1994); but I am not sure the dialogues reflect any lines of development in this respect (as is often asserted, e.g. Kahn 1996: 292 ff).

11. These issues are involved with questions of Plato's biography, e.g. the probably very important evidence of the *7th Letter* (recently discussed by e.g. Schmitz II 1985: 316 ff., Kahn 1996: 388 ff.); part of the doubts about the authenticity of the *Letter* can be met if the digression (like the lecture 'On the Good') is seen as a deliberately 'provocative mystification'; for the enumeration 1–5, *7th Letter* 342a ff., cf. *Philebus* 23d. Different layers can be traced in many dialogues, including the *Republic*. See in general the notes on 'semi-authenticity' and successive revision in Thesleff 1982, 1989. It is important to realize (1) that oral communication was still normal among sophists and philosophers in Plato's times (see e.g. Robb 1994, Nails 1995, H. Tarrant 1996, Waugh 1995); (2) that with the exception of some *Letters* and one or two odd dialogues, the Corpus Platonicum is likely to have taken shape in Plato's lifetime or very soon after his death; and (3) that most Platonic dialogues, whether intended as apology, protreptic, intellectual incitement, or philosophic training, must have been written for a sophisticated audience with well-informed persons present to appreciate and perhaps comment on hints and allusions (cf. above, n. 10, and Thesleff passim). Obviously, all dialogues were not written for the same potential audience(s); cf. e.g. Barker and Warner (eds.) 1992, Usener 1994, Gonzalez 1995. For my part, I am convinced that Plato never did (after the *Apology*) write for an anonymous general public, but for his friends and their friends. The interesting arguments of Kahn 1996 that Plato's dialogues up to the *Symposium* were designed gradually to introduce the readers (protreptically) to his metaphysical vision, are certainly insufficient. Kahn takes for granted that the dialogues were addressed to, and gratefully accepted by, a general educated readership (to whom the theory of immortal Forms would have been a greater shock than the presentation of Socrates the ever-doubting ironist); and that there are more cross-references between the dialogues than references to oral discussions in the Academy (as in the case of *Phaedo* 'developing' the thoughts of *Meno*; though occasionally Kahn admits, as 64 f. or 380 ff., that Plato may operate with different levels of readers). But this is all very problematic, like several other of his assumptions (some discussed critically already in my book of 1982, above, 145 ff.). It seems to me easier to argue (as I did) that most of the so-called 'early' dialogues were written for different audiences and different purposes after the Academy had been 'founded.' Much more careful study and pondering is needed to make sure what in the dialogues reflects a real development in thought (and style), and what are suggestions and experiments for different readers. Note also Ferber's notion (1995) of 'propädeutische Lektüre.' The ultimate aims of Plato's literary activity are still an open question; cf. Cerri 1991 (and Szlezák 1996).

Three general impressions which I have had for a very long time, but which have become acute lately, and which are connected with all of the above points, gave the ultimate impetus to this work: one is the impression that there is always something 'behind' the overtly playful realism of the dialogues; the second is my conviction that Plato always felt strongly the κοινωνία in his universe; and the third is a dissatisfaction with the current views of the nature and status of the theories of 'Forms' and 'Principles.'

There are hardly simple correct answers to any of the above problems; and perhaps few or none can ever be answered quite satisfactorily.

An approximation to truth, however, can probably be achieved by applying more systematically a combination of different approaches to Platonic studies. We are today better equipped than ever before with facts, hypotheses, and interpreting methods regarding Plato; and most serious Platonic scholars can obviously contribute with important arguments, positively or negatively.

Pluralism has indeed its advantages. My hope is a philologist's hope of being able to accumulate ever more arguments ('indications') of different kinds for a hermeneutically cumulative ('spiral') approximation to a more general agreement on how to read and interpret Plato. We have at present a mass of different authorities on Plato. Hardly any school of interpretation is totally dominating any single country or region. International communication works, if not well, at least better all the time. The complexities of Platonic studies are recognized in all or most quarters, so there is hope for an ever broader discussion and, consequently, of some consensus on central issues.

## The present approach

The present work has a philological bias. I am trying to collect a variety of evidence, especially textual evidence, for understanding what Plato 'means.' I am not so much doing mining as archaeological digging, as the saying goes: I am not primarily looking for Platonic ideas or methods relevant to modern philosophy, but for elements to reconstruct 'wie es eigentlich gewesen.' Though I find Plato a fascinating author, I am not an addicted 'Platonist'; I do not see his work as really 'paradigmatic' for our time. Yet I believe that a more correct (historically correct) understanding of Plato will also to some extent be fruitful for current philosophical and existential questions.

The problems enumerated above will be taken into account in the following: in Platonic studies, as in Plato's dialogues, all is somehow involved in all. I am focusing, however, on what I take to be an essential clue to most of my theses, namely the 'two-level model' (especially point 4, above). Cf. the Summary and Conclusions (p. 499 ff.).

---

12. *See* now Thesleff 1997 with references, below p. 519.

## [6]  Who Speaks for Plato?

This is the title of a recent volume where I am trying, in my contribution, to apply the 'two-level model' to the vexed problem of Plato's 'mouthpiece.' *See* above, n. 9.

Like several other contributors to the book, I take it for granted that each (authentic) dialogue represents Plato's views and methods in a very complex way. To detect Plato's own voice behind what is said in the dialogue, and behind how it is said, is one part of the problem; another is to interpret what Plato 'means.'

My argument goes, briefly, as follows. A Platonic dialogue always, to all intents and purposes, has a leader, and this leader is always a Philosopher: normally 'Socrates,' in most of the late dialogues another person with similar qualifications. The dialogue partners of the philosopher are philosophically less well informed, but (normally) educated and intelligent individuals easily identified as types representing various current views or attitudes. From a 'two-level' perspective, the Philosopher stands closer to stable upper-level truths. He does not possess such knowledge fully, however. Philosophy and philosophical dialectic is a continuous two-level process, a process of growing insight that goes on between the Philosopher and his partner. It is the Philosopher who speaks for Plato in the first place, but his partners offer necessary complements to the progress of the argument: their views, their protests and their comments are an essential part of this two-level dialectic. I take it that Plato is, on the whole, committed to what he makes his Socrates say, including hyperboles, more or less experimental aporias, and irony; and there are signs of his being slightly less committed to what the philosophers of the late dialogues say. But I see the actual point of his philosophy and its methods in the Philosopher's 'orientation' from the lower (human) level toward the upper level, and in the continuously varied pushes and moves toward upper-level reality.

It remains to explicate what I mean by the two-level model (Chapters III–IV).

II

## GENERAL NOTES ON CONTRASTS

### Generally human and Greek attitudes

Apart from the theory of Forms, Plato's use of contrasts and opposite concepts does not seem to have been studied. Yet this is where philosophical categorization begins, in Greece and elsewhere.

Human experience, feeling and thought, naturally operate with contrasts. Contrasts are often felt to be mutually exclusive, 'contrary' or 'polar' opposites (as white / black, heaven / earth, hot / cold, friend / enemy, life / death, truth / lie, good / evil etc.); or, introducing some elementary logic, one may speak of 'contradictory' opposites ('binary' options which can often be reduced to negations, as e.g. human / non-human, pleasant / unpleasant, true / untrue). Polar opposites are basic factors in varous ancient religious and intellectual systems traditionally called 'dualistic,' so notably in the very productive Iranian Mithraism with its early affiliations, Zoroastrianism and Zervanism. There are reflections of Iranian dualism in early Greek thought, most obviously in Anaximander and Empedocles; but the logic of ἀντικείμενα was not systematically discussed until after Plato.[13] On the whole, Greek religion and philosophy do not have a very markedly dualistic character.

It seems possible to trace, in the Greek view of the world since the earliest times, a tendency to see opposites as relational or complementary rather than pointedly polarized. For instance, Homer's characters are to a remarkable extent both 'good' and 'bad,' both divine and human (not to say multidimensional); and classical Greek sculptures are mostly meant to be looked at from all sides.

---

13. *See* in general references in Guthrie I 76 ff., II 55 ff. and Isnardi Parente 1995. The question whether opposites are substances or qualities (cf. Aristotle *Phys.* I 187a, 188a19 ff., *Gen. et Corr.* II 329b7 ff.) is probably anachronistic even in Plato's case (but cf. below, 433 ff.). For post-Platonic (Academic?) logical theories of opposites, *see* Aristotle *Categ.* 10–11 and Ps.-Archytas Π. ἀντικειμένων (15 ff. Thesleff).

[7] Without getting lost in such speculations, it should be remembered that 'harmony,' implying a (measurable) balance of contrasts, became a classicistic
[8] catchword in dealing with Greek ideas and aesthetics. Heraclitus reflected on the dynamic equilibrium of opposites, though he emphasized their never-ending internal strife; and Anaxagoras took them to be complementary.

Rather clearly, this line of thought occurs in Pythagorean metaphysics. Aristotle quotes a Pythagorean 'table' (συστοιχίαι) of ten opposites which are said to constitute the world:

limit / unlimited
odd / even
unity / plurality
right / left
male / female
rest / motion
straight / crooked
light / darkness
good / evil
square / oblong

He compares them with the doctrine of Alcmeon of Croton;[14] for Philolaus, see below (413). It has often been said that the Pythagorean table recalls the classical Chinese so-called Yang-Yin table according to which pairs such as the following form the basis of all cosmic processes:[15]

light / darkness
male / female
activity / passivity
hot / cold
dry / wet
hard / soft
odd / even

Whereas the Pythagoreans stressed the equilibrium, the Chinese saw the shifts between the opposites as a continuous series of happenings.

---

14. *Met.* A 986a, cf. *EN* 1096b. Later variations of the Pythagorean model occur in e.g. Eudorus ap. Simpl. in *Phys.* p.181 D (fr. 3–5 Mazzarelli) and Plutarch, *de Is.* 48 f. with a clear Academic bias; cf. Baltes in Dörrie and Baltes IV 402 ff., 473 ff. with further references. It is generally, and perhaps rightly, believed that Plato did not know the Pythagorean συστοιχίαι (and Philolaus' book, cf. Huffman 1993) until late, but he is very likely to have been acquainted with Pythagorean harmony doctrines in the Socratic circle; cf. below.

15. 'Tao': cf. von Fritz 1963: 249 and Guthrie I 252. There are varieties of this both in Confucianism and in Taoism. The Danish physicist Niels Bohr is said to have had Chinese philosophy in view when choosing for his motto 'Contraria sunt complementa.'

Seemingly very far from such complement doctrines, classical Greek ideology (and rhetoric) tends to polarize strongly Hellenes and barbarians, 'us' and 'the others,'[16] the good and the bad, the beautiful and the ugly, etc. (and, in Athens, the worlds of men and women). Some would perhaps see this as an expression of the Greek agonistic 'spirit of competition' or of a 'make-a-choice' attitude typical of the life in a πόλις. However this may be, the tendency to use polar opposites, polarizing, though perhaps not as dominant in advanced thought as the tendency to take opposites as relational or mutually complementary, probably contributed to what might be termed an 'either / or' argumentation in rhetoric. There seems to be a rhetorical trend in Parmenides' arguing from dichotomies for a two-world view (or ultimately a one-world one, by exclusion of the other), and perhaps also in Empedocles' dualism.[17] More evidently, the Parmenidean dichotomic method constitutes a background for 'dialectic' antilogies of the sophists, and for Academic 'dihaeretics.' All in all, classical Greece was a complex laboratory for harmonized and polarized contrasts.

## Two-level contrasts

In the present study, we are concerned with specific kinds of complementary 'opposites' which I shall call two-level contrasts. Human beings naturally tend to attach values to all contrasts, ad hoc or as a principle. From a naive point of view, most things are indeed either good or bad, now or always. In polar (contrary or contradictory) opposition, one term is valued as 'good' and the other consequently is 'bad.' In the great dualistic systems these evaluative principles are practically equal in force, and the war or tension between them never, or seldom, reaches a state of balance; or at least great efforts are required to eventually crush the forces of the evil, as in various ancient (pre-Homeric) heroic myths with more or less religious overtones (or as in the military and political propaganda of classical Greece where religion had a less universal scope).

Complementary opposites, however, can be, and perhaps tend to be, seen as a combination of a better and a less good. Looking at the two tables of complementary 'opposites' (or rather contrasts) quoted above, it will be noticed that the first term of each pair must be regarded (at least by the believers in the metaphysics implied) as being somehow preferable to or dominating the other, if not exactly as being 'better.' This is more obvious in the case of the Pythagorean table than for the Yang-Yin one which implies an eternal alternation. Surely any 'normal' Greek would regard 'right,' 'male,' 'rest,' 'straight,' 'light' and 'good' as 'better'

---

16. The 'otherness' of weird or sinister myths is pushed into the periphery by Homer, but it returns in Hesiod and especially Orphic poetry and legends. 'Otherness' in the cultural context of 5th century Greece is discussed by Hall 1989. A more or less polarized 'us / them' is certainly a fundamental contrast in human societies of all ages.

17. For rhetoric in Parmenides' poem, see Thesleff 1990²: 115.

[10] than their opposites in the table; and considering what we know of Pythagorean speculation, the same would apply to 'limit,' 'odd,' 'unit,' and 'square.'[18]

Two-level contrasts of the kind which I have in view must be kept apart from polar opposites felt to be mutually exclusive or symmetrically complementary. Every reader of the dialogues will easily notice that Plato uses polar opposites abundantly, freely and loosely in very different contexts. Mostly such opposites imply 'good' / 'bad' in accordance with ordinary Greek values: they are part of Greek linguistic usage, often with a touch of pathos or rhetoric. On the other hand, the Academic method of διαίρεσις (with its Prodicean and / or Eleatic background, *see* below, 451, 460), largely operates with such binary dichotomies where one term seemingly excludes the other. Polar opposites, however, seem to belong mainly to Plato's 'lower level': to the human, physical world around us, as will be shown below.

---

18. *See* especially Burkert 1972: 51 and passim.

# III

## PAIRS OF ASYMMETRIC CONTRASTS

### Not two worlds

It is perhaps a trivial fact—yet a fact of considerable significance to the understanding and interpretation of human activities—that ideas or concepts felt to be particularly valuable tend to push forward so as to dominate hierarchically one's thoughts and expressions. In spite of enormous variations, such highly charged ideas (Power, God, Matter, Peace, Pleasure, Right, Beauty, Love, Democracy, and so on and so forth) can be traced in practically all human attitudes. Plato of course has them (starting perhaps with καλὸς κἀγαθός and φιλοσοφία). Like everybody else, he also tends to use them in contrast to their opposites.

But what is not so trivial is the habitual combination of contrasts of a higher and lower 'charge.' It is a common belief since antiquity that Plato's universe consists of 'two different worlds,' separated (χωρίς) and even in conflict, and that the necessary contact between the two worlds formed for him a set of difficult (or according to Aristotle, insolvable) problems. This belief seems to get support from various passages in the dialogues such as *Phaedo* 79a (δύο), *Timaeus* 27d–28a (διαιρετέον), *Republic* VI 509d (δύο).[19]

It seems to me, however, that such a view is seriously misleading. It seems to me—to anticipate the following argument a bit—that Plato visualized his universe (ontologically, metaphysically, existentially, artistically, etc.) in terms of such asymmetric two-level contrasts as intimated above 394 ff. This has been claimed before, by others and by me.[20] The following is an attempt to elaborate

---

19. Cf. Plutarch, *de Def. orac.* 34, Apuleius, *de Plat.* 1.6.193 f., 1.9.200, etc., and the discussion in Dörrie and Baltes IV 256 ff., 272 ff.

20. Cf. de Vogel 1986, and several of the articles in Klagge and Smith (eds.) 1992, Gonzalez (ed.) 1995; Press 1995. Moravcsik 1992 has basically a similar view. The suggestive but narrowly founded interpretation of Freydberg 1997 (following notably Sallis) regarding Plato's 'playfulness' could be easily extended in the same direction; similarly e.g. Nummenmaa 1998, an attempt

[12] this claim and its consequences for our understanding of Plato's philosophy and such specific issues as the theories of Forms and Principal Categories.

Let me emphasize at the outset that it will be necessary to include interpretations of such intuitive 'visions' which some professional philosophers would scarcely consider very relevant, but which a philologist cannot ignore especially in documents of literary art. I repeat: I am trying to interpret not only what is 'said' but to some extent what is 'meant' in the dialogues.[21] And I shall start from very general truths.

It is very important to note, I think, not only that Plato excludes opposites from his conception of True Being and transcendent Form (below, 429 ff., 448 ff.)—there is no metaphysical Form of τὸ κακόν, τὸ αἰσχρόν, etc.—but also that his philosophy and his conception of the Universe are not built on polar opposites. His view of the world as a whole is not dualistic. His is not a 'white / black' world. There is no pointed existential or ontological (metaphysical, etc.) opposition in it between, say, light and darkness, good and evil, or truth and falsity. Even the prisoners in the Cave at least see reflections of light.

## Compare 'divine / human'

From its earliest manifestations, Plato's philosophy is oriented towards the 'good.' Considering its central issues, themes and arguments, it can be claimed that there is more rhetoric than real discussion in the dialogues of what is 'bad' or 'evil.'[22] Indeed, it is to be kept in mind that Plato nearly always is, in one sense or another, concerned with 'values,' but then, on the whole, with what is 'good' and relatively 'less good.' This could be termed an 'orientation towards ideals' (414 ff.). It seems that, for Plato, the orientation was in fact much more important than the exact fixing of the ideal. To make a preliminary illustration of this claim, let us consider one of the common contrasts in the dialogues, namely 'divine' / 'human.' Plato was no theologian, perhaps not even a religious person in the ordinary sense of the word. 'Divine / human' was for him a complementary

[13] two-level opposition where the term 'divine' has to be taken on the whole metaphorically as representing, generally, never-reached perfection of what exists on

---

by a professional psychologist and amateur Platonist to interpret Plato's theories of soul and emotions. Kahn 1996, who accepts the notion of an underlying 'vision,' does in the traditional manner consider (383 ff.) the contrast of 'being / becoming' as dualism; cf. below, n. 46.

21. The 'hermeneutic circle' is no real problem for a philologist who is used to 'spiral' argumentation. Underlying 'visions,' though on the whole implicit, can sometimes be deduced from the manner of expression; e.g. the remarks on the priority of soul in *Phaedrus* 245c ff., or in the simile of the Divided Line.

22. Consider especially *Gorgias, Phaedo* and *Republic*. The attempt in *Phaedrus* 244a ff. to explain μανία, and the rhetorical effusions in *Republic* VIII–IX, are rather exceptional cases of analyzing what is 'bad'; and the theocratic approach in *Laws* to 'evil' is perhaps not wholly and authentically Platonic.

the 'human' level only as various degrees of tentative approximations, and at the [13]
same time as representing a higher level more clearly 'influencing' the lower one
than the lower level can ever influence the higher. God and man and their relation are part of Plato's universe. He is certainly not interested in imagining a
world totally divine or totally human. He appears to take this contrast to be inherently complementary but asymmetric, with one term 'dominating' the other.

## Ten illustrative pairs in the 'earlier' dialogues

In order to illustrate this point a bit further, I have picked out ten pairs of two-level contrasts which seem to stand for some basic constituents in Plato's vision of reality. For a start, I have deliberately left out the πολυθρύλητον contrast of 'Forms' / 'particulars' to which I shall return below (p. 437). I have chosen the following:

divine / human
soul / body
leading / being led
truth / appearance
knowledge / opinion
intellect / senses
defined / undefined
stability / change
one / many
same / different

It could be argued that most or even all of these stand for various aspects of the 'divine / human' contrast. Genetically, however, they seem to come from a far wider grasp of reality than the religious one. For a 'third level' (plants, matter, etc.), *see* below, 412.

I shall try, first, to present typical examples of the occurrence of such asymmetric contrasts in the so-called 'early' and 'middle' dialogues (including *Cratylus*, *Phaedo* and *Phaedrus*), with only occasional reference to the 'later' ones. I shall return later (p. 437) to the 'late' dialogues beginning with the *Theaetetus* and *Parmenides* where new problems and approaches are faced, and also to *Republic* II—X where the two-level model is almost explicitly presented, especially in the simile of the Line. Since I take it for granted that little or nothing can be said with certainty about the relative and absolute chronology of the 'early,' 'middle,' [14]
and 'semi-authentic' dialogues,[23] I shall quote them in a varying order of ad hoc convenience.

---

23. Cf. above, n. 2 and 11.

[14] And I trust the examples are not atypical, and that occasionally adduceable counter-evidence cannot be accumulated against the overall impression that the lists below provide.

## (1) *Divine / human*

The existence of these two levels is taken for granted everywhere in the dialogues, though often conventionally and, as to θεοί and similar expressions, rather metaphorically.[24] Regarding the real character of the gods, the attitude of Plato's Socrates is agnostic, sometimes with a bantering tone, but of course without any sign of outspoken atheism (e.g. *Apology* 26b ff., 41a ff.). Anthropomorphism is censured in the well-known Presocratic manner (apart from *Republic* II–III, most explicitly though ironically in *Euthyphro*; cf. *Phaedrus* 246c where the subsequent quasi-mythic description is allegedly 'truth-like'). Individual gods occur almost exclusively in myths and similar contexts or conventional sayings (cf. *Apology* 20e where Apollo is not mentioned by name). However, though the nuances are open to debate, and though Plato obviously condemns the all-too human qualities of the gods of traditional Greek myth, it can be stated that there are indeed, unavoidably, some human features left in Plato's conception of the divine: the contrast 'divine' / 'human' is basically a complementary one. On the divine level, 'god,' 'gods' possess the excellence, knowledge, purity and powers, notably immortality and spiritual powers, that are lacking among human beings, though such qualities are after all thought of in human terms; see e.g. *Phaedrus* 246d ff., 278d ff. But, on the other hand, it is doubtful whether there can be really useful intellectual contacts between god and man other than human beings having god as a model (the ὁμοίωσις θεῷ principle, known especially from *Theaetetus* and *Republic*, cf. *Phaedrus* 246a; for μανία, see below). It is only in the probably not-wholly-authentic *Laws* and *Alcibiades* II that cultic practices, prayers, etc. are considered necessary.[25] Sometimes there may be a
[15] touch of irony even in the references to Socrates' notoriously odd δαιμόνιον, as there often is in the use of the adjective θεῖος (also θεία μοῖρα, etc.) applied to

---

24. In general, see the comprehensive discussion by Van Camp and Canart 1956 (especially on θεῖος) and the conspectus in François 1957. On the 'divine level' in Plato's thought, see also Szlezák 1998. For the apparently conventional religious beliefs of (Plato's?) Socrates, cf. Brickhouse and Smith 1994: 137 ff.

25. *Symposium* makes many references to conventional cultic practice, but even the stories of Socrates' sudden moments of 'trance' (175a, 220c, cf. 210d) are hardly meant to imply a religious revelation of philosophic matters. Socrates' δαιμόνιον (a relatively active power in *Alcibiades* I and *Theages*) was to Plato a signal, not a speaking voice. In *Phaedrus* there is a playful tone in Socrates' covering his head and his 'nympholepsy' (237a, 238cd, 241e, etc., though the δαιμόνιον gives a serious warning at 242b), surely so in the concluding prayer to Pan (hardly the right god to grant Socrates' wishes in this case). The 'inspiration' of Tynnichus, *Ion* 534d, certainly had nothing to do with philosophy (cf. below, n. 27). Socrates' seemingly futile last words in *Phaedo* (118a) are part of the pedimental composition (cf. 60a, etc.) besides being probably historically true, and hardly reveal a deeper religious conviction on Plato's part.

human matters.[26] At any rate, Plato makes it very clear that his notion of the divine differs from ordinary people's (cf. his somewhat similar handling of σοφία, σοφός). This is particularly obvious in the discussion of inspiration in *Ion* and *Phaedrus* (also *Cratylus*).[27] In *Phaedrus*, where the 'madness' of the inspired is analyzed further, the only type of inspiration taken seriously, philosophy, is being connected with ἔρως; and the same applies to philosophy notably in *Symposium* where the approach is rather different, however, and Diotima's δαίμων is not so much a symbol of 'inspired madness' as a link connecting the human and divine levels and a metaphor for human 'striving' or 'desire' for something better. In *Cratylus*, the nonsensical 'inspired etymologies' of divine matters (especially 397d ff.) must be seen against the background of a more serious acceptance of the two levels (cf. 400d–401a, 408c, 423a, 425c). The *Euthyphro* discusses the logical relations of the two levels by (ironic) elenchus which underlines the fact that it is Socrates rather than Euthyphron who knows how to approach the divine. More extensively, the *Phaedo* operates with a 'divine level' including a large use of the adjective θεῖος, not only in the discussion of immortality and in mythic contexts.[28] 'Divine / human' may be said to stand for the contrast 'everlasting / temporal' (prominent in the theory of Forms and in *Timaeus*). However, it is the living Socrates who with his λόγος dominates most dialogues, even the *Phaedo*: one might say that the Ideal Philosopher here stands for the immortality sought by never-ending argument. All in all, Plato appears to feel the divine and the human level to be somehow 'bound' together, though there is little discussion of the character of this bond except for ἔρως (almost identified with the Philosopher) in *Phaedrus* and *Symposium*.

(2) *Soul / body*

This contrast occurs in most dialogues, sometimes in passing, but always implying that soul is the most valuable term of the two, leading (cf. below, 402) and lasting longer than the body together with which it constitutes the human being.[29] Naturally, none of Plato's characters has the slightest doubt that there exists such an entity as 'soul.' In the soul, mental properties of human beings, such as intelligence (below, 6) and the cardinal virtues and vices, are present or manifested (e.g. *Republic* I 353d ff., *Charmides* 157a ff., *Amatores* 133e ff.; cf. the

---

26. Cf. Kleve 1986, and above, notes 24 and 25.

27. Cf. Tigerstedt 1969. Even the 'corybantic music' at the end of *Crito* (54d) may have a seldom noticed ironical note: could the final point of this dialogue be that Socrates is rather persuaded than convinced?

28. Cf. e.g. 58e, 80a ff., 95c, 107d ff.; also 'heaven / earth' 96cd, etc. (Van Camp and Canart 1956: 415 ff.); and cf. in general Freydberg 1997 on the rise from 'earthbound' myth. But the Idea of τὸ ἀγαθόν never becomes a god to Plato (cf. François 1957: 295 ff.); at *Republic* II 379ab (cf. 380c, X 617e) any god is identified with τὸ ἀγαθόν, 'what is good'; *Republic* VI 509c is banter.

29. For references to the vast literature on Plato's psychology, see Steiner 1992, T. Robinson (1970) 1995. Though soul is made an 'intermediate' and 'created' entity in *Timaeus* (37a ff.), it remains 'above' bodily human matters.

[16] rise to τὸ καλόν *Symposium* 210a ff.; more vaguely, *Crito* 47e, *Symposium* 218a; more specifically, διάνοια / σῶμα *Hippias Minor* 364a). The contrast soul / body is elaborated in *Gorgias* (463e ff. to the end) where Callicles argues from and for the interests of the body without being able to prove that these should be given priority, whereas Socrates forcibly defends the philosopher's orientation towards soul as the better life. The soul's immortality occurs variously as glimpses or hints (note the mythic eschatology in *Gorgias* and *Meno* and Diotima's arguments for mental reproduction in *Symposium*; with playful agnosticism *Apology* 40c ff., cf. *Crito* 44b, 54bc). In *Phaedo* it is discussed as a thesis to be defended, but it is also taken for granted although the various arguments are somehow left open.[30] More unambiguously, the immortality of the soul is 'proved' in *Phaedrus* (245c ff.) from the notions of self-movement (cf. below, 409) and ultimate cause; yet the idea of a Universal Soul is only vaguely implied (cf. below, 464), and a distinction is here made between the divine and the human soul (and the soul / body complex of both categories is illustrated, with a somewhat bizarre stuffing of associations, by the simile of the winged chariot where the driver and the two horses seem to represent the 'tripartite' soul, in itself implying a two-level conception).[31] In *Alcibiades* I 129a ff. it is argued that the human 'self' (we would perhaps say: 'personality') is composed of soul and body with soul as the leading part which gives its character to the person (130c).

(3) *Leading / being led*

This is a common contrast in everyday life. Plato makes considerable use of it, both conventionally and philosophically. It is of course a basic issue wherever political theory or, more generally, the use of power in society is discussed, as in *Gorgias* and *Republic* I (cf. also below, 408). The soul leads the body (above), knowledge
[17] leads the soul (cf. *Meno* 96e,[32] *Protagoras* 352ab, etc.), the teacher (or the dialectician) leads the pupil (or the discussion partner, e.g. *Gorgias* 455d, 458de, 461c); see the variations of this theme in *Protagoras*, *Meno* (where the idea of teaching as recollection is introduced at 81a), *Clitopho*, *Laches*; and *Alcibiades* I and *Theages* (both introducing ἔρως as a factor), *Euthydemus* and *Phaedrus* (with emphasis on the role of the soul). The ideal of the philosopher as leader of the society is sometimes alluded to (cf. *Gorgias* 521d, *Amatores* 138d ff., *Phaedrus* 252de, *Euthydemus* 291b; for the 'Proto-*Republic*,' see below, IV E 7). More abstractly, the contrast of 'leading / being led' is viewed as 'activity / passivity' (ποιεῖν / πάσχειν etc.) in vari-

---

30. None of the arguments in *Phaedo* is meant to be conclusive as such (cf. 106e–107b, and 88c ff.: what the dialogue rather 'proves' is the immortality of Socrates' λόγος); cf. also Kahn 1996: 331. The interrelation of the arguments in *Phaedo*, *Phaedrus* (*Laws*) and *Republic* is still an open question (pace Robinson 1995: 21 ff.); Glaucon's surprise at *Republic* X 608d is ironic from Plato's point of view.

31. A kind of 'tripartition' also occurs in *Protagoras* 352b; cf. the locus classicus *Republic* IV 436a ff., and below, n. 58.

32. At *Meno* 98c ff. the ὀρθὴ δόξα is ἡγημών (implying a pun on ἡγεῖσθαι 'to believe').

ous connections (e.g. *Gorgias* 476b ff., 509de, *Crito* 49a ff., *Hippias Minor* 365d ff., *Euthyphro* 10a ff., *Hippias Major* 302a, *Phaedo* 97c ff., *Phaedrus* passim); cf. the contrast ἑκών / ἄκων (e.g. *Clitopho* 407d, *Crito* 48c ff., *Hippias Minor* 370e ff., *Hippias Major* 296bc) and, more occasionally, such contrasts as 'have / need' (*Symposium* 200b ff.). A higher value normally belongs to what is here given as the first term of such contrasts: to 'lead' or 'to be active' is felt by Plato, as by all Greeks, to be generally 'better' than 'passivity' or 'being led.' The so-called Socratic paradox of 'suffering wrong' being preferable to 'doing wrong' seems to concern situations where 'right' cannot be immediately pursued and the wrongdoer is led by lower motives (i.e. less knowledge of what is 'good') than the sufferer: 'to be a victim of one's pleasures and passions' (the Aristotelian ἀκρασία) is surely not recommendable (*see* notably *Protagoras* 352d ff.). The question of causes (in a wide sense) comes in with the discussion of 'aims' of actions, or the 'model' of a craftsman which is principally 'good' (and with metaphysical extension of this notion, τὸ ἀγαθόν): so especially *Gorgias* 467e ff., 474d ff., 480c, 503e ff. (μίμησις 511a ff.), *Meno* 88e f., *Lysis* 218d–221d, *Hippias Major* 296e ff. and, in general, the treatment of the concepts φιλία (φιλοσοφία) and ἔρως in *Lysis, Symposium*, and *Phaedrus* (cf. 'middle terms,' 415 ff.). For the moving cosmic cause, see *Phaedo* 95e ff. (cf. *Phaedrus* 245c ff.); for 'Forms' as causes, *see* below, 446, 483. It is worth noting that, although the activity and leadership of the traditional gods is, however vaguely, taken for granted (cf. above, 400, and e.g. *Phaedo* 62c ff., 80a ff.; perhaps more ironically, *Cratylus* 396a ff.), they have no prominent role among the causes discussed in the dialogues.

[17]

## (4) *Truth / appearance*

The Greeks are likely to have made much use of this contrast in different kinds of argumentation and rhetoric, though the polar opposition of 'truth' and 'lie (untruth)' was certainly more often resorted to in practice.[33] For the Greeks, and notably for Plato, 'truth' was closely associated with '(true) being' (cf. Ideas, below, 441), though in a less pregnant sense 'being' includes Plato's lower level (*see* e.g. *Phaedo* 79c and especially the discussion in *Sophist* 253b ff., 460). It is clear that for Plato 'truth / appearance (including 'play')' was a basic contrast, involved not only with his theories of knowledge (below, 404) and perception (405), but with his entire manner of reasoning and his dialogue technique. It can be claimed that all of his dialogues manifest the contrast, explicitly or implicitly.[34]

[18]

---

33. The ψεύδεα ... ἐτυμοῖσιν ὅμοια of *Od.* 19.203 (cf. Hesiod, *Th.* 27) have had a long history. For 'untruth' and 'non-being,' cf. below, 412.

34. The most comprehensive discussion of Plato's conception of truth is now in Szaif 1996 who presents a kind of 'two-level model' with 'appearance' on a lower level (*see* especially 183 ff.). Cf. further e.g. Nightingale 1995: 69 ff. (on the Amphion / Zethus contrast in *Gorgias*), Parry 1996: 152 ff. (on *Republic* in particular), and Kahn 1996: 346 ff. (notably on 'true being'). It is well known that Plato does not restrict 'truth' narrowly to judgments (cf. Aristotle, *Met.* A 987b, E 1027b-1028a, etc., *De an.* III 430a); this enables him, like the Eleatics, to operate with paradigmatic ontological truth. For the complexity of Plato's truth in 'play' (including myth), cf. Freydberg 1997.

[18] More specifically, it is illustrated in his dealings with the sophists, notably in *Protagoras* where the frustrating 'hunt' for truth (search is alluded to from the beginning of the dialogue, 309a, 310c) culminates in Socrates' sophistic speech on being 'truly' (ἀληθείᾳ 343d ff.) good; but Protagoras (whose Ἀλήθεια is not explicitly mentioned, but cf. 338c, 348a and *Theaetetus* 161c, 171c, *Cratylus* 391c) and the other sophists hide behind appearances (*see* especially 314e ff., 328d, the play with styles, and Socrates' ambivalent remarks on ἡ τοῦ φαινομένου δύναμις 356d) rather more than Socrates who at least makes attempts at dialectic analyses. *Hippias Major* also elaborates this contrast (note 294a ff.), and *Cratylus* abounds in it (note especially 386de, 400d ff., 436c ff.), whereas *Hippias Minor* and *Euthydemus* are dominated by the contrast of never-reached 'truth' and polarized 'falsity' (though *Euthydemus* also refers to 'truth / play,' e.g. 283b). The 'sophistic' contrast φύσει / νόμῳ which Plato normally uses with some irony (e.g. *Gorgias* 482c ff., 489ab, *Protagoras* 337cd, also φύσει / θέσει in *Cratylus* 383a ff.; developed into the alleged aporia φύσει / διδακτόν in *Protagoras* and *Meno*; but exceptionally νόμοι / ἄνθρωποι *Crito* 54bc)[35] can be seen as a variety of 'truth / appearance.' 'Truth / fiction, myth' is another old contrast, relevant to some Presocratics, and extensively employed by Plato, especially in connection with his 'myths,' though with little explicit discussion outside the *Phaedrus* (note here the opening conversation 229c ff., the various remarks on philosophy vs. fiction beginning at 235b, and on truth vs. ὁμοιώματα 249d ff.) and the well-known chapters in *Republic* II–III, X and *Timaeus*. Some further remarks in e.g. *Phaedo* 61b ff. (cf. 65b ff., on 'truth and purity' vs. delusion), *Symposium* 198b ff., 200ab, 212a; more ironically, *Euthyphro* 5e ff. (cf. *Ion*); a playful note on εἰκών *Meno* 80c. Rhetoric represents ungrounded persuasion, not philosophical truth: cf. e.g. ἀληθές / πιθανόν at the
[19] opening of *Apology*, the use of πειθώ and πιθανόν in *Gorgias* 452e ff., the curious prominence of πείθειν in *Crito* (vs. δόξαι 46c ff.), the discussion of rhetoric in *Phaedrus* 265a, 272d ff. and elsewhere, and the entire *Menexenus*. Of particular philosophical interest is the contrast 'truth / hypothesis' which occurs in *Euthyphro* 9de, 11c and *Hippias Major* 303e; cf, *Meno* 86e ff., *Charmides* 163a, *Phaedo* 100b ff., 107b ff (cf. *Republic* VI 510b ff.). On the whole, Plato seems to think that 'truth' (whether ontological or cognitive) can be somehow reached behind, but through, 'appearances' (cf. also *Gorgias* 487e).

(5) *Knowledge / opinion*

The pointed contrast between the worlds of truth (absolute ὄν, ἀλήθεια) and belief (δόξα, πίστις which is recognized as cognate with πείθειν), which was first made by the Eleatics (cf. *Phaedrus* 262c), occurs in practically all Platonic dialogues (cf. above, 403). In more specifically epistemological contexts, Plato naturally connects 'knowledge' with truth, and 'opinion,' normally, with the level of appearance.

---

35. For κόσμος as 'cosmic,' not human 'order,' cf. *Gorgias* 439d ff., 504a ff. In *Republic* X 604d νόμος is coupled with λόγος vs. πάθος.

Disregarding now the much-debated details of the so-called ἐπιστήμη / δόξα contrast,[36] it may be noted that the most comprehensive treatment of it outside *Republic* V and *Theaetetus,* namely *Meno* 85c ff., 97a ff., gradually introduces the possibility of an ἀληθὴς δόξα on the way towards truth (*Phaedo* 66a ff. is more cryptic). Plato's terminology is notoriously inconsistent here. The first term of the contrast is normally expressed by a form of εἰδέναι (as in *Meno,* notably at 71c) or ἐπίστασθαι (ἐπιστήμη in *Meno* 97a ff., especially when specialist knowledge or 'know-how' is concerned, as in *Gorgias* 454c ff. where also μάθησις,[37] 462bc where also τέχνη contrasted to ἐμπειρία; *Protagoras* 344e ff. where also μάθησις, *Charmides* 166a ff.), also γιγνώσκειν (e.g. *Laches* 178b, *Meno* 96e, rarely γνῶσις, as *Cratylus* 440ab), whereas σοφία usually has an ironic connotation of mock-wisdom (cf. *Apology* 20d ff., *Euthyphro, Protagoras* and *Euthydemus* passim, *Meno* 70a ff., *Hippias Minor* 363a; but more seriously σοφία / ἀμαθία *Theages* 123d, σοφοί / δοξόσοφοι *Phaedrus* 275b) to be contrasted with Socratic φιλοσοφία (*see* especially *Lysis* 218ab, *Symposium* 203d ff.).[38] For πίστις in a sense corresponding to δόξα, cf. *Gorgias* 454c ff. (486c, ἡδονή 494c ff.); and ἡγεῖσθαι (e.g. *Meno* 96e), οἴεσθαι (e.g. *Charmides* 166d), φαίνεσθαι and δοκεῖν are commonly used in contrast to 'knowing (what).' For the 'madness' of the inspired, *see* above, 401 (cf. *Meno* 92b ff. etc., οἶδα / μάντις *Symposium* 173cd, ὄναρ 175de, etc.; but μαίνεσθαι is sometimes more loosely contrasted to knowing, cf. *Euthyphro* 4ab, *Alcibiades* I 111a ff.). In *Symposium* 202c ff. Diotima inserts the level of δοξάζειν with λόγος (as corresponding to φιλοσοφία) between knowledge and ignorance (cf. *Euthydemus* 286d ff., 305a ff., *Phaedrus* 238bc; and the explicit discussion in *Theaetetus* 201c ff.).

[19]

[20]

## (6) Intellect / senses

This contrast can be regarded as a logical corollary of most of the contrasts discussed so far. However, it is rather implicit in the dialogues except when it becomes pointedly ventilated in *Gorgias, Phaedrus, Symposium,* and especially *Phaedo* (and *Theaetetus* and *Republic*). Socrates, of course, always stands for intellectualism and, thus, rises above the erotic or otherwise sensual interests or feelings of his environment which, to be sure, are not alien to him: cf. in general *Lysis, Charmides, Amatores, Protagoras, Hippias Major,* and *Republic* I. In *Protagoras* 350c ff. the analysis of courage leads to a discussion of pleasure and pain and so to the famous 'hedonistic calculus' which, indeed somewhat playfully, implies the priority of measuring (356d) over passion. In *Charmides* 159a, δόξα becomes connected to αἴσθησις (cf. 167b–168c). In *Republic* I and *Gorgias* various aspects of brutality (personified by Thrasymachus and Callicles) are contrasted to the gentle intellectualism of Socrates (cf. the bantering introductions and conclusions

---

36. Discussed in every comprehensive work on Plato. It occurs also in the spuria, e.g. *Clitopho* 409c.

37. The verb μανθάνειν (or μάθημα) does not seem to occur in the 'knowledge / opinion' context,

38. On this contrast, *see* Brickhouse and Smith 1994: 30 ff.

[20] of *Republic* I and *Charmides*). In *Gorgias* (especially 494c ff., 501d ff., 513de, 521d) indulgence in pleasure in particular is being contrasted to intellectual life. This 'moralistic' attitude of Plato seems to be motivated principally by the unquestioned assumption that sense perception and passions disturb pure thought (cf. e.g. *Gorgias* 494c ff. ἐπιστήμη, 506c ff. σωφροσύνη, etc., *Phaedrus* 241ab νοῦς, 250c ff. φρόνησις; for *Phaedo, see* below), certainly not motivated by divine law or conventional morals. The *Phaedrus* has sensual seduction as one of its basic themes, and Socrates' musings on the soul and its intellectual 'driver' dominate the center (cf. above, 401). Diotima's 'ladder,' *Symposium* 210a ff., has become for all ages a symbol of sublimated intellectualism; in fact this dialogue illustrates in various ways Socrates' distancing himself from physical pleasures, although no total abstinence or refusal come into question on his part.[39] The somewhat more detailed treatment of sense perception in *Phaedo* (especially 58e ff., 64d ff., 75a ff., 79a ff.) amounts to a demonstration of the soul's proper tendency to free itself from bodily entanglements and the mixture of feelings ('opposite' reactions) which occur on the bodily level only (cf. 102b ff., also *Gorgias* 493a, etc.), while 'measuring' is an innate capacity of the soul *(Phaedo* 74d ff., below, 435, 468). Note also the fact that concrete things belonging to the prison and Socrates' person (his family, the fetters, the cup of poison, the trivial orders, etc.) and the concrete expressions of sorrow are, as it were, pushed to the beginning and end of the dialogue, whereas 

[21] the main part around the center is concerned only with λόγοι.[40] The disturbing influence of the senses is an important sub-theme in this dialogue (cf. 81b ff.).—It is interesting that the most refined of the human senses, sight, is not very much discussed in these 'earlier' dialogues (but cf. *Republic* VI, *Timaeus* 44d ff.). Socrates professes to admire the sight of beautiful bodies and sublimated sight is, by implication, an essential part of 'Diotima's mystery' (apart from *Symposium, see* notably the openings of *Lysis* and *Charmides*) and the theory of 'Forms'; but in fact the beauty of idyllic nature has only ironic appeal to Socrates (*Phaedrus* 230b ff.), and the watching of the Bendis festival (opening and end of *Republic* I) can be taken as a playful introduction to the philosophical θεωρία of the central books of *Republic*. In *Phaedo* 79a ff., however, a very clear distinction is made between the two ontological levels precisely in terms of τὸ ἀϊδές / τὸ ὁρατόν.[41] In *Phaedrus* 246c ff. gods are said to be in fact invisible. Perhaps, since Plato (especially in *Republic* and 'later') also needs the metaphor of 'seeing' for the invisible, he prefers not to emphasize or develop the idea of the 'invisible' character of the νοητά (*Phaedo* 80b, etc.) or otherwise non-concrete things that he considered to be more valuable than the concrete and variegated world around us.

---

39. This is notable especially in the case of Alcibiades, somewhat apologetically introduced by Plato; cf. the openings of *Alcibiades* I and *Protagoras*. Plato's awareness of a wide register of emotions is pointed out by Nummenmaa 1998.—In Diotima's mystery teaching, and in the central books of *Republic*, 'seeing' is of course metaphoric.

40. *See* Thesleff above, 111 ff. and 1993: 25 on the 'pedimental composition.

41. Though the adjective ἀϊδής probably alludes to Ἅιδης (cf. *Gorgias* 493b and, rather nonsensically, *Cratylus* 404b), and perhaps to εἶδος, Plato is here concerned with the 'invisible' in general.

## (7) Defined / undefined

The 'Socratic' search for definition normally amounts to finding the 'limits' or 'ends' for an indeterminate use of words. Quite often (but inconsistently) ὅρος or (δι)ορίζειν refer to such tentative 'definitions': cf. e.g. *Gorgias* 453ab (with αὐτὸ τοῦτο), 470b, 521a, *Republic* I 331d, 345c, *Phaedrus* 237d, 263d, 277b, *Charmides* 163d, *Euthyphro* 9cd. In the methodologically important *Meno*, the process of defining one single εἶδος of ἀρετή is illustrated by the image of reaching the τελευτή, the πέρας,[42] or the ἔσχατον of its σχῆμα (72a–76a). Plato's Socrates sometimes stresses the distinction between 'substance' and 'qualification, property' (τίς / ποῖος etc.): cf. *Gorgias* 448e (453e ff.), *Meno* 71a ff., 86d ff., 100b, *Symposium* 199cd, 201de, *Cratylus* 381bc, 423ab. In *Hippias Major* 300a ff. and *Euthyphro* 10e ff, this contrast is expressed by the terms οὐσία / πάθος which carry associations to a two-level model (cf. above, 402).[43] For μετέχειν, παρεῖναι, etc. in connection with the theory of Forms, *see* n. 111; for the two-level model inherent in two-level dialectic, *see* p. 451. Plato's distaste for the undefined, indeterminate, 'not yet defined' and seemingly limitless can perhaps be read from the 'mythic' simile of the sieve in *Gorgias* 493a–d: here the endless incontinence of the ἀκόλαστοι is contrasted to the controlled life of the κόσμιοι. At any rate, in his view definition is very much preferable to the indeterminate, be it 'not yet defined' or just unmeasurable, chaotic.

## (8) Stability / change

It is rather obvious that people on the whole prefer stability to ('too much') change, however appreciated variation may be. From a philosophical and social as well as generally human (and specifically biographical)[44] perspective, this was clearly and emphatically Plato's position. In dialogues with a lively setting or otherwise much movement and changes in argument, it is Socrates who is seeking stability, but often implicitly so. Thus, in *Republic* I we may note the contrasting of the attitudes of Thrasymachus and Socrates, violence and gentleness, at the center of the dialogue (336b ff.); and in the midst of the confusing movements in *Protagoras*, there are ironic glimpses of a stable εἶναι, διαμένειν vs. γίγνεσθαι in Socrates' 'sophistic' speech (344bc) which answers the great speech of Protagoras.

---

42. Cf. *Parmenides* 137d, 165a, etc. In the Pythagorean sense of metaphysical Limit, πέρας does not occur in Plato before *Philebus* (16c, 24a, etc.). In fact Philolaus has περαίνοντα vs. ἄπειρα as two classes of entities constituting the harmony (Vors. 44 B 1, Huffman 1993 ad l.), not πέρας. But this section in *Meno* may reflect indirectly the Pythagorean idea of Limit being more valuable than the Unlimited (cf. 81a ff.). Kahn 1996: 93 ff., 150 ff. argues that 'definition' was really Plato's, not Socrates', invention; he may be right about the principle of 'defining,' but cf. below, 409.

43. For οὐσία / πάθος, cf. Centrone 1995. In *Hippias Major* 294b (cf. 296b ff.), as in *Theaetetus* 182a, τὸ ποιοῦν is a pun on ποιόν (ποιότης); cf. *Cratylus* 416cd καλοῦν = καλόν. But this reflects a 'Heraclitan' view, different from Plato's classing 'activity' over 'passivity'.

44. For details about Plato's traumatic youth, *see* Thesleff above, 167 ff.; also Kahn 1996: 48 ff.

[22] 'Being / becoming' is often said to be a fundamental contrast in Plato's thought, but then 'being' is taken in its absolute sense (above, 403) which is not the dominant one. In *Euthydemus,* Socrates suddenly brings us near the end of the argument (ἐπὶ τέλει 291b) by introducing the 'kingly art' but then, ironically, falls back again into the 'labyrinth.' More explicitly, in the *Gorgias,* Socrates argues for τάξις and κόσμος in life, referring to a 'cosmic' frame (504a ff., see notably the protreptic piece 507c–508c). In the central vision of the *Phaedrus,* the gods stand still (ἔστησαν, στάσας 247bc) at the highest point of heaven. In *Symposium,* where there surely is stability (at least by implication) at the top of Diotima's ladder 207c ff., the frame stories refer to Socrates' notorious stand-stills (175ab, cf. 220cd). Unchanging Being is sometimes confronted with the world of change in contexts where Forms are not directly involved: cf. e.g. *Meno* 81a ff. (myth), *Hippias Major* 296e ff., *Charmides* 168d ff., *Phaedrus* 247e, and *Phaedo* passim (e.g. 62e, 95e ff.; here the theory of Forms, however, comes in at 65d). In *Cratylus,* the ever-present 'Heraclitan' flux (γένεσις, φορά, etc.) is, with playful frustration, contrasted to
[23] a permanence which is so difficult to reach; cf. 358e ff. (βεβαιότης), 411b–422c (μόνιμον, βέβαιον),[45] 432bc; but towards the end of the dialogue glimpses of the theory of Forms begin to offer some stability, 437a ff.; note the punning use of στάσις 426cd, cf. 438cd (with στασιάζειν).[46] The Socratic search is sometimes, more or less ironically, compared to a wandering around never-reached knowledge, cf. *Alcibiades* I 117b ff., *Hippias Minor* 376c, *Hipparchus* 228a, *Hippias Major* 304c; the δόξαι are like the statues of Daedalus: They keep moving until they are bound (δεδεμένα, παραμένει) by λογισμός, *Meno* 97d–98c; and Socrates is able to keep other people's 'statues' moving too, *Euthyphro* 11b-d (cf. 15bc). In *Meno* 80ab, the simile of the ray-fish illustrates the bringing of negative elenchus to a standstill after which constructive argumentation can begin; cf. *Phaedo* 96b, Socrates searching for the ἠρεμεῖν of knowledge. In *Phaedrus* 261d, the 'Elean Palamedes' (= Zenon?) is said to have identified like and unlike, one and many, and rest and movement (μένοντα, and φερόμενα); cf. Categories, below p. 457 ff. For Plato, it is through movement that rest can be reached.

*(9) One / many*

This contrast seems to have intrigued most Presocratics,[47] and the problem of 'unity' in particular interested the Pythagoreans and Eleatics. Plato makes a very wide use of the contrast 'one / many,' quite apart from the specific issues

---

45. Note at 418e the play with ἀγαθοῦ ἰδέα as δεσμός, κώλυμα φορᾶς.
46. Loraux 1987. It is interesting that στάσις occurs in *Republic* only in the sense of 'uproar' (unless VIII 545d στάσις / κινηθῆναι is playfully ambiguous); for the categorial sense of 'standstill' *(Parmenides* 129e, etc.) see below, 458.—Kahn 1996 (XVI, 345f, 383 ff.) regards 'being / becoming' as the central feature in Plato's philosophic vision; this is certainly a too narrow approach.
47. *See* the references in *Vors.* III DK, cf. Krämer 1959: 501 ff. For Euclides, cf. Kahn 1996: 12–15. *See* in general McCabe 1994.

connected with the 'Forms.' It is easy to note, for instance, a basic distinction between the unique Philosopher, as represented by Socrates, and the many 'others' (pointed out in *Gorgias* 472b, 475e, 521d, etc.); or, more generally, between the specialist and 'the rest' (sometimes οἱ πολλοί also in a social or political sense, cf. e.g. *Crito* 46e ff., 48a ff., *Apology* 25b, *Laches* 184de, *Phaedo* 64b, *Gorgias* 488d ff.). In all dialogues the confrontation of Socrates with one, two, or sometimes several interlocutors implies a two-level antithesis of the Philosopher who alone (however ironically or ambiguously) stands against common beliefs of the 'others' or of the 'many.' Though Plato's sympathies are with philosophy rather than with the ideas of 'others,' it can be claimed that it is, in a sense, this tension between 'one' and 'many' that motivates his philosophizing.[48] More specifically, the need of 'one' definition after 'many' mistaken attempts is discussed in *Meno* 72a ff. (cf. 77a and *Euthyphro* 6d, *Euthydemus* 282e). The relation of the whole to its parts is ventilated, somewhat cryptically, in *Protagoras* 329c ff. (cf. 349a ff., *Cratylus* 424de, *Theaetetus* 205c ff.; in *Phaedrus* 261d the Eleatic problem is playfully alluded to). Two-way dialectic implies a differentiation of ἕν and πολλά: *Phaedrus* 265d ff., 273de, 277b (cf. 249bc and *Phaedo* 78de). A Form (taken as 'Idea,' below) is always unique, versus the multitude of particulars (cf. below, 441 ff., and e.g. *Cratylus* 439c ff., *Symposium* 211ab, e); but interestingly, a Form is at the same time general in character (illustrated by the metaphor of πέλαγος versus παρ' ἑνί *Symposium* 210d).[49] It cannot be doubted that Plato's preferences lay with 'unity,' not with 'plurality,' though he was all his life struggling with the logical (and metaphysical) problems involved in this contrast.

[23]

[24]

## (10) *Same / different*

It is no far cry from 'stability' and 'unity' to the notion of 'the same.' Among the Presocratics, Heraclitus and the Eleatics especially operated with identifications, the former in paradoxes intimating a 'higher unity' beyond all change (e.g. B 15, 49a, 59 DK), the latter in their logic of 'henology' (sometimes contrasted to ἕτερον, e.g. Parmenides B 3, 8.57 f., Zenon B 1–2 DK). Some sophists (Prodicus and the erists above all) were notoriously entangled in problems of identification. Plato's Socrates professes to seek what is ταὐτόν in different uses of words: cf. *Meno* 75ab (cf. 72a ff., 75e), *Laches* 191e ff., *Amatores* 138b, *Lysis* 222bc, also *Apology* 26a ff.; and e.g. *Gorgias* 459b, 460b where 'rhetoric' is approached dihaeretically. There was a misunderstanding about this, Plato suggests. People believe that Socrates is always 'saying the same about the same trivial matters,'

---

48. Note the careful elaboration of the points of Protagoras, Callicles, and Plato's brothers who all stand for 'commonly accepted' views. Cf. Thesleff in Press (ed.) 2000: 53 ff.
49. And the 'ladder' starts with 'one,' 210a. The increasing 'width' makes 'generous philosophy' (φιλοσοφία ἄφθονος, with a pun on the meaning 'limitless') possible, 210d. Cf below, on the problems of one / many in the theory of Forms, 452 ff.

[24] cf. *Gorgias* 473a, *Symposium* 221e;[50] but in fact the λόγος of philosophy (contrary to the λόγοι of Alcibiades and others) is always about 'the same,' *Gorgias* 482a ff. (cf. 491b, 509a, 527d, *Crito* 46d); this is one of the indications of the high status of 'the same' in Plato's thought. He often contrasts τὸ αὐτό with ἕτερον (or ἄλλο), e.g. *Gorgias* 488d ff., *Protagoras* 329cd, *Ion* 531a ff., 537c ff., cf. *Charmides* 165e ff., *Alcibiades* I 129c ff., *Symposium* 207c ff. (ἕτερον secondary to τὸ αὐτό!), *Euthydemus* 301a ff.; however, ἕτερον (θάτερον) does not seem to occur as a 'categorial' term 'before' *Parmenides* (cf. below, p. 457). Moreover, Plato's Socrates appears to associate the notions of 'same' (ὁ αὐτός), 'self' (αὐτὸς ὁ, ἑαυτόν), and 'in itself' (καθ' αὐτό, etc.) in an almost mystical manner: cf. *Apology* 26c, 27e, 36c and the Delphic maxim (not explicitly quoted in *Apology*, but cf. 21a; cf. *Protagoras* 343b, *Charmides* 164e f., *Republic* IV 436bc); in *Alcibiades* I the ideas of 'taking care of oneself and 'knowing oneself (123d ff., 126a ff.) are developed into the question of what αὐτὸ ταὐτό
[25] really implies (129bc, cf. 130d); cf. the treatment of the problem of 'knowledge of knowledge' in *Charmides* (161e, 164a ff., 168a ff.) and the play with 'identification' in *Euthydemus* (e.g. 279e ff.). Having referred τὸ αὐτό to the immortal level (vs. mortal ἕτερον), Diotima passes over to the 'mystery proper' with τὸ καλόν not being any longer ἐν ἑτέρῳ τινί, but always αὐτὸ καθ' αὐτὸ μεθ' αὑτοῦ μονοειδές (*Symposium* 207c ff., 211ab). Cf. also the self-moving soul as the ultimate cause of movement in *Phaedrus* 245c (and *Laws* X 894b ff.; cf. *Theaetetus* 185de). The rise of the 'self' terminology in connection with the theory of Forms is likely to be based on Socrates' above-mentioned search for τὸ αὐτό (cf. *Euthydemus* 301a with ἕτερον, *Protagoras* 330de (cf. 360a), *Lysis* 220bc, *Meno* 72c ff., 75e, *Gorgias* 481cd, *Euthyphro* 5d, 6d, *Hippias Major* 286d, 288a, etc., and notably *Phaedo* 65 a ff., 100b ff.); see below, 442. Occasionally we encounter the distinction πρὸς αὐτό / πρὸς ἄλλο (ἕτερον) and the like, i.e. 'absolute' / 'relative': cf. *Gorgias* 451c, *Charmides* 169a ff., *Euthydemus* 281de (καθ' αὑτά), *Phaedo* 82e ff. (δι' αὑτῆς), *Cratylus* 438d ff. (δι' αὑτόν). It is easy to see that the notion of 'the same' (and 'self') is more interesting and important to Plato than 'difference' though, again, it is from the latter that the former can be reached. 'Like likes like' is a very ancient principle; similarly, the concept ἴσον, ἰσότης, is valued higher than ἄνισον (cf. e.g. *Phaedo* 74c, *Gorgias* 508a).[51] Cf, further the common association of φίλον with οἰκεῖον, ὅμοιον vs. ἀλλότριον, (e.g. *Protagoras* 345d ff., *Lysis* 214a ff., *Symposium* 186b ff.; ironically, *Euthyphro* 4b).

---

50. Also Xenophon, *Mem.* IV 4.6.
51. Plato often operates, loosely, with the 'like likes like' principle; cf. *Republic* V–VII, *Theaetetus* (beginning with the likeness of Theaitetos to Socrates, 144de), *Timaeus*, and further e.g. *Lysis* 214b ff., *Protagoras* 337cd, *Symposium* 186c (medical physics, cf. *Timaeus* 81e ff.). It goes without saying that modern approaches to the problem of 'sameness' vs. difference (e.g. Wiggins 1980) are far more sophisticated than Plato ever dreamt of being. Like 'same,' 'self' (cf. Goldin 1993), geometrical ἰσότης has a kind of mystical fascination for Plato; cf. the ἄνισα τμήματα of the Line, *Republic* VI 509d, and the problematic ἰσονομία *7th Letter* 326d, 336d. Cf. Thesleff 1984: 25 (with further references). In fact the exclusivity of Plato's Academy (in spite of its internal openness; cf. Nails 1995) and the protreptic aspect of the dialogues, may be taken as a sign of 'self-orientation'; cf. also the use of the term συνουσία (*see* des Places 1964 s.v.).

# IV

## TWO LEVELS

### Other examples

The ten pairs of unequal (asymmetric) contrasts whose occurrence was exemplified above, are in themselves only examples. It can be safely claimed, however, that they are typical examples of Plato's view of reality—remarkably enough not observed in Academic and Aristotelian theories of opposites (cf. Aristotle *De gen.* 329b ff., *Categ.* 10–11; Archytas *De oppos.*).

Several other pairs of a similar character are not uncommonly found in the so-called early and middle dialogues: take, for instance, τέχνη / ἐμπειρία in *Gorgias* (cf. the contrasts above); model / copy; good / useful (e.g. *Republic* I, *Hippias Major*); innate / taught (cf. *Meno*); heaven / earth; pure / mixed (cf. *Phaedo*); man / woman; healthy / sick; sober / drunk; introvert / extrovert (the last four especially in *Symposium*). Ultimately the mutual involvement of seriousness and play in Plato's ways of reasoning (symbolized e.g. by the contrast παιδεία / παιδιά) represents a similar double-level conception (cf. above, 389). However, the ten pairs chosen here may be taken as typically representing most other two-level pairs found in Plato. And it should be noted that examples commonly occur in so-called 'early' dialogues as well as in so-called 'middle' ones (although *Republic* and *Theaetetus* were not as a rule included in the analyses above), and indeed in the 'late' dialogues.

### Two levels—and a third?

By changing the above order a bit, the contrasts can be arranged as a series which illustrates, perhaps more suggestively than mere lists, what Plato's 'two-level vision' appears to concern:

| one | same | stable | divine | soul | leading | intellect | truth | knowledge | defined |
|---|---|---|---|---|---|---|---|---|---|
| many | different | changing | human | body | being-led | senses | appearance | opinion | undefined |

[27]  I have presented the schema approximately in this shape elsewhere.[52]

It may now be claimed that a 'third level' can be easily imagined 'beneath' the two others, and that the second level then would seem to blur into a somewhat shady general category of 'intermediates.' It is true that one could think of, for instance, the following series as a third level:

---

infinite negation chaotic vegetative matter obstructive senseless lie ignorance unmeasurable

---

It is also true that Plato sometimes seems to visualize what is here called the 'lower level' (level two) as a μέσον; note especially *Symposium* 202a ff.: as ὀρθὴ δόξα operates between φρόνησις and ἀμαθία, so does Eros between the beautiful and the ugly, between god and man (in fact inconsistent rhetoric, as if 'ignorance,' 'ugly' and 'human' were on the same level). He often admits that there is a neutral area in human life between 'good' and 'bad' (e.g. *Gorgias* 467e ff., a μεταξύ yet oriented towards good; *Protagoras* 346c–e, ironically playful; *Lysis* 216de, 220bc; *Euthydemus* 305e–306d, man between good and bad). It is sometimes said that life at its best is for Plato, as for Aristotle, a balance between opposites or extremes;[53] but then the physical reality is meant in the first place, not the basic issues of Plato's 'vision' (cf. below, 427 ff.).

[28]  No doubt, in Plato's 'late' philosophy the third level tends to receive some philosophic relevance: in *Timaeus* the infinite, unmeasurable, chaotic, senseless, obstructive 'matter,'[54] and also animals and plants; in *Parmenides, Sophist, Politicus* opposites, lie, non-being and negation; and in *Philebus* and the ἄγραφα, account is taken of the 'limitless.' In general, the focus is here on the μέσον and μέτριον. But these are after all, it seems to me, rather tentative pushes into the realm of the physical world (cf. below, 457 ff.). I am claiming that Plato's ontology was not based on a dualism of polar opposites and that the 'bottom level' did not stand for a consistent negative Principle in any sense. It may be provisionally stated here that the 'third' (or bottom) level never became an area of central interest to Plato, any more than, say, the dichotomy of virtue and vice, emphasized for the sake of argument in many dialogues, ever led to deeper reflections about the nature of the 'bad' or 'evil' (or indeed of total 'ignorance,' if there could be such a state of the soul).[55]

---

52. Thesleff 1993: 21 and elsewhere. 'Invisible / visible' is now put under 'intellect / senses,' and 'defined / undefined' has been added for reasons which will appear later (p. 470).—For Kahn 1996, *see* above, n. 46.—I do not consider the ἐπέκεινα τῆς οὐσίας (*Republic* VI 509b) relevant here.

53. This is one of the running themes of Krämer 1959 who connects it with the 'esoteric' doctrine of ἕν / ἀόριστος δυάς taken as opposites, not a two-level contrast.

54. The Aristotelian ὕλη gets an important position in post-Platonic Platonism; references in Dörrie and Baltes IV 489 ff.

55. Cf. e.g. Shorey 1903: 9 and n. 18; Jantzen 1992. Souilhé 1919, whose views I largely agree with, lays unnecessary emphasis on the 'intermediate' character of what I consider to be Plato's 'lower' level; cf. above, n. 22 and 53. For 'ideal' opposites, cf. below, 435, 448. The apparent dualism of the two 'paradigms' of life in *Theaetetus* 176e (a pointed contrast where the central issue is the ὁμοίωσις θεῷ 176b) and the Cronus myth in *Politicus* 268d–275b (where the 'world

# The two principal levels and their background in Greek thought [28]

As already intimated, we are here concerned with facts that everybody who is well acquainted with Plato's texts will recognize as basically and generally true, though perhaps not very interesting. If, however, we may take for granted that Plato intuitively and principally visualized his universe in terms of such two-level contrasts as sketched above, the consequences for our understanding of his philosophical pushes and moves might be quite considerable.

I shall proceed (as philologists are prone to do) by 'cumulative' argumentation around this hypothesis.

To begin with, let me repeat that I am a non-believer in conventional 'developmentalism' (recently associated with G. Vlastos in particular) according to which the so-called early dialogues reflect a more or less true Socratic (i.e. non-Presocratic, non-metaphysical, etc.) position, whereas Plato later, while receiving impulses from different quarters including mathematicians, Pythagoreans and other Presocratics, developed a more distinct philosophy of his own. In fact the chronology of the early and middle dialogues is still in flux, and it seems that Plato's philosophical horizon widened very early, long before dialogues such as *Crito*, *Lysis* or *Hippias Minor* were written. As I have argued in some detail [29] elsewhere, most of the intellectual cross-influences of the time are likely to have reached Plato in the late 5th century.[56]

In fact there is much in Presocratic and Socratic thought to suggest or prepare for such a Platonic two-level model as was discussed above. We already noted some parallels. It is easy to trace elements of a 'two-level vision' in all Presocratic philosophies and ways of looking at φύσις.

A common feature in all these ways of thought is the accepting of an invisible, fixed standard 'above' or 'beyond' our visible, ever-changing, unreliable world. The early Ionians speculated about ἀρχαί as rules for all change, Heraclitus introduced a λόγος, Anaxagoras a νοῦς (admittedly a somewhat separate ruling entity,

---

of Zeus' is sometimes wrongly understood as representing evil; cf. Casadio 1995, Sharples 1995, and the discussion in Rowe (ed.) 1995: 349 ff.; Nightingale 1996) is considerably more 'Platonic' than the notion of an 'evil world soul' in *Laws* X 896e–898c (as interpreted by most Platonists since Xenocrates, cf. Baltes in Dörrie and Baltes IV 399 ff.; for a monistic explication, see Hoffmann 1996: 278 ff.).

56. *See* above, notes 2, 3, 11, and p. 7 ff. It is commonly believed that Plato did not know much about Pythagoreanism before he met Archytas, but this is hardly true. Even if he had not seen any writings by Philolaus, several friends of his youth had Pythagorean interests (note at least Simmias, Cebes, Echecrates, and Antisthenes), and Isocrates' *Busiris* (XI) 28–29 is hardly later than 380 BCE. The Socratics seem to have known the tradition about Pythagoras' 'Four Speeches' (references in Thesleff 1989: 11 f.). Orphic and Pythagorean notions were current in Athens long before *Meno* was written (witness Pindar, Ion of Chios, Herodotus, Euripides, and Aristophanes, notably the *Frogs*; *see* in general Burkert 1972). As for Plato's early informants of Heraclitan and Eleatic ideas, *see* Thesleff 1982, above p. 173; for Plato's early mathematical interests, *see* below p. 509 ff. and above n. 3.

[29] yet representing the principle 'mind over matter'), the Eleatics an abstract Unity as the object of real knowledge, and the Pythagoreans a basic arithmological system and a harmony of unequal or asymmetric opposites lying 'beyond' what we see with our eyes. Even the Atomists had their Ἀνάγκη. All of these speculations had cosmic frames. Socrates and the Socratics seem to have searched for standards and limits for knowledge and standards for the 'excellence' allegedly taught by sophists. The latter operated with contrasts such as 'thing / name,' 'nature / arrangement' besides the ever-present discussion of 'good / bad.' Mathematics (and Plato's early attachment to Theodoros and Theaitetos) added to Plato's conviction that there must exist never-changing rules and forms beyond the physical world. Everyday experiences and universally accepted beliefs included 'unequal' pairs of opposites such as heaven / earth, god / man, man / woman, truth / mistake. Why not remember the predominance (in Greece) of light over darkness? Most people in Plato's environment took it for granted that 'better' individuals are always in minority, but that 'one' or 'few' are destined to rule over οἱ πολλοί, whatever aberrations there may occur in practice. The list could be easily extended (as could the list of contrasts, above).

Given all these sources of influence available to Plato in the early years of the 4th century, it is really quite natural for us to regard him as intellectually 'brought up' to a two-level vision of the universe. A truism?

[30] **Characteristics of this vision**

On closer reflection, two things are not so trivial about the specifically Platonic vision. One is its implication of a graded, terraced (not to say hierarchic), asymmetric, i.e. non-reciprocal, non-polarized relationship between a 'lower' and a (somehow related) 'higher' level, comprising all philosophy. The other is the fact that this vision is not only traceable but manifest in practically all dialogues: it is not something that Plato acquired after his alleged 'Socratic stage.' An elaboration of the first point is warranted here (for the second, see 418 ff.).

*Orientation*

Let us inspect once more the sketch of the two levels as given above (411 f.). We noted that a 'third level,' contrarily opposed to the 'first,' has little relevance in Plato's mature thought. It is a specific characteristic of the entities of Plato's first ('higher') level to be, somehow, inherent (rather than 'immanent') in the corresponding entities of the second ('lower') level, whereas vice versa is more difficult to conceive from his point of view: there are always 'ones' in 'many,' but not necessarily 'many' in every 'one'; there is something 'divine' in every 'human being' but not (in Plato's view) anything human in the ideally divine; it is the divine, unity, stability, etc. that is the 'model,' not the human, plurality, or change.⁵⁷ The first level can be said, generally, to dominate the second, whereas the second is 'oriented' towards the first. This follows both conceptually and evaluatively from Plato's premises.

To put it somewhat aristotelically, there is a 'causal' relation between the levels, even more manifestly than between Forms and particulars (cf. 445 ff., 483).

The 'doctrine' of the tripartite soul, as presented in *Republic* IV, *Phaedrus* and *Timaeus* (and indeed the Utopia of the philosophers as a leading class),⁵⁸ reflects directly the two-level vision and the idea of orientation.

It is, on the other hand, very important to note that this idea of orientation also implies some kind of accessibility from the lower level to the higher. Indeed, there is a universal κοινωνία. Again and again Plato seems to suggest that philosophy (dialectic) makes it possible to advance from the second level to the first, whereas the first level does not (or cannot?) enforce its domination, totally, on the second. Both main levels are necessary parts of Plato's view of the universe. Is the tension between them ultimately 'harmonic'?

Plato's conception of φιλο-σοφία as an 'orientation,' and of δια-λεκτική as the art of leading a dialogue towards stable truths, runs as a basic theme through his entire written work.⁵⁹ He gives us several metaphorical illustrations of this. The most explicit illustrations are Diotima's ladder with its preliminaries, and the Divided Line. Both are connected with the theory of Forms (below), but they have broader implications relevant to his two-level model.

[30]

[31]

## Eros

In the *Symposium* we are presented with a view of the universe where the 'daimonic' force of Eros (which is oriented towards the divine, as ὀρθὴ δόξα is to φρόνησις, 202a) directs the philosopher's interest from many towards 'one and the same' (210b3), from bodies towards soul, systems, and knowledge (210b ff.), from the varied to the stable, definite and ever-lasting (211a ff.), which will eventually function as a cause and enable him to produce (210d, cf. 206c ff.) not phantoms but true virtue (212a). A change of view occurs when the ladder or 'stairs' (cf. 211c) have brought the 'lover' above the level of the human body: now it is τὸ (ἐπ' εἴδει) καλόν which is the aim of the pursuit (210b ff., note the pointed back reference to σῶμα c5). The process has become an intellectual 'vision' (cf. the

---

57. A μέθεξις in a Form (below, 446) certainly does not bring with it lower level qualities to the Form.

58. *Republic* IV 436a ff., *Phaedrus* 246a ff., *Timaeus* 69c ff. and elsewhere. The leading 'part' (rather perhaps 'aspect') of the incarnated soul is always distinct from the lower parts (aspects), but there is communication between them (cf. Gill 1996: 240 ff., partly contra Irwin).

59. For the use of the word φιλόσοφος and its derivatives, *see* especially Burkert 1960, Dixsaut 1985, Nightingale 1995: 13 ff.; cf. the conspectus in des Places 1964 s.vv. and the notes on early interpretations in Dörrie and Baltes IV 231 ff.—For Plato's 'dialectic' as reasoning conducted by a philosopher towards truth, *see* above, n. 10.

[31] references to νοῦς 210a8, b2, 4, to θεωρία c3, etc.), and 'love' becomes a metaphor which functions throughout the 'mystery' only because Diotima has chosen to have καλόν still substituted for ἀγαθόν.[60] The step from the body level is a more marked one than the other steps—until the 'sudden' last revelation (210e4) which is really no step at all and which is surely meant to be 'mystifying' like the ἐπέκεινα at *Republic* VI 509b8.

## The Divided Line

The simile of the Divided Line (*Republic* VI 509d–511e) is in some respects more obscure than Diotima's Ladder, and it has been subject to a seemingly endless discussion.[61] At present we may note the following indisputable facts. The Line stands in the center of the monumental *Republic*, between the similes of the Sun and the Cave, and its style also suggests that Plato wants to give it some specific and symbolic relevance.[62] The Line is first cut into two unequal segments, and we can easily see that this cut is meant to represent what I have called Plato's

[32] two main levels. There is no 'third level' (no antithetically polarized κακόν, no 'matter,' no non-being, no ἐπέκεινα). The Line is certainly meant to be drawn vertically. The problems of the sub-division and its implications need not detain us here (cf. below, 453). Note, however, that the principle of proportional equality to be adopted in the cuts is likely to have some symbolic significance. I am quite convinced that Plato wants to emphasize above all the complexity and the mutual involvements in the relationship of the two main levels: they are indeed bound together. Thus the Line illustrates ontological, logical and epistemological aspects of a 'ladder' which in Diotima's mystery teaching is rooted in psychology and ethics.

## A philosopher's vision

The 'orientation' of everything, including the philosopher himself, towards the upper level and what is 'good,' is a theme to which Plato is always committed—I refer arbitrarily to *Gorgias* 486ab and *Republic* VI 500bc. But although a general orientation is possible for every human being (cf. *Theaetetus* 176a ff.), the philosopher alone may see a glimpse of ἀληθείας πεδίον (*Phaedrus* 248b, cf. *Symposium* 211b, etc.). Socrates' 'hope' of being taught by Euthyphron how to know the Idea of ὁσιότης (*Euthyphro* 6de) is, of course, grossly ironical.

It seems that the specific characteristics of Plato's two-level vision—its complex comprising everything that can be thought of as the subject of 'philosophy,'

---

60. Cf. τὸ ἀγαθόν *Symposium* 204e, ἀρετή 212a, and below, 444.
61. Some references below, n. 115.
62. *See* my notes on 'pedimentality,' above, p. 95 ff. The style is seriously matter-of-fact, contrary e.g. to the exuberant passage on the 'Nuptial Number,' VIII 545d ff.

the hierarchic relationship of the levels, the involvements and internal analogies of the levels so that one is practically unthinkable without the other, and the accessibility of the first level from the second—were always deeply present in Plato's mind. This vision can be said to form a very basic part of his thought. We need not be in real sympathy with it to find it interesting, potentially productive, and even innovative in certain respects.[63]

It has to be explicitly pointed out, however, that we have so far been concerned with an intuitive 'vision' only. On one hand, it is not to be identified with the patterns of artistry and artistic feeling revealed by some dialogues, although it may be reflected in some literary devices (such as 'pedimentality,' cf. above, p. 28 and pm.) or in seriousness versus humour. On the other hand, the two-level vision does not constitute any doctrinal whole whatsoever. Nor can it be factually differentiated into what we would anachronistically call metaphysics, ontology, physics, theology, psychology, epistemology, basic logic, or ethics. Rather, perhaps, Plato's vision is all of this at the same time. It is a general frame for envisaging reality, and for thought about reality. It is not a set of arguments but a philosophic position that makes philosophy possible.

[32]

[33]

## Bridging the contrasts

On closer inspection, the details of the relation between the two main levels may look quite problematic. It also seems (irrespective of the chronological problems) that Plato and his circle were from time to time, perhaps continuously, trying to analyze and explain the nature of the difference between the levels. A universal κοινωνία of reality appears to have been taken for granted (cf. e.g. *Gorgias* 507a–508b, *Symposium* 186c ff., 203a, *Phaedo* 92a ff., *Laches* 188d, 193de). The implications of philosophy at large and dialectic in particular as the only reliable means of 'bridging' the contrasts of the levels, are ventilated, explicitly and implicitly, in all dialogues. The function of the Philosopher as a 'daimonic' intermediate being between the first and the second level is, with more or less playful associations to Eros, alluded to in *Symposium, Lysis, Phaedrus, Alcibiades* I, *Theages,* and elsewhere.[64]

The fact that Plato's Socrates is the actual leader of the discussion in all dialogues 'before' the *Parmenides,* requires particular notice.[65] It is the Philosopher, in the first place Socrates in his human context—with all the confrontations, challenges, and expressions of agreement or frustration following from this—who opens the perspectives from the lower level towards the upper one. But for Plato,

---

63. 'Analogy' has often been regarded as a constitutive principle in Plato's universe (see e.g. Baltes in Dörrie and Baltes IV 360 ff.). I would rather stress the complementary ideas of 'unity over plurality,' 'sameness over otherness,' stability over change,' also 'intellect over feelings,' all relatively unpopular notions today; and on the other hand, the certainly fruitful ideas of 'involvement,' 'orientation,' and of minimizing the significance of 'evil.'

64. Cf. below, n. 110.

65. *See* now Thesleff in Press (ed.) 2000: 53 ff.

[33] the Philosopher remains a searcher. It is extremely important, as I see it, to realize that Plato was no dogmatic, but a truth-oriented visionary, constantly experimenting with new approaches.[66] This fact becomes ever more obvious from the perspectives of the two-level model.

Among the many attempts to bridge the levels and explicate their internal relations, the most explicit, ambitious and famous one was the theory of Forms.[67]

## Examples of the function of the model

The other non-trivial general fact about Plato's two-level vision is its occurrence in what is traditionally regarded as his 'early' or 'pre-middle period.' Some indications of this have already been noted.

[34] It would be easy to analyze the so-called 'middle dialogues' in terms of a two-level vision: everybody who is familiar with *Symposium, Phaedo, Phaedrus* or *Republic,* and also *Timaeus,* would probably admit this. One could, of course, regard the vision as a frame or an ornament around the theory of Forms. If one considers the theory of Forms to be primary and, indeed, the actual core of Plato's philosophy (and this has always been the view of the majority of specialists), the scope and specific features of the 'vision' are easily neglected. To be reminded of the existence in the middle dialogues (or even in *Meno* or *Gorgias,* if Platonic Forms are regarded as adumbrated in these dialogues) of such a 'vision' or 'frame,' would not be felt as particularly suggestive if one (with the majority of analytic philosophers) takes little interest in the context, background apparatus or ornament.

As a matter of fact, however, there can be found traces of the vision in all so-called early dialogues.[68] Apart from the examples referred to above (400 ff.), it can be claimed that in all these dialogues Socrates stands for (or is more or less explicitly 'oriented' towards) 'one, the same, the unchanging, the divine, soul, the leading, intellect, truth, knowledge, and definition,' in contrast to his interlocutor(s) who in various ways, like his entire environment, remains more distanced from Plato's 'higher level.' It is also worth noting that all of Socrates' interlocutors in Plato's dialogues, in spite of their shortcomings and (sometimes) pointed differences from Socrates, are 'friends' and somehow positively acceptable individuals with intellectual interests: none of them is just 'anybody,' an uneducated person (in *Meno* the slave boy is only brought in for experiment), a brute, a criminal, or simply 'bad.'

---

66. Cf. above, notes 4, 8, 11. Although a kind of two-level model subsisted in post-Platonic philosophy, notably in Stoicism, it soon became acceptable to identify the Ideal Philosopher, not with a searcher for truth, but with a σοφός.

67. *See* below 437 ff.

68. Some, of course, are thematically so specific as to have only a few traces of the vision: thus *Menexenus* which gives little more than an ironic antithesis to Platonic philosophy; and also *Clitopho* and some other of the dialogues usually considered spurious, cf. above, 351 ff. However, a detailed investigation of essentially Platonic features in the latter is needed.

The complexity of the two-level vision appears from the fact that each dialogue illustrates, or at least reflects, several of the contrasts at the same time, but with different points of emphasis.

A few examples (numbers in brackets refer to the lists p. 400–410):

## Protagoras

The rather loosely attached opening dialogue (309a–310a) directs our attention to that remarkable man, Protagoras, and so does, with much elaboration, the extensive introduction of the main dialogue (310a–317e). Thus we are successively, step by step, prepared for a confrontation of Socrates, the Philosopher, with the Great Sophist and his milieu. The contrast is more playfully and artistically (not to say artfully) wrought than the increasingly dramatic confrontation of Socrates with the rhetors in the *Gorgias*. The *Protagoras* is pointedly ironic from the beginning to the end. Socrates is alone here too: the contrast 'one / many' (9) is developed in various ways (cf. e.g. 314e–316b, 329c–331c, 349a–351a); Alcibiades' explicit support (336b–d, cf. 309b) is of little help to him. Protagoras is always supported by many. But though Socrates professes to let Protagoras dominate him, he is in fact the leader (3) of the dialogue; note also the apparent exchange of positions at the end (360e ff.). One of the most basic contrasts in this dialogue is that between truth and appearance (4), but the existence of Truth (the title of one of Protagoras' works!) is only intimated in aporetic contexts. The sophists seek appearance only, although they operate with mental rather than bodily goods (2) (cf. 313a–314c). This is brilliantly illustrated throughout the dialogue.[69] They move on the level of 'opinion' (5). So does e.g. Hippias who refers to the φύσις / νόμος contrast (4) (337cd) without seeing its deeper implications; and notably so does Protagoras himself. Even in the latter part of his great speech, which is formally a λόγος (323c, 324d), he only expresses opinions: note Socrates' remark at 331c, and the repeated use of δοκεῖ at 347a when he has finished his own sophistic antilogy. Protagoras' myth (4) tells us that it is Zeus who possesses πολιτικὴ σοφία (321d) and that man, who partakes in the divine (1) (322a), has all the cardinal ('political' 323b) virtues as a divine gift; but Protagoras then goes on to show (323c, explicitly by argued λόγος 324d) why he thinks that people regard virtue, not as innate, but as to some extent teachable (3). The great speech is certainly meant, from Plato's point of view, to be suggestively persuasive in its mildly human and culturally optimistic tone, but inconsistent and intellectually unsatisfactory on closer inspection just because it is bound to the 'lower level.' Socrates seizes upon one point, the alleged unity of virtue (9) (329c, cf. 324de), and tends in the following to stress the intellectual element (5) (6) in man, if 'truly' good (4). Most explicitly, however ironically, the question of truth is ventilated in Socrates' sophistic speech (342c–347a) which answers Protagoras' great speech

---

69. Also stylistically, cf. above, 108 f.

[35] and which forms a kind of compositional peripety in the dialogue.[70] Its allusions would be worth a more detailed analysis than have been attempted by commentators so far. Note here, apart from the 'truth' repeatedly adduced (343de, 344ab, 346e, 347a), the following: φιλοσοφία, σοφία / physical training (2) (5) (6) 342a–e; εἶναι, διαμένειν / γενέσθαι (8) 344bc; μάθησις, ἐπιστήμη / κακῶς πράττειν (5) 344e–345c; φίλον / ἀλλόκοτον (10) 345d–346b, in a complicated piece of argument, connected with ἑκών / ἄκων (3); and an interesting human μέσον below the level of 'good' (1) 346c–e (cf. the ostensible aporia at 331d–333c). 'Searching'
[36] is one of the themes of this dialogue from the beginning,[71] though Protagoras and the other sophists insist on ex cathedra teaching (3). The tentative definition (7) of courage, taken as one example of cardinal virtues (349a ff., 359a–360d), reduces all to σοφία (5).[72] The problems of ὅμοιον (and ἕν) versus ἕτερον (10) and of lower level opposites (adduced to suggest the unity and intellectual character of true virtue), are touched upon in the long central interlude (329c–338e) where even a glimpse of a Form occurs (αὐτὴ ἡ ὁσιότης 330de, cf. 360a). Protagoras here insists on a plurality of τὸ ἀγαθόν (334a–c), but he refers to the level of the senses only (6). Later, in the rather sophisticated piece of quasi-elenchus at 351b–358a, we note ἀγαθόν as contrasted to ἡδύ (6), and an occasional hint of a leading ἐπιστήμη versus lower-level θυμός and ἡδονή (and λύπη 352b) (3) (6).[73] This brings us to the so-called 'akrasia' passage and to the very interesting argument on measuring where a science of relations is intimated (6) (7): here ἡ μετρητικὴ τέχνη is explicitly contrasted to ἡ τοῦ φαινομένου δύναμις (356d); and note the play with πλέον / ἔλαττον and αὐτό / ἕτερον (10) in connection with an allusion to mathematics as σωτηρία τοῦ βίου (8) at 356e (with reference to 322b).[74] All in all, the 'message' of this many-faced dialogue to well-informed readers seems to be that the philosophical methods of the Platonic Socrates (above all dialectic, first introduced at 328e ff., cf. 335d ff., 347a ff.), including mathematics, offer more promising ways to reach stable knowledge of the good and the best life, than do sophists' lectures on such topics.—Cf. p. 399 ff., contrasts (1) (2) (3) (4) (5) (6) (7) (8) (9) (10).

## Charmides

The very charming introductory chapters of this dialogue give, as a background, what most people consider fine and pleasant: many young, good-looking happy

---

70. Thesleff 1993: 30, cf, Kahn 1996: 242 and elsewhere. Kahn is one of the few critics who emphasize the deliberately delusive traits in *Protagoras*.

71. Even hunting, 309a2, 310c; cf. 311b–314e, 316c–317c, 342a–d (ironical); and both parts agree on the need of further discussion, 361 de.

72. Probably with an ironic allusion to the sophists; cf. 309c, etc.

73. In the (perhaps) later development of the theory of tripartition of the soul (cf. above, n. 58), θυμός is the better of the two lower tendencies. For ἀγαθόν as τέλος 354bc, cf. *Gorgias* 499e, 507d, and of course *Republic* VI.

74. A suggestive passage with allusion to Pythagorean ideas; cf. also Ps.-Epicharmus, *Vors.* 23 B 56.

people, good family connections, peace, and apparent stability—against which Socrates stands out as an odd person (9). Observe his intellectualism (6) on the one hand and his recent experiences in the war on the other, and also the chaotic changes (8) in which some of the persons present will soon be involved (an implicit allusion certainly meant to be relevant). We may list here Socrates' ironic disavowal of self-control in matters of love (6) (154b), perhaps a hint that a real εἶδος is impersonal (4) (154de, 155d), his preference of soul to body (2) (ibid.), the ambiguous ποιητικός combined with φιλόσοφος as a qualification of Charmides (3) (155a), Socrates' alleged knowledge (5) (155b ff.) of a divine charm (1) against headache, the 'holistic' treatment of body and soul (2) (156a ff.), sight as the highest sense (6) (156e f.), σωφροσύνη effected by λόγοι (6) (157a ff.), and the two prominent houses of Charmides' pedigree which seem to guarantee that he is always 'first' (9) (3) (158a).[75] The subsequent issue of 'knowledge of knowledge' is adumbrated by Charmides' remark on self-knowledge (10) (5) (158cd). In the elenctic discussion that follows, Socrates first refers to a contrast between the concept σωφροσύνη and the αἴσθησις and δόξα that concern it (5) (6) (158e f.). Charmides' first attempt at a definition (7) (159b) adduces stability as a criterion (8). Socrates refutes this with reference to opposites (on the physical level, to be sure). Charmides' second attempt wrongly identifies σωφροσύνη with its effect (3) on the lower level (after Socrates has made a punning suggestion of ποιεῖ / ποῖα 160d). The third definition (161b, cf. 162c) seems to use a proposal earlier made by Critias, τὰ ἑαυτοῦ πράττειν (10). Socrates again begins his criticism with concrete examples, but now we come to the problems of the 'self' and 'same' (10) and of 'knowing that one knows' (5) (162d) which dominate the rest of the dialogue. This is a kind of peripety. In the ensuing elenctic discussion with Critias, who is challenged to activity (3), Socrates argues that it is not the good action but knowledge that is the essential characteristic of σωφροσύνη: not only self-knowledge, as Critias first suggests (165b, cf. 158cd), but perhaps 'knowledge of all knowledges including itself, and of ignorance,' as he then forces Critias to propose (166c).[76] Note in this context the thought experiments (cf. 166de, 175c) with ὅμοιος / ἕτερος (10) (165e ff.) and 'belief that one knows' (5) (166d). In a relatively sophisticated set of elenchi, Socrates goes on to doubt the self-reference of knowledge, and even its usefulness as such (on the human level) if it were possible (171de). Knowledge, like senses and opinion, is likely to have an object outside itself (5) (6) (167c–168a). The central part of the argument turns on the allegedly difficult διαίρεσις of actions πρὸς ἑαυτό / πρὸς ἄλλο (3) (10) (169a): it seems probable that Socrates' aporia (169b), whether real or not, implies that there is yet a fundamental difference between higher-level (knowledge, soul) and lower-level entities (opinion, senses). But then we come to the last definition (7): perhaps σωφροσύνη is to know what is good or bad (171d, 174b)? At any rate

[36]

[37]

---

75. Here 'one' stands over the 'dualism' of male and female, if one may toy with Pythagorean ideas; cf. below, 485 ff.

76. A much-discussed proposal, see especially Guthrie IV 168 ff. The plural ἐπιστημῶν implies technical knowledge ('know-how,' cf. Parry 1996); Critias is concerned with human matters only.

[37] happiness (εὖ πράττειν ambiguously 173d) does not follow from mere knowledge. But Socrates now feels he has just been 'moved' around the truth (8) (4)
[38] (174cd). The implication of the argument seems to be the unity of the cardinal virtues (9) which all have τὸ ἀγαθόν as their aim. The dialogue ends in apparent aporia with a promise of further research. Though Charmides admits he is in great need of Socrates' charms (1), the reader understands that he will remain in an all-too human state, even sink to brutality (note the repeated βιάζεσθαι 176cd).—Contrasts (1) (2) (3) (4) (5) (6) (7) (8) (9) (10).

## The *First Alcibiades*

I take this as an example of a dialogue which, though stylistically 'flat' and probably 'semi-authentic,'[77] contains a wide register of typical Platonic issues. In this dialogue 'one / many' (9), 'soul / body' (2), 'divine / human' (1), 'leading / being led' (3) and sublimated love (6) occur in the conceptual apparatus from the beginning. Socrates here appears as a teacher relying on his δαιμόνιον (103a, 105e, etc.) and on his elenchus. He first examines Alcibiades' lack of knowledge about what is 'better' in politics and what is 'right': Alcibiades only believes he knows this (5) (110c). It is about such things that people's opinions usually differ (10) (112a). Socrates then approaches the problem of 'one and the same' (10) (113e) through the question of the useful, the fine and the good and their opposites (on the human level), and he brings Alcibiades to aporia (116c) about his own 'different' opinions: to believe that one knows turns out to be even worse than ignorance (5) (118b). Alcibiades is made to admit that nobody has been able to teach political leadership (119b). Not even Spartan or Persian kingship would offer Alcibiades suitable standards (8) for competition or imitation, if he wants to become a true leader. The irony of the curious central speech of Socrates on the apparent greatness of Sparta and Persia (4) (6) and on the education of princes (121c–124b) seems to open itself in the Delphic maxim adduced at the end: Alcibiades should first learn to know himself, not others (5) (10); cf. *Apology* 36c. We all need education, Socrates then adds (3). We need to learn what taking care of things, friendship and concord in society implies; but Alcibiades is not able to define even that (7) (127d). It has to do with taking care of oneself (128a). The 'self' and the 'same' have to be understood (10) (129b, 130d). The human 'self' is the soul which is leading the body (2) (3) (129e ff.). Soul and its highest part, σοφία, can be seen in the human eye, and it is like god (1) (133bc). To know oneself is the true leader's and educator's first duty (134c). He and the righteous state should be oriented towards the divine (1) (134d). Only the virtuous is free to choose (135c); but it is implied at the end that Alcibiades is not, and will remain on a lower level than Socrates (although he wants an exchange of roles). The dialogue can be read as a (not-very-brilliant) Academic introduction to the
[39] use of Socratic constructive elenchus and to the philosopher-leader's orientation

---

77. Above, p. 361 ff.

towards the divine, to soul, and to knowledge (with an interesting emphasis on αὐτό).—Contrasts (1) (2) (3) (4) (5) (6) (7) (8) (9) (10).

## Apology

Even this text, though more apologetic than positively philosophical in content, presents some typical contrasts of a two-level character. It begins with the contrast of speaking the truth and speaking well (4) (17b), a commonplace which here seems to link up with the Platonic opposition of philosophy and rhetoric (as notably in *Gorgias* and *Phaedrus*). The contrast between the apparent σοφία (or rather φιλοσοφία) of Socrates which is based on knowing one's own ignorance and on dialectic, is a theme pervading the three speeches (cf. 20d–24b, 29a–30b, 33c, 38c, 41e): this is the 'knowledge / opinion' contrast (5), though technical terminology is here avoided. Furthermore, there is the 'specialist / majority' contrast (9) (24c–25a, cf. 28a, and with some irony, 36a); and, almost throughout, the 'god / man' contrast (1) (notably 25b ff.) with an interesting association of Socrates with his δαιμόνιον (31de, 40ab). Explicitly and by implication, Socrates the philosopher represents the five cardinal virtues (28b–35d), and his philosophy has a markedly social dimension (29c ff., cf. e.g. 37c–38a) although he, as (implicitly) a more noble being, is very clearly 'odd' and contrasted to 'ordinary' people (9) from the first sentence of the *Apology* to the last. Two passages offer interesting glimpses of a two-level method. At 26e–27e, a piece of Socratic elenchus achieves the grouping of apparently different things in the 'same' class (10) (τοῦ αὐτοῦ). And at 36c Socrates points out that it is more important to try to improve oneself (3) (10) (ἑαυτοῦ) than what belongs to oneself (τῶν ἑαυτοῦ), and similarly, to improve the State itself (αὐτῆς τῆς πόλεως) before concerning oneself with things that belong to it (τῶν τῆς πόλεως): the idea of a better 'self' (we might even say 'substance') is here given preference to its various 'properties.' Contrasts (1) (3) (4) (5) (9) (10).

## Hippias Minor

I take it for granted that this curious little dialogue is neither very early nor genuinely aporetic;[78] and that if it is not by Plato, it was written by somebody who was well acquainted with Plato's thought and style. Socrates the ironist is confronted with Hippias, the allegedly all-round σοφός, and the elenchus concerns 'deceiving' (ψεύδεσθαι) as reflected, principally, in the characters of Homer's Achilles and Odysseus (4). The elenchus results in little more than πλανᾶσθαι (indeed, 'deceiving': cf. 369bc, 370e, 372de, 373b, 376bc), but obviously Socrates is maintaining the initiative throughout; he is oriented towards a higher level of the λόγος (7) (8). In the second one of his 'central speeches' (372a–373a),[79] which

---

78. Cf. Szlezák 1985: 79–90; for the 'semi-authenticity,' cf. below, p. 366 f.
79. Cf. notably *Ion*, and below, p. 367 ff.

[39] functions as a kind of peripety, he contrasts his method of questioning to the sophist's manner of teaching: the former is like a medical cure of the soul (here, iron-
[40] ically, the soul of the questioner). The two-level contrast ψυχή (διάνοια) / σῶμα (2) is introduced in the opening (364a, cf. 372e f., 375e, and φιλοσοφία 363a), also 'few / many' (9) (363a, 364b, cf. 369c), and πολύτροπος as an attribute of Odysseus the deceiver (364e ff.), whereas Socrates speaks τὰ αὐτά (10) (and Hippias, if he were wise and willing, would always act κατὰ τὰ αὐτά, as Socrates insists repeatedly and ironically at 366e f.); add perhaps the playfully pointed reference at 372bc to ἓν ἀγαθόν, namely the capacity of questioning, as Socrates' sole gift. The ironically ambivalent δόξα of Hippias (5) (364b, cf. πιστευτικός 364a) seems to consist of his alleged σοφία and command of all ἐπιστῆμαι (368a–e). In his argumentation, Socrates operates with conceptual contrasts which appear to be polar opposites (cf. below, 427 ff.): φρόνησις / ἀφροσύνη, βελτίονς / πονηροτέρους (372de), ἀγαθός / κακός (373c ff.), βραδέως / ταχέως (373d). etc.; the contrast ἀληθής / ψευδής becomes blurred from the start (364e ff., cf. 367a ff., 368e). The first part of the dialogue focuses on δυνατός / ἀδύνατος (365d ff.), the second part (after the central section) on ἑκών / ἄκων, implying 'intentional' (i.e. both witting and willing) vs. 'unintentional' action (3). 'Capacity' is connected with φρόνησις (ἐπίστασθαι, σοφός) and so is 'deceit' (365d ff.); also, more ironically, Hippias' πανουργία (369a). If the capable person acts 'wittingly,' he deceives and harms 'better' (372d ff.). Since δικαιοσύνη is either a δύναμις or an ἐπιστήμη (τέχνη) of the soul (375d ff.),[80] a good man who acts wittingly and willingly is more capable of doing both right and wrong than a bad, capable and willing man (if there exist such persons, Socrates adds pointedly at 376b7). It is clear that the author's ultimate concern is logic applied to ethics, and that the apparent polarizations are used for a logical purpose: the ἀδύνατος, ἄκων, ψευδής, ἀδικῶν, and even the κακός is never consistently so, but these are properties indicating defects and shortcomings among ordinary human beings. We are probably to understand that the apparent paradox is solved if it is taken for granted that the contrasts in question (ἀληθής / ψευδής, δυνατός / ἀδύνατος, ἑκών / ἄκων, δίκαιος / ἄδικος, ἀγαθός / κακός, etc.) are here two-level contrasts implying that a truthful, capable, willingly and wittingly acting, just and good man is an ideal case who per definitionem is incapable of deceiving and doing wrong; whereas ordinary people may err in all respects but are sometimes also truthful, capable, etc. And we may suspect that Socrates is close to the ideal. Cf. also the musings on 'lie' / 'fiction' in *Republic* II 381b–383c, III 414b–415b where the mental attitude is taken to be essential—Contrasts (2) (3) (4) (5) (7) (8) (9) (10).

The early *Utopia*

[41] Whatever one thinks of Platonic chronology and the development of his thought, the conclusions to be drawn from this material taken from the extant dialogues,

---

80. Cf. *Laches* 192b, *Charmides* 168b ff., *Republic* I 346a ff., *Parmenides* 133e f. This passage in *Hippias Minor* clearly implies an earlier discussion of the issue.

is that the two-level vision belonged to Plato's philosophy from the start. At least in the terms of this vision, no decisive shift from a Socratic to a Platonic stage can be seen.

The hypothesis of an early version of Plato's political Utopia, the 'Proto-*Republic*' from the 390s, fits very well into this picture. As I have argued elsewhere,[81] the Utopia must have been a projection of Plato's early philosophy onto the notion of the Best State. The radicalism of its solutions, notably the ideas of utter specialization and of the strict unity, equality and stability among the leaders, versus pluralism and variety in the rest of society (yet all classes feeling bound together by loyalty), can be best understood from the perspectives of Plato's two-level vision. The thought-play became more complex in the final *Republic* with its cross-allusions to Aristophanes.

It is not certain, but possible (considering e.g. the emphasis on the idea of a 'cosmic order' in *Gorgias* 507c ff., cf. 504a ff.), that Plato's early Utopia included a conception of Cosmos as the ideal model for human society. However, in the final *Republic* this notion occurs in rather late contexts (VI 500b ff., IX 592ab; cf. *Timaeus* implicitly, *Politicus* 274d, *Laws* X 903b–d); and the astral speculations in *Phaedrus* and especially *Timaeus* suggest that cosmology was not an integral part of Plato's early philosophy (though mathematics was).[82]

## Some general arguments

As an overall argument for the relevance of the two-level model, it can be claimed that all or most dialogues (*Apology* and *Laws-Epinomis* are exceptions) communicate with the listener / reader on two levels, at it were (cf. also above, p. 392): there is the realistic 'protreptic' level concerned with ordinary human matters; and there are highly philosophic issues, often allusively introduced more close to the center of the work, which seem to presuppose the presence of well-informed listeners who are capable of appreciating the allusions and the reasoning. Another very different but strong argument for the relevance of this vision is the fact that the theories of 'Categories' and First Principles (below, p. 457 ff.) can be naturally explicated from it.

---

81. *See* especially below, p. 519 ff. Among those who interpret Plato's Utopia as thought-play, *see* now Freydberg 1997: 69 ff.

82. Cf. above, n. 3. I entirely agree with Kahn's view (1996, especially 143 ff., cf. also Hoffmann 1996: 19 ff.) that Plato's early philosophy was anchored in metaphysics and moralism, though I cannot follow Kahn's theory of an educational plan reflected in the dialogues.

# V

## ON POLAR OPPOSITES IN PLATO

### Opposites and two-level contrasts

In the above discussion, we have often encountered the use of polar opposites (like 'good / bad,' 'true / false,' 'dry / wet') embedded in Plato's philosophical two-level vision. It was initially suggested (p. 398) that polar opposites are used in accordance with ordinary (everyday) linguistic practice or with rhetorical pathos, but not as constitutive parts of Plato's philosophic views. Indeed, polar opposites may be freely used in argument, but they are seldom thematic, and never the actual outcome of the argument.

This chapter is intended as a slight elaboration of this point. The issue would, however, be worth a more detailed analysis than what can be carried out here. In particular, the niceties of the employment of contrary or contradictory concepts within the Academic method of 'dihaeresis,' which is in fact concerned with 'natural' conceptual distinctions[83] rather than opposites, cannot be studied here.

### Examples

*Gorgias*

It is well-known that classical Greek rhetoric has a particular predilection for antithetic expression.[84] Antitheses abound in rhetorical contexts in Plato's dialogues: see for instance the speeches in *Menexenus*, *Phaedrus*, and *Symposium*.

---

83. 'Limbs' *Phaedrus* 265e, 'slices of meat' *Hippias Major* 301b, cf. *Sophist* 246bc; Thesleff 1976: 113 f. For 'dihaeresis,' see below, p. 451.
84. See Denniston 1952: 70–77, Dover 1997: 16 f., etc.; cf. above, 54 ff.

[42]
[43]     We should therefore expect that the confrontation of Socrates with the rhetors in *Gorgias* would draw with it a wide variety of linguistic and conceptual polarizations. This is to some extent the case, though it is the philosopher's dialectic, not rhetoric, that dominates in this dialogue. However, we may take a somewhat closer look at the antitheses.

In a way, the note is struck by the first words of the dialogue (πολέμου καὶ μάχης), and then very clearly by Polus in his brief, pointedly rhetorical description of Gorgias (448c: ἐμπειρία / ἀπειρία, τέχνη / τύχη). Socrates answers with further distinctions, and these remain as a basis for the following discussion (448d–449c: ῥητορική / διαλέγεσθαι, ἐγκωμιάζειν / ψέγειν, ἐρωτᾶν / ἀποκρίνεσθαι, τίς; / ποῖα;, βραχυλογία / μακρολογία). Throughout the dialogue, his arguments are partly conducted in terms of opposites (or contrasts) such as λόγος / ἔργον 450d, ἀληθής / ψευδής 454d, εἰδώς / οὐκ εἰδώς 459b ff., γνῶναι / στοχάξεσθαι 464c, and of course quite often ἀγαθόν / κακόν (458a), καλόν / αἰσχρόν (464cd), etc. In rhetorical contexts, more or less conventional pairs of opposites occur frequently (e.g. θεοί / ἄνθρωποι, ἰδίᾳ / δημοσίᾳ, ἄνω / κάτω, πρεσβύτεροι / νεώτεροι, 461cd, 482a, 487e), and especially in Socrates' ever more protreptic arguments and speeches towards the end, 492e ff. The main theme of 'right / wrong' is first introduced by Gorgias (454b) and then taken up by Socrates (454e); similarly the questions of ἀδικεῖσθαι versus ἀδικεῖν (469b) and εὐδαίμων / ἄθλιος (470d) are introduced by Polus but instantly taken up by Socrates.

For the most part, and primarily, the use of pairs of contrasted opposites seems to be a matter of linguistic practice and style. Although polarization is part of the running argument, this practice is connected with everyday human activities and has little or no essentially philosophic content. However, in contexts where opposite concepts are applied to the philosophic themes of the dialogue and thus become thematic, they tend to lose their polarized character and approximate to Plato's two-level vision; cf. *Hippias Minor* (above, p. 423).

This can be seen in various turns in the discussion which may be considered as hints to well-informed readers. Already at 448e, the question τίς is connected with dialectic (and 'brachylogy'), and ποῖα with ἐγκωμιάζειν / ψέγειν and rhetoric: the implication seems to be that 'essence' is an issue classed higher than 'quality' (including opposites, cf. e.g. 451bc). Similar two-level contrasts are introduced e.g. by μάθησις / πίστις (454c ff., cf. εἶναι, εἰδέναι / πείθειν, δοκεῖν as connected with τὶ ἀγαθόν / τὶ κακόν 459de, etc.); the search for truth as connected with elenchus and classed first in terms of ἀγαθόν versus κακόν (458a); then τέχνη / ἐμπειρία (462bc, cf. 465a, etc.); and notably ψυχή / σῶμα as 'leading / being led' (463e) which becomes one of the dominant themes in the following. Two-level contrasts also come into the foreground in the Polus chapter; cf. e.g. the classifications culminating in τὸ βέλτιστον / τὸ ἥδιστον 464d (cf. 513de); the discussion of ἀγαθά, κακά, and τὸ μεταξύ which are rather oriented towards

[44]     the ἀγαθά 467e ff. (later more explicitly so: καλόν associated with ἡδονή but oriented towards ἀγαθόν 474d ff., cf. 503e; and τὸ ἀγαθόν as τέλος 499e f.). The paradox of ἀδικεῖσθαι / ἀδικεῖν (as such, a lower-level contrast) and εὐδαίμων / ἄθλιος 469b ff., argued together with the more pronouncedly two-level contrast

of ποιεῖν / πάσχειν⁸⁵ 476b ff., suggests that what is 'good' dominates over what is 'bad' (cf. e.g. 480c). The central issues of 'orientation' run as a basic theme through the forceful Callicles chapter where the confrontation of 'demagogy' with philosophy is explicit. Callicles at first protests that Socrates has turned things upside down (481 bc). Socrates' answer is φιλο-σοφία. Callicles' using the apparent two-level contrast φύσις / νόμος (482e ff.) is not philosophic and hence insufficient (see 488e ff. and notably 507e f.); the Ἀμφίων / Ζῆθος contrast (485e ff., cf. 500c, 506b) has a deeper symbolic relevance: it is a question of two ways of life (483b ff., 491e ff.), and there are no doubts where Socrates' sympathies lie. The κόσμιος is contrasted with the ἀκόλαστος with his ἐπιθυμίαι and his ἡδονή / λύπη (492e ff.), though, as Socrates argues rather forcibly (495e ff.), such opposites do not exclude each other in the physical world, contrary to 'good / bad,' 'health / illness,' etc. (but note the fact that what is 'present' in a 'bad' person is not the 'Form' of τὸ κακόν but τὰ κακά 498de). Life is not worth living unless it is turned towards what is best (ἀρετή 504d ff., cf. 500a ff., 506c ff. where parts of the argument are resumed); and the tyrant's life is certainly not so turned (510a ff., cf. 490d ff.). The final paradox, Socrates the 'only true politician' (521d ff.), has a similar two-level function (prepared for by the contrast εἷς / πολλοί which is frequently employed in the dialogue since 471e, see notably 488d ff.): Socrates somehow 'reaches' a higher level. And, probably with some irony, his μῦθος is turned into a λόγος (523a).

*Republic* I

It is interesting to compare the use of opposites in *Gorgias* with *Republic* I where the themes and the three-stage, climactic structure are partly similar.⁸⁶ The most obvious general differences are the following. *Gorgias* is much larger and functions as an independent work; *Republic* I, in its present form, is constructed as an introduction (προοίμιον) to Books II–X. *Gorgias* offers an increasingly dramatic confrontation of two views of life, the power-seeking political rhetorician's and the philosopher's; *Republic* I concentrates on tentative definitions of 'what is right' (δίκαιον) in a traditional 'democratic' setting, with more background and individual characterization than what we have in *Gorgias*. And *Gorgias* has many lengthy arguments or protreptic speeches and relatively little elenchus; *Republic* I has few speeches but abounds in rather strict elenchus.

*Republic* I operates with several pairs of pointedly contrasted concepts, notably δίκαιος / ἄδικος (331c ff. and passim), φίλοι / ἐχθροί (332a ff.), ὠφελεῖν / βλάπτειν (or εὖ / κακῶς ποιεῖν, etc. 332b ff.), ἀγαθοί / κακοί (or πονηροί 334c ff.), κρείττων / ἥττων (338c ff.), ἄρχοντες / ἀρχόμενοι (339c ff.), εὐδαίμων / ἄθλιος (344a ff.) more occasionally e.g. χρήσιμος / ἄχρηστος 332e ff.), θερμός /

---

85. Cf. above, n. 43.
86. Cf. above, 256 ff., 352 ff. Since few scholars now tend to separate Book I from the rest of *Republic* (see Kahn 1993), and the order *Gorgias*—*Republic* is universally taken for granted, *Republic* I is usually considered later than *Gorgias*. But the question of priority is still open.

[45] ψυχρός (335cd), ἄκων / ἑκών (336c), διδάσχειν / μανθάνειν (338b), ξύμφερος / ἀξύμφερος (339c ff.), πολιτικός / ἰδιωτικός (345e), φρόνιμος / ἄφρων (349c ff.). In the first place, they function as polarized opposites for the sake of argument. They belong to the ordinary human world and everyday linguistic classifications. In fact, the dialogue moves almost entirely on the human level. The setting and various hints suggest that Plato makes a point of Socrates now being among influential democrats where the rule of the 'stronger' (in the sense of the majority) prevails: note the opening references to persuasion and force (327c–328a); the character of the Bendis festival (also 354a); the political orientation of most of the people who meet at Cephalus'; and Thrasymachus' rudely scornful interventions (336b, etc.). The names of Polemarchus and Thrasymachus are also suggestive; friendly old Cephalus ('the Capital') soon withdraws. The dialogue ends in aporia. Socrates admits (354a–c) that his dialectic has been too 'gluttonous' (as befits a Bendis festival); and Plato's brothers remark, at the beginning of Book II, that Socrates' argument has been insufficient. We get the impression that Plato has deliberately kept his Socrates on the level of 'opinions.' The word 'philosophy' is not mentioned, though Socrates, of course, stands out as a dialectician.

On closer inspection, however, there are some traces of a two-level conception in at least some of these contrasting pairs. The basic theme of justice is viewed in terms of a kind of balance, with a successive shift of proportions following the aporias met. The simple notion of 'paying everybody his due' (with an ironic use of ἀλήθεια as 'trustworthiness' 331e f.) is complicated (334b) by the contrasts 'friends / enemies,' 'good' and 'bad' people, 'true' and 'apparent' friends (334e, pregnant), 'helping and harming,' the significance of what is 'good' (335b ff.), and the Socratic paradox that the just man will never harm anybody (335e). Thus, in the Polemarchus chapter, a δίκαιος obtains a greater specific weight than an ἄδικος. Thrasymachus (like Callicles in *Gorgias*) stands for the thesis of the right of the κρείττων (ambivalently 'stronger' and 'better') against which Socrates, ostensibly the weaker part, argues with some sophistry that leaders qua leaders, like all craftsmen, actually act in the interest of their subjects (the 'objects' of their activity, namely the 'weaker' part, 341c ff.), and not in their own interest. Thrasymachus
[46] asserts (343b ff.) that the tyrant qua ἄδικος is the happiest of men. We are probably supposed to notice that the idea of 'the right of the κρείττων' (versus ἥττων) becomes ever more clearly associated with Plato's higher level (cf. 345e ff.). In an interlude, Socrates playfully suggests (348ab) that the proportions of the eventual profit (λυσιτελές, ἀγαθά) of justice versus wrong-doing might be worked out by measuring.[87] The usefulness of justice, and hence the idea of balance, is the subject of the ensuing rather careless elenchus where justice becomes connected with knowledge and, being a virtue (350d), with the soul (353d ff.): since the proper function of the soul is to be concerned, lead, and deliberate, only the just man whose soul is just will 'live well' and be εὐδαίμων. We can see here, in glimpses and hints, how one of the terms in the contrasts employed becomes connected with the higher level, and the opposite with the lower level of Plato's vision. In particular, this applies to the only clearly thematic use of the pairs, δίκαιος / ἄδικος.

---

87. Cf. *Protagoras* 356d, *Politicus* 283e ff.

## Lysis

This dialogue may also be adduced as an interesting illustration of Plato's use of polar opposites. The extensive, somewhat bantering opening of the dialogue gives some glimpses of what we may understand as two-level contrasts: note the tension and rivalry between the lovers and their objects (with Socrates implicitly as the First Lover), and the seemingly paradoxic notions of a διάνοια in 'manic' love lyrics (205b) and of being τὰ ἐρωτικὰ σοφός (206a). By explicitly introducing φιλία as a theme of the discussion (207c), Socrates demonstrates how to lead dialectic (cf. 206c, 210e) with a very young person, Lysis. Contrasts familiar to the boy are brought to light: how is it that his parents who do love him (φιλεῖ) and wish him well, have his well-being restricted by prohibitions and punishments and even let him, a free-born child, be commanded by slaves? Generalizing polarizations such as Greeks / barbarians and men / women occur in passing (210b). The concept φιλία is viewed in terms of taking care of one's own (209c ff., cf. οἰκεῖος / ἀλλότριος 210cd), and σοφία is required here (210cd). After an interlude, Socrates enters on a more philosophic elenchus with Menexenus (212a ff.) about the relations of the subject and object of φιλία. What about the φιλεῖν / μισεῖν relation, and concepts such as φιλο-σοφία? How far can the saying 'like likes like' be applied (214a ff.)? If the 'good likes the good,' does the 'bad like' or 'hate' the 'good' or the 'bad'? By contrasting ὅμοιος / ἀνόμοιος (διάφορος), ἀγαθός / κακός (πονηρός), ὠφελία / βλαβή, and παρών / χωρίς, Socrates argues that in all φύσις (cf. 214b) a positive or constructive relationship (τροφή 215e) in fact results from polar opposites (215d f.). A long list of such 'constructive' ἐνάντια is given, beginning with πένης / πλούσιος, ἀσθενής / ἰσχυρός, κάμνων / ἰατρός. But this would give the 'antilogists' reason to ask whether ἔχθρα is not after all the polar opposite (ἐναντιώτατον) of φιλία, and δίκαιος of ἄδικος, σώφρων of ἀκόλαστος, ἀγαθός of κακός, etc. (216ab); so in what sense are such opposites constructive? From this seemingly aporetic handling of opposites on the level of the concrete physical world, Socrates proceeds to a more 'visionary'[88] (and, indeed, thematic) treatment of φιλία as an intermediate between what is classed as 'good' and 'bad.' More explicitly than above, φιλία (like ἔρως in *Symposium*) is now seen as an 'orientation' from a lower level towards a higher one. Some hints in the text (notably the παρουσία 217b ff. and τὸ ἀγαθόν as a 'final' cause 220ab) suggest that Plato expects some readers to be better informed about Academic thought than Socrates' interlocutors are.[89] The probably playful examples of a 'presence' of 'whiteness' and of τὸ κακόν (we know of course that all people tend to get white hair as time advances, but in what sense do they become 'bad'?) show that Plato operates with Forms (cf. below, 447). However, the aporia here faced (218cd), namely where and on which side to put the 'cause' of φιλία, marks a decisive change to a more metaphysical approach: we are probably to

---

88. Note ἰλιγγιῶ 216c, (ἀπο) μαντεύεσθαι 216d.
89. Note also the pointedly repeated ἐξ Ἀκαδημείας εὐθὺ Λυκείου 203ab. This 'two-level interpretation' will, on the whole, meet the arguments of Tejera 1990 against authenticity.

[47] understand that the πρῶτον φίλον (219c ff.) is, in fact, τὸ ἀγαθόν—although Socrates then focuses on the apparent efficient cause. But does the latter after all function as a cause (221a ff.)? Socrates returns to the idea that everybody wants to have the οἰκεῖον (221e), and hence to new aporias concerning ὅμοιον and ταὐτόν versus ἕτερον (222b ff.). I would conclude from all this that the dialogue is primarily intended as a piece of training in reasoning around the ambiguous concept of φιλία, where the polar opposites play a considerable part but are gradually reduced, implicitly and from the viewpoint of relatively well-informed readers, to a series of two-level contrasts. Here the lower level is 'oriented' towards the higher, and the higher level culminates in τὸ ἀγαθόν.

## Euthydemus

Here a number of opposite concepts are used by the erist brothers for their paradoxes. This is likely to have been a habitual practice among sophists of the 'eristic school.' Their first set of arguments concern σοφοί / ἀμαθεῖς (275d ff.), 'teaching / learning' and 'knowledge / ignorance.' Socrates points out to Clinias (277d ff.) that the erists use the words in senses different from (indeed opposite to, 278a) the normal meaning. He goes on to argue, with occasional employment of other opposites (μᾶλλον / ἧττων, ἀσθενής / ἰσχυρός, etc. 281c) that σοφία is always in real life preferable to ἀμαθία (279c ff.): in short, one is 'good,' the other 'bad' (281e); as yet a two-level contrast is not envisaged. However, Socrates then makes the 'protreptic' (282d, cf. 283ab) point that, granting that σοφία (or ἐπιστήμη) is
[48] teachable (282c, left open), φιλο-σοφεῖν is always important (282d). This Platonic notion of philosophy as orientation towards a perhaps unreachable σοφία is here veiled as if concerning only practical skill. Socrates then, somewhat unexpectedly, turns to the erists with the question whether there exists one ἐπιστήμη over the others which pertains to happiness and to being ἀγαθός (282e). The erists continue as before, trying to blur the differences: as one is or cannot be either σοφός or ἀμαθής (283d), so one cannot ψεύδεσθαι or ἀληθῆ λέγειν (283e ff., cf. 272b), and the ὄντα and μὴ ὄντα mix (284b, cf. 285e f.). 'Good / bad' and 'warm / cold' seem to prove the same. Even ἀντιλέγειν is impossible (285e ff.). Socrates tries to make a new, more serious approach to the problem of 'true / false' by introducing the intermediate notion of δοξάζειν (286d), but the erists continue twisting the words. Socrates then, turning to Clinias (and to Criton of the frame dialogue), resumes the issue of φιλοσοφία (288d) and, in the central section of the dialogue,[90] leads the discussion to a classification of various τέχναι (and ἐπιστῆμαι) and to the contrast ποιεῖν / χρῆσθαι (289d). There seems indeed to exist a 'highest art,' which is a 'user's and not a 'producer's art, a βασιλικὴ τέχνη (291b–d; note the connection with dialectic, cf. 290c). The erists, however, respond to this with more nonsense about 'knowing all / nothing,' 'now / always' (293b

---

90. For the pedimental structure of this dialogue, cf. above p. 111, Thesleff 1993: 31. Particularly thoughtful analyses of this section can be found in Sprague 1965 (1993), cf. 1976: 48 ff.

ff.), δυνατόν / ἀδύνατον, σιγᾶν / λέγειν (300a ff.), etc.; also 'same / different' (297d ff.) which Socrates later (301a ff.) turns into a kind of two-level contrast. In the concluding frame dialogue the φιλοσοφία issue recurs (304e ff.), probably with some allusive play about Isocrates being 'in between' good and bad (305e f.), and about the true philosopher's orientation. Thus polar opposites are used, in this dialogue, almost entirely for eristic purposes, twisting their meanings in everyday language for the sake of paradoxic assertions; but occasionally Socrates pushes them, rather allusively, in the direction of two-level contrasts. Here we can again see how the 'two-level model' is philosophically relevant to Plato.

## Phaedo

This dialogue elucidates particularly well Plato's conception of opposites and, in general, contrasts.

### Opposites

The question of opposites runs as a basic theme throughout the dialogue. Its general frame is formed by the contrasts soul / body and life / death. The former is rather clearly viewed as a two-level contrast. The latter turns around the questions of the orientation, immortality and destiny of the soul, without any specific analysis or discussion of the nature of death as a contrast to life. Somewhat loosely, death seems to be regarded as a decomposition typical of bodily matters (cf. e.g. 80bc): in this sense it is a lower level phenomenon.

Two-level contrasts are developed in various ways around the soul / body complex. Note especially 78b ff. (whereas Socrates' statement at 103b is perhaps directed against Presocratic dualism).

Manifestly polar opposites are first introduced with Socrates' brief reflections on ἡδονή / λύπη when his fetters are removed (60b). We understand that these are physical phenomena (cf. 83d, 86bc, and above, p. 406), as are tears and laughter (and indeed the hemlock and the cock; concrete issues are concentrated at the beginning and end of the dialogue). In a rhetorical context, 66b ff., the body is described as κακόν (and the soul by implication as 'good'; cf. also 78b ff. and elsewhere) which has caused much discussion of Platonic 'dualism.' But as we shall see in the context of Forms (below), a conceptual dualism in terms of pointed value contrasts is avoided. More consistently, polar opposites are discussed within the argument 'opposites arise from opposites' (70c ff.). By way of illustration, τὸ καλόν / τὸ αἰσχρόν and δίκαιον / ἄδικον are mentioned as opposites (70e που!, cf. 71a) like 'bigger / smaller,' 'stronger / weaker,' 'warm / cold,' 'awake / sleeping,' and indeed 'life / death'; but it is important to note that we are here moving solely on the physical level (ὅσαπερ ἔχει γένεσιν 70d, cf.71c, e; ἐξ ἐναντίων τὰ ἐναντία πράγματα 71a, pointed out explicitly at 103b). These are no cosmic ('metaphysic') opposites, though Presocratic conceptions figure in

[49] the background (cf. 70c, 96a ff.). Here as elsewhere Plato is unable to imagine a cosmic opposition of 'good' and 'evil.'[91]

The thesis 'opposites from opposites' is then applied to the ἀνάμνησις argument (72e ff.) which starts from the recollection of geometrical truths (with a clear reference at 73ab to the experiment known to us from the *Meno*, if not to the actual dialogue *Meno*). Socrates now adds that sense impressions (αἴσθησις 73c) of something (e.g. a lyre), may awake a memory of something different (e.g. the εἶδος of a boy); so in fact both ὅμοια and ἀνόμοια contribute to recollection (74a, cf. 76a). But it is αὐτὸ τὸ ἴσον which the soul recollects and which enables it to distinguish (and 'associate') objects (74a ff.). It is, I think, important to note here that the ἀνόμοιον (ἀνισότης 74cd) is not taken to be a Form of the same standard as αὐτὸ τὸ ἴσον: 'difference' would seem to be a characteristic of the lower level (cf. 74 ff.).

[50] The issue of opposites is again taken up in connection with the discussion of soul as a 'harmony' (85e ff., especially 91e ff.). Socrates remarks (90a) that opposites normally combine in the physical (concrete) reality; extremes are scarce (cf. 71c). A soul, however, cannot consist of opposites (92a ff.); rather, it dominates opposites (94cd, cf. 79de). Again the opposites are seen as part of Plato's lower level. Even more clearly, polar opposites are reduced to the physical world in the digression on 'natural history' (96a ff.): even Anaxagoras' Νοῦς is no sufficient explanation (αἰτία 96e) of the physical process of γένεσις / φθορά.

*Forms and opposites*

To be able to follow Socrates' final set of arguments (102b ff.), we have to consider what is said in *Phaedo* about the theory of Forms (cf. below, Chapters VI and VII).

In the (rather rhetorical) context of 65a ff., there is a reference to Forms (Ideas) of the αὐτό type: δίκαιον αὐτό, καλόν, ἀγαθόν, μέγεθος, ὑγιεία, ἰσχύς. Later, with the recollection argument, αὐτὸ τὸ ἴσον is added (74a; it is an αὐτὸ τὸ ὃ ἔστιν, 74d), still without a corresponding opposite Form: it is with the help of this τὸ ἴσον that we are able to recognize similarities and, in fact, differences (cf. ταὐτόν, below). Then at 75cd comes the interesting extension of the earlier (72e ff.) ἀνάμνησις theory to the 'earlier' (65a ff.) theory of Forms. Here τὸ ἴσον draws with it τὸ μεῖζον and τὸ ἔλαττον, apparently as supposedly innate 'means' of recognizing differences (cf. ἕτερον τι 76a); surely Plato would not at this stage have admitted that there exists a Form of 'bigger' or 'smaller.' But Socrates goes on to say that we apparently do not recollect only τὸ ἴσον (i.e. the Idea of Similarity), but all the αὐτὸ ὃ ἔστι entities which are the object of dialectic, namely αὐτὸ τὸ καλόν, ἀγαθόν, δίκαιον, ὅσιον, 'and the rest.' No opposites are mentioned. A similar picture is given at 78b ff., discussing the soul's unmixed character. However, with the renewed introduction of Forms at 100b (the πολυθρύλητα,

---

91. On this level there is alteration between ἕτερα: a pure τὸ αὐτό would be impossible, 72bc. For Presocratic dualism, cf. especially Eryximachus in *Symposium* 185e–188e.

cf. 75d, 76d), Socrates moves from the Value Forms (Ideas) mentioned before, [50] via a μέγεθος which draws with it a σμικρότης (100e, cf. 'bigger' and 'smaller,' above), and a πλῆθος, (101b) all of which seem now to function as Forms, to δυάς and μονάς (101c). Here the tentative and 'hypothetical' nature of the argument is emphasized.[92]

The final set of arguments open (102b) with an application of the contrast μέγεθος / σμικρότης introduced just before. These are now called εἴδη: the term εἶδος (later also ἰδέα, 104b, etc.) is from now on employed in a technical sense. Physical objects can partake in contrasting Forms and take their names from them (for instance, a man can be called either big or small or both, though Socrates, ironically, accepts being always 'small,' 102e); but qua Forms they seem to stand alone (102cd, cf. 103b, and below). We may safely infer from the following that Plato sees the conflict between opposites as a matter of the lower level.

An interesting key to the subsequent discussion is given by the metaphors of φεύγειν and ὑπεκχωρεῖν versus ἀπολωλέναι (102d). A Form (in this case μέγεθος [51] or σμικρότης) does not accept its opposite, nor does it 'withdraw' or 'perish'; but in a physical object which cannot partake in both of two opposite Forms, the quality in question will in fact either 'withdraw' or 'perish' (as seems to happen to Socrates the ironist). Surely, however, the metaphors are not adduced to explain the theory of Forms: Plato here begins to drive home the point that the soul may 'withdraw' but never 'perish.' The only pair of opposite Forms so far taken into account, μέγεθος and σμικρότης, does not illustrate this point particularly well. By making one of the friends present recall the earlier 'opposites from opposites' argument (103a, cf. 70c ff.), Plato induces Socrates to take a better example: 'fire' / 'snow' and 'hot' / 'cold' respectively, to which he adds 'odd' and 'even' number (103e). These examples are supposed to show that some things, owing to their typical quality ('essential' as contrasted to 'accidental' quality, to use Aristotelian terms), expel their opposites when coming in contact with them, or 'withdraw.' A typical quality, of course, is always a Form in some sense. There has been much discussion of what Plato means to take as Forms in this somewhat confused piece of argument: does, for instance, πῦρ have a Form other than τὸ θερμόν; and is περιττόν or μονάς (or ἕν) the ultimate Form of any 'odd number'?[93] 'Life' at any rate does have a Form typical of 'soul' (106d). I am inclined to think that Plato is deliberately obscure since these problems were under continuous debate in the Academy.

Though εἶδος and ἰδέα are here used as terms, and the 'conceptual' Forms (cf. below) which are now in the foreground function very similarly to Ideas, it is primarily the conceptual Forms corresponding to physical phenomena that represent opposites. As such, Ideas lack opposites. At 105d, for instance, ἄμουσος and ἄδικος seem to be mere denominations, and Plato is evidently reluctant to

---

92. Note 100b, 101d, etc.; cf. below, n. 94.
93. Cf. Nehamas 1973, and now Devereux 1994: 66 ff. Guthrie IV 357 n. 3 points out that, for Plato, the problem was ontological, not logical. And Kahn 1996: 336 n. 10 (cf. 357 f.) is certainly right in declaring (as to *Phaedo* 102b ff.) that 'immanent' opposites are no Forms; cf. below, 448.

[51] speak of negatively valued conceptual Forms. I would suggest that Plato has made these apparently new moves in the *Phaedo* as thought experiments for the sake of argument.[94]

It is very important to note that Socrates and his partners are not, in *Phaedo*, discussing or thematically developing the theory of Forms. Whether the *Phaedo* represents directly some successive stages of change in Plato's conception of Forms (as is often believed), or it reflects imperfectly the oral discussion of the issue in the Academy (I think the latter, cf. 75d, 76d, 100b, and the *Parmenides*),
[52] Plato adduces only such aspects of the theory that he thinks will illustrate his present themes: namely, the Philosopher's orientation, and the immortality of soul. This leads to thought experiments.

The arguments about 'essential' qualities are supposed to show, or suggest, that the soul, like 'fire' or 'odd number,' may withdraw from a contact with something representing its opposite (in this case the body). But the soul cannot perish, since it is by definition ('essentially') bound to higher-level entities: to 'unity,' constant 'similarity,' 'invisibility,' 'incorporeality,' etc. and, indeed, to 'life' and 'immortality,' all qualities that have been repeatedly ventilated in the previous discussion. The circularity of this 'proof' is, at least, fairly well and widely anchored in Plato's two-level vision, and in a number of extensions of the 'earlier' theory of Forms.

Plato is not concerned with details of the theory here, but he obviously extends his theory of Forms from the original Value Forms (Ideas) of the αὐτό type, over mathematical concepts and means of measuring taken over from the ἀνάμνησις theory, to various other concepts ('universals,' here called εἴδη or ἰδέαι) taken from the physical reality, which may include opposites. It is clear, however, that he wants all these abstractions to stand 'alone' on the level of Forms: not to act as opposites, not to be in conflict, perhaps to 'withdraw' but never to 'perish.' And it is also clear that he very reluctantly, if at all, operates with Forms opposite to Ideas proper: insofar as such opposites are Forms at all, they are 'conceptual' Forms without a clear metaphysical status (cf. below, 452 f.). Mark well, there is no αὐτὸ τὸ κακόν, αὐτὸ τὸ ἄδικον for Plato (cf. below, 448 ff.). He takes it for granted that there is no antagonism or conflict of opposites on the higher level. We shall return to this issue below.

---

94. Note the doubts that open the central section (84b ff.), and the rather open end of the argument developing the 'full' theory of Forms. In fact, however, the place of *Phaedo* in this 'development' is not easy to ascertain; cf. below, 452 f., 493.

# VI

## ON IDEAS AND FORMS

### The secondary status of the theory of Forms

The brief analyses made above of the argument in the *Phaedo* may serve as introduction to this chapter.

The so-called theory of Forms (Ideas), with all its alleged or real changes or ramifications, can be generally characterized as a series of attempts by Plato (and his associates) to bring what we should call a 'conceptual' apparatus into his vision of the upper level of reality, and to explicate the relations of the levels in such terms. The central position of the 'theory of Forms' in Plato's thought is easily exaggerated; indeed, Aristotle's criticism has made it appear as Plato's main doctrine. However, it constitutes only one aspect of his philosophic moves. The two levels as such, and the problems of their internal relations, always remained as foundations and frames in his thinking. The various themes and methods of the dialogues show plainly that many other aspects of his two-level vision kept in the foreground, indeed more prominently than any theory of Forms.

As a matter of fact, as has been often noted, the theory of Forms (in a large sense) is nowhere in the dialogues subject to a really thematic or systematic treatment. Even the four or five contexts where it is discussed in some detail, viz. the two sections in *Phaedo* analyzed above, *Republic* V–VII, the first part of *Parmenides*, and the central part of the *Sophist*, have ultimately other aims than a presentation of the theory: the *Phaedo* presents the Philosopher and searches for arguments to support the theory of immortality of soul, the *Republic* (like *Phaedo*) is concerned with the orientation of philosophic man, *Parmenides* criticizes an earlier version of the theory, and the *Sophist* tries to define dihaeretically the 'sophist' and non-being. Furthermore: the dialogues are never systematic philosophic treatises, and they are not likely on the whole to reflect directly the development of Plato's thought: each dialogue seems to have had its own purpose and its own potential non-professional audience whose familiarity with the issues varied from case

[53]
[54] to case. Plato seldom had reason to present his full up-to-date view of any theory he had. Without any doubt, there was an 'esoteric' discussion of Forms (Ideas), as well as of other problematic questions, going on in the Academy.[95]

This is not the place to enter into a discussion of the details of the theory of Forms, but I want to make a set of points connected with my view of Plato's two-level model.

## Notes on the terminology

The modern interpretation of Plato's 'theory of Forms' has been hampered and confused by several circumstantial facts: the lack of a thematic treatment in the dialogues; Plato's notoriously inconsistent use of terms; possible textual corruptions (on the whole not taken into account here); the allusions and ambivalent criticism possibly implied in many contexts where Forms are mentioned; the supposed lines of development in Plato's thought, methods and manners of writing; Aristotle's somewhat inconsistent and mostly adverse dealing with the theory in different places; and also the applying to Plato's thought of anachronistic categories such as 'abstraction' or 'concept,' or an anachronistic differentiation between ontological (metaphysical), epistemological, logical, and perhaps linguistic and psychological aspects of the theory.[96]

Leaving now aside the vexing details of the chronological problems, I am prepared to accept the view that the core of what I prefer to call the theory of Ideas underwent little or no change in Plato's thought between, say, the 390s and the 340s, but that there did occur changes of emphasis and that there were many accretions to the theory. The latter are clearly visible in the 'late' dialogues beginning with the *Parmenides*. This 'later' stage is also reflected in an expanding use of the term εἶδος (and to some extent ἰδέα).

[55] It is helpful for the interpretation to try to make a rough distinction between what can generally be called 'Forms,' and a core section of such entities for which I would reserve the time-honored term 'Idea' (with a capital 'I'). This differentiation

---

95. This is what πολυθρύλητα implies. Cf. *Parmenides* and *Sophist*, and what we know of Plato's pupils' attitudes to the theory.—In modern literature on Plato, the Forms are even more πολυθρύλητα, and because they keep intriguing critics (since Plato's days), their actual relevance to Plato has probably been much overrated. Different comprehensive approaches can be found, apart from Ross 1951 and Guthrie IV–V 1975–78, in Schmitz 1985, Penner 1987, Fine 1993, Devereux 1994, Dorter 1994, McCabe 1994, Blackson 1995, Szaif 1996, and Kahn 1996; cf. also the thoughtful review article by von Perger and Hoffmann 1997. The premises suggested in this study motivate a reconsideration of some aspects of the issue.

96. Most of the scholars listed in n. 95 are clearly aware of these complications, though they deal with them in different ways.

is faintly suggested by Aristotle's use of the terms εἶδος and ἰδέα, but should not be identified with it.[97]

## Forms in general

### Pre-Platonic background

First some preliminary notes on 'Forms.' No matter what terms or ways of expression Plato happens to use, and so far disregarding any consistent 'theory of Forms,' I would assign to 'Forms' all 'abstractions' of properties and things insofar as their internal relations or their relations to individual ('concrete') instances or particulars are under discussion. Such general (generic) 'names' of particular things, qualities, or manifestations (say, τὸ δίκαιον, τὰ κακά, ἀρετή, τέχνη), more or less vaguely conceived as 'universals,' are naturally employed by Plato in accordance with everyday Greek linguistic categorization. Whatever tendencies there may have been to classify things by means of such 'universals' (we shall return to this), the background of all this is difficult to ascertain in details; it is certainly Pre-Platonic.

It should be noted, for instance, that the formation of abstract nouns from the neuter of adjectives (or the infinitive) by means of the article had become very common in 'sophisticated' language since the last third of the 5th century.[98] It is also important to keep in mind that abstractions of the type of τὸ ἄπειρον, τὸ δίκαιον, properly mean '(that) what is limitless,' '(that) what is right,' which is easily felt both as a 'group' or 'class' of similar instances, and as pointing 'exactly' to the meaning of the word.

The original meaning of εἶδος and ἰδέα, '(outward) appearance,' 'shape,' often occurs in Plato alongside the secondary meanings of 'aspect' or 'type' (which are also Pre-Platonic and which sometimes lead to a vaguely periphrastic meaning, 'sort of') and besides the technical meaning of 'Form' in a Platonic sense.[99]

---

97. For the terminology in general and the traditional developmentalist view of a gradual shift in Plato's conception of Forms from 'immanence' to 'transcendence,' see the simplifying and clear-cut presentation by Ross 1951. Schmitz 1985 distinguishes, in a rather fresh manner, two main aspects which he calls 'koinonistisch' and 'isolationistisch' (II 14 f.), though his picture is blurred by his reliance on conventional chronology. A dogmatically simplified combination of Ross and Schmitz occurs in Baltes 1994. For Aristotle's views in particular, see the very different presentations by Schmitz, Fine 1993, and Isnardi Parente 1997. The 'one over many' question, problematized by Aristotle, is prominent in most modern studies (see notably McCabe 1994); for the 'intermediate' mathematicals, see below, p. 478.

98. Such nouns abound in Thucydides who has a marked preference for abstract nouns; cf. Denniston 1952: 36 f., Kahn 1996: 332 f. The notion of 'abstraction' is anachronistic if applied to such linguistic usage, but as a faint tendency towards classification the usage is interesting though mostly forgotten by those who investigate the origins of Plato's theories.

99. See the fairly full (but not complete) documentation of the occurrences in Plato, in des Places 1964 (complemented by Brandwood 1976). The 'first' occurrences of the Platonic terms are often said to be *Euthyphro* 5d, 6de, *Meno* 72c and *Hippias Major* 289d, 298b.

[56] The term εἶδος seems to have been employed for classification before Plato in some arts and crafts, notably in rhetoric and medicine,[100] and theoretical generalization was typical of Presocratic thought.

It looks, however, as if the closest we come to any theory of classification of denominations before Plato is Prodicus' search for semantic distinctions and, possibly, the historical Socrates' search for definitions. Whatever the contribution of the historical Socrates may have been (Aristotle considered it important, as we know), this search for ὅροι naturally strengthened Plato's conviction that there are common 'shapes' for all similar instances bearing the same 'name.' But although Socrates was known always to pursue 'the same' (above, 409 f.), we have no clear indications that Socrates himself or the minor Socratics had arrived at any consistent theory about this. The theory of immutable εἴδη is extremely likely to have been Plato's own. It was an aspect of his own two-level vision. An εἶδος is the 'single' and 'stable' but 'invisible' (i.e. 'divine' etc.) common shape corresponding to an indeterminate series of similar but varied phenomena.

*'Shape' rather than 'class'*

It is reasonable to ask now what made Plato adopt, for his immutable 'types,' the metaphor of εἶδος (ἰδέα), 'appearance,' rather than e.g. γένος, ὅρος, σχῆμα, φύσις, τύπος, etc. which never became terminologically fixed in this sense. The association with εἰδέναι, ἰδεῖν, presents itself naturally, but Plato rarely makes a point of it (as in *Meno* 71c, *Republic* VI 505a ff., cf. the ἰδέα of κάλλος *Republic* V 479a).[101] The best illustration of how Plato's associations run is probably found in *Meno*, a methodologically important dialogue. Socrates switches Menon's opening question about the teachability of ἀρετή into a question of τί ἐστι (versus ὁποῖόν τι 71b), and Menon answers with a series of examples which in Socrates' opinion are just like a σμῆνος, a 'swarm' of bees (72a). But, speaking of swarms, what is it, then, which is the οὐσία by which every bee 'is' a bee, though they may differ in size, position, etc.? They all have one and the same εἶδος, of course (72c). 'Shape' is here bound to the notions of 'true being,' 'one' and 'same' (upper-level notions, as we have seen). The same would apply to all different ἀρεταί, and to health, big size, strength (72de); there is certainly an 'and so forth' implied here, though Socrates does not enter into it. Εἶδος is here taken in its original sense [57] of 'appearance,' interpreted as something like 'characteristic shape,' but not as 'kind,' 'class' (which seems to be the implication of e.g. *Symposium* 210b2 ἐπ' εἴδει). An association with 'class' may have come in with the 'swarm,' but Plato soon discards it by introducing σχῆμα as a parallel to εἶδος (73e ff.; cf. the parallel εἶδος / μορφή *Phaedo* 103e). Interestingly enough, σχῆμα then becomes defined

---

100. *See* Festugière 1948: 50–53, and below, 451.
101. At *Phaedo* 75d it is αὐτὸ ὃ ἔστι which is the object of true εἰδέναι, whereas εἶδος is not introduced until 79a, and ἰδέα at 102b. This fact supports Kahn's (1996, especially 354 f.) interpretation of Forms (Ideas) as primarily definitional.

as the 'limits of a body' (στερεοῦ πέρας 76a), whereas the nature (or, as we are surely to understand, the ὅρος) of ἀρετή and the internal relations of its parts produce additional difficulties. 'What is always the same' in all instances of ἀρετή, its 'true being,' is what Plato's Socrates seems to understand as its εἶδος. But this terminology is dropped after the opening moves of the dialogue.

We need not think, as is traditionally done, that the *Meno* reflects the theory of Ideas in its making, a tentative opening 'not yet' followed up. *Meno*, I assert, was written as an Academic contribution to the 'teachability' problem, and it is full of issues about which the reader is expected to possess some previous information. Vice versa, in *Phaedo* (*see* above, 433 ff.) εἶδος and ἰδέα come in relatively late, long after the theory of Ideas has been first referred to. In fact, as every Plato student knows, they never become definitely fixed terms.

## Ideas

### Ideas as values

It is significant, however, and indeed of essential importance to note, that before the 'late dialogues,' Plato preferably introduces 'Value Forms,' or what I have called 'Ideas' proper.[102] He focuses on what is 'good,' 'fine,' 'strong,' 'healthy,' or on abstract things (such as ἀρετή or the ἀρεταί) which seem to have such implications. I take this to be a natural consequence of his two-level vision, and also of his always pronouncedly ethical inclinations: philosophy, and more generally the life of human beings, should aim at the perfect—an ideal never reached, to be sure.

Another, mostly forgotten aspect of these upper-level Values is their 'complexity.' They are typically complex entities, in spite of the fact that Plato is careful to consider them as unique. The Good as such, or what is Right, or Virtue as such, Knowledge as such, have a wide scope naturally connected with their applicability; even Similarity as such is not easily grasped as a definite unity. Plato must have been aware of this complexity though he discusses it only or chiefly in connection with ἀρετή. Indeed, the most detailed and suggestive illustration of an Idea that we have in the dialogues, Diotima's description of the Philosopher's sudden experience of τὸ πολὺ πέλαγος τοῦ καλοῦ in its purity and absoluteness (*Symposium* 210d–211b), appears to present to us the 'upper level' in its entirety. Probably it is not the analysis of concepts but the relation between the two levels in terms of Values that is one of the primary characteristics of the 'theory or Ideas.'

---

102. The specifically Platonic 'Forms' have been preferably called 'Ideas' until the translation 'Forms' replaced the latter, especially in Anglo-Saxon terminology, owing to Aristotelian influence (I believe), but with new confusions ensuing. For 'Ideas' as Values, *see* particularly Santas 1983, Dorter 1994.

[58]     It is natural, also, to infer from the two-level vision that all 'Ideas' (whatever terms used), are (in spite of the κοινωνία between the levels) somehow 'transcendent,' i.e. distinct (χωρίς) from and pointedly primary in relation to sensible things (though they are certainly not 'beyond being'): being 'divine,' invisible and attainable by intellect only, they belong entirely to the higher level in Plato's vision. They are never simply 'immanent' (as has been often asserted). This is particularly obvious if we consider the αὐτό terminology connected with the theory of Ideas.[103]

Whether or not εἶδος and ἰδέα are employed as terms, the theory of 'Ideas' operates around the question of 'what truly is' and 'is always the same' in different instances of things having the same 'name,' and how that essence is related to the instances. These questions are articulations of the two-level vision, and they can be traced in most dialogues, including some which are traditionally considered very 'early.' And I believe the complications are not exactly where most modern interpretations have found them, but elsewhere.

*Examples of Ideas of the αὐτό type*

With reference to the instances in *Phaedo* (above, p. 434 ff.), I give here a further list illustrating the varying terminology used 'before' the *Parmenides* for Ideas discussed or put in relation to concrete manifestations in the human (physical) world. The list does not aim at completeness. For chronological considerations, see below, 489 ff.. *Apology* 36c αὐτὴ ἡ πόλις, suggesting a 'theory of the State as such.'[104] At *Theaetetus* 175c αὐτῆς δικαιοσύνης τε καὶ ἀδικίας, τί ... διαφέρετον suggests a theory (σκέψις) of contrasting the two, with emphasis on the Idea of δικαιοσύνη. In *Republic* II Glaucon and Adimantus ask for the nature and effect of δικαιοσύνη (and ἀδικία) 'as such': 358b αὐτὸ καθ' αὑτὸ ἐνὸν ἐν τῇ ψυχῇ (for δικαιοσύνη etc. 'entering' the soul, cf e.g. *Gorgias* 504de), varied at d, 363a αὐτὸ δικαιοσύνη.; 366e–367d; developed by Socrates at V 472c ἐζητοῦμεν αὐτὸ [59]     δικαιοσύνη οἷόν ἐστι (cf. II 368c διερευνῆσασθαί τί ἐστιν, etc.), X 612b; but (with direct reference to the theory of Ideas) VII 517e, X 612c, 614a αὐτὴ δικαιοσύνη. Cf. *Protagoras* 360e τί πότ' ἐστιν αὐτὸ ἡ ἀρετή, *Theaetetus* 146a γνῶναι ἐπιστήμην αὐτὸ ὅ τί πότ' ἐστι (cf. *Phaedrus* 247d). The neuter αὐτό also points to an established usage in cases such as *Cratylus* 413c αὐτὸ τὸ θερμόν, supposedly present in τὸ πῦρ (cf. Forms, below, p. 447). Here the semi-nonsensical context concerns τὸ δίκαιον; for moves around the latter, see especially *Republic* I 331d ff. which starts from a search for ὅρος δικαιοσύνης but where Plato probably intentionally avoids the αὐτό terminology. Similarly *Phaedrus* 247d αὐτὴ δικαιοσύνη,

---

103. Cf. 'One' and 'Same,' above 408–410. The importance in this connection of the αὐτό (ὅ ἐστίν) terminology is often recognized (see e.g. Ross 1951: 11 ff., Blackson 1995; Kahn 1996: 335 ff. derives the entire theory of Forms from questions of definition, reflected in this terminology), but, as far as I can see, a full investigation is lacking. For exemplification, see the list below.

104. In this context, the parallel is 'Know yourself'. Certainly there is more to this than just an exhortation to withdraw from political activities; cf. *Alcibiades* I 124a–125d.

followed by σωφροσύνη, ἐπιστήμη, referring to Ideas seen by gods alone (τὴν ἐν τῷ ὅ ἔστιν ὂν ὄντως ἐπιστήμην, expressively connecting the Idea with True Being). Also *Laches* 194a (cf. 189e f.) αὐτὴ ἡ ἀνδρεία, αὐτὴ ἡ καρτέρησις, with playful personification; *Protagoras* 330cd αὐτὴ ἡ ὁσιότης coupled with ἡ δικαιοσύνη; and with other value concepts, *Charmides* 166a αὐτὴ ἡ ἐπιστήμη, αὐτὴ ἡ λογιστική, *Hippias Major* 295b αὐτὸ ... τὸ καλόν (v.l., cf. 286d, 288a ff., 292cd, etc., below). Cf. *Euthyphro* 6d ἐκεῖνο αὐτὸ τὸ εἶδος of τὸ ὅσιον, *Cratylus* 440ab αὐτὸ τὸ εἶδος of γνῶσις (but with a neutral Form, 389d αὐτὸ ἐκεῖνο ὅ ἔστιν ὄνομα, cf. p. 447).

Uses of αὐτός meaning 'self' = 'in isolation,' 'alone,' occur, of course, outside the theory, as e.g. *Phaedo* 65e αὐτῇ διανοίᾳ, 66d, 67c, 70a, *Republic* VII 525c, 526b.

For the εἶδος of ἀρετή in *Meno*, see above. The curious τὸ ἐπ' εἴδει καλόν in *Symposium* 210b probably implies 'the typical' (below, 444). In *Lysis* 219b–222b τὸ πρῶτον φίλον (which is ἐκεῖνο αὐτό, τῷ ὄντι, etc.), to all intents and purposes functions as an Idea.

The *Euthyphro* has extensive pieces of dialectic around τὸ ὅσιον (and τὸ ἀνόσιον, cf. τὸ εὐσεβές, τὸ ἀσεβές 5c, etc.), in terms partly recalling *Meno* (cf. also e.g. ὡρισμένα 9c, ὑποθέμενος 9d): note 5c–6e with εἶδος and ἰδέα; 7cd aporia about τὸ δίκαιον, τὸ ἄδικων, καλόν, αἰσχρόν, ἀγαθόν, κακόν; 11a aporia about the οὐσία when the question concerns τὸ ὅσιον ὃ τί πότ' ἐστιν; 12c–e τὸ ὅσιον as 'part' of τὸ δίκαιον. For the negative concepts, see below, p. 449. The *Hippias Major* has very similar movements around (αὐτὸ) τὸ καλόν, though very little is said of its opposite; note 286d, 289d, 297b;[105] 298b with εἶδος and ἰδέα, 289c αὐτὸ καθ' αὑτὸ καλόν.

Thus the evidence of the dialogues so far considered suggests that the theory of Ideas was principally connected with the αὐτὸ (ὅ ἔστιν) terminology and was reflected in Plato's written oeuvre from the start. The terms εἶδος and ἰδέα come in secondarily. As will be seen below, they tend to denote Forms in general, though an actual 'theory of Forms' was only gradually developed.

*Presence, participation* [60]

Although upper-level entities (above, 441), Ideas are conceived of as somehow 'present' wherever they are manifested. For the 'presence' of virtue in the soul (where it may be a δύναμις or an ἔργον, *Laches* 192b, *Hippias Minor* 375de, *Republic* I 352d ff.), cf. e.g. *Republic* II 358b (above), *Gorgias*. 504de, *Charmides* 157a, 158e, *Euthydemus* 280b. In *Laches* 189d–190b (where παραγίγνεσθαι is a kind of term, cf. des Places 1964 s.v.) the question ὅ τί πότ' ἐστιν ἀρετή leads over (190d) to ἀνδρεία as a 'part' of it. The questions of 'presence' and 'participation' were under debate in the Academy, and μέθεξις became later a kind of term for this (cf. below, 446). More concretely: *Euthydemus* 301a, *Hippias Major* 294a, c, *Phaedo* 100d 'presence' of τὸ καλόν in an object; more abstractly: *Republic* VI 509b 'presence' of τὸ ἀγαθόν in

---

105. Probably including a nonsensical play with the Simile of the Sun in *Republic* VI.

[60] knowledge and being (here upper-level entities), cf. V 476a κοινωνία. At *Gorgias* 497e, 498de we are reminded of the 'presence' of ἀγαθά in ἀγαθοί, as of κάλλος in καλοί, and of κακά in κακοί, where the plurals ἀγαθά and κακά may have an ironical bent (if the text is not corrupt), cf. 467e 'participation' in τὸ ἀγαθόν, 499e (506cd) τὸ ἀγαθόν as τέλος (as in *Republic* VI, and probably indirectly *Lysis* 220b ἐκεῖνο αὐτό, cf. *Republic* VI 510e αὐτὰ ἐκεῖνα). At *Gorgias* 487e ἔνδεια and παρουσία refer to 'manifestations' of attitudes (σοφία, αἰσχύνη) rather than to Ideas (though probably with allusion to the discussion of the 'presence' of Ideas). Similarly at *Lysis* 217b, e, it is suggested that κακοῦ παρουσία may be the cause of φίλον τοῦ ἀγαθοῦ (above, p. 431); cf. 217d 'presence' of apparent and true λευκότης in hair. All in all it seems that the παρουσία terminology, with its potential religious connotations, was well suited for Ideas of positive value.

*See* further below. For εἶδος in *Gorgias* 503de, see p. 447.

## Τὸ καλόν and the two levels

Particularly often τὸ καλόν serves as an example of an Idea. Apart from the locus classicus in *Symposium*, and the gradual shifts from τὸ καλόν to τὸ ἀγαθόν in *Republic* V–VI, and the very ironical play with the former in *Hippias Major* (above), and some other instances quoted above (including *Phaedo*, 433 ff.), note here *Cratylus* 439cd, 440b (with τὸ ἀγαθόν), *Lysis* 216c–e (similar, but covertly ironical). In *Symposium* we encounter the term εἶδος for τὸ καλόν only in the odd phrasing at 210b διώκειν τὸ ἐπ' εἴδει καλόν (the 'typical'), whereas the actual Idea is described at 211ab by the spectacular αὐτὸ καθ' αὑτὸ μεθ' αὑτοῦ μονοειδὲς ἀεὶ ὄν (in which all beautiful and fine things 'participate'); this is close to the real τέλος (211b, presumably τὸ ἀγαθόν). In *Republic* V–VI, we reach ἡ τοῦ ἀγαθοῦ ἰδέα, the μέγιστον μάθημα (VI 505a, 508e, VII 517b, 526e, 534c), through preliminary illustrations of the theory of Ideas (and 'Forms') and, more generally, via Plato's vision of the two levels. Here, after a mention in passing of opposite εἴδη

[61] (V 476a, cf. 479b, *see* below), the emphasis lies on τὸ καλόν which only the true philosopher is able to envisage: note V 476b–d (including 'participation'), followed by a lengthy discussion of the two levels of being, especially ἐπιστήμη / δόξα (with εἶδος rather as a synonym of γένος). At 478e Socrates returns to the Idea of τὸ καλόν, as seen by a philosopher alone (479a αὐτὸ μὲν καλόν καὶ ἰδέαν τινα αὐτοῦ κάλλους . . . ἀεὶ μὲν κατὰ ταὐτὰ ὡσαύτως ἔχουσαν . . . ). Then again the beginning of Book VI (484a ff.) brings us back to a wider grasp of the two-level model and the philosopher's attitude to it, as contrasted to ordinary people's lack of understanding. The theory of Ideas is part of this vision, but its focus is still on τὸ καλόν. Note especially the provocative notion of the philosopher's 'making love to' τὸ ὄν and hence 'conceiving' (490ab), which clearly presupposes Diotima's mystery teaching in the *Symposium*,[106] and the references (493e and

---

106. Cf. Thesleff 1994: 115 f.

elsewhere) back to the earlier discussion of αὐτὸ τὸ καλόν. On the whole, this section of the *Republic* seems to me to illustrate in many ways how Plato's two-level vision forms an important background to the theory of Ideas. The subsequent discussion leads, through various digressions, to the μαθήματα of true philosophers (502c); and here the Idea of Good, τὸ ἀγαθόν, is eventually approached through τὸ καλόν (and τὸ δίκαιον, cf. 505b, d, 506cd, 507b, etc.); the same is somehow implied by the simile of the Sun 507d–509d.

## *Ideas 'as such' and as the focus of orientation*

To sum up, we can trace in these instances, as in the *Phaedo* (above, 433 ff.), a 'theory of Ideas' centered on 'concepts' (substances or properties) that represent essential positive values in Plato's thought. We may assume here a vaguely axiologic hierarchy of the Ideas, culminating in the καλόν—ἀγαθόν complex as presented in *Symposium* and *Republic* V–VII.

However, it seems to me quite significant that this hierarchy of the Ideas (contrary to Forms, *see* 450 ff.) is not expressively discussed in the dialogues, apart from the placing of τὸ ἀγαθόν 'above' τὸ καλόν (notably in *Republic* VI) and the occasional differentiating of the virtues (notably in *Protagoras* and *Republic* IV). The Ideas tend to represent the 'uppermost' level of Plato's universe as such. They are clearly rooted in his moral views, in the prominence of ethics, and more generally in the two-level vision inherent in his philosophy.[107] The upper level in general, seen as Perfect Being, is in the focus of Plato's thought (cf. e.g. *Phaedo* 76de, *Timaeus* 30a and passim, *Sophist* 248e), rather more than τὸ ἀγαθόν alone. In the case of τὸ καλόν, aesthetics should not be overrated. The *Symposium* is often said to be the breakthrough of the metaphysical view of Ideas; more cautiously, it can be taken as one, perhaps the only, 'semi-public' presentation of the Philosopher's vision.[108] In Diotima's rhetoric it is truth in general and 'excellence' in particular (ἀρετή 212a5) that the philosopher reaches on the upper ontological level; and this is here viewed in terms of τὸ καλόν which is more suggestive to non-philosophers than an abstract τὸ ἀγαθόν. Plato himself was familiar with a search for positive values 'as such' ever since the *Apology*—if indeed this was his first written work surviving in its original form.[109]

---

107. The axiologic hierarchy is often pointed out (e.g. Ross 1951: 24) but not very much utilized by students of Plato's 'Forms.'

108. Kahn 1996: 339 ff. argues emphatically that the *Symposium* was planned as Plato's first public presentation of Plato's vision of reality and Forms; this may be true, though the word 'public' requires modification.—Greek καλόν is semantically close τὸ ἀγαθόν, and translations such as 'perfect' or 'fine' are often preferable to the Romantic 'beautiful' (which of course suits the theory of Eros).

109. As I argued above, p. 259 ff.

## [62] Notes on the interrelationship of the levels

At any rate, it seems that Plato was less inclined to make out the internal relation of the Ideas, than to consider them as an upper-level complex reflected (or somehow 'present') in lower-level manifestations.

The introduction of ἔρως as a bridge to the Idea of καλόν in particular was a fascinating experiment. The metaphor of course works properly only with καλόν suggesting physical beauty. A philosopher's 'love' of Truth, True Being, the Right or the Good is more difficult to make plain to the public (witness *Republic* V–VI). Plato makes two somewhat different approaches to ἔρως, one in *Phaedrus* and another philosophically more productive one in *Symposium*.[110] As already noted (443), other key terms in the discussion of the relation of Ideas to particulars are 'presence' and 'participation';[111] in principle, and quite in accordance with the [63] two-level model, such a relation is similar to the relationship between the levels seen in religious terms, e.g. ἐνθουσιασμός (ἔνθεος) or θείᾳ μοίρᾳ.[112] The ultimate τέλος is τὸ ἀγαθόν. Sometimes the Ideas occur in the dialogues, explicitly or implicitly, as 'models' (παραδείγματα) to be imitated, or as αἰτίαι.[113] The geometric 'analogies' which keep Plato's universe together are best illustrated by the Divided Line (cf. below, 453). It is again worth noting that there is no distinct gap of difference between the two levels in Plato's vision, no pointed χωρίς, no deep separation of the 'immanent' from the 'transcendent.' For the ἀνάμνησις theory and the theory of the soul, *see* below, 467; for philosophy and dialectic, *see* 451 f.

---

110. Cf. above, p. 415 f. On Eros in Plato, cf. e.g. Gräfe 1989, Feier 1990, Ferrari 1992, Kahn 1996: 4 ff., 281 ff. The vexing problem of whether *Phaedrus* is (perhaps partly) earlier than *Symposium* need not detain us here. In both dialogues the sublimating power of ἔρως lifts the individual philosopher from the human to the divine level. Also *Lysis* 220b ff. seems to operate with individual love transposed to an abstract level; cf. *Meno* 77b ff.

111. Cf. the examples above. *Phaedo* 100cd shows that the question of μετέχειν versus παρεῖναι or κοινωνεῖν was under debate in the Academy at the time when this passage was written; for κοινωνεῖν, cf. *Republic* V 476a. For μίμησις, *see* below, n. 113. It is sometimes thought that 'presence' applies only to (Socratic?) 'immanence,' not to 'transcendent' Ideas (cf. e.g. Baltes 1994: 215, Devereux 1994: 83 f.), but *see* e.g. *Republic* VI 509b, *Sophist* 247a (μέθεξις, μετέχειν, known in philosophy since Anaxagoras, is the dominant term since *Parmenides*). Kahn (1996: especially 334 ff.) has made a good case for discarding altogether the notion of 'Socratic immanence' of Forms. For the typical problem of the interrelations of τὸ θερμόν and τὸ πῦρ, see *Phaedo* 103c and especially *Cratylus* 413a (still sometimes, on loose grounds, considered an 'early' dialogue). I believe the questions of 'separation' or 'transcendence' were more problematic to others (beginning with 'Parmenides' in *Parmenides* 133a ff.) than to Plato (cf. Schmitz 1985, Devereux 1994, Baltes 1994: 221, Kahn 1996: 349 ff.): *see* the Line, below, p. 453.

112. *See* references in des Places 1964 s.vv. and above, 443 f.

113. This is a much-discussed issue; *see* e.g. Ostenfeld 1997 with references. For the Good as τέλος, see e.g. *Gorgias* 499e, *Protagoras* 354b, *Lysis* 220b, *Symposium* 211b, *Cratylus* 418e, *Republic* VI 504d. 'Imitation' has a specific footing in Pythagoreanism (cf. Aristotle, *Met.* A 987a and elsewhere; Schmitz II 1985: 9 ff.); *Symposium* 212a seems to refer to an earlier discussion of it. For παραδείγματα and αἰτίαι in dialogues 'before' *Phaedo* (91b ff.) and *Republic* (II 397b, V 472cd, VI 484c–e, 500c ff., etc.), cf. *Gorgias* 499e, 503de, 506cd, *Meno* 98a, *Euthyphro* 6de, *Hippias Major* 287c, 289d, etc. (instrumental dative), 294b (τὸ ποιοῦν), and notably the play with 'efficient' and 'final' causes in *Lysis*, above, p. 431.

## Neutral and negative Ideas and Forms

*Forms treated as Ideas*

Secondarily, then, the realm of Ideas begins to extend to more neutral concepts; or (if one prefers to see it so) Forms in a general sense take the character of Ideas. At any rate it is the Ideas, not the Forms, that constitute the dynamic center of this issue. Making the terminological distinction which is adopted here, it is doubtful what 'theories of Forms' there existed before *Parmenides* (and the central books of *Republic*), but there evidently existed a 'theory of Ideas.' Notably *Phaedo* and *Parmenides* (128e ff.) suggest that Plato's theory of Ideas was primary to any theory of Forms. Indeed, all Ideas can be termed Forms, but relatively few Forms can be termed Ideas.

The *Phaedo*, however, presents some thought experiments around the theory: I am unable to see here fragments of a consistent 'doctrine' for some reason 'withheld.' We have seen (434 ff.) how Plato here (74a ff.) introduces αὐτὸ τὸ ἴσον via the theory of ἀνάμνησις with its implication of the soul's innate capacity for measuring and comparing, and how he later, and consequently, introduces such 'Ideas' as μέγεθος, δυάς, and μονάς (101b ff.) Similarly, in *Republic* VII 524d ff. αὐτὸ τὸ ἕν is introduced; cf. VI 510d τετράγωνον αὐτό, διάμετρος αὐτή; in *Parmenides* 130b the existence of αὐτὴ ὁμοιότης is taken for granted. Elsewhere we have encountered ἐπιστήμη, λογιστική and λευκότης as occasional candidates for Ideas. However, as is said in *Parmenides* 130c, Plato's Socrates seems to be in some doubt regarding the Ideas of 'man' or 'fire' (cf. *Phaedo* 103c ff.) or 'water'; note the fact that 'Forms' as 'classes' of physical objects, 'universals,' are not under discussion at this point.

Obviously Plato's Socrates is always reluctant to apply the theory of Ideas to trivial or negatively valued concepts; cf. also *Parmenides* 129a–c (where ὃ ἔστιν ἀνόμοιον is yet accepted, as in *Phaedo* 74c). Sometimes, as in *Cratylus* 439cd (387e, 440b, 489d), *Phaedo* 66a, *Republic* VI 507b, the range of Ideas of the αὐτό type is seemingly extended to all ὄντα, but such generalizations should not be pressed: the enumerations normally begin (as at *Phaedo* 65d) with ὄντα like δίκαιον, καλόν, ἀγαθόν, and we may take it for certain that these always stay in the foreground of Plato's theory of Ideas.

*Artifacts*

The so-called 'Socratic' craftsman analogy, as represented in *Gorgias* 503de (the δημιουργός considering the εἶδος of his work), is traditionally regarded as one of the roots of the theory of Forms (Ideas). Probably it is meant to illustrate what Forms qua models are. I do not think, however, that it can be given priority to the theory of Ideas as Values of the 'in itself' type (cf. also *Meno* 72c, above, p. 440). In fact the extension of the theory of Ideas to artifacts (not mentioned in *Parmenides!*) appears to be a secondary thought experiment. In the wildly exuberant

[64] *Cratylus,* the example of the 'shuttle' is supposed to illustrate how the 'name-giver' operates (389a ff.): there is an 'ideal form' (εἶδος, cf. 389e ἰδέα) even for this everyday object, an αὐτὸ ὃ ἔστιν κερκίς on which the name-giver has modeled its name by also using the Idea (ὃ ἔστιν) of 'name.' Socrates' vision of Ideas at 439cd (440ab) and the play with the ἀγαθοῦ ἰδέα (which ultimately checks movement) at 418e plainly show that the theory of Ideas is in Plato's mind, although he here applies it to Forms (cf. below, p. 450). However, the relation of an Idea (Form) to the 'name' of a thing (i.e. the physical linguistic expression) is never seriously discussed in the dialogues (cf. *Phaedo* 102bc, 103b, *Phaedrus* 250e, *Republic* X 596a, and *7th Letter* 342a ff.).

But every artifact has, of course, a 'typical shape,' and so has (in Plato's view) every physical object—like the bee in *Meno.* Shapeless things such as 'fire,' 'water' or 'dirt' are a different matter. At *Gorgias* 503de Plato seems to operate with 'Forms,' not 'Ideas,' of artifacts, and so also in the symbolism of the Divided Line, if my interpretation is correct. We shall return to this. But in *Republic* II 380d–381b the shapes of good artifacts are changeless, as is the shape (εἶδος, ἰδέα, μορφή) of (surely not each?) god: here Forms may be said to approximate to Ideas. The much-discussed 'Ideal Bed' in *Republic* X 597a ff. (ὃ ἔστι κλινή), is perhaps made by a god, the Φυτουργός, Socrates suggests (as if dismissing the
[65] notion of a Δημιουργός at work here); but this denomination, like the example, is curious and the whole context suggestively playful.

Thus, whether or not Plato ever had a consistent theory of Forms of physical things and artifacts, it should be kept somewhat apart from his theory of Ideas.

## Ideas or Forms for opposites?

It is curious that Plato sometimes seems to allow for 'ideal' opposites to positive Ideas. It was suggested above (434 ff.) that Plato in the *Phaedo* makes use of such opposites to prop up his arguments about the 'withdrawal' of the soul after death. The physical world is full of ἐναντία, of θερμά as well as ψυχρά, ἀγαθά as well as κακά; indeed, it seems natural to speak of τὸ κακόν, τὸ ἄδικον, τὸ ψυχρόν and so on, as well as of their opposites. Plato does not seem to have an overall terminology for such concepts, corresponding to the αὐτὸ ὃ ἔστι or (secondarily) the idea (εἶδος) terminology of the theory of Ideas. For the sake of convenience, I am prepared to call all of them '(conceptual) Forms.'

In *Phaedo* (100e) we pass to the 'Idea' of μέγεθος after the mention of means of measurement taken from the ἀνάμνησις theory, and then to σμικρότης which somehow takes the function of an Idea but which is better called a 'Form'; and other 'Forms' (here called εἴδη and also ἰδέαι) follow. Things of the same 'appearance,' good or bad, can be said to have the same εἶδος (or ἰδέα) which can be taken as their 'conceptual Form.'

This way of thinking is elucidated by a rather extreme (and probably slightly playful) example in *Euthyphro* 5cd. Here τὸ ὅσιον is viewed from the perspective of τὸ ἀνόσιον: is there not a ταὐτόν ... ὅσιον αὐτὸ αὑτῷ and its opposite, which is also αὐτὸ αὑτῷ ὅμοιον καί ἔχον μίαν τινα ἰδέαν κατὰ τῆν ἀνοσιότητα πᾶν ὅ τί [65] περ ἂν μέλλει ἀνόσιον εἶναι? Euthyphron, of course, is a specialist on ἀσέβεια too. But when this issue is echoed at 6b, it is the question of αὐτὸ τὸ εἶδος ᾧ πάντα τὰ ὅσια ὅσια ἔστιν which is resumed, not the question of the ἀνοσιότης. For a short moment, the opposite of an Idea had taken the shape of an Idea. In *Lysis* 217a ff., Socrates discusses the 'presence' of κακόν and λευκότης in objects, but we are probably to understand (cf. 217de and 220bc, above, p. 431) that at least κακόν is not a real Idea. Cf. *Gorgias* 467e . . . τοιάδε . . . ἂ ἐνίοτε μὲν μετέχει τοῦ ἀγαθοῦ, ἐνίοτε τοῦ κακοῦ, ἐνίοτε δὲ οὐδετέρου. Very often (e.g. *Gorgias* 445a, *Republic* I 344c, V 472c, etc.) τὸ ἄδικον (ἀδικία) is introduced along with the search for τὸ δίκαιον (δικαιοσύνη); τὸ αἰσχρόν with τὸ καλόν once in *Symposium* (206d1); δειλία with ἀνδρεία in *Laches* (e.g. 191e) and elsewhere; and so forth.

In the *Phaedo*, as was said above (435), some 'conceptual Forms' opposite to Ideas proper (namely, ἀνομοιότης / τὸ ἴσον, σμικρότης / μέγεθος, perhaps δυάς / μονάς, ψυχρόν / θερμόν, ἄρτιον / περιττόν) tend to receive a function similar to [66] the Ideas: i.e., tend to be abstract (or rather, invisible), unique and immutable entities in which physical objects or manifestations 'have a part.' In *Symposium* 199e and *Parmenides* 133d 'brother / sister' and 'master / slave' are referred to as relational Ideas with αὐτό terminology.

This principle appears to become rather more generalized at *Republic* V 476ab. Here Socrates begins to demonstrate that ordinary citizens, contrary to true Philosophers, are unwilling and unable to see 'upper level' truths. As καλόν and αἰσχρόν are two opposites, but, Socrates says, each is one, the same λόγος applies to δίκαιον / ἄδικον, ἀγαθόν / κακόν, and πάντων τῶν εἰδῶν πέρι: each (αὐτό!) is one, but through their κοινωνία in things and in each other, they appear as many; hence he will make a distinction (χωρίς) between the φιλοθεάμονες and the φιλόσοφοι. Plato, of course, means Ideas in the first place, but these are vaguely associated with all kinds of manifestations on the lower level (cf. *Republic* III 402c). The point is not an expansion of the theory of Ideas (or a development of a theory of Forms), but the fact that the φιλοθεάμονες (contrary to φιλόσοφοι) are unable to distinguish the αἰσχρόν, ἄδικον, etc. (or what 'is not' fine, right, etc.) from what is truly καλόν or δίκαιον (cf. 479a, VII 523a ff., etc.).

Yet we can see here too a faint reflection of a 'theory of Forms' (to which we shall return below) as an enlargement of the 'theory of Ideas.' However, I find it very important to note that although Plato operates widely and freely with opposite concepts in all his dialogues, the fact is that such concepts normally refer to manifestations of opposites in the physical world (cf. above, Chapter V); note especially *Republic* VII 523a–524d. On the whole they do not receive the status of metaphysical Ideas of the αὐτὸ ὅ ἔστι type, so well known from *Phaedo* (65d etc., 78d μονοειδές as in *Symposium* 211b) and *Republic* (e.g. VI 507b, with ἰδέα). The two 'paradigms' for life in *Theaetetus* 176e are certainly no Ideas. It is also very interesting that morally or physically negative concepts, treated somehow like Ideas, occur mainly in association with their positive counterpart, and then the contextual focus or emphasis lies on the latter: the ἰδέα of ἀνοσιότης in *Euthyphro*, or the εἶδος of κακόν in *Republic* V, or the σμικρότης in *Phaedo*, are in all respects

[66] secondary to ὁσιότης, ἀγαθόν and μέγεθος respectively. In the discussion of the soul in *Republic* X (608d ff.), 'badness' (here τὸ κακόν manifested as πονηρία, μοχθηρία, ἀδικία, etc.) stands for a series of lower-level qualities or rather, perhaps, the lower level in its entirety.

I believe it can be safely inferred that these are thought experiments or loose generalizations made in passing. Plato's philosophy certainly had no place for a theory of the Idea of κακόν, an *αὐτὸ ὃ ἔστι κακόν (or an ἄκρατον τὸ κακόν, cf. Asclepios in *Met.* 77.7 Ha.).

[67] *A unique Idea versus innumerable Forms*

Socrates' visionary (ἀπὸ σκοπιᾶς) statement at the end of *Republic* IV (445c) is after all very illuminating. It seems to him now, he says, that there is only one εἶδος of ἀρετή, but innumerable ones (ἄπειρα) of κακία. As applied to ἀρετή, εἶδος is on the verge of being a technical term for αὐτὸ ὃ ἔστι Ideas (not 'yet' discussed in this context of the *Republic*, but certainly known to some of Plato's readers); but as applied to κακία, it just means 'appearances' ('types,' perhaps 'kinds'; cf. the use of εἶδος as 'Idea' and 'type' in the same passage in *Cratylus* 440ab). At the same time we can see here a glimpse of Plato's two levels: the higher level is associated with unity and the Good, the lower with plurality (cf. ἄπειρον p. 471) and imperfection.

The words εἶδος and ἰδέα retain their imprecise applications throughout Plato's written works. I suspect, since the original meaning of 'appearance' is always in use and we have seen its relevance even when typical 'Ideas' are in question, that we should sometimes try to understand εἶδος and ἰδέα as implying 'aspect' rather than 'type,' 'kind' ('class') or 'Idea.' Their application to Ideas proper is never common, and the exact sense and the connotations are not always clear. For the sense of 'aspect,' cf. e.g. *Symposium* 205b, d (one 'side' of love), *Republic* II 357c (three εἴδη of ἀγαθόν), IV 427a (a particular εἶδος of laws and government), 432b (aspects of virtue), 435c (three εἴδη of the soul, cf. IX 580d, *Phaedrus* 253c), VI 509d (two εἴδη of being, the visible and the intelligible, but γένος just before, cf. 511a and *Phaedo* 79a–d, perhaps with a pun on ἀϊδή 79a4). In *Phaedo* 98e and 100b, the other 'aspect (or kind?) of cause' mentioned is associated with τὸ ἀγαθόν (cf. 99c). In *Phaedo*, εἶδος never denotes simply 'kind.'

## Forms as 'types' or 'kinds'

We have seen how 'conceptual Forms' can take over the function of Ideas—though very occasionally and tentatively, and sometimes rather as thought experiments. The experiments with logical polarization did not get a real footing in the theory of Ideas. Neutral physical objects, including artifacts, of course have 'typical shapes,' but the passages where such 'Forms' are classed as 'Ideas' have a tentatively playful note.

## 'Kinds' in arts and crafts

Speaking of εἴδη λόγων, 'kinds of speech,' seems to have been an established practice in rhetoric (cf. *Phaedrus* 237a, d with γένος and ἰδέα; 259d, 263bc, 271d, 272a; *Republic* II 363e, 376e, III 392a, 396b, *Gorgias* 454e, 473e, *Protagoras* 338a), and medicine and other τέχναι are likely to have developed similar uses of the term. All this had probably contributed, before Plato, to a potential change in the sense or connotation of εἶδος from 'shape' or 'aspect' to 'kind.'

## Forms as 'kinds' in two-way dialectic

Evidently, some sort of theory of 'Forms' qua 'types,' 'kinds,' as distinct from 'Ideas,' began to take shape in the Academy in connection with the development of the so-called 'method of collection and division,' or 'two-way dialectic' (διαίρεσις / συναγωγή *Phaedrus* 266b). In this context the term εἶδος clearly tends to receive a technical sense of 'kind,' 'class,' which, as the simile of the Line suggests (below), can be put in some relation to the theory of Ideas. Unfortunately, not much illustration of two-way dialectic is found in the dialogues before the *Sophist*, and the dihaeretic part of the operation is always more prominent than the synagogic one. A well-known instance of 'dihaeresis' without use of the term εἶδος, is the classification of arts at *Gorgias* 464b–466a (its having some roots in Prodicus' semantics is suggested by the parody in *Protagoras* 337a–c, cf. *Charmides* 163d, 169a, 170a–171c). At *Hippias Major* 301b–e (304a), Hippias the sophist protests against the philosopher's excessive 'dihaereses,' 'choppings.' Since also the *Sophist* and *Politicus* are mainly concerned with dihaereses, the most detailed presentation of both aspects of the two-way method we have is in *Phaedrus* 265d ff. (cf. 249d, 270d, 273de, 277bc): the dialectician must be able to have in view a single ἰδέα (meaning here 'type' or 'class,' not merely 'Idea'), but to divide carefully the object in question (the complex phenomenon or rather, its 'Forms') κατ' εἴδη; in other words, he must εἰς ἕν καὶ ἐπὶ πολλὰ ... ὁρᾶν (266b). As a term, εἶδος here refers to 'typical aspects,' and probably to 'natural kinds.' The dihaeretic 'cuts' have to be properly made (indeed, we are concerned with the ideal ζῷον!). And note again (cf. above, p. 417) that this method is as such a reflection of the two-level model: higher Forms (and Ideas) as well as lower Forms which point to the physical level are involved.—Note also *Protagoras* 331c–333c where the principle of 'one over many' is brought, in elenchus, to proceed via ἐναντία and ἕτερα to a ταὐτόν. We may take it for certain that Plato and his friends operated with the 'Categories' ταὐτόν / ἕτερον (θάτερον) when developing two-way dialectic; cf. below, p. 469 ff.

Plato alludes more vaguely to the 'two-way method' in *Republic* V 454ab, 477c–478c, VI 510b, VII 532b ff., and in *Theaetetus* 147de, 148d, 157bc and especially 203e–205d. The last-mentioned passage is, on the face of it, concerned with the division of λόγος into its indivisible στοιχεῖα, but the allusions, including the use of εἶδος and ἰδέα rather in the sense of 'class,' appear to refer, though

[68]
[69]
indirectly and wryly, to two-way dialectic.[114] At *Theaetetus* 156a, the εἴδη of motion (cf. 155e πράξεις, also *7th Letter* 342d ποιήματα / παθήματα) of course imply 'kinds' rather than 'aspects' (cf. *Republic* VII 530c); cf. further 178a, 181cd, 184d, 187c. Similarly in *Cratylus*, where 'names' are analyzed, εἶδος tends to denote 'kind' besides 'Idea' (also in 440b, cf. 439cd and above, 448): cf. 386e (varying πράξεις as one εἶδος of τὰ ὄντα, cf. *Laches* 191d, though the implication is not the same as in *Republic* VI 509d, above), 389d (kinds of weaving corresponding to the εἶδος of the shuttle), 394d (the class of miracles, almost periphrastic), 411a (a class of physical phenomena, though with indirect reference to the εἶδος of ἀρετή), 424cd (εἴδη of various letters taken as 'sounds,' cf. *Theaetetus*, above). All these instances are concerned with 'analysis' in one sense or another.

*'Kinds' gradually more common?*

A renewed scrutiny of the uses of εἶδος (and ἰδέα) in *Republic* may shed some light on the meaning 'kind' gradually pushing forwards. Such a scrutiny, including a careful consideration of the contexts and the relative chronology of the various passages, cannot be undertaken here. It seems to me practically certain, however, that the sense of 'kind' is becoming more common as we approach the 'late period'; note, for instance, *Republic* II 358a, III 389b (periphrastic 'sort of,' cf. V 459d), 413d, IV 427a, V 449a, 475b, 477c–e (δύναμις seen as an εἶδος, implying 'Idea,' and a γένος τῶν ὄντων, cf. VI 507e ἰδέα), VI 510c (cf. d), VII 530c (kinds of motion, cf. above), VIII 544a–d (types of government and man), 559e ('sort of'), IX 581c, e (with γένος), 584c, X 612a.

An allusion to the 'dihaeretic' method can be found in the passage *Republic* V 476ab on positive and negative εἴδη and the κοινωνία (note a8 διαιρῶ), apparently resumed at VI 507ab. In the light of the Divided Line and X 596b (below), Plato is here concerned with a wider group of abstract entities, namely Forms seen as 'kinds' or 'universals,' which do not all reach the standard of 'Ideas'; cf. also *Cratylus* 439c ff. and *Parmenides* 135bc.

# Retrospect and partial conclusions

*Ideas, Forms as concepts, Forms as kinds*

Thus the evidence so far discussed suggests that Plato's 'theory of Forms' can be explicated, primarily, as a 'theory of Ideas': as an elaboration of the two-level

---

114. References to this complicated problem in Heitsch 1992: 29 ff., Hoffmann 1996: 36 ff. Cf. in general Schmitz' interpretation of Plato's 'elementaristic' conception of Forms (e.g. I 2 1985: 45 ff.).

vision in terms of positive values centered on τὸ καλόν and τὸ ἀγαθόν. These are seen as a rather undifferentiated group of unique, changeless, etc. entities in relation to the variability and pluralism of the physical (human) world. The terminology preferred is of the type of 'what is (truly),' 'in itself'. Occasionally the terms εἶδος and ἰδέα are employed here (apparently with specific Platonic suggestivity), and then the connotation is 'the synoptic view' which a philosopher can have of the entity in question (as e.g. of ἀρετή in *Meno*, τὸ ἀγαθόν in *Republic*; cf. *Symposium*), rather than the notion of 'type,' 'kind.' I have been terming such value entities 'Ideas.' When εἶδος (very rarely ἰδέα) takes the meaning of 'typical shape,' 'kind,' 'class' (i.e. approximately 'universal'), the background is everyday usage with specific roots probably in the terminology of some arts and crafts. This use receives some footing in the so-called two-way dialectic developed in the Academy and reflected faintly and opaquely in *Cratylus*, *Hippias Major*, *Phaedrus*, *Theaetetus*, and *Republic*, all dialogues pointing in various ways towards Plato's 'late period' (below). It is interesting that *Phaedo* does not seem to refer to this method, though 'conceptual Forms' appear occasionally. *Phaedo* is not concerned with 'kinds' or dihaereses at all, nor is *Symposium* really (but cf. 210b). But since 'kinds' must be, from Plato's point of view, abstractions somehow associated with his higher level, they may be called 'Forms' in conformance to modern Anglo-Saxon practice.

All in all, we seem to have a very large category of abstract entities, ranging from Ideas proper over 'conceptual Forms' of neutral, trivial or even negative concepts that occasionally take the function of Ideas, to Forms conceived as 'kinds.' Such Forms are entities of a lower status than Ideas. And contrary to the 'theory of Ideas,' an overall 'theory of Forms' is only in the making in connection with two-level dialectic. Its successive stages of development are difficult, if not impossible, to follow in view of the character of the evidence in the dialogues—until we reach the 'late period.'

## The Divided Line and Ideas, Forms, and Phenomena

It seems to me possible to extract some additional information from the symbolism of the Divided Line at the end of *Republic* VI (509d–511e, cf.VII 533e–534a). Its pointedly central significance as a clue to Plato's two-level vision, was emphasized above (p. 416). It illustrates the internal relations of the two main levels, here sub-divided into four, from the perspectives of ontology, physics, the philosopher's epistemology, dialectic, and psychology (to use somewhat anachronistic distinctions): to see it mainly as an illustration of the 'theory of Forms,' as is very often done, is certainly a too narrow approach. The Line should be imagined as drawn vertically, probably with the shorter segments (here 1 and 2) at the top: relative 'length' is more likely to represent here a pyramidal vision of the contrast 'few / many,' than 'relative importance'; but Plato has left this nicety open for us

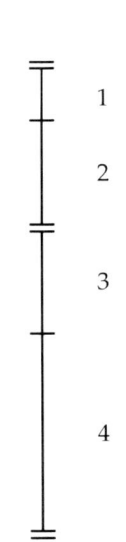

[71] to ponder.[115] At any rate, segments 1 and 2 represent the higher level of Plato's vision, 3 and 4 the lower. It seems clear that the top segment 1 is meant to stand for Ideas proper, culminating in τὸ ἀγαθόν, and segment 2 represents other εἴδη (*see* below); on the first 'visible' level, 3, we have all (?) physical objects, ζῷα etc. (510a5–7 τά τε περὶ ἡμᾶς ζῷα καὶ πᾶν τὸ φυτευτὸν καὶ τὸ σκευαστὸν ὅλον γένος); and the bottom level, 4, are the reflections of these, εἰκόνες. The geometrical principle of division applied here must be meant to illustrate the internal (geometrical) proportions and analogies that 'bind' the levels together (cf. *Gorgias* 507e–508c, and the construction of the World Soul in *Timaeus*). Plato's Socrates does not tell us how the geometrical operation is to be performed, but we may take it for granted that Plato was, and expected his informed readers to be, aware of the fact that the two middle segments of the Line 2 and 3 are by mathematical necessity equal in length. Most commentators who have realized this fact consider it irrelevant, or take Plato's intentions to be inexplicable. But why not assume here an intimation typical of Plato? I want to suggest that Plato, by choosing the simile of the doubly divided Line, may be intimating something which he makes Socrates express more explicitly later on, at *Republic* X 596a: "We are in the habit . . . of positing a single . . . form (εἶδος) in the case of the various multiplicities (τὰ πολλά) to which we give the same name (ὄνομα)" (translation by P. Shorey). The example he goes on to discuss, then, is an artifact, but apparently he means that all (generically) named objects in the physical reality are somehow represented by an εἶδος (cf. the curious φυτουργός 597d4, and φυτευτόν, σκευαστόν at segment 3 of the Line, VI 510a6; also *7th Letter* 342d).

At 510c ff. the relation between the segments 2 and 3 is 'explicated' by references to the 'hypothetic' (deductive) methods or mathematical sciences, but we need not think that the relation only applies to such sciences. The craftsman (even the 'φυτουργός') having in his mind the proper εἶδος of the object he is preparing (for this well-known and important simile, *see* especially *Gorgias* 503de, *Cratylus* 389a ff., *Timaeus* 30c ff., and above, p. 448) operates very similarly to the geometrician who (*Republic* VI 510d) may adduce visible εἴδη, though he is "not thinking of them but of those things of which they are a likeness, pursuing (his) enquiry for the sake of the square as such and the diagonal as such" (transl. Shorey); in other words (cf. 510bc), his διάνοια is based on the proper εἴδη which
[72] he has 'postulated' (or taken as ὑπόθεσις). Thus all constructive human activities (and the corresponding divine activities), all ἐπιστῆμαι and τέχναι, are concerned with intelligible εἴδη which we may call 'Forms'; and apparently there can be assumed an εἶδος for all concrete things we can point at. The whole of this heterogeneous group, including the μαθηματικά of which Aristotle speaks (and indeed, all physical things qua measurable entities have corresponding μαθηματικά, cf. below, p. 482), may well constitute what segment 2 of the Line

---

115. Plato's 'extrovert' cosmology (according to which 'heaven' must be much larger than the 'earth') could be said to speak for relative length representing importance; but the Line is not concerned with spatial dimensions. There is a vast literature on the Divided Line; I only refer to Ferber 1989: 58 ff. and elsewhere, Dörrie and Baltes IV: 343, Smith 1996, Cattanei 1996: 138ff. and Szlezák 1997¹: 213 f.

represents. Some of the Forms may function as Ideas for ordinary people, including craftsmen, technicians and artists; but only the dialectician can reach the area of the Ideas proper: hence the difference between the segments 1 and 2.[116]

If I am right, the equality of the segments 2 and 3 vaguely and symbolically points to the intimate connection between εἴδη of the lower abstract ('intelligible') level, and objects of the higher concrete ('visible') standard. If the differences in quantity, size, etc. (and indeed, the εἰδῶν συμπλοκή) are neglected, there can be (loosely) said to exist a direct correspondence between the ζῷα etc. of segment 3 and the εἴδη of segment 2 of the Line. Obviously, Plato had no reason to analyze this tentative symbolism further. From his own point of view, the involvement of higher level entities with lower level ones, an involvement which makes the philosopher's dialectic possible, is made sufficiently clear: there is no real 'separation' (χωρίς, as Parmenides suggests at *Parmenides* 130b). At the same time, however, we can see here how a 'theory of Forms,' taken as 'types,' 'kinds,' 'classes,' 'universals,' is emerging as a substructure to the earlier 'theory of Ideas': the dialectician is able to advance to the level of Ideas proper by means of a kind of 'extrapolation' from the level of 'Forms' to which he can then return, 'descend.' And a way to solve the παρουσία / κοινωνία / μέθεξις problem is opened.

## Few and unique Ideas

If there are Forms of (practically) everything, the range of Ideas is necessarily reduced to a relatively limited group of entities characterized by the dominant ἕν and ἀγαθόν.[117] The ideal ζῷον of *Timaeus* 30d, 39e presumably includes Forms (cf. below, p. 466). For instance, both ἀγαθόν and κακόν, καλόν and αἰσχρόν are to be found on level 2 but only ἀγαθόν (αὐτό) and καλόν (αὐτό) exist on level 1: here the Forms have become unique Ideas without opposites. Cf. *7th Letter* 343a where the highest level, with a different and somewhat mystifying approach, is made the 'fifth.'

---

116. Some scholars, also some who accept the geometrical truth of the equality of the segments 2 and 3 (e.g. Baltes in Dörrie and Bales IV, Baustein 108 and p. 332 ff.), take segment 2 to represent only μαθήματα (for which *see* below, p. 478); but this does not fit in with the proportions of the segments, with the contents of 3 according to 510a, with 511bc (εἴδη both at top and bottom), with the simile of the craftsman, or indeed with the four levels of soul in *Timaeus* 35c. More commonly, also in antiquity, a rather unclear distinction is made between εἴδη of a 'first' and 'second' order (cf. Alkinoos 4 who identifies the latter with Aristotle's immanent Forms). In fact εἴδεσι 510b8 and εἴδη 511c3 refer in the first place to segment 2 of the Line, i.e. 'conceptual Forms' in general. At *Republic* X 596a8 ὄνομα must refer to all 'generic' names, not only 'property names' (so Fine 1993: 112, following Crombie). And although the ἀρχὴ ἀνυπόθετος is ultimately τὸ ἀγαθόν, segment 1, being itself a line, must include other 'value Ideas'; τὸ καλόν, τὸ δίκαιον, perhaps ἀρετή, ἐπιστήμη, τὸ ἴσον.—Cf. the reference to the 'hypothetical' method in *Phaedo* 101d ff. Nehamas 1973 and Schmitz 1985 have seen many of the problems that I consider relevant here, but their approaches are very different from mine.

117. Cf. Baltes 1994: 219 f. Aristotle's ὁπόσα φύσει (*Met.* 1070a 18 f. 'natural kinds') does not include artifacts. For the post-Platonic discussion of the range of Forms or Ideas, *see* Baltes 1994: 233 ff.; for τἀγαθόν as an ultimate 'limit,' Baltes 1997.

# VII

## FORMS AND CATEGORIES*

### The impact of younger associates

As was pointed out above (p. 425), the *Republic* is likely to have received its definite shape at a fairly late date, perhaps in the 350s. It reads as a closing manifest and monument of Plato's personal experiences and convictions. At that time his younger associates in the Academy had long been contributing their own experiments, additions, and criticisms to the methods and views of their Master. Reflections of such contributions can be seen, notably, in *Phaedo, Cratylus*, and (the present version of) *Theaetetus*, but here the grip and style is still Plato's own, to judge by the majority of the dialogues in the corpus.[118]

The so-called 'late dialogues,' however, are different in many respects. The first clear signs of something new to come occur, as most commentators agree, in the *Parmenides*.[119]

### The interrelation of Ideas and Kinds

*Parmenides and new perspectives*

Whatever was the contribution of Plato's associates to the writing of *Parmenides* (I can imagine Plato writing the first part as self-criticism occasioned by an 'Eleatic

---

\*Or rather 'Basic Concepts', as I now (2009) prefer to call them.

118. Regarding these circumstances, *see* in general Thesleff 1982, above p. 351 ff. and below, p. 489. The biographic evidence also suggests that Plato met entirely new challenges after 367 BCE.

119. The marked differences between the 'earlier' and 'late' dialogues in subject, methods, setting and style, are commonplace in modern discussions of Plato. *Parmenides* does not stand out stylistically from 'earlier' dialogues but neither do, say, *Hippias Major, Sisyphus* or *Minos* (which rather clearly have to be dated to Plato's 'late period'); and for various reasons, I am still

[74] seminar' while the latter part was later added by another person, instructed by
[75] Plato), this dialogue represents a shift to the problems of Being seen as plurality, difference, and change (i.e. Plato's lower level), and as individuality,[120] which the theory of static Ideas and Forms could not easily solve and which are in the foreground in *Sophist, Politicus, Timaeus* and *Philebus* (and also *Laws*). In the *Parmenides*, 'young Socrates' (read: Plato)[121] is confronted with Eleatic thought and methods. The discussion of his 'theory of Ideas' begins (128e) with Socrates' criticism of Zenon's deliberations (127de) about ἕν and πολλά, ὅμοια and ἀνόμοια. Socrates asserts that opposite things are what they are by partaking (μετέχειν) in opposite Forms, but he cannot see how such opposite Forms could mix (συγκεράννυσθαι 129e2, πλεκομένην 130a1). The 'Forms' first mentioned are ὁμοιότης / ἀνόμοιον and ἕν / πλῆθος (129ab) which link up with Zenon's exposition. Actually they are treated as 'Ideas' (αὐτὸ καθ' αὐτὸ εἶδος, ὃ ἔστιν; cf. *Phaedo* 74cd αὐτὸ τὸ ἴσον etc., above, 434 ff.). After a generalizing formula (129c1–2 καὶ περὶ τῶν ἄλλων ἁπάντων ὡσαύτως), the aporia is resumed as concerning αὐτὰ τὰ γένη τε καὶ εἴδη, which seem to include ἕν / πολλά, ταὐτόν / ἕτερα (129cd), and στάσις / κίνησις (129el). The focusing on these εἴδη (and γένη!) is worth particular notice, and their Eleatic background is interesting (cf. *Phaedrus* 261d) though they become emphasized by 'Socrates' now reconsidering 'his' theory. When Parmenides starts his examination of Socrates' theory of the supposed 'separation' of Forms (130a), he takes αὐτὴ ὁμοιότης as his first example (in *Parmenides*, as in *Phaedo*, ὅμοιον is associated with ἴσον), but then he slips over the categories just mentioned so as to leave open whether all of them really are Ideas. The category of 'likeness' is, of course, needed later (132c ff.) to refute Socrates' notion of Ideas as 'models.' Then follows a reference to Ideas proper, τὸ δίκαιον, τὸ καλόν, etc. which are unproblematic to Socrates. But he admits he has doubts about the εἴδη of 'man,' 'fire,' and 'water'; and he strongly refuses to accept εἴδη of trivial or base things, 'hair,' 'mud,' etc., to which Parmenides remarks that he will learn when he gets older not to disdain such things. Forms of artifacts are, remarkably enough, not mentioned; but we can be rather sure that 'young Socrates' would have been in doubt about them too.[122]

In his criticism, Parmenides on the whole operates with the theory of Ideas such as we know it from (the latter half of) *Phaedo*, with the addition of the Ideas of ἐπιστήμη and ἀλήθεια (134a) and the 'relative' Ideas of 'master / slave' (133de): the emphasis is on Ideas which depend on a complement (an object of

---

prepared to defend a date 'about 362 BCE' for *Parmenides* (see above, 304 ff.) and to place *Theaetetus* before *Parmenides*. The first part of *Parmenides* rather reads as a reconsideration or as self-criticism (this is the common view, see e.g. Löhr 1990, McCabe 1994: 4 f., 75) than as self-defense (see e.g. Baltes 1994: 220 f.). The order *Republic—Parmenides* is often taken for granted, but as I argued above (331 f., etc.), *Republic* was probably finished later.

120. See now notably McCabe 1994.
121. The 'young Socrates' probably stands for Plato (as 'Aristoteles' stands for Aristotle); cf. Jatakari 1990.
122. But *Parmenides* 133d3 ὁμώνυμα may imply other kinds of ὀνόματα than those actually mentioned in the dialogue; cf. Fine 1993: 81 ff., 101 f.

an action, etc.). The criticism begins (131ab) with questions of 'participation' in terms of ὅλον / μέρος, ἕν / πολλά, ταὐτόν (ἴσον) / χωρίς (ἕτερον). The obvious point is that all or most Ideas must be seen as somehow interrelated. In order to save the theory (135bc), Parmenides proposes training by means of 'hypotheses,' the successive application of a set of assumptions and inferences to be drawn from the problems of 'being' and 'not being' 'one' and 'many.' The aspects to be applied are supposed to include (136ab) ὁμοιότης / ἀνόμοιον and στάσις / κίνησις (also γένεσις / φθορά). These recur in the actual training figures demonstrated in the latter part of the dialogue (137c ff.): besides εἶναι (οὐσία) / οὐκ εἶναι and ἕν / πολλά (also δύο, πλῆθος), and the ever-present question of μετέχειν, note here especially the following two groups of cognate 'opposites': [76]

(1) ταὐτόν (αὐτὸ ἑαυτῷ, etc.) vs. ἕτερον (ἄλλον) 138a, 139b ff., 143a, 146a, 158bc, etc., ὅμοιον / ἀνόμοιον 139e, 147c, 161a, etc., ἴσον / ἄνισον 140b, 149d, 161c, etc.

(2) στάσις (ἑστάναι, ἡσυχάζειν) vs. κινεῖσθαι (κίνησις) 138b, 145e, 156c, 162b, etc. Connected with 'motion' ('change') are γίγνεσθαι (αὐξάνεσθαι) / ἀπόλλυσθαι (φθίνειν) 156a, 163a; χρόνος 141de, 151e, 155e, etc.; πρεσβύτερον / νεώτερον 140e, 153e, etc.; μεῖζον (μᾶλλον) / ἔλαττον (ἧττον) 140b, 144b, 147c, etc. Also, ὅλον / μέρος is applied with some consistency (137c, 142d, etc.), more occasionally contrasts such as πέρας / ἄπειρον (137d, etc.), περιττά / ἄρτια (143c, etc.).

We recognize here the γένη or εἴδη which Socrates in his initial protest (129de) had refused to regard as 'mixing' together, notably ἕν / πλῆθος, ὁμοιότης / ἀνομοιότης, and στάσις / κίνησις. To start with, they were treated as Ideas, but there are several indications that Plato does not regard them as Ideas proper. Rather, they are 'Forms.' Plato takes up only ὁμοιότης (which recalls τὸ ἴσον in *Phaedo*) before he lists the typical Value Ideas; and it is only for logical reasons (cf. 137b3) that he occasionally, in the training section, makes Parmenides refer to αὐτὸ τὸ ἕν (143a, 144e, 150e, 153de); cf. the awkward definition of the 'Form' of (ὃ καλοῦμεν) ὅλον 157de. These εἴδη (γένη) are in fact rather consistently kept separate from the typical Ideas. They are contrasted pairs of complementary opposites, which is not a feature typical of Ideas. The use of the term γένος in this connection is interesting: Parmenides employs it as a somewhat vague substitute for Socrates' εἶδος, clearly suggesting 'kind' rather than 'Idea' (134b7, c6, 135a8).

With most critics, I take it for granted that Plato is here reconsidering his own earlier theory of Ideas. But he is not necessarily 'changing' it to any manifest extent. I believe he is preparing for a theory of εἰδῶν συμπλοκή, and certainly his concern is not only 'Ideas' and 'Forms.' He is moving, as it were, from segment 1 of the Divided Line to segments 2 and 3. He is now facing the variety and the opposites typical of physical reality. To cope with them, he needs a synoptic view of Being (οὐσία) in its entirety: hence he falls back on his basic vision of its two levels. He needs two-way dialectic, but also a theory of how Forms may combine: namely all the 'Forms' of segment 2, taken as 'kinds' or universals, 'names' of physical objects (though he is not yet considering artifacts). He needs a theory of how human intellect can grasp the variety of the physical world. He needs a refinement of Eleaticism to explain the problems of 'being' and 'one / [77]

[77] many,' a theory of mathematical reasoning, and a theory of the order of the Cosmos. He begins to see that there are 'kinds' (γένη) which cover both ontological levels and which so may contribute to explicating all συμπλοκή.

These are at least some of the perspectives opened by *Parmenides*, generously interpreted and taken as preceding the *Sophist, Politicus, Timaeus,* and *Philebus*. The ways Plato's own thoughts run cannot be exactly determined, especially since some of his associates are likely to have contributed to the formulations in all of these dialogues.[123] However, we can see how a number of two-level γένη grow out of his two-level model and become tools for analyzing and understanding the rules of Cosmos.

It is convenient here to discuss the *Sophist* (and *Politicus*) before *Timaeus* (and *Critias*), though the chronological order is likely to be the opposite one.[124]

## Two-level Categories in the Sophist

The divisions and classifications which abound in the *Sophist* and *Politicus* (in absurdum, really), develop suggestions that we can trace in particular in *Theaetetus* and *Parmenides*. It is interesting and probably important to note that the analyses are conducted on the abstract level throughout: they are concerned with 'kinds' (in a very general sense), or vaguely with genus vs. species, not with the relating of individual objects to 'classes,' nor with classifying specimens (as e.g. in the well-known parody of dihaereses in Epicrates, fr. 11). Yet the physical reality is continuously present, namely as a sort of reflection of the very everyday, trivial 'kinds' of being and doing brought in as illustrations (e.g. *Sophist* 221c ff., *Politicus* 282a ff.). The 'kinds' analyzed are sometimes called εἴδη (hardly at all ἰδέαι), and may of course be termed 'Forms' in English. Metaphysical Ideas figure in
[78] the background (cf. *Sophist* 238c, 239d, 253d, 254a, etc.), but an ironical distance is taken from the εἰδῶν φίλοι (*Sophist* 246bc, 248c ff.) who are unable to account for Being in its entirety.[125] The two levels, here represented by Forms and their reflections (a direct relation, if my interpretation of segments 2 and 3 of the Line is correct, above p. 453 ff.) are here seen together as a complexity (τὸ παντελὲς ὄν *Sophist* 248e) which is subject to dihaeretic (i.e. logical, conceptual, 'mereologi-

---

123. I have suggested elsewhere (e.g. above, p. 351, 1993: 34) that Plato did not himself 'write down' what is called his 'late style.' The main reason for giving dominant roles to Parmenides, the Elean Guest, Timaeus, Critias, and the anonymous Athenian, probably was that Plato was not inclined to identify himself with them to the same extent as with Socrates, who reappears in *Philebus*. Cf. also Thesleff 2000. On the whole the 'late dialogues' utilize other contemporary lines of thought current in the Academy (at least Eleaticism, Pythagoreanism, atomism, astronomy, and medicine) more manifestly than most of the 'earlier' dialogues do.

124. I still consider the relative order of *Sophist—Politicus* and *Timaeus (Critias)* an open question, though for various reasons I would prefer to take the *Timaeus* complex as preceding the *Sophist* complex; cf. above, p. 334 ff.

125. Here is certainly some self-irony on Plato's part although, as has been often assumed, there may have been stubborn conservatives among the younger generation; cf. e.g. Schmitz II 1985: 42 ff.

cal,' 'atomistic') classification. The 'cuts' of the dihaereses, though concerning εἴδη, extend to physical reality (cf. *Sophist* 246bc, 252bc, 253d).[126] We seem to have here the beginnings of a general, non-metaphysical (rather Aristotelian) theory of classification where the hierarchic dependence of the lower on the axiologically, aetiologically etc. higher is not so essential as the 'whole / part' (or 'genus / species') relation. Perhaps Plato himself was a little bit bored by all this, although he had set the ball rolling.[127]

In the *Sophist* (251d ff., cf. 237b ff.) we encounter the two-level contrasts which were tentatively applied in *Parmenides* to 'being' vs. 'non-being,' namely the ἕν / πολλά contrast (253de), ταὐτόν / θάτερον, and στάσις / κίνησις (254c ff.). Together with 'being' (οὐσία), the two latter pairs are now called the five μέγιστα γένη (254e); occasionally the terms εἶδος, ἰδέα and φύσις are also employed (cf. 255a–e). As has been often noted in recent studies, the Elean Guest uses these γένη mainly to explain the 'communion of kinds' (εἰδῶν συμπλοκή) which the theory of Ideas cannot cover as such, and especially, to offer an elegant solution to the 'Parmenidean' problem of non-being.[128]

I find it highly significant, indeed essential, that these γένη form a network different from the hierarchy of Forms and Ideas known e.g. from the Divided Line. They are 'Forms' in a very general sense only, 'invisible' (abstractions), universal classes; but they represent a different axis or dimension: they look as being 'lateral' projections of Plato's two-level model. 'Being' (οὐσία, τὸ ὄν) extends over all reality, i.e. over both main levels (cf. also *Parmenides*, especially 155e ff., 166a). Graded 'being,' a Form's 'being more truly' than a sensible particular (the relation of segments 2 and 3 of the Line), is rather irrelevant here, although the Guest plays with the partial 'unreality' of what a sophist stands for (223c, 234e ff., 260a ff,, etc.; cf. segment 4 of the Line). In addition to οὐσία, the contrasted pairs ταὐτόν / θάτερον and στάσις / κίνησις also extend over all that 'is' (note διεληλυθυῖαν *Sophist* 255e4), but every close reader of Plato (cf. Chapter IV) will understand that ταὐτόν and στάσις are more typical of the higher level, θάτερον and κίνησις of the lower. The same applies to ἕν / πολλά. The list could be easily expanded to include other two-level contrasts taken as 'Forms,' 'kinds,' 'classes' (e.g. the 'divine / human,' the 'intelligible / sensible'). But why could

---

126. For the early history of the dihaeretic method, *see* above, p. 451. Cf. e.g. *Phaedrus* 265e and *Hippias Major* 301b–e, 304a (Schmitz II 1985: 42 wrongly regards the *Hippias Major* passages as early arguments against συμπλοκή).

127. There is abundant evidence of Plato's pupils' interest in διαίρεσις. The Epicrates fragment pictures a benevolently passive Plato. The 'whole / part' problem is present in many of the so-called 'early' dialogues (cf. Kahn 1996: 172 ff.). The recently expanding discussion of Plato's late ontology does not take account of a possibly slackening commitment on Plato's part.

128. Here I only refer to Schmitz 1985, Fine 1993, McCabe 1994, O'Brien 1995, Hoffmann 1996, Seung 1996, and Szaif 1996. I find McCabe's argument particularly profitable: Plato (I would venture to say: 'Plato's research group') is in search of 'individuation' in terms of a 'mesh' of kinds (especially 222 ff.). Aristotle's hierarchic γένος / εἶδος system is somewhat different (for the latter in post-Platonic traditions, cf. Isnardi Parente 1997: 391 f.); but note Aristotle's σύνθεσις τῶν νοημάτων *De an.* III 430a 26 ff. (Fattal 1995).

[79] it not include such contrasted Forms as τὸ καλόν / τὸ αἰσχρόν, τὸ δίκαιον / τὸ ἄδικον, or indeed τὸ ἀγαθόν / τὸ κακόν? Because, I think, these are felt to be opposites, and opposites do not extend over Plato's entire realm of Being (cf. above, p. 427 ff.). Ideas (qua Ideas) do not combine. Plato needs contrasts for his dihaeretic process of analysis, but he needs contrasts that are present 'everywhere.'

The 'greatest kinds,' οὐσία, ταὐτόν / θάτερον, στάσις / κίνησις, to which we may safely add the contrast ἕν / πολλά, are certainly no 'Ideas,' and they are 'Forms' only in a very loose sense. In fact they are often classed as 'Ideas' or 'Forms' merely because their character of belonging to a different system is not recognized.[129]

This is why I would prefer to call them 'Categories.'[130] The application here of the imprecise terms εἶδος and ἰδέα has been particularly confusing.

[80] *Categories versus Ideas and Forms*

Already the alternative use of γένος suggests here an origin different from εἶδος and ἰδέα. Outside the 'late dialogues,' Plato very seldom employs the word γένος in the sense of 'conceptual class,' and all instances may be rooted in Academic technical usage.[131] The pointed contrasts, and the association of πολλά, θάτερον and κίνησις with the lower level of Plato's model, show that the theory of Forms

---

129. Cf. e.g. Cornford 1935: 273 ff., Ross 1951: 113 f., Sayre 1983: 229 ff. (who like many others translates μέγιστα as 'very important,' which misses the point of the Greek superlative), Dorter 1994: 15 f. and n. 38, Baltes 1994: 219 f., Clarke 1994, Szaif 1996: 394 ff. The Tübingen school (cf. e.g. Krämer 1982: 161 ) introduced the term 'Metaideen' (also somewhat misleading). Ancient commentators of course confuse εἶδος, ἰδέα and γένος (cf. e.g. Diog. L. III 12 ff. and 64); but Alcimus (ibid.) seems to have distinguished the search for ἀρχαί seen as 'greatest kinds' (cf. below, 476 ff.) from the search for Ideas by the hypothetical method; cf. Dörrie 1987: 308 ff. In the modern discussion, there has been little agreement on what kind of 'Ideas' or 'kinds' these γένη are; and some scholars have explicitly doubted their character of 'Forms' or 'Ideas' in any ordinary sense: so especially Peck 1952, further e.g. Schmitz I 2, 1985: 34–36, de Vogel 1986: 202, McCabe 1994: 224 ff. (cf. 222 and n. 1), Seung 1996: 185 ff., von Perder and Hoffmann 1997: 150.

130. This term has occasionally been suggested before (e.g. by Seung, *see* above, n. 129). Aristotle's κατηγορίαι have slightly different implications, though they are likely to have arisen in the same Academic context as Plato's γένη, and Plotinus (VI 1—3, especially VI 2 7.8 and 13 ff., 3.2) tends to identify the former with the latter. The Middle Platonists preferred to distinguish three Platonic 'categories': substantia, oppositional, and relational Being; cf. Krämer 1959: 282 ff., Gaiser 1963: 52 ff., 70 ff., Fine 1993: 171 ff. For a historical review of the issue of Platonic 'categories,' cf. Wyller 1981 (in Norwegian).—*See* now above, p. 457.

131. The contexts are always sophisticated (note the reference to oral discussions *Sophist* 254c4) except when γένος denotes 'families' or 'classes of living beings' (e.g. human beings, or the philosophers as a class, as *Republic* VI 501e, cf. *7th Letter* 326b). For the sense 'conceptual class,' cf. *Republic* V 477cd, *Phaedrus* 250b, 270d–271d (alternatively with εἶδος), *Theaetetus* 205b. In the *Sophist*, the term γένος is playfully introduced at the beginning (216a ff.) with reference to the Guest, to god, and to the godlike, and to the 'classes' of sophists, statesmen, and philosophers. Hoffmann 1996: 97 rightly points out that a γένος always is a 'mixture.' To identify γένος with ἰδέα or εἶδος is an old mistake (*see* e.g. des Places 1964 s.w.); for the problem, cf. *Politicus* 263ab.

is not meant. The 'greatest kinds' are tools for grouping and categorization of [80] conceptual Forms taken to represent physical reality; and indeed, if size and number (πολλά, below) are included, tools for relative measuring.

We can notice here a tendency to establish a technical terminology. It is true that the γένος / εἶδος terminology never became fixed in Plato's written works. However, the absolute ταὐτόν begins to be substituted for τὸ ἴσον (ἰσότης, also ὅμοιον, ὁμοιότης) which was first introduced as a sort of 'Idea' in *Phaedo* and *Parmenides;* subsequently the association with Ideas is lost. The contrasted ἕτερον or θάτερον[132] is just a general Category. Again, στάσις,[133] though associated with Ideas, is never termed so; and the contrasted κίνησις certainly has little to do with Ideas proper.[134]

## Politicus

In this far from identical twin of *Sophist*, the συμπλοκή is applied to the weaving of human characters and to the Statesman as a technician. New notions such as μόριον and measuring are brought in with little explicit use of the Categories, except in the Cronus myth which partly recalls the *Timaeus*.[135]

---

132. It seems that θάτερον (rather than τὸ ἕτερον) is beginning to be used since *Sophist* and *Timaeus* for the Category of 'Otherness'; but the textual tradition is hardly reliable in this case.

133. For this term, cf. above, n. 46. It never became a fixed term in the dialogues, and the meaning 'uproar' is often ambiguously present (*see* also e.g. *Politicus* 272e, 306b).

134. In *the Sophist* it tends to denote 'becoming something' (cf. McCabe 1994: 224 ff.). It includes γένεσις / φθορά (wrongly taken by Kahn 1996: 297 to be general 'Forms' of the same character as κίνησις). The Ideal ζῷον somehow 'moves' (*Sophist* 248e f., *Timaeus* 37c ff. implies that the primary circular motion of Cosmos only comes in with the creation of Time). But Plato hardly assumed a single Idea of 'Motion' (pace Baltes 1994: 216), though there are different 'Forms' of it.

135. The *Politicus* has been relatively seldom discussed, but *see* now Rowe (ed.) 1995. The differences from *Sophist* are interesting (a different finishing hand?) but cannot be followed up here. The replacing of Theaitetos with 'Young Socrates' suggests to me that we are now, more than in the *Sophist*, concerned with issues close to Plato's own commitments (cf. above, n. 121). We may note here ταὐτόν / θάτερον (ἕτερον, ἄλλο) in dihaereses (e.g. 258bc, 263a, 265c, 278bc, 285a). The terms στάσις / κίνησις do not occur as Categories (but cf. τὸ τῆς ἠρεμαίας γενέσεως εἶδος 307a; στάσις perhaps ambiguously 307c, but elsewhere clearly in the sense of 'uproar': 272e, etc.). Reflections of them can, however, be seen in the Cronus myth: here we have the two Platonic levels of a static Ideal and a created Cosmos (a ζῷον with φρόνησις 269cd); the latter has two motions (κινήσεις), κατὰ ταὐτά and ἄλλως (269e), but ἄλλως is then replaced by the bizarre notion of an ἐναντίον and μεταβολή after a sudden 'standstill' (ἔστη, ἐπαύσατο 270d). In the age of Cronus the gods were leading. In the present age of Zeus philosophy may save us (272bc, cf. 274d); and when 'difference' eventually gets the upper hand (note τῆς ἀνομοιότητος ἄπειρος πόντος 273de), god will again take the leadership; even here there is no dualism of 'good / evil' (cf. Brisson 1995[2] and the comments of Ferrari ibid. 394 n. 17). Note in general the parallels with *Timaeus* (also the two-level ψυχή 309c; and for 273e ff., cf. the myth of Protagoras in *Protagoras*, Narcy 1995). After the Cronus myth the two levels of 'divine / human' become emphasized (especially 308c ff.). The importance in this dialogue of the notions of 'model' and 'likeness' (Kato 1995) recalls the Categories of 'same' / 'different.' Note further, in *Politicus*, the concentration on 'method' (260c and passim), the problem of μέρος / εἶδος / γένος (e.g. 262ab, 363ab), the overall emphasis

## [81] Categories and the soul

### Theaetetus

We can trace the use of the Categories 'before' *Parmenides* and the *Sophist-Politicus* complex, not only as representing loosely the two levels of Plato's model (cf. above, p. 407 ff.). In the *Theaetetus*, the other background dialogue for *Sophist-Politicus*, we find the Categories connected with the soul's activities and its search for ἐπιστήμη. Having criticized at length (and with some play with the two-level model) various theories of flux versus rest,[136] Socrates extracts from Theaitetos (185c–186c) the suggestion that the soul makes use of οὐσία, τὸ ταὐτόν, τὸ ἕτερον (and no doubt 'motion' and 'rest' are involved in this process), and also ἕν and other numbers,[137] when it considers by itself τὰ κοινὰ περὶ πάντων, and what is καλόν / αἰσχρόν, ἀγαθόν / κακόν, and in general opposites.

[82] Seen from the perspective of Categories, this much-discussed passage is particularly interesting.[138] It appears to imply that the soul's ability to distinguish, compare, combine (conceptual) Forms, and apparently its capacity for two-way dialectic, is rooted in the Categories of Being, Same, Different, Rest, Motion, and Number. What is even more interesting is that these Categories are somehow inherent in the human soul. Note the fact that Socrates goes on to distinguish these mental operations from mere perception (186b–e). To judge from the context, we are here close to Plato's own views.[139]

### Phaedrus

Here, too, the brief but very pregnant 'proof' of the soul's immortality (245c–246a) contains elements which, on closer inspection, connect the soul to the Categories; so notably the opening αὐτοκίνητον / ἄλλο κινοῦν, παῦλα / κίνησις (both caused by soul), and the reference to the οὐσία of soul (e4). The impossibility of a cosmic 'standstill' (στῆναι e2) suggests that the World Soul is somehow implied.

---

on γένεσις (e.g. 260e ff., 278c, 281b ff., 283d, 287e), and the notions of μέτριον, μετρητική and τέχνη (especially 283c ff.). For the digression on acquiring knowledge, 277d–278e, see below, n. 147.

136. *Theaetetus* 152a–184b. Here κίνησις is normally used for 'change.' The term στάσις does not occur, but various forms of ἱστάναι (cf. 153a ff., where also ἡσυχία); and note the very playfully ambiguous στασιῶται 181a.

137. 185d1–2 ἀριθμός, ἄρτιον / περιττόν, also ὁμοιότης / ἀνομοιότης; cf. e.g. ἴσον 155a, ὁμιότης 158c, διαφορότης 208d ff.

138. To my knowledge, the 'psychological' point has not been noticed; cf. e.g. Shorey 1903: 33 ff., Teloh 1981: 204 ff., Burnyeat 1990: 52 ff., McCabe 1994: 151, Dorter 1994: 92 f. with further references.

139. This is suggested by the general tenor of the dialogue, and by the association of Theaitetos with 'Socrates the Younger' (147cd, cf. above, n. 121). Cf. the συλλαβαί 202b ff., Hoffmann 1996: 74 ff. In *Phaedo* 73c–75d the distinguishing of ὁμοιότης / ἀνόμοια and αὐτὸ τὸ ἴσον is said to be essential for perception and apprehension. Ebert 1974 rightly argues that Plato thought knowledge of ἰσότης as such impossible; knowledge is based on all Categories, see below, p. 467.

## The World Soul in Timaeus and Laws X

All this receives considerable elucidation if it is viewed in the light of what is said about the soul in *Timaeus*. We need not think that this rich work is in its entirety conceived or formulated by Plato alone;[140] but the basic features, curious and bizarre as they may sometimes look, the linking up with Plato's early Utopia (below, p. 519 ff.), the mystifying grip of these 'myths,' the general lines of the two-level model presented here, the vision of Cosmos as a well-ordered soul / body complex, and the pronouncedly ethical orientation of this exercise in 'physics,'—all this seems very authentically Platonic.

The symbolism of the creation of the World Soul (*Timaeus* 34b-37c) fits rather well in with the basic lines of Plato's thought. We may note here the following details. The 'mixture' that the World Soul is made of (35a ff.) consists of οὐσία (of different levels), ἀμέριστον / μεριστόν, and ταὐτόν / θάτερον. It is then divided and provided with mathematical concepts (number and proportions); and it receives two kinds of motion, κίνησις (36c). The contrast pair ἀμέριστος / μεριστός (here a two-level contrast) belongs to the theory of διαίρεσις and suggests in this context that the upper-level world of Unity and ταὐτόν represents the indivisible by including only indivisible entities (we might say Ideas);[141] number and proportions, again, are divisible. Partly, 'indivisible / divisible' stands here for the familiar ἕν / πολλά contrast. Otherwise too we recognize here the Categories of *Theaetetus, Parmenides,* and *Sophist,* except that 'standstill' (στάσις) rather naturally is not present, as such, in the soul. It can be claimed, however, that the element of 'sameness' in the soul brings it close to metaphysical 'rest' (cf. 37b4) and, indeed, that 'rest' is present in the order brought about in Cosmos (cf. e.g. 29b, 30a). And at 42e, the proper state of the Demiurge is described with the imperfect ἔμενεν (repeated by the participle μένοντος). I take it that the ταὐτοῦ φύσις (35a5) does not stand only for Ideas, but for Plato's higher level generally. Similarly, θάτερον does not represent only particulars. For instance, to reach the realm of Necessity, where 'difference' dominates, we have to make a ἑτέρα ἀρχή (48b2, cf. c). The two levels are here seen in terms of Categories.

Thus the World Soul becomes an intermediate Being (37a–c) whose function is to transfer information and activity between Plato's two levels: on one hand the realm of ταὐτόν (which is explicitly said to be 'better,' 29a, 33b), including

---

140. There has not been much discussion recently of what is eventually 'non-Platonic' in the *Timaeus-Critias* complex; cf. now Calvo and Brisson (eds.) 1997 (but, on the other hand, Taylor 1928). Rather obviously, the mathematics and astronomy of the work, and many physiological details, include contributions by Plato's contemporaries. The notion of the Creator as a Potter, a Carpenter, a Blacksmith, or perhaps a Baker (cf. *Republic* X 597 ff., 616c ff.) probably underlines Plato's somewhat ironical distance from technicalities, essential though they are for the function of the whole (cf. Schmitz II 1985: 105).

141. As to the terms ἀμέριστος / μεριστός, cf. *Theaetetus* 205cd and *Parmenides* 131c ff. In this passage in *Timaeus* they are exceptionally employed as Categories (cf. McCabe 1994: 163 ff., Baltes in Dörrie and Baltes IV 267 f. with references). The realm of the 'indivisible' vaguely stands for the upper level. Plato, of course, does not mean that all εἴδη are indivisible, nor that all ultimate ἄτμητα or ἄτομα εἴδη are Ideas (cf. *Phaedrus* 277b, *Sophist* 229d, *Politicus* 268c–e).

[83] the Perfect Being (ζῷον, 30c, 31b, 37d), the model used by the Demiurge for the soul / body complex of Cosmos,[142] and on the other hand the realm of θάτερον, the created body of Cosmos, and all that γένεσις stands for (cf. 28a ff.). The Soul's two circular motions, one closer, the other less close to ταὐτόν (i.e. like the ecliptic, 36c), are essential. Here and in the subsequent story, the contrast ταὐτόν / θάτερον is particularly prominent and effecting the principle 'like likes like.'[143]

[84] It is by its element of ταὐτόν that the Soul manifests its 'reason' (νοῦς, e.g. 46d ff., also φρόνησις 40ab). All this is very much in keeping with Plato's two-level model, only that ψυχή is now made a mediating factor, somewhat like ἔρως in *Symposium* (and cf. *Phaedrus* 245c ff.).

Like the cosmological myth in *Politicus* (above), *Laws* X has some reflections of the Categories faintly recalling *Timaeus*, though in this case the *Phaedrus* (above) offers a closer parallel. The Athenian opens his discourse on the soul (893b) with the 'standstill / motion' issue (ἔστηκε / κινεῖται, etc.) and the question of different kinds of motion; here we meet the contrasts 'one / many' (893cd, etc.) and 'self / other' (ἑαυτήν / ἕτερον 893cd, etc.). In terms of these Categories he then goes on to discuss the nature of the soul (894b ff., cf. οὐσία 896a), as if developing what was said in *Phaedrus* and *Timaeus*.[144]

The *Epinomis* is irrelevant in this context.[145]

---

142. It is usually taken for granted that this Perfect ζῷον includes all Ideas and / or Forms (cf. 51c), i.e. the segments 1 and 2 of the Divided Line; cf. Aristotle *De an*. I 2.404b19 ff., Ostenfeld 1997. I would add that there is hardly an Idea for the moving Soul, though there is a Form for it; motion comes in with the creation of Time (*Timaeus* 37c ff.) which suggests segment 2 (cf. above, n. 134). The choice of the metaphor ζῷον to cover all this is interesting. It is probably motivated by Plato's view of the 'organic' coherence of the physical world which would seem to imply the same for its upper-level counterpart, and to offer the possibility of covering by two-level dialectic the parts and the whole of both; cf. ζῷα *Republic* VI 510a. I am sure the 'Younger Socrates' who used to speak of the Ideal ζῷον according to Aristotle (*Met*. Z 1036b25 ff.) is in fact Plato; cf. above, n. 121.

143. As Aristotle remarks in the *De an*. passage quoted above (n. 142); cf. above, n. 51. See especially *Timaeus* 33b, 37a ff., 42e ff., 50bc, 61d, 63de, 81e–88e ('homeopathic' medicine), 90a–d (hymnic conclusion). On the lower levels there appear more or less 'different' kinds of motion, e.g. 40a ff. (cf. *Theaetetus* 181d, *Laws* X 893e ff.; Aristotle *Phys*. V 226a, VIII 265b–266a). Schmitz II 1985: 294 f. wrongly makes a point of the 'difficulty' of mixing θάτερον with ταὐτόν at 35a as compared with *Sophist* 259a.

144. And at 895a, as at *Phaedrus* 245e2, there is a polemical point about a 'standstill' of Cosmos; but cf. *Politicus* 270d. More clearly than *Phaedrus*, *Laws* X operates with a World Soul. The Athenian then introduces the much-debated issue of two World Souls (896e ff.) of which one, like the World Soul of *Timaeus*, moves always in the 'same' manner (ὡσαύτως etc., 898ab) and represents νοῦς, whereas the other does not. The fact that *Laws* X seems to develop the ideas of *Phaedrus* 245c–246a, without much notice taken of *Timaeus*, has been sometimes discussed; cf. notably Stenzel 1956: 16 ff.; cf. above, n. 55. In spite of the wealth of typically Platonic themes and notions in *Laws* (including also the application of the two-level model to higher education in Book XII, especially 965b ff.), I am not convinced by the earlier and recent arguments for the total authenticity of *Laws; see* references in Hoffmann 1996: 211 n. 273.

145. Much is said in the dialogue about motion and number, but the Categories do not occur. The notion of the priority of soul (and its motion) to body (980c ff.) and the general lines of cosmology and physics (981b ff.) correspond to what is said in *Timaeus*, but there are several

## Human soul in Timaeus [84]

In *Timaeus*, the individual souls meant for humans (and by degeneration for animals), are made of the same components as the World Soul, though the mixture is less 'pure' (41d–42e). It is important to note that the Demiurge gives the souls some preliminary instruction (41de), but apparently no innate knowledge of specific Ideas or Forms. When the lower 'mortal' parts of the soul are submerged in the body, where the Different and the Divisible are dominant, the task of the leading 'divine' part is to vindicate Sameness and order in the body / soul complex (notably 69b–72d). Very much as Theaitetos saw (above), the conditions of philosophical thought (διανόησις, λογισμός 47bc) consist of the use of the Categories that are inherent in the soul, and which represent the capacity to identify, distinguish, and count or measure; cf. also *Politicus* 285d–286a. In fact, interpretations [85] of the *Timaeus* on this line seem to have been current in the Academy.[146]

With my reading of the *Timaeus*, the soul possesses no innate, detailed or systematic knowledge of Forms or Ideas. It 'knows' the Categories, however, and with the aid of them and of proper instruction it can, somehow, get into contact with the Perfect Being and also make the proper divisions in the world of γένεσις. We may safely infer that the human soul is, imperfectly but potentially, capable of making calculations and divisions corresponding to those of the World Soul (37ab).[147]

## Anamnesis

It is usually, and I think rightly, taken for granted that there exists some connection between the method of μαιευτική, as presented (however playfully) in the *Theaetetus*, and the theory of ἀνάμνησις, presented in *Meno* and referred to in *Phaedo* and probably *Phaedrus* (and very loosely, *Republic* VII 516c). In the *Theaetetus*, obviously, it is not Ideas or Forms that Socrates tries to extract from Theaitetos, but definitions; but Theaitetos is aware of the Categories, and he

---

differences in details especially regarding the astral gods. I find Tarán's arguments (1975) for the authorship of Philip of Opous rather convincing.

146. Cf. Aristotle *De an.* I 2.404b16 ff., Xenocrates in Plutarch *De an. procr.* 1012a ff. (fr. 68 He.), also 1024d–f (on δυάς). Possibly this interpretation is reflected already by Alcimus in Diog. L. III 15 (cf.12). It is presented very clearly by Alcinous / Albinus *Did.* XIV; see further Dörrie and Baltes III 256 f.

147. Cf. e.g. 47bc, 71e f. At 72d ἀνασκοποῦσι may suggest the Aristotelian ἀναγωγή (cf. also the Divided Line); the aim is ταὐτόν and what it stands for. For ταὐτόν and ἕτερον in two-way dialectic, cf. above, p. 451, and also the rather intricate digression in *Politicus* 277d–278e (note ἀνάγειν 278a8). The human soul needs education and schooling (e.g. 44bc, 47c). Of course Timaeus is not modern enough to suggest that the apparent structure of the Universe is (partly) dependent on our mind's tendency to categorize and measure. The approach of the *Timaeus* to the function of the soul is cosmological and ethico-soteriological (note the conclusion 90d), not epistemological.

is an excellent mathematician. Hence it is an interesting fact that Socrates' anamnetic experiment in the *Meno* (82b–86a) concerns mathematics, measuring, what is ἴσον, μεῖζον, ἔλαττον, but not Ideas or even explicit Forms (though such have been mentioned in the dialogue).[148] It may be relevant that Socrates has earlier (75a) also pointed out his constant search for ταὐτόν. His sweeping statement that the soul appears to have known 'everything' before birth (81c) cannot be quite seriously meant: already the introductory ἀκήκοα γὰρ ἀνδρῶν τε καὶ γυναικῶν σοφῶν περὶ τὰ θεῖα πράγματα (81a) is slightly ironical, and at 86b ('if the soul has always possessed the truth, it is immortal') the logic is turned upside down. Towards the playfully ambiguous end of the *Meno* (97d ff.), it is hinted that δόξαι, however true they may be, move around like the statues of Daedalus (cf. *Euthyphro* 11b–d), but they can be fixed into ἐπιστῆμαι with the help of λογισμός, and this is what ἀνάμνησις means "as we have just seen" (98a).[149] But neither δόξαι nor ἐπιστῆμαι are really innate (98cd), so what is inherent in the soul, according to Socrates in the *Meno*, is the use of mathematical logic and, we may rather safely add, a sense of the Categories.[150]

The locus classicus for the widespread belief among Platonists in 'anamnesis' of Ideas, is the lengthy discussion in *Phaedo* (72e–77a) which seems to be based on the argument in *Meno*.[151] The discussion begins with the soul's innate capacity for distinguishing αὐτὸ τὸ ἴσον (also ὁμοιότης), ταὐτὰ / ἕτερα (also ἀνόμοιον, etc.), and for measuring (75c). This corresponds closely to what is said in *Meno* (and indeed, in *Timaeus*). Then (75cd), however, Socrates goes on to argue from the Idea of τὸ ἴσον that a knowledge (ἐπιστήμη) of the other Ideas is also innate in the soul. Like many commentators,[152] and like Cebes (77a), and very probably like Plato himself, I do not find the argument convincing at all. I would consider it a thought experiment which is not followed up. Unfortunately, it became a standard requisite of Platonism.[153]

---

148. On *Meno* 72a ff. with the slip from εἶδος to σχῆμα, see above, p. 440. The 'hypothetical' method by which Socrates then professes to define virtue (86d–87c) is 'geometrical' only in a very loose sense, as most commentators agree; but it might be said to concern segment 2 of the Divided Line.

149. Socrates has a 'vision' (ὄναρ 85c) that at least some δόξαι are innate in the soul. The curious phrasing 98a ἕως ἄν τις αὐτὰς δήσει αἰτίας λογισμῷ, appears (if the text is not corrupt) to contain adjectival αἴτιος implying that the δόξαι are 'guilty' of running away, like slaves.

150. In view of ταὐτόν 75a and δεῖσθαι, παραμένειν 97d ff. The notion of combining 'mathematics' with the preexistence of the soul is probably Pythagorean in origin; cf. *Meno* 81a ff. and below, 481. But ἀληθεῖς δόξαι 85c (cf. 86b) makes a pun of 'un-forgotten'.

151. It is usually taken for granted that 72e refers to the dialogue *Meno*; this is not absolutely certain in view of θαμά e3, but the similarities in the conduct of the argument are conspicuous enough.

152. Cf. e.g. Ross 1951: 22 ff., Chen 1992. For the thought experiments in this dialogue, cf. above, 434 ff. More correctly, Simmias at 92d makes the point that οὐσία seems to 'belong to' the soul (note the genitive αὐτῆς; here the reference to *Meno* is not clear).

153. This interpretation of ἀνάμνησις is apparently implied already by Alcimus (in Diog. L. III 15). 'Recollection' of Ideas and Forms is often taken to be a doctrine which Plato arrived at under Pythagorean influence, but later gave up; cf. e.g. Sayre 1983: 218 ff., Benson 1990, Baltes 1994: 218f., Scott 1995.

The myth of the soul's cosmic journey in the *Phaedrus* has evidently contributed to the belief that Plato regards a knowledge of the Ideas (and not only of what I have called Categories) to be innate, and hence possible to activate by ἀνάμνησις. Note, however, that only the gods (whom we may take here, as in *Timaeus*, to be astral gods) are able to contemplate the Ideas (247a–e), whereas the human soul, even in its cosmic state, has great difficulties in 'seeing' τὰ ὄντα (here 'true being') at all (248a ff.). In fact it is by the 'collecting' operation (ξυναιρούμενον 249c1) of two-way dialectic that our soul may 'recall' something of τὸ ὂν ὄντως (c4); the classing κατ' εἶδος is part of this process (249b8), whereas ἀνάμνησις only concerns what the soul possibly has 'seen.'[154]

[86]

[87]

## Categories elsewhere

It is not only in *Theaetetus, Meno, Phaedo* and *Phaedrus* that we can find some 'preliminary' reflections of the theory of Categories with which *Parmenides, Sophist* and *Timaeus* operate. Faint traces can be detected elsewhere (cf. above, p. 407 ff.).

### Cratylus and Republic IV

Wherever the roots of a specific theory of Categories are to be sought (the evidence we have in the dialogues suggests as one background the Academic discussions of two-way dialectic), two pieces of text are worth additional notice.

In the semi-serious conclusion to the *Cratylus*, the Categories seem to be alluded to as an introduction to Socrates' 'dream' about Ideas (439cd). Shall we believe, Socrates asks after all the Heraclitan excesses of the dialogue, that words represent 'standstill' or 'motion' (στάσις / φορά 438c)? 'Plurality' (πλῆθος) is no good criterion, he claims playfully. Since all words quarrel (στασιάζειν 438d, a pun again) about having their own 'similarity' to truth (ἑαυτὰ εἶναι τὰ ὅμοια τῇ ἀληθείᾳ), 'what is' (τὰ ὄντα) should apparently be sought through their kin (ξυγγενῆ, presumably the faculties of the soul are meant) and through 'themselves' (αὐτὰ δι' αὑτῶν): the 'different' (ἕτερον, ἀλλοῖον, i.e. words) denote something different.

---

154. I take it that Plato would not have subscribed to Kant's 'a priori concepts,' except for the Categories. According to the most natural interpretation of *Phaedrus* 247a–254b, the soul of man, and notably the philosopher (249a), may indeed 'remember' some true ὄντα, some part of ἀλήθεια (248b, 249b6), and notably something of eternal beauty (but no specific Ideas, 250b) and of the Perfect Being of *Timaeus*. However, it is by two-way dialectic and λογισμός (cf. 265d ff. and *Meno* 98a, above) that we attain some knowledge of them (at 249bc, read ἰόν and passive ξυναιρούμενον, both to go with εἶδος). This would not be in conflict with the epistemology Plato presents elsewhere (e.g. *Republic* V—VI). Note also that the 'Innate Sense of Right' (τὸ δίκαιον) was a sophistic notion (cf. *Protagoras* 322c ff., *Republic* I 338c ff., etc.) which Plato certainly was not prepared to endorse as such. All in all, metempsychosis was no Platonic doctrine but a 'mythic vision' that suited his rhetoric.

[87]  Truth (ἀλήθεια αὐτή) is better seen in 'itself' (αὐτήν probably to be read at 439b1) than in its reflection (εἰκών). The 'multitude' (τὰ πολλά) of words, though seemingly aiming at the 'same' (ταὐτόν), can only reflect 'motion' (ἰέναι, ῥεῖν 439c). The Categories are here rather consistently applied to two-level ontology, though the terminology is not consistent. 'Being' is seen from the perspectives of 'same / different,' 'standstill / motion,' and 'plurality'; only 'unity' is not explicitly mentioned.

[88]  In Book IV of *Republic*, again, the 'unity' of the tripartite soul is discussed in terms of (what would appear to be) the Categories. At 435c, Socrates begins his argument by stating that there are the 'same' (τὰ αὐτά) 'different' (cf. ἕτερα 436b) characters in society as in man. Since, presumably, opposite tendencies cannot coexist in the 'same' place (ταὐτόν, κατὰ ταὐτόν, πρὸς ταὐτόν), we should know whether the tendencies in our soul are the 'same' or 'many' (ταὐτόν, πλείω 436bc). Such opposites are 'standstill / motion' (ἑστάναι / κινεῖσθαι): they do not appear together in the 'same' part of an object (τὸ αὐτό, κατὰ τὸ αὐτό), though one part may stand still, another move (436cd), or a circular motion may seem to combine the contrasts (436d–437a). Here 'sameness' is, by implication, the more valuable category. This argument is then taken as a changeable 'hypothesis' (ὑποθέμενοι 437a4, note λελυμένα ἔσεσθαι 437a8) for a lengthy argument about opposite tendencies in fact coexisting in the soul (note e.g. the well-known punning στάσις 440e4), the ultimate point being (443c–e) that the different tendencies within the soul have to be harmonized so that there becomes 'one' man out of 'many' (ἕνα ... ἐκ πολλῶν 443e2). The argument is very intricate, but by adducing the Categories for a start, Plato has intimated to the attentive listener that unity and harmony within the soul (and the Best State) are indeed possible: 'unity / plurality,' 'sameness / otherness,' and 'rest / motion' do after all coexist everywhere, as they do in the soul; but the first member of the pairs is to be classed higher. In *Sophist* and *Politicus* we learn more about how such a συμπλοκή may be both understood and achieved.

## *Philebus* and πέρας / ἄπειρον

In *Philebus*, ontology-bound ethics is in the foreground. It is an interesting fact that the *Philebus* operates with the above-mentioned Categories very selectively and only in the beginning: then the new contrast πέρας / ἄπειρον takes over their function. The discussion of ἡδονή starts with some vague references to 'same / different' (ἕν / μορφὰς παντοίας 12c, ὁμοίας / διάφορον 13c, etc.), leading to the first main problem, the relation of ἕν / πολλά (14c ff.) and the identity and difference of ἑνάδες (μονάδες, also seen as Ideas or Forms, 15ab, cf. 59c).[155]

---

155. The recent discussion about *Philebus* has centered on the plurality problem and its relation to the ἄγραφα (below, p. 473 ff.); cf. e.g. Sayre 1983, Benitez 1989, Löhr 1990, Hampton 1990, Hoffmann 1996: 113 ff. But McCabe 1994: 243–257 has seen more clearly than many others the connection of the πέρας / ἄπειρον contrast with the Categories.

Having been playfully warned not to κινεῖν εὖ κείμενον (15c9), Socrates offers a [88] profuse description of how young people love to 'move' all λόγος about 'one / many' and 'same / other' (also ταὐτόν / θάτερα 15e2): but all this 'is' always there (15d8). Instead, he will recommend his own 'better way' (καλλίων ὁδός 16b5) which turns out to be two-way dialectic (16c–17a, cf. 57e–59d): to ἕν / πολλά he now adds the (clearly Pythagorean, 16c5–8) contrast πέρας / ἀπειρία (later ἄπειρον), emphasizing the importance of ἀριθμός (16d4, etc.).[156] The subsequent [89] discussion then applies πέρας / ἄπειρον, as a new pair of 'Categories' (cf. 23b), to the two-level model. However, there is also a 'mixture' of both, and a 'cause'; so after all we have four categories (εἴδη, γένη 23cd, also ἰδέα 16d7; 'four' is a playfully mystic number, as in the opening of *Timaeus*). While ἄπειρον includes πολλά and μᾶλλον / ἧττων and other opposites (24ab, etc.), τὸ πέρας is represented in τὸ ἴσον, number, and measure (25a–c). Similarly, νοῦς (and cause) is connected with to πέρας, but ἡδονή with ἄπειρον (27d–31a, cf. *Theaetetus* 156b). The 'good life,' however, is a 'mixture' (μεικτόν, cf. soul in *Timaeus*, thought, language and statemanship in *Sophist—Politicus*). To argue this, Socrates dwells at length on questions relating to opposite or contrasted feelings and reactions on the sensual level. Here, too, Plato's two-level model is obviously present throughout: cf. e.g. 54a ff. οὐσία / γένεσις, 56b ff. οἱ φιλοσοφοῦντες / οἱ πολλοί, 59c, 62ab, 64bc οἱ τοῦ ἀγαθοῦ πρόθυροι. He points out that there are more refined kinds of pleasure connected with 'purity' (ἀμεικτόν, καθαρόν, 50e ff.), namely higher level beauty (note 51c7 ἀεὶ καλὰ καθ' αὑτά, cf. 53b σμικρὸν καθαρόν / μεμειγμένον πολύ). But in human life, τἀγαθόν cannot be mere upper level-truth (61b–64a): we have to seek it in a combination of three components, κάλλος, συμμετρία, ἀλήθεια (65a).[157] In an ultimate ordering of these aspects, μέτρον (which is close to 'limit') will take the first place and ἡδοναί (close to the 'limitless') the fifth and last (66a–c).

## Concluding remarks on Categories

All in all, it would seem that the contrasts 'one / many,' 'same / other,' and 'stability / change,' all deeply rooted in Plato's philosophy, became combined and slightly systematized in discussions of the interrelation of the two main ontological levels. The first two pairs are always prominent in two-way dialectic and the

---

156. The 'young people' who love to manipulate λόγος with Categories (15d ff.) are probably those who have come forward in *Parmenides, Sophist* and *Politicus*. For the Pythagorean (Philolaic) πέρας (περαίνοντα in Philolaus) / ἄπειρον (ἄπειρα), see now Huffman 1993; cf. Isnardi Parente 1997: 472 ff. on Aristotle *Phys.* III 203a, 206b. It is to be noted that τὸ ἄπειρον does not, to Plato, mean external infinity (his Universe is limited) but limitless divisibility. For ἀριθμός (especially 15c–e), cf. *Timaeus* and Hoffmann 1996: 25 f., 126 ff.

157. Κάλλος is close to the Good (cf. 64e), as in *Symposium* and *Republic* VI; συμμετρία is the result of right measure and a combination of πέρας and ἄπειρον. The ἀλήθεια adduced at 64b perhaps refers to the result of the dialectic treatment of the entire issue.

[89] theory of Forms. With the including of 'stability / change,' they began to form a
[90] set of 'Categories': a net extending over the entire reality (οὐσία, εἶναι, ὄν, as contrasts to 'non-being'), a system inherent in human soul, and a tool for understanding reality in a large sense. For Plato the use of Categories seems to have been rather tentative. Reflections occur in *Cratylus, Theaetetus, Phaedrus,* and *Republic IV*, though the terminology remains vague. In *Parmenides, Sophist (Politicus)* and *Timaeus* the Categories are more systematically applied to ontology and psychology; but in these dialogues Plato's own role is somewhat less clear. In *Philebus* the earlier Categories are gradually replaced by the contrast 'limit / limitless.'

# VIII

## FORMS, CATEGORIES, FIRST PRINCIPLES

## The Principles as Categories

*An authentically Platonic theory?*

The partly inflamed discussion of the ἄγραφα δόγματα[158] concerns mainly the following issues:

(a) Did Plato ever propound a metaphysical theory of two basic Principles (ἀρχαί), namely ἕν and ἀόριστος δυάς (the latter representing also τὸ μέγα καὶ μικρόν), for all that 'is': number, Forms, and the physical world?

(b) If so, what exactly is the relation of Forms and numbers (or in general, mathematical concepts) to these Principles?

---

158. The vast literature up to 1981 is listed and partly discussed by Krämer 1982 (418 ff.: 181 items! I have not used the 1990 English translation of this book) and later elsewhere. After Cherniss (1944, 1945 and later) had rather unfairly repudiated the notion of 'unwritten teachings' and Ross (1951: 152 ff.) had cautiously accepted the traditions, the chief participants in the discussion were on the 'Tübingen' side Krämer (notably 1959 and 1982) and Gaiser (notably 1963 and 1968), later Szlezák (notably 1985) and Erler 1987, the 'Milanese' school of Reale (notably 1984; cf. several of the works published in the *Collana: Temi metafisici* notably by Albert [cf. Ferber 1992], Migliori, and Movia; further Cattanei 1989, 1996, Bonagura 1990), Richard 1986, Balléri-aux 1994; and with interesting modifications, Ferber (notably 1989, 1993). Their opponents have included, after Tigerstedt 1977 and Vlastos (his 'last word' 1991), notably Heitsch 1989, Brisson (1995[1], etc.), Giannantoni 1995, Isnardi Parente (especially 1993, 1995[1], and with comprehensive reconsiderations of the principal texts, 1997, 1998), von Perger and Hoffmann 1997: 117 ff.; also the more original Wieland. Outside these specific camps, various attempts have been made to interpret the ἄγραφα as genuinely Platonic: note Theiler 1964 (as usual a compact piece of learning, seldom used, and unfortunately written before Gaiser 1963), Burkert 1972: 15–28, Findlay 1974, Annas 1976, Sayre 1983 (cf. his 1993 review of Krämer), H.-G. Gadamer (*see* his recent dialogue with the esotericists in Girgenti (ed.) 1998), Schmitz II 1985: 328 ff. and 1992, de Vogel 1986: 191 ff., Gill and Mueller 1993 (both in the issue of *Méthexis* which Conrado Eggers Lan devoted to this question), and Miller 1995. The discussion will no doubt continue.

[91] (c) What was the status and chronological place of this theory in a possible development of Plato's thought?

Assuming that there are reasonable answers to (b) and (c), let us first consider the evidence for (a). Naturally, again, this will be only an aerial view of a very
[92] complicated set of sources, problems, and interpretations. Without going much into the vexing details of this issue, I am offering the 'two-level model' as a new general way of explication.

'Unity' can without any difficulty be regarded as a basic Principle in Plato's thought. But the combination of ἕν (or μονάς) with ἀόριστος δυάς, which occurs regularly in the tradition about the ἄγραφα, looks decidedly Pythagorean: the even number 'two' is, of course, constitutive of all numbers except 'one' and of most geometrical concepts except the point (an essential issue in Pythagorean arithmology), and ἀόριστος seems to allude to the Pythagorean ἄπειρον (which perhaps was originally taken from Anaximander).[159] This is no argument against an authentically Platonic origin of the theory of Principles, however. We can see in *Timaeus* and *Philebus* in particular how prepared Plato was to operate with Pythagorean ideas, and there are many other signs of this.[160] It is an interesting but seldom noticed fact that the Principles occur in Platonically-oriented Hellenistic Pythagorean texts together with various versions of the 'two-level model.'[161]

Even extreme anti-esotericists have to admit that Plato must have had continuous and detailed oral discussions about issues which he for some reason did

---

159. For Pythagorean arithmology, see the detailed discussion by Burkert 1972: 427 ff.; for ἄπειρον, ibid. 250 ff. (and above, n. 156). Cf. below, n. 179.
160. Burkert 1972 offers again abundant material. Tejera (e.g. 1984: 28, 119 ff.) rightly finds some irony in Plato's Pythagorean references, but he goes too far in rejecting Plato's reliance on Pythagorean sources. There is no reason to doubt that Pythagorean metaphysics held a fascination for Plato (cf. also Simplicius in *Phys.* 151.13 f. D, Gaiser 1963, Test. 8, Krämer 1982, Test. 2). The question is ultimately where to put the emphasis in a sometimes playfully visionary, non-dogmatic field.
161. Some observations in Dillon 1977: 118 ff. Two of the anonymous Hellenistic reports of 'Pythagorean' doctrine combine Unity with ἀόριστος δυάς: Anon.Alexandri in Diog. L. VIII 24 ff., 234 Thesleff (μονάς the sole ἀρχή which together with the Dyad as ὕλη produces number and the solid bodies; cf. the 'Dimension sequence,' below), and Anon.Photii, Phot. cod. 249, 237 Th. (similarly, referring the terms ἕν and δύο to numbers only (the line about δύο is missing from the text ed. Thesleff 1965), and adding ἰσότης and μέτρον to μονάς, and ὑπερβολή / ἔλλειψις and μᾶλλον / ἧττον to δυάς); cf. also Sextus Adv. math. X (Gaiser T 32, Krämer T 12, Isnardi Parente 1998 C 2, especially 262 ff.) which is often taken to refer to pythagorizing Academics. Traces of the same idea are found in Archytas Π. ἀρχῶν (19 Th., the second Principle 'evil'), fr. inc. 5–6 Th. (ἕν the ultimate Principle, also Thearidas 201; Butherus 59; Clinias fr. 2, 108; Brotinus 56 Th.); further Damippus 68.6 ff., Callicratides 103.11 ff., and the curious (relatively late) Ἱερὸς λόγος in Doric (especially 164.22 Th. Πρατεύς / Δυάς). The two-level model is prominent in almost all of the Pseudo-Pythagorean texts. The origin of these texts is an open question (cf. Thesleff 1961, Dillon l.c.; for recent references see Centrone 1990). I still feel that they are on the whole earlier than Eudorus and contain ideas which derive from Xenocrates' interpretation of Plato.—For other Hellenistic traditions about Platonic Principles, see Dörrie and Baltes IV 439 ff., Isnardi Parente 1997: 393 ff. 1998 (who emphasizes the fragility of the evidence).

not commit to writing.¹⁶² Several hints of an oral treatment of metaphysical questions occur in the dialogues: the well-known πολυθρύλητα at *Phaedo* 100b5 is one example of this; and the explicit reference at *Timaeus* 48c to εἴτε ἀρχὴν εἴτε ἀρχάς (cf. 53d) is worth particular notice in this connection.¹⁶³ It is also important to note that Aristotle's notorious (and singular) phrasing τὰ λεγόμενα ἄγραφα δόγματα does not imply 'dogmas' or even 'teaching' in a strict sense.¹⁶⁴ We shall return below (p. 485 ff.) to the lecture 'On the Good.'

[93]

*Notes on the sources*

Aristotle is our earliest explicit witness for the theory of two Platonic Principles.¹⁶⁵ The reliability of Aristotle has been much debated, and his accounts of the Principles and related questions may indeed look loose and inconsistent.¹⁶⁶ But though some of the later sources simply reflect Aristotle's interpretations, he is not our only early witness. It seems rather clear that Theophrastus, Dercyllides and Alexander (of Aphrodisias) had direct access to writings by some other of Plato's pupils who, like Aristotle in his now lost *De bono*, discussed the Platonic Principles more systematically: namely Speusippus, Xenocrates, Hermodorus, Hestiaeus, and possibly Heraclides.¹⁶⁷

---

162. This obvious fact was pointed out by e.g. Vlastos in 1963 (quoted by Mueller 1993: 120) and Isnardi Parente 1993: 92 f.

163. Szlezák (1985 and elsewhere) has been studying very carefully the cases where Plato seems to be 'omitting' topics reserved for oral discussion. Here is some risk for over-interpretation, as opponents have been prone to remark. But the fact remains that the dialogues do not cover Plato's philosophy in its entirety. One of the many proofs of this is Aristotle's statement *Met*. A 992a22 ff.

164. Aristotle *Phys*. IV 209b14–15. Szlezák (1993: 16 ff.) and others (e.g. Kahn 1996: 338) rightly refuse the notion of 'dogma' in this context; 'unwritten opinions' or 'tenets' would be a better translation (pace Isnardi Parente 1997: 382 n. 22, 471). Szlezák (l.c.) also emphatically denies that his own view of 'esotericism' would imply 'secrecy'; cf. below, 486 ff.

165. *See* now Isnardi Parente 1997. Gaiser's (1963: 441 ff.) collection and comments on the sources are still useful, though partly superseded by Krämer 1982: 370 ff. and Isnardi Parente 1997, 1998. The two chief contexts in Aristotle's work are *Met*. A 987a–988a and *Phys*. IV 2.209b.

166. It is often said, as Cherniss did, that Aristotle applies to Plato his own ways of thinking and a new terminology (e.g. Sayre 1983: 15). However, the core of his information about the Principles is distinct enough and, apparently, not only due to his own interpretation of the dialogues. This has been admitted by several scholars recently; cf. e.g. Cattanei 1996 (especially 128 ff.) and Isnardi Parente 1997 (especially 382) who propounds again a new variant of the somewhat complicated theories of Aristotle's partial reliance on and polemics against his contemporaries in the Academy (notably Speusippus and Xenocrates). In the following I shall focus on what is reasonably 'Platonic' in the light of the evidence so far discussed.

167. Cf. Gaiser T 8, 23 B, 30–31, Krämer T 2–3, 8, 13; Isnardi Parente 1997, 1998. For all we know, these pupils were careful to report what they believed Plato had said or 'meant' and developed their own interpretations on this 'historistic' basis, not in order to create themselves new doctrines or systems. And surely the notorious lecture 'On the Good' (below) was not their only source. For a clear, though simplifying conspectus, *see* Dillon 1977: 1–51. Aristotle appears to have been the only one of Plato's close associates to enter on a thorough criticism of his thoughts.

[94] *The Principles and the two levels*

Our main sources agree on positing Ἕν as the first Principle; Μονάς seems to be a 'pythagorizing' variant of this.[168]

The second Principle is invariably called Ἀόριστος Δυάς. There is no direct trace of this double term in the dialogues, but what it stands for looks quite Platonic, notwithstanding some varieties in the interpretations.[169] Evidently there existed no doctrinal tradition about the details, though the term was fixed as a contrast to Ἕν. However, the complex μέγα καὶ μικρόν (or μεῖζον / ἔλαττον, μᾶλλον / ἧττον) was regularly associated with it (cf. also e.g. *Phaedo* 100e–101c, *Parmenides* 149c–e; and δύο *Republic* VII 524b–d): it appears to represent the 'doubleness' of opposites, and also their apparent 'limitlessness.'

We have seen that opposites belong to the lower level of Plato's model (above, Chapter V); and notably in *Philebus* they are connected with what is 'limitless' or 'unmeasurable.' Not much imagination is needed to fit in this very general picture of the Principles with what is said in the *Timaeus* and *Philebus*. I find no real obstacles to the assumption that Plato had orally suggested something like what Aristotle reports. We shall presently return to some details.

Here I want to emphasize the mostly overlooked fact that the second Principle does not stand in equal balance to the first. It is subordinated to the first, it is asymmetric, and of a secondary rank.[170] I take it as fairly certain that we are here concerned with the two-level model.

*Principles and Categories*

Many scholars, especially the 'esotericists,' have seen a connection between the Platonic First Principles and what I have called the Categories, but have taken the latter to be secondary to the system of Principles. The Categories are then seen as Forms (Ideas), and all Forms are derived from the Principles.[171]

---

168. Cf. above, n. 161 (especially Sextus). Alexander Aphr. in *Met.* 55 ff. Ha. (Gaiser T 22 B, Krämer T 10; Isnardi Parente 1998 C 3, with detailed discussion p. 55–65) seems to operate with a source of this type where μονάς is seen as the Principle of number in the first place; ἕν is the Principle of All (56.6). For μονάς 'oneness' vs. ἕν, cf. *Phaedo* 101c (also δυάς), 105c, *Philebus* 15ab (also ἑνάς), etc.

169. The term δυάς occurs as 'twoness' (the Form of 'two') in *Phaedo* 101c (with μονάς), 104c, e, cf. *Parmenides* 149cd. The adjective ἀόριστος occurs only three times in *Laws* in irrelevant contexts. Yet it is difficult to imagine that Aristotle or any other pupil of Plato (Xenocrates? cf. n. 174) had invented a term which is so unanimously ascribed to Plato; cf. also Krämer 1959: 512 ff., Speusippus (in Proclus in *Parm.*, Pl. *Lat.* III ed. Klibansky and Labowsky, 1953: 38 ff., Gaiser T 50; cf. Burkert 1972: 63 f.) seems to have regarded ἀόριστος δυάς as genuinely Platonic since he wanted to substitute 'multitude' for it. *Epinomis* 990d ff. might be an indirect piece of evidence of how Speusippus reasoned.

170. A fact pointed out e.g. by Theiler 1964: 92 ff., Dörrie 1987: 296 ff., though they have not drawn the full consequences.

171. See e.g. Gaiser 1963 (especially 18 f., 70 ff., emphasizing the 'mathematical' aspect of all 'Categories'), Krämer 1982: 159 ff.; de Vogel 1986: 198 ff.; further references in Dörrie and Baltes IV, Baust.120, Comm. 448 ff.

To stand on firm ground, let us step out from the marshes of the theory of Forms. Just a short step is needed. I am claiming that the theory of Principles was an attempt to grasp, in 'pythagorizing' terms, the two-level Categories of ἕν / πολλά (ἀριθμός), ταὐτόν / θάτερον, στάσις / κίνησις, and indeed οὐσία (or φύσις) in its entirety. If allowance is made for some idiosyncrasies in Aristotle's interpretation, I believe this view of the Principles would free us from most of the difficulties that modern scholarship has found here. To anticipate what will be argued below, ἕν, ταὐτόν and στάσις are manifested in the first Principle, πολλά, θάτερον, and κίνησις in the second; and both together produce the harmony of what 'is': οὐσία.[172]

The first Principle is not really problematic as such, and without extra mystification the pythagorizing πέρας of *Philebus* can be put on the level of 'unity, sameness, and rest.'

The second Principle draws with it a number of complications which are, however, often exaggerated in modern studies. Rather easily and Platonically it can be taken to represent Duality as the first stage of 'plurality,' 'difference,' and 'motion.' Its qualification as 'undefined' or 'indeterminate' points in the direction of limitless 'plurality' and the pythagorizing ἄπειρον of *Philebus* which by 'mixing' with the first Principle produces a 'measurable' area.[173] We are here reminded of the realm of Necessity in *Timaeus* with its ἐκμαγεῖον. The extreme consequences of a possible identification of the second Principle with this ὑποδοχή (*Timaeus* 49a), a relatively passive (and female) τιθήνη on the verge of non-being, probably did not interest Plato very much, to judge from the dialogues. Aristotle, however, makes a point of associating the ἀόριστος δυάς with his own ὕλη, with the vague χώρα or 'receptacle' in *Timaeus*, and even with what is generally 'bad': this leads to a dualistic conception which Aristotle, as usual simplifying in order to sharpen his criticism, is not prepared to accept.[174] To Plato, the second Principle

---

172. Several Aristotelian passages do in fact suggest that Plato's Principles were associated with what I have called Categories: note *Phys.* IV 209b, *Met.* 1004b27 ff., I 1054a29 ff., N 1087b; cf. Isnardi Parente 1998 B 2a) where τὸ ἴσον and τὸ μένον (i.e. 'same' and 'standstill') occur among the characteristics of the First Principle; and Eudemus fr. 49, 60 We (Isnardi Parente 1998 B 5–6) refers to Pythagorean and Platonic discussions of κίνησις as ἀόριστος. Sextus (above, n. 161) comments on αὐτότης and ἑτερότης in relation to ἀόριστος δυάς.

173. Cf. above, n. 169. Ἀόριστος, as an attribute of the Principle Δυάς, looks like an approximation of ἄπειρος to the two-level contrast of 'defined' (including ὅρος) vs. 'undefined' (above, p. 407). The Twoness is not 'limitless' but 'not-yet defined'! For 'measure,' cf. below and n. 177.

174. See notably *Met.* A 987b20, 988a14 ff., 999a, N 1091b26 ff., *Phys.* IV 209b (cf. III 203a, Theophrastus *Met.* 6b, rightly interpreted by Schmitz II 1985: 136 and Isnardi Parente 1998: 21 ff.). Ἕν of course is universally a 'good' Principle (cf. *Met.* N 1091b, *EN* 1096a, *EE* 1218a; Isnardi Parente 1997: 446 ff., 466f, 475 ff., arguing that Aristotle took the term ἀόριστος δυάς from Xenocrates, which I find doubtful; cf. above, n. 169). This 'dualism' has often been misunderstood. E.g. Asclepios in *Met.* 77 Ha. (Isnardi Parente 1998 C 8 and p. 74) had to point out that there is no ἄκρατον τὸ κακόν in Plato's model. Already Hermodorus argued that ἀόριστος δυάς cannot be the opposite of οὐσία (*see* Simplicius in *Phys.* 248, 256 D, Gaiser T 31, Krämer T 13, Isnardi Parente 1998 B 2ab; cf. Simplicius 151.15 ff., Gaiser T 8, Krämer T 2, Isnardi Parente 1998 C 11; Dörrie 1987: 296 ff., Schmitz II 1985: 384 ff.). Xenocrates' dualism may have gone further, like Plutarch's (cf. Dillon, above, n. 161), and Plotinus followed suit (cf. *Enn.* II 4.7, III 6.16–18 on ἀόριστος δυάς).

cannot have been 'in principle' bad or evil, any more than his lower level was. But of course the rhetoric of *Timaeus* could be easily understood that way by listeners and readers.

## Principles and Ideal Numbers

Aristotle's remarks on the relation of the First Principles to Ideal Numbers and the Forms, are more problematic. Various Aristotelian passages, taken together with what Theophrastus and some later commentators state, are often interpreted to mean that Plato 'derived' Ideal Numbers from the First Principles, and the Forms from Number.[175]

It seems beyond doubt that Plato was believed, by his own pupils, to have assumed the existence of 'Ideal Numbers' and to have assumed their identification with the Pythagorean 'Decad,' the τετρακτύς $(1 + 2 + 3 + 4 = 10)$. Such a metaphysical 'Four' can be easily extracted from the *Timaeus* where 'four' occurs already as a first touch at the opening, the soul is constructed ultimately of four layers (cf. here the Line in *Republic* VI) and, notably, the physical world consists of four geometrically constructed elementary bodies (which combine in innumerable ways within the frame of a fifth).[176] We shall return presently to the 'derivation' of the metaphysical 'Four' from the Principles.

The 'objects of mathematics' (τὰ μαθηματικὰ τῶν πραγμάτων, *Met.* A 987b16, Z 1028b20), again, are placed according to Aristotle 'between' the Ideas and physical things. First, we may note that this very univocal statement corresponds to Socrates' remarks on segment 2 of the Line (above, p. 454 f.). But there is certainly more to it. Number, measure and proportions underlying the structure of Cosmos and needed for μετρητική, are intermediate entities, mediating not only between the level of Ideas and the level of physical things, but combining ultimately the Principles Ἕν and Ἀόριστος Δυάς—as the Categories or Forms respectively are, in *Timaeus*, *Sophist*, *Politicus* and *Philebus*, said to combine.[177] This is after all not so imaginative, given the notion of συμπλοκή. The Idea of 'Precision' (αὐτὸ τὸ ἀκριβές) is introduced in *Politicus* (284d). Arithmetic number (except 'One') and geometric concepts (except the 'point') include the Category of plurality.

---

175. *See* the vexing passage *Met.* A 987b7–988a:7 (Gaiser T 22 A, Krämer T 9, Isnardi Parente 1997 A 1–2) combined with Theophrastus *Met.* 6b (Gaiser T 30, Krämer T 8, Isnardi Parente 1998 B 4); cf. Aristotle *Met.* 1073a, M 1080ab, 1081a, 1083a, 1084a, 1086a , *Phys.* III 206b27 ff., Alexander Aphr. in Simplicius in *Phys.* 455.7 ff. D. In general, cf. the references in Annas 1976: 16 ff., Baltes 1994: 221, Miller 1995: 236 f., Cattanei 1996: 128 ff., Isnardi Parente 1997: 408 ff., I998: 19 ff.

176. The locus classicus is *Timaeus* 53c–57c (for the dodecahedron approximating to the sphere, *see* 55c). Cf. e.g. Aristotle *Met.* M 1083a29 ff., 1086a, *De an.* I 404b (referring to 'On Philosophy' which probably implies Plato's 'On the Good'); cf. Burkert 1972: 25 f. (pace Isnardi Parente 1997: 479 ff.) where more references are given. For the 'Dimension Sequence,' cf. below, n. 181. Isnardi Parente (l.c.) argues that 'Ideal Number' was essentially a rationalization by Xenocrates from *Timaeus*; but the notion is rather clearly implicit in *Timaeus*, given that Plato regarded the Pythagorean τετρακτύς as prior to 'creation'; cf. below. And *Timaeus* is hardly later than *Philebus* (as is sometimes thought, e.g. Schmitz II 1985: 360 ff.).

Although they are ἀίδια and ἀκίνητα, as Aristotle notes (*Met.* A 987b17–18), they are continuously 'generated' on a physical level by the interposing of ἕν on δυάς: this is how I would understand Aristotle's subsequent remarks (ibid. 22–998a2): note here ἑτέρα φύσις and γεννᾶσθαι (35 f.) applied to the level of δυάς, and ἔξω τῶν πρώτων referring to Ideal Numbers (the τετρακτύς as at M 1080b22, not 'prime numbers' or 'odd numbers' as sometimes suggested). On a higher level (namely segment 2 of Plato's Line) there are 'Forms' for such mathematicals, the objects of διάνοια.[178]

When Aristotle occasionally seems to hint that Plato's Forms 'are number,'[179] he cannot possibly mean what I have been calling 'Ideas.' What he means must be considered from a broader perspective. Above all, it is the problem of the relation of Ideal Numbers to the First Principles on one hand, and to Ideas on the other, that will concern us here.

The metaphysical 'Four' (τετρακτύς), or 'Decad,' seen as 'Ideal Numbers' (εἰδητικός ἀριθμός *Met.* M 1086a5, etc.), can, perhaps with the help of some

[97]

[98]

---

177. 'Measure' as applied to the 'indeterminate' within the two-level model, is in the foreground in these dialogues; for μετρητική in *Politicus* in particular, see Migliori 1996. 'Measuring' is normally connected with opposites in physical life: *Protagoras* 356d ff., *Phaedo* 100e ff., *De Justo* 372a ff. For (στάσις) / κίνησις as a basis for the mathematical operations in *Timaeus*, cf. Hoffmann 1996: 217 ff. The association of μέγα καὶ μικρόν and other opposites with the Ἀόριστος Δυάς can be reasonably regarded as reflecting a continuum of relative size, value, etc. which, when ἕν and πέρας are applied to it, produces measure and measurability. The Idea of Precision needed for determining the μέτριον (*Politicus* 284d) points towards Ἕν and Τἀγαθόν, but is hardly to be identified with either of these; cf. Ferber 1995: 66 ff. The 'primitive' character of this sort of mathematics has been sometimes pointed out in modern times (e.g. Mueller 1993: 128 f., Pritchard 1995): Plato was an amateur mathematician. The mathematization of the ὑπεροχή / ἔλλειψις problem seems to have followed later (see references in Gaiser T 2 B, 32, 23 B, 39–48, Krämer T 11–12, Isnardi Parente 1998 C 1–2, 12); cf. Theiler 1964: 95 ff., Dörrie and Baltes IV 344 f.: Plato's role in all this has perhaps been overemphasized.

178. For ἔξω τῶν πρώτων cf. also Isnardi Parente 1998: 63 ff. Aristotle *EN* I 1096a18 only seems to imply that there is no Form for οἱ ἀριθμοί (in plural). The much-discussed section on arithmetics and Forms, *Republic* VII 522c–526c, seems to me to fit in fairly well with a differentiation of Ideal Number (525b), Forms of mathematicals (including relative size and measure, 524b ff.), and the function of number in practical life.

179. *Met.* A 991b10 ff., M 1076a17 ff., N 1090a, etc. Scholars admit that the interpretation is largely unclear; see e.g. Annas 1976: 60 ff., Schmitz II 1985: 228, Baltes 1994: 221, Isnardi Parente 1997. Cf. notably *Met.* 1073a18 ff. 'those who accept Ideas (ἰδέας) say that they are number (ἀριθμούς), either infinitely or up to ten (δεκάδος)'; M 1086a12–13 'he who first assumed that there are Ideas (εἴδη) and that the Ideas are numbers, and that the objects of mathematics (τὰ μαθηματικά) exist, naturally separated them' (cf. 1080b). In case Plato himself is meant (which is not absolutely certain), both the latter passages may refer to Ideal Numbers, like *Phys.* III 206b32 f. At M 1081a (cf. 1083b, *EE* 1218a 17 ff.), Aristotle's polemic against those who identify the Ideas (ἰδέας) with numbers very probably concerns pythagorizing Academics such as Speusippus. It is well known that some Pythagoreans (before Archytas' times) had operated with number symbolism applied to 'forms' of physical objects ('man,' 'horse,' and so forth: Theophrastus *Met.* 6a20; one might think of the very ancient 'explication' of constellations) and even of abstract concepts, 'justice,' 'marriage,' etc. (Aristotle *Met.* A 985b): see Burkert 1972: 465 ff. I am inclined to think that Plato did not take such attempts very seriously; cf. the ironical tone of Socrates' play with the 'marriage number' at *Republic* VIII 545d ff.

[98] imagination, be 'derived' from the two basic principles of 'One' and a 'Dyad.'[180] The nearest we come to the Pythagorean τετρακτύς in any dialogue, is in *Timaeus*. Here it is interesting to see how the approach to the metaphysical 'Four' mixes an arithmetic and a geometric aspect: the pre-cosmic ordering of the four elements εἴδεσι καὶ ἀριθμοῖς (52d ff., cf. 69bc, 30a) is based on triangles and includes squares (cubes). But we may take it for granted that Plato and his friends went 'beyond' the triangle and already had operated with the 'Dimension Sequence' ('Dimensionsfolge') known from later sources:[181] a point represents 'one,' a line 'two,' a triangle 'three,' and a tetrahedron 'four'; and so we arrive at the basic constituents of our three-dimensional world. Timaeus also intimates a connection between a dodecahedron (twelve pentagons) and a sphere.[182] The numbers 1–4 have an essentially symbolic function in all this. A 'one (point)' is simply a
[99] πέρας, but 'two' already involves an element of ἄπειρον: think of a single straight 'line,' or various curved 'lines,' 'circles,' or 'spirals.' 'Three' and 'four' come naturally out of combinations of ἕν with ἀόριστος δυάς. The rest of the 'decad' only varies this pattern; and the full decad, being the basis of Greek arithmetic (besides being symbolically present elsewhere), seemed apt to close this sector of number metaphysics.

The relation of these 'Ideal Numbers' to Aristotle's μαθηματικά, i.e. (as was suggested above) the mathematical concepts of segment 2 of Plato's Line, is rather unproblematical. They seem to represent, simply, the 'Ideas' (segment 1) to which the mathematical 'Forms' can be reduced. But in what relation do they stand to other 'Ideas'?

## Principles and Ideas

Apart from Aristotle's obscure hints about 'Forms being number,' the only early evidence we have of a connection between 'Ideal Numbers' and 'Ideas' in general is Theophrastus' statement in his *Metaphysics* (6b9 ff.), following after a conspectus of Pythagorean and Academic views of First Principles (ἀρχαί). 'Plato,' he says, 'in reducing (ἀνάγειν) them (i.e. the mathematicals just mentioned) to the

---

180. Aristotle is not prepared to use such imagination; see notably his slightly unfair criticism in *Met*. M 1080a12–1086a27. Though the criticism (somewhat opaquely) involves some of Plato's associates (especially Speusippus and Xenocrates; for the 'Dimension Sequence,' see also N 1090b ff.), it seems rather clear that Plato himself had proposed some theory or vision of how numbers 'derive' from the Principles.

181. At least since Speusippus and Xenocrates (see e.g. Isnardi Parente 1997: 389), but cf. Aristotle N 1090b, Z 1036b. A Platonic origin is hardly to be doubted; cf. Alexander Aphr. in *Met*. p. 55.20 ff. (Gaiser T 22 B, Krämer T 10, Isnardi Parente 1998 C 3), Theiler 1964: 99 ff., Burkert 1972: 24 and n. 45, Annas 1976: 59 (referring to *Republic* VII 528ab, etc.), Hoffmann 1996: 258ff. (referring also to *Laws* X 894a, *Epinomis* 990e ff.). Cf. the numbers and proportions 'used' in the creation of soul, *Timaeus* 34b ff. For 'unity' as 'point,' cf. Burkert 1972: 18 n. 17.

182. *Timaeus* 55c. Cf. the triangles 'generating' a spiral-like figure at *Theaetetus* 147d ff. (below, p. 513). The geometry of the circle did not interest the Pythagoreans to the same extent as the Eastern Greek mathematicians.

Principles, would seem to connect them by attaching (ἀνάπτων) them to Ideas, [99]
and these to the numbers; and he would proceed from them (τούτων) to the Principles, and then down to the 'coming-to-be' until reaching the aforementioned entities (i.e. the mathematicals).'[183] The passage is reasonably clear if the 'numbers' (and τούτων) are taken to refer to 'Ideal Numbers.' We note here, first, a reflection of 'two-way dialectic': Theophrastus is likely to operate with an interpretation of the double process briefly described in the context of the Divided Line in *Republic* VI and VII. However, instead of one ἀρχή (*Republic* VI 510a, 511a), we have here explicitly two Principles, Ἕν and Ἀόριστος Δυάς (Theophrastus *Met.* 6a). Second, we may note the uncertainty of the interpretation (δόξειεν ἄν, 'would seem to'): Theophrastus does not fall back on a clear statement by Plato. What is particularly interesting here, is the hierarchic order ('reducing,' 'connecting,' 'attaching') of the system as Theophrastus sees it: Principles, Ideal Numbers, Ideas, Mathematicals. Perhaps Theophrastus took this interpretation from the pupils of Speusippus who (as is well known, and as Theophrastus knew) had tried to replace the Platonic εἴδη with μαθηματικά generated directly from the two Principles: Theophrastus inserted the traditional ἰδέαι. However Theophrastus or his source may have understood this, are we to understand that Plato had ended up deriving all Ideas from the Ideal Numbers? Hardly.

I want to suggest another interpretation of what Plato is likely to have had in [100]
mind. Very probably Plato's theory of First Principles did not concern the theory of Forms or Ideas to the extent that Aristotle and later sources take for granted. Aristotle on the whole overreacted on Plato's Forms and Speusippus was more interested in the μαθηματικά. Given the pythagorizing bias of the theory of Principles, it is natural that number, proportions, dimensions and measure should come into the foreground here, not the theory of Forms or Ideas. And as with the Categories, οὐσία in its entirety is meant. It is true that Plato appears to have ventilated the Principles together with Τἀγαθόν (below, p. 485 ff.). Probably, however, their focus was elsewhere: on the ontology of number, measure and measuring, and on two-level metaphysics conceived as an interplay between Categories reduced to two Principles, but ultimately concerned with the constitution of the physical world.

## A reduction of the Categories to mathematical concepts

Thus it seems preferable to visualize Plato's theory of First Principles as a reduction of the Categories to arithmetics and geometry, *more Pythagorico*. It makes sense to assume that this was, from Plato's point of view, not primarily a theory of Forms or Ideas, but a theory of the mathematical constitution of Cosmos. It is

---

183. The Greek text: Πλάτων μὲν οὖν ἐν τῷ ἀνάγειν εἰς τὰς ἀρχὰς δόξειεν ἄν ἅπτεσθαι τῶν ἄλλων εἰς τὰς ἰδέας ἀνάπτων, ταύτας δ'εἰς τοὺς ἀριθμούς, ἐκ δὲ τούτων εἰς τὰς ἀρχάς, εἶτα κατὰ τὴν γένεσιν μέχρι τῶν εἰρημένων. Cf. now the comments of Isnardi Parente 1998: 18 ff. I am not so sure that Xenocrates is Theophrastus' principal source.

[100] important to note that the four elementary bodies are discussed in the *Timaeus* under the aspect of 'Necessity' (and indeed, θάτερον), not as a work of 'Reason' (though the Demiurge has a part in the 'ordering' of things). Their connection with the realm of Ideas is a markedly loose one: Plato has chosen another 'paradigm' (47e ff.). I find it practically unthinkable that Plato ever wanted to 'derive' Ideas proper, or even the level of ταὐτόν, from a combination of Unity and Duality.[184]

He is likely to have suggested (orally) that all physical phenomena are measurable and conceivable in terms of number and proportions. By applying to this 'pythagorizing' complex the terminology of the theory of Forms (on which Aristotle seized), we may arrive at segment 2 of the Divided Line where the mathematical aspect was already brought forward by Socrates' comments, and then again by Aristotle's formulation τὰ μαθηματικὰ τῶν πραγμάτων. But if my interpretation of segment 2 is correct, it represents all the Forms corresponding to all physical phenomena. In view of what is said in *Timaeus*, Plato is likely to have assumed that this complex of Forms is, in one way or another, and ultimately via elementary geometrical bodies, reducible to the Pythagorean τετρακτύς. From the perspectives of the theory of Forms, and the somehow inherent rather than
[101] explicit plurality of segment 2, this primary 'decad' seemed to approximate to the unique and could be called 'number as such,' 'Ideal Number': it could seem to fall into segment 1 of the Line. This could easily have given rise to the tradition, traceable since Speusippus and Aristotle, that Plato in fact regarded 'Number' as primary to all Forms, including (but contrary to Plato's intentions) the Ideas. Very probably Plato himself was not prone to make such a systematizing step. Probably he thought of this more broadly and tentatively, within the frames of his two-level vision. And, as will be argued below, he was not teaching a dogma but again making a thought experiment.

All in all, by way of a general 'vision' the contrasted pair of 'Unity' versus 'Duality' (with the significant additions of 'Indeterminate' and 'Great-and-Small') can be reasonably interpreted as manifesting ultimately the 'One over Many' contrast, and at the same time the alluring τετρακτύς. But it also fitted the other two-level contrasts, notably the Categories. Unity can always be associated with Sameness, Standstill, and Limit; Duality with Difference, Motion, and the (potentially) Unlimited. There is a similar relation between Unity and Duality as between the other pairs of 'unequal' (asymmetric) contrasts. They represent the two basic levels of Plato's reality (οὐσία in a large sense). But certainly there is more of Unity on the upper level, and more of Indeterminate Duality on the lower. Pure Ἕν, however, is close to pure Ἀγαθόν (cf. p. 483), and everything is 'oriented' towards these two 'final causes'—to make an assertion that sounds more Neoplatonic than it is intended to be.

---

184. This is one of the points where I strongly disagree with the traditional Tübingen view which implies a hierarchy of Principles—Ideas / Forms—the physical world; *see* notably Krämer 1959: 246, 430 ff., Gaiser 1963: 173 ff., 190 ff.; also de Vogel 1986: 191 ff., Baltes in Dörrie and Baltes IV 450f., 458.

## Principles as Causes? [101]

The question of how to apply Aristotelian 'causes' (or rather, aetiology) to this complex, can perhaps not be definitely solved. The Tübingen scholars tend to take the ἀρχαί as 'causes' in the Presocratic sense, which would mean stressing their 'material' and 'efficient' aspects.[185] I would prefer to see them as basic constituents (ἄκρα καὶ πρῶτα, *7th Letter* 344d) of the structure of the mathematically understandable and measurable Universe and (since the human soul has the capacity for measuring, identifying and distinguishing) as prerequisites for measuring. At the same time they imply a teleological 'orientation' of the lower towards the higher, typical of Plato's two-level model: the Ἀόριστος Δυάς is subordinated to Ἕν. This may be said to mean that the Principles rather combine the 'formal' and 'final' aspects of Aristotelian causes. In fact, the idea of 'efficient [102] cause' is never very prominent in Plato's dealing with higher level entities. It is true that the higher level may have more of 'activity' (cf. above, p. 402), the Ideas are sometimes considered as αἰτίαι (implied in *Phaedo* 95d ff., etc.; cf. above, p. 446), soul is ἀρχὴ κινήσεως (*Phaedrus* 245c, etc.), and the symbolic 'Demiurge' takes the function of a Creator in *Timaeus* (28a, 46c ff., 57e, etc.) and elsewhere (cf. *Philebus* 23d ff. where the 'cause' comes in as a category of its own, above p. 471). But one cannot claim that the upper level is always or predominantly 'effecting' the lower level phenomena. Very much like the Categories, the Principles are, in my view, neither very 'efficient' nor very 'material' causes; even the generation process of regular bodies in *Timaeus* (53c ff.) is rather automatic. But of course 'aetiology' is an Aristotelian issue.

## The relation of the First Principles to Categories, Forms, and Ideas

The following simplifying table, I hope, illustrates my view of the interrelation of Ideas, Forms, Categories, and Principles; cf. the 'two-level' schema above, p. 411 f. The table also represents what I believe was a 'vision,' not a doctrinal system.

Reading the table from left to right gives a vaguely chronological aspect, but only in the sense that the theories of Categories and Principles are generally later than the theories of Ideas and Forms. There is also a slight shift from 'ethics' and the realm of Νοῦς, to physics and mathematics (the realm of Ἀνάγκη, as in *Timaeus* 48e), and so a shift of emphasis from Ἀγαθόν to Ἕν as the point of orientation. The general features of the two-level model remain the same as sketched

---

185. Cf. e.g. Krämer 1982: 153 ff., Szlezák 1997. The ἕν of course is more 'active' than δυάς, cf. e.g. Sextus *Adv. math.* X 277 (and Isnardi Parente 1998: 52). For *Timaeus* as a background for Aristotelian and later aetiology, *see* Natali 1997 with references; Isnardi Parente 1998: 68 refers also to *2nd Letter*.

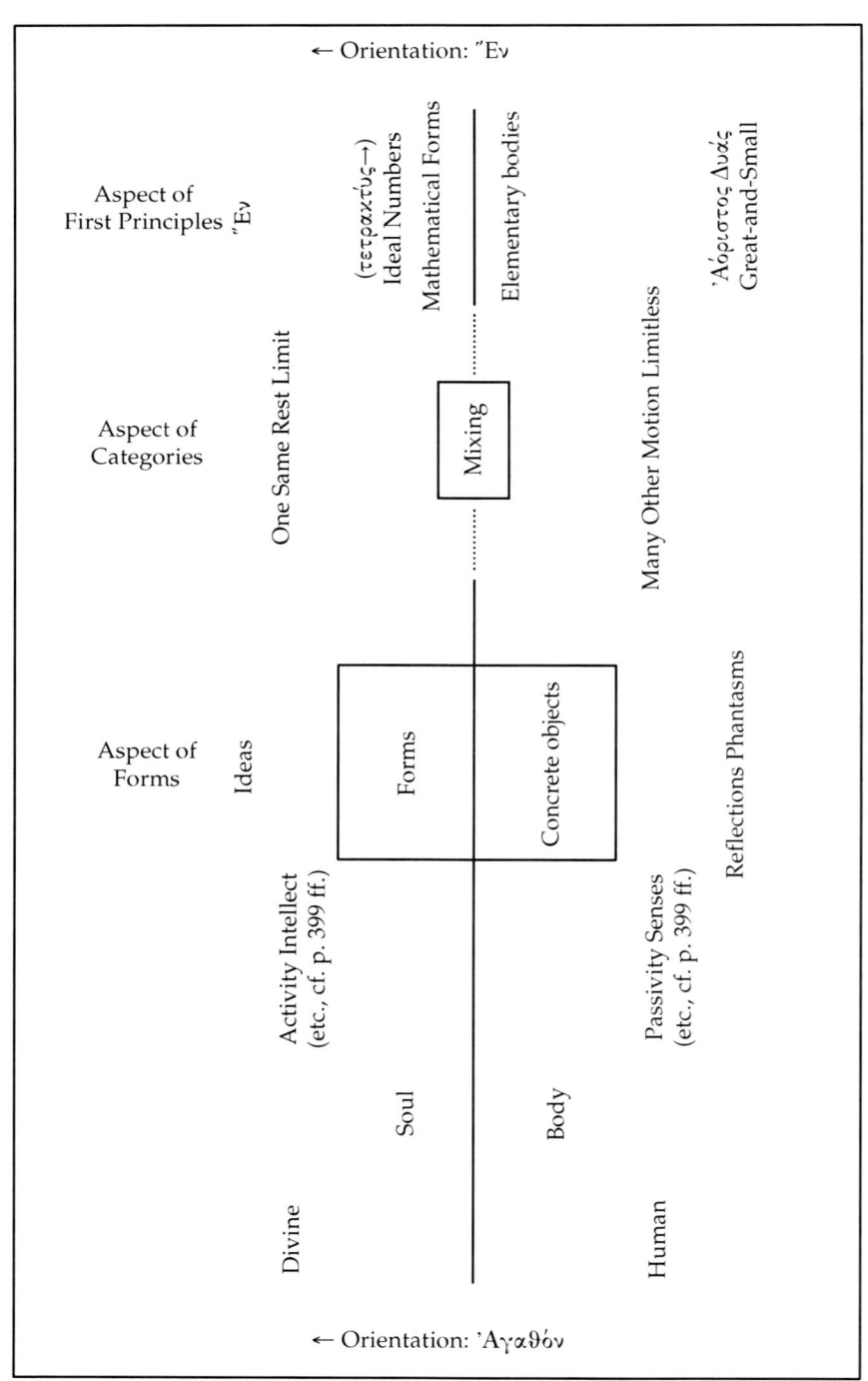

earlier in this work. But (as most scholars agree today) the issues of 'mixing' [102]
(συμπλοκή, μεῖξις) of the elements of the Universe, become more prominent in
Plato's so-called 'late philosophy.'
As a matter of fact, the original ἄγραφα δόγματα need not have been very
much more than an intuitive vision of this sort, tentatively explicated in terms of
the contrast ἕν / ἀόριστος δυάς.

## The status and chronology of the theory [104]

*'On the Good'*

The problems of Plato's notorious public ἀκρόασις 'On the Good' can be solved
reasonably well if one takes it to have been a single occasion[186] when Plato wanted
to make it clear to the Athenians that the question of τὸ ἀγαθόν is far too difficult
for a couple of hours' lecture. Plato, I believe, was teasing his public. The ultimate
Ἀγαθόν, close to Ἕν (and Πέρας), with its reflections and compromises in human life, was an ever-present and fundamental problem to Plato—nothing that
could be explicated in a public speech.
Plato had been teasing his public before: cf. notably *Menexenus*, perhaps the
'Proto-*Republic*.'[187] The 'over-difficult' digression in *7th Letter* seems to have a
similar function of a teasing 'test' (cf. 340b, 341e; πολλάκις, 342a5 of course does
not refer to Περὶ τἀγαθοῦ); cf. also *Laws* XII 968e (ἀπόρρητα / ἀπρόρρητα). Plato
professed to be speaking about what the Good is, and his public expected to be
informed about what is good in human life; instead, Plato dwelled on mathematics and astronomy and identified the Good with One.[188] No wonder the public

---

186. As argued in detail by Gaiser 1980; Isnardi Parente's skepticism (notably 1998: 7 ff.)
goes too far. Our main source is Aristoxenus *Harm. elem.* II 39 f. (Gaiser T 7, Krämer T 1, Isnardi
Parente 1998 B 1). For the later developments of the story, *see* Dörrie 1987, Baust. 1, Isnardi Parente 1998: 74 ff.. Aristotle 'used to' tell the story as an example of the audience being unprepared,
Aristoxenus says, but a repetition of the 'akroasis' is not mentioned here.

187. Above, p. 425. The lecture 'On the Good' seems to have become sometimes later confused with the 'Proto-*Republic*:' cf. Themistus *Or.* 21.245c–246a, situating the lecture in Piraeus
(Isnardi Parente 1998: 77).

188. I take it for granted that the lecture concerned not only human ἀγαθόν which is in
*Philebus* (66a–c, etc.) seen as the right measure between the two tendencies suggested by the
two-level model, but that it also referred to the metaphysical Idea of τὸ ἀγαθόν (cf. *Philebus* 60b
ff.) as the μέγιστον μάθημα (*Republic* VI 505a); and to judge from Aristoxenus, issues that we
know from *Timaeus* were included. Thus, the lecture combined the aspects of τὸ ἀγαθόν and
ἕν (cf, the Table, above); and the ἀόριστος δυάς was also implied, to judge from later sources
(Aristoxenus does not mention it, and hence many scholars deny the mention of the Principles
in this lecture; cf. Isnardi Parente 1997: 397, 1998: 8 f.).—Probably the text of Aristoxenus is somehow corrupt: ὅτε δὲ φανείησαν οἱ λόγοι περὶ μαθημάτων . . . καὶ τὸ πέρας ὅτι ἀγαθόν ἐστιν ἕν,
. . . παράδοξον ἐφαίνετο αὐτοῖς . . . The Tübingen scholars read, with Macran, <τ>ἀγαθόν and
understand, with many others, τὸ πέρας to be adverbial ('at the end'); but another possibility
would be to read, with a nominal ὅτι clause, . . . καὶ τὸ πέρας ('limit') ὅτι ἀγαθόν καὶ (corrupted
into a ligature for ἐστιν) ἕν.

[104] were puzzled.[189] However, this cannot have been the only occasion when Plato's personal disciples and friends were confronted with the details of these issues.
[105] They need not have been puzzled by the lecture at all.[190] They must have known what it was all about, and what to expect. The idea that some of them took down notes from this particular 'lecture' and later published them as presentations of Plato's late philosophy,[191] appears to me rather absurd. For all we know, Plato was not a lecturer, and his philosophy was not a public business but a dialectic process between more or less well-informed persons. What later generations considered to be his 'teaching' was a conglomerate from very many sources.

*A late and tentative theory*

The evidence discussed in this chapter, and the character of the possible reflections in the dialogues, strongly suggest to me that Plato developed the theory of Principles late in his life. This is also the opinion of the majority of those modern critics who accept it as genuinely Platonic. However, as is well known, the Tübingen scholars and their followers incline to see the theory as rooted at least in the so-called Middle Period, and also, to emphasize its very basic, indeed fundamental function in Plato's mature philosophy. The fact that he did not ventilate the theory in his dialogues is taken to be part of a deliberate policy.

We seem to be facing here a dilemma where the need for deep-going reconsiderations, and perhaps compromises, is becoming more and more urgent. Some attempts have been made in recent years. This is again a new attempt.

For my part, I have a great respect for 'Tübingen' learning, and I feel that its achievements, including the problematizing of the issue of Principles and the collecting of a wealth of material largely overlooked before, ought to be more widely recognized. I feel however, with most critics, that the extreme positions of this 'school' ought to be given up. I see no reason to deny the possibility that Plato was already at an early date playing with the contrast One / Two as a variant of 'one / many,' within the frame of his two-level vision.[192] Some of his pythagorizing

---

189. The saying Πλάτωνος ἀγαθόν, denoting something obscure and unattainable, may derive from rumours about this lecture (Thesleff below, p. 531). A reflection in Ps.-Epicharmus is quoted by Alcimus in Diog. L. III 14. But to later Platonists, Plato's Ἀγαθόν was something actively suppressed, cf. Plutarch *Dion* 14.1–3 τὸ σιωπώμενον ἀγαθόν, and Alcinous / Albinus *Didask* 27 p. 179.30 He.

190. Pace Sayre 1983: 82 f., Dörrie 1987: 279 ff., and many others. Proclus in *Parm.* 688.10 ff. Cousin (Isnardi Parente 1998 C 10), though he does not see the whole point, claims that Plato's friends were informed.

191. This idea (explicitly formulated notably by Simplicius in *Phys.* 151 D, Gaiser T 8, Krämer T 2, Isnardi Parente 1998 C 11) is often accepted by those who reconstruct Plato's 'esoteric teaching'; also e.g. Schmitz II 1985: 260 ff.

192. For instance, the fact that Socrates is often contrasted with a pair of interlocutors may possibly have some significance; and the simile of the chariot of the soul in the *Phaedrus* suggests the same. The comedian Theopompus (fr. 15 KA, Diog. L. III 26) probably hints at Academic discussions of ἕν / δύο (rather than at any specific text such as *Hippias Major* 301de, *Phaedo* 101c,

friends in the Academy (or Archytas) may have returned the ball. His interest in mathematical 'metaphysics,' in measure, and in Limit (and of course ὅρος) as dominating the Unlimited, can be traced in dialogues before the 'late' period. But I would insist that it is not until the Categories had come into the foreground in *Parmenides* and *Timaeus* that something like a theory of two-level Principles seems to take shape.[193] We have seen that the theory of Principles can be reasonably interpreted as secondary to the employment of the Categories: it represents a reduction of the two-level Categories to the 'mathematical' constituents of the world. Here at least we may detect a rough chronological line or shifts of emphasis in Plato's thought (though not necessarily an actual 'development').

Surely one should expect the central books of the *Republic* with their rather esoteric—and certainly not very 'early'—musings about τὸ μέγιστον μάθημα, to have been somewhat more explicit on two ἀρχαί (and not only one, as 510b4), if Plato at that stage had had the theory clearly present in his mind. He refers to Forms of mathematicals, and possibly he implies the τετρακτύς, but this is not reduced to two Principles. I have argued elsewhere (cf. below, 489 ff.) that the *Republic* was not finished before the 350s, and I take it to be a manifestation of Plato's genuinely personal thought. In *Parmenides, Sophist, Politicus* and *Timaeus* (*Critias*) he allows others to interfere; in *Philebus* he (as 'Socrates') is back again, but not yet propounding a theory of ἕν / ἀόριστος δυάς. The *Parmenides, Sophist, Politicus, Timaeus*, and even the *Philebus*, are suggestive of the theory in the making, rather than of a final coherent view of ἕν versus ἀόριστος δυάς with its μέγα καὶ μικρόν.

Thus I prefer to conclude that the final theory of Principles did not take shape before the mid-350s, and that it was not entirely a product of Plato's own thought.

Consequently, and contrary the original Tübingen view (which still has its defendants),[194] I would claim that the theory of the two-level Principles was a late 'pythagorizing' intellectual adventure, an experiment. It was not, I believe, a doctrine of fundamental significance to Plato. Like so many other of Plato's visions, whether playfully suggestive or more seriously elaborated, it was hardly a part of a consistently wrought doctrinal 'system.' In the light of recent discussions of Plato's aporetically suggestive manner, the burden of proof lies—now more than ever—with those who argue for a 'system.' In this connection there may be a place for accepting Plato's many-leveled irony and thought-play. Those who

---

or *Republic* VII 524bc). The dichotomy of man in Aristophanes' myth (*Symposium* 192d ff.) is probably irrelevant (pace Reale in Girgenti (ed.) 1998: 104 f.).

193. Traces of oral discussions about the Principles can be seen in *Timaeus* 48c, 53d (cf. 54c), but I am not prepared to endorse the Tübingen interpretation of the central books of *Republic* as implying the full theory of First Principles (accepted also by e.g. Ferber 1989, Mueller 1993: 120 ff.). Sometimes *Phaedo, Phaedrus, Theaetetus*, even *Protagoras* and *Cratylus*, are included among the dialogues supposed to build on this theory (e.g. Krämer 1982, Kranz 1986). In my view, only *Philebus* brings us close to it.

194. *See* the discussion in *Méthexis* 1993 and Girgenti (ed.) 1998 (especially Reale and Krämer). Szlezák, Erler and others have taken a more cautious position.

[107] have recently proposed something like the latter approach to the Principles are in my opinion on the right track.¹⁹⁵ After all, Plato was not Aristotle. Unfortunately this leaves a back door wide open to subjective interpretations. Let us try to make them intersubjective.

With the above assumptions, the pieces find their places. One reason why the theory of Principles remained an ἄγραφον probably was its late appearance in Plato's thought: surely he was always prepared to use thought-play in his writings. I am willing to grant to Tübingen that Plato felt this vision to be too difficult to reach by any short-cut, too abstract (even more so than the subject of *Philebus*), and even too close to his innermost convictions of what is important in philosophy, to be suited for presentation in writing. The theory was 'esoteric' in this sense, not 'secret.'¹⁹⁶ Perhaps it was not really ready for dialectic treatment, not even for oral dialectic. But dialectic is losing its grip in the posthumous *Laws*. Let me add that I am inclined to think that the *Timaeus-Critias* complex remained a draft not intended for 'publication' in its present shape; and yet it has only hints of the two Principles.¹⁹⁷

*An episode?*

The theory of First Principles, as sketched by Plato's friends and followers, appears in fact to have been an episode of minor importance in the history of Platonism. Apart from some Hellenistic Pseudo-Pythagorean texts and some symbolism in Plutarch (all probably deriving from Xenocrates), it has left few traces in the philosophy before Plotinus. Even to Plotinus and his followers, the Principles meant no central doctrine.¹⁹⁸

It is the consistently realized 'two-level model' and its elaborations in various directions that was to become one of Plato's lasting contributions to human thought.

---

195. This line has been argued, with widely varying emphasis, by e.g. Findlay 1974, Schmitz II 1985: 227 ff., Ferber 1989 and 1993 (the objections of Isnardi Parente, e.g. 1995: 98 n. 15, are hardly to the point), Gill and Mueller 1993, Miller 1995 (who misleadingly speaks of 'teachings'). Even the skeptical minimalist Brisson (e.g. 19951: 120) admits that the ἄγραφα might have been 'spiritual exercises.'

196. Note Plato's conviction, explicitly emphasized in *7th Letter* (341c, 344d, repeatedly adduced by Szlezák, e.g. 1993, 1997) that there are serious basic issues about Being and φύσις which cannot be attained except by long συνουσία. Cf. above, n. 51. On the loose difference between 'exoteric' and 'esoteric,' cf. Aristotle *Pol.* II 1278b31, and LSJ s. vv.

197. Cf. Thesleff above, p. 337 ff. I would speak of mere 'hints,' pace Szlezák 1997.²

198. Cf. e.g. Theiler 1964, Krämer 1964, Dörrie 1987 (especially 277); they do not consider the Pseudo-Pythagorica (for which see above, n. 161). For the 'dyadic' symbolism in Plutarch, see Dillon 1977: 199 ff. (considering Xenocrates as Plutarch's chief source). For Plotinus, the principal poles are the Ἕν—Ἀγαθόν and the Ὕλη. Very occasionally Plotinus refers to the δυάς (at V 1.5 even misleadingly). For later Neopythagoreans and Neoplatonists, and the Commentators of Aristotle, the Platonic Principles are part of the history of philosophy. I admit that the assertions of this paragraph are controversial; but this is not the place for detailed argumentation.

# IX

## NOTES ON CHRONOLOGY

### The coherence of the Corpus

For reasons elaborated elsewhere (*see* above, p. 387 ff.), I have considered the absolute and relative chronology of the so-called 'early' and 'middle' dialogues to be an open question. The relative lateness of the so-called 'late' dialogues can, however, be regarded as an established fact although here too the internal order is under debate. For some dialogues, notably *Theaetetus, Parmenides* and *Republic*, stylistic and other indications suggest a proximity to the late group. On the other hand, cases such as *Hippias Major, Sisyphus* or *Minos* prove beyond reasonable doubt that dialogues of the 'early Socratic' type were being written late in Plato's life, whether by Plato himself or (rather) by his associates in the Academy.[199] It seems impossible, in fact, to distinguish clearly between authentic and spurious texts in the Corpus: whether we want to or not, we have to work with a sliding scale from reasonably acceptable authenticity, over what I have called 'semi-authenticity,' to total spuriousness.

Plato's 'two-level vision,' such as I have tried to sketch in terms of ten asymmetric contrasts (p. 397–436), appears to cover all of the 'certainly' authentic texts in the Corpus, and at least some of the semi-authentic ones (e.g. *Hippias Major, Alcibiades* I). As far as this general vision is concerned, I can find no clues suggesting a chronological order, or even a rough clustering of any chronological relevance. The fact that all of the ten pairs are not equally prominent in all dialogues is easier to explain from changes in themes or audience (cf. below) than from a development in time.

The occurrence of the two-level model does, however, point to one fact of general significance to the chronology of the dialogues: I mean the fact that the

---

199. For details, *see* Thesleff above, p. 147 ff. (and 1989). My theses were meant as hypotheses for further testing.

[108]
[109] Corpus appears as a somehow coherent whole even in this respect. Except for a few odd pieces (most flagrantly *Eryxias* and *Axiochus*)[200] the two-level model functions as a Platonic background pattern in all dialogues. There are no clear instances of 'early Socratic dialogues' by Plato without this pattern. At least from this general perspective, a 'Socratic stage' cannot be distinguished from one or several 'Platonic' ones.

## Problems with a refined analysis

As is the case with all points of tenet or method or style in Plato's dialogues, mere statistics are not very helpful. Mere statistics of the occurrence of the pairs of contrast discussed in this work cannot determine the relative chronology. Perhaps a more refined analysis of how these pairs are used can be expected to shed some light on the order in which the passages were composed?

In 1982, I recommended for such analyses what I called a 'method of confrontation.'[201] A painstakingly detailed comparison of two passages where the same issue is treated and of the context and tone of the passages, would perhaps tend to reveal which of them was written first. I tried this method on the discussion of ἀνδρεία in *Laches* and *Protagoras*, but had to admit that although there was a slight balance of evidence for the order *Protagoras—Laches*, the problem was really a *non liquet*. And yet in this case the passages are very similar, but not identical (so as to suggest a direct copying).

When the approaches to the same theme are manifestly different, when we have to reckon with another mood of writing and another purpose or potential audience for the dialogue, the comparison is even more difficult. This appears to be often, even normally, the case with Plato's dialogues. Sometimes revisions or re-writings of originally Platonic sketches may also come into question. Add to all this the fact that the dialogues are philosophical dramas where the issues are not treated as problems to be gradually, explicitly, and definitely solved. The leader of the discussion ('Socrates' or his stand-in) normally 'knows more' and often withholds some information required for a systematic treatment of the issue (cf. p. 389). We have to take it for granted that Plato seldom or never gives an explicitly 'full' account of his position in regard to any question of philosophic relevance.

[110] Even addicted developmentalists are now more aware of these circumstances than they used to be in the heyday of mechanically analytic interpretation. Yet a general warning against chronological conclusions from thematic shifts in the dialogues is warranted.

---

200. Add *Menexenus* which functions as an ironical Platonic antithesis to Platonism, and probably the rather un-Platonic *Demodocus* (and of course *Halcyon*). The digression of *7th Letter* (342a ff.) reflects, however wryly, the two-level model.

201. *See* above, p. 192 ff., 246.

Many of the themes that we have encountered above have a very doubtful [110] relevance as chronological criteria. Take for instance ἔρως, Soul, Being as True Being, Sense perception, or Definition.

## Eros

As a 'bridge' between the two levels (cf. p. 399 ff., 415 ff.), Eros is approached very differently in *Lysis, Phaedrus* and *Symposium*, and also in *Alcibiades* I and *Theages*. None of these cases can be said to argue beyond or really 'replace' any of the others, with regard to chronology, though notably *Phaedrus* and *Symposium* proceed from commonplace standpoints to a 'Socratic' (i.e. Platonic) one, both actually complementing the other without mutual references. Only in *Republic* VI, what would appear to be the teaching of Diotima is brought to a playful paradox, so as to suggest the order *Symposium—Republic* VI.

## Soul

The question of the soul (cf. p. 401 f., 464 ff.), its 'aspects' ('parts'), its function, the arguments for its immortality and existence outside the body, are in the foreground in many contexts. Plato's soul myths are variously elaborated; and, if elaboration (and sophistication) is taken as a criterion, they suggest the order *Apology—Gorgias—Meno—Phaedo—Phaedrus—Republic* X, while the cosmological myth of *Timaeus* stands in some rather loose relation both to the *Phaedrus* and to *Republic* X. This relative order (with *Republic* X possibly as the last in the series) is acceptable on other grounds too, but not necessarily deducible from the degree of elaboration or sophistication alone. The immortality arguments as we have them in *Phaedo, Phaedrus, Republic* X and *Laws* X would suggest the order *Republic* X—*Phaedo—Phaedrus—Laws* X if it is not observed that Glaucon's surprise at *Republic* X 608d is meant as irony. The ensuing 'proof' in *Republic* X is, like the set of arguments in *Phaedo,* a thought experiment with obviously broader implications than the point allegedly demonstrated; in *Republic,* the issue is about the higher-level function of the good and the non-composite, while the immortality of the soul is, from Plato's point of view, certainly self-evident. The idea of self-movement in *Phaedrus* (and *Laws* X) is probably the closest we can come in Plato's explicit thought to a real criterion for the immortality of the soul. The tripartition of the soul, again, may appear as a new 'discovery' in *Republic* IV, then taken up as the myth of the horses and the driver in *Phaedrus* and in the physiology of *Timaeus* (especially 61c ff.). It is reflected, however, in *Protagoras* (352ab) which few would date after *Republic* IV; and what is after all argued in *Republic* IV is the parallelism between the three functions of the human soul and the three main classes of Plato's State (illustrated but in fact taken for granted). The two lower tendencies are activated in the incarnated soul only. It is doubtful whether the lack of references to tripartition in the theoretical arguments of *Phaedo* and [111] *Republic* X or in the eschatological myths can be used as a criterion of chronology.

[111]    *True Being*

The distinguishing of 'True Being' from 'Being' that extends over the entire reality ('Existing' or 'Being the case' versus 'Not being' or 'Non-Being') is equally difficult (cf. p. 403 ff., 457 ff.). Without much sophistication, both occur in most dialogues (though in *Protagoras* 344a ff. a specific point is made of 'Being / Becoming'). Both are rooted in Greek linguistic practice (cf. e.g. idioms such as ὄντως, ἔστιν οὕτως), and in philosophy, at least since Parmenides (who is usually said not to have seen the different senses of εἶναι). The Eleatic approach of *Parmenides* (followed up in *Sophist)* brought the problems of absolute vs. relative Being into the foreground; in this respect *Parmenides* and the *Sophist* stand apart from the rest of the dialogues.

*Senses*

Sense impressions, perception and sensuality do always in Plato's thought belong to the 'lower,' i.e. bodily level (cf. p. 405 f.), although sight has at least a metaphorical connection with upper-level truth. The manifestly different stand taken on bodily things in various Platonic contexts has functioned as a traditional but elusive criterion of chronology. Notably the apparent appreciation of pleasure in dialogues such as *Protagoras, Symposium, Phaedrus* or *Philebus* has been adduced as contrasting to the more rigid condemnation of hedonism and sensuality in *Gorgias, Phaedo, Republic* and *Laws*. And it has been often noted that the discussion of sense perception in *Theaetetus*, and Parmenides' warning in *Parmenides* to young Socrates not to disdain the seemingly futile, seem to anticipate the more open-minded interest in physical matters in the 'late' dialogues. The latter trend is probably true. But the varying attitude to bodily feelings and emotions is rather more a question of the themes chosen and of mood and rhetoric than a chronological trend. There is no real ground for the common assumption that Plato's 'middle period' was characterized by an ascetic aversion to bodily matters or pleasure. I have emphasized above that Plato's philosophy (except for the eschatological myths) always presupposes the body as a lower-level condition for the soul's activities, and that he always took for granted that the intellect of a good person should dominate the senses and the feelings.

*Definition*

The search for definitions (cf. p. 407) could be seen superficially as a sign of relative earliness: this seems to be the implication of Aristotle's remark on the origin of the theory of Forms; and many of the so-called early dialogues operate with this theme. On closer inspection the issue is far more complex. The *Apology*, for instance, has no sign of definition-seeking (apart from the general question of who is σοφός), *Meno* and *Protagoras* introduce this theme only gradually, *Gorgias* and *Republic* start from it but soon abandon it, and two dialogues which are certainly not 'early,' *Theaetetus* and *Hippias Major*, concentrate on it from the beginning to the end. *Non liquet*, again.

# Forms and Categories as Criteria

*Forms and Ideas*

From the earliest days of research on Platonic chronology, the theory of Forms (Ideas) has figured as a well-established criterion for the ordering of the dialogues. Especially after the introduction of stylometry as a cross-support, it became the habit among developmentalists to claim that the early dialogues have no sign of the theory, or at the most show reflections of some very preliminary attempts to build up the theory. The middle dialogues are supposed to give, together, a 'full' picture of it. How, then, the development was reflected in details and, notably, what became of the theory in Plato's late period, has been the subject of endless discussions. In fact even this generally accepted criterion has led to no generally accepted consensus about the delimitation of the three main groups, or the order of composition of the dialogues within them.

The main faults of this reasoning are again in the reading of the dialogues as tracts supposed to reflect directly the progress of Plato's thought. It is generally admitted, though, that Plato nowhere gives a systematic account of the theory of Forms and that his terminology is, here as usual, inconsistent (cf. p. 437 ff.).

The above discussion of Ideas and Forms as upper-level entities of Plato's vision motivates the following remarks on the chronological aspect:

'Ideas' (i.e. unique value concepts of the αὐτὸ ὅ ἔστιν type) always occur in Plato's philosophy, though seldom very prominently. Their adduction in the argument of *Symposium, Phaedo, Phaedrus* and *Republic*, and occasionally elsewhere,[202] seems to depend on specific circumstances and is not, as such, very relevant to chronology.

Thought experiments with neutral and negative (opposite) concepts treated as 'Ideas' are likely to be secondary (447 ff.). Thus *Phaedo, Euthyphro, Parmenides, Republic* (V and elsewhere) and, if artifacts are included, *Cratylus* and *Republic* X, appear as relatively 'advanced' dialogues (cf. below, 494 ff.). It is interesting that *Parmenides* does not refer to Ideas of artifacts.

'Forms' as a larger class of entities 'below' the level of Ideas, can be said to occur in all dialogues, if a theory or a terminology is not sought. It seems to me difficult to ascertain even here a single line of development. However, at least the establishment of 'two-way dialectic' (p. 451) appears to have given rise to a theory of lower Forms as 'kinds' (universals) which can be put in some relation to the metaphysical

---

202. Note also *Meno, Euthyphro, Cratylus* and *Theaetetus* as examples of dialogues where Ideas have some relevance in the argument.

[113] Ideas. The two-way method is not mentioned in *Phaedo*, but it is clearly reflected in *Republic* (book V onwards), *Theaetetus*, *Phaedrus*, *Hippias Major*, and *Cratylus*. Such 'kinds' get a prominent role in *Parmenides* and notably *Sophist* and *Politicus*. It would seem that *Theaetetus*, *Hippias Major*, *Phaedrus* and *Cratylus* are in this respect 'on the verge' of the late period, and that the central books of *Republic* (notably the Divided Line) present rather explicitly a combination of the theories of Ideas and Forms.

## Terms

A carefully minute consideration of the terminology used might give additional clues. Within the frames of this work it can only be said that εἶδος, and to some extent ἰδέα, appears to receive wider applications in *Phaedo*, *Cratylus*, *Republic* and the late dialogues (beginning with *Parmenides*). These terms are becoming more common, and they can be used for two-level 'Categories,' a process resulting in further confusions for posterity.

In the methodologically important *Meno* (p. 440), εἶδος qua Idea is given pointedly the connotation of 'shape' while the connotation of 'kind' figures vaguely in the background, which suggests that 'Forms' have begun to be discussed at the time; so here is another indication of the relative order *Meno—Phaedo*.

## Categories

What I have called 'Categories' (better: 'Basic Concepts') occur occasionally all over Plato's oeuvre (p. 407 ff., 457 ff.). They function more systematically in connection with the two-way dialectic (note *Cratylus*), the theory of soul in *Theaetetus*, *Phaedrus*, *Republic* IV, and *Timaeus*, and notably in connection with the Eleatic analyses in *Parmenides*, *Sophist* and *Politicus*. In *Philebus* they begin to be replaced by the Pythagorean 'categories' πέρας / ἄπειρον. This would suggest, again (cf. 471), that *Cratylus*, *Theaetetus*, *Phaedrus* and (parts of) *Republic* are 'on the verge' of the late period, and that *Philebus* is later than *Sophist* and *Politicus*.

The theory of 'Principles' (473 ff.) can be considered a late development of the theory of two-level Categories. They belong in the context of *Philebus* and *7th Letter*.

# Can chronological conclusions be drawn?

We have few or no reliable means of determining the exact degree of explicitness of the theories of Forms (Ideas) and Categories as reflected in the dialogues, or the real changes in Plato's visions that lie behind the written evidence. Yet it seems to me possible to approach the problem of chronology from a general hypothesis of the different functions of the dialogues.

As I have sometimes suggested elsewhere,[203] most of the dialogues were probably intended to be read (or 'performed') to closed audiences of friends and their friends, where well-informed people were supposed to be present. Plato did not normally write for a totally anonymous public (as most poets, dramatists, orators and historians were inclined to do). The 'reported' ('narrated') dialogue type was originally meant to be protreptic and to have a somewhat wider distribution than the directly 'dramatic' one (though at least *Theaetetus* and *Parmenides*, and probably *Republic*, *Gorgias* and *Phaedrus*, manifest a change of plan). The 'late' dialogues (except the posthumous *Laws*) have a more esoterically Academic character. From several circumstances it can be inferred that none of the dialogues as we have them (except the *Apology*) is from the time before 387 BCE (when Plato decided to settle down in Academeia), though at least *Gorgias* is likely to reflect ideas of the 390s. And, to repeat a claim that I have often made, dialogues of the 'Socratic' character continued to be written at least until the 350s.

Now, within this seemingly confusing pattern a few tentative steps can be made. For instance: *Euthyphro*, *Hippias Major* and *Cratylus* appear to play with a rather 'advanced' conceptual and terminological apparatus relating to the two-level model and the theory of Forms. These dialogues are not of the protreptic (reported) type. If they were written principally for an Academic audience, their exuberantly provocative tone must be meant to stimulate thinking around issues such as the theory of Ideas. The nature of an Idea was ventilated, rather plainly and without much sophistication, in the methodologically interesting and likewise non-protreptic *Meno*. I would see here a slight (to be sure, a very slight) hint that *Meno* was written earlier. The *Phaedo*, again, while apparently developing some of the notions reflected in *Meno*, operates with a series of thought experiments that appear to be addressed to well-informed Academics, in spite of the 'exoteric' character of this dialogue. Its theme may suggest that it was designed as the last of the set of protreptic dialogues of the reported type, concerned with the 'historical Socrates.' The *Theaetetus*, which manifests a shift from the protreptic to a more esoteric type of dialogue, is also otherwise 'on the verge' of the late period that begins with *Parmenides*.[204] Here we encounter the Categories, two-way dialectic connected with Forms, and a seemingly awakening interest in lower-level phenomena put in relation to abstractions (including mathematics). *Parmenides* introduces a new dimension. It takes account of the theory of Ideas such as it is represented in *Phaedo* in particular. I have given some reasons for dating *Parmenides* about 362 BCE.[205]

Even if hints such as those presented above can contribute to the establishing of a hypothetical chronology, the places of *Phaedrus* and *Republic* are very problematic.

---

203. E.g. Thesleff 1993: 40, 2000; for the general picture, cf. above p. 352, below 499 ff. and 1989 with references.
204. This hardly needs arguing; cf. above, p. 300 ff.
205. Thesleff above, p. 304 ff.

[115]     For *Phaedrus*, my theory of revision would offer a reasonable clue.[206] The allusions to astral theology, to a theory of soul recalling the *Timaeus*, to two-way dialectic systematically applied, and a long series of other details, associate the *Phaedrus* with the late dialogues. The literary grip, however, the tenor and two of the main themes, oratory and love, recall the exoteric, protreptic type of dialogue and Plato's polemics with the rhetoricians (*Gorgias* and *Symposium*). Perhaps the early version of *Phaedrus* was written as a reported dialogue in the 380s or even earlier, while the revision was made after 370, and probably after the revision of *Theaetetus*.

For the *Republic*, I am now very decidedly inclined to propose a hypothesis which cannot be argued in detail here. The evidence I have collected in various connections[207] suggests that the early Utopia from the 390s (the 'Proto-*Republic*') was gradually expanded with the addition of the present *Republic* I, the opening speeches of book II, book IV, and with most of the ideas now present in the central books and the concluding myth. Nothing of this accretion (except perhaps *Republic* I) was 'published,' however, until Plato late in his life, perhaps in the 350s when the Sicilian experiment was over on his part, decided to collect the entire complex as a 'final' manifestation of his philosophy: as a monument of the Ideal State and Ideal Man, the Philosopher; a substitution, perhaps, for the piece missing after the *Politicus* (the Φιλόσοφος), but never written. This hypothesis would explain much, including the mass of heterogeneous contents yet composed as a coherent whole, and the shift from a very exoteric beginning to a partially esoteric exposition hardly meant for 'publication' outside the Academy. The final work would represent only and purely Plato's 'own' and personal philosophy as he saw it as contrasted to the Eleatic, Pythagorean, mathematical, cosmological, physiological and legislative interests of his associates in the Academy. The *Philebus* would be still later, a semi-personal document (hence 'Socrates' is back again). The *Laws*, then, was the Academy's up-to-date version for a more general
[116]   use of the never-published *Republic*.

These tentative steps would lead to the following chronological grouping of the dialogues, which is only a slight modification of what was suggested above, p. 245 ff.:

390s down to 387 BCE:
 ('Proto-*Republic*'), *Apology*, (*Gorgias*), *Menexenus*[208]
Between 387 and 367 BCE:
 (a) Most of the reported dialogues, ending up in *Phaedo*.
 (b) Some dramatic dialogues, such as *Gorgias, Meno, (Laches?), Cratylus, Euthyphro*, on the whole later than (a), but with *Meno* before *Phaedo*, and ending up in *Theaetetus* and *Phaedrus*.

---

206. Above, p. 317 ff. The extensive and very many-sided recent discussion of this dialogue (see e.g. Rossetti ed. 1992) has not contributed much to the question of dating. But the arguments of Tomin 1997 for a very early date are symptomatically interesting and partly relevant.

207. References below, p. 519 ff.

208. For *Menexenus*, the authenticity (contrary to, say, *Clitopho*) and the date soon after 387 are beyond reasonable doubt.

Later 360s and 350s:

(a) Minor dramatic dialogues, including some semi-authentic ones such as *Alcibiades* I, *Hippias Major*.

(b) 'Late' dialogues (all written down by others than Plato), beginning with *Parmenides* (362 BCE) and *Timaeus-Critias*, then *Sophist-Politicus* and (again more close to Plato) *Philebus*; also *7th Letter* (soon after 354 BCE).

(c) Final composition of *Republic* (mainly by Plato himself).

Soon after 347 BCE:

*Laws* and *Epinomis*; probably most spurious *Letters*; perhaps *Alcibiades* II.[209]

---

209. Cf. above, p. 377. I am not prepared now to suggest more precise dates for the 'semi-authentic' dialogues beginning with *Clitopho* (351 ff.).

# X

## SUMMARY AND CONCLUSIONS

It can be taken for certain that the dialogues reflect, partially and indirectly, the discussions in Plato's environment and the Academy. Since the dialogues are not tracts where Plato sp eaks in his own voice, but artistic and often ironically or humorously dramatic pieces, and since their intended audiences and purposes probably vary from piece to piece, Plato's philosophical positions are not very easily extracted from them.

It can be argued (cf. p. 392) that, in a Platonic dialogue, reasoning proceeds by 'cooperative' (two-level) dialectic between the leader of the dialogue and his less well informed partner whose protests, criticism or consent is a necessary part of the intellectual drama in question. Evidently the leader of the dialogue (normally Socrates) stands closer to Plato than the other characters do. When similar ideas recur in the protagonist's pronouncements or hints in different dialogue contexts, they can be safely regarded as Plato's own.

Thus interpreted and reduced to its foundations, Plato's philosophy can be considered a fairly homogeneous whole, except for some of the new challenges and moves that come in with the 'late' dialogues. The *Republic* appears to be a rather late manifestation of what is essentially 'Platonic' in form and content.

In this work, I am not primarily interested in distinguishing lines of development of tenets, methods, approaches, or the literary technique within the main Corpus of dialogues, or in reconstructing a possible system of doctrines or a plan lying behind the written texts, or in analyzing the subtle details of Plato's thought and art.

Instead, I am claiming (by 'cumulative' argument) that Plato had, from the start, a rather coherent philosophical vision. There is much to say for the relative homogeneity of the Corpus. The 'two-level vision,' I assert, became elaborated in

[118] various directions but functioned always as a basis and frame for Plato's thought and literary expression. It can also be used as a clue to the understanding of the dialogues.

It is essential to realize, however, that this two-level vision was an intuitive pattern only, a crude frame for what Plato felt and wanted to say—not a set of doctrinal or aesthetic rules. The refinements of his intellectual argument, his irony and his artistry of course cannot be reached merely by analyzing the functions of this vision. Yet I would claim that the two-level model constitutes a prerequisite for a real understanding of Plato's oeuvre: it is a more comprehensive and better founded frame than the traditional contrasting of 'Being' and 'Becoming,' or of Forms versus particulars.

∞∞ O ∞∞

Plato's two-level vision can be grasped in a series of contrasts which have their roots in pre-Platonic thought and common human ways of experiencing the world, but which in Plato's case have very specific implications. These contrasts are not felt to be polar opposites. The manifestation of opposites as polarization (hot / cold, white / black, good / evil) belongs, in Plato's view, to the physical world around us. This world is not all that exists.

Plato's thought always includes the invisible as a complement to the concrete. In the objects of his thinking and reasoning, the 'abstract' and the 'concrete' side tend to become contrasted, but not polarized. His two-level contrasts represent the invisible versus the visible, the ideal good versus the less good, perfection versus the imperfect, the primary versus the secondary. Thus, such contrasts are asymmetric. Sometimes polar contrasts are treated as two-level contrasts and then receive a deeper philosophical relevance (Chapter V).

Typically, two-level contrasts are, like 'divine / human' (where 'divine' is a metaphor rather than a religiously experienced truth), complementary and asymmetrically balanced in the sense that the 'lower' member is felt to be dependent on the 'higher' one while both are necessary parts of a functioning universe.

Taken together, Plato's two-level contrasts tend to form what I have called a 'two-level model.' A third ('bottom') level, though occasionally appearing especially in Plato's late philosophy, is of little relevance; even less relevant is an alleged 'super-level' (ἐπέκεινα in *Republic* VI).

The model is not restricted to particular facets or aspects of Plato's thought, or to what we should call either ontology or epistemology, logic, psychology, cosmology, etc. It covers his thought, and also its literary expression, in its entirety.

[119] ∞∞ O ∞∞

Analyses of a number of dialogues are presented to illustrate the function of the two-level model (Chapter IV–V). I take it that several well-known issues of

Plato's philosophy and artistry are elucidated by this model. Some of these issues are not discussed in detail in this work. A few aspects will be mentioned below; for additional references, *see* the Index.

⦁⦁⦁ ○ ⦁⦁⦁

I have given some attention to the so-called theory of Forms (VI–VIII). It seems that this complex can be regarded as a series of elaborations of the conceptual aspect of the two-level model. Its importance to Plato has probably been exaggerated ever since Aristotle directed his criticism towards it.

Plato's primary vision was, and remained, the two-level model. Ideas and Forms as 'abstractions' fitted intuitively this vision, but the details of the relationship between Forms, and between Forms and particulars, were not easily explicated in a logically satisfactory way; hence the dialogues reflect only tentative attempts around the issue. In these moves, the part played by Plato's associates was surely significant, though difficult for us to ascertain.

It is convenient to distinguish 'Ideas,' i.e. positive value concepts of the 'in itself' type, from 'Forms' in general, i.e. abstractions functioning as 'universals' or 'kinds.' Both are upper-level entities as contrasted to the phenomena and particulars of the lower level. 'Ideas' are unique, changeless, lacking opposites, and culminating in τὸ καλόν and τὸ ἀγαθόν. The internal relation of Ideas is not really discussed in the dialogues; rather, they are seen as a complex representing the highest level in its entirety. 'Forms,' however, may include plurality, change, and opposites; but from a human perspective some of them may occasionally take the character of Ideas. Ideas are hierarchically 'above' Forms in general. The relation of Ideas and Forms to each other and to the concrete world is illustrated by the Divided Line.

The term εἶδος (less frequently ἰδέα) is freely employed for both Ideas and Forms, besides denoting 'outward appearance,' 'shape,' type, or (periphrastically) 'sort of.' As terms, εἶδος and ἰδέα were perhaps primarily used to denote Forms, not Ideas. The word εἶδος appears more frequently in sophisticated 'Academic' contexts. Together with other indications, this suggests (a) that 'Ideas and Forms' were under continuous debate in Plato's Academy, and (b) that no very definite theory took shape in Plato's days.

The discussion of Ideas and Forms can be regarded as a series of tentative but ambitious attempts to grasp one aspect of the relation of the levels in Plato's vision.

Ideas were always part of Plato's philosophy, though they are not very much ventilated in the dialogues. The only presentation of Ideas which was obviously meant for non-Academic readers is Diotima's speech in *Symposium* which focuses on τὸ καλόν in a very suggestive manner.

Forms, however, though always present in the dialogues, seem to be secondarily considered as entities requiring a theory of their own 'below' the level of Ideas. I have not been able to follow the rise of a distinct 'theory of Forms,' but

[120] I have noted more or less tentative reflections of it in various dialogues (*see* the Index s.v. Forms). There are more of such reflections in the dialogues which for different reasons seem to be close to the 'late' ones (notably in *Phaedo, Euthyphro, Cratylus, Theaetetus, Phaedrus*). The Divided Line in *Republic* VI rather certainly implies a kind of theory of Forms as distinct from Ideas.

One important step towards developing a theory of Forms was 'two-way dialectic' (p. 451). This became a popular method in Academic training (perhaps after *Phaedo*).

Ideas are sometimes said to be 'models' for imitation, as Forms of artifacts are models for craftsmen (though the importance of the 'craftsman analogy' has perhaps been exaggerated). More commonly the entire upper level functions as the model for orientation. The relation of Ideas and Forms to particulars is normally described as 'presence' or 'participation' (cf. the notion of ἐνθουσιασμός p. 443 ff.). Parmenides' (and Aristotle's) query about χωρισμός is no real problem to Plato whose two main levels are a priori interconnected. This connection is metaphorically described as a geometrical analogy.

With my interpretation of the Divided Line (p. 453), there are Forms for all physical phenomena and things that can be individualized, including artifacts. But there are only a few Ideas, no real Ideas for 'motion' or 'plurality,' and certainly no Ideas (except in playful thought experiments) for negative notions such as 'violence,' 'ignorance,' or indeed 'evil.' The 'Intelligible Being' (ζῷον) of *Timaeus* is probably meant to include all Ideas and Forms.

However, the details of this continuously debated issue are deliberately left open by Plato (or 'Socrates the Younger,' according to Academic jargon).

∘⊙∘ ◯ ∘⊙∘

[121] This work also discusses the 'Forms' which in the *Sophist* are called μέγιστα γένη and which I would prefer to characterize as two-level 'Categories,' not Forms proper (Chapters VII and VIII). 'Being' (in a loose sense), and the contrasts 'One / many,' 'same / other' and 'rest / motion,' occur in practically all dialogues in more or less suggestive contexts; sometimes they are associated with the soul (below). With the Eleatic approach of *Parmenides*, however, they begin to be systematically applied to ontology, cosmology and physics. Whether the development of such Categories is entirely due to Plato's initiative or not, they can be reasonably explained as representing, as such, the two-level model.

By the new 'pythagorizingly' ontological approach to ethics in *Philebus*, very different from *Timaeus*, the Categories are made to include the similarly two-level contrast 'limit / limitless' which later in the dialogue replaces the former.

The passages which concern the soul's innate capacities seem to reveal that Plato thought the human soul to possess from birth a knowledge of the two-level Categories, which make thinking possible, but not a knowledge of Ideas or Forms proper. Such knowledge can only be reached in life by a dialectical process.

As a Category, 'Being' (οὐσία, εἶναι, ὄν) is contrasted to 'Non-Being' and covers the entire reality of Plato's two levels. The restricted, absolute sense of 'True Being' (versus 'becoming,' 'appearance,' etc. of the lower level) is found in practically all dialogues, but does not seem to occur with derivatives of εἶναι representing a Category. This specific problem is not, however, studied here.

⁘⦁⁘

Plato's vexing so-called 'unwritten views' (ἄγραφα δόγματα) concerning the First Principles (Chapter VIII) must, in accordance with the present approach, be explained as a 'pythagorizing' extrapolation from the two-level Categories. It is argued here that the theory of First Principles was a thought experiment which may have had early roots but grew up rather late as a part of Plato's attempts to develop philosophy (including the theories of Forms) in a mathematical direction. Like the two-level Categories, the Principles form a 'system' different from and only loosely connected with Forms.

Here again the impact of Plato's friends is on the whole impossible to distinguish from Plato's own position.

The lecture 'On the Good' was a late occasion designed to demonstrate provocatively to the public how difficult this issue is.

⁘⦁⁘

Chronology is not in the focus in this work. I take it that very little can be said with certainty about the absolute dates and relative order of the dialogues, except for the relative lateness of the so-called 'late' group. On the whole, the analyses presented here tend to confirm my hypotheses of above, p. 245 ff. about different purposes and audiences being more relevant as explanations of the different approaches and degrees of explicitness than is any alleged line of development of doctrines or methods. However, sophisticated passages designed for more esoterically Academic use (and perhaps partly written down by other Academics) suggest a successively increasing interest in two-way dialectic and a theory of Forms 'below' Ideas. The theory of Categories (and of First Principles) is also a rather late issue. The final composition of the monumental *Republic* seems to have taken place in the 350s, as a manifestation of Plato's philosophy. The return of 'Socrates' in *Philebus* may reflect an even later approximation to Plato's own position.

As a general rule, it can be claimed that the more 'esoteric' dialogues (which on the whole tend to be later than the 'exoteric' ones, though the details are unclear) seem to reflect somewhat more directly the progress of Plato's and his Academy's thought.

⁘⦁⁘

[122]  The specific problems enumerated p. 387–391 have been constantly present in these Studies. As outcomes of the discussion, the following may now be said:

(1) and (10): Before progress can be made in questions of chronology, we need reasonable hypotheses as to the purposes, audiences, and manner of publication of the dialogues. All dialogues, also the 'reported' (narrated) ones originally designed for a more protreptic use, were intended to be read to audiences where relatively well-informed persons were present. The directly 'dramatic' pieces were on the whole designed for more esoterically Academic use (references to this issue also p. 494 ff. and p. 541 ff.).

(2): There is no 'early Socratic stage' in Plato's oeuvre.

(3) and (4): The two-level model was basic and central in Plato's thought, and it always included what we would call 'metaphysics.' He operated with more or less tentative thought experiments within this model, in cooperation with his associates.

(5): There were no 'esoteric' doctrines, but a number of issues which Plato did not think worth communicating to larger audiences; and behind the written texts, there was a continuous oral discussion of relevant problems.

(6) and (7): It is absolutely essential to try to understand 'holistically' and in context what is said in the dialogues.

(8) and (9): Socrates (or his stand-in) represents the Philosopher (Plato) in continuous two-level debate with his associates and opponents. Plato saw 'dialectic' as philosopher-led ('two-level') dialogue proceeding from premises to results or to refutation.

[123]  (11): The *Republic* was Plato's main work, a life-long personal project finished very late and standing somewhat apart from the Eleatic, Pythagorean, cosmological, physical, legislative, etc. experiments in which he as an elderly man took part together with some younger members of the Academy.

∘∘∘ ○ ∘∘∘

The two-level model, as sketched here—I repeat this again—is certainly no simple doctrinal, methodological, or artistic principle or set of principles that could be used, as such, to explain Plato's thought and art. It is an intuitive 'vision' which offers only crude basic patterns and frames for the structures of Plato's thinking, feelings, intuitions, and intentions, from his youth to his old age, and for our understanding of them.

This two-level vision seems, however, to open significant perspectives, from Plato's point of view, and perhaps from ours.

To make a final summary of the explicit and implicit points of this work, I want to emphasize the following:

Plato's dialogue art, where intellectual and emotive strands are always interwoven, sometimes with suggestive settings, is as such a two-level process which may open itself too easily to restricted or anachronistic interpretations. The dialogues are not really 'concerned' with the concrete realities which they overtly reflect: their realism is often misleading. One of the theses of this work is that, in order to understand Plato's intentions, we ought to read the dialogues holistically with constant regard to the 'orientation' of the lower level towards upper-level stable but abstract truths.

Such a holistic view of the dialogues with their two levels implies, for instance, that issues of Plato's philosophy traditionally differentiated—ontology, epistemology, logic, psychology, ethics, cosmology, etc.—have to be regarded in their complexity as related aspects of Plato's two-level vision.

The two-level model also implies a universal κοινωνία: there is no real χωρισμός between the levels.

The dynamics of the two-level model imply that the two levels are always in interaction. What happens in the physical world are lower-level phenomena which Plato finds less interesting than theory, general principles, and abstractions.

Human beings at their best (men and women) are intellectuals, indeed potential philosophers; Plato's interests focus totally on such individuals. Every moderately gifted intellectual is in principle able to ennoble himself or herself with the help of proper instruction and the soul's capacity of rising towards the higher, i.e. a rather more intellectual ('noetic') level. Such personal improvement is always more important than a doubtfully achieved improvement of society.

Plato was pessimistic regarding the majority's intellectual resources. For most people, he surmised, the process of ennobling oneself is hardly worth trying, beyond the rising above simple brutality. In a specialized society, such as was his Utopian ideal, everybody will find his / her place, provided that all are brought to accept the actual dominance by the intellectuals. The substitution of the traditional aristocracy with an intellectual elite is an interesting thought experiment.

Thus we cannot expect from Plato a real sympathy with the non-gifted, the weak, the unlucky, the outcast, or otherwise handicapped individuals. He was born to a world different from ours. Maybe his openness to humanity, revealed by the dialogues and superimposed on deeply-rooted ethical standards, can encourage modern readers to develop their own sympathies for the ordinary, the non-elite, or the weak. This was hardly what Plato intended. Plato rather wished to shift his readers' fascination away from lower-level brutality, emotionalism, and irrationalism (obviously current not only in human society and ordinary life but also in poetry and arts of all kinds) to intellectualism. More deplorable, perhaps, considering his own emotional register, is Plato's apparent lack of understanding of the positive potentials of human feelings in general, apart from ἔρως.

In Plato's view, the bodily ties, feelings and emotions, i.e. lower-level factors, are not only unavoidable but necessary even for an ideally good life; but they have always to be kept in check by the intellect. Human life at its best is a constant 'orientation' from the human level towards order and the (metaphorically) divine. Evil is no active force: evil is imperfection and the chaotic state of lower-level tendencies getting the upper hand.

It is a very remarkable fact that Plato's entire philosophy, in spite of its depth, its wealth, and its many dimensions, does not on closer inspection seem to offer a single definite solution to any problem. All questions are somehow left open.

[124] Plato's ideal Philosopher ('Socrates' whose personality is illuminated in most dialogues) is no sophist, no pulpit teacher; nor is he a divinely inspired priest or poet. His δαιμόνιον has its restricted limits. However, because of his orientation towards upper-level stability and truth, he is able to conduct 'two-level' dialectic with suitable partners so as to enrich both himself and his partners (and the readers of the dialogues) with ever larger ranges of (theoretical, logically acceptable) knowledge. Ultimately everything aims to what is 'good' (i.e. 'appropriate'), ideal καλόν and ἀγαθόν.

[125] Philosophy in this sense is a continuous search. It is a dialectic search involving open-ended pushes and moves by the leader of the dialogue, and consent or objections and criticism by both parties. This dialectical process, exemplified in the dialogues, covers both levels of Plato's reality, and may hybristically move 'beyond' reality. The ontological scope of the model contributed significantly to all aspects of philosophy—without offering doctrinal solutions. What is essential in this early Academic debate, is the continuous experimenting with new approaches within the two-level model.

This internal openness of Academic reasoning around ultimately unsolved problems is, in spite of its exclusivity, one of Plato's great gifts to posterity—a posterity which only in recent years has begun to appreciate it fully.

Too often, over the centuries, have Plato's thought experiments been understood as his convictions or as revelations of profound truths.

# Articles

# THEAITETOS AND THEODOROS [147]

The Athenian Theaitetos seems to occupy a secure position in the history of Greek mathematics ever since Eva Sachs, a pupil of Wilamowitz, established it in the beginning of this century.[1] I shall argue here that skepticism regarding his achievements, and a reconsideration of his function in Plato's dialogue, are warranted. The problem of Theaitetos, as I see it, offers very typical examples of the crystallizing of old hypotheses into quasi-facts later used for building new hypotheses, a process all too common in classical scholarship.[2]

Theaitetos is now generally thought to have lived ca. 414–369 BCE. The evidence is precarious apart from what can be deduced from Plato's *Theaetetus*. In Eudemus' list of geometricians he is mentioned together with Leodamas of Thasos, a very shadowy figure, and Archytas of Tarentum, as belonging to the same generation as Plato.[3] According to a confused piece of information in Hesychius and Suda (*see* below), he had been teaching in Heracleia, and Heracleia on the Pontus was the home city of Plato's pupil Heraclides (born not earlier than ca. 400 BCE). And various sources attribute to him discoveries concerning irrational numbers and regular solids, which are reflected in Euclid, Books X and XIII, and consequently he is sometimes thought to have written essential parts of these Euclidean texts. [148]

Though the dialogue situation of *Theaetetus* is very probably fictitious, we have no reason whatever to doubt that the presentation of the young Theaitetos

---

1. Sachs 1914; independently, with similar conclusions, Vogt 1909/10: 97–155, 1913/14: 9–29; endorsed by Heath, Brumbaugh, van der Waerden, and practically everybody who has written on Plato's *Theaetetus* since then. *See* also the comprehensive RE articles on 'Theaitetos' and 'Theodoros' by K. von Fritz 1934: 1351 ff., 1811 ff.; Heller's (1967: 55 ff.) conspectus, and the discussion of Academic mathematics by Gaiser in Ueberweg 1983 and F. Lasserre, De Léodamas de Thasos à Philippe d' Oponte 1987.

2. I have ventilated this set of problems before, notably in my *Studies in Platonic Chronology*, above p. 300 ff. (cf. Thesleff 1989: 18 n. 67), without being able to shake the consensus about Theaitetos.

3. Proclus, In Eucl. *Elem.* I, Prol., II p. 64 ff. Friedländer, Eudemus fr. 133 W; Lasserre 1987 argues that the list derives from Philip of Opous, not Eudemus.

[148] approximates to historical truth. A nonsensical distortion of facts known to the readers (as, say, in *Menexenus*) would have been pointless here; but the reappearance of Theaitetos in the *Sophist* and *Statesman* has, of course, no pretensions to historicity. We may take it for granted that Theaitetos was a youngster of less than 17 years in 399 BCE.[4]

The fixing of the death of Theaitetos in 369 BCE is mainly based upon the following four considerations:

(a) The *Theaetetus*, at least in its present form and including its present prologue, is a fairly late dialogue.
(b) The writing of the prologue was occasioned by Theaitetos' death.
(c) The battle at Corinth referred to must be that of 369 BCE, not 394 BCE as Zeller and others have suggested.
(d) Theaitetos' achievements in mathematics, as reflected in Euclid and elsewhere, must have taken a long time to accomplish.

If, however, (d) does not apply, as I shall argue below, it is more natural to interpret (a)–(c) differently.

[149] (a) It is true that *Theaetetus* as we have it cannot be an early dialogue. Clearly it links up with the 'critical' dialogues *Parmenides*, the *Sophist*, and the *Statesman*.[5] But very probably it has been revised and re-written from an earlier draft of the *Charmides* type.[6] And even if this were not the case, and we have the text as it was originally composed, Plato is much more likely to have introduced, as Socrates' partner, a long-since dead friend whom he saw from an idealizing perspective (indeed very much like Charmides), than a scholar from his own Academic environment whom many readers would know well. The only obvious counter-argument would be 'Aristotle' in *Parmenides*, but he appears in a 5th century disguise and is not really individualized at all.[7]

(b) A close reading of the prologue and the subsequent presentation of Theaitetos (to 148b) does not suggest to me that the writing of the dialogue was occasioned by the death of Theaitetos. Plato may have had other reasons for

---

4. This is the dramatic date of *Theaetetus* (142c, 210d). The implications of μειράκιον, beardlessness (168e), etc. are discussed by Sachs 1914: 25 f., Lasserre 1987: 462. If Theaitetos in reality was very much younger than this it is, apart from other difficulties, reasonable to ask why Plato takes so much trouble to explain the circumstances of Socrates meeting Theaitetos. Unlike *Parmenides* and *Timaeus*, the setting of the *Theaetetus* was within checking reach of contemporary readers; for 'Aristotle,' see below, n. 7.

5. This is a consensus of post-Zellerian scholarship, which I am fully prepared to accept; cf. Thesleff above, p. 306 ff.

6. I argued this above, p. 300 ff.; cf. 1989: 18. H. Tarrant (in a paper known to me from a draft) has added more arguments.

7. A play with masks is part of the game in Platonic dialogues; cf. the following note and the references in Thesleff above. For 'Socrates J:r,' see note 23. In fact the *Theaetetus* reflects the beginning of the curious 'split' of Socrates in some later dialogues (including the *Hippias Major*).

introducing him (below, p. 516). But if we assume as a possibility that one reason was his recent death, a date as late as the 360s would seem rather odd after all. A fact not often observed, which makes me suspicious from the start, is the remarkable vitality of Socrates' old friends, Euclides and Terpsion (note 142a, 143ab): in 369 Euclides may have been well over 80.[8] And then there is nothing to indicate that Plato thought of Theaitetos as ever having reached the age of 45 or more. He reached manhood, to be sure (ἄνδρα 142b, ἡλικίαν [military age!] 142d), but ἐλλόγιμον in the *vaticinium* of Socrates (142d) playfully alludes to his interest in ἄλογα, I believe (cf. again p. 516), and does not as such imply an advanced age.

(c) Eva Sachs[9] made an effort to prove that the battle at Corinth (142a, τὴν μάχην 142b) where Theaitetos was mortally wounded, was a notorious one, and that it occurred in 369 when the Athenians were allied with the Spartans against Thebes. She made it plain, no doubt, that one of the battles in the Isthmian war of 369 was a more important event than earlier critics had thought, and that 45-year-old intellectuals could have taken part in this campaign. She notes that Xenophon (*Hell*. VI 5.49) describes the Athenians' enthusiasm and decision to assist Sparta πανδημεί. And there are additional circumstances which she does not mention but which may suggest that members of Plato's circle were engaged in these operations: Iphicrates assembled his troops in Academeia (Xen. ibid., somewhat differently Diod. *Sic*. XV 68); Chabrias took command (Diod. ibid.);[10] and Dionysius of Syracuse supplied auxiliary forces (Xen. VII 1.20,28; Diod. XV 70).

Yet thinking of a battle in the Corinthian war around 390 BCE seems more natural after all: Sachs sweeps this possibility aside on quite insufficient grounds.[11] We happen to know that there was a detachment of Athenian hoplites under Callias cooperating with Iphicrates' mercenary peltasts in the famous battle when a Spartan regiment was completely defeated (Xen. *Hell*. IV 5.11–18, cf. Demosth. IV 24; Diod. *Sic*. XIV 68, 91 ff. seems to confuse facts). Whatever Xenophon's πανδημεί may imply for the year 369, Theaitetos is somewhat more likely to be found among Callias' hoplites. The chronology of the events around 390 has been subject to some dispute; today the Spartan disaster is dated not earlier than 392,

---

8. Obviously Plato avoids introducing living persons into his dialogues (Thesleff above, 178, 301 ff.). Euclides perhaps was still active about 370 BCE, though one may wonder about the long walks implied in the opening scene of *Theaetetus*. He is said to have made Socrates' acquaintance before the Peloponnesian War (Gell. 7, 10); at any rate he is likely to have been much older than Plato. In *Parmenides* 127b the 65-year-old Parmenides is described as εὖ μάλα ἤδη ... πρεσβύτης, and in *Epistle* VII 338c Plato considers himself a γέρων at that age. The Athenian of the *Laws* stands (and walks) closer to Speusippus than to Plato.

9. Sachs 1914: 22 ff.

10. Chabrias seems to have been a personal acquaintance of Plato's, according to the anecdotes in Diog. L. III 20,23 f. Plato's alleged pro-Spartan sympathies should not be overrated: he was taken prisoner by the Spartans in 387 (*see* now the Academic Index, Gaiser (ed.) 1988: 165 ff.).

11. Her chief target was the view of Schultess and Zeller that the dialogue was an early work, and Zeller and his contemporaries dated 'proelium illud nobilissimum' in 394 BCE.

[150]   and Iphicrates' subsequent operations on the Isthmus (Xen. *Hell.* IV 5.19) are thought to have extended to at least 390.¹² And Plato's τὴν μάχην of course refers
[151]   to the battle where Theaitetos received his wounds, not to the fact that this battle was particularly famous.

(d) Although many mathematicians have reached their peak of brilliance at an early age – can we really trust a young geometrician of 25 years or less with all the discoveries and activities attributed to Theaitetos by the historians of mathematics? The consensus of modern scholarship would point to a simple "No."

I would insist, however, that this consensus is mistaken. "No other branch of history offers such temptations to conjectural reconstruction as does the history of mathematics."¹³ Students of Theaitetos have too readily yielded to such temptations.

Let us consider, first, what Plato tells us in the mathematical passage, *Theaetetus* 147c–148c.

Theodoros had been drawing (ἔγραφε) figures, showing (ἀποφαίνων) that lines whose squares have the area of three or five square foot, are incommensurable with the side of a one foot square; and he had proceeded from case to case until he reached the side of a seventeen square foot square where he "somehow met with complications" (ἐν δὲ ταύτῃ πως ἐνέσχετο).¹⁴ In modern times there has been considerable discussion about what Theodoros was in fact doing, how he 'proved' the irrationality of √3 ... √17 (except for the rational numbers, √4, √9, √16), and why he stopped at √17.¹⁵ I cannot see why he should have 'proved' anything at all. The easiest way to explain his procedure was suggested by
[152]   H. J. Anderhub in a curious book called 'Joco–Seria' which, as a matter of course, has not been taken seriously by specialists.¹⁶

Anderhub interpreted the passage approximately as follows: Theodoros must have been well acquainted with the 'theorem of Pythagoras' and with the irrationality of √2 as seen in the relation of the side to the diagonal of a square.¹⁷

---

12. The dating of the Spartan defeat in 392 by Judeich 1926: 147 A. 6, may still be too early; cf. Griffith 1950: 252, Accame 1951: 108 ff.

13. *See* Burkert 1972: 404.

14. Cf. ἐνέχεσθαι ἀπορίῃσι Hdt I 190. The participle προαιρούμενος is curious: what did he choose? Should one read προαγόμενος? Cf. below, n. 29.

15. It is commonly and wrongly assumed that ἔγραφε means 'proved' (note also the imperfect tense). *See* the references in n. 1 and notably Heath's (1921: 1202 ff.) History and van der Waerden's Science awakening (I have used the second German edition, 1966: 235 ff.); add Heller's (1956: 1 ff.) comprehensive discussion; further references in Anderhub (next note), Burkert 1972: 463 n. 81 and Brown 1969: 359 ff.

16. Anderhub 1941: 161–224; preliminary notes in Wochenschrift für klassische Philologie 1918 (49/50): 598 f. Anderhub rightly insists that γράφειν cannot mean 'to prove.' The spiral was also drawn by S. Moraïtes in his Modern Greek Plato edition (1913) but he did not see the consequences (Anderhub 222). Heller 1956 adopts a variant of Anderhub's spiral as an illustration, but presumes that Theodoros had given a one hour's lesson on the subject of irrationality.

17. For the evidence, *see* now Burkert 1972: 428 ff., 462 f.

Making the diagonal of a one foot square one side of a right-angled triangle, and preserving one foot as the length of the other side, Theodoros was able to 'show' that the hypotenuse of this triangle must have the length of the side of a three square foot square (because 2 + 1 = 3), and that the new hypotenuse could not be measured in terms of one foot. Remember: the Greeks did not normally operate with fractions. Then he drew the next right-angled triangle, using the former hypotenuse as one side and again a one foot line as the other side. Obviously this √4 foot hypotenuse measured 2 feet. And then he proceeded to draw a spiral-like figure where only √9 and √16 could be seen to be commensurable with one foot.

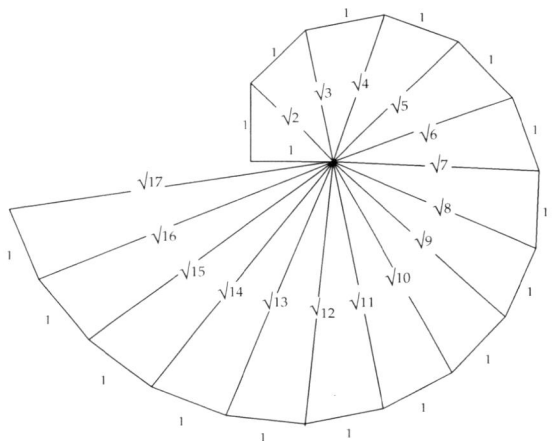

He stopped at √17 because the √18 triangle would have intruded into his first triangle.[18] I am sure Anderhub was right. There is an additional indication of this, never observed in this connection as far as I know. The only evidence we have of Theodoros' mathematical studies which is seemingly independent of this Platonic passage, is a somewhat cryptic statement on spirals in Proclus. A ἕλιξ, Proclus says, is a mixed line which does not consist of parts, so Theodoros the mathematician wrongly took it to be a 'κρᾶσις based on lines.'[19] Modern scholars do not seem to have noticed the connection with *Theaetetus*. Without knowing it, Anderhub drew the relevant figure illustrating what Proclus meant. Proclus

---

18. The sum of the inner angles of the √2 – √18 triangles would amount to 364.783 degrees, the √17 one reaching 351.150 (and certainly somewhat further, if drawn in sand). I am indebted to my son-in-law Henrik Segercrantz for these calculations.

19. Proclus, In Eucl. *Elem.* I, p. 117.25–118.8 Friedländer, discussing the nature of curves. I understand κρᾶσις ἐπὶ τῶν γραμμῶν to mean a mixture made 'on the basis' of or 'out of' straight lines.

[153] probably had access to an old tradition about the historical Theodoros having studied triangle-based spirals and Plato having referred to such figures orally and in the dialogue. The Anonymous Commentator on *Theaetetus*, as usual, is not so well informed.[20]

I also find it important to note that throughout the dialogue Theodoros is depicted as an adherent of φαινόμενα, and indeed of Protagoras, who is known to have opposed theoretical geometry.[21] We should definitely not expect any 'proofs' from Theodoros. And shall I add that I am not a believer in the legend of Plato receiving instruction from him in Cyrene?[22]

[154] Plato's Theaitetos, however, is a more theoretically and philosophically-minded person.

Since an infinite number of roots appeared (ἐφαίνοντο) to exist—the spiral could be made to grow *ad infinitum*—, he and the Younger Socrates (who probably stands for Plato)[23] looked for a common term for all irrational roots versus rational ones.[24] They divided all numbers into two classes,[25] square numbers (τετράγωνον, ἰσόπλευρον) and 'oblong' numbers (προμήκη, ἑτερομήκη), and returning to geometry, 'defined' (ὡρισάμεθα) the lines corresponding to square numbers as μῆκος, and the lines corresponding to oblong numbers as δυνάμεις, because they are not arithmetically, but by their geometrical 'potency,' commensurable with the lines of the former class. "And similarly with the solids," Theaitetos adds.

So Plato says, simply, that Theaitetos and his friend defined geometrical commensurability by means of a new generalizing classification of number, i.e. (as we would say) by introducing 'roots.' The old classification into odd/even was substituted by a more sophisticated one. Presumably, the Pythagoreans had operated with the notion of square and oblong 'gnomon' numbers long before the 390s,[26] but we have no reason to doubt that Theaitetos had a share in generalizing the concept of ἑτερομήκης ἀριθμός. Plato at any rate found the idea suggestive of his own metaphysical category of θάτερον versus ταὐτόν I find it practically certain that the play with ἴσον and ἕτερον in *Theaetetus* alludes to the two Platonic

---

20. Diels-Schubart 1905: Col. 25 ff., p. 18 ff. Various unreliable guesses are offered at Col. 34 ff., discussed and rejected by Anderhub 1941: 183 f. Obviously Platonists in the 2nd century BCE(?) were bewildered by the passage.

21. Theodoros is old and intellectually lazy, though interested in 'appearances' (e.g. 143e, 144bc, 147d, 162ab, 168e, 177c, 180b; 162e is ironical in view of 165a), and he is called upon to defend the tenets of his 'friend,' Protagoras (161b, 162a, 171c, 179a). – For Protagoras, see DK 80 B 7, Arist. *Met.* B 998a, cf. Plat. *Prt.* 318de. The outburst of 'Protagoras' in *Theaetetus* 162e about the need of proofs is certainly ironical from Plato's perspective.

22. Diog. L. III 6, cf. II 103 and above, p. 174.

23. *See* the article by Jatakari 1990: 29 ff.

24. This is clearly the implication of 147d8–e1 where ταύτας refers to τρίποδος, πεντέποδος and ἑπτακαιδεκάποδος.

25. Note the application of the method of διαίρεσις, cf. συλλαβεῖν d9.

26. *See* in general Burkert 1972: 427 ff., and for the terminology, Lasserre 1987: 466 ff. with references.

principles of the Same and the Different (later linked up with Ἕν and Δυάς), [154] which constitute measure and knowability on various levels.²⁷

Theodoros and Theaitetos had been 'measuring' the sides of their triangles; [155] finding a common μέτρον is a central topic in the dialogue.²⁸ The methods of geometrical measuring cannot have been very refined in those days, but Plato's contemporaries are likely to have used an approximative method sometimes called 'reciprocal subtraction.'²⁹

Then we have the interesting statements of Eudemus (in an Arabic text of Pappos, overlooked by Wehrli), which are sometimes thought to represent a tradition independent of Plato. There it is said in connection with a reference to the dialogue that Theaitetos "divided the most generally known irrational lines according to the different [i.e. geometric, arithmetic, and harmonic] means," perhaps using the terms μέση (medial), ἐκ δυοῖν ὀνομάτοιν (binomial surd) and ἀποτομή (subtractive binomial surd); and that he "assumed two lines commensurable in square and proved that if he took between them a line in ratio according to geometric proportion (the geometric mean), then the line named the medial was produced, but if he took (the line) according to harmonic proportion (the harmonic mean), then the apotome was produced."³⁰

---

27. For ἴσον / ἕτερον cf. 143e, 144d ff., 148ab, 155a, 158c ff., 181c ff., 185b ff., 189a ff., 203e, 208d; μέγα / σμικρόν 152d, 155a, 172bc; ἕν/δύο, πολλά, ἄπειρον 146d ff., 154cd, 156a, 185b ff.; κίνησις, δύναμις, ποιεῖν 147d ff., 152e, 156a ff., 181b ff. (ποιότης! 182ab), 185c ff., 197c; Theaitetos the γεννικός (γενναῖος) somehow representing 'generation' of numbers and λόγοι 144d, 146d, 149a ff., 156cd, 158e ff. Plato's world is a κρᾶσις of unequal opposites (cf. 152d and Theodoros' spiral); his 'two-level model' (Thesleff above) is presented in the digression 172c–177c.– The *locus classicus* for the metaphysics of the Same versus the Different is *Timaeus* 35a ff., cf. the μέγιστα γένη, *Sophist* 254cd. I shall not enter into the question of oral teaching, but note the abundant references to γράφειν 143a–c, as if Plato wanted to remind his readers that the μεταξὺ τῶν λόγων (cl) are indeed δυνάμεις in their own way (147e9). For an attentive interpretation of *Theaetetus*, where an attempt is made to give the mathematical passages their proper philosophical bearing, see Brown 1969 (above, n. 15) who, however, shares the conventional view of Theaitetos' achievements in geometry.

28. Cornford's (1935) commentary, useful in its time, is of little help in these matters; see notably Friedländer III² 1960: 151, and Brown 1969. For μετρητική, cf. *Protagoras* 356e–357b (with metaphysical allusions similar to *Theaetetus*!), *Statesman* 283c–287b, also *Gorgias* 508a ff.

29. Cf. Eucl. X 2 ff. and see e.g. Heath I 206 ff., Brumbaugh 1954: 54 f., Heller 1956: 23 ff., Junge (1958): 42–44; Burkert 1972: 459; Brown 1969: 363–365; Lasserre 1987: 447 ff., 476 ff.; each making a somewhat different approach. An illustrative example is given by van der Waerden 1966: 208. In Arist. *Top*. VIII 158b33 ff. ἀνταναίρεσις probably means the same as ἀνθυφαίρεσις in Euclid. The notions of ἔλλειψις (ἐνδεία) / ὑπεροχή (ὑπερβολή) belonged to geometry in Plato's days; cf. *Prt*. 357a, *Men*. 87a, *R*. VIII 546c, and the methods for 'squaring' the circle from Hippocrates of Chios onwards, and the 'Golden Section' (see especially Burkert 1972: 452 f.); cf. also the 'Divided Line,' *R*. VI 509d ff. with its metaphysical διαιρέσεις. Possibly the use of the verb προαιρεῖσθαι in *Tht*. 147d7 has something to do with all this, but cf. above, n. 14.

30. Junge-Thomson 1930: 63 ff., 72 ff., 138 ff., and Junge's comments p. 15–17; fr. D 3–4 Lasserre 1987 (with comments, p. 467 ff.). For the terms, cf. Eucl. *Elem*. X 21 ff., 47 ff., 73 ff.; cf. also Ps.-Arist. *De lineis insec*. 968b13 ff., which may reflect an earlier tradition. For the Pythagorean or at least pre-Platonic origins of the three 'means' as represented in *Timaeus* (31cd, 36a, cf. *Epin*. 991a), see Burkert 1972: 440–42 and Brown 1975: 173 ff. Von Fritz 1934: 1354 ff. and some later critics (van der Waerden 1966: 275 ff. among them, also Lasserre l.c. in spite of his generally cautious interpretation) have made too much of this notice in Pappos.

[156] It is doubtful what 'proving' means in the latter quotation even if the translation from Arabic is literally correct. Proportionals of the 'arithmetic' and 'geometric' type were easily obtained from Theodoros' triangles, and for the *apotome* one might think of the traditional construction of the 'Golden Section' by means of 'cut-offs' from a right-angled triangle though in fact the geometrical constructions needed for illustrating a harmonic mean (2 √2 to 1 + √2) by ἀποτομαί of three lines, (a − b): (b − c) = a : c, are not very sophisticated.

Apparently it was known in the Academy that Theaitetos used to classify various combinations of surds, i.e. δυνάμει commensurable lines, in relation to the three means. But assuming this does not mean accepting that he systematized the doctrine of surds as we have it in Euclid.

In the dialogue, Theaitetos' function is to act as an intelligent discussion partner with Socrates (cf. the slave boy in *Meno*), well versed in geometry and ἄλογα, and prepared to use λόγοι as well, potentially an ideal philosopher. But as far as I can see, Plato or Eudemus give no further hints about his achievements in the study of irrationals.[31]

Now Euclid's Book X, which contains the theory of incommensurability and surds, may indeed somehow represent the essentials of what the historical Theaitetos thought in this matter. Ancient sources seem to take this for granted, and it seems to fit in with other pieces of evidence which can be gathered from the historians of mathematics from Eudemus onwards.[32] But to infer that Theaitetos 'wrote' Euclid X, or at least formulated the main part of its propositions and [157] proofs, is a modern idea.[33] I can see no reason at all for accepting this view. The Academy had fostered many prominent mathematicians before Euclid's times.[34] Supposing that Theaitetos died as a young man, surely Plato, the 'architect' of Academic geometry,[35] would have been able to transmit his dead friend's visions

---

31. For λόγοι, cf. συλλαβαί 202b ff. (also συλλαβεῖν 147d), and ἄρρητα 152c, 155e, 156b (with ἄλογα, 202b ff.); cf. above, n. 27. Elsewhere in Plato no manifest allusions occur to Theaitetos' studies: *see* the critical remarks of Lasserre 1987: 487 ff. (who, however, accepts *Laws* VII 820c and *Epin.* 990d as 'fragments').

32. After Sachs, the evidence was recorded by von Fritz 1934: 1353 ff. (who did not know Thomson's Pappos, above, n. 30). Cf. also the rather negative evidence of the Testimonia collected by Stamatis in his new B. T. edition of Euclid, Book X (1972).

33. Sachs 1914: 11–13, 41–42. It is reflected very clearly in van der Waerden (e.g. 1966: 271–91) with his tendency to dogmatic conclusions. Even the generally cautious von Fritz insists that Theaitetos offered Euclidean proofs (e.g. 1934: 1358). Lasserre 1987: 464 is wisely skeptical about the possibility of reconstructing Theaitetos' formulations.

34. Menaechmus, Dinostratus, Athenaeus, Hermotimus, Theudius (who actually published a book of 'Elements'), and Eudoxus, to mention just a few; *see* now Lasserre 1987. Eudoxus' relation to Theaitetos is a matter of conjecture. The sweeping statements of Proclus, In Eucl. *Elem.* I, p. 67 Friedländer Ἑρμότιμος . . . τὰ ὑπ' Εὐδόξου προηυπορημένα καὶ Θεαιτήτου προήγαγεν ἐπὶ πλέον (probably from Eudemus), p. 68 . . . Εὐκλείδης . . . πολλὰ μὲν τῶν Εὐδόξου συντάξας πολλὰ δὲ τῶν Θεαιτήτου τελεωσάμενος (probably his own addition), have very little relevance.

35. The new Dicaearchus text published by Gaiser 1988, comments on the development of mathematics and μετρολογία in the Academy, ἀρχιτεκτονοῦντος . . . τοῦ Πλάτωνος (Col. 1 Υ. 4 ff., p. 152) and emphasizing the role of Eudoxus in developing the ὁρισμοί (cf. *Tht.* 148a8 and Gaiser p. 348). Plato, of course, was not himself very active as a mathematician.

of irrationality and commensurability to younger generations who were capable of elaborating the theories and giving them a fixed written form. Perhaps, too, Plato was the only transmitter of the tradition about Theodoros' ἕλιξ.

Theaitetos' other speciality is said to have been the construction of the five regular solids. The evidence was discussed in detail by Sachs,[36] who argued a point later doubted by very few, namely that Theaitetos made his discoveries mainly after Plato had written the *Republic*, where (VII 528a ff.) Socrates remarks on the deplorable state of stereometry, and before the *Timaeus* where the theory of the solids is implied (31b–34a, 53c–55c, cf. *Epin.* 990d). Euclid's Book XIII would largely derive from Theaitetos' work on the solids. Again, I think, the moderns have gone far too far.

The brief reference to stereometry in *Theaetetus* (148b) certainly points to Theaitetos' activities in this field though, as such, it only implies that Theaitetos and his friend 'saw' that the same rule of δυνάμει commensurability must apply to the relation of the edges to the volume of cubes, pyramids, etc.[37] The rest of the ancient sources referring to Theaitetos' studies of the solids do not suggest more than that he was able to construct and explain the cube, the regular tetrahedron, the octahedron, the icosahedron, and the dodecahedron.[38]

If no proofs or systematized theories are required, this is not so very remarkable. The theory of the cube (6 squares) and the tetrahedron (4 equilateral triangles) had been well known for a long time, the dodecahedron (12 regular pentagons) had been an object of wonder among the Pythagoreans and before,[39] and the octahedron (8 equilateral triangles) was easily, the icosahedron (20 equilateral triangles) possibly, derived from the tetrahedron. It is reasonable, however, to infer that Theaitetos applied his knowledge of reciprocal subtraction and ἀποτομαί to the construction of the icosahedron and the dodecahedron and, hence, to the regular pentagon.[40] But as far as I can see, there is no evidence of his producing the system of regular solids as we have it in Euclid XIII.

Plato's *Republic* took shape gradually, and I find it quite plausible that Glaucon's and Socrates' complaints about stereometry in Book VII reflect the state of affairs in the late 370s.[41] But to force Theaitetos' alleged discoveries of the 'five

---

36. Sachs 1917, especially 146 ff.; cf. Sachs 1914: 40.
37. von Fritz 1934: 1360 seems to admit this.
38. The evidence collected by Sachs is discussed with critical cautiousness by von Fritz 1934: 1363 ff. and Lasserre 1987: 492 ff. (who emphasizes the intermediary role of Hermotimus). The most explicit piece of information is a Scholium on Euclid, Book XIII, where it is stated that the octahedron and the icosahedron are Θεαιτήτου.
39. Burkert 1972: 460.
40. *See* von Fritz 1934: 1369–71; Junge 1958 (above, n. 29). The 'Golden Section' was used in antiquity for constructing the pentagon. The Anonymous Commentator, Col. 41 ff. (p. 28 Diels-Schubart), in explaining *Tht.* 148b, starts from arithmetic (which is probably correct) but proceeds by guesses and hardly supplies historically reliable information.
41. R. VII 528b–d: Glaucon remarks that "this subject (i.e., of the third dimension) does not appear to have been investigated yet," and Socrates gives some reasons why this is so, one being that "the investigators need a director," and "as things are now, seekers in this field would be

[158] Platonic bodies' in between that date and 369 BCE, is simply to overinterpret a series of hypotheses. And surely we should expect Plato, who was not afraid of anachronisms, to have made more than a casual reference to τὰ στερεά in *Theaetetus* if his friend had made such remarkable progress just before the dialogue was written.

In my view, it can be rather safely concluded that Theaitetos only laid the foundations for stereometry by trying to generalize the rules for square roots to cubic roots and by studying the properties of the regular solids. After the 380s,

[159] Eudoxus and some others actually built the system eventually laid out in *Timaeus, Epinomis,* in various Aristotelian passages, and in Euclid. And so Theaitetos the stereometrician will have to take a similar step backwards in history as Theaitetos the irrationalist. I am not, however, questioning his brilliance in relation to his contemporaries.

Finally, there is the odd notice in Hesychius and Suda about Theaitetos having taught in Heracleia.[42] A mistake, similar to the emerging of 'Theaitetos of Rhegion,'[43] is quite possible. Still, Theaitetos may have visited Heracleia in the 390s; he was a friend of Euclides of Megara, and Heracleia was a Megarian colony. The awkward fact that Theaitetos is not mentioned in the Philodemic list of members of Plato's Academy traditionally known as the 'Academicorum Index,' has sometimes been taken to indicate that he was working abroad and not in Athens.[44] My explanation of why he does not appear in the list is different.

I am inclined to think that Theaitetos lived ca. 415–390 BCE and that the explicitness of his discoveries has been exaggerated by modern interpreters. Plato's reasons for introducing him and Theodoros in *Theaetetus* may be looked for along the general lines suggested by Malcolm Brown.[45]

---

too arrogant to submit to this guidance" (translation by P. Shorey). This reproach surely would not apply to the promising young geometrician of *Theaetetus*. For the date of the *Republic*, cf. Thesleff above, p. 286, 331.

42. Suda ends by having two Theaitetoses, the Athenian who was an ἀστρολόγος etc. and a pupil of Socrates and who taught in Heracleia, and the Heracleote, who was a pupil of Plato.

43. Iambl. V P 172; here Theocles is meant, cf. ibid. 130.

44. Cf. Lasserre 1987: 434. For the Academicorum Index, see now Suppl. Plat., (above, n. 35), Col. 5.32 ff., and Gaiser's comments p. 443 ff. (also p. 15 f., 90, on Lasserre's solutions). Nor does Dicaearchus mention Theaitetos.

45. In the article referred to above, n. 15. *See* also above, n. 27.

# THE EARLY VERSION OF PLATO'S *REPUBLIC**  [149]

The theory of the "Proto-*Republic*" is an uncomfortable one. Those who have seen it mentioned tend to dismiss it offhand, chiefly because it does not fit in with their views of Plato's development, and certainly because so very few specialists have endorsed it. And were not Hirmer (1897) and Adam (1902, followed by Usher 1973 and many others) able to refute definitely the notion that Aristophanes' Ecclesiazusae might refer to Plato, rather than vice versa?

No, they were not. The theory has been revived recently.[1] The following is an attempt to restate my position regarding the issue of Plato's early Utopia, by adding a few more arguments and by developing some of the consequences of the theory for our understanding of Plato's public relations and his early philosophy. As I see it, the question demands an extensive (and 'philological') treatment and probing from as many angles as possible. It is largely a matter of circumstantial evidence.

The main arguments for the existence of an early Platonic Utopia are the following.

(i) Although the *Republic*, as we have it in our manuscripts, forms a monu- [150] mental, pedimentally composed unity,[2] it is not likely to have been a monolith

---

*Variants of this paper were read in 1994 in Columbia SC (*The Rosamond Kent Sprague Lecture* II), Chicago, New York, and Athens, and in 1995 at a conference in Gammel Vraa (Denmark). I am particularly indebted to the friendly help and criticism from Ian Mueller, Debra Nails, Jerry Press, Rosamond Sprague, and two anonymous referees.

1. Cf. Nails 1995: 116–122, developing the theses of Thesleff 1982 (above, p. 145 ff.) and id., 1989: 10–15.

2. Contrary to earlier attempts to analyze the *Republic* into parts, it has been customary in recent years to underline its structural unity. For the 'pedimental' composition, *see* above, 83 ff. and G. A. Press 1993: 27 f., with context.

[150] from the start. The dialogue is usually taken as typical of Plato's 'Middle Period,' and so the commonly accepted date of composition is 'about 375 BCE.' As a matter of fact, however, this conventional view is a loose compromise among a wide variety of considerations. There are no unambiguous clues to the dating. The different blocks of the work may well originate in different periods and contexts, and the final editing probably took place rather late, after Plato's Sicilian adventures were over.[3] It is quite possible, indeed feasible considering the structure of the work, that the Utopia (Callipolis) belongs to its earliest layers.

(ii) Aulus Gellius, a usually well-informed author, reports that Xenophon was said to have opposed the ideas of Plato's *Republic*, having read the "approximately two books which had first reached the public."[4] Hence, Gellius continues, Xenophon put forward a different view of a good government in the *Cyropaedia*, which occasioned Plato to remark (*Laws* III 694c) that Cyrus was not educated at all. Gellius' source probably had in mind the opening section of the *Cyropaedia* and Book VIII, which present a theory of the Best State in a Persian setting, with some apparent reminiscences of Plato's Utopia.[5] The date of the *Cyropaedia* is usually put rather late because of the references in the epilogue (VIII 8); but if this is a postscript, the bulk of the text may well, like the *Anabasis*, have been written in Skillous in the 380s when Xenophon cannot possibly have seen the final *Republic*.

What is really intriguing here, is the mention in Gellius of 'approximately two books.' This is irrelevant to his basic story which concerns the relations
[151] of Plato and Xenophon. Gellius is quoting an unnamed author who obviously did not mean the beginning of the *Republic* (as Gellius knew it), from Book I to somewhere about the end of Book II or the opening of Book III, since these sections could not have provoked what we read in the *Cyropaedia*. Very probably Gellius' source was well-informed enough to know, or to assume, that Xenophon had been using an earlier, shorter version of Plato's political Utopia, a text which he perhaps had not seen but which he presumed to be of 'about' two papyrus scrolls in length, like the Peripatetic epitome we happen to know of (below, p. 159).

(iii) In the opening of Plato's *Timaeus* (17c 19b), we read what purports to be a constricted but complete summary of the λόγοι περὶ πολιτείας that Socrates had presented to the same audience the day before. The summary covers the essentials of the political proposals of Books II–III and V of the *Republic*:

---

3. This is one of the theses of Thesleff 1982; *see* further below.
4. *NA* XIV 3.3, note *duobus fere libris, qui primi in volgus exierant.* Cf, below, Aristotle.
5. Especially I 1.1, deficiencies of all Greek constitutions, cf. Plato. *Seventh Letter* 326ab (below); I 2.15, schools of justice; VIII 1–2: loyalty aiming at common εὐδαιμονία, Guardians, σχολή, training for ἀρετή and justice, respect for women (1.27 f.), strict specialization of the crafts (2, 5–6). Xenophon does not appear to know Isocrates' *Busiris* (below) which may have been published earlier.

| Timaeus | Republic |
|---|---|
| 17cd The specialization of the trades in the Best State and the need of specialized soldiers as Guardians | II 369b–374d |
| 17d–18a The mild and violent, spirited and philosophic nature required for Guardians | II 374d–376c |
| 18a The education (τροφή) of the Guardians will consist of γυμναστική, μουσική, and μαθήματα proper for them [no details given but note 19de on μίμησις and poetry] | II 376c–III 412b, VII 521c–531c (cf. VI 502c–506b) |
| 18b The Guardians would have no private property but live modestly on common public funds, devoting themselves to ἀρετή and σχολή | III 416d–417b (and more loosely V 461e–466d), cf. II 374b–e |
| 18c Equality of women and men | V 451d–457c |
| 18cd The strange proposal of community of women and children | V 457c–458c, 461dc |
| 18dc Eugenics: the secret manipulation of sexual unions | V 459a–460b, cf. III 415bc |
| 19a Good offspring to be reared, bad offspring to be sent to their proper class | V 460c–461c, cf. III 415bc |

The summary begins where Socrates in our text of the *Republic* takes over, after the speeches of Plato's brothers (II 368c), and it ends before the discussion of philosophy and philosophic man begins (V 472a). There is in *Timaeus* no reference to the issues of Book IV (happiness as a balance of virtues in the state and the soul) or to the detailed criticism of myth in Books II and III (377d–398b), though note the hint 19de; and the education of the (yet undifferentiated) Philosopher-Guardians is only mentioned in passing (18a), though μαθήματα are included (elaborated in *Republic* VII 521c ff., cf. VI 502c–506b). The main distinction is that between the Guardians of society and the rest.

The framing of the summary involves some obvious fiction and deliberate mystification. It is particularly interesting that the summary only deals with a specific part of our *Republic* and, moreover, that it does not correspond exactly even to this part, although it is explicitly said to be complete. "This is all that was said yesterday," we are assured (19ab), before Socrates goes on to say that he would now like to see the Ideal City in action (which leads first to the Atlantis story). The mock-pedantic and pointed restriction to what we know as parts of the *Republic*, put in a different context, must have some significance. Why could Plato not just refer to the ideas of 'Socrates' as presented in the *Republic*? On the other hand, if Plato had wanted to operate with pure fiction, it would have been easy for him to create a summary of a previous discussion which would have fitted his present theme much better than the summary given in the *Timaeus* actually does.

[152] We shall never know all the implications of this mystification. But by reason of what we seem to know, it is difficult to avoid the assumption that Plato makes Socrates refer to an existing version of his Utopia, without such later accretions as readers of the *Timaeus* presumably knew of: oral or written additions that would too readily associate with Plato's activities in the Academy and in Syracuse. He simply made a reference to his early Utopia of equality and communism among the leading class, a Utopia which included little or no explicit discussion of philosophical issues. Such a static Utopia, projected into prehistory, gave him somehow a suitable starting point for the dynamics of the Atlantis story, the Egyptian fabulations (cf. Isocrates, below), and indeed the cosmic background of all this, rooted as it is in constant κίνησις.[6] In other words, I presume Plato is here playing with the 'approximately two books' known to the source of Gellius.

[153] The fiction of the lecture having been given 'the day before' to the same company (though one is now missing due to ἀσθένεια, like Plato is in the *Phaedo*) may imply that the earlier version had not been published in the manner of the more widely known dialogues and, consequently, that it did not have a fixed literary setting. It is also important to note that the language of the relevant portions of the present *Republic* II–III and V has features of Plato's 'late style':[7] so if the utopian part of this dialogue represents an earlier layer, it has not come to us in its original shape. This original shape need not even have been dialogic (below).

(iv) The existence of an early version of Plato's Utopia is partially confirmed by Aristophanes' *Ecclesiazusae* (about 392 BCE). To skeptics it should be remarked at the outset that those who deny that Aristophanes might have had Plato in mind probably have not considered all the parallels found—or the existing indications that Plato had a distinct political philosophy before 388 BCE, long before the *Republic* received its final shape, or the fact that a comic parody is likely to exaggerate and disfigure to the point of sheer nonsense, or how Plato would react on an earlier parody of his views. Plato's own sense of humour may well account for the comic tones and allusions in *Republic* V and elsewhere in the dialogue, even if he had himself set the ball rolling and Aristophanes had already made him the subject of public mockery.[8]

The most conspicuous parallels with our text of the *Republic* are the following:

| *Ecclesiazusae* | *Republic* |
|---|---|
| 1–240 Opening arguments of Praxagora for the need of reform and rule of women, ending in statement: εὐδαιμονοῦντες τὸν βίον διάξετε | (Εὐδαιμονία given as background motivation for the utopia, IV 419a ff., V 465d ff., 473c) |

---

6. Movement is typical of both soul and body of the Cosmos.
7. References above, p. 86 ff., 286.
8. And he knows that mockery subsides with time, V 452b e. The reflections of comedy in the *Republic* have been often noted, and hence some critics tend to interpret the entire Utopia as satire. More commonly, Plato is said to play ironically with ideas originally advanced by Aristophanes.

The Early Version of Plato's *Republic*  523

| | | |
|---|---|---|
| 441–442 Women are both intellectual and productive | Cf. esp. V 454d–456a (VII 540c) | [153] |
| 556–568 No social injustice | Cf. 416d–417b (V 462bc) | |
| 571–582 Chorus introducing Praxagora's proposals by addressing her: "Collect your philosophic knowledge (πυκνὴν φρένα φιλόσοφον φροντίδα ἐπισταμένην) for the benefit of your sisters (φίλαι); for the thoughts of your revolutionary speech (καινὴ γλώττης ἐπίνοια) will bring much happiness, joy, and help to the life of our citizens. It is time to show what you can. For our city needs some clever innovation (σοφοῦ τινος ἐξευρήματος). Go on with what has never been done or said before . . ." | Cf. Socrates' reluctance in Book V to present his proposal of community of woman and children, under the supervision of philosophers | [154] |
| Praxagora: | | |
| 583–585 I know my advice is good (χρηστὰ διδάξω) and for the women's part revolutionary (καινοτομεῖν). | Cf. above | |
| 589 Try to understand my thought (ἐπίστασθαι τὴν ἐπίνοιαν) | | |
| 590–604 All property shall be common | V. passim | |
| 605–608 There will be plenty of everything | Cf. II 372ab | |
| 609–610 Old laws not needed | Cf. V 462a | |
| 613–615 Free love, community of women | V 451d–461c | |
| 615–618 External beauty not decisive | Cf. V 474dc | |
| 635–645 Fathers will not recognize their offspring | V 457d, 461c–e, 463c | |
| 651–652 Slaves as farmers | (Note σχολή of Guardians, II 374b–e and passim; cf. *Timaeus* 18b; cf. further III 415a, e, V 466b: farmers the lowest class) | |
| 656–672 No quarrels and lawsuits | III 405bc, V 464d–465d | |
| 678–680 Recital of epic poetry to make children courageous | Cf. V 468cd (and II/III) | |
| 673–688 (cf. 715) Common meals; the city will become like one single home (μίαν οἴκησιν, εἰς ἓν ἅπαντα) | III 416de, V 462a–464d | |

It is a new (583 ff.) 'philosophic' theory of communism and community of women and children that is the chief target of Aristophanes' parody. He makes his heroine Praxagora present her communistic manifesto (571–688) together with a plan for women's takeover. The latter follows by Aristophanic logic from the deplorable political conditions in Athens (171 ff.), from the need of justice for all, and from the notion of the equality of the sexes. But the points of contact with

[155] the relevant sections of the *Republic* (II–III and V) are unmistakable.[9] Note especially the emphasis on the 'philosophic' nature of the proposal (571 ff., 589).

Specific questions are the possible indirect reflection of Pythagorean ideas in this context, and Antisthenes' role here. The figuring of Antisthenes and other Socratics in Aristophanes' scenery cannot be excluded, and the idea of philosophizing women has a Pythagorean flavor.[10] The main target, however, of the parody is likely to be Plato. When Praxagora first addresses her public, in the disguise of a pale young man (427 ff.), she is acting a young, effeminate, intellectual revolutionary. Here she probably represents Plato (aged thirty-five or less). She represents a philosopher (not a 'sophist'). In fact, verse 571 gives the only occurrence of the word φιλόσοφος or its derivatives in the entire Aristophanic Corpus, including the *Clouds* and all the fragments: and we know that Plato, apparently more emphatically than the other Socratics, made a special point of φιλοσοφία. And there is an additional indication, surely not popular among Platonists, of the presence of Plato in the *Ecclesiazusae*: he seems to figure here, indirectly in the shape of a 'pervert,' in the hint at the risks of free love resulting in a kiss by Aristyllus the fellator (647).[11]

[156] (v) It is fairly generally agreed that Isocrates in his Essay XI, the *Busiris*, includes Plato (typically unnamed) among the "well-known philosophers" who have used the Egyptian institutions (allegedly founded by King Busiris) as their model when speaking about the organization of society and constitutions.[12] The institutions referred to are the strict specialization of trades and the division of society into three main classes, priests, soldiers and workers; the ascetic communal life of the two first for the benefit and happiness of all (also imitated but

---

9. Nails 1995: 117–121, discusses several of the points and sums up the arguments for the priority of Plato. It is not necessary to repeat them here.

10. For Antisthenes, *see* my notes 1989, 11 f. and below. The Ps.-Pythagorean 'Four Speeches' (Iambl. VP 37–57, p. 178–183 Thesleff) give a relatively early reflection of Pythagorean social ethics, but they do not have very much in common with Plato's Utopia (cf. below). Possibly Plato also referred to the three Graiae who share everything ('Speech' IV 55), cf. *Ecclesiazusae* 446 451, 877 ff. (Isocrates' *Busiris* 29 suggests a knowledge of the 'Speeches'); cf. further the pointed διασπᾶν, *Republic* V 462b, 464c, *Ecclesiazusae* 1076, and 'Speech' II 49. At any rate, note the explicit statement in Aristotle, *Politics* II 1266a34 (cf. 1274b9): before Plato, nobody had put forth the idea of community of women and children (though Phaleas had proposed community of property): and it is pronouncedly a καινὴ ἐπίνοια, according to Aristophanes 573 f.

11. *Etym. Magn.* s.v. (referring in fact to Aristophanes; cf. also Eusthatios; Edmonds 1957: 717n, 719) explains Aristyllus as hypocoristic for Aristocles, and this is said by some sources to have been Plato's original name (Diog. L. III 4, 43). The reference in *Ecclesiazusae* 647 is to an effeminate young man, and καλαμίνθη 648 is perfume (not in the first place ordure), cf Usher ad 1. But in the nonsensical context of Plutus 311 ff. Aristyllus can be taken to "follow still his mother" (i.e. to preach feminism?), though he has been punished (in *Ecclesiazusae?*); note here μινθώσομεν (perversity is probably implied), and note also the tone of the hypocoristic name form. Plato's homosexual inclinations, as well as Aristophanes' populistic attitude to 'perverts,' are well known.

12. XI 16–23. It may be relevant that Isocrates writes λέγειν ἐπιχειροῦντας which suggests recent attempts; Pythagoras (mentioned later, 28–29) is not meant in the first place.

misused, according to Isocrates, by the military cast in Sparta); and the special training and σχολή reserved for the intellectuals (the priests in Isocrates' account). It is the intellectuals as a class who are the leaders (not the King). The point of Isocrates is to characterize the mythic King Busiris as a benefactor of mankind, against the rhetor and anti-intellectualist Polycrates who, in a recent speech and following Greek traditions, had made him rather a criminal. A 'report' or even a criticism of the contents of Plato's *Republic* is not intended by Isocrates' fiction, and so it is understandable that nothing is said about the community of women and children. However, we can detect some close parallels with the summary in *Timaeus* (cf. below, p. 536). There is nothing in particular in Isocrates' text that would suggest his use of the full version of the *Republic*. Rather, it reads as a projection of suitably selected parts of Plato's Utopia upon a vague picture of Egyptian society.[13]

The date of *Busiris* is open to dispute. It is often dated by the *Republic*, i.e. 'soon after 375 BCE'; but Eucken (1983) who finds difficulties with the chronology, admits that Isocrates might have seen the *Republic* "im Stadium der Abfassung." In fact, a date in the 380s is plausible.[14] In that case it must be the 'Proto-*Republic*' that Isocrates has in mind. And perhaps Plato, in his usual playful manner, is answering Isocrates (much later) by putting his Utopia into a 'true' Egyptian context, and by making Socrates enumerate in the *Timaeus* (with a pedantry more typical of Isocrates than of Plato) the issues of 'yesterday's speech.'[15]

○○○ ○ ○○○

---

13. Pace Eucken; *see* the next note. The 'Proto-*Republic*' is likely to have contained some criticism of poetry (cf. *Busiris* 38–40, *Timaeus* 18a προσήκει), but Isocrates added his own comments on Egyptian medicine (22) and religion (24–29, with an ironical note on Pythagoras). I have argued elsewhere (in a paper read to the Nordic 'Platonselskabet,' 1997) that Isocrates did not know more of Egyptian society than what Herodotus reports, and that he identified the Egyptian 'priests' with the philosophers of Plato's Utopia, attributing to the former such Platonic notions as fitted Herodotus' picture. In this essay, Isocrates still avoided a confrontation with Plato (whether he or somebody else, perhaps Plato himself, was the first to assert that Plato had drawn on Egyptian models). In attacking Polycrates, Isocrates saw an ally in Plato whose Utopia probably had referred to the detractors of philosophy (cf. e.g. *Republic* III 407c).

14. Eucken 1983: 180 f., does not accept the 'Proto-*Republic*' theory. Note, however, that the formal addressee of the *Busiris*. Polycrates, had left Athens for Cyprus about 390 BCE, and we do not hear from him later. The ultimate purpose of Isocrates is to defend 'philosophy' against the (certainly recent) attacks by Polycrates and his Athenian sponsors (notably Anytus). The praise of Egypt, also but inconsistently undertaken by Polycrates, is understandable from the fact that both Cyprus and Athens were allies of Egypt (King Acoris) in the 380s; the renewed contacts between Athens and Egypt after 363 BCE (King Tachos) are obviously irrelevant here. The note on the behavior of the Spartans, *Busiris* 19–20, also points to the 380s. And *Busiris* fits in with Isocrates' earlier interests in fictitious culture and myth, also reflected in Helen (X), rather than with his engagement in contemporary politics, beginning with the Panegyricus (IV) of 380 BCE.

15. Isocrates' using Plato's *Apology* extensively in his *Antidosis* (XV) of 354 BCE is a good example of the slow movements in the 'dialogue' between Plato and Isocrates.

[157] Thus we may take it as a fairly well grounded hypothesis that Aristophanes in 392 BCE knew, and expected some in his audience to know, of a recent communistic and 'feministic' political manifesto by young Plato. The contents of this proposal corresponded to the summary in the *Timaeus*, and so it presumably represented the 'approximately two books' of Gellius, and the ideas to which Isocrates refers.[16]

It is quite possible, in my view rather probable, that Plato had originally presented his manifesto at an informal gathering, as a speech in his own name – not in the name of Socrates, though later the distinction between the two was naturally blurred. There is nothing to suggest that young Plato wrote only dialogues; on the contrary, the *Apology, Menexenus* and the extensive use of speeches in some dialogues point to an early familiarity with rhetoric. If the 'Proto-*Republic*' was a speech, it is even more understandable that Plato's ideas were soon abroad, and copies may have been immediately taken (cf. 'Lysias' in *Phaedrus*) whether he wanted it or not.[17]

[158]

I shall discuss below the additional information given by the *Seventh Letter*. First, however, it is fair to ask what other reflections there are, in 4th century sources, of Plato's Utopia or, in general, of his *Republic*.

The intra–Academic discussion of Plato's political theories is not easily traced until we come to the *Timaeus, Politicus*, and *Laws*. The somewhat ambiguous evidence of the *Apology, Gorgias, Menexenus* and *Theaetetus* will be considered below. A βασιλικὴ τέχνη is unexpectedly and humorously introduced at the center of the *Euthydemus* (291b), possibly with allusion to Isocrates.[18] Young men dreaming of power occur in several dialogues, including *Alcibiades* I and *Theages*. It looks, however, as if Plato were avoiding the theme of the Utopia in his written dialogues until it suddenly turns up in the *Timaeus*. Certainly this does not mean that *Timaeus* was written immediately after the *Republic*.

The opening of *Parmenides* seems to allude to *Republic* I, but I am not so sure[19] that the criticism of the theory of Forms applies to the *Republic* version of it. Even the *Politicus* does not demonstrably take account of a published version of the

---

16. For some further references and considerations, *see* Nails 1995: 114 ff.

17. The anecdote in Themistus (23.296ed) about the protreptic effect of the *Republic* on Plato's woman pupil Axiothea, rather applies to the 'Proto-*Republic*' if it is not just a redoubling of the story about the Gorgias and the Corinthian farmer (ibid., cf. Riginos 1976: 183 f.) which probably derives from Aristotle.

18 Since Isocrates the 'semi-politician' (305dc) is very probably alluded to at the end of the dialogue, one might think of the 'Cyprian Essays' (below). Cf. also 289d λογοποιοί: Antisthenes is not likely to be meant here.

19. Pace myself, above p. 306 and many others. The frame story of *Republic* I occurs in several variants, cf. below, n. 26

*Republic*: the myth of metals occurs at 269b ff. (271a ff.), but the treatment of, say, βασιλική τέχνη (259c ff., 277c ff.) and μίμησις has a slightly different basis (note 301c, 303a), and the attitude to legislation (293e ff,) corresponds to that of the *Laws* without reference to the Utopia. The various kinds of government (291c ff.) are dealt with in a manner very different from the *Republic*. Strictly speaking, the *Laws* does not presuppose the existence of a written *Republic*, either; but it is oriented to Plato's Utopian City in very many ways, most explicitly in the chapter on ideal communism which suits gods, not men (V 739b ff.). At any rate, the existence of the *Republic* as a written text soon after Plato's death cannot be doubted.

Several of Plato's younger associates took up the theory and practice of lawgiving, but as far as we know only Aristotle took up the theme of the communistic Utopia.[20] In his *Politics*, Aristotle criticizes Plato's Utopian proposals extensively, comparing them to the *Laws* and, somewhat unfairly, presenting both as Plato's political teachings without taking account of his philosophical motivations. He has seen a written version of the *Republic*, though obviously it was not a favorite text with him.[21] For his criticism, he may have used the epitome of Plato's Πολιτεία in two (!) books which belonged to his and Theophrastus' library (Diog. L. V 22, 43).[22]

Among the pupils of Aristotle, notably Theophrastus, Dicaearchus and Aristoxenus studied the theory of constitutions in the footsteps of their master but, as far as we can see, with no direct reference to Plato. We are now in the vicinity of Zeno the Stoic to whom we shall return presently.

But what about the early extra-Academic discussion of the *Republic*? After all, should we not expect the early Utopia and the monumental final work to have left more marks in contemporary debate, than those we have seen so far? A scrutiny of our sources gives a meager result which is, however, not without some interest.

---

20. For Aristotle, *see* the next note. Some Ps.-Platonic *Letters* (notably VIII) refer to lawgiving, and several of Plato's pupils wrote on political theory and laws, apparently developing themes of the Platonic Laws. Xenocrates also wrote on Kingship (for Alexander the Great). The only philosopher known to have written a commentary or tract on Plato's *Republic*, apart from Aristotle and before the late Hellenistic period, is Clearchos of Soloi, a pupil of Aristotle (cf. Dörrie-Baltes III 1993: 44 f., 202 ff.); but his main interests were the Line and the Nuptial Number.

21. In Book II of the *Politics*, Aristotle almost entirely avoids the philosophical aspects of the *Republic*, though occasional echoes of Books VIII–IX of the latter suggest that he knows the final version (and note τὸ κομψόν II 1265a 12). Elsewhere, he rarely refers to this work (cf. Bonitz.' Index). The most interesting quotations, apart from the discussion in the *Politics*, are two passages in *EN* (I 1095a31, V 1132a20 ff.) alluding to the Divided Line, and a passage in the *Rhetorics* (III 1406b32 ff.) where three examples of Platonic similes are given, from *Republic* V, VI, and X.

22. Was this a text of the 'Proto-*Republic*' which the source of Gellius had in mind? No wonder antiquity knew several incipits for the *Republic* (cf. Thesleff above, p. 232 and below, n. 26). Theophrastus also wrote 'On the Best Constitution,' in addition to works on kingship and laws, but he certainly did not develop Plato's utopian ideas any more than Aristotle did. For Clearchos, *see* n. 20, for Aristoxenus n. 30.

[159] Disregarding Xenophon, the only 'minor Socratic' of relevance here is Antisthenes.²³ He wrote several essays or dialogues about social ethics and also [160] kingdom, βασιλεία. Without going into the vexed details of reconstruction and chronology, it can be safely stated that Antisthenes' mythic heroes, Herakles and Cyrus the Great, stand very far from Plato's Philosopher-King, and also that his Proto-Cynic ideals of ἐγκράτετα, αὐτάρκεια, τὰ αὑτοῦ πράττειν, σωφροσύνη, and δικαιοσύνη, may at most have given impulses to his younger contemporary Plato's conception of the Best City and the Best Man. Antisthenes seems to have known the tradition about the Four Speeches of Pythagoras with their emphasis on the internal harmony and loyalty of a Pythagorean city and the active role of women. Antisthenes 'the dog' may figure in a playful context in the *Republic* (II 376ab), and his Laconism may be reflected in certain traits of Plato's version of the Guardians of the Best City.²⁴ Plato, however, was no admirer of Spartan brutality. And, again, the education and particularly the μαθήματα of the philosophers, so essential to Plato, meant little or nothing to Antisthenes. On the other hand, there is no direct trace of an Antisthenean polemic against Plato's political theory, either. Although Plato put more emphasis on φιλοσοφία than Antisthenes was inclined to do, perhaps the fact is that his 'Proto-*Republic*' was basically so close to Antisthenes' own idea of the Just City that the latter found no reason to laugh, with Aristophanes, at the politics of young Σάθων. This might explain the character of the allusions to Antisthenes in the *Ecclesiazusae*. Probably Antisthenes never saw the final *Republic*.

Later, however, Plato's Utopia provoked a sarcastically exaggerated answer from Diogenes of Sinope, the Cynic. The role of Diogenes as an intermediate link between the Πολιτεῖαι of Plato and Zeno the Stoic has been very seldom noted. To be sure, the authenticity of the fragments of Diogenes' Πολιτεία in the recently restored and reinterpreted Herculaneum papyri is under debate.²⁵ [161] Assuming that the papyrus reports at least an authentic tradition about what Diogenes had said, if not the original wording, and whatever backing Diogenes had found in Antisthenes, it would seem that one of his sources of inspiration was Plato. Partly like Zeno after him, Diogenes appears to have argued for radical

---

23. See G. Giannantoni's extensive collection of material and references in his *Socraticorum Reliquiae* (with some additions in *SSR*); cf. above, n.10. Several of the titles attributed to Antisthenes (and also Aeschines, Simon, and Simmias) suggest themes found in the *Republic,* but except for myths there is nothing to point to Utopian contents. Possibly it was Antisthenes who first introduced the idea of an Ideal King into philosophy (cf. Diog. L. VI 15); the idea was elaborated in different ways by Xenophon, Isocrates, Plato and his pupils, and the Stoics.

24. Cf. above, n. 10. For Antisthenes 'the dog,' cf. Eubulus fr. 85 KA.

25. For the earlier discussion, *see* Ferguson 1975: 95. Andria-Dorandi's text of Philodemus' account (II 1983: 466–468, cf. III 1985: 416 f., 487–494) and then in *SSR*. Dorandi (following Höistad 1948) defends the authenticity of Diogenes' *Politeia* in Goulet-Cazé and R. Goulet (eds) 1993: 57–68. I am inclined to take the Πολιτεία to be a Hellenistic 'reconstruction' of authentic traditions, presumably on the basis of Zeno's account. Cf. the platonizing 'reconstructions' of early Pythagorean ideas in the Hellenistic Pseudo-Pythagorean texts (ed. Thesleff 1965). But the question requires further scrutiny.

communism, equality of the sexes, free love, and community of children; and [161]
he accepted incest, masturbation in public, cannibalism, and total anarchy in the
name of concord, peace, and love. This Arch-Cynic Utopia meant an extremist
radicalization of some of Plato's ideas, but at the same time a pointed rejection of
his basic premises: the notion of a city state with stable institutions, the division
into classes and trades, and above all, the education and social responsibility
of the Leaders, the philosophers. We cannot of course determine the degree of
ironically sarcastic thoughtplay in Diogenes' proposals; at least Zeno seems to
have found serious logic in them. More humorously than Zeno, and probably
inspired by Diogenes, Krates the Cynic (Diog. L. VI 85) wrote a satirical poem
about his bag, Πήρη, as representing a chaotic cosmopolitan paradise, the only
πόλις needed. There is no evidence that the Cynics had ever bothered to read
anything by Plato. Presumably Diogenes took a stand on the ideas orally dis-
seminated about the early Utopia.

Xenophon rather clearly alludes to some Platonic dialogues, and the *Republic* is sometimes automatically counted among these. However, apart from the
'Proto-*Republic*' story related by Gellius, and except some possible reminiscences
of Book I, the alleged traces of the *Republic* in Xenophon's works disappear on
closer scrutiny.[26]

Plato's relations with Isocrates is another much-discussed issue. Like Anti- [162]
sthenes, Isocrates was some ten years Plato's senior. He was Plato's only serious rival as an educator of an intellectual elite. And he insisted on calling his
educational programme φιλοσοφία, which must have irritated Plato ever since
Isocrates had begun his regular teaching in Athens in the late 390s. 'Right philosophy' meant something different to Plato (below). It is well known that Isocrates
and Plato allude to each other in various connections, though most of the details
are controversial; the references are seldom (and never on Isocrates' part) explicitly clear, and Plato maintains an ironical distance. However, the controversies

---

26. *Republic* I is, at any rate, to be distinguished from the 'Proto-*Republic*', and there are several indications of the existence of an earlier version of it as a separate dialogue (pace Kahn
1993: 131–142) before it became incorporated with the final work. The opening of Xenophon's
*Symposium* seems to allude to the former, and reminiscences of it seem to occur in *Memorabilia*
IV 4 (cf. also the openings of Plato's *Symposium* and *Parmenides*), unless a common source (Antisthenes?) lies behind all this. Elsewhere Xenophon does not operate with ideas reminiscent of the
*Republic*, hardly even in the women chapter of his Spartan Constitution (I 3–10, and certainly not
in the last chapter on Kings, XV). The discussion of political leadership in *Memorabilia* III 6–7 is
closer to *Alcibiades* I (or *Theages*), though Socrates' partners are Glaucon and Charmides respectively. The βασιλική τέχνη at IV 2.11 suggests the *Euthydemus*, though the partner of Socrates is
Euthydemus, son of Diocles, not the erist. The remarks on the decline of Athens at III 5.13–17
and on the misery of tyrants at IV 2.38 f. are commonplaces; cf. the theme of the Hiero (where, at
10.1–8, the φύλακες occur as a kind of Secret Service in the manner of *Laws* VI 758a ff. rather than
of the *Republic*). A passage on μίμησις in art, *Memorabilia* III 10, surely need not be a loan from the
text of our *Republic*. And when, in IV 6, Xenophon makes an evident attempt to turn 'philosophical,' τὸ ἀγαθόν is defined as τὸ ὠφέλιμον (8) and καλόν as χρήσιμον (9), and the presentation of
the 'hypothetical method' (13–14) has nothing in common with *Republic* VI. In fact, as has been
often noted, Xenophon often appears to represent an earlier 'Socratic' position than Plato.

[162] between the two have probably been very much exaggerated by later critics. It seems that Isocrates in addition to Plato's early Utopia refers at least to the *Gorgias* and *Phaedrus*, and in his old age he was well acquainted with Plato's *Apology*. Naturally it was rhetoric, not dialectic, that interested him. At the time when he wrote the *Busiris*, he saw in Plato an ally against the detractors of 'philosophy.'[27] And when Plato had founded the Academy, the two operated on very different levels. If, however, Isocrates had known the final *Republic*, he might be expected to have referred to it in his three 'Cyprian Essays' from about 370 BCE, Ad Nicoclem (II), Nicocles (III), and Euagoras (IX), which all deal with the best constitution and the education of the King. Indeed, it is usually taken for granted that Isocrates has the *Republic* in view here. I find this extremely unlikely and all the supposed allusions easy to explain otherwise.[28] I am prepared to infer that Isocrates, at this

[163] stage, knew only the 'Proto-*Republic*' which did not consider Kingship at all, but regarded the philosophers as a class. The specific issues of Plato's Utopia such as communism were of course totally irrelevant in this Cyprian context. As a matter of fact, there are no clear allusions to the *Republic* complex in any of Isocrates' writings from the 370s, 360s, or even the 350s. This may have some bearing on the dating of the final *Republic*. Only in his open letter to Philip II, written in 346 when Isocrates was ninety and Plato was dead, he may be thinking of the *Republic* when declaring that empty eulogies of a King (such as others have written) are as useless as are the Νόμοι and Πολιτεῖαι written by the sophists.[29]

But there had certainly been other sophists around who 'wrote' Πολιτεῖαι: Hippodamus, Phaleas, and perhaps Protagoras among them.[30] In Plato's *Protagoras*,

---

27. Cf. above, n. 14. Isocrates is even prepared to allow for μαθήματα in education (23) which he otherwise rather rejects (*see* especially *Antidosis* 261 ff.).

28. The most comprehensive discussions of the relations of Isocrates and Plato are by Ries (1959) and Eucken (1983, above n. 14). Though Eucken often corrects Ries, he is still too ready to see marks of a 'dialogue' or even polemics between Isocrates and his contemporaries. He is probably right in inferring (5 ff., 251 f., 269) that Isocrates' first pamphlet against rival schools, Adversus Sophistas (XIII) of about 390 BCE, considers the Socratics as a group where Antisthenes stands out but where Plato as yet plays no distinct part; indeed, Isocrates had no specific reasons to refer to Plato in this context (cf. XIII 9–10) even if he knew the 'Proto-*Republic*'. The same seems to me to apply to the Helen (X) where the opening criticism hardly includes Plato in particular. Occasional echoes of *Gorgias* and *Phaedrus* seem to occur later, and Plato's *Apology* is clearly being used in the *Apodosis* (XV, a late work), without a trace of criticism.—The alleged parallels of the 'Cyprian Essays' with the *Republic* (cf. Eucken 1983: 216–268), such as μετέχειν τῶν ἰδεῶν in connection with ἀρεταί (III 29–30), may suggest a vague acquaintance with Academic terminology, but nothing more. It is typical of this line of arguing that Isocrates' praise of τυραννίς as τὸ κάλλιστον τῶν ὄντων (IX 40, Eucken 268) is considered as polemic against Plato's metaphysical Form of the Good and his negative view of the tyrant.

29. V 12. Isocrates' use of the word σοφιστής is sometimes very imprecise, e.g. XV 268. Allusions to Plato's *Laws* seem to occur in the Panathenaicus (XII) of 339 BCE, cf. Eucken 1983: 42 ff. and elsewhere.

30. Aristoxenus, who himself wrote on constitutions, is reported (Diog. L. III 37, fr. 67 We.) to have found the essentials of the *Republic* (i.e. the Utopia?) in Protagoras' Ἀντιλογικά; possibly Aristoxenus saw traces of radical ideas which he interpreted in his slanderous manner, anti-Platonically. But there was a dialogue attributed to Criton, named Πρωταγόρας ἢ Πολιτικός (Diog. L. II 121).

the sophist presents the growth of human society where the τέχναι have an essential function (especially 322b–e): though most critics think that Plato had not 'yet' conceived *Republic* II, I would insist that the opposite might as well be true. At any rate we are far from Plato's Utopia here. Again, of a more 'pythagorizing' type is the Pseud-Epicharmean Πολιτεία in trochaic tetrameters said to have been written by the musician Chrysogonus (mid-4th century):[31] in the two brief fragments we have, it is emphasized that mathematics and θεῖος λόγος direct a good life and good τέχναι. Somewhat similarly (though not without some allusive play) Socrates asserts towards the end of *Protagoras* (356e) that σωτηρία τοῦ βίου depends on μετρητική; cf, also the 'nuptial number' in *Republic* VIII (546a–547a). Such pythagorizing sophistry, however, has no direct bearing on Plato's Utopia, nor have the other remains of sophistic literature that we know of.[32]

The fragments of Middle Comedy might also be expected to shed some light on the possible discussion of the *Republic*. We have more than 20 fragments, many of them from Alexis, in which Plato and his Academy are mentioned or certainly alluded to. Hellenistic critics (and detractors) have evidently been looking for such references, so the material is likely to cover the ground fairly well. Probably or possibly the *Phaedrus, Gorgias, Phaedo* and *Symposium* were known.[33] It is therefore noteworthy that the comedians do not seem to make fun of Plato's monumental *Republic*, after Aristophanes had used the Utopia for his own ends in his *Ecclesiazusae*. Amphis (fr. 8 KA) and Alexis (41–42) wrote plays called Γυναικοκρατία, but they seem to link up with Aristophanes, not (at least not directly) with Plato: presumably the later examiners of comedy would have notified it if Plato had figured here (since Plato was known to be a target of Middle Comedy). However, there was a saying, Πλάτωνος ἀγαθόν, denoting something entirely obscure or unattainable. The saying is found e.g. in Amphis (6) and Alexis (98), both mid-4th century comedians, and somewhat, later in Philippides (6). Does this indicate, as many critics have thought, that Book VI of the *Republic* was known to the Athenian public? Hardly. It is more natural to assume that the saying originated in rumours about Academic discussions, and especially in Plato's notorious lecture 'On the Good.'[34] Plato's Sun, Line, or Cave did not become slogans, nor indeed did Plato the feminist or Plato the Ὁμηρομάστιξ. Perhaps we ought to accept as a fact that Plato's dialogues were not so widely read and discussed by his contemporaries, as is often believed.

---

31. Vors. 23 B 56 57 DK; cf. *Epinomis* 977c–978a. On the whole, the Pseud-Epicharmea seem to be influenced by Academic thought rather than vice versa.

32. Cf. Kerferd 1981: 139, 162.

33. For *Phaedrus*, cf. Alexis fr. 20 KA, 247–248, Eubulus 20, Philemon 126, Philyllius 20, Timocles 6, Timotheus 2 (but the 'winged Eros' of course occurs in art too); *Gorgias*, Antiphanes 198, Philetaerus 17; *Phaedo*, Kratinus J:r 10, Theopompus 16 (or an allusion to 'On the Good'?); *Symposium*, Alexis 247–248, Anaxandrides 62, Strattis 27–33. Further possible allusions include the *Laws* (VI 761c) in Antiphanes 298. Unfortunately Plato's βιβλίον ἐμβρόντητον which is "like pepper" (Ophelion 3) cannot be identified. See below, p. 547.

34. For K. Gaiser's (1980) interpretation of 'On the Good' and arguments for regarding it as a deliberate challenge of the Athenian public, see above p. 485 f. and Thesleff 1993: 39 f. More remote allusions to Plato's ἀγαθόν seem to occur in Clearchus 3 KA and Philemon 74.

[165] But the silence of our sources in the case of Plato's *Republic* may have a particular bearing on the question of his public relations.

⸻ ◯ ⸻

It has appeared so far that the signs we have, from the first half of the 4th century, of Plato's Utopia being known and discussed outside the Academy—Aristophanes' *Ecclesiazusae*, Isocrates' *Busiris*, the source used by Gellius, probably Plato's Timaeus, and Diogenes of Sinope – all point to an early version of the *Republic*. Indeed, there are no clear indications of the existence of the final work before, say, 350 BCE.

In the light of these facts, the picture of Plato's early activities which is given in the opening part of the *Seventh Letter* is quite interesting. It is of little consequence if these are or are not Plato's ipsissima verba (I think they are), since the writer is obviously well informed and expects his readers to know various specific circumstances; and his point is to defend Plato's and Dion's intentions and undertakings in Syracuse, and to state the fact that there is no easy short cut to philosophy – taking for granted that Plato had a philosophy of his own already in the 390s. The description of the events before the first voyage to Sicily (in 388 BCE) amounts to the statement (327a) that Plato began to instruct Dion out of his well-grounded conviction that only *true* philosophy will reform human life and society. This philosophical education brought Dion into conflict with Italian and Sicilian practice (327b), which contributes to explaining the unfortunate happenings after the death of Dionysius I (in 367 BCE).

The review of events between ca. 407 and 388 BCE (324b–326e) has a very reliable ring, and the omissions may be intentional. Plato's political hopes and frustrations, the shock he felt at the trial and death of Socrates, and his 'dizziness' looking from outside at the shortcomings of all existing types of government, are presented in a vivid, personal, and convincing manner. And as in *Gorgias* (512c ff.), but unlike the basic conception in the final *Republic*, Plato's viewpoint is principally Athenian.

[166] In that situation (i.e. in the late 390s), says Plato, he came to the conviction that only a "marvelous arrangement of luck" could change things: "And I felt compelled to declare, while recommending right philosophy, that it is by this that one is enabled to discern all political and individual justice; so evil will not cease from the classes of mankind until the class of those who are right and true philosophers attain political leadership, or else the class of those who hold power in the cities becomes by some divine dispensation really philosophic" (326ab, Bury's translation).

It is usually thought that the *Letter* simply refers to the famous passage in Book V (473d) of our *Republic*, at the end of the chapter on women, equality and the Just State, with the sole difference that the *Letter* speaks of the philosophers as a class, whereas Socrates in the *Republic* speaks of Philosopher-Kings (introduced just before, at 473b). Though the *Letter* appears to echo some of the wording in

*Republic* V, it is more natural to infer that the *Letter* actually reports what was said in Plato's early Utopia. A theory of Philosopher-Guardians as a class (γένος), the elite of the Guardians of the Ideal City, would better suit Plato's thought before he met Dion, than a theory of Philosopher-Kings: and indeed, what we read in our Republic up to that crucial passage,[35] as in *Timaeus*, and in Aristophanes and Isocrates, is a theory of the former kind. The *Letter* (note 326d) also implies that Plato's deliberations about the degeneration of constitutions (i.e. what we read in Books VIII-IX of our *Republic*) were caused by his experiences in the West.

Moreover, the curious formulation "I was forced" or "compelled to declare" (326a5) suits the reluctance of a young moralist presenting a very odd theory, as well as it may appear to suit the reluctance of old Socrates at *Republic* V 472a–474b. But the latter passage is rather clearly written post festum: Plato knows, and expects his readers to know, the surge of doubt and laughter that the proposal has already awakened. After all, the λέγειν ἠναγκάσθην and its context in the *Letter* suggest an oral declaration by Plato in a situation of political and moral frustration, more naturally than it applies to the fictitious situation in which Socrates speaks, though indeed under some pressure (cf. notably 472a, 473c).

What, then, does the ὀρθὴ φιλοσοφία involve which the *Letter* says Plato had been "recommending" or "praising"? The *Letter* seems to state that Plato felt bound to put forth his thesis of the philosophers' rule, at the time and as the consequence of his arguing for right philosophy as the only way to a right conception of justice.[36] On a superficial reading, and assuming that the writer of the *Letter* expresses himself confusedly besides being confused about chronology, one might take the 'recommendation' of right philosophy to refer to the subsequent central books of the *Republic* (end of V to VII). Up to the crucial passage 473cd, no such recommendation or praise has occurred in the latter.[37] However, why not trust the *Letter*?

o-o-o- O -o-o-o-

---

35. At *Republic* III 414b the φύλακες παντελεῖς (in plural) are distinguished from the ἐπίκουροι, but Kings come in at V 473b (ἑνός-δυοῖν – ὅτι ὀλιγίστων). In the *Letter*, the emphasis on Plato's theoretical (σκοπῶν 325e, περιμένειν 326a) engagement in politics, is surely meant as a contrast to the eventual πράττειν that he admits he recommended to Dion (327a).

36. In the *Letter* (326a6), the present participle ἐπαινῶν points to a situation (caused by the political development in Athens) where arguments about the nature of philosophy necessitated arguments about the derivation from philosophy of a theory of justice. For the use of this verb in debates, cf. *Republic* II 358d. Plato seems to be referring to a more general discussion in early 4th century Athens about the status of philosophy, a discussion where Plato had reason to profile himself, not only in relation to people like Polycrates, Thrasymachus, or 'Callicles,' but also perhaps against the loose conception of φιλοσοφία as advocated by Isocrates (but cf. above, n. 13).

37. The only contexts where philosophy is mentioned in our text of the *Republic*, before the rather unexpected pronouncement at V 473cd, are the discussion of the double 'dog like' nature of Philosopher-Guardians in Books II (374e 376c) and III (410c–412a, *Timaeus* 17d–18a), a remark

[167] Those who are prepared to take a critical distance from the traditional view of Plato's philosophical development[38] will find a particular challenge in the question what Plato meant by philosophy in the 390s.

Let us assume (as I am sure we have to) that Plato did *not* begin his philosophic career as a writer of short, playfully aporetic dialogues in the so-called Socratic manner, trying to define what virtue is. Let us assume that the developmentalist picture of Plato gradually abandoning Socratic openness, betraying [168] his Socratic legacy, and becoming a metaphysician and totalitarian only after his experiences in the West, is *totally misleading*. Let us assume that the 'Socratic' dialogues, as we have them, were composed after the founding of the Academy, and that they have other purposes than to depict accurately the ways Socrates reasoned.[39] Let us assume, instead, that Plato began as an intensely committed moralist with 'metaphysical' inclinations, however deep his admiration was of the Socratic method.

The *Apology* (though also an apology of the Socratics and of Plato himself) of course focuses on what Plato thought the historical Socrates has said (or meant) in 399, and here φιλοσοφία implies mainly a Socratic examination of the opinion of others to reach the truth and to abandon the untrue (cf. 23d, 28e, 29cd); this is an essential aspect of what Plato later called 'dialectic' (below). But even here the social responsibility of the philosopher's criticism is emphasized, and an occasional hint of the need of a theory of the State is given (36c). More specifically, the issue of τὸ δίκαιον is introduced in what we know as Book I of the *Republic*. Whenever this book (the *Thrasymachus*) may have taken definite shape,[40] it is likely to illustrate the 'dialectic' moves around the definition of justice which occurred in the Socratic circle: witness the *Clitopho* and several of the writings of Antisthenes. Plato's early fascination by geometry is intimated by Theaetetus 147c–148c where the 'Younger Socrates' appears to stand for young Plato.[41] Moreover, the *Gorgias* certainly has its roots in the 390s, though it probably (like the *Theaetetus*) received its present form later.[42] Here the question of right and wrong is one of the basic themes, and the conflict between philosophy and political rhetoric is envisaged, partly, in rhetorical terms; but some metaphysical aspects are also to be observed, notably in the very pregnant statement 507c–508c. *Gorgias* probably illustrates what Plato meant by 'right philosophy' at the time

---

on the detraction of philosophy (III 407c), and a remark in passing on philosophical women (V 456a). The introduction of the Form of Justice at V 472c (with 'αὐτό terminology') includes no 'praise.' In the final work, the ἀληθινὴ φιλοσοφία is only gradually introduced (cf. VI 487a ff., VII 521 bc).

38. The problems of Platonic chronology are now in a flux: *see* my studies above and 1989, J. A. Howland 1991: 189–214, Nails 1995 and G. A. Press 1996: 511 f

39. This is one of my basic theses.

40. For the 'separatist' view and a very tentative dating, *see* above, 256 ff.; 1989, 11 n. 36, 14 f.; above, n. 26.

41. *See* Jatakari 1990: 29–45.

42. References above, 309 f. and in Thesleff 1989, 7 n. 28.

of his presentation of the Utopia: a fearless 'dialectic' search into the ontological (cosmic, metaphysical) foundations of ethics, perhaps with an ironical sideglance at Isocrates' non-committal conception of 'philosophy,' but with its pathos directed against influential anti-intellectualists such as Anytus (cf. the *Apology*, also *Meno*). The *Phaedo*, where the importance of ὀρθὴ φιλοσοφία and its metaphysical dimension is made explicit,[43] hardly reflects as such Plato's early thought; but the account of Socrates' search for metaphysical standards (96a–100a) rather naturally applies to young Plato, not to the historical Socrates. We may safely assume that Plato's own philosophy had begun to take shape in the 390s.

To Plato, dialectic seems always to mean philosopher-conducted dialogic pushes and moves, preferably in the form of questioning and answering.[44] The *Republic* does not offer much illustration of strict dialectic (after Book I); but Plato presumably regarded a philosopher's thesis put forward in a context of criticism and controversy or a push from hypotheses towards ἀνυπόθετα (*Republic* VI 510b, 511b) as 'dialectic' to all intents and purposes. If the Utopia of the final *Republic* is such a move (explicitly provoked as it is by Thrasymachus and Plato's brothers), the early Utopia may well have been 'dialectic' in the same sense (though we do not know exactly who provoked it). However, there is more of philosophy in it.

At a first glance, the Utopia of the 'Proto-*Republic*' does not look particularly philosophic. Does Aristophanes call it a 'philosophical' scheme simply because it was set forth by a philosopher, as Isocrates also seems to imply? Or did Plato himself present it as 'philosophy'? The latter does make better sense, as we shall see.

It is true that the Spartan institutions provided some parallels or even models for Plato. But his Spartan sympathies were ambivalent.[45] Strict equality and loyalty on the top level of society among the ὅμοιοι (*pares*, 'peers') is a very ancient idea found all over the world, and it must have been known as a traditional ideal in Athens too. Slogans such as 'justice for all,' ἰσονομία, or ὁμόνοια belonged to the political debate of classical Athens. Community of property had been proposed by Phaleas. Plato, however, went much farther than any Greeks had ever gone in theory or practice. The 'Proto-*Republic*' is even less likely to have been intended as a political pamphlet or blueprint than the final *Republic* was, however revolutionary its thoughts may have looked. Plato cannot have been so naive, even as a young man, as to believe in its implementation as such. And the 'Proto-*Republic*' referred to classes only, not to a Philosopher-King or anybody else who might start a coup d'état: who was supposed to do something for the implementation?

---

43. E.g. 64a ff., 68c ff., 78b ff., 84b. The 'School of Tübingen' tends to emphasize the esoteric traits in Plato's 'right philosophy' more than I am prepared to do for this early stage.
44. I have argued this in a contribution to G. A. Press (ed.) 2000: 53 ff.
45. *See* Tigerstedt 1965: 244 ff., who however slightly overrates Plato's Spartan sympathies. Plato certainly agreed with Isocrates in despising Spartan brutality. In *Protagoras* 342c–343b we find ironical play with Spartan anti-intellectualism.

[170] 'Socrates,' the only true politician (*Gorgias* 521d)? Or those who follow up Socrates' mission (*Apology* 39cd)? No, the Utopia sounds like pure theory. And it was not just a radicalization of current ideas for improvement of society, whether playful or not. It is in fact arguable that Plato's early Utopia, seen in the light of the *Seventh Letter* (and also the *Ecclesiazusae*), was what the Utopia purports to be in the final *Republic*: a theory of ideal justice that arose from a moral indignation at all kinds of selfishness and brutality, from a dissatisfaction with all existing forms of government, and from a search for a philosophic framework for true social ethics. The Utopia tells us what the Ideal City *ought* to be *if* it is constructed in accordance with what Plato regarded as fundamental philosophical premises. It is only from this perspective that the radicalism of its solutions become really understandable.

In the final work, the foundations of Plato's theory of the Ideal City appear as ethical, psychological and educational considerations (especially in Book IV and from the latter part of Book VII onwards) and as glimpses of certain rather complicated metaphysical truths at the important center, from the latter part of Book V to the first part of Book VII, with τὸ ἀγαθόν, the μέγιστον μάθημα as the pivot (VI 505a). The Ideal City is a manifestation of the Good and other ideal qualities such as the cardinal virtues, unity, sameness, and stability; and the philosopher-leaders' methods of reaching the appropriate knowledge of these ideal qualities is a prerequisite for the establishment of the Ideal City.[46] These methods are described as μαθήματα culminating in 'dialectic' (VII 531c ff.). But the same conception would seem to work in the early Utopia, though with far less elaboration of detail. The pointedly ethical excellence of the ruling class is based on

[171] the selection of suitable individuals[47] and on philosophy. The details of this philosophy remain rather unspecified in our sources. It is said to imply leniency towards 'natural friends' (*Timaeus* 17d, cf. *Ecclesiazusae*)[48] and complete devotion to ἀρετή (*Timaeus* 18b, *Busiris* 21, 23), φρόνησις (*Busiris* 21, cf. *Ecclesiazusae*), ascetic responsibility and σχολή from other tasks (*Timaeus* 18b, *Busiris* 21); and Isocrates states (*Busiris* 22), almost certainly by inference from Plato, that the philosophy of the ruling class includes νομοθετῆσαι and τὴν φύσιν τῶν ὄντων ζητῆσαι. The education of the future Guardians is essential (*Timaeus* 18a, *Busiris* 23 and 38–43, also Gellius). We may take it that the early Utopia reserved γυμναστική (for obvious reasons substituted by medicine in *Busiris*), μουσική and relevant μαθήματα, (ἀστρολογία, λογισμός, γεωμετρία according to Isocrates) for the training of all Guardians before the differentiation of the Soldiers from the Leaders (cf. *Republic* III 414ab; Isocrates 15–16 makes King Busiris separate the three main classes, priests, soldiers and laborers, from the start). Furthermore, admitting that Plato's early Utopia is likely to have taken for granted a search into the φύσις τῶν ὄντων

---

46. The application of the theory of the tripartite soul to the theory of society implies that a clear distinction is made between the two classes of Guardians.

47. Their character is a matter of φύσις not strictly inherited, since there is a certain social mobility (*Timaeus* 19a); the new genealogical myth, the myth of metals (III 414a–d), is a ψεῦδος for soothing and persuading, whether it belonged to the early Utopia or not.

48. Cf. the Isocratic ideal of humanity; also *Busiris* 20, and *Ecclesiazusae*.

and μαθήματα as parts of the philosophical pursuits of the Guardians, the very [171] prominent principles of unity, specialization and balance between unequals (in particular the ὁμόνοια and mutual understanding between the rulers and the ruled) can in fact be explained as rooted in Platos philosophical ontology: Unity, Sameness and Stability versus Plurality, Difference and Change can be taken as covertly basic ideas in the early Utopia.

I would see here an early reflection of what I have elsewhere called Plato's 'two-level model.'[49] This is not the place to go into the details. A few points have to be emphasized, however. I am careful to note that the model cannot, at any stage, have been a fixed or systematically formulated doctrine. It was rather an intuitive 'vision' of a two-level universe, a frame for thinking and understanding the nature of things, a vision that had taken shape in Plato's mind not long after the death of Socrates, if not before. It can be naturally derived from Presocratic thought, Socrates' search for unchanging definitions, and mathematical truths.[50] [172] Its constituents are pairs of contrast, such as one/many, same/different, stability/change, invisible/visible, divine/human, intellect/senses, truth/appearance, where the contrasts are not felt to be polar opposites, but where the first term is conceived as better, more important, leading, and in all respects primary in relation to the second, both main levels yet being necessary parts of a 'harmoniously' constructed whole (as are the συστοιχίαι in Pythagorean metaphysics).[51] Such a two-level vision can actually be traced as a background in all Platonic dialogues. As I see it, the theory of Forms, the μέγιστα γένη of the late dialogues, and the pythagorizing First Principles of the ἄγραφα δόγματα, are due to secondary elaborations of this model.

This is what Plato's 'right philosophy' very probably comprised. And if applied to the problem of the Best State (and its cosmic paradigm) and to justice in human society and the individual, Plato's model would rather naturally produce something like the basic pattern we seem to have in the 'Proto-*Republic*': the upper level of society manifesting unity, stability and theoretical knowledge, the lower level representing plurality and practical skill, everybody specializing and yet feeling bound together and acting for the benefit of the whole. The theory of the ascetic, altruistic Philosopher-Guardians as a united and 'communistic' ruling class, contrasted to the variety of the lower classes, can be best explained against the background of this model.[52]

---

49. *See* above, p. 387 ff.
50. For the early (!) death of Theaitetos and Plato's early geometrical interests, *see* my notes p. 509 ff.
51. Aristotle *Met.* A 986ab, *EN* 1096b, 1106b29, etc.
52. In addition to the all-pervading notions of Unity, Stability and Knowledge (on the upper level of society), note e.g. the double nature of the Philosopher-Guardians (yet undifferentiated from Soldiers. *Republic* II 374e ff., etc.): a philosopher (i.e. dialectician) is able to recognize and reject. What is known and φίλον is of the class of the 'same'; and philosophy is always about τὰ αὐτά, as Socrates remarks in a pregnant context in *Gorgias* (482ab, misunderstood by ordinary Athenians, cf. *Gorgias* 490e, *Symposium* 221e; Xenophon, *Memorabilia* IV 4.6). The fact that there is no sign of political or social utopianism in the *Apology* or *Gorgias* (or indeed in any

[172]    We need not feel shocked at the totalitarianism of such a theory, never applied and not really applicable to real life. Indeed, it bears the stamp of the youthfulness of its author.

[173]    ┈┈┈ ○ ┈┈┈

Thus I find it reasonable to assume that the Utopia was a manifestation of experimental dialectic, part of Plato's arguing for 'right philosophy' in the mid-390s. But the Utopia was no success. It aroused more laughter and skepticism than real understanding. Plato laid the sketch of his Best City aside, and avoided the theme for a long time. The *Apology* and the first version of the *Gorgias* perhaps took shape in this atmosphere of attack and disdain from many quarters. If (as seems very plausible) Plato travelled to the West in 388, after the death of his friend Theaitetos,[53] in the hope of learning more about Pythagorean institutions and philosophy, he came back enriched by rather different experiences. Above all, he had met Dion.

Now he definitely turned his back on Athenian politics: the *Menexenus* (its date in or soon after 387 is firm) reads as a funeral oration to Athenian chauvinism. With some grim irony, the speaker is Aspasia, and at the end there is a promise of more fine political λόγοι from her; but, to be sure, her role was soon taken over by another woman, Diotima. Does the 'feminism' of the Utopia figure in the background?

The Academy was being founded, in fact extra muros to keep a distance from the city. The activities of the Academy, the schooling and training of philosophers, and the writing of dialogues, absorbed Plato's time for the next twenty years. Issues of political theory were certainly ventilated, and the idea of a real Philosopher-King may have entered Plato's mind.[54] But it was not until the unexpected death of Dionysius I of Syracuse in 367, that the remote possibility of the implementation of at least a Second Best City seemed to present itself. Plato was summoned to assist Dion.

The character and design of the final *Republic*, its different layers, and the internal tensions in it,[55] are best explained by the hypothesis of an early

---

dialogue 'before' the *Republic* and *Timaeus*) obviously is no argument against the early date of the Utopia: Plato had reasons for avoiding this theme.

53. Cf. p. 173 ff. and above, n. 50.

54. Antisthenes seems to have introduced the idea of a Philosopher-King (cf. above, n. 23), but the King remains in a mythic disguise (cf. Isocrates' *Busiris* and Xenophon's *Cyropaedia*); in his 'Cyprian Essays', Isocrates applies the idea to contemporary politics. For Plato, it was Dion who symbolized something of the kind: cf, *Republic* VI 499b–d, 502a, *Phaedrus* 252c–e (*Philebus* 30cd, 33b). This gives a terminus post quem for *Republic* V 473b. The teachability of the ἀρετή of political leaders as a class is 'debated' e.g. in *Meno* (89b ff., 91a ff); in *Alcibiades* I it applies to a single leader.

55. For the tensions in the *Republic* interpreted as part of an overall design, see e.g. the widely different approaches of Reeve 1988, and P. W. Rose 1992. Some other recent critics tend to place the final *Republic* into the context of Plato's later 'cosmopolitan' thought, without arguing for specific

'Proto-*Republic*', followed by a long public silence on the issue. This silence may account for the lack of traditions about Plato's political and educational views being subject to further public criticism or mockery: it was the 'Proto-*Republic*' that, perhaps against Plato's wish, continued to awaken occasional interest. If I am right, the complex thought-play of the Utopia and its philosophic basis remained in the background of Plato's mind throughout his life, and its partial implementation became a source of frustration and rethinking. Perhaps it was this interference by practice that eventually—at certain inspired and/or desperate moments after 360—motivated the composition of the *Republic* as we have it: a monument of a theory of man and society at their Best, a theory never tested nor really testable, and a monument never meant to be 'published' outside the Academy.[56]

---

dates, e.g. Laks 1990: 209–229; Trampedach 1994. If the theory of the 'Proto-*Republic*' is accepted, the successive accumulation of the blocks of the final work, and the possible re-writing of large portions of the text, require renewed scrutiny from a post-developmentalist point of view. It is worth considering, for instance, how the theory of the tripartite soul was applied here (cf. above, n. 46); how Books IV and VIII–IX became connected; how the different versions of the theory of Forms took shape in Books V, VI and X; and how Plato's Sicilian experiences became reflected in the work (note the fact that Dion reached the age of fifty about 358 BCE; cf. VII 540a, often taken to refer to Plato's own age). *See* the preliminary observations, some of them very hypothetical, above, p. 285 ff., 331 ff.

56. It is almost always taken for granted that the *Republic* was meant for immediate publication. But was there a public for a work of this scope and of such refinement of thought, style, and composition? It is true that large portions read as if intended for a general audience, but then much would remain un-understandable, and the overall design would require the constant presence of well-informed commentators (an arrangement more natural for the shorter dialogues). The posthumous and more exoteric *Laws* became at any rate oriented towards this monument. What 'protreptic' and 'publication' might have meant, concretely, in Plato's environment is the underlying theme in many recent studies. The question is certainly worth detailed scrutiny.

# PLATO AND HIS PUBLIC[1]

The theme of this paper is based on an apparent paradox: Is it conceivable that Plato, one of the most influential philosophers ever, with obvious interests in society and public life, did not seek publicity himself?

First, the problem of orality. It is well known today that 4th century Greek authors still worked on the verge of orality, and the recent discussion of literacy vs. orality in ancient Greece has often included Plato. In the steps of Eric Havelock,[2] several scholars have claimed (but with very different emphasis) that some or all of the dialogues must have been orally presented or 'performed' in the first place, before the manuscript was copied and put in circulation as a written work. However, with Aristotle 'the Reader' (ὁ ἀναγνωστής, as he was called) the final step was taken to literate philosophy.

This general picture does not change if (with Douglas Kelly and others) one makes a rough distinction between 'public' and 'private' literature. Such authors who appear to address a closed audience in the first place, Xenophon and—to some extent—Isocrates among them, usually do have a more general public in view. And so is Plato said to have.[3] He differs, however. It seems that Plato did not even want to address a general public—not as a rule. Plato wrote for very specific audiences.

This would appear to be an extraordinary claim, at first sight. Are not at least the Socratic dialogues written for 'all of us,' as most Platonists seem to have loosely taken for granted even if they accept a limitation of the first audience? To take just three recent examples. Charles Kahn, who wants to save something of the old developmentalist interpretation of Plato, thinks that Plato was deliberately and 'proleptically' preparing his readers (i.e. the sophisticated part of the Athenian public) to accept more advanced pieces of philosophy; the 'early dialogues' serve this purpose. The Tübingen scholar Thomas Szlezák, who takes

---

1. This is a substantially revised version of a paper presented, at conferences in Finland, in Swedish (1999, published as Thesleff 2000, as Jørgen Mejer may recall) and English (2001, unpublished).
2. *See* Havelock 1963 (etc.) and 1982; cf. also Robb 1994.
3. *See*, e.g., Usener 1994; for Plato, *see* especially 190 ff.; 228f. More cautiously, Kelly 1996.

[289] it for granted that Plato's real philosophy was taught esoterically, insists that the dialogues were written 'for everybody.' And one of his antagonists, Joachim
[290] Dalfen, agrees on this single point: Plato wanted to be read and heard, since he wanted to influence ("weil er wirken wollte").[4] Such beliefs are in various ways misleading, in my view. I think we have to face the fact that Plato's philosophy, even in its written form, was not a public activity. And note: Beginning with the Milesians, Greek philosophers (contrary to 'sophists') had an esoteric bent, though individual thinkers such as Empedocles, Anaxagoras and Socrates blurred the picture.

Even the closest parallels to Plato's writings we have, the remains of the *Socratica Minora*, differ from Plato in several respects. The best known of them, Xenophon's *Socratic Dialogues*, seem to represent a general trend typical of all the *Minora*: direct or indirect praise of their hero, the consistently wise and virtuous Socrates; apology of him against contemporary slander; samples of the good advice (even in very practical matters) he gave to all who ask for it; and stimulating or entertaining anecdotes about him, or stories told by him. However odd as a person, he is a guru.

Plato was not the first to write Socratic dialogues.[5] At least Antisthenes had preceded Plato as a Socratic writer: Antisthenes had obvious ambitions to make a public figure himself and to influence his contemporaries, and he was by some ten years Plato's senior. Without entering here into the frustrating questions of the intertextual relationships of Antisthenes, Xenophon and Plato, I take it for granted that Plato, as the literary artist he was, wished not only to emulate but to write better and more interesting dialogues than the *Minores*. Though he had a more restricted public in view, he naturally chose for private literary communication the narrated (reported) dialogue which the *Minores* normally used. Narrated dialogues are easy to read prima vista. In five out of eight certainly authentic cases, Plato makes Socrates himself the narrator. This seems to have been the prevailing practice in Socratic literature (though Xenophon makes the report in his own name).

However—and this is an indisputable truth we have to face—Plato's Socrates is certainly not the type of a wise, old teacher and counselor, an example for the young, that the average Athenian of the Anytus category would have appreciated, or the idealized sage that Xenophon and probably even Antisthenes liked to introduce to the public. Consider the dialogue *Charmides*, to take just one example. In spite of its elegant setting, and its seemingly both playful and serious ἀπορίαι, the dialogue would hardly have functioned as an apology of Socrates and his circle, or even as protreptics to philosophy, if it had reached an unprepared general public who expected a positive answer to the simple

---

4. Kahn 1996; Szlezák 1993, first published in Italian, cf. Szlezák 1991: 51: "Platone scriveva per tutti"; Dalfen 1998: 79: "Platon wollte gelesen bzw. gehört werden, weil er wirken wollte."

5. *See* in general Vander Waerdt 1994; for the texts, *see* Giannantoni 1990.

question of what σωφροσύνη is (cf. the *Clitopho*), and who loathed the kind of people—Critias, Charmides and the rest—with whom Socrates is here on such friendly terms. On the contrary, if put as such into the hands of an ordinary Athenian citizen, it would rather have lessened than increased the popularity of its author—apparently a *Socrates redivivus* whose new *Phrontistêrion* perhaps just ought to be set on fire like the old one. We need not think of the general public only, but also and particularly of people of influence such as Callicles of the *Gorgias* who surely is meant to represent a common view when he declares (485A ff.) that it is ridiculous for a grown-up man to philosophize like Socrates, "hiding in a corner, whispering with three or four youngsters . . .". And Socrates admits he has to turn into a demagogue to make himself heard and understood by Callicles. He professes to do so in the *Gorgias*—as in the *Protagoras* he becomes a sophist. But in the *Charmides*, even an introductory excuse for his choice of company had not made Socrates' λόγος more palatable to people who agreed with Callicles, or with Strepsiades, the unfortunate father in Aristophanes' *Clouds*. Compare again with Xenophon's Socrates, a slightly odd person, but always politically and even socially correct, and always very comprehensible to ordinary readers.

All of Plato's dialogues, the narrated as well as the dramatic ones, include passages or sections which are simply not comprehensible without an apparatus of background knowledge of Socratic/Platonic philosophy. Or at least, such passages require the presence of somebody who is prepared to offer additional explication. Plato's Socrates is almost explicit on this point towards the end of *Phaedrus* (273e f., 275c ff., 278cd). This very obviously implies a situation of oral communication within a limited, chosen audience. Some mathematical passages require drawing of figures. And some of the dialogues require a close attention by the audience for hours, perhaps (as in the case of the *Republic*) for several successive days. There is some *ben trovato* truth in the malicious story (Diog. L. 3.37) that "when Plato read the dialogue 'On the Soul' [the *Phaedo*], Aristotle alone stayed to the end; the rest of the audience got up and went away."

Among Plato's dialogues, only the *Symposium* introduces a Socrates who meets all the expectations for a hero of philosophy, an intellectual of a morally faultless character, representing the ideals of all virtues, placed in the center of a splendid Athenian social occasion, in a brilliant literary setting, and indeed, for once revealing a clear and positive doctrine. The *Symposium* is both apologetic, laudatory, protreptic, and somehow constructive. To Charles Kahn,[6] the *Symposium* is Plato's first attempt to present his theory of Forms to a general Athenian readership who has been 'proleptically' prepared for it by earlier dialogues. Please note, however: The very idea of an exclusive mystery, brought forward and underlined in various ways, suggests that even the *Symposium* is addressed in the first place to listeners who know what to make of the initiation. But no

---

6. Kahn 1996: 329 ff.

[292] doubt the dialogue stands out among the *Platonica,* as its Xenophontic counterpart does on its own side.

The *Apology,* however, stands out as Plato's only writing which is certainly directed to a general public: namely the same, anonymous public as the orators, the sophists, the historians, the dramatists, and apparently the other Socratics addressed, directly or indirectly. The *Apology* is a public speech (or a set of three speeches). Essentially, it follows the rules of the logographic speeches to which the Athenian public was well accustomed. It is simply an apology of Socrates (though published *post festum*), with little protreptic, and with no advanced philosophy to challenge sophisticated readers. With his *Apology,* Plato is acting just like any Socratic, or any logographer.

Compare, on the other hand, the curious *Menexenus* with its mock-patriotic funeral speech. It is hardly thinkable that Plato wanted to have the speech recited as such, publicly, to the Athenians,[7] or had taken the risk of letting it be read publicly with its present bizarre frame which makes the parody obvious. The *Menexenus* is a good example of Plato's deliberate limiting of his public.

There is a trend in Plato's literary production away from the narrated dialogue form to the direct dramatic form. The majority of the dialogues of the corpus are of the dramatic type. I am not entering now into the details of the vexed chronological issues, but I think I have made this general tendency sufficiently clear in a book published in 1982.[8]

All of the so-called 'late dialogues' are dramatic in form, and indeed Academic in content. But the atmosphere of all the dialogues is in fact dialectic in the Platonic sense. The partners of Socrates (or of his stand-in in the late dialogues) are regularly provoked to further 'searching together' (κοινῇ ζητεῖν, cf. *Laches* 201A). The dialogue situation is as such a sign of the restricted audience Plato has in view. Plato never makes his Socrates talk on the *agora,* or with 'anybody.'

The oral presenting or performing of a Socratic dialogue in dramatic form requires a specific, somehow closed audience who knows the characters and types beforehand and does not need much introduction to clarify the fictitious situation. The audience ought to know what is to be expected, to 'know the rules' of the game. We can easily imagine such readings or performances to have been common in closed gatherings of Socratics soon after the death of their Master, during Plato's visit to Megara, for instance, and later in Athens; and we [293] can also imagine such performances to have become institutionalized in Plato's Academy. It has sometimes been suggested that there could have been public performances of Plato's dramatic dialogues in Athens.[9] I do not think this hypothesis can be taken seriously. Apart from other difficulties, we never hear of any institution for this, a theatre open for public prose dramas (the Academy

---

7. Though a naive reader could easily miss the point of the speech. Cicero *Orat.* 44.151 informs us that it was in his days recited in Athens at patriotic festivals. Cf. the speech of 'Lysias' in *Phaedrus* where the context is necessary for the correct interpretation.

8. Above, p. 147 ff.

9. E.g., Ryle 1966: 32 ff.

was not an open institution); the Athenians did not know the rules for Socratic dramas.

But the publishing of dramatic dialogues entails additional complications. Dramatic dialogues could hardly be published as such, without introductory frames, if there was no institution (like the theatre) to handle them. One obvious obstacle to a direct publication of dramatic dialogues lies in the curious and interesting fact that character *sigla* had not yet been invented:[10] i.e. signs in the manuscript margin to distinguish the speakers, such as we find in the codices from late antiquity and onwards, and again in our printed editions: 'ΣΩ' for 'Socrates,' 'ΚΑΛ' for 'Callicles,' 'ΓΟΡ' for 'Gorgias,' and so forth. We know for certain that in Hellenistic manuscripts (papyri) the change of speaker was still noted only by a little line in the margin (or occasionally by a 'χοροῦ' in drama). This worked all right as long as the manuscript was meant for reading by a stage-manager or actors who were prepared to take account of the dialogue indicators in the text (such as vocative addresses) and to apply their intuition and inspiration to the context. And it worked all right with Socratic dialogues where only two speakers occur. But when several persons are involved in a lively conversation, as for instance in the *Laches*, it is sometimes difficult to see, without the *sigla* in the margin, who is saying what, unless you have first studied the text closely—or unless you happen to be the author. Indeed, here is one indication that the dramatic dialogues were originally read by the author himself and obviously, then, not to a general, open audience.

Note at the opening of the *Gorgias*, for instance, how easily the identity of the speakers is confused when there are no *sigla* to help. In fact there is one utterance (at 448A) which is certainly meant to be Socrates,' though all our manuscripts, and all editors, attribute it to Gorgias. But, as I have argued elsewhere, there are signs of the *Gorgias* having had originally a narrated form which prevented such mistakes.[11]

Once the Academy had been established, and the writing of dramatic dialogues had become an institutionalized practice there, the frame narrative with its inserenda, 'I said,' 'He answered,' 'Callicles remarked,' etc., could be easily be dropped. The opening of the *Theaetetus* tells us in so many words how this could be done. I find it possible that the same had happened to the *Laches*. When written down in its present form, it required an audience who knew the rules of the game, and the presence of the author himself or a reader or director who knew the text and could direct the flow of the dialogue correctly.

Much of this remains unclear to us, to be sure, as Plato's notorious play with masks and allusions very often is (Euclides as the author of *Theaetetus*, for instance). I am not going into this now. I only want to emphasize that the mask-play is an additional indication of a deliberate restriction of the audience for the dialogues—the dramatic as well as the narrated ones.

---

10. Above, p. 210 referring to Andrieu 1954 and Turner 1971.
11. References in Thesleff 1989: 7 n. 28. On this issue, see H. Tarrant 1996. See also below, p. 551.

[294] The contents of the *Theaetetus* certainly do not appeal to a general public. But the *Gorgias* would seem to have such an appeal; at least it has passages with a public bearing. In fact, there is the story of the Corinthian farmer who heard somebody read the *Gorgias*, and was so taken by it that he threw away his mattock and walked straight away to Athens to hear more.[12] If the story is not simply a fiction, it seems quite possible that a rhetor could present suggestive sections of a Platonic dialogue, such as Socrates' 'demagogic' effusions towards the end of *Gorgias*, at public gatherings somewhere in Greece. Plato, alas, did not write for Corinthian farmers. He addressed his protreptics to limited audiences, as can be seen for instance at the conclusions of the *Apologia* and the *Euthydemus* (cf. also *Clitopho*).

The Platonic dramatic dialogues are, on the whole, even less exoteric than the narrative ones—with one notable exception: the *Crito*. There are several oddities in this dialogue which have been noted by recent critics.[13] However they be explained, the *Crito* is very far from being a typical Platonic piece of writing.

But then there is the *Republic*, one of the most famous and most hotly debated dialogues in the Platonic Corpus. Was the *Republic* really not meant for publication, for reading to an unprepared general audience, or at least for private reading by every Greek with a bent for 'philosophy' in some sense? My answer is "No," but with one important reservation. Plato had, unintentionally, published a part of the work at an early date, namely the Utopia which now occupies large sections of Books II, III and V of our present text. I have tried to prove, elsewhere,[14] that the 'Proto-*Republic*' was a sketch, read by Plato (in his own name, not in Socrates'), in the mid-390s, to an audience who found it sufficiently shocking to memorize, have it put down in writing, and copied. The *Republic*, as we have it, is likely to be a product of accretion of material over many years. The final composition probably came about fairly late (say, in the 350s). I interpret the work as a monument over Plato's thought for internal use in the Academy, or for persons well acquainted with the Academy. A general, open public in Athens [295] or elsewhere is certainly not likely to have enjoyed listening to the entire work, over several days, and it could not have been able to appreciate the niceties of its composition, style, and thoughts (when there was no theatrical apparatus for it). It has parts, of course, that would have had an appeal to a large audience, but would such an audience be able to fathom the contexts and the coherence of this magnificently pedimental composition, which ultimately carries Socrates' arguments and makes them comprehensible?

---

12. Them. *Or.* 23.296cd. Here a similar legend is told about the protreptic effect of the *Republic* (the 'Proto-*Republic*'? cf. Them. *Or.* 21.245c) upon Plato's woman pupil Axiothea; Riginos (1976) 183f. is skeptical.

13. The lively discussion around the *Crito.* seems to continue (some older references in Thesleff 1982 above, 355 ff.; 1989: 7f.). Few scholars have noted the implications of the theme of πείθειν and the (possibly ironic) reference to Corybantic music at the end.

14. For a relatively recent summary of my arguments, *see* above, p. 519 ff. *Phaedrus* 228A–E illustrates how speeches could be memorized and written down in Plato's days.

Plato never held any public office at Athens. And his withdrawal to a kind [295] of exclusivity in the Academy, *extra muros*, is one sign out of many of his lack of interest in direct publicity. From this perspective, too, we may understand his often attested unwillingness to communicate his philosophy to unprepared listeners.[15] Nobody believes today that he would have liked himself to be, in Syracuse or elsewhere, the Philosopher on the Throne. He only wished to influence by philosophy (as he understood philosophy) people like Dion, or Dionysius II, or Hermias of Scepsis. He wanted political leaders to learn to think philosophically, dialectically, with a view to metaphysics. But he did not address Athenians specifically: none of the prominent Academics of the first generation were Athenians, except Speusippus, Plato's nephew.

I tried once to trace all the possible reflections of Plato's works in the remains of 4th century literature before Aristotle.[16] The result was meager but not uninteresting. Intertextual references, of course, are not common in ancient literature, and they are often difficult to identify. But Plato's thought and art should have left some manifest traces in contemporary authors, if his dialogues were widely known and discussed. I found very few echos of Plato, and even fewer obvious references to Plato's dialogues. Much of what is commonly thought to be references to Platonic passages in Isocrates and Xenophon, could as well and more naturally derive from common sources, or are just commonplaces. The Utopia was known, at least by hearsay, and so was Book I probably, but other parts of the *Republic* are not mentioned, let alone discussed. In a little-known fragment by the comedian Ophelion somebody seems to suggest that a Platonic text (βιβλίον Πλάτωνος) produces a peculiar smell when it is burnt—which (if my interpretation is correct) does not imply very much of respect for Plato's writings.[17]

There was a saying current in the latter half of the fourth century, Πλάτωνος ἀγαθόν, meaning something very obscure and unattainable.[18] Some scholars have derived the saying from what Socrates says at the end of Book VI of the *Republic*, but I would certainly prefer to connect it with Plato's notorious lecture Περὶ ἀγαθοῦ, 'On the Good.'

This lecture, 'On the Good,' has been the subject of much controversy in recent years.[19] In my view, it can be rather confidently stated that Plato gave such a [296]

---

15. This is one of the well-documented theses of Szlezák 1985.
16. Some references above, p. 526 ff. The entire material has not so far been published.
17. Ophelion fr. 3 (KA): †Λιβυκὸν πέπερι θυμίαμα καὶ βιβλίον/Πλάτωνος ἐμβρόντητον.
18. Clear instances of the saying are found in Middle Comedy: Amphis fr. 6 (KA); Alexis fr. 98 (KA); somewhat later, Philippides fr. 6 (KA). A reflection of the saying is found in Ps.-Epicharmus, quoted by Alcimus in Diog. L. 3.14. But to later Platonists, Plato's Ἀγαθόυ was something actively suppressed, cf. Plut. *Dio*. 14.2 (τὸ σιωπώμενον ἀγαθόν) and Alcinous, *Introductio in Platonem* 27 (179.30 He.): πάνυ γοῦν ὀλίγοις τῶν γνωρίμων καὶ τοῖς γε προκριθεῖσι τῆς περὶ τοῦ ἀγαθοῦ ἀκροάσεως μετέδωκεν.
19. Recent references to this complicated issue above, p. 478 ff., especially 485. The basic ingredients in the story come from Aristotle (partly via Theophrastus and Aristoxenus) and Hermodorus (Plato's biographer, later elaborated by many others, including Proclus and Simplicius). The parallel with the digression in the *Seventh Letter* is more instructive than most scholars

[296] lecture, and that this was one of his few appearances in public (after the times of the 'Proto-*Republic*'), and probably his last. It belonged to his late period. It was a single occasion (not a set of lectures), and Plato had announced it as a public lecture on τὸ ἀγαθόν; but his audience, who had expected to be told how to lead a good life, were gravely disappointed since Plato referred to metaphysics, to mathematics, and apparently to his 'unwritten views' about First Principles. Compare the discussion in the *Philebus* (certainly an esoteric dialogue) of the good life in the light of the Pythagorean Pinciples 'Limit' and 'The Unlimited.' I am sure Plato was deliberately obscure when he lectured 'On the Good' to the Athenians. He wanted his lecture to be provocative in a very specific sense. He wanted to make his audience see that the question of what is ultimately 'good' is far too difficult to be treated in an hour's public lecture: Πλάτωνος ἀγαθόν was not easy to reach. In a similar manner, in the *Seventh Letter* (342a–344d), Plato produces a dense piece of reasoning about various aspects of Being, the so-called philosophical digression, to show what young Dionysius could not possibly have picked up during his brief interviews with Plato. Here, too, Plato is provocatively obscure (which of course has contributed to modern scholars' athetizing the letter). Plato's 'true philosophy' did, indeed, have metaphysical and methodological bents which were hopelessly difficult to communicate directly. It demanded dialectical training during a long συνουσία, 'being together,' as Plato and his Socrates often point out.[20] He could not propagate his true philosophy to the general public even if he wanted to.

Aristotle, on the other hand, is known to have divided his own teaching into 'acroamatic' sessions (later called 'epoptic' or 'esoteric') and 'exoteric' ones, that is popularizing lectures (often held in the afternoon).[21] His published dialogues seem to have been of the exoteric kind. Aristotle believed more sincerely than Plato in the usefulness of 'publishing' philosophical thoughts and arguments, and of doing it in written form. He saw in the Platonic (and / or Socratic) dialogue a vehicle for such popularizing (as Cicero did very much later).

In Plato's case we can at the most speak of 'semi-exoteric' dialogues: the *Symposium*, and perhaps two or three more. I would not, however, count the *Phaedo* among them. Contrary to the *Symposium*, the *Phaedo* has, from the beginning to the end, an inward bent of almost Pythagorean exclusivity; and Socrates' different [297] λόγοι do not amount to a generally acceptable and easily palatable demonstration of the soul's immortality. As is implied in the central part of the dialogue, it is Socrates' λόγοι that must live on.

---

seem to think. Cf. also Düring 1957: 360: "Aristoxenus' story gives us a glimpse of the difference which really existed between the discourses of the common sophists and the highly technical discussions in the Academy. It was during these years that the break occurred between general education and scientific knowledge, and a new mode of expression, scientific prose, took shape."

20. Cf. e.g. *Apology* 20a; *Protagoras* 335bc; *Republic* 6.493b, 495c; *Theaetetus* 150de; *Laws* 12.968c; *Seventh Letter* 341c, 344d; with an emphasis on divine intervention, *e.g. Theages* 129e ff.

21. Gell. *NA* 20.5, and others. *See* the references in Düring 1957: 426–43.

Plato's so-called 'late dialogues' all have a decidedly 'esoteric' character, disregarding perhaps certain isolated sections such as the Atlantis story of the *Critias* (which is left unfinished). But the posthumously published *Laws* is an anomalous work in several respects; and here a definite step is taken from orality to literacy.

And note, finally, as an argument worth closer study, that most Platonic dialogues use the literary device of gradually focusing the listener's interest, often via a change of scene, onto a private discussion between the Philosopher and one or two other persons.

⸻ ○ ⸻

I have been trying to argue, or to accumulate some support to my claim, that Plato deliberately avoided a confrontation with an open, anonymous public. Plato was very much in favor of 'narrowcasting,' instead of broadcasting.

Much more could be said on this issue. As a preliminary conclusion, we may surmise that Plato's original public consisted of the kind of people he makes his Socrates meet in the dialogues: closed groups of intellectuals, or potential intellectuals, or well-established people of some influence, or their sons. The dialogues were meant to be read to such groups, by the author himself, or at least in the presence of well-informed experts who were prepared to give additional information and to continue the discussion. And also as an artist, Plato was an elitist, whether we want him to be one or not.

But, of course, the very idea of writing down texts in a literarily refined form proves that Plato had in mind something more than a single occasion for dialectic reasoning, i.e. more than one single orally performed 'seminar.' It seems that the dialogues tend to move on two levels of communication.[22] There is the ordinary human level with its lively coloring, its shortcomings and its ἀπορίαι, which may appeal to less well-informed listeners and may sometimes have a protreptic, 'propaedeutic' function; and there is a philosophical core, often in the center of the dialogue, which by hints and allusions searches the area of interest of the better informed. It is perhaps this inner circle of philosophically minded readers that Plato hopes will be able to utilize the message of the dialogue in further dialectic reasoning, and to read the text again to suitable, chosen, outer circles.

In that sense, Plato did speak to larger audiences, though not 'to all if us.' He did it in a very indirect way—like the Socrates he wanted to rejuvenate. His own anonymity is a sign as good as any of this indirect approach. He wished to speak to distinct groups of people where he could seek personal confrontation or agreement. And he did this through the medium of friends who understood his play with masks and allusions—though in some late dialogues he may already have given the initiative over to others. At any rate, the essentially oral character of

---

22. References in Thesleff above p. 389 n. 8. The two-level communication, so typical of Plato, lost its *raison d'être* when literacy took over.

[298] Plato's art of dialogue facilitated the restriction of his audience, even the restriction of the 'outer circle.'

The misunderstanding and misinterpretation of Plato began when the dialogues came into the hands of people who lacked the direct or indirect contact with their author, who did not understand the context, and who did not know how to deal with the texts: that is, when the dialogues were published and put into general circulation (a process that may have begun in Plato's lifetime). The long story of mistakes about Plato will certainly never be finished.

In the ancient world, Plato's dialogues affected public life to a minimal extent; and why this was so has perhaps become somewhat clear from what I have said. We may deplore the dialogues' enigmatic elusiveness and their exclusiveness, their elitism; but we have to admit that their dynamics lie somewhere in the tension between their two general levels of communication, the appeal to an outer circle (yet a limited circle!), and the appeal to better informed inner elite: a never-ending appeal to dialectic as Plato understood it; a philosopher-conducted dialogue between intellectuals.

# A SYMPTOMATIC TEXT CORRUPTION:
## PLATO, *GORGIAS* 448a5

Papyrologists know that the change of speaker was rarely and inconsistently noted in manuscripts of ancient dialogue texts. A line in the margin may occur, occasionally some other mark, but names or so-called character sigla ('singulae litterae'), such as we are used to (ΑΓ, ΚΛ, ΚΑΛ, ΣΩ), were not normally employed. Perhaps codicologists know when the sigla began to be regularly adopted. This must have been at a time when dialogue texts were professionally copied for new readers who were expected to cope with the written dialogues on their own. In the Hellenistic age, the practice was still unknown, as far as I can see. I have argued elsewhere that the lack of character sigla has some bearing on the question of in what way, and for what audiences, the Platonic dialogues were originally meant to be presented.[1]

A well-established public institution such as the Greek theater had no difficulties in using manuscripts lacking character sigla. Those who studied the written texts, stage directors and actors, were from the start acquainted with the distribution of the roles, and little training was needed to identify them. Nor was the change of speaker a big problem with pieces of simple dramatic prose dialogue where only two characters appear, such as some of Plato's texts. If a third person occasionally turns up (as in, say, the opening of *Hippias Minor* and again at 373a–c), a vocative address helps with the identification. And when a dialogue is carried by a narrative, there is normally no problem at all in determining who said what. This literary practice was well known since Homer, and the Socratics adopted it at an early date.[2] Such texts could be read by anybody outside the public institutions.

Most of Plato's literarily wrought dialogues are of the narrative ('reported') kind. They were probably meant for (relatively) large audiences, and the text could be put in circulation beyond the immediate control of the author. The narrator, and through him the reader, can easily manage the flow of the dialogue even when

---

1. Thesleff 2002: above, p. 544 f. The absence in ancient manuscripts of names or sigla for dialogue speakers was argued in detail by Andrieu 1954: 209–229, 283, 307 f.; cf. Turner 1971: 15. I do not know of any counter-evidence.

2. Details in Thesleff 1982: above, p. 199 ff.; Vander Waerdt 1994.

[252] several characters are involved in a lively discussion (as in *Protagoras, Symposium, Euthydemus* or *Phaedo*).³

However, a few of Plato's directly "dramatic" dialogues present obvious difficulties to a reader who has no character sigla for orientation. The *Gorgias* is a glaring example. I shall focus here on a single passage where the problem of character identification has led to a corruption of the text. I see this detail, which I have previously noted only in passing, as a very strong support for my hypothesis that the *Gorgias* was originally a narrated dialogue, later revised and expanded and rewritten in dramatic form.⁴

The introductory discussion (447a–448b) has a two-stage setting. The text (Burnet's OCT edition) runs as follows:

> ΚΑΛ. Πολέμου καὶ μάχης φασὶ χρῆναι, ὦ Σώκρατες,     **447**
> οὕτω μεταλαγχάνειν.
> ΣΩ. Ἀλλ᾽ ἦ, τὸ λεγόμενον, κατόπιν ἑορτῆς ἥκομεν καὶ
> ὑστεροῦμεν;
> ΚΑΛ. Καὶ μάλα γε ἀστείας ἑορτῆς· πολλὰ γὰρ καὶ καλὰ     **5**
> Γοργίας ἡμῖν ὀλίγον πρότερον ἐπεδείξατο.
> ΣΩ. Τούτων μέντοι, ὦ Καλλίκλεις, αἴτιος Χαιρεφῶν ὅδε,
> ἐν ἀγορᾷ ἀναγκάσας ἡμᾶς διατρῖψαι.
> [253]   ΧΑΙ. Οὐδὲν πρᾶγμα, ὦ Σώκρατες· ἐγὼ γὰρ καὶ ἰάσομαι.     **b**
> φίλος γάρ μοι Γοργίας, ὥστ᾽ ἐπιδείξεται ἡμῖν, εἰ μὲν δοκεῖ,
> νῦν, ἐὰν δὲ βούλῃ, εἰς αὖθις.
> ΚΑΛ. Τί δέ, ὦ Χαιρεφῶν; ἐπιθυμεῖ Σωκράτης ἀκοῦσαι
> Γοργίου;     **5**
> ΧΑΙ. Ἐπ᾽ αὐτό γέ τοι τοῦτο πάρεσμεν.
> ΚΑΛ. Οὐκοῦν ὅταν βούλησθε παρ᾽ ἐμὲ ἥκειν οἴκαδε· παρ᾽
> ἐμοὶ γὰρ Γοργίας καταλύει καὶ ἐπιδείξεται ὑμῖν.
> ΣΩ. Εὖ λέγεις, ὦ Καλλίκλεις. ἀλλ᾽ ἆρα ἐθελήσειεν ἂν
> ἡμῖν διαλεχθῆναι; βούλομαι γὰρ πυθέσθαι παρ᾽ αὐτοῦ τίς ἡ     **c**
> δύναμις τῆς τέχνης τοῦ ἀνδρός, καὶ τί ἐστιν ὃ ἐπαγγέλλεταί
> τε καὶ διδάσκει· τὴν δὲ ἄλλην ἐπίδειξιν εἰς αὖθις, ὥσπερ σὺ
> λέγεις, ποιησάσθω.
> ΚΑΛ. Οὐδὲν οἷον τὸ αὐτὸν ἐρωτᾶν, ὦ Σώκρατες. καὶ γὰρ     **5**
> αὐτῷ ἓν τοῦτ᾽ ἦν τῆς ἐπιδείξεως· ἐκέλευε γοῦν νυνδὴ ἐρωτᾶν
> ὅτι τις βούλοιτο τῶν ἔνδον ὄντων, καὶ πρὸς ἅπαντα ἔφη
> ἀποκρινεῖσθαι.
> ΣΩ. Ἦ καλῶς λέγεις· ὦ Χαιρεφῶν, ἐροῦ αὐτόν.
> ΧΑΙ. Τί ἔρωμαι;     **10**
> ΣΩ. Ὅστις ἐστίν.
> ΧΑΙ. Πῶς λέγεις;     **d**

---

3. But contrary to other Socratics, Plato seems always to have preferred closed audiences; *see* above, p. 541 ff.
4. First argued in 1982 above, p. 234 f; also 1989: 7 n. 28 with further references.

ΣΩ. Ὥσπερ ἂν εἰ ἐτύγχανεν ὢν ὑποδημάτων δημιουργός, [253]
ἀπεκρίνατο ἂν δήπου σοι ὅτι σκυτοτόμος· ἢ οὐ μανθάνεις ὡς
λέγω; 5
ΧΑΙ. Μανθάνω καὶ ἐρήσομαι. Εἰπέ μοι, ὦ Γοργία,
ἀληθῆ λέγει Καλλικλῆς ὅδε ὅτι ἐπαγγέλλῃ ἀποκρίνεσθαι ὅτι
ἄν τίς σε ἐρωτᾷ;
ΓΟΡ. Ἀληθῆ, ὦ Χαιρεφῶν· καὶ γὰρ νυνδὴ αὐτὰ ταῦτα **448**
ἐπηγγελλόμην, καὶ λέγω ὅτι οὐδείς μέ πω ἠρώτηκε καινὸν
οὐδὲν πολλῶν ἐτῶν.
ΧΑΙ. Ἦ που ἄρα ῥᾳδίως ἀποκρινῇ, ὦ Γοργία.
ΓΟΡ. Πάρεστι τούτου πεῖραν, ὦ Χαιρεφῶν, λαμβάνειν. 5
ΠΩΛ. Νὴ Δία· ἂν δέ γε βούλῃ, ὦ Χαιρεφῶν, ἐμοῦ.
Γοργίας μὲν γὰρ καὶ ἀπειρηκέναι μοι δοκεῖ· πολλὰ γὰρ ἄρτι
διελήλυθεν.
ΧΑΙ. Τί δέ, ὦ Πῶλε; οἴει σὺ κάλλιον ἂν Γοργίου
ἀποκρίνασθαι; 10
ΠΩΛ. Τί δὲ τοῦτο, ἐὰν σοί γε ἱκανῶς; b
ΧΑΙ. Οὐδέν· ἀλλ᾽ ἐπειδὴ σὺ βούλει, ἀποκρίνου.
ΠΩΛ. Ἐρώτα.

Thus, at the opening, Socrates and Chaerephon arrive too late to an epideictic [254] performance by Gorgias, perhaps at a gymnasium. Then Callicles (447b7–8) invites them to his home where Gorgias is staying during his visit to Athens, and the ensuing debate seems to be carried on there.[5] The situation recalls the settings of some narrative dialogues (notably *Protagoras, Symposium* and *Republic*), but nothing is explicitly said in the text of *Gorgias* about a change of place. This is of no factual importance here, though we may feel that something is missing.

Another, more interesting feature is the lack of clear indications of who the speaker is—assuming that there are no character sigla. Callicles opens the dialogue, but the unprepared reader will not know this before there comes the vocative address in Socrates' second rejoinder (447a7). This same reader will also find it hard to identify the speaker at 447b1 as Chaerephon, until he has read on a bit, and perhaps reflected on what has been said. Similar difficulties occur now and again in the following pages. At 448a5 there comes a stumbling block which no editors and commentators seem to have noticed.

The immediate context is this. Socrates has suggested to Chaerephon (who knows Gorgias personally, 447b2) that he might try to interrogate Gorgias about 'who (or what) he is' (ὅστις ἐστίν, 447d1), as if he were asking a maker of shoes who he is (answer: a cobbler). Chaerephon begins (447d6) by asking if it is true, as Callicles has just said (447c5–8), that Gorgias is prepared to answer all questions. Gorgias self-consciously declares (448a1–3) that nobody has asked him any new questions in many years. "So you will find it easy to answer?," Chaerephon suggests (448a4).

---

5. For the earlier discussion of the possible change of place, *see* Guthrie IV 1975: 285; *see* further Fussi 2000: 45–49.

[254] Gorgias replies to this, according to all our manuscripts and editions (448a5): Πάρεστι τούτου πεῖραν, ὦ Χαιρεμῶν, λαμβάνειν. This must mean something like "Here is an opportunity to make a test of this, Chaerephon." Now, πάρεστι meaning 'here is a chance' is good colloquial Attic, a bit peculiar in the mouth of the pompous Gorgias, but possible. The noun πεῖρα, including the phrase πεῖραν λαμβάνειν, is normally constructed with persons or with qualities or attitudes that can be tested in persons.[6] The following speaker in fact understands τούτου
[255] personally, as if referring to Gorgias. This speaker is Polus, an associate of Gorgias, again a new character (whose identification, by the way, is not immediately obvious from the context). He interferes (448a6–8): "Yes, certainly, but please (try) me! For Gorgias seems to decline: he has been speaking so much a while ago." And Chaerephon now starts to interrogate Polus. Gorgias only reappears at 448d, as Socrates' interlocutor.

We note that Polus not only understands τούτου personally and substitutes it with ἐμοῦ, but also he does not find Gorgias as prepared to be 'tried,' 'tested,' as the Πάρεστι reply, put in his mouth, would imply. Polus understands Gorgias to have declined (ἀπειρηκέναι 448a7), apparently judging from his attitude. Indeed, Gorgias is certainly not interested in a πεῖρα. It is very peculiar that he would instantly offer himself to a testing by this minor Socratic, Chaerephon. After all, Gorgias has only claimed that he knows answers to all questions, and that people always keep asking him the same things (448a2–3). He is bored. Later it takes Socrates some time (448d–449c) to persuade Gorgias to undergo his elenchus.

These specific complications disappear if the Πάρεστι comment is given to Socrates instead of Gorgias. Then Socrates would be following up what he said to Chaerophon before (447cd): "Go on, Chaerephon! Here is a chance to test this (namely, whether Gorgias finds it easy to answer) and him (namely, Gorgias himself)." Socrates does not say αὐτοῦ. But the genitive τούτου may have a double implication:[7] it refers to Chaerephon's tentative ῥᾳδίως ἀποκρινῇ (448a4), but at the same time to Gorgias. Socrates is ironical: this is not going to be easy, but surely Gorgias is worth examining. To test persons (rather than things) is typical of Socrates. Polus overhears this remark, does not see the irony, and interferes by stressing the personal aspect of τούτου: "rather test me!"

The emendation of the post-Platonic ΓΟΡ into ΣΩ is easily done. What makes this very minor correction of the text tradition interesting, is that it corroborates the aforementioned hypothesis of a secondary change in the dialogue technique of the *Gorgias*.[8] According to Plato's narrative practice, the narrator of the dialogue, here presumably Socrates himself, is likely to have commented on the setting, notably in this introductory section. He gave sufficient hints of who says what, and
[256] how—note for instance that Gorgias evidently does not listen to the discussion between Callicles, Chaerephon and Socrates until Chaerephon (447d6) turns to him.

---

6. Most of the 20 occurrences in the Platonic corpus refer to persons only. For *Laches* 189b, see below, n. 7.
7. Cf. *Laches* 189b where πεῖρα is constructed with two genitives, σαυτοῦ and ἀρετῆς.
8. Above, n. 4.

With the establishment of the text, and the later adoption of the sigla, the Πάρεστι comment was *automatically* attributed to Gorgias who had made the statement at 448a1–3 and whom Chaerophon addresses at 448a4. But in fact the only utterance by Gorgias at the beginning of the dialogue seems to be the pompous statement at 448a1–3, with its special effect and its implication of boredom.

We can only speculate about what made Plato and the early Platonists drop the 'inserenda,' the μεταξὺ τῶν λόγων, and make the dialogue directly dramatic. This is likely to have happened in Plato's lifetime. In *Theaetetus,* where the process is explicitly referred to (142c–143c), the ultimate motivation was probably the successively more Academic contents of the dialogue which made the literary apparatus superfluous. Here the fiction of Euclides of Megara being the 'writer' who had several times been verifying, and making additions to, Socrates' narrative (ibid.), is a piece of Platonic play that does not entirely open itself to us. But the speakers of this dialogue, in its directly dramatic form, were easily identified by a reader, in this case a slave (143c), who has rehearsed the reading beforehand. We may presume that slaves were trained for reading in the Academy. At any rate the author, or somebody who knew the text well, was present at the performance and prepared to give the necessary instructions to the reader and his listeners. Remember: oral communication still dominated in the Early Academy.

However, the *Gorgias* is not a strictly Academic writing even in its present form. It has quite a protreptic tone, and Socrates in a way turns into an orator (as in *Protagoras* he has, in the end, changed position with the sophist). There may be some symbolic truth in the story about the Corinthian farmer who had listened to the *Gorgias* (presumably some part of it) and become so impressed that he marched straight on to Athens to hear more.[9] Yet there are ingredients alluding to Academic practice, such as the dihaereses at 462c–466a; and Socrates' discussion with Polus and Callicles especially (beginning at 481b) includes important philosophical points. Most pertinently, the section 506c–509c looks almost like a manifesto of Platonic philosophy. Some scholars have pointed out features in *Gorgias* which were hardly intended for the general public.[10] I imagine that the *Gorgias* was gradually expanded and elaborated as Plato's personal defense of philosophy until it became a useful textbook for Academic training.

Thus, while the dialogue still preserved much of Plato's specific non-Academic concerns from the 390s (Athenian politics, the influence of rhetors, the attack of Polycrates, apology of Socrates, and a general appeal to educated Athenians), the inserenda, which were useful for non-Academics only, could be left out from this new version.[11] But the hints about the background and the speakers had to be given orally.

---

9. Themistius *Or.* 23, 296cd.

10. E.g., Szlezák 1985: 191–207. The dialectic of the 'tyrannical' and 'dishonest' Socrates of this dialogue (*see* Babut 1992: 59–110, Beversluis 2000: 291–376) can, after all, only contribute to a fairly refined sort of protreptic (contrary to, say, *Euthydemus* which also ends with a protreptic note).

11. As tended to happen in *Republic* II–X and *Parmenides*. I have not basically changed my view of this process, as argued in 1982 (above, n. 2).

[257]    A somewhat similar case is the *Laches* (cf. the narrative *Charmides*) which cannot be dealt with here.[12] If the *Gorgias* had perhaps originally been addressed to a somewhat larger audience, the dialogue was now habitually presented by a trained reader to chosen audiences of intellectuals—where Corinthian farmers, alas, had no place. In Plato's lifetime, the dialogues were not on the whole intended for the general market, i.e., copied for publication, though some of the narrative pieces had a larger appeal. Plato's manuscripts, and especially the dramatic pieces, were not meant to be studied in a literate society by new readers unacquainted with the text. Thus the mistake with the attribution of *Gorgias* 448a5 is symptomatic of three trends on which I have commented recently:[13] the slide in Plato's dialogue technique from narrative to dramatic form; the preference for oral presentation in Plato's environment; and Plato's deliberate withdrawal from publicity. All lead to additional complications for our understanding of his allusions and moods.

---

12. Possibly some dialogues were performed dramatically by students in Plato's Academy; cf. Thesleff above, p. 209 f, with references; doubted by de Vries 1984 143–145. Public performances in Plato's Athens, as suggested by Gilbert Ryle, are rather out of the question.

13. In the studies published above. Addition 2009: I have argued later that by changing from narrative to dramatic form, Plato also made his grip more personal in *Gorgias* while distancing himself from the historical Socrates (cf. again *Laches* versus *Charmides*, etc.).

# BIBLIOGRAPHY

Aalders, G. J. D. "The authenticity of the Eighth Platonic Epistle reconsidered." *Mnemosyne* 22 (1969): 233–257.

———. "Political thought and political programs in the Platonic epistles." *Pseudepigrapha* I, Entretiens sur l'antiquité classique 18. Geneva: Foundation Hardt (1972): 145–187.

Accame, Silvio. *Ricerche intorno alla Guerra corinzia*. Collana di studi greci 20. Napoli: Libreria Scientifica, 1951.

Adam, J. *The 'Republic' of Plato: edited with critical notes, commentary and appendices by J. A.* Cambridge: Cambridge University Press, 1902. New edition with introduction by D. A. Rees, I–II, Cambridge: Cambridge University Press, 1965.

Adam, R. "Über die Echtheit und Abfassungszeit des platonischen Alkibiades I." *Archiv für Geschichte der Philosophie* 14 (1901): 40–65.

———. "Über die platonischen Briefe." *Archiv für Geschichte der Philosophie* 23 (1909): 29–52.

Allan, D. J. "The Problem of Cratylus." *American Journal of Philology* 75 (1954): 271–287.

———. "Aristotle and the *Parmenides*". Ingemar Düring and G. E. L. Owen (eds.), *Aristotle and Plato in the Mid-Fourth Century: Papers of the Symposium Aristotelicum, Held at Oxford in August 1957*. Göteborg, 1960: 133–144.

Allen, Reginald E. "Anamnesis in Plato's *Meno* and *Phaedo*." *Review of Metaphysics* 13, (1959/60): 165–174.

———, (ed.). *Studies in Plato's 'Metaphysics.'* New York: Humanity Press, 1965. First British edition. London: Routledge, 1965. Reprint 1968.

———. *Plato's 'Euthyphro' and the Earlier Theory of Forms*. London: Routledge, 1970.

Alline, H. *Histoire du texte de Platon*. Bibliothèque de l'École des Hautes Études 218. Paris, 1915.

Allmann, H. "Über die beste Erziehung: Zum Dialog 'Kallias' des Sokratikers Aischines." *Philologus* 16 (1972): 213–253.

Alrivie, J. J. "Les prologues du Théétète et du Parménide." *Revue de Métaphysique & Morale* 76 (1971): 6–23.

Aly, W. *Volksmärchen, Sage und Novelle bei Herodot und seinen Zeitgenossen*. Göttingen: Vandenhoeck & Ruprecht, 1921. Reprinted with appendix, 1969.

———. "Formprobleme der frühen griechischen Prosa." *Philologus Supplement* 21.3. Leipzig, 1929.

Ammann, Adolf N. *-ΙΚΟΣ bei Platon. Ableitung und Bedeutung mit Materialsammlung*. Freiburg: Druckerei, 1953.

Anderhub, J. H. *Joco-Seria aus den Papieren eines reisenden Kaufmanns*. Wiesbaden-Biebrich: Kalle, 1941.

Anderson, F. H. *The argument of Plato*. London: Dent & Sons, 1934.
Andria, R. G., and T. Dorandi. "Philodemus." Gabriele Giannantoni, *Socraticorum Reliquiae* II (1983): 466–468, III (1985): 416 f., 487–494.
Andrieu, J. *Le dialogue antique. Structure et présentation*. Collection D'Études Latines, Serie scientifique, 29. Paris: Les Belles Lettres, 1954.
Annas, Julia. *Aristotle's 'Metaphysics,' Books M and N*. Translated with introduction and notes. Oxford: Clarendon Press, 1976.
Apelt, Otto. [Review of] Hans von Arnim, *De reipublicae Platonis compositione ex Timaeo illustranda* (1898/99). *Archiv für Geschichte der Philosophie* 14 (1901): 408–415.
———. [Review of] Hans Raeder, *Platons philosophische Entwickelung* (1905). *Neue Jahrbücher für das Klassische Altertum* 11 (1908): 73–78.
———. *Platonische Aufsätze*. Leipzig: Teubner, 1912. Reprint Aalen, 1975. Reprint New York: Arno Press, 1976.
———. *Platon, Sämtliche Dialoge*, herausgegeben von Otto Apelt. I–VII. Leipzig 1913–1919. 2. Auflage. 1922–.
Archer-Hind, R. D. (ed.). *The 'Phaedo' of Plato*. Edited with introduction, notes and appendices by R.D.Archer-Hind. London; New York: Macmillan, 1894.
Arieti, J. A. *Interpreting Plato: The Dialogues as Drama*. Lanham: Rowman & Littlefield, 1991.
———. "How to Read a Platonic Dialogue." Francisco J. Gonzalez (ed.), *The Third Way: New Directions in Platonic Studies*. Lanham: Rowman & Littlefield, 1995: 119–132.
Arnim, Hans von. *De Platonis dialogis. Quaestiones chronologicae*. Vorlesungsverzeichnis der Universität Rostock für das Winter Semester, 1896.
———. *De reipublicae Platonis compositione ex Timaeo illustranda*. Programm Rostock, 1898/99.
———. "Die Verwertbarkeit der sprachstatistischen Methode zu chronologischen Schlüssen." *Zeitschrift für das österreichisches Gymnasium* 51 (1900): 481–492.
———. *Sprachliche Forschungen zur Chronologie der platonischen Dialoge*. Sitzungsberichte der Philosophisch-Historischen Classe der Kaiserlichen Akademie der Wissenschaften, Bd. 169.3 Wien, 1912.
———. *Platons Jugenddialoge und die Entstehungszeit des Phaidros*. Berlin: Teubner, 1914.
———. "Plato's *Lysis*." *Rheinisches Museum* 71 (1916): 364–387.
———. *Xenophons Memorabilien und Apologie des Sokrates*. Det Kongelige Danske Videnskabernes Selskab, Historisk-filologiske Meddelelser VIII, 1. Copenhagen: Host & Son, 1923.
———. *Die sprachliche Forschung als Grundlage der Chronologie der platonischen Dialoge*. Sitzungsberichte der Philosophisch-Historischen Classe der Kaiserlichen Akademie der Wissenschaften zu Wien 210:4, 1929.
Ast, Friedrich. *Lexicon Platonicum, sive vocum Platonicarum index*. I–III. Classic Books, 1835. Reprint Lipsiae: Libraria Weidmanniana, 1969.
Atkins, J. W. H. *Literary Criticism in Antiquity. A Sketch of its Development*. I-II. New York: Peter Smith, 1952.
Ausland, H. W. "On Reading Plato Mimetically." *American Journal of Philology* 118:33 (1997): 371–416.
Austin, Marion J. "Plato as a Writer of Imaginary Conversations." *The Classical Journal* 17 (1921): 243–266.
Babut, D. "ΟΥΤΟΣΙ ΑΝΗΡ ΟΥ ΠΑΥΣΕΤΑΙ ΦΛΥΑΡΩΝ: Les Procédés dialectiques dans le Gorgias et le dessin du dialogue." *Revue des Études Grecques* 105 (1992): 59–110.

Baer, Eva. *Die historischen Angaben der Platonbriefe VII und VIII im Urteil der modernen Forschung seit Eduard Meyer.* Dissertation. Humboldt-Universität. Berlin, 1957.

Bal, B. H. *Plato's ascese in de Phaedo.* Weert: Smeets, 1950.

Baldry, H. C. "Plato's Technical Terms." *Classical Quarterly* 31 (1937): 141–150.

Balleriaux, O. "Les dialogues de Platon et les AGRAPHA DOGMATA. Le Parménide et le Sophiste à la lumière des doctrines non écrites." *L'Antiquité Classique* 63 (1994): 299–307.

Bally, C. *Traité de stylistique française.* I–II. Heidelberg, 1921.

Baltes, Matthias. "Idee (Ideenlehre)." *Real-Lexikon für Antike und Christentum* (1994): 213–238.

———. "Is the Idea of the Good in Plato's *Republic* Beyond Being?" M. Joyal (eds.), *Studies in Plato and the Platonic Tradition. Essays Presented to J. Whittaker*, Aldershot 1997: 3–23.

———. *See* also Heinrich Dörrie.

Barford, R. *The Criticisms of the Theory of Forms in the First Part of Plato's 'Parmenides'.* Dissertation. Indiana University 1971: DA XXXI, 1970: 6655A–6656A.

———. "The Context of the Third Man Argument in Plato's *Parmenides*." *Journal of the History of Philosophy* 16 (1978): 1–11.

Barker, A. and M. Warner (eds.). *The Language of the Cave.* Edmonton: Academic Printing & Publishing, 1992.

Baron, C. *De Platonis dicendi genere.* Thèse, Faculte des lettres de Paris, 1891.

———. "Contributions à la chronologie des dialogues de Platon." *Revue des Études Grecques* 10 (1897): 264–278.

Bartoletti, V. "Un frammento di dialogo socratio." *Studi Italiani di Filologia Classica* 31 (1959): 100–103.

Beare, J. I. "A New Clue to the Order of the Platonic dialogues." *Essays & Studies presented to William Ridgeway.* Cambridge (1913): 27–61.

Begemann, A. W. *Plato's 'Lysis.' Orderzoek naar de plaats van den dialoog in het oeuvre.* Dissertation. Vrije Universiteit. Amsterdam: Buijten & Schipperheijn, 1960.

Belfiore, E. S. *'Imitation' and Book X of Plato's 'Republic.'* Dissertation. University of California (1978): DA XXXIX 1978: 2911A–2912A.

Benardete, S. "The Right, the True, and the Beautiful." *Glotta* 41 (1963): 54–62.

———. "χρή and δεῖ in Plato and others." *Glotta* 43 (1965): 285–298.

Bengtson, H. *Griechische Geschichte von den Anfängen bis in die römische Kaiserzeit. Handbuch der Altertuwissenscheft* III 4. 2. Auflage. München, 1960.

Benítez, E. E. *Forms in Plato's 'Philebus.'* Revised edition. Assen: Van Gorcum, 1989.

Benn, A. W. "The Later Ontology of Plato." *Mind* XI (1902): 31–53.

Benson, H. H. "Meno, the Slave-Boy and the Elenchos." *Phronesis* 35 (1990): 128–158.

Berti, E. "Una nuova ricostruzione delle dottrine non scritti di Platone." *Journal of Metaphysics* 19 (1964): 546–557. German translation in: Jürgen Wippern, *Das Problem der ungeschriebenen Lehre Platons.* Darmstadt: Wissenschaftliche Buchgesellschaft 1972): 240 ff.

———. [Review of] Hans J. Krämer, *Arete bei Platon und Aristoteles* (1959) and *Der Ursprung der Geistesmetaphysik* (1964). *Rivista Critica di Storia della Filosofia* 20 (1965): 231–235.

Berve, Helmut. *Dion.* Abhandlungen der Geistes- und Sozialwissenschaftlichen Klasse; 1956, Nr. 10. Mainz: Akademie der Wissenschaften und der Literatur, 1957.

———. [Review of books on Dion]. *Gnomon* 35 (1963): 375–382.

Beversluis, J. *Cross-Examining Socrates: A Defense of the Interlocutors in Plato's Early Dialogues*. Cambridge: Cambridge University Press, 2000.
Bezzel, Chris. "Zur Struktur des platonischen Frühdialogs (*Euthyphron*)." *Zeitschrift für philosophische Forschung* 17 (1963): 42–65.
Billig, L. "Clausulae and Platonic chronology." *Journal of Philology* 35 (1920): 225–256.
Blackson, Thomas A. *Inquiry, Forms, and Substances: A Study in Plato's Metaphysics and Epistemology*. Dordrecht: Kluwer Academic, 1995.
Billings, Grace H. *The Art of Transition in Plato*. Dissertation. Chicago, 1920.
Blass, Friedrich W. *Die attische Beredsamkeit*. I–III. Leipzig, 1887. II–III. Leipzig: Teubner, 1874–1880. 2nd edition: 1892. Three Volumes bound into two: 1898.
———. Die *Rhythmen der attischen Kunstprosa: Isokrates, Demosthenes, Platon*. Leipzig: Teubner, 1901.
———. "Über die Zeitfolge von Platons letzten Schriften." *Apophoreton* XLVII, Berlin: Weidmannsche Buchhandlung (1903): 52–66.
Blaszczak, Wenzel. *Götteranrufung und Beteuerung*. Dissertation. Breslau, 1932.
Bloedow, E. F. "Aspasia and the Mystery of the *Menexenus*." *Wiener Studien* 9, (1975): 32–48.
Blois, L. de. "Some Notes on Plato's Seventh Epistle." *Mnemosyne* 32 (1979): 268–283.
Bloom, Allan. *The Republic of Plato*. Translated with notes, an interpretative essay, and a new introduction (1968). 2nd edition. New York: Basic Books, 1991.
Bluck, R. S. *Plato's Life and Thought: With a Translation of the 'Seventh Letter.'* London: Routledge, 1949.
———. "The Origin of the 'Greater Alcibiades.'" *The Classical Quarterly* 3 (1953): 46–52.
———. "On τραγιχή: Plato, *Meno* 76e." *Mnemosyne* 14 (1961): 289–295.
———. *Plato's 'Meno'*. Edited with introduction and commentary. Cambridge: Cambridge University Press, 1961.
Boder, Werner. *Die Sokratische Ironie in den platonischen Frühdialogen*. Studien zur antiken Philosophie 3. Amsterdam: Grüner, 1973.
Bodrero, E. "Dello stilo di Protagora." *Rendiconti di Accademie Lincei* 12 (1903): 103–121.
Böhme, R. *Von Sokrates zur Ideenlehre. Beobachtungen zur Chronologie des platonischen Frühwerks*. Dissertation. Berlin: Francke, 1959.
Bolton, R. H. *Studies in Plato's 'Cratylus.'* Dissertation. University of Michigan (1973): 168 p. [microfilm].
Bonagura, Patrizia. "Il Filebo come una 'summa' del pensiero metafisico platonico." *Rivista di filosofia neo-scolastica* 82 (1990): 543–577.
Bos, C. A. *Interpretatie vadershap en datering van Alcibiades Major*. Dissertation. Amsterdam, 1970.
Bovet, Pierre. *Le dieu de Platon d'apres l'ordre chronologique des dialogues*. Paris: Kündig and Alcan, 1902.
Brandwood, Leonard. "Analysing Plato's Style with an Electronic Computer." *Bulletin of the Institute of Classical Studies of the University of London* 3 (1956): 45–54.
———. *The Dating of Plato's Work by the Stylistic Method*, I–II. Dissertation. University of London, 1958 (typed copy).
———. "Plato's 7th letter." *Revue de L'Organisation international pour l'étude des langues anciennes par ordinateur* (R.E.L.O. Liège 1969): 1–25.
———. *A Word Index to Plato*. Leeds: Maney and Son, 1976.
———. *The Chronology of Plato's Dialogues*. Cambridge: Cambridge University Press, 1990.

Brecht, F. J. "Sokratische Dialektik." *Neue Jahrbücher für Wissenschaft und Jugendbildung* 11 (1935): 30–47.
Breitenbach, H. R., F. Buddenhagen, A. Debrunner, and F. Von der Mühl (eds). "Diogenis Laerti Vita Platonis." *Juvenes dum sumus*. Aufsätze zur klassischen Altertumswissenschaft 49. Versammlung deutscher Philologen und Schulmänner. Basel, 1907.
Breitenbach, H. R. "Xenophon (6): Xenophon von Athen." *Paulys Real-Encyclopädie der classischen Altertumswissenschaft* IXA (1967): 1569–2051.
Breitholtz, Lennart. *Die dorische Farce im griechischen Mutterland vor dem 5. Jahrhundert. Hypothese oder Realität?* Acta Universitatis Gothoburgensis 66:4. Stockholm: Almqvist & Wiksell, 1960.
Brès, Yvon. *La psychologie de Platon*. Publications de la Faculté des Lettres et Sciences humaines de Paris-Sorbonne. Série "Recherches," t. 41. Thèse, Presses Universitaires de France, 1968.
Brickhouse, T. C. and N. D. Smith. *Plato's Socrates*. Oxford: Oxford University Press, 1994. Reprint New York Routledge, 2004.
Brinkmann, A. *Quaestiones de dialogis Platoni falso adscriptis*. Dissertaton. Bonn, 1891.
———. "Ein Brief Platons." *Rheinisches Museum* 66 (1911): 226–230.
Brisson, Luc. *Le Même et l'Autre dans la structure ontologique du Timée de Platon. Un commentaire systématique du Timée de Platon*. Publications de l'Universitie de Paris X Nanterre, Lettres et Sciences Humaines, Série A: Thèses et Travaux, No. 23. Paris: Klincksieck, 1974. International Plato Studies 2, Sankt Augustin: Academia Verlag, 1994.
———. "Platon 1958–1975 (Bibliographie)." *Lustrum* 20 (1977): 5–305. Göttingen: Vandenhoeck et Ruprecht, 1979.
———. "Platon 1975–1980." Avec la collaboration de H. Joannidi. *Lustrum* 25 (1983): 31–320.
———. "Interprétation du mythe du Politique." Christopher J. Rowe (ed.), *Reading the 'Statesman'. Proceedings of the Third Symposium Platonicum*. International Plato Studies 4. Sankt Augustin: Academia Verlag (1995): 349–363.
———. "Premises, Consequences, and Legacy of the Esotericist Interpretation of Plato." *Ancient Philosophy* 15 (1995): 117–134.
Bröcker, Walter. "Plato über das Gute." *Lexis* 2 (1949): 47–66. Reprint Jürgen Wippern, *Das Problem der ungeschriebenen Lehre Platons*. Darmstadt: Wissenschaftliche Buchgesellschaft (1972): 217–239.
———. "Der philosophische Exkurs in Platons siebentem Brief." *Hermes* 91 (1963): 416–425.
———. *Platos Gespräche*. Frankfurt am Main: Klostermann, 1964. 2. Augflage, 1967. 3. Auflage, 1985. 4. Auflage, 1990. 5. Auflage, 1999.
———. "Nachtrag zum philosophischen Exkurs im Platons siebenten Brief." *Hermes* 93 (1965): 132.
Brommer, P. ΕΙΔΟΣ et ΙΔΕΑ. *Étude sémantique et chronologique des oeuvres de Platon*. Philosophia critica 1. Dissertation. Assen, 1940.
Brown, Malcolm S. and James Coulter. "The Middle Speech of Plato's 'Phaedrus'." *Journal of the History of Philosophy* 9 (1971): 405–423.
Brown, Malcolm S. "*Theaetetus:* Knowledge as Continued Learning." *Journal of the History of Philosophy* 7 (1969): 357–379.
———. "Pappus, Plato and the Harmonic Mean." *Phronesis* 20 (1975): 173–184.

Bruell, C. "Socratic Politics and Self-Knowledge. An Interpretation of Plato's 'Charmides'." *Interpretation* 6 (1977): 141–203.

Brumbaugh, R. S. *Plato's Mathematical Imagination: The Mathematical Passages in the Dialogues and Their Interpretation.* Indiana University Publications: Humanities Series 29, 1954.

Brünnecke, H. *De Alcibiade II qui fertur Platonico.* Dissertation. Göttingen, 1912.

Bruns, Ivo. *Das literarische Porträt der Griechen im fünften und vierten Jahrhundert vor Christi Geburt.* Berlin: Hertz, 1896.

———. "Attische Liebestheorien und die zeitliche Folge des platonischen Phaidros sowie der beiden Symposien." *Neue Jahrbucherftir das Klassische Altertum* 5 (1900): 17–37.

Buccellato, M. *La retorica sofistica negli scritti di Platone.* (Studi sofistico-platonici). Pubblicazioni delle *Rivista critica di storia della filosofia* 2. Fratelli Bocca Roma, 1953.

———. "Studi sul dialogo platonico." *Rivista critica di storia della filosofia* 18 (1963): 527–560.

Buchheit, V. *Untersuchungen zur Theorie des Genos epideiktikon von Gorgias bis Aristoteles.* Habilitationsschrift (Saarbrücken 1957). München, 1960.

Buchmann, Klara. "Die Stellung des Menon in der platonischen Philosophie." *Philologus* Supplementband 29, Heft 3 (1936).

Burkert, Walter. "Platon Oder Pythagoras? Zum Ursprung des Wortes 'Philosophie'." *Hermes* 88 (1960): 159–177.

———. *Weisheit und Wissenschaft. Studien zu Pythagoras, Philolaos und Platon.* Erlanger Beiträge zur Sprach- und Kunstwissenschaft 10. Nürnberg: Carl, 1962.

———. *Lore and Science in Ancient Pythagoreanism.* Translated by Edward L. Minar, Jr. Cambridge, MA.: Harvard University Press, 1972.

Burnet, John. *Platonism.* Berkeley: University of California Press, 1928.

Burnyeat, Myles F. "Socratic Midwifery, Platonic Inspiration." *British Institue of Classical Studies* 24 (1977): 7–16.

———. *The 'Theaetetus' of Plato.* Translation by M. J. Levett. Indianapolis: Hackett, 1990.

Bury, Robert G. *The 'Philebus' of Plato.* Edited with introduction, notes, and appendices. Cambridge: Cambridge University Press, 1897.

———. *Plato, The 'Symposium.'* Cambridge: Heffer, 1909; 1932.

Cadiou, R. "Le Philèbe et le théatre." *Revue des Études Grecques* 65 (1952): 302–311.

Cahn, Steven M. "A Puzzle Concerning the *Meno* and the *Protagoras.*" *Journal of the History Philosophy* 11 (1973): 535–537.

Caizzi, Fernanda D. *Antisthenis fragmenta.* Milan: Istituto editoriale Cisalpino, 1966.

Calvo, Tomás and Luc Brisson (eds.). *Interpreting the 'Timaeus-Critias.' Proceedings of the IV Symposium Platonicum.* Selected Papers, International Plato Studies 9. Sankt Augustin: Academia Verlag, 1997.

Campbell, Lewis. (Rev). *The 'Sophistes' and 'Politicus' of Plato.* With a revised text and English notes. Oxford: Oxford University Press, 1867.

———. *The 'Theaetetus' of Plato.* With a revised text and English notes. Oxford: Oxford University Press, 1883.

———. "On the Position of the *Sophistes, Politicus,* and *Philebus* in the Order of the Platonic Dialogues" and "On Plato's Use of Language." *Plato's 'Republic'.* Oxford: Clarendon Press, 1894: 46–66, 165–340.

———. *Plato's 'Republic'*. The Greek text edited with notes and essays by Benjamin Jowett and Lewis Cambell, II. Oxford: Clarendon Press, 1894. Reprint Manchester, NH: Ayer, 1994.

———. "On the Place of the *Parmenides* in the Chronological Order of the Platonic Dialogues." *Classical Review* 10 (1896): 129–136.

Capelle, Annemarie. "Platonisches im Grösseren Hippias". *Rheinisches Museum*, 99 (1956): 178–190.

Capizzi, Antonio. *Platone nel suo tempo: l'infanzia della filosofia e i suoi pedagoghi*. Filologia e Critica 50. Roma, 1984.

Carlini, A. "Alcuni dialoghi pseudoplatonici e l'Accademia di Arcesilao." *Annali di Scuola Normale di Pisa* 31 (1962): 33–63.

Carter, B. E. "The Function of the Myth of the Earthborn in the *Republic*." *Classical Journal* 48 (1952): 297–302.

Casadio, Giovanni. "The Politicus Myth (268d–274e) and the History of Religions." *Kernos* 8 (1995): 85–95.

Casertano, Giovanni. *Il nome della cosa. Linguaggio e realtà negli ultimi dialoghi di Platone*. Napoli: Loffredo, 1996.

Caskey, Elizabeth G. "Again—Plato's *Seventh Letter*." *Classical Philology* 69 (1974): 220–227.

Cattanei, Elisabetta. "Per una rilettura dei libri M e N della Metafisica di Aristotele alla luce delle 'dottrine non scritti' di Platone e dei loro sviluppi nel pensiero dell'Accademia antica." *Rivista di Filosofia Neo-scolastica* 81 (1989): 543–558.

———. *Enti matematici e metafisica. Platone, l'Accademia e Aristotele a confronto*. Milano: Vita e Pensiero, 1996.

Cauer, P. "Platons Menon und sein Verhältnis zu Protagoras und Gorgias." *Rheinisches Museum* 72 (1917/18): 284–306.

Centrone, Bruno. *Pseudopythagorica Ethica. I trattati morali di Archita, Metopo, Teage, Eurifamo*. Elenchos Collana 17. Napoli: Bibliopolis, 1990

———. "Πάθος e οὐσία nei primi dialoghi di Platone." *Elenchos* 16 (1995): 129–152.

Cerri, Giovanni. *Platone sociologo della communicazione*. Milano: il Saggiatore, 1991.

Chantraine, Pierre. "La stylistique greque." *Actes du premier Congrès Internationale des Assocations des études classiques* (1950): 339–360.

———. *Études sur le vocabulaire grec*. Études et commentaires 24. Paris: Klincksieck, 1956.

Chen, Ludwig C. H. *Acquiring Knowledge of the Ideas. A Study of Plato's Method in the 'Phaedo', the 'Symposium', and the Central Books of the 'Republic'*. Stuttgart: Steiner, 1992.

Cherniss, Harold. *Aristotle's Criticism of Plato and the Academy, Vol. I*. Baltimore: John Hopkins University Press, 1944.

———. *The Riddle of the Early Academy*. Berkeley: University of California Press, 1945.

———. [Review of] P. Brommer, ΕΙΔΟΣ et ΙΔΕΑ. *Étude sémantique et chronologique des oeuvres de Platon* (1940). *American Journal of Philology* 68 (1947): 126–133.

———. "A Much Misread Passage of the *Timaeus* (49c7–50b5)." *American Journal of Philology* 75 (1954): 113–130.

———. "The Relation of the *Timaeus* to Plato's Later Dialogues." *American Journal of Philology* 78 (1957): 225–266.

———. "*Timaeus* 38a8–b5." *Journal of Hellenic Studies* 77 (1957): 18–23.

———. "Plato 1950–1957." *Lustrum* 4 (1959): 5–308; 5 (1961): 323–648.

Chevalier, Jacques. "Note sur la chronologie des oeuvres de Platon, et sur leur exégèse a l'époque contemporaine." Thèse, Lyon (1914). Id., *La notion du nécessaire chez Aristote et chez ses prédécesseurs, particulièrement chez Platon*. Paris: Libraire Félix Alcan, 1915: 191–222.

Chiappelli, Alessandro. "Le Ecclesiazuse di Aristofane e la Repubblica di Platone." *Rivista di Filologia* 11 (1883): 161–273; 15 (1887): 343–352.

———. "Über die Spuren einer doppelten Redaktion des platonischen Theaitetos." *Archiv für Geschichte der Philosophie* 17 (1904): 320–333.

Christ, W. "Platonische Studien." *Abhandlungen der philosophisch-historische Classe der Königlichen Bayerschen Akademie der Wissenschaften* 17 (1886): 453–512.

Chroust, Anton-Hermann. "Xenophon, Polycrates and the 'Indictment of Socrates'." *Classica & Mediaevalia* 16 (1955): 1–77.

———. *Socrates: Man and Myth*. London: Routledge, 1957

———. "The Organization of the Corpus Platonicum in Antiquity." *Hermes* 93 (1965): 34–46.

Clark, Pamela M. "The Greater Alcibiades." *The Classical Quarterly* 5 (1955): 231–240.

Clarke, Patricia. "The Interweaving of the Forms with One Another: *Sophist* 259e." *Oxford Studies in Ancient Philosophy* XII (1994): 35–62.

Classen, Carl J. *Sprachliche Deutung als Triebkraft platonischen und sokratischen Philosophierens*. Zetemata. Monographien zur klassischen Altertumswissenschaft Heft 22. München: Beck, 1959.

Clavaud, Robert. *Le Ménèxene de Platon et la rhétorique de son temps*. Paris: Les Belles Lettres, 1980.

Clay, Diskin. "The Origins of the Socratic Dialogue." Paul A. Vander Waerdt, ed.. *The Socratic Movement*. Ithaca: Cornell University Press, 1994: 23–47.

Cobb, William S. "Anamnesis, Platonic Doctrine or Sophistic Absurdity?" *Dialogue* 12 (1973): 604–628.

Cohen, Maurice H. "The Aporias in Plato's Early Dialogues." *Journal of the History of Ideas* 23 (1962): 163–174.

Colli, Giorgio. "Lo sviluppo del pensiero politico di Platone." *Nuova Rivista Storica* 23 (1939): 169–192, 449–476.

Conroy, D. L. *Plato's Early Theory of Knowledge*. Dissertation. University of Massachusetts (1974): DA XXXV, 1975: 6190A–6191A.

Cornford, Francis M. *Plato's Theory of Knowledge. The 'Theaetetus' and the 'Sophist' of Plato Translated With a Running Commentary*. London: Routledge, 1935. Reprint New York: Liberal Arts Press, 1957.

———. *Plato and Parmenides. Parmenides' 'Way of Truth' and Plato's 'Parmenides' translated with an introduction and a running commentary*. London: Kegan Paul, Trench, Trubner & Co. Ltd., 1939 and New York: Harcourt, Brace and Company, 1939; Reprint London: Routledge, 1949, 1950, 1958, 1964, 1968, 1977, 1980.

———. *Plato, The 'Republic'*. Translation with introduction and notes. Oxford: Oxford University Press, 1941.

Corte, M. de. "La question platonicienne." *Review de Philosophie* 7 (1938): 501–531.

Coulter, James A. "Plato and Sophistic Myth. Studies in Plato's *Apology* and *Symposium*." Summary of Dissertation in *Harvard Studies of Classical Philology* 67 (1963): 307 f.

———. "The Relation of the Apology of Socrates to Gorgias' Defense of Palamedes and Plato's Critique of Gorgianic Rhetoric." *Harvard Studies of Classical Philology* 68 (1964): 269–304.

———. "*Phaedrus* 279a: The Praise of Isocrates." *Greek Roman & Byzantine Studies* 8 (1967): 225–236.
Cox, D. R. and Brandwood, L. "On a Discriminatory Problem Connected with the Works of Plato." *Journal of the Royal Statistical Society* Series B, 21 (1959): 195–200.
Crain, Paulus. *De ratione quae inter Platonis Phaedrum Symposiumque intercedat*. Dissertation. Leipzig: Teubner, 1906.
Croiset, Maurice. (ed.). *Platon. Oeuvres complètes*, T. I. Introduction, 1–13. Collection Budé. Paris: Les Belles Lettres, 1921.
Crombie, I. M. *An Examination of Plato's Doctrines, I–II*. London: Routledge, 1962–63.
———. "Ryle's New Portrait of Plato." *Philosophical Review* 78 (1969): 362–373.
Dain, Alphonse. *Leçon sur la stylistique greque*. Paris, 1941.
Dalfen, Joachim. "Gedanken zur Lektüre platonischer Dialoge." *Zeitschrift fur philosophischer Forschung* 29 (1975): 169–194.
———. "Wie, von wem und wann wollte Platon gelesen werden? Eine Nachlese zu Platons Philosophiebegriff." *Grazer Beiträge* 22 (1998): 29–79.
Davies, John K. *Athenian Propertied Families 600–300 BC*. Oxford: Clarendon Press, 1971.
de Groot, Albert W. *A Handbook of Antique Prose Rhythm*. Groningen: Wolters, 1918.
———. *Der antike Prosarhythmus*. Groningen: Wolters, 1921.
———. *La prose métrique des anciens*. Collection d'Études Latines, 2. Paris: Les Belles Lettres, 1926.
de Magalhâes-Vilhena, Vascos M. *See* Magalhâes-Vilhena, Vascos M. de.
de Vogel, Cornelia J. "La dernière phase du platonisme et l'interpretation de M. Robin." *Studia varia Carolo Guilielmo Vollgraff a discipulis oblata*. Amsterdam: North-Holland (1948): 165–178.
———. "Problems Concerning Later Platonism." *Mnemosyne* (IV) 2 (1949): 197–216, 299–318. Reprint: de Vogel, *Philosophia, Vol. I: Studies in Greek Philosophy* with the title "Problems Concerning Plato's Later Doctrine." Assen (1970): 256–95. German translation in: Jürgen Wippern, *Das Problem der ungeschriebenen Lehre Platons*. Darmstadt: Wissenschaftliche Buchgesellschaft (1972): 41–87.
———. "The Legend of the Platonizing Aristotle." Ingemar Düring and G. E. L. Owen (eds.), *Aristotle and Plato in the Mid-Fourth Century: Papers of the Symposium Aristotelicum, Held at Oxford in August 1957*. Göteborg, 1960: 248–256.
———. "Two Major Problems Concerning Socrates." Θ-Π (*Theta-Pi*. A Journal for Greek and Early Christian Philosophy. Leiden: Brill) 2 (1973): 18–39.
———. *Rethinking Plato and Platonism*. Mnemosyne, Supplement 92. Leiden: Brill, 1986.
de Vries, Gerrit J. *Untersuchungen über die Sperrung von Substantiv und Attribut in der Sprache der attischen Redner*. Dissertation. Göttingen, 1938.
———. *Spel bij Plato*. Amsterdam: Noord-Hollandsche Uitg. Mij, 1949.
———. "Isocrates' Reaction to the *Phaedrus*." *Mnemosyne* 6 (1953): 39–45.
———. "A New Indication For the Date of the *Phaedrus*?" *Mnemosyne* 16 (1963): 286 f.
———. "Novellistic Traits in Socratic Literature." *Mnemosyne* 16:1 (1963): 35–42.
———. *A Commentary on the 'Phaedrus' of Plato*. Amsterdam, 1969.
———. "Isocrates in the *Phaedrus*. A Reply." *Mnemosyne* 24 (1971): 387–390.
———. "Platonic Dialogues Performed?" *Mnemosyne* 37 (1984): 143–145.
Deane, Philip. "Stylometrics Do Not Exclude the *Seventh Letter*." *Mind* 82 (1973): 113–117.

Demos, Raphael. *The Philosophy of Plato*. New York: Scribner's Sons, 1939. Reprint New York: Octagon Books, 1966.

Denkinger, M. "L'énigme du Nombre de Platon et la Loi des dispositifs de M. Diès." *Revue des Études Grecques* 68 (1955): 38–76.

Denniston, John D. *Greek Prose Style*. Oxford: Clarendon Press, 1952. Reprint London: Duckworth, 2007.

———. *The Greek Particles*. 2nd edition. Oxford: Clarendon Press, 1954. New edition. Indianapolis: Hacket, 1996.

Derbolav, Josef. *Der Dialog 'Kratylos' im Rahmen der platonischen Sprach- und Erkenntnisphilosophie*. Saarbrücken: West-Ost-Verlag, 1953.

———. *Platons Sprachphilosophie im 'Kratylos' und in den späteren Schriften*. Darmstadt: Wissenschaftliche Buchgesellschaft, 1972.

des Places, Édouard. *Études sur quelques particules de liaison chez Platon*. Collection d'Etudes anciennes. Paris: Les Belles Lettres, 1929.

———. "Style parlé et style oral chez les écrivains grecs." *Mélanges Bidez*, Bruxelles: Institut pour Philologie et Histoire Orientales, (1934): 267–286.

———. "Les dernières années de Platon." *L'Antiquité Classique* 7 (1938): 169–200.

———. "Un livre nouveau sur les Lettres de Platon." *Revue de Philologie* 66 (1940): 127–135.

———. *Pindare et Platon*. Bibliothèque des archives de philosophie. Quatrième section. Philosophie ancienne 1. Paris: Beauchesne, 1949.

———. "Phrase et période chez Platon." *Actes du Premier Congrès de la Fédération Internationale des Associations d'Études Classiques*, Paris 1950. Paris: Klincksieck (1951): 364–366.

———."L'authenticité des Lois et de l'Epinomis." *L'Antiquité Classique* 21 (1952): 376–383.

———, (ed.). *Platon, Oeuvres complètes*, T.XII. 2. *Les Lois*, livres XI–XII, texte établi par A. Diès. *Epinomis*, texte établi par É. des Places. Collection Budé. Paris: Les Belles Lettres, 1956.

———. "La langue philosophique de Platon." *Siculum Gymnasium* 14 (1961): 71–83.

———. *Platon, Oeuvres complètes*, T.XIV: 1–2. *Lexique de la langue philosophique et religieuse de Platon*. Collection Budé. Paris: Les Belles Lettres, 1964.

Detel, W. "Zur Argumentationsstruktur im ersteren Hauptteil von Platons Aretedialogen." *Archiv für Geschichte der Philosophie* 55 (1973): 1–29.

———. "Die Kritik an den Definitionen im zweiten Hauptteil der platonischen Aretedialoge." *Kant-Studien* 65 (1974): 122–134.

———. "Bemerkungen zum Einleitungsteil einiger platonischer Frühdialoge." *Gymnasium* 82 (1975): 308–314.

Devereux, D. L. "Separation and Immanence in Plato's Theory of Forms." *Oxford Studies in Ancient Philosophy* 12 (1994): 63–90. Reprint *Fine* (1999): 192–214.

Díaz Tejera, A. "Ensayo de un metodo lingüístico para la cronología de Platon." *Emerita* 29 (1961): 241–286.

———. "Die Chronologie der Dialoge Platons." *Das Altertum* 11 (1965): 79–86.

Diels, H. and W. Schubart. *Anonymer Kommentar zu Platons Theätet*. Pap. 9782 nebst 3 Bruchstücken philosophischen Inhalts. Unter Mitwirkung von J. L. Heiberg. Berliner Klassikertexte 2. Berlin, 1905.

Diès, Auguste. "La transposition platonicienne." *Annales de Institut Supérieur de Philosophie*, Université de Louvain. Tome II (1913): 265–308.

―――, (ed.). *Platon, Oeuvres complètes,* T.VIII.2: *Théétète,* texte établi par A.D. Collection Budé. Paris: Les Belles Lettres, 1924.

―――, (ed.). *Platon, Oeuvres complètes,* T.VIII.3: *Le Sophiste,* texte établi par A.D. Collection Budé. Paris: Les Belles Lettres, 1925.

―――. *Autour de Platon. Essais de critique et d'histoire. I. Les Voisinages; Socrates. II. Les Dialogues; Esquisses Doctrinales.* Paris: Beauchesne, 1927.

―――, (ed.). *Platon, Oeuvres complètes,* T.VI: *La République.* I–III, texte établi par E. Chambry avec introduction de Auguste Diés. Collection Budé. Paris: Les Belles Lettres, 1932.

―――, (ed.). *Platon, Oeuvres complètes,* T.IX.1: *Le Politique.* Texte établi et traduit. Collection Budé. Paris: Les Belles Lettres, 1935.

―――, (ed.). *Platon, Oeuvres complètes,* T.IX.2: *Philèbe.* Text établi. Collection Budé. Paris: Les Belles Lettres, 1941.

―――, (ed.). *Platon, Oeuvres complètes,* T.XI.1: *Les Lois,* livres I–II, texte établi par Édouard des Places avec introduction de Auguest Diés et L. Gernet. Collection Budé. Paris: Les Belles Lettres, 1951.

Diesendruck, Z. *Struktur und Charakter des platonischen Phaidros.* Wien/Leipzig: Braumüller, 1927.

Dieterle, R. *Platons 'Laches' und 'Charmides.' Untersuchungen zur elenktisch-aporetischen Struktur der platonischen Frühdialoge.* Dissertation. Freiburg, 1966.

Dihle, Albrecht. *Studien zur griechischen Biographie.* Abhandlungen der Akademie der Wissen- schaften in Göttingen, Philologisch-Historische Klasse, Dritte Folge 37. Göttingen: Vandenhoeck & Ruprecht, 1956.

Diller, H. "Probleme des platonischen *Ion.*" *Hermes* 83 (1955): 171–187.

Dillon, John. "Comments on John Moore's Paper [1973]." J. M. E. Moravcsik (ed), *Patterns in Plato's Thought.* Dordrecht: Reidel (1973): 72–77.

―――. *The Middle Platonists, 80 BC to AD 220.* Ithaca: Cornell University Press, 1977. Revised edition by London: Duckworth, 1996.

Dittenberger, W. "Sprachliche Kriterien für die Chronologie der platonischen Dialoge." *Hermes* 16 (1881): 321–345.

Dittmar, Heinrich. *Aischines von Sphettos: Studien zur Literaturgeschichte der Sokratiker, Untersuchungen und Fragmente.* Philologische Untersuchungen 21. Berlin, 1912.

Dixsaut, Monique. *Le naturel philosophe. Essai sur les dialogues de Platon.* Paris: Les Belles Lettres/Vrin, 1985.

Dodds, E. R. "Plato and the Irrational." *Journal of Hellenic Studies* 65 (1945): 16–25.

―――. *Plato, 'Gorgias.'* A revised text with introduction and commentary. Oxford: Clarendon Press, 1959.

Dönt, Eugen. "Die Stellung der Exkurse in den pseudo-platonischen Dialogen." *Wiener Studien* 76 (1963): 27–51.

―――. "'Vorneuplatonisches' im Grossen Alkibiades." *Wiener Studien* 77 (1964): 37–51.

―――. "Bemerkungen zu Platons Spätphilosophie und zu Philipp von Opus." *Wiener Studien* 78 (1965): 45–57.

―――. *Platons Spätphilosophie und die Akademie. Untersuchungen zu den platonischen Briefen, zu Platons 'ungeschriebene Lehre' und zur Epinomis des Philipp von Opus.* Sitzungsberichte der Philosophisch-Historischen Classe der Kaiserlichen Akademie der Wissenschaften 251:3. Böhlaus: Österreichische Akademie der Wissenschaften, 1967.

Döring, A. "Eudoxos von Knidos, Speusippos und der Dialog Philebos." *Vierteljahrsschrift für wissenschaftliche Philosophie und Soziologie* 27 (1903): 113–129.

Döring, Friedrich. *De Legum Platonicarum compositione.* Dissertation. Leipzig, 1907.
Döring, Klaus. "Über den Sophisten Polyxenos." *Hermes* 100 (1972): 29–42.
Dornseiff, F. "Platons Politeia Buch I." *Hermes* 76 (1941): 111 f.
Dörrie, Heinrich and Baltes, Matthias. *Der Platonismus in der Antike.* I–IV. Stuttgart-Bad Cannstatt: Frommann-Holzboog, 1987–1996.
Dorter, Kenneth. "Imagery and Philosophy in Plato's *Phaedrus.*" *Journal of the History of Philosophy* 9 (1971): 279–288.
———. *Form and Good in Plato's Eleatic Dialogues.* Berkeley: University of California Press, 1994.
Dover, Kenneth J. "The Date of Plato's *Symposium.*" *Phronesis* 10 (1965): 2–20.
———. *Aristophanes, 'Clouds.'* Edited with introduction and commentary. Oxford: Clarendon Press, 1968.
———. *Lysias and the 'Corpus Lysiacum'.* Sather Classical Lectures 39. Berkeley: University of California Press, 1968.
———. *The Evolution of Greek Prose Style.* Oxford: Clarendon Press, 1997.
Droste, P. *De adjectivorum in ειδής et in ώδης desinentium apud Platonem usu.* Dissertation. Marburg, 1886.
Duchemin, Jaqueline. "Remarques sur la composition du 'Gorgias'." *Revue des Études Grecques* 56 (1943): 265–286.
———. "Platon et l'héritage de la poésie." *Revue des Études Grecques* 68 (1955): 12–37.
Dümmler, Ferdinand von. *Akademika. Beiträge zur Literaturgeschichte der Sokratischen Schulen.* Giessen: Ricker, 1889.
———. *Chronologische Beiträge zu einigen platonischen Dialogen aus den Reden des Isokrates.* Programm zur Rektoratsfeier der Universität Basel. Basel: Reinhardt, 1890.
Duncan, R. B. *The Role of the Concept of Philia in Plato's Dialogues.* Dissertation. Yale University (1969): DA XXX, 1970: 3499 A–3500A.
Düring, Ingemar. *Herodicus the Cratetean. A Study in Anti-Platonic Tradition.* Kungliga Vitterhets Historie och Antikvitets Akademiens Handlingar 51:2. Stockholm: Wahlström & Widstrand, 1941.
———. "Aristotle and Plato in the Mid-Fourth Century." *Eranos* 54 (1956): 109–120.
———. *Aristotle in the Ancient Biographical Tradition.* Studia Graeca et Latina Gothoburgensia 5. Göteborg: Garland, 1957. Reprint Taylor & Francis, 1987.
Düring, Ingemar and G. E. L. Owen (ed's.), *Aristotle and Plato in the Mid-Fourth Century: Papers of the Symposium Aristotelicum, Held at Oxford in August 1957.* Studia Graeca et Latina Gothoburgensia. Göteborg, 1960.
Dušanić, Slobodan. "L'académie de Platon et la paix commune de 371 av. J.-C." *Revue des Études Grecques* 92 (1979): 319–347.
Dyer, L. "Plato as a Playwright." *Harvard Studies in Classical Philology* 12 (1901): 165–180.
Ebert, Theodor. *Meinung und Wissen in der Philosophie Platons. Untersuchungen zum 'Charmides', 'Menon' und 'Staat'.* Berlin: De Gruyter, 1974.
Eberz, Jakob. *Über den Philebos des Platon.* Dissertation. Würzburg: Borst, 1902.
———. "Die Einkleidung des platonischen Parmenides." *Archiv für Geschichte der Philosophie* 20 (1907): 81–95.
———. "Die Tendenzen der platonischen Dialoge *Theaitetos, Sophistes, Politikos.*" *Archiv für Geschichte der Philosophie* 22 (1909): 252–263, 456–492.
———. "Die Bestimmung der von Platon entworfenen Trilogie Timaios, Kritias, Hermokrates." *Philologus* 69 (1910): 40–50.

———. "Platons Gesetze und die sizilische Reform." *Archiv für Geschichte der Philosophie* 25 (1912): 162–174.
Eckert, Wilhelm. *Dialektischer Scherz in den früheren Gesprächen Platons*. Dissertation. Erlangen: Nürnberg, 1911.
Edelstein, L. "The Function of the Myth in Plato's Philosophy." *Journal of the History of Ideas* 10 (1949): 463–481.
———. *Plato's 'Seventh Letter.'* Philosophia Antiqua 14. Leiden: Brill, 1966
Edmonds, John M. *The Fragments of Attic Comedy*, 1. Leiden: Brill, 1957.
Effe, B. "Platons Charmides und der Alkibiades des Aischines von Sphettos." *Hermes* 99 (1971): 198–208.
Egermann, Franz. *Die platonischen Briefe VII und VIII*. Dissertation. Berlin, Wien 1928.
———. "Platonische Spätphilosophie und Platonismen bei Aristoteles." *Hermes* 87 (1959): 133–142.
Ehlers, Barbara. *Eine vorplatonische Deutung des sokratischen Eros. Der Dialog Aspasia des Sokratikers Aischines*. Zetemata 41. München: Beck, (1966).
Ehrenfels, Frida von. "Zur Deutung der platonischen 'Hochzeitszahl'." *Archiv für Geschichte der Philosophie* 44 (1962): 240–244.
Eichholz, D.E. "The Pseudo-Platonic dialogue *Eryxias*." *The Classical Quarterly* 29 (1935): 129–149.
Else, Gerald. F. *The Structure and Date of Book 10 of Plato's 'Republic.'* Abhandlungen der Heidelberger Akademie der Wissenschaften 3, Philosophisch-Historische Klasse. Heidelberg: Winter, 1972.
Engelhardt, F. G. *De periodorum Platonicorum structura, I–II*. Programmschriften. Gymnasium Gedanensis 1853, 1864.
Enkvist, Nils E., John Spencer and Michael Gregory (eds). *Linguistics and Style*. Language and language learning 6. London: Oxford University Press, 1964.
Erbse, Hartmut. "Die Architektonik im Aufbau von Xenophon's Memorabilien." *Hermes* 89 (1961): 257–287.
———. "Platon und die Schriftlichkeit." *Antike und Abendland* 11 (1962): 7–20.
———. "Über Platons Methode in den sogenannten Jugenddialogen." *Hermes* 96 (1968): 21–40.
———. "Platons Urteil über Isokrates." *Hermes* 99 (1971): 183–197.
———. "Zur Entstehungszeit von Platons 'Apologie des Sokrates'." *Rheinisches Museum* 118 (1975): 22–47.
Erler, M. *Der Sinn der Aporien in den Dialogen Platons: Übungsstücke zur Anleitung im philosophischen Denken*. Untersuchungen zur antiken Literatur und Geschichte 25. Berlin: De Gruyter, 1987.
———. "Episode und Exkurs in Drama und Dialog. Anmerkung zu einer poetologischen Diskussion bei Platon und Aristiteles." Anton Bierl al. (eds.), *Orchestra. Drama, Mythos, Bühne*. Stuttgart: Teubner (1994): 318–330.
Eucken, Christoph. *Isokrates: Seine Positionen in der Auseinandersetzung mit den zeitgenössischen Philosophen*. Untersuchungen zu antiken Literatur und Geschichte 19. Berlin: De Gruyter, 1983.
Evans, D. W. *Plato's 'Minos,' 'Hipparchus,' 'Theages' and 'Lovers:' A Philosophical Interpretation*. Dissertation. Pennsylvania State University (1976): DA XXXVII, 1976: 2939A–2940A.
Fackeldey, Hubert. *Zur Einheit des platonischen 'Timaios.'* Dissertation. Köln, 1958.
Fattal, M. "La composition des concepts dans la De anima (III,6) d'Aristote." *Commentaires grecs et arabes. Revue des Études Grecques* 108 (1995): 371–387.

Feier, J. *L'Éros platonicien*. Jérusalem: Éditions Academon, 1990.
Ferber, Rafael. *Platos Idee des Guten*. Sankt Augustin: Richarz, 1984. 2nd edition 1989.
———. *Die Unwissenheit des Philosophen oder warum hat Plato die "ungeschriebene Lehre" nicht geschrieben?* Sankt Augustin: Academia Verlag, 1991.
———. [Review of] Karl Albert, *Über Platons Begriff der Philosophie*, 1989. *Gnomon* 64 (1992): 662–667.
———. "Hat Plato in der 'ungeschriebene Lehre' eine 'dogmatische Metaphysik und Systematik' vertreten?" Einige Bemerkungen zum Status Quaestionis. *Méthexis* 6 (1993): 37–53.
———. "Für eine propädeutische Lektüre des Politicus." Christopher J. Rowe (ed.), *Reading the 'Statesman'*. *Proceedings of the Third Symposium Platonicum*. International Plato Studies 4. Sankt Augustin: Academia Verlag, 1995: 63–75.
Ferguson, John. *Utopias of the Classical World: Aspects of Greek and Roman Life*. London: Thames and Hudson, 1975.
Ferrari, G. R. F. "Platonic Love." In: Richard Kraut (ed.), *The Cambridge Companion to Plato*. Cambridge: Cambridge University Press, 1992: 248–272.
———. "Myth and Conservatism in Plato's *Statesman*." Christopher J. Rowe (ed.), *Reading the 'Statesman'*. *Proceedings of the Third Symposium Platonicum*. International Plato Studies 4. Sankt Augustin: Academia Verlag, 1995: 389–397.
Festa, N. "Note sull'arte di Platone." *La Cultura* 31 (1912): 406–409, 434–443, 465–476.
Festugière, A.-J. "Sur un passage difficile du Protagoras." *Bulletin de la Correspondence Hellènique* 70 (1946): 179–186.
———. *Hippocrate, L'Ancienne Médicine*. Introduction, traduction et commentaire. Études et Commentaires 4. Paris: Klincksieck, 1948. Reprint New York: Arno Press, 1979.
———. *Les trois 'protreptiques' de Platon: 'Euthydème,' 'Phédon,' 'Epinomis.'* Paris: Vrin, 1973.
Field, G. C. *Plato and his Contemporaries. A Study in Fourth-Century Life and Thought*. London: Methuen, 1930; 2nd edition 1953; 3rd edition 1967. Reprint Whitefish: Kissinger Publishing, 2007.
———. *The Philosophy of Plato*. Oxford 1949; 2nd edition 1969.
Findlay, J. N. *Plato: The Written and the Unwritten Doctrines*. London: Routledge, 1974.
Fine, Gail. *On Ideas: Aristotle's Criticism of Plato's Theory of Forms*. Oxford: Clarendon Press, 1993.
Finley, M. I. *Aspects of Antiquity*. New York: Viking Press, 1968. Reprint London: Penguin, 1972, 1991.
Fischer, J. L. *The Case of Socrates*. Rozpravy Čeckoslovenske Akademie Věd, Řada Společensk. Věd LXXIX 8. Prague: Nakladatelstvi Českolovenske Academia Ved, 1969.
Flacelière, R. "À propos du 'Banquet' de Xénophon." *Revue des Études Grecques*. 74 (1961): 93–118.
Flashar, Helmut. *Der Dialog Ion als Zeugnis platonischer Philosophie*. Berlin: Akademie-Verlag, 1958.
———. *Platon, Ion*. Griechisch-deutsch herausgegeben. München: Heimeran, 1963.
Fossum, Andrew. "Hapax Legomena in Plato." *American Journal of Philology* 52 (1931): 205–231.
Fowler, Roger. (ed.). *Essays on Style and Language: Linguistic and Critical Approaches to Literary Style*. London: Routledge, 1966.
Fox, Marvin. "The Trials of Socrates: An Interpretation of the First Tetralogy." *Archiv für Philosophie* 6 (1956), 226–261.

François, Gilbert. *Le polythéisme et l'emploi au singulier des mots* θεός, δαίμων *dans la littérature grecque d'Homère à Platon*. Bibliothèque de la Faculté de Philosophie et Lettres de l'Université de Liège 147. Paris, 1957.
Frank, Alfons. *Vorsicht und Behutsamkeit gegenüber Mensch und Gott in der Sprache Platos.* Eine sprachpsychologische Untersuchung. Dissertation. Würzburg. München, 1937.
Frank, Erich. *Plato und die sogenannten Pythagoreer*. Ein Kapitel aus der Geschichte des griechischen Geistes. Halle: Niemeyer, 1923. 2nd edition, Tübingen: Niemeyer, 1962.
Freydberg, Bernard. *The Play of the Platonic Dialogues*. Literature and the Sciences of Man 12. New York: Lang Publishers, 1997.
Friedländer, Paul. *Der Grosse Alcibiades,* I–II. Bonn, 1921–23.
———. "Socrates Enters Rome." *American Journal of Philology* 66 (1945): 337–351.
———. *Platon* I–III. Berlin: De Gruyter, 1960–1964. 3 Auflage, 1975.
Fries, C. "Zur Vorgeschichte der platonischen Dialogform." *Rheinisches Museum* 82 (1933): 145–161.
Freis, Richard. (ed.). *The Progess of Plato's Progress*. ΑΓΩΝ Supplement 2, 1969.
Friis Johansen, Karsten. *Studier over Platons Parmenides i dens forhold til tidligere platoniske dialoger*. With an English summary. Dissertation. København, 1964.
Fritz, Kurt von. "Die Ideenlehre des Eudoxos von Knidos und ihr Verhältnis zur platonischen Ideenlehre." *Philologus* 82 (1927): 1–26.
———. "Die Lebenszeit des Eudoxos von Knidos." *Philologus* 85 (1930): 478–481.
———. "Zur Frage der Echtheit der xenophontischen Apologie des Sokrates." *Rheinisches Museum* 80 (1931): 36–68.
———. "Platon, Theaetet und die antike Mathematik." *Philologus* 87 (1932): 40–62, 136–178.
———. "Theaitetos" (2). *Paulys Real-Encyclopädie der classischen Altertumswissenschaft* V A (1934): 1351–1372.
———. "Theodoros" (31). *Paulys Real-Encyclopädie der classischen Altertumswissenschaft* V A (1934): 1811– 1825.
———. "Pythagoras." *Pauly's Real-Encyclopädie der classischen Altertumswissenschaft* 24 (1963): 171–209.
———. "Die philosophische Stelle im siebten platonischen Brief und die Frage der 'esoterischen' Philosophie Platons." *Phronesis* 11 (1966): 117–153.
———. "Zur Frage der esoterischen Philosophie Platons." *Archiv für Geschichte der Philosophie* 49 (1967): 255–268.
———. *Platon in Sizilien und das Problem der Philosophenherrschaft*. Berlin: De Gruyter, 1968.
Frutiger, Perceval. *Les mythes de Platon*. Étude philosophique et littéraire. Thèse Genève, Paris 1930. Reprint New York: Arno Press, 1976.
Fussi, Alessandra. "Why is the *Gorgias* So Bitter?" *Philosophy and Rhetoric* 33 (2000): 39–58.
Gadamer, Hans-Georg al. (eds.). *Idee und Zahl: Studien zur platonischen Philosophie*. Abhandlungen der Heidelberger Akademie der Wissenschaften, Philologisch-historische Klasse 2. Heidelberg: Winter, 1968.
———. *Idee und Wirklichkeit in Platons Timaios*. Sitzungsberichte der Heidelberger Akademie der Wissenschaften, Philologisch-historische Klasse 2. Heidelberg: Winter, 1974.

Gagarin, Michael. "The Purpose of Plato's *Protagoras.*" *Transactions and Proceedings of the American Philological Association* 100 (1969): 133–164.
Gaiser, Konrad. *Protreptik und Paränese bei Platon.* Untersuchungen zur Form des platonischen Dialogs. Tübinger Beiträge zur Altertumswiss 40. Stuttgart: Kohlhammer, 1959.
———. *Platons ungeschriebene Lehre.* Studien zur systematischen und geschichtlichen Begründung der Wissenschaften in der platonischen Schule. Stuttgart: Klett, 1963.
———. "Platons Menon und die Akademie." *Archiv für Geschichte der Philosophie* 46 (1964): 241–292. Reprint: Jürgen Wippern, *Das Problem der ungeschriebenen Lehre Platons.* Darmstadt: Wissenschaftliche Buchgesellschaft (1972): 329–393.
———. "Platons Farbenlehre." *Synusia:* Festgabe für Wolfgang Schadewaldt. Pfullingen (1965): 173–222. Reprint *Gesammelte Schriften* (2004), 451–499.
———. "Quellenkritische Probleme der indirekten Platonüberlieferung." Hans-Georg Gadamer al. (eds.), *Idee und Zahl,* Abhandlungen der Heidelberger Akademie der Wissenschaften, Philologisch-historische Klasse 2. Heidelberg: Winter, 1968: 31–84. Reprint *Gesammelte Schriften* (2004): 205–263.
———, (ed.). *Das Platonbild.* Zehn Beiträge zum Platonverständnis. Hildesheim: Olms, 1969.
———. *Name und Sache in Platons 'Kratylos'.* Abhandlungen der Heidelberger Akademie der Wissenschaften, Philologisch-Historische Klasse 3. Heidelberg: Winter, 1974.
———. "Plato's Enigmatic Lecture 'On the Good'." *Phronesis* 25 (1980): 5–37.
———. "La teoria dei principî in Platone." *Elenchos* 1 (1980): 45–75.
———, (ed.). *Philodems Academica.* Die Berichte über Platon und die Alte Akademie in zwei herkulanensischen Papyri. Supplementum Platonicum I. Stuttgart-Bad Cannstatt: Frommann-Holzboog, 1988.
Gartmann, Georg. *Der pseudoplatonische Dialog Eryxias.* Dissertation. Bonn, 1949.
Gauss, Hermann. *Philosophischer Handkommentar zu den Dialogen Platos* I–III. Bern: Lang, 1952–1960.
Gautier, Léopold. *La langue de Xénophon.* Thèse. Geneva: Georg & Co., 1911.
Geach, P. T. "Plato's *Euthyphro.* An Analysis and Commentary." *The Monist* 50 (1966): 369–382.
Gebhardt, Ernst. *Polykrates' Anklage gegen Sokrates und Xenophons Erwiderung.* Dissertation. Frankfurt, 1957.
Geffcken, Johannes. *Griechische Literaturgeschichte.* I–II, Von Demokritos bis Aristoteles. II A, Text und Anmerkungen. Bibliothek der Klassischen Altertumswiss IV. Heidelberg: Winter, 1926, 1934.
———. "Studien zu Platons Gorgias." *Hermes* 65 (1930): 14–37.
Geiszler, Aloys. *Über die Idee der platonischen Apologie des Sokrates.* Dissertation. C.J. Beckers Universitäts-Buchdruckerei, 1905.
Gercke, Alfred. "Die Analyse als Grundlage der höheren Kritik." *Neue Jahrbücher für das klassische Altertum* 7 (1901): 81–112.
———. "Eine Niederlage des Sokrates." *Neue Jahrbücher für das klassische Altertum* 41 (1918): 145–191.
Gerson, Lloyd. P. *The unity of Plato's Parmenides.* Dissertation. University of Toronto (1975): DA XXXVIII; (1977): 3557A–3558A.
Giangrande, G. "L'epistola platonica X." *Studi Italiani di Filologia Classica* 24 (1950): 181–186.
———."La Epistola platonica I." *Rivista Filologia Classica* 32 (1954): 353–371.

Giannantoni, Gabriele. "Il primo libro della Repubblica di Platone." *Rivista critica di storia della filosofia* 12 (1957): 123–145.
———. *Socratis et Socraticorum Reliquiae* I–IV. Napoli: Bibliopolis, 1983–1985. 2nd edition, *Socratis et Socraticorum Reliquiae* (SSR), ibid., 1990.
———, al. *La Tradizione Socratica: Seminario di Studi.* Memorie dell'Istituto Italiano per gli Studi Filosofici 25. Napoli: Bibliopolis, 1995.
Gifford, Edwin H. *The 'Euthydemus' of Plato.* With revised text, introduction, notes and indices. Oxford: Clarendon Press, 1905. Reprint New York: Arno Press, 1973.
Gigon, Olof. "Studien zu Platons Protagoras." *Phyllobolia.* (Schwabe, 1946): 91–152.
———. *Sokrates: Sein Bild in Dichtung und Geschichte.* Bern: Francke, 1947.
———. *Platon.* Bibliographische Einführungen in das Studium der Philosophie 12. Bern: Francke, 1950.
———. "Das Einleitungsgespräch der Gesetze Platons." *Museum Helveticum* 11 (1954): 201–230. Reprint *Studien zur antiken Philosophie* (1972): 155–187.
———. "Platons Euthyphron." *Westöstliche Abhandlungen.* R. Tschudi überreicht. Wiesbaden (1954): 6–38. Reprint *Studien zur antiken Philosophie* (1972): 188–225.
———. [Review of] Marion Sorelh, *Der platonische Dialog Hippias Major* (1953). *Gnomon* 27 (1955): 14–20.
Gill, Christopher. *Plato's Use of Characters in His Dialogues.* Dissertation. Yale University (1970): DA XXXI, (1971): 6574A.
———. "The Death of Socrates." *The Classical Quaterly* 23 (1973): 25–28.
———. "Platonic Dialectic and the Truth-Status of the Unwritten Doctrines." *Méthexis* 6, (1993): 55–72.
———. *Personality in Greek Epic, Tragedy, and Philosophy. The Self in Dialogue.* Oxford, Clarendon Press, 1996, 1998.
Giordano, D. "Il Cratilo di Platone." *Vichiana: Rassegna di Studi Classic* 1 (1964): 390–406.
Girgenti, Giuseppe (ed.). *La nuova interpretazione di Platone.* Un dialogo tra Hans-Georg Gadamer e la scuola di Tubinga-Milano (Tübingen, 3th Sept. 1996). Introduzione di Hans-Georg Gadamer. Milano: Rusconi, 1998.
Gleisberg, K. *De vocabulis tragicis quae apud Platonem inveniuntur.* Dissertation. Breslau, 1909.
Goedeckemeyer, Albert. "Die Reihenfolge der platonischen Schriften." *Archiv für Geschichte der Philosophie* 22 (1909): 435–455.
Goldin, Owen. "Self, Sameness, and Soul in *Alcibiades* I and the *Timaeus.*" *Freiburger Zeitschrift für Philosophie und Theologie* 40 (1993): 5–19.
Goldschmidt, Victor. *Essai sur le 'Cratyle': Contribution à l'Histoire de la Pensee de Platon.* Paris: Vrin, 1940. Reprint Paris: Vrin, 1982.
———. *Les Dialogues de Platon.* Structure et méthode dialectique. Thèse. Paris: Presses Universitaires de France, 1947. 3me édition 1971.
———. *Le paradigme dans la dialectique platonicienne.* Thèse complém. Paris: Presses Universitaires de France, 1947.
———. "Sur le problème du 'système' de Platon." *Rivista Critica di Storia di Filosofia* 5 (1950): 169–178. Also in: *Questions Platoniciennes,* (1970): 23–33.
———. "Temps historique et temps logique dans l'interpretation des systèmes philosophiques." *Proceedings of 11th International Congress of Philosophy* 12, Amsterdam (1953): 7–13. Also in: *Questions Platoniciennes,* (1970): 13–21.
———. *Questions Platoniciennes.* Paris: Vrin (Bibliothèque d'Histoire de la Philosophie), 1970.

Gomme, A. W. "The Structure of Plato's *Crito*." *Greece & Rome* 5 (1958): 45–51.
Gomperz, Heinrich. "Über die Abfassungszeit des platonischen Kriton." *Zeitschrift für Philosophie und philosophische Kritik* 109 (1896): 176–179.
———. "Isokrates und die Sokratik." *Wiener Studien* 27 (1905): 163–207; 28 (1906): 1–42.
———. "Die Anklage gegen Sokrates in ihrer Bedeutung für die Sokratesforschung." *Neue Jahrbücher für das Klassische Altertum* 53 (1924): 129–173.
———. "Plato's System of Philosophy." Gilbert Ryle (ed.), *Proceedings of the Seventh International Congress of Philosophy*. Oxford: Oxford University Press (1931): 426–431.
Gomperz, Theodor. "Platonische Aufsätze, I: Zur Zeitfolge platonischer Schriften." *Sitzungsberichte der Philosophisch-Historischen Classe der Wissenschaften zu Wien* 114 (1887): 741–768.
———. *Griechische Denker*, II. Leipzig: Veit & Company, 1902.
Gonzalez, Francisco J. "Self-knowledge, Practical Knowledge, and Insight. Plato's Dialectic and the Dialogue Form." *The Third Way*, (1995): 155–187.
———, (ed.). *The Third Way. New Directions in Platonic Studies*. Lanfield: Rowman & Littlefield, 1995.
Görgemanns, Herwig. *Beiträge zur Interpretation von Platons Nomoi*. Zetemata 25. München, 1960. Also in: Dissertation. Würzburg, 1959.
Gosling, J. C. B. *Plato*. London: Routledge, 1973.
Gottschalk, H. B. [Review of] Konrad Gaiser, *Protreptik und Paränese bei Platon* (1959) and *Platons ungeschriebene Lehre* (1963). *Erasmus* 16 (1964): 419–422.
———. *Heraclides of Pontus*. Oxford: Oxford University Press, 1980.
Gould, John. *The Development of Plato's Ethics*. Cambridge: Cambridge University Press, 1955. Reprint New York: Russell & Russell, 1972.
Goulet-Cazé, Marie-Odile and Richard Goulet (eds.). *Le cynisme ancien et ses prolongements*. Actes du colloque international du CNRS (1991). Paris: Presses Universitaires de France, 1993.
Graeser, Andreas. "Kritische Retraktationen zur esoterischen Platon-Interpretation." *Archiv für Geschichte der Philosophie* 56 (1974): 71–87.
———. "Zur Logik der Argumentationsstruktur in Platons Dialogen Laches und Charmides." *Archiv für Geschichte der Philosophie* 57 (1975): 172–181.
Gräfe, Steffen. *Der gespaltene Eros. Platons Trieb zur Weisheit*. Europäische Hochschulschriften, R.20. Philosophie, Bd. 219. Frankfurt am Main: Klosterman, 1989.
Greene, W. C. "The Spirit of Comedy in Plato." *Harvard Studies in Classical Philology* 31 (1920): 63–123.
———. "The Spoken and the Written Word." *Harvard Studies in Classical Philology* 60 (1951): 23–59.
———. "The Paradoxes of the *Republic*." *Harvard Studies in Classical Philology* 63 (1958): 199–216.
Griffith, G. T. "The Union of Corinth and Argos (392–386 B. C.)." *Historia* 1 (1950): 236–256.
Griswold, Charles L., Jr. (ed.). *Platonic Writings, Platonic Readings*. London: Routledge, 1988. Reprint University Park: Pennsylvania State University Press, 2007.
Groag, Emil. "Platons Lehre von den Seelenteilen, I–II." *Wiener Studien* 35 (1913): 323–352; 37 (1915): 118–141.
———. "Zur Lehre vom Wesen der Seele in Platos Phaedrus und im X.Buche der Republik." *Wiener Studien* 37, (1915): 189–222.
Grote, George. *Plato and the Other Companions of Sokrates*, I–III. London: Murray, 1865. 2nd edition, 1867. Reprint Charleston: BookSurge Publishing, 2004.

Grube, George M. A. "On the Authenticity of the *Hippias Major.*" *The Classical Quarterly* 20, (1926): 134–148.

———. "The Logic and Language of the *Hippias Major.*" *Classical Philology* 24 (1929): 369–375.

———. *Plato's Thought.* London: Methuen, 1935.

———. "Thrasymachus, Theophrastus, and Dionysius of Halicarnassus." *American Journal of Philology* 73 (1952): 251–267.

Grünwald, E. *Sprichwörter und sprichwörtliche Redensarten bei Plato.* Programmschriften. Berlin, 1893.

Gulley, Norman. "Ethical Analysis in Plato's Earlier Dialogues." *The Classical Quarterly* 2, (1952): 74–82.

———. "Plato's Theory of Recollection." *The Classical Quarterly* 4 (1954): 194–213.

———. *Plato's Theory of Knowledge.* London: Methuen, 1962. Reprint 1973.

———. "The Authenticity of the Platonic Epistles." *Pseudepigrapha* I, Entretiens sur l'antiquité classique 18. Geneva: Foundation Hardt (1972): 103–30; discussion 31–143.

Gundert, Hermann. "Die Simonides-Interpretation in Platons Protagoras." *Hermeneia.* Festschrift Otto Regenbogen, Heidelberg: Winter (1952): 71–93.

———. "Platon und das Daimonion des Sokrates." *Gymnasium* 61 (1954): 513–531.

———. *Der platonische Dialog.* Bibliothek der klassischen Altertumswissenschaften, Neue Folge, 2. Reihe, Bd. 26. Heidelberg: Winter, 1968.

———. "Zum philosophischen Exkurs im 7. Brief." Hans-Georg Gadamer al. (eds.), *Idee und Zahl: Studien zur platonischen Philosophie.* Abhandlungen der Heidelberger Akademie der Wissenschaften, Philologisch-Historische Klasse 2. Heidelberg: Winter (1968): 85–105.

———. *Dialog und Dialektik: Zur Struktur des platonischen Dialogs.* Studien zur antiken Philosophie 1. Amsterdam: Grüner, 1971.

Gundert, Hermann, Klaus Dörring, and Felix Preishofen (eds.). *Platonstudien.* Studien zur antiken Philosophie 7. Amsterdam: Grüner, 1977.

Guthrie, W. K. C. "Plato's Views on the Nature of the Soul." *Entretiens sur l'antiquité classique,* Foundation Hardt 3 (1957): 3–21. Reprint: Gregory Vlastos (ed.), *Plato: A Collection of Critical Essays* II. Garden City: Anchor Books/Doubleday, (1971): 230–43. Reprint: T. M. Robinson, *Plato's Psychology,* 2nd edition. Toronto: University of Toronto Press, 1995.

———. *A History of Greek Philosophy.* Vol 1–6. Cambridge: Cambridge University Press, 1962–1981.

Haack, Joannes. *De Reipublicae Platonis priore editione.* Dissertation. Griefswald, 1917.

Haag, Adelheid. *Hippias Major. Interpretation eines pseudoplatonischen Dialogs.* Dissertation. Tübingen, 1973.

Haag, Erich. *Platons 'Kratylos.' Versuch Einer Interpretation.* Tübinger Beiträge zur Altertumswiss 19. Stuttgart: Kohlhammer, 1933.

Hackforth, Reginald. *The Authorship of the Platonic Epistles.* Cambridge: Cambridge University Press, 1913. Reprint 1985.

———. "The Modification of Plan in Plato's *Republic.*" *The Classical Quarterly* 7 (1913): 265–272.

———. *The Composition of Plato's 'Apology.'* Cambridge: Cambridge University Press, 1933.

———. *Plato's Examination of Pleasure*: *A Translation of the 'Philebus' With Introduction and Commentary.* Cambridge: Cambridge University Press, 1945.

———. "Immortality in Plato's *Symposium*." *The Classical Review* 64 (1950): 43–45.
———. *Plato's 'Phaedrus.'* Translated with an introduction and commentary. Cambridge: Cambridge University Press, 1952. Reprint 1972.
———. *Plato's 'Phaedo.'* Translated with introduction and commentary. Cambridge: Cambridge University Press, 1955. Reprint 1972.
Hagen, Benno von. *Num simultas intercesserit Isocrati cum Platone*. Dissertation. Jenae: Neuenhahn, 1906.
Hager, Fritz-Peter. "Vom sokratischen Zweifel zur platonischen Gewissheit. Ein beispielhafter Weg des Philosophierens." *Museum Helveticum* 34 (1977): 99–121.
Hall, Edith. *Inventing the Barbarian: Greek Self-Definition Through Tragedy*. Oxford University Press, 1989. Reprint 1991.
Halliwell, S. [Review of] Richard Kraut (ed.), *The Cambridge Companion to Plato* (1992). *Dialogos* 1 (1994): 128–134.
Hammer-Jensen, Ingeborg. "Apologien og Euthyphron." *Nordisk Tidsskrift for Filologi* 14 (1905/06): 116–120.
———. "Demokrit und Plato." *Archiv für Geschichte der Philosophie* 23 (1910): 92–105; 211–229.
Hampton, Cynthia M. *Pleasure, Knowledge, and Being: An Analysis of Plato's 'Philebus.'* SUNY Series in Ancient Greek Philosophy. New York: University of New York Press, 1990.
Hansen, Mogens H. "Hvorfor henrettede athenerne Sokrates?" *Museum Tusculanum* 40–43 (1980): 55–82. Reprint Thested: Klassikerforeningens Kildehæfter, 1991.
Happ, Heinz. *Hyle. Studien zum aristotelischen Materie-Begriff*. Berlin and New York: De Gruyter, 1971
Harder, Richard. "Plato und Athen." *Neue Jahrbücher für Wissenschaft und Jugendbildung* 10 (1934): 492–500.
———. *Platons Kriton*. Berlin: Weidmann, 1934.
Harris, W. A. *Plato as a Narrator: A Study in the Myths*. Dissertation. John Hopkins University, 1892.
Harrison, E. L. "Plato's Manipulation of Thrasymachus." *Phoenix* 21 (1967): 27–39.
Hartland-Swann, John. "Plato as Poet. A Critical Interpretation." *Philosophy* 26 (1951): 3–18, 131–141.
Harward, J. *The Platonic Epistles*. Translated with introduction and notes. Cambridge: Cambridge University Press, 1932.
Haslam, M. W. "A Note on Plato's Unfinished Dialogues." *American Journal of Philology* 97 (1976): 336–339.
Hathaway, R. "Sceptical Maxims about the 'Publication' of Plato's Dialogues." ΑΓΩΝ, Supplement 2 (1969): 28–42.
Havelock, Eric. *Preface to Plato*. Cambridge, MA: Belknap Press of Harvard University Press, 1963. Reprint 2006.
———. *The Literate Revolution in Greece and Its Cultural Consequences*. Princeton: Princeton University Press, 1982.
Havers, W. *Handbuch der erklärenden Syntax. Ein Versuch zur Erforschung der Bedingungen und Triebkräfte in Syntax und Stilistik*. Indogermanische Bibliothek. Abt. 1. Reihe 1. Bd. 20. Heidelberg: Winters, 1931.
Heath, Thomas L. *A History of Greek Mathematics*, I. Oxford: Clarendon Press, 1921. Reprint Mineola: Dover Publications, 1981.
Hedenius, Ingemar. "Kommentar till Platons *Gorgias*." *Platon: 'Gorgias.'* Copenhagen: Gyldendal (1977): 137–184.

Heidel, William A. *Pseudo-Platonica.* Dissertation. University of Chicago. The Friedenwald Company, 1896.
———. "On Plato's *Euthyphro.*" *Transactions of the American Philological Society* 31 (1900): 163–181.
———. *Plato's 'Euthyphro.'* With introduction and notes. American Book Company, 1902.
Heikel, I. A. "Bemerkungen zur Sprachstatistik und zur sogenannten Stylometrie." *Eranos* 4 (1900): 11–19.
Heintzeler, Gerhard. *Das Bild des Tyrannen bei Platon.* Tübinger Beiträge zur Altertumswissenschaft 3. Stuttgart: Kohlhammer, 1927.
Heitsch, Ernst. "Timiotera." *Hermes* 117 (1989): 278–287.
———. *Wege zu Platon: Beiträge zum Verständnis seines Argumentierens.* Göttingen: Vandenhoeck & Ruprecht, 1992.
Hell, G. "Zur Datierung des siebenten und achten platonischen Briefes." *Hermes* 67 (1932): 295–302.
Heller, Siegfried. "Ein Beitrag zur Deutung der Theodoros-Stelle in Platons 'Theaetet'." *Centaurus* 8 (1956): 1–58.
———. "Theaetets Bedeutung als Mathematiker." *Sudhoffs Archiv für Geschichte der Medizin und der Naturwissenschaften* 51 (1967): 55–78.
Helmbold, W. C. and W. B. Holther. *The Unity of the 'Phaedrus.'* University of California Publications in Classical Philology 14, No. 9 (1952): 387–417.
Hentschke, Ada B. *Politik und Philosophie bei Plato und Aristoteles: Die Stellung der Nomoi im platonischen Gesamtwerk und die politische Theorie des Aristoteles.* Frankfurter Wissenschaftliche Beiträge, Kulturwissenschaftliche Reihe 13. Klostermann, 1971. Reprint 2004.
Hermann, Alf. *Untersuchungen zu Platons Auffassung von der Hedone.* Ein Beitrag zum Verständnis des platonischen Tugendbegriffes. Hypomnemata 35. Göttingen: Vandenhoeck & Ruprecht, 1972.
Hermann, Karl F. *Geschichte und System der platonischen Philosophie*, I. Heidelberg: Winter, 1839. Reprint New York: Arno Press, 1976.
Hiestand, Max. *Das sokratische Nichtwissen in Platons ersten Dialogen.* Eine Untersuchung über die Anfänge Platons, Dissertation. Orell Fussli, 1923.
Hildebrandt, Kurt. *Platon. Logos und Mythos.* Berlin: De Gruyter, 1959.
Hinske, Norbert. "Zur Interpretation des platonischen Dialogs Laches." *Kant-Studien* 59 (1968): 62–79.
Hintikka, Jaakko. "Knowledge and Its Objects in Plato." J. M. E. Moravcsik (ed.), *Patterns in Plato's Thought.* Dordrecht: Reidel (1973): 1–30.
Hirmer, J. "Entstehung und Komposition der platonischen Politeia." *Jahrbücher für classische Philologie*, Supplement 23. Leipzig (1897): 579–678.
Hirschberger, Johannes. "Die Phronesis und die Philosophie Platons vor dem Staate." *Philologus*, Supplement 25, 1. Leipzig: Dietrich, 1932.
Hirzel, Rudolf. *Der Dialog. Ein literaturhistorischer Versuch*, I. Stuttgart: Hirzel, 1895.
———. *Über das Rhetorische und seine Bedeutung bei Plato.* Stuttgart: Hirzel, 1871.
Hitchcock, D. L. "The Role of Myth and Its Relation to Rational Argument in Plato's Dialogues." Dissertation. Claremont Graduate School (1973): DA XXXV; (1974): 1701A–1702A.
Hoerber, Robert. G. "Plato's *Hippias Major.*" *The Classical Journal* 50 (1955): 183–186.
———. "Plato's *Euthyphro.*" *Phronesis* 3 (1958): 95–107.
———. "Plato's *Lysis.*" *Phronesis* 4 (1959): 15–28.

———. "Plato's *Meno*." *Phronesis* 5 (1960): 78–102.
———. "Plato's *Lesser Hippias*." *Phronesis* 7 (1962): 121–131.
———. "The Socratic Oath 'By the Dog'." *Classical Journal* 58 (1963): 268–269.
———. "Plato's *Greater Hippias*." *Phronesis* 9 (1964): 143–155.
———. "Plato's *Laches*." *Classical Philology* 63 (1968): 95–105.
Höfer, H. *De particulis Platonicis capita selecta*. Dissertation. Bonn, 1882.
Hoffmann, Ernst. "Der gegenwärtige Stand der Platon-Forschung." Eduard Zeller, *Die Philosophie der Griechen in ihrer geschichtlichen Entwicklung*, II. Leipzig: Reisland (1922): 1051–1086. Reprint Hildesheim: Olms, 1990.
———. *Platon*. Zürich and München: Artemis, 1950.
Hoffmann, Michael. *Die Entstehung von Ordnung. Zur Bestimmung von Sein, Erkennen und Handeln in der späteren Philosophie Platons*. Beiträge zur Altertumskunde 81. Berlin: Teubner, 1996.
Hoffmann, Michael and Mischa von Perger. "Ideen, Wissen und Wahrheit nach Platon. Neue Monographien." *Philosophische Rundschau* 44 (1997): 113–151.
Hofmann, Johann B. "Wege und Ziele der umgangssprachlichen Forschung." *Bayerische Blätter für das Gymnasial-Schulwesen* 62 (1926): 317–326.
———. *Lateinische Umgangssprache*. 2nd edition. Indogermanische Bibliothek 1.1.17. Heidelberg: Winter, 1936.
———. *Lateinische Syntax und Stilistik*. Neubearbeitet von Anton Szantyr. Handbuch der Altertumswissenschaft II.2.2. Müchen: Beck, 1965.
Hoopes, J. P. "An interpretation of Plato's *Euthyphro*." Dissertation. Vanderbilt University (1967): DA XXVIII, 1968: 4212A.
Horn, Ferdinand. *Platonstudien. Neue Folge*. Wien: Hölder, 1904.
Horn, Hans- Jürgen. *Hippias Major. Untersuchungen zur Echtheitsfrage des Dialogs*. Dissertation. Köln, 1964.
Horneffer, Ernest. *Der junge Platon*. Giessen: Töpelmann, 1922.
Hornsby, R. "Significant Action in the *Symposium*." *The Classical Journal* 52 (1956): 37–40.
Howald, Ernst. "Der alte Platon." *Festgabe für H. Blümner*. Zürich (1914): 272–286.
———. *Platons Leben*. Zürich: Fussli, 1923.
Howland, Jacob A. "Re-reading Plato. The Problem of Platonic Chronology." *Phoenix* 45 (1991): 189–214.
———. *The Paradox of Political Philosophy. Socrates' Philosophical Trial*. Lanham: Rowman & Littlefield, 1998.
Howland, R. L. "The Attack on Isocrates in the *Phaedrus*." *The Classical Quarterly* 31, (1937): 151–159.
Huby, Pamela M. "The *Menexenus* Reconsidered." *Phronesis* 2 (1957): 104–114.
Huffman, C. *Philolaus of Croton. Pythagorean and Presocratic. A Commentary of the Fragments and Testimonia with Interpretative Essays*. Cambridge: Cambridge University Press, 1993. Reprint 2006.
Humbert, J. "Le pamphlet de Polycratès et le Gorgias de Platon." *Revue de Philologie* 5 (1931): 20–77.
———. "Remarques sur la structure de la phrase de Platon." *Actes du Congrès de l'Association G. Budé*, 1953. Paris (1954): 189–192.
———. *Socrate et les petits socratiques*. Paris: Presses Universitaires France, 1967.
Hyland, Drew A. *Finitude and Transcendence in the Platonic Dialogues*. Albany: SUNY Press, 1995.

Ickler, Hans-Theodor. *Der platonische Menexenos*. Tübinger Beiträge zur Altertumswissenschaft, Heft 41. Stuttgart: Kohlhammer, 1961.
———. *Platons sogenanntes 'Hypothesis-Verfahren'*. Dissertation. Universität Marburg, Fachbereich Altertumswissenschaft, 1973.
Ilting, Karl-Heinz. "Aristoteles über Platons philosophische Entwicklung." *Zeitschrift für philosophische Forschung* 19 (1965): 377–392.
———. "Platons 'ungeschriebene Lehren': Der Vortrag 'über das Gute'." *Phronesis* 13 (1968): 1–31.
Immisch, Otto. "Zum gegenwärtigen Stande der platonischen Frage." *Neue Jahrbucher für das Klassische Altertum* 3 (1899): 440–465, 549–561, 612–628.
———. "Die antike Angaben über die Entstehungszeit des platonischen Phaidros." *Berichte über die Verhandlungen der Königlichen Sächsischen Gesellschaft der Wissenschaften zu Leipzig, Philologisch-historische Klasse* 56 (1904): 213–251.
———. "Der erste platonische Brief, mit einer Einleitung über den Zweck und einer Vermutung über die Entstehung der platonischen Briefsammlung." *Philologus* 72 (1913): 1–41.
———. "Neue Wege der Platonforschung." *Neue Jahrbucher für das Klassische Altertum* 35 (1915): 545–572.
Ingenkamp, Heinz G. "Laches, Nikias und platonische Lehre." *Rheinisches Museum* 110 (1967): 234–247.
———. *Untersuchungen zu den pseudoplatonischen Definitionen*. Klassisch-philologische Studien Heft 35. Wiesbaden: Harrassowitz, 1967.
Irwin, Terence. *Plato's Ethics*. Oxford: Oxford University Press, 1995.
———. *Plato's Moral Theory: The Early and Middle Dialogues*. Oxford: Oxford University Press, 1977.
Isenberg, Meyer W. "The Unity of Plato's *Philebus*." *Classical Philology* 35 (1940): 154–179.
Isnardi Parente, Margherita. "Note al dialogo pseudoplatonico Anterastai." *La Parola del Passato* 9 (1954 [a]): 137–143.
———. "Una nota al Minosse pseudoplatonico." *La Parola del Passato* 9 (1954 [b]): 45–53.
———. "Sugli apocrifi platonici Demodoco e Sisifo." *La Parola del Passato* 9, (1954 [c]): 425–431.
———. "L'Accademia e le Lettere platoniche." *La Parola del Passato* 10 (1955): 241–273.
———. "Un discorso consolatorio del corpus Platonicum." *Rivista critica di storia della filosofia* 16 (1961): 33–47.
———. "Per l'interpretazione dell'excursus filosofico della VII epistola platonica." *La Parola del Passato* 19 (1964): 241–290.
———. "La VII epistola e Platone esoterico." *Rivista critica di storia della filosofia* 24 (1969): 416–431.
———. *Filosofia e politica nelle lettere di Platone*. Napoli: Guida, 1970.
———. "Platone e il problema degli ágrapha." *Méthexis* 6 (1993): 73–93.
———. "Criteri e metodi per una nuova raccolta delle testimonianze sugli 'Agrapha Platonica'." *Rivista critica di storia della filosofia* 50 (1995): 73–87.
———. "Pitagorismo di Crotone e pitagorismo accademico." *Archivio Storico per la Calabria e la Lucania* 62 (1995): 5–25.
———. "Testimonia Platonica (I). Per una raccolta dei principali passi della tradizione indiretta riguardante i λεγόμενα ἄγραφα δόγματα. Le testimonianze di Aristotele." *Atti della Accademia Nazionale dei Lincei* 394. *Classe di Scienze Morali, Storiche e Filologiche, Memorie S.* IX, Vol. VIII.4. Roma (1997): 371–487.

———. "Testimonia Platonica (II) di età ellenistica e di èta imperiale." *Atti della Accademia Nazionale dei Lincei* 395. *Classe di Scienze Morali, Storiche e Filologiche, Memorie* S. IX, Vol. X.1. Roma (1998): 3–120.
Jackson, H. "Plato's Later Theory of Ideas." *Journal of Philology* 10 (1882–1886): 253–98; 11: 287–31; 13: 1–40 and 242–72; 14: 173–230.
———. "The Supposed Priority of the *Philebus* to the *Republic*." *Journal of Philology* 25 (1897): 65–82, 290–298.
Jaeger, Werner. [Review of ] A. E. Taylor, *Plato. The Man and his Work* (1926). *Gnomon* 4 (1928): 1–11
———. *Diokles von Karystos: Die griechische Medizin und die Schule des Aristoteles.* Berlin, 1938. Reprint 1963.
———. *Paideia: The Ideals of Greek Culture,* Volume II: *In Search of the Divine* and Volume III: *The Conflict of Cultural Ideals in the Age of Plato.* Translated from the German by Gilbert Highet. Oxford: Oxford University Press, II 1943 and III 1944. Reprint II–III, 1986. German version: *Die Formung des griechischen Menschen* II–III. Berlin, 1954–55.
Jäger, G. *'Nus' in Platons Dialogen.* Hypomnemata 17. Göttingen: Vandenhoeck & Ruprecht, 1967.
Janell, W. "Quaestiones Platonicae." Dissertation. *Jahrbücher für klassische Philologie*, Supplementum 26 (1901): 263–336.
———. "Über die Echtheit und Abfassungszeit des Theages." *Hermes* 36 (1901): 427–439.
Janson, T. "The Problems of Measuring Sentence-Length in Classical Texts." *Studia Linguistica* 18 (1964): 26–36.
Jantzen, Jörg. "Das philosophische Problem des Bösen. Platon und die ontologische Tradition." *Philosophisches Jahrbuch* 99 (1992): 74–90.
Jatakari, Tuija. "Der jüngere Sokrates." *Arctos* 24 (1990): 29–45.
Jecht, R. *De usu particulae ἤδη in Platonis dialogis qui feruntur.* Dissertation. Halle, 1881.
Joël, Karl. *Der echte und der xenophontische Sokrates,* I–II. R. Gaertner, 1893–1901.
———. "Der λόγος Σωκρατικός." *Archiv für Geschichte der Philosophie* 9 (1896): 50–66.
———. "Platons sokratische Periode und der 'Phaidros'." *Philosophische Abhandlungen für M. Heinze.* Berlin (1906): 78–91.
———. "Zu Platons Laches." *Hermes* 41 (1906): 310–318; 42 (1907): 160.
———. "Zur Entstehung von Platons Staat." *Festschrift zur 49. Versammlung Deutscher Philologen und Schulmänner.* Berkhouser, (1907): 295–323.
Joly, Henri. *Le renversement platonicien. Logos, Epistémè, Polis.* Paris: Vrin, 1974.
Joly, Robert. "Platon et la médecine." *Bulletin de l'Association G. Budé* 4 (1961): 435–451.
Jowett, Benjamin. *The Dialogues of Plato.* Translated into English with analyses and introductions, I–V. 3rd edition revised and corrected. Oxford: Oxford University Press,1892.
Judeich, W. "Die Zeit der Friedensrede des Andokides." *Philologus* 81 (1926): 141–154.
———. "Athen und Theben vom Königsfrieden bis zur Schlacht bei Leuktra." *Rheinisches Museum* 76 (1927): 171–197.
Junge, Gustav and William Thomson. *The Commentary of Pappus on Book X of Euclid's 'Elements.'* Arabic text and translation with introductory remarks, notes and a glossary of technical terms. Harvard Semitic Series 8. Cambridge, MA: Harvard University Press, 1930.

Junge, Gustav "Von Hippasus bis Philolaus." *Classica & Mediaevalia* 19 (1958) : 41–72.
Kahn, Charles H. "Plato's Funeral Oration: The Motive of the *Menexenus*." *Classical Philology* 58 (1963): 220–234.
———. "Language and Ontology in the *Cratylus*." Edward N. Lee, Alexander P. D. Mourelatos and Richard M. Rorty (eds.), *Exegesis and Argument, Studies Presented to Gregory Vlastos*. Assen: Van Gorcum, (1973): 152–176.
———. "Plato and the Unity of the Virtues." W. H. Werkmeister (ed.), *Facets of Plato's Philosophy*. Assen: Van Gorcum (1976): 21–39.
———. "Did Plato Write Socratic Dialogues?" *The Classical Quarterly* 31 (1981): 305–320.
———. "Proleptic Composition in the *Republic,* or Why Book I Was Never a Separate Dialogue." *The Classical Quarterly* 43 (1993): 131–142.
———. *Plato and the Socratic Dialogue: The Philosophical Use of a Literary Form*. Cambridge: Cambridge University Press, 1996.
Kaimio, Maarit. (ed.). *Filosofen och publiken. Rapport från Platonsällskapets femtonde symposium, Helsingfors 3–6 juni 1999*. Helsinki, 2000.
Kakridis, Johannes T. *Der thukydideische Epitaphios. Ein stilistischer Kommentar*. Zetemata 26. München: Beck, 1961. Reprint 1996.
Kallenberg, H. "'Ὅτι und ὡς bei Platon als Hilfsmittel zur Bestimmung der Zeitfolge seiner Schriften." *Rheinisches Museum* 68 (1913): 465–476.
Kaluscha, W. "Zur Chronologie der platonischen Dialoge." *Wiener Studien* 26 (1904): 190–204.
Kamlah, Wilhelm. *Platons Selbstkritik im Sophistes*. Zetemata 33. München: Beck, 1963.
Kapp, E. "Sokrates der Jüngere." *Philologus* 79 (1924): 225–233.
———. "The Theory of Ideas in Plato's Earlier Dialogues." *Ausgewählte Schriften*, Berlin (1968): 55–150.
Kato, Shinro. "The Role of Paradeigma in the *Statesman*." Christopher J. Rowe (ed.), *Reading the 'Statesman.' Proceedings of the Third Symposium Platonicum*. International Plato Studies 4. Sankt Augustin: Academia Verlag (1995): 162–172.
Kelly, Douglas. "Oral Xenophon." Ian Worthington (ed.), *Voice into Text: Orality and Literacy in Ancient Greece*. Leiden: Brill (1996): 149–63.
Kemmer, Ernst. *Die polare Ausdrucksweise in der griechischen Literatur*. Beiträge zur historischen Syntax der griechischen Sprache 15. Würzburg: Stuber, 1903.
Kennedy, George. *The Art of Persuasion in Greece*. London: Routledge and Princeton: Princeton University Press, 1963.
Kerferd, G. B. *The Sophistic Movement*. Cambridge: Cambridge University Press, 1981.
Kerschensteiner, Jula. "Zum Gebrauch von σύν und ξύν bei Platon." *Münchener Studien zur Sprachwissenschaft* 1 (1952): 29–45. Nachdruck, München (1956): 28–41.
———. *See also* Neumann.
Kesters, Hubert. *Plaidoyer d'un Socratique contre le Phèdre de Platon: XXVIe Discours de Thémistius*. Louvain: Nauwelaerts, 1959.
Kiock, A. *De Cratyli Platonici indole ac fine*. Dissertation. Breslau, 1913.
Kirk, G. S. "The Problem of *Cratylus*." *American Journal of Philology* 72 (1951): 225–253.
Kirk, W. "*Protagoras* and *Phaedrus*: Literary Techniques." *Studies Presented to David Moore Robinson II*. St. Louis (1953): 593–601.
Klagge, James C. and Nicholas D. Smith (eds.). *Methods of Interpreting Plato and his Dialogues*. Oxford Studies in Ancient Philosophy, Supplementary Volume. Oxford, Clarendon Press, 1992.

Kleemann, A. von. "Platonische Untersuchungen II." Menon. *Archiv für Geschichte der Philosophie* 21 (1908): 50–75.

Klein, Jacob. *A Commentary on Plato's 'Meno.'* University of North Carolina Press, 1965. Reprint Chicago: University of Chicago Press, 1998.

Kleve, Knut. "The unum venerabilissimum and Plato's mystical style (Parm. 142a)." *Symbolae Osloenses* 37 (1961): 88–95.

———. "The Daimonion of Socrates." *Studi Italiani di Filologia Classica* 79 (1986): 5–18.

Kolár, A. "De Platonis eurhythmia." *Charisteria* Thaddaeo Sinko oblata. Warszawa (1951): 107–120.

Koller, H. *Die Komposition des platonischen Symposions.* Dissertation. Zürich, 1948.

Kopetsch, G. *De verbalibus in* τος *et* τέος *Platonicis dissertatio.* Programmschriften. Lyck, 1860.

Koster, W. J. W. *Le mythe de Platon, de Zarathoustra et des Chaldéens.* Étude critique sur les relations intellectuelles entre Platon et l'Orient. Mnemosyne Bibliotheca Classica Batava, Supplement 3. Leiden: Brill, 1951.

Krämer, Hans J. *Arete bei Platon und Aristoteles.* Zum Wesen und zur Geschichte der platonischen Ontologie. Heidelberg: Winter, 1959. Abhandlungen der Heidelberger Akademie der Wissenschaften. Philosophisch-historische Klasse 1959.

———. "Die platonische Akademie und das Problem einer systematischen Interpretation der Philosophie Platos." *Kant-Studien* 55 (1964): 69–101.

———. "Retraktationen zum Problem des esoterischen Platon." *Museum Helveticum* 21 (1964): 137–167.

———. *Der Ursprung der Geistesmetaphysik.* Untersuchungen zur Geschichte des Platonismus zwischen Platon und Plotin. Amsterdam: Grüner, 1964.

———. "Die grundsätzlichen Fragen der indirekten Platonüberlieferung." In: Hans-Georg Gadamer al. (eds.), *Idee und Zahl: Studien zur platonischen Philosophie.* Abhandlungen der Heidelberger Akademie der Wissenschaften, Philologisch-historische Klasse 2. Heidelberg: Winter (1968): 106–150.

———. "Neues zum Streit um Platons Prinzipentheorie." *Philosophische Rundschau* 27 (1980): 1–38.

———. *Platone e i fondamenti della metafisica. Saggio sulla teoria dei principi e sulle dottrine non scritte di Platone con una raccolta dei documenti fondamentali in edizione bilingue e bibliografia.* Introduction et traduzione di Giovanni Reale. Metafisica e storia della metafisica 1. Milano: Vita e Pensiero, 1982.

Kranz, Margarita. *Das Wissen des Philosophen. Platons Trilogie Theaitet, Sophistes und Politikos.* Dissertation. Tübingen, 1986.

Kratzsch, S. *Platos Grosser Alkibiades.* Eine echtheitskritische Untersuchung. Dissertation. Jena, 1964.

Kraus, Oskar. *Platons Hippias Minor.* Versuch einer Erklärung. Akademisches Antiquariat. Prague: Taussig & Taussig, 1913.

Kraut, Richard. (ed.). *The Cambridge Companion to Plato.* Cambridge: Cambridge University Press, 1992. Reprint 1993, 1995, 1996, 1997, 1999.

Kretschmer, Paul. [Review of] Hans von Arnim, *Die Sprachliche Forschung* (1929). *Glotta* 20 (1932): 232.

Krüger, G. *Der Dialog Theages.* Dissertation. Greifswald, 1935.

Kube, Jörg. TEXNH *und* APETH: *Sophistisches und platonische Tugendwissen.* Berlin: De Gruyter, 1969.

Kucharski, Paul. *Les chemins du savoir dans les derniers dialogues de Platon.* Paris: Presses Universitaires de France, 1949.

———. "La rhétorique dans la Gorgias et le Phèdre." *Revue des Études Grecques* 74 (1961): 371–406.

———. "Sur l'évolution des méthodes du savoir dans la philosophie de Platon." *Revue Philosophique* 155 (1965): 427–440.

Kühn, Helmut. "The True Tragedy: On the Relationship Between Greek Tragedy and Plato." *Harvard Studies in Classical Philology* 52 (1941): 1–40, 53 (1942): 37–88.

———. "Platonische und antiplatonische Platoninterpretation." *Philosophische Rundschau* 24 (1977): 187–203.

Kühn, J. H. [Review of] Ernst Gebhardt, *Polykrates' Anklage* (1957). *Gnomon* 32 (1960): 97–107.

Kühner, Raphael, Friedrich Blass and Bernhard Gerth. *Ausführliche Grammatik der griechischen Sprache. Satzlehre.* I–II. Hannover: Hahnsche Buchhandlung, 1898–1904.

Kühner, Raphael and Friedrich Blass. *Ausführliche Grammatik der griechischen Sprache. Elementarlehre und Formenlehre.* I–II. Hannover: Hahnsche Buchhandlung, 1890–1892.

Kuiper, Wolter E. J. *De Lysidis dialogi origine, tempore, consilio.* Dissertation. Amsterdam: Zwolle, 1909.

Laborderie, Jean. *Le Dialogue platonicien de la maturité.* Paris: Les Belles Lettres, 1978.

———. "La forme du dialogue platonicien de la maturité." *L'information littéraire* 12 (1960): 64–70.

Lafrance, Y. "Le Platon de Gilbert Ryle." *Revue philosophique de Louvain* 69 (1971): 337–369.

Laks, A. "Legislation and Demiurgy: On the Relationship between Plato's *Republic* and *Laws*." *Classical Antiquity* (Berkeley) 9 (1990): 209–229.

Lammermann, K. *Von der attischen Urbanität und ihrer Auswirkung in der Sprache.* Dissertation. Göttingen, 1935.

Landmann, Michael. *Elenktik und Maieutik.* Bonn: Bouvier, 1950.

Lanzalaco, A. "Il convenzionalismo platonico del Cratilo." *Acme* 8 (1955): 205–248.

Lasserre, François. "'Ερωτικοὶ λόγοι." *Museum Helveticum* 1 (1944): 169–178.

———, (ed.). *Die Fragmente des Eudoxos von Knidos.* Herausgegeben, übersetzt und kommentiert. Texte und Kommentare 4. Berlin, 1966.

———. *De Léodamas de Thasos à Philippe d'Oponte. Temoignages et fragments.* La Scuola di Platone 2. Napoli: Bibliopolis, 1987.

Lasso de la Vega, J. S. "En el centenario de Platón. Consideraciones en torno a la 'cuestión platónica'." *Cuadernos de Filologia clásica* (Madrid, Universitas Complutensis) 8 (1975): 9–75.

Lattanzi, G. M. "Il significato e l'autenticità del Menesseno." *La Parola del Passato* 8 (1953): 303–306.

Laudien, A. "Platons Apologie des Sokrates." *Neue Jahrbucher für das Klassische Altertum* 34 (1914): 180–191.

Lavely, J. H. "The Turning Point in Plato's Life." *Boston University Journal* 22 (1974): 32–36.

Ledger, Gerard R. *Re-counting Plato. A Computer Analysis of Plato's Style.* Oxford: Clarendon Press, 1989. Reprint 1990.

Lehnert, Georg. "Bericht über die rhetorische Literatur (1907–1914). Plato." *Jahresbericht über die Fortschritte der klassischen Altertumswissenschaft ('Bursian')* 248 (1935): 34–47.

Leisegang, Hans. *Die Platondeutung der Gegenwart.* Wissen und Wirken 59. Karlsruhe: Braun, 1929.
———. "Platon (1)." *Paulys Real-Encyclopädie der classischen Altertumswissenschaft* 20 (1950): 2342–2537.
Levi, Adolfo. "Questioni platoniche." *Revue de Philologie* 66 (1940): 110–126.
———. "I miti platonici." *Rivista Critica di Storia della Filosofia* 1 (1946): 197–225.
Levin, D. N. "Some Observations Concerning Plato's *Lysis*." *Essays in Ancient Greek Philosophy*. New York: Anton & Kustas, (1971): 231–258.
Levinson, R. B. *In Defense of Plato*. Cambridge: Cambridge University Press, 1953.
———. "Plato's *Phaedrus* and the New Criticism." *Archiv für Geschichte der Philosophie* 46 (1964): 293–309.
Levison, M., Andrew Q. Morton, and A. D. Winspear. "The *Seventh Letter* of Plato." *Mind* 77 (1968): 309–325.
Liebrucks, Bruno. "Das Problem der Entwicklung bei Platon." *Zeitschrift für Religions- und Geistesgeschichte* 1 (1948): 352–355.
———. *Platons Entwicklung zur Dialektik*. Untersuchungen zum Problem des Eleatismus. Frankfurt am Main: Klostermann, 1949.
Lier, Hans. *Untersuchungen zur Epinomis*. Dissertation. Marburg: Lahn, 1966.
Liminta, Maria T. *Il problema della bellezza. Autenticità e significato dell' Ippia maggiore di Platone.* Scienze umane 30. Milano: Celuc, 1974.
Lloyd, A. C. "Plato's Later Dialogues." *Philosophy Quarterly* 3 (1953): 244–247.
Lloyd, G. E. R. *Polarity and Analogy. Two Types of Argumentation in Early Greek Thought.* Cambridge: Cambridge University Press, 1966. 1971. Reprint Indianapolis: Hackett, 1992.
Lodge, Rupert C. *The Philosophy of Plato*. London: Routledge, 1956.
Loepfe, Alfred. *Die Wortstellung im griechischen Sprechsatz erklärt an Stücken aus Platon und Menander.* Dissertation. Freiburg in der Schweiz: Paulusdruckerei, 1940.
Loewenclau, Ilse von. "Mythos und Logos bei Platon." *Studium Generale* 11 (1958): 731–741.
———. *Der platonische Menexenos*. Tübinger Beiträge zur Altertumswissenschaft, Heft 41. Stuttgart: Kohlhammer, 1961.
Löhr, Gebhard. *Das Problem des Einen und Vielen in Platons 'Philebos'*. Hypomnemata 93. Göttingen: Vandenhoek & Ruprecht, 1990.
Lönborg, Sven E. "The Chronology of the Platonic Dialogues." *Theoria* 5 (1939): 141–160.
———. *Platons Eros*. Det sjunde brevet och Symposion. Svenska Humanistiska Förbundets skrifter, no. 49. Stockholm: Norstedt, 1939.
Loraux, Nicole. "Socrate contrepoison de l'oraison funèbre." *L'Antiquité Classique* 43 (1974): 172–211.
———. "Cratyle à l'épreuve de stasis." *Revue de Philosophie Ancienne* 5 (1987): 49–69.
Lottich, O. *De sermone vulgari Atticorum maxime ex Aristophanis fabulis cognoscendo.* Dissertation. Halle, 1881.
Louis, Pierre. *Les métaphores de Platon*. Thèse. Rennes, Paris 1945.
Luccioni, Jean. *La pensée politique de Platon.* Publications de la Faculté des Lettres d'Alger, 30. Paris, 1958.
Luce, J. V. "The Date of the *Cratylus*." *American Journal of Philology* 85 (1964): 136–154.
———. "The Theory of Ideas in the *Cratylus*." *Phronesis* 10 (1965): 21–36.
Luise Reinhard. *Die Anakoluthe bei Platon*. Philologische Untersuchungen 25. Berlin: Weidmann, 1920 (expanded edition). Originally "Observationes criticae in Platonem." Dissertation. Berlin, 1916.

Luther, Wilhelm. *Die Schwäche des geschriebenen Logos.* Ein Beispiel humanistischer Interpretation, versucht am sogenannten Schriftmythos in Platons Phaidros. *Gymnasium* 68 (1961): 526–548.
Lutoslawski, Wincenty. "Über Echtheit, Reihenfolge und logische Theorien von Platos drei ersten Tetralogien." *Archiv für Geschichte der Philosophie* 9 (1895): 67–114.
———. *Sur une nouvelle méthode pour déterminer la chronologie des dialogues de Platon.* Mémoire lu le 16 mai 1896 à l'Institut de France. Paris: Welter, 1896.
———. *The Origin and Growth of Plato's Logic.* With an account of Plato's style and the chronology of his writings. London, New York, Bombay: Longmans, Green and Co., 1897.
———. "Principes de stylométrie." *Revue des Études Grecques* 11 (1898): 61–81.
———. "Plato's Change of Mind." *Proceedings of the 10th International Congress of Philosophy.* 1, fasc. 2, Amsterdam (1949): 1076–1080.
MacClintock, Stuart. "More on the Structure of the *Philebus.*" *Phronesis* 6 (1961): 46–52.
Maddalena, Antonio. *Platone, 'Lettere.'* A cura di A. Maddalena. Bari: Laterza, 1948.
Magalhães-Vilhena, Vasco M. de. *Le problème de Socrate: Le Socrate historique et le Socrate de Platon.* Paris: Presses Universitaires de France, 1952.
———. *Socrate et la légende platonicienne.* Paris: Presses Universitaires de France, 1952.
Maier, Heinrich. *Sokrates: Sein Werk und seine geschichtliche Stellung.* Tübingen: Mohr, 1913. Reprint Scientia Auflage, 1985.
Malcolm, J. "On the Place of the *Hippias Major* in the Development of Plato's Thought." *Archiv für Geschichte der Philosophie* 50 (1968): 189–195.
Manasse, E. M. "Bücher über Platon. Werke in deutscher Sprache," *Philosophische Rundschau.* Beiheft 1–2. Tübingen, 1957–1961.
———. "Bücher über Platon. Werke in französischer Sprache." *Philosophische Rundschau.* Beiheft 7. Tübingen, 1976.
Mannsperger, D. "Zur Sprache der Dialektik bei Platon." Hellmut Flashar and Konrad Gaiser (ed.), *Synusia: Festgabe für Wolfgang Schadewaldt.* Pfullingen: Neske, 1965: 161–171.
Manuwald, Bernd. "Lust und Tapferkeit: Zum gedanklichen Verhältnis zweier Abschnitte in Platons Protagoras." *Phronesis* 20 (1975): 22–50.
Marasco, G. "Osservazioni su Nicia in Platone." *Atene & Roma* 20 (1975): 56–60.
Markowski, Hieronymus. *De Libanio Socratis defensore.* Breslauer philologische Abhandlungen 40. Breslau, 1910. Reprint Hildesheim: Olms, 1970.
Marschall, Theodore. *Untersuchungen zur Chronologie der Werke Xenophons.* Dissertation. München, 1928.
Marten, R. Οὐσία *im Denken Platons.* Monographien zur philosophischen Forschung 29. Meisenheim, 1962.
Martens, H. H. *Die Einleitungen der Dialoge "Laches" und "Protagoras".* Untersuchungen zur Technik des platonischen Dialoges. Dissertation. Kiel, 1954.
Martin, Gottfried. *Platons Ideenlehre.* Berlin: De Gruyter, 1973.
Martin, Josef. *Symposion: Die Geschichte einer literarischen Form.* Studien zur Geschichte und Kultur des Altertums 17. 1–2. Paderborn: Schöningh, 1931.
Masaracchia, A. "Il 'Carmide' de Platone." *Maia* 3 (1950): 161–180.
Mathieu, G. "Les premiers conflicts entre Platon et Isocrate et la date de l'Euthydème." *Mélanges G. Glotz*, II. Paris: Presses Universitaires de France (1932): 555–564.
Mattingly, H. B. "The Date of Plato's *Symposium.*" *Phronesis* 3 (1958): 31–39.

McCabe, Mary M. *Plato's Individuals.* New Jersey: Princeton University Press, 1994.
McDonald, John M. S. *Character-portraiture in Epicharmus, Sophron, and Plato.* Dissertation. Columbia University, Sewanee 1931.
McGilp, I. F. "The Unity of Plato's Political Thought." Dissertation. University of British Columbia (1974): DA XXXV, 1975: 7352A.
McKirahan Jr., Richard. D. *Plato and Socrates: A Comprehensive Bibliography 1958–1973.* New York: Garland, 1978.
Meinhardt, P. *De forma et usu iuramentorum, quae inveniuntur in comicorum Graecorum et Platonis, Xenophontis, Luciani sermone.* Dissertation. Jena, 1892.
Meiser, K. "Kritische Beiträge I. Ist Platon der Verfasser des Dialoges Kriton?" *Abhandlungen aus dem Gebiete der klassischen Altertumswissenschaft, für W. von Christ.* München: Beck, (1891): 5–8.
Meissner, Helmut. *Der tiefere Logos Platons.* Heidelberger Forschungen 21. Heidelberg: Winter, 1978.
Meister, M. *De Axiocho dialogo.* Dissertation. Breslau, 1915.
Menzel, A. "Untersuchungen zum Sokrates-Processe." *Sitzungsberichte der Philosophisch-Historischen Classe der Kaiserlichen Akademie der Wissenschaften zu Wien* 145:2, 1902. Wien, 1903.
Méridier, Louis. *Platon, Oeuvres complètes,* T.V.1. *Ion—Ménexène—Euthydème,* texte établi par L. M. Collection Budé. Paris, 1931.
———. *Platon, Oeuvres complètes,* T.V.2 *Cratyle,* texte établi par L. M. Collection Budé. Paris, 1931.
Merlan, Phillip. "Form and Content in Plato's Philosophy." *Journal of the History of Ideas* 8 (1947): 406–430.
———. *Studies in Epicurus and Aristotle.* (Appendix p. 98–104; The Life of Eudoxus). Klassisch-Philologische Studien, Heft 22. The Hague: Nijhoff, 1960.
———. "War Platons Vorlesung Das Gute einmalig?" *Hermes* 96 (1968): 705–709. Reprint: Phillip Merlan, *Kleine philosophische Schriften.* Hildesheim: Olms, (1976): 259–73.
Mesk, E. "Anklagerede des Polykrates gegen Sokrates." *Wiener Studien* 32 (1911): 56–84.
Meyer, Edward. *Geschichte des Altertums,* Bd. V. Stuttgart, 1902.
Meyer, G. "Die stilistische Verwendung der Nominalkomposition im Griechischen." *Philologus Supplement* 16.3. Leipzig, 1923.
Meyer, Thomas. *Platons Apologie.* (Dissertation. Tübingen) Tübinger Beiträge zur Altertumswissenschaft 42. Stuttgart: Kohlhammer, 1962.
Michaelson, S. and Andrew Q. Morton. "The New Stylometry. A One-word Test of Authorship for Greek Writers." *The Classical Quarterly* 22 (1972): 89–102.
———. "The Authorship and Integrity of the Platonic Epistles." *Revue International de Philosophic* 103 (1973): 3–9.
———. "Elision as an Indicator of Authorship in Greek Writers." *Revue de L'Organisation international pour l'étude des langues anciennes par ordinateur* (R.E.L.O. Liège 1973): 33–56.
———. "Things Ain't What They Used To Be: A Study of Chronological Change in Greek Writers." Alan Jones and R. F. Churchhouse (eds.), *The Computer in Literary and Linguistic Studies: Proceedings of the Third International Symposium.* Cardiff: University of Wales Press, (1976): 78–84.
Michaelson, S., Andrew Q. Morton and D. A. Gillies. "The Problem of Plato." *Revue de L'Organisation international pour l'étude des langues anciennes par ordinateur* (R.E.L.O. Liège 1977): 1–28.

Migliori, Maurizio. *L'uomo fra piacere, intelligenza e Bene: Commentario storico-filosofico al'Filebo di Platone*. Studi e Testi 28. Milano: Vita e Pensiero, 1993.

———. *Arte politica e metretica assiologica: Commentario storio-filosofico al'Politico di Platone*. Prefazione di Hans J. Krämer. Studi e Testi 52. Milano: Vita e Pensiero, 1996.

Miller, Mitchell. "The Choice Between the Dialogues and the 'Unwritten Teachings': A Scylla and Charybdis for the Interpreter?" Francisco J. Gonzalez (ed.), *The Third Way: New Directions in Platonic Studies*. Lanham: Rowman & Littlefield (1995): 225–244.

Milobenski, E. "Zur Interpretation des platonischen Dialogs Kriton." *Gymnasium* 75 (1968): 371–390.

Momigliano, A. "Il Menesseno." *Rivista di Filologia e di Istruzione Classica* 8 (1930): 40–53.

Montuori, M. *Socrates. Physiology of a Myth*. London Studies in Classical Philology 6. Amsterdam: Geiben Publishing (Brill), 1981.

———, (ed.). *The Socratic Problem. The History, the Solutions, from the 18th Century to the Present Time*. Philosophica 4. Amsterdam: Gieben Publishing (Brill), 1992.

Moore, John D. "The *Symposium* and Plato's development." Dissertation. Stanford University (1969): DA XXX, (1969): 1156A–1157A.

———. "The Relation between Plato's *Symposium* and *Phaedrus*." J. M. E. Moravcsik (ed.), *Patterns in Plato's Thought*, Dordrecht: Reidel 1973: 52–71.

———. "The Dating of Plato's *Ion*." *Greek, Roman and Byzantine Studies* 15 (1974): 421–439.

Moravcsik, J. M. E. (ed.). *Patterns in Plato's Thought: Papers Arising out of 1971 West Coast Greek Philosophy Conference*. Dordrecht: Reidel, 1973.

———. "Plato's Method of Division." Moravcsik (ed.), *Patterns in Plato's Thought*, 1973: 158–180.

———. *Plato and Platonism. Plato's Conception of Appearance and Reality in Ontology, Epistemology and Ethics, and its Modern Echoes*. London: Blackwell, 1992.

Moreau, Joseph. *La construction de l'idéalisme platonicien*. Thèse. Paris, 1939.

———. "Les thèmes platoniciens de l'Ion." *Revue des Études Grecques* 52 (1939): 419–428.

———. "Le Platonisme de l'Hippias Majeur." *Revue des Études Grecques* 54 (1941): 19–42.

———. "Platon et la connaissance de l'âme." *Revue des Études Anciennes* 55 (1953): 249–257.

Morrison, J. S. "Meno of Pharsalus, Polycrates, and Ismenias." *The Classical Quarterly* 36 (1942): 57–78.

———. "The Origins of Plato's Philosopher-Statesmen." *The Classical Quarterly* N. S. 8 (1958): 198–218.

———. "Four notes on Plato's *Symposium*." *The Classical Quarterly* 14 (1964): 42–55.

Morrow, Glenn. R. *Studies in the Platonic Epistles*. With a translation and notes. Illinois Studies in Language and Literature 18, 3–4. Urbana: University of Illinois Press, 1935.

———. "Plato's Conception of Persuasion." *Philosophical Review* 62 (1953): 234–250.

———. "The Demiurge in Politics: The *Timaeus* and the *Laws*." *Proceedings of the American Philolosophical Association* 27 (1953–4): 5–23. Nicholas D. Smith (ed.), *Plato: Critical Assessments*. London: Routledge (1998): 309–324.

———. "Aristotle's Comments on Plato's *Laws*." Ingemar Düring and G. E. L. Owen (eds.), *Aristotle and Plato in the Mid-Fourth Century: Papers of the Symposium Aristotelicum, Held at Oxford in August 1957*. Göteborg, 1960: 145–162.

———. *Plato's Cretan City: A Historical Interpretation of the 'Laws.'* Princeton: Princeton University Press, 1960.
Morton, Andrew Q. and James McLeman. *Paul, the Man and the Myth: A Study in the Authorship of Greek Prose.* London: Hodder and Stoughton, 1966.
Morton, Andrew Q., James McLeman and Alban D. Winspear. *It's Greek to the Computer.* Montreal: Harvest House, 1971.
Motte, A. "Pour l'authenticité du Premier Alcibiade." *L'Antiquité Classique* 30 (1961): 5–32.
Moutafakis, N. J. "Plato's Emergence in the *Euthyphro*." *Apeiron* 5 (1971): 23–31.
Moutsopoulos, Evanghélos. *La Musique dans l'oeuvre de Platon.* Thèse. Paris: Presses Universitaires de France, 1959. Reprint 1992.
Movia, G. *Apparenze Essere e Verità. Commentario storico-filosofico al 'Sofista' di Platone.* Prefazione di Hans J. Krämer, introduzione di Giovanni Reale. Studi e Testi 16. Milano: Vita e Pensiero, 1991.
Mras, K. "Plato's Phaedrus und die Rhetorik." *Wiener Studien* 37 (1915): 88–117.
Mueller, Ian. "The Esoteric Plato and the Analytic Tradition." *Méthexis* 6 (1993): 115–134.
Mugler, Charles. *La Physique de Platon.* Études et Commentaires 35. Paris: Klincksieck, 1960.
Müller, Carl W. "Weltherrschaft und Unsterblichkeit im pseudoplatonischen Theages und in der Eudemischen Ethik." Peter Steinmetz (ed.), *Politeia und Respublica.* Palingenesia 4. Wiesbaden: Steiner (1969): 135–147.
———. *Die Kurzdialoge der Appendix Platonica.* Studia et testimonia antiqua 17. München: Fink, 1975.
Müller, Friedrich. *Stilistische Untersuchung der Epinomis des Philippos von Opus.* Dissertation. Berlin, 1928.
Müller, Gerhard. *Der Aufbau der Bücher II und VII von Platons Gesetzen mit Beiträgen zur Einzelerklärung und einem Exkurs über Gesetze 732d-734e.* Dissertation. Königsberg: Weida, 1935.
———. "Die Philosophie im pseudoplatonischen VII. Brief." *Archiv für Philosophie* 3 (1949): 251–276. Reprint: Gerhard Müller, Andreas Graeser, and Dieter Maue (eds.), *Platonische Studien.* Heidelberg: Winter (1986): 146–171.
———. *Studien zu den platonischen Nomoi.* Zetemata 3. München: Beck, 1951. Reprint 1968.
———. "Die Mythen der platonischen Dialoge." *Nachrichten der Giessener Hochschulgesellschaft* 32 (1963): 77–92. Reprint: Gerhard Müller, Andreas Graeser, and Dieter Maue (eds.), *Platonische Studien.* Heidelberg: Winter (1986): 110–125.
———. "Philosophischer Dialogkunst Platons (an Beispiel des Charmides)." *Museum Helveticum* 33 (1976): 129–161.
Münscher, Karl. "Isokrates (2)." *Pauly's Real-Encyclopädie der classischen Alterumswissenschaft* 9 (1916): 2146–2227.
Murley, Clyde. "Plato's *Phaedrus* and Theocritean Pastoral." *Transactions and Proceedings of the American Philological Association* 71 (1940): 281–295.
———. "Techniques of Modern Fiction in Plato." *Classical Journal* 50 (1954): 281–287.
Murray, James S. "Interpreting Plato on Sophistic Claims and the Provenance of the 'Socratic Method'." *Phoenix* 48 (1994): 115–134.
Muthmann, Fritz. *Untersuchungen zur "Einkleidung" einiger platonischen Dialoge.* Dissertation. Bonn: Rheinische Friedrich-Wilhelms-Universität, 1961.
Mutschmann, Hermann. "Zu Platons Charmides." *Hermes* 46 (1911): 473–478.

———. "Zur Datierung des platonischen Lysis." *Wochenschrift für klassische Philologie* (1918): 429–431.
Myres, John L. *Herodotus, Father of History*. Oxford: Clarendon Press, 1953. Reprint 1999.
Nagel, Werner. "Zur Darstellungskunst Platons insbesondere im Dialog Laches." *Serta philologica Aenipontana*. Innsbrucker Beiträge zur Kulturwissenschaft 7–8. Innsbruck (1962):119–142.
Nails, Debra. *Agora, Academy, and the Conduct of Philosophy*. Philosophical Studies Series 63. Dordrecht: Kluwer Academic Publishers, 1995.
———. "Tidying the Socratic Mess of a Method." *Southwest Philosophy Review* 13:2 (1997): 1–14. *1st Arizona Colloquium in Ancient Philosophy: Socrates*. Tucson, 1996.
Narcy, Michel. "La critique de Socrate par l'Étranger dans le Politique." Christopher J. Rowe (ed.), *Reading the 'Statesman.'* *Proceedings of the Third Symposium Platonicum*. International Plato Studies 4. Sankt Augustin: Academia Verlag (1995): 227–235.
Natali, Carlo. "Le cause del Timeo e la teoria delle quattre cause." Tomás Calvo and Luc Brisson (eds.), *Interpreting the 'Timaeus'-'Critias.'* *Proceedings of the IV Symposium Platonicum*. Sankt Augustin: Academia Verlag (1997): 207–213.
Natorp, Paul. "Platons Phaidros." *Philologus* 48 (1889): 428–449, 583–628.
———. "Über Grundansicht und Entstehungszeit von Platos Gorgias." *Archiv für Geschichte der Philosophie* 2 (1889): 394–413.
———. "Über die Methode der Chronologie platonischer Schriften nach sprachlichen Kriterien." *Archiv für Geschichte der Philosophie* 11 (1898): 461–464.
———. "Untersuchungen über Platons Phaidros und Theaitet." *Archiv für Geschichte der Philosophie* 12 (1899): 1–49, 159–186; 13 (1900): 1–22.
———. "Plato's *Phaedrus*." *Hermes* 35 (1900): 385–436.
———. *Platos Ideenlehre*. Leipzig: Meiner 1903. 2nd edition, 1921. Reprint 1994.
———. "Zur philosophischen Frage." *Deutsche Literaturzeitung* 32 (1911): 1669–1677.
Nawratil, Karl. "Platon in Ägypten." *Zeitschrift für philosophische Forschung* 28 (1974): 598–603.
Nehamas, Alexander. "Predication and Forms of Opposites in the *Phaedo*." *Review of Metaphysics* 26 (1973): 461–491.
Neumann, Willy and Jula Kerschensteiner. *Platon: Briefe*. Griechisch-deutsch herausgegeben von Willy Neumann bearbeitet von Jula Kerschensteiner. München: Heimeran, 1967.
Nickel, Rainer. *Xenophon*. Erträge der Forschung 111. Darmstadt: Wissenschaftliche Buchgesellschaft, 1979.
Nielsen, G. Rangel "Om forholdet mellem Aristophanes 'Ekklesiazusai' og Platons 'Stat'." *Nordisk Tidsskrift for Filologi* 3 R. 11 (1902/03): 49–73.
Niewöhner, F. W. *Dialog und Dialektik in Platons 'Parmenides.' Untersuchungen zur sogenannten platonischen 'Esoterik'*. Monographien zur philosophischen Forschung 78. Meisenheim am Glan: Hain, 1971. Also in Dissertation. Bochum.
Nightingale, Andrea W. *Genres in Dialogue. Plato and the Construct of Philosophy*. Cambridge: Cambridge University Press, 1995.
———. "Plato and the Origin of Evil: The *Statesman* Myth Reconsidered." *Ancient Philosophy* 16 (1996): 65–91.
Nock, Arthur D. "Word-coinage in the Hermetic Writings." *Coniectanea Neotestamentica* 11 (1947): 163–178.
Nolte, Albert. *Sprachstatistische Beispiele aus den früheren platonischen Schriften und aus Ariosts Orlando furioso*. Göttingen: Hubert, 1914.

Norden, Eduard. *Die antike Kunstprosa vom 6. Jahrhundert v. Chr. bis in die Zeit der Renaissance,* I. Leipzig: Teubner, 1898. 1915. 5th edition by Darmstadt: Wissenschaftliche Buchgesellschaft, 1958.

———. *Agnostos Theos: Untersuchungen zur Formengeschichte religiöser Rede.* Leipzig: Teubner, 1913.

Novák, Jan V. "Platon und die Rhetorik." Jahrbücher für Klassische Philologie. *Philologus* Supplement 13 (1883): 441–540.

Novotný, František. "῝Οτι und ὡς in Platons Briefen." *Rheinisches Museum* 69 (1914): 742–744.

———. *Platonis epistulae commentariis illustratae.* Edited. Brno: Opera Facultatis Philosophicae Universitatis Masarykianae Brunensis, 1930.

———. *Plato, Epinomis Commentariis Illustrata.* Edited. Prague: Academiae Scientiarum Bohemoslovenicae, 1960.

Nummenmaa, Tapio. *Divine Motions and Human Emotions in the Philebus and in the Laws. Plato's Theory of Psychic Powers.* Commentationes Humanarum Litterarum 112. Helsinki: Societas Scientiarum Fennica, 1998.

O'Brien, Denis. *Le Non-Être: Deux Études sur le Sophiste de Platon.* International Plato Studies 6. Sankt Augustin: Academia Verlag, 1995.

O'Brien, Michael J. "The Unity of the Laches." *Yale Classical Studies* 18 (1963): 133–147.

Oehler, K. "Der entmythologisierte Platon. Zur Lage der Platonforschung." *Zeitschrift für Philosophische Forschung* 19 (1965): 393–420. Reprint: Oehler, *Antike Philosophie,* München: Beck, (1969): 66–94. Reprint: Jürgen Wippern, *Das Problem der ungeschriebenen lehre Platons.* Darmstadt: Wissenschaftliche Buchgesellschaft (1972): 95–129.

———. "Neue Fragmente zum esoterischen Platon." *Hermes* 93 (1965): 397–407.

Ojeman, M. R. "Assent in Plato's Respublica." *The Classical Bulletin* 4 (1957): 57.

Oldfather, W. A. "The date of Plato's *Laws.*" *American Journal of Philology* 44 (1923): 275 f.

Olzscha, Friedrich T. *Platons Tugendlehre als Kriterium für die die Chronologie seiner Dialoge.* Programmschriften. Zwickau: Zwickauer Zeitungs-(Amtsblatt-)Druckerei, 1910.

Orth, E. "Urteile über Platons Stil." *Philologische Wochenschrift* (1933): 1020–1023.

Ostenfeld, E. "The Role and Status of the Forms in the *Timaeus.* Paradigmatism Revised?" Tomás Calvo and Luc Brisson (eds.), *Interpreting the 'Timaeus'-'Critias.' Proceedings of the IV Symposium Platonicum.* Sankt Augustin: Academia Verlag (1997): 167–177.

Oświecimski, S. "The Enigmatic Character of Some of Plato's Apocrypha." *Eos* 66 (1978): 31–40.

———. "The Acephalous Dialogues." *Eos* 67 (1979): 55–67.

Owen, G. E. L. "The Place of the *Timaeus* in Plato's Dialogues." *The Classical Quarterly* N. S. 3 (1953): 79–95.

Paleikat, Jorge. "Métodos científicos para determinar a autenticidade e a ordem de publicação dos diálogos platónicos." *Organon: Revista da Facultade de Filosofia.* Universidade do Rio Grande do Sul 1 (1956): 47–63, 3 (1959): 31–40.

Palm, Jonas. *Über Sprache und Stil des Diodoros von Sizilien: Ein Beitrag zur Beleuchtung der hellenistischen Prosa.* Lund: Gleerup, 1955.

Panagiotou, Spiro. "Lysias and the date of Plato's *Phaedrus.*" *Mnemosyne* 28, (1975): 388–398.

———. "The Relative Order of Plato's *Parmenides* and *Theaetetus.*" *Classical Philology* 76 (1981): 37–39.
Parente, *See* Isnardi.
Parmentier, L. "La chronologie des dialogues de Platon." *Bulletins de la Classe des Lettres*, Académie Royal de Belgique (1913): 147–173.
Parry, Richard D. *Plato's Craft of Justice*. SUNY Series in Ancient Greek Philosophy. New York: State University of New York Press, 1996.
Pasquali, Giorgio. *Le lettere di Platone*. Sonsoni: Firenze, 1938. 2nd edition, 1967.
Patzer, Harald. "Die philosophische Bedeutung der Sokratesgestalt in den platonischen Dialogen." *Parusia, Studien zur Philosophie und zur Problemgeschichte des Platonismus*. Festgabe für Johannes Hirschberger, herausgegeben Von Kurt Flash. Frankfurt am Main (1965): 21–43.
Pavlu, Josef. *Alcibiades prior quo iure vulgo tribuatur Platoni*. Dissertationes Philologae Vindobonenses 8. Wien: Deuticke, 1905.
———. "Der pseudoplatonische Dialog Theages." *Wiener Studien* 31 (1909): 13–37.
———. *Der pseudoplatonische Kleitophon*. Jahresbericht des Gymnasiums, Programmschriften. Znaim, 1909.
———. *Die pseudoplatonischen Zwillingsdialoge Minos und Hipparch*. Programmschriften. Wien, 1910.
———. *Die pseudoplatonische Gespräche über Gerechtigkeit und Tugend*. Dissertation. Programmschriften Staatsgymmnasiums. Im 3. Bezirk: Wien, 1913.
———. "Zur pseudoplatonischen Epinomis." *Commentationes Vindobonenses* 2 (1936): 29–55.
———. "Zur Abfassungszeit der pseudoplatonischen Epinomis." *Wiener Studien* 55 (1937): 55–68.
———. "Der pseudoplatonische Grössere Hippias." *Wiener Studien* 59 (1941): 35–60.
Peck, A. L. "Plato and the μέγιστα γένη of the *Sophist*." *The Classical Quarterly* 64 N. S. 2 (1952): 32–56.
Penner, Terry. *The Ascent from Nominalism. Some Existence Arguments in Plato's Middle Dialogues*. Philosophical Studies Series 37. Dordrecht: Reidel, 1987.
Perger, M. von. *See* Hoffmann, Michael.
Perls, Hugo. *Plato. Seine Auffassung vom Kosmos*. Bern: Francke, 1966.
Perpeet, W. "Der systematisierte Platon." *Philosophische Rundschau* 10 (1962): 253–271.
Peters, H. *Platons 'Lysis.' Untersuchungen zur Problematik des Gedankenganges und zur Gestalt des Kunstwerks*. Dissertation. Kiel, 1968.
Pfister, F. "Ein Kompositionsgesetz der antiken Kunstprosa." *Philologische Wochenschrift* (1922): 1195–1200.
———. "Der Begriff des Schönen und das Ebenmass." *Würzburger Jahrbücher für die Altertumswissenschaft* 1 (1946): 341–358.
Pfleiderer, Edmund. *Zur Lösung der Platonischen Frage*. Freiburg I. B.: Mohr, 1888.
———. *Socrates und Plato*. Tübingen: Laupp, 1896.
Philip, J. A. "The Platonic Corpus." *Phoenix* 24 (1970): 296–308.
Philipp, H. "Zur Chronologie des Platonischen Dialogs Kritias." *Berliner philologische Wochenschrift* 33 (1913): 1119–1120.
Philippson, R. "Akademische Verhandlungen über die Lustlehre." *Hermes* 60 (1925): 444–481.
Plass, P. "'Play' and Philosophic Detachment in Plato." *Transactions and Proceedings of the American Philological Association* 98 (1967): 343–364.

Pohlenz, Max. *Aus Platos Werdezeit*. Philologische Untersuchungen. Berlin: Weidmann, 1913.

———. "Nochmals Platons Lysis." *Nachrichten von der Königlichen Gesellschaft der Wissenschaften zu Göttingen, Philologisch-historische Klasse* (1917): 560–588.

Pohlenz, Max. [Review of] Hans von Arnim, *Platons Jugenddialoge und die Entstehungszeit des Phaidros* (1914) and Otto Immisch, "Neue Wege der Platonforschung" (1915). *Göttingische gelehrte Anzeigen* 178 (1916): 241–282.

———. [Review of] Ulrich von Wilamowitz-Moellendorff, *Platon* (1919 [Zweite Auflage 1920]). *Göttingische gelehrte Anzeigen* 183 (1921): 1–30.

———. [Review of] Dorothy Tarrant, *The 'Hippias Major' attributed to Plato* (1928). *Gnomon* 7 (1931): 300–307.

Popper, Karl R. *The Open Society and Its Enemies: The Spell of Plato*. Volume I. London: Routledge, 1945, 1947, 1962, 1965. 5th Revised edition. 1990. 2002.

Pöschl, Victor, Helga Gärtner, und Waltraut Heyke. *Bibliographie zur antiken Bildersprache*. Bibliothek der klassischen Altertumswissenschaften, Neue Folge 1. Heidelberg: Winter, 1964.

Praechter, K. *See* Ueberweg.

Preiswerk, R. *Neue philologische Untersuchungen zum I. Buch des platonischen Staates*. Dissertation. Zürich: Freiburg i.d. Schweiz, 1939.

Press, Gerald A. (ed.), *Plato: Dialogues. New Studies and Interpretations*. Lanham: Rowman & Littlefield, 1993.

———, "Knowledge as Vision in Plato's Dialogues." *Journal of Neoplatonic Studies* 3 (1995): 61–89.

———. "Plato's Dialogues as Enactments." Francisco J. Gonzalez (ed.), *The Third Way: New Directions in Platonic Studies*. Lanham: Rowman & Littlefield (1995): 133–152.

———, "The State of the Question in the Study of Plato." *The Southern Journal of Philosophy* 34 (1996): 507–532. Reprint: Nicholas D. Smith (ed.), *Plato, Critical Assessments*, Volume I. New York: Routledge, 1998.

———, (ed.), *Who Speaks for Plato? Studies in Platonic Anonymity*. Lanham: Rowman & Littlefield, 2000.

Prior, William J. "Plato's Intellectual Development. A Critique of the Owen Thesis." Dissertation. University of Texas, Austin (1975): DA XXXVI, 1976: 6755A–6756A.

———. *Unity and Development in Plato's Metaphysics*. La Salle: Open Court Publishing Co., and Kent: Croom Helm Ltd., 1985.

Pritchard, Paul. *Plato's Philosophy of Mathematics*. International Plato Studies 5. Sankt Augustin: Academia Verlag, 1995.

Puech, A. *Étude littéraire de quelques dialogues de Platon*. Revue des Cours et Conférences 34 (1932): 35 (1933–34). Paris: Bouivier.

———. "Quelques remarques sur l'art de la composition dans les Dialogues de Platon." *Comptes Rendus de l'Académie des Inscriptions et Belles-Lettres* (1940): 319–322. Paris: Picard.

Quincey, J. H. "Another Purpose for Plato, Republic I." *Hermes* 109 (1981): 300–315.

Raeder, Hans. *Platons philosophische Entwickelung*. Leipzig: Teubner, 1905.

———. "Über die Echtheit der platonischen Briefe." *Rheinisches Museum* 61 (1906): 427–471, 511–542.

———. "Alkidamas und Platon als Gegner des Isokrates." *Rheinisches Museum* 63 (1908): 495–511.

———. "Note sur la chronologie platonicienne." *Bulletin de l'Association G. Budé* 9 (1925): 15–20.

———. *Platons Epinomis*. Kongel. Danske Videnskabernes Selskab, Historisk-filologiske Meddelelser 26.1. København: Munksgaard, 1938.

———. *Platons planlegte Dialog Philosophos*. Studier fra Sprog- og Oldtidsforskning udgivne af det Filologisk-Historiske Samfund 207. København: Munksgaard, 1948.

———. *Platoniske Stadier*. Kongel. Videnskabernes Selskab, Filosofiske Meddelelser 2.5 (with a summary in English). København: Munksgaard, 1950.

———. *Platon und die Rhetoren*. Filosofiske Meddelelser Danske Videnskabernes Selskab 2.6. København: Munksgaard, 1956.

Randall Jr., John H. *Plato, Dramatist of the Life of Reason*. New York: Columbia University Press, 1970. Reprint 1973.

Raubitschek, A. E. "Damon." *Classica et Mediaevalia* 16 (1955): 78–83.

Raven, John E. *Plato's Thought In The Making. A Study of the Development of His Metaphysics*. Cambridge: Cambridge University Press, 1965. Reprinted by Westport: Greenwood Press, 1985.

Reale, Giovanni. *Per una nuova interpretazione di Platone*. Milano, 1984 (and 21 editions).

———. "In che cosa consiste il nuovo paradigma storico-ermeneutico nella interpretazione di Platone." *Méthexis* 6 (1993): 135–154.

Rees, D. A. "Bipartition of the Soul in the Early Academy." *Journal of Hellenic Studies* 77 (1957): 112–118.

———. [Introduction to new edition] *The 'Republic' of Plato*, edited by James Adam (q. v.), I. Cambridge: Cambridge University Press, 1965.

Reeve, C. D. C. *Philosopher-Kings: The Argument of Plato's 'Republic.'* Princeton: Princeton University Press, 1988. 1992. Reprint Indianapolis: Hackett: 2006.

Regenbogen, O. "Bemerkungen zur Deutung des platonischen Phaidros." *Miscellanea Acadademica Berolinensia* 2, 1. Berlin (1950): 198–219. Also in: *Kleine Schriften*, München: Beck (1961): 269 ff.

Rehork, A. *Untersuchungen zu Platons Auffassung von der Hedone*. Ein Beitrag zum Verständnis des platonischen Tugendbegriffes. Hypomnemata 35. Göttingen: Vandenhoeck & Ruprecht, 1972.

Reich, Hermann. *Der Mimus*, I.1–2. Berlin: Weidmann, 1903.

Reinhard, Luise. *Die Anakoluthe bei Platon*. Philologische Untersuchungen 25. Berlin: Weidmann, 1920.

Reinhardt, Karl. *Platons Mythen*. Bonn: Cohen, 1927.

Rezzani, Maria. *Note e ricerche intorno al linguaggio di Platone*. Il pensiero antico 1.3. Padova: Cedam, 1959.

Ribbing, Sigurd. *Genetische Darstellung der platonischen Ideenlehre*, I–II. Leipzig, 1863–64.

Richard, Marie-Dominique. *L'Enseignement oral de Platon*. Une nouvelle interprétation du Platonisme. Préfacier Pierre Hadot. Paris: Cerf, 1986.

Richards, Herbert P. *Platonica*. London: Richards, 1911.

Rick, Hubert. "Der Dialog Charmides." *Archiv für Geschichte der Philosophie* 29 (1916): 211–234.

———. *Neue Untersuchungen zu platonischen Dialogen*. Bonn: Röhrscheid, 1931.

Riddell, James. "A Digest of Platonic Idioms." Riddell (ed.), *The Apology of Plato*. Oxford: Clarendon Press (1867):110–244. Reprint Amsterdam: Hakkert, 1967.

Ries, Klaus. *Isokrates und Platon im Ringen um die Philosophie*. Dissertation. München, 1959.

Riginos, Alice Swift. *Platonica. The Anecdotes Concerning the Life and Writings of Plato.* Columbia Studies in the Classical Tradition, vol 3. Leiden: Brill, 1976.
Rist, John M. "The Order of the Later Dialogues of Plato." *Phoenix* 14 (1960): 207–221.
———. "Plato's 'Earlier Theory of Forms'." *Phoenix* 29 (1975): 336–357.
Ritter, Constantin. *Untersuchungen über Plato.* Stuttgart: Kohlhammer, 1888.
———. *Neue Untersuchungen über Platon.* München: Beck, 1910. Reprint Manchester, NH: Ayer, 1976.
———. *Platon. Sein Leben, seine Schriften, seine Lehre*, I–II. München: Beck, 1910–1923. Reprint Manchester, NH: Ayer, 1976.
———. "Bericht über die in den letzten Jahrzehnten über Platon erschienenen Arbeiten." *Jahresbericht über die Fortschritte der klassischen Altertumswissenschaft* ('Bursians') 161 (1913): 1–72, 187 (1921): 1–227, 191 (1922): 79–305, 195 (1923): 1–94, 220 (1929): 37–108, 225 (1930): 121–168.
———. "Die Abfassungszeit des Phaidros, ein Schiboleth der Platonerklärung." *Philologus* 73 (1914–16): 321–373.
———. *Platons Dialog Phaidros.* Übersetzt, erläutert und mit ausführlichem Register versehen. Philosophische Bibliothek 152. Leipzig: Meiner, 1922. 2. Auflage in: Otto Apelt, *Platon, Sämmtliche Dialoge* II.
———. "Unterabteilungen innerhalb der zeitlich ersten Gruppe platonischer Schriften." *Hermes* 70 (1935): 1–30.
Rivaud, Albert. *Platon, Oeuvres complètes, Tome X. Timée-Critias.* Texte établi par Albert Rivaud. Collection Budé. Paris: Les Belles Lettres, 1925.
———. "Platon auteur dramatique." *Revue d'Histoire de la Philosophie* 1 (1927): 125–151.
Robb, Kevin. *Literacy and 'Paideia' in Ancient Greece.* New York: Oxford University Press, 1994.
Robert, Carl. "Aphoristische Bemerkungen zu den Ekklesiazusen des Aristophanes." *Hermes* 57 (1922): 321–356.
Robin, Léon. *La théorie platonicienne des idées et de nombres.* Paris: Alcan, 1908.
———. *La théorie platonicienne de l'amour.* Thèse. Paris: Alcan, 1908. Reprint 1933.
———. *Platon, Oeuvres complètes,* T.IV.1: *Phédon,* texte établi par L. R. Collection Budé. Paris: Les Belles Lettres, 1926.
———. *Platon, Oeuvres complètes,* T.IV.2: *Le Banquet,* texte établi par L. R. Collection Budé. Paris: Les Belles Lettres, 1929.
———. *Platon.* Paris: Alcan, 1938.
———. *Platon, Oeuvres complètes,* T.IV.3: *Phèdre,* texte établi par L. R. Collection Budé. Paris: Les Belles Lettres, 1947.
Robinson, Richard. *Plato's Earlier Dialectic.* Ithaca: Cornell University Press, 1941. 2nd edition. London: Oxford University Press, 1953. Reprint 1984.
———. "Plato's *Parmenides.*" *Classical Philology* 37 (1942): 51–76, 159–186.
———. "Forms and Error in Plato's *Theaetetus.*" *Philosophical Review* 59 (1950): 3–30.
Robinson, T. M. *Plato's Psychology.* Phoenix Supplement Vol. 8. Toronto: University of Toronto Press, 1970. New edition, 1995.
Rochol, Hans. *Der allgemeine Begriff in Platons Dialog Parmenides.* Erörterung eines Einwandes gegen den Platonismus (nebst einigen Skizzen zu demselben Dialog). Monographien zur philosophischen Forschung 137. Meisenheim am Glan: Hain, 1975.
Rodier, Georges. *Études de philosophie greque.* Paris: Vrin, 1926.
Roeper, Augustus. *De dualis usu Platonico.* Dissertation. Bonn, 1878.

Rohatyn, Dennis A. "Struktur und Funktion in Buch X von Platons Staat: Ein Überblick." *Gymnasium* 82 (1975): 314–330.
Romilly, Jacqueline de. "Réflexions sur le courage chez Thucydide et chez Platon." *Revue des Études Grecques* 93 (1980): 307–323.
Ronnet, Gilberte. *Étude sur le style de Démosthène dans les discours politiques.* Thèse. Paris: Boccard, 1951.
Rose, Herbert J. "A Colloquialism in Plato, *Rep.* 621b8." *Harvard Theological Review* (1938): 91–92.
Rose, Lynn E. "On Hypothesis in the *Cratylus* as an Indication of the Place of the Dialogue in the Sequence of Dialogues." *Phronesis* 9 (1964): 114–116.
Rose, Peter W. *Sons of the Gods, Children of Earth.* Ithaca: Cornell University Press, 1992.
Rosen, Stanley. *Plato's 'Symposium.'* New Haven: Yale University Press, 1968. 1987. Reprint New Haven: St Augustine Press, 1999.
———. *Plato's 'Sophist.' The Drama of Original and Image.* New Haven: Yale University Press, 1983.
Rosenmeyer, Thomas. G. "The Family of Critias." *American Journal Of Philology* 70 (1949): 404–410.
———. "Platonic Scholarship 1945–1955." *Classical World* 50 (1957): 173–199.
Ross, W. David. *Plato's Theory of Ideas.* Oxford: Clarendon Press, 1951.
———. "The Date of Plato's *Cratylus.*" *Revue International de Philosophie* 9 (1955): 187–196.
Rossetti, Livio. "'Socratica' in Fedone di Elide." *Studi Urbinati* 47, Series B (1973): 364–381.
———. "Spuren einiger Erotikoi Logoi aus dec Zeit Platons." *Eranos* 72 (1974): 185–192.
———. "Alla ricerca dei *logoi sokratikoi* perduti (II)." *Rivista di Studi Classici* 23 (1975): 87–99; (III), ibid. 361–381.
———. "Tracce di un λόγος Σωκρατικός alternativo al Critone a al Fedone platonici." *Atene e Roma* 20 (1975): 34–43.
———. "Ricerche sui 'Dialoghi socratici' di Fedone e di Euclide." *Hermes* 108 (1980): 183–200.
———, (ed.). *Understanding the 'Phaedrus': Proceedings of the II Symposium Platonicum.* International Plato Studies 1. Sankt Augustin: Academia Verlag, 1992.
Röttger, G. *Studien zur platonischen Substantivbildung.* Dissertation Keil. Kieler Arbeiten zur klassischen Philologie 3. Würzburg, 1937.
Roussel, Louis. "Grec ancien parlé." *Annuaire de l'Institut de Philologie et d'Histoire Orientales* (Mélanges Gregoire I) 9 (1949): 511–515. Bruxelles: Université Libre.
Rowe, Christopher J. (ed.). *Plato, 'Phaedo.'* Cambridge: Cambridge University Press, 1993.
———, (ed.). *Reading the 'Statesman.' Proceedings of the Third Symposium Platonicum.* International Plato Studies 4. Sankt Augustin: Academia Verlag, 1995.
Rudberg, Gunnar. *Kring Platons Phaidros.* Svenskt Arkiv för Humanistiska Avhandlingar 1. Göteborg: Eranos Verlag, 1924.
———. "Zur Personenzeichnung Platons." *Symbolae Osloenses* 6 (1928): 17–32.
———. "Das dramatische Element bei Platon." *Symbolae Osloenses* 19 (1939): 1–13.
———. "Zu den literarischen Formen der Sokratiker." *Dragma Martino P. Nilsson dedicatum, Acta Instituti Romani Regni Sueciae.* 2.1. Lund (1939): 419–429.
———. "Zum platonischen Thrasymachos." *Symbolae Osloenses* 23 (1944): 1–6.

———. *Gedanke und Gefühl*. Prolegomena zu einer hellenischen Stil-betrachtung. Symbolae Osloenses Supplement 14. Oslo, 1953.
———. "Protagoras—Gorgias—Menon. Eine platonische Übergangszeit." *Symbolae Osloenses* 30 (1953): 30–41.
———. *Platonica selecta*. Stockholm: Almqvist & Wiksell, 1956.
Runciman, Walter G. "Plato's *Parmenides.*" *Harvard Studies in Classical Philology* 64 (1959): 89–120. Reprint: R. E. Allen (ed.), *Studies in Plato's Metaphysics*. New York: Humanity Press (1965): 149–184. First British edition. London: Routledge, 1965. Reprint 1968.
———. *Plato's Later Epistemology*. Cambridge: Cambridge University Press, 1962.
Rutherford, R. B. *The Art of Plato. Ten Essays in Platonic Interpretation*. London: Duckworth, 1995. Reprint Cambridge: Harvard University Press, 1998.
Rutherford, W. G. *The New Phrynichus*. London, 1881. German Translation by A. Funck, "Zur Geschichte des Attizismus." *Jahrbücher für klassische Philologie*, Supplementband 13 (1883): 355–399.
Ryle, Gilbert. "Plato's *Parmenides.*" *Mind* 48 (1939), 139–51, 303–25. Reprinted with an afterword in: R. E. Allen (ed.), *Studies in Plato's Metaphysics*. New York: Humanities Press, (1965): 145–147. First British edition. London: Routledge, 1965. Reprinted 1968.
———. *Plato's Progress*. Cambridge: Cambridge University Press, 1966.
———. "Plato's Progress: Counter-Queries." Richard Freis (ed.), "The Progess of Plato's Progress." ΑΓΩΝ Supplement 2 (1969): 72–75.
Sachs, Eva. *De Theaeteto Atheniensi mathematico*. Dissertation. Berlin, 1914.
———. *Die fünf platonischen Körper*. Zur Geschichte der Mathematik und der Elementenlehre Platons und der Pythagoreer. Philologische Untersuchungen 24. Berlin: Weidmann, 1917. Reprint Manchester, NH: Ayer, 1975.
Sansone, David. "Plato and Euripides." *Illinois Classical Studies* 21 (1996): 35–67.
Santas, G. "The Form of the Good in Plato's *Republic.*" John P. Anton and Anthony Preus (eds.), *Essays in Ancient Greek Philosophy*, II. Albany: SUNY Press (1983): 232–263.
Santillana, George de. "Eudoxus and Plato: A Study in Chronology." *Isis* 32 (1940; published 1949): 248–262.
Saunders, S. A. *Studies in Plato's Style in the First Tetralogy*. Dissertation. University of Iowa (1974): DA XXXV, 1975: 4470A.
Saunders, Trevor J. *Bibliography on Plato's 'Laws,' 1920–1970*, with additional citations through May, 1975. New York: Arno Press, 1976.
Saupe, W. *Die Anfangsstadien der griechischen Kunstprosa in der Beurteilung Platons*. Dissertation. Leipzig, 1916.
———. "Neue Probleme der Platonforschung." *Helikon* 7 (1967): 537–545.
Sayre, Kenneth M. *Plato's Late Ontology: A Riddle Resolved*. Princeton: Princeton University Press, 1983. Reprinted with a new introduction and essay, "Excess and Deficiency at *Statesman* 283C–285C". Las Vegas: Parmenides Publishing, 2005.
———. [Review of ] Hans J. Krämer, *Plato and the Foundations of Metaphysics* (1990). *Ancient Philosophy* 13 (1993): 167–184.
Schadewaldt, W. "Platon und Kratylos: ein Hinweis." Palmer and Hamerton-Kelly (eds), *Philomathes*, Essays in honor of Phillip Merlan. The Hague: Nijhoff (1971): 3–11.
Schaerer, René. *La question platonicienne. Étude sur les rapports de la pensée et de l'expression dans les dialogues*. Mémoires de l'Université de Neuchâtel 10. (Neuchâtel 1938.) 2e edition revue et augmentée d'une postface: A la recherché de Platon. Paris: Secrétariat de l'université, 1969.

———. "La composition du Phédon." *Revue des Études Grecques* 53 (1940): 1–50.
———. "La structure des dialogues métaphysiques de Platon." *Revue International de Philosophie* 9 (1955): 197–220.
Schanz, Martinus. *Novae commentationes Platonicae.* Programmschriften. Würzburg: Wirceburgi, 1871.
———. "Zur Entwickelung des platonischen Stils." *Hermes* 21 (1886): 439–459.
Scheidweiler, F. "Zum platonischen Phaidros." *Hermes* 83 (1955): 120–122.
Schiassi, G. "La questione del Menesseno platonico." *Rendiconti dell' Istituto Lombardo, Classe di Lettere*, Vol. 96 (1962): 37–58.
Schilling, Kurt. *Platon. Einführung in seine Philosophie.* Monographien zur philosophischen Forschung, Bd 3/4. Wurzach: Gryphius Verlag, 1948.
Schleiermacher, Friedrich. *Platons Werke.* I–III [6 volumes]. Berlin: Akademie Verlag, 1804–1828. I. 1. Einleitung also in: Konrad Gaiser, *Das Platonbild.* Zehn Beiträge zum Platonverständnis. Hildesheim: Olms (1969): 1–32.
Schmalenbach, Herman. "Macht und Recht. Platons Absage an die Politik (zugleich zur Entstehungsgeschichte der Apologie und des Kriton)." *Natur und Geist*, Festschift für F. Medicus. Zürich: Rentsch (1946): 183–209.
Schmalzriedt, Egidius. *Platon. Der Schriftsteller und die Wahrheit.* München: Piper, 1969.
Schmeken, H. "Eine Schülerarbeit aus der mittleren Akademie." *Philosophische Jahrbuch* 60 (1950): 20–30.
Schmid, Wilhelm. *Geschichte der griechischen Literatur*, I.3. Handbuch der Altertumswissenschaft 7.1.3. München: Beck, 1940.
Schmidt, Ernst G. "Die drei Arten des Philosophierens." Zur Geschichte einer antiken Stil- und Methodenscheidung. *Philologus* 106 (1962): 14–28.
Schmitz, Hermann. *Die Ideenlehre des Aristoteles.* I 1–2–II. Bonn: Bouvier, 1985.
Schneidewin, M. "Ein Versuch über die Rätsel des platonischen Parmenides." *Neue Jahrbucher für das Klassische Altertum* 37 (19), (1916): 379–401.
Schofield, M. "Eudoxus in the *Parmenides.*" *Museum Helveticum* 30 (1973): 1–19.
Scholl, Maximilianus. *De verborum lusu apud Platonem.* Programmschriften. Bayreuth, 1899.
Scholl, Nikolaus. *Der platonische Menexenos.* (Dissertation. Frankfurt, 1957.) Termi e Testi 5. Roma: Edizioni di storia e letteratura, 1959.
Schöne, Richard. *Über Platons Protagoras. Ein Beitrag zur Lösung der platonischen Frage.* Leipzig: Breitkopf und Hartel, 1862.
Schubert, F. "Zur mehrfachen praefixalen Zusammensetzung im Griechischen." *Xenia Austríaca* I Festschrift zur 42. Versammlung deutscher Philologen und Schulmänner in Wien. Wien (1893): 193–258.
Schuhl, Pierre-Maxime. *Études sur la fabulation platonicienne.* Paris: Presses Universitaires de France, 1947.
———. "Remarques sur la technique de la répétition dans le Phédon." *Revue des Études Grecques* 41 (1948): 373–380. Reprint *Études platoniciennes.* Paris: Presses Universitaires de France (1960): 118–125.
———. "Platon. Quinze années d'études platoniciennes." *Congrès de l'Association G. Budé* (1953). *Actes du Congrès*, Paris (1954): 149–169.
———. *Études platoniciennes.* Paris: Presses Universitaires de France, 1960.
Schultess, F. *Die Abfassungszeit des platonischen Theaitet.* Programmschriften des protestantischen Gymnasiums. Strassburg, 1875.
Schulz, W. "Das Problem der Aporie in den Tugenddialogen Platos." *Die Gegenwart der Griechen im neueren Denken*, Festschrift für Hans-Georg Gadamer. Tübingen: Mohr (1960): 261–275.

Schwarz, E. "Kallisthenes Hellenika." *Hermes* 35 (1900): 106–130.
Schwessinger, Agnes. "Eigenart und Eigengesetzlichkeit in Platons Kunst." *Philologus* 80 (1925): 225–297.
Schwyzer, Eduard. *Griechische Grammatik,* I–II. Handbuch der Altertumswissenschaft II.1.1–2. München: Beck, 1950, 1953.
Scott, Dominic. *Recollection and Experience. Plato's Theory of Learning and its Successors.* Cambridge: Cambridge Univeristy Press, 1995.
Sease, Victor W. *The 'Cratylus.' Plato and the Doctrine of the Academy.* Dissertation. University of Califfornia, Berkeley (1966): DA XXVII, 1967: 4234A–4235A.
Selvers, Friedrich. *De mediae comoediae sermone.* Dissertation. Münster, 1909.
Sesonske, A. "Ryle on the *Republic.*" Richard Freis (ed)., *The Progress of Plato's Progress.* ΑΓΩΝ Supplement 2 (1969): 63–71.
Setti, G. "Il linguaggio dell'uso commune presso Aristofane." *Museo italiano di antichità classica* 1 (1885): 113–130.
Seung, T. K. *Plato Rediscovered. Human Value and Social Order.* Lanham: Rowman & Littlefield, 1996.
Shankman, Steven. (ed.). *Plato and Postmodernism.* Glenside: Aldine Press, 1994.
Sharples, R. W. "Plato, Plotinus and Evil." *Bulletin of the Institute of Classical Studies* 40 (1995): 171–181.
Shiner, Roger A. *Knowledge and Reality in Plato's 'Philebus.'* Assen: Van Gorcum, 1974.
Shorey, Paul. "The Interpretation of the *Timaeus.*" *American Journal of Philology* 9 (1888): 395–418.
———. *The Unity of Plato's Thought.* Chicago: University of Chicago Press, 1903. Reprint New York: Garland Press, 1980.
———. [Review of] Hans von Arnim, *Sprachliche Forschungen zur Chronologie der platonischen Dialoge* (1912). *Classical Philology* 7 (1912): 490–492.
———. *Plato, The 'Republic,' with an English Translation.* I–II. London, The Loeb Classic Library 1930–1935. London and Cambridge: Heinemann and Harvard University Press, 1963.
———. *What Plato Said.* Chicago: University of Chicago Press, 1933. Reprint 1978.
Siebeck, H. "Zur Chronologie der platonischen Dialoge." *Jahrbücher für classische Philologie* 131, (1885): 231–254.
Simeterre, R. "La chronologie des oeuvres de Platon." *Revue des Études Grecques* 58 (1945): 146–162.
Sinaiko, Herman. L. *Love, Knowledge and Discourse in Plato: Dialogue and Dialectic in 'Phaedrus,' 'Republic,' 'Parmenides.'* Chicago: University of Chicago Press, 1965.
Singer, Kurt. *Platon, der Gründer.* München: Beck, 1927.
Skemp, J. B. *Plato's 'Statesman.' A Translation of the 'Politicus' of Plato With Introduction, Essays and Footnotes.* London: Routledge, 1952. Reprinted by London: Duckworth, 2002.
———. "On the Date of the *Timaeus* of Plato." *Proceedings of the Cambridge Philological Society* 183 (1954/55): 32.
Smith. N. D. "Plato's Divided Line." *Ancient Philosophy* 16 (1996): 25–45.
———. *See* also Brickhouse, Klagge.
Socher, Joseph. *Über Platons Schriften.* München: Lentner, 1820.
Solignac, Aimé. "Vues nouvelles sur la dernière philosophie de Platon." *Archives de Philosophie* 34 (1971): 475–493.
Solmsen, Friedrich. *Die Entwicklung der aristotelischen Logik und Rhetorik.* Neue Philologische Untersuchungen 4. Berlin: Weidmann, 1929.

———. "Platos Einfluss auf die Bildung der mathematischen Methode." *Quellen und Studien zur Geschichte der Mathematik* I (1929): 93–107. Reprint: Konrad Gaiser (ed.), *Das Platonbild*. Zehn Beiträge zum Platonverständnis. Hildesheim: Olms (1969): 125–139.

———. "*Republic* III 389b2–d6. Plato's Draft and the Editor's Mistake." *Philologus* 109 (1965): 182–185.

Sordi, Marta. "A proposito di uno scritto politico del 401–400 a.C.: il Περὶ πολιτείας della Pseudo Erode." *Rivista di Filologia* 83 (1955): 175–198.

Soreth, Marion. *Der platonische Dialog Hippias Major*. Dissertation. Marburg, 1953. Zetemata. Monographien zur klassischen Altertumswissenschaft 6. München: Beck, 1953.

———. "Zur relativen Chronologie von Menon und Euthydem." *Hermes* 83 (1955): 377–379.

Souilhé, Joseph. *La notion platonicienne d'intermédiaire dans la philosophie des dialogues*. Thèse Poitiers. Paris: Librairie F. Alcan, 1919.

———. *Platon, Oeuvres complètes*, T.XIII.1 *Lettres*, texte établi et traduit. Collection Budé. Paris: Les Belles Lettres, 1926.

———. *Platon, Oeuvres complètes*, T.XIII.2: *Dialogues suspects*, texte établi et traduit. Collection Budé. Paris: Les Belles Lettres, 1930.

———. *Platon, Oeuvres complètes*, T.XIII.3: *Dialogues apocryphes*, texte établi et traduit. Collection Budé. Paris: Les Belles Lettres, 1930.

Sparshott, F. "Critical Notices." *Canadian Journal of Philosophy* 22 (1992): 411–426.

Specchia, Ottorino. *Platone, Epinomis*. Introduzione testo critico e commento. Quaderni di Cultura e Scuola 1. Firenze: Le Monnier, 1967.

Sprague, Rosamund Kent. *Plato's Use of Fallacy. A Study of the 'Euthydemus' and Some Other Dialogues*. London: Routledge, 1962.

———. *Plato, 'Euthydemus.'* With translation, introduction and notes. Library of Liberal Arts 222. Indianapolis: Hackett, 1965. Reprinted 1993.

———. *Plato's Philosopher-King. A Study of the Theoretical Background*. Columbia: University of South Carolina Press, 1976.

———. "Platonic Unitarianism, or What Shorey Said." *Classical Philology* 71 (1976): 109–112.

Stark, R. "Platons Dialog 'Euthyphron'." *Annales Universitatis Saraviensis* 1 (1952): 144–159.

Stefanini, L. *Platone*. I–II. Seconda edizione aggiornata. Padova: Cedam, 1949.

Steidle, Werner. "Der Dialog Laches und Platons Verhältnis zu Athen in den Frühdialogen." *Museum Helveticum* 7 (1950): 129–146.

Steinen, H. von den. "Sokrates und Platon." *Deutsche Neue Rundschau* 64 (1953): 248–275.

Steiner, Peter. M. *Psyche bei Platon*. Neue Studien zur Philosophie 3. Göttingen: Vandenhoeck & Ruprecht, 1992.

Stenzel, Bertha "Is Plato's *Seventh Epistle* Spurious?" *American Journal Philology* 74 (1953): 383–397.

Stenzel, Julius. *Literarische Form und philosophische Gehalt des platonischen Dialoges*. Jahresbericht der Schlesischen Gesellschaft für vaterländische Kultur. Breslau, 1916. Also in: *Kleine Schriften zur Griechischen Philosophie*. Darmstadt: Gentner (1956): 32–47.

———. *Studien zur Entwicklung der platonischen Dialektik von Sokrates zu Aristoteles: Arete und Diairesis*. Breslau: Trewendt und Granier, 1917. 2nd edition: Leipzig, 1931. English Translation: 1940. Reprint Darmstadt: Wissenschaftliche Buchgesellschaft, 1961. 1974.

———. *Zahl und Gestalt bei Platon und Aristoteles*. Leibzig Berlin, 1924. 2nd edition: 1933. Darmstadt: Wissenschaftliche Buchgesellschaft, 3, 1959. Bad Homburg vor der Höhe: Gentner, 1959.

———. *Kleine Schriften zur griechischen Philosophie*, herausgegeben von Bertha Stenzel. Darmstadt: Wissenschaftliche Buchgesellschaft, 1956.

Stephanides, Basilius C. *Die Stellung von Platons Politikos zu seiner Politeia und den Nomoi*. Dissertation Universität Heidelberg. Heidelberg: Rössler & Herbert, 1913.

Stern, Harold S. "Plato's Funeral Oration." *The New Scholasticism* 48 (1974): 503–508.

Stevens, P. T. "Colloquial Expressions in Euripides." *The Classical Quarterly* 31 (1937): 182–191. Reprint Hermes, Einzelschriften 38. Wiesbaden: Steiner (1976): 1–72.

———. "Colloquial Expressions in Aeschylus and Sophocles." *The Classical Quarterly* 39 (1945): 95–105.

Stewart, John A. *The Myths of Plato*. London; New York: Macmillan, 1905. Reprint London: Open Gate Press, 1960; 1970. Reprint Whitefish: Kessinger Publishing, 2006; 2007.

Stöcklein, Paul. *Über die philosophische Bedeutung von Platons Mythen*. Philologus Supplement 30, Heft 3. Leipzig: Dieterich, 1937.

Strycker, É de. "Chronique platonicienne (1929–1934)." *L'Antiquité Classique* 4 (1935): 227–243.

———. "L'authenticité du Premier Alcibiade." *Les Études Classiques* 11 (1942): 135–151.

Susemihl, Franz. *Die genetische Entwickelung der platonischen Philosophie, einleitend dargestellt*. I–II. Leipzig: Teubner, 1855–1860.

Sybel, L. von. *Platons Technik an Symposion und Euthydemos nachgewiesen*. Programmschriften. Marburg, 1889.

Sykutris, J. "Sokratikerbriefe." *Pauly's Real-Encyclopädie der classischen Altertumswissenschaft* Supplement 5 (1931): 981–987.

Szaif, Jan. *Platons Begriff der Wahrheit*. Symposion 104. Freiburg: Alber, 1996. Revised edition: 1998.

Sze, C. V. P. *Plato's 'Republic' I. Its Function in the Dialogue as a Whole*. Dissertation. Yale University (1971): DA XXXII, 1972: 6951A.

Szlezák, Thomas A. "Unsterblichkeit und Trichotomie der Seele im zehnten Buch der Politeia." *Phronesis* 21 (1976): 31–58.

———. "Dialogform und Esoterik. Zur Deutung des platonischen Dialogs 'Phaidros'." *Museum Helveticum* 35 (1978): 18–32.

———. "Probleme der Platoninterpretation." *Göttingische Gelehrte Anzeigen* 230 (1978): 1–37.

———. "The Acquiring of Philosophical Knowledge According to Plato's *Seventh Letter*." *Arktouros. Hellenic Studies presented to B. M. W. Knox*. Berlin–New York (1979): 354–363.

———. *Platon und die Schriftlichkeit der Philosophie*. Interpretation zu den frühen und mittleren Dialogen. Berlin: De Gruyter, 1985.

———. *Come leggere Platone*. Presentazione di Giovanni Reale. Milano: Vita e Pensiero, 1991. German version: *Platon Lesen*. Stuttgart: Holzboog, 1993. Reprinted as: *Reading Plato*, edited translation by Graham Zanker. London: Routledge, 1999.

———. "Zur üblichen Abneigung gegen die Agrapha Dogmata." *Méthexis* 6 (1993): 155–174.

———. [Review of] Giovanni Cerri, *Platone sociologo della communicazione* (1991). *Gnomon* 68 (1996): 589–593.

———. "Das Höhlengleichnis (Buch VII 514a-521b und 539d-541b)." Otfried Höffe (hrsg.), *Platon, 'Politeia.'* Berlin: Akademie Verlag (1997): 205–228.
———. "Über die Art und Weise der Erörterung der Prinzipien in Timaios." Tomás Calvo and Luc Brisson (eds.), *Interpreting the 'Timaeus'–'Critias.'* Proceedings of the IV Symposium Platonicum. Sankt Augustin: Academia Verlag (1997): 195–203.
———. "Von der τιμή der Götter zur τιμιότης des Prinzips." Aristoteles und Platon über den Rang des Wissens und seiner Objekte. Fritz Graf (hrsg.), *Ansichten griechischer Rituale: Festschrift für Walter Burkert* (1996). Stuttgart: Teubner (1998): 420–439.
Tack, Erwin. *Die sogenannten Platonzeugnisse bei Aristoteles.* Dissertation. Kiel: Selbstverlag, 1970.
Tarán, Leonardo. *Academica. Plato, Philip of Opus, and the Pseudo-Platonic Epinomis.* Memoir 107. Philadelphia: American Philosophical Society, 1975. 1978.
Tarrant, Dorothy. "The Art of Plato." *Classical Review* 40 (1926): 104–112.
———. *The 'Hippias Major' Attributed to Plato.* With introductory essay and commentary. Cambridge: Cambridge University Press, 1928. Reprint New York: Arno Press, 1973. Reprint Manchester, NH: Ayer, 1988.
———. "The Pseudo-Platonic Socrates." *The Classical Quarterly* 32 (1938): 167–173.
———. "Imagery in Plato's *Republic.*" *The Classical Quarterly* 40 (1946): 27–34.
———. "Style and Thought in Plato's Dialogues." *The Classical Quarterly* 42 (1948): 28–34.
———. "Plato's Use of Quotations and Other Illustrative Material." *The Classical Quarterly* N. S. 1 (1951): 59–67.
———. "Metaphors of Death in the *Phaedo.*" *Classical Review* N. S. 2, (1952): 64–66.
———. "Plato as Dramatist." *Journal of Hellenic Studies* 75 (1955): 82–89.
———. "Plato's Use of Extended Oratio Obliqua." *The Classical Quarterly* N. S. 5 (1955): 222–224.
———. "More Colloqialisms, Semi-proverbs, and Word-play in Plato." *The Classical Quarterly* N. S. 8 (1958): 158–160.
———. "The Touch of Socrates." *The Classical Quarterly* N. S. 8 (1958): 95–98.
Tarrant, Harold. "Orality and Plato's Narrative Dialogues." Ian Worthington (ed.), *Voice into Text. Orality and Literacy in Ancient Greece.* Leiden: Brill (1996): 129–147.
Taylor, Alfred E. *Varia Socratica: First Series.* St. Andrews University Publications 9. Oxford: Parker, 1911. Reprint New York: Garland Press, 1987.
———. *Plato. The Man and His Work.* London: Methuen, 1926. 2nd edition. London, 1927. 3rd edition. Oxford: Clarendon Press, 1928. 4th edition, 1937. Reprint New Haven: Meridian Books, 1956. Reprint Mineola: Dover Publications, 2001.
———. *A Commentary on Plato's 'Timaeus.'* Oxford: Clarendon Press, 1928.
———. *Plato, 'Philebus' and 'Epinomis.'* Translation and introduction. Edited by Raymond Klibansky with the co-operation of Guido Calogero and A. C. Lloyd. London: Nelson, 1956. Reprint Folkestone: Dawsons, 1972.
———. *Plato, The 'Sophist' and the 'Statesman.'* Translation and introduction. Edited by Raymond Klibansky and Elizabeth Anscombe. London: Nelson, 1961. Reprint New York: Barnes & Noble, 1971.
Teichmüller, Gustav. *Über die Reihenfolge der platonischen Dialoge.* Leipzig: Köhler, 1879.
———. *Literarische Fehden im vierten Jahrhundert v. Chr.* I–II. Breslau: Koebner, 1881–84.
Tejera, Victorino. *Plato's Dialogues One by One. A Structural Interpretation.* New York: Irvington, 1984.

———. "On the Form and Authenticity of the *Lysis*." *Ancient Philosophy* 10 (1990): 173–191.

———. *Rewriting the History of Ancient Greek Philosophy*. Contributions in Philosophy, 59. Westport: Greenwood Press, 1997.

Telle, Heidemarie. *Formen der Beweisführung in den platonischen Frühdialogen*. Habelts Dissertationsdrucke. Reihe Klassische Philologie 22. Halbelt: Bonn, 1975.

Teloh, H. *The Development of Plato's Metaphysics*. University Park: Pennsylvania State University Press, 1981.

———. *The Ontology of Plato's 'Hippias Major.'* Dissertation. University of Wisconsin, Madison (1972): DA XXXIII, 1972: 2432A.

Theiler, W. "Einheit und unbegrenzte Zweiheit von Plato bis Plotin." Jürgen Mau and Ernst G. Schmidt (eds.), *Isonomia: Studien zur Gleichheitsvorstellung im griechischen Denken*. Deutsche Akademie der Wissenschaften zu Berlin. Institut für Griechisch-Römische Philosophie. Veröffentlichung 9. Berlin: Akademie Verlag (1964): 89–109.

Thesleff, Holger. *Studies on Intensification in Early and Classical Greek*. Commentationes Humanarum Litterarum 21.1. Helsinki: Societas Scientiarum Fennica, 1954.

———. *Studies on the Greek Superlative*. Commentationes Humanarum Litterarum 21.3. Helsinki: Societas Scientiarum Fennica, 1955.

———. *An Introduction to the Pythagorean Writings of the Hellenistic Period*. Acta Acadademiae Aboensis. Series A. Humaniora 24, 3. Åbo: Åbo Akademi, 1961.

———. *The Pythagorean Texts of the Hellenistic Period*. Collected and edited. Acta Acadademiae Aboensis. Series A. Humaniora 30, 1. Åbo: Åbo Akademi, 1965.

———. "Scientific and Technical Style in Early Greek Prose." *Arctos* N. S. 4 (1966): 89–113.

———. "Stimmungsmalerei oder Burleske? Der Stil von Platons Phaidros 230bc und seine Funktion." Societas Philosophica Fennica. *Arctos* N. S. 5 (1967): 141–155.

———. *Studies in the Styles of Plato*. Acta Philosophica Fennica 20. Helsinki: Societas Philosophica Fennica, 1967. Reprint: *Platonic Patterns: A Collection of Works by Holger Thesleff*, Las Vegas: Parmenides Publishing (2009): 1–142.

———. "Colloquial Style and Its Use in Plato's Later Works." *Arctos* 7 (1972): 219–227.

———. "The Date of the Pseudo-Platonic *Hippias Major*." *Arctos* 10 (1976): 105–117.

———. "The Interrelation and Date of the Symposia of Plato and Xenophon." *Bulletin of the Institute of Classical Studies* 25 (1978): 157–170.

———. "Notes on Unio Mystica in Plotinus." *Arctos* 14 (1980): 101–114.

———. *Studies in Platonic Chronology*. Commentationes Humanarum 70. Helsinki: Societas Scientiarum Fennica, 1982. Reprint: *Platonic Patterns: A Collection of Works by Holger Thesleff*, Las Vegas: Parmenides Publishing (2009): 143–382.

———. "Plato and Inequality" Iro Kajanto (ed.), *Equality and Inequality of Man in Ancient Thought: Papers Read at the Colloquium in Connection with the Assemblée Generale of the Federation Internationale des Études Classiques Held in Helsinki in August, 1982*. Commentationes Humanarum Litterarum 75. Helsinki: Societas Scientiarum Fennica (1984): 17–29.

———. "Platonic Chronology." *Phronesis* 34 (1989): 1–26.

———. "Presocratic Publicity." Sven-Tage Teodorsson (ed.), *Greek and Latin Studies in Memory of Cajus Fabricius*. Studia Graeca et Latina Gothoburgensia 54. Göteborg: Acta Universitatis Gothoburgensis (1990): 110–121.

———. "Theaitetos and Theodoros." *Arctos* 24 (1990): 147–159. Reprint: *Platonic Patterns: A Collection of Works by Holger Thesleff*, Las Vegas: Parmenides Publishing (2009): 509–518.

———. "In Search of Dialogue." Gerald Press (ed.), *Plato's Dialogues: New Studies and Interpretations*. Lanham: Rowman & Littlefield (1993): 259–266.

———. "Looking for Clues. An Interpretation of Some Literary Aspects of Plato's 'Two-Level Model'." Gerald Press (ed.), *Plato's Dialogues: New Studies and Interpretations*. Lanham: Rowman & Littlefield (1993): 17–45.

———. "The Early Version of Plato's *Republic*." *Arctos* 31 (1997): 149–174. Reprint: *Platonic Patterns: A Collection of Works by Holger Thesleff*, Las Vegas: Parmenides Publishing (2009): 519–540.

———. *Studies in Plato's Two-Level Model*. Commentationes Humanarum Litterarum 113. Helsinki: Societas Scientiarum Fennica, 1999. Reprint: *Platonic Patterns: A Collection of Works by Holger Thesleff*, Las Vegas: Parmenides Publishing (2009): 383–508.

———. "För vem skrev Platon?" Maarit Kaimio (ed), *Filosofen och publiken*. Rapport från Platonsällskapets femtonde symposium, Helsingfors 3–6 juni 1999. Helsinki (2000): 1–15.

———. "The Philosopher Conducting Dialectic." Gerald Press (ed.), *Who Speaks for Plato?* Lanham: Rowman & Littlefield (2000): 53–66.

———. "Plato and His Public." Bettina Amden al. (eds.), *Noctes Atticae: 34 Articles on Graeco-Roman Antiquity and its Nachleben: Studies Presented to Jørgen Mejer*. Copenhagen: Museum Tusculanum Press (2002): 289–301. Reprint: *Platonic Patterns: A Collection of Works by Holger Thesleff*, Las Vegas: Parmenides Publishing (2009): 541–550.

———. "A Symptomatic Text Corruption: Plato, *Gorgias* 448a5." *Arctos* 37 (2003): 251–257. Reprint: *Platonic Patterns: A Collection of Works by Holger Thesleff*, Las Vegas: Parmenides Publishing (2009): 551–556.

Thiersch, Friedrich. *Über die dramatische Natur der platonischen Dialoge*. Abhandlungen der Bayrischen Akademie der Wissenschaft, Philosophisch-philologische Klasse 2. München, 1837.

Thomson, William. *See* Junge, Gustav (1930).

Thurnher, Rainer. *Der siebente Platonbrief*. Versuch einer umfassenden philosophischen Interpretation. Monographien zur philosophischen Forschung 125. Meisenheim am Glan: Hain, 1975.

Thurow, Reinhard. *Der platonische Epitaphios*. Untersuchungen zur Stellung des 'Menexenos' im platonischen Werk. Dissertation. Tübingen: Stuttgatt, 1968.

Tielsch, Elfriede. *Die platonischen Versionen der griechischen Doxalehre*. Ein philosophisches Lexikon mit Kommentar. Monographien zur philosophischen Forschung 58. Meisenheim am Glan: Hain, 1970.

Tigerstedt, Eugène N. *The Legend of Sparta in Classical Antiquity*, I. Acta Universitatis Stockholmiensis, Stockholm Studies in History of Literature 9. Stockholm: Almqvist & Wiksell, 1965.

———. *Plato's Idea of Poetical Inspiration*. Commentationes Humanarum Litterarum 44, 2. Helsinki: Societas Scientiarum Fennica, 1969.

———. *The Decline and Fall of the Neoplatonic Interpretation of Plato: An Outline and Some Observations*. Commentationes Humanarum Litterarum 52. Helsinki: Societas Scientiarum Fennica, 1974.

———. *Interpreting Plato*. Acta Universitatis Stockholmiensis, Stockholm Studies in History of Literature 17. Stockholm: Almqvist & Wiksell, 1977.

Tomin, Julius. "Plato's First Dialogue." *Ancient Philosophy* 17 (1997): 31–45.

Toomer, G. J. [Review of] François Lasserre, *Die Fragmente des Eudoxos von Knidos* (1966). *Gnomon* 40 (1968): 334–337.

Totok, Wilhelm and Schröer, Helmut. *Handbuch der Geschichte der Philosophie*, I. Altertum. Frankfurt am Main: Klostermann, 1964.
Tracy, H. L. "Plato as Satirist." *Classical Journal* 33 (1937): 153–162.
Trampedach, K. *Platon, die Akademie und die zeitgenossische Politik*. Hermes Einzelschriften 66, 1994.
Trenkner, Sophie. *Le style καί dans le récit attique oral*. Assen: Van Gorcum, 1960.
Trense, P. *De attributi eiusque collocationis usu Platonico*. Dissertation. Rostock, 1901.
Treves, P. "Polykrates (7)". *Pauly's Real-Encyclopädie der classischen Altertumswissenschaft* 21 (1952): 1736–1752.
Tuckey, T. Godfrey. *Plato's 'Charmides.'* Cambridge: Cambridge University Press, 1951.
Turner, Eric G. *Greek Manuscripts of the Ancient World*. Oxford: Clarendon Press, 1971. Reprint London: University of London, Institute of Classical Studies, 1987.
Ueberweg, Friederich. *Untersuchungen über die Echtheit und Zeitfolge Platonischer Schriften und über die Hauptmomente aus Plato's Leben*. Wien, 1861.
Ueberweg, Friederich and Praechter, Karl. *Grundriss der Geschichte der Philosophie*, I Teil: Die Philosophie des Altertums. 13 Auflage. Basel. Tübingen: Mittler, 1953.
———, [Praechter's additional pages denoted by asterisk *]
Untersteiner, M. "Studi platonici. Il 'Carmide'." *Acme* 18 (1965): 19–67.
Usener, Sylvia. *Isokrates, Platon und ihr Publikum. Hörer und Leser von Literatur im 4. Jahrhundert v. Chr.* Scripta Oralia 63. Altertumswissenschaftliche Reihe 14. Tübingen: Narr, 1994.
Usher, S. "Individual Characterization in *Lysias*." *Eranos* 63 (1965): 99–119.
Ussher, R. G. *Aristophane's 'Ecclesiazusae.'* Edited with introduction and commentary. Oxford: Clarendon Press, 1973. Reprint London: Duckworth, 2007.
Van Camp, J. and Canart, P. *Le sens du mot θεῖος chez Platon*. Université de Louvain, Recueil de travaux d'histoire et de philosophie, 4e Série, 9. Louvain, 1956.
Vanachter, Yvonne. "Un aspect du style de Platon. Essai d'une interprétation chronologique et psychologique." *L'Antiquité Classique* 15 (1946): 83–95.
van der Waerden, Bartel L. *Erwachende Wissenschaft*. Basel: Birkhäuser, 1966.
Vander Waerdt, Paul A. (ed.). *The Socratic Movement*. Ithaca: Cornell University Press: 1994.
Vanhoye, A. "Deux pages poétiques de Platon (Banquet, 203b–203e)." *Les Études Classiques* 20 (1952): 3–21.
Verdam, H. D. "De ordine, quo Platonis dialogi inter se succedunt." *Mnemosyne* 44 (1916): 255–294.
———. "Quo ordine Isocratis 'Busiris' 'Adversus Sophistas' et 'Helena' orationes inter se succedant et quid Plato ad eas respondent." *Mnemosyne* 44 (1916): 373–395.
———. "Quid Plato responderit ad Polycratis orationem in Socratem." *Mnemosyne* 45 (1917): 189–204.
———. "Quo tempore Phaedrus Platonicus scriptus sit." *Mnemosyne* 46 (1918): 383–402.
———. "Qua aetate Plato Theaetetum dialogum scripserit." *Mnemosyne* 47 (1919): 171–186.
Verdenius, W. J. *Mimesis. Plato's Doctrine of Artistic Imitation and Its Meaning to Us*. Philosophia antiqua 3. Leiden: Brill, 1949. Reprint 1962, 1972.
Versenyi, L. "Plato's *Lysis*." *Phronesis* 20 (1975): 185–198.
Vicaire, Paul. *Platon, critique littéraire*. Thèse Paris. Études and commentaries 34. Paris: Klincksieck, 1960.

———. *Platon, Lachès et Lysis*. Édition avec l'introduction et le commentaire. Collection Érasme. Textes grecques 7. Paris: Presses Universitaires de France, 1963.
Vink, C. *Plato's Eerste Alcibiades. Een onderzoek naar zijn authenticiteit*. Dissertation. Amsterdam, 1939.
Violette, R. "Avènement du language de la doctrine des Idées chez Platon." *Revue des Études Grecques* 90 (1977): 296–313.
Vlastos, Gregory. "The Third Man Argument in the *Parmenides*." *The Philosophical Review* 63 (1954): 319–349. Reprint: R. E. Allen (ed.), *Studies in Plato's Metaphysics*. New York: Humanity Press (1965): 231–291 (with postscript 1963). First British edition. London: Routledge, 1965. Reprint 1968.
———. "Socratic Knowledge and Platonic 'Pessimism'." *The Philosophical Review* 66 (1957): 226–238.
———. [Review of ] Hans J. Krämer, *Arete bei Platon und Aristoteles* (1959). *Gnomon* 35 (1963): 641–655.
———. "Anamnesis in the *Meno*." *Dialogue* 4 (1965/66): 143–167. Reprint Jane Mary Day (ed.), *Plato's 'Meno' in Focus*. New York: Routledge 1994: 88–111. Reprint 2000, 2001, 2002. Digital Print: 2003.
———. *Platonic Studies*. Princeton: Princeton University Press, 1973. 2nd edition with corrections: 1981.
———. *Socrates. Ironist and Moral Philosopher*. Cornell Studies in Classical Philology 50. Ithaca: Cornell University Press, 1991.
Vogt, H. "Die Entdeckungsgeschichte des Irrationalen nach Platon." *Bibliotheca Mathematica* III, Folge 10 (1909/10): 97–155; Folge 14 (1913/14): 9–29.
Voigtländer, H.-D. [Review of] Hans J. Krämer, *Arete bei Platon und Aristoteles* (1959). *Archiv für Geschichte der Philosophie* 45 (1963): 194–211.
———. [Review of] Konrad Gaiser, *Protreptik und Paränese bei Platon* (1959). *Archiv für Geschichte der Philosophie* 45 (1963): 68–75.
———. [Review of] Thomas Meyer, *Platons Apologie* (1962). *Gnomon* 35 (1963): 537–543.
Vollenhoven, D. H. T. "The Course of Plato's Development." *Melange Philosophique* offerts en homage aux Congressistes par l'Union des Societés de Philosophie des Pays Bas. Bibliothéque du X. Congrès International de Philosophie, Volume II. Amsterdam (1948): 1–16.
Vourveris, K. J. "Ὁ παιδεύων διάλογος." Πλάτων 6 (1954): 4–16.
Vretska, Karl. "Typische und polare Darstellung bei Platon." *Symbolae Osloenses* 30 (1953): 42–55.
———. "Platons Demokratenkapitel (Pol. VIII, 13, p. 559d ff.). Untersuchung seiner Form." *Gymnasium* 62 (1955): 407–428.
———. "Platonica I." *Gymnasium* 63 (1956): 406–420.
———. "Platonica II." *Wiener Studien* 69 (1956): 154–161.
———. "Platonica III." *Wiener Studien* 71 (1958): 30–54.
———. "Zu Form und Aufbau von Platons Symposion." *Serta Philologica Aenipontana*. (Innsbrucker Beitrage zur Kulturwissenschaft) 7–8. Innsbruck (1962): 143–156.
———. "Zu Platon, Symposion 183a." *Wiener Studien* 75 (1962): 22–27.
Waddington, Charles. *La Philosophie Ancienne et la Critique Historique*. Paris: Librairie Hachette, 1904.
Wake, W. C. "Sentence Length Distributions of Greek Authors." *Journal of the Royal Statistical Society*, Series A, 120 (1957): 331–346.

Walbe, Ernestus. *Syntaxis Platonicae specimen.* Dissertation. Bonn, 1888.
Waldenfels, B. *Das sokratische Fragen. Aporie, Elenchos, Anamnesis.* Monographien zur philosophischen Forschung 26. Meisenheim am Glan: Hain, 1961.
Walsdorff, Friedrich. *Die antiken Urteile über Platons Stil.* Klassisch-philologische Studien, Heft 1. Leipzig, 1927.
Warburg, Max. *Zwei Fragen zum Kratylos.* Neue Philologische Untersuchungen 5. Berlin: Weidmann, 1929.
Waugh, Joanne. "Neither Published Nor Perished. The Dialogues as Speech, not Text." Francisco J. Gonzalez (ed.), *The Third Way: New Directions in Platonic Studies.* Lanham: Rowman & Littlefield (1995): 61–77.
Webster, Thomas B. L. "A Study of Greek Sentence Construction." *American Journal of Philology* 62 (1941): 385–415.
———. *Art and Literature in Fourth Century Athens.* London: The Athlone Press, 1956.
———. *Studies in Later Greek Comedy.* 2nd edition. Manchester: Manchester University Press and New York: Barnes & Noble, 1970. New edition. Westport: Greenwood Press, 1981.
Wedberg, Anders. *Plato's Philosophy of Mathematics.* Stockholm: Almqvist & Wiksell, 1955. Reprint Westport: Greenwood Press, 1977.
Weerts, Emil. *Plato und der Heraklitismus. Ein Beitrag zum Problem der Historie im platonischen Dialog.* Philologus Supplement 23, Heft 1 (1931).
Wehrli, Fritz. "Der erhabene und der schlichte Stil in der poetisch-rhetorischen Theorie der Antike." *Phyllobolia für von der Mühll,* Basel (1946): 9–34.
———. *Die Schule des Aristoteles 7: Herakleides Pontikos.* Basel: Schwabe, 1953.
———. "Herakleides der Pontiker." *Pauly's Real-Encyclopädie der classischen Altertumswissenschaft,* Supplement 11 (1968): 675–686.
Weil, Raymond. *"L'Archéologie" de Platon.* Études et Commentaires 32. Paris: Klincksieck, 1959.
———. "La place du Premier Alcibiade dans l'oeuvre de Platon." *L'Information Littéraire* 16 (1964): 75–84.
Weinstock, Heinrich. *De Erotico Lysiaco.* Dissertation. Münster, 1912.
Welch, C. "The *Euthyphro* and the Forms." *Giornale di Metafisica* 22 (1967): 228–244.
Werner, Guilelmus. *De Anterastis dialogo Pseudoplatonico.* Dissertation Giessen. Darmstadt, 1912.
Wichmann, Ottomar. *Platon. Ideelle Gesamtdarstellung und Studienwerk.* Darmstadt: Wissenschaftliche Buchgesellschaft, 1966.
Wickert, L. "Zur Frage der Echtheit des dritten platonischen Briefes." *Rheinisches Museum* 93 (1950): 383 f.
Wieland, Wolfgang. *Platon und die Formen des Wissens.* Göttingen: Vandenhoeck & Ruprecht, 1982. 1999.
Wiggins, David. *Sameness and Substance.* London: Blackwell 1980. Reprinted in a revised and expanded version: *Sameness and Substance Renewed.* Cambridge: Cambridge University Press, 2001.
Wilamowitz-Moellendorff, Ulrich von. *Platon.* Sein Leben und seine Werke. I–II. Zweite Auflage. Berlin: Weidmannsche Buchhandlung, 1920
Wiles, Ann M. *Plato's Theory of Forms. A critical analysis.* Dissertation. University of Virginia (1974): DA XXXV, 1974: 3068A.
Willi, Walter. *Versuch einer Grundlegung der platonischen Mythopoiie.* Zürich: Füssli, 1925.

Wilpert, Paul. "Neue Fragmente aus Περὶ τἀγαθοῦ." *Hermes* 76 (1941): 225–250.
———. "Die Stellung des Timaios im platonischen Korpus." *Actes du XIème Congrès International de Philosophie*, vol. 12. Bruxelles 1953. Amsterdam (1953): 71–76.
Windelband, Wilhelm. *Geschichte der alten Philosophie*. 2. Auflage. München: Beck, 1894.
———. *Platon*. Frommanns Klassiker der Philosophie 9. Stuttgart: Frommann, 1900.
Windelband, Wilhelm and Goedeckemeyer, Albert. *Geschichte der abendländischen Philosophie im Altertum*. Handbuch der Altertumswissenschaft 1, Band 5,1. Vierte Auflage. München: Beck, 1923.
Wippern, Jürgen. *Das Problem der ungeschriebenen Lehre Platons*. Beiträge zum Verständnis der platonischen Prinzipienphilosophie. Wege der Forschung 186. Darmstadt: Wissenschaftliche Buchgesellschaft, 1972.
Wirth, A. "Platons Lysis nach 394 v. Chr. entstanden." *Archiv für Geschichte der Philosophie* 9 (1896): 163 f.
Wishart, D. and S. V. Leach. "A Multivariate Analysis of Platonic Prose Rhythm." *Computer Studies in the Humanities and Verbal Behavior* 3 (1970): 90–99.
Witte, Bernd. *Die Wissenschaft vom Guten und Bösen. Interpretationen zu Platons 'Charmides.'* Untersuchungen zur antiken Literatur und Geschichte 5. Berlin: De Gruyter, 1970.
Witte, K. *Platon*. Band I, *'Politeia'* I–II. Erlangen: Junge, 1949.
Wolf, Erik. *Plato's 'Apologie.'* Neue Philologische Untersuchungen 6. Berlin: Weidmann, 1929.
———. *Griechisches Rechtsdenken*, IV.1. *Platon, Frühdialoge und Politeia*. Frankfurt am Main: Klosterman, 1968.
———. *Griechisches Rechtsdenken*, IV.2. *Platon, Dialoge der mittleren und späteren Zeit, Briefe*. Frankfurt am Main: Klosterman, 1970.
Wolff, Hans M. *Plato, Der Kampf ums Sein*. Berkeley: University of California Press, 1957.
Woodruff, Paul B. *Two Studies in Socratic Dialectic. The 'Euthyphro' and the 'Hippias Major.'* Dissertation. Princeton University (1973): DA XXXIV, 1974: 7285A–7286A.
Wörle, Andrea. *Die politische Tätigkeit der Schüler Platons*. Göppinger akademische Beiträge 112. Lauterburg: Kümmerle, 1981.
Worthington, Ian. (ed.). *Voice into Text. Orality and Literacy in Ancient Greece*. Mnemosyne Supplements 157. Leiden: Brill, 1996.
Wunderlich, Hermann. *Unsere Umgangssprache in der Eigenart ihrer Satzfügung dargestellt*. Weimer und Berlin: Felber, 1894.
Wundt, Max. *Platons Leben und Werk*. Jena: Diederichs, 1914.
———. *Platons 'Parmenides.'* Tübinger Beiträge zur Altertumswissenschaft 25. Stuttgart: Kohlhammer, 1935.
———. "Die Zeitfolge der platonischen Gespräche." *Zeitschrift für philosophische Forschung* 4 (1949): 29–56.
Wyller, Egil A. "Platons *Ion*." Versuch einer Interpretation. *Symbolae Osloenses* 34 (1958): 19–38.
———. *Platons Parmenides in seinem Zusammenhang mit Symposion und Politeia*. Interpretationen zur platonischen Henologie. Skrifter utgitt av Det Norske Videnskaps-Akademi i Oslo, Historisk-filosofisk Klasse, 1959, 1. Oslo: Aschehough, 1960.
———. "The Architectonic of Plato's Later Dialogues." *Classica & Mediaevalia* 27 (1966): 101–115.
———. "The Parmenides is the Philosopher. A Thesis Concerning the Inner Relatedness of the Late Platonic Dialogues." *Classica & Mediaevalia* 29 (1968): 27–39.

———. *Der späte Platon*. Tübinger Vorlesungen 1965. Hamburg: Meiner, 1970.

———. *Enhet og annethet. En historisk og systematisk studie i henologi*. I–III. Oslo: Dreyer, 1981.

Zeise, Hans. *Der Staatsmann: Ein beitrag zur Interpretation des Platonischen Politikos*. Philologus Supplement 31.3. Leipzig: Dieterich'sche Verlagsbuchhandlung, 1938.

Zekl, Hans G. *Platon, Parmenides*. Philosophische Bibliothek 279. Hamburg, 1972.

Zeller, Eduard. *Platonische Studien*. Tübingen, 1839. Reprinted by Hildesheim: Olms, 1968. Reprinted by New York: Arno Press, 1976. VDM, 2007. Facsimile edition: Manchester, NH: Ayer, 1976.

———. *Die Philosophie der Griechen*. I–II. Tübingen, 1844–46. New revised and expanded editions: II.12 1859. II.13 1875. II.14 1889. II.15 1992 (with additions on Plato by Ernst Hoffman).

———. "Die deutsche Litteratur über die sokratische, platonische und aristotelische Philosophie 1896." *Archiv für Geschichte der Philosophie* 13 (1900): 272–303.

Zucker, Friedrich. *Der Stil des Gorgias nach seiner inneren Form*. Sitzungsberichte der Deutschen Akademie der Wissenschaften, Klasse für Sprache 1956. Berlin, 1956.

Zuckert, Catherine. *Postmodern Platos: Nietzsche, Heidegger, Gadamer, Strauss, Derrida*. Chicago: Univeristy of Chicago Press, 1996.

Zürcher, J. *Das Corpus Academicum in neuer Auffassung dargestellt*. Paderborn: Schöningh, 1954.

# INDEX

**A**

absolute 410, 463
abstract expression 56-, 65, 438-, 439n98
Academeia 268, 302; cf. Academy
Academy xvi-, 11, 14, 17-, 177-, 207, 209, 212, 231, 234, 272, 309, 388n3, 390n11, 431n89, 435-, 438, 457, 467, 474n161, 478, 479n179, 480, 487, 489, **495**, 499, 501-, 504, 518; cf. associates of Plato
accumulation 137, 141; *see* expansive style
active / passive 394, 402-, 429, 483-, 483n185
Acumenus 322
Adimantus 168n23, 268, 271n303, 286, 306, 338
Aegina 176
Aeschines of Sphettus 34, 37, 41, 45-, 46n135, 169n32, 173n48, 181, 205-, 208, 236n215, 258n267, 267n294, 269n296, 276n314, 278, 283, 298, 298n426, 311, 328, 355n644, 368n691
Aeschines the Orator 56n175
Aesopus 203n138
aesthetics 188; cf. literature, poetry
Aetna 175n59
affected style 56-
Agatharchides 63n198
ἀγαθόν (τό), ἀγαθός 182n80, 253n253, 284n348, 299, 317, 372, 375, 401n28, 403, 408n45, 416, 420-, 428, 431-, **443-**, 447, **453-**, 455, 462, 471, **481-**, 485-, 485n188, 506, 536; cf. Plato, 'On the Good'
Agathon 144, 261n278, 268, 270, 288n368
Agesilaus, Agesipolis 303n446
agnosticism 400, 402; cf. religion

ἄγραφα δόγματα 191, 412, 470n155, 473-, 503
αἰσχρόν 398, 449
αἴσθησις 290n374, 291, 303n449, 338n588, 345n618–619, 405; cf. senses
αἰτία *see* cause, causality
ἀκέφαλος 205n146, 236
ἄκλητος 270n299
ἀκόλαστος 407, 429
'akrasia' 402-, 420
ἀκριβές (τό) 478
Albinus 237n221, 467n146
Alcibiades 114, 135, 169n30, 179, 206n149, 240-, 274n309, 327, 360-, 362-
Alcidamas 320
Alcimus 237n221
Alcmeon 394
Ἀλήθεια (Protagoras) 404, 419
ἀλήθεια 416, 458-, 468n150; cf. knowledge, truth
Alexamenus 34, 203
Alexander Aphr. 475
Alexander the Great 239, 377
Alexis 345n616; *see* comedy
allegorism 239
ἄλλος cf. ἕτερος
allusions xvi, 178, 180, **183-**, 257-, 370-, 375, 504
ἀμαθία 412, 432; cf. knowledge
Ammon 239, 377
anachronism 179, 182, 184, 241n237, 389n7, 417, 438; cf. allusions
ἀνάγκη 414, 477, 482, 483; *see* necessity
ἀναγωγή 467n147
analogy 417n63, 446, 454, 502
analytic methods 389, 418; *see* interpretation

anamnesis 187-, 187n108, 188n111, 291, 301n439, 310, 312-, 360, 363, 434-, 448, 467-
Anaxagoras 58, 168, 332n555, 394, 413-, 434
Anaxandrides 373; cf. comedy
Anaximander 393, 474
Andocides 55, 204
ἀνδρεία 192-; see courage; cf. virtue
anecdotes 203-
Anniceris 176n60
anonymous partners 327
Antalcidas 265-, 276
antilogies 45-, 48n145, 205-
Antiphon of Rhamnus 204
Antiphon the Rhetor 55, 114
Antiphon, stepbrother of Plato 168n23, 269, 271n303
ἀντικείμενα 393, 427-
Antisthenes 37, 64n201, 181, **206-**, 266-, 342, 353-, 367-, 370, 524, 528, **542**
antithesis 56, 65
Anytus 178-, 179n72, 260, 261n278, 310-, 355, 357n653
ἀόριστος 473-; cf. principles
ἄπειρος 439, 450, 463n135, 470-, 474
ἀποβλέπειν 284n348
Apollo 235n211, 400
Apollodorus of Phaleron 114, 242, 290n381, 327, 327n546
apologetic tendency 16, 171, 212, 262, 283, 305, 347, 355, 357-
aporia 191, 198, 249n243, 300n434, 313, 357n652, 362, 366-, 392
ἀπόρρητα, ἀπόρρητα 485
appearance 403-
ἀρχαί 413, 462n129, 473-, 479-, 483, 487; see principles
Arcesilaus 376-
Archelaus of Macedon 239, 377
Archilochus 202
Archinus 321n521
Archytas 59, 175-, 175n59, 182, 336n577, 413n56, 487
ἀρετή 416, 419, 440-, 443, 450; see virtue
Arion 175n57
Aristides (J:r) 361
Aristides (S:r) 179, 360

Aristippus (S:r) 206n148, 345n616
Aristocles 253n252
Aristodemus 285
Aristophanes of Athens 114, 181, 204, 252-, 260, 262, 268, 284, 288n368, 413n56, 425, **522-**
Aristophanes of Byzantion 185
Aristophon 280
Aristoteles 269, 271, 305-
Aristotle 58, 116, 170, 184, 189, 205-, 254n254, 306, 332, 345n616, 367, 527
— on forms 437-, 454-
— on principles **475-**
Aristoxenus 173, 485-
Aristyllus 253, 253n252, 524n11
art, Plato's attitude towards 7
artifacts 447-, 454-, 455n117, 458, 493
artistry 389, 397, 419, 499-, 504; see literary art
arts and crafts 30, 280, 389, 440, 451-, 504; cf. poetry
ascetism 187; cf. hedonism
Aspasia 101, 283, 288, 328, 328n548–549, 354
aspect 439-, 450
associates of Plato 457-, 460n123, 460n125, 465n140, 471n156, 475n167, 478, 480n180–181, 487-, 495-, 501-; cf. Academy
astronomy 349, 465n140, 469, 485, 495-, 536-; cf. cosmology, mathematics
asymmetric contrasts 397-, 411, 414, 476, 482, 500; see two levels
atheism 400; see religion
Athenian Guest 340
Athenian politicians 188, 310-, 311n483, 360
Atlantis 336n576
ἄτομα 465n141
atomist 414
audience 390n11, 437, 457, 489, 495, 499, 503; cf. publication
authenticity 10-, 126n332, 127-, 141, 147, 150, 167, 201-, 210, 217, 219-, 230n202, **235-**, 346, **351**, 378-, 388n2, 390, 489-
αὐτός (ὁ), αὐτό, ταὐτόν 402, 407, **409-**, 421, **434-, 442-,** 447, **457-,** 465-, 477n172, 493; cf. ἕτερος

Index 611

**B**
bad 477; cf. evil, κακός
beauty 406-, 469n154, 471; cf. καλός
being (and becoming) 397n20, 398, 402-, **407-**, 420, 434-, **440-**, **458-**, 467, 472, 477, 482, **492**, 503; cf. εἶναι, οὐσία
big / small 435, 448, 459
biography 390n11, 407, 457n118
body *see* soul
βραχυλογία 281
Bryson 354
Burlesque cf. play

**C**
Callias 178, 258, 264n286, 267-
Callicles 103, 135, 234, 256-, 261n278, 272
Callistratus 257-, 375
categories 451, **457-**, 462-, 476-, 481, 487, **493-**, 502-; cf. concepts, kinds, principles
cause, causality 402-, 410, 415, 431-, 434, 446, 470-, 482-
Cave, simile of 416
Cebes 169, 206n148, 268, 289
central sections 28, 36, 38-, **46-**, 95, 98, 104, 115-, 129-, 131-, **138**, 389n8, 406
Ceos 334
Cephalus of Clazomenae 269, 271n303, 306-
Cephalus of Syracuse 96, 135, 257-, 306-
Ceremonious style 61-, 137
Chabrias 334
Chairemon 209n159
Chairephon 103, 268, 327n546, 378
change of scene *see* setting
chaotic 412
characterization of speakers 34, 39, 132-, 141n352, 212, 358, 504-
— Socrates 16-, 29-, 36-, 40-, 45-, 50, 95-, 131-
characters, choice of 213, 267-, 380, 389, 392, 418, 499; cf. interlocutors
Charmides 168, 268, 298-, 306
χώρα 477
χωρίς 397, 442, 446, 446n111, 455, 459, 502
χρῆσις *see* usefulness
chronology of Plato's writings 10-, 41, 142-, **165-**, 186-, **381-**, 388, 413, 438, 457, 460n124, **489-**, 503-

χρόνος 459, 463n134
Cimon 177n65, 282
class 440-, 451-, 460, 462-; cf. forms, kinds
clausulae 214-, 218, 243, 335n571–572, 343n607
Clinias 268, 270
Clitophon 129, 258n265, 353
cluster stylometry 230
colloquial style 51-, 136
comedy 52, 171, 181-, 255n258, 277n325, 288n368, 291, 348n629, 373, 531, 547; cf. Aristophanes
communism 252-
community *see* one / many
composition technique 27-, 131, **137-**, **201-**, 210-, 240, **271-**, 285, 289, 318; cf. pedimental composition
— climactic 28n79, 138
— haphazarded 126n329
— rhythm 35, 95, 132
computers, electronic 215, 222, 240
concepts 438, 457, 462, 499; cf. categories, forms, kinds
conceptual forms 435-, 448-, 453, 463
conclusions 35, 48-, 138-
confrontation of dialogues 192-, 246, 273, 490
Confucianism 394n15
Conon 179
contents, arguments from 167, 186-, 214, 246, 273-
context xvi, 3, 389, 504, 541-
contrasts 393-, 397-, 417, 500
conversation 33-, 53-, 136, 201-; cf. composition technique
conversational style, semi-literary 53-, 136; cf. colloquial style
Corinthian farmer 276n314, 285n351
Corinthian war 173, 176, 278
Corpus Platonicum 210, 230n202, 232, 235-, 242, 246, 390n11, 489; *see* Plato
corybants 356n646, 368
cosmology 187, 267n295, 292, 319, 323-, 344, 454n115, 460, 463n135, 465-, 471n156, 483; cf. κόσμος
courage 192-, 278n329, 282, 312; cf. virtue

crafts *see* arts
Crantor 338n583, 378
Cratylus 168, 173n47
creation 401n29, 465-, 483; cf. δημιουργός
Critias 37n110, 168, 179, 203, 261n278, 268-, 298-, 336, 340; cf. characters
Criton 169n32, 206n148, 268, 293, 344, 355, 357
Cronus 344
criteria *see* contents, dialogue technique, external, internal, style
cross-references in the Corpus 184-, 340; *see* allusions
Ctesippus 268, 293, 297
culmination cf. central sections, pedimental composition
cultic practices 400; *see* religion
curses 61
Cyrene 174
Cyrus 254

**D**
Daedalus 371
δαίμων, δαιμόνιον 119, 319-, 363- 401, 415-, 417, 422-, 506
δαιμόνιον of Socrates 187n107, 206n 150, 239, 268, 271, 319, 361-, 368, 400, 400n25, 423, 506
Damon 359
dates *see* chronology
decad cf. τετρακτύς
deceiving 432-; cf. fiction, lie
defined, definition 256, 279, 357n652, 407, 411, 436, 440, 443, 477, 492-; cf. ὅρος
Delium 206n149, 358-
Delos 172n44
δημιουργός 447-, 465-, 465n140, 480-
democracy 172n43, 178n67, 179, 257n263, 258n265, 266, 355, 430; cf. political theory, politics
Democritus 59
Demodocus 376
Demosthenes 56n175
Dercyllides 475
description 39; cf. dialogue technique, report
development of Plato's philosophy **147-**, 151-, **165-**, 175n54, 186-, 199,

**216-**, 245-, 388, 413, 490, 493-; cf. interpretation
developmentalism 388, 389n7, 390n11, 413, 490, 493, 541
dialectic, διαλέγεσθαι xvii, 18, **29-**, 188, 293-, 323-, 389-, 390n10, 392, 395, **414-**, 432, 434, 455, 486, 488, 499, 504-, 535
— two-way dialectic 409, **451-**, 464, 467n147, 469-, 481, 493-, 502
dihaeretics, διαίρεσις 103, 121-, 341-, 380, 395-, 421, 427, 451, 460, 465
— dihaeretic method 59, 188, 273, 315n499, 340n597, 341-, 342n604, 373, 395-, 427-, 451, 460-
dialogue, early history of 202-
dialogue technique 28-, 131-, 167, 199-, 239-, 246, 271, 289, 338-, 359
— dialogue approximating to monologue 41-, 140, 201-, 211, 340n593
— fictitious dialogue 38
— report 15-, 17-, 36-, 131-
Dicaearchus 517n35, 518n44, 527
dichotomy, binary 393, 396
didactic tendency cf. exercise, teaching, teachability
dihegematic dialogue *see* reported dialogue
δίκαιος, δίκαιον, δικαιοσύνη 257, 261, 279n331, 279, 286, 310, 353-, 363, 373, 429-, 433-, 439, 449, 458, 469n154; cf. virtue
dimensions 480, 483
Dio Chrysostom 353, 373n711
Diogenes Laertius 167n21
Diogenes of Apollonia 58
Diogenes of Sinope 528-
Dion 175-, 182-, 266, 319, 332-, 337, 341n599, 346-, 375
Dionysius I of Syracuse 175-, 183, 332
Dionysius II of Syracuse 183, 242-, 332, 334
Dionysodorus 268, 294n399
Diotima 114-, 266, 283-, 406, 410, 415-, 501
direct dialogue *see* dramatic dialogue
discussion 33-
Dissoi logoi 58

Divided Line 415-, **453-**, 478-, 502
divine / human 398-, 402, 406, **408-**, 411, 414-, 423, 442, 446, 463n135, 467
doctrines 388; cf. dogmaticism, system of doctrines, ἄγραφα δόγματα
dodecahedron 478n176, 480
dogmaticism 388, 418, 481
Dorian cities 177
Doris of Locri 175n56
δόξα 198, 263, 275n311, 288, 312-, 359, 360, 366, 371, 402n32, **404-**, 408, 412, 419, 432, 468; cf. ἐπιστήμη
drama 28, 34-, 208-, 249n24, 288n368; cf. comedy, tragedy
dramatic dialogues 15, **27-**, **199-**, 200-, 234, 274, 279, 305, **309-**, 318, 357-, 495, 504, 545-; cf. composition technique
dramatic elements 389, 490
dry / wet 394
dualism 393-, 395, 397-, 412, 433-, 477
dubia cf. authenticity; see semi-authenticity
δυάς 268, 317n505, 435, 447, 473-, 476n169, 488n198

E
early dialogues 152-, 171, 187, 200, 213n173, 216-, 246, 369, 388, 390n11, 399, 418, 457n119, 489-; cf. chronology
E.C. (external criteria) 167-, 245-, 273
Echecrates 175n57, 289
editing see publication, revision
education 177, 187, 269, 277-, 279-, 286, 360-, 364; cf. teaching, teachability
Egypt 174, 254-, 319-, 337, 524-
εἰδέναι 405, 440
εἶδος 435, 438-, 494, 501; see forms, ἰδέα
εἰδῶν φίλοι 460
εἶναι 407, 492; cf. ὄν, being
ἐκμαγεῖον 477
Elean philosophers 204, 340; cf. Parmenides, Zenon
Eleatics 29-, 173, 339-, 396, 408, 413-, 457-, 492
elenchus, ἔλεγχος 29-, 201-, 274n307, 343n605, 362, 365-, 376, 390n11, 402, 408, 422; cf. dialectic

emotions 139, 406n39, 417n63, 505; cf. pathetic style, senses
Empedocles 393-, 395
ἐμπειρία 411
encomium 269, 299n428, 303n446
endings of dialogues 35n101, 48, 138-, 213
ἐνθουσιασμός 446, 502; cf. divine / human, inspiration
ἐπέκεινα 412n52, 416, 500
Ephippus 354n640
Epicharmus 267n295, 531
Epicrates 182, 342, 460-, 461n127
ἐπιστήμη 193-, 299-, 310, 328-, 357, 371, **404-**, 432, 458-, 464, 468; cf. knowledge
epitaphios see funeral speech
ἐπιτηδεύματα 284
erists 29-, 204, 263, 268, 292-, 293n395, 295, 432
ἔρως, Eros 45, 188, 270-, 283-, 301n439, 319-, 324-, 365-, 400-, 412, **415-**, 417, 422, 431, 446-, 491, 505; see love
Erotikoi logoi 45
Eryximachus 114, 322
eschatology 49, 187, 272, 282, 287, 290-, 312-, 323-, 378; cf. soul, immortality
esoteric writings, esotericism 11, 18, 20, **152-**, 169n31, 191, 212, 270-, 283, 304-, 333, 340n592, 348, 360-, 366, 376, 388, 438, 475n164, 476, **486-**, 486n189, 486n191, 488, 503-; cf. exoteric, oral doctrines, ἄγραφα δόγματα
ethics 277; cf. political theory, virtue
etymologies 42, 315-
Euagoras 179n72
Eubulides 303
Euclides of Megara 19n60, 45n134, 172-, 206, 209n161, 242, 289n371, 301, 303, 325, 328
εὐδαίμων 430
Eudemus 289n372, 302, 515-
Eudicus 99
Eudoxus 12n20, 59, 302, 306n465, 321n521, 332, 337, 345, 362n670, 372-, 375
Euenus 204
Eupolis 258n267, 267n294, 360
εὖ πράττειν 422

Eurytus 175n55
Euthydemus son of Diocles 294
Euthydemus the erist 268, 294, 317
Euthyphron 316, 371
evil 412, 417n63, 434, 463n135, 474n161, 502, 505; see κακός
evolution see developmentalism
exercise 205, 296, 299-, 305, 309, 376; cf. dialectic
exoteric, exoteric writings 37, 209, 309, 340n592, 349, 352, 357, 366, 377, 546; cf. esotericism
expansive style 63-, 137
experiments in thought 388n4, 389, 392, 408, 412, 416-, 421, 424, 431-, **434-**, 446-, 450-, 457-, 468-, 472, 482, **486-**, 502-, 505-; cf. irony, play, orientation, vision
explicitness cf. implicitness
'extra muros' theme 271, 318, 324-

**F**
feelings cf. senses
fees for instruction 263, 275
fiction 404, 424
fifth element 346n621, 349n635
fire 435-, 442, 446n111, 447-, 458
forgeries 12, 238-; cf. authenticity, pseudepigraphy
formal criteria see composition technique, dialogue technique, setting, style
forms 388n5, 391, 399, 409-, 418, 420-, 431-, **434-**, 450-, 460-, 473, **493-**, 501-; cf. Ideas, ἰδέα, kinds
— theory of 149-, 187, 191, 288-, 290-, 304-, 370-
formulae of reply 215-, 226-
frame dialogue 40-, 207-, 232-, 260, 265, 268, 272-, 289, 293, 301, 310, 326-; cf. composition technique
funeral speech 231, 265

**G**
G.C. (general considerations) 273-
Gellius 254, 520
generation of numbers 478-; cf. dimensions

γένεσις 407-, 433-, 459, 464n135, 466, 471; cf. being
genetic view cf. developmentalism
γένος 440-, 444, 450-, 459-, 461-, 462n129-; cf. class, kinds
geometry 416-, 434, 446, 454-, 468n148, 480-; see mathematics
γίγνεσθαι 277n320-321; see being
γιγνώσκειν, γνῶσις 405; cf. knowledge
Glaucon 96, 135, 168n23, 206n148, 256n260, 268, 271n303, 286, 306, 327, 338
Glaucus 94
gods cf. divine / human, religion
good 394-, 398, 441; cf. ἀγαθόν
Gorgias 55, 57-, 114, 114n300, 182, 256-, 259n273, 267n295, 276n314-315, 280-, 312, 321; cf. characters
Guardians 252
gymnasium 177, 269, 273, 366n681

**H**
Hades 284n346, 292
hapax legomena 67, 215, 220-, 240
hard / soft 394
harmony 394, 415, 425, 470; cf. κοινωνία
ἑαυτόν cf. self
ἡδονή 420, 428, 433, 470-, 492; cf. senses
hedonism 187, 267n295, 282n337, 284-, **289-, 345-**, 372-, 420, 429, 433, **470-**; cf. senses
'hedonistic calculus' 277, 281, 420
ἑκών / ἄκων 403, 420, 424, 430
Hellenes / barbarians 395-
ἕν ''Εν 408-, 412n53, 447, 455, 458-, 461, **473-**, 481, 483-, 485-; cf. principles, unity, one / many
ἑνάς 470, 476n168
henology 305-, 307n468, 317n505, 339, 409
Heraclides of Pontus (J:r) 315-, 475
Heraclides of Pontus (S:r) 206n148, 315-, 371
Heraclitanism 168, 170, 173
Heraclitus 63, 78n231, 140n348, 168-, 173, 394, 408, 413-; see Heraclitanism
Herakles 303n446
hermeneutics 391, 398n21

Hermippus 173n47
Hermocrates 336n576
Hermodorus 169n29, 172n42–43, 182, 243, 475, 477n174
Hermogenes 173n47
Herodicus of Babylon 236
Herodicus of Leontini 280
Herodotus 60, 202
Hesiod 288n368, 395n16, 403n33
Hestiaeus 475
ἕτερος **409-**, 421, 434-, 451, **458-**, 463n132, **465-**
hiatus 55, 67, 214, 218, 243, 343n607, 346n622
Hippias 45, 82, 99, 109, 128, 182, 203, 322, 367-, 373-, 419; cf. characters
Hippocratics 58, 440, 446n143
Hippocrates, friend of Socrates 280
Hippocrates of Chios 59n185
— of Kos 58n182, 208, 237, 280
Hippodamus 530
Hippothales 268
historians 37, 45, 202
historical style 61, 137
holism 389n8, 504
ὅλον / μέρος 409, 459, 461n127
Homer 63, 202, 208, 237, 239, 253, 283, 288n368, 368-, 374, 393-, 403n33, 423; cf. poetry
homoerotics 524n11
ὅμοιος (ἀνόμοιος) 410, 420, 431, 434, 447, 458-, 465
ὁμοίωσις 400-, 409-, 412n55, 420, 431, 434, 447, 458-
ὅρος 407, 440-, 487; *see* defined
hot / cold 394
human 398-; cf. divine / human
ὕβρις 322n528
ὕλη 198, 412n54, 474n161, 477, 488n198
ὑπεροχή 277, 479n177
ὑποδοχή 477
Hyperides 63
hypomnemata 171, 204, 207-, 242n238, 376
hypophora, ὑποφορά 38, 203-
Hypothekai 45
hypothesis 391, 404, 443, 454-, 455n116, 459, 462n129, 468n148, 470

hypothetical method 312-, 313n493, 360, 370, 404, 443, 454-, 462n129, 468n148

I
I.C. (internal criteria) 273; cf. contents
ἰδέα, Ideas 416, 434-, **437-**, 450, 455, 458-, **462-**, 478-, 480-, 482-, 493-, 501-; cf. forms
ideal numbers 478-, 478n176
ideal philosopher 292-, 310; cf. philosophers
ideal state 187n105, 231, 251-, 256n260, 333, 337; cf. political theory
ἰδεῖν 440
ignorance 412, 432; *see* ἀμαθία
imagery 9, 47, 52, 67, 140-; cf. style markers
imitation cf. μίμησις
immanence 414, 439n97, 442, 446n111; cf. παρουσία
immortality 187, 284n346, 290-, 319, 364, 378, 402; cf. eschatology, soul
implicitness 188-, 246, 257, 299, 314
infinite 412
innate knowledge 467-, 502; cf. knowledge
inscriptions 62
inserenda 40, 206-, 209, 233, 274n307
inspiration 42-, 140, 368-, 371-, 400-, 446-; cf. ἐνθουσιασμός, divine / human
intellect 405-, 411, 505; cf. νοῦς, knowledge
intellectual style 57-, 136-
intentions of Plato 389n7, 390n11, 391-, 398, 504; cf. publication, purpose of dialogues
interlocutors 32, 36
interludes 34-; *see* composition technique
intermediate 412, 465
interpolation 242, 370; cf. authenticity
interpretation cf. 'schools' of Plato interpretation
— history of xiii-, 7-, 142, 147-, 186-, 215-, 387-, 490-
— new methods xviii, 21-, 141-, **165-**, **245-**, 273-, **309-**, 351-, 381, **387-**, **437-**, **457-**, 499, 504
intertextual references 185

introductions *see* opening sections
intuition cf. vision
invisible 406, 412n52, 413-, 442, 500;
　cf. sight, abstract expression
Ion of Chios 37, 203
Iphicrates 278, 302
Iranian religion 393
irony 52, 97, 213, **268-**, 389, 392, 400-, 419, 487-; cf. play
Isles of the Blessed 284n346
Ismenias 184, 258n266, 310-
Isocrates 19, 55, 64n201, 114n300, 177, 180, 254-, **262-**, 275, 294, 320, 413n56, 433, 522-, **529-**
ἴσος, ἰσότης 410, **434-**, 455n161, **458-**, 468, 474n161, 477n172; cf. ὅμοιος
ἰσονομία 410n51
Italy 174-; cf. Archytas, Pythagoreanism

**K**

κακός, κακία 398-, 412, 416-, 428-, 431, 433, 449-, 462, 474n161, 505
καλός, (τὸ) καλόν **284-**, 295, 372-, 397, 401-, 405, 415, **443-**, 453, 455, 458, 462
κερκίς 448
Kings 524-; cf. Royal Art
kinds 450-, 457-, 459-, 494, 501; cf. class, concept, forms
κίνησις 459-, 464-; cf. στάσις
know-how 421n76
knowledge / opinion 404-, 411, 421-, 432-, 462n139
knowledge, theory of 188, **193-**, 263, 311-, 325, 392, **403-**, 412, 416, 420-, **432-**, 464, **467-**, 502
　— philosopher's knowledge 392; cf. soul
　— know yourself 410, 421-, 442n104
Koiné 139n345
κοινῇ ζητεῖν 357, 360, 544
κοινωνία 391, 415-, 417, 442-, 444, 446n111, 449, 455, 505
κόσκινος 287n363
κόσμος 404n35, 408, 425, 454n115, 459, 463n135, 464-, 471n156; cf. cosmology

**L**

Laches 135, 358-

language of Plato 9-
language cf. style, stylometry
　— homogeneity of 227-
　— theory of 314-, 325; cf. etymologies
late dialogues, 'late style' 8, **19-**, 63-, 98, 120, **139-**, 211-, 216, 227, 243, 285, 301n437, 305n459, 315-, 318, 324, **331-**, 340, 347n624, 380, 392, 417, 438, 441, 443, 453, **457-**, 460n123, 549;
　cf. chronology, onkos style
late group of dialogues 148-, 154-, 191, 207, 211-, 216-, **331-**
'Law of Affinity' (Lutoslawski) 217
'Law of Parmentier' 178, 303
lawgiving, laws 62, 179, 334n565, 344, 355-, 527; cf. legal style
leading / being led 402-, 411, 422, 428
lecture, 'lecturer's monologue' 41-, 140-, 201, 211, 246, 252, 315, 340, 347-
legal style 62, 137
legends 47; cf. myths
Leo of Byzantion 236n216, 243, 378
levels 391-, 395-, 411-
Libanius 178-
lie 403, 412
light / darkness 394
likeness cf. ὅμοιος, ἴσος
limit / unlimited 394, 476
line *see* Divided Line; cf. dimensions
linguistic criteria *see* style, stylometry
literal vs. literary interpretation 389; cf. artistry
literary art of Plato **9-**, 54, 57, **199-**, 211, 246, 272, 276-, **283-**, 289-, 295-, 295n406, 370n699; cf. composition technique
literary criteria cf. dialogue technique, setting, style
literary criticism applied to Plato 9-
literature, criticism of 323, 346n621; cf. poetry
literature, Plato's attitude towards 7
Locri 175, 184, 334
logic 187-, 189, 277, 296-, 341, 366-, 375
logography 37, 45, 60
λόγος 401, 403-, 405, 410, 413, 419, 471n156; cf. dialectic
love, theory of 188, 231, 270, 283-, 301, 312, 324-; *see* ἔρως, φιλία

Lucian 236
Lyceum 268-, 271, 293, 296, 370n698
Lysias 55, 118-, 179, 182, 204, 260, 263, 276n315, 318-, 322, 353
Lysimachus 241, 358-
Lysis 268-

## M
Macrology 30, 46, 49, 281
madness cf. μανία
Magians 174n53, 175n54
maieutics 29n83, 187n103, **301-**, 303, 313-, 361, 365, 467
male / female 394-; cf. women
μᾶλλον / ἧττον 471, 473-, 474n161; see more / less
μανία 319, 322, 325n543, 368-, 400-
many 408-, 414, 450, 454, 458-, 470-, 477; cf. one / many
μαστροπεία 301n439
μάθημα 444-, 455n116
— μέγιστον μάθημα 444, 485n188, 487
mathematics, μαθήματα 59, 175, 175n54, 188, 267n295, 274, 284, 287, 302, 313n491, 349n635, 370n697, 388n3, 403, 413-, 416, 420, 453-, 460, 465n140, 468, 476n171, 478-, 479n177, **481-**, 509-
μάθησις 405
matter 412; cf. ὕλη
measuring 277, 290n379, 346n623, 405-, 420, 430, 436, **463**, 463n135, 471, 477-, 479, 483
medicine 440, 466; cf. Hippocratics
— medical style 58, 78
μέγα καὶ μικρόν 473-
Megalopolis 334
Megara 172-, 356n648
'Megarian period' of Plato 148, 172, 300n434
Megarian philosophy 172-, 209n161, 300n434, 303n445, 307n471, 329, 376
μέγεθος 434-, 448-; see big / small
μέγιστα γένη 461, 502; cf. categories, kinds
Melesias 359n657, 360
Meletus 260, 370n701
Melissus 58

memoirs 37, 203, 204, 208
Menedemus 342
μένειν 407-
Menexenus 268, 328
μέσον 345, 349, 412, 420, 465
metaphors cf. imagery
metaphysics 187, 287-, 305n456, 345n618; cf. forms, ontology, principles
metempsychosis 469n154; see reincarnation
μέθεξις (μετέχειν) 407, 415n57, 443, 446n111, 455, 458-; see participation
methods 21-, l65-, 192, 243-, 490
μετρητική cf. measuring
μέτριος 412, 464n135, 471, 474n161, 479n177
'middle period' 154-, 170, 191, 200, 216-, 251, 332n554, 418
midwifery see maieutics
military service 168, 173
Miltiades 282
mime 34, 173n48, 205, 209
Mimesis, mimetic, μίμησις 7, 16-, 34, 37, **86-**, 95-, 136, 200n131, 304, 317, 332, 403, 414, **446-**, 446n113, 458, 463n135, 502; cf. orientation
'mimetic' dialogue 200
mirror 362n669
μισολογία 292n391, 359
Mithaecus 267n295
mixing 394, **458-**, 462n131, 465, 467, 471, 476, 485
model, of craftsman 403, 415, 447, 458, 463n135, 502
μονάς 435, 447, 470-, 474, 476n169
monologue 41-, 44-, 131; cf. dialogue approximating to monologue
more / less 459, 471, 474n161, 493
motion cf. stability / change, κίνησις
mouthpiece of Plato cf. characters
multitude see many
music 288, 359; cf. poetry
Myrto 359n657
mysteries 270n300, 312, 319, 378
mystification 316, 379-
myths 11n15, 19n63, **47-**, 138, 189, 203, 211, 274, 282, 287n363, 333, 335-, 344, 368, 378, **400-**, 401n28, 402, 404, 429

—mythic narrative style 60, 137

**N**
name 439-, 448, 455n116, 458n122
narrated dialogue *see* reported dialogue
narrative cf. dialogue technique
Naxos 370
necessity 414, 477, 483; cf. ἀνάγκη
negation 412, 447-, 459-; cf. being
Neoplatonists 358; cf. Plotinus
Nicias 135
νοητόν 406
νόμος 282, 284; cf. lawgiving
νοῦς 405-, 413-, 416, 434, 466, 471, 482-
number 464, 471; cf. ἕν, ideal numbers, odd / even, one / many, mathematics

**O**
oaths 61
obstructive 412
Occelos 336n577
odd / even 394, 435, 459, 474; *see* mathematics
Odysseus 367
Old Oligarch *see* Ps.-Xenophon
Olympic games 176n60, 183n88
ὄν, ὄντως 444, 460-, 469, 492; cf. εἶναι, being
one / many 408-, 411, 414, 417n63, 419-, 428, 451, 459-, 470-, 481-; cf. ἕν, unity
onkos style 63-, 137, 139-, 141-, 212, 285
ontology 284, 306-, 388, 397, 416-, 461n127, 500; cf. being
open ends 138
opening sections 36, 39, 46, 49-, 131; cf. composition technique, frame dialogue
opinion cf. δόξα
opposites 411, 424, 448-, 458-, 462, 464, **470-**, 476-, 479n177, 493
— contrary opposites 393-, 427
— polar opposites 54, 69, 393-, 395-, **427-**, 500
orality, oral communication, oral doctrines xvi, 151-, 181, 184, 187, 191, **198, 231-**, 255, 346-, 359, 379, 388-, 388n6, 390n11, 436, 438, 462n131, **474-**, 482, **485-**, 487n193,

499, **541-**, 555; cf. ἄγραφα δόγματα, publication, audience, esotericism
oratio obliqua 41, 68
oratory 45, 54, 204, 266, 279, 281; cf. rhetoric
orientation 392, 398, 414-, 418 , 428-, 431-, 445, 483-, 505-
Orion, grammarian 315
Orphics, orphic beliefs 292, 395n16, 413n56
otherness 395, 409; cf. ἕτερος
οὐσία 440, 443, 459-, 471, 477, 477n174, 482; *see* being
οὐσία / πάθος 407; cf. being, εἶναι

**P**
παιδεία *see* education
παιδεραστία 291n384
παιδιά *see* play
pairs, pairs of contrast 268-, 271, 286, 357n652, 399-; cf. contrast
palinody 319-
Pan 400n25
Panaetius 237
papyrus fragments of prose dialogue 206n148
παράδειγμα 339, 446
paradoxes 375-
parainesis 46
paraphrase, of the Iliad 141
Parmenides 63, 116, 172-, 269, 305-, 308, 342-, 395; cf. characters
parody cf. play
παρουσία (παρεῖναι) 294-, 296, 297n421, 407, 414, 431, 439n97, 442-, 444, 446n111, 449, 455
participation 407, 415n57, 443-, 446-, 455, 458-
particles 220, 222-
Pasiphon 243
pastiche 207, 266, 283, 318, 321
pathetic style 56-, 136-
pedimental composition 28, 138, 240, 389n8, 400n25, 406, 416n62, 432n90; cf. central sections
πείθειν *see* persuasion
πέλαγος 409, 441
peltasts 278, 302

πέρας / ἄπειρον 346n622, 407, 441, 459, 470-, 476-, 479n177, 480, 485-, 485n188, 494
performance of dialogues 205, 209, 231, 309; *see* publication
Pericles 282; *see* Athenian politicians
periods, rhetorical 55, 68
Peripatos 296, 370n698
Peripeteia 28, 46, 138; *see* central sections
Περὶ τἀγαθοῦ *see* Plato, 'On the Good'
Persia 254, 266, 310, 362, 422
personification 68
persons, choice and characterization of 211-, 267-, 345, 358
persuasion 97-, 119, 140-, 404, 430; cf. Psychagogy
Phaedon 46n135, 112, 112n294, 169n32, 178, 205-, 237n220, 242, 270, 280, 289, 366n682
Phaedrus 322, 324n533
φαίνεσθαι 403-
Phaleas 253n251, 530
Phidias 280
Philebus 345
φιλία 297n417, 324, 403, 410, 431-; cf. ἔρως
Philip of Opous 126n332, 128n333, 243, 348-
Philistion 336n576
Philolaus 175n55, 336n577, 394n14, 407n42, 413n56, 471n156
philological methods xiv, 389, 391, 398, 413
philosopher, ideal searcher 392, 409, 416-, 422-, 449, 496, 506
philosophers as leaders 174, 251-, 286; cf. ideal philosopher
philosophy, φιλοσοφία xvii, **261**, 263, 291n384, 365, 392, 397, **415**-, 423-, 432-, 449, 496, **505-, 529-**
— philosophy as approach and method 397, 413, 415-, 429, 432, 505-
φιλοθεάμων 449
φρόνησις 406, 412, 466, 536; cf. knowledge
physical (reality) 187, **411-**, 431, 433-, **459-**, 463, 471, 478-, 481-, 492, 500, **504-**

physics 187; cf. cosmology
φύσις / νόμος 282, 404, 413, 461, 467
φυτουργός 448, 454
Pindar cf. poetry
πίστις 275n311, 404-; cf. δόξα
πλανᾶσθαι 388n4, 423; cf. experiments in thought
Plato
— autobiographical information 169n29, 174n52, 287, 347
— biographical facts and problems 167-, 184-, 234-, 251n248, 287, 378-, 390n11
— Corpus Platonicum coherent 246, 489-
— dynamics and shortcomings 504-
— late works 19, 41, 63-, 132, 139-, 142
— oral teaching 20
— Platonic Texts *see* Index of Platonic of Texts 625
Πλάτωνος ἀγαθόν 486n189, 531
play xvii, **9**, 42, 47-, 60, **96-**, 98, 118-, 132, 136, 138-, 140-, 171, 191, **211-**, 218-, 272, **292-**, 313n492, **314-**, 320, 328, 342, **366-**, 389-, 392, 397n20, 401, 403-, 411-, 419, 474n160, **487-**; cf. irony
pleasure cf. hedonism
Plotinus 322n527, 369, 477n174, 488
plurality cf. πολλά, many
Plutarch 167n21
poetry 35, 57, 60n190, 63-, 69, 140-, 179, 188, 253, 286, 288, 367-, 377, 505
ποιεῖν / πάσχειν cf. active / passive
ποιότης 407n43
Polemarchus 96, 257
polishing of texts 231-, 235n212; cf. publication
political theory, politics 168, 174-, 187, 261, 292-, 353-, 364-
politicians cf. Athenian
πολλά, οἱ πολλοί 409, 414, 451, 454, 458-, 470-; cf. ἕν, number, one / many
Polus 257
πολυθρύλητος 434, 438n95, 475
Polyaenus 206n148
Polyclitus 280

Polycrates of Athens, the rhetor 16, **178**, 258, 260, 274-, 278, 310-, 327, 355-
Polycrates of Samos 311
Polygnotus 280
Polyxenus 305
'post festum' theme 213n174, 270, 359n661
Πρατεύς 474n161
prayers 61
presence cf. παρουσία
Presocratics 58, 413-, 433
principles (metaphysical) 152, 188n109, 191, 253, 270n297, 274, 277, 291n387, 304, 317n505, 344n609, 345-, 391, 412n53, 413, 462n129, **473-**, 483, 487, 494, **503**; cf. esotericism, oral communication, ἄγραφα δόγματα
Proclus 237n220, 250
Prodicus 45, 109, 182, 203, 396, 409, 440, 451; cf. characters
progress cf. developmentalism
prolepsis 388n2, 388n5, 389n6, 425n82, 541
Prometheus 282
προοίμια νόμων 126-, 334n564, 379
propaedeutic 390n11
proportions 416, 430, 454, 478, 481-
Protagoras 109, 135, 168n27, 203-, 280-, 312, 316, 327, 419-, 530-
Protarchus 345
Proto-Republic 519-; cf. *Republic*
protreptic 16-, 20n68, 46, 48, 128, 138, 152, 171, 203, 208, 212, 283, 293, 314, **353-**, 366, 390n11, 410n51, 425, 432-, 495
proverbs 52, 69
Ps.-Pempelos 63n198
Ps.-Xenophon 203n140
pseudepigraphy 231n204, 239, 242; cf. authenticity
pseudonymity 208
psychagogy 98, 119, 140, 142; *see* persuasion
psychology 398n20, 401; cf. soul
publication, public, purpose of dialogues xvi, **185-**, 207-, **231-**, 241, 246, 249n243, 259-, 264, 309, 333-, 335-, 376, 381, 390-, 398, **439-**, 445n108, 457, **485-**, 495-, 504-, **541-**

punishment 282
purity 411, 467, 471
purpose 202n132, 212, 219, 241, 246, 265-, 305, 309, 314, 333, 336n574
Pyrilampes 168n23
Pythagoras, Pythagoreanism, Pythagoreans 169-, 175, 182, 267n295, 289, 298n424, 313, **336-**, 341, 345-, 349n635, 378-, 380, **394-**, 413-, 420n74, 421n75, 460n123, 468, 468n150, 468n153, 471, 471n156, **474-, 478-**, 479n179, 482, **486-**, 502-, 524
Pythodorus 269

Q
qualification 407, 428, 435-
question and reply 29-, 43-, 201-; cf. dialectic
— strict 33, 59
questioning, questions, cf. elenchus
quotation 50, 69; cf. hypophora

R
readers 425; cf. audience
reading 209-, 307; cf. writing; *see* orality, publication
reality 472; cf. οὐσία, physical
reason *see* knowledge, νοῦς, φρόνησις
receptacle 477
reincarnation 187, 287n363, 291-, 312-, 323n531, 469n154; cf. soul
relative 410, 449, 458, 462n130
religion 179, 187, 261n278, 262n282, 267n295, 311n482, 363-, 367-, 377, 400-; cf. divine / human
reply, formulae of 31, 40; cf. question and reply
report, two- or three-stage 212n170, 273, 290, 305, 308, 327
reported dialogue 15-, 18, 36-, 132, 200-, 265-, 267-, 310, 357, 365, 376, 495, 504; *see* dialogue technique
rest / motion 394; cf. στάσις; *see* κίνησις
retardation 35, 97
revision 14-, 167, 217, 219, 230-, 230n202, 246, 300, 310, 315n498, 318, 322, 325-, 333, 370, 390, 490, 496; cf. authenticity
revision of dialogues 390, 490, 496

rhapsodes 261n278
rhetoric, rhetorical style, rhetors 38, 44, **54**-, 61, 114n300, 136-, 141, 209, 257-, 272, 279-, 294, 310, **318**-, 325, 327-, 353, 380, 395, 398, 403-, 423, **427**-, 440; cf. oratory
rhythm *see* composition technique
right / left 394
right / wrong 428
Royal Art 293-, 299, 341n599, 432, 532-

S

same / different (other) 409-, 411, 417n63, 422-, 442, 465, 470, 477n172; cf. categories; *see* αὐτός
Sappho 202
scenery cf. setting
σχῆμα 440-
σχολή 325n543, 335, 536
school accumulation 242
'schools' of Plato interpretation 387-
scientific style 58, 60n198
secrecy 475n164, 488
secretary 217, 243, 333
seduction 406; cf. deceiving
self 402, 410, 421-, 443; *see* αὐτός
self-knowledge 362, 365
semi-authenticity 242-, 351-, 390n11, 399, 422, 455n116, 489-; cf. authenticity
sense perception cf. αἴσθησις
senseless 412
senses 291-, 304, 338, 345-, **405**-, 433-, 465, 492
separation cf. χωρίς
settings 211-, 231, 246, 267-, 389n8, 407-; cf. composition technique
shape 439-, 448
Sicily 19n60–61, 19, 305, 319n515, 334, 341, 348, 366; cf. Syracuse
— Plato's voyages to 173-, 182-, 212, 249, 255, 267, 319, 323, 326, 331-, 336-, 379
sight 405-, 415, 422, 440, 452-, 469, 492
sigla, speakers' sigla 16n46, 207n153, 210, 234, 305, 545, 551-
similes cf. imagery
Simmias 169, 206n148, 268, 289, 324n533
Simon 206n148
Simonides 47

slave 418, 458
Socrates
— as a historical person 169-, 173, 179, 212, 259-, 289n372, 352-, 358-, 388n3, 407-, 440
— as leader of dialogues 417-, 460n123, 490, 503-
— as leader of Platonic discussions 210, 345, 357
— as narrator of dialogues 270
— in the dialogues 95-, 102-, 108-, 118-, 128, **132**-, 168-, 392, **417**-, 490, 504
— 'rejuvenated' 270, 302n441, 302, 306, 307, 340, 358n657
Socrates the Younger 270n297, 306, 340, 340n595, 458n121, 463n135, 464n139, 466n142, 502, 534
Socratic paradox 403, 430
'Socratic period' xvi, 153-, 170-, 191, 199-, 210, 238, 277n318, 357n652, 366-, 369, 374, 388, 413-, 489-, 495, 504, 534; cf. early dialogues
Socratic λόγοι 169, 181, 203-, 208, 231, 243, 246, 261, 300n436, 376, 378n725
Socratics 34, 37, 170-, 205-, 231, 259, 261, 263, 269n296, 287, 321, 353-, 388n3, 413-, 440
soldiers 261n278
solemnity 61-, 137
σοφία, σοφός 401, 405, 418n66, 419-, 422-, 432, 468; cf. knowledge, virtue
sophists 46, 109, 168, 171, 188, 203-, 270-, 276-, 311-, 353-, 395, 414, 419-, 461
Sophron 34, 205, 209
σωφροσύνη 298-, 406, 421; cf. virtue
soul (and body) 187, 274-, 287, 319, 324, 325n543, **401**-, 410, 411, 415, 421-, 430, **433**-, 455n116, 463n135, **464**-, 467-, 470, 491-
Sparta 176-, 179, 278, 362n670, 422, 535
specialists 409, 423, 425, 448-, 505; cf. arts and crafts
speeches 42, 44-, 114-, 201-, 210, 249-, 271-, 283-, 320-; cf. funeral speech, myths, rhetoric, oratory
Speusippus 242n238, 316, 342, 345n616, 377, 475-, 481, 547; cf. associates of Plato

sport 319n515
spuria *see* authenticity
spuriousness 236-; cf. authenticity
square / oblong 394
stability / change **407-**, 411, 417n63, 421, 457-, 464-, 470, **476-**; cf. categories, στάσις
στάσις / κίνησις **407-**, 458-, 461, 463-, 463n135, 469-; cf. categories
statesmanship cf. political theory
statistics, statistics of language 220-; *see* stylometry
Stesimbrotus 37, 203
Stoic philosophy, Stoicism 239, 366, 370n698, 377, 418n66
straight / crooked 394
structure of dialogue cf. composition technique, dialogue technique
style 21-, 25, 70, **135-**, 167, 211-, 243, 272, 293, 352, 356-, 374-, 389n8, 416n62, 419n69, 422, 428, 490
style, of Plato, in the view of ancient authors 7, 62-
— change of style 83, 96-
— classes of style 22, 51-
— in relation to thought 7, 10, 135-, 142
— "late style" 98, 139-, 142
— patterns of style 21
— shades of style 22
— style markers 22-, 51-, **64-**, 71-, 217
stylistic groups 219-
stylometry 7-, 63, 141-, 145-, 166, 172, 188n111, 190, 199-, 211-, 213-, 240, 246, 335, 344, 351, 388, 490, 493, 495-
sublimation cf. love
substance 407, 462n130
Sun, simile of 416, 443n105, 445
συμμετρία 471
συμπλοκή 455, 459-, 463, 478, 485
symbolism in use of characters 213n175, 257, 286, 296, 307; cf. allusions
συμβουλεύεσθαι 357, 376
συναγωγή 390n10, 451-; cf. two-way dialectic
συνουσία 283, 307n468, 357-, 361, 363-, 390n10, 410n51, 488n196

συστοιχίαι 394
symposia, symposion literature 45-, 267-, 284n344
synoptic dialectic 390n10, 453, 459
Syracuse 175-, 334, 348; cf. Sicily
system of doctrines 10-, 388, 417, 475n167, 487, 493
systematic disposition 315, 345
systematic view of Plato's philosophy cf. developmentalism

T
Tao 394n15
Tarentum 175n59
Taureas 271
ταὐτόν / θάτερον 410, 451, 458-, 461-; cf. categories; *see* αὐτός, ἕτερος
τάξις 408
teaching, teachability 177-, 179, 187, 212, 271-, **277**, 279-, 295-, 309-, **354-**, 357-, 367-, **402-**, 419-, 432, 440-, **474-**, 486, 488n195; cf. education, dialectic
τέχνη 405, 411, 428, 432, 451, 454, 464n135; cf. arts and crafts
technical style 58-; *see* scientific style
τέλος 420n73, 428, 444, 446, 446n113
terms, philosophical 58, 70, 220-, 438-, 494
τετρακτύς, holy four 471, 478-, 487
tetralogies 151n10, 185, 213, 235-, 336n574
θάτερον 410, 463n132; cf. ταὐτόν; *see* ἕτερος
θεία μοῖρα 355, 363, 368, 400-, 446; cf. divine / human
Theaitetos 269, 301-, 328-, 340, 414
Thebes 356
θεῖος cf. divine / human
thematic criteria *see* contents
Themistius 179n71, 233
Themistogenes 242
Themistocles 179, 282
Theodectes 19n61
Theodoros of Cyrene 175, 269, 340, 414, 509-
Theophrastus 475, 477-, 480-
Theopompus the Comedian 191n120

θεωρία 406, 416; *see* sight
θερμός 435, 442, 446n111
Theuth 174n53, 319-
'third man' argument 306, 339
Thracia 271, 314n496
Thrasybulus 179n72, 257-
Thrasyllus 235-
Thrasymachus 96, 135, 256-, 261n278, 263, 272, 352-
Thucydides the historian 45, 55, 61n193, 114n300, 202, 276n315, 439n98
Thucydides the politician 360
θυμός 420n73
τιθήνη 477
Timaeus Locrus 120n316
Timaeus of Locri 175, 336, 340
Timocrates 311n479
Timotheus 373
τίς / ποῖος 407
tragedy 63, 169, 211, 288n368, 290-; cf. comedy, drama, poetry
transcendence 439n97, 442, 446n111
transition 27, 31
triads 12n20, 28n79
trichotomies 348-
trilogies 20, 185, 213, 300, 336, 340n593, 344, 346
tripartite soul *see* soul
truth, ontological or cognitive 403-
truth / appearance 403-, 411, 416-, 432-, 469-, 469n154; cf. knowledge
Tübingen school of 389n6, 473-, 473n158, 482n184, 483-, 485n188, 486-; *see* oral communication, esotericism, ἄγραφα δόγματα
two levels 393-, 537
two-way dialectic 409-, 451-, 469-, 480-, 493
tympanon *see* pedimental composition
Tynnichus 368, 400n25
τύπος, type 439-, 450-
tyrants 258n265, 267n295, 332, 364

U
unitarian view of Plato's philosophy 151-, 190, 250-, 305n457, 318n509, 332n559, 333n563, 388n2–3; cf. developmentalism, revision

unity 394, 409, 414, 473-; cf. αὐτός, ἕν, one / many
universals 436, 439, 452
unmeasurable 412, 476
unwritten doctrines *see* oral communication, ἄγραφα δόγματα
use of an art 293-, 295n404, 297n421, 314n495, 316
usefulness 284
Utopia 424-, 505, 519-; cf. ideal state; *see* Plato, *R*

V
value 395-, 397-, 436, 441-
variation 31-, 64, 95, 211-; cf. style markers
vegetative 412
virtue, innate or teachable 152, 187, 193, 261, 275, 298, 310, 357, 401-, 419, 427-, 432, 441, 536; cf. teaching, ἀρετή
vision, of two levels 46-, 136-, 388n5, **397-**, 411-, **414-**, 431, 437, 442, 445n108, 450, 467, 468n149, 480n180, 485, 499-; cf. sight
vocabulary *see* style markers
vulgarisms 52, 57, 72, 75, 96, 128

W
wandering 408; cf. πλανᾶσθαι
weaving 341, 344
women 113n295, 252-, 394-, 411, 414, 477, 505
world soul 338, 344; cf. soul
writing 173, 191-, 191n120, 209, 230-, 243n241, 253, 317-, 319, 325-, 329, 388n6, 393; cf. audience, esotericism, orality

X
Xanthippa 113, 268, 271
Xenocrates 378, 474-, 477n174, 481n183
Xenophon 34, 37, 41, 45, 52, 54-, 63, 170, 178-, **180-**, 205-, 230n202, 258-, 260, 269-, 276, 283, 354-, 373, 520, **526**, **529**, 542; *see* Ps.-Xenophon

Y
Yang–Yin 394

## Z

Zalmoxis 298, 325n539
Zenon of Elea 58, 116, 173, 203n138, 269, 326, 364, 408, 458; cf. characters
Zenon the Stoic 306n465
Zervanism 393
ζῷον, the perfect 451, 454-, 463n134–135, 466, 502
Zoroastrianism 393

# INDEX OF PLATONIC TEXTS

N.B. The titles of the writings are abbreviated as in LSJ and listed in alphabetical order according to the abbreviations.

*Alc. 1 (Alcibiades I)* 12, 129, 233, 352, 361-, 422-
— 129a ff. 402
*Alc. 2 (Alcibiades II)* 12, 129, 239-, 352, 377-
*Alkyon* see *Halcyon* 14n32
*Amat. (Amatores)* 12, 129, 352, 365
*Ap. (Apology)* 17, 101, 170-, 173, 180n73, 231, 249-, 259-, 263-, 423, 445, 544
*Ax. (Axiochus)* 13, 220-, 223-, 226-, 238, 352, 378
*Chrm. (Charmides)* 18, 38-, **107-**, 268, 298-, 420-
*Clit. (Clitopho)* 12, 129-, 256n260, 352-, 418n68
*Cra. (Cratylus)* 17, 42-, 105-, 233, 314-, 408-, 447
— 438c ff. 469
*Cri. (Crito)* 17, 100, 173, 352, 355-, 404, 546
— 54d 401n27
*Criti. (Critias)* 19, 120-, 335-, 337; cf. *Ti*
*Def. (Definitiones)* 14, 238, 352, 377
*Demod. (Demodocus)* 13, 352, 376
*Ep. (Epistulae)* 1–6, 8–13 in general 13-, 130, 236, 239, 352, 378-
*Ep. (Epistulae)* 7 13, 124, 168, 174-, 216, 255, 346-, 532-; cf. *Seventh Letter*
*Epigr. (Epigrams)* 236
*Epin. (Epinomis)* 20, 127-, 216, 243, 341n598, 348n630, 349, 466n145
— 990d ff. 476n169
*Erx. (Eryxias)* 12, 130, 240, 352, 366

*Euthd. (Euthydemus)* 18, 38-, 109-, 268, 292-, 432-
*Euthphr. (Euthyphro)* 17, 105, 171n39, 172n41, 352, 369-, 443
— 5c-6b 448-
*Grg. (Gorgias)* 15, 17, 101-, 234-, 237-, 256-, 258, 267-, 274-, 309-, 427-, 495, 545, 551
— 448e ff. 428
— 463e ff. 402, 451
— 503de 447-
— 507c-508c 48
*Halc. (Halcyon)* 202, 227, 236, 238, 352, 378
*Hipparch. (Hipparchus)* 12, 128, 240, 352, 374-
*Hp.Ma. (Hippias Major)* 12, 128, 212, 240-, 352, 372-, 443
— 301b-e 451
*Hp.Mi. (Hippias Minor)* 16, 99, 171, 171n39, 352, 366-, 423-
*Ion* 16, 99, 171, 171n39, 233, 352, 367-
*Just. (De Justo)* 12, 128, 205, 352, 376-
*La. (Laches)* 16-, 99, 190, 192-, 352, 357-
*Lg. (Laws)* 14, 20, 125-, 241, 333-, 348-, 466n144, 496-
— X 893b ff. 466-
— 896e ff. 413n55
*Ly. (Lysis)* 15, 18, 38-, 106-, 171n38, 268, 295-, 431-
— 217a ff. 449
*Men. (Meno)* 15, 17, 103-, 235, 310-, 434, 495-
— 71b-76a 440-

— 72a-76a  407
— 80a ff.  408, 468
— 97d ff.  408, 468
*Min. (Minos)*  12, 130, 352, 375
*Mx. (Menexenus)*  15, 17, 101, 265-, 276,
    327-, 418n68, 485, 490n200, 496n208,
    538
'On the Good'  347-, 485-, 503, 547-
*Phd. (Phaedo)*  15, 18, 38-, 111-, 172,
    233, 237-, 268, 288-, 341n598, 433-,
    447-, 495-
— 72e-77a  468-
— 92d  486n152
*Phdr. (Phaedrus)*  14, 19, 118-, 189, 212, 216,
    231-, 233, 317-, 494-
— 245c ff.  402, 464, 469
— 246c ff.  400, 469n154
— 465d ff.  451
*Philosophus*  20, 341, 343n605, 496
*Phlb. (Philebus)*  15, 20, 123-, 212, 341n598,
    344-, 470-, 476, 487n193, 496-
*Plt. (Politicus)*  20, 122-, 172, 339-, 463, 496
— 268d ff.  412n55, 463n135
*Prm. (Parmenides)*  15, 18, 38-, 115-, 189,
    207, 212, 216, 233, 269, 304-, 334-,
    341n598, 446n111, 457-, 495-
— 129a-130a  447
*Prt. (Protagoras)*  18, 38-, 108-, 192-, 232-,
    258, 267-, 276-, 327, 419-, 463n135
— 331c-333c  451
— 344bc  407
— 352b ff.  402-, 402n31
*R. (Republic)*  14-, 18-, 38, 83-, 207, 216,
    231-, 237-, 250-, 256-, 285-, 331-,
    341n598, 390, 424-, 452, 457, 485, 487,
    495-, 504, **519-**
— I  429-
— II  380d-381b  448
— IV  435c ff.  470
    — 445c  450-
— V-VI  444-
— V  476ab  449, 452
— VI  509d-511e  416-, 453-
— VII  523a-524d  449
— VIII  545d ff.  416n62, 479n179
— X  596a  454, 455n116
    — 597a ff.  448
    — 608d  491

*Seventh Letter (7th Letter)*  390n11; *see*
    *Ep. 7*
— 340b ff.  485
— 341c ff.  488n196
— 343a  455
*Sis. (Sisyphus)*  12, 130, 240-, 352, 375
*Smp. (Symposium)*  15, 18, 38-, 113-, 233,
    237-, 258, 266-, 283-, 326-, 341n598,
    444-, 543-
— 202a  415
— 210a ff.  406, 415-, 441-
*Sph. (Sophist)*  20, 121-, 172, 339-, 460-
*Thg. (Theages)*  12, 129, 352, 364-
*Tht. (Theaetetus)*  14, 18, 116-, 172, 189, 207,
    216, 232-, 269, 300-, 328, 334-, 495
— 147d ff.  480n182
— 152a ff.  464n136
— 176a  416
— 176e  412n55, 449
— 185c-186c  464
— 203e-205d  451
*Ti. (Timaeus)*  19, 119-, 251-, 335-, 341n598,
    343-, 465-, 476, 478, 480, 488, 467n147,
    520-
— 34b ff.  455n116, 465-, 480n181
*Virt. (De Virtute)*  12, 128, 352, 376-

• Also available from Parmenides Publishing •

## PRE-SOCRATICS

*By Being, It Is: The Thesis of Parmenides* by Néstor-Luis Cordero

*To Think Like God: Pythagoras and Parmenides. The Origins of Philosophy.* Scholarly and fully annotated edition by Arnold Hermann

*The Illustrated To Think Like God: Pythagoras and Parmenides. The Origins of Philosophy.* Over 200 full color illustrations. By Arnold Hermann

*The Legacy of Parmenides: Eleatic Monism and Later Presocratic Thought* by Patricia Curd

*Parmenides and the History of Dialectic: Three Essays* by Scott Austin

*'Parmenides, Venerable and Awesome': Proceedings of the International Symposium* edited by Néstor-Luis Cordero

*The Route of Parmenides: Revised and Expanded Edition, With a New Introduction, Three Supplemental Essays, and an Essay by Gregory Vlastos* by Alexander P.D. Mourelatos

## PLATO

*God and Forms in Plato* by Richard D. Mohr

*Image and Paradigm in Plato's* Sophist by David Ambuel

*Interpreting Plato's Dialogues* by J. Angelo Corlett

*One Book, the Whole Universe: Plato's Timaeus Today* edited by Richard D. Mohr

*The Philosopher in Plato's* Statesman by Mitchell Miller

*Platonic Patterns: A Collection of Studies* by Holger Thesleff

*Plato's Late Ontology: A Riddle Resolved* by Kenneth M. Sayre

*Plato's Parmenides: Text and Translation* by Arnold Hermann and Sylvana Chrysakopoulou

*Plato's Universe* by Gregory Vlastos

## ARISTOTLE

*One and Many in Aristotle's Metaphysics—Volume 1: Books Alpha-Delta* by Edward C. Halper

*One and Many in Aristotle's Metaphysics—Volume 2: The Central Books* by Edward C. Halper

## HELLENISTIC PHILOSOPHY

*A Life Worthy of the Gods: The Materialistic Psychology of Epicurus* by David Konstan

*Plotinus The Platonist: A Comparative Account of their Mysticism, Epistemology, Metaphysics, and Ethics* by David J. Yount

## ETHICS

*Sentience and Sensibility: A Conversation about Moral Philosophy* by Matthew R. Silliman

## AUDIOBOOKS

*The Iliad* (unabridged) by Stanley Lombardo

*The Odyssey* (unabridged) by Stanley Lombardo

*The Essential Homer* by Stanley Lombardo

*The Essential Iliad* by Stanley Lombardo